Revisiting America
Readings in Race, Culture, and Conflict

Susan Wyle

Stanford University

D0209259

PEARSON

Prentice
Hall

Upper Saddle River, New Jersey 07458

Library of Congress Cataloging-in-Publication Data

Revisiting America: readings in race, culture, and conflict / [edited by] Susan Wyle.
   p. cm.
   ISBN 0-13-029305-9
  1. Readers—United States. 2. United States—Civilization—Problems, exercises, etc.
3. English language—Rhetoric—Problems, exercises, etc. 4. Report writing—
Problems, exercises, etc. 5. College readers. I. Wyle, Susan.
   PE1127.H5R45 2004
    808'.0427—dc21   2003012589

Senior Acquisitions Editor: Corey Good
VP, Editor-in-Chief: Leah Jewell
Editorial Assistant: Steven Kyritz
Media Editor: Christy Schaack
Executive Marketing Manager: Brandy Dawson
Marketing Assistant: Allison Peck
Prepress and Manufacturing Buyer: Mary Ann Gloriande
Interior Design: John P. Mazzola
Cover Design: Robert Farrar-Wagner
Cover Art: John Gast, "American Progress," 1872. *A woman in a white robe is the symbol of progress. She floats over the prairie holding a school book and a coil of telegraph wire, which she is stringing out behind her. On the ground below, Native Americans and bison run in front of her. Behind her are signs of "progress": trains, ships, and settlers.* Corbis.
Director, Image Resource Center: Melinda Reo
Manager, Rights and Permissions: Zina Arabia
Interior Image Specialist: Beth Boyd-Brenzel
Photo Researcher: Jane Sanders
Image Permission Coordinator: Craig A. Jones
Composition/Full-Service Project Management: Kari C. Mazzola and John P. Mazzola
Printer/Binder: Courier Companies, Inc.
Cover Printer: Phoenix Color Corp.

Pearson Education LTD.
Pearson Education Singapore, Pte. Ltd
Pearson Education, Canada, Ltd
Pearson Education–Japan
Pearson Education Australia PTY, Limited

Pearson Education North Asia Ltd
Pearson Educación de Mexico, S.A. de C.V.
Pearson Education Malaysia, Pte. Ltd
Pearson Education, Upper Saddle River, NJ

10 9 8 7 6 5 4 3 2 1
ISBN 0-13-029305-9

Contents

Thematic Contents

Race and Racism

By and About Native Americans

Race, Culture, and Conflict in the West

Slavery and the Civil War

Issues of Immigration

Speeches

Biography and Autobiography

Poverty and Wealth

Literary Selections

Preface

Revisiting America: Readings in Race, Culture, and Conflict is a composition reader designed for first-year college students. Roughly organized chronologically, this text offers readings on myriad racial and cultural struggles in past and present America. The philosophy behind this reader is that a combination of primary, secondary, and literary sources will encourage students to think critically about the issues that have shaped the world around them, issues that take root in the early history of the United States and that continue to be important in contemporary society. These readings will encourage students to think more deeply about cultural and historical issues that offer opportunities for further study and research. This textbook also seeks to offer students a glimpse into the power of language, written and spoken, in shaping ideas, attitudes, and policies when conflicts arise. *Revisiting America* is not intended to give a full history of all the conflicts of race, class, and gender in the United States, but rather to offer some key readings that will encourage students to think and write critically and to pursue research topics generated by the readings, discussion questions, and writing suggestions in each chapter.

I have included a number of primary and secondary sources that are not widely published, in addition to readings with which teachers and students may be more familiar. For example, students can read Tituba's own trial testimony from the Salem Witch Trials, Custer's outspoken opinion about Native Americans, and the writings of Luther Standing Bear; readers can peruse Junipero Serra's letter to Father Juan Andrés as well as historian Richard White's revisionist view of the mission system; and writers can study the speeches and rhetorical devices of presidents, feminists, Vietnam protesters, and African American civil rights activists in the context of both literary texts and researched essays. These primary, secondary, and literary selections invite students to challenge their own assumptions about race, culture, and conflict in the United States, and to expand, through self-reflection, journal writing, critical reading, analytical essays, comparison essays, and researched arguments, their own understanding of both past and contemporary society in America.

The "Introduction" to this text covers a number of important aspects of reading and writing, including tips on finding and using primary sources, the differences between primary and secondary sources, how to search the Web for accurate and unusual collections, and a brief discussion of fallacies and the evaluation of arguments.

Chapter 1, "Early Conflicts on the Eastern Shore," includes readings that range from a scholarly discussion of the Pocahontas myth to the trial testimonies of the Salem Witch Trials, addressing issues of race, gender, slavery, and freedom in colonial America.

Chapter 2, "The Native Americans versus the Newcomers," offers opposing perspectives from Native Americans, U.S. presidents, and scholars about the loss of Indian lands, the assimilation of Native Americans into white "civilization," and the process of Indian relocation under Presidents Jefferson and Jackson.

Chapter 3, "Conflicts on the Way West," includes a wide variety of primary and secondary sources dealing with the racial, social, and gender -based conflicts experienced by the men and women who traveled West.

Chapter 4, "Slavery and the Civil War," examines the experiences of slaves and freedmen, soldiers and women, politicians and writers who participated in many different aspects of the Civil War.

Chapter 5, "Conflicts in California: The Missions, the Gold Rush, and Chinese Exclusion," offers a variety of writings that portray the conflicts between the Catholic missions and early Californians, the struggles of men and women who followed the lure of gold, and the experience of the Chinese who built the railroad and then faced a series of exclusion laws.

Chapter 6, "Poverty, Wealth, and the American Dream," includes essays, letters, poetry, and congressional testimony about the experiences of the poorest immigrants and the wealthiest Americans in the late nineteenth and early twentieth century.

Chapter 7, "The Depression and the Two World Wars on the Home Front," uses visual and textual arguments, media selections, and propaganda posters to examine some of the economic, political, and racial hardships of the Depression and the two world wars.

Chapter 8, "Civil Rights, Protest, and Foreign Wars," looks at the writings and speeches of women, minorities, and civil rights leaders in the 1960s and 1970s and also examines the rhetoric of politicians and presidents sending troops to Vietnam and the Gulf War.

Chapter 9, "Conflicts Past and Conflicts Present," offers more recent twentieth century and twenty-first century readings that deal with a variety of contemporary issues, including conflicts of gender, race, and immigration, all of which find their roots in issues and events represented in earlier chapters of the text. In addition, this chapter offers written and visual text selections by authors and artists responding to the terrorist attacks of September 11.

Each chapter starts with a brief introduction that provides historical background and "Before You Read" questions for students to keep in mind while reading the selections. Each selection is accompanied by background information on the author, post-reading "Discussion Questions," and post-reading "Writing Suggestions." Each chapter ends with final "Writing Suggestions" and suggestions for "Further Research on the Web."

Acknowledgments

I have received so much support and encouragement in completing this project that it is hard to know where to start my list of acknowledgments.

I would very much like to thank the folks at Prentice Hall, including Leah Jewell, Corey Good, John Ragozzine, and Steven Kyritz for their original interest in this project and for their time and patience in seeing the project through all of its phases. In addition, great thanks are due to permissions researcher Kathleen Karcher for her tireless work, and to production editor/compositor Kari Callaghan Mazzola, who pulled the whole project together with amazing skill and energy!

I would especially like to thank my research assistant, Mike Bordoni, Stanford class of 2006, for his remarkable work above and beyond the call of duty; his help on every aspect of the final draft was invaluable over the course of two summers.

I would also especially like to thank my whole family and Kinji Imada for their ongoing interest, encouragement, and research contributions, and my friends Patti Edelemeier, Jim Hankey, Gladie Kirkman, Michael Lowenstein, and Julie Wood, for the same. Special thanks go to Melanie Bean for her years of friendship, encouragement, and advice, and for her invaluable proofreading skills! In addition I would like to thank John and Maeve Manning for their help in collecting both historical and artistic materials. And, of course, great thanks to the Italian ladies for years of encouragement and hugs—grazie!

At Stanford, I would like to thank all my colleagues in the Program in Writing and Rhetoric—especially Ann Watters, Ron Rebholz, Wendy Goldberg, Joyce Moser, and Marjorie Ford—for continued support, suggestions, guidance, and feedback. Also, warm thanks go to Ardel Thomas for all of the above, in addition to her excellent editing and proofreading help. I would also like to thank Andrea Lunsford and Marvin Diogenes for their interest in and encouragement for this project, and my thanks also go to George Brown and Chris Rovee from the English department for their daily support. In the Creative Writing department I would like to thank Simone DiPiero for the summer use of his beautiful office and David MacDonald for his encouragement and help with literary selections. And finally, I would like to thank Cristina Huerta for her remarkable patience and unending help with all things technical!

In addition, I owe great thanks to archivists Elena Danielson, Cissie Hill, and Carol Leadenham for all their help in collecting materials from the Hoover Archives. Thanks also go to Maggie Kimball, Stanford University archivist, for her help with the materials from Green Library Special Collections.

For the portions of this text that address the American West, I owe a special debt of gratitude to all the staff at Hunewill Guest Ranch in Bridgeport, California—thanks go to Jan Hunewill for her suggestions about materials pertaining to women in the West; to wrangler and cowboy Art Black, who contributed not only text ideas but also the illustration of the modern cowboy for Chapter 9; and to the entire Cleeland band for caring about this project and discussing it over all the Memorial Day weekends!

I would also like to thank my reviewers, who took the time to read the manuscript and to make so many helpful suggestions: Judy E. Sneller, South Dakota School of Mines & Technology; Neil W. Bernstein, Duke University; Robert A. Henderson, Southeastern Oklahoma State University; Richard Goldman, West Virginia University; Deidre Lashgari, California Polytech; Deborah Kirkman, University of Kentucky; Kenneth C. Hawley, University of Kentucky; Marsha Urban, University of Nevada–Reno; Holly A. Wheeler, Monroe Community College; Karin E. Westman, Kansas State University.

And last but not least, thanks to all of the students in my writing classes who added their ideas and gave such good feedback about the assignments and readings in this text.

Susan Wyle

Introduction

This book is designed to give you new perspectives on the major conflicts that have shaped the culture and history of the United States. *Revisiting America* offers a variety of readings that shed new light on some of the major issues of race, culture, and conflict. By offering multiple perspectives on these conflicts, *Revisiting America* will enable you to analyze and respond to readings that will challenge previous assumptions and that will supplement your current understanding of life in America. As you broaden your understanding of these themes and issues, your own research and writing skills will begin to reflect the divergent views that characterize the written and oral history of conflict in the United States.

The readings presented in the chapters of this book date from the seventeenth century to the present. Some of the readings are scholarly articles that will give you background information about the conflicts that shaped American culture and history; other readings include personal writings, diaries, and speeches of individuals who were part of the panorama of American history. Some of the chapters include visual materials, such as political cartoons, advertisements, and propaganda posters, all of which add a new dimension to our understanding of visual rhetoric.

The nine chapters of *Revisiting America* move chronologically from the late 1600s to the new millennium, and each chapter focuses on a small number of topics related to race, culture, or conflict. Chapter 1 includes new insights into the well-known story of Pocahontas, such as the Powhatan Nation's response to the mythology of the story, and also offers a variety of readings to help you learn more about the Salem Witch Trials. Chapter 2 presents not only the early presidents' beliefs about the role of Native Americans in the newly developing nation, but also the beliefs and feelings of various Native American writers and speakers. Chapter 3 describes the conflicts on the way West, including the role of Mormon pioneers. In Chapter 4, the readings about the Civil War include not only the famous speeches of Abraham Lincoln and Jefferson Davis, but also the diaries of slaves and of Southern and Northern women who dressed as men to join the Confederate and Union Armies. Chapter 5 challenges some of the basic assumptions about the role of the missionaries in California, in addition to presenting a variety of perspectives on the lives of the men and women who rushed for gold in 1849 and the Chinese Exclusion laws passed after the building of the railroad. Chapter 6 presents the writings of nineteenth-century industrialists along with the writings of some of the poorest Americans: Carnegie and Rockefeller express opinions about wealth and its distribution, which are challenged by the experiences of the newest immigrants, described in their letters to the *Daily Forward* newspaper. Chapter 7 offers a variety of perspectives on the two world wars and the Depression, including a number of visual arguments, such as advertisements and propaganda posters from World War I and II. Chapter 8 explores the unrest in America during the 1950s, 1960s, and 1970s, and includes the writings of feminist leaders, government officials, student protesters, and civil rights leaders. Finally, Chapter 9 presents readings and political cartoons depicting current conflicts—from feminist concerns to racial and immigration issues to terrorism and issues raised by September 11.

A Note on Terminology

As you explore the various readings, discussion questions, and writing suggestions in this book, you will notice that the names of different ethnic groups change depending on the historical context of the piece and the particular author's terminology. Although currently the terms "Native Americans" and "American Indians" are used most often by Native Americans, many of the early authors used the term "Indians," so I have maintained the authors' terminology in those selections to maintain historical accuracy. When authors refer to African Americans as blacks, I have also used the term "blacks," and when authors from earlier decades describe "Hispanic" peoples, I have used the term "Hispanic" rather than "Latino." The issue of ethnic groups renaming themselves reflects the desire of these groups to move away from the labels given them by a dominant culture: These changes in terminology reflect the very conflicts in race, culture, and conflict that *Revisiting America* addresses.

Evaluating Sources

The readings in each chapter seek to illuminate the topics more fully, so that you can "read around" a subject and look at it from a number of different angles. As you begin to see how readings about major topics of conflict differ so vastly, you will want to research topics fully, using a wide range of sources to investigate the variety of materials that address an issue.

What Are Primary and Secondary Sources?

Revisiting America uses a number of primary and secondary sources, so it may be helpful to define more clearly how these sources differ. While scholars offer varying definitions of primary sources, in general, a primary source is an original document, letter, testimony, photo, map, or other piece of evidence that in and of itself is your text. A secondary source is usually crafted by the researcher from primary sources and other secondary sources. For example, the actual trial testimony of Tituba, a slave woman accused of witchcraft, is a primary source that you may study and about which you can draw your own conclusions (see Chapter 1). But David Levin's *What Happened in Salem?* is a secondary source, because Levin wrote a book—using letters, trial testimonies, and other primary sources—to answer the question he poses in the title of his book (see Chapter 1).

Primary and secondary sources used together can enlighten you in a way that is not possible with just one or the other. For example, a scholarly essay about the Salem Witch trials can give you historical information about what happened at the trials, but the testimony of Tituba can offer you a more immediate understanding of her experience. Her actual testimony allows you to see more clearly what she endured at the hands of her questioners and to study her own words and the strategy she used to elude capital punishment.

The combined use of primary and secondary sources also allows you to create a more interesting, complex essay or argument for your own readers. Say, for example, that you are writing a research paper about General Custer and his famous Last Stand. If you read Custer's journals and incorporate his words into your analysis of his decision to attack the Indians at Little Big Horn, your readers will get a much deeper sense of who Custer was and of how and why he made his decisions. The challenge facing you as a writer is to weave the primary and secondary sources together to offer solid evidence from the secondary sources and rich, interesting, and colorful materials from the primary sources. It may be difficult to prove a major assertion with primary sources only, but an essay or argument that lacks the immediacy of a primary source may lack concrete detail or human interest.

Before you read *Revisiting America*, you should visit the Web sites listed below, which are authored by the University of California at Berkeley and Yale University. Both of these Web sites offer a comprehensive description of primary and secondary sources, and they will also give you a good idea of the kinds of sources available on-line:

Yale University Library Primary Source Research
www.library.yale.edu/ref/err/primsrc.htm

UC Berkeley Library Research Using Primary Sources: Primary Sources on the Web
www.lib.berkeley.edu/TeachingLib/Guides/PrimarySources.html

Evaluating Internet Sources

While the Internet is an invaluable research aid, Internet users need to be wary about which sources they use and which facts they believe to be credible. A number of questions can help you evaluate whether or not your Internet source seems trustworthy. First, you need to look at the source itself—who is the author of the site, or which organization has sponsored the site? The Web site address will give you the first clue; you can tell a great deal about the origin of the site from its suffix:

.org indicates that the site belongs to a nonprofit organization.

.net indicates that the site belongs to a news or network organization.

.com indicates that the site is a commercial site.

.gov indicates that the site is a government site.

.edu indicates that the site belongs to an educational organization.

Once you have determined the origin of the site, it will be helpful to ask yourself the following questions about each Web site before you use any of the information you find on the Internet:

1. Who is the author? Is the author listed or identified? Why might this author be reliable? Might the author be biased? What are the author's qualifications?
2. When was the site last updated? (You can find this information by looking at the date at the bottom of the Web page.)
3. What kinds of information does the site present? What kinds of links does the site offer? Does the site explain the source of its information? Is the site supported by advertisers who might present biased information? Does the site offer facts and sources for its information, or does the material on the site seem unsupported?
4. What kinds of persuasive strategies does the site use? Does it use visual or musical components to draw you in? Does the music or artwork that accompanies the site add valid information or not?
5. What kind of language does the site use? Do the authors of the site use biased, overly strong terms, or does the language of the site reflect a more neutral tone? What can you learn from the tone and diction used in the site's written materials?

"Reading" Visual Sources

Revisiting America includes a number of visual images, including drawings, posters, and editorial cartoons. As you look at these images, take the time to look at all the details the artist has arranged. Look at the background, the foreground, the smallest details you can find, inch by inch, and then look again at the whole picture. Ask yourself what the artist was trying to convey and consider some of the questions at the top of page 5 as you look at the images.

1. Is the artist criticizing or praising the subject at hand?
2. Does the visual image contain implied arguments?
3. What small details give you clues to the meaning of the visual image?
4. Does the artist rely on humor to make an argument?
5. Is the image attempting to depict historically accurate events, or is the artist expressing his or her own emotions?
6. What assumptions is the artist making about his or her audience?
7. What can you learn about the world of the artist from the visual piece?
8. What emotions does the visual image draw from you?

　　To practice "reading" pictures carefully, let's look at the political cartoon (circa 1909) below, which criticizes the idea of women's suffrage, and then consider the questions at the top of page 6.

E. W. Gustin/Courtesy of the Library of Congress

1. How do you know that the woman shown in the center of the picture is a suffragette?
2. How do you know that the cartoonist is not sympathetic to women's suffrage?
3. How do the details of the woman's clothing affect the representation of her character?
4. How has the artist depicted the husband in the picture?
5. What does the cat feel about the woman going out the door on Election Day?
6. What small details can you find that make the picture of this family even more chaotic than it seems at first?
7. What does this cartoon imply about what life in America would be like if women were to be granted the right to vote?

Evaluating Arguments

A variety of written, visual, and oral arguments are included in *Revisiting America*, and as you read these arguments it will be important to maintain a critical stance and to examine different arguments with an eye toward their factual and emotional honesty.

Before you read an argument, consider the author's purpose and intended audience so that you can be aware of motives, biases, or even hidden agendas. For example, when you read Franklin Delano Roosevelt's "Pearl Harbor Address" (in Chapter 7), the speech will make more sense to you if you consider the context: the isolationist feelings of the American people before Pearl Harbor, and Roosevelt's task of convincing the public and the Congress that the time to declare war on Japan had arrived. And when Jefferson Davis states in his Inaugural Address (in Chapter 4) that the North has violated the South's constitutional rights and that therefore the South has every right to secede from the Union, you need to consider his arguments in light of the political and economic conflicts surrounding his inauguration as President of the new Confederate States.

Different sources are important for different reasons; just because a source may be biased does not mean that you cannot learn from it. Other sources may be more neutral, such as scholarly essays about subjects that do not seem to impact the life or fortunes of the author directly. However, even scholarly sources have many different biases, so it is important to read a number of different types of sources when you read about any one person or event. News media sources are notoriously inconsistent when reporting about identical events, as you can see in the media coverage of President Herbert Hoover's response to the Bonus Expeditionary Force, as covered by *Time Newsmagazine* and the *San Francisco Examiner* (in Chapter 7). The examples illustrate the need for students of history and of contemporary culture to be wary of taking any one account of an event as "the" truth.

A Look at Fallacies

When evaluating arguments, you may find it helpful to be familiar with some commonly used methods of persuasion that appear with surprising frequency in arguments from many different historical times. What are fallacies? Fallacies are dishonest patterns of persuasion, which seek to persuade not with fair, supported, unbiased facts, but rather with exaggerated appeals to emotion, faulty reasoning, or dishonesty. Some common fallacies include the following:

1. Non-Sequitur: The practice of drawing conclusions based on questionable facts or no facts at all describes the fallacy non-sequitur, which in Latin means "does not follow." For example, when Colonel Karl Bendetsen claimed that the Japanese Americans on the West Coast had to be interned in relocation camps, he gave as evidence the fact that they had *not* held celebrations for the Emperor's birthday and that there had been "no substantial evidence of manifestation of nationalistic fervor exhibited by any Japanese group in the United States since the outbreak of the war." From this data, he concluded that "this attitude may be and can be a most ominous thing." (See Chapter 7.) The fact that the Japanese in America had *not* held demonstrations of loyalty for the Japanese Emperor should not have led to the conclusion that their silence was ominous; however, Bendetsen used this reasoning to convince members of the Commonwealth Club of California that people of Japanese descent were so dangerous that they had to be interned in relocation camps immediately.

2. Appeal to the Bandwagon Instinct: A rhetorician using this method of persuasion tries to get popular backing for an idea by claiming that everyone else has supported and still does support the idea. For example, George Fitzhugh, responding to the Declaration of Independence, writes in *Sociology of the South* (in Chapter 4) in defense of the institution of slavery that "life and liberty have been sold in all countries, and in all ages, and must be sold so long as human nature exists." He argues that because slavery has existed before, it is part of human nature and must continue to exist forever.

3. Hasty Conclusion: The term *hasty conclusion* covers a number of different kinds of fallacies, all of which draw conclusions from insufficient evidence, false evidence, or no evidence at all. When President Jackson gave his address to Congress in 1835 about relocating the Indians (see Chapter 2), he stated that "It seems now to be an established fact that they can not live in contact with a civilized community and prosper." Here Jackson concluded that—despite the success of many tribes in the southern portion of the United States who had indeed prospered by adopting European ways in farming, education, and religion—the Indian could never live and prosper with "civilized" whites. By failing to give any proof for his conclusions, he was also guilty of using undocumented assertions. Another example of the use of undocumented assertions and insufficient evidence can be found in the 1941 *Time Magazine* article, "How to Tell your Friends from the Japs," (in Chapter 7), which offered "a few rules of thumb—not

always reliable" to tell the Chinese and the Japanese peoples apart. The piece claimed that "Japanese are hesitant, nervous in conversation, and laugh loudly at the wrong time," and that "Most Chinese avoid horn-rimmed spectacles." *Time Magazine* later apologized for the publication of this fallacy-riddled piece.

4. Either/Or: An either/or argument presents only two possibilities out of a broad range of choices. When President George W. Bush described his plans for war in Afghanistan, he stated that "Every nation, in every region, now has a decision to make. Either you are with us, or you are with the terrorists" (see Chapter 9). Many listeners felt that the lines of this argument were drawn too sharply, because Bush did not leave room for those who were not for the terrorists but who also were against bombing Afghanistan. Either/or arguments ignore any middle ground, and are thus dishonest in their form of persuasion.

5. *Ipse Dixit*: Translated from Latin, *ipse dixit* means "he said it himself," and as a fallacy refers to an appeal to authority that is weak or inappropriate. The appeal to authority can be a powerful argumentative strategy, but when the authority is not an appropriate person to offer evidence or support for the argument, this fallacy constitutes a weak type of evidentiary support. For example, in *My Life on the Plains* (in Chapter 3), when General George Custer criticizes others for their interpretations of the character of the Indians, he establishes himself as the authority best equipped to explain the true character of the Indian. Custer claims that the Indian is "so far as all knowledge goes, as he ever has been, a savage in every sense of the word . . . one whose cruel and ferocious nature far exceeds that of any wild beasts of the desert." General Custer here sets himself up as an authority on the Indian character, when in fact his limited contact with and limited knowledge about the range of Indian tribes and customs in the United States made him a poor authority on Indians.

6. Appeals to Emotion: While most good arguments do contain some appeals to our emotions, some arguments attempt to use appeals to emotions like fear, guilt, greed, prejudice, or hatred in dishonest ways to promote dishonest arguments. For example, when Senator James Blaine wanted to join the popular movement to exclude Chinese workers from the United States in 1879, he wrote that ". . . we have the right to exclude immigration which reeks with impurity and which cannot come to us without plenteously sowing the seeds of moral and physical disease, destitution, and death" (see Gyory, in Chapter 5). While the Chinese had originally been recruited and welcomed to work on the railroads, once they became economic competitors the arguments against the Chinese were based on emotion rather than on reason or evidence. Similarly, when Senator Joseph McCarthy gave his speech at Wheeling, West Virginia in 1950, he claimed that the State Department was "thoroughly infested with Communists," and that the United States was "engaged in a final, all-out battle between communistic atheism and Christianity." Lacking proof, McCarthy instead relied on fear of communism to persuade his listeners of the prevalence of "card-carrying Communists" in the State Department. Relying entirely on

emotional appeals, the arguments against Chinese workers and State Department employees were nevertheless effective and devastating for those who were excluded or accused.

As you examine the different essays, arguments, literary works, and visual images in *Revisiting America*, please do revisit America. This textbook is only a starting point for reading and writing about your own understanding of America, past and present.

Early Conflicts
on the Eastern Shore

The early period of the American colonization of the New World is a good moment in history to begin our study of the different genres of writing that address the topics of race, culture, gender, and conflict in American history. All of the readings in this chapter are important to the study of early conflicts in the New World, as explorers developed their own interpretations of the truth and of history, and as reality and interpretation often took sharply divergent paths. Part of the challenge of understanding American culture is to see these conflicts from as many angles as possible, and to try to develop an understanding of the importance of reading *around* an issue to see all sides. Studying both primary and secondary sources, letters and diaries, essays and fiction allows us, as readers and writers, to gain access to a much broader understanding of the conflicts that dominated this period of American history. As you read the different types of writing in this chapter and the chapters to follow, start to think about how your own writing and research will benefit from integrating more sources, different genres, different voices, and different points of view. Ask yourself as you read the following selections how the issues of race, gender, and conflict in the sixteenth century are related to similar issues today. Look for the connections between our past and our present, and try to begin to draw the arc that links us to those who have come before us.

For the early Jamestown settlers and the Puritans who followed them, the New World was a dangerous and difficult place, and early writings show how hard it was for these new settlers to survive without the aid of the native inhabitants. However, the myths and stories that have grown up around these early times are often based on fantasy; they are so much more complicated than they seem at first glance that these stories provide a rich field of study for critical reading and thinking and for accurate researching of historical topics. To begin an examination of racial conflicts in the early Puritan period, you can look at Ronald Takaki's "The 'Tempest' in the Wilderness," in which he discusses the fact that Europeans thought of New World inhabitants as savages. He explains that Shakespeare, writing for an audience who thought of New World inhabitants as little more than beasts, portrayed the New World savage in the character of Caliban in *The Tempest*. In this case, the genre of drama played an important role in reflecting and shaping the views of white Europeans toward the "savages" in the New World. You can ask yourself whether the cultural assumptions of this time have changed dramatically today or not—how do we perceive the peoples of "third world" countries, for example? Are we still guilty of "the racialization of savagery?"

Another important literary representation of race appears in the story of Pocahontas, a story that many American schoolchildren have read or seen on film, most recently with the release of Disney's 1995 film, *Pocahontas*. The standard myth of Pocahontas is that she saved John Smith's life and that she risked her own to do so. Pocahontas has been represented as the beautiful young Indian maiden who loved a white man so much she gave up her life and her family for him. The truth of the historical incident is vastly different from this myth, although we may never know exactly what happened. However, we can study the way in which this myth has manifested itself in our national consciousness. How has the history of the Pocahontas myth affected native peoples? How has the story affected the beliefs of generations of schoolchildren? How has the story contributed to racial stereotypes? Three of the readings in this chapter will expose you to the range of responses to the Pocahontas story today: Rayna Green's essay offers an entirely new perspective on the Pocahontas myth. Jacquelyn Kilpatrick's essay, which analyzes the Disney film *Pocahontas* and the role the film plays in the education of children, is followed by the Powhatan Nation's response to the film's historical inaccuracy. All of these sources give you, as a student of American literary culture, a chance to see how complicated the recording of one historical situation can become, and how writing, stories, language, and film can work together to distort or to clarify historical and contemporary issues.

Another very important historical event in Puritan New England—the trial and hanging of the Salem witches in 1692—illuminates conflicts between both gender and race: Tituba, a black slave girl, was blamed for the "outbreak" of witchcraft that victimized so many young girls and older women. Although a few men were convicted of being witches, most of the accused were women. Because New Englanders of the seventeenth century believed so strongly in the existence of the Devil, the trials did not try to prove that the Devil existed but simply that certain Salem townspeople were guilty of consorting with the Devil through witchcraft. Central to the accusations was the belief in "spectral evidence," a belief that held that the Devil could appear in the guise of a human being, thus disguised as a member of the community. The irony of the trials was that if an accused man or woman confessed to witchcraft, the accused was then considered to be reclaimed into the Christian community and therefore saved; those who confessed were not hanged. However, those innocent citizens who refused to confess to witchcraft were actually hung, or, in one case, pressed to death with large stones. The variety of readings in this chapter will provide several lenses through which to view the trials at Salem: These works of fiction and non-fiction allow you to explore the history of the victimization of blacks and women, issues that remain central to Americans today. The study of conflicts of race and culture in the witch trials begins with a scholarly introduction to the topic by David Levin, and then moves on to the primary source of the chilling trial testimony of Sarah Good. Elaine Breslaw analyzes the role of Tituba in the trials, and this selection includes the actual trial testimony of Tituba herself.

A look at early American conflicts of race and culture would not be complete without mentioning the American Revolution, one of the largest conflicts in the history of the New World. Thomas Jefferson's Declaration of Independence provides a wonderful starting point to discuss the principles of the founding fathers. The irony of these principles is clarified by Richard Hofstadter's description and history of slavery in the North, before, during, and after the Civil War. These texts give you some context in which to understand the early period of racial conflicts on the eastern shore. While slavery never became as deeply rooted in the North as it did in the South, slaves were originally brought into the United States through the northern sea ports, and many northerners owned slaves in the seventeenth and eighteenth centuries. The combination of primary and secondary sources here should help you begin to develop a critical ability to read documents with a sense not only of their historical importance, but also of the importance of the links between past conflicts and present issues. As you read this chapter, look for the continuity between the treatment of Native Americans, African Americans, and women in the earliest years of our nation and the ongoing struggles American society faces today.

Before You Read

1. Write a brief paragraph about your current impressions of the meeting between the pilgrims and the inhabitants of the New World. What can you remember about the relations between the two groups? Do you think of this early time as one of conflict or of cooperation?
2. Freewrite briefly about your beliefs and feelings about witchcraft. What are your associations with the witches of Salem? What are your associations about witchcraft in North America today?
3. Have you seen the Disney movie *Pocahontas*? Before reading the selections in this chapter, write down your impressions of the movie. Did you like or dislike it? Why or why not?

4. Make a list of the facts you believe to be true about slavery in the United States. Work in groups and see if you can answer some of the questions below:

    Where did slavery start in the United States?
    When did slavery end?
    How did the lives of indentured slaves and slaves brought from Africa differ?

5. Think about what the Declaration of Independence means to you as a citizen or as a resident of the United States of America. Even if you do not remember specific articles of the Declaration, jot down your memories of what you have learned about this important early document.

The "Tempest" in the Wilderness

The Racialization of Savagery

RONALD TAKAKI

Ronald Takaki, professor of ethnic studies at the University of California, Berkeley, is the author of numerous books, including *Strangers from a Different Shore*. In his book *A Different Mirror: A History of Multicultural America*, Ronald Takaki writes that he has chosen in this book to look closely at America's "racial and cultural diversity—Native Americans as well as peoples from different 'points of departure' such as England, Africa, Ireland, Mexico, Asia, and Russia." In this selection from *A Different Mirror*, Takaki examines how the early Puritan and English encounters with Indians set the stage for the "racialization of savagery." Takaki also explores Shakespeare's 1611 production of *The Tempest* as a "masquerade for the creation of a new society in America," and explains how some viewers saw the character of Caliban as the representative of the "savage" Indians encountered by early New Englanders.

In their first encounters with Europeans, the Indians tried to relate the strangers to what was familiar in their world. Traditional Penobscot accounts had described the earth as flat and surrounded by ocean, the "great salt water," *ktci-sobe-k*. Beyond this body of water, there were other islands and countries inhabited by "tribes of strangers." The Indians of Massachusetts Bay, according to early reports by the English, "took the first ship they saw for a walking island, the mast to be a tree, the sail white clouds, and the discharging of ordnance for lightning and thunder. . . ." They were seized by curiosity. By word of mouth, the fantastic news spread, and the "shores for many miles were filled with this naked Nation, gazing at this wonder." Armed with bows and arrows, some of them approached the ship in their canoes, and "let fly their long shafts at her . . . some stuck fast, and others dropped into the water." They wondered why "it did not cry." The native people were struck by the "ugliness" and "deformity" of the strangers—their "white" complexions, hair around their mouths, the eyes with "the color of the blue sky." They tried to identify the visitors. According to Roger Williams, the Indians in Rhode Island used the term *Manittoo*, meaning "god," to describe excellence in human beings and animals. When they saw the English arriving on their ships, they exclaimed: "*Mannittowock*. They are Gods."

Indian dreams had anticipated the coming of the strangers. In New England, an old Wampanoag story told about a wise chief foretelling the arrival of Europeans: "On his death-bed he said that a strange white people would come to crowd out the red men, and that for a sign, after his death a great white whale would rise out of the witch pond below. That night he died . . . and the great white whale rose from the witch pond." Another version of this story recounted how the old man was describing his approaching death when suddenly "a white whale arose from the water off Witch Pond." The chief said: "That's a sign that another new people the color of the whale [would arrive], but don't let them have all the land because if you do the Indians will disappear." In Virginia, a Powhatan shaman predicted that "bearded men should come take away their Country & that there should be none of the original Indians be left, within an hundred & fifty years." Similarly, an Ojibwa prophet had a dream many years before actual contact between the two peoples: "Men of strange appearance have come across the great water. Their skins are white like snow, and on their faces long hair grows. [They came here] in wonderfully large canoes which have great white wings like those of a giant bird. The men have long and sharp knives, and they have long black tubes which they point at birds and animals. The tubes make a smoke that rises into the air just like the smoke from our pipes. From them come fire and such terrific noise that I was frightened, even in my dream."

Shakespeare's Dream about America

"O brave new world that has such people in't!" they heard Miranda exclaim. The theatergoers were attending the first performance of William Shakespeare's *Tempest*. This play was first presented in London in 1611, a time when the English were encountering what they viewed as strange inhabitants in new lands. The circumstances surrounding the play determined the meaning of the utterances they heard. A perspicacious few in the audience could have seen that this play was more than a mere story about how Prospero was sent into exile with his daughter, took possession of an island inhabited by Caliban, and redeemed himself by marrying Miranda to the king's son.

Indeed, *The Tempest* can be approached as a fascinating tale that served as a masquerade for the creation of a new society in America. Seen in this light, the play invites us to view English expansion not only as imperialism, but also as a defining moment in the making of an English-American identity based on race. For the first time in the English theater, an Indian character was being presented. What did Shakespeare and his audience know about the native peoples of America, and what choices were they making in the ways they characterized Caliban? Although they saw him as "savage," did they racialize savagery? Was the play a prologue for America?

The Tempest, studied in relationship to its historical context, can help us answer these questions. While *Othello* also offers us an opportunity to analyze English racial attitudes, as Winthrop Jordan has demonstrated so brilliantly, our play is a more important window for understanding American history, for its story is set in the New World. Moreover, the timing of *The Tempest* was crucial: it was first performed after the English invasion of Ireland but before the colonization of New England, after John Smith's arrival in Virginia but before the beginning of the tobacco economy, and after the first contacts with Indians but before full-scale warfare against them. This was an era when the English were encountering "other" peoples and delineating the boundary between "civilization" and "savagery." The social constructions of both these terms were dynamically developing in three sites—Ireland, Virginia, and New England.

One of the places the English were colonizing at the time was Ireland, and Caliban seemed to resemble the Irish. Theatergoers were familiar with the "wild Irish" onstage, for such images had been presented in plays like *Sir John Oldcastle* (1599) and *Honest Whore* (1605). Seeking to conquer the Irish in 1395, Richard II had condemned them as "savage Irish, our enemies." In the mid-sixteenth century, shortly before the beginning of the English migrations to America, the government had decided to bring all of Ireland under its rule and encouraged private colonization projects.

Like Caliban, the Irish were viewed as "savages," a people living outside of "civilization." They had tribal organizations, and their practice of herding seemed nomadic. Even their Christianity was said to be merely the exterior of strongly rooted paganism. "They are all Papists by their profession," claimed Edmund Spenser in 1596, "but in the same so blindly and brutishly informed for the most part as that you would rather think them atheists or infidels." To the colonists, the Irish lacked "knowledge of God or good manners." They had no sense of private property and did not "plant any Gardens or Orchards, Inclose or improve their lands, live together in settled Villages or Townes." The Irish were described as lazy, "naturally" given to "idleness" and unwilling to work for "their own bread." Dominated by "innate sloth," "loose, barbarous and most wicked," and living "like beasts," they were also thought to be criminals, an underclass inclined to steal from the English. The colonists complained that the Irish savages were not satisfied with the "fruit of the natural unlaboured earth" and therefore continually "invaded the fertile possessions" of the "English Pale."

The English colonizers established a two-tiered social structure: "Every Irishman shall be forbidden to wear English apparel or weapon upon pain of death. That no Irishman, born of Irish race and brought up Irish, shall purchase land, bear office, be chosen of any jury or admitted witness in any real or personal action." To reinforce this social separation, British laws prohibited marriages between the Irish and the colonizers. The new world order was to be one of English over Irish.

The Irish also became targets of English violence. "Nothing but fear and force can teach duty and obedience" to this "rebellious people," the invaders insisted. While the English were generally brutal in their warfare practices at that time, they seemed to have been particularly cruel toward the Irish. The colonizers burned the villages and crops of the inhabitants and relocated them on reservations. They slaughtered families, "man, woman and child," justifying their atrocities by arguing that families provided support for the rebels. After four years of bloody warfare in Munster, according to Edmund Spenser, the Irish had been reduced to wretchedness. "Out of every corner of the woods and glens they came creeping forth upon their hands, for their legs would not bear them. They looked anatomies of death; they spake like ghosts crying out of their graves." The death toll was so high that "in short space there were none almost left and a most populous and plentiful country suddenly left void of man and beast." The "void" meant vacant lands for English resettlement.

The invaders took the heads of the slain Irish as trophies. Sir Humphrey Gilbert pursued a campaign of terror: he ordered that "the heads of all those . . . killed in the day, should be cut off from their bodies and brought to the place where he encamped at night, and should there be laid on the ground by each side of the way leading into his own tent so that none could come into his tent for any cause but commonly he must pass a lane of heads. . . . [It brought] great terror to the people when they saw the heads of their dead fathers, brothers, children, kinsfolk, and friends. . . ." After seeing the head of his lord impaled on the walls of Dublin, Irish poet Angus O'Daly cried out:

> *O body which I see without a head,*
> *It is the sight of thee which has withered up my strength.*
> *Divided and impaled in Ath-cliath,*
> *The learned of Banba will feel its loss.*
> *Who will relieve the wants of the poor?*
> *Who will bestow cattle on the learned?*
> *O body, since thou art without a head,*
> *It is not life which we care to choose after thee.*

The English claimed that they had a God-given responsibility to "inhabit and reform so barbarous a nation" and to educate the Irish "brutes." They would teach them to obey English laws and stop "robbing and stealing and killing" one another. They would uplift this "most filthy people, utterly enveloped in vices, most untutored of all peoples in the rudiments of faith." Thus, although they saw the Irish as savages and although they sometimes described this savagery as "natural" and "innate," the English believed that the Irish could be civilized, improved through what Shakespeare called "nurture." In short, the difference between the Irish and the English was a matter of culture.

As their frontier advanced from Ireland to America, the English began making comparisons between the Irish and Indian "savages" and wondering whether there might be different kinds of "savagery."

The parallels between English expansionism in Ireland and America were apparent. Sir Humphrey Gilbert, Lord De La Warr, Sir Francis Drake, and Sir Walter Raleigh participated in both the invasion of Ireland and the colonization of the New World. The conquest of Ireland and the settlement of Virginia were bound so closely together that one correspondence, dated March 8, 1610, stated: "It is hoped the plantation of Ireland may shortly be settled. The Lord Delaware [Lord De La Warr] is preparing to depart for the plantation of Virginia." Commander John Mason conducted military campaigns against the Irish before he sailed to New England, where he led troops against the Pequots of Connecticut. Samuel Gorton wrote a letter to John Winthrop, Jr., connecting the two frontiers: "I remember the time of the wars in Ireland (when I was young, in Queen Elizabeth's days of famous memory) where much English blood was spilt by a people much like unto these [Indians]. . . . And after these Irish were subdued by force, what treacherous and bloody massacres have they attempted is well known."

The first English colonizers in the New World found that the Indians reminded them of the Irish. In Virginia, Captain John Smith observed that the deerskin robes worn by the Indians did not differ much "in fashion from the Irish mantels." Thomas Morton noticed that the "Natives of New England [were] accustomed to build themselves houses much like the wild Irish." Roger Williams reported that the thick woods and swamps of New England gave refuge to the Indians engaged in warfare, "like the bogs to the wild Irish." Thus, in their early encounters, the English projected the familiar onto the strange, their images of the Irish onto the native people of America. Initially, "savagery" was defined in relationship to the Irish, and the Indians were incorporated into this definition.

The Tempest, the London audience knew, was not about Ireland but about the New World, for the reference to the "Bermoothes" (Bermuda) revealed the location of the island. What was happening onstage was a metaphor for English expansion into America. The play's title was inspired by a recent incident: caught in a violent storm in 1609, the *Sea Adventure* had been separated from a fleet of ships bound for Virginia and had run aground in the Bermudas. Shakespeare knew many of the colonizers, including Sir Humphrey Gilbert and Lord De La Warr. One of his personal friends was geographer Richard Hakluyt, author of widely read books about the New World. The future of Englishmen lay in America, proclaimed Hakluyt, as he urged them to "conquer a country" and "to man it, to plant it, and to keep it, and to continue the making of Wines and Oils able to serve England."

The scene of the play was actually the mainland near the "Bermoothes"—Virginia. "The air breathes upon us here most sweetly," the theatergoers were told. "Here is everything advantageous to life." "How lush and lusty the grass looks! how green!" Impressed by the land's innocence, Gonzalo of *The Tempest* depicted it as an ideal commonwealth where everything was as yet unformed and unbounded, where letters, laws, metals, and occupations were yet unknown. Both the imagery and the language revealed America as the site of Prospero's landing: it was almost as if Shakespeare had lifted the material from contemporary documents about the New World. Tracts on Virginia had described the air as "most sweet" and as "virgin and temperate," and its soil *"lusty"* with meadows "full of *green grass.*" In *A True Repertory of the Wracke*, published in 1609, William Strachey depicted Virginia's abundance: "no Country yieldeth goodlier *Corn*, nor more manifold increase. . . . [W]e have thousands of goodly *Vines*." Here was an opportunity for colonists to enhance the "fertility and pleasure" of Virginia by "cleansing away her woods" and converting her into "goodly meadow."

Moreover, the play provided a clever clue that the story was indeed about America: Caliban, one of the principal characters, was a New World inhabitant. "Carib," the name of an Indian tribe, came to mean a savage of America, and the term *cannibal* was a derivative. Shakespeare sometimes rearranged letters in words ("Amleth," the name of a prince in a Viking era tale, for example, became "Hamlet"), and here he had created another anagram in "Caliban."

The English had seen or read reports about Indians who had been captured and brought to London. Indians had been displayed in Europe by Christopher Columbus. During his first voyage, he wrote: "Yesterday came [to] the ship a dugout with six young men, and five came on board; these I ordered to be detained and I am bringing them." When Columbus was received by the Spanish court after his triumphal return, he presented a collection of things he had brought back, including some gold nuggets, parrots in cages, and six Indians. During his second voyage in 1493, Columbus again sent his men to kidnap Indians. On one occasion, a captive had been "wounded seven times and his entrails were hanging out," reported Guillermo Coma of Aragon. "Since it was thought that he could not be cured, he was cast into the sea. But keeping above water and raising one foot, he held on to his intestines with his left hand and swam courageously to the shore. . . . The wounded Carib was caught again on shore. His hands and feet were bound more tightly and he was once again thrown headlong. But this resolute savage swam more furiously, until he was struck several times by arrows and perished." When Columbus set sail with his fleet to return to Spain, he took 550 Indian captives. "When we reached the waters around Spain," Michele de Cuneo wrote matter-of-factly, "about 200 of those Indians died, I believe because of the unaccustomed air, colder than theirs. We cast them into the sea."

Similarly, English explorers engaged in this practice of kidnapping Indians. When Captain George Waymouth visited New England in 1605, he lured some Abenakis to his ship; taking three of them hostage, he sailed back to England to display them. An early seventeenth-century pamphlet stated that a voyage to Virginia was expected to bring back its quota of captured Indians: "Thus we shipped five savages, two canoes, with all their bows and arrows." In 1614, the men on one of Captain John Smith's ships captured several Indians on Cape Cod. "Thomas Hunt," Smith wrote, ". . . betrayed four and twenty of these poor savages aboard this ship, and most dishonestly and inhumanely . . . carried them with him to Maligo [Málaga] and there for a little private gain sold. . . those savages for Rials of eight." In 1611, according to a biographer of William Shakespeare, "a native of New England called Epnew was brought to England . . . and 'being a man of so great a stature' was showed up and down London for money as a monster." In the play, Stephano considered capturing Caliban: "If I can recover him, and keep him tame, and get to Naples with him, he's a present for any emperor. . . ." Such exhibitions of Indians were "profitable investments," literary scholar Frank Kermode noted, and were "a regular feature of colonial policy under James I. The exhibits rarely survived the experience."

To the spectators of these "exhibits," Indians personified "savagery." They were depicted as "cruel, barbarous and most treacherous." They were thought to be cannibals, "being most furious in their rage and merciless . . . not being content only to kill and take away life, but delight to torment men in the most bloody manner . . . flaying some alive with the shells of fishes, cutting off the members and joints of others by piecemeal and broiling on the coals, eating the collops of their flesh in their sight whilst they live." According to Sir Walter Raleigh, Indians had "their eyes in their shoulders, and their mouths in the middle of their breasts." In *Nova Brittania*, published in 1609, Richard Johnson described the Indians in Virginia as "wild and savage people," living "like herds of deer in a forest." One of their striking physical characteristics was their skin color. John Brereton described the New England Indians as "of tall stature, broad and grim visage, of a blacke swart complexion."

Indians seemed to lack everything the English identified as civilized—Christianity, cities, letters, clothing, and swords. "They do not bear arms or know them, for I showed to them swords and they took them by the blade and cut themselves through ignorance," wrote Columbus in his journal, noting that the Indians did not have iron. George Waymouth tried to impress the Abenakis: he magnetized a sword "to cause them to imagine some great power in us; and for that to love and fear us."

Like Caliban, the native people of America were viewed as the "other." European culture was delineating the border, the hierarchical division between civilization and wildness. Unlike Europeans, Indians were allegedly dominated by their passions, especially their sexuality. Amerigo Vespucci was struck by how the natives embraced and enjoyed the pleasures of their bodies: "They . . . are libidinous beyond measure, and the women far more than the men. . . . When they had the opportunity of copulating with Christians, urged by excessive lust, they defiled and prostituted themselves." Caliban personified such passions. Prospero saw him as a sexual threat to the nubile Miranda, her "virgin-knot" yet untied. "I have used thee (filth as thou art) with humane care," Prospero scolded Caliban, "and lodged thee in mine own cell till thou didst seek to violate the honor of my child." And the unruly native snapped: "O ho, O ho! Would't had been done! Thou didst prevent me; I had peopled else this isle with Calibans."

To the theatergoers, Caliban represented what Europeans had been when they were lower on the scale of development. To be civilized, they believed, required denial of wholeness—the repression of the instinctual forces of human nature. A personification of civilized man, Prospero identified himself as mind rather than body. His epistemology was reliant on the visual rather than the tactile and on the linear knowledge of books rather than the polymorphous knowledge of experience. With the self fragmented, Prospero was able to split off his rationality and raise it to authority over the "other"— the sensuous part of himself and everything Caliban represented.

But could Caliban, the audience wondered, ever become Christian and civilized? The Spanish lawyer Juan Gines de Sepulveda had justified the Spanish conquest of Indians by invoking Aristotle's doctrine that some people were "natural slaves." The condition of slavery, Sepulveda argued, was natural for "persons of both inborn rudeness and of inhuman and barbarous customs." Thus what counted was an ascriptive quality based on a group's nature, or "descent."

On the other hand, Pope Paul III had proclaimed that Indians, as well as "all other people" who might later be "discovered" by "Christians," should not be deprived of their liberty and property, even though they were outside the Christian faith. Christopher Columbus had reported that Indians were "very gentle and without knowledge of . . . evil." He added: "They love their neighbors as themselves, and have the sweetest talk in the world, and gentle, and always with a smile." In *The Tempest*, Gonzalo told theatergoers: "I saw such islanders . . . who, though they are of monstrous shape, yet, note, their manners are more gentle, kind, than of our human generation you shall find many—nay, almost any." Thus, Indians were not always viewed as brutish by nature: they could be acculturated, become civilized through "consent."

Indeed, Caliban seemed educable. Prospero had taught him a European language: "I . . . took pains to make thee speak, taught thee each hour one thing or other. When thou didst not, savage, know thine own meaning, but wouldst gabble like a thing most brutish." Defiantly, the native retorted: "You taught me language, and my profit on't is, I know how to curse. The red plague rid you for learning me your language." Clearly, Caliban was no mere victim: capable of acculturation, he could express his anger. A Virginia tract stated that the colonists should take Indian children and "train them up with gentleness, teach them our English tongue." In the contract establishing the Virginia Company in 1606, the king endorsed a plan to propagate the "Christian Religion to such people" who as yet lived in "darkness and miserable ignorance of the true knowledge and worship of God." Three years later, the Virginia Company instructed the colony's governor to encourage missionaries to convert Indian children. They should be taken from their parents if necessary, since they were "so wrapped up in the fog and misery of their iniquity." A Virginia promotional tract stated that it was "not the nature of men, but the education of men" that made them "barbarous and uncivil." Every man in the new colony had a duty to bring the savage Indians to "civil and Christian" government.

All of these cultural constructs of Indians at this point in time were either the fantasy of Shakespeare or the impressions of policymakers and tract writers in London. What would happen to these images on the stage of history?

The first English settlement in the New World was in Virginia, the home of fourteen thousand Powhatans. An agricultural people, they cultivated corn—the mainstay of their subsistence. Their cleared fields were as large as one hundred acres, and they lived in palisaded towns, with forts, storehouses, temples, and framed houses covered with bark and reed mats. They cooked their food in ceramic pots and used woven baskets for storing corn: some of their baskets were constructed so skillfully they could carry water in them. The Powhatans had a sophisticated numbering system for evaluating their harvests. According to John Smith, they had numbers from one to ten, after which counting was done by tens to one hundred. There was also a word for "one thousand." The Powhatan calendar had five seasons: "Their winter some call *Popanow*, the spring *Cattaapeuk*, the sommer *Cohattayough*, the earing of their Corne *Nepinough*, the harvest and fall of the leafe *Taquitock*. From September until the midst of November are the chief Feasts and sacrifice."

In Virginia, the initial encounters between the English and the Indians opened possibilities for friendship and interdependency. After arriving in 1607, the first one hundred and twenty colonists set up camp. Then, John Smith reported, came "the starving time." A year later, only thirty-eight of them were still alive, hanging precariously on the very edge of survival. The reality of America did not match the imagery of the New World as a garden; the descriptions of its natural abundance turned out to be exaggerated. Many of the English were not prepared for survival in the wilderness. "Now was all our provision spent . . . all help abandoned, each hour expecting the fury of the savages," Smith wrote. Fortunately, in that "desperate extremity," the Powhatans brought food and rescued the starving strangers.

A year later, several hundred more colonists arrived, and again they quickly ran out of provisions. They were forced to eat "dogs, cats, rats, and mice," even "corpses" dug from graves. "Some have licked up the blood which hath fallen from their weak fellows," a survivor reported. "One [member] of our colony murdered his wife, ripped the child out of her womb and threw it into the river, and after chopped the mother in pieces and salted her for his food, the same not being discovered before he had eaten part thereof." "So great was our famine," John Smith stated, "that a savage we slew and buried, the poorer sort took him up again and ate him; and so did diverse one another boiled and stewed with roots and herbs."

Hostilities soon broke out as the English tried to extort food supplies by attacking the Indians and destroying their villages. In 1608, an Indian declared: "*We hear you are come from under the World to take our World from us.*" A year later Governor Thomas Gates arrived in Virginia with instructions that the Indians should be forced to labor for the colonists and also make annual payments of corn and skins. The orders were brutally carried out. During one of the raids, the English soldiers attacked an Indian town, killing fifteen people and forcing many others to flee. Then they burned the houses and destroyed the cornfields. According to a report by commander George Percy, they marched the captured queen and her children to the river where they "put the Children to death . . . by throwing them overboard and shooting out their brains in the water."

Indians began to doubt that the two peoples could live together in peace. One young Indian told Captain John Smith: "[We] are here to intreat and desire your friendship and to enjoy our houses and plant our fields, of whose fruits you shall participate." But he did not trust the strangers: "We perceive and well know you intend to destroy us." Chief Powhatan had come to the same conclusion, and he told Smith that the English were not in Virginia to trade but to "invade" and "possess" Indian lands.

Indeed, Smith and his fellow colonists were encouraged by their culture of expansionism to claim entitlement to the land. In *The Tempest*, the theatergoers were told: "I think he will carry this island home in his pocket and give it his son for an apple." Prospero declared that he had been thrust forth from Milan and "most strangely" landed on this shore "to be the lord on't." Projecting his personal plans and dreams onto the wilderness, he colonized the island and dispossessed Caliban. Feeling robbed, Caliban protested: "As I told thee before, I am subject to a tyrant, a sorcerer, that by his cunning hath cheated me of the island." But the English did not see their taking of land as robbery. In *Utopia*, Sir Thomas More justified the appropriation of Indian lands: since the natives did not "use" the soil but left it "idle and waste," the English had "just cause" to drive them from the territory by force. In 1609, Robert Gray declared that "the greater part" of the earth was "possessed and wrongfully usurped by wild beasts . . . or by brutish savages." A Virginia pamphlet argued that it was "not unlawful" for the English to possess "part" of the Indians' land.

But the English soon wanted more than just a "part" of Indian territory. Their need for land was suddenly intensified by a new development—the cultivation of tobacco as an export crop. In 1613, the colony sent its first shipment of tobacco to London, a small but significant four barrels' worth. The exports grew dramatically from 2,300 pounds in 1616 to 19,000 the following year, and to 60,000 by 1620. The colonists increasingly coveted Indian lands, especially the already cleared fields. Tobacco agriculture stimulated not only territorial expansion but also immigration. During the "Great Migration" of 1618–1623, the colony grew from four hundred to forty-five hundred people.

In 1622, the natives tried to drive out the intruders, killing some three hundred colonists. John Smith denounced the "massacre" and described the "savages" as "cruel beasts," who possessed "a more unnatural brutishness" than wild animals. The English deaths, Samuel Purchas argued, established the colonists' right to the land: "Their carcasses, the dispersed bones of their countrymen . . . speak, proclaim and cry, This our earth is truly English, and therefore this Land is justly yours O English." Their blood had watered the soil, entitling them to the land. "We, who hitherto have had possession of no more ground than their [Indian] waste, and our purchase . . . may now by right of War, and law of Nations," the colonists declared, "invade the Country, and destroy them who sought to destroy us." They felt they could morally sweep away their enemies and even take their developed lands. "*We shall enjoy their cultivated places. . . . Now their cleared grounds in all their villages (which are situated in the fruitfulest places of the land) shall be inhabited by us.*"

In their fierce counterattack, the English waged total war. "Victory may be gained in many ways," a colonist declared: "by force, by surprise, by famine in burning their Corn, by destroying and burning their Boats, Canoes, and Houses . . . by pursuing and chasing them with our horses, and blood-hounds to draw after them, and mastives to tear them." In 1623, Captain William Tucker led his soldiers to a Powhatan village, presumably to negotiate a peace treaty. After he concluded the treaty, he persuaded the Indians to drink a toast, but he served them poisoned wine. An estimated two hundred Indians died instantly, and Tucker's soldiers then killed another fifty and "brought home part of their heads." In 1629, a colonist reported, the English forced a hostile Indian leader to seek peace by "continual incursions" and by "yearly cutting down, and spoiling their corn." The goal of the war was to "root out [the Indians] from being any longer a people."

What happened in Virginia, while terrible and brutal, was still based largely on the view that Indian "savagery" was cultural. Like the Irish, Indians were identified as brutal and backward, but they were not yet seen as incapable of becoming civilized because of their race, or "descent." Their heathenism had not yet been indelibly attached to distinctive physical characteristics such as their skin color. So far at least, "consent" was possible for Indians. What occurred in New England was a different story, however, and here again, the play was preview.

Although the theatergoers were given the impression that Caliban could be acculturated, they also received a diametrically opposite construction of his racial character. They were told that Caliban was "a devil, a born devil" and that he belonged to a "vile race." "Descent was determinative: his "race" signified an inherent moral defect. On the stage, they saw Caliban, with long shaggy hair, personifying the Indian. He had distinct racial markers. "Freckled," covered with brown spots, he was "not honored with human shape." Called a "fish," he was mockingly told: "Thy eyes are almost set in thy head." "Where should they be set else? He were a brave monster indeed if they were set in his tail." More important, his distinctive physical characteristics signified intellectual incapacity. Caliban was "a thing of darkness" whose "nature nurture [could] never stick." In other words, he had natural qualities that precluded the possibility of becoming civilized through "nurture," or education. The racial distance between Caliban and Prospero was inscribed geographically. The native was forced to live on a reservation located in a barren region. "Here you sty [to lodge, to place in a pig pen or sty] me in this hard rock," he complained, "whiles you do keep from me the rest o' the island." Prospero justified this segregation, charging that the "savage" possessed distasteful qualities, "which good natures could not abide to be with. Therefore wast thou deservedly confined into this rock, who hadst deserved more than a prison." The theatergoers saw Caliban's "sty" located emblematically at the back of the stage, behind Prospero's "study," signifying a hierarchy of white over dark and cerebral over carnal.

This deterministic view of Caliban's racial character would be forged in the crucible of New England. Five years after the first performance of *The Tempest*, Captain John Smith sailed north from Virginia to explore the New England coast, where again he found not wild men but farmers. The "paradise" of Massachusetts, he reported, was "all planted with corn, groves, mulberries, savage gardens." "The sea Coast as you pass shews you all along large Corne fields." Indeed, while the Abenakis of Maine were mainly hunters and food gatherers dependent on the natural abundance of the land, the tribes in southern New England were horticultural. For example, the Wampanoags, whom the Pilgrims encountered in 1620, were a farming people, with a representative political system as well as a division of labor, with workers specializing in arrowmaking, woodwork, and leathercrafts.

The Wampanoags as well as the Pequots, Massachusetts, Nausets, Nipmucks, and Narragansets cultivated corn. As the main source of life for these tribes, corn was the focus of many legends. A Narraganset belief told how a crow had brought this grain to New England: "These Birds, although they do the corn also some hurt, yet scarce one *Native* amongst a hundred will kill them, because they have a tradition, that the Crow brought them at first an *Indian* Grain of Corn in one Ear, and an *Indian* or French bean in another, from the Great God *Kautantouwits* field in the Southwest from whence . . . came all their Corn and Beans." A Penobscot account celebrated the gift of Corn Mother: during a time of famine, an Indian woman fell in love with a snake in the forest. Her secret was discovered one day by her husband, and she told him that she had been chosen to save the tribe. She instructed him to kill her with a stone ax and then drag her body through a clearing. "After seven days he went to the clearing and found the corn plant rising above the ground. . . . When the corn had born fruit and the silk of the corn ear had turned yellow he recognized in it the resemblance of his dead wife. Thus originated the cultivation of corn."

These Indians had a highly developed agricultural system. Samuel de Champlain found that "all along the shore" there was "a great deal of land cleared up and planted with Indian corn." Describing their agricultural practices, he wrote: "They put in each hill three or four Brazilian beans [kidney beans]. . . . When they grow up, they interlace with the corn . . . and they keep the ground very free from weeds. We saw there many squashes, and pumpkins, and tobacco, which they likewise cultivate." According to Thomas Morton, Indians "dung[ed] their ground" with fish to fertilize the soil and increase the harvest. After visiting the Narragansets in Rhode Island, John Winthrop, Jr., noted that although the soil in that region was "sandy & rocky," the people were able to raise "good corn without fish" by rotating their crops. "They have every one 2 fields," he observed, "which after the first 2 years they let one field rest each year, & that keeps their ground continually [productive]." According to Roger Williams, when the Indians were ready to harvest the corn, "all the neighbours men and women, forty, fifty, a hundred," joined in the work and came "to help freely." During their green corn festival, the Narragansets erected a long house, "sometimes a hundred, sometimes two hundred feet long upon a plain near the Court . . . where many thousands, men and women," gathered. Inside, dancers gave money, coats, and knives to the poor. After the harvest, the Indians stored their corn for the winter. "In the sand on the slope of hills," according to Champlain, "they dig holes, some five or six feet, more or less, and place their corn and other grains in large grass sacks, which they throw into the said holes, and cover them with sand to a depth of three or four feet above the surface of the ground. They take away their grain according to their need, and it is preserved as well as it be in our granaries." Contrary to the stereotype of Indians as hunters and therefore savages, these Indians were farmers.

However, many colonists in New England disregarded this reality and invented their own representations of Indians. What emerged to justify dispossessing them was the racialization of Indian "savagery." Indian heathenism and alleged laziness came to be viewed as inborn group traits that rendered them naturally incapable of civilization. This process of Indian dehumanization developed a peculiarly New England dimension as the colonists associated Indians with the Devil. Indian identity became a matter of "descent": their racial markers indicated inerasable qualities of savagery.

This social construction of race occurred within the economic context of competition over land. The colonists argued that entitlement to land required its utilization. Native men, they claimed, pursued "no kind of labour but hunting, fishing and fowling." Indians were not producers. "The *Indians* are not able to make use of the one fourth part of the Land," argued Reverend Francis Higginson in 1630, "neither have they any settled places, as Towns to dwell in, nor any ground as they challenge for their owne possession, but change their habitation from place to place." In the Puritan view, Indians were lazy. "Fettered in the chains of idleness," they would rather starve than work, William Wood of Boston complained in 1634. Indians were sinfully squandering America's resources. Under their irresponsible guardianship, the land had become "all spoils, rots," and was "marred for want of manuring, gathering, ordering, etc." Like the "foxes and wild beasts," Indians did nothing "but run over the grass."

The Puritan possession of Indian lands was facilitated by the invasion of unseen pathogens. When the colonists began arriving in New England, they found that the Indian population was already being reduced by European diseases. Two significant events had occurred in the early seventeenth century: infected rats swam to shore from Samuel de Champlain's ships, and some sick French sailors were shipwrecked on the beaches of New England. By 1616, epidemics were ravaging Indian villages. Victims of "virgin soil epidemics," the Indians lacked immunological defenses against the newly introduced diseases. Between 1610 and 1675, the Indian population declined sharply—from 12,000 to a mere 3,000 for the Abenakis and from 65,000 to 10,000 for the southern New England tribes.

Describing the sweep of deadly diseases among the Indians, William Bradford reported that the Indians living near the trading house outside of Plymouth "fell sick of the smallpox, and died most miserably." The condition of those still alive was "lamentable." Their bodies were covered with "the pox breaking and mattering and running one into another, their skin cleaving" to the mats beneath them. When they turned their bodies, they found "whole sides" of their skin flaying off. In this terrible way, they died "like rotten sheep." After one epidemic, William Bradford recorded in his diary: "For it pleased God to visit these Indians with a great sickness and such a mortality that of a thousand, above nine and a half hundred of them died, and many of them did rot above ground for want of burial."

The colonists interpreted these Indian deaths as divinely sanctioned opportunities to take the land. John Winthrop declared that the decimation of Indians by smallpox manifested a Puritan destiny: God was "making room" for the colonists and "hath hereby cleared our title to this place." After an epidemic had swept through Indian villages, John Cotton claimed that the destruction was a sign from God: when the Lord decided to transplant His people, He made the country vacant for them to settle. Edward Johnson pointed out that epidemics had desolated "those places, where the English afterward planted."

Indeed, many New England towns were founded on the very lands the Indians had been living on before the epidemics. The Plymouth colony itself was located on the site of the Wampanoag village of Pawtuxet. The Pilgrims had noticed the village was empty and the cornfields overgrown with weeds. "There is a great deal of Land cleared," one of them reported, "and hath beene planted with Corne three or foure yeares agoe." The original inhabitants had been decimated by the epidemic of 1616. "Thousands of men have lived there, which died in a great plague not long since," another Pilgrim wrote; "and pity it was and is to see so many goodly fields, and so well seated, without men to dress and manure the same." During their first spring, the Pilgrims went out into those fields to weed and manure them. Fortunately, they had some corn seed to plant. Earlier, when they landed on Cape Cod, they had come across some Indian graves and found caches of corn. They considered this find, wrote Bradford, as "a special providence of God, and a great mercy to this poor people, that here they got seed to plant them corn the next year, or else they might have starved." The survival of these pallid strangers was so precarious that they probably would have perished had it not been for the seeds they found stored in the Indian burial grounds. Ironically, Indian death came to mean life for the Pilgrims.

However, the Puritans did not see it as irony but as the destruction of devils. They had demonized the native peoples, condemning Indian religious beliefs as "diabolical, and so uncouth, as if . . . framed and devised by the devil himself." The Wampanoags of Martha's Vineyard, wrote Reverend Thomas Mayhew in 1652, were "mighty zealous and earnest in the Worship of False gods and Devils." They were under the influence of "a multitude of Heathen Traditions of their gods . . . and abounding with sins."

To the colonists, the Indians were not merely a wayward people: they personified something fearful within Puritan society itself. Like Caliban, a "born devil," Indians failed to control their appetites, to create boundaries separating mind from body. They represented what English men and women in America thought they were not—and, more important, what they must not become. As exiles living in the wilderness far from "civilization," the English used their negative images of Indians to delineate the moral requirements they had set up for themselves. As sociologist Kai Erikson explained, "deviant forms of behavior, by marking the outer edges of group life, give the inner structure its special character and thus supply the framework within which the people of the group develop an orderly sense of their own cultural identity. . . . One of the surest ways to confirm an identity, for communities as well as for individuals, is to find some way of measuring what one is *not*." By depicting Indians as demonic and savage, the colonists, like Prospero, were able to define more precisely what they perceived as the danger of becoming Calibanized.

The Indians presented a frightening threat to the Puritan errand in America. "The wilderness through which we are passing to the Promised Land is all over fill'd with fiery flying serpents," warned Reverend Cotton Mather. "Our Indian wars are not over yet." The wars were now within Puritan society and the self: the dangers were internal. Self-vigilance against sin was required, or else the English would become like Indians. "We have too far degenerated into Indian vices. The vices of the Indians are these: They are very lying wretches, and they are very lazy wretches; and they are out of measure indulgent unto their children; there is no family government among them. We have [become] shamefully Indianized in all those abominable things."

To be "Indianized" meant to serve the Devil. Cotton Mather thought this was what had happened to Mercy Short, a young girl who had been a captive of the Indians and who was suffering from tormenting fits. According to Mather, Short had seen the Devil. "Hee was not of a Negro, but of a Tawney, or an Indian colour," she said; "he wore an high-crowned Hat, with straight Hair; and had one Cloven-foot." During a witchcraft trial, Mather reported, George Burroughs had lifted an extremely heavy object with the help of the Devil, who resembled an Indian. Puritan authorities hanged an English woman for worshiping Indian "gods" and for taking the Indian devil-god Hobbamock for a husband. Significantly, the Devil was portrayed as dark complected and Indian.

For the Puritans, to become Indian was the ultimate horror, for they believed Indians were "in very great subjection" of the Devil, who "kept them in a continual slavish fear of him." Governor Bradford harshly condemned Thomas Morton and his fellow prodigals of the Merrymount settlement for their promiscuous partying with Indians: "They also set up a maypole, drinking and dancing about it many days together, inviting the Indian women for their consorts, dancing and frisking together like so many fairies." Interracial cavorting threatened to fracture a cultural and moral border—the frontier of

Puritan identity. Congress of bodies, white and "tawney," signified defilement, a frightful boundlessness. If the Puritans were to become wayward like the Indians, it would mean that they had succumbed to savagery and failed to shrivel the sensuous parts of the self. To be "Indianized" meant to be decivilized, to become wild men.

But they could not allow this to happen, for they were embarking on an errand to transform the wilderness into civilization. "The whole earth is the Lord's garden and he hath given it to the sons of men [to] increase and multiply and replenish the earth and subdue it," asserted John Winthrop in 1629 as he prepared to sail for New England. "Why then should we stand starving here for the places of habitation . . . and in the meantime suffer a whole Continent as fruitful and convenient for the use of man to lie waste without any improvements."

Actually, Indians had been farming the land, and this reality led to conflicts over resources. Within ten years after the arrival of Winthrop's group, twenty thousand more colonists came to New England. This growing English population had to be squeezed into a limited area of arable land. Less than 20 percent of the region was useful for agriculture, and the Indians had already established themselves on the prime lands. Consequently, the colonists often settled on or directly next to Indian communities. In the Connecticut Valley, for example, they erected towns like Springfield (1636), Northampton (1654), Hadley (1661), Deerfield (1673), and Northfield (1673) adjacent to Indian agricultural clearings at Agawam, Norwottuck, Pocumtuck, and Squakheag.

Over the years, the expansion of English settlement sometimes led to wars that literally made the land "vacant." During the Pequot War of 1637, some seven hundred Pequots were killed by the colonists and their Indian allies. Describing the massacre at Fort Mystic, an English officer wrote: "Many were burnt in the fort, both men, women, and children. . . . There were about four hundred souls in this fort, and not above five of them escaped out of our hands. Great and doleful was the bloody sight." Commander John Mason explained that God had pushed the Pequots into a "fiery oven," "filling the place with dead bodies." By explaining their atrocities as divinely driven, the English were sharply inscribing the Indians as a race of devils. This was what happened during King Philip's War of 1675–1676. While one thousand English were killed during this conflict, over six thousand Indians died from combat and disease. Altogether, about half of the total Indian population was destroyed in southern New England. Again, the colonists quickly justified their violence by demonizing their enemies. The Indians, Increase Mather observed, were "so *Devil driven* as to begin an unjust and bloody war upon the English, which issued in their speedy and utter extirpation from the face of God's earth." Cotton Mather explained that the war was a conflict between the Devil and God: "The Devil decoyed those miserable savages [to New England] in hopes that the Gospel of the Lord Jesus Christ would never come here to destroy or disturb His *absolute empire* over them."

Indians, "such people" of this "brave new world," to use Shakespeare's words, personified the Devil and everything the Puritans feared—the body, sexuality, laziness, sin, and the loss of self-control. They had no place in a "new England." This was the view trumpeted by Edward Johnson in his *Wonder-working Providence*. Where there had originally been "hideous Thickets" for wolves and bears, he proudly exclaimed in 1654, there were now streets "full of Girls and Boys sporting up and down, with a continued concourse of people." Initially, the colonists themselves had lived in "wigwams" like Indians, but now they had "orderly, fair, and well-built houses . . . together with Orchards filled with goodly fruit trees, and gardens with variety of flowers." The settlers had fought against the Devil, who had inhabited the bodies of the Indians, Johnson observed, and made it impossible for the soldiers to pierce them with their swords. But the English had violently triumphed. They had also expanded the market, making New England a center of production and trade. The settlers had turned "this Wilderness" into "a mart." Merchants from Holland, France, Spain, and Portugal were coming here. "Thus," proclaimed Johnson, "hath the Lord been pleased to turn one of the most hideous, boundless, and unknown Wildernesses in the world in an instant . . . to a well-ordered Commonwealth."

But, in a sense, all of these developments had already been acted out in *The Tempest*. Like Prospero, the English colonists had sailed to a new land, and many of them also felt they were exiles. They viewed the native peoples as savages, as Calibans. The strangers occupied the land, believing they were entitled to be "the lord on't."

Still, in Shakespeare's fantasy, race as a social construction had not yet been firmly formed, and Caliban's qualities as "other" not yet definitely fixed by race. What happened in history, however, was a different story.

The English possessed tremendous power to define the places and peoples they were conquering. As they made their way westward, they developed an ideology of "savagery," which was given form and content by the political and economic circumstances of the specific sites of colonization. Initially, in Ireland, the English had viewed savagery as something cultural, or a matter of "consent": they assumed that the distance between themselves and the Irish, or between civilization and savagery, was quantitative rather than qualitative. The Irish as "other" was educable: they were capable of acquiring the traits of civilization. But later, as colonization reached across the Atlantic and as the English encountered a new group of people, many of them believed that savagery for the Indians might be inherent. Perhaps the Indians might be different from the English in kind rather than degree; if so, then the native people of America would be incapable of improvement because of their race. To use Shakespeare's language, they might have a "nature" that "nurture" would never be able to "stick" to or change. Race or "descent" might be destiny.

What happened in America in the actual encounters between the Indians and the English strangers was not uniform. In Virginia, Indian savagery was viewed largely as cultural: Indians were ignorant heathens. In New England, on the other hand, Indian savagery was racialized: Indians had come to be condemned as a demonic race, their dark complexions signifying an indelible and inherent evil. Why was there such a difference between the two regions? Possibly the competition between the English and the Indians over resources was more intense in New England than in Virginia, where there was more arable land. More important, the colonists in New England had brought with them a greater sense of religious mission than the Virginia settlers. For the Puritans, theirs was an "errand into the wilderness"—a mission to create what John Winthrop had proclaimed as "a city upon a hill" with the eyes of the world upon them. Within this economic and cultural framework, a "discovery" occurred: the Indian "other" became a manifest devil. Thus savagery was racialized as the Indians were demonized, doomed to what Increase Mather called "utter extirpation." Once the process of this cultural construction was under way, it set a course for the making of a national identity in America for centuries to come.

Discussion Questions

1. How did the early explorers describe the Native Americans? What was the dominant tone in their descriptions of the "savages"? How does Shakespeare's character, Caliban, represent seventeenth-century beliefs about Native Americans?

2. What kinds of arguments did the colonists use to justify their taking of Indian lands? Consider the evolution of this attitude—how did it change or stay the same over the next 200 years of colonization of the New World?

Writing Suggestions

1. Remembering what you have read about the early colonists' attitudes toward the "savages" of the New World, put yourself in the position of a sailor on one of Columbus's ships, and write a letter home to your family, describing the people you have just seen in the East Indies. Keep in mind your audience, purpose, and tone for this letter home and use description and narration to bring the world you have just seen to life.

2. First, make a list of Takaki's major points about Columbus's descriptions and attitudes about the native inhabitants of the New World. Then, go to your local or university library and check out the journals of Christopher Columbus. One good edition is *Journals and Other Documents on the Life and Voyages of Christopher Columbus*, edited by Samuel Eliot Morison, published by The Heritage Press.

Read some of Columbus's early journal entries and, using Takaki's claims about the racialization of savagery as a starting point, write a three-page essay about Columbus's personal responses to the Indians of the New World. What kinds of descriptions did Columbus send home? What kinds of assumptions did Columbus take for granted about his audience's beliefs about "the savages"? What cultural beliefs of his times do you see reflected in his letters? Do you see any different attitudes from those described by Takaki? Use specific quotes from Columbus and Takaki in your essay so that your reader can fully understand your points.

The Pocahontas Perplex

The Image of Indian Women in American Culture

RAYNA GREEN

Rayna Green is well-known for her museum exhibitions at the Smithsonian and for her work as director of the American Indian Program at the National Museum of the American Indian at the National Museum of American History. Green, who is Cherokee, holds a Ph.D. from Indiana University in folklore and American studies. In "The Pocahontas Perplex," which appeared in 1975 in the *Massachusetts Review*, Green examines the image of Indian women in American culture, focusing on the role of Pocahontas and the way in which American fantasies about Pocahontas have worked to distort a true picture of Native American women.

In one of the best known old Scottish ballads, "Young Beichan" or "Lord Bateman and the Turkish King's Daughter" as it is often known in America, a young English adventurer travels to a strange, foreign land. The natives are of a darker color than he, and they practice a pagan religion. The man is captured by the King (Pasha, Moor, Sultan) and thrown in a dungeon to await death. Before he is executed, however, the pasha's beautiful daughter—smitten with the elegant and wealthy visitor—rescues him and sends him homeward. But she pines away for love of the now remote stranger who has gone home, apparently forgotten her, and contracted a marriage with a "noble" "lady" of his own kind. In all the versions, she follows him to his own land, and in most, she arrives on his wedding day whereupon he throws over his bride-to-be for the darker but more beautiful Princess. In most versions, she becomes a Christian, and she and Lord Beichan live happily ever after.

In an article called "The Mother of Us All," Philip Young suggests the parallel between the ballad story and the Pocahontas–John Smith rescue tale. With the exception of Pocahontas' marriage to John Rolfe (still, after all, a Christian stranger), the tale should indeed sound familiar to most Americans nurtured on Smith's salvation by the Indian Princess. Actually, Europeans were familiar with the motif before John Smith offered his particular variant in the *Generall Historie of Virginie* (1624).

Francis James Child, the famous ballad collector, tells us in his *English and Scottish Popular Ballads* that "Young Beichan" (Child #40) matches the tale of Gilbert Beket, St. Thomas Aquinas' father, as well as a legend recounted in the *Gesta Romanorum*, one of the oldest collections of popular tales. So the frame story was printed before 1300 and was, no doubt, well distributed in oral tradition before then. Whether or not our rakish adventurer-hero, John Smith, had heard the stories or the ballad, we cannot say, but we must admire how life mirrors art since his story follows the outlines of the traditional tale most admirably. What we do know is that the elements of the tale appealed to Europeans long before Americans had the opportunity to attach their affection for it onto Pocahontas. Whether or not we believe Smith's tale—and there are many reasons not to—we cannot ignore the impact the story has had on the American imagination.

"The Mother of Us All" became our first aristocrat, and perhaps our first saint, as Young implies. Certainly, the image of her body flung over the endangered head of our hero constitutes a major scene in national myth. Many paintings and drawings of this scene exist, and it appears in popular art on everything from wooden fire engine side panels to calendars. Some renderings betray such ignorance about the Powhatan Indians of Virginia—often portraying them in Plains dress—that one quickly comes to understand that it is the mythical scene, not the accuracy of detail that moved artists. The most famous portrait of Pocahontas, the only one said to be done from life (at John Rolfe's request), shows the Princess in Elizabethan dress, complete with ruff and velvet hat—the Christian, English lady the ballad expects her to become and the lady she indeed became for her English husband and her faithful audience for all time. The earliest literary efforts in America, intended to give us American rather than European topics, featured Pocahontas in plenty. Poems and plays—like James Nelson Barber's *The Indian Princess*; or, *La Belle Sauvage* (1808) and George Washington Custis' *The Settlers of Virginia* (1827), as well as contemporary American novels, discussed by Leslie Fiedler in *The Return of the Vanishing American*—dealt with her presence, or sang her praises from the pages of literary magazines and from the stages of popular playhouses throughout the east. Traditional American ballads like "Jonathan Smith" retold the thrilling story; schoolbook histories included it in the first pages of every text; nineteenth century commercial products like cigars, perfume and even flour used Pocahontas' name as come-on; and she appeared as the figurehead for American warships and clippers. Whether or not she saved John Smith, her actions as recounted by Smith set up one kind of model for Indian-white relations that persists—long after most Indians and Anglos ceased to have face-to-face relationships. Moreover, as a model for the national understanding of Indian women, her significance is undeniable. With her darker, negatively viewed sister, the Squaw—or, the anti-Pocahontas, as Fiedler calls her—the Princess intrudes on the national consciousness, and a potential cult waits to be resurrected when our anxieties about who we are make us recall her from her woodland retreat.

Americans had a Pocahontas Perplex even before the teenage Princess offered us a real figure to hang the iconography on. The powerfully symbolic Indian woman, as Queen and Princess, has been with us since 1575 when she appeared to stand for the New World. Artists, explorers, writers and political leaders found the Indian as they cast about for some symbol with which to identify this earthly, frightening, and beautiful paradise; E. McClung Fleming has given one of the most complete explications of these images. The misnamed Indian was the native dweller, who fit conveniently into the various traditional folkloric, philosophical and literary patterns characteristic of European thought at the time. Europeans easily adopted the Indian as the iconographic representative of the Americas. At first Caribbean and Brazilian (Tupinamba) Indians, portrayed amidst exotic flora and fauna, stood for the New World's promises and dangers. The famous and much-reproduced "Four Continents" illustrations (circa, early 16th century) executed by artists who had seen Indians and ones who had not, ordinarily pictured a male and female pair in America's place. But the paired symbol apparently did not satisfy the need for a personified figure, and the Indian Queen began to appear as the sole representation for the Americas in 1575. And until 1765 or thereabouts, the bare-breasted, Amazonian Native American Queen reigned. Draped in leaves, feathers, and animal skins as well as in heavy Caribbean jewelry, she appeared aggressive, militant, and armed with spears and arrows. Often, she rode on an armadillo, and stood with her foot on the slain body of an animal or human enemy. She was the familiar Mother-Goddess figure—full-bodied, powerful, nurturing but dangerous—embodying the opulence and peril of the New World. Her environment was rich and colorful, and that, with the allusions to Classical Europe through the Renaissance portrayal of her large, naked body, attached her to Old World History as well as to New World virtue.

Her daughter, the Princess, enters the scene when the colonies begin to move toward independence, and she becomes more "American" and less Latin than her mother. She seems less barbarous than the Queen; the rattlesnake (Jones's "Don't Tread On Me" sign) defends her, and her enemies are defeated by male warriors rather than by her own armed hand. She is Britannia's daughter as well as that of the Carib Queen, and she wears the triangular Phrygian cap and holds the liberty pole of her later, metamorphosed sister, Miss Liberty (the figure on the Statue of Liberty and the Liberty dime). She is young, leaner in the Romanesque rather than Greek mode, and distinctly Caucasian, though her skin remains slightly tinted in some renderings. She wears the loose, flowing gowns of classical statuary rather than animal skins, and Roman sandals grace her feet. She is armed, usually with a spear, but she also carries a peace pipe, a flag, or the starred and striped shield of Colonial America. She often stands with The Sons of Liberty, or later, with George Washington.

Thus, the Indian woman began her symbolic, many-faceted life as a Mother figure—exotic, powerful, dangerous, and beautiful—and as a representative of American liberty and European classical virtue translated into New World terms. She represented, even defended America. But when real Indian women—Pocahontas and her sisters—intruded into the needs bound up in symbols and the desires inherent in daily life, the responses to the symbol became more complex, and the Pocahontas perplex emerged as a controlling metaphor in the American experience. The Indian woman, along with her male counterparts, continued to stand for the New World and for rude native nobility, but the image of the savage remained as well. The dark side of the Mother-Queen figure is the savage Squaw, and even Pocahontas, as John Barth suggests in *The Sotweed Factor*, is motivated by lust.

Both her nobility as a Princess and her savagery as a Squaw are defined in terms of her relationships with male figures. If she wishes to be called a Princess, she must save or give aid to white men. The only good Indian—male or female, Squanto, Pocahontas, Sacagawea, Cochise, the Little Mohee or the Indian Doctor—rescues and helps white men. But the Indian woman is even more burdened by this narrow definition of a "good Indian," for it is she, not the males, whom white men desire sexually. Because her image is so tied up with abstract virtue—indeed with America—she must remain the Mother Goddess-Queen. But acting as a real female, she must be a partner and lover of Indian men, a mother to Indian children, and an object of lust for white men. To be Mother, Queen and lover is, as Oedipus' mother, Jocasta, discovered, difficult and perhaps impossible. The paradox so often noted in Latin/Catholic countries where men revere their mothers and sisters, but use prostitutes so that their "good" women can stay pure is to the point here. Both race conflict and national identity, however, make this particular Virgin-Whore paradox more complicated than others. The Indian woman finds herself burdened with an image that can only be understood as dysfunctional, even though the Pocahontas perplex affects us all. Some examination of the complicated dimensions of that image might help us move toward change.

In songs like "Jonathan Smith," "Chipeta's Ride" and others sung in oral tradition, the Indian woman saves white men. In "Chipeta's Ride," she even saves a white woman from lust-enraged Indian males. Ordinarily, however, she rescues her white lover or an anonymous male captive. Always called a Princess (or Chieftain's Daughter), she, like Pocahontas, has to violate the wishes and customs of her own "barbarous" people to make good the rescue, saving the man out of love and often out of "Christian sympathy." Nearly all the "good" Princess figures are converts, and they cannot bear to see their fellow Christians slain by "savages." The Princess is "civilized"; to illustrate her native nobility, most pictures portray her as white, darker than the Europeans, but more Caucasian than her fellow natives.

If unable to make the grand gesture of saving her captive lover or if thwarted from marrying him by her cruel father, the Chieftain, the Princess is allowed the even grander gesture of committing suicide when her lover is slain or fails to return to her after she rescues him. In the hundreds of "Lover's Leap" legends which abound throughout the country, and in traditional songs like "The Indian Bride's Lament," our heroine leaps over a precipice, unable to live without her loved one. In this movement from political symbolism (where the Indian woman defends America) to psychosexual symbolism (where she defends or dies for white lovers), we can see part of the Indian woman's dilemma. To be "good," she must defy her own people, exile herself from them, become white, and perhaps suffer death.

Those who did not leap for love continued to fall in love with white men by the scores, and here the sacrifices are several. The women in songs like "The Little Mohea," "Little Red Wing," and "Juanita, the Sachem's Daughter" fall in love with white travellers, often inviting them to share their blissful, idyllic, woodland paradise. If their lovers leave them, they often pine away, die of grief, or leap off a cliff, but in a number of songs, the white man remains with the maiden, preferring her life to his own, "civilized" way. "The Little Mohea" is a prime example of such a song.

> As I went walking for pleasure one day,
> In the sweet recollection, to dwell time away.
> As I sat amusing myself on the grass,
> Oh, who should I spy but a fair Indian lass.
> She walked up behind me, taking hold of my hand,
> She said, "You are a stranger and in a strange land,
> But if you will follow, you're welcome to come
> And dwell in my cottage that I call my home."
> My Mohea was gentle, my Mohea was kind.
> She took me when a stranger and clothed me when cold.
> She learned me the language of the lass of Mohea.
> "I'm going to leave you, so farewell my dear.
> The ship's sails are spreading and home I must steer."
> The last time I saw her she was standing on the strand,
> And as my boat passed her she waved me her hand.
> Saying "when you have landed and with the one you love,
> Think of pretty Mohea in the coconut grove."
> I am home but no one comes near me nor none do I see,
> That would equal compare with the lass of Mohea.
> Oh, the girl that I loved proved untrue to me.
> I'll turn my course backward far over the sea.
> I'll turn my course backward, from this land I'll go free,
> And go spend my days with the little Mohea.

Such songs add to the exotic and sexual, yet maternal and contradictorily virginal image of the Indian Princess, and are reminiscent of the contemporary white soldier's attachments to "submissive," "sacrificial," "exotic" Asian women.

As long as Indian women keep their exotic distance or die (even occasionally for love of Indian men), they are permitted to remain on the positive side of the image. They can help, stand by, sacrifice for, and aid white men. They can, like their native brothers, heal white men, and the Indian reputation as healer dominated the nineteenth century patent medicine business. In the ads for such medicines, the Indian woman appears either as a helpmate to her "doctor" husband or partner or as a healer herself. In several ads (and the little dime novels often accompanying the patent medicine products), she is the mysterious witch-healer. Thus, she shares in the Caucasian or European female's reputation for potential evil. The references here to power, knowledge, and sexuality remain on the good side of the image. In this incarnation, the Princess offers help in the form of medicine rather than love.

The tobacco industry also capitalized on the Princess' image, and the cigar-store figures and ads associated with the tobacco business replicate the Princess figures to sell its products. Cigar-store Princesses smile and beckon men into tobacco shops. They hold a rose, a bundle of cigars, or some tobacco leaves (a sign of welcome in the colonial days), and they smile invitingly with their Caucasian lips. They also sell the product from tobacco packages, and here, like some of the figures in front of the shops, Diana-like or more militant Minerva (Wonder-Woman)-like heroines offer the comforts of the "Indian weed." They have either the rounded, infantile, semi-naked (indicating innocence) bodies of Renaissance angels or the bodies and clothes of classical heroines. The Mother Goddess and Miss Liberty peddle their more abstract wares, as Indian Princesses, along with those of the manufacturer. Once again, the Princess comforts white men, and while she promises much, she remains aloof.

But who becomes the white man's sexual partner? Who forms liaisons with him? It cannot be the Princess, for she is sacrosanct. Her sexuality can be hinted at but never realized. The Princess' darker twin, the Squaw, must serve this side of the image, and again, relationships with males determine what the image will be. In the case of the Squaw, the presence of overt and realized sexuality converts the image from positive to negative. White men cannot share sex with the Princess, but once they do so with a real Indian woman, she cannot follow the required love-and-rescue pattern. She does what white men want for money or lust. In the traditional songs, stories, obscene jokes, contemporary literary works, and popular pictorializations of the Squaw, no heroines are allowed. Squaws share in the same vices attributed to Indian men—drunkenness, stupidity, thievery, venality of every kind—and they live in shacks on the edge of town rather than in a woodland paradise.

Here, Squaws are shamed for their relationships with white men, and the males who share their beds—the "squaw men," or "bucks," if they are Indian—share their shame. When they live with Indian males, Squaws work for their lazy bucks and bear large numbers of fat "papooses." In one joke, a white visitor to a reservation sees an overburdened squaw with ten children hanging on her skirts. "Where's your husband?" the visitor demands. "He ought to be hung!" "Ugh," says the squaw, "pretty well-hung!" They too are fat, and unlike their Princess sisters, dark and possessed of cruder, more "Indian" features. When stories and songs describe relationships with white men, Squaws are understood as mere economic and sexual conveniences for the men who—unlike John Smith or a "brave"—are tainted by association with her. Tale after tale describes the Indian whores, their alcoholic and sexual excesses with white trappers and hunters. A parody of the beautiful-maiden song, "Little Red Wing," speaks of her lewd sister who "lays on her back in a cowboy shack, and lets cowboys poke her in the crack." The result of this cowboy-squaw liaison is a "brat in a cowboy hat with his asshole between his eyes." This Squaw is dark, and squat, and even the cigar-store Indians show the changes in conception. No Roman sandals grace their feet, and their features are more "Indian" and "primitive" than even their male counterparts. The cigar-store squaws often had papooses on their backs, and some had corrugated places on their hips to light the store patrons' matches. When realities intrude on mythos, even Princesses can become Squaws as the text of the ragtime song, "On an Indian Reservation," illustrates.

> On an Indian reservation, far from home and civilization,
> Where the foot of Whiteman seldom trod.
> Whiteman went to fish one summer,
> Met an Indian maid—a hummer,
> Daughter of Big-Chief-Spare-the-rod.
> Whiteman threw some loving glances, took this maid to Indian dances,
> Smoked his pipe of peace, took chances living in a teepee made of fur.
> Rode with her on Indian ponies, bought her diamond rings, all phonies,
> And he sang these loving words to her:
> Chorus:
>> You're my pretty little Indian Napanee.
>> Won't you take a chance and marry me.
>> Your Daddy Chief, 'tis my belief,
>> To a very merry wedding will agree.
>> True, you're a dark little Indian maid,
>> But I'll sunburn to a darker shade,
>> I'll wear feathers on my head,
>> Paint my skin an Indian red,
>> If you will be my Napanee.
> With his contact soon he caught her,
> Soon he married this big chief's daughter,
> Happiest couple that you ever saw.
> But his dreams of love soon faded,
> Napanee looked old and jaded,
> Just about like any other squaw.
> Soon there came papoose in numbers, redskin yells disturbed his slumbers,
> Whiteman wonders at his blunders—now the feathers drop upon his head.
> Sorry to say it, but he's a-wishing, that he'd never gone a-fishing,
> Or had met this Indian maid and said:
> Chorus:

The Indian woman is between a rock and a hard place. Like that of her male counterpart, her image is freighted with such ambivalence that she has little room to move. He, however, has many more modes in which to participate though he is still severely handicapped by the prevailing stereotypes. They are both tied to definition by relationships with white men, but she is especially burdened by the narrowness of that definition. Obviously, her image is one that is troublesome to all women, but, tied as it is to a national mythos, its complexity has a special piquance. As Vine Deloria points out in *Custer Died For Your Sins*, many whites claim kinship with some distant Indian Princess grandmother, and thus try to resolve their "Indian problem" with such sincere affirmations of relationships.

Such claims make it impossible for the Indian woman to be seen as real. She does not have the power to evoke feeling as a real mother figure, like the black woman, even though *that* image has a burdensome negative side. American children play with no red mammy dolls. She cannot even evoke the terror the "castrating (white) bitch" inspires. Only the male, with upraised tomahawk, does that. The many expressions which treat of her image remove her from consideration as more than an image. As some abstract, noble Princess tied to "America" and to sacrificial zeal, she has power as a symbol. As the Squaw, a depersonalized object of scornful convenience, she is powerless. Like her male relatives she may be easily destroyed without reference to her humanity. (When asked why he killed women and children at Sand Creek, the commanding general of the U.S. Cavalry was said to have replied, "nits make lice.") As the Squaw, her physical removal or destruction can be understood as necessary to the progress of civilization even though her abstracted sister, the Princess, stands for that very civilization. Perhaps the Princess had to be removed from her powerful symbolic place, and replaced with the male Uncle Sam because she confronted America with too many contradictions. As symbol and reality, the Indian woman suffers from our needs, and by both race and sex stands damned.

Since the Indian so much represents America's attachment to a romantic past and to a far distant nobility, it is predictable but horrible that the Indian woman should symbolize the paradoxical entity once embodied for the European in the Princess in the tower and the old crone in the cave. It is time that the Princess herself is rescued and the Squaw relieved of her obligatory service. The Native American woman, like all women, needs a definition that stands apart from that of males, red or white. Certainly, the Native woman needs to be defined as Indian, in Indian terms. Delightful and interesting as Pocahontas' story may be, she offers an intolerable metaphor for the Indian-white experience. She and the Squaw offer unendurable metaphors for the lives of Indian women. Perhaps if we give up the need for John Smith's fantasy and the trappers' harsher realities, we will find, for each of us, an image that does not haunt and perplex us. Perhaps if we explore the meaning of Native American lives outside the boundaries of the stories, songs, and pictures given us in tradition, we will find a more humane truth.

Discussion Questions

1. Review what Green has said about the Pocahontas myth as a model "for the national understanding of Indian women." What are the characteristics of the Princess as portrayed in the ballads, novels, and art of England and colonial America? What are the characteristics of the Squaw, according to Green? In discussion groups, consider your own exposure to film, art, or other representations of Indian women. Do you agree or disagree that this duality between Princess and Squaw has been the American model of Indian women? Why or why not?

2. Green states that American folk songs "add to the exotic and sexual, yet maternal and contradictorily virginal image . . . reminiscent of the contemporary white soldier's attachments to submissive, sacrificial, exotic Asian women." Discuss this statement in terms of Disney's animated Pocahontas film. Do you agree or disagree with Green's statement?

Writing Suggestions

1. Rent a western movie by director John Ford, such as *The Searchers*, and write a three-page analysis of the role of Native American women in the movie. Respond to Green's claims that Indian women are often portrayed as either the evil squaw or the sexually unavailable princess in terms of the movie. Answer some of the following questions in your paper:

    What kinds of Native American women appear in the film?

    How are they portrayed?

    What do they look like physically?

    What is the role of these women in the plot?

    How are they treated by the white men or women in the movie?

    What kinds of stereotypes do you see in the portrayal of the Native American women?

2. Green argues that we must "explore the meaning of Native American lives outside the boundaries of the stories, songs, and pictures given us in tradition." Pick one Native American historical figure, such as Geronimo or Sacajewa, and write a three-to-five page research paper with the most recent scholarly text and Web sources you can find. Answer the following research questions in your paper:

    How was this historical figure represented in American folk art and music?

    What more realistic scholarship has been conducted recently, and how do your studies of this person reflect a more realistic view of his or her life?

    A good Internet resource for information or research subject ideas for this assignment is the Smithsonian Museum's Encyclopedia Web site:

    http://www.si.edu/resource/faq/nmai/start.htm

Disney's "Politically Correct" Pocahontas

JACQUELYN KILPATRICK

Jacquelyn Kilpatrick is professor of literature at Governor's State University in University Park, Illinois. She attended California State University in Fresno and went on to get her Ph.D. at the University of California at Santa Cruz in 1996. Kilpatrick teaches and writes about Native American film and film-makers, and about the multicultural history of the United States. She has also hosted a course at Governor's State University, where many of today's major Native American writers discuss their works with students. In this essay, written for *Cineaste* magazine, Kilpatrick objects to Disney's portrayal of Pocahontas in the controversial 1995 Disney film.

When I walked into the theater to see *Pocahontas*, I had my choice of venue. It was playing on three of six screens, and the line waiting to get in never seemed to diminish. Later, I looked at the film section of the local paper and found that somewhere in the vicinity the movie was starting every fifteen minutes. Now that was a depressing thought.

In an interview with *The New York Times*, Eric Goldberg, the film's codirector (with Mike Gabriel), said, "We've gone from being accused of being too white bread to being accused of racism in *Aladdin* to being accused of being too politically correct in *Pocahontas*. That's progress to me." As much as I wanted to like Disney's production, I must disagree with Goldberg. Instead of progress in depicting Native Americans, this film takes a step backwards— a very dangerous step because it is so carefully glossed as "authentic" and "respectful."

The visual is emotionally more compelling than the written word, to say nothing of being more accessible, and since few people will read about Pocahontas, this film will exist as "fact" in the minds of generations of American children. They will believe in the Romeo and Juliet in the wilds of North America that Disney has presented, which, as Robert Eaglestaff, principal of the American Indian Heritage School in Seattle, has said, is much like "trying to teach about the Holocaust and putting in a nice story about Anne Frank falling in love with a German officer."

It might seem a moot point at best to debate the authenticity or reality of an animated film in which a tree speaks words of wisdom and the protagonist guides her canoe over a deadly looking waterfall without mussing her hair. If this were a story about a fictional character in a fictional situation, I would agree. I like Mickey Mouse, too. But Pocahontas was a real woman who lived during the pivotal time of first contact with the outside force that would ultimately decimate her people. Although we know of her only from the English reports, and some of the details are a bit hazy, there are some facts that are well supported. For one thing, she was not a voluptuous young woman when she met John Smith but a ten- to twelve-year-old girl, and John Smith was a thirty-something mercenary who more resembled a brick than a blonde Adonis.

Smith's report of Pocahontas's brave act in saving his life was nowhere to be found in his initial description of his capture by Powhatan in 1608, surfacing only eight years later in a letter to the queen. There are a couple of possibilities to explain why that might have been. He could have been embarrassed, given the macho community of Jamestown boys, to admit a child had saved his life, or he might have stolen the story, possibly from the account published around the same time about Juan Ortiz and the Utica woman who saved him about eighty years before Smith met Pocahontas.

Assuming she did save his life, it could have been her idea, or it could have been her father's. If Powhatan had his own reasons for wanting Smith to live, he might have instructed her to do as she did to save face. Smith's report said she wanted her father to keep him alive but in captivity so he could make bells and beads for her, which, according to John Gould Fletcher (*John Smith—Also Pocahontas*, 1928), would have provided a cover story to eliminate the censure of the tribe for Powhatan's benevolent act and which would have been in keeping with their traditions.

Assuming Smith stole the story, he could have done so because he turned into a chronicler of his adventures in the New World after it became clear he was not going to be able to return to America to have more of them. He tried repeatedly to return, but even the first settlers in New England were happy to accept his advice but refused his company.

What we do know of Pocahontas is that she met John Smith in 1608, was probably responsible for some trading between the settlers and her people, was kidnapped and raped by the English but later married a tobacco planter named John Rolfe, had a son in 1615 and sailed to England in 1616. She was introduced to Ben Jonson and made such an impression that he wrote her into one of his comedies, *The Staple of News*; she attended a court masque that he wrote and evidently impressed the king and queen as well. She attempted to return home but became ill on the voyage and had to turn back to England, where she died, probably of smallpox, at the age of twenty-two. We have no idea how she or her people felt about any of this, except that some of the contemporary reports said she died "of a broken heart."

That's a pretty interesting story, but not the sort of thing animated Disney films are known for. For one thing, it's much too violent and sad. According to James Pentecost, the film's producer, the changes that were made were due to the fact that Pocahontas's real story was simply too long. He said, "We decided to dramatize what we felt was the *essence* of Pocahontas." Now the logic may be a little tough to follow here, but evidently what that means is that they changed her age, her body, and gave her a motive for her actions that boils down to going gaga over the first white man she sees.

Ignoring for a moment the very non-PC nonfeminist content of that change, there lies within it a very old stereotype of Native American women. In hundreds of films made during the last century, Indian women have been seen sacrificing themselves and their tribal communities for their white loves. I'm sure the irony is unintentional in *Pocahontas* as she paddles her canoe along, having just refused to marry the stereotypically stoic and noble Kocoum, singing about the change that is waiting "just around the river bend." The change that waits is another man and another culture in the form of John Smith.

The Disney folks have made much of the fact that Pocahontas is the driving force of this movie, which is, I suppose, to mean it makes some sort of feminist statement. She does sing to John about living naturally in tune with the Earth—also skirting dangerously close to another stereotype, that of the "natural ecologist"—but does she have to do it in an off-the-shoulder miniskirt? And I would love to see a report on the physics of her body. Would she, like Barbie, fall over if really given those dimensions? Glen Keane, the film's supervising animator, researched the paintings of the real Pocahontas but wasn't very impressed, so he made a few "adjustments." Besides her beautiful "more Asian" eyes, he gave her a body with a wasp waist, sexy hips and legs, and breasts that are *truly* impressive. He says, "Some people might see her as sexy, but she's not Jessica Rabbit. I think she looks rather athletic." Uh huh. Mel Gibson (the voice of John Smith) put it more succinctly when he said, "She's a babe." Or, what the heck, maybe she's just drawn that way.

To give the Disney folk their due, they apparently made some effort to be nonoffensive, hiring Native Americans to work on the film and to act as consultants. Unfortunately, there seems to have been some miscommunication of concept. The Disney people were making an animated film about a fictional character. They knew she was fictional because they created her. The Native Americans on the team had other interests. Russell Means, the voice of Powhatan, likes the film even though they were willing to take his advice about a detail such as the father referring to Pocahontas as Daughter instead of her name, but were unwilling to change important aspects of the image of the Indians as warlike, as established by the return from war at the beginning of the film. He says, "There are scenes where the English settlers admit to historical deceit. . . . Their animated settlers say they are here to rob, rape, pillage the land and kill Indians. This is the truth that Disney is entrusting with children while the rest of Hollywood won't trust that truth with adults."

As a mixedblood woman, I too am concerned with the truth of the colonization of America, but establishing another stereotype isn't the way to go about it. Even given that Disney's animated characters are by nature larger than life, the English in the film are extremely one-dimensional in their bumbling greed. As Terry Russio, a screenwriter for Disney, said, "You can judge the sentiments of the country by who you can confidently make fun of. Nowadays the ultimate villain, I suppose, would be a fat, white male terrorist who ran a Fortune 500 company on the side." That fairly well describes the governor in *Pocahontas*, a description which renders the history of first contact literally cartoonish.

Disney also hired Shirley (Little Dove) Custalow-McGowan, a Powhatan who travels through Virginia teaching the history and culture of her people, to work as consultant for the film. When she saw the early rushes, she said, "My heart sorrowed within me. . . . Ten-year-old Pocahontas has become twenty-year-old Pocahontas. The movie was no longer historically accurate."

According to the film's producer, James Pentecost, all this talk about historical accuracy is somewhat irrelevant. He believes that "Nobody should go to an animated film hoping to get an accurate depiction of history." Okay, I'll buy that, as long as you're talking about *The Lion King*, but Pocahontas was real, and most people have heard her name even if they know nothing about her reality. Most of the adults who view this film, however, will not have the background to judge whether it is accurate or not, and since the hype has been toward the "political correctness" of the film, I would think they'd be more apt to trust it than not. And those are the adults. What about the children? As Linda Woolverton, screenwriter for *Beauty and the Beast* and *The Lion King* said, "When you take on a Disney animated feature, you know you're going to be affecting entire generations of human minds." In this case, the effect is one more misconception advertised in the guise of authenticity and respect for Native American values.

As Custalow-McGowan said, "History is history. You're not honoring a nation of people when you change their history."

Discussion Questions

1. How does the Disney text change the story of the relationship between Pocahontas and John Smith? What is the main "argument" of the Disney story? How is this argument conveyed in the plot changes?

2. Some have charged that the Disney producers are guilty of the sin of omission in their telling of the story of Pocahontas for a mass film audience. Which historical facts does the Disney text leave out? Do you approve or disapprove of the omissions you have noticed?

3. Discuss the ways in which Disney movies had an impact on your life as you grew up. Which films had the most effect on you? Do you feel that they colored your perception of reality, or do you feel that Disney as an entertainer has the right to change the facts for the purpose of entertainment? For example, do you mind that Disney changed the stories of Pocahontas and Anastasia, or do you think the movies worked well as entertainment and did not need to be historically correct?

Writing Suggestions

1. Write a two-page analysis of Kilpatrick's argument. Consider her sources, evidence, examples, and tone, and state whether or not you feel she makes her arguments effectively. Use specifics from her piece to back up your assertions about the value of her arguments and evidence.

2. After reading all the materials on Pocahontas, build from your ideas developed in the discussion questions for this selection, and write a movie review of Disney's 1995 film, answering some of the following questions:

    Do you think Disney was justified in changing the film for children?
    Would you recommend this film for children?
    What key elements do you think should have been added, if any?
    How is Disney's film more or less appropriate for children than the real story?

The Pocahontas Myth

POWHATAN NATION RESPONSE / CHIEF ROY CRAZY HORSE

The Powhatan Nation is an American Indian Nation located on a reservation in Burington County in New Jersey. The number of original Powhatans was greatly reduced after the arrival of Europeans on the East Coast of North America, but some descendants of the original Powhatans still remain. Forefathers of the current Powhatan Nation members were primarily Rappahannocks from Virginia and Nanticokes from Delaware. Joining forces with a number of different tribes, the Powhatan Nation came together in the 1960s and was officially recognized as nation by the State of New Jersey in 1980. In 1982 the tribe was given the Rankokus Indian Reservation, on 350 acres of formerly state-owned land. The Powhatan Nation maintains a Web site at <http://www.powhatan.org/index.html>. On this Web site the Powhatans explain that one of their goals, in addition to educating "the non-Indian community about our traditional ways," is to "dispel the widely heard Pocahontas 'myth.'" With these goals in mind, they have posted the following article on-line and have also written a new play entitled *The One Called Pocahontas*. You can learn more about the goals and beliefs of the Powhatan Nation at their Web site, in addition to reading more articles by Chief Roy Crazy Horse.

In 1995, Roy Disney decided to release an animated movie about a Powhatan woman known as "Pocahontas." In answer to a complaint by the Powhatan Nation, he claims the film is "responsible, accurate, and respectful."

We of the Powhatan Nation disagree. The film distorts history beyond recognition. Our offers to assist Disney with cultural and historical accuracy were rejected. Our efforts urging him to reconsider his misguided mission were spurned.

"Pocahontas" was a nickname, meaning "the naughty one" or "spoiled child." Her real name was Matoaka. The legend is that she saved a heroic John Smith from being clubbed to death by her father in 1607—she would have been about 10 or 11 at the time. The truth is that Smith's fellow colonists described him as an abrasive, ambitious, self-promoting mercenary soldier.

Of all of Powhatan's children, only "Pocahontas" is known, primarily because she became the hero of Euro-Americans as the "good Indian," one who saved the life of a white man. Not only is the "good Indian/bad Indian theme" inevitably given new life by Disney, but the history, as recorded by the English themselves, is badly falsified in the name of "entertainment."

The truth of the matter is that the first time John Smith told the story about this rescue was 17 years after it happened, and it was but one of three reported by the pretentious Smith that he was saved from death by a prominent woman.

Yet in an account Smith wrote after his winter stay with Powhatan's people, he never mentioned such an incident. In fact, the starving adventurer reported he had been kept comfortable and treated in a friendly fashion as an honored guest of Powhatan and Powhatan's brothers. Most scholars think the "Pocahontas incident" would have been highly unlikely, especially since it was part of a longer account used as justification to wage war on Powhatan's Nation.

Euro-Americans must ask themselves why it has been so important to elevate Smith's fibbing to status as a national myth worthy of being recycled again by Disney. Disney even improves upon it by changing Pocahontas from a little girl into a young woman.

The true Pocahontas story has a sad ending. In 1612, at the age of 17, Pocahontas was treacherously taken prisoner by the English while she was on a social visit, and was held hostage at Jamestown for over a year.

During her captivity, a 28-year-old widower named John Rolfe took a "special interest" in the attractive young prisoner. As a condition of her release, she agreed to marry Rolfe, who the world can thank for commercializing tobacco. Thus, in April 1614, Matoaka, also known as "Pocahontas," daughter of Chief Powhatan, became "Rebecca Rolfe." Shortly after, they had a son, whom they named Thomas Rolfe. The descendants of Pocahontas and John Rolfe were known as the "Red Rolfes."

Two years later in the spring of 1616, Rolfe took her to England where the Virginia Company of London used her in their propaganda campaign to support the colony. She was wined and dined and taken to theaters. It was recorded that on one occasion when she encountered John Smith (who was also in London at the time), she was so furious with him that she turned her back to him, hid her face, and went off by herself for several hours. Later, in a second encounter, she called him a liar and showed him the door.

Rolfe, his young wife, and their son set off for Virginia in March of 1617, but "Rebecca" had to be taken off the ship at Gravesend. She died there on March 21, 1617, at the age of 21. She was buried at Gravesend, but the grave was destroyed in a reconstruction of the church. It was only after her death and her fame in London society that Smith found it convenient to invent the yarn that she had rescued him.

History tells the rest. Chief Powhatan died the following spring of 1618. The people of Smith and Rolfe turned upon the people who had shared their resources with them and had shown them friendship. During Pocahontas's generation, Powhatan's people were decimated and dispersed and their lands were taken over. A clear pattern had been set which would soon spread across the American continent.

It is unfortunate that of this sad story, which Euro-Americans should find embarrassing, Disney makes "entertainment" and perpetuates a dishonest and self-serving myth at the expense of the Powhatan Nation.

Discussion Questions

1. The Powhatan Nation's statement came from a Web site on the Internet. What kinds of problems might this source have as a research tool? For example, how could you verify the following statement?

    Most scholars think the "Pocahontas incident" would have been highly unlikely, especially since it was part of a longer account used as justification to wage war on Powhatan's Nation.

    How could you find out more about the Powhatan Nation, and what other members of that nation might feel about Disney's movie?

2. Look at the diction and resulting tone in the Powhatan Nation's statement. Which words give the piece its particular tone? Do you think that this piece stands as an effective argument? Does the tone add or detract from the argument? Why or why not?

Writing Suggestions

1. Using a search engine such as Google, Altavista, or Lycos, search for film reviews of Disney's film *Pocahontas*. If you are working in a group, ask each group member to search on a different search engine so that you can compare search results. Print out the film reviews you have found, and then summarize the variety of opinions you have found in a two-page analysis.

2. Using your survey of film reviews, and your knowledge of some of the complexities of the issues involved in the making of the film, write a critical analysis of one of the reviews. You might address some of the following questions:

    Did the reviewer take into account the feelings of the Powhatan Nation?

    Did the reviewer address some of the controversial aspects of the making of this film?

    Did the reviewer use appropriate details to back up his or her assertions?

    Did the reviewer give examples that made the review come alive?

    Be specific, and use quotes from the review to back up your own assertions about the reviewer's essay.

What Happened in Salem?

Introduction

DAVID LEVIN

In addition to his book *What Happened in Salem?*, David Levin wrote many articles about the witch hunts in New England. Levin received his Ph.D. in English from Harvard University in 1955 and went on to teach English at Stanford University for nineteen years. He then became the Commonwealth Professor of English and the Thomas Jefferson Professor of Arts and Sciences at the University of Virginia. The author of five books and numerous articles, Professor Levin died in 1999. Much of Levin's writing focused on the complicated events surrounding the Salem Witch trials, including the role of Cotton Mather and other elders at the trials. In the following introduction to *What Happened in Salem?* Levin summarizes the major events of and controversies about the trials.

I

Between June 10 and September 22, 1692, nineteen Massachusetts men and women and two dogs were hanged for witchcraft, and one man was pressed to death for refusing to plead to the indictment. When the executions came to an end, fifty-five people had confessed that they were witches, and a hundred and fifty were in jail either waiting to be tried or enduring, as several convicted women did, reprieves granted them so that infants they had already conceived would not be executed with them. It would be easy to dismiss this episode merely as a horrible example of "superstition," as a curious delusion of a curiously demented people; but no one can reach a reasonable judgment without taking history into account, and that means trying to understand the ideas and beliefs which to people of the time seemed to justify the Salem executions.

Toward the end of the seventeenth century, belief in the reality of witchcraft was virtually universal. In European countries both Catholic and Protestant, thousands of "witches" had been executed. Despite important advances toward modern science, few people had thought of criticizing current theology in the light of the newest scientific discoveries. No one used Newton's law of gravitation[1] to challenge Cotton Mather's remarks about the aerial activities of "legions of devils." The "invisible world" was still, for most people,

---

[1] Set forth in the *Principia*, 1687.

50

a real one. Even the few articulate critics of the Salem trials did not deny the existence of witchcraft; they attacked the methods used by the Salem judges. The intellectual leaders and, so far as we know, the mass of the people read their Bibles literally, accepting without question the Mosaic pronouncement (Exodus 22. 18): "Thou shalt not suffer a witch to live."

The crime of witchcraft consisted in entering into a contract or "covenant" with the Devil. Belief in a real and energetic Devil was therefore the major premise on which seventeenth-century thinkers based their measures against witchcraft. The Devil was an angel who had rebelled against God and fallen from grace; he worked "in continual opposition to the designs of God." This protracted campaign was doomed to failure, for God was omnipotent, but for reasons of His own God allowed the Devil certain powers over men until the millennium, the beginning on earth of the Kingdom of God. Among other powers, the Devil and his legions were allowed to afflict individuals or communities with special trials or adversities from time to time. At all times the Devil tempted men and women to sin, to transgress against the will of God. Not only could he tempt men to isolated acts of sin; he could go farther and invite them to join a covenant binding all the covenantors to work together against "the children of God." In most of his actions the Devil was, of course, invisible; only the results of his work could be seen. It was the Devil and his invisible hellhounds who entered and controlled the body of a "possessed"— an insane—person. But the Devil and his evil spirits were not always invisible; once a witch had entered the fatal covenant, the Devil or one of his agents could assume the witch's shape when tormenting some other human being.

Although belief in witchcraft and the Devil's evil power was not, in the seventeenth century, restricted to any single branch of Christianity, certain tenets made the Puritan in England and America especially sensitive to Devils and witches, and frontier conditions in New England aggravated this sensitivity. The Puritans believed in the doctrine of original sin, which informed them that they were worms, dogs, potential colleagues of the Devil until the grace of God was, by God's free gift, poured into them. Cotton Mather was not preaching unusual doctrine when he reminded his congregation that "we should every one of us be a *dog* and a *witch* too, if God should leave us to ourselves. It is the mere *grace* of God, the *chains* of which refrain us from bringing the *chains of darkness* upon our souls." Knowing that for all practical purposes he belonged to the Devil anyway, the sincere Puritan who had not yet experienced the gift of God's grace was engaged in a constant struggle to find the weak spots in the "chains of darkness" which held him temporarily and threatened to bind him forever. He wanted no more connection with the Devil than he was born with; conscious of his sinfulness, he wanted to repent, to exorcise the Devil, to be prepared for the gift of grace if and when it came.

The Puritans' struggle against the Devil was external as well as internal. Those who had already experienced the influx of grace knew that their mission was to advance the Bible Commonwealth and also to strike down the

Devil wherever he appeared too boldly among their unregenerate brethren. The New England Puritans and some other Englishmen believed, moreover, that the Devil's last and most powerful stronghold was in the wilds of North America. This conviction was supported by the presence of "barbarous savages," the antics of whose medicine men savored of witchcraft; and some Puritans reasoned that Satan and his legions would carefully patrol the heathen and Catholic frontier to defend it against any expansion of the Bible Commonwealth. "If any are scandalized," one English minister wrote, "that *New England*, a place of as serious piety, as any I can hear of under Heaven, should be troubled so much with witches; I think, 'tis no wonder; where will the Devil show most malice, but where he is hated, and hateth most . . . ?" At the same time, the Puritans, schooled in Old Testament history, believed that God visits terrible judgments upon His wayward people. As one means of inflicting this punishment, God permitted the Devil and his witches to torment not only the guilty but their neighbors and countrymen; the Puritans knew that God sometimes chastised a whole nation for the sins of its most wicked citizens.

The Puritans knew, too, that the Devil had little time left before the millennium; one minister estimated that Antichrist had only about twenty years more in which to win converts and torture mankind. The experience of those who had lived through the years from 1684 to 1692 seemed to justify the text Cotton Mather chose for a sermon in the summer of 1692: "Woe to the Inhabitants of the Earth, and of the Sea; for the Devil is come down unto you, having great Wrath; because he knoweth, that he hath but a short time." In 1684, James II had revoked the old charter of Massachusetts Bay, by which the colony had been largely self-governing. In 1688, the French and Indians had made new attacks on the frontier settlements, thus starting a costly war that lasted for years; the colonists suspected Andros, the hated royal governor, of conniving with the Indians; the shops were closed on the "pagan" Christmas Day; an old woman in Boston confessed to witchcraft and was hanged. During the next four years the Indian wars continued; even after the Glorious Revolution in England had turned out King James II in favor of William of Orange, the colony failed to win back its old charter and had to accept a compromise providing for a royally appointed governor. In 1692, the magistrates discovered a witchcraft conspiracy in Salem Village, and while the scope of the plot seemed to be growing the people learned that a devilish earthquake had killed seventeen hundred in Jamaica. The Devil seemed to be striking on several fronts at once.

2

When in February, 1692, Elizabeth Parris, eleven-year-old daughter of the minister at Salem Village, and her cousin Abigail Williams began having violent fits, they behaved as had afflicted children in Sweden in 1669, and the Goodwin children who were bewitched in Boston in 1688. These Goodwin

children, whose woes Cotton Mather described in a book about their bewitchment, had been

> handled with . . . many sorts of ails. . . . Sometimes they would be deaf, some-
> times dumb, and sometimes blind, and often, all this at once. One while their
> tongues would be drawn down their throats; another while they would be
> pulled out upon their chins, to a prodigious length. They would have their
> mouths opened to such a wideness, that their jaws went out of joint; and
> anon they would clap together with a force like that of a spring-lock.

Samuel Parris and the doctors he consulted could compare the symptoms of
his daughter and niece with accounts of the earlier bewitchments. When they
learned, too, that the girls had been taking lessons in palmistry from Tituba,
a West Indian slave in the Parris family, they were sure that the Devil had
made some converts in Salem Village. Moving cautiously, Parris called in
some fellow ministers and asked their advice. They suggested fasting and
prayer, the method Cotton Mather had used in curing the Goodwin children
four years earlier. They planned on meeting at the Parris house for a fast day,
and suggested that he keep the matter quiet.

Parris evidently tried to follow the ministers' advice about comparative
secrecy, but one of his parishioners advised Tituba's husband that a witchcake—made with the urine of the afflicted—would cure the girls. This cake,
Parris believed, was the people's real invitation to the Devil, for the good Puritan was forbidden to use the Devil's means, even in fighting against him. Actually, there were more worldly reasons why the affliction spread. On several
earlier occasions the Salem Village doctor had diagnosed bewitchment, and
there had been no excitement. But this time the victims were girls who were
known to have toyed with the dangerous "preternatural"; their tormentors
were more persistent; and above all, there was reason to believe that the Devil
was making an all-out attack on New England in general and Salem Village
in particular.

Besides the general tribulations of New England, Salem Village had its
own special problems: boundary disputes with neighboring Topsfield, a rep-
rimand from the General Court of Massachusetts Bay (for an uncharitable attitude toward the minister), a bitter quarrel with the minister over who should
supply his firewood, and personal wrangles over true title to certain lands.
(One of the first few people accused of witchcraft was Rebecca Nurse, a deaf
old woman whose family had for years been contending with the Putnams in
a fight for land title.) Then, when the first accused woman confessed in open
court, she named her "confederates"; other confessors soon told a weird story
of witches' sabbaths held in Salem Village, and implied that they were partners in a well-planned diabolical conspiracy, using Salem Village as a central
operations base.

Tituba's public confession set the fatal pattern to which the accusations
and trials conformed during the hectic months that followed. The afflicted

girls, whose number came to include all those who had watched Tituba's exhibitions of palmistry, continued to enjoy notoriety and public solicitude. Although Cotton Mather offered to take them into his home and try to cure them by prayer, as he had cured the Goodwin children, they remained in Salem Village, where they appeared in court to testify against the people they "cried out upon." When anyone questioned the validity of their accusations, the judges could always point to a penitent witch or two who had confirmed the girls' charges.

The sheriff served the first warrants on February 29, 1692, and Tituba appeared before the magistrates, John Hawthorne and Jonathan Corwin, on the first of March. The three women first accused were likely candidates for the role of witches: Tituba was, of course, a West Indian and a conjurer; Sarah Good was a destitute, wizened, pipe-smoking hag; Sarah Osborne had been suspected of immorality and had not been attending church, though attendance was compulsory. As the number of accusations increased after Tituba's confession, the afflicted accused not only old women, but also some men whom the people might find reason to suspect, and at least six children.

By the time the new governor, Sir William Phips, arrived from London on May 14, the jails were crowded, the Salem court clerk had recorded hundreds of pages of frightening testimony, and the friends of both accused and afflicted were clamoring for trials. Governor Phips had to act fast. He had the attacking Indians to contend with, and the witchcraft accusations were increasing so rapidly that he could not wait for the General Court to convene and pass a law providing for judges to try the cases. The growing number of confessions was also alarming; some official government action, some executions, might show the Devil that his enemies were in no way submissive; and state action might discourage the weak-willed from signing the Devil's book. On May 29, Governor Phips appointed a Special Court of Oyer and Terminer, a court empowered to "hear and determine" cases, with Lieutenant-Governor William Stoughton as chief justice.[2]

The court scheduled the first trial for June 2—three months after the first arrest—and on that day convicted Bridget Bishop, whom Stoughton sentenced to hang. This trial must have caused some dissension among the judges, for Nathaniel Saltonstall resigned his seat, and the court adjourned until June 29. It seems that the judges wanted moral backing; presumably for their guidance, Governor Phips sent the colony's ministers a request for procedural advice. Before the ministers had delivered this "Return," Governor Phips left Boston for a summer campaign against the Indians, and on June 8, Stoughton, as acting governor, ordered the execution of the woman he himself had sentenced six days before. For the rest of the summer Stoughton served both is acting governor and chief justice. A learned man,

---

[2]The other Judges were Samuel Sewall, Bartholomew Gedney, Wait Winthrop, Nathaniel Saltonstall, John Richards, William Sergeant, and—after Saltonstall resigned—Jonathan Corwin.

thoroughly orthodox in his theology, he believed in vigorously prosecuting the witches. When he and his court received the ministers' rather equivocal advice on June 15, they proceeded as before, admitting all kinds of testimony, but professing not to rely wholly on what was called spectral evidence: testimony that a specter in shape of the accused had tormented the accuser or demanded that he sign the Devil's book.

After the court reassembled on June 29, the trials moved rapidly, for they consisted mostly in the reading of depositions taken earlier from witnesses at "examinations" conducted by the magistrates. Five witches were hanged on July 19; five more on August 19; and eight on September 22. On September 19, Giles Cory, an old man who did not want his heirs to be deprived of his property by a bill of attainder, had to pay for his foresightedness; refusing to plead either guilty or not guilty, he avoided conviction but had to endure being pressed to death under increasing weights of stone as the sheriff, in accordance with British common law, tried to force him to answer the indictment.

During August and September more and more people of all ranks came to suspect that there had been "a going too far" in the witch hunt and trials. Many of those who watched the hangings on August 19 shouted objections against the execution of George Burroughs and John Proctor. In court, several courageous witnesses testified that someone had prompted one of the afflicted girls to cry out the right name in making an accusation; others, that one afflicted girl said she made her accusations "for sport." Some embarrassingly logical critics began to ask why it was that the government had not executed any of the witches who confessed, and rumors said that the sheriff had won some confessions by using force. The common people began to lose confidence in the judges after discovering that some "respectable" people who had been accused were not prosecuted, and that others who had been arrested had managed to escape. Mrs. Thatcher, the mother-in-law of Judge Jonathan Corwin, was repeatedly accused, but no one arrested her; Nathaniel Saltonstall, the judge who had resigned, remained at liberty even though someone had cried out upon him; and many believed the rumor that Lady Phips herself had been accused. At the same time, some of the colony's leading thinkers and most of the socially prominent people were amazed and frightened that such men and women as Saltonstall, Lady Phips, and Mrs. Thatcher—persons "of good conversation"—had been accused at all.

At the end of the summer, when Sir William Phips made his second grand entrance as governor of the colony, he found that witchcraft had again forced him to face an explosive situation. During the summer the affliction had spread to Andover, and officials had captured at least one witch in Maine. Cotton Mather was now convinced that the Devil's strategy was subtly to divide God's people—by "*devices*, of perhaps a finer thread than was ever yet practiced among the world," to force them so far "into a *blind man's buffet*" that they were "even ready to be *sinfully*, yea hotly and madly, mauling one another in the *dark*." By this time it was clear that there was open disagreement between some of the judges on the one hand, and the ministers and several laymen on the other. Governor Phips was alarmed by the dissension and the accusations of "unblamable" persons. He consulted Increase Mather, his most trusted adviser, and learned that the burning issue was the court's admission of spectral evidence. Before the twelfth of October, a week after Increase Mather read the ministers an essay demonstrating the unreliability of spectral evidence, Governor Phips prohibited the arrest "without unavoidable necessity" of any more accused persons; he forbade further executions, pending orders from the King; and he tried to persuade William Stoughton to change the court's methods, to stop relying on the testimony of the bewitched. Stoughton apparently refused, for Phips dismissed the court before the end of the month.

With the fall of the Court of Oyer and Terminer the "witchcraft delusion," at least in its most harmful form, came to an end. There were no more executions, and Phips ordered the jailers to release some prisoners on bail. In November the General Court passed a law creating a Superior Court to judge the remaining cases. With new instructions charging them to give very little weight to spectral evidence, the jurors convicted only three of fifty-two persons tried in January. Stoughton condemned these three and signed the death warrants of five others, four of them confessing witches, who had been granted reprieves; but Phips stayed all the executions. The Court sat again in April, but there were no more convictions, and in May Phips signed a general pardon. The period of penitence began soon afterward, though not before some of the sufferers had their revenge on Samuel Parris, whom they banished from the Salem Village pulpit. In 1697, the General Court proclaimed a fast day, and Samuel Sewall stood in church to hear his own confession of error read to the congregation; several of the jurors who had convicted witches asked public pardon on the same day. During the next ten years there were other personal apologies, and in 1711 a resolution of the General Court reversed the bills of attainder against all the executed witches whose families had sought to have the bills revoked.

3

The sudden reversal of public opinion and official action on Salem witchcraft did not mean that most people renounced their belief in the existence of witches. The central issue in 1692 was not whether witches existed, or whether to execute them, but how to discover them. Once Increase Mather and fourteen other ministers had demonstrated that not only spectral evidence but all the testimony of the afflicted was unreliable, there was no really just basis for convicting a witch except a free confession. At the end of the year, therefore, even those who believed that some of the condemned "witches" had been guilty could offer no consistent formula for distinguishing the guilty from the innocent. Although witchcraft was still a real danger, the crime of spilling innocent blood came to be more frightening than the crime of suffering a witch to live.

Why had the ministers failed to speak out against spectral evidence before October? They had spoken, but in a confused whisper rather than a cry of clear conviction. From the very beginning they cautioned the judges not to rely too heavily on spectral evidence, since the Devil could, they said, assume the shape of an innocent person while tormenting a victim. They saw, too, that by June 15 the list of alleged witches had grown almost too large to be credible. Yet the tales of confessors, which agreed with each other in the few details they gave, multiplied almost as rapidly as the number of accusations. Such confessors as William Barker and Deliverance Hobbs seemed to prove that the Devil and his three hundred-odd witches had to be stopped quietly. What the ministers wanted most of all from an accused witch was a confession; let the sheriff execute the witch while the minister extricated the soul of the victim. If the defendant did not plead guilty, then the court had to proceed according to the best light it had, and pray for guidance. True, witchcraft was a crime of the invisible world, but God had commanded His people in this world to destroy witches. There must be some way for the enlightened in the visible world to discover and punish the other-worldly criminals. Although the Devil could impersonate an innocent person, the ministers believed that lie did not often do so. Thus spectral evidence, while not conclusive of the defendant's guilt, seemed to be reasonable grounds for "presumption" or suspicion; along with other, corroborative evidence, it might help convict a witch.

Seeing that the accusations did not cease after months of trials, and that after twenty executions the basic dilemma remained unsolved, such different men as Increase Mather and Thomas Brattle the merchant began to wonder how much reliance on spectral evidence was "too much." The ministers came to see that the Devil was making almost as much headway through confusion and dissension as he could make by trying to convert New Englanders to witchcraft. Endorsing Increase Mather's *Cases of Conscience*, the ministers denounced spectral evidence and turned wholly to exhortation as a means of inducing their congregations to combat the Devil. Yet it would be a mistake to think that by this book Increase Mather and the other ministers intended to repudiate the judges. They still believed in witchcraft; they still believed that New England was the target of a large-scale witchcraft conspiracy. This book was not a condemnation but an admonition to the judges. It announced that the ministers would not support any further convictions based on the testimony of the afflicted, but it did not say that all those already executed had been innocent. Increase Mather was careful to assure the reader that he himself would have convicted George Burroughs after hearing the evidence against him; that "there was more than that which is called *specter evidence* for the conviction of the persons condemned."

The documents of five trials appear in this collection. The trials include all the kinds of evidence offered in court against the Salem witches. In choosing them, I have also tried to present a cross section of the kinds of people who were convicted and executed in 1692. Bridget Bishop, a widow who had remarried, was the proprietress of a little tavern. Gaudy in her dress, she had long been the subject of community gossip. She had been accused of witchcraft in 1680. Sarah Good, the wife of a propertyless farm worker, was unpopular because of her slothfulness, her sullen temper, and her poverty; she had recently taken to begging, an occupation the Puritans detested. Susanna Martin of Amesbury was an outspoken woman who answered with defiance the slander that had centered around her ever since she was accused of witchcraft in 1669. John Proctor, a farmer who was master of one of the afflicted girls, had won the respect of most of his neighbors; but his honestly vehement expression of skepticism did not help him in 1692. George Burroughs was the only minister tried for witchcraft. As minister at Salem Village in the early 1680s, he had suffered the usual bickering between this parish and its pastor; after a sharp quarrel with some of his parishioners over debts they said he owed them, he had left Salem Village for a small parish in Maine.

The controversy over who was to blame for the Salem executions has continued in historical writing ever since Cotton Mather, in the first history of Salem witchcraft, blamed the Devil. But aside from this search for heroes and villains, other questions remain unsolved. How large a part did spectral evidence play in some of the convictions? In a trial involving the invisible world, where did "spectral" evidence end and "concrete," human evidence begin? What was the psychology of the afflicted girls? Of the confessed witches? Were any of the condemned witches really "guilty"? The materials of the Salem witchcraft trials are worth studying today not only for the historical exercise of reconstructing human drama, but also because the problem of dealing with heresy and even conspiratorial opinion seems to be a perennial one, as does the question of assigning to individuals responsibility for collective error.

Discussion Questions

1. How does Levin define the "crime of witchcraft"? What role did the Devil play in the Puritan understanding of witchcraft? What were the particular Puritan beliefs about the qualities of the Devil?

2. What was "spectral evidence" and why was it so important in the trials?

3. Consider the root of the word *spectral*, derived from the Latin word *spectrum*, meaning *apparition*. List as many other words as you can that derive from the root verb *spectare*, which means *to look at* (*spectacle*, for example). How do the words all relate to the original meaning and the use of the word *spectral* as pertaining to evidence?

Writing Suggestions

1. Write a personal essay describing your concept of who or what "the Devil" is. You could include childhood images that haunted you about the Devil, or media or film representations that colored your picture of the Devil, or you could write a more philosophical view of what the concept of "the Devil" means to you. Use concrete descriptions and vivid details to show what this word "conjures up" in your mind.

2. First, look up "Salem Witch Trials" on Google, Lycos, or Yahoo. Brainstorm, as a group, different key words you might use to search the Internet for more sites about the witch trials. (For example, you might try "spectral evidence," or "Reverend Parrish" to get more specific information.) Then make a list comparing the ways each site emphasizes different information. What kind of information is offered? What are the link names? What kinds of historical summaries does each site offer? What categories of information does each site offer? When were the sites updated? Remember to look at the domain names of each site. Is the site labeled ".com," ".gov," or ".edu"? In other words, is the origin of the site an organization, a government agency, or a university? Next, look at Purdue's "Evaluating Internet Sources" guidelines, at <http://owl.english. purdue.edu/handouts/research/r-evalsource4.html>. Finally, write an analytical essay comparing the high quality sites you have found with those you feel are less credible. Answer the question: Which sites are the best sources for writing a research essay about the witch trials in Salem? As evidence for your conclusions, consider the following questions:

What are the differences between these sites?
How did you reach your conclusions?
What criteria did you use in evaluating the sources?
What kinds of authorities does each site offer?
Where did you find corroborating evidence between sites?

Records of Salem Witchcraft

Trial Testimony

SARAH GOOD

Sarah Good was one of the first three women of Salem to be accused of witchcraft. Sarah was arrested on February 29, 1692, but she was not tried until June 29. Below is the chilling record of her trial. Sarah was hanged on Gallows Hill on July 19, 1692, and is perhaps best known for her final statement to Reverend Noyes, who tried to get her to confess just before her hanging. She said to him: "I am no more witch than you are wizard. If you take my life away, God will give you blood to drink." Many years later, Reverend Noyes did indeed die of a hemorrhage in his mouth.

Examination of Sarah Good

The examination of Sarah Good before the worshipfull Assts John Harthorn Jonathan Curran

(H.) Sarah Good what evil Spirit have you familiarity with
(S. G.) None
(H.) Have you made contracte with the devil
Good answered no.
(H.) Why doe you hurt these children
(g) I doe not hurt them. I scorn it.
(H.) Who doe you imploy then to doe it.
(g) I imploy no body
(H) What creature do you imploy then.
(g) no creature but I am falsely accused.
(H) why did you go away muttering from Mr Parris his house.
(g) I did not mutter but I thanked him for what be gave my child.
(H) have you made no contract with the devil.
(g) no.
(H) desired the children all of them to look upon her and see if this were the person that had hurt them and so they all did looke upon her, and said this was one of the persons that did torment them—presently they were all tormented.
(H) Sarah Good do you not see now what you have done, why doe you not tell us the truth, why doe you thus torment these poor children
(g) I doe not torment them.

(H) who do you imploy then.

(g) I imploy nobody I scorn it.

(H) how came they thus tormented

(g) what doe I know you bring others here and now you charge me with it

(H) why who was it.

(g) I doe not know but it was some you brought into the meeting house with you.

(H) wee brought you into the meeting house.

(g) but you brought in two more.

(H) who was it then that tormented the children.

(g) it was osburn.

(H) what is it you say when you go muttering away from persons houses

(g) if I must tell I will tell.

(H) doe tell us then

(g) if I must tell, I will tell, it is the commandments. I may say my commandments I hope.

(H.) what commandment is it.

(g) if I must tell I will tell, it is a psalm.

(H) what psalm.

(g) after a long time shee muttered over some part of a psalm.

(H) who doe you serve

(g) I serve God

(H) what God doe you serve.

(g) the God that made heaven and earth. though shee was not willing to mention the word God. her answers were in a very wicked spitfull manner. reflecting and retorting against the authority with base and abussive words and many lies shee was taken in it was here said that her husband had said that he was afraid that she either was a witch or would be one very quickly. the worsh. Mr. Harthon asked him his reason why he said so of her, whether he had ever seen any thing by her, he answered no, not in this nature, but it was her bad carriage to him, and indeed said he I may say with tears that shee is an enemy to all good.

Salem Village March the 1st 169½

Written by Ezekiell Chevers

Salem Village March the 1st 169½[1]

---

[1]According to the Old Style calendar still in use in England at this time, the legal year began on March 25. Thus, this date, which was March 1, 1692, as we now count, was technically March 1, 1691. The double designation 169½ was often employed, reflecting both legal and popular usage.

Discussion Questions

1. Discuss in groups whether or not you have ever been falsely accused of any crime, misdemeanor, or even misbehavior. How did you react? Were you able to argue logically against your accusers? Were you able to marshal effective evidence? Consider how your experience might help you to put yourself in the place of Sarah Good.

2. First, as a group discuss the series of questions posed to Sarah Good by her examiners. Look at the pattern and repetition of the questions, and then, imitating the examiners' rhetorical strategy, design your own set of questions for a contemporary "trial" of an "accused" class member. (For example, you could ask the accused member "Why did you cheat on that test?") Design the questions for two questioners and one accused person, and then conduct the "trial." Afterwards, discuss how all members of the mock trial felt. You can vary this exercise by gender: Try having two male questioners and one female accused, and then reverse the genders so that the women are the examiners and the man is the "accused." How do the gender changes affect the feelings of the trial, if at all?

Writing Suggestions

1. Consider your responses to the second discussion question for this selection, and then write a brief analysis of the language used by Sarah Good's questioners. What strategies did they use to try to get Sarah to confess? For example, you might count the number of times prosecutors asked Sarah Good the same questions. Were these questioning strategies effective? Consider the purpose of the interviewers. How does the tone of their questions reflect an awareness of their audience and the historical period they were living in?

2. Imagine that you are Sarah Good's defense attorney, and that you can examine her in front of a jury. As an attorney, what might your strategy be in questioning Sarah? Which assumptions of the jury are you trying to question? Which evidence or lack of it are you trying to showcase? Write a series of questions that you would ask her, and then write a brief analysis of why you feel these questions would contribute to a verdict of "innocent" for Sarah Good.

The Reluctant Witch

Fueling Puritan Fantasies

ELAINE G. BRESLAW

Elaine G. Breslaw is the author of numerous articles and books about colonial and revolutionary America, and she has written widely on the subject of the Salem witch trials and the trial of Tituba, the black slave woman who was accused of witchcraft. Currently adjunct professor of history at the University of Tennessee, Breslaw taught for many years at Morgan State University and at the Johns Hopkins University School of Continuing Studies. In the selection below, taken from Breslaw's book, *Tituba, Reluctant Witch of Salem*, Breslaw argues that Tituba, rather than falling prey to the accusations leveled against her, "improvised a new idiom of resistance by overtly submitting to the will of her abuser while covertly feeding his fears of a conspiracy."

Tituba an Indian woman brought before us by Const[able] Jos Herrick of Salem upon Suspition of Witchcraft by her Commited according to the Compl't of Jos. Hutcheson & Thomas putnam etc. of Salem Village as appears p Warrant granted Salem 29 febr'y 1691/2 . . .

    —In Paul Boyer and Stephen Nissenbaum, eds., *Salem Witchcraft Papers*

On the last day of February 1692, a leap year, Joseph Hutchinson, Edward and Thomas Putnam, and Thomas Preston appeared before Salem magistrates John Hathorne and Jonathan Corwin to make complaints against the three accused women for "suspition of Witchcraft." They charged that Sarah Osborne, Tituba, and Sarah Good had been using occult means to injure four girls over a period of two months. Four girls—Betty Parris, Abigail Williams, Ann Putnam, and Elizabeth Hubbard, all under eighteen years of age—added their testimony to support the complaints. Thus began the legal process that focused attention on Tituba and would eventually lead to the imprisonment of more than one hundred people over a period of nine months and the execution of twenty between June 19 and September 22. A few more would die in prison from exposure and disease, adding a gruesome note to the death toll from this witch scare. Tituba would escape with her life, but she would spend thirteen months in a crowded, foul-smelling and filthy Boston prison, unsure of her fate.

Tituba's subsequent testimony confirmed the worst fears of a diabolical presence and gave the Salem worthies reason to launch a witchhunt. She supplied the essential legal evidence required to begin the process of communal exorcism, to purge the community of its collective sin. Without her testimony the trials could not have taken place. Thus it was only after Tituba began to confess that the witchhunt began in earnest. In her fantasies of an evil power, the Indian woman confirmed that the Devil was now among them.

Witchcraft was a crime against God in the European world and, therefore, a heresy, but in England it was treated as a social crime. English laws of 1542 and 1604 made it a capital offense to invoke an evil spirit, to use magic to hurt or kill people, find lost treasure, harm cattle, or to "provoke unlawful love," among other anti-social activities. The penalty for such acts was a year's imprisonment for the first offense and death for the second. As in all criminal cases in the English world, the legal process in identifying and prosecuting persons accused of witchcraft followed a standard sequence. It began with a formal complaint presented by members of the community, a preliminary hearing to investigate the charges, the presentation of an indictment against the accused, and finally trial by a jury of freeholders of that county. The somewhat vague Massachusetts laws of 1641 and 1642, which governed events in 1692, were seemingly based on a combination of the English laws and Old Testament prohibitions. They prescribed death "If any man or woman be a witch (that is hath consulteth with a familiar spirit)." Massachusetts generally followed English procedures; a jury trial was mandatory before the punishment could be inflicted.

Magistrates John Hathorne and Jonathan Corwin, after hearing the complaints of Joseph Hutchinson, Edward and Thomas Putnam, and Thomas Preston in Salem, followed the standard procedure and issued warrants on February 29, 1692, to arrest the three accused women. Constable Joseph Herrick was also ordered to search Tituba's and Osborne's possessions for "images and such like" as evidence and to bring the women to Ingersoll's Tavern at 10:00 the next morning for questioning. No incriminating artifacts were found in their possession. Constable George Locker was sent to arrest Sarah Good and bring her too to the tavern.

Samuel Parris must have felt a certain satisfaction when Joseph Herrick appeared at his door to arrest Tituba. He was angry at her defiance of his authority by participating in an occult ritual. A day or two before he had beaten his servant woman to force a confession about her role in the making of the witchcake. She contritely admitted her guilt in that ritual and hoped that the matter would end there. Parris was not satisfied with that minimal confession and demanded more details about her knowledge of occult practices and of others involved in this incident. She told him of Mary Sibley's participation. His immediate response to the imputations of witchcraft on the part of one of his supporters in his conflict with the Village has not been recorded. At first Parris appeared to ignore the implications of Sibley's role. But Sibley was not forgotten; he would deal with her later and in a less punitive fashion.

When questioned later about her familiarity with witchcraft practices, Tituba admitted to having learned about occult techniques in Barbados. Her mistress in her own country, she said, had taught her how to reveal the cause of witchcraft and also how to protect herself against that evil power. Such knowledge was intended to help defend herself against the malevolence of others, but not to do harm herself. To Parris she denied being a witch or taking part in the pain experienced by the girls, even though she had admitted to participation in an occult ritual. Tituba did not understand Parris's insistence that she was responsible for the children's distress. She had not meant to hurt Betty, but to help the little girl. Why, when her intentions were good, was she accused of causing Betty's illness?

Tituba's initial reluctance to respond to Parris's accusations of witchcraft followed from a difference between folk and Christian theological notions regarding magic. Tituba, drawing on folklore, made a distinction between protective and healing powers and evil intent, between white magic and black magic, or what could be perceived among some tribal cultures as the difference between sorcery and the magical work of healers and curers like obeahs and shamans. In Tituba's mind witchcraft was equated with the European idea of maleficium, the commission of an evil act. Because she had no evil intent in manufacturing the witchcake, Tituba denied that she was a witch.

Parris, on the other hand, assumed evil intent. In his mental world all occult powers were evil because they were derived from devilish associations. Tituba, in the tradition of most ordinary folk, as well as Indians and Africans, focused on the effect of the ritual rather than the origins of her power. Parris, concerned with the assumed Satanic source of her magical power, began with a different set of premises. Participation in magic was a form of blasphemy—it violated God's commandments—that could not be left unchallenged.

This "disjunction" between theological and popular notions of witchcraft did not matter until people turned to the legal system for protection against the magic of the cunning folk. Judicial policy required concrete evidence of diabolism to convict. Magistrates were under pressure to accommodate the law to the needs of the populace: to revise the rules of evidence and make it easier to punish those accused. But the legal system, influenced by clerical concerns, seldom succumbed to popular lore and few people were indicted for witchcraft; only a small number of those were found guilty. Parris's use of the courts to punish Tituba for her countermagic created an intellectual crisis in New England that finally forced a convergence of the two disparate traditions. Popular views as articulated by his Indian woman servant and then reformulated by others in the community ultimately brought about changes in the legal definitions and theological assumptions regarding witchcraft.

Parris seemed determined to prove Tituba's guilt and bring her to trial. In his worldview, dabbling in the occult signified witchcraft and Tituba's participation in the preparation of the rye meal-urine mixture was sufficient evidence of involvement in a Satanic pact. Perhaps he was concerned about his own image as a clerical leader and the imputation of a diabolical presence in his household. The behavior of the two girls Betty and Abigail, as well as of Tituba, was his responsibility. Tituba's improper approach to the problem of evil cast doubt on Parris's ability to maintain order in his own house. Had he somehow compromised himself by neglecting his duties to force obedience from this dependent? To control unacceptable behavior, strict discipline and punitive action were sometimes necessary and socially approved. He would not be faulted for beating either servants or children. Instead of punishing the girls, Parris elected to discipline Tituba. In so doing, by blaming Tituba for the misfortune of his family, he was able to uphold the stereotype of the Indian as Devil worshiper while distancing himself from the taint of association with the evil force she represented.

Parris's treatment of his servant woman to force an admission of complicity with the Devil was in the tradition of the European inquisitors who used torture to elicit confessions. He was rewarded with similar results. To prevent further punishment, Tituba reluctantly promised to do as he demanded and name others who were involved. Unaware of the potential consequences, he turned her over to the magistrates to answer more questions regarding the details of her devilish alliance. She would be punished as much for defying his ministerial and paternal authority as for her alleged dabbling in the occult.

The hearing was to be held at Ingersoll's Tavern on March 1. The spectacle of three women revealing the titillating details of witch activities attracted a considerable number of Salem inhabitants. By early morning, the crowd of onlookers waiting to observe the investigation had grown too large to fit into the tavern and the examinations were moved to the meeting house. The curious as well as the witnesses and their families crowded into the building. The three accused women were brought into the meeting room one at a time.

Sarah Good, who in appearance fit the popular mental and physical image of a witch—an abrasive middle-aged female of low social position who was frequently involved in conflicts with others—was the first to be questioned. Even though she was the mother of a five-year-old and was pregnant at the time, Good was thirty-eight years old and looked haggard. She was not helped by her reputation. She was known and feared for her sharp tongue, avoided attendance at church, and only grudgingly accepted the assistance of her apparent betters when she was destitute. No images had been found in her possession, but she was assumed guilty of the charge of familiarity with evil spirits and bluntly asked about her association with the Devil. She denied any diabolical contact. Asked why she hurt the children, Sarah Good vehemently denied all allegations and explained, in defense of her absence from church, that she lacked adequate clothing.

The girls, listening to her denials, began to complain of painful pinching and, crying out, accused Sarah Good of tormenting them at that moment. She denied being responsible for their distress. If not her, who then was torturing the girls? asked the magistrates. Good suggested that it was the other accused woman, Sarah Osborne. The girls, temporarily recovering their composure, agreed that it was Osborne, a reasonable assumption since she too had been arrested and was being held for questioning.

Osborne, who like Good had habitually missed church services, was brought into the room after Good. Unaware that the other woman had implicated her, Osborne too denied being in league with the Devil or doing anything to hurt the children. She complained that she was more likely to be bewitched than be a witch because of her past troubles. Sarah Osborne reflected on a dream when she too had been pricked by an appearance which she described as "a thing like an indian," in an artful allusion to the Puritan stereotype of the Devil as Indian. Another time she heard voices telling her not to go to church, which she had resisted. The voices and the remembered dream were taken as evidence not of a bewitchment but of a guilty association with invisible specters. Guilt would be the presumption in almost all the hearings to follow.

Tituba was brought forward last to answer her accusers in the meeting house. Parris's act in submitting his servant woman to legal action pushed Tituba to the forefront of the witchscare and set the stage for the extraordinary persecution that would follow her reluctant confession. It is possible that if the Indian woman had maintained silence during the subsequent interrogation, that witchhunt might not have occurred, or, at the least, would have followed a different course. She reluctantly and hesitatingly took the lead in implicating others beyond the boundaries of the Salem community and established the framework of a fictional conspiracy of witches linked to the Devil through a written pact. Her story would then be embellished by the fantasies, fears, and cultural biases of other witnesses, but she provided the raw material from which they could weave even more elaborate narratives.

Her earlier questioning at Parris's hands convinced her that the truth, so cherished by her Puritan mentors, would fail her as a defense in court. She had every reason to sense that her successful facade as an acculturated servant would crumble in the face of this blatantly hostile legal procedure. The truthful denial of association with the evil presence not only failed to provide protection, it was treated as an act of defiance. Her rejection of Parris's suggestion that she was in league with the Devil had challenged his authority in spiritual matters and he was determined to exact retribution. Moreover, her admission of guilt to an act of white magic in fashioning the witchcake had had grotesque results. It frightened the girls into more bizarre behavior and enraged Parris. Another means of defense had to be devised if Tituba were to escape extreme punishment.

After a preliminary and weak denial of familiarity with the Devil or of causing harm, Tituba reluctantly confessed. She fulfilled her promise to Parris and began to respond positively to the accusations and charges. She confessed to consorting with the Devil, blaming Sarah Good and Sarah Osborne for forcing her to take part in a plot to hurt the children, and proceeded to elaborate on a fantastic chronicle describing a coven of witches in Boston, suggesting with telling detail how Satanic power had infiltrated their Salem community. The girls quieted as they listened with astonishment to her extraordinary story, an account of witchcraft so inspired and singular that it appeared to be plausible. It was not, as some earlier historians have suggested, the "incoherent nonsense" of a confused slave woman. It was a carefully crafted tale that provided satisfactory answers to the questions in the seventeenth-century mind. Tituba explained the cause of the calamities. She also created a new aura of mystery about the events in Salem. The more credulous the magistrates appeared to be, the more richly embroidered the tale became. The reluctant witch had captured her audience.

It is impossible to determine exactly what Tituba was thinking on that March 1, 1692 day when she was forced to admit to having made a Satanic pact. Her decision may have been influenced by what happened in other cases of witchcraft in Boston and how those others accused were treated by the authorities in the recent past. She may well have been aware that between 1680 and 1692, during the time she had lived in Massachusetts, only one person had been executed for witchcraft. Those accused of other crimes and who demonstrated penitence by humbly confessing to their sins were treated sympathetically. In most criminal trials in Massachusetts, "magistrates from the start were lenient with penitent offenders." Tituba probably thought she had only to demonstrate true repentance for her past behavior to end her trial.

Few people in New England received harsh punishment for the crime of witchcraft. Executions had virtually ended in 1663 with the hanging of Rebecca and Nathaniel Greensmith. Tituba probably knew nothing of these earlier events that predated her arrival. On the other hand, not too long after the Indian woman had landed in Boston, Mary Hale had been indicted by the provincial court for familiarity with the Devil and bewitching a man to death. There was insufficient evidence and the court found her not guilty in March of 1681. Two years later Mary Webster was also tried and found not guilty of witchcraft. Tituba probably knew about Elizabeth Morse who was convicted in 1680 but managed to avoid execution. In June of 1681 Morse, after her husband's sorrowful petition, was reprieved but confined to her home and the meeting house. Tituba may also have heard about Joseph Fuller of Springfield who in 1683 had at first confessed to praying to the Devil and then retracted that confession. He was, however, found not guilty of the charge but whipped for lying. Thus any knowledge of the experiences of other accused persons indicated that the worst Tituba could expect for confessing even a lie might be a beating. The death penalty for witchcraft, in spite of the law, was a rare occurrence and was imposed only once in New England while Tituba was there prior to the Salem witchscare.

That recent incident of execution, however, was more ominous. The allegations against Goodwife Glover, an Irish woman who, in 1688, had received a great deal of attention in the Boston community, ran contrary to earlier experiences. The Goodwin children, like Betty Parris and Abigail Williams, had exhibited strange behaviors and Goodwife Glover was suspected of bewitching them. Glover did confess and was subsequently convicted and executed.

But the Glover execution was unusual and Tituba, if she knew about it, may have expected that her own earlier blameless life, unlike that of Goody Glover, would afford some leniency.

On the other hand, the Parris family had moved to Salem before the Goodwin children had been "possessed" and it is possible that Tituba was not aware of the disposition of the Glover trial and her execution. In that case Tituba's knowledge of how accused witches were treated by the authorities came from the experiences of those who were either exonerated, received minimum punishment, or were reprieved. Confession, she expected, would satisfy Parris's grim determination to find a scapegoat for his daughter's troubles and did not necessarily entail either prison or death.

Quite likely she also hoped that confessing to supernatural power would intimidate her tormentors into leaving her alone. Such a threat might at least temporarily protect her from physical punishment. Claims of occult power were not unusual ploys by servants and slaves whose repertoire of resistance tended to be more passive than active. Invoking the Devil, like the use of violence by the dispossessed, was one of those extra-legal weapons used by powerless people who would challenge law and authority. Tituba devised an even more imaginative use of that kind of resistance to protect her life.

Her decision to comply with Parris's orders to confess gave new meaning to a technique that had been used successfully by other slaves to avoid punishment. Depending on the gullibility of their victims, the implied threat in the slaves' claim to magical power could provide protection against excessive abuse. In Tituba's case, Parris's insistence that she had made a pact with the Devil not only forced her to claim occult power, but it also opened the possibility of deflecting attention from herself by accusing others of complicity in a witches' coven. Tituba improvised a new idiom of resistance by overtly submitting to the will of her abuser while covertly feeding his fears of a conspiracy. An admission of sin, even though a lie, followed by repentance became a workable tactic of resistance that others would follow.

As is typical of witchcraft interrogation in all cultures, Tituba's questioners provided her with clues as to what her answers should be. Since those accused of witchcraft were usually innocent of the charges, such testimonies were more often an affirmation of the questioners' ideas about witchcraft than a revelation of the accused witches' particular beliefs and practices. A good part of Tituba's testimony was a direct response to those questions. She certainly understood some of what they wanted her to say and did give them the evidence needed to pursue their suspicions, but she also added details and notions that were not implied in the questions and set off a broader investigation than they had intended. Tituba's testimony was not merely the frightened response of a simple slave woman to the hints put forth by the magistrates, but an effective manipulation of their deepest fears. The impact of that confession triggered the witchhunt that defied all past experience with witchhunting in New England. In the process Tituba also led an assault on gender roles, social rank, and the clergy's authority, an attack that would be pursued relentlessly by the "afflicted" girls and the other confessors.

On the surface, in this cautious exchange between Tituba and her accusers, she seemed to ally herself with the Puritan theological notions of demonic evil, collaborating to assist in the process of purifying their society. But something more was at work. Hidden in that confession was not so much a Puritan concept of evil but one derived from non-Christian cultures; a set of ideas that was at once familiar and strange. The anomaly of this aberration heightened the fear of an invasive presence.

When asked if she ever saw the Devil, Tituba acknowledged that "the devil came to me and bid me serve him." Who else did she see, asked the interrogator? Because she now knew he wanted others involved, Tituba answered, there were four women and a man. And who were they? Tituba identified two likely women who fit the popular image of a witch, Sarah Osborne and Sarah Good, both quarrelsome and somewhat disreputable, but already accused by the girls and thus understood by the magistrates as potential conspirators. The other three she did not know, but one was a tall man from Boston.

The man, according to Tituba's story, had visited her once before in late December or early January at the time that the children had first exhibited the bizarre symptoms. He appeared to her one night just as she was going to sleep. The Salem magistrates missed her cue. The dream was not even reported in the official record of her testimony taken by Ezekiel Cheever. It does appear in a more detailed report written by Jonathan Corwin. In Corwin's version she told them that the man-like shape came to her "Just as I was goeing to sleep . . . this was when the children was first hurt."

Tituba's nightmare of that evil presence may well have triggered memories of her earlier Barbados life, where dreams among both African and American Indians were thought to be the work of spirits and interpreted as omens of things to come. That ominous dream of an evil presence would be confirmed, in her mind, by the continuing illness of the children in the household and her own current misfortune to be identified with witchcraft. She sensed that Parris's wrath was the cause of Betty's problems, that the minister's continuing jeremiads against the ungrateful community and his terrifying warnings of future evils were taking their toll on the mental health of his daughter. By couching her accusation in the form of a sleep reference, in line with Indian beliefs in the identification of dreams as omens, she tried to inform others of Parris's evil ways. Her subversive suggestion was ignored.

Dreams were not significant elements in Puritan theology. They took her nightmare not as a visionary omen or spiritual experience but an actual occurrence that involved the specters of people they had to identify. Magistrates Hathorne and Corwin focused their questions on the activities of this odd group of creatures who inhabited the diabolical realm brought down to earth. "What is this appearance you see? . . . What did it say to you? . . . What did you say to it?" they asked.

Responding to their probing, Tituba embellished her story even more. The creatures all met in Boston at night where the five evil ones, including Sarah Good and Sarah Osborne, threatened her if she did not hurt the children. Tituba introduced a new element in witchcraft testimony, a witches' coven attended by the specters of people both known and unknown to her. The startled examiners paused to question her about this strange, distant meeting. Witchcraft accusations traditionally involved people known to each other, an aggrieved party usually could be suspected of causing harm to others. But Tituba told them that strangers were involved.

The interrogation of the other two accused women, Osborne and Good, had followed conventional tactics. In the face of continued denials, they had been asked in a prescribed sequence about the spirits they were familiar with, why they hurt the children or whom they used for that purpose, and finally about a covenant with the Devil. This procedure changed with the questioning of Tituba. The examiners did not immediately pursue the issue of a satanic pact. They were distracted by her complex tale of an experience that took her from Boston back to Salem with orders to kill the children and of a specter that changed shape from that of a man to a dog and a hog. Joining this party of phantoms were a yellow bird, rats, a wolf and a cat, four women, and a hairy imp.

Additional details were elicited from Tituba on the dress and physical appearance of this group. Tituba specified that Osborne had a familiar with the head of a woman and two legs and wings similar to one previously described by Abigail. The tall man wore black clothes. One of the unidentified Boston women, Tituba said, wore a black hood over a white silk hood with a top knot. The other, a shorter person, had a serge coat and white cap. Tituba stated that she had seen the taller woman in Boston when she had lived there, but did not know her name. The silk clothing of the tall woman would indicate that Tituba had a person of higher class in mind; the shorter woman in wool and a white cap wore the dress of the more ordinary folk.

Sumptuary laws in Massachusetts prohibited men, women, and children from dressing in clothing made out of finer material. By order of October 14, 1651, the Massachusetts General Court had forbidden people of "meane condition" from wearing the "garbe of gentlemen" or women of the same rank from wearing "silke or tiffany hoodes or scarfes, which though allowable to persons of greater estates, or more liberal education, yet, we cannot but judge it intolerable in persons of such like condition." The description of the woman in silk and the man in black were, therefore, veiled references to respectability and an attempt to identify maleficium with higher social status. The man's black clothing carried a connotation of dignity and formality. The silk worn by the "tall woman" denoted wealth.

Tituba's extraordinary message to her examiners was to look among the elite for the evil beings. That message, delivered in a discrete and artful attack on the social class system, opened the way to the accusation of women of respectable sainthood, beginning with Martha Corey and Rebecca Nurse on March 19 and 23, respectively. The convictions of these women would be eloquent testimony to the force of Tituba's suggestion that women eligible to wear silk could be witches. Her hints regarding the dangers hidden among the obviously respectable were confirmed and reinforced by Parris's sermons later that month and by his early April warning that the Devil could lurk among the apparent saints. Her testimony confirmed the predictions of reformers who had reminded their congregations of an impending catastrophe if the community continued on its worldly path.

The strange, tall, white-haired man Tituba claimed to see wearing black clothes could fit many respectable, elderly men in the community dressed in their Sunday meeting clothes. In the imagination of some other confessed witches, obsessed by the rhetoric of race and in their fantasies of satanic Indians, this tall Boston mystery man would be transformed into a tawny or black man. But he was clearly a white man in Tituba's recorded testimony, a devious reference to Samuel Parris, a clergyman with strong connections to Boston. In effect this part of her testimony triggered a search for an appropriate male scapegoat. The result, discussed in the next chapter, was a widening of the witchhunt to include men; the arrest, conviction, and execution of several men; and the hanging of one clergyman, George Burroughs.

Whatever her intent, the consequence of Tituba's accusation in this community where words were believed to have the force of action, was to challenge the principle of social rank and raise the possibility of clerical misconduct. No one would be more likely to resent the special privilege of that class than a slave in the house of a Congregational minister. But Tituba's rudimentary anti-clericalism probably did not exist in isolation. She spoke to resentments against the special privilege and influence of the clergy harbored by other ordinary people, particularly young women. They would give vent to their hostility in later testimonies and confessions as they adapted and reformulated Tituba's stories to fit their own situations. Thus others, sensing the possible subversive message of a respectable white man leading a witch's coven, transformed Tituba's suggestion of an evil stranger into a parody of their own church rites—an indirect attack on the congregational ideal.

Questioned further about this strange group of people, Tituba said that they all met in Boston the night before. And how had they traveled there? Tituba described the ride through the night on "stickes," with Osborne and Good behind her. The man had appeared to her earlier that same evening while she was washing the lean-to room. This, she acknowledged, was her second encounter with the diabolical creature; he was the same one who appeared two months before in her dream.

The nightmarish story continued. Sometime during the morning of February 29, she was forced to pinch Elizabeth Hubbard at Dr. Grigg's house, where "the man brought her to me and made me pinch her." She regretted causing the child pain but could not stop doing so because they, "pull mee & hall me to . . . pinch the childr, & I am very sorry for itt." That night, Tituba testified, Good and Osborne had taken her spirit to Boston where they told her to "hurt the children." After returning to Salem, riding their "stickes or poale," with Good and Osborne behind her holding on to one another, Tituba was taken to the Putnams' household where they made her "hurt the Child," Ann, holding a knife to her throat, and then back to her own house to torment Abigail Williams and Betty Parris. All this time Tituba reported that she had tried to resist and had struggled against the overwhelming strength of the five evil ones. They in turn were assisted by a variety of strange creatures including the wolf that had scared Elizabeth Hubbard.

Suddenly, Elizabeth Hubbard, who was sitting in the Meeting House listening to the questioning, panicked at Tituba's graphic description of these evil beings and a verification of her complaint about a wolf. She fell into "an extreame fit." Pandemonium broke loose as the other girls began to cry out. Tituba was so overcome by this reaction to her story that she appeared to be "once or twice taken dumb herself." As Tituba drew into a trance-like silence, the hysteria of the girls heightened. The questioning could not continue. The first examination ended abruptly.

Tituba's behavior at the end of the first day of testimony was unusual for anyone steeped in English folklore. The trance, as a form of possession, was not characteristic of English witchcraft practice; only those bewitched by evil forces were as a rule possessed. Since the Reformation at least, in English and European beliefs, victims exhibited strange symptoms brought on by the power of the witches, but witches themselves did not go into a trance any more than priests did in the exercise of their duties.

The case was otherwise in the African and Indian rituals in Barbados in the 1670s, where possession by the spirit resulting in a trance was a traditional part of the shaman's or obeah's function in fighting evil. In Tituba's Amerindian world, such a trance was a familiar part of magico-religious healing ceremonies. During those rites the shaman used the trance as a shield in a battle with the spirits and to establish contact with the lost souls of the sick ones. Now, no doubt frightened by the hysterical response of the girls, she reverted to this technique of her earlier world that offered spiritual protection against the evil presence.

Such behavior was not part of the witch's arsenal in the Puritan seventeenth-century world. The Puritans of Tituba's time referred to a religious ceremony that involved a trance as conjuring and associated it with Devil worship. Tituba's penitent tone and regret for the pain she had inflicted, however, was so convincing to her listeners that the sudden loss of vision and hearing during her examination was taken to mean that she herself was bewitched by the others. It was not necessarily her intent to claim to be a victim. It was others like Thomas Putnam who excused her behavior as bewitchment, explaining that Tituba "was her self very much afflicted." That misunderstanding of her behavior, one of several such confusing encounters, added to Tituba's credibility as a witness.

The next day, March 2, in her second official examination, calm temporarily prevailed and Tituba was finally asked about a covenant with the man. The story became even more elaborate, with Tituba seemingly taking more deliberate steps to frighten her listeners. She said the man had told her he was God. He wanted her to serve him for six years and to hurt the children. In return for signing the pact with him, she would be protected from harm and would receive "many fine things." Asked why she had not informed Parris of these happenings and requested his assistance, Tituba explained that she was sworn to secrecy by the two Salem women, who threatened her life if she revealed their diabolical powers. She was afraid the man "would Cutt [her] head off" if she told. Fear for one's physical safety was an emotion that Puritans could sympathize with.

The officials were shocked and possibly secretly gratified by Tituba's acknowledgment of a covenant with the Devil. They took it as confirmation of their worst fears. Puritan divines had always required evidence not of maleficium—evil action—but of a Satanic influence to convict people of witchcraft. Thus their questioning of suspected witches usually concentrated on their involvement with this diabolical presence and of a conspiracy resulting from it. As a result, the courts were usually unable to secure convictions of accused witches who knew nothing of such a pact. Tituba ostensibly gave them the needed evidence.

This questioning regarding a diabolical pact corresponded with a drive for moral reform that had occupied the clergy since 1675. A transcendent evil force fit what the ministers conceived as an atmosphere of "Provoking Evils" that was threatening their society. Any proof of that evil gave substance to their complaints. Tituba's testimony of a diabolical conspiracy provided a new forum with which the clergy could express their dissatisfaction with the state of religious convictions in Massachusetts. A witchhunt to ferret out the malefactors could prove that the decline in religious zeal had opened the door to Satan.

On the surface, Tituba's answers regarding this pact do appear to be responses to questioning regarding the theological concepts of the covenant of grace and its inversion, the Devil's pact. This notion of the covenant was a major element in Puritan theology and society and Tituba must have absorbed some of its meaning. The covenant idea was central to Puritan social and theological life—it authorized and regulated the relations between the saints and their God, between the congregation and its minister, and between the members of the community and the magistrates. A pact with Satan violated the covenant with God, parodied the very notion of the covenant, and put the community in jeopardy of punishment for those transgressions.

On the other hand, the contractual relationship was also basic to the institutional life of an English community and was an important factor in the lives of the servant class in America. Tituba's reference to a contract on a piece of paper, a contract that stipulated a limited number of years of service and with its promise of material rewards, is more reminiscent of a servant's indenture than that of a Satanic conspiracy. Under such a contract, that she knew protected English servants and indentured Indians, Tituba would have a limited time of servitude—about six or fewer years—and could expect payment in goods or money as freedom dues at the end of that time. With such a contract she could benefit from some additional legal protection from abuse by a master.

Tituba probably knew little about the sophisticated concept of a Devil's pact, which existed only in the minds of her more educated interrogators. Nor did she necessarily conceptualize a Devil's sabbat, that "nightmare of learned witch lore." But she would have been well versed in the institution of servitude and the various levels of bondage in colonial society. Her answers to the question of what kind of "covenant" she had made with "that man that came to you?" was to voice her discontent with her present status and talk about her whimsical hopes for the future embodied in a piece of paper that she could sign. Tituba's response to their questioning was easily the reaction of a slave to the suggestion of a written agreement that could improve her life on earth.

She was not alone in this kind of reaction to her social standing. Dissatisfaction with their lot in life was a common theme in several later testimonies. William Barker expected the Devil to pay his debts so that he and his family could live comfortably. Elizabeth Johnson, a widow in somewhat difficult financial circumstances, was promised money. Mercy Lewis, a destitute servant in Thomas Putnam's household, in her "afflictions" was offered gold and many fine things by the Devil. Abigail Hobbs struck a bargain with the Devil to serve only two years in return for "fine clothes." But she complained that when the Devil did not fulfill his part of their bargain, she refused to sign a new contract obliging her to serve him for another four years. Hobbs, who had lived in the Burroughs family when they had been in Salem, was clearly disappointed in her treatment at the hands of her master. Her subsequent identification of George Burroughs as a diabolical creature was surely a metaphor for his lack of integrity to his servants. So too, Tituba's hopes for freedom from bondage to Samuel Parris were reflected in this promise of a contract with a limited term of servitude.

It took a few more leading questions before Tituba, responding to the magistrates' additional promptings regarding a Devil's book, gave her inquisitors more reason to wonder about what was happening in their community. The contract on a piece of a paper became a book with many marks. Now, mindful of the power she had to create anxiety and probably with malice in mind, Tituba had added a few more people to the supposed Satanic pact. When asked how many names she saw in the book, she said there were nine marks in the book. It was sufficient evidence to arouse her questioners to the enormity of the conspiracy and further fuel their fears of a pervasive diabolical presence.

Whether Tituba understood the theological implications of her testimony is not clear. That she frightened those who heard her story is evident from the immediate hysterical reaction of the audience. Their fear was clearly demonstrated. That she fully grasped the import of a plot to ruin their Godly commonwealth and destroy Christ's church is questionable. What she told them is what she understood about the evil presence—a combination of notions from a variety of sources, some religious, some derived from an eclectic folklore, and some from the substance of her own frightening dreams about evil beings that may well have belonged to her memory of Indian beliefs.

The story told by Tituba is a blending of elements from several sets of witchcraft beliefs. The book, of course, was an artifact of literate societies only and the Devil a part of Christian theology. They would not be found in the pre-colonial Amerindian or African cultures. But the strong link to Satanism, the evil force, with its promise of power over others, was surprisingly rare in the English folk tradition or in New England. Few persons giving testimony in witchcraft cases in Massachusetts mentioned the Devil. In responding to the hints regarding Satan suggested by the questioners, and tuned to the nuances of this questioning, Tituba described the Devil as she was cued, but she also added a few non-Puritan variations on the source of evil that inadvertently heightened the sense of diabolical invasion. Under the stress of questioning, Tituba began to fall back on her knowledge of Indian and Creolized folklore notions.

In tribal or folk traditions, magical power was derived from the ability to manipulate the mystical elements of the universe for one's own purposes, whether good or evil. That power did not require a separate motivating spiritual element. Among South American Indians, for instance, such evil power was believed to be inherent in individuals and required no intermediary spiritual force as in the concept of the Devil. For Indians like the Arawaks, evil power could exist in different degrees of strength. The most potent evil spirit, the most feared source of evil, was a kenaima. Unlike the Christian Devil, the power of the kenaima existed in a real person of flesh and blood and not of spirit. In the American Indian manner, Tituba gave the evil presence substance as a persona, identifiable in her testimony as a respectable white man living in the distant community of Boston. That suggestion led to a hunt for a man as the personification of the Devil, shifting some of the investigation away from the traditional woman as witch and leaving men more vulnerable to accusation.

Her testimony, apart from the reference to the Devil and his book, is not particularly English or even European in substance, but formed part of a universal assumption about the occult. She sketched a rather generic portrait of a witch who could fly through the air, take animal or human form, and submit to oaths and ordeals involving other spirits; she hinted at the efficacy of magical techniques without going into details. These were all common characteristics of witches from Africa to Asia and throughout America. Amerindians of Guyana on the coast of South America, for instance, believed that "the spirit may be passed from the body of its proper owner into that of any animal, or even into any inanimate object." So Tituba described the metamorphosis of Sarah Good's spirit into a hog and a dog.

She also saw animals change into the tall man and then back again into animals, sometimes into a hog and sometimes into "a great black dogge," in a manner typical of both the European witch and the evil South American kenaima who had the power to put his spirit into the body of any animal he wished, even mythic animals. But her choice of animal, a dog, as the alter ego of her respectable man, reflected a "sub-genre of insults" common in New England. To be a dog "was to lack precisely those qualities which defined ruling men: intellect, independence, and godliness." Tituba's tall man was a parody of the godly. Her commitment to him was to be written in her blood—a symbol associated with many forms of witchcraft that both renewed fears of Indian cannibalism and reminded them of the blood-sucking witches of medieval legends. To Tituba, however, that blood oath may have been part of her memory of her earlier life in Barbados, of Africans who sealed compacts with their blood.

One almost universal quality of witch belief was the supposed ability of witches to fly through the air on a stick or pole. Both European and African traditions contained folklore of night-riding witches on sticks. The idea is so ancient that it is found in the oldest Hindu beliefs as well as in medieval Jewish lore and in Greek and Roman mythology. The object of all such nocturnal trips was to attend secret meetings and to take part in cannibalistic rituals. Although the witches' meeting is a common feature of witchcraft lore, some characteristics associated with the idea were not shared. Tituba's testimony contained some significant variations from the European or African model.

During her first two examinations on March 1 and 2, Tituba drew on common traditions when she told the magistrates of a ride on a "sticke" to Boston, with Osborne and Good behind her to meet the other witches she could not name. But Tituba could not give any detail of those rides, refusing to respond to the interrogator's prompting to describe the roadways. She denied seeing "trees nor path, but was presently there." This description was somewhat different from the Anglo-African model of a witch on a pole sailing over the clouds to a meeting to plot harm to others. Tituba knew Boston because she had lived there with the Parrises and was also familiar with the road to Salem. During the second day of questioning, responding to some unidentified prompting, she appeared to retract part of her earlier statement about actually being in Boston at the meeting of the witches. "I was goeing & then Came back againe[.] I was never att Boston," she said. There was an echo of the folklore of American Indians in those words.

Many Indians of North and South America believed in a dream soul that could leave the body during sleep and visit faraway places without the use of a prop. Integral to this belief is the idea that all tangible objects have two parts, a body and a spirit, which separate during sleep and death. During sleep the spirit side can return to the physical object. Events that occur during that dream state are considered real, tangible happenings. Thus Tituba's story of a witch meeting was shaped by the idea of a dream-like state, during which her spirit traveled to a distant city, leaving her body behind. In keeping with her artful use of Puritan notions, however, when describing these events, she carefully included an unnecessary but familiar artifact from European folklore—the witch's pole or stick, an early version of the broomstick. Nonetheless, she tried to tell her interrogators that it was not her physical presence that went to Boston—"I was never att Boston"—but that her spirit had left her temporarily.

While they could ignore the notion of a dream spirit, the Puritans could not mistake the site of the witch's meeting. Tituba placed it in Boston—outside the Salem community. By locating the evil source outside of the community, Tituba again reverted to Indian ideas. She may have been evoking the Guyanese concept of the evil persona that is rarely of the same village as his victim. Thus the evil forces feared by the Indians of the Circum-Caribbean area, including the Arawak, emanate from sources outside the immediate group and remain there. Tituba saw her evil beings stationed in Boston, not Salem. Her story, at least in outline, followed the tradition of South American Indian folklore. Her hearers, however, misunderstanding her allusions, reinterpreted these unfamiliar notions.

Puritans, obsessed with the intrusion of evil power into their own community, would later transform Tituba's suggestion of a distant meeting and a plan to cause harm to the children to a meeting held within the confines of their village, led by a stranger who mocked Puritan religious rites. From the beginning of April through the trial of George Burroughs in August, all accusers described this meeting as taking place near Parris's house. Abigail Hobbs, for instance, described such a meeting in a field near the Parris household, and Abigail Williams said she saw a great number of persons at a similar mock sacramental meeting in the village. The Puritans thus reshaped Tituba's vision to fit their own version of a Satanic presence. But the concept of the Indian kenaima, the evil stranger, had entered into Puritan thought. They retained the vision of an outside force that could be blamed for the evil among them, an idea that in turn would propel the witchhunt into unexpected paths.

One other Caribbean import in Tituba's testimony is the hairy imp: "a thing all over hairy, all the face hayre & a long nose . . . with two Leggs, itt goeth upright & is about two or three foot high." This creature could be an Irish Leprechaun but, more likely, it too was based on the Guyanese evil kenaimas, often described as little people who lived in the depths of the forest and came out at night to attack people. The description also fits the evil spirit of the Ashanti of West Africa called Sasabonsam, a monster supposedly covered with long hair, having blood-shot eyes, and known to sit on the branches of a tree dangling his legs. In Jamaica the Creole spirit came to be known as a duppy, "a malicious vindictive, imp-like spirit that haunts forests and burying grounds, a figure very likely derived from a combination of African and Amerindian beliefs." Tituba relied on the prototype of an evil presence found among societies in the Caribbean rather than the English idea. Nonetheless, the Indian and English concepts of magic and evil were close enough to allow some unfamiliar details of Tituba's story to be reinterpreted and incorporated into their English framework of belief.

Tituba also added details that were not implied in the questions. She spoke of a yellow bird and later of a green and white bird and a black dog, of two rats (cats in a second version of her testimony) both red and black, and of a hog. The yellow bird would appear in many other testimonies and hallucinations, as would the dog. The bird in particular probably had special significance for Tituba. Among the Arawak Indians of Guiana, birds were taken as magical messengers. The goatsucker or nightjar, the supernatural ancestor of Tituba's clan, with its weird piercing call at night, was held in particular awe by many Guiana Indians. Were these birds of her fantasy a memory of her earlier existence and an attempt to draw on her guardian spirit for assistance? Whatever her intent, others found these allusions useful for their own purposes.

There was abundant material in her fantastic story for the other accused witches to draw on, and much of what she said reappeared with variations in subsequent confessions. By the end of the second day she had already given the Salem authorities many reasons to fear a Satanic presence. Over the course of the next three days she continued to confirm her story, as she repeated most of the details given at the beginning.

Tituba had lived in a Barbados society among Africans and Amerindians who incorporated the trance, image-magic, divination, and similar techniques into their religious ceremonies. As an Amerindian, her world was informed by similar behavior and she proved in 1692 that she could draw on that residual knowledge when expedient. In March of 1692 Tituba found it useful to emerge from her role as a docile Puritan servant woman and demonstrate the native American side of her identity. It both fascinated and repelled her listeners. But they listened and absorbed the information needed to exorcise the Devils from their community, an evil presence that only Tituba could help them locate.

Her confession in turn was made that more easily because of cultural differences regarding the use of language. Distortion of the truth did not carry the same negative meaning among American Indians as it did in Puritan societies, where deception for personal gain or to save one's life was equated with Satanic practices. Puritans who confessed falsely endangered their souls. On the other hand, in Indian cultures a reluctance to contradict others and the use of metaphoric language were cultivated as diplomatic arts. What was to Indians a polite embellishment was understood by Puritans as a lie. To protect herself in Massachusetts the Indian woman reverted to those remembered concepts and familiar practices, as she cunningly confessed to promoting an evil conspiracy that had merely been suspected.

During the five days of testimony, Tituba and the two other women were taken to jail in Ipswich, about ten miles away from the Salem village meeting house. Daily the constables, on horseback, brought the women back to the village for additional questioning. At some time during that five-day period, they were subjected to at least one minute and humiliating search of their naked bodies, including the genital area, for signs of a "witches' teat" or some mark from which, according to legend, the Devil or his familiars suckled their converts. Such marks had been used traditionally both in England and in New England as empirical evidence of a diabolical association. The examining women thought they saw some tell-tale sign on Tituba, but it could just as well have been the wounds from a beating shortly before the hearings. It was not there on reexamination.

The two Sarahs continued to maintain their innocence. But with each session Tituba confirmed with more certainty the evil presence, as she faithfully repeated her early testimony. The Reverend Hale was convinced of her honesty because he assumed she could not have remembered all those extraordinary details if she had been lying. Finally satisfied that she could offer no more information, on March 7 the magistrates sent Tituba and the other two to Boston to await trial and punishment. Sarah Osborne would die in prison on May 10, 1692; Sarah Good would be tried, found guilty, and hanged on July 19. Tituba outlived them, her confession serving as a shield against any immediate drastic action.

By March 5 the magistrates had most of the pieces of their Satanic plot: evidence of the Devil's book, a cabal of night-riding witches, and incidents of maleficium. They lacked only a few elements of their diabolical fantasy. Tituba did not offer any information about sexual orgies or cannibalism, or suggest that her witches' coven had any relation to the Christian religious ceremonies. Neither concept entered into Indian lore. Such ideas were too distant from Tituba's worldview to appear in her description of evil acts. She was either not asked about them or chose to ignore what was foreign to her understanding. Details on some of these notions would come in later testimonies as Tituba's story was reformulated by the beliefs of those steeped more deeply in English folklore and Christian theology.

Thomas Newton, the Attorney General preparing the first cases for trial, considered bringing her back to Salem as a witness for the June 2 court when the first trial of Bridget Bishop was conducted. There is no record that he did so, or that his recommendation to separate the witnesses from the prisoners was followed. Communication and the exchange of information between the two groups continued. By the beginning of June Tituba's testimony apparently was no longer necessary; the details had entered into the folklore of New England witchcraft. Other witnesses, reformulating and embellishing her fantasy of a Satanic pact, would provide sufficient evidence to condemn the innocent to death.

If Tituba had had revenge in mind for her own enslavement, she could not have found a more effective weapon against the community than her fantastic story of a witches' meeting in Boston to plot harmful acts, a compact with an evil being, and a suspicious book with nine names. The magistrates interpreted the details of that confession as proof that the diabolical presence had invaded their community. Tituba had fueled their fantasies of a Satanic plot. As she awaited news of her fate in a Boston jail, the next stage in this witchhunt, to find those unnamed conspirators and reveal the extent of Satan's influence, was about to begin.

Discussion Questions

1. What is Breslaw's central argument about Tituba's motivation for her confession? Do you agree with Breslaw's claim that Tituba's confession, rather than being the testimony of a confused servant woman, was actually "a carefully crafted tale that provided satisfactory answers" to the questions of the Puritans about the mysterious events in Salem?
2. What does Breslaw mean when she says that Tituba "lead an assault on gender roles, social rank, and the clergy's authority"? What process resulted in this widening attack on the different strata of Puritan society?

Writing Suggestions

1. After you have considered the first discussion question for this selection, analyze Tituba's testimony carefully, and then write a two-to-three page paper responding to Breslaw's claim that the trial testimony was "a carefully crafted tale that provided satisfactory answers." Agree or disagree with Breslaw's claims, arguing closely from Tituba's own words and sequence of statements.
2. Research other incidents of false confession. You could search both the library and the Web for "false confession," and take one other famous case. Write a three-page essay comparing the motivations of Tituba and another historical figure, and consider the following questions: What were the motivations of the accused? What kinds of social pressures came to play in each case? What effects did the confessions have on the surrounding communities?
3. Research the occurrence of the malicious "imp" figure in African, Amerindian, and Caribbean cultures. Write an essay describing the role of the "kenaima," "sasobansam," and the Creole "duppy" in the folklore of these countries. Alternatively, trace the appearance of this type of figure in Tituba's testimony, and compare her descriptions to what you found in your research about these malicious imps found in African and Amerindian folklore.

The Declaration of Independence

THOMAS JEFFERSON

Born in 1743 in Albemarle County, Virginia, Thomas Jefferson came from a landed family of some social standing and attended the College of William and Mary. Thomas Jefferson was a member of the Continental Congress, governor of Virginia, ambassador to France, secretary of state, vice-president, and finally, the third president of the United States, serving from 1801 to 1809. Jefferson is well-known for his early accomplishments in drafting the text of the Declaration of Independence and later, as president, for his purchase of the Louisiana Territory from Napoleon in 1803. He wrote the Declaration of Independence in 1776, when he was just thirty-two years old. His words and phrases have passed the test of time, and you will recognize many parts of this Declaration as you read. The following is Jefferson's first draft of the Declaration of Independence. Some of the words, phrases, and paragraphs in the first draft were revised or deleted in subsequent drafts.

A DECLARATION BY THE REPRESENTATIVES OF THE UNITED STATES OF AMERICA, IN GENERAL CONGRESS ASSEMBLED.

When in the course of human events, it becomes necessary for one people to dissolve the political bands which have connected them with another, and to assume among the powers of the earth the separate and equal station to which the laws of nature and of nature's God entitle them, a decent respect to the opinions of mankind requires that they should declare the causes which impel them to the separation.

We hold these truths to be self evident: that all men are created equal, that they are endowed by their Creator with inherent and unalienable rights; that among these are life, liberty, and the pursuit of happiness; that to secure these rights, governments are instituted among men, deriving their just powers from the consent of the governed; that whenever any form of government becomes destructive of these ends, it is the right of the people to alter or to abolish it, and to institute new government, laying its foundation on such principles, and organizing its powers in such form, as to them shall seem most likely to effect their safety and happiness. Prudence, indeed, will dictate that governments long established should not be changed for light and transient causes; and accordingly all experience hath shown that mankind are more disposed to suffer while evils are sufferable, than to right themselves by abolishing the forms to which they are accustomed. But when a long train of abuses and usurpations, begun at a distinguished period and pursuing invariably the same object, evinces a design to reduce them under absolute despotism, it is their right, it is their duty to throw off such government, and to provide new guards for their future security. Such has been the patient sufferance of these colonies; and such is now the necessity which constrains them to expunge their former systems of government. The history of the present king of Great Britain is a history of unremitting injuries and usurpations, among which appears no solitary fact to contradict the uniform tenor of the rest, but all have in direct object the establishment of an absolute tyranny over these states. To prove this, let facts be submitted to a candid world for the truth of which we pledge a faith yet unsullied by falsehood.

He has refused his assent to laws the most wholesome and necessary for the public good.

He has forbidden his governors to pass laws of immediate and pressing importance, unless suspended in their operation till his assent should be obtained; and, when so suspended, he has utterly neglected to attend to them.

He has refused to pass other laws for the accommodation of large districts of people, unless those people would relinquish the right of representation in the legislature, a right inestimable to them, and formidable to tyrants only.

He has called together legislative bodies at places unusual, uncomfortable, and distant from the depository of their public records, for the sole purpose of fatiguing them into compliance with his measures.

He has dissolved representative houses repeatedly and continually for opposing with manly firmness his invasions on the rights of the people.

He has refused for a long time after such dissolutions to cause others to be elected, whereby the legislative powers, incapable of annihilation, have returned to the people at large for their exercise, the state remaining, in the meantime, exposed to all the dangers of invasion from without and convulsions within.

He has endeavored to prevent the population of these states: for that purpose obstructing the laws for naturalization of foreigners, refusing to pass others to encourage their migrations hither, and raising the conditions of new appropriations of lands.

He has suffered the administration of justice totally to cease in some of these states refusing his assent to laws for establishing judiciary powers.

He has made our judges dependent on his will alone for the tenure of their offices, and the amount and payment of their salaries.

He has erected a multitude of new offices, by a self-assumed power and sent hither swarms of new officers to harass our people and eat out their substance.

He has kept among us in times of peace standing armies and ships of war without the consent of our legislatures.

He has affected to render the military independent of, and superior to, the civil power.

He has combined with others to subject us to a jurisdiction foreign to our constitution and unacknowledged by our laws, giving his assent to their acts of pretended legislation for quartering large bodies of armed troops among us; for protecting them by a mock trial from punishment for any murders which they should commit on the inhabitants of these states; for cutting off our trade with all parts of the world; for imposing taxes on us without our consent; for depriving us of the benefits of trial by jury; for transporting us beyond seas to be tried for pretended offenses; for abolishing the free system of English laws in a neighboring province, establishing therein an arbitrary government, and enlarging its boundaries, so as to render it at once an example and fit instrument for introducing the same absolute rule into these states; for taking away our charters, abolishing our most valuable laws, and altering fundamentally the forms of our governments; for suspending our own legislatures, and declaring themselves invested with power to legislate for us in all cases whatsoever.

He has abdicated government here withdrawing his governors, and declaring us out of his allegiance and protection.

He has plundered our seas, ravaged our coasts, burnt our towns, and destroyed the lives of our people.

He is at this time transporting large armies of foreign mercenaries to compleat the works of death, desolation and tyranny already begun with circumstances of cruelty and perfidy unworthy the head of a civilized nation.

He has constrained our fellow citizens taken captive on the high seas to bear arms against their country, to become the executioners of their friends and brethren, or to fall themselves by their hands.

He has endeavored to bring on the inhabitants of our frontiers, the merciless Indian savages, whose known rule of warfare is an undistinguished destruction of all ages, sexes and conditions of existence.

He has incited treasonable insurrections of our fellow citizens, with the allurements of forfeiture and confiscation of our property.

He has waged cruel war against human nature itself, violating its most sacred rights of life and liberty in the persons of a distant people who never offended him, captivating and carrying them into slavery in another hemisphere, or to incur miserable death in their transportation thither. This piratical warfare, the opprobrium of INFIDEL powers, is the warfare of the CHRISTIAN king of Great Britain. Determined to keep open a market where MEN should be bought and sold, he has prostituted his negative for suppressing every legislative attempt to prohibit or to restrain this execrable commerce. And that this assemblage of horrors might want no fact of distinguished die, he is now exciting those very people to rise in arms among us, and to purchase that liberty of which he has deprived them, by murdering the people on whom he also obtruded them: thus paying off former crimes committed against the LIBERTIES of one people, with crimes which he urges them to commit against the LIVES of another.

In every stage of these oppressions we have petitioned for redress in the most humble terms: our repeated petitions have been answered only by repeated injury.

A prince whose character is thus marked by every act which may define a tyrant is unfit to be the ruler of a people who mean to be free. Future ages will scarcely believe that the hardiness of one man adventured, within the short compass of twelve years only, to lay a foundation so broad and so undisguised for tyranny over a people fostered and fixed in principles of freedom.

Nor have we been wanting in attentions to our British brethren. We have warned them from time to time of attempts by their legislature to extend a jurisdiction over these our states. We have reminded them of the circumstances of our emigration and settlement here, no one of which would warrant so strange a pretension: that these were effected at the expense of our own blood and treasure, unassisted by the wealth or the strength of Great Britain: that in constituting indeed our several forms of government, we had adopted one common king, thereby laying a foundation for perpetual league and amity with them: but that submission to their parliament was no part of our constitution, nor ever in idea, if history may be credited: and, we appealed to their native justice and magnanimity as well as to the ties of our common kindred to disavow these usurpations which were likely to interrupt our connection and correspondence. They too have been deaf to the voice of justice and of consanguinity, and when occasions have been given them, by the regular course of their laws, of removing from their councils the disturbers of our harmony, they have, by their free election, reestablished them in power. At this very time too, they are permitting their chief magistrate to send over not only soldiers of our common blood, but Scotch and foreign mercenaries to invade and destroy us. These facts have given the last stab to agonizing affection, and manly spirit bids us to renounce forever these unfeeling brethren. We must endeavor to forget our former love for them, and hold them as we hold the rest of mankind, enemies in war, in peace friends. We might have been a free and a great people together; but a communication of grandeur and of freedom, it seems, is below their dignity. Be it so, since they will have it. The road to happiness and to glory is open to us, too. We will tread it apart from them, and acquiesce in the necessity which denounces our eternal separation!

We therefore the representatives of the United States of America in General Congress assembled, do in the name, and by the authority of the good people of these states reject and renounce all allegiance and subjection to the kings of Great Britain and all others who may hereafter claim by, through or under them; we utterly dissolve all political connection which may heretofore have subsisted between us and the people or parliament of Great Britain: and finally we do assert and declare these colonies to be free and independent states, and that as free and independent states, they have full power to levy war, conclude peace, contract alliances, establish commerce, and to do all other acts and things which independent states may of right do.

And for the support of this declaration, we mutually pledge to each other our lives, our fortunes, and our sacred honor.

We, therefore, the representatives of the United States of America in General Congress assembled, appealing to the supreme judge of the world for the rectitude of our intentions, do in the name, and by the authority of the good people of these colonies, solemnly publish and declare, that these united colonies are, and of right ought to be free and independent states; that they are absolved from all allegiance to the British crown, and that all political connection between them and the state of Great Britain is, and ought to be, totally dissolved; and that as free and independent states, they have full power to levy war, conclude peace, contract alliances, establish commerce, and to do all other acts and things which independent states may of right do.

And for the support of this declaration, with a firm reliance on the protection of divine providence, we mutually pledge to each other our lives, our fortunes, and our sacred honor.

Discussion Questions

1. Jefferson argues in the Declaration of Independence for "certain inalienable rights." Make a list of all the rights the colonists were arguing for in this document. Then review the different essays you have read in this chapter, and discuss in groups the discrepancies between the rights claimed as "inalienable" and the treatment of Native Americans, women, and slaves in the years before and during the writing of the Declaration. What kinds of cultural assumptions could Jefferson make about his audience? How do you account for the discrepancies you have found?

2. Consider the struggles of minorities and women today. Are Jefferson's "inalienable rights" more available for these groups today? Discuss the ways in which the United States has made progress toward "liberty and justice for all," and also consider the ways the United States as a country needs to work toward assuring the rights of all individuals.

Writing Suggestions

1. Analyze the paragraph at the bottom of page 85 and the paragraph at the top of this page, which Jefferson left out of the final version of the Declaration of Independence. Consider Jefferson's audience and legal training. Write an essay in which you offer an explanation for his argumentative strategy in leaving out this section of his original text. Obtain and read a copy of the final version. Which version do you find more effective? Why? Be specific and quote from both versions as you analyze the differences.

2. Review your responses to the second discussion question for this selection. Then write a personal essay in which you discuss the ways in which the United States has made progress toward "liberty and justice for all," and also consider the ways the United States as a country needs to work toward assuring the rights of all individuals. Use examples from your own life and from current events, and be specific.

3. Research Jefferson's complicated history with slavery, and write a paper in which you compare Jefferson's original comments about slavery in the first draft of the Declaration of Independence with his own history as slave owner. Consider his famous words, "All men are created equal," and address what he might have meant by these words, considering that he refused to give up his slaves. How did he justify keeping his own slaves, and what were his relationships with these slaves?

Black Slavery

Richard Hofstadter was a prolific writer of American history, and he won the Pulitzer Prize in history for *The Age of Reform*, 1955, and the Pulitzer Prize for nonfiction for *Anti-Intellectualism in American Life*, 1963. Hofstadter, who died in 1970, was Professor of History at Columbia University for many years, and he also taught briefly at Cambridge. In the selection below, which was taken from Hofstadter's book *America at 1750: A Social Portrait*, he discusses the role of slavery in colonial America.

North of Maryland slavery was not vital to the economy as it was in the South; the treatment of slaves in the North, therefore, illuminates many of the social differences between the two sections, and has a distinct interest for the social and moral history of the Northern colonies. The North, however, cannot be treated as a unit, since in some colonies, such as New York, slaves were relatively numerous while in others, notably in New England, they were few. New York was slow in drawing white settlers until after mid-century, and the shortage of labor led to a considerable use of slaves; indeed it is possible that in the early Dutch days it was slave labor that enabled the colony to survive. Most of the first slaves were not from Africa but were reimported from Curaçao in the Dutch West Indies. It was a profitable system: in the 1640s it cost only a little more to buy a slave than to pay a free worker's wages for a year. Although the slave system in the Dutch West Indies was brutal, in New Netherland the institution was not particularly harsh. Many slaves there had a kind of half freedom under which they enjoyed personal liberty in return for an annual payment to the West India Company and an occasional stint of labor for it. They were allowed to testify in court, an effort was made to convert them to Christianity, and free Negroes were permitted to own freeholds and to intermarry. Still, the desire of slaves for liberty did not flag, and a considerable number of runaways, sometimes assisted by whites, fled to the neighboring English colonies.

After the English took control of New Netherland in 1664, a brisk and highly profitable trade in skilled slaves was carried on. Most slaveholders in the province were flourishing small farmers or small artisans who, in the absence of an adequate supply of free labor, needed moderately skilled help, and were able to pay the rising prices for slaves. A partial census of 1755 showed a widely diffused slave population, most owners having only one or two slaves, only seven New Yorkers owning ten or more. Among the largest lots held were those of the elder Lewis Morris with 66 slaves on his large estate and the first

Frederick Philipse, an affluent landowner, with about 40. Such men could work gangs of slaves on their manors, but slaves were also sought by other wealthy men for the comfort and prestige a substantial staff of domestic servants would bring. William Smith, for example, was reputed to keep a domestic staff of 12 or more to run his New York City household, and other leading citizens traveled with Negro footmen. But the main body of slaves was employed by small proprietors, and, learning a wide variety of skills, worked chiefly in the towns, in the service trades and the shipyards, in the shops of coopers, tailors, bakers, weavers, masons, and other craftsmen. From the first the competition of black labor was resented by whites. Competition in the labor market was intensified by the slave owners' widespread practice of putting out their slaves for hire, under-cutting white laborers who were paid twice the slaves' wages. On most New York farms slaveholding was uneconomical: the growing season was relatively short, and idle slaves would have to be maintained during the long winter months. Small proprietors also had little space to house a slave family, and on small premises slave children would be a liability rather than an asset. In New York sterility in a female slave was at a premium. Nonetheless, slavery persisted; white labor was in short supply, and selected black labor was skillful and productive.

Miscegenation, which began in New York under the Dutch, yielded such a number of persons of mixed blood in the colony that by the end of the seventeenth century slave status had to be defined not by color but by the status of the mother. Some light-colored runaways won freedom by passing into the white population. Bargaining between blacks and their white lovers inevitably took place, as slaves found themselves in a position to ask for money or goods, even in some cases for manumission. Yet even under the relatively open system of slavery that prevailed, family structure was weak and there were a large number of broken and female-headed families.

The New York slave, suspended in an awkward equipoise between complete bondage and half freedom, was often restive. Slave controls, reflecting persistent nervousness in the white population, were quite rigid. Aside from private punishments that could be administered by masters, such public controls were meant to put sharp limits on the temptations slaves would face. After 1702, flogging was prescribed if three slaves gathered together on their own time. They were not permitted to gamble or to buy liquor, though liquor was often sold to slaves by tavern keepers, nor could they engage in trade without their masters' consent. Fires were a frightening problem in the eighteenth-century towns, and blacks were commonly suspected of arson. With hired-out slaves coming and going in the city, the opportunities for arson were considerable; the perpetrators of arson were always hard to trace, and arson could be used to conceal theft. The penalty for committing arson, consequently, was death.

A special cause of slave restiveness arose from the presence in New York of a considerable number of Spanish Negroes, captured in the wars with Spain, condemned as prizes, and sold into slavery without regard to their prior status. Apparently some of the Spanish Negroes had been freemen. They were resentful and rebellious at having been re-enslaved, and some played a role in the New York slave conspiracy of 1712. Although slaves were entitled to and indeed usually received real and not *pro forma* trials, serious offenses were punished with harsh sentences intended to be effective deterrents. The killing of a white person by a black was punished by torture followed by execution, a sentence which courts did not hesitate to impose. Yet for lesser offenses, slaves in New York as in several other colonies enjoyed an exemption which grew out of their value as property: whites could be executed for certain categories of theft, but slaves could not.

New England was more important as the major carrier of the slave trade to the mainland colonies than as a user of slave labor. Principle was not, however, at issue. From the very beginning the Puritans had sought to solve their labor shortage by enslaving Indians for limited terms of service, or Negroes, and in 1645 Emanuel Downing, John Winthrop's brother-in-law, expressed the hope that slaves could be supplied because the colony would never thrive "until we get . . . a stock of slaves sufficient to do all our business." In the early days even Roger Williams condoned slavery; at the peak of the eighteenth-century slave trade, the New England slavers were men of great wealth and respectability in their communities. Small numbers of slaves were brought to such major ports as Boston, Newport, and Salem and some were sent into the communities of the interior. The typical New England slaveholding was one or two slaves per family, although there were a few large owners in the Narragansett country, farmers who engaged in dairying and stock raising on parcels of land ranging from three hundred to two or three thousand acres and employing from a half-dozen to forty slaves, indispensable for such large-scale enterprises. For comfort and convenience, as well as for status, leading village families might own a domestic slave or two, and the generality and respectability of the practice is underlined by the presence of slaves in such prominent and upright ministerial families as those of Jonathan Edwards, Ezra Stiles, and the Mathers. Even Judge Samuel Sewall who wrote an early and prophetic anti-slavery tract held slaves. John Adams, who found the practice repugnant and held no slaves, recalled: "The best men in my vicinity thought it not inconsistent with their character." Besides domestic service and family farm labor, slaves were employed in a wide variety of occupations, skilled and unskilled, in the shops of blacksmiths, tanners, and carpenters, the offices of printers, in distilleries, ropewalks, iron forges, lumbering, shipbuilding, and other industries. Partly in the hope of escaping slavery, Negroes also went to sea. As a source of cheap and reasonably skilled labor, Negroes were probably more important to the New England economy than their small numbers would lead one to expect.

In the small-scale slaveholding pattern of New England, blacks were often the familiar associates of their masters, and New England slavery, with this pattern of intimacy and an ethos of personal restraint, lacked the harshness of slavery in the Southern colonies or New York. New England masters, though on occasion they became nervous about their slaves, did not suffer the constant terror of Negro uprisings that afflicted planters in the South and the West Indies. There were, to be sure, some rumors of insurrection, some slaves plotted to burn Charlestown, Massachusetts, in 1741, and there were occasional panics over arson. And many slaves ran away. The desire for freedom that was so generally manifest among the slaves of the colonial era was not quenched by the comparative mildness of New England slavery.

The machinery of control in New England, though less rigid than elsewhere, was elaborate enough. On pain of being classified as runaways, slaves were forbidden to wander beyond the town limits without a pass from their masters or some other authority. Ferrymen were prohibited from transporting slaves across rivers, householders from entertaining them, tavern keepers from selling them liquor. Slaves were forbidden to remain on Boston Common after sunset, and a law of 1728 in Massachusetts prevented them from buying provisions from country people. Small thefts were punishable by whipping, not more than twenty lashes, and if the amount stolen was large, the guilty slave, especially in Rhode Island, might be punished by banishment—a dire penalty, because it usually meant that the slave would be sold into the West Indies. Slaves were subject to a nine o'clock curfew. They were forbidden to build bonfires, out of fear of arson. Striking a white person was punished by severe whipping. To prevent masters from freeing old and decrepit slaves who would then have to be supported at the public expense, laws required them to support their former slaves and not permit them to become public charges.

In spite of laws against miscegenation, it was quite common in New England. While there is no accurate general measure, some sense of the prevalence of miscegenation is given by the records of Rhode Island, which show that in 1782 the 3,806 Negroes in the colony included 464 mulattoes, or nearly one-eighth of the Negro population.

As elsewhere, the Negro family was gravely injured by slavery, even though many masters attempted to accommodate slaves by sanctioning marriages. Sometimes a mother and her children were sold away from their husband and father, sometimes children were sold or even given away from their parents. A petition to the Massachusetts legislature by a group of Boston Negroes in 1773 expressed their plight poignantly and with an adroit appeal to Christian pieties: "The endearing ties of husband and wife we are strangers to for we are no longer man and wife than our masters or mistresses think proper. . . . Our children are also taken from us by force and sent many miles from us where we seldom see them again there to be made slaves of for life which sometimes is very short by reason of being dragged from their mothers' breasts. How can a slave perform the duties of a husband to a wife or parent to his child? How can a husband leave master and work and cleave to his wife? How can the wife submit themselves to their husbands in all things? How can the child obey his parents in all things?"

Discussion Questions

1. Compare what you learned in elementary school, junior high, and senior high school about slavery. Did anyone learn about slavery as an economic factor in the Puritan communities? Did you know about the holding of slaves in the North well into the eighteenth century? Which aspects of Hofstadter's discussion of slavery were new to you?

2. Compare the attitudes of northern slaveholders toward black slaves with the Puritans' attitudes toward the Indians. What kinds of similarities or differences do you find in the treatment of slaves and Indians? When Indians were kept as slaves, were they treated similarly to black slaves? You can also discuss the treatment of black slave women in comparison to the treatment of Indian women—what differences, if any, do you find in black and Indian women's experiences with the white colonists and slaveholders?

Writing Suggestions

1. The problem of contemporary slave dealing has recently surfaced in the media and has also become an important topic of concern in the United Nations. Estimates vary, but by all accounts, millions of men, women, and children have been sold into forced labor or prostitution all over the globe.

    Research three current newspaper or magazine articles dealing with forced labor, child slavery, or the sex slave trade, and write a three-page paper reporting on what these three articles offer in the way of information about the current slave trade. You can use a print or electronic index of the *New York Times, Los Angeles Times, Time, Newsweek,* or other news magazine to begin your research. Another good site to use is Academic Universe, if your university subscribes to this Web site, which offers news from all major newspapers around the world. The Web address for Academic Universe is <http://web.lexis-nexis.com/universe>.

    In your paper, compare and contrast the sources and facts that the articles use, and try to assess the reliability of the sources. Is one better than the others? Why? How do the tones differ in each article? Which article seems to offer the most factual information? How do the different articles add to your knowledge about this issue?

2. Hofstadter writes that a petition to the Massachusetts legislature in 1773 on the part of black slaves appealed to "Christian pieties" to end the separation of families sold into slavery on different estates. Research the results of this appeal, and write a three-page paper about what happened to slavery in Massachusetts after 1773. When did slavery become illegal in Massachusetts? Who was instrumental in bringing about its end? Which black and white leaders led the movement to end slavery in Massachusetts?

Chapter 1: Writing Suggestions

1. Review the readings in this chapter, and then write a two-to-three-page personal essay answering the following questions:

    Which readings touched you the most and changed your perceptions about early North American history?

    What were your reactions to these readings, and why did they surprise or interest you?

    Specifically, what were your personal responses, and how have the readings caused you to rethink some of your assumptions about New England history? Use both personal details and details from the texts.

2. Reflect on what Ronald Takaki means by the phrase "racialization of savagery." Then look at several magazines and newspapers that are covering civil wars or conflicts in Third World countries. Examine the language of the reporting. What kinds of verbs, nouns, and adjectives do the writers use? Do you find any "racialization of savagery" in the reporting of conflicts in Third World countries, or is the reporting similar to the reporting of conflicts in the United States or Europe? Write a paper analyzing the language in three newspaper or magazine accounts dealing with conflicts in a Third World country, expanding on the questions above.

3. Using your library resources, research the question of female slavery further. In addition to library sources, you can also look at the sources available at the Duke University Web site <http://scriptorium. lib.duke.edu/collections/african-american-women.html>. This site will give you access to many sources and will also offer links to other sources about women and slavery in the United States. Another good site to check is the Smithsonian Institution <http://www.si.edu/search/>. Also search using the terms "women and slavery" to connect to many interesting sites.

    In your paper, answer one of the following research questions, or develop a question of your own:

    How did female slaves participate in slave revolts?

    Which revolts were most successful, and how did women help?

    How did the Underground Railway operate to help slave women escape with their children? Were women able to take their children with them?

4. Review Levin's and Breslaw's different approaches to the historical interpretation of the Salem witch trials. Write a three-page paper in which you compare and contrast their interpretations. What does each offer? Which do you find more interesting? Which more helpful? What differences in fact and evidence do they offer?

Chapter 1: Further Research on the Web

To pursue your research on the Internet, explore some of the following sites:

Pocahontas
http://www.iath.virginia.edu/vcdh/jamestown/Pocahontas.html

Salem
http://www.salemweb.com/
http://etext.lib.virginia.edu/salem/witchcraft/

Slavery
http://www.coloradocollege.edu/Dept/HY/HY243Ruiz/Research/politics.html
http://memory.loc.gov/ammem/aaohtml/exhibit/aopart1.html#01a

Declaration of Independence
http://www.nara.gov/exhall/charters/declaration/dechist.html
http://memory.loc.gov/const/declar.html

2

The Native Americans versus the Newcomers

This chapter begins with the tumultuous period of the Indian wars and the forced relocation of the five Southern tribes who were destined to endure the Trail of Tears, as the long march to Oklahoma came to be known. These tribes included the Cherokee, Creek, Choctaw, Chickasaw, and Seminole. In this chapter you can begin the process of looking at the importance of language and argument in justifying political decisions and racist policies. How has our government justified policies such as the annexation of native lands? How is language used to soften or cover the reality of national policies? How do government policies and presidential speeches today reflect rhetorical strategies similar to those of the eighteenth century? To answer some of these questions we can look at the relationship between the native Indian tribes and the U.S. government and settlers as an example of a period of time in which language and policy were interlinked to promote the desires of the white government. A careful examination of the writings of presidents and philosophers at this time reveals a recurring ambivalence on the part of the white "conquering race" toward the American Indians. On the one hand, many of the leading spokesmen of the eighteenth and nineteenth centuries considered the Indians to be wild and uncivilized "savages," while on the other hand, these same leaders professed a great interest in the native customs and culture of the tribes they often called their "brothers." The emotionally complex writings of both political leaders and writers of literature reveal this inability to fully come to terms with what happened to the native tribes under the white man's rule, and these writings also offer an opportunity for you to review the logic and evidence used in the arguments justifying the taking of lands and lives from Native Americans. As you read the following selections, ask yourself how language helps cover the rapaciousness of the policy of manifest destiny and the essential lack of respect for the "savages."

The first selection in this chapter is Michael Rogin's "Liberal Society and the Indian Question." Rogin explains for us the ambivalence of the policy setters and "white fathers," whose language reveals both a patronizing attitude toward their "brothers" and a complete lack of understanding of the culture and desires of the Indians. We then move to a key primary source—Jefferson's famous "Policy of Civilization and Assimilation." A study of this policy reveals Jefferson's logic and ambivalence firsthand, and allows you to look at the rhetorical devices and use of language to justify removing Indians from their own lands. Another president who was intent on his Indian Policy was Andrew Jackson, the man who initiated the forced removal of many Native American tribes, resulting in the Trail of Tears. You can look at Jackson's own arguments for removal of the Indians in his "Message to Congress" in 1865. This speech offers ample opportunity to study the justification and reasoning used by the "white man" in removing Native Americans from their lands, and lays the foundation for a study of political speeches throughout the history of the United States, speeches that announced annexations of land, declarations of war, and justifications for military interventions. As you study more speeches throughout this text, these early presidential writings about Native Americans will give you an interesting base from which to compare later speeches and rhetorical techniques of politicians throughout U.S. history.

While the writings of the conquerors are well-represented in texts, too often American scholarly publications have given only cursory coverage to Native American writings and oral histories, which offer a rich field of powerful oral and written interpretations of the struggle between Native Americans and whites. We will look at the speeches of Native speakers who were present at major battles and traveled to Washington to speak to the government. By comparing the arguments of the U.S. presidents with those of Native American leaders, we can reach a fuller, more accurate view of this complex and multifaceted period of American history. Different strategies of argument and expression show us the remarkably dissimilar approaches taken by whites and Native Americans in communicating their desires.

We begin with Frederick W. Turner III's introduction to *I Have Spoken*. Turner argues strongly for a re-vision of history, this time including the darker side of the white man's coming—the Native American histories. We then go to the primary sources and the oral histories themselves: The speeches of Chief Red Cloud and Chief Black Hawk tell a very different side of the history of "manifest destiny." The power of language comprising simpler sentences and vivid imagery presents both another angle of historical vision on the loss of Indian lands and an example of an alternative style of argument and communication. Luther Standing Bear's eloquent "What the Indian Means to America" serves as an example of writing that incorporates both the Native style and the style of one educated in white schools. Luther Standing Bear describes the destruction of the land by the whites and explains how only the Indians truly understand and are part of the land.

Next we look at an excerpt from one of the most famous captivity narratives from the seventeenth century, *Narrative of the Captivity and Restoration of Mrs. Mary Rowlandson*. Rowlandson's writings not only offer a fascinating account of her life with the Indians after she was captured, but also are representative of many of the beliefs that exacerbated relationships between whites and Indians during this period.

To see how past conflicts replay themselves in a contemporary setting, we end this chapter with a current piece of writing, Ruth Rosen's editorial about the controversy of Albert Mechau's 1930s-era mural "Dangers of the Mail," which features a full-scale massacre of white men while white women are being attacked by Indians. Mechau's mural now covers the wall of a federal office building in Washington, D.C. Many feel that the representation of Native Americans is so offensive that it should be removed or covered, while others argue that the painting represents early twentieth-century beliefs and should be studied as a representation of white thought about Native Americans in the early twentieth century.

As you read the selections in this chapter, ask yourself how language and writing have played important roles in preserving, presenting, and misrepresenting this period of history. Do you think a conquered people can ever rewrite history from their own point of view? What is the importance of oral and written argumentation in the representation of controversial acts? How has your perception of the loss of Native American lands changed with a study of the writings of both whites and Native Americans?

Before You Read

1. While white settlers often claimed that Indians were "savage" and "uncivilized," they admired many qualities of these same "red brothers." Consider the abundance of sports teams and commercial and military products that carry Native American names, such as the "Atlanta Braves," the "Jeep Cherokee," or the "Tomahawk Cruise Missile." List as many product or military names as you can that refer to Native American names or words. What qualities are the advertisers or the military trying to promote by using Native American names?

2. Think about your own definition of the word "civilized." What qualities do you think a "civilized" nation must have? Make a list of these qualities, and refer back to this list as you read some of the selections in the chapter referring to the white man's desire to "civilize" Native Americans.

3. Freewrite briefly about the conflict between the Native Americans and the early American government and settlers. Write anything that comes to your mind, both facts you know and questions you have about this period.

Liberal Society and the Indian Question

MICHAEL PAUL ROGIN

Michael Paul Rogin (1937–2001), a graduate of both Harvard and the University of Chicago, authored many books, including *The Intellectuals and McCarthy* (1967), *Fathers and Children: Andrew Jackson and the Subjugation of the American Indian* (1975), *Subversive Genealogy: The Politics and Art of Herman Melville* (1983), *Ronald Reagan, the Movie, and Other Episodes in Political Demonology* (1987), *Blackface, White Noise: Jewish Immigrants in the Hollywood Melting Pot* (1996), and *Independence Day, or How I Learned to Stop Worrying and Love Enola Gay* (1998). Rogin taught for over thirty years at the University of California, where he was the Chancellor's Professor of Political Science. In the following selection from *Fathers and Children*, Rogin discusses the conflict of early American statesmen who wrote about and discussed the harsh treatment of their "Indian brothers" while rationalizing their subjugation at the same time.

Our conduct toward these people is deeply interesting to our national character.

—*Andrew Jackson, First Annual Message to Congress, December 1829*

"In the beginning," John Locke wrote, "all the world was America." Then men relinquished the state of nature, freely contracted together, and entered civil society. That was not the way it began, in America. True, settlers came to escape the corruption and traditional restraints of Europe, to begin again, to return to the state of nature and contract together. They aimed, as Hamilton put it in the *Federalist Papers*, to build a state based on "reflection and choice" rather than "accident and force." But while the origins of European countries were shrouded by "the chaos of impenetrable antiquity," America clearly began not with primal innocence and consent but with acts of force and fraud. Indians were here first, and it was their land upon which Americans contracted, squabbled, and reasoned with one another. Stripping away history did not permit beginning without sin; it simply exposed the sin at the beginning of it all. The dispossession of the Indians, moreover, did not happen once and for all in the beginning. America was continually beginning again on the frontier, and as it expanded across the continent, it killed, removed, and drove into extinction one tribe after another.

The years spanned by Andrew Jackson's life were the great years of American expansion. Born on the frontier, Jackson joined the movement west as a young man. In the years of his maturity and old age, from Jefferson's

Presidency to the Mexican War, expansion across the continent was the central fact of American politics. Two-thirds of the American population of 3.9 million lived within fifty miles of the ocean in 1790. In the next half-century 4.5 million Americans crossed the Appalachians, one of the great migrations in world history. The western states contained less than three percent of the U.S. population in 1790, twenty-eight percent in 1830. In two decades the west would become the most populous region of the country.

Indians inhabited in 1790 almost all the territory west of the original thirteen states. If America were to expand and take possession of the continent, they would have to be dispossessed. Indians had not mattered so much, in the history of Europeans in the English new world, since the colonial settlements. They would never matter so much again. Indian removal was Andrew Jackson's major policy aim in the quarter-century before he became President. His Indian wars and treaties were principally responsible for dispossessing the southern Indians during those years. His presidential Indian removal finished the job. Martin Van Buren, Jackson's ally and successor, listed Indian removal as one of "the old Hero's" major achievements. During the years of Jacksonian Democracy, 1824–1852, five of the ten major candidates for President had either won reputations as generals in Indian wars or served as Secretary of War, whose major responsibility in this period was relations with the Indians. Historians, however, have failed to place Indians at the center of Jackson's life. They have interpreted the Age of Jackson from every perspective but Indian destruction, the one from which it actually developed historically.

125,000 Indians lived east of the Mississippi in 1820. Seventy-five percent of these came under government removal programs in the next two decades. By 1844 less than 30,000 Indians remained in the east, mainly in the undeveloped Lake Superior region. Most of the eastern tribes had been relocated west of the Mississippi; the total population of Indians indigenous to the east had declined by one-third.

How reconcile the destruction of the Indians with the American self-image? This problem preoccupied statesmen of the period. "The great moral debt we owe to this unhappy race is universally felt and acknowledged," Secretary of War Lewis Cass reported in 1831. John Tipton, land speculator, Indian agent, and Indiana Senator, explained, "There is something painful in the reflection that these people were once numerous, and that by our approach they have been reduced to a few. It is natural that we should feel averse to the admission that the true causes of their decline are to be found among *us*." In our relations to the Indians, wrote Van Buren, "we are as a nation responsible *in foro conscientiae* to the opinions of the great family of nations, as it involves the course we have pursued and shall pursue towards a people comparatively weak, upon whom we were perhaps in the beginning unjustifiable aggressors, but of whom, in the progress of time and events, we have become the guardians, and, as we hope, the benefactors."

Van Buren and the others felt the eyes of the world on America. They needed to demonstrate that our encounter with the Indians, "the most difficult of all our relations, foreign and domestic, has at last been justified to the world in its near approach to a happy and certain consummation." They needed to justify—the Puritan word means save for God—a society built on Indian graves.

American rhetoric filled the white–Indian tie with intimate symbolic meaning. Indians were, every treaty talk insisted, our "friends and brothers." "Our red brethren" were the "voice of nature" in "the human family." "Members of the great American family," they were, like us, "descendants of Adam." "We take an interest in your fate," Secretary of War Calhoun told one tribe, "as you were the first proprietors of this happy country." But white Americans had displaced "this unhappy race—the original dwellers in our land." In the words of Virginia Congressman Thomas Bouldin,

> I think they are a noble, gallant, injured race. I think they have suffered nothing but wrong and injury from us, since the Anglo-Saxon race . . . first landed in this country. . . . Sir, a melancholy overcasts my mind whenever I think of this too probable issue in regard to the red man—his gradual but entire extinction. . . . Many of our first families and most distinguished patriots are descended from the Indian race. My heart compels me to feel for them for some of my nearest relations (not that I have myself any of their blood) are descended from the Indian race.

Yet Bouldin insisted that whites must continue to dispossess their brothers. Norman O. Brown writes,

> The comic wearing of the Indian mask, in the Boston Tea Party, or Tammany's Wigwam, is the lighter side of a game, a ritual, the darker side of which is fraternal genocide. Indians are our Indian brothers; one of the ten lost tribes of Israel; the lost sheep we came to find: now unappeased ghosts in the unconscious of the white man.

The European psyche in the new world, D. H. Lawrence believed, contained the Indian brother as an inner double. Early American painting often portrayed this theme. Benjamin West's serene, classical portrait of Colonel Guy Johnson reveals on closer inspection a dark, shadowy Indian half hidden behind him. An Indian horseman fights with a white in Charles Deas' turbulent painting; horses and human limbs inextricably intertwined, the two men are locked in *The Death Struggle*.

Indians could not remain "unappeased ghosts," however. The south, bound in slavery, was prey to visions of violent, immoral possession. Southerners like Bouldin often rooted authority in unredeemed force and contaminated inheritance. Whites must take Indian land, Bouldin suggested, but the process was contaminated at the core. The fraternal conflict of Indians and whites contained no moral resolution. But neither the south nor the country as a whole could rest with such a birthright. Whites developed, as they took Indian land, a powerful, legitimating cultural myth. America's expansion across the continent, everyone agreed, reproduced the historical evolution of mankind. "The first proprietors of this happy country" were sometimes said to be the first people on earth. Early in time, they were also primitive in development. Human societies existed along a unilinear scale from savagery to civilization. As civilization advanced westward, it must inevitably displace savagery.

"The unfortunate sons of nature," said the young John Quincy Adams, "had no cause of complaint" against the Plymouth founders.

> What is the right of a huntsman to the forest of a thousand miles, over which he has accidentally ranged in quest of prey? . . . Shall the exuberant bosom of the common mother, amply adequate to the nourishment of millions, be claimed exclusively by a few hundreds of her offspring? Shall the lordly savage not only disdain the virtues and enjoyments of civilization himself, but shall he controul the civilization of the world? . . . Shall the fields and valleys, which a beneficent God has formed to teem with the life of innumerable multitudes, be condemned to everlasting barrenness.

The Indian was the brother with original title to the land. But, explained Hugh Henry Brackenridge, "there is no right of primogeniture in the laws of nature and of nations." Whites followed the biblical injunction to "subdue and replenish" the earth; "the lordly savage" did not. In sole possession of "the exuberant bosom of the common mother," he lived in a "state of nature," and gained "subsistence from spontaneous productions." Agricultural people represented a superior stage of development; they had the God-given right to dispossess hunters from their sovereignty over nature.

The evolution of societies from savagery to civilization was identical to the evolution of individual men. The Indian was the elder brother, but he remained in the "childhood" of the human race. "Barbarism is to civilization," wrote Francis Parkman, "as childhood is to maturity." Indians were "children of nature." They were "part of the human family" as children, children who could not mature. Their replacement by whites symbolized America's growing up from childhood to maturity. Winthrop Jordan writes,

> The Indian became for Americans a symbol of their American experience; it was no mere luck of the toss that placed the profile of an American Indian rather than an American Negro on the famous old five-cent piece. Confronting the Indian in America was a testing experience, common to all the colonies. Conquering the Indian symbolized and personified the conquest of American difficulties, the surmounting of the wilderness. To push back the Indian was to prove the worth of one's own mission, to make straight in the desert a highway for civilization.

Not the Indians alive, then, but their destruction symbolized the American experience. The conquest of the Indians made the country uniquely American. But this conquest was, in the language Americans used, a conquest of their own childhoods. Jordan is right: America identified at once with the conquered and the conquering. The Indians—that "much-injured race" who were once "the uncontrolled possessors of these vast regions"— became a symbol of something lost, lost inevitably in the process of growing up.

America was born with the modern age, with discovery and expansion, Protestant reformation, and bourgeois development. Liberalism—to identify the modern impulse by its name in political thought—transformed European societies; it operated on a state of nature in America. Americans were, in Tocqueville's phrase, "born equal." There was "no right of primogeniture in the law of nature" (Brackenridge), and none took deep root in America. America had no feudal past. It lacked a hereditary nobility, a long-established church, a standing army, and a peasantry bound to the soil. Settlers lived by the covenants of God with man and men with each other. They reproduced in westward migration their self-imposed exile from mother country. The wilderness exposed them to the dangers of domination by nature. Fleeing European traditional ties, they set out self-consciously to conquer the wilderness, and to people the land with God-fearing, self-reliant families.

Liberalism encountered resistance in Europe, first from feudalism and then from revolutionary socialism. But the Europeans who settled America were confronted with no alternatives to liberal uniformity save the psychically charged presences of "the black race within our bosom . . . [and] the red on our borders." Subculture conflict and historical change mark white American history. Nevertheless, the country lacked the historical bases for political alternatives to liberalism, and radical historians who search for such alternatives mistake the American experience. Liberalism reached everywhere in white America; the resistance it encountered came from within.

Modernism enforced, throughout the west, a monumental, systematic ordering of external and internal worlds. It separated men from the customary universe as they had historically experienced it, and from their own spontaneous emotional life. It generated anger at buried parts of the self and their images in the world. It also generated nostalgia. Underneath the "ambitious expansionism" of modern Western societies, writes Henry Baudet in *Paradise on Earth*, "with their economic savoir faire, their social ideology, and their organizational talents," lies "a psychological disposition out of all political reality. It exists independently of objective facts, which seem to have become irrelevant. It is a disposition that leads [its adherent] 'to die' rather than 'to do,' and forces him to repent of his wickedness, covetousness, pride and complacency." The worldly orientation, Baudet argues, points to history and practical consequences, the inner disposition to a primitiveness beyond history.

The first is expansive, the second regressive. The regressive inner disposition, Baudet believes, has fastened on images of the noble savage, the garden of Eden, and paradise on earth. In America "aggressive expansionism" encountered the regressive impulse as a "political reality." That is the precise meaning ante-bellum Americans gave to their destruction of the Indians, and it is the meaning we shall give to it here.

At the outset the contrast between expansionist, liberal America's self-conception and its image of the Indians seems clear enough. Liberalism insisted on the independence of men, each from the other, and from cultural, traditional, and communal attachments. Indians were perceived as connected to their past, their superstitions, and their land. Liberalism insisted upon work, instinctual repression, and acquisitive behavior; men had to conquer and separate themselves from nature. Indians were seen as playful, violent, improvident, wild, and in harmony with nature. Private property underlay liberal society; Indians held land in common. Liberal relations were based, contractually, on keeping promises and on personal responsibility. Indians, in the liberal view, were anarchic and irresponsible. Americans believed that peaceful competitiveness kept them in touch with one another and provided social cement. They thought that Indians, lacking social order, were devoted to war.

Disastrously for the liberal self-conception, however, its distance from primitive man was not secure. At the heart of ambitious expansionism lay the regressive impulse itself. Indians were in harmony with nature; lonely, independent liberal men were separated from it, and their culture lacked the richness, diversity, and traditional attachments necessary to sustain their independence. Liberalism generated a forbidden nostalgia for childhood—for the nurturing, blissful, primitively violent connection to nature that white Americans had to leave behind.

They did not have to leave it behind forever. The west healed the division between Indian childhood and adult white maturity. America did not create its history in closed space. It returned to childhood on the frontier. There Americans, as they understood their history, began again; there they regenerated themselves and their society in heroic Indian combat. There they created a uniquely American identity, emancipated from old-world forms and wilderness savagery. They then took upon themselves, to recall Van Buren's words, the obligations of "benefactors" and "guardians." In paternal benevolence toward their "red children," white fathers redeemed the debt to the childhood they replaced. What meaning can be given to a policy of death and dispossession, centrally important to American development, which is justified by the paternal benevolence of a father for his children?

Indian dispossession, as experienced by the whites who justified it and carried it out, belongs to the pathology of human development. Indians remained, in the white fantasy, in the earliest period of childhood, unseparated from "the exuberant bosom of the common mother." They were at once symbols of a lost childhood bliss and, as bad children, repositories of murderous, negative fantasies. Psychoanalytic theory suggests that the infant at the breast and the small child experience world-destroying rage at separation from the mother, dependence upon her, and fear of her loss. Culture affects the resolution of separation anxiety, and liberal culture lacked libidinal ties to replace those forsaken in childhood. Suspicious of the pleasure principle, it inhibited the mature enjoyments which sustain loving interdependence and quiet primitive rage. Liberalism accentuated regressive pressures on the mature, isolated ego. The encounter with Indians and the virgin land returned America to the natural world. Projecting primitive rage onto Indians, independent adult whites revenged themselves for their own early loss. The Indian's tie with nature was broken, literally by uprooting him, figuratively by civilizing him, finally by killing him.

Replacing Indians upon the land, whites reunited themselves with nature. The rhetoric of Manifest Destiny pictured America as a "young and growing country"; it expanded through "swallowing territory," "just as an animal eats to grow." Savagery would inevitably "be swallowed by" civilization. Whites imaginatively regressed, as they described expansion, to fantasies of infant omnipotence. They entertained the most primitive form of object relations, the annihilation of the object through oral introjection.

Expansion, whites agreed, inevitably devoured Indians; only paternal governmental supervision could save the tribes from extinction. Paternalism, however, met white needs better than Indian ones. The new American world undermined the authority provided by history, tradition, family connection, and the other ties of old European existence. Political authority, as Locke demonstrated against Sir Robert Filmer, must derive from interactions among free men, not from paternal relations. But Indians were not liberal men. The paternal authority repressed out of liberal politics returned in Indian paternalism.

This paternalism was badly contaminated by the destructive maturing process from which it grew. It required children to have no independence or life of their own. Either a man had "independence of mind and action," Jackson explained to his ward, or he "becomes the real tool in the hands of others, and is wielded, like a mere attamaton, sometimes, without knowing it, to the worst of purposes." In their paternalism toward Indians, white policy-makers indulged primitive longings to wield total power. They sought to regain the primal infant–mother connection from a position of domination instead of dependence. Explicitly the father was to break the child's tie to nature so the child could grow up. The actual language and practice substituted for the tie to nature a total, infantilized dependence upon the white father and the fragmented workings of liberal marketplace and bureaucracy.

Discussion Questions

1. How did the white statesmen justify the need to conquer Native Americans, despite a sense of sorrow at the plight of the Native Americans? What kinds of reasoning did the statesmen offer for the necessity of removing Native Americans from their native lands? What assumptions did these early politicians make about "civilization" and "savages"?

2. Discuss in groups what Rogin means when he says, "Whites developed, as they took Indian land, a powerful, legitimating cultural myth. American's expansion across the continent, everyone agreed, reproduced the historical evolution of mankind." Discuss this statement—how did expansion, according to Rogin, mirror the evolution of mankind?

Writing Suggestions

1. Examine the language of John Quincy Adams as he speaks about the Native Americans, as quoted in Rogin's chapter. Then write a two-page paper in which you analyze Adams's argument, examining the diction, imagery, and logic Adams uses to persuade his readers that the whites had every right to take the Indian lands. Consider Adams's audience, and state in your paper whether or not his argument would have been persuasive to this audience. What kinds of appeals does Adams make? What reasons does he offer for the need to take over the "everlasting barrenness" of undeveloped lands?

2. Rogin states that whites "developed, as they took Indian land, a powerful, legitimating cultural myth," that justified the idea that as "civilization advanced westward, it must inevitably displace savagery." Read the following two selections in this chapter: Thomas Jefferson's "Policy of Civilization and Assimilation," and Andrew Jackson's "Message to Congress." Then write a three-page paper in which you analyze both Jefferson's and Jackson's statements about the taking of Indian lands in relationship to Rogin's article. Use Jefferson and Jackson to examine Rogin's arguments, and agree or disagree that these two statesmen exemplify the "legitimating cultural myth" that Rogin states was so necessary to justify the taking of lands. Look closely at the language of Jefferson and Jackson, and use specific quotes from each to illustrate your points.

Policy of Civilization and Assimilation

THOMAS JEFFERSON

Born in 1743 in Albemarle County, Virginia, Thomas Jefferson came from a landed family of some social standing, and attended the College of William and Mary. Thomas Jefferson was the third president of the United States, serving from 1801 to 1809. Jefferson is well-known for his role in drafting the text of the Declaration of Independence and later for his purchase of the Louisiana Territory from Napoleon in 1803. Many students of history will also recognize Jefferson's name in connection with Monticello, his beautiful mountaintop home. Recently, scholars have been fascinated by Jefferson's complex character, and by the inconsistencies in his own life when compared with his famous written lines, "all men are created equal." With regard to Native Americans, particularly, Jefferson seemed torn between admiration for the Native American cultures and his own belief that those very cultures must give way to the white man's dominance. In the following excerpt from a letter to Benjamin Hawkins, his ideas about the future of Indians in the new Republic demonstrate some of these interesting contradictions in Jefferson's character.

"I consider the business of hunting as already become insufficient to furnish clothing and subsistence to the Indians. The promotion of agriculture, therefore, and household manufacture, are essential in their preservations, and I am disposed to aid and encourage it liberally. This will enable them to live on much smaller portions of land, and, indeed, will render their vast forests useless but for the range of cattle; for which purpose, also, as they become better farmers, they will be found useless, and even disadvantageous. While they are learning to do better on less land, our increasing numbers will be calling for more land, and thus a coincidence of interests will be produced between those who have land to spare, and want other necessaries, and those who have such necessaries to spare, and want lands. This commerce, then, will be for the good of both, and those who are friends to both ought to encourage it. . . . In truth, the ultimate point of rest and happiness for them is to let our settlements and theirs meet and blend together, to intermix, and become one people.

"Incorporating themselves with us as citizens of the United States, this is what the natural progress of things will, of course, bring on, and it will be better to promote than to retard it. Surely it will be better for them to be identified with us, and preserved in the occupation of their lands, than be exposed to the many casualties which may endanger them while a separate people. I have little doubt, but that your reflections must have led you to view the various ways in which their history may terminate, and to see that this is the one most for their happiness. And we have already had an application from a settlement of Indians to become citizens of the United States. It is possible, perhaps probable, that this idea may be so novel as that it might shock the Indians, were it even hinted to them. Of course, you will keep it for your own reflection; but, convinced of its soundness, I feel it consistent with pure morality to lead them towards it, to familiarize them to the idea that it is for their interest to cede lands at times to the United States, and for us thus to procure gratifications to our citizens, from time to time, by new acquisitions of land."

Discussion Questions

1. In what ways do you think Jefferson succeeds or fails in his arguments for the Indians ceding lands to the whites? Consider the following:

    What evidence does he offer, and what evidence does he leave out?
    What kinds of logical fallacies do you see in his arguments?
    What large assumptions is he making?
    How is he defining the phrase "for the good of both"?

2. Jefferson says it is "consistent with pure morality" to persuade the Indians to cede land to the whites. How does he support this line of reasoning?

3. How has the government's position toward Native American lands changed since Jefferson's time? Do you think the federal government now makes more of an effort to accommodate tribal land rights, or do you think the attitude toward tribal land rights has stayed the same?

Writing Suggestions

1. Review your answers to the first discussion question, and then write a three-page paper in which you analyze Thomas Jefferson's "Policy of Civilization and Assimilation" for soundness of argument and logic. Answer some of the following questions in your essay:

    What are Jefferson's central arguments?
    What evidence does he offer, and what evidence does he leave out?
    What kinds of logical fallacies do you see in his arguments?
    What large assumptions is he making?
    How is he defining the phrase "for the good of both"?
    Do you find him persuasive or not?

2. Research a current debate about land between the Federal Government and a Native American tribe. Try different key words in your search, such as "Tribal Issues," "Native Americans and Land," or "Federal Government and Native American Tribes." You can look for these current legal battles in the indexes of the *New York Times* or the *Wall Street Journal*, or you could look for the same issues on Academic Universe, Lexis Nexis. (See the Introduction to this book for more information on using the Internet for research.) Research both sides of the issue, and take a stand for what you believe should be the solution. Create a thesis that argues for your ideal resolution of the controversy. Deal with your opposition by stating their positions clearly, and then refute or concede each point with your own evidence. Use at least five sources, including quotes from Native American representatives and those representing the U.S. government. Also look for sources that would not have as strong a bias in favor of one side or the other—try to find neutral sources that seem to acknowledge the complexities of the problem.

Seventh Annual Message to Congress
Indian Removal

ANDREW JACKSON

Andrew Jackson was president of the United States from 1829 to 1837, and he is well-known for his role in the House of Representatives, his brief stay in the Senate, and, most particularly, his role as general in the War of 1812, in which he defeated the British in New Orleans. Jackson is less well-known for his now very controversial role in the removal of the Native Americans from their lands, especially the forced relocation of the Cherokee nation from its southern homelands. In the following extract from Jackson's "Seventh Annual Message to Congress" (December 7, 1835), he explains that the Indians cannot be "civilized" and thus must be removed from their lands and placed in protected reservations.

The plan of removing the aboriginal people who yet remain within the settled portions of the United States to the country west of the Mississippi River approaches its consummation. It was adopted on the most mature consideration of the condition of this race, and ought to be persisted in till the object is accomplished, and prosecuted with as much vigor as a just regard to their circumstances will permit, and as fast as their consent can be obtained. All preceding experiments for the improvement of the Indians have failed. It seems now to be an established fact they can not live in contact with a civilized community and prosper. Ages of fruitless endeavors have at length brought us to a knowledge of this principle of intercommunication with them. The past we can not recall, but the future we can provide for. Independently of the treaty stipulations into which we have entered with the various tribes for the usufructuary rights they have ceded to us, no one can doubt the moral duty of the Government of the United States to protect and if possible to preserve and perpetuate the scattered remnants of this race which are left within our borders. In the discharge of this duty an extensive region in the West has been assigned for their permanent residence. It has been divided into districts and allotted among them. Many have already removed and others are preparing to go, and with the exception of two small bands living in Ohio and Indiana, not exceeding 1,500 persons, and of the Cherokees, all the tribes on the east side of the Mississippi, and extending from Lake Michigan to Florida, have entered into engagements which will lead to their transplantation.

The plan for their removal and reestablishment is founded upon the knowledge we have gained of their character and habits, and has been dictated by a spirit of enlarged liberality. A territory exceeding in extent that relinquished has been granted to each tribe. Of its climate, fertility, and capacity to support an Indian population the representations are highly favorable. To these districts the Indians are removed at the expense of the United States, and with certain supplies of clothing, arms, ammunition, and other indispensable articles; they are also furnished gratuitously with provisions for the period of a year after their arrival at their new homes. In that time, from the nature of the country and of the products raised by them, they can subsist themselves by agricultural labor, if they choose to resort to that mode of life; if they do not they are upon the skirts of the great prairies, where countless herds of buffalo roam, and a short time suffices to adapt their own habits to the changes which a change of the animals destined for their food may require. Ample arrangements have also been made for the support of schools; in some instances council houses and churches are to be erected, dwellings constructed for the chiefs, and mills for common use. Funds have been set apart for the maintenance of the poor; the most necessary mechanical arts have been introduced, and blacksmiths, gunsmiths, wheelwrights, millwrights, etc., are supported among them. Steel and iron, and sometimes salt, are purchased for them, and plows and other farming utensils, domestic animals, looms, spinning wheels, cards, etc., are presented to them. And besides these beneficial arrangements, annuities are in all cases paid, amounting in some instances to more than $30 for each individual of the tribe, and in all cases sufficiently great, if justly divided and prudently expended, to enable them, in addition to their own exertions, to live comfortably. And as a stimulus for exertion, it is now provided by law that "in all cases of the appointment of interpreters or other persons employed for the benefit of the Indians a preference shall be given to persons of Indian descent, if such can be found who are properly qualified for the discharge of the duties."

Such are the arrangements for the physical comfort and for the moral improvement of the Indians. The necessary measures for their political advancement and for their separation from our citizens have not been neglected. The pledge of the United States has been given by Congress that the country destined for the residence of this people shall be forever "secured and guaranteed to them." A country west of Missouri and Arkansas has been assigned to them, into which the white settlements are not to be pushed. No political communities can be formed in that extensive region, except those which are established by the Indians themselves or by the United States for them and with their concurrence. A barrier has thus been raised for their protection against the encroachment of our citizens, and guarding the Indians as far as possible from those evils which have brought them to their present condition. Summary authority has been given by law to destroy all ardent spirits found in their country, without waiting the doubtful result and slow process of a legal seizure. I consider the absolute and unconditional interdiction of this article among these people as the first and great step in their melioration.

Halfway measures will answer no purpose. These can not successfully contend against the cupidity of the seller and the overpowering appetite of the buyer. And the destructive effects of the traffic are marked in every page of the history of our Indian intercourse. . . .

Discussion Questions

1. What justifications does Jackson give for Indian removal? Make a list of his assertions about the character of the Indians, such as "All preceding experiments for the improvement of the Indians have failed." Analyze his evidence. Do you think he argues logically?

2. Now, compare his logic with that of Jefferson in his "Policy of Civilization and Assimilation." What strategies of argument do the two presidents have in common? What justifications do they both use? What kinds of evidence do they present?

Writing Suggestions

1. Jackson states in his speech that the Congress has promised "that the country destined for the residence of this people shall be forever secured and guaranteed to them." Research the fate of the Native Americans under Jackson's presidency. Use a variety of sources, including Native American perspectives, neutral scholarly historical sources, and primary sources such as Chief Black Hawk's "Surrender Speech." In your paper, consider the promises Andrew Jackson made about the fate of the Indians, and then research what actually happened in light of these promises.

2. On the Internet, go to the home page of The Hermitage, Andrew Jackson's family plantation in Tennessee, now open to the public: <http:/www.thehermitage.com/>. Look closely at this site, and follow all the links. Then, write an analysis of this site as a source for historical information about Jackson and his life. Answer some of the questions below as you assess the worth of this site as a research tool:

   Who produced the Web site?

   What did you learn from the site that you had not read elsewhere?

   What kind of links does this site offer? Do they offer historical background?

   What kinds of sources are cited?

   What aspects of Jackson's presidency are missing from the site? What areas of Jackson's life are highlighted?

   What information does the site offer about Native Americans? What information does it offer about slavery?

   Overall, how would you rate the site as a historical source?

I Have Spoken

Introduction

FREDERICK W. TURNER III

Frederick W. Turner III was a professor of English and folklore at the University of Massachusetts until he retired in 1980. He is perhaps best-known for his anthology of Native American essays and stories, *The Portable North American Indian Reader* (1977). He also wrote *Beyond Geography: The Western Spirit against the Wilderness* (1980) and *Spirit of Place: The Making of an American Literary Landscape* (1989). Turner also wrote the Introduction to a collection of Native American speeches entitled *I Have Spoken* (1971), edited by Virginia Armstrong. In this Introduction, which appears below, he argues strongly for a more inclusive approach to American history, an approach that includes the voices of the vanquished as well as the victors.

The knowledge of history is always sheerly potential.

—Johan Huizinga

History, history! We fools, what do we know or care? History begins for us with murder and enslavement, not with discovery. No, we are not Indians but we are men of their world. The blood means nothing; the spirit, the ghost of the land moves in the blood, moves the blood. It is we who ran to the shore naked, we who cried, "Heavenly Man!" These are the inhabitants of our souls, our murdered souls that lie . . . . agh.

—William Carlos Williams

[*I Have Spoken*] is so unusual a book that we have to find keys to it wherever we can. Thus two inscriptions here, one from a Dutch historian, the other from a white American physician and poet. Doubtless there are others, and if I were an Indian, I should probably find my keys among the sayings of the grandfathers. But I am white, and this book, though it can with considerable profit be read by anybody, should be of greatest interest to white Americans who conquered the Indian and settled on his lands.

In the first inscription, Huizinga refers to the fundamental difference between the conditions of knowledge in the physical sciences and mathematics on the one hand, and history on the other. In the first areas, knowledge is actual, given, and (to students of these areas) known. Yet the knowledge of history is always in a state of becoming and is entirely dependent upon the uncovering and interpretation of the materials that make it up. There is no History waiting for us like some giant and architecturally perfect edifice that we will at long last discover in the tangled growth of an intellectual forest. History does not exist for us until and unless we dig it up, interpret it, and put it together. Then the past comes alive, or, more accurately, it is revealed for what it has always been—a part of the present. The materials of *I Have Spoken*, recondite surely for most of us, constitute an important piece of our common history, unearthed and made actual.

The second inscription sounds one of Williams' major themes: the anti-historical bias of American culture and white Americans' ignorance of how much we actually share with those whom in our arrogance and fear we dispossessed. No, we are not Indians, but we are men of the same continent. We are humans, moving upon the same landscape, and in that large perspective differences of blood and customs seem dwarfed. In that same perspective we can see through Williams' words that it is true that it was the Europeans who ran naked to these shores—naked of any knowledge of the land or of its inhabitants; that naked as were those who hailed Columbus, we too brought so little to the settling of this New World. And it is true also that if the Indian was at first disposed to see us as gods (though later as demons), we in our way saw the red men as children of paradise (though later merely as children of a Great White Father). In *I Have Spoken* we can begin to see ourselves through the eyes of another race of men, and this should be an important part of the process of understanding the history which man has made upon this continent.

It becomes clearer with each passing year that this is precisely the greatest need of all Americans: a continental history. By this I mean a whole, fully integrated history of this continent from the granitic base of the land mass itself, up through the layers of soil to the grasses and plants, the trees, the huge geological configurations; the animals who lived and died out and those that still live; the first men who, following those animals, crossed the widening and narrowing land strait; the rise of cultures here and their myths which describe for us how it felt to stand defenseless in a gigantic landscape and then how the people of those cultures learned to propitiate their world; and finally, the coming of the European and what he has done since he settled in with his imported implements and ideas, his slaves, his dreams. An enormous undertaking, this five billion year history, but one that must be seriously begun if we are to understand who we are and where we ought to be headed.

In the past few years, indeed, such a project has been begun on many fronts. Think here of writers such as Frank Waters and Peter Farb whose books have sketched for us some of the major features of that ur-history; of the explorations of the natural world and man's place in it in the works of Joseph Wood Krutch, Loren Eisley, and Peter Matthiessen; of Charles Nichols' rescue of the slaves' narratives; and of the new poetry of the earth of Gary Snyder. These are hopeful signs, threads stretching back to earlier writers who began on this task years ago—Whitman, Daniel Brinton, George Bird Grinnell—but whom we seem to have forgotten. I remember being intrigued some years ago by a line in Edmundo O'Gorman's book, *The Invention of America*, where he writes an entry in the imaginary diary of the North American continent: "At long last, someone has arrived to discover me!" We need to construct such a diary, using both recoverable materials and the powers of our imaginations.

It is in this connection that Indian history—*their* history, not our version of it—becomes so important. In it we see the potential for the recovery of that primal past which will, if we but surrender ourselves to its lessons, explain much about ourselves and our world that now seems almost desperately unknowable. Wherever Indian history survives and wherever we encounter the remnants of it, we move closer to the rhythms of our land, rhythms which we are divorced from, as the Sioux Luther Standing Bear pointed out years ago:

> The white man . . . does not understand America. He is too far removed from its formative processes. The roots of the tree of his life have not yet grasped the rock and the soil. The white man is still troubled by primitive fears; he still has in his consciousness the perils of this frontier continent, some of its fastnesses not yet having yielded to his questing footsteps and inquiring eyes. He shudders still with the memory of the loss of his forefathers upon its scorching deserts and forbidding mountaintops. The man from Europe is still a foreigner and an alien. And he still hates the man who questioned his path across the continent.
>
> But in the Indian the spirit of the land is still vested; it will be until other men are able to divine and meet its rhythm. Men must be born and reborn to belong. Their bodies must be formed of the dust of their forefathers' bones.

This is no accident, nor is the scarcity of Indian history which makes clear this condition. Without invoking the spectre of conspiracy, I say that there has been among whites a planned destruction of the past—or at any rate, all of it that did not illustrate the national mythology. This fact became clear to some in the 1920s when certain folklorists set about in earnest to collect Afro-American traditions. The collections of those traditions bear the unmistakable marks of mutilation, suppression, and attempted obliteration. In short, their condition reflects back upon a people careless of its past and so unaware of its present. In recent years the attempt to recover America's black past has been renewed with an urgency born of desperation, for it has only been through riots, bombings, and murders that we have come to see that an understanding of the past is vital to a sense of the present.

Much the same is true of that part of the past that concerns the Indian. Here, too, the destruction of tribal traditions was a planned, concerted effort carried out over long years by such diverse agents as missionaries, army officers and soldiers, school teachers and bureaucrats. Collections of Indian history until the late years of the last century were random ones, usually interspersed in documents written for other purposes, and many of the best of these, interestingly enough, were written by Europeans whose sense of history was more developed than that of a people busily engaged in making over a New World in its own image.

This attempted destruction of the African and Indian pasts can also be understood as a consequence of our physical subjugation of these peoples: the victors write the histories; the vanquished are rendered historyless. It was this and something more. In the white man's opinion, oral history was non-history, a bundle of foolish superstitions without authority or value. Worse, such traditions seemed to be the very things which stood most in the way of the psychological subjugation of blacks and red men. Thus the history of the New World was to be begun again, this time from the top down: written history from the white point of view, fixing its attention on economic trends, trade agreements, election processes, military engagements, and diplomatic entanglements.

When this rewriting was completed to, say, World War II, white Americans could look back upon a past that seemed by this arrangement neat, orderly, glorious, and—yes—perhaps divinely necessary. The structure was entirely coherent and self-explanatory. School children learned it with the same ease and nonchalance that they learned to spell "Mississippi." It has become the fate of these school children to guess that there must have been yet another kind of history, a deep, dark, subterranean stream of history running all this time under the bright ribbon of that version of the continental past they were given in their formative years. The events of the past decade in particular have shown them in violent and oblique ways that their knowledge of themselves and of the land they live on is terribly incomplete. The long-silenced voices of the blacks and of the Indian have risen to challenge the words of the textbooks. And to these has been added the wordless voice of the land itself, crying out against the continued despoilment of it, threatening to turn finally upon the despoilers and swallow them whole like the *vagina dentata* of Indian legend.

But by this time these school children (that is, we ourselves) were all but incapable of reading the emerging record of the substratum of New World history. Our minds and ears were closed; oral history still seemed less than authentic; and the histories of the Afro-Americans and Indian less important on the world stage than the Plymouth Rock–Washington litany. The result has been that while we have been coerced into surmising that our view of ourselves was not the only one possible, we have not yet been able to really look through other angles of vision. So apparitional is our sense of history that it is only with the greatest difficulty, if at all, that we can imagine, for example, the Sioux leader Red Cloud standing before a packed house at the Cooper Union—that same Cooper Union where Lincoln had spoken in 1860—and making the kind of tough, forceful, and eloquent speech that is reproduced here (Speech #168). This is not only a failure of our imaginations (disastrous enough in itself), it is crucial ignorance. It is a divorce from the whole reality of our land. In its final stage it expresses itself in a propensity to see ourselves as agents and principal actors in world history and all others as props in our production. Elevated to the level of foreign and domestic policy, as this view in fact has been, such a sense of history results in tyranny and genocide.

Discussion Questions

1. How does Turner interpret John Huizinga's quote—"The knowledge of history is always sheerly potential"—in relationship to the history of Native Americans?

2. Turner says, "The victors write the histories, the vanquished are rendered historyless." He goes on to say that we have no true history of the United States unless we hear the history of those who were conquered. Consider what you learned in high school about the struggles between whites and Native Americans. Discuss in groups what you did or did not learn about the history of Native Americans from the "historyless." Did you read transcribed speeches of Native American leaders? Did you read contemporary Native American authors? Assess your own education in light of Turner's claims, and use specific examples in your discussion.

Writing Suggestions

1. As a group assignment, write a rebuttal to Turner. Pretend you are sending him a letter in which you disagree with his arguments, and, for the purposes of this exercise, gather specific evidence to support your contention that he wrongly accuses the white "victors" of rewriting history. Even if you do agree with Turner, try to visualize the arguments of those who oppose his views. Brainstorm in groups and list these arguments, and then write the letter.

2. Turner argues for as complete a knowledge of historical roots as possible. Research your own family history to find out as much as you can about how your family came to live in America. You can ask your family for help or use an Internet site that offers help in tracing family trees.

   Then, write an essay reflecting on the process of becoming American, and define what that means to you. Discuss what the process of immigration meant to your family, and record the kinds of changes and struggles your extended family went through. What kinds of family stories have been passed down to you, and how do they affect your perception of yourself? You can answer some of the following questions as you write your rough draft of the paper:

   Did you immigrate to the United States yourself, or were you born here?

   Were your grandparents or parents born in America? If not, how did they come to America?

   What do they know of their country of origin?

   What stories were told to them about their family history?

   What kinds of family personality traits do you see in yourself?

Address to President Grant

CHIEF RED CLOUD

Chief Red Cloud (1822–1909) of the Oglala Sioux played an important role in the Plains Wars, and is generally acknowledged to have helped force the U.S. Government into negotiations after the failure of the army's campaigns against the Sioux in 1865. Although Red Cloud was a fierce warrior, eventually he was forced to accept reservation status for the Sioux, and he lived long enough to see the loss of Indian lands and freedoms. However, Red Cloud was able to fight for the rights of his people throughout his life. In the 1880s, for example, he exposed the illegal practices of Pine Ridge Indian Agent Valentine McGillycuddy—who misused his power over the distribution of government food and supplies for the Indians of Pine Ridge—and McGillycuddy was fired. Red Cloud was in contact with Eastern reform movement leaders, and he himself often spoke to white audiences about the plight of Native Americans. In the speech below, Red Cloud addresses President U.S. Grant in Washington in June of 1870.

My Brothers and my Friends who are before me today: God Almighty has made us all, and He is here to hear what I have to say to you today. The Great Spirit made us both. He gave me lands and He gave you lands. You came here and we received you as brothers. When the Almighty made you, He made you all white and clothed you. When He made us He made us with red skins and poor. When you first came we were very many and you were few. Now you are many and we are few. You do not know who appears before you to speak. He is a representative of the original American race, and first people of this continent. We are good, and not bad. The reports which you get about us are all on one side. You hear of us only as murderers and thieves. We are not so. If we had more lands to give to you we would give them, but we have no more. We are driven into a very little island, and we want you, our dear friends, to help us with the Government of the United States. The Great Spirits made us poor and ignorant. He made you rich and wise and skillful in things which we know nothing about. The good Father made you to eat tame game and us to eat wild game. Ask any one who has gone through to California. They will tell you we have treated them well. You have children. We, too, have children, and we wish to bring them up well. We ask you to help us do it. At the mouth of Horse Creek, in 1852, the Great Father made a treaty with us. We agreed to let him pass through our territory unharmed for fifty-five years. We kept our word. We committed no murders, no depredations, until the troops came there. When the troops were sent there trouble and disturbance arose. Since that time there have been various goods sent from time to time to us, but only once did they reach us, and soon the Great Father took away the only good man he had sent us, Col. Fitzpatrick. The Great Father said we must go to farming, and some of our men went to farming near Fort Laramie, and were treated very badly indeed. We came to Washington to see our Great Father that peace might be continued. The Great Father that made us both wishes peace to be kept; we want to keep peace. Will you help us? In 1868 men came out and brought papers. We could not read them, and they did not tell us truly what was in them. We thought the treaty was to remove the forts and that we should then cease from fighting. But they wanted to send us traders on the Missouri. We did not want to go on the Missouri, but wanted traders where we were. When I reached Washington the Great Father explained to me what the treaty was, and showed me that the interpreters had deceived me. All I want is right and justice. I have tried to get from the Great Father what is right and just. I have not altogether succeeded. I want you to help me to get what is right and just. I represent the whole Sioux nation, and they will be bound by what I say. I am no Spotted Tail, to say one thing one day and be bought for a pin the next. Look at me. I am poor and naked, but I am the Chief of the nation. We do not want riches, but we want to train our children right. Riches would do us no good. We could not take them with us to the other world. We do not want riches, we want peace and love.

The riches that we have in this world, Secretary [of the Interior Jacob] Cox said truly, we cannot take with us to the next world. Then I wish to know why Commissioners are sent out to us who do nothing but rob us and get the riches of this world away from us! I was brought up among the traders, and those who came out there in the early times treated me well and I had a good time with them. They taught us to wear clothes and to use tobacco and ammunition. But, by and by, the Great Father sent out a different kind of men; men who cheated and drank whisky; men who were so bad that the Great Father could not keep them at home and so sent them out there. I have sent a great many words to the Great Father but they never reached him. They were drowned on the way, and I was afraid the words I spoke lately to the Great Father would not reach you, so I came to speak to you myself; and now I am going away to my home. I want to have men sent out to my people whom we know and can trust. I am glad I have come here. You belong in the East and I belong in the West, and I am glad I have come here and that we could understand one another. I am very much obliged to you for listening to me. I go home this afternoon. I hope you will think of what I have said to you. I bid you all an affectionate farewell.

Discussion Questions

1. Imagine the audience and the rhetorical situation Red Cloud faced as he made his speech in 1870. How does he address his audience, and how does he try to draw parallels between the white man and the "red man" right away? What rhetorical strategy is he using here? What is his tone? What kinds of imagery does he use?

2. What kinds of differences between the values of Native Americans and the values of whites does Red Cloud point out? What insights about Native American life can you gain from Red Cloud's speech?

Writing Suggestions

1. Review your answers to the first discussion question for this selection. Then write an analytical paper examining Red Cloud's speech, detailing what makes the speech so effective. What imagery does Red Cloud use? How does his tone lend credence to his argument? What is tough about his speech? What do you find forceful?

2. Red Cloud was well-known for his success in exposing the dishonesty and brutality of Valentine McGillycuddy, one of the Indian agents responsible for delivering food and supplies to the Pine Ridge Reservation. Research the subject of Indian agents on the reservations, and write a research paper about the role of the Indian agents on the reservations, focusing primarily on one or two famous Indian agents. Answer some of the following questions in your paper:

    What kind of power did these agents have in their jobs?

    What were their responsibilities?

    What kinds of altercations occurred between white agents and Native Americans?

    What kind of government supervision was in place to observe the agents?

Surrender Speech

CHIEF BLACK HAWK

Chief Black Hawk was the leader of the Sac and Mesquakie Indians in Northern Illinois, and he fought for his land and his people against such military officers as Zachary Taylor and Jefferson Davis. Black Hawk fought for months against Jackson's troops, who were ordered to round up the Sac-Mesquakie in 1832; he was captured and imprisoned after most of his people were slaughtered in the fighting between the U.S. Army and the Indians. In the following speech, delivered in 1832, Black Hawk says goodbye to his people and to his life as a free man.

You have taken me prisoner with all my warriors. I am much grieved, for I expected, if I did not defeat you, to hold out much longer, and give you more trouble before I surrendered. I tried hard to bring you into ambush, but your last general understands Indian fighting. The first one was not so wise. When I saw that I could not beat you by Indian fighting, I determined to rush on you, and fight you face to face. I fought hard. But your guns were well aimed. The bullets flew like birds in the air, and whizzed by our ears like the wind through the trees in the winter. My warriors fell around me; it began to look dismal. I saw my evil day at hand. The sun rose dim on us in the morning, and at night it sunk in a dark cloud, and looked like a ball of fire. That was the last sun that shone on Black Hawk. His heart is dead, and no longer beats quick in his bosom. He is now a prisoner to the white men; they will do with him as they wish. But he can stand torture, and is not afraid of death. He is no coward. Black Hawk is an Indian.

He has done nothing for which an Indian ought to be ashamed. He has fought for his countrymen, the squaws and papooses, against white men, who came, year after year, to cheat them and take away their lands. You know the cause of our making war. It is known to all white men. They ought to be ashamed of it. The white men despise the Indians, and drive them from their homes. But the Indians are not deceitful. The white men speak bad of the Indian, and look at him spitefully. But the Indian does not tell lies; Indians do not steal.

An Indian who is as bad as the white men, could not live in our nation; he would be put to death, and eat [sic] up by the wolves. The white men are bad school-masters; they carry false looks, and deal in false actions; they smile in the face of the poor Indian to cheat him; they shake them by the hand to gain their confidence, to make them drunk, to deceive them, and ruin our wives.

We told them to let us alone; but they followed on and beset our paths, and they coiled themselves among us like the snake. They poisoned us by their touch. We were not safe. We lived in danger. We were becoming like them, hypocrites and liars, adulterers, lazy drones, all talkers, and no workers.

We looked up to the Great Spirit. We went to our great father. We were encouraged. His great council gave us fair words and big promises, but we got no satisfaction. Things were growing worse. There were no deer in the forest. The oppossum and beaver were fled; the springs were drying up, and our squaws and papooses without victuals to keep them from starving; we called a great council and built a large fire. The spirit of our fathers arose and spoke to us to avenge our wrongs or die. . . . We set up the war-whoop, and dug up the tomahawk; our knives were ready, and the heart of Black Hawk swelled high in his bosom when he led his warriors to battle. He is satisfied. He will go to the world of spirits contented. He has done his duty. His father will meet him there, and commend him.

Black Hawk is a true Indian, and disdains to cry like a woman. He feels for his wife, his children and friends. But he does not care for himself. He cares for his nation and the Indians. They will suffer. He laments their fate. The white men do not scalp the head; but they do worse—they poison the heart, it is not pure with them. His countrymen will not be scalped, but they will, in a few years, become like the white men, so that you can't trust them, and there must be, as in the white settlements, nearly as many officers as men, to take care of them and keep them in order.

Farewell, my nation. Black Hawk tried to save you, and avenge your wrongs. He drank the blood of some of the whites. He has been taken prisoner, and his plans are stopped. He can do no more. He is near his end. His sun is setting, and he will rise no more. Farewell to Black Hawk.

Discussion Questions

1. Black Hawk's speech was translated and then transcribed, but we can still look at the patterns of his language and his speech, knowing that it may differ from what he actually said in his own language. Look at Black Hawk's speech and discuss the most important message that Black Hawk wants to convey to the white man. Make a list of the comparisons Black Hawk makes between the whites and the Indians. What does he hope to achieve by this comparison of attributes?

2. Compare Black Hawk's analysis of the character of the white man with Andrew Jackson's analysis of the character of the Indian in his "Message to Congress." What kinds of accusations does each man make about the other's race? How does each man assess the character of the other race? Trace the polarities of opinion found in these two speeches.

Writing Suggestions

1. Review your answers to the first discussion question for this selection. Then write a three-page paper in which you analyze Black Hawk's speech, considering some of the following questions:

    Where does the power in the speech come from?
    What kind of language does Black Hawk use?

    Analyze Black Hawk's imagery, and look at the length of his sentences. Incorporate into your paper a personal response to Black Hawk's words, describing the impact of his speech on you.

2. Research the Black Hawk War and the Sac-Patawatomi tribe. Write a review of three different Internet sources you have found about Black Hawk, his struggle against the U.S. troops, and the history of his people. Analyze each source for bias, completeness of information, links, use of secondary and primary sources, and kinds of data. Which source do you find most reliable and informative, and why?

What the Indian Means to America

LUTHER STANDING BEAR

Luther Standing Bear (1868–1947), a member of the Teton Sioux tribe, wrote eloquently about the plight of the American Indian under U.S. government rule. Standing Bear attended the government Indian School at Carlisle, Pennsylvania, and he experienced firsthand the loss of individual freedom, the prohibition of the use of his native language, and the lack of understanding on the part of the white man of native culture and of the strong connection to native lands. The following selection, in which Standing Bear explains the Indians' relationship to the land, is from his third book, *Land of the Spotted Eagle*, written in 1933.

The feathered and blanketed figure of the American Indian has come to symbolize the American continent. He is the man who through centuries has been moulded and sculpted by the same hand that shaped its mountains, forests, and plains, and marked the course of its rivers.

The American Indian is of the soil, whether it be the region of forests, plains, pueblos, or mesas. He fits into the landscape, for the hand that fashioned the continent also fashioned the man for his surroundings. He once grew as naturally as the wild sunflowers; he belongs just as the buffalo belonged.

With a physique that fitted, the man developed fitting skills—crafts which today are called American. And the body had a soul, also formed and moulded by the same master hand of harmony. Out of the Indian approach to existence there came a great freedom—an intense and absorbing love for nature; a respect for life; enriching faith in a Supreme Power; and principles of truth, honesty, generosity, equity, and brotherhood as a guide to mundane relations. . . .

The white man does not understand the Indian for the reason that he does not understand America. He is too far removed from its formative processes. The roots of the tree of his life have not yet grasped the rock and soil. The white man is still troubled with primitive fears; he still has in his consciousness the perils of this frontier continent, some of its fastnesses not yet having yielded to his questing footsteps and inquiring eyes. He shudders still with the memory of the loss of his forefathers upon its scorching deserts and forbidding mountaintops. The man from Europe is still a foreigner and an alien. And he still hates the man who questioned his path across the continent.

But in the Indian the spirit of the land is still vested; it will be until other men are able to divine and meet its rhythm. Men must be born and reborn to belong. Their bodies must be formed of the dust of their forefathers' bones.

The attempted transformation of the Indian by the white man and the chaos that has resulted are but the fruits of the white man's disobedience of a fundamental and spiritual law. The pressure that has been brought to bear upon the native people, since the cessation of armed conflict, in the attempt to force conformity of custom and habit has caused a reaction more destructive than war, and the injury has not only affected the Indian, but has extended to the white population as well. Tyranny, stupidity, and lack of vision have brought about the situation now alluded to as the "Indian Problem."

There is, I insist, no Indian problem as created by the Indian himself. Every problem that exists today in regard to the native population is due to the white man's cast of mind, which is unable, at least reluctant, to seek understanding and achieve adjustment in a new and a significant environment into which it has so recently come.

The white man excused his presence here by saying that he has been guided by the will of his God; and in so saying absolved himself of all responsibility for his appearance in a land occupied by other men.

Then, too, his law was a written law; his divine decalogue reposed in a book. And what better proof that his advent into this country and his subsequent acts were the result of divine will! He brought the Word! There ensued a blind worship of written history, of books, of the written word, that has denuded the spoken word of its power and sacredness. The written word became established as a criterion of the superior man—a symbol of emotional fineness. The man who could write his name on a piece of paper, whether or not he possessed the spiritual fineness to honor those words in speech, was by some miraculous formula a more highly developed and sensitized person than the one who had never had a pen in hand, but whose spoken word was inviolable and whose sense of honor and truth was paramount. With false reasoning was the quality of human character measured by man's ability to make with an implement a mark upon paper. But granting this mode of reasoning be correct and just, then where are to be placed the thousands of illiterate whites who are unable to read and write? Are they, too, "savages"? Is not humanness a matter of heart and mind, and is it not evident in the form of relationship with men? Is not kindness more powerful than arrogance; and truth more powerful than the sword?

True, the white man brought great change. But the varied fruits of his civilization, though highly colored and inviting, are sickening and deadening. And if it be the part of civilization to maim, rob, and thwart, then what is progress? . . .

After subjugation, after dispossession, there was cast the last abuse upon the people who so entirely resented their wrongs and punishments, and that was the stamping and labeling of them as savages. To make this label stick has been the task of the white race and the greatest salve that it has been able to apply to its sore and troubled conscience now hardened through the habitual practice of injustice.

But all the years of calling the Indian a savage has never made him one; all the denial of his virtues has never taken them from him; and the very resistance he has made to save the things inalienably his has been his saving strength—that which will stand him in need when justice does make its belated appearance and he undertakes rehabilitation.

All sorts of feeble excuses are heard for the continued subjection of the Indian. One of the most common is that he is not yet ready to accept the society of the white man—that he is not yet ready to mingle as a social entity.

This, I maintain, is beside the question. The matter is not one of making over the external Indian into the likeness of the white race—a process detrimental to both races. Who can say that the white man's way is better for the Indian? Where resides the human judgment with the competence to weigh and value Indian ideals and spiritual concepts; or substitute for them other values?

Then, has the white man's social order been so harmonious and ideal as to merit the respect of the Indian, and for that matter the thinking class of the white race? Is it wise to urge upon the Indian a foreign social form? Let none but the Indian answer!

Rather, let the white brother face about and cast his mental eye upon a new angle of vision. Let him look upon the Indian world as a human world; then let him see to it that human rights be accorded to the Indians. And this for the purpose of retaining for his own order of society a measure of humanity. . . .

The spiritual health and existence of the Indian was maintained by song, magic, ritual, dance, symbolism, oratory (or council), design, handicraft, and folk-story.

Manifestly, to check or thwart this expression is to bring about spiritual decline. And it is in this condition of decline that the Indian people are today. There is but a feeble effort among the Sioux to keep alive their traditional songs and dances, while among other tribes there is but a half-hearted attempt to offset the influence of the Government school and at the same time recover from the crushing and stifling regime of the Indian Bureau.

One has but to speak of Indian verse to receive uncomprehending and unbelieving glances. Yet the Indian loved verse and into this mode of expression went his deepest feelings. Only a few ardent and advanced students seem interested; nevertheless, they have given in book form enough Indian translations to set forth the character and quality of Indian verse.

Oratory receives a little better understanding on the part of the white public, owing to the fact that oratorical complications include those of Indian orators.

Hard as it seemingly is for the white man's ear to sense the differences, Indian songs are as varied as the many emotions which inspire them, for no two of them are alike. For instance, the Song of Victory is spirited and the notes high and remindful of an unrestrained hunter or warrior riding exultantly over the prairies. On the other hand, the song of the *Cano unye* is solemn and full of urge, for it is meant to inspire the young men to deeds of valor. Then there are the songs of death and the spiritual songs which are connected with the ceremony of initiation. These are full of the spirit of praise and worship, and so strong are some of these invocations that the very air seems as if surcharged with the presence of the Big Holy.

The Indian loved to worship. From birth to death he revered his surroundings. He considered himself born in the luxurious lap of Mother Earth and no place was to him humble. There was nothing between him and the Big Holy. The contact was immediate and personal, and the blessings of Wakan Tanka flowed over the Indian like rain showered from the sky. Wakan Tanka was not aloof, apart, and ever seeking to quell evil forces. He did not punish the animals and the birds, and likewise He did not punish man. He was not a punishing God. For there was never a question as to the supremacy of an evil power over and above the power of Good. There was but one ruling power, and that was *Good*.

Of course, none but an adoring one could dance for days with his face to the sacred sun, and that time is all but done. We cannot have back the days of the buffalo and the beaver; we cannot win back our clean bloodstream and superb health, and we can never again expect the beautiful *rapport* we once had with Nature. The springs and lakes have dried and the mountains are bare of forests. The plow has changed the face of the world. Wi-wila is dead! No more may we heal our sick and comfort our dying with a strength founded on faith, for even the animals now fear us, and fear supplants faith.

And the Indian wants to dance! It is his way of expressing devotion, of communing with unseen power, and in keeping his tribal identity. When the Lakota heart was filled with high emotion, he danced. When he felt the benediction of the warming rays of the sun, he danced. When his blood ran hot with success of the hunt or chase, he danced. When his heart was filled with pity for the orphan, the lonely father, or bereaved mother, he danced. All the joys and exaltations of life, all his gratefulness and thankfulness, all his acknowledgments of the mysterious power that guided life, and all his aspirations for a better life, culminated in one great dance—the Sun Dance.

When the Indian has forgotten the music of his forefathers, when the sound of the tomtom is no more, when noisy jazz has drowned the melody of the flute, he will be a dead Indian. When the memory of his heroes are no longer told in story, and he forsakes the beautiful white buckskin for factory shoddy, he will be dead. When from him has been taken all that is his, all that he has visioned in nature, all that has come to him from infinite sources, he then, truly, will be a dead Indian. His spirit will be gone, and though he walk crowded streets, he will, in truth, be—*dead!*

But all this must not perish; it must live, to the end that America shall be educated no longer to regard native production of whatever tribe—folk-story, basketry, pottery, dance, song, poetry—as curios, and native artists as curiosities. For who but the man indigenous to the soil could produce its song, story, and folk-tale; who but the man who loved the dust beneath his feet could shape it and put it into undying, ceramic form; who but he who loved the reeds that grew beside still waters, and the damp roots of shrub and tree, could save it from seasonal death, and with almost superhuman patience weave it into enduring objects of beauty—into timeless art!

Regarding the "civilization" that has been thrust upon me since the days of reservation, it has not added one whit to my sense of justice; to my reverence for the rights of life; to my love for truth, honesty, and generosity; nor to my faith in Wakan Tanka—God of the Lakotas. For after all the great religions have been preached and expounded, or have been revealed by brilliant scholars, or have been written in books and embellished in fine language with finer covers, man—all man—is still confronted with the Great Mystery.

So if today I had a young mind to direct, to start on the journey of life, and I was faced with the duty of choosing between the natural way of my forefathers and that of the white man's present way of civilization, I would, for its welfare, unhesitatingly set that child's feet in the path of my forefathers. I would raise him to be an Indian!

Discussion Questions

1. Luther Standing Bear points out that, while the white man may have the "ability to write his name on a piece of paper," he is lacking in other qualities. What kinds of defects does he find in the white man's character and society?

2. Why does Luther Standing Bear feel that the elements of song, art, and dance are so vital to the American Indian? What effect did the white man's coming have on these artistic aspects of the Indians' lives?

Writing Suggestions

1. List the arguments Standing Bear makes about the white man's treatment of the Native American. How has the white man tried to change the Native American? What has the white man tried to take away from the Native American? What has been the result?

   Now, write a paper comparing Standing Bear's arguments with those found in Chief Black Hawk's speech. Although the two men lived many years apart, there are many similarities in the charges they bring against the white man. Compare the two men's arguments, and trace the evolution of Chief Black Hawk's arguments forward to 1933 when Standing Bear wrote *Land of the Spotted Eagle*.

2. Luther Standing Bear knew firsthand the experience of attending a government school run for Native American children. Research Standing Bear's life before and during the time he attended the government school at Carlisle, Pennsylvania. You can look at his books, *My Indian Boyhood* or *Stories of the Sioux,* for more information on Standing Bear's experiences. You can also look for more information on the Internet on the government-run schools for Native Americans. Write a paper in which you answer some of the following research questions:

   Which rights were taken away from the Native American children in these schools?

   How were the children treated?

   What did Standing Bear feel about his school?

   What were the stated goals of the Carlisle School, and did the educators achieve these goals?

Captivity and Restoration

The Twentieth Remove

MARY ROWLANDSON

Mary Rowlandson's captivity narrative remains a classic piece—a harrowing description of captivity and survival. Captured by Indians in Lancaster, Massachusetts, during King Philip's War in 1675, Mary Rowlandson and her six-year-old daughter were taken from their burning home by a group of Pocasset, Wampanoag, and Nipmuc Indians. Her life may have been spared because of her ransom value: She was the wife of a minister, and her captors may have expected to get a good ransom for her. In fact, a number of efforts were made to rescue her, and, after 12 weeks of captivity, Mary Rowlandson returned to Boston. Her narrative was published in 1682, and was one of the most widely read pieces of literature of her time. In the excerpt below, Rowlandson describes the twentieth "remove"—the last of the journeys made by Rowlandson and her captors during the time of her captivity.

It was their usual manner to remove, when they had done any mischief, lest they should be found out: and so they did at this time. We went about three or four miles, and there they built a great *Wigwam*, big enough to hold an hundred *Indians*, which they did in preparation to a great day of Dancing. They would say now amongst themselves, that the *Governour* would be so angry for his loss at Sudbury, that he would send no more about the Captives, which made me grieve and tremble. My Sister being not far from the place where we now were, and hearing that I was here, desired her master to let her come and see me, and he was willing to it, and would go with her: but she being ready before him, told him she would go before, and was come within a Mile or two of the place; Then he overtook her, and began to rant as if he had been mad; and made her go back again in the Rain; so that I never saw her till I saw her in *Charlestown*. But the Lord requited many of their ill doings, for this *Indian* her master, was hanged afterward at *Boston*. The *Indians* now began to come from all quarters, against their merry dancing day. Among some of them came one *Goodwife Kettle*. I told her my heart was so heavy that it was ready to break: so is mine too, said she, but yet said, I hope we shall hear some good news shortly. I could hear how earnestly my Sister desired to see me, and I as earnestly desired to see her: and yet neither of us could get an opportunity. My Daughter was also now about a mile off, and I had not seen her in nine or ten weeks, as I had not seen my Sister since our first taking. I earnestly desired them to let me go and see them: yea, I intreated, begged, and perswaded them, but to let me see my Daughter; and yet so hard hearted were they, that they would not suffer it. They made use of their tyrannical power whilst they had it: but through the Lord's wonderful mercy, their time was now but short.

On a Sabbath day, the Sun being about an hour high in the afternoon, came Mr. John Hoar *(the Council permitting him, and his own foreward spirit inclining him) together with the two forementioned Indians,* Tom *and* Peter, *with their third Letter from the Council.* When they came near, I was abroad: though I saw them not, they presently called me in, and bade me sit down and not stir. Then they catched up their Guns, and away they ran, as if an Enemy had been at hand; and the Guns went off apace. I manifested some great trouble, and they asked me what was the matter? I told them, *I thought they had killed the* English-man (for they had in the mean time informed me that an *English-man* was come), they said, *No*; They shot over his Horse, and under, and before his Horse; and they pusht him this way and that way, at their pleasure, shewing what they could do: Then they let them come to their *Wigwams.* I begged of them to let me see the *English man*, but they would not. But there was I fain to sit their pleasure. When they had talked their fill with him, they suffered me to go to him. We asked each other of our welfare, and how my Husband did, and all my Friends? He told me they were all well, and would be glad to see me. Amongst other things which my Husband sent me, there came a pound of *Tobacco:* which I sold for nine shillings in Money: for many of the *Indians* for want of *Tobacco*, smoaked *Hemlock*, and *Ground-Ivy*. It was a great mistake in any, who thought I sent for *Tobacco*: for through the favour of God, that desire was overcome. I now asked them, whither I should go home with Mr. *Hoar?* They answered *No*, one and another of them: and it being night, we lay down with that answer; in the morning, Mr. *Hoar* invited the *Saggamores* to Dinner; but when we went to get it ready, we found that they had stollen the greatest part of the Provision Mr. *Hoar* had brought, out of his Bags, in the night: *And we may see the wonderfull power of God, in that one passage, in that when there was such a great number of the* Indians *together, and so greedy of a little good food; and no* English *there, but Mr.* Hoar *and myself: that there they did not knock us in the head, and take what we had: there being not only some Provision, but also Trading-cloth, a part of the twenty pounds agreed upon: But instead of doing us any mischief, they seemed to be ashamed of the fact, and said, it were some* Matchit Indian *that did it.* Oh, that we could believe that there is nothing too hard for God! God shewed his Power over the Heathen in this, *as he did over the hungry Lyons when* Daniel *was cast into the Den.* Mr. *Hoar* called them betime to Dinner, but they ate very little, they being so busie in dressing themselves, and getting ready for their Dance: which was carried on by eight of them, four *Men* and four *Squaws*; My master and mistriss being two. He was dressed in his Holland shirt, with great Laces sewed at the tail of it, he had his silver Buttons, his white Stockins, his Garters were hung round with Shillings, and he had Girdles of *Wampom upon his head and shoulders.* She had a Kersey Coat, and covered with Girdles of *Wampom* from the Loins upward: her armes from her elbows to her hands were covered with Bracelets; there were handfulls of Neck-laces about her neck, and severall sorts of Jewels in her ears. She had fine red Stockins, and white Shoos, her hair powdered and face painted Red, that was alwayes before Black. And all the Dancers were after the same manner. There were two other singing and knocking on a Kettle for their musick. They keept hopping up and down one after another, with a Kettle of water in the midst, standing warm upon some Embers, to drink of when they were dry. They held on till it was almost night, throwing out *Wampom* to the standers by. At night I asked them again, if I should go home? They all as one said No, except my Husband would come for me. When we were lain down, my Master went out of the *Wigwam*, and by and by sent in an *Indian* called *James the Printer*, who told Mr. *Hoar*, that my Master would let me go home tomorrow, if he would let him have one pint of Liquors. Then Mr. *Hoar* called his own *Indians*, *Tom* and *Peter*, and bid them go and see whither he would promise before them three: and if he would, he should have it; which he did, and he had it. Then *Philip* smelling the business cal'd me to him, and asked me what I would give him, to tell me some good news, and speak a good word for me. *I told him, I could not tell what to give him, I would anything I had, and asked him what he would have?* He said, two Coats and twenty shillings in Mony, and half a bushel of seed Corn, and some Tobacco. I thanked him for his love: but I knew the good news as well as the crafty *Fox*. My Master after he had had his drink, quickly came ranting into the *Wigwam* again, and called for Mr. *Hoar*, drinking to him, and saying, *He was a good man:* and then again he would say, *Hang him, Rogue:* Being almost drunk, he would drink to him, and yet presently say he should be hanged. Then he called for me, I trembled to hear him, yet I was fain to go to him, and he drank to me, shewing no incivility. He was the first *Indian* I saw drunk all the while that I was amongst them. At last his *Squaw* ran out, and he after her, round the *Wigwam*, with his money jingling at his knees: But she escaped him: But having an old *Squaw* he ran to her: and so through the Lords mercy, we were no more troubled that night. *Yet I had not a comfortable nights rest: for I think I can say, I did not sleep for three nights together.* The night before the Letter came from the Council, I could not rest, I was so full of feares and troubles, God many times leaving us most in the dark, when deliverance is nearest: yea, at this time I could not rest, night nor day. The next night I was overjoyed, Mr. *Hoar* being come, and that with such good tidings. The third night I was even swallowed up with all thoughts of things, *viz.* that ever I should go home again; and that I must go, leaving my Children behind me in the *Wilderness;* so that sleep was now almost departed from mine eyes.

On *Tuesday morning* they called their *General Court* (as they call it) to consult and determine, whether I should go home or no: And they all as one man did seemingly consent to it, that I should go home; except *Philip*, who would not come among them.

But before I go any further, I would take leave to mention a few remarkable passages of providence, which I took special notice of in my afflicted time.

1. *Of the fair opportunity lost in the long March, a little after the* Fort-fight, *when our* English Army *was so numerous, and in pursuit of the* Enemy, *and so near as to take several and destroy them: and the* Enemy *in such distress for food, that our men might track them by their rooting in the earth for Ground-nuts whilest they were flying for their lives.* I say, that then our Army should want Provision, and be forced to leave their pursuit and return homeward: and the very next week the *Enemy* came upon our *Town,* like Bears bereft of their whelps, or so many ravenous Wolves, rending us and our Lambs to death. But what shall I say? God seemed to leave His People to themselves, and order all things for His own holy ends. *Shall there be evil in the City and the Lord hath not done it? They are not grieved for the affliction of* Joseph, *therefore shal they go Captive, with the first that go Captive. It is the Lords doing, and it should be marvelous in our eyes.*

2. *I cannot but remember how the* Indians *derided the slowness, and dulness of the* English *Army, in its setting out.* For after the desolations at *Lancaster* and *Medfield,* as I went along with them, they asked me when I thought the *English* Army would come after them? I told them I could not tell: It may be they will come in *May,* said they. Thus did they scoffe at us, as if the *English* would be a quarter of a year getting ready.

3. *Which also I have hinted before, when the* English *Army with new supplies were sent forth to pursue after the enemy, and they understanding it, fled before them till they came to* Baquaug *River, where they forthwith went over safely: that that River should be impassable to the* English. I can but admire to see the wonderfull providence of God in preserving the heathen for farther affliction to our poor Countrey. They could go in great numbers over, but the *English* must stop: God had an over-ruling hand in all those things.

4. *It was thought, if their corn were cut down, they would starve and dy with hunger: and all their Corn that could be found, was destroyed, and they driven from that little they had in store, into the Woods in the midst of Winter;* and yet how to admiration did the Lord preserve them for his Holy ends, and the destruction of many still amongst the *English!* Strangely did the Lord provide for them; that I did not see (all the time I was among them) one Man, Woman, or Child, die with hunger.

Though many times they would eat that, that a Hog or a Dog would hardly touch; yet by that God strengthened them to be a scourge to His People.

The chief and commonest food was Ground-nuts: They eat also Nuts and Acorns, Harty-choaks, Lilly roots, Ground-beans, and several other weeds and roots, that I know not.

They would pick up old bones, and cut them to pieces at the joynts, and if they were full of wormes and magots, they would scald them over the fire to make the vermine come out, and then boile them, and drink up the Liquor, and then beat the great ends of them in a Morter, and so eat them. They would eat Horses guts, and ears, and all sorts of wild Birds which they could catch: also Bear, Venison, Beaver, Tortois, Frogs, Squirrels, Dogs, Skunks, Rattlesnakes; yea, the very Bark of Trees; besides all sorts of creatures, and provision which they plundered from the *English.* I can but stand in admiration to see the wonderful power of God, in providing for such a vast number of our Enemies in the *Wilderness*, where there was nothing to be seen, but from hand to mouth. Many times in a morning, the generality of them would eat up all they had, and yet have some further supply against what they wanted. It is said, *Psal.* 81. 13, 14. *Oh, that my People had hearkened to me, and* Israel *had walked in my wayes, I should soon have subdued their Enemies, and turned my hand against their Adversaries.* But now our perverse and evil carriages in the sight of the Lord, have so offended Him, that instead of turning His hand against them, the Lord feeds and nourishes them up to be a scourge to the whole Land.

5. *Another thing that I would observe is, the strange providence of God, in turning things about when the* Indians *were at the highest, and the* English *at the lowest.* I was with the Enemy eleven weeks and five dayes, and not one Week passed without the fury of the Enemy, and some desolation by fire and sword upon one place or other. They mourned (with their black faces) for their own losses, yet triumphed and rejoyced in their inhumane, and many times devilish cruelty to the *English.* They would boast much of their Victories; saying, that in two hours time they had destroyed such a *Captain,* and his *Company* at such a place; and such a *Captain* and his *Company* in such a place; and boast how many *Towns* they had destroyed, and then scoffe, and say, *They had done them a good turn, to send them to Heaven so soon.* Again, they would say, *This summer that they would knock all the Rogues in the head, or drive them into the Sea, or make them flie the Countrey:* thinking surely, *Agag*-like, *The bitterness of Death is past.* Now the Heathen begins to think all is their own, and the poor Christians hopes to fail (as to man) and now their eyes are more to God, and their hearts sigh heaven-ward: and to say in good earnest, *Help Lord, or we perish.* When the Lord had brought his people to this, that they saw no help in any thing but himself: then he takes the quarrel into his own hand: and though they had made a pit, in their own imaginations, as deep as hell for the Christians that Summer, yet the Lord hurll'd themselves into it. And the Lord had not so many wayes before to preserve them, but now he hath as many to destroy them.

But to return again to my going home, where we may see a remarkable change of Providence: At first they were all against it, except my Husband would come for me; but afterwards they assented to it, and seemed much to rejoyce in it; some askt me to send them some Bread, others some Tobacco, others shaking me by the hand, offering me a Hood and Scarfe to ride in; not one moving hand or tongue against it. Thus hath the Lord answered my poor desire, and the many earnest requests of others put up unto God for me. In my travels an *Indian* came to me, and told me, if I were willing, he and his *Squaw* would run away, and go home along with me: I told him *No*: I was not willing to run away, but desired to wait Gods time, that I might go home quietly, and without fear. And now God hath granted me my desire. O the wonderfull power of God that I have seen, and the experience that I have had: *I have been in the midst of those roaring Lyons, and Salvage Bears, that feared neither God, nor Man, nor the Devil, by night and day, alone and in company: sleeping all sorts together, and yet not one of them ever offered me the least abuse of unchastity to me, in word or action.* Though some are ready to say, I speak it for my own cred-it; *But I speak it in the presence of God, and to His glory.* Gods power is as great now, and as sufficient to save, as when he preserved *Daniel* in the Lions den; or the three *Children* in the fiery Furnace. I may well say as his *Psal.* 107. 1, 2, *Oh give thanks unto the Lord for He is good, for his mercy endureth for ever.* Let the Redeemed of the Lord say so, whom He hath redeemed from the hand of the Enemy, especially that I should come away in the midst of so many hundreds of Enemies quietly and peacably, and not a Dog moving his tongue. So I took my leave of them, and in coming along my heart melted into tears, more then all the while I was with them, and I was almost swal-lowed up with the thoughts that ever I should go home again. About the Sun going down, Mr. *Hoar,* and my self, and the two *Indians* came to *Lan-caster,* and a solemn sight it was to me. There had I lived many comfortable years amongst my Relations and Neighbours, and now not one *Christian* to be seen, nor one house left standing. We went on to a Farm house that was yet standing, where we lay all night: and a comfortable lodging we had, though nothing but straw to ly on. The Lord preserved us in safety that night, and raised us up again in the morning, and carried us along, that be-fore noon we came to *Concord.* Now was I full of joy, and yet not with out sorrow: joy to see such a lovely sight, so many *Christians* together, and some of them my Neighbours: There I met with my Brother, and my Brother in Law, who asked me, if I knew where his Wife was? Poor heart! he had helped to bury her, and knew it not; she being shot down by the house was partly burnt: so that those who were at *Boston* at the desolation of the *Town,* and came back afterward, and buried the dead, did not know her. Yet I was not without sorrow, to think how many were looking and longing, and my own Children amongst the rest, to enjoy that deliverance that I had now received, and I did not know whither ever I should see them again. Being recruited with food and raiment we went to *Boston* that day, where I met with my dear Husband, but the thoughts of our dear Children, one being dead, and the other we could not tell where, abated our comfort each to other. I was not before so much hem'd in with the merciless and cruel Heathen, but now as much with pittiful, tender-hearted and compassionate Christians. In that poor, and destressed, and beggerly condition I was received in, I was kind-ly entertained in severall Houses: so much love I received from several (some of whom I knew, and others I knew not) that I am not capable to declare it. But the Lord knows them all by name: *The Lord reward them seven fold into their bosoms of his spirituals, for their temporals!* The *twenty pounds* the price of my redemption was raised by some *Boston* Gentlemen, and Ms. *Usher,* whose bounty and religious charity, I would not forget to make mention of. Then Mr. *Thomas Shepard* of *Charlestown* received us into his House, where we con-tinued eleven weeks; and a Father and Mother they were to us. And many more tender-hearted Friends we met with in that place. We were now in the midst of love, yet not without much and frequent heaviness of heart for our poor Children, and other Relations, who were still in affliction. The week following, after my coming in, the Governour and Council sent forth to the *Indians* again; and that not without success; for they brought in my Sister, and Good-wife Kettle: Their not knowing where our Children were, was a sore tryal to us still, and yet we were not without secret hopes that we should see them again. That which was dead lay heavier upon my spirit, than those which were alive and amongst the Heathen; thinking how it suffered with its wounds, and I was in no way able to relieve it; and how it was buried by the Heathen in the *Wilderness* from among all Christians. We were hurried up and down in our thoughts, sometimes we should hear a report that they were gone this way, and sometimes that; and that they were come in, in this place or that: We kept enquiring and listening to hear concerning them, but no certain news as yet. About this time the Council had ordered a day of publick *Thanks-giving:* though I thought I had still cause of mourning, and being unsettled in our minds, we thought we would ride toward the *Eastward*, to see if we could hear anything concerning our Children. And as we were riding along (God is the wise disposer of all things) between *Ipswich* and *Rowley* we met with Mr. *William Hubbard*, who told us that our Son *Joseph* was come in to Major *Waldrens*, and another with him, which was my Sisters Son. I asked him how he knew it? He said, the Major himself told him so. So along we went till we came to *Newbury*; and their Minister being absent, they desired my Husband to preach the *Thanks-giving* for them; but he was not willing to stay there that night, but would go over to *Salisbury*, to hear further, and come again in the morning; which he did, and Preached there that day. At night, when he had done, one came and told him that his Daughter was come in at *Providence:* Here was mercy on both hands: Now hath God fulfilled that precious Scripture which was such a comfort to me in my distressed condition. When my heart was ready to sink into the Earth (my Children being gone I could not tell whither) and my knees trembled under me, *And I was walking through the valley of the shadow of Death:* Then the Lord brought, and now has fulfilled that reviving word unto me: Thus saith the Lord, *Refrain thy voice from weeping, and thine eyes from tears, for thy work shall be rewarded*, saith the Lord, *and thy shall come again from the Land of the Enemy*. Now we were between them, the one on the *East*, and the other on the *West*: Our Son being nearest, we went to him first, to *Portsmouth*, where we met with him, and with the Major also: who told us he had done what he could, but could not redeem him under *seven pounds;* which the good People thereabouts were pleased to pay. The Lord reward the Major, and all the rest, though unknown to me, for their labour of Love. My Sisters Son was redeemed for *four pounds*, which the Council gave order for the payment of. Having now received one of our Children, we hastened toward the other: going back through *Newbury*, my Husband Preached there on the *Sabbath-day*: for which they rewarded him many fold.

On *Munday* we came to Charlestown, where we heard that the Governour of *Road-Island* had sent over for our Daughter, to take care of her, being now within his Jurisdiction: which should not pass without our acknowledgments. But she being nearer *Rehoboth* than *Road-Island*, Mr. *Newman* went over, and took care of her, and brought her to his own House. And the goodness of God was admirable to us in our low estate, in that he raised up passionate Friends on every side to us, when we had nothing to recompance any for their love. The *Indians* were now gone that way, that it was apprehended dangerous to go to her: But the Carts which carried Provision to the *English* Army, being guarded, brought her with them to *Dorchester*, where we received her safe: blessed be the Lord for it, *For great is his Power, and he can do whatsoever seemeth him good.* Her coming in was after this manner: She was travelling one day with the *Indians*, with her basket at her back; the company of *Indians* were got before her, and gone out of sight, all except one *Squaw*; she followed the *Squaw* till night, and then both of them lay down, having nothing over them but the heavens, and under them but the earth. Thus she travelled three dayes together, not knowing whither she was going: having nothing to eat or drink but water, and green *Hirtle-berries*. At last they came into *Providence*, where she was kindly entertained by several of that *Town*. The *Indians* often said, that I should never have her under *twenty pounds*: But now the Lord hath brought her in upon free-cost, and given her to me the second time. The Lord make us a blessing indeed, each to others. Now have I seen that Scripture also fulfilled, *Deut.* 30. 4, 7. *If any of thine be driven out to the outmost parts of heaven, from thence will the Lord thy God gather thee, and from thence will he fetch thee. And the Lord thy God will put all these curses upon thine enemies, and on them which hate thee, which persecuted thee.* Thus hath the Lord brought me and mine out of that horrible pit, and hath set us in the midst of tender-hearted and compassionate Christians. It is the desire of my soul, that we may walk worthy of the mercies received, and which we are receiving.

Our family being now gathered together (those of us that were living) the South Church *in* Boston *hired an House for us: Then we removed from Mr.* Shepards, *those cordial Friends, and went to* Boston, *where we continued about three quarters of a year: Still the Lord went along with us, and provided graciously for us.* I thought it somewhat strange to set up Housekeeping with bare walls; but as *Solomon* says, *Mony answers all things*; and that we had through the benevolence of Christian-friends, some in this *Town*, and some in that, and others: And some from *England*, that in a little time we might look, and see the House furnished with love. The Lord hath been exceeding good to us in our low estate, in that when we had neither house nor home, nor other necessaries, the Lord so moved the hearts of these and those towards us, that we wanted neither food, nor raiment for our selves or ours, *Prov.* 18. 24. *There is a Friend which sticketh closer than a Brother.* And how many such Friends have we found, and now living amongst? And truly such a Friend have we found him to be unto us, in whose house we lived, *viz.* Mr. *James Whitcomb*, a Friend unto us near hand, and afar off.

I can remember the time, when I used to sleep quietly without workings in my thoughts, whole nights together, but now it is other wayes with me. When all are fast about me, and no eye open, but his who ever waketh, my thoughts are upon things past, upon the awfull dispensation of the Lord towards us; upon his wonderfull power and might, in carrying of us through so many difficulties, in returning us in safety, and suffering none to hurt us. I remember in the night season, how the other day I was in the midst of thousands of enemies, & nothing but death before me: It is then hard work to perswade myself, that ever I should be satisfied with bread again. But now we are fed *with the finest of the Wheat,* and, as I may say, *with honey out of the rock.* In stead of the Husk, we have the fatted Calf. The thoughts of these things in the particulars of them, and of the love and goodness of God towards us, make it true of me, what David said of himself, *Psal. 6. 6. I watered my couch with my tears.* Oh! the wonderfull power of God that mine eyes have seen, affording matter enough for my thoughts to run in, that when others are sleeping mine are weeping.

I have seen the extrem vanity of this World: One hour I have been in health, and wealth, wanting nothing: But the next hour in sickness and wounds, and death, having nothing but sorrow and affliction.

Before I knew what affliction meant, I was ready sometimes to wish for it. When I lived in prosperity, having the comforts of the World about me, my relations by me, my Heart chearfull: and taking little care for any thing; and yet seeing many, whom I preferred before my self, under many tryals and afflictions, in sickness, weakness, poverty, losses, crosses, and cares of the World, I should be sometimes jealous least I should have my portion in this life, and that Scripture would come to my mind, *Heb. 12. 6. For whom the Lord loveth he chasteneth, and scourgeth every Son whom he receiveth.* But now I see the Lord had his time to scourge and chasten me. The portion of some is to have their afflictions by drops, now one drop and then another; but the dregs of the Cup, the Wine of astonishment: like a sweeping rain that leaveth no food, did the Lord prepare to be my portion. Affliction I wanted, and affliction I had, full measure (I thought) pressed down and running over; yet I see, when God calls a Person to any thing, and through never so many difficulties, yet he is fully able to carry them through and make them see, and say they have been gainers thereby. And I hope I can say in some measure, As *David* did, *It is good for me that I have been afflicted.* The Lord hath shewed me the vanity of these outward things. That they are the *Vanity of vanities, and vexation of spirit,* that they are but a shadow, a blast, a bubble, and things of no continuance. That we must rely on God himself, and our whole dependence must be upon him. If trouble from smaller matters begin to arise in me, I have something at hand to check my self with, and say, why am I troubled? It was but the other day that if I had had the world, I would have given it for my freedom, or to have been a Servant to a Christian. I have learned to look beyond present and smaller troubles, and to be quieted under them, as *Moses* said, *Exod. 14. 13. Stand still and see the Salvation of the Lord.*

FINIS

Discussion Questions

1. Mary Rowlandson's writing is part narrative, part religious tract. How do you think the inclusion of so many Biblical quotes affected the popularity of the narrative when it was published? What could Rowlandson assume about the values and beliefs of her audience? What does her tone tell us about her audience and the world she comes from?

2. How does Rowlandson's writing relate to Jefferson's and Jackson's beliefs about Native Americans? Where do you see similarities in her earlier writings to their later discussions of Native Americans, especially concerning the idea of "civilization" versus "savagery"?

Writing Suggestions

1. At the end of her tale, Mary Rowlandson writes that although she had born such afflictions, she could see that she had gained greater perspective: "If trouble from smaller matters begin to arise in me, I have something at hand to check myself with, and say why am I troubled?" Do you think she is unusual in this response to past troubles overcome, or do you feel this is a common response from people who have survived great disasters? Write an essay reflecting on your own experience with a very difficult situation, and, starting with Rowlandson's quote, discuss what happened to your perspective after your traumatic experience. Did your perspective change? Did you become stronger? More fearful? More or less confident about your ability to survive hardship? Can you relate to Rowlandson's lesson from her captivity, or does it seem unrealistic to you?

2. The captivity narrative as a genre became very popular after Mary Rowlandson published her accounts. Research another story of a white woman taken captive by Native Americans: You can use the search term "Captivity Narratives" on either the Internet or in your library catalog. Write a five-page paper about the experience of the woman (or women) you have chosen to research. You might consider some of the following questions to help organize your paper:

    How was the woman taken captive? Was she alone, or with other white women? At what age was she taken, and how long was she held captive?

    What kind of adaptation did she make to captivity? Did she speak well of her captors?

    Did she wish to return to the white world when she was rescued? (Some white women chose to stay with the Indian tribes who had taken them hostage.)

    Did she write a journal at the time of her captivity, or did she write the account later when she came home? What tone does the journal take? How did she feel about her treatment at the hands of her captors?

The War to Control the Past

RUTH ROSEN

Ruth Rosen is a staff writer for the *San Francisco Chronicle*, and she wrote the piece below for the Open Forum page of the December 29, 2000 edition of the paper. Rosen discusses the controversy over Albert Mechau's 1930s-era mural "Dangers of the Mail," which appears on the fifth floor of a federal government building in Washington, D.C. As you read her arguments, think about what you would suggest to resolve the controversy she describes.

The fight over our nation's memory is nothing less than a struggle for political control of the country's future. Americans may be famous for their historical amnesia, but they are passionately divided about how they want their nation's history told.

Some would like to erase our country's crimes and tell a story of triumphant and virtuous democracy. Others would like to evoke a history of victimization. But in between are those who believe that the democratic promise of America, magnificent as it is, is still unfolding, and still a work in progress.

The war to control the past has reached new levels of ferocity. Two new struggles over the historical representation of indigenous people have reignited the ever-simmering history wars.

As always, the question is: Who should decide what is accurate *and* acceptable?

One of these battles is being fought in Kansas, where a development company is poised to build an $861 million Wonderful World of Oz theme park and resort. If built, the project would be organized around L. Frank Baum's 1900 fantasy about a little girl swept by a tornado to a magical world, the Land of Oz.

So what's the problem? Well, it turns out that L. Frank Baum, then editor and publisher of the Aberdeen Saturday Pioneer, was a rabid racist who repeatedly called for the "total annihilation" of all Native Americans. In 1890, for example, an editorial declared, "The Pioneer has before declared that our only safety depends upon the total extermination of the Indian. Having wronged them for centuries we had better, in order to protect our civilization, wipe out these untamed and untamable creatures from the face of the earth."

To add insult to injury, the theme park is to be built upon former Shawnee land, contaminated by pollutants from the manufacture of munitions. The developers have promised to clean up the site.

139

What should be done? The land won't be returned to the Shawnee people. So if there is to be a theme park, what should it teach those who enter the magical tour of Oz?

Teach the truth. There are lessons to be learned in both the biography of the author and his creation. Children should learn that settlers of European descent conquered and stole the land of indigenous people. Children should also learn that Baum was hardly alone in believing in the inferiority of the native people he called "whining curs" and that many Americans simultaneously defended the ideal of democracy even as they waged campaigns against minorities or immigrants.

At the same time, kids should relish the wonderful world that Baum created. In the land of Oz, a motley but delightful cast of characters—a little girl, a tin man, a cowardly lion—transcended their differences, and reached the Emerald City—together.

Nothing could be more American. In 1890, Baum loathed Indians, but 10 years later created a world as diverse and complex as the nation in which he lived. By showing the young both sides of this tale, we teach them about the complicated nature of our past.

Meanwhile, another battle over history is simmering in Washington, D.C. This historical debate swirls around a 13-foot-wide canvas hung in the Ariel Rios Building, which has received historic landmark status. Painted by Colorado artist Frank Albert Mechau, "Dangers of the Mail" depicts Indians attacking and scalping white people. It also includes graphic images of Indians looming over a dozen naked pioneer women, as well an Indian stabbing a white man in the back.

It's offensive, no question about it. It reflects the unquestioned view of indigenous people as savage barbarians who inhibited settlers' heroic effort to "open up" the west. But westward expansion also resulted in the theft of Indian lands, as well as the near extinction of Native Americans.

Since the canvas cannot be removed from the fragile, thin wall—or from the building—what should be done? Should it be covered? This is what some Native American activists have proposed.

There is another solution. Teach a different story. Keep the picture, but educate the public about the genocide of indigenous people. Include a plaque or sign that explains how this painting, commissioned by the Works Progress Administration during the Great Depression, reflects how white settlers viewed Indians—as savages that needed to be eliminated. Tell viewers that mail delivery was dangerous precisely because it came through lands that Native Americans defended from those who would "settle" them.

The difference between the theme park and the painting is that one already exists, while the other can still be created. If they are careful, the creators of the theme park can juxtapose Frank Baum's racist attitudes with the important fable he inserted into the American imagination.

The painting, however, already exists. To cover up an artifact from the past may feel good, but it also wipes out an important part of our nation's history. Better to recast the story than to erase this evidence. Here is a painting that shows, with excruciating detail, how pioneers accused native peoples of the very cowardly and savage behavior for which they, in fact, were responsible.

Unpleasant truths do not destroy a nation's social fabric. The real danger to a democracy comes from an official history that sanitizes the past in order to justify the status quo. George Orwell understood the magnitude of this threat, quoting Big Brother in his classic novel, "1984": "Who controls the past, controls the future; who controls the present controls the past."

Discussion Questions

1. Discuss Rosen's proposal to "teach the truth" by integrating lessons about American racism into the Wonderful World of Oz theme park. What do you think should be done with the theme park that is to be built on former Shawnee land? Should history lessons about conflict between the Native Americans and the whites be integrated into the park? In general, what do you think theme parks should do: Should they educate and amuse at the same time, or should they be designed solely for the purpose of amusement?

2. Discuss the writing strategies Rosen uses to make her arguments. Where does she put her thesis? How does she develop her points? What kinds of details does she use, and how do these details inform the tone of the piece? Did you feel that her argument was effective? Why or why not?

Writing Suggestions

1. Reread Rosen's editorial about the controversy over Albert Mechau's mural "Dangers of the Mail." Then, write your own letter to the editor of the *Washington Post*, explaining what you think should be done with the mural. While you may appeal to emotion in your argument, try to keep your tone neutral and to use some historical facts as part of your argument.

2. Rosen writes that L. Frank Baum, famous author of *The Wizard of Oz*, "was a rabid racist who repeatedly called for the 'total annihilation' of

Native Americans." Research Baum's life, and write an analysis of his attitudes toward Native Americans and his reasons for saying in his newspaper, "we had better . . . wipe out these untamed and untamable creatures from the face of the earth." What were the historical conditions at the time? Where had Baum encountered Native Americans? What incidents or political leanings led to such strong statements?

Chapter 2: Writing Suggestions

1. Research the history of one Native American tribe over the past thirty years. Then write an analysis of the tribe's current situation. Has the health and welfare of the tribe improved? Are more of the tribe's students attending college? Has the tribe received additional federal funding?
2. Write a four- or five-page research paper about the controversies regarding the newly gained Native American rights to run gambling casinos on native lands. Take a stand on whether or not this gambling should be legal, and argue your position using a variety of sources.
3. Research the paintings of George Catlin, Charles Russell, or Frederick Remington. Write an analysis of one of these painters, tracing his portrayal of Native Americans. What kinds of situations did the artist portray in painting Native Americans? Were the paintings realistic or romantic? How is conflict portrayed in the paintings? There are books in most libraries about the men who painted the frontier and the American West, and information about the painters and some of these paintings can also be found on the Internet. You can search the Web by using the name of the artist.
4. Write a comparison essay on this question: Are today's justifications for occupying lands similar to the justifications given by whites for taking Indian lands? First, list the justifications given by Jackson, Jefferson, and other statesmen quoted by Rogin. Then examine current political rhetoric justifying displacement of people in an occupied territory (e.g., Bosnia, Africa, Israel and Palestine, etc.). Compare the political rhetoric you find regarding today's struggles over land with the political rhetoric of the founding fathers. Use specific examples and quote politicians from both eras.

Chapter 2: Further Research on the Web

To pursue your research on the Internet, explore some of the following sites:

Native American Treaties
http://www-libraries.colorado.edu/ps/gov/us/native.htm
http://carbon.cudenver.edu/public/library/reference/nam.html

Smithsonian Institution
http://www.si.edu/resource/faq/nmai/start.htm

Mary Rowlandson
http://www.bio.umass.edu/biology/conn.river/mary.html

Jefferson and Native American Policy
http://etext.lib.virginia.edu/jefferson/quotations/jeff1300.htm

Native Americans
http://falcon.jmu.edu/~ramseyil/native.htm

3

Conflicts on the Way West

This chapter will introduce you to a variety of writings about cultural and racial conflicts that arose as the Western frontier moved steadily toward the shores of the Pacific Ocean. The history of the westward movement has generally been told in terms of white settlers fighting the Indians, as the pioneers struggled to make their way across the Great Plains and the mountains to the sunnier shores of California and Oregon. But, as we will see in this chapter, the struggles that ensued in North America during the nineteenth and into the twentieth centuries were far more complicated than most history books have led us to believe. Recently, numerous historians have been writing a more inclusive version of the westward movement, and some of these historians are represented in this chapter. As you read, try to keep in mind the differences we discussed earlier between primary, secondary, and literary sources. The questions below may help you consider the material more carefully:

Which new perspectives on history can you gain from these sources?

What assumptions are challenged as you read this material?

What are the strengths and weaknesses of each source?

How do these sources contradict each other? How do they complement each other?

How can you find a fuller picture of any of the topics in this chapter?

How can you weigh the varying accounts of history to get a fuller, more accurate picture of what really happened?

How can you relate the lessons of history to what is going on in our country today?

Historical writers have offered many theories about the role of the frontier in American history and the American psyche. Frederick Jackson Turner gave his speech "The Significance of the Frontier in American History" in 1893 at the Chicago World's Fair. He said that the existence of the frontier was instrumental in the development of the American character. He claimed that when the frontier came to an end, so did the "first epoch of American history."

N. Scott Momaday, a Pulitzer Prize winning author, approaches the history of the West from a different angle: He describes the difficulty of understanding, seeing, and thus "believing" in the complexity of the West as it really is and was. His essay, "The American West and the Burden of Belief," uses three biographical stories to show how different perception and reality really are; his discussion of George Armstrong Custer's inability to see the beauty of the Indian way of life is particularly moving. Next, using General Custer's autobiography as a primary source to elucidate Momaday's claims, you can look into Custer's mind in the selection from *My Life on the Plains*, in which Custer's writings about Indians explain some of his fanaticism about killing "savages." You thus have a chance to rethink the Custer myth and to look more closely at the personal writings of the mythologized hero/villain of so many films and stories.

The next selection in this chapter attempts to throw some light on the variety and richness of Native American cultures and traditions, which have received very little attention in most texts. For example, most Americans know the story of black slavery under white plantation owners, but few know the story of the Five Civilized tribes who kept slaves and modeled their laws and slave codes on the white antebellum farmers and slave owners of the East coast. In Quintard Taylor's "Slavery in the Antebellum West, 1835–1865" from *In Search of the Racial Frontier*, he describes the importance of slaves to the Cherokee nation in particular, stressing the role of slaves not only in running Cherokee farms, but also in helping their Cherokee masters to survive the long Trail of Tears. You can see the hidden side of an already complicated story and can begin to appreciate how many written records and historical facts have simply never surfaced or been recorded in history books.

As the philosophy of "manifest destiny" swept the American political scene in the 1840s, politicians were quick to appeal to the belief expressed by *Morning News* editor John L. O'Sullivan: It was "our manifest destiny to overspread the continent." Words became an important tool in the process of expansion, and treaties were often used to gain land and safe passage for settlers. The Mexican-American War officially ended with one such treaty, and the next selection, "The Treaty of Guadalupe Hidalgo," serves to show exactly how some of the rights of Mexican citizens were eclipsed during the Mexican-American War. This source allows you to see firsthand how the diction of treaties can change according to political whims.

The chapter next offers information about some of the other groups involved in conflicts as the West began to open up. John W. Ravage's excerpts from *Black Pioneers* offer a new look at the variety of roles played by black men and women on the western frontier. In the introduction to his book *The Gathering of Zion*, Wallace Stegner takes an interesting look at the challenges and the contributions of the Mormons as they went west. In the selection from *A Life in*

Bondage, Ann Eliza Young's account of her marriage to Brigham Young and her experiences with polygamy shows a negative side of Mormon life.

A more modern scholarly piece by Anne M. Butler reveals a rarely discussed aspect of women in the West: the surprisingly high rate of incarcerated women, especially black women, and the unfair treatment of these women at the hands of the law. Butler's research techniques and writing give you a chance to look at a model for integrating primary and secondary sources in a research paper, and also give you a glimpse of the range of research opportunities available in tracing the roots of race and gender conflicts in America.

We cannot leave the West without paying some attention to one more genre of writing: the dime novel, which came into popularity in the second half of the nineteenth century, and which shaped the beliefs of Easterners about the westward experience dramatically. One of the most famous dime novelists, Edward Wheeler, had never been West, but his stereotyped and mythical heroes, outlaws, and heroines so appealed to his audiences that the truthfulness of the stories was never called into account. Wheeler wrote thirty-three novels about his outlaw hero Deadwood Dick, and in this chapter we look at the beginning of *Deadwood Dick, the Prince of the Road.* Students of history and literature can enjoy and analyze the tremendous appeal these dime novels held for Eastern audiences.

The importance of research, and of writing about that research, becomes clear as these truths surface. As writers and researchers, our ability to uncover and publish a fuller record of our complex culture and history highlights the importance of excellent writing and researching skills. The variety of accounts here may encourage you to do more research on these controversial topics to try to understand how such varying accounts could all be part of one historical period.

Before You Read

1. Freewrite about the topic of religious persecution in the history of the United States. What do you know about the original Puritan goals in coming to the United States? What other groups suffered religious persecution as the West was opened to more and more groups? What does the separation of Church and State mean to you?

2. When you think of racial conflicts in the opening of the West, which groups do you think of? Write down a list of your impressions, noting which groups were in conflict. After you have read some of the selections in this chapter, come back and reassess your list.

3. What does the term *manifest destiny* mean to you? What associations do you have with this term? Do you know when it originated or who first coined this phrase? Think about what impact this philosophy had on the course of American history.

The Significance of the Frontier in American History

FREDERICK JACKSON TURNER

Frederick Jackson Turner (1861–1932) graduated from the University of Wisconsin in 1884 and received a Ph.D. in history from Johns Hopkins University in 1890. A scholar and professor, he taught both at the University of Wisconsin and Harvard until 1924. Turner presented his ideas of the frontier in his thesis, "The Significance of the Frontier in American History," in Chicago in 1893. At the time, the speech made very little impact on the group of historians he was addressing. Gradually, however, historians began to debate his assertions and assumptions about the importance of the frontier to the American character, and today his ideas are challenged and discussed by many scholars, some of whom feel that a number of influences, such as immigration and industrialization, played just as important a role in what Jackson called "American development."

In a recent bulletin of the Superintendent of the Census for 1890 appear these significant words: "Up to and including 1880 the country had a frontier of settlement, but at present the unsettled area has been so broken into by isolated bodies of settlement that there can hardly be said to be a frontier line. In the discussion of its extent, its westward movement, etc., it can not therefore, any longer have a place in the census reports." This brief official statement marks the closing of a great historic movement. Up to our own day American history has been in a large degree the history of the colonization of the Great West. The existence of an area of free land, its continuous recession, and the advance of American settlement westward, explain American development.

Behind institutions, behind Constitutional forms and modifications, lie the vital forces that call these organs into life and shape them to meet changing conditions. The peculiarity of American institutions is, the fact that they have been compelled to adapt themselves to the changes of an expanding people—to the changes involved in crossing a continent, in winning a wilderness, and in developing at each area of this progress out of the primitive economic and political conditions of the frontier into the complexity of city life. Said Calhoun in 1817, "We are great, and rapidly—I was about to say fearfully—growing!" So saying, he touched the distinguishing feature of American life. All peoples show development; the germ theory of politics has been sufficiently emphasized. In the case of most nations, however, the development has occurred in a limited area; and if the nation has expanded, it has met other growing peoples whom it has conquered. But in the case of the

United States we have a different phenomenon. Limiting our attention to the Atlantic coast, we have the familiar phenomenon of the evolution of institutions in a limited area, such as the rise of representative government; the differentiation of simple colonial governments into complex organs; the progress from primitive industrial society, without division of labor, up to manufacturing civilization. But we have in addition to this a recurrence of the process of evolution in each western area reached in the process of expansion. Thus American development has exhibited not merely advance along a single line, but a return to primitive conditions on a continually advancing frontier line, and a new development for that area. American social development has been continually beginning over again on the frontier. This perennial rebirth, this fluidity of American life, this expansion westward with its new opportunities, its continuous touch with the simplicity of primitive society, furnish the forces dominating American character. The true point of view in the history of this nation is not the Atlantic coast, it is the great West. Even the slavery struggle, which is made so exclusive an object of attention by writers like Professor von Holst, occupies its important place in American history because of its relation to westward expansion.

In this advance, the frontier is the outer edge of the wave—the meeting point between savagery and civilization. Much has been written about the frontier from the point of view of border warfare and the chase, but as a field for the serious study of the economist and the historian it has been neglected.

The American frontier is sharply distinguished from the European frontier—a fortified boundary line running through dense populations. The most significant thing about the American frontier is, that it lies at the hither edge of free land. In the census reports it is treated as the margin of that settlement which has a density of two or more to the square mile. The term is an elastic one, and for our purposes does not need sharp definition. We shall consider the whole frontier belt, including the Indian country and the outer margin of the "settled area" of the census reports. This paper will make no attempt to treat the subject exhaustively; its aim is simply to call attention to the frontier as a fertile field for investigation, and to suggest some of the problems which arise in connection with it.

In the settlement of America we have to observe how European life entered the continent, and how America modified and developed that life and reacted on Europe. Our early history is the study of European germs developing in an American environment. Too exclusive attention has been paid by institutional students to the Germanic origins, too little to the American factors. The frontier is the line of most rapid and effective Americanization. The wilderness masters the colonist. It finds him a European in dress, industries, tools, modes of travel, and thought. It takes him from the railroad car and puts him in the birch canoe. It strips off the garments of civilization and arrays him in the hunting shirt and the moccasin. It puts him in the log cabin of the Cherokee and Iroquois and runs an Indian palisade around him. Before long he has gone to planting Indian corn and plowing with a sharp stick; he shouts the war cry and takes the scalp in orthodox Indian fashion. In short, at the frontier the environment is at first too strong for the man. He must accept the conditions which it furnishes, or perish, and so he fits himself into the Indian clearings and follows the Indian trails. Little by little he transforms the wilderness, but the outcome is not the old Europe, not simply the development of Germanic germs, any more than the first phenomenon was a case of reversion to the Germanic mark. The fact is, that here is a new product that is American. At first, the frontier was the Atlantic coast. It was the frontier of Europe in a very real sense. Moving westward, the frontier became more and more American. As successive terminal moraines result from successive glaciations, so each frontier leaves its traces behind it, and when it becomes a settled area the region still partakes of the frontier characteristics. Thus the advance of the frontier has meant a steady movement away from the influence of Europe, a steady growth of independence on American lines. And to study this advance, the men who grew up under these conditions, and the political, economic, and social results of it, is to study the really American part of our history. . . .

The Frontier Furnishes a Field for Comparative Study of Social Development

At the Atlantic frontier one can study the germs of processes repeated at each successive frontier. We have the complex European life sharply precipitated by the wilderness into the simplicity of primitive conditions. The first frontier had to meet its Indian question, its question of the disposition of the public domain, of the means of intercourse with older settlements, of the extension of political organization, of religious and educational activity. And the settlement of these and similar questions for one frontier served as a guide for the next. The American student needs not to go to the "prim little townships of Sleswick" for illustrations of the law of continuity and development. For example, he may study the origin of our land policies in the colonial land policy; he may see how the system grew by adapting the statutes to the customs of the successive frontiers. He may see how the mining experience in the lead regions of Wisconsin, Illinois, and Iowa was applied to the mining laws of the Rockies, and how our Indian policy has been a series of experimentations on successive frontiers. Each tier of new States has found in the older ones material for its constitutions. Each frontier has made similar contributions to American character, as will be discussed farther on.

But with all these similarities there are essential differences, due to the place element and the time element. It is evident that the farming frontier of the Mississippi Valley presents different conditions from the mining frontier of the Rocky Mountains. The frontier reached by the Pacific Railroad, surveyed into rectangles, guarded by the United States Army, and recruited by the daily immigrant ship, moves forward at a swifter pace and in a different way than the frontier reached by the birch canoe or the pack horse. The geologist traces patiently the shores of ancient seas, maps their areas, and compares the older and the newer. It would be a work worth the historian's labors to mark these various frontiers and in detail compare one with another. Not only would there result a more adequate conception of American development and characteristics, but invaluable additions would be made to the history of society.

Loria, the Italian economist, has urged the study of colonial life as an aid in understanding the stages of European development, affirming that colonial settlement is for economic science what the mountain is for geology, bringing to light primitive stratifications. "America," he says, "has the key to the historical enigma which Europe has sought for centuries in vain, and the land which has no history reveals luminously the course of universal history." There is much truth in this. The United States lies like a huge page in the history of society. Line by line as we read this continental page from west to east we find the record of social evolution. It begins with the Indian and the hunter; it goes on to tell of the disintegration of savagery by the entrance of the trader, the pathfinder of civilization; we read the annals of the pastoral stage in ranch life; the exploitation of the soil by the raising of unrotated crops of corn and wheat in sparsely settled farming communities; the intensive culture of the denser farm settlement; and finally the manufacturing organization with city and factory system. This page is familiar to the student of census statistics, but how little of it has been used by our historians. Particularly in eastern States this page is palimpsest. What is now a manufacturing State was in an earlier decade an area of intensive farming. Earlier yet it had been a wheat area, and still earlier the "range" had attracted the cattle herder. Thus Wisconsin, now developing manufacture, is a State with varied agricultural interests. But earlier it was given over to almost exclusive grain-raising, like North Dakota at the present time.

Each of these areas has had an influence in our economic and political history; the evolution of each into a higher stage has worked political transformations. But what constitutional historian has made any adequate attempt to interpret political facts by the light of these social areas and changes?

The Atlantic frontier was compounded of fisherman, fur-trader, miner, cattle-raiser, and farmer. Excepting the fisherman, each type of industry was on the march toward the West, impelled by an irresistible attraction. Each passed in successive waves across the continent. Stand at Cumberland Gap and watch the procession of civilization, marching single file—the buffalo following the trail to the salt springs, the Indian, the fur-trader and hunter, the cattle-raiser, the pioneer farmer—and the frontier has passed by. Stand at South Pass in the Rockies a century later and see the same procession with wider intervals between. The unequal rate of advance compels us to distinguish the frontier into the trader's frontier, the rancher's frontier, or the miner's frontier, and the farmer's frontier. When the mines and the cow pens were still near the fall line the traders' pack trains were tinkling across the Alleghenies, and the French on the Great Lakes were fortifying their posts, alarmed by the British trader's birch canoe. When the trappers scaled the Rockies, the farmer was still near the mouth of the Missouri. . . .

Land

The exploitation of the beasts took hunter and trader to the west, the exploitation of the grasses took the rancher west, and the exploitation of the virgin soil of the river valleys and prairies attracted the farmer. Good soils have been the most continuous attraction to the farmer's frontier. The land hunger of the Virginians drew them down the rivers into Carolina, in early colonial days; the search for soils took the Massachusetts men to Pennsylvania and to New York. As the eastern lands were taken up migration flowed across them to the west. Daniel Boone, the great backwoodsman, who combined the occupations of hunter, trader, cattle-raiser, farmer, and surveyor—learning, probably from the traders, of the fertility of the lands on the upper Yadkin, where the traders were wont to rest as they took their way to the Indians, left his Pennsylvania home with his father, and passed down the Great Valley road to that stream. Learning from a trader whose posts were on the Red River in Kentucky of its game and rich pastures, he pioneered the way for the farmers to that region. Thence he passed to the frontier of Missouri, where his settlement was long a landmark on the frontier. Here again he helped to open the way for civilization, finding salt licks, and trails, and land. His son was among the earliest trappers in the passes of the Rocky Mountains, and his party are said to have been the first to camp on the present site of Denver. His grandson, Col. A. J. Boone, of Colorado, was a power among the Indians of the Rocky Mountains, and was appointed an agent by the Government. Kit Carson's mother was a Boone. Thus this family epitomizes the backwoodsman's advance across the continent. . . .

Composite Nationality

First, we note that the frontier promoted the formation of a composite nationality for the American people. The coast was preponderantly English, but the later tides of continental immigration flowed across to the free lands. This was the case from the early colonial days. The Scotch-Irish and the Palatine Germans, or "Pennsylvania Dutch," furnished the dominant element in the stock of the colonial frontier. With these peoples were also the freed indentured servants, or redemptioners, who at the expiration of their time of service passed to the frontier. Governor Spottswood of Virginia writes in 1717, "The inhabitants of our frontiers are composed generally of such as have been transported hither as servants, and, being out of their time, settle themselves where land is to be taken up and that will produce the necessarys of life with little labour." Very generally these redemptioners were of non-English stock. In the crucible of the frontier the immigrants were Americanized, liberated, and fused into a mixed race, English in neither nationality nor characteristics. The process has gone on from the early days to our own. Burke and other writers in the middle of the eighteenth century believed that Pennsylvania was "threatened with the danger of being wholly foreign in language, manners, and perhaps even inclinations." The German and Scotch-Irish elements in the frontier of the South were only less great. In the middle of the present century the German element in Wisconsin was already so considerable that leading publicists looked to the creation of a German state out of the commonwealth by concentrating their colonization. Such examples teach us to beware of misinterpreting the fact that there is a common English speech in America into a belief that the stock is also English.

Industrial Independence

In another way the advance of the frontier decreased our dependence on England. The coast, particularly of the South, lacked diversified industries, and was dependent on England for the bulk of its supplies. In the South there was even a dependence on the Northern colonies for articles of food. Governor Glenn, of South Carolina, writes in the middle of the eighteenth century: "Our trade with New York and Philadelphia was of this sort, draining us of all the little money and bills we could gather from other places for their bread, flour, beer, hams, bacon, and other things of their produce, all which, except beer, our new townships begin to supply us with, which are settled with very industrious and thriving Germans. This no doubt diminishes the number of shipping and the appearance of our trade, but it is far from being a detriment to us." Before long the frontier created a demand for merchants. As it retreated from the coast it became less and less possible for England to bring her supplies directly to the consumer's wharfs, and carry away staple crops, and staple crops began to give way to diversified agriculture for a time. The effect of this phase of the frontier action upon the northern section is perceived when we realize how the advance of the frontier aroused seaboard cities like Boston, New York, and Baltimore, to engage in rivalry for what Washington called "the extensive and valuable trade of a rising empire." . . .

Growth of Democracy

But the most important effect of the frontier has been in the promotion of democracy here and in Europe. As has been indicated, the frontier is productive of individualism. Complex society is precipitated by the wilderness into a kind of primitive organization based on the family. The tendency is anti-social. It produces antipathy to control, and particularly to any direct control. The tax gatherer is viewed as a representative of oppression. Professor Osgood, in an able article, has pointed out that the frontier conditions prevalent in the colonies are important factors in the explanation of the American Revolution, where individual liberty was sometimes confused with absence of all effective government. The same conditions aid in explaining the difficulty of instituting a strong government in the period of the confederacy. The frontier individualism has from the beginning promoted democracy.

The frontier States that came into the Union in the first quarter of a century of its existence came in with democratic suffrage provisions, and had reactive effects of the highest importance upon the older States whose peoples were being attracted there. An extension of the franchise became essential. It was *western* New York that forced an extension of suffrage in the constitutional convention of that State in 1821; and it was *western* Virginia that compelled the tide-water region to put a more liberal suffrage provision in the constitution framed in 1830, and to give to the frontier region a more nearly proportionate representation with the tide-water aristocracy. The rise of democracy as an effective force in the nation came in with western preponderance under Jackson and William Henry Harrison, and it meant the triumph of the frontier—with all of its good and with all of its evil elements. . . .

So long as free land exists, the opportunity for a competency exists, and economic power secures political power. But the democracy born of free land, strong in selfishness and individualism, intolerant of administrative experience and education, and pressing individual liberty beyond its proper bounds, has its dangers as well as its benefits. Individualism in America has allowed a laxity in regard to governmental affairs which has rendered possible the spoils system and all the manifest evils that follow from the lack of a highly developed civic spirit. In this connection may be noted also the influence of frontier conditions in permitting lax business honor, inflated paper currency and wild-cat banking. The colonial and revolutionary frontier was the region whence emanated many of the worst forms of an evil currency. The West in the War of 1812 repeated the phenomenon on the frontier of that day, while the speculation and the wild-cat banking of the period of the crisis of 1837 occurred on the new frontier belt of the next tier of States. Thus each one of the periods of lax financial integrity coincides with periods when a new set of frontier communities had arisen, and coincides in area with these successive frontiers, for the most part. The recent Populist agitation is a case in point. Many a State that now declines any connection with the tenets of the Populists, itself adhered to such ideas in an earlier stage of the development of the State. A primitive society can hardly be expected to show the intelligent appreciation of the complexity of business interests in a developed society. The continual recurrence of these areas of paper-money agitation is another evidence that the frontier can be isolated and studied as a factor in American history of the highest importance. . . .

Intellectual Traits

From the conditions of frontier life came intellectual traits of profound importance. The works of travelers along each frontier from colonial days onward describe certain common traits, and these traits have, while softening down, still persisted as survivals in the place of their origin, even when a higher social organization succeeded. The result is that to the frontier the American intellect owes its striking characteristics. That coarseness and strength combined with acuteness and inquisitiveness; that practical, inventive turn of mind, quick to find expedients; that masterful grasp of material things, lacking in the artistic but powerful to effect great ends; that restless, nervous energy; that dominant individualism, working for good and for evil, and withal that buoyancy and exuberance which comes with freedom—these are traits of the frontier. Since the days when the fleet of Columbus sailed into the waters of the New World, America has been another name for opportunity, and the people of the United States have taken their tone from the incessant expansion which has not only been open but has even been forced upon them. He would be a rash prophet who should assert that the expansive character of American life has now entirely ceased. Movement has been its dominant fact, and, unless this training has no effect upon a people, the American energy will continually demand a wider field for its exercise. But never again will such gifts of free land offer themselves. For a moment, at the frontier, the bonds of custom are broken and unrestraint is triumphant. There is not *tabula rasa*. The stubborn American environment is there with its imperious summons to accept its conditions; the inherited ways of doing things are also there; and yet, in spite of environment, and in spite of custom, each frontier did indeed furnish a new field of opportunity, a gate of escape from the bondage of the past; and freshness, and confidence, and scorn of older society, impatience of its restraints and its ideas, and indifference to its lessons, have accompanied the frontier. What the Mediterranean Sea was to the Greeks, breaking the bond of custom, offering new experiences, calling out new institutions and activities, that, and more, the ever retreating frontier has been to the United States directly, and to the nations of Europe more remotely. And now, four centuries from the discovery of America, at the end of a hundred years of life under the Constitution, the frontier has gone, and with its going has closed the first period of American history.

Discussion Questions

1. What does Turner claim created a particularly American character? How did the frontier and civilization mix to create this character?
2. Think about Turner's statement that the American frontier is now gone. Do you agree with this statement, or do you feel that Americans have found new frontiers? Explain.

Writing Suggestions

1. Frederick Jackson Turner claims that the taming of the frontier has created essential intellectual traits of the American character. Write a personal essay in which you describe what you think the "American character" is, and argue for or against the role of the taming of the frontier in the creation of this American character.

2. Turner calls Daniel Boone the "essential" American frontiersman. Research the life of Daniel Boone, and then write a three-page paper relating Boone's life and character to Turner's thesis. How did Boone exemplify Turner's idea of the essential frontiersman? What events and struggles did Boone endure and triumph over? How did Boone help to "tame" the wilderness, and why did Turner name him as the true example of the frontiersman?

The American West and the Burden of Belief

N. SCOTT MOMADAY

N. Scott Momaday won the Pulitzer Prize for his first novel, *House Made of Dawn*. A Kiowa Indian who was raised on the reservations and pueblos of the Southwest, Momaday is a prolific writer of essays, books, and poems and is one of the most influential Native American authors of our time. He currently teaches English and fiction writing as the Regents Professor at the University of Arizona in Tucson. In the following selection, which appears in Geoffrey Ward's book *The West*, Momaday blends poetry and story-telling into his historical essay, exemplifying the style that has made his work so popular today.

I

West of Jemez Pueblo there is a great red mesa, and in the folds of the earth at its base there is a canyon, the dark red walls of which are sheer and shadow stained; they rise vertically, to a remarkable height. You do not suspect that the canyon is there, but you turn a corner and the walls contain you; you look into a corridor of geologic time. When I went into that place I left my horse outside, for there was a strange light and quiet upon the walls, and the shadows closed upon me. I looked up, straight up, to the serpentine strip of the sky. It was clear and deep, like a river running across the top of the world. The sand in which I stood was deep, and I could feel the cold of it through the soles of my shoes. And when I walked out, the light and heat of the day struck me so hard that I nearly fell. On the side of a hill in the plain of the Hissar I saw my horse grazing among sheep. The land inclined into the distance, to the Pamirs, to the Fedchenko Glacier. The river which I had seen near the sun had run out into the endless ether above the Karakoram range and the Plateau of Tibet.

—*The Names*

When I wrote this passage, some years ago, it did not seem strange to me that two such landscapes as that of northern New Mexico and that of central Asia should become one in the mind's eye and in the confluence of image and imagination. Nor does it seem strange to me now. Even as we look back, the partitions of our experience open and close upon each other; disparate realities coalesce into a single, integrated appearance.

This transformation is perhaps the essence of art and literature. Certainly it is the soul of drama, and historically it is how we have seen the American West. Our human tendency is to concentrate the world upon a stage. We construct proscenium arches and frames in order to contain the thing that is larger than our comprehension, the plane of boundless possibility, that which reaches almost beyond wonder. Sometimes the process of concentration results in something like a burden of belief, a kind of ambiguous exaggeration, as in the paintings of Albert Bierstadt, say, or in the photographs of Ansel Adams, in which an artful grandeur seems superimposed upon a grandeur that is innate. Or music comes to mind, a music that seems to pervade the vast landscape and emanate from it, not the music of wind and rain and birds and beasts, but Virgil Thomson's "The Plow That Broke the Plains," or Aaron Copland's "Rodeo," or perhaps the sound track from *The Alamo* or *She Wore a Yellow Ribbon*. We are speaking of overlays, impositions, a kind of narcissism that locates us within our own field of vision. But if this is a distorted view of the West, it is nonetheless a view that fascinates us.

And more often than not the fascination consists in peril. In *My Life on the Plains*, George Armstrong Custer describes a strange sight:

> I have seen a train of government wagons with white canvas covers moving through a mirage which, by elevating the wagons to treble their height and magnifying the size of the covers, presented the appearance of a line of large sailing vessels under full sail, while the usual appearance of the mirage gave a correct likeness of an immense lake or sea. Sometimes the mirage has been the cause of frightful suffering and death by its deceptive appearance.

He goes on to tell of emigrants to California and Oregon who, suffering terrible thirst, were deflected from their route by a mirage, "like an *ignis fatuus*," and so perished. Their graves are strewn far and wide over the prairie.

This equation of wonder and peril is for Custer a kind of exhilaration, as indeed it is for most of those adventurers who journeyed westward, and even for those who did not, who escaped into the Wild West show or the dime novel.

For the European who came from a community of congestion and confinement, the West was beyond dreaming; it must have inspired him to formulate an idea of the infinite. There he could walk through geologic time; he could see into eternity. He was surely bewildered, wary, afraid. The landscape was anomalously beautiful and hostile. It was desolate and unforgiving, and yet it was a world of paradisal possibility. Above all, it was wild, definitively wild. And it was inhabited by a people who were to him altogether alien and inscrutable, who were essentially dangerous and deceptive, often invisible, who were savage and unholy—and who were perfectly at home.

This is a crucial point, then: the West was occupied. It was the home of peoples who had come upon the North American continent many thousands of years before, who had in the course of their habitation become the spirit and intelligence of the earth, who had died into the ground again and again and so made it sacred. Those Europeans who ventured into the West must have seen themselves in some wise as latecomers and intruders. In spite of their narcissism, some aspect of their intrusion must have occurred to them as sacrilege, for they were in the unfortunate position of robbing the native peoples of their homeland and the land of its spiritual resources. By virtue of their culture and history—a culture of acquisition and a history of conquest—they were peculiarly prepared to commit sacrilege, the theft of the sacred.

Even the Indians succumbed to the kind of narcissism the Europeans brought to bear on the primeval landscape, the imposition of a belief—essentially alien to both the land and the peoples who inhabited it—that would locate them once again within their own field of vision. For the Indian, the mirage of the ghost dance—to which the concepts of a messiah and immortality, both foreign, European imports, were central—was surely, an *ignis fatuus*, and the cause of frightful suffering and death.

II

George Armstrong Custer had an eye to the country of the Great Plains, and especially, to those of its features that constituted a "deceptive appearance." As he stealthily approached Black Kettle's camp on the Washita River, where he was to win his principal acclaim as an Indian fighter, he and his men caught sight of a strange thing. At the first sign of dawn there appeared a bright light ascending slowly from the skyline. Custer describes it sharply, even eloquently:

> Slowly and majestically it continued to rise above the crest of the hill, first appearing as a small brilliant flaming globe of bright golden hue. As it ascended still higher it seemed to increase in size, to move more slowly, while its colors rapidly changed from one to the other, exhibiting in turn the most beautiful combinations of prismatic tints.

Custer and his men took it to be a rocket, some sort of signal, and they assumed that their presence had been detected by the Indians. Here again is the equation of fascination and peril. But at last the reality is discovered:

> Rising above the mystifying influences of the atmosphere, that which had appeared so suddenly before us and excited our greatest apprehensions developed into the brightest and most beautiful of morning stars.

In the ensuing raid upon Black Kettle's camp, Custer and his troopers, charging to the strains of "Garry Owen," killed 103 Cheyenne, including Black Kettle and his wife. Ninety-two of the slain Cheyenne were women, children, and old men. Fifty-three women and children were captured. Custer's casualties totaled one officer killed, one officer severely and two more slightly wounded, and eleven cavalrymen wounded. After the fighting, Custer ordered the herd of Indian ponies slain; the herd numbered 875 animals. "We did not need the ponies, while the Indians did," he wrote.

In the matter of killing women and children, Custer's exculpatory rhetoric seems lame, far beneath his poetic descriptions of mirages and the break of day:

> Before engaging in the fight orders had been given to prevent the killing of any but the fighting strength of the village; but in a struggle of this character it is impossible at all times to discriminate, particularly, in a hand-to-hand conflict such as the one the troops were then engaged in the squaws are as dangerous adversaries as the warriors, while Indian boys between ten and fifteen years of age were found as expert and determined in the use of the pistol and bow and arrow as the older warriors.

After the fighting, too, Black Kettle's sister, Mah-wis-sa, implored Custer to leave the Cheyenne in peace. Custer reports that she approached him with a young woman, perhaps seventeen years old, and placed the girl's hand in his. Then she proceeded to speak solemnly in her own language, words that Custer took to be a kind of benediction, with appropriate manners and gestures. When the formalities seemed to come to a close, Mah-wis-sa looked reverently to the skies and at the same time drew her hands slowly down over the faces of Custer and the girl. At this point Custer was moved to ask Romeo, his interpreter, what was going on. Romeo replied that Custer and the young woman had just been married to each other.

In one version of the story it is said that Mah-wis-sa told Custer that if he ever again made war on the Cheyenne, he would die. When he was killed at the Little Bighorn, Cheyenne women pierced his eardrums with awls, so that he might hear in the afterlife; he had failed to hear the warning given him at the Washita.

In the final paragraph of *My Life on the Plains*, Custer bids farewell to his readers and announces his intention "to visit a region of country as yet unseen by human eyes, except those of the Indian—a country described by the latter as abounding in game of all varieties, rich in scientific interest, and of surpassing beauty in natural scenery." After rumors of gold had made the Black Hills a name known throughout the country, General (then Lieutenant Colonel) George Armstrong Custer led an expedition from Fort Abraham Lincoln into the Black Hills in July and August 1874. The Custer expedition traveled six hundred miles in sixty days. Custer reported proof of gold, but he had an eye to other things as well. He wrote in his diary:

> Every step of our march that day was amid flowers of the most exquisite colors and perfume. So luxuriant in growth were they that men plucked them without dismounting from the saddle. . . . It was a strange sight to glance back at the advancing columns of cavalry and behold the men with beautiful bouquets in their hands, while the headgear of the horses was decorated with wreaths of flowers fit to crown a queen of May. Deeming it a most fitting appellation, I named this Floral Valley.

In the evening of that same day, sitting at mess in a meadow, the officers competed to see how many different flowers could be picked by each man without leaving his seat. Seven varieties were gathered so. Some fifty different flowers were blooming in Floral Valley.

Imagine that Custer dreamed that night. In his dream he saw a man approaching on horseback, approaching slowly across a meadow full of wildflowers. The man drew very close and stopped, sitting straight up on the horse, holding Custer fast in his gaze. There could be no doubt that he was a warrior, and fearless, though he flourished no scalps and made no signs of fighting. His unbound hair hung below his waist. His body was painted with hail spots, and a white bolt of lightning ran down one of his cheeks, and on his head he wore the feathers of a red-backed hawk. Except for moccasins and breechcloth he was naked.

"I am George Armstrong Custer," Custer said, "called Yellowhair, called Son of the Morning Star."

"I am Curly," the man said, "called Crazy Horse."

And Custer wept for the nobility and dignity and greatness of the man facing him. And through his tears he perceived the brilliance of the meadow. The wildflowers were innumerable and more beautiful than anything he had ever seen or imagined. And when he thought his heart could bear no more, a thousand butterflies rose up, glancing and darting and floating around him, to spangle the sky to become prisms of the sun. And he awoke serene and refreshed in his soul.

George Armstrong Custer sees the light upon the meadows of the Plains, but he does not see disaster lurking at the Little Bighorn. He hears the bugles and the band, but he does not hear or heed the warning of the Cheyenne women. All about there is deception; the West is other than it seems.

III

In 1872, William Frederick Cody was awarded the Medal of Honor for his valor in fighting Indians. In 1913, U.S. Army regulations specified that only enlisted men and officers were eligible to receive the Medal of Honor, and Cody's medal was therefore withdrawn and his name removed from the records. In 1916, after deliberation, the army decided to return the medal, having declared that Cody's service to his country was "above and beyond the call of duty."

Ambivalence and ambiguity, like deception, bear upon all definitions of the American West. The real issue of Cody's skill and accomplishment as an Indian fighter is not brought into question in this matter of the Medal of Honor, but it might be. Beyond the countless Indians he "killed" in the arena of the Wild West show, Cody's achievements as an Indian fighter are suspect. Indeed, much of Cody's life is clouded in ambiguity. He claimed that in 1859 he became a pony express rider, but the pony express did not come into being until 1860. Even the sobriquet "Buffalo Bill" belonged to William Mathewson before it belonged to William Frederick Cody.

Buffalo Bill Cody was an icon and an enigma, and he was in some sense his own invention. One of his biographers wrote that he was "a man who was so much more than a western myth." One must doubt it, for the mythic dimension of the American West is an equation much greater than the sum of its parts. It would be more accurate, in this case, to say that the one dissolved into the other, that the man and myth became indivisible. The great fascination and peril of Cody's life was the riddle of who he was. The thing that opposed him, and perhaps betrayed him, was above all else the mirage of his own identity.

If we are to understand the central irony of Buffalo Bill and the Wild West show, we must first understand that William Frederick Cody was an authentic western hero. As a scout, a guide, a marksman, and a buffalo hunter, he was second to none. At a time when horsemanship was at its highest level in America, he was a horseman nearly without peer. He defined the plainsman. The authority of his life on the Plains far surpassed Custer's.

But let us imagine that we are at Omaha, Nebraska, on May 17, 1883, in a crowd of 8,000 people. The spectacle of the "Wild West" unfolds before us. The opening parade is led by a twenty-piece band playing "Garry Owen," perhaps, or "The Girl I Left Behind Me." Then there comes an Indian in full regalia on a paint pony. Next are buffalo, three adults and a calf. Then there is Buffalo Bill, mounted on a fine white horse and resplendent in a great white hat, a fringed buckskin coat, and glossy thigh boots. He stands out in a company of cowboys, Indians, more buffalo, and the Deadwood Stage, drawn by six handsome mules, and the end is brought up by another band, playing "Annie Laurie" or "When Johnny Comes Marching Home." Then we see the acts—the racing of the pony express, exhibitions of shooting, the attack on the Deadwood Stagecoach, and the finale of the great buffalo chase. Buffalo Bill makes a stirring speech, and we are enthralled; the applause is thunderous. But this is only a modest beginning, a mere glimpse of things to come.

What we have in this explosion of color and fanfare is an epic transformation of the American West into a traveling circus and of an American hero into an imitation of himself. Here is a theme with which we have become more than familiar. We have seen the transformation take place numberless times on the stage, on television and movie screens, and on the pages of comic books, dime novels, and literary masterpieces. One function of the American imagination is to reduce the American landscape to size, to fit that great expanse to the confinement of the immigrant mind. It is a way to persist in our cultural being. We photograph ourselves on the rim of Monument Valley or against the wall of the Tetons, and we become our own frame of reference. As long as we can transform the landscape to accommodate our fragile presence, we can be saved. As long as we can see ourselves on the picture plane, we cannot be lost.

Arthur Kopit's play *Indians* is a remarkable treatise on this very subject of transformation. It can and ought to be seen as a tragedy, for its central story is that of Buffalo Bill's fatal passage into myth. He is constrained to translate his real heroism into a false and concentrated reflection of itself. The presence of the Indians is pervasive, but he cannot see them until they are called to his attention.

BUFFALO BILL: Thank you, thank you! A great show lined up tonight! With all-time favorite Johnny Baker, Texas Jack and his twelve-string guitar, the Dancin' Cavanaughs, Sheriff Brad and the Deadwood Mail Coach, Harry Philamee's Trained Prairie Dogs, the Abilene County Girls' Trick Roping and Lasso Society, Pecos Pete and the—

VOICE: *Bill.*

BUFFALO BILL: (Startled.) Hm?

VOICE: Bring on the Indians.

BUFFALO BILL: What?

VOICE: The *Indians.*

BUFFALO BILL: Ah . . .

Solemnly the Indians appear. In effect they shame Buffalo Bill; they tread upon his conscience. They fascinate and imperil him. By degrees his desperation to justify himself—and by extension the white man's treatment of the Indians in general—grows and becomes a burden too great to bear. In the end he sits trembling while the stage goes completely black. Then all lights up, rodeo music, the glaring and blaring; enter the Rough Riders of the World! Buffalo Bill enters on his white stallion and tours the ring, doffing his hat to the invisible crowd. The Rough Riders exit, the Indians approach, and the lights fade to black again.

At five minutes past noon on January 10, 1917, Buffalo Bill died. Western Union ordered all lines cleared, and, in a state of war, the world was given the news at once. The old scout had passed by. Tributes and condolences came from every quarter, from children, from old soldiers, from heads of state.

In ambivalence and ambiguity, Cody died as he had lived. A week before his death, it was reported that Buffalo Bill had been baptized into the Roman Catholic Church. His wife, Louisa, was, however, said to be an Episcopalian, and his sister Julia, to whom he declared, "Your church suits me," was a Presbyterian. Following his death there was a controversy as to where Cody should be buried. He had often expressed the wish to be buried on Cedar Mountain, Wyoming. Notwithstanding, his final resting place is atop Mount Lookout, above Denver, Colorado, overlooking the urban sprawl.

IV

DECEMBER 29, 1890

Wounded Knee Creek

In the shine of photographs
are the slain, frozen and black
on a simple field of snow.
They image ceremony:
women and children dancing,
old men prancing, making fun.
In autumn there were songs, long
since muted in the blizzard.
In summer the wild buckwheat
shone like fox fur and quillwork,
and dusk guttered on the creek.
Now in serene attitudes
of dance, the dead in glossy
death are drawn in ancient light.

On December 15, 1890, the great Hunkpapa leader Sitting Bull, who had opposed Custer at the Little Bighorn and who had toured for a time with Buffalo Bill and the Wild West show, was killed on the Standing Rock reservation. In a dream he had foreseen his death at the hands of his own people.

Just two weeks later, on the morning of December 29, 1890, on Wounded Knee Creek near the Pine Ridge agency, the Seventh Cavalry of the U.S. Army opened fire on an encampment of Big Foot's band of Miniconjou Sioux. When the shooting ended, Big Foot and most of his people were dead or dying. It has been estimated that nearly 300 of the original 350 men, women, and children in the camp were slain. Twenty-five soldiers were killed and thirty-nine wounded.

Sitting Bull is reported to have said, "I am the last Indian." In some sense he was right. During his lifetime the world of the Plains Indians had changed forever. The old roving life of the buffalo hunters was over. A terrible disintegration and demoralization had set in. If the death of Sitting Bull marked the end of an age, Wounded Knee marked the end of a culture.

> I did not know then how much was ended. When I look back now from the high hill of my old age, I can still see the butchered women and children lying heaped and scattered all along the crooked gulch as plain as when I saw them with eyes still young. And I can see that something else died there in the bloody mud, and was buried in the blizzard. A people's dream died there. It was a beautiful dream. . . .

—Black Elk

In the following days there were further developments. On January 7, 1891, nine days after the massacre at Wounded Knee, a young Sioux warrior named Plenty Horses shot and killed a popular army officer, Lieutenant Edward W. Casey, who wanted to enter the Sioux village at No Water for the purpose of talking peace. The killing appeared to be unprovoked. Plenty Horses shot Case in the back at close quarters.

On January 11, two Sioux families, returning to Pine Ridge from hunting near Bear Butte, were ambushed by white ranchers, three bothers named Culbertson. Few Tails, the head of one of the families, was killed, and his wife was severely wounded. Somehow she made her way in the freezing cold a hundred miles to Pine Ridge. The other family—a man, his wife, and two children, one an infant—managed to reach the Rosebud agency two weeks later. This wife, too, was wounded and weak from the loss of blood. She survived, but the infant child had died of starvation on the way.

On January 15 the Sioux leaders surrendered and established themselves at Pine Ridge. The peace for which General Nelson A. Miles had worked so hard was achieved. The Indians assumed that Plenty Horses would go free, and indeed General Miles was reluctant to disturb the peace. But there were strong feelings among the soldiers. Casey had been shot in cold blood while acting in the interest of peace. On February 19, Plenty Horses was quietly arrested and removed from the reservation to Fort Meade, near Sturgis, South Dakota.

On March 27, General Miles ordered Plenty Horses released to stand trial in the federal district court at Sioux Falls. Interest ran high, and the courtroom was filled with onlookers of every description. The Plenty Horses trial was one of the most interesting and unlikely in the history of the West. Eventually the outcome turned upon a question of perception, of whether or not a state of war existed between the Sioux and the United States. If Plenty Horses and Casey were belligerents in a state of war, the defense argued, then the killing could not be considered a criminal offense, subject to trial in the civil courts.

General Nelson A. Miles was sensitive to this question for two reasons in particular. First, his rationale for bringing troops upon the scene—and he had amassed the largest concentration of troops since the Civil War—was predicated upon the existence of a state of war. When the question was put to him directly he replied, "It was a war. You do not suppose that I am going to reduce my campaign to a dress-parade affair?" Second, Miles had to confront the logically related corollary to the defense argument, that, if no state of war existed, all the soldiers who took part in the Wounded Knee affair were guilty of murder under the law.

Miles sent a staff officer, Captain Frank D. Baldwin, to testify on behalf of Plenty Horses' defense. This testimony proved critical, and decisive. It is a notable irony that Baldwin and the slain Casey were close friends. Surely one of the principal ironies of American history is that Plenty Horses was very likely to have been the only Indian to benefit in any way from the slaughter at Wounded Knee. Plenty Horses was acquitted. So too—a final irony—were the Culbertson brothers; with Plenty Horses' acquittal, there was neither a logical basis for nor a practical possibility of holding them accountable for the ambush of Few Tails and his party.

We might ponder Plenty Horses at trial, a young man sitting silent under the scrutiny of curious onlookers, braving his fate with apparent indifference. Behind the mask of a warrior was a lost and agonized soul.

As a boy Plenty Horses had been sent to Carlisle Indian School in Pennsylvania, the boarding school founded by Richard Henry Pratt, whose obsession was to "kill the Indian and save the man." Carlisle was the model upon which an extensive system of boarding schools for Indians was based. The boarding schools were prisons in effect, where Indian children were exposed to brutalities, sometimes subtle, sometimes not, in the interest of converting them to the white man's way of life. It was a grand experiment in ethnic cleansing and psychological warfare, and it failed. But it exacted a terrible cost upon the mental, physical, and spiritual health of Indian children.

Plenty Horses was for five years a pupil at Carlisle. Of his experience there he said:

> I found that the education I had received was of no benefit to me. There was no chance to get employment, nothing for me to do whereby I could earn my board and clothes, no opportunity to learn more and remain with the whites. It disheartened me and I went back to live as I had before going to school.

But when Plenty Horses returned to his own people, they did not fully accept him. He had lost touch with the old ways; he had lived among whites, and the association had diminished him. He rejected the white world, but he had been exposed to it, and it had left its mark upon him. And in the process he had been dislodged, uprooted from the Indian world. He could not quite get back to it. His very being had become tentative; he lived in a kind of limbo, a state of confusion, depression, and desperation.

At the trial Plenty Horses was remarkably passive. He said nothing, nor did he give any sign of his feelings. It was as if he were not there. It came later to light that he was convinced beyond any question that he would be hanged. He could not understand what was happening around him. But in a strange way he could appreciate it. Indeed he must have been fascinated. Beneath his inscrutable expression, his heart must have been racing. He was the center of a ritual, a sacrificial victim; the white man must dispose of him according to some design in the white man's universe. This was perhaps a ritual of atonement. The whites would take his life, but in the proper way, according to their notion of propriety and the appropriate. Perhaps they were involving him in their very notion of the sacred. He could only accept what was happening, and only in their terms. With silence, patience, and respect he must await the inevitable.

Plenty Horses said later:

> I am an Indian. Five years I attended Carlisle and was educated in the ways
> of the white man. . . . I was lonely. I shot the lieutenant so I might make a place
> for myself among my people. Now I am one of them. I shall be hung and the
> Indians will bury me as a warrior. They will be proud of me. I am satisfied.

But Plenty Horses was not hanged, nor did he make an acceptable place for
himself among his people. He was acquitted. Plenty Horses lived out his life
between two worlds, without a place in either.

Perhaps the most tragic aspect of Plenty Horses' plight was his silence, the
theft of his language and the theft of meaning itself from his ordeal. At Carlisle
he had been made to speak English, and his native Lakota was forbidden,
thrown away, to use a term that indicates particular misfortune in the Plains
oral tradition, where to be "thrown away" is to be negated, excluded, eliminated. After five years Plenty Horses had not only failed to master the English language, he had lost some critical possession of his native tongue as well.
He was therefore crippled in his speech, wounded in his intelligence. In him
was a terrible urgency to express himself—his anger and hurt, his sorrow and
loneliness. But his voice was broken. In terms of his culture and all it held
most sacred, Plenty Horses himself was thrown away.

In order to understand the true nature of Plenty Horses' ordeal—and a
central reality in the cultural conflict that has defined the way we historically see the American West—we must first understand something about the nature of words, about the way we live our daily lives in the element of language.
For in a profound sense our language determines us; it shapes our most fundamental selves; it establishes our identity and confirms our existence, our
human being. Without language we are lost, "thrown away." Without names—
language is essentially a system of naming—we cannot truly claim to be.

To think is to talk to oneself. That is to say, language and thought are practically indivisible. But there is complexity in language, and there are many
languages. Indeed, there are hundreds of Native American languages on the
North American continent alone, many of them in the American West. As
there are different languages, there are different ways of thinking. In terms of
what we call "worldview," there are common denominators of experience
that unify language communities to some extent. Although the Pueblo peoples
of the Rio Grande valley speak different languages, their experience of the
land in which they live, and have lived for thousands of years, is by and large
the same. And their worldview is the same. There are common denominators
that unify all Native Americans in certain ways. This much may be said of
other peoples, Europeans, for example. But the difference between Native
American and European worldviews is vast. And that difference is crucial to
the story of the American West. We are talking about different ways of thinking, deeply different ways of looking at the world.

The oral tradition of the American Indian is a highly developed realization of language. In certain ways it is superior to the written tradition. In the

oral tradition words are sacred; they are intrinsically powerful and beautiful. By means of words, by the exertion of language upon the unknown, the best of the possible—and indeed the seemingly impossible—is accomplished. Nothing exists beyond the influence of words. Words are the names of Creation. To give one's word is to give oneself, wholly, to place a name, than which nothing is more sacred, in the balance. One stands for his word; his word stands for him. The oral tradition demands the greatest clarity of speech and hearing, the whole strength of memory, and an absolute faith in the efficacy of language. Every word spoken, every word heard, is the utterance of prayer.

Thus, in the oral tradition, language bears the burden of the sacred, the burden of belief. In a written tradition, the place of language is not so certain.

Those European immigrants who ventured into the Wild West were of a written tradition, even the many who were illiterate. Their way of seeing and thinking was determined by the invention of an alphabet, the advent of the printed word, and the manufacture of books. These were great landmarks of civilization, to be sure, but they were also a radical departure from the oral tradition and an understanding of language that was inestimably older and closer to the origin of words. Although the first Europeans venturing into the continent took with them and held dear the Bible, Bunyan, and Shakespeare, their children ultimately could take words for granted, throw them away. Words, multiplied and diluted to inflation, would be preserved on shelves forever. But in this departure was also the dilution of the sacred, and the loss of a crucial connection with the real, that plane of possibility that is always larger than our comprehension. What follows such loss is overlay, imposition, the distorted view of the West of which we have been speaking.

V

My children, when at first I liked the whites,
My children, when at first I liked the whites,
I gave them fruits,
I gave them fruits.

—Arapaho

Restore my voice for me.

—Navajo

The landscape of the American West has to be seen to be believed. And perhaps, conversely, it has to be believed in order to be seen. Here is the confluence of image and imagination. I am a writer and a painter. I am therefore interested in what it is to see, how seeing is accomplished, how the physical eye and the mind's eye are related, how the act of seeing is or can be expressed in art and in language, and how these things are sacred in nature, as I believe them to be.

Belief is the burden of seeing. And language bears the burden of belief rightly. To see into the heart of something is to believe in it. In order to see to this extent, to see and to accomplish belief in the seeing one must be prepared. The preparation is a spiritual exercise.

In order to be perceived in its true character, the landscape of the American West must be seen in terms of its sacred dimension. "Sacred" and "sacrifice" are related. Something is made sacred by means of sacrifice; that which is sacred is earned. I have a friend who wears on a string around his neck a little leather pouch. In the pouch is a pebble from the creek bed at Wounded Knee. Wounded Knee is sacred ground, for it was purchased with blood. It is the site of a terrible human sacrifice. It is appropriate that my friend should keep the pebble close to the center of his being, that he should see the pebble and beyond the pebble to the battlefield and beyond the battlefield to the living earth.

The history of the West, that is, the written story that begins with the record of European intervention, is informed by tensions that arise from a failure to see the West in terms of the sacred. The oral history, the oral tradition that came before the written chronicles, is all too often left out of the equation. Yet one of the essential realities of the West is centered in this still living past. When Europeans came into the West they encountered a people who had been there for untold millennia, for whom the landscape was a kind of cathedral of their spiritual life, the home of their deepest being. It had been earned by sacrifice forever. But the encounter was determined by a distortion of image and imagination and language, by a failure to see and believe.

George Armstrong Custer could see and articulate the beauty of the Plains, but he could not see the people who inhabited them. Or he could see them only as enemies, impediments to the glory for which he hungered. He could not understand the sacred ceremony, the significance of the marriage he was offered, and he could not hear the words of warning, nor comprehend their meaning.

Buffalo Bill was a plainsman, but the place he might have held on the picture plane of the West was severely compromised and ultimately lost to the theatrical pretensions of the Wild West show. Neither did he see the Indians. What he saw at last was a self-fabricated reflection of himself and of the landscape in which he had lived a former life.

The vision of Plenty Horses was that of reunion with his traditional world. He could not realize his vision, for his old way of seeing was stolen from him in the white man's school. Ironically, just like the European emigrants, Plenty Horses attempted by his wordless act of violence to persist in his cultural being, to transform the landscape to accommodate his presence once more, to save himself. He could not do so. I believe that he wanted more than anything to pray, to make a prayer in the old way to the old deities of the world to which he was born. But I believe too that he had lost the words, that without language he could no longer bear the burden of belief.

The sun's beams are running out
The sun's beams are running out
The sun's yellow rays are running out
The sun's yellow rays are running out
We shall live again
We shall live again

—Comanche

They will appear—may you behold them!
They will appear—may you behold them!
A horse nation will appear.
A thunder-being nation will appear.
They will appear, behold!
They will appear, behold!

—Kiowa

Discussion Questions

1. What does Momaday mean when he refers to "the burden of belief" in this essay? Does he ever specifically define the term?
2. What does Momaday claim about Buffalo Bill and the problem of seeing the West clearly? How do his facts about Buffalo Bill relate to the idea of "the burden of belief," which he discusses throughout the essay?
3. Discuss Plenty Horse's dilemma—what caused his lack of location in either a white or an Indian world? Does his situation relate at all to Native American students today?

Writing Suggestions

1. Momaday writes his essay using a variety of rhetorical styles and writing techniques. Write an essay in which you analyze his essay, arguing for or against his techniques of mixing dream sequences, songs, primary sources, dialogue, and third-person research writing. Did you find this kind of writing effective? Why or why not?
2. Do you know of instances where a student's first language has been forbidden in the classroom? Do you believe it is better to learn a new language by total immersion, or is it better for students to learn a second language gradually? Write a personal essay in response to these questions, and relate your discussion to the experience of Plenty Horses and other Indian children at government-run schools.

My Life on the Plains

GEORGE ARMSTRONG CUSTER

General George Armstrong Custer, best known for his demise at the controversial battle of Little Big Horn, was an author as well as a Civil War cavalry leader and renowned Indian fighter on the Great Plains. His writings, originally published serially in *The Galaxy* magazine in May of 1872, describe the Seventh Cavalry's battles against the Plains Indians from 1867 to 1869. In the following selection from *Wild Life on the Plains and Horrors of Indian Warfare*, Custer describes both the physical terrain of the Great Plains and his interpretation of the psyche and character of the American Indian.

If the character given to the Indian by Cooper and other novelists, as well as by well-meaning but mistaken philanthropists of a later day, were the true one; if the Indian were the innocent, simple-minded being he is represented, more the creature of romance than reality, imbued only with a deep veneration for the works of nature, freed from the passions and vices which must accompany a savage nature; if, in other words, he possessed all the virtues which his admirers and works of fiction ascribe to him, and were free from all the vices which those best qualified to judge assign to him, he would be just the character to complete the picture which is presented by the country embracing the Wichita mountains. Cooper, to whose writings more than to those of any other author are the people speaking the English language indebted for a false and ill-judged estimate of the Indian character, might well have laid the scenes of his fictitious stories in this beautiful and romantic country.

It is to be regretted that the character of the Indian as described in Cooper's interesting novels is not the true one. But as, in emerging from childhood into the years of a maturer age, we are often compelled to cast aside many of our earlier illusions and replace them by beliefs less inviting but more real so we, as a people, with opportunities enlarged and facilities for obtaining knowledge increased, have been forced by a multiplicity of causes to study and endeavor to comprehend thoroughly the character of the red man. So intimately has he become associated with the Government as ward of the nation, and so prominent a place among the questions of national policy does the much mooted "Indian question" occupy, that it behooves us no longer to study this problem from works of fiction, but to deal with it as it exists in reality. Stripped of the beautiful romance with which we have been so long willing to envelop him, transferred from the inviting pages of the novelist to the localities where we are compelled to meet with him, in his native village, on the war path, and when raiding upon our frontier settlements and lines of travel, the Indian forfeits his claim to the appellation of the *"noble* red man." We see him as he is, and, so far as all knowledge goes, as he ever has been, a *savage* in every sense of the word; not worse, perhaps, than his white brother would be similarly born and bred, but one whose cruel and ferocious nature far exceeds that of any wild beast of the desert. That this is true no one who has been brought into intimate contact with the wild tribes will deny. Perhaps there are some who, as members of peace commissions or as wandering agents of some benevolent society, may have visited these tribes or attended with them at councils held for some pacific purpose, and who, by passing through the villages of the Indian while *at peace*, may imagine their opportunities for judging of the Indian nature all that could be desired. But the Indian, while he can seldom be accused of indulging in a great variety of wardrobe, can be said to have a character capable of adapting itself to almost every occasion. He has one character, perhaps his most serviceable one, which he preserves carefully, and only airs it when making his appeal to the Government or its agents for arms, ammunition, and license to employ them. This character is invariably paraded, and often with telling effect, when the motive is a peaceful one. Prominent chiefs invited to visit Washington invariably don this character, and in their "talks" with the "Great Father" and other less prominent personages they successfully contrive to exhibit but this one phase. Seeing them under these or similar circumstances only, it is not surprising that by many the Indian is looked upon as a simple-minded "son of nature," desiring nothing beyond the privilege of roaming and hunting over the vast unsettled wilds of the West, inheriting and asserting but few native rights, and never trespassing upon the rights of others. This view is equally erroneous with that which regards the Indian as a creature possessing the human form but divested of all other attributes of humanity, and whose traits of character, habits, modes of life, disposition, and savage customs disqualify him from the exercise of all rights and privileges, even those pertaining to life itself. Taking him as we find him, at peace or at war, at home or abroad, waiving all prejudices, and laying aside all partiality, we will discover in the Indian a subject for thoughtful study and investigation. In him we will find the representative of a race whose origin is, and promises to be, a subject forever wrapped in mystery; a race incapable of being judged by the rules or laws applicable to any other known race of men; one between which and civilization there seems to have existed from time immemorial a determined and unceasing warfare—a hostility so deep-seated and inbred with the Indian character, that in the exceptional instances where the modes and habits of civilization have been reluctantly adopted, it has been at the sacrifice of power and influence as a tribe, and the more serious loss of health, vigor, and courage as individuals.

Discussion Questions

1. In "The American West and the Burden of Belief," N. Scott Momaday pro-
    poses an alternate version of history that might have taken place—Custer
    meets Crazy Horse and weeps "for the nobility and dignity and great-
    ness of the man." Reading Custer's own writings about the Indians, do
    you think Custer felt any of these feelings in real life? What sorts of feel-
    ings do you think Custer conveys in his writings?
2. What does Custer object to in the writings of Cooper and other novelists
    describing the Indians?

Writing Suggestions

1. Make a list of Custer's assertions about the "savage red man's" character.
    Review Jackson's speech about the relocation of the Indians, and make a
    list of his assertions about the character of the Indians. Then, write a short
    comparison paper about Jackson's and Custer's arguments about the char-
    acter of the Indians. What similarities do you find in the two men's argu-
    ments? What kinds of evidence do they use to back up their claims? What
    similar beliefs do they hold about the Indians? What differences do you
    find in the arguments? Does one seem more well-reasoned than the other?
2. Although Custer's Last Stand is usually equated in American history with
    the idea of bravery and patriotism, recent research has challenged this
    idea and many historians have pointed out that Custer needlessly sacri-
    ficed the lives of his men because he refused to obey orders; instead of
    waiting for reinforcements to arrive, he charged the large Indian en-
    campment at Little Big Horn, and, vastly outnumbered by Indian troops,
    died along with all of his men.
        To see how Custer was portrayed earlier in American history, check
    out or rent the classic 1942 movie about General Custer, *They Died with
    Their Boots On*, starring Errol Flynn. Then write an analysis of the movie,
    answering the following questions:

    How does this movie portray General Custer?

    How does it mythologize him?

    Which character traits are stressed?

    How are the Indians portrayed in the film?

    What role does his wife play in the film?

    How does the director use music, lighting, and plot to bring out a particular
    view of Custer?

    What feeling did you take away from the movie about Custer and his Last
    Stand?

Slavery in the Antebellum West, 1835–1865

QUINTARD TAYLOR

Quintard Taylor is professor of history at the University of Oregon, Eugene. Taylor has studied African Americans in the American West extensively, and is the author of more than twenty articles on blacks in the West. He has also served as a consultant for numerous documentaries about blacks in the West, and he is the author of *The Forging of a Black Community: A History of Seattle's Central District, 1870 Through the Civil Rights Era* (1994). His second book, *In Search of the Racial Frontier* (1998), looks at the experiences of African Americans during the settlement of the West. In the selection that follows—an excerpt from the chapter "Slavery in the Antebellum West, 1835–1865" from the book *In Search of the Racial Frontier*—Taylor examines some little-known aspects of slavery in the Indian Territory.

Few western historians link slavery with the youngest of the nation's regions. When the Civil War began in 1861, only four western states—Texas, Kansas, California, and Oregon—had been admitted to the Union, and the Euro-American inhabitants of the vast territories considered themselves physically and psychologically removed from slavery's debate. The West's claims of innocence on slavery, however, are muted by the presence of black bond servants in virtually every state and territory prior to the Civil War and by the intense local debates about its suitability in Oregon, California, Utah, and "bleeding" Kansas, where political discourse gave way to armed conflict in the 1850s. The ninety-eighth meridian, which stretched across the plains from Dakota Territory to central Texas, represented the farthest advance of plantation agriculture. It did not, however, bar some mutation of the servile institution in the West. The region was saved from slavery by the demands of white free-soil farmers, who were always more numerous than proslavery advocates and slaveholders, rather than by geography or westerners' commitment to universal liberty.

Before 1861 most African Americans came West as slaves. Yet in such a large, diverse region the importance of slavery in the states and territories differed markedly. Texas, where the Old South met the western frontier, had by far the largest slave population. The 1860 U.S. census reported 182,556 bondspeople, 30 percent of the state's total population. With the influx of "refugeed" slaves from neighboring states during the Civil War, Texas's total servile population surpassed 250,000 by April 1865.

Texas was the exception in the West because its economic and political elite embraced a slave-based economy and society before 1836. But slavery emerged in other western areas. The Five Nations, like Texas, had an economy that rested largely on slave labor. Indian Territory in 1860 had seven thousand slaves, who constituted 14 percent of the total population. Slavery was legal in one other territory, Utah, although only twenty-nine of its fifty-nine black inhabitants were slaves in 1860. Slavery was outlawed in the remainder of the states and territories. Yet the historical record is replete with accounts of bond servants held from Washington Territory to New Mexico.

The discussion of slavery in the West begins in Texas, the heart of the region's slave regime. After the Texas war of independence slaveholding Anglo-Americans poured into the republic. Slaveholders unapologetically proclaimed both the agricultural need for black labor and their right to own their fellow human beings. "I have no doubt," District Court Judge C. A. Frazier told an Upshur County grand jury in 1860, "of the right of a civilized and Christian nation to capture the African wherever he may be found and subject him to labor, enlightenment and religion, than I have of one of our people to capture a wild horse on the prairies of the West, and domesticate and reduce him to labor." Austin's *Texas State Gazette* editor John Marshall, was more direct. Arguing that slavery was growing too slowly in Texas, Marshall in 1858 called for the reopening of the African slave trade. "Until we reach somewhere in the vicinity of two million slaves," declared Marshall, "such a thing as too many slaves in Texas is an absurdity."

Slaves resided in virtually all of Texas's 105 counties in 1860, but they were concentrated in three regions of the state. The oldest slaveholding area, the Austin colony, extended inland from the Gulf Coast along the cotton-, rice-, sugarcane-producing lowlands of the Brazos and Colorado rivers. Slaveholders also favored southeast Texas, around San Augustine County, and the northeastern corner of the state near the Arkansas and Louisiana borders. Some of these counties quickly obtained black majorities. In 1850 six predominantly black counties stretched along the Brazos and Colorado. Ten years later thirteen Texas counties were predominantly black.

This labor system produced a harsh daily physical routine described by one former Texas slave as work from "can see to can't see." There was little division of labor based on gender or age. Women, men, and children alike harvested the crops, picking cotton, pulling corn, or cutting sugarcane, and performed the numerous chores associated with nineteenth-century farming. Slave men handled the heaviest work of plowing, felling trees, and digging ditches; female slaves planted corn and cotton, drove horses, and hoed cotton, corn, and vegetable gardens. Children began with such jobs as gathering firewood, hauling water, and knocking down old cotton stalks and, as they grew older, assumed responsibilities for tending livestock. Just as some male slaves were allowed to develop special skills, such as blacksmithing and carpentry, or became carriage drivers and butlers, some slave women specialized as cooks, laundresses, maids, seamstresses, and spinners.

Much of the work routine of Texas slaves paralleled that of bondspeople east of the Sabine River, but some slaves worked in the state's emerging cattle industry. African slave stock grazers from the cattle-raising region of the Gambia River in West Africa were part of the expansion of the livestock industry in colonial South Carolina, passing their herding skills down through generations and steadily across the Gulf Coast states to Texas. These skills and those acquired from Mexican vaqueros, themselves descendants of colonial-era mestizo, mulatto, black, and Indian cattle herders, gave Texas slaves considerable cattle-growing experience on the southwest frontier.

Usually assigned the task of catching and tending wild cattle in the Gulf Coast brush country, slave cowboys used lariats to produce long trains of steers led by oxen and trailed by baying dogs. The Civil War governor of Texas, Francis Richard Lubbock, relied on his five bondsmen to tend the two thousand cattle on his ranch near Houston. Lubbock allowed one of them, a man named Willis, to acquire cattle and horses while still a slave so that he could purchase freedom for himself and his family. James Taylor White, the first Texas "cattle baron," used black drovers for the thousands of heads of cattle he owned in Liberty County, while Amanda Wildy reported her dependence on black slave cowboys when she told a court in 1854, that "it will require the service of the principal part of the horses and negroes to take care of and manage [her] stock of cattle." African Americans constituted the majority of cowboys in Texas by the early 1850s, according to one historian, and in an activity that foreshadowed the famous post–Civil War cattle drives to Kansas, they trailed herds of cattle to Mexico and New Orleans.

Plantation life for Texas slaves demanded the harshest, least remitting toil under the most oppressive social pressures, but it also afforded the greatest opportunity for the development of family life. Familial ties provided love, individual identity, and a sense of personal worth from people like themselves rather than from anglo Texans. In 1839 Albert, one of Ashbel Smith's slaves, strenuously objected to even briefly leaving his family. Smith's plantation overseer, M. S. Tunnel, reported to his employer: "Albert got home, safely, on Monday night. He takes the separation from his family to heart considerably." "I haven't forgot you nor I never will forget you as long as the world stands, even if you forget me," wrote Fannie, a Harrison county slave woman, in 1862 to her husband, Norfleet, who was away with his owner, a Confederate officer. "If I never see you again, I hope to meet you in Heaven."

Plantations set the norm for much of antebellum Texas society, but 54 percent of the state's slaves lived on farms with fewer than twenty bondspeople, and one-fourth of the slaveholders owned only one slave. Significant sections of east and central Texas considered unsuitable for cotton cultivation developed an agricultural economy centered on small-scale wheat and corn production. Slaves on these farms fared no better. Their material condition depended upon the affluence of their owners. Slaves of impoverished farmers shared the poverty of their masters. Although masters and slaves often worked side by side, such slaveowners were no more and no less considerate of the welfare of their slaves than the planters.

Unless they lived in plantation country, small farm slaves had few opportunities to mingle with other African Americans. Those on the frontier saw few other people, black or white. In such settings black slaves and their white owners developed a mutual dependence born of necessity. The much-feared Comanche made no distinction between black and white frontier settlers. As Kenneth W. Porter remarked, the Comanche saw people dressed similarly, using identical tools and weapons, living in comparable houses and often in the same house. Because of their basic lifestyle and cultural similarity, the Comanche regarded whites and blacks with antipathy and contempt and killed men and captured women and children with scant regard to color. Conversely, many black slaves (and free blacks), embraced a hatred and fear of the plains raiders with as much fervor as white frontier settlers.

Urban slaves, although only 6 percent of Texas bondspeople, nonetheless formed a distinct population. Galveston and Houston, the largest cities in antebellum Texas, each had more than 1,000 black slaves while several hundred lived in Austin and San Antonio. The urban black slave population grew proportionately with the cities. Occasionally these urban populations established churches and other community institutions. Galveston slaves, for example, founded Baptist and Methodist churches housed in substantial buildings seating 350 worshipers. The majority of these slaves were house servants, but others worked on farms outside the cities or as cooks, teamsters, hotel waiters, carpenters, bricklayers, and boatmen. A small number of skilled slaves worked in flour mills, sawmills, and brickyards. The growth of the skilled slave artisan class prompted white groups, such as the Houston Mechanics Association, to adopt a resolution in 1858 declaring their opposition to "the practice adhered to by some, of making contracts with the negro mechanics to carry on work, as a contractor."

Most white urban Texans worried more about the social latitude black people assumed in the cities than their occupations. One Austin ordinance enacted in 1855 granted the "city marshal and his assistants . . . control and supervision of the conduct, carriage [sic], demeanor and deportment of any and all slaves living, being, or found within the city limits," and another forbade "any white man or Mexican" from "making associates" of black slaves. City laws called for slave patrols, the regulation of assemblies, and the prohibition of gambling or the possession of liquor and weapons. Yet some urban slaves openly flouted these bans, prompting one Austin newspaper editor in 1854 to declare in disgust that he "almost imagines himself in the land of amalgamation, abolition meetings, and woman's rights conventions." Other slaves challenged the limits of their servile status by openly defying whites. Urban slaves, according to historian Paul Lack, commonly disregarded the groveling courtesies demanded by "polite" racial etiquette and instead used loud and profane language and engaged in insubordination and disorderly conduct. One bondsman was quoted in an Austin paper: "[L]et any white man tell him to stop his mouth, and see if he would not give him hell." Describing his visit to Houston in 1863, a British observer was surprised to see "innumerable Negros and Negresses parading about the streets in the most outrageously grand costumes." Galveston's slaves celebrated the city's May Day parade by driving their owner's carriages and riding their horses.

Most Texas slaves were not openly defiant, but many sought every opportunity to escape. The problem was far more acute than in the Old South. Texas was bordered on three sides by sparsely populated regions that offered the possibility of escape: Indian Territory to the north, the western frontier, and Mexico. Of the three border regions Mexico posed the greatest concern to slaveholders. "Sometimes someone would come 'long and try to get us to run up North and be free," declared San Antonio slave Felix Haywood. "We used to laugh at that. There was no reason to run up North. All we had to do was to walk . . . south, and we'd be free as soon as we crossed the Rio Grande." Haywood's view confirmed Mexico's image as a haven for fugitive slaves dating back to the Texas war of independence. Many blacks fled with the retreating Mexican Army and settled just below the Rio Grande in Matamoros. A colony of former slaves on the international border prompted other blacks to strike out south for freedom. If they reached the Rio Grande, Mexicans often helped their river crossing.

Four thousand fugitives lived south of the Rio Grande by 1855. Mexico welcomed them because officials believed they and Native Americans discouraged further American incursion. The symbol of this black-Indian-Mexican nexus was the border settlement created by the Seminole Indian chief Wild Cat, who led a band of 200 Indians and blacks into Coahuila in 1850. The Mexican government allowed this band to create a colony in the Santa Rosa Mountains eighty miles southwest of the Rio Grande border community of Piedras Negras. There Wild Cat welcomed other fugitives from Texas and Plains Indians. South Texas slaveholders demanded an end of the colony. Mexico has "long been regarded by the Texas slave," according to the *San Antonio Ledger* in 1852, "as his El Dorado for accumulation, his utopia for political rights, and his Paradise for happiness." After a series of meetings in San Antonio and other South Texas towns, slaveholders raised twenty thousand dollars for an expedition to recapture runaways. In October 1855 they sent Texas Ranger Captain James H. Callahan and 130 men to Mexico ostensibly to "chastise hostile Indians" but in fact to attack Wild Cat and his followers and return as many fugitive slaves as possible to Texas. The expedition failed when a combined Mexican-Indian-black force drove the intruders out of the region.

Mexican opposition to slaveholder efforts to retrieve fugitives generated reprisals against Tejanos. With their loyalty to Texas already suspect, it took very little "evidence" to persuade slaveholders that Tejanos were abolitionists.

In September 1854, when Anglo citizens learned that transient Tejanos near Seguin were enticing bondsmen to run away, they quickly passed a resolution declaring that no peon could enter or live in Guadalupe County. Austin residents took similar action. In October 1854, after a "respectable citizen" had observed a Mexican camp where slaves and tejanos "smoked, drank, gambled and made love," the local citizens in a resolution declared that Mexican laborers instilled "false notions of freedom," and made slaves "discontented and insubordinate." The city subsequently expelled all Tejanos except those identified by "respectable citizens." Colorado and Matagorda counties drove out their Mexican populations two years later, when county officials linked Tejanos to an abortive insurrection. In all, the Mexican "abolitionist" scare affected more than ten counties in south-central Texas.

The Civil War ended black bondage in Texas but not before its servile population grew dramatically during the conflict. While black southerners from Virginia to Louisiana were gaining their freedom with the approach of Union armies after January 1, 1863, Texas instead received nearly seven thousand additional bondspeople during the last years of the war as slaveholders from throughout the Confederacy fled to the state. "It looked like everybody in the world was going to Texas," ex-slave Allen Manning recalled as he described mothers carrying children on their backs and fathers tending wagons and livestock. "We would have to walk along side all the time to let the wagons go past, all loaded with folks going to Texas."

The refugee flight, which continued into 1865, only delayed the inevitable. On June 19, 1865, Union forces landed at Galveston, where Major General Gordon Granger issued General Order No. 3 ending slavery in the last state of the former Confederacy. The day of Texas emancipation was from that point called Juneteenth. As news of emancipation spread throughout Texas, the reactions were predictable. "Soldiers, all of a sudden, was everywhere—coming in bunches, crossing and walking and riding. Everyone was singing. We was all walking on golden clouds," recalled Felix Haywood of San Antonio. Many newly freed slaves, however, were sobered by an uncertain future. As Haywood succinctly put it, "We knowed freedom was on us, but we didn't know what to do with it . . . Freedom could make folks proud but it didn't make them rich." Yet few former slaves wished for the return of slavery. H. C. Smith spoke for many of them in 1867: "Freedom, in poverty . . . and tribulations, even amidst the most cruel prejudice, is sweeter than the best fed or the best clothed slavery in the world."

Indian Territory comprised the second-largest slaveholding region in the West. The Cherokee, Creek, Choctaw, Chickasaw, and Seminole entered the region after the Indian removal treaties of the 1830s, and they brought slaves with them. Of the five hundred Indian nations that inhabited the United States, the Five Nations were virtually the only Indians holding blacks in bondage. Moreover, only a minority in each tribe were slaveholders. Yet for this minority, which often was each tribe's political and economic elite, slavery was a profitable labor system and a proud source of identification with the planter culture of the Old South. Slavery in much of Indian Territory was a microcosm of the peculiar institution in the United States, differing only in that the owners were "red" rather than "white." However, that is not the entire story. Slaveholding varied among the five tribes. The Cherokee, with their stringent slave codes, regulations on free blacks, and laws against black–Indian intermarriage, exhibited "the strongest color prejudice of any Indians." Black slaves among the Seminole had wide latitude of action and considerable influence within tribal society.

Slavery among Native Americans predated European arrival on the North American continent. Numerous Indian people regularly enslaved other native people from opposing tribes. By the 1600s the Cherokee, Creek, and other southeastern Indians welcomed runaway black slaves because initially neither group harbored suspicions about the racial inferiority of the other. Moreover, the black newcomers brought important skills. Fugitive slaves served as interpreters and negotiators with whites; they also knew how to repair guns and traps, to shoe horses, to improve agricultural methods, to spin and weave, to make butter, and to build houses, barns, and wagons.

By the 1670s white traders had become permanent residents among the Cherokee, Creek, Choctaw, and Chickasaw. Although the traders learned the Indian languages, adopted some native customs, and took wives from among their hosts, they also created the first plantations and purchased black slaves to work them. The biracial children of the traders inherited the plantations and became the first generation of prominent mixed-blood landholders. These people were far less sympathetic to fugitives from neighboring white plantations.

By 1800 the Cherokee and Creek had established plantation agriculture and its labor system, black slavery, both of which challenged the traditional Indian values of communal property and wealth sharing. Alexander McGillivray, a Creek chief, set the pattern of large-scale landholding when he developed a plantation that by 1793 included 60 slaves and three hundred head of cattle. In 1802 a visitor to the Cherokee Nation described large plantations worked by black slaves. One early northwest Georgia plantation, Chieftains, owned by Major Ridge, a full-blooded Cherokee, had a spacious two-story eight-room house with front and back verandas and a brick fireplace at either end. His 30 slaves, acquired "to do the harder work about the premises," cultivated three hundred acres of corn, cotton, tobacco, wheat, and oats and an orchard of seventeen hundred fruit trees. By 1810 the total population of the Cherokee Nation stood at 12,395, including 583 bondspeople.

Slavery had become so fixed in Cherokee and Creek society by 1819 that various laws, remarkably similar to those of the white South, were devised to regulate black behavior and protect the institution. In 1819 the Cherokee

General Council adopted the first slave codes. These laws prohibited slaves from purchasing liquor or engaging in unsupervised trade. The council also established patrols to monitor the slave community. In 1824 the council outlawed marriage between blacks and Indians, but not between Indians and whites. Creek laws, which first appeared in 1824, were less draconian than the Cherokee statutes, but they also provided a legal foundation for slavery and discrimination. One law barred slaves from owning property while another banned marriages between blacks and Indians. Slaves could not be educated or become citizens of the nation. Censuses in 1833 for the Creek and 1835 for the Cherokee, the last enumerations taken when the majority of the tribes still resided in the East, revealed 22,694 Creek with 902 slaves and 16,542 Cherokee who possessed 1,592 black slaves. The Cherokee and Creek had chosen slaveholding as the path toward social progress.

This path, however, did not assure these native people security in their ancient lands. In 1829, according to one account, a black slave found a gold nugget in northwest Georgia, touching off the first gold rush of the nineteenth century and ultimately precipitating the events that removed the Cherokees and four other southern tribes to Indian Territory. When President Andrew Jackson refused to uphold the U.S. Supreme Court ruling in *Worcester v. Georgia*, he opened Cherokee territory to thousands of gold seekers and land speculators. The subsequent policy of relocating the Cherokee to Indian Territory eight hundred miles to the West made possible an orderly and dignified retreat.

The saga of the Trail of Tears is too well known to be recounted here. Less well known is that among the native people who emigrated were hundreds of black slaves, including 175 who perished on the journey with the Cherokee. Slaves who traveled along the Trail of Tears performed labor that reduced the suffering experienced by slaveholding Indians during the removal. They hunted game, worked as teamsters, cooks, and nurses, tended livestock on the trail, and guarded the camps at night. After arrival they cleared and fenced fields, built houses and barns, constructed docks, and planted crops. With slave labor, Indian planters cleared more acreage and made more improvements on their lands than did their impoverished kinsfolk. Seventy thousand Indians and their bond servants migrated to a vast new domain of woodland and prairie "west of Arkansas," where the newcomers overwhelmed the indigenous "wild tribes," pushing them into the western part of the territory. This rich land, protected from white intrusion by the federal government, evolved into a plantation society that, like the Old South, was politically and culturally dominated by a minority of affluent Indian landowners. Typical of this dominant group was George Lowery's family. The Lowerys left their "comfortable" estate in northwest Georgia in September 1838 with 30 slaves. Five months later the family settled eight miles south of Tahlequah, the capital of the Western Cherokee Nation,and their slaves soon had several hundred acres under cultivation. In time Lowery built a "substantial house" on the land he now called Greenleaf Plantation. Benjamin Marshall, a Creek, took his family of 8 and 19 slaves from central Georgia to Indian Territory in December 1835. Five years later Benjamin Love, a Chicasaw from Holly Springs, Mississippi, emigrated west leading a party that included 340 slaves, 95 of whom he owned.

Slaveholding Indians held a tremendous advantage in reestablishing their prosperity and wealth in the new land. Josiah Gregg, a trader who frequently crossed Indian Territory on his way to Santa Fe, remarked on the contrast between the "occasional stately dwelling, with an extensive farm attached, and the miserable hovels of the indigent, sometimes not ten feet square, with a little patch of corn, scarce[ly] large enough for a garden." Gregg also noted: "Most of the labor among the wealthier classes of Cherokees, Choctaws, Chickasaws, Creeks and Seminoles, is done by negro slaves."

Despite Gregg's comment, the Seminoles devised a different relationship with their slaves. The Indian agent Wiley Thompson reported in 1835 that a Seminole "would almost as soon sell his child as his slave. . . . The almost affection of the Indian for his slave, the slave's fear of being placed in a worse condition, and the influence which the negroes have over the Indians, have all been made to subserve the views of government." This "influence" inspired a pattern of social relations between master and servant that began in Florida and continued in Indian Territory. Black slaves lived in separate villages, often remote from their owners. They were annually required to produce for their masters predetermined amounts of Indian corn, usually about ten bushels. In return they were allowed to keep the rest of the crop along with stocks of horses, cattle, and hogs, all of which were their property. The frequent warfare along the frontier necessitated that the blacks remain armed. In this social milieu it was not surprising that two blacks, John Caesar and Abraham, became trusted advisers to Seminole chiefs. Abraham, for example, was the uncle-in-law of Principal Chief Micanopy in Florida and later in Indian Territory.

When the Seminole were finally defeated by U.S. troops in 1842, thirty-three hundred were removed to Indian Territory. They included five hundred blacks, the largest percentage (18 percent) of persons of African ancestry in any of the Five Nations. The Seminole slaves resumed in the West their pattern of autonomous living, owning livestock, and carrying weapons. Such freedom dismayed other Indian slaveholders, who feared the demeanor of Seminole blacks would encourage rebelliousness among their slaves.

The work of black slaves for other nations in Indian Territory differed little from their southern past. Blacks cleared and improved land, split rails, built fences, plowed, planted and harvested cotton, tended livestock and cultivated vegetables, rice, and corn. Female slaves cooked, operated spinning wheels, cleaned, and cared for children. Male and female slaves produced tools, cotton and woolen cloth; knitted stockings, gloves, and scarves; and tanned hides for shoes and harnesses. Since the Indians had few mechanics, blacks, slave and free, often served as the artisans and blacksmiths. The wealthier Indians had slave coachmen, butlers, and maids. Black slaves were used as saltworks operatives, ferrymen, and stevedores, who loaded and unloaded steamships and flatboats. One group of Cherokee slaves constituted the majority of the crew of Joseph Vann's steamboat *Lucy Walker*.

Indian Territory slaves developed one special skill: They were language translators. John Cowaya, a Seminole slave, spoke Spanish, English, and Seminole. He was the interpreter for several Seminole chiefs in Florida, Indian Territory, and Mexico between 1835 and 1860. An unnamed African American woman in 1832 translated for Washington Irving and Charles Latrobe when they visited the home of a Cherokee farmer. One commentator wrote of another black female interpreter for the Cherokee: "The spectacle seems strange . . . no doubt, the coal black girl speaking both English and Cherokee and keeping the old woman informed as to what was being said."

To give a "sense of the white man's meaning" suggests that many African American slaves moved comfortably between the worlds of red and white. But some African American slaves, having lived among Indian people for generations, knew no other language and culture. They adopted Indian dress, followed the Indian diet, used native medicine, carried tomahawks and club axes, and practiced Indian modes of agriculture. These blacks even celebrated Indian holidays and festivals, attended "ball plays" and "bangas" (dances), and on occasion participated in syncreatic church services. At North Fork Town (Creek Nation) in January 1842, Lieutenant Colonel Ethan Allen Hitchcock observed Creek, mixed-bloods, and blacks in prayer and psalm singing. His description of the service revealed an odd mixture: The language was Creek, the music typical of Southern Baptist or Methodist services, and the lyrics were those of an old slave spiritual. Another observer described Chickasaw slaves in 1837 as "picturesque looking Indian negroes, with dresses belonging to no country but partaking of all."

As in the Old South, many slaves resisted their Indian masters. This resistance became evident soon after Indian Removal. The most famous fugitive from Indian Territory, Henry Bibb, fled upon the death of his Cherokee owner. Bibb eventually arrived in Michigan, where he wrote *The Life and Adventures of Henry Bibb*, a popular nineteenth-century slave narrative. Other black slaves exploited both the journey west and unsettled frontier conditions to make their escapes. Some fugitives went north to Kansas Territory; others took their chances with Plains Indians. The greatest opportunities lay in the vast Indian Territory itself. Slaves of the Creek, Cherokee, Choctaw, and Chickasaw fled to the Seminole Nation, at the center of the territory. Other fugitives sought temporary refuge within their own sparsely populated nations, often joining runaway groups from neighboring Missouri, Arkansas, and Louisiana. "Our country is traversed," lamented the *Cherokee Advocate* in 1846, "by numbers of slaves who have escaped from their rightful owners, either of the Nation, or the State [s] or the Creek Country."

Slaves also rebelled against their owners. The Cherokee Nation saw three uprisings in 1841, 1842, and 1850. The 1842 "revolt" eventually included Creek and Choctaw slaves as well as Cherokee bondspeople. In November 1842 about two dozen slaves from Cherokee plantations attempted a mass escape. At a predetermined hour and on the signal of a particular song, the insurrectionists took horses, mules, several rifles, ammunition, food, and supplies and started for Mexico, spurred on by the "rumor" that there was a settlement of free blacks along the Rio Grande. Indian officials blamed the rumor on "some renegade Mexican [who claimed] that far away over the setting sun was a country where slavery did not exist and was not tolerated by law." That settlement did exist at Matamoros, but the slaves would never reach it. They headed southwest toward New Mexico, then part of the Mexican nation, pursued by forty Cherokee slave catchers.

When the fugitives entered the Creek country, other slaves joined them, bringing the total number to thirty-five. Creek slave catchers, meanwhile, joined the Cherokee pursuers and caught the fleeing party just south of the Canadian River. The blacks fought off their pursuers although two were killed and twelve captured. Driven off, the Creek and Cherokee pursuing parties returned for reinforcements. Fifteen miles beyond the battle site the fugitives encountered Choctaw slave traders with eight recently captured runaways, including five children. They killed the slave catchers and brought the Choctaw runaways into their group. Recognizing the potential for general unrest, the Cherokee Council dispatched a force of one hundred men to capture the slaves and return them to the Cherokee Nation. On November 26 the Cherokee militia overtook the slaves on the plains three hundred miles from their former plantations and seven miles north of the Red River. Two fugitives escaped, but the remaining thirty-one surrendered to the Cherokee militia.

On the eve of the Civil War Indian people held 7,367 black slaves. African slavery was firmly established among these nonwhite peoples. In contrast with Texas, however, their liberation came quickly in the war. Three Indian nations, the Cherokee, Creek, and Seminole, sent soldiers to fight for both the Union and the Confederacy, engulfing the territory in the national conflict while pitting Indian against Indian in an intratribal warfare that historian Alvin Josephy called the "little civil war." By the fall of 1861 two Confederate Cherokee Indian regiments were created, one commanded by Stand Watie and the other under John Drew. Before the end of the year Drew and most of his regiment, nearly a thousand men, joined the Union forces, which accepted "all persons, without reference to color . . . willing to fight for the American flag . . . and the Federal Government." The Indian "Federals" in fact attracted nearly one thousand fugitive slaves, primarily from the various nations but also from neighboring Confederate states. Indian Territory freedman Chaney McNair remembered Union troops gathering up "four or five hundred" slaves in the territory to take to Kansas. When the group arrived, "most all the negro men folks joined the Northern Army and the women were put to work in the fields." Fugitives from the territory joined the First Kansas Colored Infantry and fought against their former masters at Honey Springs and Cabin Creek. Meanwhile loyal Cherokee met on February 21, 1863, to issue an emancipation proclamation, making them the only tribe to end slavery before 1865.

The horrific impact of the war on Indian Territory, where proportionately more lives were lost and more refugees created than in any Union or Confederate state, ironically accounted for more slaves gaining their freedom than the Cherokee proclamation. Several hundred African Americans fled north with loyal Indians, such as the Creek chief Opothlayahola, who led three thousand Union supporters to safety in Kansas in 1861 after fending off numerous attempts by white and Indian Confederate soldiers to capture the refugee party. Far more slaves escaped from pro-Confederate Indians en route to Texas or the southern part of the Choctaw and Chickasaw nations to protect their property. Other slaves fled owner-abandoned farms and plantations for nearby woods and hills until Confederate forces rounded them up and transferred them to Fort Gibson. As the war continued, these refugees "piled in[to Fort Gibson] from everywhere" according to freedwoman Rochelle Ward. Living conditions deteriorated rapidly, and by 1863 blacks were "cooking in the open, sleeping most anywhere, making shelter . . . out of cloth scraps and brush, digging caves along the river bank to live in." When Union officials occupied the fort in 1863, they found five hundred black refugees. Unable to persuade the blacks to leave the area for Kansas and bound by the Emancipation Proclamation to free them, the U.S. Army provided supplies for the remainder of the war. Given the chaotic conditions in the Indian nations, few blacks remained in bondage when the fighting ended in 1865.

Discussion Questions

1. What is Taylor's central thesis, and where do you find it in this piece? How does he organize and support his argument? Map out his strategy and organization on paper.

2. Discuss the varieties of experiences black slaves had in the different tribes of the Five Nations. What points does Taylor make about the treatment of slaves in the Seminole tribe compared to the Cherokee tribe, for example?

3. Discuss in groups how Cherokee slaveholding evolved, and to what extent white society and early Indian societies were similar in their patterns of slaveholding.

Writing Suggestions

1. Review your responses to the first discussion question, and then write an analysis of Taylor's argument and style. Analyze his thesis, topic sentences, and organization. How does he sustain his argument while giving a wealth of information? How does he achieve unity in this piece? How does he link different portions of his writing together? How does he begin and end his chapter? Include your response to his writing—did you find it effective or not?

2. Some African American spokespersons today are calling for financial reparations for black enslavement. At the same time, Native Americans are also calling for restitution of lands and property taken by the U.S. government during the Indian Wars. Write a personal essay in which you address the concerns of both of these groups. Argue for what you think should or should not be done to compensate these two groups, and consider the complicated issue of whether or not Native Americans should compensate blacks, too, since some Indian tribes held slaves.

3. Research the use of black slaves by Cherokee Indians in the nineteenth century. Write a five-page research paper answering some of the following questions:

    How were the slaves treated?

    What kinds of rules and laws did the Cherokee formulate for treatment of slaves?

    What kinds of similarities and differences do you find in the Indian slaveholders' and white slaveholders' treatment of black slaves?

The Treaty of Guadalupe Hidalgo

Articles VIII, IX, XI, XII

The Treaty of Guadalupe Hidalgo, ratified in 1848, was the document that officially marked the end of the Mexican–American War. Although it promised to safeguard the rights of Mexicans living in the disputed areas of Texas, California, and other southwestern states, Congress never passed the key articles that would have protected the civil and religious rights of Mexican nationals. The selection below shows not only the treaty that Congress did pass, but also the version of Article IX that was modified by Congress.

Article VIII

Mexicans now established in territories previously belonging to Mexico, and which remain for the future within the limits of the United States, as defined by the present treaty, shall be free to continue where they now reside, or to remove at any time to the Mexican Republic, retaining the property which they possess in the said territories, or disposing thereof, and removing the proceeds wherever they please, without their being subjected, on this account, to any contribution, tax or charge whatever.

Those who shall prefer to remain in the said territories, may either retain the title and rights of Mexican citizens, or acquire those of citizens of the United States. But they shall be under the obligation to make their election within one year from the date of the exchange of ratifications of this treaty; and those who shall remain in the said territories, after the expiration of that year, without having declared their intention to retain the character of Mexicans, shall be considered to have elected to become citizens of the United States.

In the said territories, property of every kind, now belonging to Mexicans, not established there, shall be inviolably respected. The present owners, the heirs of these and all Mexicans who may hereafter acquire said property by contract, shall enjoy with respect to it, guarantees equally ample as if the same belonged to citizens of the United States.

Article IX

The Mexicans who, in the territories aforesaid, shall not preserve the character of citizens of the Mexican Republic, conformably with what is stipulated in the preceding article, shall be incorporated into the Union of the United States and be admitted, at the proper time (to be judged of by the Congress of the United States) to the enjoyment of all the rights of citizens of the United States according to the principles of the Constitution; and in the mean time shall be maintained and protected in the free enjoyment of their liberty and property, and secured in the free exercise of their religion without restriction.

[*One of the amendments of the Senate struck out Article 10.*]

Article XI

Considering that a great part of the territories which, by the present Treaty, are to be comprehended for the future within the limits of the United States, is now occupied by savage tribes, who will hereafter be under the exclusive control of the Government of the United States, and whose incursions within the territory of Mexico would be prejudicial in the extreme; it is solemnly agreed that all such incursions shall be forcibly restrained by the Government of the United States, whensoever this may be necessary; and that when they cannot be prevented, they shall be punished by the said Government, and satisfaction for the same shall be exacted; all in the same way, and with equal diligence and energy; as if the same incursions were meditated or committed within its own territory against its own citizens.

It shall not be lawful, under any pretext whatever, for any inhabitant of the United States, to purchase or acquire any Mexican or any foreigner residing in Mexico, who may have been captured by Indians inhabiting the territory of either of the two Republics, nor to purchase or acquire horses, mules, cattle or property of any kind, stolen within Mexican territory by such Indians.

And, in the event of any person or persons, captured within Mexican Territory by Indians, being carried into the territory of the United States, the Government of the latter engages and binds itself in the most solemn manner, so soon as it shall know such captives being within its territory, and shall be able so to do, through the faithful exercise of its influence and power, to rescue them and return them to their country, or deliver them to the agent or representative of the Mexican Government. The Mexican Authorities will, as far as practicable, give to the Government of the United States notice of such captures; and its agent shall pay the expenses incurred in the maintenance and transmission of the rescued captives; who, in the mean time, shall be treated with the utmost hospitality by the American authorities at the place where they may be. But if the Government of the United States, before receiving such notice from Mexico, should obtain intelligence through any other channel, of the existence of Mexican captives within its territory, it will proceed forthwith to effect their release and delivery to the Mexican agent, as above stipulated.

For the purpose of giving to these stipulations the fullest possible efficacy, thereby affording the security and redress demanded by their true spirit and intent, the Government of the United States will now and hereafter pass, without unnecessary delay, and always vigilantly enforce, such laws as the nature of the subject may require. And finally, the sacredness of this obligation shall never be lost sight of by the said Government, when providing for the removal of the Indians from any portion of the said territories, or for its being settled by citizens of the United States; but on the contrary special care shall then be taken not to place its Indian occupants under the necessity of seeking new homes, by committing those invasions which the United States have solemnly obliged themselves to restrain.

Article XII

In consideration of the extension acquired by the boundaries of the United States, as defined in the fifth Article of the present treaty, the Government of the United States engages to pay to that of the Mexican Republic the sum of fifteen Millions of Dollars.

Immediately after this treaty shall have been duly ratified by the Government of the Mexican Republic, the sum of three millions of dollars shall be paid to the said Government by that of the United States at the city of Mexico, in the gold or silver coin of Mexico. The remaining twelve millions of dollars shall be paid at the same place and in the same coin, in annual instalments of three millions of dollars each, together with interest on the same at the rate of six per centum per annum. This interest shall begin to run upon the whole sum of twelve millions, from the day of the ratification of the present treaty by the Mexican Government, and the first of the instalments shall be paid at the expiration of one year from the same day. Together with each annual instalment, as it falls due, the whole interest accruing on such instalment from the beginning shall also be paid.

Article IX Before Senate Amendment

Article IX

The Mexicans who, in the territories aforesaid, shall not preserve the character of citizens of the Mexican Republic, conformably with what is stipulated in the preceding Article, shall be incorporated into the Union of the United States, and admitted as soon as possible, according to the principles of the Federal Constitution, to the enjoyment of all the rights of citizens of the United States. In the mean time, they shall be maintained and protected in the enjoyment of their liberty, their property, and the civil rights now vested in them according to the Mexican laws. With respect to political rights, their condition shall be on an equality with that of the inhabitants of the other territories of the United States and at least equally good as that of the inhabitants of Louisiana and the Floridas, when these provinces, by transfer from the French Republic and the Crown of Spain, became territories of the United States.

The same most ample guaranty shall be enjoyed by all ecclesiastics and religious corporations or communities, as well in the discharge of the offices of their ministry, as in the enjoyment of their property of every kind, whether individual or corporate. This guaranty shall embrace all temples, houses and edifices dedicated to the Roman Catholic worship; as well as all property destined to its support, or to that of schools, hospitals and other foundations for charitable or beneficent purposes. No property of this nature shall be considered as having become the property of the American Government, or as subject to be, by it, disposed of or diverted to other uses.

Finally, the relations and communication between the Catholics living in the territories aforesaid, and their respective ecclesiastical authorities shall be open, free and exempt from all hindrance whatever, even although such authorities should reside within the limits of the Mexican Republic, as defined by this treaty; and this freedom shall continue, so long as a new demarcation of ecclesiastical districts shall not have been made, conformably with the laws of the Roman Catholic Church.

Discussion Questions

1. Article XI of the treaty is devoted to describing what will happen to the Indians still living in the newly ceded areas. Politically, how would Article XI help the United States to convince the Mexicans to sign the treaty? What kind of protections does the U.S. government offer Mexicans?
2. What does the original Article IX state about Mexicans' right to become U.S. citizens? How did Congress change these rights by changing the wording in the revised Article IX?

Writing Suggestions

1. Look carefully at the language in Article XI. Can you restate the meaning in plain words? Rewrite this part of the treaty in plain language, and then write a brief essay about the diction used in the treaty and the effect of this word choice on readers. Why do you think the government used the language it did for this treaty? How might the wording benefit the writers?
2. Find the text of a current U.S. treaty with another country by searching this Web site: <http://fedlaw.gsa.gov/legal20.htm>. Then, analyze the wording of the treaty for clarity or ambiguity, noting diction, organization, and use of abstract versus concrete words. Write an essay discussing the treaty, answering some of the following questions:

   What motivations lie behind the wording of the treaty?
   Does the treaty seem clear, or does it seem wordy and ambiguous?
   Can you understand the treaty, and do you think others will understand it?
   What parts of the treaty are open to interpretation? How could this interpretation affect the results of the treaty?

Black Pioneers

Images of Black Experience
on the North American Frontier

JOHN W. RAVAGE

John W. Ravage taught at the University of Wyoming in the Communications Department and is the author of *Black Pioneers: Images of Black Experience on the North American Frontier*. In the following excerpts from *Black Pioneers*, Ravage offers us a new look at the variety of roles played by black men and women on the western frontier.

Introduction: Moving Westward and Northward

The institution of slavery in America—while not unusual in human history—was nonetheless unique in the way it was practiced in the seventeenth through the nineteenth centuries. To begin with, never before had such large numbers of people been ripped from their homelands and transported over vast distances for delivery to a destination so alien to and so far removed from their origins. Neither had any other group been enslaved with such exclusivity to their masters with no hope of release. Even the ancient Greeks and Romans granted education and freedom as eventual rewards to their slaves.

In the American colonies and, later, the slave states and in eighteenth-century Canada, there was virtually no legal escape from bondage. In time, these enslaved people lost much of their individual national identity not only through systematic exclusion from their owners' society but also through permanent subjugation through the force of law.

The system, however, did not last forever. For various complex political, religious, and social reasons, institutionalized—and governmentally approved—slavery in the United States came to an end in the middle of the nineteenth century; in Canada it occurred somewhat earlier. In both countries, black citizens were given the same choices open to all free men and women to pursue their own goals in whatever ways they could. Although racial prejudice did not come to an end with Abraham Lincoln's signature on the Emancipation Proclamation or the Canadian laws outlawing slavery in the early 1800s, many of the previously existing barriers erected to stem the progress of ex-slaves were reduced if not removed entirely.

As a result, many individuals of African and West Indian descent chose to remain in the South out of familiarity or a sense of obligation, if nothing else. Oddly, some had apparently chosen to fight for the Confederacy and, by doing so, paid allegiance to the soil that they came to call their own.* Others took fate by the coattails and moved to the more industrialized North in search of better-paying jobs. A few decided to relocate to the border states, where slower life-styles blended with governments that were more accepting than the deep South. The Underground Railroad served to spirit thousands from the middle and deep South across the border into southern and western Canada and other compass points less well known.

Fewer still were pulled into the western migration that was sweeping the country at the time. Much was going on in the Old West of both the States and Canada that stretched from Kansas to California and from Alberta to New Mexico: gold in California, British Columbia, and the Yukon; cattle in Texas and the Indian territories; railroad construction by Union Pacific, Northern Pacific, Canadian Pacific, and Burlington Northern across the Great Plains; the Indian wars; bands of raiders left after the end of the Civil War. There were mountains and passes waiting to be explored and conquered by men and women courageous or foolhardy enough to try. At sea, there were fisheries in the Sandwich Islands and northern Pacific and Atlantic Oceans. Opportunities for those with able bodies and minds seemed to abound, and thousands of former slaves decided to try for their shares of the American dream.

Essentially, the migratory patterns of African Americans from the Old South followed the railways that were gradually connecting heretofore isolated areas; many railways followed original American Indians' trails. Some of the earliest job opportunities available to these new emigrants were on the trains as porters, butchers, waiters, cooks, service personnel, loaders, and baggage clerks—about any job except those already taken by the European immigrants who had arrived earlier and had the "front end" occupations of engineers, firemen, and station clerks.

Ultimately, the job of conductor became almost the sole domain of a black man if he stayed at it long enough. Still, there were other jobs to be had and men and women willing to take them, whatever they were.

Many of these job hunters stopped and stayed along the train routes, creating niches in the growing economics of the small towns that sprang up to meet the demands of the railroads. By 1900, for instance, the overwhelming majority of barbers in the country were African American—a fact often overlooked by historians and authors in general.

---

*Researchers into the history of African Americans who are U.S. citizens eventually stumble across vague references to black men who fought on the side of the Confederacy. Although assiduous scholars have searched diligently for the evidence, not one has found a "mustering out" list of any "Negro" soldiers from southern regiments. Still, the stories persist. The stories most likely grew out of the action of the Virginia legislature in 1865, which tried to establish two black state units. The Civil War ended prior to the enactment of the bill. If, however, records of these soldiers were to be found, it would be solid evidence of how deeply the system of slavery became ingrained in those on both sides of the practice—creating some previously enslaved individuals so accommodated to the system that they thought it worthy of defense. Maybe no one will ever know the truth.

The way west for these newly relocated citizens was inextricably mixed with the movement of others also searching for personal success and unique challenges. Immigrant Irish, Chinese, English, Scottish, Scandinavian, German, and Russian workers were just beginning an influx that would peak within fifty years. Also in the mix were French Canadians who could trace their fur-trapping ancestors back into the 1700s.

As opportunities for employment began to stratify, entrepreneurs and hustlers dominated the economic life of the new cities and towns; unskilled laborers were forced to gravitate toward labor-intensive positions like working cattle or heavy industrial jobs; women were less likely to find employment as a result of social stereotyping, and they were primarily untrained workers to begin with. Blacks, Chinese, Japanese, Indians, and individuals of "mixed blood" were at the bottom of the job ladder, having to take whatever was left over.

Or so it seemed to historians of the early twentieth century as they looked back on those times. As with all such generalizations, there were many and varied exceptions—for example, the actual roles played by African Americans. Late in the twentieth century, we are only beginning to realize the full range of activities in which the pioneers of the vast two-thirds of our continent engaged. Heretofore, prejudices, myopia, cultural insensitivity, invalid surveys—call them what you will—have dominated much of the examination of this period of American history. We have often seen what we wanted to see rather than what was there. The popular media of the time—as well as a pervasive longing for a sense of identity—compounded the problem by producing stories about heroes who either never existed or were dramatically modified to appeal to the sentiments of mainly white readers of newspapers, buyers of pennydreadfuls, motion picture audiences, and—much later—television viewers.

As perspectives became distorted, it was nearly impossible to separate fact from fiction. Minorities became less and less important in history texts, popular entertainments, and casual conversations. Nonwhites ceased to exist, essentially, in these aspects of our nation's history. Slavery, to book and pennydreadful readers (and television and film viewers of the twentieth century), became little more than a dramatic device—a piece of theater that white readers barely could imagine let alone experience.

In all fairness, this erasure of nonanglos from our background as a nation was probably not done solely through malevolence; it may not have been simple oversight either. Rather, it seems that much of the history of this continent involved "superior" invading forces from foreign cultures taking life and property from those who were already living here. In order to avoid a depressing self-concept, the dominant, white society has systematically sought to justify these acts of aggression. After all, it does not fit well with the "American ideal" to think that theft, rape, and—at times—wanton destruction were the principal means by which we grew and prospered as a nation. There must be—the explanation goes—a better rationale behind all of this evil-doing to justify the success of our social, technological, and economic experiment.

This self-defensive attitude of Manifest Destiny has a calming effect for many. For example, it encourages the acceptance of the inevitability of one society's domination by another as "growth" or "natural law." This rationale is far more pleasing to some than the alternatives: that one group was merely stronger, more technically advanced, or richer than those it came to dominate.

So, by design or omission, plan or default, our cultural heritage has been rewritten to conform to what we think is true rather than to what actually happened. It is not the first time (nor the first society) in which words have been used in an attempt to alter facts, but the result has been a particularly effective restructuring of facts.

In actuality, African Americans played the same roles in the development of western North America as did other ethnic groups. They fought and died, raised children, killed and were killed, smuggled, lied, whored; they were God-loving and God-fearing, lawmen and outlaws, mountaineers and townspeople; millionaires and paupers; they built cities and towns and destroyed them, too; they danced, cried, fought Indians, protected travelers, and so forth.

"Colored" men and women were assigned, in the spirit of the times, to relatively insignificant places in society, since their numbers made it impossible for them to be ignored totally. Menial occupations became jobs they could hold without offending the more numerous nonblacks who populated cities and towns. In this environment, human individuality mutated into stereotypic "facts," as servants, laborers, dissemblers, and shufflers were invariably interpreted in novels, textbooks, stories, and films of African descendants. "It's in their blood," the saying went.

In fact, former slaves and their progeny were spending their days and nights much the same as their fair-skinned compatriots of the time. For every white con man, there was a black one; for every asian laundryman, there was a black one—or a white one, for that matter. Life was as complex for people then as it is now, and those who experienced it were just as hard-pressed to exist and grow as are many today.

"The West"

We, who profess to be Christians, and boast of the peculiar advantages we enjoy by means of an express revelation of our duty from heaven, are in effect these very untaught and heathen countries. With all our superior light, we instill into those, whom we call savage and barbarous, the most despicable opinion of human nature. We, to the utmost of our power, weaken and dissolve the universal tie, that binds and unites mankind. . . . Good God! may the time come when thou shalt stretch out thy strong arm, and say to his mighty deluge, which is sweeping myriads and myriads to enthraldom and a degraded servitude, who are entitled to equal rights and privileges with ourselves, hitherto shalt thou come, and no further, and here shall thou proud waves be stayed!

—Ogden, 1905

North America was, in many ways, segmented in its attractiveness to emigrants, especially those recently freed from slavery. The trans-Mississippi West became a lure to some who sought to leave the Old South and find success and prosperity, and their presence in northern and eastern parts of the United States and Canada dates from the seventeenth and eighteenth centuries. Farms and plantations of the South and the domestic quarters of French Canada ("New France") became the main residences of former slaves, and their presence was part of the social and political realities over more than two centuries.

Riding along on the migratory routes were the stereotypes and myths that seem to accompany all newcomers into areas populated with large numbers of earlier settlers. If the South had myths based on appearance, religion, skin color, and educational levels, so did the West.

In colonial times, for example, areas west of New York and Philadelphia were "terra incognita," and Canada was a haven for traitors, rascals, Royalists, and runaways, as far as many residents of the States were concerned.

By the nineteenth century, Ohio, Indiana, and Tennessee were the outermost reaches of U.S. expansion. By mid-century, large-scale migration west and north, across the Great Plains, had changed the lines once again.

The trans-Mississippi West became a relatively concise designation for "the West" when the U.S. military fort system began in earnest with the construction of Fort Atkinson to protect river traffic on the Missouri in 1819. Consistent with the military's mission to protect travelers, barges, and small communities, the fort system was expanded when Congress authorized construction of railroads across the Plains. Fort Laramie and Fort Hall, plus other installations in the Southwest, were established to control the American Indians who were resisting incursions into and through their historical lands. Additionally, these outposts protected wagon trains heading toward the west coast as well as an enlarged web of railroads that would serve the growing cattle empires of the West and Southwest.

Eventually, U.S. forts and the military would become centers for new communities when some travelers tarried and a few enlisted mens' families did not return to their homes back East.

As a result, the West as a concept came to typify the last frontier of the United States' part of the continent. In the process, it became not only a place but also a mystic, marvelous, mythological part of the American psyche, which was celebrated in song, dance, story, and film. It became a cultural identifier uniquely dissimilar to the urbanity of New York City, the industrial dynamism of Chicago, or the agricultural fiefdoms of pre–Civil War Georgia.

The West became a unique, if generalized, part of this continent's history and culture. It became the place from which, according to observers like historian Frederick Jackson Turner, we sprang as a nation: a strong, open, wonder-filled place that permeates our modern life and stimulates our self-concepts, industry, and even religions. In our popular mythology, it was populated with characters of strength, durability, and purpose—and they were almost all white.

It wasn't like that at all—hence, the reason for this book. Instead of settling for "myth," we need to know the facts of our past. Reality, truth, and historical perspective are more important and revealing than fiction—no matter how dramatically structured—in helping us assess the past, and they may help us to understand who we are, where we came from, and—most important—where we are going.

The Western Period

The West, at bottom, is a form of society, rather than an area. It is the term applied to the region whose social conditions result from the application of older institutions and ideas to the transforming influences of free land.

(From Turner 1929:278)

What is "the West," anyway? Tangled up in our cultural myths about pioneers, wagon trains, Indian skirmishes, cavalry outposts, land-grabbers, gold rushes, vast spaces, gunfighters, and bad men (and women) are the realities of life in those times and places.

James Beckworth

Not many black men rose to the level of "legendary" in the American West, but Dark Sky (James Beckworth's Sac Indian name) was an exception. In fact, Beckworth's life was exceptional in so many ways as to truly earn the appellation "heroic."

A freed slave and the son of a white, transplanted St. Louis blacksmith, "Sir Jennings Beckwoth" (note the variant spelling) spent his first years in the fur-trading era of the early 1800s watching and listening to the tall tales of those mainly French-Canadian explorers who came down the Missouri and Mississippi Rivers for trade, recreation, and human contact. In 1824 he asked his father* what he should do with his life, and was told to follow his yearnings. Later that year he signed on with William H. Ashley's expedition out of St. Louis as a wrangler and body servant. It was only a short association since, within a year, he was an independent trapper buying "mounts" (an old term for furs) from the Pawnees. His lot was cast forever.

Beckworth ventured westward in search of the mountains, sharing the vast areas of the Great Plains and Northwest with white mountain men like Jim Bridger, Kit Carson, and Jedidiah Smith. He also roamed throughout the Southwest, the Cascades, and the Dacotah Territory fighting Indians, Mexicans, and the weather. He was not the only African American to take up this solitary trade: Edward Rose and Dred Scott—whose slavery indenture was upheld by the U.S. Supreme Court in later years—also sought their fortunes in the high mountains.

---

*James Beckworth's slave master was also his father. The resulting light skin was possibly one reason he was readily accepted into the business of trading.

Beckworth's achievements in the wilds of the West culminated in his becoming "chief of chiefs" of the Crow Indian nation in 1834 for seven years—an almost unheard of honor for any non-Indian. He married "Sue," a Santee woman; "discovered" the pass in northern California/Nevada that bears his name; and pioneered the Oregon Trail through Crow country. In later years, he opened a bar and other businesses in a small village on Cherry Creek that would become Denver, Colorado.

His exploits are recorded in his autobiography, which blends factual stories of his adventures with the garrulous and often outrageous tales that mountain men perfected into an art form.

Cowhands and Ranch Hands

No one knows when the first black man took up a lariat or applied for a piece of land to call his own under the open reaches of the sky west of the Mississippi River. One thing is certain, however, it was earlier than most think. Edmund Flagg, writing in 1838 of his earlier trip of two years to the Far West, witnessed masters unloading barges of black slaves on the banks of the Missouri River in preparation for their journey to distant quarters of the Rocky Mountains and Plains territories.

Exact numbers are hard to derive, but it is safe to say that thousands of black men rode the trails of the American West from the mid-1800s through the early part of the twentieth century. If the thousands of military men, "exoduster" farmers, and other emigrants from the historic South are included in the count, there were, clearly, tens of thousands of African American men, women, and children in the West during the "cattle kingdom" years from 1860 to 1910—and this number does not take into consideration the people who moved northward into Canada.

Today, African American cowboys are portrayed in motion pictures, television programs, and magazine articles, but how the early historians could have missed the existence of this many people remains an intriguing mystery, as does the omission of black exploits in the stories and songs of the day.

Another misconception about African American cowhands is that they were all menial laborers. In fact, many were competent and skilled workers, certainly more experienced than the young men (usually teenagers) who worked under them. Coming, as many of these men did, from southern farms and plantations, they were especially skilled in training and vetting horses. When herding cattle, black cowhands often "rode point," which was a position of honor since the rider would be ahead of the dust clouds stirred up by the cattle.

Although often interpreted as a menial position, cooks were an important component of life on the range. They faced hungry and demanding cowboys daily. Cowboying was a tough and boring grind for the young men riding herd; and, with towns and settlements often tens of miles distant from the trail, they could become unruly and difficult to control. Consequently, cooks had to prepare a variety of appetizing meals as well as find ways of distracting youthful goings-on that could range from baking fresh fruit pies (a challenge since dry larders were the main source of "fresh" food) to making treats of candy and sweet drinks.

Cooks were employed for their combined skills in food storage and preparation, a knowledge of sources of comestibles on the trail, and a general ability to control their rambunctious young comrades. Nearly every ranch of any size knows of multitalented black cooks who worked there—often for decades. Their contributions are a part of the historical record in virtually every place where cattle was king and the cowboy was knight-errant.

Another accomplishment of the African American cowboy was his musical talents. Cooks, especially, were often accomplished players of fiddles, harmonicas, and guitars. Most noteworthy cow-country musicians were black cowboys—contrary to the images of singing cowboys fostered in western films of the 1930s and 1940s. The popularized, legendary singing cowboy* was most likely a derivation of former slaves, now cowboys, who had brought with them the southern practice of using the musical sounds of a human voice to calm nervous cattle.

Women of the West

If the roles for black men were affected by the racism and prejudice of others, those for black women were even more affected. Given the societal restrictions placed upon women in general in the nineteenth century, it is truly surprising to find women who stood out in the crowd with their accomplishments. Although some chose a life-style that might be deemed less than salutary in nature—this was the West, after all—there were those who, through their success and determination, became the inspiration for other black women.

Some Positive Experiences

The number of documented ex-slave women who came west is small since most were the wives and daughters of men whose names—if recorded at all—were forgotten over time. Mary Fields, however, was a noteworthy exception.

A native of Tennessee (born a slave circa 1832), Mary Fields moved to Montana in the company of Ursuline nuns after escaping slavery. Because she left the care of the nuns when she was a teenager, her life in not recorded in great detail. What is known, however, ranks her among the most interesting, individualistic, and determined women of the era.

---

*In motion pictures of the 1930s and 1940s, actor-singers Gene Autry and Roy Rogers were the most well-known. Herb Jefferies, a black singer and producer of movies with black casts, preserved the historical origins of those men who sang to cattle to quiet them.

Six feet tall and weighing two hundred pounds, with a girth to match, she brooked little challenge in her various jobs. Barkeeper, mail carrier,* brawler, whorehouse owner, and a cigar-smoking, Wells Fargo shotgun rider in Montana and northern Wyoming (maybe even swinging north into Canada on occasion), she was a composite of personality traits necessary for survival in those days and places. Her high spirits and tough life-style cast her as a truly unforgettable character of the American West.

If one state has remained in people's imagination as symbolic of the Rocky Mountain West, it is surely Colorado. Prospering and growing with the gold and silver booms of the mid-nineteenth century, Colorado saw a wild mélange of railroaders, mountain men, cowboys, whores, ranchers, miners, hoteliers, lawmakers, soldiers, guides, hunters, entrepreneurs, philanthropists, teachers, newspaper editors, ministers, and more. And all these were black.

Among those who dedicated their lives to the betterment of others, in ways most people would find difficult to emulate, was "Aunt" Clara Brown.

Born a slave in Spotsylvania County, Virginia, in 1806, she was sold as a three-year-old to a Mr. Brown from Logan, Kentucky. Although the history is cloudy, she found her way to Kansas Territory as an "exoduster" in the great out-migration of black southerners during the late 1850s, apparently heading west with those caught up in the Rocky Mountain gold rush. Noted for her kindness and gentle nature, she was often referred to as "the angel of the Rockies" during her travel toward what is now Colorado.

Central City, the destination of her wagon train, was a rough-and-tumble boomtown in the Rockies. As a town it was a more suitable place for rugged miners and their ways of life than for a fortyish black woman who wanted to found an African Methodist Episcopal church, be active in Sunday school programs, and acquire property.

A frugal woman who kept her own counsel, she began to acquire inexpensive land around Central City as well as around the cattle and Indian town of Denver, consisting at the time of little more than canvas-covered buildings and tepees around Cherry Creek.

She frequently grubstaked miners who had no other means of support while they looked for gold in the mountains west of Denver, and was repaid handsomely for her kindness and generosity by those who struck pay dirt. She used any profits to continue her philanthropy among the needy and to increase her landholdings.

Nature and Lady Luck were not kind to Clara Brown. In one of the periodic great floods that sweep down out of the foothills west of Denver, the records of her landholdings were washed away. She could not prove ownership and subsequently lost title to much of her property. In addition, there

---

*One of the more common occupations of early black settlers in the West was that of postmaster. Apparently, this was not a job coveted by resident whites, probably due to its long hours and low pay. Many areas of the West, however, could boast of the black men and women who opened post offices in far-flung settlements.

were dishonest business rivals who found her vulnerable to their unscrupulous deals; especially when her property records were lost. Eventually, she had nothing left but her kind and charitable ways, but no one whom she had helped at one time or another let her suffer the privations of hunger or lack of love.

Whether rich or poor, landholder or not, "Aunt" Clara Brown became one of the true legends of the Rocky Mountains in the past century.

Mary Ellen Pleasant, an early pioneering woman, was better known as "Mammy Pleas." She resented the appellation, considering it an overly familiar form of address. Called an "angel of the West" by many for her work with troubled and abused women, men, and children, she was a mercurial businesswomen known far more widely than in her home base of San Francisco in the late 1800s.

A self-proclaimed capitalist, she was partners with Thomas Bell, cofounder of the first Bank of California. As a businesswoman, Mary Ellen was most likely cunning, cynical, and calculating, but she was also soft-hearted by nature in helping many individuals in need of financial or personal support. An intriguing rumor: she may have murdered Thomas Bell and plotted to kill his foster son.

Her statement, "I am a theater in myself," was a self-admission of having a complex character. She used large sums of money (how and where obtained is uncertain) to aid fugitive slaves and freedmen. She fed them, found occupations for them, and financially backed them in numerous small businesses. She was also a leader in the protection of abused women, building and supporting safe havens for them in California.

Whatever her true motivations, Mary Ellen Pleasant carved herself an indelible niche in western American history.

Some Adverse Experiences

Traditionally, the criminal stereotype is a male. Throughout history, the majority of incarcerated individuals in North America—and the world in all probability—have been men. However, there have been black women who were apprehended and sentenced to prison.

Eliza Stewart was sentenced in 1899 to the territorial prison at Laramie, Wyoming, for shooting at her paramour—and missing. A large woman, recorded in prison documents as "weighing over 200 pounds," Eliza served time in the equivalent of a federal penitentiary for an assault for which few, if any, white women were ever charged. She served one year, nine months, and was released.

Caroline Hayes was sentenced a second time to the penitentiary for one year, nine months for an unspecified crime. Oddly, a mere two weeks after her release, she was again arrested for stealing two fifty-cent blankets from a local store. This time she was incarcerated in the local jail and then sent home to Cheyenne, Wyoming.

The issue, of course, was not that these crimes were particularly heinous or a major threat to public safety. Some women were put in jail for stealing bread or small articles of clothing. Clearly, their crime was that of "stepping out of bounds," by not heeding social expectations of standards of behavior set by the white majority for both black men and women.

Few women—regardless of skin color—served full terms in these prisons. Most were released after a few months because of ill health, for good behavior, or for being pregnant.*

Discussion Questions

1. How does Ravage claim that common misconceptions about the roles of minorities in the American West came about? What different kinds of publications contributed to these misconceptions? What kinds of evidence does Ravage offer for his assertions?

2. Ravage writes that "Today, African American cowboys are portrayed in motion pictures, television programs, and magazine articles," but that early historians failed to record the importance of the black cowboys. Do you agree or disagree with this statement that African American cowboys are currently portrayed in the media? In groups, discuss various examples of African American cowboys you have seen in movies, magazines, or television programs.

Writing Suggestions

1. Write an essay in which you analyze Ravage's statement that "Today, African American cowboys are portrayed in motion pictures, television programs, and magazine articles." Building on your responses to the second discussion question, browse through some current and recent back issues of magazines in your library that cover subjects such as ranching, the West, American history, or American culture. Alternatively, browse the Internet to see what kinds of sites you can find about African American cowboys. Then describe the information you found, explaining how African American cowboys are portrayed today in the media and on the Internet.

---

*How a woman could become pregnant while in a territorial prison, completely isolated from wardens, guards, and other prisoners is a reasonable question. Unless they were pregnant prior to being imprisoned, the answer is obvious: they weren't that isolated. Whatever the stated reasons may have been, officials were apparently eager to release their female charges as soon as possible.

2. In arguing that "African Americans played the same roles in the development of western North America as did other ethnic groups," Ravage states that "our cultural heritage has been rewritten to conform to what we think is true rather than to what actually happened." Ravage goes on to explain the many roles that African American men and women played in the development of the West that have not appeared in most traditional histories of the United States.

    For this assignment, first go to your college library and research any available material on black pioneers. Look at both older and more recent historical analyses—you may need to look at books on the West in general if you cannot find any books specifically about blacks in the West. Then write an essay in which you respond to Ravage's assessment of the lack of written history of black pioneers.

    What kinds of materials did you find? Did you find materials on black women pioneers? Did you find a difference in older texts and more recent texts? Did you have trouble finding any information on black pioneers? Write up your results, comparing them directly to the information Ravage offers about the variety of roles played by black men and women in the West. Conclude by agreeing or disagreeing with Ravage's claims about written history and black pioneers.

The Gathering of Zion

The Story of the Mormon Trail

WALLACE STEGNER

Wallace Stegner (1909–1993) wrote many short stories, novels, and nonfiction works, many of them dealing with Western history and the Mormons in the West, including *Mormon Country* and *Beyond the Hundredth Meridian*. He won a National Book Award for *The Spectator Bird* in 1976 and a Pulitzer Prize for *Angle of Repose* in 1971. He was also director of Stanford University's Creative Writing Program. Stegner was born in Iowa, but spent much of his youth in Utah and later lived in California for many years. In the selection below, from his introduction to *The Gathering of Zion: The Story of the Mormon Trail* (1964), Stegner explains the importance of the Mormons to the opening and development of the West.

Introduction: The Way to the Kingdom

Close to the heart of Mormondom, as close as the beehive symbol of labor and cohesiveness that decorates the great seal of Utah, is the stylized memory of the trail. For every early Saint, crossing the plains to Zion in the Valleys of the Mountains was not merely a journey but a rite of passage, the final, devoted, enduring act that brought one into the Kingdom. Until the railroad made the journey too easy, and until new generations born in the valley began to outnumber the immigrant Saints, the shared experience of the trail was a bond that reinforced the bonds of the faith; and to successive generations who did not personally experience it, it has continued to have sanctity as legend and myth.

It is fully, even monotonously, documented. Attics and archives are crammed with its records, for in addition to the official journals authorized by a history-conscious church, it seems that every second Mormon emigrant kept a diary, and every Mormon family that has such a diary cherishes it as part of the lares and penates. Great-granddaughters edit the jottings of their pioneer ancestors as piously as they go to the temple to be baptized for the dead, and if great-grandfather was too occupied to keep notes, his recollective yarns will be gathered up and published as reminiscences, with a genealogical chart to show all the branches and twigs that have sprung from the pioneer root. Any people in a new land may be pardoned for being solicitous about their history: they create it, in a sense, by remembering it. But the tradition of the pioneer that is strong all through the West is a cult in Utah.

Symbols of the trail rise as naturally out of the Mormon mind as the phrase about making the desert blossom as the rose—and that springs to Mormon lips with the innocent ease of birdsong. Those symbols—white bows of covered wagons, horned cattle low-necked in the yoke, laboring files of handcarts, booted and bearded pioneers, sunbonneted Mothers of Zion—are recurrent, if not compulsive, in Mormon art, which runs strongly to monumental sculpture and is overwhelmingly historical in emphasis. One might expect to find artistic treatment of Joseph's revelations from God or His angels, the early persecutions and martyrdoms, the massacre at Haun's Mill, the assassination of Joseph and Hyrum Smith in Carthage Jail. But these things, though remembered, have not emerged as abiding symbols. Instead, one finds the trail.

No responsible historian can afford to underestimate the literalness of Mormon belief. These emigrants were convinced that they went not merely to a new country and a new life, but to a new Dispensation, to the literal Kingdom of God on earth. In the years between Joseph's vision and its fulfillment, persecution and hardship discouraged many, and others fell away into apostasy, but what might be called the hard core of Mormonism took persecution and suffering in stride, as God's way of trying their faith. Signs and wonders accompanied them, their way was cleared by divine interventions. Rivers opportunely froze over to permit passage of their wagons, quail fell among their exhausted and starving camps as miraculously as manna ever fell upon the camps of the Israelites fleeing Pharaoh, the sick (even sick horses) upon whom the elders laid their hands rose up rejoicing in health, the wolves that dug up Oregonian and California graves and scattered Gentile bones across the prairies did not touch the graves of the Lord's people. If they were blessed with an easy passage, they praised God for His favor; if their way was a via dolorosa milestoned with the cairns of their dead, they told themselves they were being tested, and hearkened to counsel, and endured.

Patience Loader, a girl who could not have been more aptly named, said it for all of them in the journal she kept across the plains in 1856: "It seemed the Lord fitted the back for the burden. Every day we realized that the hand of God was over us and that he made good his promises unto us day by day. ... We know that his promises never fail and this we prooved day by day. We knew that we had not strength of our own to perform such hardships if our heavenly Father had not help us. ...."

The Lord fitted the back for the burden. And however heavy or light the burden, it was on the trail that the back was generally shaped. Especially for those who had not come through the early drivings and burnings (and this means nearly every Mormon emigrant after the evacuation of Kanesville in 1852) the crossing of the plains provided a testing that most proselytes welcomed. The Kingdom of God should not be too easily come at. Those who felt such things must have understood that the hard trail was both religiously and artistically right: a labor to be performed, difficulties to be overcome, dangers to be faced, faithfulness to be proved, a great safety to be won. Welsh converts aware of their own folklore might have remembered the heroes who after great trouble arrived at the Isle of Glass and succeeded in making their way across to it on a sword-edge bridge.

Having endured, and crossed to safety, they began at once to transform their experience into myth. In this they were aided by the patriarchal character of Mormon society. The head of the family then was, and in theory still is, a sun around which revolved planetary wives and offspring. The abjuration to be fruitful and multiply—good practical doctrine in a desert wilderness and at a time when numbers meant strength—was reinforced by the spiritual doctrine that the more numerous a man's offspring were, the greater would be his glory in heaven. When the patriarch was also a pioneer, one of those who had most suffered for the faith, filial pride as well as filial duty tended to magnify him.

So long as any were still alive, pioneers were a revered club in Utah, and the club included not only the exclusive members of the original 1847 party and the 1856 handcart companies, but anyone who had crossed into Utah before the coming of the railroad. The one universally celebrated Mormon holiday is Pioneer Day, July 24, the day on which Brigham Young entered Salt Lake Valley. The honorific societies based on inheritance are not called Sons and Daughters of Nauvoo, or Sons and Daughters of the Three Witnesses, but Sons and Daughters of the Utah Pioneers. Their principal activity is an assiduous collecting and memorializing of the history of the migration and settlement. In their loving memorials, the men and women who came out the hard way look like photographs taken by infra-red light, imposing but transparent and unreal. They loom taller as time passes; their harsh and violent qualities soften; their beards achieve a Mosaic dignity; they walk through Mormon history with the tread of Jacob or Abraham.

Mormonism was in several ways—and its persecutors rightly felt it so— antipathetic to the unlicked democracy out of which it grew. Far from separating church and state, it made them synonymous. ("Theoretically," said Apostle Franklin D. Richards in 1880, "Church and State are one. If there were no Gentiles and no other Government there would be no Civil Law.") Instead of celebrating the free individual, it celebrated the obedient group. For the will of the people it substituted the will of God as announced by the priesthood. Its internal elections showed only one slate, its votes were not choices between competing candidates but "sustaining votes" for candidates proposed by the hierarchy—and it took a bold man to vote Nay. Its shibboleths were not the catchwords of republicanism, but were lifted from the patriarchal vocabulary of the Old Testament, especially Isaiah. What they went to build in the Great Basin was not a state, not a republic, but a Kingdom. Hierarchic, theocratic, patriarchal, this strange descendant of New England puritanism was in some ways wildly un-puritan—or seemed so. For ever since some time in the 1830s the doctrine of plural marriage had been secretly making its way among them. Not an indulgence but a divine command, it had been revealed privately by Joseph to his most confidential counselors, had been put into writing in 1843 for the eyes of the High Council and of Joseph's difficult wife Emma, and had finally been publicly admitted in 1852. As if all this were not enough, the Mormons tended to vote solid in state and national elections, and as a "closed" society surrounded by an open one, they had a tendency to attract outlaws looking for asylum, to breed fearful rumors, and to infuriate the Gentiles with their smug assumption that they alone held the keys of truth, they alone were the chosen of the Lord.

And yet in at least one way Mormonism was profoundly of its time and place: its movement was inevitably westward beyond the frontiers. The pioneering itch troubled Mormon flesh and spirit quite as much as did the contemporary religious stirrings, the talking and interpreting in tongues, the magical hearings, the millennial hopes, the revelations, the direct interventions of God in man's affairs. If the martyrdom of Joseph and Hyrum Smith assured the persistence of this sect, which doctrinally was a pastiche of the revivals that had swept New York State's "burned-over ground" in the 1820s, the combination of millennialism and the westward movement assured its growth. All but one of the splinter sects that refused to follow when the mass of Mormondom went west were shortly extinct; that one, though it was headed by Joseph's wife Emma and her sons, remained essentially dormant. The main body of Mormonism chose to fulfill its millennial destiny by moving with the current that carried the nation west, and in good part because of that choice, it throve. Millennium and Manifest Destiny turned out to be hardly more than variant spellings for the same thing.

Nothing so emphasizes Mormonism's simultaneous identity with and separation from the tide of western expansion as its presence on wheels in the Platte valley during all the years from 1847 to the completion of the transcontinental railroad. It was part of the tide—but across the Platte from most of it; it was going the same direction—but stepping short. Looking for an escape from the Missouri "pukes" and the Illinois mobbers and the other agents of Manifest Destiny, the Mormons were in fact inextricably entangled with them. They built up their own solidarity and morale by listening disapprovingly to the language of Missouri wagontrains. When the gold that their own young men helped to discover pulled fortune-hunters toward California in thousands, the Mormons were not only caught in the rush, but profited by it, sold it cattle and fresh teams, vegetables and flour, melons and the homemade whiskey called Valley Tan. They solidified themselves in their chosen valley on the profitable trade of their enemies. Fleeing America, they fled it by that most American of acts, migration into the West.

So there are more than theological reasons for remembering the Mormon pioneers. They were the most systematic, organized, disciplined, and successful pioneers in our history; and their advantage over the random individualists who preceded them and paralleled them and followed them up the valley of the Platte came directly from their "un-American" social and religious organization. Where Oregon emigrants and argonauts bound for the gold fields lost practically all their social cohesion en route, the Mormons moved like the Host of Israel they thought themselves. Far from loosening their social organization, the trail perfected it. As communities on the march they proved extraordinarily adaptable. When driven out of Nauvoo, they converted their fixed property, insofar as they could, into the instruments of mobility, especially livestock, and became for the time herders and shepherds, teamsters and frontiersmen, instead of artisans and townsmen and farmers. When their villages on wheels reached the valley of their destination, the Saints were able to revert at once, because they were town-and-temple builders and because they had their families with them, to the stable agrarian life in which most of them had grown up.

They built a commonwealth, or as they would have put it, a Kingdom. But the story of their migration is more than the story of the founding of Utah. In their hegira they opened up southern Iowa from Locust Creek to the Missouri, made the first roads, built the first bridges, established the first communities. They transformed the Missouri at Council Bluffs from a trading post and an Indian agency into an outpost of civilization, founded settlements on both sides of the river and made Winter Quarters (now Florence, a suburb of Omaha) and later Kanesville (now Council Bluffs) into outfitting points that rivaled Independence, Westport, and St. Joseph. They defined the road up the north side of the Platte that is now the route of both U.S. 30 and the Union Pacific Railroad. Their guide books and trail markers, their bridges and ferries, though made for the Saints scheduled to come later, served also for the Gentiles: according to Irene Paden in *The Wake of the Prairie Schooner*, a third of the California and Oregon travel from 1849 on followed the Mormon Trail.

That is to say, the Mormons were one of the principal forces in the settlement of the West. Their main body opened southern Iowa, the Missouri frontier, Nebraska, Wyoming, Utah. Samuel Brannan's group of eastern Saints who sailed around the Horn in the ship *Brooklyn*, and the Mormon Battalion that marched 2,000 miles overland from Fort Leavenworth to San Diego, were secondary prongs of the Mormon movement; between them, they contributed to the opening of the Southwest and of California. Battalion members were at Coloma when gold gleamed up from the bedrock of Sutter's millrace. Battalion members crossed the Sierra in the spring of 1847 when the dismembered bodies of the Donner Party victims were still scattered through their ghastly camps. Battalion members opened for wagons the Hensley route around the north end of Great Salt Lake that California trains increasingly took after 1850. And Brigham Young's colonizing Mormons, taking to wheels again after the briefest stay, radiated outward from the Salt Lake, Utah, and Weber Valleys and planted settlements that reached from Northern Arizona to the Lemhi River in Idaho, and from Fort Bridget in Wyoming to Genoa in Carson Valley under the loom of the Sierra, and in the Southwest down through St. George and Las Vegas to San Bernardino.

With much of this activity, central though it is to the story of western settlement, this book has nothing to do. Neither does it concern itself, except for the indispensable summary of event and belief, with the history of Mormonism before the expulsion from Nauvoo. Because that early history is hardly credible, and because the Mormon faith has seemed to historians in need of explanation, apologetics, or ridicule, books dealing with any aspect of Mormon history have had a tendency to go over the whole ground from the Hill Cumorah to the Edmunds-Tucker Act. A history of the Mormon Trail is subject to the same temptations. In electing otherwise, I have had to make some arbitrary limitations, choices, and definitions.

The Mormon Trail ends in Salt Lake City, but where does it begin, and how many branches does it have, and how shall we compute its duration? From the time of Joseph Smith's first visions, he and the church he founded were in motion; and the church stayed in motion, with short breathing spaces in Ohio, Missouri, and Illinois, until it found its sanctuary in the mountains. Does a proper discussion of the Mormon Trail begin at the Hill Cumorah, near Palmyra, New York, where the angel showed young Joseph the golden plates and chose him, out of all men in these latter days, to receive the true priesthood? Or at Manchester, New York, where Joseph organized six members into what he then called the Church of Christ, on April 6, 1830? Or at Kirtland, Ohio (now a suburb of Cleveland), the site of the first divinely ordered Gathering and of the first temple, from which Joseph and his diminished faithful fled in a fog of apostasy, bankruptcy, and criminal charges resulting from the prophet's ill-advised experiments in the banking business? Or at Independence, Missouri, where a colony of Mormons made a short-lived attempt to build the Kingdom, only to be driven out by settlers suspicious of their groupiness and their potentially Abolitionist vote? Or at Far West, Missouri, and the near-by town they called Adam-ondi-Ahman, from which they were driven bloodily in the fall and winter of 1838–1839? Or at Nauvoo the Beautiful, on the Mississippi, where for a few years they flourished, where they built their second temple and a city over which Joseph ruled like an oriental potentate, and from which they were again driven, almost before their crowding feet had settled the temple's truss floor? Or at Winter Quarters on the Missouri, where they built a transient town of huts and dugouts from which, next year, they started on the 1,032-mile traverse of the wilderness that brought them finally to safety?

This is a strange, often incredible, sometimes terrible story, and it has been told so generally by partisans full of piety, hatred, or paranoia that it would be worth trying to tell it again. But not here, and not so long as Dale L. Morgan has it in his mind to tell it. For purposes of simplification, this narrative begins at Nauvoo in the last months of 1845; its primary subjects are the Mormon migration from the bank of the Mississippi to the bank of City Creek in Salt Lake Valley, and the Gathering of Zion that took place over essentially the same route during the next twenty-two years.

There is one extension of the trail that cannot be ignored. The peculiar Mormon commandment known as the Gathering of Zion had effective implementation and devoted agents. In the very agony of their exodus from Nauvoo, elders obediently left wives and families to make their way as they could, and turned back eastward to do missionary work in the "black counties" and the textile cities of England; and once Zion was established and the Gathering reinstituted, the trickle of European converts that had formerly run by gravity toward Nauvoo was put under pressure, with pumping stations at New Orleans (later New York or Boston or Philadelphia) and at some frontier staging point, generally Council Bluffs or Florence. Between 1847 and 1868, the last year of overland emigration by trail, nearly 50,000 British, Scandinavian, and German converts were pumped along that pipeline into Salt Lake City.* During the peak year of 1855 it was said that a third of all the emigrants from the British Isles to the United States were Mormons. Because for a very large proportion of Utah's early settlers the Mormon Trail began at the Liverpool docks, I have given some space to the structure of conversion and emigration that the Mormons developed before 1840 and matured in the 1850s, and I have followed at least one party of European Saints from Liverpool all the way to the valley.

From the Missouri west, despite the assertion of many journals and many histories that the Mormons were breaking a new road, the trail was known and traveled before they came. Both sides of the Platte valley, that almost inescapable level highway into the West, had been an Indian travel route for generations. Traders between Fort Laramie and the Missouri River posts had sometimes traveled the north bank. The missionaries who in 1844 built a mission to the Pawnee on Loup Fork had used it. The Stevens Party of 1844 had gone that way. According to George R. Stewart, there had been wagons up the north bank as early as 1835.

From Fort Laramie to just beyond South Pass the Mormon Trail, Oregon Trail, and California Trail were synonymous. From South Pass to Fort Bridger the Mormon Trail followed the older fork of the Oregon–California Trail. West from Fort Bridger on through Echo, Weber, and East Canyons and over the Wasatch to Salt Lake Valley, the Mormon pioneers were following the dim and barely passable route that Lansford Hastings had so lamentably sold to

*Figures for Mormon immigration, like many of the data of Mormon history, are profuse but contradictory. Mr. Earl Olsen of the Church Historian's Office supplies a figure of 68,028 for the emigration of European Saints between 1847 and 1868, but this is almost surely the total influx into the Salt Lake Valley, and therefore must include many from the Missouri frontier and from the United States. Kate B. Carter's compilation in *Heart Throbs of the West* adds up to 46,972, but Mrs. Carter is not always reliable in such details. Unfortunately the most reliable tabulation, that by James Linforth in the notes to Piercy's *Route from Liverpool to Great Salt Lake Valley* (1855) ends with the year 1854. A combination of Linforth's figures and later figures from Gustive Larson's *Prelude to the Kingdom* gives a total of 47,099, which is close enough to Mrs. Carter's total to substantiate the general order of magnitude her summary suggests.

the Donner-Reed party of 1846. There was nothing at all new about the Mormon Trail except the two hundred miles across western Iowa and the little loop at the very western end known as Golden Pass, which circumnavigated the difficulties of Big and Little Mountains and came into Salt Lake Valley through Parley's Canyon instead of through Emigration. It was opened in 1850 as a toll road, but maintenance problems in the canyon caused it to be abandoned after only a brief period of use.

What was new about the Mormon migration was that it was the permanent hegira of a whole people—grandparents, parents, children, flocks and herds, household goods and gods. In the composition of its wagontrains, the motives that drove them, the organization and discipline of the companies, it differed profoundly from the Oregon and California migrations. These were not groups of young and reckless adventurers, nor were they isolated families or groups of families. They were literally villages on the march, villages of a sobriety, solidarity, and discipline unheard of anywhere else on the western trails, and not too frequent in the settled United States.

Moreover, the Mormon Trail was a two-way road to an extent that neither the California nor the Oregon Trail was. It saw a steady eastward traffic in elders headed for the mission fields, a constant flow of wagons and strong teams going back to pick up supplies and new converts at the Missouri, or to meet faltering companies, generally at some point between the last crossing of the North Platte and Fort Bridger, and help them on in to Salt Lake. After 1861 the immigration was handled largely by Church trains that came east from Salt Lake, picked up passengers and freight at the Missouri, and returned the same season. Few California or Oregon emigrants gave a thought to people coming after them, unless they feared a company behind them might pass them and use up the grass. There are recorded instances of their destroying rafts and ferries to prevent their use by other groups. Not so the Mormons. The first thought of the pioneer company was to note good campgrounds, wood, water, grass, to measure distances and set up mileposts. They and succeeding companies bent their backs to build bridges and dig down the steep approaches of fords. They made rafts and ferry boats and left them for the use of later companies—and twice left men with them to make an honest dollar ferrying the Gentiles. They threw rocks off the road on the tough stretch between Fort Laramie and the Mormon Ferry at modern Casper, Wyoming; they cut and grubbed the abominable willows in the East Canyon bottoms. By the improvements they made in it, they earned the right to put their name on the trail they used.

Thus it is not primarily the route, but the people who traveled it, and how, and why, that is my subject. My betters have been before me at least part of the way. It is a brave man who attempts to tell the story of the Mormon expulsion from Nauvoo after Bernard DeVoto's brilliant account in *The Year of Decision, 1846*. Yet I must attempt it, for Nauvoo is where the trail began. Fortunately for me, DeVoto's account follows the Mormons west of

Winter Quarters only in brief summary. There are objective and dependable histories of the pioneer and later companies west of the Missouri, but most are either narrowly focused, as are Dale Morgan's meticulous studies of the ferries on the North Platte, or are inclined to treat the migration incidentally, a part of the larger history of Mormonism or as part of the western movement. The most detailed histories of the trail itself have been written in the spirit of celebration and faith-promotion, and though most of them make extensive use of journals, they end by dehumanizing the emigrants almost as much as do the debunkers who see the migration as a movement of dupes led by blackguards. For the celebrators characteristically enlarge and mythify, and hence falsify, people who in their lives were painfully and complicatedly human. They leave out matters that they or the Church authorities feel to be embarrassing, they wash out of the mouths of Brigham Young, Heber Kimball, and others the strong language that stress and humor sometimes put there, they minimize frictions and gloss over personal animosities.

I should prefer to deal with the Mormon pioneers, if I can, as human beings of their time and place, the earlier ones westward-moving Americans, the latter ones European converts gripped by the double promise of economic betterment and eternal life. Suffering, endurance, discipline, faith, brotherly and sisterly charity, the qualities so thoroughly celebrated by Mormon writers, were surely well distributed among them, but theirs also was a normal amount of human cussedness, vengefulness, masochism, backbiting, violence, ignorance, selfishness, and gullibility. So far as it is possible, I shall take them from their own journals and reminiscences and letters, and I shall try to follow George Bancroft's rule for historians: I shall try to present them in their terms and judge them in mine. That I do not accept the faith that possessed them does not mean I doubt their frequent devotion and heroism in its service. Especially their women. Their women were incredible.

Discussion Questions

1. Stegner writes that Mormonism was in several ways "antipathetic to the unlicked democracy out of which it grew." Discuss this claim, using the evidence Stegner offers in this selection. Do you agree with Stegner? How were the Mormons threatening to some of the pioneers and other white Americans?

2. Stegner writes that the "Mormons were one of the principal forces in the opening of the West." Discuss the various contributions the Mormons made in opening up the frontier. Compare their successes with those of other groups. What kinds of advantages does Stegner claim the Mormons had over other pioneers? Which characteristics allowed them to achieve so much?

Writing Suggestions

1. Look on Lexis-Nexis for a recent account of the celebration of Pioneer Day, July 24, which celebrates Brigham Young's arrival in Salt Lake City. Write an essay in which you analyze the article you have selected. What aspects of history does it recount? Does it support Stegner's assertion that the Mormons were key to opening up the West? What is the tone of the article? Are the Mormons respected in the article? Does the topic of religious freedom appear in the article? Who wrote the article?

2. One of the more controversial aspects of Utah becoming a state of the Union was that the federal Government refused to allow Utah to join the Union unless it banned the practice of polygamy. Do some research on how the Mormons were forced by the U.S. government to give up their practice of polygamy, and then argue whether you feel the actions taken by the Government in the late nineteenth century were just or not. In a three-page essay, argue for or against the government actions, and discuss the question of freedom of religion and polygamy.

A Life in Bondage

ANN ELIZA YOUNG

Ann Eliza Young was forced into marriage with Brigham Young when she was 22 and he was 61. She was a fierce opponent of polygamy, and after she was able to divorce Young, she spent nine years on the lecture circuit preaching the evils of polygamy. In 1875 she wrote her memoirs, *A Life in Bondage,* in which she details her life before and after her marriage to Brigham Young. Her story was one of the first exposés about polygamy, and her outspoken criticism of the practice helped to force the Mormons to abandon plural marriage in order to become a state in the Union. In the selection that follows, from *A Life in Bondage*, Ann Eliza Young describes some of the psychological difficulties of mothers and daughters marrying the same man.

To the Mormon Wives of Utah

I Dedicate this Book to you, as I consecrate my life to your cause.

As long as God gives me life I shall pray and plead for your deliverance from the worse than Egyptian bondage in which you are held.

Despised, maligned, and wronged; kept in gross ignorance of the great world, its pure creeds, its high aims, its generous motives, you have been made to believe that the noblest nation of the earth was truly represented by the horde of miscreants who drove you from State to State, in early years, murdering your sons and assassinating your leaders.

Hence, you shrink from those whom God will soon lead to your deliverance, from those to whom I daily present your claims to a hearing and liberation, and who listen with responsive and sympathetic hearts.

But He will not long permit you to be so wickedly deceived; nor will the People permit you to be so cruelly enslaved.

Hope and pray! Come out of the house of bondage! Kind hearts beat for you! Open hands will welcome you! Do not fear that while God lives you shall suffer uncared for in the wilderness! This Christian realm is not "Babylon," but THE PROMISED LAND!

Courage! The night of oppression is nearly ended, and the sun of liberty is rising in the heavens for you.

—Ann Eliza Young

To the Wives of Brigham Young

Should this book meet your eyes, I wish you most distinctly to understand that my quarrel is not with you. On the contrary, the warmest and tenderest feelings of my heart are strongly enlisted in your favor. As a rule, you have been uniformly kind to me. Some of you I have dearly loved. I have respected and honored you all. My love and respect have never failed, but have rather increased with separation. I think of you often with the sincerest sympathy for your helpless condition, bound to a false religion, and fettered by a despotic system; and I wish from the depths of my heart that I could bring you, body and soul, out from the cruel bondage, and help you to find the freedom, rest, and peace which have become so sweet to me since my eyes have been opened to the light of a true and comforting faith.

Since I have left Utah, I know that some of you have censured me severely, and have joined in personal denunciations. But I know that you are actuated by a mistaken zeal for the cause which you feel yourselves bound to sustain. You, no doubt, regard my course with horror. I look upon your lives with pity.

I have taken the liberty of describing your characters and situations. I was not prompted by the slightest animosity toward you, but because the public are interested in you, and curious concerning you, and I felt that I could give to the world a true story of your lives, and, at the same time, do you justice, and let you be seen as you are in my eyes, which are not dimmed by prejudice.

I was driven to the course I am pursuing by sheer desperation, as some of you, with whom I have exchanged confidences, well know. The motives which have been attributed to me, and the charges that have been made against me, are as utterly false and foreign to my nature as darkness is to light. You, at least, should not misjudge me. You should know me better, and you do. Even your bitter prejudice, and your disapprobation of the step I have taken, cannot make you believe me other than I am. You know that apostasy from Mormonism does not necessarily degrade a person, and sink them at once to the lowest depths of infamy.

If, as is taught,—and as I suppose you believe,—I have lost the light of the gospel, and departed from "the faith once delivered to the saints," am I not rather deserving your compassion than your censure? Your own hearts and consciences must answer that.

The women of Utah should know that I shall vindicate their rights, and defend their characters, at all times and in all places. Their sorrow has been my sorrow; their cause is my cause still. My heart goes out to them all, but more especially to you. *You* have been my companions and my sisters in tribulation. Now our paths diverge. I go on the way that I have chosen alone, while you stay sorrowing together. I wish I had the power to influence you to throw off the fetters which bind you, and to walk triumphantly forth into the glories of a faith, whose foundation is in God the compassionate Father, whose principles are those of a tender mercy, whose ruling spirit is love. Alas! I cannot do it; but I pray that the good Father in His infinite mercy may open your eyes to His glory, and lead you forth His children to do His blessed will.

—Ann Eliza Young

Chapter XIX: The Mysteries of Polygamy—What the Wives Could Tell

Incestuous Intermarriages.—A Widow and her Daughters married to the same Man.—"Marrying my Pa."—The "U.S." Government Conniving at Mormon Iniquities.—Beastly Conduct of Delegate George Q. Cannon.—Polygamists Legislating for Bigamists.—Mother and Daughter fighting for the same Man!—It is Wicked to Live with an Old Wife.—A *Young* lover Ninety Years Old!—A Bride *Eleven* years Old!—Brides of Thirteen and Fourteen Years!—I receive an "Offer" when Twelve Years Old!—Old Ladies at a Discount: Young Women at a Premium.—Respect for the Silver Crown of Age.—Heber gives his Opinion.—"Why is She making such a Fuss?"—Seeing One's Husband Once a Year.—The Rascality of Orson Hyde towards his Wife.—When Rival Wives make Friends.—A Very Funny Story about an Apostle and his Wife.—Rights of the First Wife: Brigham Young in a Fix.—He treats an Early Wife to a Dance.—Amelia in the Shade.—The Prophet becomes Frisky.—Poor, neglected Emmeline.—How Polygamy was once Denied.—A Mistake which a French Lady Made.—Milk for Babes.

The marriage of mother and daughter to one man was of so common an occurrence that it ceased to be regarded as anything out of the ordinary course of events.

I had some schoolmates, two sisters, whose mother was married to a Mr. McDonald, and when she gave herself to him, it was with the express understanding that the daughters should be sealed to him as soon as they were of a proper age. The little girls knew of the arrangement, and used to talk very openly of "marrying Pa," and in very much the same way they would speak of their intention to take tea with a friend.

That mother must have taken a great deal of comfort with her children! Fancy her feelings; knowing that she was bringing up her daughters as wives for her own husband!

Wives and mothers, living outside of polygamy, can anything be more revolting to your ideas of womanly purity, more thoroughly opposed to all the sweet tenderness of the maternal instinct, than cases like this? And yet, horror-stricken as you are by them, they are by no means exceptional, but are of frequent occurrence. And it is in your own country that these outrages against all womanhood occur, under your own government, upheld by your own chosen legislators—tacitly, at least—since in this time, as in the days of Christ's actual presence on earth, those who are not for are against. And if your government and its rulers refuse to do, or even fail to do without refusing, anything to eradicate this foul blot upon national purity and honor, why, they are in so far encouraging its presence, and rendering it daily more difficult of eradication.

For the tide of evil that set so strongly in those terrible days of 1856 has never been stayed. It still rolls on with all the added filth and abomination which it has gathered in its course, until it is one reeking mass of the foulest impurities.

Incest, murder, suicide, mania and bestiality are the chief "beauties" of this infamous system, which are so glowingly alluded to by its eloquent expounders and defenders.

And George Q. Cannon, one of its ablest apostles,—himself a practical polygamist, being the husband of four living wives, three of whom he grossly neglects,—goes to Washington from Utah as Congressional Delegate from that Territory, and helps to make the laws which send George Smith, of Massachusetts, to State Prison for three years for the crime of having two wives! Is it that bigamy is a punishable offence, and polygamy is not? If so, George Smith has only to take two more wives and he can, perhaps, enjoy the confidence of the government and the protection of its laws as fully as the Apostolic George Q.

If the gentleman in Memphis, Tennessee, who has recently been indicted for marrying his deceased wife's niece had only married six of his own nieces, he might now be enjoying his liberty and his youthful brides' society, with all the freedom which is accorded to Bishop Johnson, of Utah—that is, if he, too, had lived among the Saints in Utah.

The relation between mother and daughter, when one becomes the rival of the other, is by no means the pleasantest in the world, and it is usually the case that the mother has much the worse time. She sees herself neglected for a younger and fairer woman by the man in whose service she has expended both youth and beauty, and sees the daughter whom she has so carefully and tenderly nurtured, and who should now be her stay, and her comfort, and the pride of her maternal heart, usurping her place in her husband's affection and in her home, and striking a blow at her happiness that is fatal. She can turn neither to husband nor daughter for comfort, and the religion which should be her stay is but a mockery, since it brings all the misery and desolation into her wrecked life.

The leaders of her religion teach openly that it is not right for husbands to live with their wives after they are advanced in years; and they also teach that a man is marriageable until he is a hundred years old. This has always been a strong point with them, and in urging polygamy, in the "Reformation" times, they used to advise the young girls to choose for their husbands men of experience, who would have the power of resurrecting them, rather than a young man whose position in the church was not fixed. They carried the practice of this doctrine to the same extreme that they carried everything else. One enthusiastic elder secured for a wife a girl of eleven years, and brides of thirteen and fourteen were often seen, especially in Southern Utah, where the excitement was most intense, and rose almost to frenzy. I was about twelve years of age, and my father had several offers for me from different church dignitaries; but however easily he might be beguiled himself into the snares set by the lecherous leaders of Mormonism and polygamy, he had no idea of making his little girl a victim; and though I was duly advised by teachers and catechists to marry into polygamy when I was a little older, I gave very little heed to the advice, and set about making my own romance, just as girls everywhere do, in my imagination.

It is painful to one used to the finer courtesies of life to see how age is neglected in Utah, and the want of respect that is shown towards it, especially towards women, who have passed out of the sunshine years of life, and are entering the shadow. When I came East, one of the strangest things to me was the deference that was paid to age, it was so unlike anything I had been used to; and when I saw an old couple clinging together, with no dread shadow of polygamy between them, with only the prospect of death to part them, I have been thrilled through and through with the sweetest, strangest emotion. I could scarcely believe my own senses; it seemed impossible that in this world such devotion could exist, and I could only wonder and weep, and thank God that, in the world that I had been taught to look upon as so wicked and depraved, there was such a thing as love, and devotion, and thoughtful care for women, and that every added wrinkle or silver hair brought more tender care and tenderer devotion. In the light of affection like this, well-tried and long-enduring, the hateful form of polygamy would rise up before me more monstrous, more hideous, more revolting than ever.

Think, in contrast to this, of a woman who has lived with her husband during all the years of her fresh and mature womanhood, being left alone, when she becomes deserted by the husband whom she has loved so well and so long, at the command of the priesthood! Heber Kimball used to say, when he knew of a woman grieving over the neglect of her husband, "What is she making such a fuss for? She has no business with a husband." Who can blame the disciples when the leader sets the example? Brigham Young's first living wife,—his only real and legal wife,—a woman of his own age, is entirely neglected by him, and long ago ceased to be his wife but in name.

Sometimes these old and middle-aged ladies do not see their husbands once a year, and yet they may not live half a mile apart. A few years since, at a large party at the Social Hall in Salt Lake City, Orson Hyde, one of the twelve apostles, met the wife of his youth, the mother of many of his children. He had escorted some of the younger wives there, and she came with a friend. It chanced that they were seated near each other at the table, and were compelled to speak; they shook hands, exchanged a very commonplace greeting, and that was all that passed between them. Neither is this an isolated case; it very often occurs that an elderly lady attends a party with friends, and meets her husband there with one or more younger wives; and sometimes both she and they have to watch their mutual husband while he plays the agreeable to some young girl who has taken captive his wandering fancy, and whom he intends to make the next addition to his kingdom.

It is then that wives, who have heretofore been rivals, join their forces against a common enemy; and the young woman who is engaging the attentions of the already much-married but still marriageable *beau*, is sure to suffer at the hands of the new allies, who have so recently struck hands in a common cause. She, of course, knows this instinctively, and she revenges herself by "drawing" on her admirer by every art in her power, until he becomes so marked in his devotion that the entire company know, as well as the wives themselves, what his intentions are; and, in addition to the pique caused by his neglect, they have to endure the congratulations of friends upon the approaching alliance. In cases like this, the first wife does not feel so much pain as the younger one, and the whilom favorite, who, no matter how she has snubbed her before, comes now to seek her sympathy. She would be something more than human, if, with the sadness of her heart was not mingled a little feeling of pleasure that she was getting her revenge in seeing the jealousy and suffering of her late rival.

To return to the encounter between Hyde and his wife. There is a little romance attached to their separation which I have just been reminded of. When Joseph Smith first taught polygamy, and gave the wives as well as the husbands opportunity to make new choice of life-partners, Mrs. Hyde, at that time a young and quite prepossessing woman, became one of the Prophet's numerous fancies, and he took great pains to teach her most thoroughly the principles of the new celestial doctrines. It was rumored, at the time, that she was an apt and willing pupil. Hyde was away on a mission at the time, and when he returned, he, in turn, imbibed the teachings of polygamy also, and prepared to extend his kingdom indefinitely. In the mean time it was hinted to him that Smith had had his first wife sealed to himself in his absence, as a wife for eternity. Inconsistent as it may seem, Hyde was in a furious passion. Like many other men, he thought it no harm for him to win the affection of another man's wife, and make her his "celestial" spouse; but he did not propose having *his* rights interfered with even by the holy Prophet whose teachings he so implicitly followed, and he swore that if this was true he would never live with her again. But he did live with her for several years after the exodus from Nauvoo and the settlement of Utah. Finally, the old affair was revived, and I think Brigham himself informed his apostle that she was his wife only for time, but Joseph's for eternity; and as she was no longer young, and other wives were plentiful, he left her to care for herself as best she could.

Although the Mormons have from the very commencement been very fond of parties, and of amusements generally, they are much more enjoyed by the men than by the women, although both attend. Occasionally some very curious scenes are witnessed, which, after all, are not at all amusing to the persons most nearly concerned. For instance: a man takes two wives to a ball, and, if he be a lover of peace, he is at his wits' ends how to preserve it. He must treat each one alike, as nearly as possible; dance with each one an equal number of times, and see that each one is equally well served at supper. The beginning of sorrow comes with the vexed question, which he shall dance with *first*. That, however, is quite easily settled, since custom, or, rather, Mormon etiquette, demands that he shall give the older wife the preference. It may be she is not the favorite; but that does not matter: on this one point etiquette is rigid, and even the Prophet himself dare not defy it.

He had invited Amelia, the present favorite, and Emmeline, whose place in the priestly heart Amelia had taken, to attend a ball with him. It was a very strange thing to do, for generally, when Amelia went with him, he devoted himself exclusively to her. But on this occasion he had brought Emmeline along, too. Early in the evening, one of the committee of management came bustling up, with a "Brother Brigham, won't you dance?"

"Well, I suppose so," was the reply. Then he hesitated for a moment. There sat both Emmeline and Amelia, the former looking quietly unconscious, yet wondering very much, as she afterwards told me, "what Brother Brigham would do," and enjoying his dilemma immensely, while the latter looked very stately and dignified, and also threatening. There stood the Prophet, inclination pulling him one way, etiquette and duty the other. He hesitated a moment longer; then, walking up to Emmeline, said, ungraciously and gruffly, "Come along and dance;" and, without offering her his arm, walked on to the floor, leaving her to follow.

As is the custom at balls which Brigham and Amelia grace with their presence, one of his satellites instantly begged for the honor of Amelia's hand in the dance, and led her at once as *vis-à-vis* to her husband. During the entire dance he did not address one word to Emmeline, and was evidently made very wretched by the demeanor of Amelia, who snubbed him most decidedly, and would take no notice of all his attempts to win her back to good humor.

At the end of the dance he led Emmeline to her seat as hastily as possible, left her without a word, and endeavored, with all the art which he possessed, to propitiate his angry favorite. Presently, the ubiquitous manager was at his elbow again:—

"Another cotillon, Brother Brigham; will you dance again?"

"With pleasure," answered the delighted President. Then, turning quickly to Amelia, he offered his arm in the most impressive manner, saying,—

"*Now* I will dance with my wife;" and led her off in triumph, as pleased as any young fellow at the opportunity of showing his devotion to her. He was vivacity itself during the dance, and finally succeeded in coaxing a smile from the capricious tyrant of his heart. As deeply hurt as Emmeline was by his rude boorishness of manner towards herself, and the insult conveyed to her by the remark to Amelia, which she overheard, she could not help being pleased at seeing the punishment he was receiving at the hands of the outraged favorite.

A system that engenders feelings like this can surely not be called, with any degree of propriety, a heavenly system, and religion is outraged every time its name is used in connection with it. It panders to the baser passions of men, and crushes the graces of Christian faith and charity out of every woman's heart. It engenders malice, and strife, and envyings, and hatred, and backbiting, and all that is worst in the masculine or feminine heart. It makes men selfish and mean, and women wretched and degraded. It takes from one the dignity and poise which come from absolute self-control, and from the other the sweet, refined, womanly assurance which comes from self-respect. Talk of its "celestial" origin! It is the devil's own device for rendering men and women both less godlike and pure. And the cunning of his device is shown in the religious mask which he puts upon its frightful face, and the Christian robes with which he hides its horrible deformity.

It began by deception, it has been fostered by lies.

When the first rumor of its existence as a religious ordinance among the American Saints was first exciting Europe, and the American missionaries were assuring their converts that the rumor was false, and was started by their enemies to injure them and their cause, the most eloquent and remarkable denial of it was made by the Apostle John Taylor, at *Boulogne-sur-Mer*, where there was at that time quite a large and successful mission.

The Apostle Taylor was the husband of five wives, all living in Salt Lake; yet that slight matter did not hinder him from most emphatically repudiating the charge brought against the church. He quoted from the Book of Mormon, dwelling particularly on the passage that expressly commands that a man shall have but *one* wife; then mentions the Bible command that a man shall take a wife and cleave to her *only*; and made the sermon so strong and so convincing that no further proof was asked by those who heard him. His manner was impressive. He was sorrowful, he was indignant, he was reproachful; he was eloquent, and fervent, and almost inspired, thought those who heard him. He was logical and convincing in what he said. In short, he was a consummate hypocrite, lying in the name of God to a confiding people, with a smooth tongue and an unblushing face.

He employed a French lady—one of his converts, and a most charming and cultured person—to translate the sermon for him into her own language. He then had it published, and distributed largely through the country. Very many were kept from apostatizing by this tract, and a large number announced their intention of at once gathering to Zion. Among them was the lady who had translated the sermon for Taylor, and who, influenced by the spirit of the discourse, and the seeming earnestness of the missionary, had become more zealous than ever in her devotion to her new and ardently beloved faith.

Imagine, if you can, her horror, on reaching Utah, at the social state of affairs which found her there, and discovered that she not only had been grossly deceived, but, in her ignorance, had helped to deceive so many others; for it was through the influence of her translation of Taylor's denial that nearly all the party with whom she emigrated had come.

She apostatized at once, but she was conscience-stricken at the part she had so unwittingly played, and could not be comforted. A more remorseful, grief-stricken woman was never seen, and she felt all the more deeply the harm that had been wrought, when she saw how powerless she was to undo it. No effort of hers could ever bring these unhappy people from the infamous community in which they found themselves, and a part of which they were destined to become. For with them, the men especially, as with all others who remain under the baleful influence long, the end was certain. They first endured, and then embraced; pity was left out altogether, although God knows there is no condition that calls for pity as does that of the polygamous wife. The lady herself left Utah, but her people were forced to remain. I wonder how those poor wives, decoyed into a strange country by priestly promises, and deceived by priestly lying, could bear ever again to look in the face, or listen to the voice, of the man who had so wickedly misled them.

When the missionaries were asked why they denied so stoutly the existence of the system, when it must be sooner or later discovered that they were falsifying, they excused themselves by saying that the people could not then stand such strong doctrine, and they must give them only what they could safely take; that in good time the Lord would open their hearts to receive his truth,—the "good time" which the brethren referred to being after they had left their own country, crossed the United States, and put themselves outside the pale of civilization, and were literally in the power of the church. When they had gone so far that retreat was impossible, then they would tell them the truth, knowing that they could not choose but listen.

As long as they possibly could they denied it in the missions abroad, but, by-and-by, it became so notorious that it must be acknowledged; and in the face of all the denial, all the asseverations that there was no such institution, and, according to the laws of God and man there could be no such institution, the *Millennial Star* suddenly published the "Revelation," having given no warning of what it was about to do.

The excitement among the Mormons through Europe, in England especially, was intense, and it took all the eloquence and sophistry of the entire missionary board to prevent a general apostasy. Hundreds did leave the church, and many more were on the point of doing so. But the ingenuity of the Mormon Elders, which seems never to fail them, came to their rescue. They explained that this "Revelation" forced no one into polygamy; it only established it as a church institution that might be availed of by anyone who chose to enter the "Celestial Kingdom," but that it was entirely optional. In fact, the same arguments that were used to win single and special converts were used to convince the masses; and, strange as it may seem, all this sophistry had actual weight, and many worthy and sensible men and women stayed by the church who would have abandoned it in disgust, had they known the truth as it was forced upon them afterwards. But, as I said a little while since, the system begun in deception and fraud fattened on lies and treachery. May it meet with a speedy death, brought on by a surfeit of its favorite food.

Discussion Questions

1. What kind of persona does Ann Eliza Young try to establish in her preface, "To the Wives of Brigham Young"? What is her central message to these wives? What kind of tone does Young use when she describes the details of polygamy? Does her tone make you more or less sympathetic to her cause?

2. Of what does Young accuse U.S. legislators? What does she want the government to do about polygamy? What irony does she describe concerning George Cannon, the congressional delegate from Utah?

Writing Suggestions

1. Write an analysis of Young's argument: Examine her tone, diction, evidence, and examples. Do you find her to be a strong and persuasive writer or not? Would you have been moved by her accounts if you were a reader in the nineteenth century? Why or why not?

2. Although polygamy is now illegal, thousands of Mormons still favor plural marriage, claiming that it is part of their religious beliefs and that they should be allowed to have multiple wives. Currently, legal battles are occurring to challenge the practice, and accusations have been made against polygamous husbands, including child abuse, rape, and incest. Write a research paper in which you examine some of the complexities of this situation, and argue for your solution to this legal battle. You will need to address some of the following issues:

    Should husbands who practice polygamy be imprisoned?

    Is there evidence to back up the claims of child abuse and incest?

    What rights are protected under the freedom of religion clause in the U.S. Constitution?

Gendered Justice in the American West

Women of the Prison World

ANNE M. BUTLER

Anne M. Butler is a professor of history at Utah State University, and she is also coeditor of the Western Historical Quarterly. She has written a number of books and articles about women in the American West, including *Daughters of Joy, Sisters of Mercy: Prostitutes in the American West* and *Gendered Justice in the American West*, a book in which she explores western women and their relationships to violence, both in and out of prison. In the following selection, Chapter 3 from *Gendered Justice in the American West*, Butler explores the female prison population in the West in the nineteenth century, focusing on the effects of race and gender as applied to women's prison sentences and the treatment of women at the mercy of the early western judicial system.

> I am wear of this dreary imprisonment . . . my health is failing . . . and [I] feel that I could not live long to indure [*sic*] what a prisoner must undergo.
> —Mollie Forsha, Nevada State Penitentiary, 1874

The generic term "the woman prisoner" does little to illuminate a clear definition of the western women who went to the penitentiary. No single western woman typified the female inmate. They shared characteristics, but women prisoners also reflected diversity. Overarching issues of race, class, and gender helped to etch a basic prisoner profile, but perhaps the most universal marker of these women sprang from the perverse legal treatment they encountered in the courts.

Life in the prison world brought its own set of assaults, but the constraints that women prisoners faced began outside the penitentiary. Women, regardless of whether they were "respectable" or "fallen," the majority or the minority, shared a common gender designation that placed them at jeopardy. Minority and ethnic women in the West struggled with one set of risks, those of the emerging white middle class with another.

If a woman accumulated a record of minor offenses or earned an unsavory name with the local police, these weighed heavily against her when she was charged with major felonies. A woman with a public identity had already challenged the existing social structure and required firmer chastisement. A string of arrests, county jail time, negative newspaper reports—all these made women—regardless of race or ethnicity—from the so-called vice community easy targets for conviction and imprisonment in the penitentiary.

Ida Jones, an African American prostitute in Denver, Colorado, had attracted just such unfavorable public notice by the time she faced a murder charge in August 1890. Her earlier skirmishes, which stemmed from an ongoing feud within the Market and Blake Streets vice community, brought her to the attention of the Denver authorities. Apparently angered by her neighbors' part in a fall 1889 arrest for maintaining a house for "lewd women and common prostitutes and wicked, deluded, lascivious men," Ida Jones struck back. Once released from jail, Jones made a destructive sweep through her accusers' home. Not only did the owner, Lizzie Ames, claim that Jones broke all the windows but Ames listed in detail the fourteen dollars and ten cents worth of destroyed possessions—five plates, six meat platters, three cups, four saucers, one bed, one washstand, and two yards of wallpaper. Ida Jones made her fury known in the neighborhood.

Within two weeks, Jones again faced charges of "keeping a lewd house and place for the practice of fornication." On this occasion, eight area residents, including Lizzie Ames, her husband, and two others from the recently besieged Blake Street address, appeared as witnesses for the state. Among the other men and women of the vice district, Ida Jones had crossed a line into unacceptable behavior. She had not only offended noncriminal Denverites but had discredited herself among members of her own community, a dangerous circumstance for one who lived within society's marginal groups. An outcast from both the "respectable" and the "nonrespectable" of Denver, Jones floundered along with virtually no public backing as her legal troubles escalated.

By the time Ida Jones came to criminal court in 1890 charged with murder, her problems mushroomed beyond her black neighbors and drew in one of the best-known white families in the Denver vice neighborhood. The Ryan/Wallace family, prominent brothel and saloon owners, testified for the state against Ida in the murder of Stephen Zemmer. The mother of the family, Jane Elizabeth Wallace Ryan, her daughters, Julia Wallace and Annie Ryan, along with the youngest child, Buddy Ryan, joined a long list of witnesses from the Market/Blake Streets area.

The cluster of subpoena addresses issued for Ida's various arrests showed her troubles centered in her neighborhood, close to the property of the Wallace family. Most state witnesses lived within a four block range of the Wallace Saloon at 1937 Blake Street, where John "Buddy" Ryan received his summons, while officials delivered Laura Reed's to her residence "up the alley." Laura's alley address meant her prostitute's crib, rented from the Wallaces, who kept a number of these shacks behind their saloons. Laura Reed, working outside the safety of a well-managed house of prostitution and among the lower strata of western prostitutes, made a wise choice to cooperate with the powerful Jane Wallace Ryan. Ryan, a former owner of brothels and cribs in Cripple Creek, Colorado, had moved her family business to Denver, where, with her three daughters and son, she expanded her vice operations.

With one of the most influential white families in the vice district aligned against Jones, the issue of race increased her precarious position with Denver authorities. A black prostitute could not hope for the same considerations her white counterparts often negotiated. After all, in the late 1800s, Annie Ryan, daughter of Jane Elizabeth Wallace Ryan, shot the bartender, her paramour, in her saloon but did not go to the penitentiary. And early in the twentieth century, Rosie O'Grady, a white prostitute and drinking friend of at least one city detective, killed Clarence Sears, her African American lover and was acquitted. Authorities often exhibited contradictory attitudes toward the white vice community, indulging it on one hand, punishing it on the other.

African Americans in the vice districts confronted a less flexible and forgiving power structure. This, even though minority people in the late nineteenth and early twentieth centuries, strapped for economic options, responded to the encouragement of white male patrons to operate small vice establishments. Regardless, no privileged outcome awaited Ida Jones. In her case, the attitude of the police toward blacks in Denver brothels and saloons crept into the paper work drawn up for the fifteen witnesses, with two notations for state's witness W. L. Swoap, identified as a "Good Black." As usual, authorities willingly called on members of a red light district for testimony that would aid the prosecution, but held dear the negative racial and cultural biases that kept certain groups at the edges of citizenry.

A Kentuckian transplanted to Denver, Ida Jones, who could neither read nor write and counted no allies among the many witnesses, was lost before she entered the court. Her attorney's attempt to have four other women charged with premeditated murder failed, and Ida faced a jury of twelve white men. By the time the judge delivered his jury instructions, which included the suggestive remarks that jurors should "not allow the fact that the prisoner has been in the habit of practicing fornication," or "the prevalence . . . of crime in the community . . . prejudice your mind against the prisoner," the court had sealed the fate of Ida Jones. Her public identity melded with her crime to send the young woman to the Colorado State Penitentiary for a term of fifteen years.

In keeping with the dynamic for incarcerated women, Jones disappeared from the minds of Denver residents for the next nine years. Denverites did not worry about Ida Jones again until she returned to their community. Discharged from prison on 13 August 1899, Ida Jones surfaced again in the city court records in October 1901. Referred to as "Black Ida," Jones had returned to the old neighborhood of Market Street, where one Charles Peterson accused her of stealing two hundred dollars. This case dragged out over the next ten months; Ida, convicted in March 1902, apparently felt she knew enough about local justice and by August police listed her as a fugitive. Reporting the event the newspaper described Ida Jones, now only about thirty-seven years old, as "the most dangerous and vicious woman in Denver."

"Dangerous and vicious" women such as Ida Jones stirred up public censure, but those very qualities empowered Jones to withstand the environment she found inside the Colorado penitentiary. Her experiences with customers, neighbors, and competitors gave her some preparation for the world behind bars. It seems unlikely that the penitentiary, with its many abuses, surprised Ida Jones and when it did, she possessed a reservoir of knowledge about life for marginal women to sustain her. If anything helped her to survive nine years of confinement, a near record among imprisoned women, it must have been the "dangerous and vicious" qualities that infused her spirit.

Other women entered the prison world without as much of this critical grit. These women, accustomed to a private existence, lacked the personal advantage of physical and mental combat with male public authority before imprisonment. They collided unexpectedly with the law and fell from the good graces of their own communities. These women lacked the insight about the realities of an unrestrained male hierarchy that might have helped them to adjust quickly. Ill-prepared for the masculine community around them, some faltered both in spirit and health, stunned by a world they had never imagined to inhabit.

On 3 June 1888, Prisoner no. 1270, a forty-four-year-old houseworker from Illinois, concluded that the first nine months of her twenty-five-year sentence to the Nebraska State Penitentiary had been more than enough. At 6:30 in the morning, she, a woman of "temperate habits" and no previous convictions, committed suicide by cutting her throat. She left little personal record of herself, only that she had lived in Nebraska since the age of fourteen, had a "poor" education and a Methodist background, and had pleaded "not guilty" to a charge of murder. She listed her politics as "none," and her family as "nobody." Beyond these dreary, brief notations in the convict register, Prisoner no. 1270 left no indication of the circumstances that prompted her to slit her own throat as the early daylight touched her cell.

Unlike this prisoner, others managed to live out their terms, but often they faced a shorter sentence or drew strength from the knowledge that family members continued to pursue legal options that might lead to freedom. Still, for some women the events that led to imprisonment grew out of the utterly improbable. Such appeared to be so in the case of a mother and daughter from Wyoming.

In 1904, Viola Biggs, a stenographer, and her mother, Anna E. Trout, a forty-two-year-old dressmaker, entered the penitentiary at Rawlins, Wyoming, convicted on charges of kidnapping. During the previous year and a half, Viola Biggs had struggled with a mounting domestic crisis, but nothing that foreshadowed a criminal trial, conviction, and penitentiary time for the young wife. The same could be said of her mother, the law-abiding Anna Trout, caught up in the collapse of her daughter's marriage.

In May of 1903, John Biggs, Viola's husband of six months, abandoned his pregnant wife. Biggs immediately notified the family physician that he would not cover any medical expenses for the coming birth and also conveyed the same message to local merchants about bills for Viola and the child. On 16 August, twenty-year-old Viola gave birth to a son; she named him Leonard. John Biggs did not attend the birth, never came to see the infant, and, as he had declared, paid nothing in support. In early September, Viola, deserted by her husband and without economic means, directed her mother, Anna Trout, to take three-week-old Leonard to Denver and place him for adoption.

At the train depot, Anna Trout chanced to encounter none other than the errant father, who knew the purpose of his mother-in-law's Denver trip but neither protested nor tried to prevent her departure. Shortly, in what appears to have been an impulsive gesture, perhaps symptomatic of most of his life decisions, John Biggs filed kidnapping charges against his wife and her mother. Basing his claim on a statute that gave fathers the right of guardianship of a minor child in preference to the mother, Biggs found the Casper, Wyoming, district attorney receptive to the case. In short order, Viola Biggs and Anna Trout came to trial before a judge who disallowed the substantial testimony of various Casper residents, ready to document John Biggs's refusal to support a son he openly acknowledged as his own.

Viola Biggs's troubles began with a husband who abandoned her almost immediately after their marriage. They mounted as the summer of 1903 moved forward and Viola had neither emotional nor economic support. These difficulties paled in comparison to the results produced by a court that permitted only the father's voice and penalized the mother's action on behalf of the infant.

Although the appellate court reversed the decision, the wheels of corrective justice ground slowly. Mother and daughter entered the penitentiary in February of 1904. The higher court rendered its opinion in April, but the two women remained in the Rawlins prison until the end of August. In the meantime, the men of this episode—the father, the district attorney, and the judge—lived on in Casper, while it remained unclear who cared for baby Leonard Biggs. It was not his mother and grandmother, serving penitentiary time for trying to guarantee his upbringing within a family environment of Viola's choosing.

Well into the twentieth century, middle-class white women continued to feel the impact of a legal system that could take on decidedly western hues. This could occur especially in those cases when a woman ignored the pressures to conform to male expectations. Such forces apparently fueled the criminal conviction of Ella Smith, a stock raiser and freighter from Wyoming.

In May 1908, Ella went on trial in Big Horn County, Wyoming. State's witnesses agreed they had known Smith, a Texas transplant, for about seven years as an independent business owner in their Wyoming community. She established a solid reputation as a hard worker, who handled all the heavy outdoor labor required of one raising horses and running a freighting business. Apparently, however, she offended the powerful stockmen, whose association in nearby Johnson County had a few years earlier conducted an infamous western range war. Ella Smith, who had resisted mounting pressures from the stockmen to abandon her business, found herself charged with misbranding stock.

At her trial, Ella Smith admitted rounding up two colts off the open range and branding them, but explained why she had good reason to believe the animals belonged to her. Smith pointed out that the animals had been ranging in a common stock area, and that she did not hide the colts from anyone. In broad daylight, she drove them over a public road through town to a barn, where she finished the branding.

She also detailed her efforts to compensate rancher John M. Baldwin, after she learned he was accusing her of the theft. Surely, Ella Smith heard whispers from the stockmen's association in the charges, as she hurried to deflect further trouble by offering Baldwin the colts, other horses, or money. She must have recognized the seriousness of her situation when Baldwin told her he would settle if he could, but the stockmen would not allow it.

On the witness stand, the neighbor, John Baldwin, readily agreed that Ella Smith tried to end the dispute in advance of any criminal charges, coming to see him before he swore out a warrant. Baldwin testified that Smith acknowledged the branding and told him she thought she owned those particular colts. If he felt otherwise, she offered to make monetary restitution or give him horses from her herd. Baldwin admitted he told Smith the matter had gone too far to be resolved, but hedged on what he might have revealed about the role of the stockmen's association in her troubles.

Smith's attorney offered a spirited defense, pointing to his client's long record in the community, the openness of her actions, the lack of criminal intent, and the vagueness of the lease lines in the area where the horses of several people ranged. In an unfriendly court, attorney Ridgley protested repeatedly as the judge allowed wide conjecture and hearsay evidence from the state's witnesses. Of thirty-one times that the defense attorney objected or moved for dismissal, the judge overruled Ridgley twenty-eight times, while the district attorney was overruled on three of five objections.

Despite the vigor of her attorney, Ella Smith went to the penitentiary at Rawlins for misbranding stock. If her attorney had planned through his many objections to pave the way for a reversal from the appeals court, such did not happen. Smith served her full sentence of eighteen months, perhaps, as a single parent, determined to do so for the young daughter who awaited her return. Ella Smith, who had ridden the range for weeks at a time, singlehandedly thrown colts to the ground for branding, and managed a freighting business, had crossed gender and economic lines, an offense to her neighboring stockmen.

They softened their response more than Wyoming stockmen of an earlier era who lynched their female competition, Ella "Cattle Kate" Watson, during the 1888 Johnson County War. Perhaps hesitant to repeat a nineteenth-century vigilante action, local cattle barons still devised ways to retain control of the stock industry. Whether by death or imprisonment, women received clear signals about the limits of gender in western enterprise. In the nineteenth century, economic opposition from the local stockmen meant death for "Cattle Kate" Watson. In the twentieth century, it meant penitentiary time for Ella Smith.

Like Ida Jones, Viola Biggs, Anna Trout, Ella Smith, and perhaps Prisoner no. 1270, many women went to a penitentiary under questionable circumstances, convicted on circumstantial or manipulated evidence. Because the women came largely from groups with limited political and economic status, prosecuting attorneys, judges, and juries, usually white males, acted with a free hand to bring about convictions. Local jurisdictions moved quickly, often denying poorly informed defendants a chance to organize a case or locate witnesses. Families and friends saw women tried and convicted before legal assistance could be mobilized. The power of those orchestrating the procedures swept over the women with such force that the accused had neither time nor means to question or affect the outcome. Whether truly guilty or truly innocent of the charges, women barely caught a glimpse of due process.

A weak understanding of the legal system and the language used there further hurt the women. Their grasp of the formal statutes was often sketchy or incorrect, their understanding of the courtroom events even more fragmented. Many did not read or write, few had more than a rudimentary education—situations that kept them confused during court proceeding. In 1888, Lizzie Gibson, an African American woman, incriminated herself, admitting she stole $1.50. But since she took the money by pushing a door open and reaching into a house, Lizzie thought she had not been breaking and entering; Lizzie went to the Texas penitentiary for two years, although within three days of her trial local citizens began petitions on her behalf.

Other women, even if not schooled in the refinements of the law, fully realized the dangers for black persons who faced the nineteenth-century court system. Susan Wallace, whose "agony . . . suffered . . . in jail . . . almost bereft her of her reason," knew not only that harsh time awaited in the Texas penitentiary but that her six small children faced an uncertain future with their mother imprisoned. Wallace, the only support of her youngsters, had taken a silver plate, a shawl, and a hat from the white family for whom she worked. She defended her actions by reason of her long service to the white woman, who over a period of three months paid the servant a total of twenty-five cents. The jury convicted the black woman of the theft, then asked for a pardon before she could be transported to the penitentiary.

In support of the state, juries tended to uphold arrest and trial procedures of court officers; they feared acquittals undercut the decisions of their elected officials. To distance themselves from responsibility in a blatantly unfair or questionable case, juries often used the "instant" citizens' petition as a way to undo their own actions.

For example, jurors in Reno, Nevada, asserted in their 1877 petition for Maggie Hart that they had convicted her based on the promise of the district attorney that the woman would be immediately pardoned. In his summation, the prosecutor demanded a guilty verdict, not because of evidence against Maggie Hart in an arson case, but to disprove public rumor that Washoe County could not get a conviction. Jurors claimed that the "declaration and promise of the district attorney . . . was taken into consideration while . . . rendering their verdict, and that verdict . . . was . . . with the distinct understanding that a petition for her pardon . . . be at once circulated." While the jury, comfortable within the confines of home and community, may have agonized over the turn of events, in October 1877 it was Maggie Hart who went to the state penitentiary for a one-year sentence.

Whether juries such as this one wanted to acknowledge their role or not, such trials for women increased the immediate local power of state officers and agencies. While pardon and parole boards then mulled over the particulars at their leisure, women served long months and years inside male penitentiaries. In the cases of Susan Wallace and Maggie Hart, state authorities showed little interest in jury reversals of sentiment; Susan Wallace went to the penitentiary for two years and Maggie Hart still had no action on her pardon application by June 1878.

In some cases, local politics, rather than issues of justice, influenced both the convictions and the pardons. For example, in the case of Essie Sara, her attorney, J. S. Hill, charged that the trial judge made public statements of his determination to convict the defendant and used incorrect courtroom procedures. From the firm of Fly and Davidson, another attorney wrote that although he did not know the woman or the case, he believed the governor could rely on certain local citizens, including a former member of the legislature, in the request "to undo what has been done by *our* county court."

Local political rivalries explained some of the actions taken by whites on behalf of black women. In 1892 when Sarah Thomas, a chambermaid at a hotel in Belton, Texas, went to the penitentiary for receiving stolen goods, almost one hundred citizens signed a clemency petition for her. George Pendleton, her white attorney, introducing the black citizen who carried the petition to the governor, asserted that Sarah was "poorly defended and probably innocent." A second lawyer from the Pendleton firm demonstrated that politicians saw executive clemency less as an issue of justice, and more as political opportunity. D. R. Pendleton recommended Sarah's pardon because he told the Texas governor, James Hogg: "if you can possibly take up this case . . . it will help your cause here wonderfully with the Negroes. We have some few in line already, some on the fence and some for Clark. However, Curry will be here soon and I am afraid of his influence with them."

Whether the convictions were against black women or poor white women, whether they oozed with the tensions of local political competition or court corruption, each involved keeping the woman in the local jail for a lengthy period, assessing her with a heavy fine, and threatening her with or committing her to the penitentiary. Regardless of the jockeying between court official and local politicos, the result for women meant public censure and questionable justice; for the community it meant greater awareness of just who retained political and social control. At least that appeared to be the thinking of Texas attorney G. I. Turnley, who endorsed a pardon from fines for a young black couple convicted of unlawful fornication. Turnley asked for relief for the local pair, who scraped by raising corn and cotton, because he

believed the executive action, "would have a good effect upon other uninformed and ignorant negroes."

Juries, instruments of the judiciary, reinforced a double-edged system of
punishment and "sympathy" that further intensified the hold courts maintained over women and a white system held over black citizens. Knowledge
of such matters circulated widely in poor communities, where residents enjoyed, at best, an uneasy truce with the law. The possible punitive outcome of
a clash with the law guided the choices of some, when confronted with the
force of the legal authorities.

In 1888, African American Minnie Mitchell, mother of three small children, went to the Texas penitentiary for two years, charged with concealing
stolen property. A year later, she received a pardon when the trial judge and
prosecuting attorney filed on behalf of the "honest and hard working girl," because of "new evidence" that revealed Minnie had been protecting her eleven-
year-old sister, who had taken a ring. Minnie understood about the Susan
Wallaces of her world and knew it possible for her sister to join other black
youngsters incarcerated at the Huntsville prison. Mitchell, aware that under
the ordinary mechanisms of punishment a black child could and would go to
the penitentiary, chose defense of her family over personal security and risked
the dangers of imprisonment.

Not every woman had the opportunity to make such well-thought-out
choices. Texan Amanda Roads, a former slave said to be "old and feeble,"
served two years for "not returning money she had found." Roads, convicted of what appeared to have been no true crime, received a pardon in 1883.
Close to the same date, another Texas inmate, Lena Gayhart, "a young German girl, not knowing English," was also pardoned. Charged with a grand larceny offense of stealing over twenty dollars, Gayhart served a year in the
penitentiary before officials acknowledged the prisoner could not understand
the proceedings and had no chance to secure witnesses for her defense. On the
day of the conviction, jury members signed a petition for Gayhart's pardon because they "doubted the justice of their verdict."

Four years later, questionable trial practices in Texas continued to haunt
women, especially African Americans. On 19 November 1887, authorities arrested Ellen Smith, "an ignorant but honest and industrious colored woman,"
and took her immediately to the courtroom. She had no "opportunity to obtain advice or know her rights," and was convicted on her own testimony of
maiming a hog. Smith's "confession" consisted of explaining how one dog
(not necessarily hers) attacked the swine, but a second, which Smith had tied
up, broke loose and did the damage. On this evidence and without understanding self-incrimination or how such a civil case might be resolved, Smith
was convicted.

Regardless of the western location or the trial procedures, the process
of arrest and conviction threw women off balance. They exercised limited
control in the legal negotiations, as they received their first lessons in the
power of the courts. Town and county officials moved swiftly for arrest and

conviction. Although court officers often willingly threw themselves into the appeals process for a woman convict, they initiated such action only after women had been detained for long periods in some type of custodial care. Thus, at the local level, women experienced the first phase of transformation into a female prisoner. They then faced a new world of power, one fueled by race, class, and gender imperatives, inside the penitentiary.

Race, the first of these forces, shaded prisons with the many hues of women of color. At the Kansas penitentiary, at least 150 of 200 women received between 1865 and 1906 were black. In Missouri between 1865 and 1871, of approximately 110 women who went to the penitentiary, thirty-seven were clearly black, while the racial designation of twenty-six could not be determined. Depending on the race of individuals in the latter group, between 34 percent and 57 percent of the Missouri women prisoners were black. Between 1866 and 1872, sixty-seven women, sixty-four of whom were African American, entered the Louisiana state prison system. Of 107 women prisoners in the Iowa prison at Anamosa between 1883 and 1907, eighteen, or almost 20 percent, were black, but the racial heritage of another thirty-four, or 23 percent, could not be determined with certainty. In Montana, of sixty identified women who entered prison between 1890 and 1910, twenty-nine were African Americans. Even Idaho, with its small number of women prisoners across time, reported that between 1903 and 1904, of its three female inmates, two were African Americans. Of Arizona's twenty-eight women held at the Yuma prison, fourteen, or 50 percent, were Mexican American and six, or approximately 21 percent, were African American. None of these states included any Asian women in the registers. Regardless of western location, African American women, against whom the state often used slight criminal evidence, went to state penitentiaries in proportionately greater numbers than females of other groups.

These figures, though they might not be precise, aligned with one of the first surveys about criminal statistics in the United States. According to findings from the 1910 census, African Americans equaled 10.7 percent of the total national population, but 21.9 percent of all committed prisoners in the country. In addition, the ratio for incarcerated black women (418.3 per 100,000) soared almost six times above the corresponding ratio for white women (70 per 100,000). Overall, in proportion to total population figures, eleven times as many African American women as Caucasian women were committed for larceny and about thirty-three times as many for crimes of assault. In crimes designated as "moral offenses," black women went to prison about five times more frequently than white women. Although sectional differences might be thought to skew the survey results, in every geographic region, including the West, the percentage of African American women incarcerated, relative to the area's demography, surpassed that of any other group, including black males. Arrest and conviction practices that favored some white women tipped prisoner statistics against black women and thus artificially inflated their appearance of criminality.

More than just the greater likelihood for imprisonment, other factors influenced the time served for nonwhite women. In Nebraska, between 1869 and 1910, of ninety females sentenced to the penitentiary, fifty-one were African American women, nine white, one Native American, one Hispanic, and the racial identity of twenty-eight women could not be ascertained with certainty. Of the nine white women, four were released early through good time credit, one spent her sentence in and out of the insane asylum, one died in prison, and three received pardons, two of these from murder and manslaughter convictions. A dressmaker sentenced to life was pardoned after two years, and a prisoner serving a year for manslaughter received not parole but a pardon after nine months. Of the fifty-two black women, none saw the penitentiary gates swing open before the expiration of their sentences through a good time allowance and none received pardons. Of the twelve incarcerated for crimes of violence, only one served less than one-half to three-quarters of the full sentence.

In Arkansas, these racial distinctions in time served also prevailed. A sampling of 270 women prisoners, from among those imprisoned at some time between 1881 and 1915, showed that eighteen whites had been sentenced to the penitentiary, in contrast to 252 African American women. Among these, prisoner files could be identified for sixty-eight women, six whites and sixty-two blacks.

Of the white inmates, one, Sarah Weidner, a fifty-eight-year-old woman, served twenty months of a five-year term for murder and died in the prison hospital of heart failure. Two young white women were transferred to a correctional home for girls, one the day after arrival at the penitentiary. One white woman was pardoned after serving two and a half years of a four-year sentence, one after serving five months of a twelve-month term, and one was pardoned after three weeks.

African American women did not experience so lenient a release and pardon system. Of the sixty-two black women, fifty-two served at least until expiration of term through good time, one died in prison, and nine received pardons. Unlike the white women, whose pardons arrived promptly, only two blacks served less than half the full sentence. Four of the African American women secured pardons after imprisonment of several years—thirteen out of a fifteen-year sentence, six out of seven years, eight out of ten.

In 1910, all thirty-seven Arkansas women prisoners were African American. This prompted one citizen to protest the figures, noting the high incarceration numbers conflicted with the fact that "the negroes are far in the minority in population." He complained about this imbalance and felt sure that "statisticians" would use the biennial report of the penitentiary superintendent to "'prove' the depravity and criminality of the negro." He asserted that it was "well known . . . that white women are convicted for every crime, . . . receive penitentiary sentences, but are pardoned forthwith." Further, he claimed the governor boasted that no white woman would be within the walls during his administration. White women received gubernatorial pardons with such "frequency as to excite the disgust of even the white daily papers and the court itself."

Black women not only faced incarceration more often and served hefty portions of their sentences but their punishment had community application as well. For example, at the age of seventeen, Caroline Williams, an African American woman from Lamar County, Texas, entered the penitentiary on a life sentence for murder. Nearly sixteen years later, the supervising sergeant endorsed her application for a pardon, acknowledging Williams's generally satisfactory conduct. His main argument, however, concerned the impact her release would have on the other convicts at the camp. He stressed that the "long time ones" looked "with eagerness" to marking fifteen years in the penitentiary, as they anticipated that anniversary would automatically bring them freedom. The sergeant did not fear that "criminals" who had "paid their debt to society" would be wronged by unduly severe terms or that a crime might not be adequately punished. Rather, he worried that disappointing those prisoners with lengthy sentences would endanger discipline. Caroline Williams received her pardon, and Texas conveyed a message about its power to black communities, both free and imprisoned.

Race guaranteed that African American women faced a daunting set of legal procedures. Under a rubric that defined all female criminals as "unfit," the nonwhite became more unfit, until a whole set of racial imperatives underscored the practices inside the prisons. The penitentiary served as one more societal location where black women found that race propelled a wide spectrum of policies reinforcing social, economic, and political control over minority groups.

At the same time, the punishment of women functioned as a way to weave folk controls through ethnic families. Using the powerful oral network of the black and Hispanic communities, mothers, aunts, grandmothers, and sisters imposed familial restrictions on children before youngsters stumbled across inflexible racial rules. Drawing on the bitter experiences of their communities, these women of color tried to blunt the racism of the dominant culture as they sought to protect their own families. This was exactly the desired outcome in the perspective of the dominant culture, with its many-faceted strategies for racial control.

Along with race, the infrastructure of punishment also incorporated class assessment into the treatment of women prisoners. Class designations, however, slipped across a slick surface, shifting as convenient for officials. Judgments appeared based on impression and circumstance, as much as on rigid definition. In St. Louis several missionaries petitioned for the release of Mary Godfrey because the inmate had "proved by her general conduct that she is not of the class of females usually found in such places." What they meant by this assertion, they did not feel compelled to explain. In the New Mexico penitentiary, Mexican American women dominated in numbers, but received fewer privileges than Anglo women. But in nearby Texas, authorities segregated Spanish-speaking women with white inmates, giving both significantly

better living accommodations and work assignments than the larger group
of black females. Also in Texas a petitioner argued that Mrs. W. J. Stewart, a
white woman, deserved a pardon because her father was, "a *gallant Confederate Soldier* and served the entire war." Local determinations within western
regions and the personnel managing the women prisoners apparently influenced class designations.

In Utah, Belle Harris despised the humiliation she felt when the war-
den's wife brought women visitors to stare at the "polygamous prisoner."
At the same time, Belle failed to see the irony in herself when she protested
vehemently that she had to share her small quarters and "eat at the same
table" with a "common prostitute." Belle complained in her journal, "She is
one of the lowest classes though she acts very well so far." Loneliness and
motherhood quickly showed the two outcasts they had more in common
than they thought, and Belle grieved when her new friend departed through
an early release.

The social thinker Kate Richards O'Hare saw more precisely that class distinctions inside the prison reflected those of the outside world. Among the
women at the Missouri penitentiary, federal and political prisoners respectively ranked as the "upper class" and the "aristocracy," while third place
went to those who "disposed of undesirable husbands." O'Hare, herself a
political prisoner, referred to the African American inmates as "colored girls"
and somewhat regally reported that one said it a shame that women like
"Miss Emma [Goldman] and Miss Kate" had to be in a penitentiary. Nonetheless, an appreciation for the common suffering marked O'Hare's interaction
with all the women prisoners, and she actively cultivated relationships
throughout the cell block.

Although constrained by her own sense of class, O'Hare looked with little regard to women outside the prison walls. About two months into her
term, she wrote, "I am not particularly optimistic concerning the average
middle class woman." Her criticism stemmed from the fact that "not a
woman's club or the women of one church have ever shown one gleam of interest in this institution." She complained particularly about the wives of
prison administrators as middle-class women who should have felt some attachment to female inmates.

Despite the reluctance of noncriminal middle-class women to identify
with prisoners, the inmates themselves understood the importance of class
rhetoric in their incarceration. For example, twenty-eight-year-old Dolly
Brady freely admitted working as a prostitute, but called on her "long and
honest residence," affirmed by any man who "ever policed the district in
which she lived," as reason for clemency. Brady, of Cheyenne, Wyoming, described herself as one with "lax" morals, but never indulging in larceny and
robbery, "for which she . . . had many opportunities." Yet, her attorney told
the governor that Brady's petition was "much more difficult than the ordinary applicant . . . because of the common lack of reputation and conscience
in people of her class." Dolly Brady, no doubt, would have objected to such

a description of herself. Clearly, she had defined standards for herself that met her understanding of so-called better class and expected the "respectable" men of the community to vouch for her record.

Dolly Brady's claim to executive clemency may have been enhanced because the crime committed inside her brothel involved an Asian. Clyde M. Watts, court reporter at Brady's trial, informed the governor that a Japanese customer came to Dolly's house, paid her five dollars, and went to bed with the woman. Watts remembered that, according to the trial testimony, "she got up and went out in the sitting room and . . . told [them] to throw the Jap out and take what he had." Dolly's friends in Cheyenne may have thought it unnecessary for her to serve two years in the penitentiary for a robbery and beating inflicted on a Japanese client. The pardon and parole board may have recoiled at the thought of a white woman, regardless of her own class definitions, engaging in sexual relations with an Asian man. However racial and class forces mingled in this case, the governor did not accommodate the petition; Dolly Brady served her full sentence in the Wyoming penitentiary.

A woman might be able to enhance her own class standing with authorities, if she could demonstrate that the object of her crime ranked lower on the social ladder than she. Jane Taylor's lawyer used this argument when seeking a pardon for his client. Although the Winnemucca, Nevada, woman was convicted on a charge of assault with intent to kill, her lawyer argued that "it would have been a blessing to the community if she had been a better shot." Winnemucca citizens joined in the petition, noting that although Jennie was "a woman of the town," she was known for her "strict honesty," "very many redeeming qualities," and "generous contributions for the relief of the afflicted."

The concept of class gave certain women an edge when entangled in criminal matters. In 1909, Herbert S. Hadley, the governor of Missouri, intervened at the local police level when some of his constituency objected to the police treatment of Hildegarde Hallon, a St. Louis woman arrested on charges of forgery. The complaints came to Hadley in letters, immediately heightening the importance of the protest and underscoring the muscle of literate voters. Not only did Hadley inquire about the use of excessive force by police but he challenged the wisdom of disturbing the woman after dark, when the arrest could have been postponed until daylight hours. Particularly, Hadley wanted to know if it had ever been the practice of the St. Louis department "to arrest persons who clearly do not belong to the criminal class."

He might better have asked the forty-three women—eleven whites and thirty-two blacks—at that time incarcerated in the Missouri penitentiary. Their definitions of place and rank inside their own communities certainly did not mesh with the governor's. Within their own cultures and families, women formulated attitudes about position and status that had little or no connection to those of a white male politician or the public agencies surrounding his office.

Not surprisingly, police dropped the forgery charges against Hildegarde Hallon, and she did not need to call on her race and class as bargaining chips

in the penitentiary. The few women of the middle class—armed with education, paid legal counsel, and strong political purpose—who entered prison
endured great deprivation, but they had sufficient social and economic backing to gain some advantage with prison authorities. Better food, cleaner housing, more access to officials—these were the typical benefits for high profile
political prisoners. After prison these women looked to the prospect of reconstructing the fabric of their lives, using their prison time as a badge of
courage and a vehicle for public discourse about reform. For western ethnic
women, however, dismissed as "low class," a penitentiary sentence reinforced
stereotypes held by the dominant society.

While race and class stratified prisoner life for differing groups of women,
gender dominated the female experience inside the walls. If anything, it reminded women of their shared dilemma and helped the few housed together in any prison to forge common bonds. Gender ruled as the unspoken
vulnerability of all imprisoned women. Seldom did women prisoners overlook
that reality.

In 1896, Minnie Snyder, a native of New York, stood trial in Wyoming because her husband shot and killed a rancher, John Rooks. Minnie's husband,
Peter, whirled and fired blindly into a fast-pursuing mob, in what appeared
to be another clash between newcomer sheep ranchers and local cattlemen.
The judge rejected the Snyders' pleas of self-defense, suggested the mob
should have lynched the couple, dismissed incriminating evidence given by
the cattle vigilantes themselves, labeled the husband and wife the "evil-doers,"
and sent them off to the penitentiary for terms of ten and six years respectively. Not content with this statement, the judge, aiming his sentencing comments directly at Minnie Snyder, said: "A woman, that is a good woman, is
respected in every community, but a woman, when she uses her tongue can
stir up more mischief and do more damage in a community than any one. . . .
It is one of the saddest of things to sentence a woman to the penitentiary, but
my duty is [so] clear."

As the judge finished sentencing Minnie, he declared the country around
Lander safe for a "good woman," but that Minnie had "gone too far" in standing by her husband's side during the crisis. Since the notion of standing by
one's husband represented a central tenet of marriage in the nineteenth century, one wonders how Minnie could have extricated herself from the court's
double jeopardy.

Within a year, friends of the Snyders began to circulate pardon petitions
for the imprisoned pair. Countering the censure of Minnie as one who offended gender sensibilities, these petitions placed the inmate back inside the
circle of good womanhood as "delicate and kind in disposition . . . and always obedient to her aged parents." Two years later, Minnie's mother wrote
to the governor that her daughter's health in prison had deteriorated and expressed fear the young woman would not survive much longer. Despite these
appeals, Minnie Snyder, who apparently took no part in the shooting death
of John Rooks, did not elude the gender culpability defined by the judge; she

received no gubernatorial pardon and remained in the penitentiary at Rawlins, Wyoming, until 29 August 1901, when she was released and moved to Deadwood, South Dakota, to await her husband.

Race, class, and gender outlined the configurations of the woman prisoner profile. Women inmates shared another common element, that of youthfulness. The usual woman prisoner's age fell between eighteen and thirty. For example, from among the extant records for women inmates in Colorado between 1884 and 1909, ages for seventy-two prisoners can be determined. Twenty-two prisoners were over the age of thirty, while fifty women, or nearly 70 percent, were between eighteen and thirty. In Iowa, from 1893 to 1907, from among 107 women prisoners, seventy women or 65 percent showed ages between sixteen and thirty. In Arizona, no woman over thirty was incarcerated at Yuma.

Youthfulness marked the female inmates, imprisoned through their most potentially rebellious years, at ages when society preferred an ordered community of women committed to marriage and motherhood. For young women who challenged that structure, or even thought of doing so, the conditions in the penitentiary suggested the possible consequences.

Those consequences often meant life-changing experiences for young women. Sarah Crook, aged sixteen, escaped from the Texas penitentiary. Crook, sentenced to twelve years for murder, took flight to Louisiana, where Texas officials tracked her in May of 1878. If the authorities apprehended her, Crook certainly faced the same penalty as had Louisiana inmate Alice Dunbar, ten years earlier. In 1868, Dunbar bolted from a prison superintendent's office, after serving almost a full year of an eighteen-month sentence. Authorities captured her in 1871 and returned her to the state prison system. Upon completion of her outstanding six months, Dunbar received her discharge. Officials added no time for the 1868 flight; just as during the recently past days of slavery, this fifty-one-year-old black woman, stripped to the waist and flogged, paid for her escape.

Occasionally, in the cases of very young girls, one or two citizens or attorneys raised a voice of protest on behalf of the child. For example, in Santa Fe, New Mexico, in 1881, a fight between two twelve-year-old girls—one white and one black—resulted in charges, conviction, and jail time for the latter. After the encounter, the father of the white girl, W. H. Gray, secured the arrest of the black child, Mary Elizabeth Washington McKiev. Mary Elizabeth was placed in the county jail and the next day required to appear before justice of the peace García Ortiz.

After listening to Gray and securing the "confession of the . . . little girl," Justice Ortiz found the child guilty and fined her a total of seven dollars and fifty cents. When the child could not pay her fine, Justice Ortiz returned her to the county jail. An attorney, M. S. Breeden, who immediately took the case, wrote in his petition, "considering the respective ages of these *two children* . . . this is a case which calls *loudly* for *Executive Clemency*." The acting governor heard Breeden's call and responded by granting a pardon. The bonding of

Hispanics and Anglos against African Americans does not appear to have been confined to the Texas penitentiary but spilled over into New Mexico as well. A local social or political alliance across race lines apparently impelled these adult men to react so vigorously to a quarrel between two children.

New Mexico was not the only jurisdiction willing to punish children with prison time. Other young girls went to penitentiaries as well. In 1880 Henrietta Waideman, "less than sixteen years of age," left the Texas prison system. Four years later, Mary Jane Watson, a fourteen-year-old girl convicted of the theft of a diamond ring, departed, with a reminder that her parole would be revoked for any criminal violation. These teenagers, African Americans, mingled with the general inmate population and worked beside the adults. Although this situation exposed them to violence and sexual abuses, it may also have given them the encouragement and protection of older inmates.

On occasion, local authorities intervened before a child actually entered the penitentiary. Such occurred for Ophelia LeCour, sentenced to the penitentiary at the age of fourteen. Charged with theft, LeCour, who may have been white, received a pardon while still in the county jail. In 1890, in Texas, Susan Bates, "under sixteen years of age," was convicted of perjury and sentenced to five years in the house of corrections. A year and a half later, her attorney, using the written verdict from Bates's trial, demonstrated that the confinement of the inmate at the Huntsville penitentiary violated the judgment of the local court. The lawyer simply placed the embarrassing matter before Governor James Hogg, who signed the pardon two days after receipt of the documents.

Petty theft, "stealing" a diamond ring, perjury—such charges lodged against children and adolescents underscored the controlling purpose of the law. Under what circumstances did officials secure the "confessions" of these children? Certainly intimidation and the desire to frighten children into "good behavior" were among the motivations for placing youngsters inside penitentiaries. These episodes, especially involving children from African American and Hispanic families, again indicated the intention that youngsters learn early about the authority of the state.

Whether adolescent, young woman, or older person, the majority of women committed or faced charges of small crimes against property. A local jail would have been the more appropriate place to serve the brief sentences that should have accompanied such minor offenses. But in high numbers women went to penitentiaries for misdemeanors or nonviolent crimes. For example, in Kansas between 1865 and 1901, forty-six women entered the penitentiary for violent crimes and 105 for nonviolent ones. In Missouri between 1865 and 1871, ten women faced penitentiary time for violent actions and seventy-eight for nonviolent ones. In Arkansas between 1901 and 1906, eighteen women were committed for nonviolent crimes and seven for violent offenses. The nonviolent charges against inmates included grand larceny, accessory to burglary, bigamy, adultery, forgery, slander, perjury, possessing counterfeit coin, and concealing or receiving stolen property.

Grand larceny charges, a common cause for women's imprisonment, often did not meet the usual statutory definition of theft in excess of a twenty-dollar value. Of fourteen former slave women confined to the Huntsville, Texas, penitentiary in 1867, thirteen had been imprisoned on thievery charges (the fourteenth woman gave her husband a pick axe to help him escape from prison). The stolen items included a hog, a nightgown, a pair of drapes, a petticoat, a pair of stockings, and $1.00. Only two women clearly stole an amount to equal a grand larceny charge. One had confessed to her crime after physical torture, and Polly Ann Jennings admitted her theft of eighty dollars, money owed by her white "mistress" who refused to pay the wages due her.

These Texas women came to the attention of William Sinclair, an inspector for the Bureau of Refugees, Freedmen, and Abandoned Lands, who examined the Huntsville penitentiary early in 1867. Sinclair sought executive clemency for approximately 225 former slaves, whom he felt were held against all justice. Sinclair wrote to his superior that the "trivial nature of the crimes charged against them and the severity of the punishment already inflicted . . . should be . . . a sufficient argument for their release."

The case of Caroline Johnson, a free woman from Galveston County, Texas, demonstrated what Sinclair meant. In June 1866, the district court convicted Johnson for the theft of a woman's skirt, valued at three dollars. Nothing in her pardon petition revealed how long Johnson awaited trial in Galveston County before this conviction. William Sinclair, however, noted that most of the Huntsville prisoners had been detained six months to a year in a county jail before trial and that the local time served did not count toward the penitentiary sentence.

Johnson offered Sinclair no particular explanation for the crime, and he recorded only that the prisoner indicated the skirt had been taken from her "mistress." Sinclair hoped he could secure an immediate release for Johnson and the others arguing, "Had they half the funds that many a greater rascal has they would not remain in prison one week."

Despite his goals, Sinclair did not succeed, at least for Caroline Johnson. Not until 20 December 1867 was a pardon petition entered for her. It indicated that the law under which Johnson had been convicted no longer existed. The punishment for her crime had changed from two years in the penitentiary to one year in the county jail, with a possible fine of one hundred dollars. Ten months after William Sinclair interceded for Caroline Johnson and her companions at Huntsville, the Galveston woman received a full pardon. A former slave who eked out a slim living as a domestic worker, Johnson lacked an advocate until this federal officer intervened, and time diminished his success. The impact of her lengthy imprisonment and the questions surrounding her guilt, not only touched her life but rippled through her Texas community.

After all, citizens knew about the court events inside a local jurisdiction. Each person had reason to view the speedy and fickle conduct of the courts with wariness. For example, on 19 November 1866, Amanda Hawkins, a black woman laboring as a farmer in Fayette County, Texas, was indicted for "theft of money," convicted the next day, and sentenced to two years in the penitentiary. In April 1868, in response to a gubernatorial inquiry about Hawkins, a court clerk admitted that no one could find the original indictment, making it impossible to confirm the size of the theft. Hawkins herself had told an investigator at the penitentiary that the amount was $2.50, a sum far below that required for a grand larceny indictment. Charged under vague circumstances for a misdemeanor, Hawkins had virtually no time to assemble a defense, went immediately to the penitentiary, and stayed there almost a year and a half before any official raised questions about her incarceration.

Amanda Hawkins's experience pointed to how rarely major theft accounted for the convictions rendered against women. Rather, women's nonviolent crimes tended to reflect the limited economics of their lives. For women with little education or closed out of western industrial growth, occupational choices stayed narrow. Some jobs were seasonal, none especially lucrative. From region to region, women worked as servants, housekeepers, prostitutes, waitresses, hotel maids, seamstresses, laundresses, cooks, cleaning women, and field hands. Even as the West matured and its economy shifted, the general trend for women to have lower-paying jobs remained steady.

Women with lesser economic options typically associated with men of the same financial standing. Sometimes women's crimes grew out of their connection to these husbands and partners, although which party acted as the instigator of the wrongdoing remained unclear. On one afternoon in Denver, Mary Caffieri and her husband conspired in the theft of oriental rugs from two different establishments. She went to the Colorado penitentiary for two concurrent five-year terms.

Gertie Smith also had connections to Denver crime, where she and her partner Edward Martin operated a shell game. When they moved on to Rawlins, Wyoming, they traveled with Pearl Smith and James Murphy. In Rawlins the two women, who were not related, were charged with distracting store clerks while the men shoplifted. Although the evidence against Gertie and Pearl was circumstantial, they, along with their male companions, went to the Laramie penitentiary for two years.

Frequently, single and married women depended on the economic support of a male partner, whether he obtained it by legal or illegal means. If a husband died or deserted his family, a woman had few opportunities to earn a sufficient income to maintain the home. Poor women, often the only support of several little children, stole food, jewelry, small sums of money. They pilfered a few clothes and household goods. Occasionally they wrote a threatening letter, tried to pass a forged check, or disturbed a church service. When apprehended, they had no money for attorneys and fines, because it was their poverty that made thievery a solution in the first place. Overall, the punishments meted out for these illegalities far surpassed the crimes themselves.

When a woman's transgression included the violation of moral rules, then another layer of social punishment awaited her. Any charge connected to human intimacy—adultery, fornication, bigamy, prostitution—brought strict penalties for women from all cultures. Those penalties often translated into costly fines, the price for sexual misbehavior.

Actually price proved to be exactly what transgressors in morals charges lacked—the price of the fine. Across the era, fines and court costs ranged from $100 to more than $300, handsome fees for women who supported themselves by doing housework or field labor. Without the financial means to pay county fines, prostitutes and poor women, frequently abandoned by the men who were their sexual partners, faced the threat of penitentiary time for carnal offenses.

Even if a woman had not strayed across society's moral boundaries, she might find herself ensnared in charges connected to vice. In 1896 officials in Bonham, Texas, sought remission of a $200 fine for Melia Edwards, a black woman who had worked in the community for years. Edwards's former husband brought the complaint for keeping a disorderly house, a charge for which there appeared to be no foundation. Nonetheless, once she was convicted and could not produce the fine, Melia Edwards went to the county work farm.

The danger of punishment intensified in a morals charge if men and women crossed racial lines, regardless of the gender mix of the couples. In 1881 Sallie Wheeler, an African American mother of four young children and only support for her family, was fined $250 after her conviction for fornication with a white man. The woman had no way to pay a fee of that magnitude and remained incarcerated until county officials wanted her released to care for her children. Nothing in her record indicated whether her male partner had also been charged.

Such was not the case for Texan Ella Anderson, convicted of adultery with a white man and sentenced to a convict labor camp to work off her fine of $300. The camp contractor set the female convict labor rate at thirty dollars per year; Ella Anderson faced a ten-year sentence for adultery. Her partner, a white man, also convicted, served five years, because the same contractor valued male labor at sixty dollars per year. Six years after Ella Anderson went to a work camp, her county attorney filed a pardon petition, arguing that on a misdemeanor the woman had been removed from the local jurisdiction and treated like a state felon. Whatever the circumstances of their union, both Ella Anderson and her white partner gave many years of their lives for ignoring current sexual taboos.

Fifteen years later, eighteen-year-old Dora Meredith, a white woman, went to the Huntsville penitentiary and served seven months of a two-year sentence for an "unlawful marriage to a negro." Attorneys argued unsuccessfully for her immediate pardon on the grounds that her "unnatural white parents" had advised the "girl of very low . . . intelligence" and from a "family . . . of a . . . debasing nature" to enter the marriage. Dora's lawyers determined the only appeal that could be made for a white woman in this situation had to be based on the concept of female stupidity that opened the way for the corrupting influence of others. This gave explanation to the choice of a white woman and a black man to cast aside both popular opinion and legal restrictions against unions across racial lines.

In conclusion, women who came to the penitentiaries of the West often left behind a life that had placed them in an untenable position with local law enforcement officials. Despite the difficulties their public lives generated, these women may have enjoyed some advantage inside the prison because their experiences had forced them to negotiate the rocky road of male authority. The prison world contained new challenges, but public women came equipped with knowledge of their own survival skills and were ready to use them.

Women prisoners who had led private lives, where they resided securely inside the boundaries of acceptable gender conduct, had more lessons to learn in prison. They had to adjust to an unexpected physical environment and to a type of masculine power that they would have liked to deny. Some made the necessary transition; others did not.

Regardless of whether a woman came from a private or public life, few women confronted an evenhanded legal system. Tried in the public press with the language of morality, women had little formal knowledge about the forces that moved quickly to imprison them. Improper court proceedings, excessive sentences for trivial crimes, lengthy time served—all these existed, if they did not indeed prevail. Although their crimes fell largely into nonviolent misdemeanor categories and often reflected the poverty of their lives, women went to male penitentiaries.

The various inequities intensified when the prisoners were women of color. African Americans particularly, in relation to their numbers, went to penitentiaries more often than women from other groups. They served longer sentences and received less leniency through the pardon and parole system.

Class imperatives also influenced the treatment of women prisoners. Across racial lines, economically disadvantaged women made up the prison rosters. The experiences of middle-class and wealthy women with the criminal justice system seems explained by their near-total exclusion from prisoner records. If women of economic means committed crimes, adjudication was reached for many before they entered western penitentiaries. Women inside the prisons were subjected to arbitrary class assignment by those who supervised them. Within the context of the prison community, women also had their own rules for designating class.

The forces of race, class, and gender shaped the dynamics of penitentiary time. Moreover, these forces cascaded down on the heads of young women, twisting the contours of their adult lives. If they survived the penitentiary, none would forget its special hardships for women. None would want her kith and kin to travel that road. Despite that feeling, women entered male penitentiaries in the West. From the Dakotas to Texas, from Kansas to Idaho, in small cells and on work farms, they became the women of the western prison world.

Discussion Questions

1. Examine Butler's assertion that "regardless of western location, African American women, against whom the state often used slight criminal evidence, went to state penitentiaries in proportionately greater numbers than females of other groups." What kinds of figures and evidence does she give to support this assertion? Do you find her evidence compelling? Why or why not?

2. Butler writes of children incarcerated for petty crimes. Discuss the controversy, which continues today, about whether or not violent youths should be treated as adults or as children in the courts. Do you think children under eighteen who are guilty of violent crimes should or should not be tried as adults? What changes do you see that have taken place since the times of the early western justice system? Which problems remain in our justice system today?

Writing Suggestions

1. Write a three-page essay in which you analyze Butler's argumentation in this selection. Consider her use of topic sentences and primary and secondary sources, and her strategy for proving her points. How does she support her assertions with evidence? How does she weave primary and secondary sources together to substantiate her assertions? How does she introduce her sources?

2. Butler's assertion that black women were incarcerated at much higher rates than white women is echoed by a number of judicial system critics today. Research the current status of women in prison in your state, looking at percentages of women incarcerated by race, age, socioeconomic background, and any other factors you find interesting. What kinds of crimes have these women committed, and what is the length of their sentence? Does race seem to make a difference in sentencing, or have judicial conditions improved today compared to the inequalities of the nineteenth century? Write your findings in a researched report, using clear topic sentences that relate clearly to your thesis.

Deadwood Dick, the Prince of the Road

Fearless Frank to the Rescue

EDWARD WHEELER

Dime novels originated in the second half of the nineteenth century, when these tales of adventure and intrigue sold for a dime. Some of the most popular dime novels were about the West, and Edward Wheeler's series about Deadwood Dick was the most popular dime novel series of all. Published by Beadle and Adams, these novels played a major role in establishing the myths and romantic tales about the West. Written by an easterner who had never even seen the West, the Deadwood Dick series incorporated popular current events into the texts, portraying history in a unique, if not accurate, fashion. Edward Wheeler wrote thirty-three Deadwood Dick novels between 1877 and 1884. In the first chapter of *Deadwood Dick, the Prince of the Road*, Wheeler introduces us to some of the colorful characters who will play parts in the story.

On the plains, midway between Cheyenne and the Black Hills, a train had halted for a noonday feed. Not a railway train, mind you, but a line of those white-covered vehicles drawn by strong-limbed mules, which are most properly styled "prairie schooners."

There were four wagons of this type, and they had been drawn in a circle about a camp-fire, over which was roasting a savory haunch of venison. Around the camp-fire were grouped half a score of men, all rough, bearded, and grizzled, with one exception. This being a youth whose age one could have safely put at twenty, so perfectly developed of physique and intelligent of facial appearance was he. There was something about him that was not handsome, and yet you would have been puzzled to tell what it was, for his countenance was strikingly handsome, and surely no form in the crowd was more noticeable for its grace, symmetry, and proportionate development. It would have taken a scholar to have studied out the secret.

He was of about medium stature, and as straight and square-shouldered as an athlete. His complexion was nut-brown, from long exposure to the sun; hair of hue of the raven's wing, and hanging in long, straight strands adown his back; eyes black and piercing as an eagle's; features well molded, with a firm, resolute mouth and prominent chin. He was an interesting specimen of young, healthy manhood, and, even though a youth in years, was one that could command respect, if not admiration, wheresoever he might choose to go.

One remarkable item about his personal appearance, apt to strike the be-holder as being exceedingly strange and eccentric, was his costume—buck-skin throughout, and that dyed to the brightest scarlet hue.

On being asked the cause of his odd freak of dress, when he had joined the train a few miles out from Cheyenne, the youth had laughingly replied:

"Why, you see, it is to attract bufflers, if we should meet any, out on the plains 'twixt this and the Hills."

He gave his name as Fearless Frank, and said he was aiming for the Hills; that if the party in question would furnish him a place among them, he would extend to them his assistance as a hunter, guide, or whatever, until the desti-nation was reached.

Seeing that he was well armed, and judging from external appearances that he would prove a valuable accessory, the miners were nothing loth in ac-cepting his services.

Of the others grouped about the camp-fire, only one is specially noticeable, for, as Mark Twain remarks, "the average of gold-diggers look alike." This person was a little, deformed old man; hump-backed, bow-legged, and white-haired, with cross eyes, a large mouth, a big head, set upon a slim, crane-like neck; blue eyes, and an immense brown beard, that flowed downward half-way to the belt about his waist, which contained a small arsenal of knives and revolvers. He hobbled about with a heavy crutch constantly under his left arm, and was certainly a pitiable sight to behold.

He too had joined the caravan after it had quitted Cheyenne, his advent taking place about an hour subsequent to that of Fearless Frank. His name he asserted was Nix—Geoffrey Walsingham Nix—and where he came from, and what he sought in the Black Hills, was simply a matter of conjecture among the miners, as he refused to talk on the subject of his past, present or future.

The train was under the command of an irascible old plainsman who had served out his apprenticeship in the Kansas border war, and whose name was Charity Joe, which, considering his avaricious disposition, was the wrong handle on the wrong man. Charity was the least of all old Joe's redeeming characteristics; charity was the very thing he did not recognize, yet some wag had facetiously branded him Charity Joe, and the appellation had clung to him ever since. He was well advanced in years, yet withal a good trailer and an expert guide, as the success of his many late expeditions into the Black Hills had evidenced.

Those who had heard of Joe's skill as a guide, intrusted themselves in his care, for, while the stages were stopped more or less on each trip, Charity Joe's train invariably went through all safe and sound. This was partly owing to his acquaintance with various bands of Indians, who were the chief cause of an-noyance on the trip.

So far we see the train toward the land of gold, without their having seen sight or sound of hostile red-skins, and Charity is just chuckling over his usual good luck:

"I tell ye what, fellers, we've hed a fa'r sort uv a shake, so fur, an' no mistake 'bout it. Barrin' thar ain't no Sittin' Bulls layin' in wait fer us, behead yander, in ther mounts, I'm of ther candid opinion we'll get through wi'out scrapin' a ha'r."

"I hope so," said Fearless Frank, rolling over on the grass and gazing at the guide, thoughtfully, "but I doubt it. It seems to me that one hears of more butchering, lately, than there was a month ago—all on account of the influx of ruffianly characters into the Black Hills!"

"Not all owing to that, chippy," interposed "General" Nix, as he had immediately been christened by the miners—"not all owing to that. Thar's them gol danged copper-colored guests uv ther government—they're kickin' up three pints uv the'r rumpus, more or less—consider'bly less of more than more o' less. Take a passel uv them barbarities an' shet 'em up inter a prison for three or thirteen yeers, an' ye'd see w'at an impression et'd make, now. Thar'd be siveral less massycrees a week, an' ye wouldn't see a rufyan onc't a month. W'y, gentlefellows, thar'd nevyar been a ruffian, ef et hedn't been fer ther cussed Injun tribe—not *one*! Ther infarnal critters ar' ther instignators uv more deviltry nor a cat wit nine tails."

"Yes, we will admit that the reds are not of saintly origin," said Fearless Frank, with a quiet smile. "In fact I know of several who are far from being angels, myself. There is old Sitting Bull, for instance, and Lone Lion, Rain-in-the-Face, and Horse-with-the-Red-Eye, and so forth, and so forth!"

"Exactly! Every one o' 'em's a danged descendent o' ther old Satan, hisself."

"Layin' aside ther Injun subjeck," said Charity Joe, forking into the roasted venison, "I move thet we take up a silent debate on the pecooliarities uv a deer's hind legs; so heer goes!"

He cut out a huge slice with his bowie, sprinkled it over with salt, and began to devour it by very large mouthfuls. All hands proceeded to follow his example, and the noonday meal was dispatched in silence. After each man had fully satisfied his appetite and the mules and Fearless Frank's horse had grazed until they were full as ticks, the order was given to hitch up, which was speedily done, and the caravan was soon in motion, toiling along like a diminutive serpent across the plain.

The afternoon was a mild, sunny one in early autumn, with a refreshing breeze perfumed with the delicate scent of after-harvest flowers wafting down from the cool regions of the Northwest, where lay the new El Dorado—the land of gold.

Fearless Frank bestrode a noble bay steed of fire and nerve, while old General Nix rode an extra mule that he had purchased of Charity Joe. The remainder of the company rode in the wagons or "hoofed it," as best suited to their mood—walking sometimes being preferable to the rumbling and jolting of the heavy vehicles.

Steadily along through the afternoon sunlight the train wended its way, the teamsters alternately singing and cursing their mules, as they jogged along. Fearless Frank and the "General" rode several hundred yards in advance, both apparently engrossed in deepest thought, for neither spoke until, toward the close of the afternoon, Charity Joe called their attention to a series of low, faint cries brought down upon their hearing by the stiff northerly wind.

"'Pears to me as how them sound sorter human like," said the old guide, trotting along beside the young man's horse, as he made known the discovery. "Jes' listen, now, an' see if ye ain't uv ther same opinion!"

The youth did listen, and at the same time swept the plain with his eagle eyes, in search of the object from which the cries emanated. But nothing of animal life was visible in any direction beyond the train, and more was the mystery, since the cries sounded but a little way off.

"They *are* human cries!" exclaimed Fearless Frank, excitedly, "and come from some one in distress. Boys, we must investigate this matter."

"You can investigate all ye want," grunted Charity Joe, "but I hain't a-goin' ter stop ther train till dusk, squawk or no squawk. I jedge we won't get inter their Hills any too soon, as it ar'."

"You're an old fool!" retorted Frank, contemptuously. "I wouldn't be as mean as you for all the gold in the Black Hills country, say nothin' about that in California and Colorado."

He turned his horse's head toward the north, and rode away, followed, to the wonder of all, by the "General."

"You needn't; I do not want any of your wishes. I'm going to search for the person who makes them cries, an' ef you don't want to wait, why go to the deuce with your old train!"

"There ye err," shouted the guide; "I'm going ter Deadwood, instead uv ter the deuce."

"*Maybe* you will go to Deadwood, and then, again, maybe ye won't," answered back Fearless Frank.

"More or less!" chimed in the general—"consider'bly more of less than less of more. Look out thet ther allies uv Sittin' Bull don't git ther *dead wood* on ye."

On marched the train—steadily on over the level, sandy plain, and Fearless Frank and his strange companion turned their attention to the cries that had been the means of separating them from the train. They had ceased now, altogether, and the two men were at a loss what to do.

"Guv a whoop, like a Government Injun," suggested "General" Nix; "an' thet'll let ther critter know thet we be friends a-comin'. Par'ps she'm g'in out ontirely, a-thinkin' as no one war a-comin' ter her resky!"

"She, you say?"

"Yas, she; fer I calkylate 'twern't no *he* as made them squawks. Sing out like a bellerin' bull, now an' et ar' more or less likely—consider'bly more of less 'n less of more—that she will respond!"

Fearless Frank laughed, and forming his hands into a trumpet he gave vent to a loud, ear-splitting "hello!" that made the prairies ring.

"Great whale uv Joner!" gasped the "General," holding his hands toward the region of his organs of hearing. "Holy Mother o' Mercy! don't do et ag'in b'yee—don' do et; ye've smashed my tinpanum ail inter flidners! Good heaven! ye hev got a bugle wus nor enny steam tooer from heer tew Lowell."

"Hark!" said the youth, bending forward in a listening attitude.

The next instant silence prevailed, and the twain anxiously listened. Wafted down across the plain came in faint piteous accents the repetition of the cry they had first heard, only it was now much fainter. Evidently whoever was in distress was weakening rapidly. Soon the cries would be inaudible.

"It's straight ahead!" exclaimed Fearless Frank, at last. "Come along, and we'll soon see what the matter is!"

He put the spurs to his spirited animal, and the next instant was dashing wildly off over the sunlit plain. Bent on emulation, the "General" also used his heels with considerable vim, but alas! what dependence can be placed on a mule! The animal jolted, with a vicious nip back at the offending rider's legs, and refused to budge an inch.

On—on dashed the fearless youth, mounted on his noble steed, his eyes bent forward, in a sharp scrutiny of the plain ahead, his mind filled with wonder that the cries were now growing more distinct and yet not a first glimpse could he obtain of the source whence they emanated.

On—on—on; then suddenly he reins his steed back upon its haunches, just in time to avert a frightful plunge into one of those remarkable freaks of nature—the blind canal, or, in other words, a channel valley washed out by heavy rains. These the tourist will frequently encounter in the regions contiguous to the Black Hills.

Below him yawned an abrupt channel, a score or more of feet in depth, at the bottom of which was a dense chaparral thicket. The little valley thus nestled in the earth was about forty rods in width, and one would never have dreamed it existed, unless they chanced to ride to the brink, above.

Fearless Frank took in the situation at a glance, and not hearing the cries, he rightly conjectured that the one in distress had again become exhausted. That that person was in the thicket below seemed more than probable, and he immediately resolved to descend in search. Slipping from his saddle, he stepped forward to the very edge of the precipice and looked over. The next second the ground crumbled beneath his feet, and he was precipitated headlong into the valley. Fortunately he received no serious injuries, and in a moment was on his feet again, all right.

"A miss is as good as a mile," he muttered, brushing the dirt from this clothing. "Now, then, we will find out the secret of the racket in this thicket."

Glancing up to the brink above to see that his horse was standing quietly, he parted the shrubbery, and entered the thicket.

It required considerable pushing and tugging to get through the dense undergrowth, but at last his efforts were rewarded, and he stood in a small break or glade.

Stood there, to behold a sight that made the blood boil in his veins. Securely bound with her face toward a stake, was a young girl—a maiden of perhaps seventeen summers, whom, at a single glance, one might surmise was remarkably pretty.

She was stripped to the waist, and upon her snow-white back were numerous welts from which trickled diminutive rivulets of crimson. Her head was dropped against the stake to which she was bound, and she was evidently insensible.

With a cry of astonishment and indignation Fearless Frank leaped forward to sever her bonds, when like so many grim phantoms there filed out of the chaparral, and circled around him, a score of hideously painted savages. One glance at the portly leader satisfied Frank as to his identity. It was the fiend incarnate—Sitting Bull!

Discussion Questions

1. Dime novels were written for entertainment, not accuracy. What kinds of stereotypes can you identify in this selection? Compare the diction Wheeler uses to describe Fearless Frank as opposed to the diction he uses to describe the Indians. Look at nouns, adjectives, and verbs. How does language help establish the stereotyped characters? Discuss in groups why these stereotyped characters might appeal to Wheeler's audience.

2. What impression will Wheeler's readers have of Sitting Bull? Compare Wheeler's description of Sitting Bull with Custer's description of the "savage" and then consider the writings by Native Americans you read in Chapter 2. Discuss in groups how dime novels may have affected eastern readers' perceptions of the character of Native Americans.

Writing Suggestions

1. Review your answers to the first discussion question, and then write an analysis of Wheeler's writing, addressing the following issues: Which stereotypes does Wheeler establish in this selection, and how does he use language to establish these stereotypes? For example, how does the diction Wheeler uses to describe Fearless Frank compare to the diction he uses to describe the Indians? (Look at nouns, adjectives, and verbs.) How does Wheeler's language define the stereotyped qualities of these characters?

2. On the Internet, research the history and character of the dime novels, and then write your own first chapter of a dime novel. Remember to look closely at tone, diction, plot, and character development in two or three of the dime novels you find on the Internet. Try to mimic these characteristics in your own dime novel, and remember, accuracy and truth were not as important to dime novel plots as were adventure, romance, and action! You can start your search for information about dime novels at <http://www.sul.stanford.edu/depts/dp/pennies/home.html>.

Chapter 3: Writing Suggestions

1. Using the readings in this chapter as background, write a personal essay
    in which you discuss your current concept of the American West of the
    nineteenth century, compared to your concept of the West before you read
    any of the materials in the chapter. You might make a list of your first set
    of feelings and impressions about the West, and then make a second list
    of ideas and impressions that now come to mind. Then work the com-
    parison together to make an interesting and concrete personal essay that
    gives your readers a real sense of your own feelings and ideas about the
    American West in the nineteenth century. You could discuss your re-
    sponses and thoughts about a number of different issues in this essay, in-
    cluding the conflicts of race, gender, religions, and cultures that
    characterized the "opening" of the West.

2. We have read a few essays in this chapter about women on the way West
    and some of the trials they faced. Research further a particular aspect of
    women in the West, and write a research essay about women's roles in, for
    example, one of the following areas:

    women in mining

    women in prostitution

    women as prisoners in the West

    women as nuns in the West

    women in captivity

    women as wives in polygamous marriages

    women in businesses

    women as ranchers

    Your library should have a number of new books about women, by
    women, which have been published in recent years. You can also search
    on the Internet for "women in the West" or "women pioneers."

3. Ravage states that early images and advertisements in magazines such
    as *Harper's Weekly* "were scurrilously racist, portraying African Ameri-
    cans as unable to speak well, reason intelligently, or conduct themselves
    with socially acceptable manners or mores." If your college or university
    has a subscription, you will be able to go to *Harper's Weekly* on-line, at
    <http://app.harpweek.com>. If you cannot log into this site, you can also
    try to get old copies of *Harper's Weekly* at your library. Research the state-
    ment above, and write an essay in which you corroborate or challenge
    Ravage's statement. Answer some of the questions listed at the top of
    page 251 in your essay.

What variety of images of blacks were portrayed in *Harper's Weekly?*

What kinds of work positions were blacks shown holding?

Were black women portrayed? How?

What attitude did advertisers and publishers take toward blacks?

Were there any illustrations of blacks as cowboys, miners, or ranchers?

Alternatively, write a research paper about the variety of roles blacks played in the West, roles which were not portrayed in the media of the time. Using some of the essays in this chapter as starting points, research a specific black man or woman who played an important role in the early West, or research the larger question of blacks' true roles and contributions in early western frontier life. Some possible topics include the following:

Black women and business

Black prostitutes

Black cowboys

Black buffalo soldiers

Black miners

Black ranchers

Black explorers

Blacks and violence

4.   Beginning with information from the selection by Ravage and from the selection by Butler, write a research paper about the relationship between race, gender, and incarceration in the American West. Research the assertions by both Ravage and Butler that black women were incarcerated for crimes for which white women were not incarcerated, and that their treatment in the jails differed from that of white women. You can research the lives of specific women incarcerated in federal penitentiaries and the general question of black versus white women in Western jails.

5.   Look at the cover of this textbook, which shows a painting by John Gast called "American Progress," completed in 1872. Write a paper in which you analyze the arguments about Manifest Destiny in this painting. Look carefully at all the details in the painting, and use specific descriptions to answer some of the following questions:

What idea of progress does the painter show?

What kind of racial conflict or coexistence is reflected in the painting?

Which details are stressed in the painting?

How many different groups are represented in the painting?

What does the dominant figure represent? What is she holding in her hand?

Chapter 3: Further Research on the Web

To pursue your research on the Internet, explore some of the following sites:

New Perspectives on the West at PBS
http://www.pbs.org/weta/thewest

History of Kansas and the Frontier
http://history.cc.ukans.edu/heritage

Photographs of the American West
http://www.nara.gov/nara/nn/nns/amwest.html

Women and the American West
http://www.library.csi.cuny.edu/westweb/pages/women.html

Custer and Military History
http://leav-www.army.mil/history/custer.htm
http://www.custermuseum.org

Treaty of Guadalupe Hidalgo
http://www.loc.gov/exhibits/ghtreaty

4

Slavery and the Civil War

In Chapter 4 we examine one of the greatest conflicts in the history of the United States—a civil war that split the nation into pro-slavery and abolitionist camps, pitted brother against brother, and almost caused the end of the republic that the founding fathers had worked so hard to form. At stake for the South was a way of life in which "cotton was king" and slave labor was key to the economy. Wealthy plantation owners and their less wealthy neighbors who owned no slaves at all came together to create the Confederate Army and to defend the Southern way of life against what they considered an unconstitutional display of power by the federal government. Following the lead of South Carolina, the states of Mississippi, Florida, Georgia, Louisiana, and Texas declared that they were seceding from the Union. Virginia, Arkansas, Tennessee, Missouri, and North Carolina followed suit shortly after. When Confederate troops took control of Fort Sumter in April of 1861, Lincoln called the Northern militia to arms, and the Civil War began. Between 1861 and 1865, well over half-a-million Southern and Northern soldiers lost their lives. The infrastructure of the south lay in ruins—farms, factories, and railroads were destroyed, as were large sections of many Southern cities. But the Union remained intact, and in 1865 slaves were legally freed by the 13th Amendment to the Constitution.

What were the documents, speeches, stories, and writings that accompanied this war?

How did the two sides justify their beliefs?

How did both sides call soldiers and civilians into supportive action?

What fundamental arguments did the Northern and Southern states put forth about the constitutionality of slavery and secession?

As students of writing you can study a rich field of primary and secondary sources from the period of the Civil War itself, in addition to reading new historical perspectives on the political, social, and economic implications of this war. The speeches of presidents, letters of soldiers, and diaries of women who fought alongside their husbands all give you a chance to see the varying points of view and perspectives of those who fought so hard for what they believed. These writings address basic questions of liberty and freedom: Should the Confederate states be allowed to secede? Should slavery be abolished? Which rights should be accorded people of all races? Who is an American citizen, and what rights should those citizens have? And finally, what rights are worth dying for? These questions remain vital to all Americans today, and in fact emotions still run high in southern states where some citizens feel that the Confederate symbols belong on the state flag and that Confederate generals should be honored with large public monuments and state holidays. Others consider these tributes to the Confederacy an affront to the feelings of African Americans who were enslaved until the Emancipation Proclamation freed them.

This chapter begins with Jefferson Davis's "Inaugural Address," which represents the official southern government's views about the Civil War. As president of the new confederacy, Jefferson Davis gives an impassioned speech to the new Confederate Congress, explaining the goals and beliefs of the southern states who banded together to secede from a nation they felt was infringing on their rights under the Constitution. In contrast, celebrating the view of the Union, Abraham Lincoln's famous "Gettysburg Address" gives you a chance not only to study the famous speech for its rhetorical strategies and euphonious rhythms, but also to examine the way the speech highlights the key issues facing Americans at the time of the war—the central questions of what it meant to be American and how Americans would come to define "liberty and justice for all." George Fitzhugh's "Proslavery Defense" delineates a vastly different set of beliefs about slavery and helps give you some hindsight into what the southern gentry felt about their world.

Differing interpretations of the Civil War and its causes emerged after the war was over, as Alan T. Nolan explains in his selection, "The Anatomy of the Myth," in which he analyzes the romantic Lost Cause interpretation of the Civil War. Of course, the lives of slaves were *not* romantic, contrary to southern mythology, as we can see in Sojourner Truth's excerpt from *Narrative of Sojourner Truth*, which describes her life before she escaped slavery, and which gives you a chance to hear the voice and the concerns of a woman who dealt not only with the abuses of slavery by her white masters, but also with the anger of other slaves who envied her position in the white household.

The primary sources in Edwin S. Redkey's excerpts from *A Grand Army of Black Men* represent yet another point of reflection for the Civil War: What were the experiences of those black men who fought alongside whites to free the South from slavery? What prejudice did they encounter in the Northern armies?

Women's roles in the Civil War ranged from tending the home fires to actually fighting in the infantry and cavalry. Elizabeth D. Leonard's selection from *All the Daring of the Soldier* relates the stories of a surprising number of women who fought in both armies, dressed as men, and who were often not discovered to be women until their deaths or until the end of the war when they went back into women's clothes.

Two additional primary sources give us more important information about the Civil War. In a letter to the editor in *Harper's Weekly* from the spring of 1865, an unknown author extols the virtues of primary source documents like a civil war soldier's diary, part of which is included in the letter. In this selection you can read both documents, the letter describing the soldier's diary and selections from the diary itself.

And finally, we look at Ambrose Bierce's powerful short story, "An Occurrence at Owl Creek Bridge," which complements the primary and secondary sources in this chapter. The story stands as both an example of anti-war propaganda and as a literary tour de force whose imagery, flashbacks, dialogue, and descriptions exemplify the short-story writer at his best.

All of the selections in this chapter aim to give you several different angles from which to view the conflicts of the Civil War. These readings present a vision that varies dramatically depending on the race and gender of the writer.

Before You Read

1. Have you seen the movie *Gone with the Wind*? If so, jot down your impressions from the movie about the South, slavery, and the Civil War. What kind of feeling did you take away from the movie about Civil War history?

2. What have you learned about the roles black and white women played during the Civil War? How have these women been portrayed in your history books, or in movies you may have seen about the war?

3. How do you perceive the legacy of slavery in contemporary American society? Does slavery and its history still play any part in your assumptions and thoughts about American history?

Inaugural Address of the President of the Provisional Government

JEFFERSON DAVIS

Jefferson Davis (1808–1889) was born in Kentucky and educated at Transylvania University in Lexington before going on to the U.S. Military Academy and service in the U.S. Army. He fought in the Mexican War and, after his resignation from the army in 1835, he served as U.S. senator from Mississippi from 1835 to 1845. He then served as a congressman from 1845 to 1846 and again from 1857 to 1861. When Mississippi seceded from the Union in 1861, Davis withdrew from the Senate, and on February 18, 1861, he was made provisional president of the new Confederate States. He was elected to office the same year for a six-year term, and went on to lead the Confederacy during the Civil War. He appointed General Robert E. Lee and worked to raise funds and encourage industrial production throughout the war. Davis was a firm believer in the legitimacy of the Confederacy and never wavered from his opposition to the federal government's attempt to stop the secession. He was finally captured at Irwinville, Georgia, on May 10, 1865, and was imprisoned from 1865 to 1867 for treason. He was released on bond, and in 1868 the federal government dropped the case against him. After the war he wrote, traveled, and worked at a number of failed business ventures, but he remained very popular in the South. After he died in New Orleans in 1889, his final remains were moved to Richmond, the capitol of the Confederacy. The selection that follows is Davis's Inaugural Address, dated February 18, 1861.

Gentlemen of the Congress of the Confederate States of America, Friends, and Fellow-citizens: Called to the difficult and responsible station of Chief Magistrate of the Provisional Government which you have instituted, I approach the discharge of the duties assigned to me with humble distrust of my abilities, but with a sustaining confidence in the wisdom of those who are to guide and aid me in the administration of public affairs, and an abiding faith in the virtue and patriotism of the people. Looking forward to the speedy establishment of a permanent government to take the place of this, which by its greater moral and physical power will be better able to combat with many difficulties that arise from the conflicting interests of separate nations, I enter upon the duties of the office to which I have been chosen with the hope that the beginning of our career, as a Confederacy, may not be obstructed by hostile opposition to our enjoyment of the separate existence and independence we have asserted, and which, with the blessing of Providence, we intend to maintain.

Our present political position has been achieved in a manner unprecedented in the history of nations. It illustrates the American idea that governments rest on the consent of the governed, and that it is the right of the people to alter or abolish them at will whenever they become destructive of the ends for which they were established. The declared purpose of the compact of the Union from which we have withdrawn was to "establish justice, insure domestic tranquillity, provide for the common defense, promote the general welfare, and secure the blessings of liberty to ourselves and our posterity;" and when, in the judgment of the sovereign States composing this Confederacy, it has been perverted from the purposes for which it was ordained, and ceased to answer the ends for which it was established, a peaceful appeal to the ballot box declared that, so far as they are concerned, the Government created by that compact should cease to exist. In this they merely asserted the right which the Declaration of Independence of July 4, 1776, defined to be "inalienable." Of the time and occasion of its exercise they as sovereigns were the final judges, each for itself. The impartial and enlightened verdict of mankind will vindicate the rectitude of our conduct; and He who knows the hearts of men will judge of the sincerity with which we have labored to preserve the Government of our fathers in its spirit.

The right solemnly proclaimed at the birth of the United States, and which has been solemnly affirmed and reaffirmed in the Bills of Rights of the States subsequently admitted into the Union of 1789, undeniably recognizes in the people the power to resume the authority delegated for the purposes of government. Thus the sovereign States here represented have proceeded to form this Confederacy; and it is by abuse of language that their act has been denominated a revolution. They formed a new alliance, but within each State its government has remained; so that the rights of person and property have not been disturbed. The agent through which they communicated with foreign nations is changed, but this does not necessarily interrupt their international relations. Sustained by the consciousness that the transition from the former Union to the present Confederacy has not proceeded from a disregard on our part of just obligations, or any failure to perform every constitutional duty, moved by no interest or passion to invade the rights of others, anxious to cultivate peace and commerce with all nations, if we may not hope to avoid war, we may at least expect that posterity will acquit us of having needlessly engaged in it. Doubly justified by the absence of wrong on our part, and by wanton aggression on the part of others, there can be no cause to doubt that the courage and patriotism of the people of the Confederate States will be found equal to any measure of defense which their honor and security may require.

An agricultural people, whose chief interest is the export of commodities required in every manufacturing country, our true policy is peace, and the freest trade which our necessities will permit. It is alike our interest and that of all those to whom we would sell, and from whom we would buy, that there should be the fewest practicable restrictions upon the interchange of these commodities. There can, however, be but little rivalry between ours and any manufacturing or navigating community, such as the Northeastern States of the American Union. It must follow, therefore, that mutual interest will invite to good will and kind offices on both parts. If, however, passion or lust of dominion should cloud the judgment or inflame the ambition of those States, we must prepare to meet the emergency and maintain, by the final arbitrament of the sword, the position which we have assumed among the nations of the earth.

We have entered upon the career of independence, and it must be inflexibly pursued. Through many years of controversy with our late associates of the Northern States, we have vainly endeavored to secure tranquillity and obtain respect for the rights to which we were entitled. As a necessity, not a choice, we have resorted to the remedy of separation, and henceforth our energies must be directed to the conduct of our own affairs, and the perpetuity of the Confederacy which we have formed. If a just perception of mutual interest shall permit us peaceably to pursue our separate political career, my most earnest desire will have been fulfilled. But if this be denied to us, and the integrity of our territory and jurisdiction be assailed, it will but remain for us with firm resolve to appeal to arms and invoke the blessing of Providence on a just cause.

As a consequence of our new condition and relations, and with a view to meet anticipated wants, it will be necessary to provide for the speedy and efficient organization of branches of the Executive department having special charge of foreign intercourse, finance, military affairs, and the postal service. For purposes of defense, the Confederate States may, under ordinary circumstances, rely mainly upon the militia; but it is deemed advisable, in the present condition of affairs, that there should be a well-instructed and disciplined army, more numerous than would usually be required on a peace establishment. I also suggest that, for the protection of our harbors and commerce on the high seas, a navy adapted to those objects will be required. But this, as well as other subjects appropriate to our necessities, have doubtless engaged the attention of Congress.

With a Constitution differing only from that of our fathers in so far as it is explanatory of their well-known intent, freed from sectional conflicts, which have interfered with the pursuit of the general welfare, it is not unreasonable to expect that States from which we have recently parted may seek to unite their fortunes to ours under the Government which we have instituted. For this your Constitution makes adequate provision; but beyond this, if I mistake not the judgment and will of the people, a reunion with the States from which we have separated is neither practicable nor desirable. To increase the power, develop the resources, and promote the happiness of the Confederacy, it is requisite that there should be so much of homogeneity that the welfare of every portion shall be the aim of the whole. When this does not exist, antagonisms are engendered which must and should result in separation.

Actuated solely by the desire to preserve our own rights, and promote our own welfare, the separation by the Confederate States has been marked by no aggression upon others, and followed by no domestic convulsion. Our industrial pursuits have received no check, the cultivation of our fields has progressed as heretofore, and, even should we be involved in war, there would be no considerable diminution in the production of the staples which have constituted our exports, and in which the commercial world has an interest scarcely less than our own. This common interest of the producer and consumer can only be interrupted by exterior force which would obstruct the transmission of our staples to foreign markets—a course of conduct which would be as unjust, as it would be detrimental, to manufacturing and commercial interests abroad.

Should reason guide the action of the Government from which we have separated, a policy so detrimental to the civilized world, the Northern States included, could not be dictated by even the strongest desire to inflict injury upon us; but, if the contrary should prove true, a terrible responsibility will rest upon it, and the suffering of millions will bear testimony to the folly and wickedness of our aggressors. In the meantime there will remain to us, besides the ordinary means before suggested, the well-known resources for retaliation upon the commerce of an enemy.

Experience in public stations, of subordinate grade to this which your kindness has conferred, has taught me that toil and care and disappointment are the price of official elevation. You will see many errors to forgive, many deficiencies to tolerate; but you shall not find in me either want of zeal or fidelity to the cause that is to me the highest in hope, and of most enduring affection. Your generosity has bestowed upon me an undeserved distinction, one which I neither sought nor desired. Upon the continuance of that sentiment, and upon your wisdom and patriotism, I rely to direct and support me in the performance of the duties required at my hands.

We have changed the constituent parts, but not the system of government. The Constitution framed by our fathers is that of these Confederate States. In their exposition of it, and in the judicial construction it has received, we have a light which reveals its true meaning.

Thus instructed as to the true meaning and just interpretation of that instrument, and ever remembering that all offices are but trusts held for the people, and that powers delegated are to be strictly construed, I will hope by due diligence in the performance of my duties, though I may disappoint your expectations, yet to retain, when retiring, something of the good will and confidence which welcome my entrance into office.

It is joyous in the midst of perilous times to look around upon a people united in heart, where one purpose of high resolve animates and actuates the whole; where the sacrifices to be made are not weighed in the balance against honor and right and liberty and equality. Obstacles may retard, but they cannot long prevent, the progress of a movement sanctified by its justice and sustained by a virtuous people. Reverently let us invoke the God of our fathers to guide and protect us in our efforts to perpetuate the principles which by his blessing they were able to vindicate, establish, and transmit to their posterity.

With the continuance of his favor ever gratefully acknowledged, we may hopefully look forward to success, to peace, and to prosperity.

Discussion Questions

1. What kinds of assumptions can Davis make about his audience? How does his audience awareness manifest itself in his speech? Discuss how his arguments rest on certain shared assumptions between author and audience and isolate specific arguments that illustrate this fact. Slavery as an issue is markedly absent from Davis' speech—address this absence in your discussions.
2. In his Inaugural Address, Davis appeals to many emotions as he takes office. Make a list of the different appeals to emotions he uses, and, in groups, discuss the effectiveness of this technique for his purpose and his audience.

Writing Suggestions

1. After the Civil War was over, Jefferson Davis wrote a history of the war called *Rise and Fall of the Confederate Government*, published in 1881. In this book Davis wrote, "The object of this work has been from historical data to show that the Southern States had rightfully the power to withdraw from a Union, into which they had, as sovereign communities, voluntarily entered." Write a personal essay in which you respond to both Davis's Inaugural Address and his later statement about the freedom of states to secede, agreeing or disagreeing with his reasons for secession from the Union. Argue for either the rights of the states who wished to secede, or for the importance of freeing the slaves and maintaining the Union, and be specific about your personal reasons for your stance.
2. Write a paper in which you compare Jefferson Davis's arguments in his speech to the arguments found in the Declaration of Independence. Analyze the two pieces for purpose, diction, tone, audience awareness, and argumentation, and then write your paper, answering some of the following questions in your comparison:

    Which piece do you find more effective?
    Which piece has stronger argumentation?
    Which piece moved you more?
    What similarities do you find in the pieces? What differences?
    What ironies do you find in this comparison?

The Gettysburg Address

ABRAHAM LINCOLN

Abraham Lincoln (1809–1865) was the sixteenth president of the United States, elected first in 1860 and again in 1864. Lincoln, who was born in Hardin County, Kentucky, has achieved heroic status in American history books, both for his role in freeing the slaves with the Emancipation Proclamation in 1862, and for his leadership in the Civil War, which dominated his presidency. Just after General Lee's surrender, Lincoln was assassinated by John Wilkes Boothe in 1865. The selection below, Lincoln's famous "Gettysburg Address," was delivered at the dedication of the Gettysburg National Cemetery on November 19, 1863. This brief speech is one of the most famous in American history, and it crystallizes Lincoln's ideals for a united nation.

Four score and seven years ago our fathers brought forth on this continent a new nation, conceived in liberty and dedicated to the proposition that all men are created equal. Now we are engaged in a great civil war, testing whether that nation or any nation so conceived and so dedicated can long endure. We are met on a great battlefield of that war. We have come to dedicate a portion of that field as a final resting-place for those who here gave their lives that that nation might live. It is altogether fitting and proper that we should do this. But in a larger sense, we cannot dedicate, we cannot consecrate, we cannot hallow this ground. The brave men, living and dead who struggled here have consecrated it far above our poor power to add or distract. The world will little note nor long remember what we say here, but it can never forget what they did here. It is for us the living rather to be dedicated here to the unfinished work which they who fought here have thus far so nobly advanced. It is rather for us to be here dedicated to the great task remaining before us—that from these honored dead we take increased devotion to that cause for which they gave the last full measure of devotion—that we here highly resolve that these dead shall not have died in vain, that this nation under God shall have a new birth of freedom, and that government of the people, by the people, for the people shall not perish from the earth.

Discussion Questions

1. How does Lincoln use his setting to add power to his speech? Where and when does he refer to the setting in his talk? How does Lincoln move

from the concept of the men who died and are buried at Gettysburg to the larger issues facing the nation? Look for diction that broadens his message—which words, specifically, help him make that transition?

2. Lincoln's speech is not only a tribute to those who have already died in the Civil War, but it is also an argument. Reframe his argument into a single sentence—what is the central point he argues in this speech?

Writing Suggestions

1. Lincoln was a master speaker and rhetorician, using words and language to appeal to his audience of U.S. citizens. Read the information below, and then write a paper in which you analyze Lincoln's persuasive and rhetorical devices in the Gettysburg Address:

    Lincoln uses a number of classical rhetorical devices to make his speech rhythmic and powerful. One of these devices is parallelism, the use of repeated similar words, phrases, or clauses in order to stress an idea. Look for Lincoln's use of parallelism in the speech. How many times does he use this rhetorical device? What is the effect on the listener? How does his use of repeated structures of language affect his argument?

    Antithesis is the use of a type of parallel structure, but it highlights opposite ideas or words. Find Lincoln's use of antithesis in the speech, and comment on the effectiveness of this technique in your paper.

    Consider Lincoln's audience, not only those people present at the cemetery but also citizens throughout the United States who would read the speech in the newspapers the next day. How does Lincoln gear his speech to the larger audience? What emotional appeals does Lincoln make to that larger audience?

2. Now, using your work from the assignment above, write your own persuasive speech about an issue of importance in your community or in the world, imitating Lincoln's style. Think about the different strategies Lincoln has used, and then write a short piece that incorporates his patterns of language, his appeal to his audience, and his rhetorical techniques.

The Proslavery Defense

GEORGE FITZHUGH

George Fitzhugh (1806–1881) was a Virginia lawyer and plantation owner who became well-known for his defense of slavery through his writings, including *Sociology of the South, or the Failure of Free Society* (1854) and *Cannibals All! or Slaves without Masters*. Fitzhugh openly criticized the principles of the Declaration of Independence in his proslavery arguments. In the selection that follows, "The Proslavery Defense," taken from *Sociology of the South*, Fitzhugh claims that the Preamble of the Declaration of Independence was "verbose, false, newborn, and unmeaning" and that its principles cannot be used to argue against the institution of slavery.

"We hold these truths to be self-evident, that all men are created equal; that they are endowed by their Creator with certain inalienable rights, that among them, are life, liberty, and the pursuit of happiness; that to secure these rights governments are instituted among men, deriving their just powers from the consent of the governed; that whenever any form of government becomes destructive of these ends it is the right of the people to alter or abolish it, and to institute a new government, laying its foundation on such principles, and organizing its powers in such form, as to them shall seem most likely to effect their safety and happiness."

It is, we believe, conceded on all hands, that men are not born physically, morally, or intellectually equal,—some are males, some females, some from birth, large, strong and healthy, others weak, small and sickly—some are naturally amiable, others prone to all kinds of wickedness—some brave, others timid. Their natural inequalities beget inequalities of rights. The weak in mind or body require guidance, support and protection; they must obey and work for those who protect and guide them—they have a natural right to guardians, committees, teachers or masters. Nature has made them slaves; all that law and government can do, is to regulate, modify and mitigate their slavery. In the absence of legally instituted slavery, their condition would be worse under that natural slavery of the weak to the strong, the foolish to the wise and cunning. The wise and virtuous, the brave, the strong in mind and body, are by nature born to command and protect, and law but follows nature in making them rulers, legislators, judges, captains, husbands, guardians, committees and masters. The naturally depraved class, those born prone to crime, are our brethren too; they are entitled to education, to religious instruction, to all the means and appliances proper to correct their evil propensities, and all their failings; they have a right to be sent to the penitentiary,—for there, if they do not reform, they cannot at least disturb society. Our feelings, and our consciences teach us, that nothing but necessity can justify taking human life.

We are but stringing together truisms, which every body knows as well as ourselves, and yet if men are created unequal in all these respects, what truth or what meaning is there in the passage under consideration? Men are not created or born equal, and circumstances, and education, and association, tend to increase and aggravate inequalities among them, from generation to generation. Generally, the rich associate and intermarry with each other, the poor do the same; the ignorant rarely associate with or intermarry with the learned, and all society shuns contact with the criminal, even to the third and fourth generations.

Men are not "born entitled to equal rights"! It would be far nearer the truth to say, "that some were born with saddles on their backs, and others booted and spurred to ride them,"—and the riding does them good. They need the reins, the bit and the spur. No two men by nature are exactly equal or exactly alike. No institutions can prevent the few from acquiring rule and ascendancy over the many. Liberty and free competition invite and encourage the attempt of the strong to master the weak; and insure their success.

"Life and liberty" are not "inalienable"; they have been sold in all countries, and in all ages, and must be sold so long as human nature lasts. It is an inexpedient and unwise, and often unmerciful restraint, on a man's liberty of action, to deny him the right to sell himself when starving, and again, to buy himself when fortune smiles. Most countries of antiquity, and some, like China at the present day, allowed such sale and purchase. The great object of government is to restrict, control and punish man "in the pursuit of happiness." All crimes are committed in its pursuit. Under the free or competitive system, most men's happiness consists in destroying the happiness of other people. This, then, is no inalienable right.

The author of the Declaration may have, and probably did mean, that all men were created with an equal title to property. Carry out such a doctrine, and it would subvert every government on earth.

In practice, in all ages, and in all countries, men had sold their liberty either for short periods, for life, or hereditarily; that is, both their own liberty and that of their children after them. The laws of all countries have, in various forms and degrees, in all times recognised and regulated this right to *alien* or sell liberty. The soldiers and sailors of the revolution had aliened both liberty and life, the wives in all America had aliened their liberty, so had the apprentices and wards at the very moment this verbose, newborn, false and unmeaning preamble was written.

Mr. Jefferson was an enthusiastic speculative philosopher; Franklin was wise, cunning and judicious; he made no objection to the Declaration, as prepared by Mr. Jefferson, because, probably, he saw it would suit the occasion and supposed it would be harmless for the future. But even Franklin was too much of a physical philosopher, too utilitarian and material in his doctrines, to be relied on in matters of morals or government. We may fairly conclude, that liberty is alienable, that there is a natural right to alien it, first, because the laws and institutions of all countries have recognized and regulated its alienation; and secondly, because we cannot conceive of a civilized society, in which there were no wives, no wards, no apprentices, no sailors and no soldiers; and none of these could there be in a country that practically carried out the doctrine, that liberty is inalienable.

Discussion Questions

1. Fitzhugh makes a large leap in logic from the statement that men and women are created "some from birth, large, strong, and healthy, others weak, small and sickly . . ." to the statement that "their natural inequalities beget inequalities of rights." Fitzhugh tries to give examples to justify his reasoning. Discuss in groups how successful he is in this attempt. How well does his argument apply to the justification of slavery? How would his reasoning affect the lives of different individuals in your class? Which of you would have rights and which would not?

2. Review Jefferson's speech, "Policy of Civilization and Assimilation" and Jackson's speech, "Message to Congress," both in Chapter 2. What similarities in reasoning do you find between Fitzhugh's discussion of inequality of mankind and Jackson and Jefferson's justifications for the treatment of Native Americans?

Writing Suggestions

1. Write a personal response to Fitzhugh, letting your feelings and emotions rule your writing. Let your tone emerge freely, and respond to all of his major assertions about "alienable" rights and the necessity for slavery.

2. Review your answers to the first discussion question for this selection. Then write an analysis of Fitzhugh's attempt to justify slavery. Express your opinion of his logic, his use of analogies, his assumptions, and his conclusions. How does he take his audience into consideration? How would his audience be likely to react to his arguments? How well does his analogy apply to the justification of slavery? Do you think an audience of his time would have found his evidence convincing or not? Why? Quote from both the Declaration of Independence and Fitzhugh's writing as you compose your essay.

The Anatomy of the Myth

ALAN T. NOLAN

Alan T. Nolan is the author of *Lee Considered* and *The Iron Brigade*, and is the editor of *Giants in Their Tall Black Hats*. He is also the co-editor (with Gary Gallagher) and contributor to *The Myth of the Lost Cause and Civil War History*. The selection below, "The Anatomy of the Myth," is the chapter written by Nolan for *The Myth of the Lost Cause and Civil War History*, which is a collection of essays by nine Civil War historians who discuss their belief that the "Lost Cause Myth," promoted by southern writers, historians, and civilians, is a false attempt to rationalize the secession and the Civil War. The Lost Cause Myth suggests that the South was outnumbered from the beginning in its heroic fight for states rights, and that the Civil War was a heroic attempt to fight for freedom against impossible odds. In this selection, Nolan explains exactly what elements made up the myth and tackles each of these elements in his arguments against "The Myth of the Lost Cause."

In the period 1861–1865, there was a major war in the United States of America (USA). The antagonists were the "North," that is, the United States except for eleven states, and the "South," which claimed to have seceded, that is, withdrawn from the United States to form a new nation, the Confederate States of America (CSA). The citizens of both sides were of the same Caucasian race and national and ethnic origins. They were committed to democratic political principles and were blessed with an unusually rich geography. The Confederate states had an African-American slave labor system. Although it was racist, the North's labor system was free, except in the border states of Kentucky, Missouri, Maryland, and Delaware and in the District of Columbia. Northern people in the main were antagonistic to slavery. The two sides had been unable politically to resolve sectional disagreements.

The United States refused to recognize the existence of the Confederate States of America as a nation. The Confederate states promptly recruited armies and claimed as their own all property within their borders that had been the property of the United States of America; in many cases, the Confederate states seized that property by force. Ultimately, the United States refused to surrender Fort Sumter in Charleston, South Carolina. Thereupon Confederate and South Carolina forces attacked the fort and forced its surrender. Then, in President Abraham Lincoln's words, the war came.

The war ended in 1865 within a period of several weeks after the surrender at Appomattox, Virginia, of Gen. Robert E. Lee's Army of Northern Virginia, the CSA's most prominent army. The United States successfully reclaimed the eleven seceded states and the United States of America survived. During the course of the war and as a consequence, slavery was abolished and African Americans were emancipated. The people of the Confederate States of America were left free by the United States government. There were no large-scale arrests or punishments. As stated by Samuel Eliot Morison, "By 1877, all of the former Confederate states were back in the Union and in charge of their own domestic affairs, subject only to the requirements of two constitutional amendments (Articles XIV and XV) to protect the freedmen's civil rights." Within a few years of the surrender at Appomattox, former Confederate leaders were serving in high offices in the United States government. According to Morison, white supremacy continued in a different form, "as numerous lynchings in rural districts indicated; and presently 'Jim Crow' would emerge" to intimidate and control the Southern Negro.

The war had been enormously destructive. More than six hundred thousand American men, soldiers from both the USA and CSA, died in the war. Thousands more were wounded, many of whom were disabled for life. The destruction of property was also vast.

The foregoing carefully phrased, simple declarative statements are believed to be undisputed as accurately describing the central aspects of the event generally called today the American Civil War. Despite the undisputed essentials, the war is surrounded by vast mythology. Indeed, it is fair to say that there are two independent versions of the war. On one hand there is the *history* of the war, the account of what in fact happened. On the other there is what Gaines Foster calls the "Southern Interpretation" of the event. This account, "codified" according to Foster, is generally referred to by historians today as "the Lost Cause." This version, touching almost all aspects of the struggle, originated in Southern rationalizations of the war. Then it spread to the North and became a national phenomenon. In the popular mind, the Lost Cause represents the national memory of the Civil War; it has been substituted for the *history* of the war.

The Lost Cause is therefore an American legend, an American version of great sagas like *Beowulf* and the *Song of Roland*. Generally described, the legend tells us that the war was a mawkish and essentially heroic and romantic melodrama, an honorable sectional duel, a time of martial glory on both sides, and triumphant nationalism.

Cambridge political scientist D. W. Brogan, a keen and detached observer of the United States, has written that "the country that has a 'history,' dramatic, moving and tragic, has to live with it—with the problems it raised but did not solve, with the emotions that it leaves as a damaging legacy, with the defective vision that preoccupation with the heroic, with the disastrous, with the expensive past fosters."

In the case of the Confederacy, the past was indeed expensive. James M. McPherson has briefly summarized the ultimate consequences of the war in

terms of its impact on the South: "The South was not only invaded and conquered, it was utterly destroyed. By 1865, the Union forces had . . . destroyed
two-thirds of the assessed value of Southern wealth, two-fifths of the South's
livestock, and one-quarter of her white men between the ages of 20 and 40.
More than half the farm machinery was ruined, and the damages to railroads
and industries were incalculable . . . Southern wealth decreased by 60 percent."

Leaders of such a catastrophe must account for themselves. Justification
is necessary. Those who followed their leaders into the catastrophe required
similar rationalization. Clement A. Evans, a Georgia veteran who at one time
commanded the United Confederate Veterans organization, said this: "If we
cannot justify the South in the act of Secession, we will go down in History
solely as a brave, impulsive but rash people who attempted in an illegal manner to overthrow the Union of our Country."

Today's historians did not, of course, coin the term "Lost Cause." It goes
back almost to the events it characterizes. An early use of the term occurred in
1867 when Edward A. Pollard, the influential wartime editor of the *Richmond Examiner*, published *The Lost Cause: The Standard Southern History of the War of the
Confederates*. It is a full-blown, argumentative statement of the Confederate point
of view with respect to all aspects of the Civil War. The character of Pollard's insights may be judged from a quotation from another of his books, *Southern History of the War*, published in 1866, in which he wrote of the sectional disagreement
in this way: "The occasion of that conflict was what the Yankees called—by one
of their convenient libels in political nomenclature—slavery; but what was in fact
nothing more than a system of Negro servitude in the South . . . one of the mildest
and most beneficent systems of servitude in the world."

The origins and development of the Lost Cause legend have been the concern of several excellent modern books, including Thomas L. Connelly's *The
Marble Man: Robert E. Lee and His Image in American Society*; Gaines M. Foster's *Ghosts of the Confederacy: Defeat, the Lost Cause, and the Emergence of the
New South, 1865 to 1913*; and *Lee's Tarnished Lieutenant: James Longstreet and His
Place in Southern History* by William Garrett Piston. These studies establish
that the purpose of the legend was to foster a heroic image of secession and
the war so that the Confederates would have salvaged at least their honor
from the all-encompassing defeat. Thus the purpose of the legend was to hide
the Southerners' tragic and self-destructive mistake. The creators of the myth,
certain Confederate leaders, prominent among them Jubal A. Early, William
N. Pendleton, and Rev. J. William Jones, and the Virginia Cult, intentionally
created the principles and misinformation of the Lost Cause.

The victim of the Lost Cause legend has been *history*, for which the legend has been substituted in the national memory.

My purpose here is not to retell the story of the origin and development
of the legend. I am more concerned with its historicity. Thus I will catalogue
the assertions of the Lost Cause and compare them to the *history* of the Civil
War experience. The goal is to correct the national memory by refuting the
Lost Cause legend and reestablishing the war as *history*.

The Lost Cause

The Lost Cause as Advocacy

As has been suggested, the Lost Cause was expressly a rationalization, a cover-up. It is, therefore, distinctly marked by Southern advocacy. As pointed out by Michael C. C. Adams in *Our Masters the Rebels*, long before the secession crisis, Southerners "came to see themselves as representing a minority within the nation." One reason for this was "the need to justify the existence of slavery . . . even before the abolitionist attack from the North, Southerners began the defense of slavery as a social system that provided unique benefits, both for the slaves whom it placed under the fatherly care of a superior race and for the master who was given the freedom from toil necessary to the creation of a superior culture." In short, Southerners were placed in a defensive posture before the war, and this has never changed.

The advocacy aspect of the Southern legend has been express on the part of Southern spokesmen. On the back page of the April 1880 issue of the *Southern Historical Society Papers*, as well as in other issues, the following advertisement for subscriptions appears above the name of Rev. J. William Jones, D.D., secretary of the Southern Historical Society of Richmond, Virginia: "[The contents] will make our Papers interesting to all lovers of historic truth and simply INVALUABLE to those who desire to see vindicated the name and fame of those who made our great struggle for constitutional freedom." Writing whose purpose is to "vindicate" the "name and fame" of the South's "great struggle" plainly proceeds from an advocacy premise.

Douglas Southall Freeman, one of the twentieth century's most prominent historians of the war, was also quite candid regarding his concerns. In *The South to Posterity*, Freeman published a critical bibliography of works about the war. He acknowledged that he was "interested to ascertain which were the books that seemed to have made new protagonists for the South." He states that his effort is to identify the books "that have brought a new generation of Americans to understanding of the Southern point of view." Freeman clearly identified himself as an advocate, and his advocacy marked his view of the war, General Lee, and other Confederate leaders. His books have been highly influential with other historians and the American public.

The Claims of the Legend

Slavery Was Not the Sectional Issue. According to the legend, slavery was not the critical issue between the sections. Slavery was trivialized as the cause of the war in favor of such things as tariff disputes, control of investment banking and the means of wealth, cultural differences, and conflict between industrial and agricultural societies. In all events, the South had *not* seceded to protect slavery!

Kenneth M. Stampp observes that Southern spokesmen "denied that slavery had anything to do with the Confederate cause," thus decontaminating it and turning it into something that they could cherish. "After Appomattox, Jefferson Davis claimed that 'slavery was in no wise the cause of the conflict' and Vice President Alexander H. Stephens argued that the war 'was not a contest between the advocates or opponents of that Peculiar Institution.'" The denial that slavery protection had been the genesis of the Confederacy and the purpose of secession became "a cardinal element of the Southern apologia," according to Robert F. Durden. He finds that "liberty, independence and especially states rights were advanced by countless Southern spokesmen as the hallowed principles of the Lost Cause." And James L. Roark notes that postwar Southerners manifested "a nearly universal desire to escape the ignominy attached to slavery."

The Abolitionists as Provocateurs. The status of the abolitionists in the legend is a corollary to the principle that slavery was not the cause of secession. In the context of the legend, the abolitionists' image is negative. They are seen as troublemakers and provocateurs—virtually manufacturing a disagreement between the sections that was of little or no interest to the people and had little substance.

The South Would Have Given Up Slavery. Another of the assertions of the Lost Cause is that the South would have abandoned slavery of its own accord. It was simply a question of time. If the war was about slavery, it was unnecessary to the elimination of slavery because it would have died a natural death. From this premise, it is claimed that the war was foolish, a vain thing on the part of the North.

The Nature of the Slaves. Given the central role of African Americans in the sectional conflict, it is surely not surprising that Southern rationalizations have extended to characterizations of the persons of these people. In the legend there exist two prominent images of the black slaves. One is of the "faithful slave"; the other is of what William Garrett Piston calls "the happy darky stereotype." It is interesting that the faithful slave had a more or less official status in the Confederate myth. In a message to the Confederate Congress in 1863 in which he attacked the Emancipation Proclamation, President Davis called the slaves "peaceful and contented laborers." It was the uniform contention of Southern spokesmen—the press, the clergy, and the politicians—that the slaves liked their status. Fiction writers from Thomas Nelson Page, James Dixon, and Joel Chandler Harris to Walt Disney and Margaret Mitchell in our own time carried this view well into this century. In the 1930s, Hollywood's slaves were invariably happy in their slavery and affectionate toward their uniformly kind and indulgent masters. Indeed, evidenced by the 1940 film *Santa Fe Trail*, Hollywood embraced the full range of Lost Cause stereotypes: the abolitionists, the slaves, and the valiant Southern men.

The Nationalistic/Cultural Difference. Having eliminated slavery as the source of sectional contention, the South created a nationalistic/cultural basis for the disagreement. This theory was instituted on the eve of the war and became a staple of the Lost Cause during and after it. An extensive statement of the argument appeared in June 1860 in the *Southern Literary Messenger.*

Northerners were said to be descended from the Anglo-Saxon tribes that had been conquered by the Norman cavaliers. The cavaliers were, of course, the ancestors of the Southerners according to this theory. It was written that the cavaliers were "descended from the Norman Barons of William the Conqueror, a race distinguished in earliest history for its warlike and fearless character, a race in all times since renowned for its gallantry, chivalry, honor, gentleness, and intellect." As described in *Why the South Lost the Civil War*, "Without its own distinctive past upon which to base its nationality, the Confederacy appropriated history and created a mythic past of exiled cavaliers and chivalrous knights."

The Military Loss

Like the apologists who created the "stabbed-in-the-back" myth to explain Germany's defeat in World War I, Lost Cause spokesmen sought to rationalize the Southern military loss. This presented a confusing and sometimes contradictory set of assertions, the first of which simply manipulated semantics: the Confederates had not really been defeated, they had instead been overwhelmed by massive Northern manpower and materiel. This was presented with a suggestion that the North's superior resources constituted Yankee trickery and unfairness. Furthermore, the South's loss was said to be inevitable from the beginning; the fact of loss was somehow mitigated in the myth because it was said that winning had been impossible. If the Confederacy could not have won, it somehow did not lose. On the other hand, the myth asserted that had the South won at Gettysburg, it would have won the war. The loss at Gettysburg was attributed to Lt. Gen. James Longstreet. The "Longstreet-lost-it-at-Gettysburg" thesis was presented in this way by Rev. J. William Jones, secretary of the Southern Historical Society. He wrote that "the South would have won at Gettysburg, and Independence, but for the failure of *one man*" (emphasis in original).

Another Lost Cause rationale for the loss at Gettysburg was Stonewall Jackson's death earlier in 1863.

The Idealized Home Front. In the context of the Lost Cause, Southern culture is portrayed as superior. William Garrett Piston finds the prewar South "blessed" in the myth, peopled by cavalier aristocrats and martyrs along with the fortunate happy darkies. Gaines Foster sees "grace and gentility" attributed to the South in the myth. The planter aristocracy, the other whites, and blacks are pictured as united in defense of the South's humane, superior culture. The "moonlight and magnolias" culture as described by Foster is fully displayed in *Gone with the Wind*, America's favorite Civil War story. That story idealized the men and women of the plantation class, suggested the superior valor of Southern manhood, and is strongly peopled with happy slaves and gentle and indulgent masters.

The Idealized Confederate Soldier. Piston writes that the Lost Cause legend "developed a romanticized stereotype of the Confederate soldier." He was invariably heroic, indefatigable, gallant, and law-abiding. It is not my intent in any way to disparage the common soldier of the Confederacy. In many ways he was the principal victim of the Lost Cause myth. Nor do I contend that the majority of Confederate soldiers believed they were fighting to preserve slavery. In fact, they were, but many of them thought in terms of defending their homeland and families and resisting what their leaders had told them was Northern aggression.

The Lawfulness of Secession. The Lost Cause doctrine endlessly asserted that secession was a constitutional right. Moreover, because it was lawful, those supporting it were not rebels or traitors; there had not been a rebellion or revolution. The premise of this contention was that because the Constitution was silent on the issue, withdrawal from the Union was permitted. It was argued that the states had entered into a compact from which they had the right to withdraw.

The Saints Go Marching In. Another characteristic of the Lost Cause legend appears in its characterizations of Southern military leaders. These men, at least the successful ones, are not evaluated simply in terms of their military and leadership skills and combat effectiveness. Although they are surely given such credit, they are also presented as remarkable and saintly creatures, supermen. Generals Lee and Stonewall Jackson are the primary examples of this phenomenon. The Lee hagiography is surely well known. Douglas Southall Freeman, his leading biographer, whose treatment has been highly influential with all other Lee writers, goes to great lengths to picture Lee as Christlike. Lee's supreme, God-like status was established almost immediately after the war. As early as 1868 he was described in a Southern publication as "bathed in the white light that falls directly upon him from the smile of an approving and sustaining God." The apotheosis had advanced by 1880, when John W. Daniel, who had served on Lt. Gen. Jubal Early's staff, wrote that: "The Divinity in his bosom shown translucent through the man and his spirit rose up to the god-like." A group of twentieth-century writers including Gamaliel Bradford, Clifford Dowdey, and Freeman have carried this image of Lee well into our own time.

Stonewall Jackson is also presented as more than an effective soldier. Early Lost Cause writers like Robert Lewis Dabney and John Esten Cooke presented him as a deeply religious, mystical, eccentric, and brilliant military leader of Olympian proportions. This was also the thrust of Englishman G. F. R. Henderson's writing in 1898. The neo-Confederate writers of the Lost Cause in this century—people like James I. Robertson, Jr.—are, if anything, more elaborate in their tributes to Jackson than were his early biographers. Robertson's 1997 biography describes Jackson as a "spiritual prince," "standing alone on a high pedestal," and he says that Jackson's devotion to God, duty, and country "remain treasured legacies of the American people just as they are inspirations to people everywhere." This work approvingly quotes the following tribute paid by one of Jackson's subordinate officers: "He was indeed a soldier of the cross."

National Park Service personnel conduct a tour of the grounds at Guiney Station, Virginia, including the building in which Jackson died. These affairs are in the nature of pilgrimages, with candlelight and lugubrious readings of accounts of the general's death, not unlike the reading of Christ's Passion and death on Palm Sunday at a Roman Catholic mass.

Currently, a third Confederate general officer, Nathan Bedford Forrest, is in the midst of his apotheosis in the hands of contemporary neo-Confederates and the merchants who sell Civil War materials. God, it seems, also had him by the hand.

As pointed out hereafter, the Lost Cause characterizations of Confederate generals also had a negative category reserved for those like Longstreet who did not fit the myth.

Civil War History

Slavery as the Sectional Issue

The assertion by the Lost Cause spokesmen of the insignificance of slavery in the sectional conflict seems outrageous and disingenuous in the light of nineteenth-century American political history, of which Southern spokesmen were and are well aware. Although muted in the early years of the United States, the sectional slavery disagreement emerged full-blown prior to 1820 in connection with the issue of admitting Missouri to the Union. In the midst of a fierce national debate, Congress passed the Missouri Compromise in 1820. This legislation admitted Missouri as a slave state, Maine as a free state, and prohibited slavery in the territory north of Missouri's southern boundary, that is, latitude 36°30'. At an increasingly accelerated pace during the years between 1820 and Lincoln's election in 1860, the issue of slavery divided the sections in a long series of political crises ranging from the location of a transcontinental railroad to the Wilmot Proviso, which would have prohibited slavery in territory acquired in the Mexican War. These crises also concerned such issues as the Mexican War itself, the congressional gag rule, the admission of other states to the Union, slavery in the District of Columbia, popular sovereignty and the Kansas-Nebraska territory, the Compromise of 1850, the rise of a sectional political party, the sectional division of the Democratic Party, the dispute over the admission of Kansas as a state, and the increase of rhetorical and physical violence between representatives of the sections. Indeed, Don E. Fehrenbacher does not exaggerate in asserting that the prewar tendency of nearly all public controversy to fall into line with the slavery question bespeaks the power with which that question gripped the minds of the American people."

Also plainly contradicting the Lost Cause assertion of the irrelevancy of slavery are the prewar statements of the Southern leaders themselves. Jefferson Davis had frequently spoken to the United States Senate about the significance of slavery to the South and had threatened secession if what he perceived as Northern threats to the institution continued. In 1861, Confederate Vice President Stephens in his famous Charleston speech characterized the "great truth" of slavery as the "foundation" and "cornerstone" of the Confederacy. The Confederate Constitution also disclosed the role of slavery. It contained many verbatim repetitions of the Constitution of the United States but also included marked departures from the national document in Article 1, Section 9, and Article 4 by providing for protection of "the right of property in slaves." In spite of these facts, the Southerners' contention that slavery had nothing to do with the war was widely accepted in the postwar North and became part of the Civil War legend in the popular mind. This belief was advanced by such prominent twentieth-century historians as Charles and Mary Beard, Avery Craven, and James G. Randall, influenced surely in part by their own racism. Others also set slavery aside as the critical concern of the Confederacy and critical issue of the war.

Recent scholarship seems at last to acknowledge the pervasive role of slavery in secession and the war. Thus Bertram Wyatt-Brown describes the "desperate commitment of Southern whites to hold black Americans forever in their power." On the other hand, in Fehrenbacher's words, the North "insisted on the value and sanctity of the union" and "there was a growing opinion of the Northern people that slavery was inconsistent with the destinies of the republic." D. W. Brogan, the United Kingdom commentator, has concluded that "the South was demanding of the North what it was less and less willing to give—theoretical and as far as possible practical equality for the peculiar institution." The Southerners, he concluded, "seceded over one thing and fought over one thing, slavery."

The Abolitionists

It is doubtless true that the Abolitionists were difficult. Reformers are always painful people, simply because they will not "go along" and they demand the reluctant attention of those who are going along, frequently provoking an unpleasant sense of guilt among the latter. But it is now early in the twenty-first century. An overwhelming majority of Americans have long believed in Lincoln's words that "If slavery is not wrong, nothing is wrong." The substantial point would seem to be that the Abolitionists were right one hundred fifty years ago. In a historical sense, there would seem to be no excuse for their lingering negative reputation.

The South Would Have Given Up Slavery

This contention overlooks a number of plain historical facts, including the mid-century agitation for the acquisition of Cuba and the filibustering about Central and South American territories. It also overlooks the increasingly more restrictive provisions that the slave states enacted affecting the institution of slavery. In the interest of protecting slavery at all costs, Southern states struck down such American constitutional premises as freedom of speech, freedom of the press, and similar assumptions like privacy of the mails. In regard to free speech and the First Amendment, for example, Virginia in 1849 made it a criminal offense to *state* "that owners had not the right of property in their slaves." And Missouri prohibited the publication of anti-slavery materials. It appears that Allan Nevins spoke accurately when he said: "The South, as a whole, in 1846–1861 was not moving toward emancipation but away from it. It was not relaxing the laws which guarded the system, but reinforcing them. It was not ameliorating slavery, but making it harsher and more implacable. The South was further from a just solution of the slavery problem in 1830 than it had been in 1789. It was further from tenable solution in 1860 than it had been in 1830."

There is simply no evidence tending to show that the South would have voluntarily abandoned slavery. The evidence is that the Southern states had openly abridged the Constitution of the United States, especially the Bill of Rights, in behalf of the institution.

The Nature of the Slaves

In order to respond to the image of the faithful slave and happy darky portrayed in the legend, one may start with the *Official Records*. One of the biggest problems facing Federal logisticians was how to handle the slaves fleeing in wholesale numbers to the Federal lines as those lines advanced southward. As early as December 4, 1861, Secretary of State William H. Seward was forced to instruct Maj. Gen. George B. McClellan that "Persons claimed to be held to service or labor under the laws of the State of Virginia frequently escape from the lines of the enemy's forces and are received in the lines of the Army of the Potomac and are received with the military protection of the United States."

Further contradiction of the myth appears in the numerous accounts by Federal soldiers of assistance rendered to them by slaves in the field. And Benjamin Quarles, Dudley Cornish, and others have reminded us that approximately 180,000 African Americans, mostly former slaves, were enlisted in the armies of the United States and many of them fought and died for this country.

The Nationalistic/Cultural Difference

Kenneth Stampp has commented on this fiction. "Fundamentally," he writes, "the Confederacy was not the product of a genuine southern nationalism. Indeed, except for the institution of slavery, the South had little to give it national identity, and the notion of a distinct southern culture was largely the figment of the romantic imagination of a handful of intellectuals and pro-slavery propagandists." Grady McWhiney and other of today's historians share this opinion.

The Military Analysis

The suggestion that somehow the South was not defeated is, of course, counterfactual. In fact, Federal armies seized the ports and major cities of the Confederacy, decimated its armies in battle, destroyed its logistical facilities, and ultimately roamed at will through the Confederacy. There was no magic or hocus-pocus in the Confederacy's military defeat. Nor do serious historians credit the contention that the defeat of the Confederates was a foregone conclusion.

Historians concede the North's advantage in population and the capacity to make war but reject the inevitable loss tradition and its premise in regard to men and material wealth. Historians today generally believe that the South could have won the Civil War. In 1956, the leading Southern historian, Bell I. Wiley, wrote the following:

> In the years since Appomattox, millions of Southerners have attributed Confederate defeat to the North's overpowering strength. This is a comforting conclusion and is not without a substantial basis of fact. . . . But the North also faced a greater task. In order to win the war, the North had to subdue a vast country of nine million inhabitants while the South could prevail by maintaining a successful resistance. To put it another way, the North had to conquer the South while the South could win simply by outlasting its adversary. By convincing the North that coercion was impossible or not worth the effort. The South had reason to believe that it could achieve independence; that it did not do so was as much, if not more, due to its own failings as to superior strength of the North.

A 1960 volume edited by David Donald contained the opinions of other distinguished professional historians who also argued that the defeat of the South was not a foregone conclusion and that it could have won. More recently, Richard Beringer, Herman Hattaway, Archer Jones, and William Still expressed the same view. They note that "No Confederate army lost a major engagement because of a lack of arms, munitions or other essential supplies," and summarize the case as follows:

> By remarkable and effective efforts the agrarian South did exploit and create an industrial base that proved adequate with the aid of imports to maintain suitably equipped forces in the field. Hence the Confederate Army suffered no crippling deficiency in weapons or supplies. Their principal handicap would be numerical inferiority. But to offset this lack Confederates fought the first major war in which both sides armed themselves with rifles and had the advantage of a temporary but very significant surge in the power of the tactical defensive. In addition, the problem of supply in a very large but thinly settled region was a powerful aid to the strategic defensive. Other things being equal, Confederate military leadership were confident that if the Union did not display Napoleonic genius, the tactical and strategic power of the defensive could offset the Northern numerical superiority and presumably give the South a measure of military victory adequate

to maintain its independence. In short, the task of the North was literally gigantic. It was the task of organizing and harnessing its superior resources and committing them to warfare on a financial scale that was historically unprecedented. The South too had a similar organizing job to do but inertia was on the South's side and would have been fatal to the North. The North had the necessity to conquer. The South could have won simply by not being conquered. It did not have to occupy a foot of ground outside its own borders.

With further reference to the military claims of the Lost Cause, the "Longstreet-lost-it-at-Gettysburg" thesis is based on the concept of the "high tide at Gettysburg": The Confederate loss at Gettysburg decided the war. This, too, is a myth; it disregards the remaining almost two years of fighting as well as Vicksburg, Missionary Ridge, Nashville, and Sherman's March to the Sea. Jeffry Wert responds in this volume to the scapegoating of Longstreet regarding Gettysburg. And the Jackson death thesis is also invalid. His death was clearly a blow to the Confederacy, but to point to that single 1863 event as decisive apart from the conduct of the war as a whole is simply unreasonable.

The Idealized Home Front

The typical moonlight and magnolias view of Southern society is highly distorted from a historical standpoint. Bertram Wyatt-Brown accurately notes that the Edenic view of the antebellum South ignores what he calls the "darker side of honor."

> Individuals and sometimes groups spoke out against popular forms of injustice and honor—duels, summary hangings, mob whippings. These efforts at reform seldom received public acclamation and support. Even historians, whether native to the South or not, have not seen these expressions of public will and private esteem as part of a total cultural pattern. Instead they have been labeled tragic aberrations, or techniques by which the planter class manipulated lesser, more virtuous folk. Gentility, the nobler, brighter feature of Southern ethics has been a more congenial topic. Certainly it was the model that Southerners have publicly revered and exalted.

The last three chapters of Wyatt-Brown's *Southern Honor* discuss some of the dark sides of the Southern ethos under the suggestive titles "Policing Slave Society: Insurrectionary Scares," "Charivari and Lynch Law," and "The Anatomy of a Wife-Killing." Contrary to the legend's picture of a unified and committed Southern people, we also know today that the South was bitterly divided politically on issues like the Confederate military draft, control of the Southern armies, and requisition of supplies for the armies. Furthermore, there was a high degree of strife and conflict that marked the political culture, the military establishment, and the personal relationships of Confederate leaders. Wiley remarks that "strife was the Confederacy's evil genius and no major organization or activity escaped its crippling influence."

The Idealized Confederate Soldier

The historical records simply do not bear out the idealized picture of the Confederate common soldier. Piston notes that "Desertions reached nightmare proportions during and after the [Antietam] campaign. Perhaps as many as 20,000 men left the army either before it crossed the Potomac or prior to the fight at Antietam. Significantly, desertions increased after the Confederates returned to Virginia." Lee's communications confirmed these typical soldier problems. Writing to Jefferson Davis from Hagerstown, Maryland, on September 13, 1862, before Sharpsburg, Lee stated: "One great embarrassment is the reduction of our ranks by straggling, which it seems impossible to prevent with our present regimental officers. Our ranks are very much diminished—I fear from a third to one half of the original numbers." Lee described the state of the army after the battle in a letter dated September 21: "Its present efficiency is greatly paralyzed by the loss to its ranks of the numerous stragglers. . . . A great many men belonging to the Army never entered Maryland at all; many returned after getting there, while others who crossed the river kept aloof. The stream (of stragglers) has not lessened since crossing the Potomac." The next day Lee advised Davis that "A great deal of damage to citizens is done by stragglers, who consume all they can get from the charitable and all they can take from the defenseless, in many cases wantonly destroying stock and property." What Douglas Southall Freeman calls "mass desertion" was a source of losses to Lee's army after Gettysburg as well. Reporting to President Davis on July 27, 1863, Lee stated that "There are many thousand men improperly absent from this army." Less than a month later Lee informed Davis that "General Imboden writes that there are great numbers of deserters in the valley, who conceal themselves successfully from the small squads sent to arrest them." On the same day, August 17, Lee ordered Imboden to collect and send back deserters from the valley in northwest Virginia and Lee reported that according to reports that he was receiving from North Carolina, there was "an organization of deserters . . . a formidable and growing evil there." These men, according to Secretary of War James A. Seddon, were engaged in "dangerous combinations and violent proceedings." Desertions from the Confederate Army of Tennessee in the western theater "climbed at an alarming rate" after the Confederate victory at Chickamauga.

The Lawfulness of Secession

The Northern people did not, of course, concede the Southern contention regarding the legality of secession. Lincoln addressed the question in his first inaugural speech: "I hold, that in contemplation of universal law, and the Constitution, the Union of the states is perpetual. Perpetuity is implied, if not expressed, in the fundamental law of all national governments." On the issue of a compact of sovereign states, he said: "Again, the United States would not be a government proper but an association of states in the status of a contract merely, can it, as a contract be peaceably unmade by less than all of the parties who made it? One party to a contract may violate—break it, so to speak, but does it not require all to lawfully rescind it?" But the issue could not be reduced to a theoretical, abstract argument or be legalistically resolved. In practical terms, the South was asserting a right to revolution, a right Americans acknowledged. But the North in practical terms was unwilling to allow the nation to perish. The real issue regarding secession was whether, under the circumstances, it was just or unjust.

The Saints Go Marching In

The legend's image of Lee is at odds with the facts. He was not antislavery as the image claims; he was a strong believer in the institution. His secession, following Virginia, was not inevitable, but a calculated act of will in highly ambiguous circumstances. His aggressive, offensive generalship cost his army disproportionate, irreplaceable, and excessive casualties, which led to his being caught in a fatal siege. Contrary to the legend of his magnanimity, he was hateful and bitter toward the North during and after the war. His persistence in continuing the war after he realized the South was defeated was costly in the lives of his men as well as the Yankees and not necessarily a creditable act. In the postwar period, he was less of a healer than he was a conventional advocate of Southern positions.

Historically, Jackson was clearly an effective soldier. He was also fanatical, like Oliver Cromwell among the Irish, killing people zestfully for the glory of God. He was zealously pietistic, but advocated a no prisoners, black flag war, seriously proposing this to Virginia's governor and proposing that he embark on such a campaign himself.

In many ways Forrest, although an able soldier, seems a strange hero for twentieth-century Americans. His personal fortune resulted from slave trading. He looked on as his troops helped massacre black Union soldiers at Fort Pillow after they had surrendered. After the war he became a prominent Ku Klux Klan leader. To a thoughtful or humane person, he seems an anomalous hero.

The Lost Cause Legacy to History

Taken together, the elements of the Myth of the Lost Cause created the Southern image that was sought. Slavery and the slavery disagreement were excluded from that image. There had been a distinctive and superior Southern culture, benign and effective in its race relations. That culture was led by wise and superior men who seceded because they sought freedom from an oppressive Northern culture, an effort that failed because of overwhelming Northern power. The warfare itself was a contest of honor and martial glory in which the chivalrous and valorous Southerners pursued a sort of Arthurian tournament, seeking Southern independence.

The Lost Cause version of the war is a caricature, possible, among other reasons, because of the false treatment of slavery and the black people. This false treatment struck at the core of the truth of the war, unhinging cause and effect, depriving the United States of any high purpose, and removing African Americans from their true role as the issue of the war and participants in the war, and characterizing them as historically irrelevant. With slavery exorcised, it appeared that the North had conducted itself within the Union so as to provoke secession and then bloodily defeated the secessionists in war so as to compel them to stay in the Union against their will.

The historical image of the war is, of course, quite different. It says that the seceding states were dominated by a cruel and wrongful slavery. As evidenced by the prewar political discord, the nature of the compromise efforts on the eve of Fort Sumter—all of which concerned the legal status of slavery—and the prewar statements of Southern political leaders, slavery was *the* sectional issue. Southern political leaders led their states out of the Union to protect slavery from a disapproving national majority. Although slaveholders constituted a distinct minority of Southern people, a majority of these people were committed to the institution for African Americans. The North went to war to defeat secession. The Civil War, therefore, presented three issues: (1) however flawed the circumstances, human freedom was at stake; (2) the territorial and political integrity of the United States was at stake; and (3) the survival of the democratic process—republican government of, by, and for the people—was at stake.

Secession was not therefore heroic—it was mean and narrow and a profound mistake. Its leaders were wrong and authored a major tragedy for the American people. Dismantling the United States in 1861 would not have benefited either the North or the South. On the contrary, it would have led to constant conflict over such things as access to the Mississippi River and the rights of the two nations to the territories, and it would have established the precedent that a loser in a democratic election may successfully resort to warfare, as Lincoln discussed in his Gettysburg Address. The warfare itself, in which African Americans participated in behalf of the North, was cruel and terribly destructive to the people of both sides.

Confederate sympathizers today contend that the secessionists acted in good faith; this presumably means that they thought that they were doing the right thing. It would seem that this is neither here nor there in a historical sense. Leaders of all kinds of destructive causes—causes with wholly negative values—have thought they were right. It would be inflammatory to identify examples of this in modern times, but surely they occur to us. The historical question is whether, in good faith or bad, the movement that was led was positive or negative, humane or inhumane?

The Lost Cause treatment of the role of slavery in the war and its view of African Americans as subhumans not to be taken seriously formed the prelude to the myth of Reconstruction, another historical legacy of the Lost Cause. As portrayed in D. W. Griffith's *Birth of a Nation* and its updated Margaret Mitchell version, the Reconstruction myth identified the freedmen variously as shiftless fools, corrupt political connivers, or despoilers of the virtues of white women. Reconstruction was pictured as a cynical exploitation of African Americans by cynical schemers. The Ku Klux Klan existed as the shield of justice and the virtue of Southern women. This Negrophobic Reconstruction myth has been so dominant that a man as intelligent and humane as Shelby Foote commented negatively about Reconstruction in Ken Burns's Civil War television series.

The Political Legacy

The political legacy of the Lost Cause had two signal aspects. On one hand, its development facilitated the reunification of the North and South. Ex-Confederates saw the acceptance of the myth by Northerners as "signs of respect from former foes and Northern publishers [which] made acceptance of reunion easier. By the mid-80s, most southerners had decided to build a future within a reunited nation. The North had . . . acknowledged the heroism and nobility of the Confederate effort, the honor of the South" so that "Southerners would be totally at ease in the union."

The second aspect of the political legacy concerned the status of African Americans. The virulent racism that the North shared with the South, in spite of Northern antislavery views, was a premise of the Lost Cause and the principal engine of the North's acceptance of it. The reunion was exclusively a white man's phenomenon and the price of the reunion was the sacrifice of the African Americans. Indeed, the reunion of the white race was expressly at the expense of the freedmen. The Compromise of 1877 gave the presidential election to Rutherford B. Hayes and the Republicans on the promise that Federal troops—the blacks' only shield—would be withdrawn from the South. The blacks were abandoned, the states of Confederacy were "redeemed" by the empowerment of the former Confederate political leadership, and Articles XIV (equal protection of the law) and XV (voting rights), constitutional products of the war, were permitted to atrophy for a hundred years. In short, the success of the teachings of the Lost Cause led to the nation's abandoning even its half-hearted effort to protect African Americans and bring them into the United States as equal citizens. Jim Crow, lynch law, and disfranchisement followed.

Epilogue

As has been said, the Lost Cause legacy to history is a caricature of the truth. This caricature wholly misrepresents and distorts the facts of the matter. Surely it is time to start again in our understanding of this decisive element of our past and to do so from the premises of history unadulterated by the distortions, falsehoods, and romantic sentimentality of the Myth of the Lost Cause.

Having swept away the counterfactual Myth of the Lost Cause, a historian may briefly state the history of the Civil War as follows.

The eleven states that seceded and became the Confederate States of America did so in order to protect the institution of African slavery from a perceived political threat from the majority of the people of the United States who disapproved of the institution. Although slaveholders were a minority in each of the Confederate states, the slaveholding planter class dominated the politics and culture and tastes of those states and led them into secession and armed rebellion against the United States.

African slavery was an inhumane, reactionary, uneconomic labor system, disapproved of by the civilized people of the world. Most of the slaves disliked their status and took any opportunity to escape slavery, despite the fact that if caught they risked flogging, branding, and other severe punishments or death. The slave states before the war effected legal provisions that plainly violated the United States Constitution's Bill of Rights in an effort to secure the institution of slavery. Furthermore, prior to secession, Southern people who objected to slavery were isolated, silenced, and driven out of the slave states.

Having seceded, the eleven states raised armies and claimed the property and institutions of the United States that were within their borders. If the United States failed to surrender those properties voluntarily, the Confederates seized them by force of arms. When the United States in 1861 refused to surrender Fort Sumter in Charleston Harbor, the fort was attacked and taken by Southern arms. This started the war. Under the leadership of President Abraham Lincoln, an unusually skilled and inspirational politician, the United States defended itself against the Confederate rebellion over the next four years and ultimately reclaimed the territory of the eleven seceded states by military force.

The war was cruel, costly, and devastating, killing in excess of six hundred thousand American men, Northern and Southern, and wounding many, many more. It also was highly destructive to the Southern economy. African Americans also participated in the war; many escaped slavery; 180,000 of them fought in the United States military forces and thousands of others assisted the United States in logistical and supporting ways and in sheltering and taking care of Federal soldiers in Confederate territory. As a consequence of the war, slavery was abolished and constitutional amendments were effected which prohibited slavery (the Thirteenth), guaranteed equal protection of the law (the Fourteenth), and provided for universal male suffrage (the Fifteenth). At the conclusion of the war, the eleven states resumed their places in the Union. There occurred a brief period during which the United States attempted to reform Southern political life by drawing into it the freed slaves and protecting them from persecution and discrimination. The Southern people persistently opposed these efforts, often pursuing cruel and violent acts against the freed people. White Northerners, who were also intensely racist, ultimately abandoned the effort to ensure the protection of the freed people. The United States soldiers were withdrawn from the South. The Confederate leadership returned to power in the former Confederate states and succeeded in institutionalizing the discriminatory and violent treatment of the freed people and excluding them from political life.

Appendix

Because *Gone with the Wind,* both the book and the movie, has been so popular and so widely known and I have been negative about them, I should explain my view. I do not require the reader to choose between Abraham Lincoln and Clark Gable, but I offer examples of Mitchell's great story as very bad history, essentially a Lost Cause statement:

The Slaves. In the story, they are pictured as unintelligent, passive, and faithful to the always indulgent "Old Massa." The implication is that the war was not about slavery and the message is also that the slaves were well treated, happy, and did not care whether they were slaves or free people. As has been pointed out, the fact is that the war was all about slavery—the South seceded to protect slavery—and the slaves knew this and were overwhelmingly supportive of the North.

The Yankee Soldier. The reader may recall the scene in which a snaggletoothed, evil-looking Federal soldier has entered Tara to steal. Scarlett shoots him on the steps to protect herself from his rather obvious intent to assault her. The implication is that the Yankees were bush-whackers or guerrilla warriors—bad people who were gratuitously and randomly upsetting the genteel and benign Southern culture. There were, of course, atrocities committed during the Civil War, as is true in all wars, but such activity was relatively insignificant and, more to the point, there were Southern perpetrators of atrocities in the North as well as in the South, just as there were Federal perpetrators. A particularly interesting fact concerns Pennsylvania as Lee's army was en route to Gettysburg. The Confederate soldiers captured black people, including children and free blacks, and sent them South into slavery.

The Southern Armies. The reader may recall pictures of the ragged, forlorn Southern army, marching through the streets of Atlanta in its attempt to defend the city. The myth is that the defeat of the South was inevitable, that it was simply overwhelmed by massive Northern materiel and manpower and could not have won the war. The consensus among serious historians today discredits this myth. A recent study by a group of professional historians makes this observation: "No Confederate army lost a major engagement because of lack of arms, munitions or other essential supplies."

The Vigilantes. There is a scene in which Leslie Howard, as Ashley Wilkes, and his fellow Southern protagonists secretly go out armed immediately after the war to "clean out" the encampment of homeless former slaves. Howard is wounded in the struggle. This, of course, is the nascent Ku Klux Klan, and it is presented in a manner wholly sympathetic to the idea of vigilantes and the necessity of their existence in order to protect good white people from the former slaves, who are bad black people.

After the War. As indicated by its title, the book extends into the early period of Reconstruction. It depicts the freed black people as arrogant and crude and the Southern whites who cooperated with the social revolution of the war as vicious and evil. The implication again is that the Yankees had replaced the chivalrous and benign Southern people with evil Southern people. Reconstruction was, in fact, a flawed process, but it had its idealistic side. Moreover, the failures were caused by Southern intransigence as much as by Northern errors.

Discussion Questions

1. First list the major arguments Nolan makes in "The Anatomy of the Myth." Then, look at the organizational strategy he uses in arranging this selection. Map out the organization of this selection in groups, and discuss how this organization does or does not contribute to Nolan's central argument.

2. Discuss in groups what your previous education and exposure to films and television programs about the Civil War have taught you. Do you feel your impressions of the Civil War have been influenced by historians of the "Lost Cause" school, or do you see the Civil War more in the unromanticized light that Nolan seeks to show us? Do you agree with his assertions? Do you feel the theories of the "Lost Cause" scholars have validity or not?

Writing Suggestions

1. Building on your answers to the first discussion question for this selection, write an analysis of Nolan's essay, examining his organizational strategy and its relationship to his argument. Does his organization contribute or not to the power of his argument? How does his organization add to or detract from his arguments? Do you feel this essay would have been more or less effective with a different kind of organization? Explain.

2. Sentiment for the Confederacy remains strong today in some southern states. In a number of southern states, such as South Carolina, Mississippi, and Georgia, recent controversy has arisen about flying the Confederate flag or state flag with a Confederate symbol integrated into the flag. Research on the Web the current practices and arguments concerning the Confederate flag, and then write an opinion piece about whether or not these southern states should fly a separate Confederate flag or a flag with a Confederate symbol in it. Discuss both sides of the issue in your paper, but take a stand on what you believe is the best policy, and be specific in your argumentation.

Narrative of Sojourner Truth

SOJOURNER TRUTH

Sojourner Truth (1797–1893) was born a slave in New York, on the estate of a Dutch slave-holding family. Originally named Isabella Baumfree, she was sold to several owners before she arrived at the household of John Dumont in 1810. Her time there is described in the selection below, taken from *Narrative of Sojourner Truth*, which she wrote with the help of a white woman, Olive Gilbert, in 1850. After New York became a free state in 1827, Isabella began her travels, changing her name to Sojourner Truth. She met Frederick Douglass in Massachusetts and he persuaded her to join the abolitionist lecture circuit, which she followed for many years. She was a great orator, and became well-known all over the country. During the Civil War, she nursed wounded soldiers and performed a variety of war duties. She was invited to the White House by President Lincoln, and later became involved in the black self-determination movement, urging blacks to move West.

Her Standing with Her New Master and Mistress

Had Mrs. Dumont possessed that vein of kindness and consideration for the slaves, so perceptible in her husband's character, Isabella would have been as comfortable here, as one had *best* be, if one *must* be a slave. Mr. Dumont had been nursed in the very lap of slavery, and being naturally a man of kind feelings, treated his slaves with all the consideration he did his *other* animals, and *more*, perhaps. But Mrs. Dumont, who had been born and educated in a non-slaveholding family, and, like many others, used only to workpeople, who, under the most stimulating of human motives, were willing to put forth their every energy, could not have patience with the creeping gait, the dull understanding, or see any cause for the listless manners and careless, slovenly habits of the poor down-trodden outcast—entirely forgetting that every high and efficient motive had been removed far from him; and that, had not his very intellect been crushed out of him, the slave would find little ground for aught but hopeless despondency. From this source arose a long series of trials in the life of our heroine, which we must pass over in silence; some from motives of delicacy, and others, because the relation of them might inflict undeserved pain on some now living, whom Isabel remembers only with esteem and love; therefore, the reader will not be surprised if our narrative appears somewhat tame at this point, and may rest assured that it is not for want of facts, as the most thrilling incidents of this portion of her life are from various motives suppressed.

One comparatively trifling incident she wishes related, as it made a deep impression on her mind at the time—showing, as *she* thinks, how God shields the innocent, and causes them to triumph over their enemies, and also how she stood between master and mistress. In her family, Mrs. Dumont employed two white girls, one of whom, named Kate, evinced a disposition to 'lord it over' Isabel, and, in her emphatic language, 'to *grind her down.*' Her master often shielded her from the attacks and accusations of others, praising her for her readiness and ability to work, and these praises seemed to foster a spirit of hostility to her, in the minds of Mrs. Dumont and her white servant, the latter of whom took every opportunity to cry up her faults, lessen her in the esteem of her master and increase against her the displeasure of her mistress, which was already more than sufficient for Isabel's comfort. Her master insisted that she could do as much work as half a dozen common people, and do it well, too; whilst her mistress insisted that the first was true, only because it ever came from her hand but half performed. A good deal of feeling arose from this difference of opinion, which was getting to rather an uncomfortable height, when, all at once, the potatoes that Isabel cooked for breakfast assumed a dingy, dirty look. Her mistress blamed her severely, asking her master to observe 'a fine specimen of Bell's work!'—adding, 'it is the way *all* her work is done.' Her master scolded also this time, and commanded her to be more careful in future. Kate joined with zest in the censures, and was very hard upon her. Isabella thought that she had done all she well could to have them nice; and became quite distressed at these appearances, and wondered what she should do to avoid them. In this dilemma, Gertrude Dumont (Mr. D.'s eldest child, a good, kind-hearted girl of ten years, who pitied Isabel sincerely), when she heard them all blame her so unsparingly, came forward, offering her sympathy and assistance; and when about to retire to bed, on the night of Isabella's humiliation, she advanced to Isabel, and told her, if she would wake her early next morning, she would get up and attend to her potatoes for her, while she (Isabella) went to milking, and they would see if they could not have them *nice*, and not have 'Poppee,' her word for father, and 'Matty,' her word for mother, and all of 'em, scolding so terribly.

Isabella gladly availed herself of this kindness, which touched her to the heart, amid so much of an opposite spirit. When Isabella had put the potatoes over to boil Getty told her she would herself tend the fire, while Isabel milked. She had not long been seated by the fire, in performance of her promise, when Kate entered, and requested Gertrude to go out of the room and do something for her, which she refused, still keeping her place in the corner. While there, Kate came sweeping about the fire, caught up a chip, lifted some ashes with it, and dashed them into the kettle. Now the mystery was solved, the plot discovered! Kate was working a little too fast at making her mistress's words good, at showing that Mrs. Dumont and herself were on the right side of the dispute, and consequently at gaining power over Isabella. Yes, she was quite too fast, inasmuch as she had overlooked the little figure of justice, which sat in the corner, with scales nicely balanced, waiting to give all their dues.

But the time had come when she was to be overlooked no longer. It was Getty's turn to speak now. 'Oh, Poppee! oh, Poppee!' said she, 'Kate has been putting ashes in among the potatoes! I saw her do it! Look at those that fell on the outside of the kettle! You can now see what made the potatoes so dingy every morning, though Bell washed them clean!' And she repeated her story to every new comer, till the fraud was made as public as the censure of Isabella had been. Her mistress looked blank, and remained dumb—her master muttered something which sounded very like an oath—and poor Kate was so chop-fallen, she looked like a convicted criminal, who would gladly have hid herself (now that the baseness was out), to conceal her mortified pride and deep chagrin.

It was a fine triumph for Isabella and her master, and she became more ambitious than ever to please him; and he stimulated her ambition by his commendation, and by boasting of her to his friends, telling them that '*that* wench' (pointing to Isabel) 'is better to me than a *man*—for she will do a good family's washing in the night, and be ready in the morning to go into the field, where she will do as much at raking and binding as my best hands.' Her ambition and desire to please were so great, that she often worked several nights in succession, sleeping only short snatches, as she sat in her chair; and some nights she would not allow herself to take any sleep, save what she could get resting herself against the wall, fearing that if she sat down, she would sleep too long. These extra exertions to please, and the praises consequent upon them, brought upon her head the envy of her fellow-slaves, and they taunted her with being the '*white folks' nigger.*' On the other hand, she received a larger share of the confidence of her master, and many small favors that were by them unattainable. I asked her if her master, Dumont, ever whipped her? She answered, 'Oh yes, he sometimes whipped me soundly, though never cruelly. And the most severe whipping he ever give me was because I was cruel to a cat.' At this time she looked upon her master as a *God*; and believed that he knew of and could see her at all times, even as God himself. And she used sometimes to confess her delinquencies, from the conviction that he already knew them, and that she should fare better if she confessed voluntarily: and if any one talked to her of the injustice of her being a slave, she answered them with contempt and immediately told her master. She then firmly believed that slavery was right and honorable. Yet she *now* sees very clearly the false position they were all in, both masters and slaves; and she looks back, with utter astonishment, at the absurdity of the claims so arrogantly set up by the masters, over beings designed by God to be as free as kings; and at the perfect stupidity of the slave, in admitting for one moment the validity of these claims.

In obedience to her mother's instructions, she had educated herself to such a sense of honesty, that, when she had become a mother, she would sometimes whip her child when it cried to her for bread, rather than give it a piece secretly, lest it should learn to take what was not its own! And the writer of this knows, from personal observation, that the slaveholders of the South feel it to be a *religious duty* to teach their slaves to be honest, and never to take what is not their own! Oh consistency, art thou not a jewel? Yet Isabella glories in the fact that she was faithful and true to her master; she says, 'It made me true to my God'—meaning, that it helped to form in her a character that loved truth, and hated a lie, and had saved her from the bitter pains and fears that are sure to follow in the wake of insincerity and hypocrisy.

As she advanced in years, an attachment sprung up between herself and a slave named Robert. But his master, an Englishman by the name of Catlin, anxious that no one's property but his own should be enhanced by the increase of his slaves, forbade Robert's visits to Isabella, and commanded him to take a wife among his fellow-servants. Notwithstanding this interdiction, Robert, following the bent of his inclinations, continued his visits to Isabel, though very stealthily, and, as he believed, without exciting the suspicion of his master; but one Saturday afternoon, hearing that Bell was ill, he took the liberty to go and see her. The first intimation *she* had of his visit was the appearance of her master, inquiring 'if she had seen Bob.' On her answering in the negative, he said to her, 'If you see him, tell him to take care of himself, for the Catlins are after him.' Almost at that instant, Bob made his appearance; and the first people he met were his old and his young masters. They were terribly enraged at finding him there, and the eldest began cursing, and calling upon his son to '*Knock down* the d____d black rascal;' at the same time, they both fell upon him like tigers, beating him with the heavy ends of their canes, bruising and mangling his head and face in the most awful manner, and causing the blood, which streamed from his wounds, to cover him like a slaughtered beast, constituting him a most shocking spectacle. Mr. Dumont interposed at this point, telling the ruffians they could no longer thus spill human blood on *his* premises—he would have 'no niggers killed there.' The Catlins then took a rope they had taken with them for the purpose, and tied Bob's hands behind him in such a manner, that Mr. Dumont insisted on loosening the cord, declaring that no brute should be tied in *that* manner, where *he* was. And as they led him away, like the greatest of criminals, the more humane Dumont followed them to their homes, as Robert's protector; and when he returned, he kindly went to Bell, as he called her, telling her he did not think they would strike him any more, as their wrath had greatly cooled before he left them. Isabella had witnessed this scene from her window, and was greatly shocked at the murderous treatment of poor Robert, whom she truly loved, and whose only crime, in the eye of his persecutors, was his affection for her. This beating, and we know not what after treatment, completely subdued the spirit of its victim, for Robert ventured no more to visit Isabella, but like an obedient and faithful chattel, took himself a wife from the house of his master. Robert did not live many years after his last visit to Isabel, but took his departure to that country, where 'they neither marry nor are given in marriage,' and where the oppressor cannot molest.

Isabella's Marriage

Subsequently, Isabella was married to a fellow-slave, named Thomas, who had previously had two wives, one of whom, if not both, had been torn from him and sold far away. And it is more than probable, that he was not only allowed but encouraged to take another at each successive sale. I say it is probable, because the writer of this knows from personal observation, that such is the custom among slaveholders at the present day; and that in a twenty months' residence among them, we never knew any one to open the lip against the practice; and when we severely censured it, the slaveholder had nothing to say; and the slave pleaded that, under existing circumstances, he could do no better.

Such an abominable state of things is silently tolerated, to say the least, by slaveholders—deny it who may. And what is that religion that sanctions, even by its silence, all that is embraced in the *'Peculiar Institution'*? If there *can* be any thing more diametrically opposed to the religion of Jesus, than the working of this soul-killing system—which is as truly sanctioned by the religion of America as are her ministers and churches—we wish to be shown where it can be found.

We have said, Isabella was married to Thomas—she was, after the fashion of slavery, one of the slaves performing the ceremony for them; as no true minister of Christ *can* perform, as in the presence of God, what he knows to be a mere *farce*, a *mock* marriage, unrecognized by any civil law, and liable to be annulled any moment, when the interest or caprice of the master should dictate.

With what feelings must slaveholders expect us to listen to their horror of amalgamation in prospect, while they are well aware that we know how calmly and quietly they contemplate the present state of licentiousness their own wicked laws have created, not only as it regards the slave, but as it regards the more privileged portion of the population of the South?

Slaveholders appear to me to take the same notice of the vices of the slave, as one does of the vicious disposition of his horse. They are often an inconvenience; further than that, they care not to trouble themselves about the matter.

Discussion Questions

1. What does Isabella recount about her early feelings toward her master as "a God"? How did she later come to feel about this attitude of slave to master?
2. How do the details in this primary source help clarify Isabella's struggles? Which details from the reading stand out in your mind?

Writing Suggestions

1. Write a journal response to the following question: What argument does Isabella make by narrating the story of Robert, who loved her but was forbidden to see her? Of what is she persuading her audience in this small story? How does this story make her writing even more effective?

2. Review Fitzhugh's writings earlier in this chapter. List his major arguments. Then, write an analysis of Sojourner Truth's life as a reflection of Fitzhugh's statements. How and when do Isabella's masters show their agreement with Fitzhugh? What are the specific results in Sojourner's life of the philosophy of Fitzhugh and those who agreed with his arguments?

A Grand Army of Black Men

Letters from African-American Soldiers in the Union Army, 1861–1865

EDWIN S. REDKEY

Edwin S. Redkey is a retired professor of history at the State University of New York at Purchase. Redkey is the editor of *A Grand Army of Black Men: Letters from African-American Soldiers in the Union Army, 1861–1865*, and also wrote *Black Exodus: Black Nationalist and Back-to-Africa Movements, 1890–1910* (1969), and was Scholar-in-Residence (1992–1993) at the New York City Library Schomburg Center, where he conducted further research in black history in America. In the following selection from *A Grand Army of Black Men*, Redkey gives us a glimpse of what kinds of struggles black soldiers fought on and off the battlefield. The selection includes Redkey's "Introduction" and a sample of letters from men who wrote not only about the war but also about their struggles for equality within the Union Army and in the United States.

Introduction: For Freedom and Equality

For a century after the Civil War, most Americans thought that blacks had done little or nothing to win their freedom from slavery. During the Civil Rights Movement of the 1950s and 1960s, renewed study of African-American history corrected that old ignorance and showed that almost 200,000 black soldiers (and thousands of black sailors) had served the Union. But most interested people thought that those soldiers were newly freed slaves, capable only of labor, afraid of battle, illiterate, and ignorant of the more complex issues of the war.

Forgotten were the thousands of free black men from the Northern states who had fought not only to free the slaves and serve the Union but also to show the world that they, as much as any other men, deserved to be full partners in the United States. From Vermont and Maryland, from Massachusetts and Iowa, from every one of the Union states, they had put on blue uniforms to show their patriotism and manhood. From 1863 to 1865 they had marched and fought, suffered and died from rebel bullets and army diseases, just as the white troops had done. Whites did not know or care that these Northern black soldiers were different from the slaves, that they could read and write as well as most whites, that they were prepared to struggle not only against rebellion in the South but against racism everywhere.

These brave, free black men let the nation know how they felt about the war. A few were college-trained, many had a public school education, and some were just learning to read and write. They wrote to their friends and families, but few of those letters have survived. They also wrote to army and government officials; many of those official letters were saved in the National Archives. They wrote most often to black and abolitionist newspapers to tell their friends at home about their experiences, their fears, and their hopes. This book is a selection of such letters published by newspapers during the war years.

The writers of these "letters to the editors" told about the many sides of army life. They began by telling about the training days in camp; they proceeded to the marching, digging, raiding, and fighting that made their war. They wrote about comrades, mostly brave, some dead; about officers, mostly white, some gallant, others racist; about Southerners, black and white. They told of the diseases that killed so many soldiers. They described in detail their raids behind Confederate lines, their charges against rebel trenches, and their wounds from Southern guns. And they told of their triumphal marches into Charleston, Wilmington, and Richmond, capital of the defeated Confederacy.

The newspaper letters also told why the black troops were fighting; more than anything else, they wanted to earn their rights as Americans. For many years free blacks had been denied the equality proclaimed in the Declaration of Independence. By joining the army, by fighting willingly and dying bravely, African Americans wanted to earn both respect and citizenship.

Their letters told of the many racist insults they suffered and what they did to endure them. They complained of bad treatment by white officers, soldiers, and civilians, both South and North. The worst of those insults was the government's decision to give black soldiers reduced pay. Instead of the thirteen dollars paid whites, blacks got only seven dollars each month. Thousands of them protested and refused to accept any pay at all until they could get the same pay as whites. Letter after letter told why they took no pay; despite the suffering of their families at home, they would take no government money until they got equality. Despite criticism from their white officers, from civilian leaders, and from some of their black comrades, they kept up their boycott of the paymaster until Congress finally voted them equal pay.

Through all their letters flows a current of dignity and pride. There is an unmistakable note of achievement and self-confidence. They could join with Private Charles T. Brown when he wrote soon after the valiant attack by black troops against Petersburg, Virginia, "What a glorious prospect it is to behold this grand army of black men, as they march at the head of their column over the sacred soil of Virginia. They cause what few inhabitants yet remain to look and wonder."

The United States government was slow to enlist blacks in the war effort. The war had been under way for a year when, in the summer of 1862, Congress authorized President Abraham Lincoln to use black soldiers at his discretion. He and most other whites doubted that blacks could or would fight as well as whites. Furthermore, he had to consider the prejudices of the border states—slave states that remained in the Union and feared that enlisting blacks would undermine their "peculiar institution." As a result, Lincoln refused at first to use his new authority. But as the war dragged on and Union victories seemed to come too seldom, the President risked using black troops. They would serve in all-black regiments led by white officers, and they would face the hardships of racism as well as the hazards of war. But they would have the chance to show that they were men equal to any and patriots worthy of citizenship in the nation of their birth.

The first black regiments were raised in the fall of 1862, after Lincoln announced the Emancipation Proclamation. Around the edges of the Confederacy, Federal forces had established important bases that served to harass the rebels and to squeeze the Southern lifeline of supplies from abroad. Especially strong bases had been built on the islands near Charleston, South Carolina, and in Louisiana. The first three black regiments were mustered in New Orleans by November. They were composed mostly of free blacks who had a long tradition of militia training, and who originally had their own black officers. A fourth regiment was formed in Kansas, on the border of a slave state, Missouri; it was mustered into Federal service in January 1863. Also mustered that same month was the fifth black regiment, recruited in the Sea Islands of South Carolina. This was the regiment of ex-slaves described in the classic book *Army Life in a Black Regiment*, written by its white colonel, Thomas Wentworth Higginson.

Lincoln's Emancipation Proclamation, which took effect in January 1863, announced his intention to use black soldiers more actively, and he soon authorized state governors in New England to enlist new black regiments. Massachusetts, led by abolitionist Governor John Andrew, quickly created three such units; they were soon matched by Rhode Island and Connecticut. Because the black population of New England was small, men for these regiments came from free black communities all across the North, from as far west as Illinois and Iowa.

These communities had been founded during the era of the Revolutionary War. Starting with Massachusetts, the Northern states had gradually abolished slavery by 1804. The Northwest Ordinance of 1787 guaranteed that the new states north of the Ohio River would also be free. By 1860 about 210,000 free persons of color lived in the Northern states, mostly in eastern cities and in the parts of other states closest to the slave states, such as the southern portions of Pennsylvania, Ohio, Indiana, and Illinois. Some of the people had been born in slavery but had been given their freedom or run away to the North. Many young men from those black settlements joined the Union Army.

Although they were legally free, blacks in the North suffered much discrimination. Most could only work as unskilled laborers or farmers. Only in New England and New York could they vote, and they could not serve on juries or in the state militias—duties required of white citizens. Public schools spread rapidly across the North in the years before the Civil War, but most of them refused to admit blacks. Despite these handicaps, a small but growing number of free African Americans found ways to get an education, usually at their own expense. Those were the men who would write the letters collected in this book.

The 1850s were difficult years for Northern blacks. A new, harsh Fugitive Slave Law went into effect in 1850. It allowed "slave chasers" to accuse any black of being a runaway slave and would not allow the accused to testify in his or her own defense. As a result an unknown number of free people were taken away to the South. For fear of being kidnapped and sent to the South, many others thought about leaving the United States for Canada, Haiti, or Liberia. This fear grew after 1857, when the Supreme Court ruled in the Dred Scott case that "blacks had no rights that whites were bound to respect," and that they had no rights to be citizens of the United States.

Black leaders spoke out against these injustices. Besides vigorously campaigning to abolish slavery, they organized conventions and wrote petitions to get citizenship and civil rights. But with powerful political forces supporting slavery, it seemed by 1861 that there was little hope for change. Even Frederick Douglass, the bold speaker and writer for black freedom and equality, began to despair for his people. When finally the Federal government started enlisting black soldiers, he immediately began traveling across the North as a recruiter, urging, "Men of Color: To Arms!" By fighting for the Union, blacks could strike a blow against slavery and, at the same time, demonstrate their worthiness to be citizens. Many of the men who wrote the letters in this book joined the army because of Douglass and other black leaders, such as Martin R. Delany, John M. Langston, and many clergymen, who recruited in almost every black settlement in the North.

The first Northern black regiments were raised by Massachusetts, Connecticut, and Rhode Island. But in order to deal more effectively with the training and leadership of black units, the Federal government in May 1863 established the Bureau of Colored Troops. Northern agents began energetically recruiting recently freed slaves in Southern areas held by Union troops. The War Department decreed that henceforth all new black regiments, even though they might be recruited and sponsored by Northern states, would be administered together and labeled "United States Colored Troops" (USCT). Eventually, all black regiments with the exception of those from Massachusetts and Connecticut were designated "USCT." Most were infantry regiments (USCI), some were in the cavalry (USCC), and a few were in the heavy artillery (USCHA).

The army's use of black troops, especially those from the Northern states, varied from region to region, from commander to commander. Some, such as General William T. Sherman, virtually refused to employ them at all. Others used them for garrison and rear-guard duty, for construction details, or in labor battalions. But some generals, especially Benjamin Butler, came to believe firmly in the military abilities of black soldiers and used them in combat. Butler late in 1862 mustered black militia regiments in Louisiana and later used black troops in Virginia and North Carolina during the attacks on Petersburg,

Richmond, and Wilmington. In addition to serving in the Gulf Coast and Tidewater regions, Northern black soldiers were used extensively in combat in the Department of the South—coastal South Carolina, Georgia, and Florida—where union forces worked to close the ports and inlets against Confederate blockade runners.

Most whites doubted that blacks would make good soldiers. They reasoned that blacks could not be relied on to fight their "superiors," the white troops of the Confederacy. This belief was put to rest in the spring and summer of 1863, however, when African-American troops began to prove their skill and courage in battle. Black regiments fought and died bravely on May 27 at Port Hudson, Louisiana, a rebel fortress in the swamps near the Mississippi River. A few days later Confederates tried to overwhelm a Union base where black troops were being trained at Milliken's Bend, Louisiana. In hand-to-hand combat those fresh recruits drove off their attackers and won the praise of generals and the press. In July a black regiment helped rout Confederate troops at Honey Springs in the Indian Territory. The next day, July 18, 1863, the 54th Massachusetts Infantry led the bold but futile assault on Fort Wagner, near Charleston, South Carolina. Other major battles in which colored troops acquitted themselves well included the first attack on Petersburg, Virginia, on June 15, 1864, and the engagement at Nashville, Tennessee, on December 14–15, 1864.

When the Union began using African-American troops in combat, the Confederates announced that they would consider any black soldier they could capture not as a prisoner of war but as a fugitive slave. Furthermore, many Southerners announced unofficially that they would execute any black soldier they captured. With this threat hanging over them, the Union's black troops understood what their fate might be if they surrendered. Confederate General Nathan B. Forrest made this threat very real on April 12, 1864, when his cavalry attacked a Union base at Fort Pillow, Tennessee. Both white and black defenders surrendered to Forrest's men, but the Confederates proceeded to shoot their prisoners, especially the blacks. After that, whenever black soldiers went into combat they understood that surrender might mean death. So they were determined to fight all the harder, and their battle cry was "Remember Fort Pillow!"

But even the rebels were impressed by the courage of black soldiers. In desperation during the last weeks of the war, the Confederate government authorized the South's state governors to enlist their own black troops. Nothing much came of the decision; the war was virtually lost by then, and Southerners feared what might happen if they armed their slaves. Union soldiers often reported seeing black soldiers in Confederate units, but there is no solid evidence to confirm these sightings. Probably what they saw was black servants of rebel officers; even though technically civilians, such servants sometimes joined in the fighting to defend their masters. But racism deprived the South of possible further help from blacks who might have fought for the Confederacy in return for their freedom.

Racism was also strong in the Union Army. Black soldiers endured a variety of insults and hardships at the hands of white soldiers and officers. Officers of the early regiments from Louisiana were black, but they were soon pressured to resign. Only at the end of the war did the Federal government decide that African Americans could lead troops in combat. This meant that almost all black soldiers served under white officers. The men resented this; they knew that some of their own number were as skilled and experienced as many of the whites promoted over them.

As soon as the war ended, several African-American regiments were transferred from Virginia to Texas to establish Federal control there and to guard against trouble from Mexico, which was then under French domination. Elsewhere, black soldiers served as occupation troops in various communities and for varying lengths of time. By the end of 1865 most of the Northern black troops had been discharged and had returned to civilian life.

The letters collected here tell in the black soldiers' own words what they experienced and what they hoped for. Their words reveal the texture of their struggles: struggles against an armed enemy and struggles against ever present racism. Bravery, fear, boredom, exhilaration, piety, despair, danger, triumph—all these and more fill the letters, which are an eloquent window on an important chapter of the past.

For the Rights of Citizens

James Henry Hall enlisted in the 54th Massachusetts Infantry at his first opportunity. When a recruiter came to his city in February 1863, he left his job as a barber in Philadelphia, even though he was thirty-eight years old, almost too old to be a soldier. With his regiment he fought at James Island, at Fort Wagner, and at Olustee; and he went without pay to protest the army's racism. By August 1864 he told newspaper readers why he was fighting: "If we fight to maintain a Republican Government, we want Republican privileges." He added, "We do not covet your wives nor your daughters, nor the position of political orator. All we ask is the proper enjoyment of the rights of citizenship, and a free title and acknowledged share in our own noble birthplace." Whatever else Hall and his fellow soldiers might be fighting for, they were fighting for their rights as Americans.

When the African-American soldiers of the Union Army thought about why they were fighting, American citizenship came first. Some wrote about their desire to free the slaves, and probably all of them wanted to see their brothers and sisters free from bondage. Many of them had been slaves themselves, and more had slave relatives; they knew from experience the pains of slavery. Those who had lived in the Northern states also wanted slavery abolished because it reinforced racism; whites could justify discrimination against free blacks by pointing out that slavery had made them inferior. But most soldiers' letters do not focus on emancipation. President Lincoln had already issued the Emancipation Proclamation before these soldiers had enlisted, so they had no need to argue for abolition. Instead, they argued that they were fighting to show that they deserved full equality and citizenship.

For the short term, they wanted equality in the army. Many soldiers resented the fact that they could not have black officers. The black officers of the colored militia regiments in Louisiana were forced to resign. All the officers appointed to lead the United States Colored Troops were white. The enlisted men resented the fact that, while many white soldiers were promoted to officer ranks as a reward for their skill and bravery in battle, blacks were not allowed to lead, no matter how excellent they might be. The army commissioned a few African-American chaplains and doctors, but the key positions of leadership were closed. A month before the fighting stopped, to help recruit new men, Dr. Martin R. Delany was made a major. Only after the fighting had stopped and the soldiers were being discharged did a few battle-tested men win promotion to lieutenant. But through most of the war, commissions were off-limits to black soldiers. Fighting for equality in the army, they wanted their own officers.

For the longer term, African-American soldiers fought for full citizenship in the United States. Even most Northern states put restrictions on free blacks. Some prohibited them from even moving into the state. Other states would not let them serve on juries or testify in court. And some would not let them attend public schools. In Philadelphia and Washington, D.C., they could not ride the streetcars. President Lincoln and many other whites had urged them to leave the country and settle in Liberia or Haiti. And the Supreme Court had ruled in 1857 that they were not citizens of the United States, that they had no rights that white men must respect. Although many Republican politicians said that African Americans were indeed citizens, the matter would not be finally settled until after the war. The black soldiers were eager to fight for the Union to show whites that they deserved full citizenship rights.

The most important of those rights was the right to vote. With political power, blacks could work for equality in other areas. Only six of the Northern states allowed African Americans to vote, and in some of those states that right was restricted to those who owned property. Free blacks in general and black soldiers in particular resented the fact that immigrants from Europe could vote soon after their arrival, while blacks who had lived here all their lives could not. Many of those immigrants voted for the Democratic party and against the war policy of President Lincoln. These "Copperheads" urged peace with the Confederacy and rioted when asked to fight for freedom for the slaves. This outraged black soldiers who strongly endorsed Lincoln's goal of freeing the slaves and who risked their lives to defeat the Confederacy. When disloyal whites had the franchise, why shouldn't loyal blacks vote?

Under the leadership of Frederick Douglass, a "National Convention of Colored Men" met in Syracuse, New York, in October 1864. Several of the delegates were army men. The flag on the platform was the battle flag of the First Louisiana Native Guards, who had proven their valor at Port Hudson, the first major battle for black troops. "We want the elective franchise in all the states," read the convention's address to the American people. Whites had once argued that blacks should not vote, because they were not required to serve in the military. Now, they served willingly on many fronts. "Are we good enough to use bullets, and not good enough to use ballots? May we defend rights in time of war, and yet be denied the exercise of those rights in time of peace?" Through the letters from African-American soldiers ran echoes of this question, this call for the right to vote.

The letters selected for this chapter focus on the call for equality, for the rights of citizens. The soldiers demanded suffrage justice in the courts, equal access to schools, street-cars, and jobs, and they wanted black officers. They had earned these things, not only for themselves but for their race.

Letter 88

(J. H. B. P., [Corporal,] 55th Massachusetts Infantry, Morris Island, South Carolina, May 24, 1864; CR, June 11, 1864) This letter was written by Corporal John H. B. Payne, a thirty-year-old schoolteacher from Bellefontaine, Ohio. He claimed that even though the promises of freedom and civil rights had been broken in the past, at least the pay of white and black troops had been equal. But more important than equal pay, he wanted the right to vote and be voted for.

. . . I am not willing to fight for anything less than the white man fights for. If the white man cannot support his family on seven dollars per month, I cannot support mine on the same amount.

And I am not willing to fight for this Government for money alone. Give me my rights, the rights that this Government owes me, the same rights that the white man has. I would be willing to fight three years for this Government without one cent of the mighty dollar. Then I would have something to fight for. Now I am fighting for the rights of white men. White men have never given me the rights that they are bound to respect. God has not made one man better than another; therefore, one man's rights are no better than another's. They assert that because a large proportion of our race is in bondage we have a right to help free them. I want to know if it was not the white man that put them in bondage? How can they hold us responsible for their evils? And how can they expect that we should do more to blot it out than they are willing to do themselves? If every slave in the United States were emancipated at once, they would not be free yet. If the white man is not willing to respect my rights, I am not willing to respect his wrongs. Our rights have always been limited in the United States. It is true that in some places a colored man, if he can prove himself to be half-white, can vote. Vote for whom? The white man. What good do such rights ever do us—to be compelled always to be voting for the white man and never to be voted for?

Now, the white man declares that this is not our country, and that we have no right to it. They say that Africa is our country. I claim this as my native country—the country that gave me birth. I wish to know one thing, and that is this: Who is the most entitled to his rights in a country—a native of the country or the foreigner? This question can be very easily answered. Now there are foreigners who have flooded our shores. They bring nothing with them but antagonistic feelings to rule and order, and they are without the rudiments of education, and yet they can train their children to be law-abiding citizens. In their own country mis-rule reigns. Generally very poor, they have no leisure for the cultivation of their hearts' best feelings; for in their case, poverty degrades human nature. In this country their social influence is much greater than in their own. Here every avenue to distinction is open to them. The foreigner, when he enters this country, enters into life in an age full of a progressive spirit in the elective franchise. Such persons are the first to take up an offensive position against the Government, instead of marching under the banner of the Prince of Peace. Such people have ruled this country too long already.

The ignorant Irish can come to this country and have free access to all the rights. After they have gained their rights, they cannot appreciate them. They then want to bully the Government. They soon get tired of living under the laws of the country and commence to mutiny, riot, ransack cities, murder colored children, and burn down orphan asylums, as was done in New York. Is the power to be given to such men to direct and govern the affairs of the Union, on which the weal or woe of the nation depends? This is productive of moral degradation and becomes one of the fruitful sources of evil in our land, from which we shall suffer most severely unless some plan is specially adopted to check its onward course. How can this nation ever expect to prosper? I wonder that God does not bring on them present deluge and disaster. I do not wonder at the conduct and disaster that transpired at Fort Pillow. I wonder that we have not had more New York riots and Fort Pillow massacres.

Liberty is what I am struggling for; and what pulse does not beat high at the very mention of the name? Each of us, with fidelity, has already discharged the duties devolving on us as men and as soldier. The very fact of such a union on grounds so commonly and deeply interesting to all, undoubtedly cannot always fail, by the blessing of God, to exert a hallowed influence over society, well fitted to break up alike the extremes of aristocratic and social feeling, which too often predominate in society, and to beget unity, love, brotherly kindness, and charity. . . .

Letter 89

("Sergeant," 54th Massachusetts Infantry, Morris Island, South Carolina, August 26, 1864; The Liberator, October 4, 1864) Although the 54th Massachusetts Regiment had many officers who were abolitionists and competent military leaders, the simple fact that they were white created problems for the black soldiers. This regiment had earned glory in the charge on Fort Wagner in July 1863, and its officers earned fame for their devotion to the cause of abolition. But, as "Sergeant" writes here, that was not good enough: The men wanted officers of their own color and the possibility of commissions for themselves.

Charleston is not ours yet, but no doubt will soon be. And why? Because the country needs an important victory, and somehow it is a religious or superstitious belief with me that this country will be saved to us (black men) yet. I say I believe this; but it is not a mere blind belief. I know that we shall have to labor hard, and put up with a great deal before we are allowed to participate in the government of this country. I am aware that we in the army have done about all we can do, and that to you civilians at home falls the duty of speaking out for all—as we have done the fighting and marching, and suffered cold, heat, and hunger for you and all of us.

My friend, we want black commissioned officers; and only because we want men we can understand and who can understand us. We want men whose hearts are truly loyal to the rights of man. We want to be represented in courts martial, where so many of us are liable to be tried and sentenced. We want to demonstrate our ability to rule, as we have demonstrated our willingness to obey. In short, we want simple justice. I will try to be plainer: There are men here who were made sergeants at Camp Meigs (Readville), who have had command of their companies for months. Can these men feel contented when they see others, who came into the regiment as second lieutenants, promoted to captaincy, and a crowd of incompetent civilians and non-commissioned officers of other regiments sent here to take their places? Can they have confidence in officers who read the Boston *Courier* and talk about "Niggers"? . . .

Discussion Questions

1. In Letter 88, Corporal Payne writes, "If every slave in the United States were emancipated at once, they would not be free yet." Why would emancipated slaves not be free? What is Payne arguing for in his letter?

2. Do you find any prejudice on the part of Payne himself? How does he use his feelings about the Irish to argue for the rights of black men? Do you find his arguments convincing or not? How are they similar or not to arguments used against the blacks by whites?

Writing Suggestions

1. Write a letter home from a black soldier to his parents in the North. Base your themes in this letter on the material you have read in this selection, but be creative in your descriptions of the trials and triumphs you have experienced as a black soldier in the Union army.

2. What kinds of problems did the letters of free blacks reveal? What did the black soldiers want from their government? Research the experience of black men in the Northern armies. Then, write a paper in which you refer to the letters posted from Morris Island and explain what kinds of experiences blacks in the Army endured compared to their white counterparts.

All the Daring of the Soldier

Women of the Civil War Armies

ELIZABETH D. LEONARD

Elizabeth D. Leonard is an associate professor of history at Colby College in Maine, a Junior Research Fellow in American History, and director of women's studies. Her areas of study include women's history and women's culture and nineteenth century U.S. history, including women in the Civil War. Her book *All the Daring of the Soldier: Women of the Civil War Armies*, from which the following selection is taken, explores the many roles women played during the Civil War, including their activities as soldiers and spies for both the North and the South.

To "Don the Breeches, and Slay Them with a Will!"

A Host of Women Soldiers

A sister-soldier's greeting to you, for I too have been, and was, until a few months ago, a soldier.
>   —Miss Nellie A. K., quoted in *The Life of Pauline Cushman*, 1864

Sarah Emma Edmonds, Jennie Hodgers, and Rosetta Wakeman are three among hundreds of women who dressed as men, adopted male identities, and enlisted in the armies of the Union and the Confederacy during the Civil War. Needless to say, many women who envisioned a military role for themselves in connection with the war, particularly when wanting to defend their homes, did not ultimately enlist as soldiers, although some seemed to come quite close to doing so. A group of women in December 1864 wrote to the Confederate Secretary of War, James Alexander Seddon, requesting—probably not facetiously—that he sanction their organization of a "full regiment of *ladies*, between the ages of 16 and 40," to be armed and "equipped to perform regular service in the Army of the Shenandoah Valley," notably for purposes of local defense. "Our homes have been visited time and again by the vandal foe," wrote Irene Bell, Annie Samuels, and ten other women. "We have been subjected to every conceivable outrage & suffering," for which they blamed "the incompetency of the Confederate Army upon which we depend for defence." In consequence, wrote the women, "we propose to leave our hearthstones, to endure any sacrifice, any privation for the ultimate success of our Holy Cause." Should the Secretary of War approve their plan, Bell and the others concluded, "please favor us by sending immediately properly authenticated orders for the carrying out of our wishes.

301

All arrangements . . . have been effected & we now only wait [for] the approval of the War department."

Many other women, privately and publicly, expressed a similarly strong desire to join the army. In an 1862 letter to the Adjutant General of the Wisconsin National Guard, a Mrs. S. Ann Gordon asked if there was any way she might join the army as a nurse in order to be with her husband, a soldier in the 10th Wisconsin. Although she requested a nurse's position, Gordon clearly believed herself to be soldier material. "As most ladies are considered delicate," she told the Adjutant General, "excuse me for saying that for some weeks past I have accustomed myself to from two to 4 miles walk every day and endure it with very slight fatigue. I have not seen any sickness in twenty years, and I think I should make an enduring soldier." And Louisiana's Sarah Morgan was undoubtedly not the only woman to confide her martial aspirations to her diary: "Oh! if I were only a man," Morgan wrote. "Then I could don the breeches, and slay them with a will! If some few Southern women were in the ranks," she insisted, "they could set the men an example they would not blush to follow."

As we already know, not all women who actually "don[ned] the breeches" during the war served as soldiers. Some, like Mrs. L. A. McCarty, disguised themselves as men for the sole purpose of engaging in espionage and resistance activity. Arrested in March 1862 while en route to the Confederacy in possession of an item of contraband ordnance, a quantity of contraband medicine, and a weapon tucked into her baggage, McCarty became for a brief time an inmate at "Fort Greenhow," where she caught Rose Greenhow's attention. "Quite an excitement was created throughout the prison . . .," wrote Greenhow later, "by the arrest of a woman in male attire at the hotel of a man named Donnelly, in Washington. . . . She was very handsome, and was a woman of some cultivation and scientific attainments . . . a keen observer, and both spoke and wrote well."

The vast majority of women who dressed as men during the war, however, did so in order to enlist, and as the stories of Edmonds, Hodgers, and Wakeman (like that of Deborah Sampson) indicate, sustaining an imposture as a male soldier was possible even over an extended period of time. As far as we know, not one of these women was discovered conclusively to be a woman by any observer during the period of her service. Fellow soldiers may have had some suspicions based on the women's relatively small stature, their beardlessness, their more highly pitched voices, and so forth, but in none of these cases is there any indication that such suspicions progressed any further. Rather, we know that Edmonds confessed her sex to her friend Jerome Robbins; that Hodgers lived out the bulk of her life, half a century beyond the end of the war, as a male laborer; and that Wakeman took her identity to the grave. How was it possible for these and so many other women to maintain their impostures, not infrequently for years at a time?

Certain features of mid-nineteenth-century military life and culture helped make cross-gender "passing" possible. For one thing, although in theory

women had to overcome the obstacle of a physical examination in order to enlist in the army, in practice the recruitment exam was often quite perfuncto-
ry, and thus rarely constituted a serious barrier to a woman's enlistment. This
is not to say that there were no army guidelines designed to make the examination process meaningful, for indeed there were. "In passing a recruit," one
regulation stipulated,

> the medical officer is to examine him stripped; to see that he has free use of
> all his limbs; that his chest is ample; that his hearing, vision and speech are
> perfect; that he has no tumors, or ulcerated or cicatrized legs; no rupture or
> chronic cutaneous affection; that he has not received any contusion, or wound
> of the head, that may impair his faculties; that he is not subject to convul-
> sions; and has no infectious disorder that may unfit him for military service.

Moreover, after being examined as a raw recruit, the soldier who was accepted into the service was supposed to undergo a second examination upon joining his regiment.

But thanks to the combination of an equally inexperienced medical staff
and the rush of so many soldiers to enlist, in the first part of the war in particular an army recruit rarely faced a physical examination "more rigorous
than holding out his hands to demonstrate that he had a working trigger finger, or perhaps opening his mouth to show that his teeth were strong enough
to rip open a minié ball cartridge." According to one soldier, the recruitment
examination he received from the "fat, jolly old doctor" assigned to perform
it was both typical and absurd. "He requested me to stand up straight," the
soldier recalled,

> then gave me two or three little sort of "love taps" on the chest, turned me
> round, ran his hands over my shoulders, back, and limbs, laughing and talk-
> ing all the time, then whirled me to the front, and rendered judgment on me
> as follows: "Ah, Capt. Reddish! I only wish you had a hundred such fine
> boys as this one! He's all right, and good for the service."

According to historian Bell Wiley's research, of two hundred federal regiments who were the subject of an investigation by the watchdog United States
Sanitary Commission towards the end of 1861, 58 percent were cited as failing to have made even a pretense of examining the health of their recruits at
the time of their enlistment. At least one examiner had a reputation for being
able to evaluate ninety recruits per hour. From this perspective alone, it is no
wonder that women were often able to slip into the ranks undetected.

Women soldiers who evaded or made it through the physical examination
process soon discovered that many of the features of regular Civil War army
life also provided effective shields against the discovery of their sex. Army
life in the 1860s was significantly different from army life in the late twentieth century. For one thing, recruitment was rarely if ever followed by anything resembling modern-day boot camp with its intensive physical training.

Rather, the focus was generally on learning how to drill. Wrote one Pennsylvania soldier after six months in the army: "The first thing in the morning is drill, then drill, then drill again. Then drill, drill, a little more drill. Then drill, and lastly drill. Between drills, we drill and sometimes stop to eat a little and have a roll-call." In new units at least, "drilling" meant learning how to handle, load, and fire guns and how to parry and thrust with a bayonet, practicing simple maneuvers, and marching. In the early weeks of their military service, women soldiers' efforts, like those of their male comrades, centered on such gender-neutral exercises. Of course, women soldiers also had to learn to carry their own gear, which typically included a gun, a bayonet and scabbard, ammunition, blankets, a canteen, clothing, stationery, photographs, toiletries, and a mending kit, plus equipment for cooking and eating rations. But once they grew accustomed to the forty to fifty pounds of matériel they had to carry, as many men also needed to accustom themselves, women soldiers rarely had to fear that additional biologically based differences in physical strength would lead to their disclosure.

Moreover, camp life, although intimate in some ways, allowed for sufficient freedom of movement to enable women soldiers to avoid notice when bathing and dealing with other personal matters. Civil War soldiers lived and slept in close proximity to one another, but they rarely changed their clothes. Furthermore, they passed the bulk of their time, day and night, out of doors, where they also attended to their bodily needs. Thus, a female soldier could often maintain a certain amount of physical distance from her comrades, which was particularly important in connection with her toilet. Prevailing standards regarding modesty in such matters worked in a woman soldier's favor, writes the editor of Sarah Rosetta Wakeman's papers, Lauren Burgess, "ensur[ing] that no one would question a shy soldier's reluctance to bathe in a river with his messmates or to relieve himself in the open company sinks [long trenches soldiers dug for sanitation purposes wherever they camped]."

Of course, attending to one's personal needs on the march or in battle was a rather different matter. Though generally loose-fitting for the sake of easy sizing (and thus beneficial to the woman soldier trying to disguise her physical form), Civil War soldiers' uniforms consisted of many pieces, overlaid with a great deal of equipment—or "impedimenta," as Wiley calls it. Much of this clothing and equipment had to be removed if a woman did not want to soil herself, and at least one modern student of the phenomenon of women soldiers during the Civil War has argued persuasively that in order to avoid detection while on the march or on the field, women soldiers simply drank as little as possible given the weather conditions to which they were exposed, and if they could not get away to some private place to relieve themselves, just went ahead and did so in their clothing, as discreetly as possible, while on the move. Regarding the question of menstruation, one suspects that many women soldiers, who often became lean and athletic in the service, simply stopped menstruating. Those who continued to do so simply had to find ways to dispose of the evidence of their menstrual periods: bloody rags that they probably managed either to burn or bury themselves, or to combine surreptitiously with similar-looking "laundry" from soldiers wounded in battle.

That there were so many young men and even boys in the ranks during the Civil War also helped women soldiers avoid exposure. Whereas armies composed only of fully mature men might have been less tolerant of the odd enlisted man whose build was slighter or whose cheeks were strangely smooth, Civil War armies drew their soldiers from a wide range of age groups. Despite various regulations to the contrary, untold numbers of boys seventeen and younger lied about their ages and joined the Union and Confederate armies as regular soldiers. The presence of so many youngsters who looked and sounded similar to women provided women soldiers with an added measure of security.

Rigid codes of dress typical of the mid-nineteenth century also reinforced an assumption among Civil War soldiers that "if it wore pants, it was male." Wrote one soldier after he discovered that a former comrade was a woman, "A single glance at her in her proper character leads me to wonder how I ever could have mistaken her for a man, and I readily recall many things which ought to have betrayed her, except that no one thought of finding a woman in a soldier's dress." In 1902 Captain Ira B. Gardner, formerly of the 14th Maine, recalled enrolling a woman soldier in his company who went on to serve for two years before he realized his mistake. "If I had been anything but a boy, I should have probably seen from her form that she was a female," Gardner wrote, but clearly the woman's clothes had been enough to deceive him. Dominant mid-century notions about differences in men's and women's capabilities had a similar result: women were considered unfit for military service in consequence of their presumed physical, emotional, and intellectual weaknesses (though such presumed weaknesses clearly did not apply to working-class and slave women). Thus, few expected to find them in the ranks or thought to look for them there. Interestingly, there is considerable evidence to suggest that women soldiers, who knew what signs to watch for, recognized each other with relative ease.

Almost certainly the bulk of women who served as soldiers during the Civil War were never discovered. Some, like Jennie Hodgers, were discovered only years after their military service had come to an end. According to a Chicago *Times-Herald* story published shortly after "his" death, a coroners examination revealed that Civil War veteran "Otto Schaffer" was a woman. "Schaffer" had spent many years after the war in Butler County, Kansas, living as a hermit. One day a major thunderstorm caused "Schaffer" to take shelter in his cabin moments before a bolt of lightning demolished it. Neighbors found the body on the floor and called the coroner, who became aware of "Schaffer's" secret while he was preparing the body for burial. Perhaps because "Schaffer" was known to have participated in so many battles during the war, local veterans rose to the occasion and gave "him" a soldier's burial, during which they honored the veteran's remains with a final gun salute.

A somewhat different case is that of Emma A. B. Kinsey. Whether or not she ever actually served in the Civil War military, her husband later in life claimed that she had. An undated memo at the National Archives notes his request for information regarding her service. According to the memo, Kinsey's widower claimed that his late wife had reached the rank of lieutenant colonel with the 40th New Jersey Infantry before she received an honorable discharge from the regiment's commander, Augustus Fay, Jr., in July 1865. The author of the memo in turn insisted that Kinsey's name was not to be found on the rolls of the 40th New Jersey. Needless to say, however, the fact that her name did not appear on the rolls hardly precludes the possibility of her having served: like other women soldiers, Emma Kinsey would have enlisted under an alias that her husband may not have known.

Other women soldiers' identities came to light shortly after they received their discharges as men. In 1863 a Detroit newspaper described the arrest of a discharged soldier on suspicion of being a woman. Following her arrest, Ida Remington of Rochester, New York—who was still wearing her uniform—informed police that she had served with the 11th New York for two years through several battles, including the September 14, 1862, battle of South Mountain in Maryland, where the 11th New York helped to foil General Lee's plans for a successful invasion of the North; and the bloodbath at nearby Antietam that came a few days later. Because she had already left the army, authorities had no cause to hold her, and upon her release, the article noted, Remington left town. "Her whole story . . ." the article concluded, "shows that 'when a woman will, she will,' regardless of consequences."

Women soldiers sustained their impostures through all sorts of complicated situations and sometimes for the duration of their postwar lives. Still, there were circumstances during the war under which exposure became virtually unavoidable. Certainly any situation that caused her to come under close scrutiny put a woman soldier's imposture in jeopardy. One woman soldier is mentioned in the letter an Indiana cavalryman wrote to his wife in February 1863: "We discovered last week a soldier who turned out to be a girl," he wrote, and who had already been in service for almost two years, during which time she was wounded twice. "Maybe she would have remained undiscovered for a long time if she hadn't fainted. She was given a warm bath which gave the secret away."

In some cases, an unexpected encounter with a particularly observant family member or friend was enough to put an end to a woman soldier's career. In October 1862 the Owensburg, Kentucky, *Monitor* remarked on the commotion that the discovery of a woman soldier had provoked among the men of the 66th Kentucky. During her four weeks with the regiment, the woman had apparently conducted herself in such a way as to allay suspicions among her comrades about her sex. But an unexpected visit by her uncle to the regiment's camp—he had probably come to see others in the regiment whom he might have known from his community—led to her undoing. When he recognized her, her uncle saw immediately to her discharge.

In February 1863 the Detroit *Advertiser and Tribune* reported that authorities had arrested one Mary Burns after she was recognized by an acquaintance, and had dismissed her from the service. Burns, it seems, had—with his knowledge—followed her lover into the 7th Michigan Cavalry under the alias "John Burns" and had succeeded in maintaining her disguise for two weeks. Similarly, a woman who enlisted with her brother in a Confederate regiment by using the pseudonym "Joshua Clarke" was quickly recognized by someone who knew her and discharged. Upon her departure, "Private Clarke" expressed her determination to reenlist as soon as possible in a different regiment, and one suspects that the lessons she learned as a result of having been discovered once only helped her to disguise herself more effectively in the future. In contrast, Marian Green of Michigan was forced to return home after several weeks, not because someone unexpectedly recognized her, but because her fiancé, whom she had followed into the army against his will, chose to inform her unhappy parents that she was with him.

Some women soldiers inadvertently gave themselves away by displaying behavior that aroused observers' suspicions about their sex. When Sarah Collins of Wisconsin cut her hair, donned men's clothes, and enlisted with her brother after the war broke out, she hoped to have an opportunity to engage the enemy in battle. Instead, she failed to make it out of town with her regiment. Described as a "robust girl" for whom the soldier's life should have presented few challenges she could not meet, Collins nevertheless aroused suspicion—and brought on her dismissal—by her "unmasculine manner of putting on her shoes and stockings." Similarly, shortly after the war, in his history of wartime Secret Service activities, Albert Richardson wrote of a twenty-year-old woman who served with the 1st Kentucky Infantry for three months before the regimental surgeon guessed that she was a woman. "She performed camp duties with great fortitude," wrote Richardson, "and never fell out of the ranks during the severest marches." Nevertheless, her "feminine method of putting on her stockings" gave her away. A particularly careless female recruit in Rochester, New York, unwittingly exposed herself as a woman when in a brief moment of awkwardness she was seen trying to pull her pants on over her head. Sources indicate that when Lizzie Cook of Iowa tried to enlist with her brother at St. Louis, she gave herself away by displaying surprisingly refined table manners. And despite being "inspected, accepted, and sworn in" with her regiment and participating fully in the regiment's establishment of its initial camp site near Cincinnati—"handling lumber, doing sentry duty, &c."—one young woman who followed her brother into the 3rd Ohio Infantry lasted only two weeks before she provoked suspicion by displaying an unusual degree of familiarity with him.

Sometimes a woman soldier aroused observers' suspicions for reasons that they later failed to record. When Civil War nurse and soldier relief activist Mary Livermore wrote her memoirs, she recalled her encounter with an unidentified woman enlisted in the 19th Illinois, the initial regimental home of John and Nadine Turchin. On a visit to the regiment, Livermore wrote, she had been observing a drill when an officer approached her and asked her if she noticed anything peculiar about the appearance of one of the soldiers drilling. Immediately, Livermore claimed, she realized that the soldier was a woman. After sharing her thoughts with the officer, who had suspected the masquerade himself, Livermore then watched as the woman soldier was called out of the ranks and charged with being an impostor. "There was a scene in an instant," Livermore recalled.

> Clutching the officer by the arm, and speaking in tones of passionate entreaty, she begged him not to expose her, but to allow her to retain her disguise. Her husband had enlisted in his company, she said, and it would kill her if he marched without her. "Let me go with you!" I heard her plead. "Oh, sir, let me go with you!"

The woman's pleas were in vain, however, and shortly thereafter she attempted suicide by jumping into the Chicago River, only to be rescued by a police officer and placed in a charity home where Livermore found her depressed and incapable of being comforted. "It was impossible to turn her from her purpose to follow her husband," wrote Livermore. Some days later the woman disappeared from the home, presumably with the intention of finding her way back into the ranks.

Though it did not ultimately prove so in the cases of Jennie Hodgers or Rosetta Wakeman, landing in a hospital as a result of illness or a battle wound was, not surprisingly, the most common precursor of discovery. In July 1862 seventeen-year-old Mary Scaberry of Columbus, Ohio, enlisted as "Charles Freeman" in Company F of the 52nd Ohio. Sixteen weeks later, when she was admitted to the general hospital at Louisville, Kentucky, the doctors diagnosed "Freeman" not only with "remittent fever" but also with "sexual incompatibility," and on December 13 Scaberry received her discharge. In July 1863 the feminist reform journal *The Sibyl*, which had published an article on Kady Brownell at New Bern, published one in which it described the discovery of a woman in the ranks of the 1st Kansas Infantry. The unnamed woman, who had been with the regiment for almost two years and who had reportedly participated in a dozen battles and skirmishes, had just died in the hospital, her sex having been revealed upon examination. The article described her as "rather more than average size for a woman, with rather strongly marked features" such that "with the aid of man's attire she had quite a masculine look." According to the article, the unnamed woman had a good reputation as a soldier, and was remembered by the men of her regiment with respect and affection for being "as brave as a lion in battle" and for never having failed to perform her duty under any conditions. "She must have been very shrewd," the article continued, "to have lived in the regiment so long and preserved her secret so well." In January 1864 *The Sibyl* noted the arrival in Louisville, Kentucky, of a sixteen-year-old Canadian woman who had already been in the army for a year and a half. The article associated this young woman with a number of regiments, claiming that she had fought in several battles and had been wounded more than once. Each time the authorities discovered her sex, they mustered her out of the service. Each time she convalesced, she mustered back in from some other location. Despite her foreign heritage and her repeated discovery and dismissal, the article made clear, this young woman was "bound to fight for the American Union."

One young woman who enlisted in the 2nd East Tennessee Cavalry regiment in mid-1862 survived for five months without being discovered. Despite having experienced the grisly December contest at Stones River, Tennessee, for control of Nashville's supply lines which saw almost thirteen thousand Union casualties (Confederate losses were equally severe), the woman masquerading as "Frank Martin" was wounded in the shoulder, and a medical examination revealed her secret and resulted in her discharge. "Martin," however, showed no signs of giving up on her determination to be a soldier, and as soon as she was able she reenlisted, this time in the 8th Michigan, with which she served as an orderly sergeant and a scout for several more months, during which time some evidence suggests that her sex again became known but was ignored. A journal of the time described "Martin" as about eighteen years of age in 1863, amiable, loquacious, and "quite small" with auburn hair, blue eyes, and a fair complexion that had become tanned from months of living outdoors.

Other cases of female soldiers being discovered as a consequence of hospitalization are abundant. In October 1863 an article in *Frank Leslie's Illustrated Newspaper* commented that authorities had recently detected the presence of a twelve-year-old girl posing as a drummer in the ranks of a Pennsylvania regiment, with which she had already seen five battles. Now ill with typhoid fever and a patient at the Pennsylvania Hospital in Philadelphia, the girl— whom a later source identified with the alias "Charles Martin"—was scheduled to go home. In August 1864 the *New York Herald* republished an article that had originally appeared in the Memphis *Argus* and which described a nineteen-year-old woman from Long Island, New York, named Fanny Wilson. Wilson, whose identity had been discovered in Memphis, claimed to have served for two years in the 24th New Jersey Infantry regiment before she fell sick, her sex was revealed, and she was discharged. A brief interlude as a ballet dancer at a theater in Cairo, Illinois, preceded Wilson's return to the ranks, this time as a member of the 3rd Illinois Cavalry, with whom she served until her sex was detected again and she was sent north. Two days later the *Herald* published a story about Mary Wise, a "female private" of the 34th Indiana Volunteers. Wise, the article claimed, had participated in several battles in the western theater and been wounded three times, most recently by a bullet in her shoulder at Lookout Mountain in Tennessee. Upon being taken to a hospital, Wise's sex was discovered and she, like so many others, was mustered out of the service.

During October 1863 both the Wellsburg, West Virginia, *Weekly Herald* and *Frank Leslie's Illustrated Newspaper* published articles about a native of

Minnesota named Frances Clayton (alternately "Clalin") who enlisted with her husband in a Minnesota regiment in 1861 and served with him for about a year until she was wounded, and her husband was killed, while engaging in a bayonet charge at the late December 1862 battle of Stones River. Clayton was hospitalized with a bullet in her hip, and an examination led to the discovery of her sex and her eventual discharge. Prior to that, however, Clayton had concealed her sex successfully, in part because she displayed personal habits that marked her as a soldier—drinking, smoking, chewing tobacco, and swearing—and partly because she unfailingly performed her duty in all sorts of weather both on the field and when on guard or picket duty. Her fellow soldiers considered Clayton "a good fighting man"; the author of one of the articles described her as a "very tall, masculine looking woman, bronzed from exposure to the weather" with a "masculine stride" and a "soldierly carriage." The article also noted that once she had recovered from her wound, the widowed Clayton had made her way back to her former regiment, ostensibly to recover some papers belonging to her husband, but probably in the hope of reenlisting. Instead, she was sent home.

Many women soldiers' identities came to light after they were captured by the enemy. Such was the case with a woman who appears in the sources alternately as "Amy Clarke" and "Anna Clark." According to a December 1862 article in the Jackson *Mississippian*, Amy Clarke of Iuka, Mississippi, was thirty years old when she enlisted with her husband in a Confederate cavalry regiment, fighting with him until his death at the battle of Shiloh, whereupon she left the regiment and reenlisted in the 11th Tennessee. It was during her second period of enlistment, the article claimed, that Clarke was wounded in battle and captured by the federals, who discovered her sex and tried to put an end to her army career (in the same inconclusive manner that federal officials had attempted to put a stop to Confederate women's espionage activities) by sending her beyond the Confederate lines.

In fact, the *Mississippian* was not the first paper to report the Clarke story. A few days earlier the Cairo, Illinois, *City Gazette* had noted the discovery in the ranks of the 11th Tennessee of a "Mrs. Anna Clark," the widow of one Walter Clark and a native of Luka [sic], Tennessee. "Not above medium height, rather slight in build, features effeminate but eye full of resolution," the article commented, Clark had been taken prisoner as a private in the Confederate army only to have her masquerade—perpetrated under the alias "Richard Anderson"—discovered. To her federal captors Clark purportedly explained that when her husband had enlisted early in the war, she had tried to manage their home without him but had not been particularly successful. In addition, in his absence (he subsequently died in the service, though the article did not say under what circumstances), Clark had fallen in love with a trooper in a Louisiana cavalry regiment. Procuring a horse for herself, Clark had enlisted in her lover's company and for four months had remained at his side until the demands of a life on horseback made her yearn for the infantry, for which she considered herself better suited. Joining the 11th Tennessee as

"Richard Anderson," Clark served the Confederate army for another half year, by her own account performing such "prodigies of valor" as "having to stand upon the dead body of a comrade to obtain a sight of the enemy, upon whom she continually emptied the contents of her musket," until Yankee soldiers took her and some of her fellow Confederates prisoner. Now, her imposture having been exposed, she asked to be returned south, where she promised to resume her female identity and stay out of the ranks. The *City Gazette* article concluded with the news that Clark was expected to be sent on to Vicksburg shortly. According to one source, a short time after her arrival in Vicksburg, this determined Confederate woman was seen making plans to reenlist. Another source indicates that Clarke/Clark succeeded in doing so—undoubtedly under a different name—only to be discovered again in Tennessee in August 1863, by which time she had achieved the rank of lieutenant.

Union nurse Anna Morris Holstein wrote of a Confederate woman artillery sergeant captured in the summer of 1864 near Port Royal, Virginia, not far from Belle Boyd's hometown of Martinsburg. This woman, Holstein pointed out, "was the *last* to leave the gun" when the troops were captured by the federals. When Annie Wittenmyer wrote her 1892 memoir of her work as a nurse and a leader in wartime soldier relief, she recalled coming across a wounded woman soldier in the hospital where she was working. According to Wittenmyer, this unnamed Union woman had been with her regiment for over a year before being captured by the Confederates after the September 1863 battle of Chickamauga and sent beyond federal lines with the note "As Confederates do not use women in war [*sic*], this woman, wounded in battle, is returned to you." Wittenmyer, who recommended that the woman return home once she was healed and forget about any future military service, noted that the woman instead swore her determination to reenlist as soon as possible. In 1934 the *New York Times* published a story about a woman known as Florena (alternately "Florina") Budwin who had enlisted in an unidentified Union regiment with her husband. Having served with him in battle for some time, Budwin was subsequently captured by the Confederates with her husband, and together they were transferred to the crowded, inadequately supplied, and critically unsanitary Confederate prison at Andersonville, Georgia, where Budwin's husband—like almost thirteen thousand other Union soldiers—died. Late in 1864, following a transfer to another prison in Florence, South Carolina, Budwin herself became ill. Discovered in the hospital to be a woman, she was released from the prison only upon her death in January 1865. After the war, Budwin was buried at the National Cemetery in Florence along with other federal soldiers who had died in prison there, her simple tombstone listing only her name. Budwin was not as lucky as one "Madame Collier," who had enlisted with a federal regiment from eastern Tennessee and whose exposure as a woman while imprisoned at Belle Isle, Virginia—the second-largest Confederate prison after Andersonville—led to her safe removal to the north under a flag of truce.

Frances Hook also devoted herself to the Union cause, serving under the name of "Frank Miller." Described by one contemporary source as "of about medium height, with dark hazel eyes, dark brown hair, rounded features, and a feminine voice and appearance," Hook enlisted with her brother in the 65th Illinois Home Guards shortly after the outbreak of the war, and served three months without discovery before being mustered out. Brother and sister then reenlisted in the 90th Illinois Infantry and fought together until Hook's brother was killed at the battle of Shiloh in April 1862. Hook remained with the regiment after her brother's death, however, until she was taken prisoner by the Confederates at Florence, Alabama, probably in late 1863. In an escape attempt some weeks later, Frances Hook took a bullet in her left leg, and when Confederate authorities examined her, they discovered her sex and promptly sent her to Nashville in a February 1864 prisoner exchange. There, Union officials hospitalized Hook until she was well enough to travel, then sent her north. According to an April 1864 article, during her captivity Hook received a letter from Confederate President Jefferson Davis offering her a lieutenant's commission if she would join the Confederate army. Hook, claimed the article, responded in the negative, informing Davis that she "preferred to fight as a private soldier for the stars and stripes, rather than be honored with a commission from the Rebs." Whether or not Hook resumed her military service under a different name once her wound healed is unknown.

Of course, some women soldiers simply chose for personal reasons to reveal their identity after a period of service. Such was the case with Sarah Malinda Pritchard Blalock (alternately "Blaylock"). Born in Alexander County, North Carolina, in 1839 and married in 1856 to William ("Keith") McKesson Blalock, Malinda Blalock followed her husband in March 1862 into Company F of the 26th North Carolina, posing as Keith's younger brother and using the alias "Sam Blalock." Enlisting for three years or the duration of the war, Malinda Blalock received a bounty of fifty dollars.

Whether or not she saw fighting during her brief tenure with the 26th North Carolina is unclear: at least one source indicates that Blalock fought in three major battles and may even have been wounded before she left the service. Malinda Blalock was only with her regiment for about a month, however, and the more persuasive evidence suggests that her service as a soldier did not take her beyond the boundaries of the 26th's camp. Nevertheless, during her weeks with the regiment, Malinda Blalock learned the drill and did exemplary duty as a new soldier, earning an early spot on the regiment's honor roll. Her service might have been more protracted had her husband not received a discharge, as a consequence of a probably feigned disability: Keith Blalock claimed to have a hernia and severe sumac poisoning. In fact, Malinda Blalock's husband was a Unionist at heart who seems to have enlisted in order to avoid conscription and who had planned to desert until he found that it was more difficult to do so than he had expected. In any case, once her husband received his medical discharge, Malinda Blalock immediately confessed her imposture to the company's commander—and the future governor of North Carolina—Zebulon Vance. Vance dismissed her right away, demanding that she return the bounty money she had accepted under false pretenses. Malinda and Keith Blalock subsequently returned home to take up the work of Unionist resistance in North Carolina and eastern Tennessee, leading raids and escorting prison escapees to safety. Malinda Blalock died in 1903.

A woman soldier's sex necessarily came to light, of course, if—as happened on very rare occasions—she became visibly pregnant while in the service, though some continued to hide their true identity until the delivery of the child. In December 1864 the Sandusky, Ohio, *Commercial Register* reported a "strange birth" in the Confederate army. "We are credibly informed," wrote the article's Yankee author with obvious glee,

> that one day last week, one of the rebel officers in the "bull pen," as our soldiers call it: otherwise, in one of the barracks in the enclosure on Johnson's Island [prison on Lake Eric in Ohio], in which the rebel prisoners are kept, gave birth to a "bouncing boy." This is the first instance of a father giving birth to a child we have heard of; nor have we read of it "in the books."

Pregnancy in the ranks was not confined to the Confederate army: according to one source, Union General William S. Rosecrans became outraged when an unnamed sergeant under his command *"was delivered of a baby*, which," he irately noted, "is in violation of all military law and of the army regulations." On August 21, 1862, Civil War nurse Harriet Whetten reported in her diary the discovery of a woman among the hospitalized Union soldiers in her care, and to whom she had just brought some jelly. "She is obliged to go home for a womanly reason," Whetten noted. According to Lauren Burgess, at least six pregnant women soldiers went undiscovered until their babies were born, including one who went into labor while on picket duty and another who fought at the bloody battle of Fredericksburg in December 1862—and was promoted for her valor there from corporal to sergeant—not long before she gave birth. Wrote a soldier in this woman's regiment to his family at home: "What use have we for women, if soldiers in the army can give birth to children?"

Death, of course, offered a belated opportunity for the detection of a woman soldier's true identity, but it did not guarantee it, as the story of Rosetta Wakeman attests. Most female soldiers' corpses underwent the same cursory burial on the field or on the grounds of the hospital as did those of their male counterparts. On July 17, 1863, however, when Brigadier General William Hays reported on the burial of the dead at Gettysburg, he noted that among those he counted was a "female (private) in rebel uniform." At least one woman's body went undiscovered at the Shiloh battleground in Tennessee until 1934, when Mancil Milligan unearthed the remains of several Civil War soldiers while planting in the flower bed of his home on the outskirts of the Shiloh National Military Park. Summoning the authorities, Milligan observed the excavation of the bones of nine soldiers, one of whom was determined to have been a woman, along with bits of the soldiers' uniforms and gear, and the ammunition that killed them. The bones, including those of the woman, were subsequently reinterred at the National Cemetery.

The final revelation of at least one woman soldier's true identity—Frances Day, who served with the 126th Pennsylvania under the alias "Frank Mayne"—seems to have come at the very moment of her demise. Day enlisted as a nine months' recruit at Mifflin, Pennsylvania, on August 5, 1862, and mustered in at Harrisburg on August 9. Eighteen years old at the time of her enlistment, with "complexion light, eyes light, hair light," Day deserted the regiment about three weeks later, despite having received a rapid promotion to sergeant. Apparently Day had followed her lover, William Fitzpatrick, into Company F of the 126th, but when Fitzpatrick died of an illness while in camp, Day went absent without leave. According to the author of the 126th Pennsylvania's regimental history, Day resurfaced much later in the war as a soldier in the Far West. When she was mortally wounded and unable to conceal her sex any longer, she told her story to a comrade, explaining that the "abandon and despair" she had experienced when Fitzpatrick died had driven her to reenlist.

Because the information surrounding so many women soldiers' stories is so limited, it is often impossible to know precisely how an individual woman's imposture was revealed. An unidentified nineteen-year-old woman enlisted as "John Williams" in Company H of the 17th Missouri Infantry in October 1861, only to be discharged a few days later. Her service record reads simply, "Discharged (Proved to be a Woman)." In April 1862 at Natchez, Mississippi, a woman using the alias "William Bradley" mustered in to Company G of an organization of Louisiana volunteers known as "Miles's Legion." Though she signed on for the duration of the war, "Bradley" was discharged at the end of June. The remarks on her service record for June 30 indicate only that she was "mustered in through mistake, was of female sex." In July 1862 *Frank Leslie's Illustrated Newspaper* reported the frustration of a woman from Chenango County, New York—the same region where Rosetta Wakeman had worked as a boatman—who had repeatedly attempted to join the army, first following her husband into the 61st New York as a nurse but then, having become separated from the regiment and being without resources, posing as a man and joining a Pennsylvania regiment. By some unknown means her imposture was detected, however, and she was discharged, after which she wandered about in desperation until a group of sympathetic soldiers underwrote her trip home. "The woman's sex could easily have been discovered," the article boasted with all the confidence of hindsight. "Voice, looks, actions and shape were all tell-tales, yet she had successfully passed guards and broke through orders." And a March 1864 article in the Platteville, Wisconsin, *Witness* reported the return from the army of Georgianna Peterman, a native of Ellenboro, Wisconsin, who had served for two years as a drummer in the 7th Wisconsin Infantry. "She lives in Ellenboro," the article noted, "is about twenty years old, wears soldier clothes, and is quiet and reserved."

We know little, too, about the means by which the true identity of "John Hoffman" of Battery C, 1st Tennessee Artillery (Union), became known. In September 1864 the *Richmond Daily Examiner* reported without explanation the discovery in Nashville, Tennessee, that "John Hoffman" was in fact Louisa Hoffman, a native of New York City and a "very good looking and respectable soldier girl." Hoffman disclosed that she had initially served with the 1st Virginia Cavalry up through the second battle of Bull Run in August 1862, and had then, switching her allegiance to the Union, taken a position as a cook with the 1st Ohio Infantry before deciding to join the artillery corps. Possibly the revelation of her sex while in Nashville ended Hoffman's career as a soldier; given her history, it is more likely that she went on to find a new regimental home somewhere else.

In February 1865 the *Richmond Whig* reported, also without bothering to explain, the discovery of a woman named Mollie Bean in the ranks of the 47th North Carolina. Bean, who used the alias "Melvin Bean," had been picked up a few days earlier for questioning and had told investigators that she had been with the regiment for over two years and had been wounded twice in the service. Although the *Whig* presumed that others in her company knew that Bean was a woman, there is no reason to believe that they did.

Clearly a key reason why we know of the wartime service of so many women soldiers is that they received so much attention in the newspapers when their impostures were exposed. Indeed, newspaper notices relating to women's military service during the Civil War continued to appear years after Appomattox. In 1896 an article appeared in the St. Louis *Star* which considered the case of Mary Stevens Jenkins (alternately "Mary Owens Jenkins"). Jenkins, the article claimed, had been a Pennsylvania schoolgirl when the war broke out. Although a schoolgirl, Jenkins was also in love with a young man identified as William Evans, whom she followed into the army. For approximately two years Jenkins served with William Evans in Company K of the 9th Pennsylvania Infantry under the alias "John Evans." After William died in battle, Jenkins remained with the regiment and continued in the service, possibly being wounded on several occasions. It is not clear whether her sex was ever discovered while she was in the service: the sources disagree. In any case, after the war Jenkins married a coal miner named Abraham Jenkins. When she died, in about 1881, Jenkins was buried in a village graveyard in Ohio. Shortly thereafter, the St. Louis *Star* noted, when the story of her military service became widely known, Jenkins's grave was quickly decorated by local veterans with honors equal to those bestowed upon any other of the grass-grown mounds."

In 1898 the Charlestown, West Virginia, *Farmer's Advocate* printed a poignant article about Mary Walters, who had followed her husband, William—without his knowledge—into the 10th Michigan Infantry. Wounded at Antietam in the fall of 1862, Mary Walters had refused the advice she received from the doctor who examined her and discovered her sex, namely, that she return home. Instead, as soon as she was well enough, Walters returned to her regiment. Only when her husband disappeared while on a scouting expedition did Walters apply for a discharge and go home to Michigan. Meanwhile, William was wounded in the head and lost his memory, making a reunion of the two unlikely. Thirty-four years later, however, a bizarre set of circumstances conspired to bring them together again. "The happy couple," the article concluded, "have returned to Michigan where they will spend the remaining years of their lives." In 1915 the *New York Times* published a piece that mentioned Mary Siezgle, the wife of a soldier in the 44th New York Infantry who had first entered the military ranks as a nurse but had soon exchanged her skirts for the uniform of a soldier in order to fight the enemy directly. According to the article, Siezgle's battlefield experience included Gettysburg. In 1920 a Raritan, New Jersey, newspaper noted the death of Elizabeth Niles, who, it claimed, "with close-cropped hair and a uniform, concealed her sex and is said to have fought beside her husband through the civil war." A newlywed at the time of the war's outbreak, the article continued, Niles had followed her husband Martin into the 4th New Jersey and had acted the soldier's part through a number of engagements, her sex remaining undiscovered to the end of her service.

Snippets of material about various other women soldiers appear in a variety of sources, modern and otherwise. We learn, for example, about Lizzie Compton, whose sex was detected after she was wounded and who claimed, upon discovery, to have enlisted at the age of fourteen and to have served for eighteen months in seven different regiments, pursuant to the repeated discovery of her sex. We learn, too, of Margaret Henry and Mary Wright, Southern women discovered in uniform shortly before the end of the war, when they were captured by federal authorities while in the act of burning the bridges around Nashville; Catherine E. Davidson of Sheffield, Ohio, who after her discharge told interviewers that she had seen her lover killed at Antietam, where she herself sustained a wound; Satronia Smith Hunt, who enlisted with her husband in an Iowa regiment and who, after he died in battle, remained in the regiment until the end of the war, unwounded and her sex undetected; and Annie Lillybridge of Detroit, who enlisted in the 21st Michigan in order to be near her fiancé, but who managed to hide her identity even from him until she was disabled by a wound in her arm and was discharged following the discovery of her sex. Especially if we assume that the majority remained undetected, it is clear that an impressive array of women joined the armies of the Union and the Confederacy in the guise of men, and that as long as they were able to sustain their impostures, they commonly fulfilled with fierce determination the responsibilities they had assumed as soldiers. As in the cases of women spies, resistance activists, army women, and daughters of the regiment, the individual women soldiers for whom we have the most substantial documentation are only a small proportion of those who felt compelled to "don the breeches" and serve as men.

Discussion Questions

1. Leonard discusses a variety of motivations for the women who joined the Union and Confederate armies as "male" imposters. What were these motivations? What conclusions about women's civilian lives during the Civil War might we draw from the variety of motivations discussed?

2. Leonard writes that one reason the women were so rarely detected as "imposters" was that men simply did not expect to find them in the Army: "Women were considered unfit for military service in consequence of their presumed physical, emotional, and intellectual weaknesses. . . ." Discuss some of the ironies of these beliefs. According to Leonard, how did women perform in the field? What kinds of tasks did they do? How did men's assumptions about women differ from women's beliefs about their own abilities?

Writing Suggestions

1. The question of women participating in active combat in the American military forces remains very controversial to this day. Write a personal opinion paper on this issue, responding to the following question: Should women military personnel be allowed to take part in combat duty in the air, on land, and on the high seas?

   State your thesis clearly at the beginning of your paper, respond to your opposition (those who argue the other side), and be specific with your examples and evidence.

2. Research the role of women in the Civil War, not only as soldiers but also as spies. Many women were involved in espionage in both the North and the South. Write a research essay in which you explain the role these women spies played in the Civil War, and profile the careers of at least two women in detail. You can start your research with the author of this selection, Elizabeth Leonard. You can also look on the Web for information about women spies in the Civil War at <http://scriptorium.lib. duke.edu/women/cwdocs.html> and <http://intellit.muskingum. edu/intellsite/civwar_folder/civwarconfwomen.html>.

A Soldier's Story

HARPER'S WEEKLY

Harper's Weekly was one of the earliest American weekly magazines, published first in June of 1850. The magazine quickly attracted a following of 50,000, who could read articles by famous American authors, including Mark Twain and Jack London. Artists like Winslow Homer and Frederic Remington also appeared on the pages of *Harper's Weekly*, which remains a popular magazine in America today. *Harper's Weekly* covered all the major political events of its times, so the Civil War held an important place on the its pages. In the letter below, the name of the author who wrote to the editor of *Harper's Weekly* in 1865 is not given, but we can assume that this person was a writer and researcher who was deeply impressed by the value of primary sources and was determined to capture for posterity the selection from the Civil War soldier's diary that follows. The diary was written by a Yankee soldier in 1865, the last year of the Civil War.

Mr. Editor,

I send you a bit of veritable history—a leaf from a soldier's diary in the last campaign. The testimony of an eye-and-ear witness, the personal record and experience of one man is always valuable. But every man in the army has his story or report to give. Collect a hundred thousand such reports, and you have the history of a campaign. Not the dry official report of the general or corps commander, nor even the flaming rhetorical descriptions of "our correspondent." Here, as nothing was done for glory, so nothing is written for effect. But the simple incidents of a soldier's life, told naturally as they fell out, are forever linked with the brightest and the darkest page in a nation's history.

To the writer, of course, and to his family and friends, not to the great public, such a record is most valuable. It will instruct the present, and be an heir-loom to future generations. And to himself it remains a cherished memento of dear-bought experience. A note taken on the spot is a wonderful refresher of memory. The mere telling from day to day of what he did and where he was brings up a host of incidents, a thousand associations, just as the items of a business man's experience lay open at a glance his whole plan and economy of life. All common men in the midst of great actions are poets, and write poetically; that is, truthfully. A bold stroke or two, no matter how rough the writing may be, paints the image to the mental eye, and gives the scenery of war and battle. And as the scene changes and shifts, and unrolls itself to the gaze of the actor and spectator, he is made a participant in all the fortunes of the fight, in all the passions of the combatants, while the glory or disgrace of the action is keenly felt as his own. In after-life he lives over again in memory the battles through which he passed, and how he fought all day and marched all night in one of those flank movements which his General was so famed for executing. He remembers that in such an action or skirmish a bullet ticked him, and a comrade was either wounded or killed; that on such a night he worked in the trenches in the rain, or was detailed as picket-guard; and that another time he lay with his regiment a long time under a broiling sun, and lay close to keep clear of rebel bullets and shells falling thick about him. He is fond of telling over "hair-breadth" escapes, his "moving accidents" by flood and field, and his particular "peril" in the "imminent deadly breach." In short, the whole art of writing or story-telling, to the private soldier, consists in putting the greatest quantity of life and action into the fewest possible words.

April 13.—Pleasant morning.—Left for our regiment at 8 o'clock; marched to Alexandria at 10 o'clock; took the cars, got to our regiment at Rappahannock station at 5 o'clock.

April 17.—Sunday.—Cloudy, cold morning.—Worked all day building our tents.—Cleared off in the afternoon—heavy fall of snow on the mountains.

April 18.—Cold morning.—Finished our hose and moved into it—four of us all together.

April 22.—Frosty morning, but pleasant.—The regiment presented Colonel Woodard with a splendid horse, saddle, and bridle, worth $305.

May 4.—Started for the front.—Marched across the Rapidan at 9 o'clock; camped and got our breakfast; marched to the front and camped for the night.

May 5.—Drawn up in line of battle.—Marched into the woods and laid down.—Four companies went out skirmishing.—At 9 o'clock, drawn up in line of battle; 12 o'clock, charged the rebel lines.—Lost a good many boys.—Colonel Woodard wounded.

May 6.—Started at 4 o'clock; marched out two miles to the rebel lines, formed in line of battle, and laid down.—Laid all day: shells passed over us pretty thick.—Rebs charged our right wing: drove it in.—Withdrew to our breast-works.

May 7.—At sunrise the rebs made a charge on our centre, but we drove them back: sharp-shooters firing at us, we charged on them and drove them back to their breast-works.—They shelled us all day.—Left at 9 o'clock to reinforce the left wing.

May 8.—Marched all night down through Spottsylvania.—Went into the fight at 10 o'clock, made two charges on the rebs, got drove back—loss very heavy.—Rested.—Ordered out in front: only 200 men left.—Stand picket all night.

May 9.—Pleasant morning.—Started early, marched out, formed a line of battle.—Laid down.—Laid all day in the hot sun, with our straps on.—

Attacked the rebs a little before night, drove them back, then laid down and slept.

May 10.—Pleasant morning.—The battle commenced anew at noon, lasted till 9 o'clock, when we passed to the front to support the skirmishers.— Staid there until dark; drew back, lay down for the night.

May 11.—Cloudy, looks like rain.—Skirmish firing commenced early.— Just commenced to rain a little.—Ten o'clock, moved back into the woods, and stopped.—Laid there all day and all night, until 4 o'clock.—Rained nearly all night.

May 13.—Started at daylight, marched one mile, stopped and wrote a letter home at 11 o'clock.—Built a line of breast-works—rained a good deal— put up tents and laid down.—Called up at 10 o'clock, and marched all night in the mud.

May 14.—Stopped at 5 o'clock, made our coffee, and ate our breakfast.— Laid there all day and all night; rained a good deal.—Drew three days' rations.—A good deal of fighting through the day: got shelled some.

May 17.—Cloudy.—All quiet along the lines this morning.—Sick to-day: building fortifications.

May 18.—Warm morning.—The battle opened at sunrise; very heavy artillery firing.—Fired all the forenoon.—Got letters from home—sent a letter home. Threatening rain.—Go on picket: rained some in the night.

May 19.—Cloudy.—All quiet on the line.—Our boys changed papers with the rebs this morning.—Wrote a letter home—Relieved from picket at 9 o'- clock: laid behind breast-works all night.

May 23.—Cloudy and cool.—All quiet this morning.—We are in Bowling Green, beginning to move forward.—Marched nine miles, forded the North Anna River at 2 o'clock.—The rebs attacked us at 6 o'clock.—Fought an hour and a half: whipped them.

May 28.—Pleasant morning.—Started at sunrise, marched 10 miles, crossed the Pamunky River, and formed a line of battle: threw up breast-works.

June 3.—Rainy morning.—The battle opened at six o'clock.—Continual roar of musketry and artillery until evening: rained all the time.—I was on the skirmish line from 9 to 5: balls and shells fell thick all around me.

June 6.—Cloudy, but warm. Stopped at 6 o'clock near Cold Harbor.— Cooked our breakfast, washed, got a letter from home: ordered to pack up and go on picket at evening.—Got a good night's sleep.

June 7.—Cool and cloudy.—The boys go in swimming in the mill-pond.— Went out on picket at 8 o'clock: relieved at sundown. Marched five miles and bivouacked for the night.

That will do for the present. The notes have a sameness, like the duties which the soldier has to perform. But they give some idea of a campaign which the boys commonly describe as "forty days under fire." O ye civilians and pen-and-ink generals, who manage the war at home and sketch imaginary campaigns over cigars and wine and the daily papers, while you speculate on the rising glory of the country, and the great names of the war, never forget the poor private soldier, nor despise these "short and simple annals" of his existence!

Discussion Questions

1. What does the author of the letter to the editor claim are the benefits of reading a soldier's diary? What does this author mean when he states, "But the simple incidents of a soldier's life . . . are forever linked with the brightest and the darkest page in a nation's history"? Does this statement still make sense for our times? Why or why not?

2. What is the tone of the author's letter to the editor? Which specific words date this piece? (Consider the author's diction.) Who do you think *Harper's Weekly* readers were—what audience was this writer aiming for? Did you find the author's comments instructive or not when you read the soldier's diary itself?

Writing Suggestions

1. Review the diary carefully, and then write your own analysis, for a current or peer audience, of what the diary taught you about the daily life of this Yankee soldier. Reading between the lines, what did you discover about life as a soldier, or about this particular soldier? How did this primary source add to your knowledge and understanding of the Civil War?

2. Review the on-line site of *Harper's Weekly*, which you can find at <http://www.harpweek.com>. Research other articles or art selections about the Civil War that are posted on-line, and then write a review of this Civil War section of Harpweek, answering some of the following questions:

    Would you recommend this site as a valid historical research site? Why or why not?

    What was most helpful? What kinds of information did you find?

    Was the organization and content of the site easy to access?

    What did you not like about the site?

    How did this site change or add to your understanding of the Civil War?

An Occurrence at Owl Creek Bridge

AMBROSE BIERCE

Ambrose Bierce, born in Ohio in 1842, fought in the Civil War before eventually moving to San Francisco, where he lived and wrote until his mysterious disappearance into Mexico in 1913. Bierce is famous not only for the short story that follows, "An Occurrence at Owl Creek Bridge," but also for his biting wit and satirical commentary, which he displayed in the San Francisco column "The Prattler" and as editor of the San Francisco newspaper *The Wasp*. Bierce was estranged from his family when he took off for Mexico in 1913, and the circumstances of his death remain a mystery. In the short story that follows, Bierce displays his mastery of imagery and symbolism as he tells the story of the wartime hanging of a Confederate civilian.

I

A man stood upon a railroad bridge in northern Alabama, looking down into the swift water twenty feet below. The man's hands were behind his back, the wrists bound with a cord. A rope closely encircled his neck. It was attached to a stout cross-timber above his head and the slack fell to the level of his knees. Some loose boards laid upon the ties supporting the rails of the railway supplied a footing for him and his executioners—two private soldiers of the Federal army, directed by a sergeant who in civil life may have been a deputy sheriff. At a short remove upon the same temporary platform was an officer in the uniform of his rank, armed. He was a captain. A sentinel at each end of the bridge stood with his rifle in the position known as "support," that is to say, vertical in front of the left shoulder, the hammer resting on the forearm thrown straight across the chest—a formal and unnatural position, enforcing an erect carriage of the body. It did not appear to be the duty of these two men to know what was occurring at the center of the bridge; they merely blockaded the two ends of the foot planking that traversed it.

Beyond one of the sentinels nobody was in sight; the railroad ran straight away into a forest for a hundred yards, then, curving, was lost to view. Doubtless there was an outpost farther along. The other bank of the stream was open ground—a gentle slope topped with a stockade of vertical tree trunks, loopholed for rifles, with a single embrasure through which protruded the muzzle of a brass cannon commanding the bridge. Midway up the slope between the bridge and fort were the spectators—a single company of infantry in line, at "parade rest," the butts of their rifles on the ground, the barrels inclining slightly backward against the right shoulder, the hands crossed upon the stock. A lieutenant stood at the right of the line, the point of his sword upon the ground, his left hand resting upon his right. Excepting the group of four at the center of the bridge, not a man moved. The company faced the bridge, staring stonily, motionless. The sentinels, facing the banks of the stream, might have been statues to adorn the bridge. The captain stood with folded arms, silent, observing the work of his subordinates, but making no sign. Death is a dignitary who when he comes announced is to be received with formal manifestations of respect, even by those most familiar with him. In the code of military etiquette silence and fixity are forms of deference.

The man who was engaged in being hanged was apparently about thirty-five years of age. He was a civilian, if one might judge from his habit, which was that of a planter. His features were good—a straight nose, firm mouth, broad forehead, from which his long, dark hair was combed straight back, falling behind his ears to the collar of his well fitting frock coat. He wore a moustache and pointed beard, but no whiskers; his eyes were large and dark gray, and had a kindly expression which one would hardly have expected in one whose neck was in the hemp. Evidently this was no vulgar assassin. The liberal military code makes provision for hanging many kinds of persons, and gentlemen are not excluded.

The preparations being complete, the two private soldiers stepped aside and each drew away the plank upon which he had been standing. The sergeant turned to the captain, saluted and placed himself immediately behind that officer, who in turn moved apart one pace. These movements left the condemned man and the sergeant standing on the two ends of the same plank, which spanned three of the cross-ties of the bridge. The end upon which the civilian stood almost, but not quite, reached a fourth. This plank had been held in place by the weight of the captain; it was now held by that of the sergeant. At a signal from the former the latter would step aside, the plank would tilt and the condemned man go down between two ties. The arrangement commended itself to his judgement as simple and effective. His face had not been covered nor his eyes bandaged. He looked a moment at his "unsteadfast footing," then let his gaze wander to the swirling water of the stream racing madly beneath his feet. A piece of dancing driftwood caught his attention and his eyes followed it down the current. How slowly it appeared to move! What a sluggish stream!

He closed his eyes in order to fix his last thoughts upon his wife and children. The water, touched to gold by the early sun, the brooding mists under the banks at some distance down the stream, the fort, the soldiers, the piece of drift—all had distracted him. And now he became conscious of a new disturbance. Striking through the thought of his dear ones was a sound which he could neither ignore nor understand, a sharp, distinct, metallic percussion like the stroke of a blacksmith's hammer upon the anvil; it had the same ringing quality. He wondered what it was, and whether immeasurably distant or near by—it seemed both. Its recurrence was regular, but as slow as the tolling of a death knell. He awaited each new stroke with impatience and—he knew not why—apprehension. The intervals of silence grew progressively longer; the delays became maddening. With their greater infrequency the sounds increased in strength and sharpness. They hurt his ear like the thrust of a knife; he feared he would shriek. What he heard was the ticking of his watch.

He unclosed his eyes and saw again the water below him. "If I could free my hands," he thought, "I might throw off the noose and spring into the stream. By diving I could evade the bullets and, swimming vigorously, reach the bank, take to the woods and get away home. My home, thank God, is as yet outside their lines; my wife and little ones are still beyond the invader's farthest advance."

As these thoughts, which have here to be set down in words, were flashed into the doomed man's brain rather than evolved from it the captain nodded to the sergeant. The sergeant stepped aside.

II

Peyton Fahrquhar was a well to do planter, of an old and highly respected Alabama family. Being a slave owner and like other slave owners a politician, he was naturally an original secessionist and ardently devoted to the Southern cause. Circumstances of an imperious nature, which it is unnecessary to relate here, had prevented him from taking service with that gallant army which had fought the disastrous campaigns ending with the fall of Corinth, and he chafed under the inglorious restraint, longing for the release of his energies, the larger life of the soldier, the opportunity for distinction. That opportunity, he felt, would come, as it comes to all in wartime. Meanwhile he did what he could. No service was too humble for him to perform in the aid of the South, no adventure too perilous for him to undertake if consistent with the character of a civilian who was at heart a soldier, and who in good faith and without too much qualification assented to at least a part of the frankly villainous dictum that all is fair in love and war.

One evening while Fahrquhar and his wife were sitting on a rustic bench near the entrance to his grounds, a gray-clad soldier rode up to the gate and asked for a drink of water. Mrs. Fahrquhar was only too happy to serve him with her own white hands. While she was fetching the water her husband approached the dusty horseman and inquired eagerly for news from the front.

"The Yanks are repairing the railroads," said the man, "and are getting ready for another advance. They have reached the Owl Creek bridge, put it in order and built a stockade on the north bank. The commandant has issued an order, which is posted everywhere, declaring that any civilian caught interfering with the railroad, its bridges, tunnels, or trains will be summarily hanged. I saw the order."

"How far is it to the Owl Creek bridge?" Fahrquhar asked.

"About thirty miles."

"Is there no force on this side of the creek?"

"Only a picket post half a mile out, on the railroad, and a single sentinel at this end of the bridge."

"Suppose a man—a civilian and student of hanging—should elude the picket post and perhaps get the better of the sentinel," said Fahrquhar, smiling, "what could he accomplish?"

The soldier reflected. "I was there a month ago," he replied. "I observed that the flood of last winter had lodged a great quantity of driftwood against the wooden pier at this end of the bridge. It is now dry and would burn like tinder."

The lady had now brought the water, which the soldier drank. He thanked her ceremoniously, bowed to her husband and rode away. An hour later, after nightfall, he repassed the plantation, going northward in the direction from which he had come. He was a Federal scout.

III

As Peyton Fahrquhar fell straight downward through the bridge he lost consciousness and was as one already dead. From this state he was awakened—ages later, it seemed to him—by the pain of a sharp pressure upon his throat, followed by a sense of suffocation. Keen, poignant agonies seemed to shoot from his neck downward through every fiber of his body and limbs. These pains appeared to flash along well defined lines of ramification and to beat with an inconceivably rapid periodicity. They seemed like streams of pulsating fire heating him to an intolerable temperature. As to his head, he was conscious of nothing but a feeling of fullness—of congestion. These sensations were unaccompanied by thought. The intellectual part of his nature was already effaced; he had power only to feel, and feeling was torment. He was conscious of motion. Encompassed in a luminous cloud, of which he was now merely the fiery heart, without material substance, he swung through unthinkable arcs of oscillation, like a vast pendulum. Then all at once, with terrible suddenness, the light about him shot upward with the noise of a loud splash; a frightful roaring was in his ears, and all was cold and dark. The power of thought was restored; he knew that the rope had broken and he had fallen into the stream. There was no additional strangulation; the noose about his neck was already suffocating him and kept the water from his lungs. To die of hanging at the bottom of a river!—the idea seemed to him ludicrous. He opened his eyes in the darkness and saw above him a gleam of light, but how distant, how inaccessible! He was still sinking, for the light became fainter and fainter until it was a mere glimmer. Then it began to grow and brighten, and he knew that he was rising toward the surface—knew it with reluctance, for he was now very comfortable. "To be hanged and drowned," he thought, "that is not so bad; but I do not wish to be shot. No; I will not be shot; that is not fair."

He was not conscious of an effort, but a sharp pain in his wrist apprised him that he was trying to free his hands. He gave the struggle his attention, as an idler might observe the feat of a juggler, without interest in the outcome. What splendid effort!—what magnificent, what superhuman strength! Ah, that was a fine endeavor! Bravo! The cord fell away; his arms parted and floated upward, the hands dimly seen on each side in the growing light. He watched them with a new interest as first one and then the other pounced upon the noose at his neck. They tore it away and thrust it fiercely aside, its undulations resembling those of a water snake. "Put it back, put it back!" He thought he shouted these words to his hands, for the undoing of the noose had been succeeded by the direst pang that he had yet experienced. His neck ached horribly; his brain was on fire, his heart, which had been fluttering faintly, gave a great leap, trying to force itself out at his mouth. His whole body was racked and wrenched with an insupportable anguish! But his disobedient hands gave no heed to the command. They beat the water vigorously with quick, downward strokes, forcing him to the surface. He felt his head emerge; his eyes were blinded by the sunlight; his chest expanded convulsively, and with a supreme and crowning agony his lungs engulfed a great draught of air, which instantly he expelled in a shriek!

He was now in full possession of his physical senses. They were, indeed, preternaturally keen and alert. Something in the awful disturbance of his organic system had so exalted and refined them that they made record of things never before perceived. He felt the ripples upon his face and heard their separate sounds as they struck. He looked at the forest on the bank of the stream, saw the individual trees, the leaves and the veining of each leaf—he saw the very insects upon them: the locusts, the brilliant bodied flies, the gray spiders stretching their webs from twig to twig. He noted the prismatic colors in all the dewdrops upon a million blades of grass. The humming of the gnats that danced above the eddies of the stream, the beating of the dragon flies' wings, the strokes of the water spiders' legs, like oars which had lifted their boat—all these made audible music. A fish slid along beneath his eyes and he heard the rush of its body parting the water. He had come to the surface facing down the stream; in a moment the visible world seemed to wheel slowly round, himself the pivotal point, and he saw the bridge, the fort, the soldiers upon the bridge, the captain, the sergeant, the two privates, his executioners. They were in silhouette against the blue sky. They shouted and gesticulated, pointing at him. The captain had drawn his pistol, but did not fire; the others were unarmed. Their movements were grotesque and horrible, their forms gigantic. Suddenly he heard a sharp report and something struck the water smartly within a few inches of his head, spattering his face with spray. He heard a second report, and saw one of the sentinels with his rifle at his shoulder, a light cloud of blue smoke rising from the muzzle. The man in the water saw the eye of the man on the bridge gazing into his own through the sights of the rifle. He observed that it was a gray eye and remembered having read that gray eyes were keenest, and that all famous marksmen had them. Nevertheless, this one had missed. A counter-swirl had caught Fahrquhar and turned him half round; he was again looking at the forest on the bank opposite the fort. The sound of a clear, high voice in a monotonous singsong now rang out behind him and came across the water with a distinctness that pierced and subdued all other sounds, even the beating of the ripples in his ears. Although no soldier, he had frequented camps enough to know the dread significance of that deliberate, drawling, aspirated chant; the lieutenant on shore was taking a part in the morning's work. How coldly and pitilessly—with what an even, calm intonation, presaging, and enforcing tranquility in the men—with what accurately measured interval fell those cruel words: "Company! . . . Attention! . . . Shoulder arms! . . . Ready! . . . Aim! . . . Fire!" Fahrquhar dived—dived as deeply as could. The water roared in his ears like the voice of Niagara, yet he heard the dull thunder of the volley and, rising again toward the surface, met shining bits of metal, singularly flattened, oscillating slowly downward. Some of them touched him on the face and hands, then fell away, continuing their descent. One lodged between his collar and neck; it was uncomfortably warm and he snatched it out. As he rose to the surface, gasping for breath, he saw that he had been a long time under water; he was perceptibly farther downstream—nearer to safety. The soldiers had almost finished reloading; the metal ramrods flashed all at once in the sunshine as they were drawn from the barrels, turned in the air, and thrust into their sockets. The two sentinels fired again, independently and ineffectually. The hunted man saw all this over his shoulder; he was now swimming vigorously with the current. His brain was as energetic as his arms and legs; he thought with the rapidity of lightning: "The officer," he reasoned, "will not make that martinet's error a second time. It is as easy to dodge a volley as a single shot. He has probably already given the command to fire at will. God help me, I cannot dodge them all!" An appalling splash within two yards of him was followed by a loud, rushing sound, DIMINUENDO, which seemed to travel back through the air to the fort and died in an explosion which stirred the very river to its deeps! A rising sheet of water curved over him, fell down upon him, blinded him, strangled him! The cannon had taken a hand in the game. As he shook his head free from the commotion of the smitten water he heard the deflected shot humming through the air ahead, and in an instant it was cracking and smashing the branches in the forest beyond. "They will not do that again," he thought; "the next time they will use a charge of grape. I must keep my eye upon the gun; the smoke will apprise me—the report arrives too late; it lags behind the missile. That is a good gun." Suddenly he felt himself whirled round and round—spinning like a top. The water, the banks, the forests, the now distant bridge, fort and men, all were commingled and blurred. Objects were represented by their colors only; circular horizontal streaks of color—that was all he saw. He had been caught in a vortex and was being whirled on with a velocity of advance and gyration that made him giddy and sick. In few moments he was flung upon the gravel at the foot of the left bank of the stream—the southern bank—and behind a projecting point which concealed him from his enemies. The sudden arrest of his motion, the abrasion of one of his hands on the gravel, restored him, and he wept with delight. He dug his fingers into the sand, threw it over himself in handfuls and audibly blessed it. It looked like diamonds, rubies, emeralds; he could think of nothing beautiful which it did not resemble. The trees upon the bank were giant garden plants; he noted a definite order in their arrangement, inhaled the fragrance of their blooms. A strange roseate light shone through the spaces among their trunks and the wind made in their branches the music of Æolian harps. He had no wish to perfect his escape—he was content to remain in that enchanting spot until retaken. A whiz and a rattle of grapeshot among the branches high above his head roused him from his dream. The baffled cannoneer had fired him a random farewell. He sprang to his feet, rushed up the sloping bank, and plunged into the forest. All that day he traveled, laying his course by the rounding sun. The forest seemed interminable; nowhere did he discover a break in it, not even a woodman's road. He had not known that he lived in so wild a region. There was something uncanny in the revelation. By nightfall he was fatigued, footsore, famished. The thought of his wife and children urged him on. At last he found a road which led him in what he knew to be the right direction. It was as wide and straight as a city street, yet it seemed untraveled. No fields bordered it, no dwelling anywhere. Not so much as the barking of a dog suggested human habitation. The black bodies of the trees formed a straight wall on both sides, terminating on the horizon in a point, like a diagram in a lesson in perspective. Overhead, as he looked up through this rift in the wood, shone great golden stars looking unfamiliar and grouped in strange constellations. He was sure they were arranged in some order which had a secret and malign significance. The wood on either side was full of singular noises, among which—once, twice, and again—he distinctly heard whispers in an unknown tongue. His neck was in pain and lifting his hand to it found it horribly swollen. He knew that it had a circle of black where the rope had bruised it. His eyes felt congested; he could no longer close them. His tongue was swollen with thirst; he relieved its fever by thrusting it forward from between his teeth into the cold air. How softly the turf had carpeted the untraveled avenue—he could no longer feel the roadway beneath his feet! Doubtless, despite his suffering, he had fallen asleep while walking, for now he sees another scene—perhaps he has merely recovered from a delirium. He stands at the gate of his own home. All is as he left it, and all bright and beautiful in the morning sunshine. He must have traveled the entire night. As he pushes open the gate and passes up the wide white walk, he sees a flutter of female garments; his wife, looking fresh and cool and sweet, steps down from the veranda to meet him. At the bottom of the steps she stands waiting, with a smile of ineffable joy, an attitude of matchless grace and dignity. Ah, how beautiful she is! He springs forwards with extended arms. As he is about to clasp her he feels a stunning blow upon the back of the neck; a blinding white light blazes all about him with a sound like the shock of a cannon—then all is darkness and silence!

Peyton Fahrquhar was dead; his body, with a broken neck, swung gently from side to side beneath the timbers of the Owl Creek bridge.

Discussion Questions

1. Bierce himself fought in the Union Army. Do you think he takes a side in this story in favor of the Union or the Confederacy? Why or why not?
2. Reread the opening paragraphs of the story. What variety of diction does Bierce use? What is the effect of this diction on the reader? How and where does the diction change later on in the story?

Writing Suggestions

1. Bierce uses a number of symbolic elements to make the story more meaningful for the reader. Write an essay in which you answer the question: What symbolism can you find in the story? Consider colors, sounds, and setting. How does this symbolism contribute to Bierce's argument?
2. Ambrose Bierce led a very colorful life, including a stint as editor of the San Francisco newspaper *The Wasp*. At the end of his life, Bierce disappeared into Mexico, never to be seen again. Currently, historians are still not sure what happened to Bierce. Research his life and disappearance, and write a paper in which you discuss the mystery surrounding Bierce's last years.

Chapter 4: Writing Suggestions

1. Look back over all the selections you have read in this chapter. Then write a personal essay reflecting on the myths and multiple versions of "truth" that emerge in these writings. Which of these readings challenged your previous beliefs about slavery and the Civil War? Which of the readings confirmed your beliefs? How has your impression of the Civil War changed after studying these texts?

2. The proslavery movement had a number of vocal and enthusiastic supporters. Research this movement and analyze some of the arguments used by two or three different well-known writers of the time, such as those writers whose works appear in the nineteenth century anthology of proslavery writings: *Cotton Is King and Pro-Slavery Arguments*. Look for other sources in your library, and use at least two secondary sources by modern historians writing about this movement.

3. The Civil War is a complicated and interesting period of history, with many possibilities for research and exploration. Write a five-page research paper on one of the following topics (or a topic of your own choice), using at least seven sources from your library or from government or educational sources on the Internet, some of which are listed at the end of this chapter for your reference. Some possible research topics include the following:

    Abraham Lincoln and the abolition of slavery
    The Underground Railroad
    Blacks in the Confederate or Union armies
    Black and white abolitionist movements
    Andersonville Prison
    General Sherman's career in the Civil War
    General Lee's career in the Civil War
    General Grant's career in the Civil War
    The life of Jefferson Davis
    Battles at sea during the Civil War
    The constitutionality of secession
    The role of slavery in the southern economy
    Southern military strategies that led to defeat
    Women's roles as spies for both the South and the North
    Women soldiers in both armies
    The importance of individual military battles such as those at Gettysburg or Antietam
    Medical practices during the war
    Art, music, and poetry created during the Civil War

4. Rent the movie *Gone with the Wind*, and as you watch the movie, keep in mind the various selections you have read in this chapter and the vastly different views of Davis, Lincoln, Fitzhugh, Nolan, and Truth. Then write a review of the Selznick film production of *Gone with the Wind*, analyzing where the Selznick production falls in the range of representation of slavery, white slave owners, Confederate versus Yankee soldiers, and southern women. Where are the movie's strengths and weaknesses? Where do you think the movie takes liberties with history? Does it matter to you whether or not the movie is historically accurate? Do you find it a great movie or not? Why?

Chapter 4: Further Research on the Web

To pursue your research on the Internet, explore some of the following sites:

Abolition and Slavery

http://www.cwc.lsu.edu/cwc/links/slave.htm
http://sunsite.utk.edu/civil-war/warweb.html
http://memory.loc.gov/amem/cwphtml/cwphome.html

Slavery and Slave Narratives

http://memory.loc.gov/amem/snhtml/snhome.html
http://scriptorium.lib.duke.edu/slavery/

Abraham Lincoln

http://www.whitehouse.gov/history/presidents/al16.html
http://lincoln.lib.niu.edu/
http://memory.loc.gov/ammem/alhtml/alhome.html

Jefferson Davis

http://www.ruf.rice.edu/~pjdavis/jdp.htm

5

Conflicts in California
The Missions, the Gold Rush, and Chinese Exclusion

The study of primary and secondary sources in this chapter will show you a California you may not have read about or seen before—a complicated, violent, beautiful, and multiracial region where women dressed as men and worked in the mines, where Chinese laborers were imported and then sent home with no recourse, where more Indians were killed by whites and disease than in any other state of the union, and where literary greats like Mark Twain and Bret Harte found materials to last them a lifetime of writing.

The history of conflicts in California is related to the conflicts played out elsewhere in the United States concurrently and in earlier centuries. The subjugation of native peoples, the quest for land, gold, and power, and the exploitation of immigrant labor were all issues that had already surfaced in other geographical regions of America. The history of conflicts in California, however, combines unique elements that deserve special study. Many questions present themselves for students reading and writing about American history and culture:

> What do the writings of Father Junipero Serra offer us in answer to the question: Were the missions a curse or a blessing for the Indians of California?
>
> How were the myth and the reality of the experiences of those who came West in search of Gold expressed in literature, letters, advertisements, and diaries?
>
> How have historical writings treated the Gold Rush and the myth of the Argonauts who made California famous?
>
> What kinds of race and class conflicts arose during and after the building of the transcontinental Railroad?

This chapter begins with a look at the California mission system and Father Junipero Serra. On the one hand, Father Serra's supporters point to his religious dedication, his self sacrifice in the face of tremendous physical and emotional hardship, and his success in converting the Indians to Christianity. On the other hand, recent scholarship reminds us that the Indians were tortured, shackled in chains, starved, and punished if they did not willingly adopt the Franciscans' religion. In these selections, you have a chance to look at the missions and the missionary movement from two points of view: Father Serra's letter to Father Juan Andrés offers a rare view of the thoughts and feelings of one of the earliest missionaries in California, while revisionist historian Richard White's essay describes a mission system under Father Serra's rule that differs vastly from the one described in Father Serra's letter.

The romanticization of the mission system is also the subject of Gutiérrez's essay "Myth and Myopia," which addresses the complex relationship of Hispanics and whites. Looking back to earlier days to explore the way in which Hispanics in California and the Southwest became marginalized and invisible, Gutiérrez's essay takes us backward and forward in time, creating a picture of conflicts old and new. Gutiérrez writes of the tendency to romanticize life in early California under the mission system and brings up the irony of Helen Hunt Jackson's successful novel *Ramona*, which was intended to portray the cruel treatment of the Indians under the U.S. government, but which, with its romantic portrayal of life under the Spanish mission system, instead lured thousands of tourists to see the beautiful California sights and missions described in her novel. In an excerpt from *Ramona* we can see the evocative power of fiction, which in this case backfired and romanticized the mission system instead of drawing attention to the plight of the Indians.

To understand the voices and writings of the men and women who were drawn to the promises of gold first found at Sutter's Mill, we next read Kevin Starr's selection from *Americans and the California Dream*. Starr's lively and informative style offers us an excellent example of researched writing. Starr explains the joys and miseries of the reality of life in California, detailing the journeys and trials of those who came to get rich. He discusses the few who succeeded, and describes the change in emphasis from mining to farming, a change that set the stage in California for the development of the railroad.

Men did not always come alone to mine for gold; some brought wives and sisters, others brought prostitutes or women whom they met along the trail. To understand more clearly the range of women's experiences, you can look at Dee Brown's excerpt from *The Gentle Tamers*, which explains the somewhat limited range of options open for women in the West, one of which was prostitution. You can observe the tone and discourse from a piece written in 1958, appreciating the context from which the piece emerges and the historical information it gives us about conflicts between men and women.

Bret Harte adds his voice to the mix of writings about the Gold Rush in "The Luck of Roaring Camp." Harte explores a world in which issues of gender, race, class, and hardship dominate the story of an orphaned baby cared for by the rough crew of Roaring Camp.

Central to the development of the West after the first wave of gold miners was the development of the transcontinental railroad. Different genres and different voices portray the recurring issues of immigration laws, dominance, helplessness, and courage that typified the Chinese experience in California in the nineteenth century. These issues are discussed by Andrew Gyory in his selection from *Closing the Gate*, where he explains the influence of politicians and the media in passing the Chinese Exclusion Laws after the railroad was completed and Chinese labor became a threat instead of a boon to big business. The text of the Chinese Exclusion Act itself gives you a chance to see the wording and organization of the act, and to compare this text to previous government documents that took away the rights of other groups in other centuries. In addition, the Thomas Nast political cartoon from *Harper's Weekly* in 1871, "The Chinese Question," gives us a firsthand look at some of the arguments about the treatment of the Chinese workers and illustrates the role that political cartoonists played in the late nineteenth century.

Finally, to end this chapter we look at Sui Sin Far's short story "In the Land of the Free," which offers us a moving fictional account of the terrible hardships encountered by Chinese families in America in the late 1800s.

As you read the selections in this chapter, reflect on the roots of our current multicultural identities, not only in California but also throughout the United States. How did immigration labor shape the building of the railroad? How did the railroad change the shape of America and American history? What kinds of labor and racial problems today find their roots in the nineteenth century settling of California? And how does the myth of the Gold Rush continue to express itself today?

Before You Read

1. Consider the role of Chinese immigrants in the development of America. What do you know about the history of Chinese immigration and exclusion? What associations do you have with the idea of the Chinese in California? What roles have you seen Chinese immigrants play in movies? What have you learned about the construction of the Central Pacific Railroad and immigrant labor?

2. Write a brief paragraph of your thoughts and images about the California Gold Rush—include ideas or thoughts about men, women, stereotypes, racism, and so on. Then write a paragraph about ideas you hold about California today. What do you know about the Golden State and its history? What do you think of when you hear the word California? Freewrite and allow whatever thoughts that come to appear in your paragraph.

To Father Juan Andrés

JUNIPERO SERRA

Father Junipero Serra, born in Mallorca and schooled by the Franciscans, was both a priest and a professor of theology by the age of twenty-four. However, he felt a strong calling to travel to Mexico, where he worked for many years as a missionary with the Indians. In 1767 Serra was appointed head of the missions in Baja California, and, at the request of the governor, the next year he began the long process of building missions in Alta California, which we know now as the state of California. These missions had two purposes: to spread Christianity to the Indians, and to expand Spain's economic and political base in the New World. Father Serra is a particularly controversial figure in California history, and the Vatican's 1987 beatification of Father Serra has recently given new life to the debate about his life and his work. In the letter that follows, Father Serra writes of his arrival in San Diego and his early impressions of the "heathen land."

The meeting of the land and sea expeditions at San Diego; scurvy among the sailors; friendliness of the Indians; the diary; the need of missionaries; the qualifications these should have and the equipment they should bring. Written at San Diego, July 3, 1769.

+

Hail Jesus, Mary, Joseph!

Very Reverend Father Guardian Fray Juan Andrés.

Venerable Father and my dear Sir:

I am writing this letter in this Port and new Mission-to-be of San Diego, some hundred leagues within the heathen land of California. Here I have with me Fathers Crespí, Viscaíno, Parrón and Gómez, all in good health, thank God, and at the orders of Your Reverence, as our father and lord.

We came together here in separate groups, a few at a time. Fathers Viscaíno and Gómez came first, arriving by the packet boat *San Antonio*; then Father Parrón in the *San Carlos*, which, starting a month and a half before the *San Antonio*, arrived twenty days after it. The third on the list was Father Crespí, with the first part of the land expedition; and I was the last to join them here, the day before yesterday, with the Governor and the rest of the said expedition.

As regards the missions already in existence, Father Professor Palóu who is now their President, as I wrote in my last letters to Your Reverence before beginning this journey—which fact appeared to confirm to me why Your Reverence had nominated him as President—no doubt will report to Your Reverence the state of affairs and all that has happened since the visit of His Most Illustrious Lordship to Loreto. He was still expected to come when I left.

Before starting, I drew up a memorandum putting down all the matters that, in my mind, had to be laid before the said gentleman so that everything might be in good order. I was informed before leaving Christian parts that all my suggestions were approved of. Blessed be God.

As regards our present undertaking: the expedition by sea was a disaster. As a matter of fact both ships landed at this port, but neither of them is in condition to proceed to Monterey. Owing to the faulty condition of the barrels, the *San Carlos* suddenly found itself without water. They put in to the coast and procured some water but of poor quality. The crew took sick with scurvy—or Loanda sickness—and since their arrival at this port, they all died, with the exception of one sailor and a cook.

Of the volunteers, or Migueletes, from Catalonia, three died, and many are sick with little hope of recovery. The worst of all was that the crew of the *San Antonio*, which was ready to sail from here to Monterey, arriving here in good health, went to the assistance of the *San Carlos* and were themselves infected, and eight of their number died. Therefore the gentlemen here came to the decision that the said *San Antonio*, also called *El Príncipe*, must return to the Port of San Blas and that from there it should bring a double crew, so that on returning, both ships may be manned and continue their voyage.

The third packet boat, the *San Joseph*, we imagine must have already set sail for the same destination. On it comes Father Murguía; that is on the supposition that his mission at Santiago de los Coras was placed by His Most Illustrious Lordship in the care of Father Baeza, a secular priest, and nephew of Father Fray Buenaventura. If the ship lands here in good condition, and ready to go ahead, although it was the last to leave, it will be the first to get to Monterey.

I regret that my time is all too short to write more extensively. Arriving the day before yesterday, about noon, after a tiresome journey, I am being pressed by the report that the boat sails this very night. That is why I am not sending to Your Reverence the diary of my journey which lasted among the infidels a little less than one month and a half. We met with no hostile demonstrations, in fact just the reverse. On many occasions we were regaled by the gentiles— reversing the proverb, "The stingy man gives more than the naked man," because these naked Indians gave us more than many stingy men would have given us.

Naked indeed are all the males among the gentiles, be they children or adults, throughout all this country, without any exception. They go just as their mothers brought them into the world. And they have given us, on many occasions, food—not that we needed it, since, thank God, we came with plenty. Father Crespí and his companions of the expedition, by the way, experienced dire hunger on the road. They arrived at this port emaciated, and five of their Indians died on the way from extreme want.

On the first opportunity that presents itself after this, I will send you the said diary. In the letter enclosed with this, I promise our Father Commissary General a copy of the diary, on condition that if I cannot have it duplicated here, I will ask Your Reverence to order a good transcript to be made there. Not that it is worth anybody's attention, but it may help to a knowledge of these lands that had never before been trodden by a Christian foot. It will show how rich is the harvest of souls that might easily be gathered into the bosom of our holy Mother the Church and, it would appear, with very little trouble.

I asked them in different places if they would like me to stay with them, and their answer was always yes.

Here there are no Apaches, and no enemies other than the spiritual ones. Thus with apostolic zeal and the grace of God, it seems to me that we may work to our hearts' content, and our Lord God will accomplish the promise made to our Seraphic Father Saint Francis that, at the mere sight of his sons, in these last centuries, the gentiles will be converted. It was fulfilled in what happened at the new mission of San Fernando de Velicatá, to which Father Campa is appointed, as I wrote to Your Reverence, I think, in my last letter.

And so, my Reverend Father Guardian, we need ministers and more ministers, now that God Our Lord has put in the hands of our holy College the care of so bounteous a harvest.

Of those who are up here three have asked me repeatedly to be returned to the College. They are. Fathers Villumbrales, Medinaveytia and Basterra. It seems to me advisable that permission be granted in order not to spread their discouragement to others. As to poor Father Morán, he richly deserves the rest that his age requires.

Of the five that are here, within a few days Fathers Crespí and Gómez will both set out to accompany the expedition; I will stay here for some time, and wait and see if I will take ship from here in the *San Joseph*. My intentions are to rest a little after my continuous journeyings—the distance from here to Loreto is about 250 leagues—and also to give a helping hand to these good Fathers in the foundation and organization of the new mission here. We will start work on it as soon as all the excitement caused by the setting out of the land expedition subsides.

Land here is plentiful and good, and a river goes with it. Although not long ago it had flowing water, at present—this being the driest part of the year—there is no water running in it. But there are still large and good pools. And so as regards the material side of things it seems that quite a good mission can be established. Besides there are so many vines grown by nature and without human help that it would mean little expense to follow the example of our good father Noe.

There are roses of Castile and trees in abundance; above all a large population of gentiles, both in this locality and in the surrounding country. They visit us frequently, but first they put aside their bows and arrows. May God grant both us and them His holy grace so that soon they may all become Christians.

To sum it all up, my intention is that as ministers of the mission here, Fathers Murguía and Parrón, should remain; for the Mission of San Buenaventura, that has to follow this, Fathers Gómez and Viscaíno; and for Monterey Mission, Father Crespí and I.

Here it is quite cold, and my tunics—well, they are both about falling to pieces. Although on the way up here I took particular care to mend them. So I ask you especially that, at the first opportunity, you assist us in this matter. The tunics should be made of the thickest sackcloth that can be found.

As regards anything more, thanks be to God, I want for nothing but the prayers of many, that His Divine Majesty deign to grant me pardon for my numerous and great sins, and enable me to become a worthy minister of the Holy Gospel. And so I ask for the prayers of our holy Community both for myself and for all my brethren here. You in turn I will always remember in my own poor and lukewarm prayers.

Those who are assigned to come to this country should be sure to bring with them good blankets. With regard to those who come to missions already established, blankets will be superfluous. In this way it seems to me that blankets should be specified more for the missions than for the missionaries, that is if they are not already earmarked for a specified destination. And I am referring here to the missions yet to be founded, when our numbers are increased, and when the older missions are furnished with a second minister, for they have been too long with only one.

I intended to speak of many other things to Your Reverence; but there is no time for more. This however I will add: I consider that the missions to be founded in these parts will enjoy many advantages over the old ones, as the land is much better and the water supply is more plentiful. The Indians especially of the west coast seem to me much more gifted; they are well set up, and the Governor looks upon most of them as likely Grenadier Guards because they are such stoutly built and tall fellows.

To sum up, those who are to come here as ministers should not imagine that they come for any other purpose than to put up with hardships for the love of God and the salvation of souls. In a desert like this it is impossible for the old missions to come to the help of the new ones. The distances are great and the intervening spaces are peopled by gentiles. In addition to this, the almost complete lack of communication by sea makes it necessary that they endure, especially at the beginning, many and dire hardships. But to a willing heart all is sweet, *amanti suave est.*

Much more, beyond compare, did these poor Indians cost my Lord Jesus Christ. May His most holy Majesty keep Your Reverence, and all of you, and every one of the members of your holy Community—to whom I recommend myself with much affection—for many years in health and in His holy grace.

From this port among the infidels, and the projected Mission of San Diego, in California, July 3, 1769.

Kissing the hand of Your Reverence,

Your most affectionate and devoted subject and servant in Jesus Christ,

Fray Junípero Serra

Discussion Questions

1. From Father Serra's letter to Father Andrés, you can deduce a number of elements that made up the experience of the early Spanish missionaries in California. In groups, discuss some of the hardships and emotional states revealed by Father Serra's letter. If you were to read Father Serra's description alone, what would your impression be of the Indians' reception of the missionaries? What does his letter as a whole convey about Indian attitudes toward the padres?

2. What does Father Serra mean, after describing his own fatigue, cold, and hardships, when he says, "Much more, beyond compare, did these poor Indians cost my Lord, Jesus Christ"? What assumptions can you infer about Father Serra's attitudes from this statement?

Writing Suggestions

1. Write a brief essay analyzing Father Serra's use of language—his diction, metaphors, and tone. How does his use of metaphor affect your understanding of his purpose in California? What words does he use to describe the Indians? How does his word choice clarify his beliefs about the land he is visiting? Include in your essay your personal response to his letter—what impressions of California and Father Serra's experiences there do you come away with?

2. The beatification of Father Serra has generated a great deal of controversy in recent years. Research the process of Father Serra's beatification by researching the topic on Academic Universe. Read the arguments of both those for and those opposed to making Father Serra a saint. Then write your own opinion essay on the topic, arguing why or why not Father Serra should achieve sainthood in the Catholic Church.

"It's Your Misfortune and None of My Own"

A New History of the American West

RICHARD WHITE

Richard White is the author of several books about the history of the American West, including *The Middle Ground* and *The Roots of Dependency*. Previously the McClelland Professor of History at the University of Washington, he is now Margaret Byrne Professor of American History at Stanford University. White's work in the field of environmental history has earned him many awards, including the MacArthur Foundation Fellowship Award in 1995. In the following selection from *"It's Your Misfortune and None of My Own": A New History of the American West*, White discusses the treatment of the Indians by the Spanish missionaries in Alta California.

California

The Spanish had known of California well before they moved to secure the area from imperial rivals. Spanish sailors had visited Alta California, as the area north of present Baja California was known, as early as 1542, when Juan Rodríguez Cabrillo died while looking for the Northwest Passage. More than two centuries later, in 1769, the Spanish set out to establish a string of missions, presidios, and towns along the coast that Cabrillo had only glimpsed through the ocean fog. By 1770 they had two presidios: one at Monterey and the other at San Diego. In 1769, Fray Junipero Serra began establishing the 21 missions which would eventually stretch from San Diego to San Francisco Bay. In 1774, Juan Bautista de Anza succeeded in traveling overland to California from Sonora, thus providing the new province with a land link as well as a sea link with older settlements. Anza duplicated the trip in 1775–1776, bringing west the settlers who founded San Francisco in the fall of 1776. A nearly simultaneous attempt by Fray Silvestre Vélez de Escalante and Fray Francisco Atanásio Domínguez to reach Monterey from Santa Fe in 1776 failed. The Franciscans and their party spent most of their time wandering around Utah. Anza's success led the Spanish in 1779 to attempt to secure the Gila-Colorado route from Sonora to California by erecting a presidio and two missions among the Yuma Indians who lived along the Colorado.

Although largely successful, the attempt to secure California did gain the Spanish some new Indian enemies. The Yumas, who had first been visited by the Jesuit Father Kino in 1698, initially welcomed Franciscan missionaries. They expected trade goods and spiritual power, but they were unprepared for the Franciscan zeal for reorganizing their lives. Nor had they anticipated

340

the lust for property of the soldiers who accompanied the Franciscans. When the friars set about rearranging Yuma landholdings, and settlers and soldiers allowed their cattle to ruin both Yuma crops and the mesquite trees from which Yumas gathered food, the Yumas rebelled. They destroyed the missions, the settlements, and the presidio and cut California off from Mexico. The Spanish retaliated with punitive expeditions to kill Yumas, but they never did reoccupy the lower Colorado. The Yumas had blocked Spanish attempts to reorder Indian lives on the Colorado, but in California a massive reconstruction of Indian society was underway.

In California the Spanish created a way of life quite distinct from that of Texas or New Mexico. At a time when missions were crumbling elsewhere in the northern territories, missions formed the heart of the social order in California. Missionaries, aided by soldiers, gathered virtually the entire coastal population of California Indians south of San Francisco Bay into their missions. The missionaries worked not only to convert them, baptizing nearly 54,000 Indians in all, but also to "reduce" them from their "free and undisciplined" state to a regulated and disciplined condition. In the eyes of the Franciscans who supervised them, the California missions were humanitarian endeavors.

The missions controlled land, livestock, and labor. As in New Mexico, the missionaries instructed the neophytes (as baptized Indians were called) in a wide variety of new skills. Indian weavers, brick makers, blacksmiths, farmers, shepherds, and vaqueros—cattle drovers—created the California economy, and the missions prospered on their labor. At their height, the mission herds numbered more than 400,000 cattle, 60,000 horses, and 300,000 sheep and goats. The Indians did not, however, freely bestow the labor that maintained the missions. It was forced labor. Neophytes could not leave the missions, where the priests attempted to exercise absolute authority over them. If Indians persistently refused to work or resisted orders, they faced the lash, stocks, or irons. If neophytes fled the missions, soldiers were sent to retrieve them and whip them publicly. The results of Indian labor did not personally enrich the missionaries. The proceeds became part of the communal wealth of the mission, but the missionaries decided how these proceeds would be allocated. Under the mission system, Indians controlled neither their own labor nor its proceeds.

The cost of this wholesale transformation of Indian life was horrifying. During the mission period the Indian population between San Diego and San Francisco declined from 72,000 to 18,000, most of it from introduced diseases aggravated by the poor sanitation, the lack of medical care, the change in diet, and the often harsh social discipline of the missions. As the anthropologist Alfred Kroeber summarized the results, "The Fathers . . . were saving souls only at the inevitable cost of lives." If dying because of the actions of saintly men had advantages over dying at the hands of sinners, the mission Indians were lucky people indeed.

Discussion Questions

1. In groups, discuss White's account of the missionaries compared to the pic-ture portrayed by Father Serra. What specific "horrifying" transformation does White describe? Look back at Father Serra's letter. What hints of the changes that White describes can you find in Father Serra's letter?

2. Imagine that Father Serra could be present to respond to Richard White's account of "forced labor," and the "stocks and irons" the Indians were subject to. How might Father Serra justify the actions of the missionar-ies? What differences in assumptions and beliefs would characterize a conversation between these two men?

Writing Suggestions

1. The Internet is a rich source of information and photographs about the California Mission system. Review the following four Web sites:

    http://www.cmp.ucr.edu/exhibitions/missions
    http://library.monterey.edu/mcfl/mission.html
    http://www.pbs.org/weta/thewest/people/s_z/serra.htm
    http://www.sfmuseum.org/bio/jserra.html

    Then write a paper comparing the Web sites, discussing some of the fol-lowing aspects:

    What characteristics are unique to each Web site? Are the sites biased or do they present both sides of the issue?

    How are they arranged differently? Which are easy to navigate?

    Does one work better for you than another, and if so, why?

    How complete are the sites? Which site has the best links?

    Do these sites deal with the controversy over Father Serra and the mission-ary system?

2. Richard White and many other historians have written about the experi-ence of the California Indians under missionary influence and control. While some historians claim that the missionaries brought salvation and order to Indian lives, others claim that the Spanish missionaries brought death and destruction to Indian communities. Research this controversial topic. Write a research paper that tries to answer the following questions:

    What were the different motivations behind the establishment of the missions?

    What was the California mission system's economic and sociological impact on Indian communities?

    Did the mission system bring benefits to the Indians?

    Was the mission system cruel and violent in its control of the Indians?

    What happened to Indian life after the demise of the mission system?

Myth and Myopia

Hispanic Peoples and Western History

DAVID G. GUTIÉRREZ

David G. Gutiérrez is associate professor of history at the University of California at San Diego. His interests include the history of the American Southwest, and he has written *Walls and Mirrors: Mexican Americans, Mexican Immigrants,* and *The Politics of Ethnicity.* In addition, he is the editor of *Between Two Worlds: Mexican Immigrants in the United States.* In the following selection, taken from *The West* by Geoffrey Ward, Gutiérrez writes about the polarized and fantasized American vision of the Mexican population of the United States.

When my paternal great-grandparents Antonio Gutiérrez and Lola Gallardo Camucci met and began courting in Los Angeles in the early years of this century, they probably had little sense of themselves as actors in a sweeping historical drama. Indeed, in many ways, they were just doing what came naturally. Like so many immigrants from Mexico, Antonio had come to the United States from his home in Yucatán to work on one of the West's rapidly expanding railroads, and he naturally gravitated to the old Mexican American neighborhood surrounding Los Angeles's central plaza that had been established when the region was still part of the Spanish empire. Drawn by the familiar sounds of Mexican music and Spanish conversation, the welcome aromas of savory Mexican food, and by a network of Mexican American-run mom-and-pop restaurants, stores, and saloons, Antonio entered a world that at least in some ways must have felt similar to the world he had left behind. However many butterflies he may have felt when he met Lola, be must have felt fairly at home in her world in Los Angeles's ethnic Mexican enclave.

It was just as natural for Lola to be attracted to Antonio. After all, unions between Spanish-speaking people from "Old Mexico" and Hispanic inhabitants of Texas, New Mexico, and California had been almost an everyday occurrence ever since Spanish colonists had begun settling the northern frontier in 1598. Although Antonio was more darkly complected than Lola, probably spoke a slightly different variant of Spanish, and most likely grew up following different customs than those familiar to Mexican Californians, it was not at all uncommon or unusual that the two should fall in love and decide to marry. Thus, when my great-grandparents married in 1905 and had their first son, my grandfather, on Valentine's Day, 1906, they were simply repeating a pattern that had helped to sustain a significant and unbroken Hispanic presence in the region over more than three centuries.

While these events must have seemed perfectly natural and normal to Lola and Antonio and to people like them who lived in Los Angeles's expanding Mexican barrios, my great-grandparents began their life together in a social world that was far removed from the experience of most of their Anglo-American neighbors. Indeed, even though Lola's family had lived in southern California for generations, and Antonio was part of an immigrant influx that would soon increase the Mexican population of the Southwest by more than a million people, ethnic Mexicans seemed invisible to most Americans.

On one level, this inability to "see" Mexicans like my great-grandparents can be explained as the more or less logical result of the severe social polarization between ethnic Mexicans and Americans that occurred in the West after the United States annexed Mexico's northern territories in 1848. Over the years, this tendency toward mutual avoidance contributed to the gradual emergence of neighborhoods so segregated along ethnic lines that Mexican Americans and Anglo-Americans rarely came into direct contact with one another. By the turn of the century, the social distance between the two groups had grown so great that many Anglo-Americans had come to believe that Mexicans had simply disappeared. There was, however, much more to this story. Although residential segregation provides at least a partial explanation for the gradual disappearance of Mexicans from the social landscape of the West, the erasure of ethnic Mexicans from American consciousness was part of a longer, more complicated process.

Before the early nineteenth century, Americans had little reason to think about the Spanish-speaking inhabitants of the trans-Mississippi West. Although some harbored vaguely negative opinions about Hispanics—a legacy of British prejudice against Spain, laced with their own distaste for the practice of miscegenation between Spaniards and Indians in Latin America—such attitudes were of little practical consequence. But once American trappers, traders, and travelers began to eye Mexican territory for themselves in the 1820s and 1830s, their casually negative attitudes about Mexicans began to harden into more serious stereotypes that, in turn, helped provide a rationale for territorial expansion.

Among the most influential shapers of public opinion on life on the northern Mexican frontier was Richard Henry Dana, whose *Two Years Before the Mast* (published in 1840) introduced a generation of Americans to life in Mexican California. Although Dana expressed qualified admiration for some aspects of *Californio* society, he ultimately dismissed the Mexican Californians as "thriftless, proud, and very much given to gaming" and therefore utterly unworthy of holding such valuable territory. "In the hands of an *enterprising* people," he mused, "what a country this might be." Other Americans were more brutal in their assessments. After a visit to Taos, New Mexico, in 1846, New Englander Rufus Sage was moved to write that "there are no people on the continent of America, with one or two exceptions, more miserable in condition or despicable in morals than the mongrel race inhabiting New Mexico. . . . Half naked and

scantily fed . . . [and] possessed of little moral restraint and interested in nothing but the demands of present want, they abandon themselves to vice, and
prey on one another and those around them." After a visit to Mexican California, another traveler from New England, Thomas Jefferson Farnham, voiced
similar opinions. "Thus much for the Spanish population of the Californias,"
he noted,

> in every way a poor apology of European extraction; as a general thing, in-
> capable of reading or writing, and knowing nothing of science or literature,
> nothing of government but its brutal force, nothing of virtue but the sanc-
> tion of the Church, nothing of religion but ceremonies of the national ritu-
> al. Destitute of industry themselves, they compel the poor Indian to labor
> for them, affording him a bare savage existence for his toil, upon their plan-
> tations and the fields of the Missions. In a word, Californians are an imbe-
> cile, pusillanimous, race of men, and unfit to control the destinies of that
> beautiful country.

Ironically, the pervasiveness of negative attitudes among the few Americans who actually had had direct contact with Mexicans presented expansionists with some nettlesome problems when the debate over possible
westward expansion into Mexican lands began to heat up during the 1840s.
Given the increasing tension over the potential expansion of slavery into newly
acquired territories and Americans' general sensitivity about racial issues, the
possible incorporation into U.S. society of large numbers of such seemingly
racially and culturally inferior people raised troubling questions. Indeed, once
war erupted between the United States and Mexico, public discussion about
"what to do" with the region's mixed-blood Spanish-speaking population became a key political issue.

Journalists, politicians, and members of the general public all advanced
different theories about what was to become of people who might come with
any annexed territory. Some of the more idealistic advocates of continental
expansion argued that, with proper training in the principles of republicanism, most Mexicans eventually could be integrated into American society.
Others were not so optimistic. Convinced, as another observer suggested, that
Mexicans were "scarcely a visible grade, in the scale of intelligence, above the
barbarous tribes by whom they are surrounded," many Americans believed
that, like Indians, Mexicans either should be removed to reservations or exterminated altogether. Most expansionists, however, simply tried to sidestep
the tricky question by predicting vaguely that the indigenous populations of
the West would somehow "recede" or "fade away" before the advance of
American civilization. New York senator Daniel Dickinson, for example, simply dismissed Mexicans as one part of "the fated aboriginal races, who can neither uphold government [n]or be restrained by it; who flourish only amid the
haunts of savage indolence, and perish under, if they do not recede before,
the influences of civilization. . . . Like their doomed brethren, who were once

spread over the several States of the Union, they are destined by laws above human agency to give way to a stronger race from this continent or another."

Such attitudes played a powerful role in ordering interethnic relations in the West after the Mexican War. Although the United States officially guaranteed by treaty that Mexican nationals who came with the transfer of territory would be granted "all the rights of American citizens" (including suffrage, religious freedom, and protection of their private property), when issues of control over economic resources and political power arose—as they soon did in California, New Mexico, and Texas—it became clear that most American settlers had no intention of observing, much less protecting, Mexicans' personal or property rights. While it is true that pockets of Spanish-speaking people in South Texas, northern New Mexico, and southern California were able to hold their own and maintain some social and political influence for a short period after the war, widespread racial antagonism, the imposition of new legal and taxation systems, the crushing pressure of squatters, and subsequent loss of much of their land combined to push ethnic Mexicans to the margins of society. As a result, by the late 1870s and early 1880s the vast majority of this first generation of Mexican Americans had been divested of their property, politically disfranchised, and socially ostracized and segregated as a racialized minority. As Texan Juan Seguín noted after experiencing the brunt of these processes himself, Mexicans in the West had been reduced to "foreigners in their native land."

Although the specific circumstances of the erosion of Mexican Americans' political and economic position varied from place to place, a pattern soon became distressingly clear. Local elites gradually lost their lands to taxes, lawyers' fees, and squatters, and as their land base dwindled, so did their ability to intercede on behalf of working-class Mexican Americans who had once looked to them for leadership. Events in Nueces County, Texas, provide a good illustration of these processes at work. While in 1835 Mexican landowners held title to fifteen large land grants covering tens of thousands of square acres, by 1859 only one of the original grants remained in Mexican hands.

The more successful Anglo-Americans were in marginalizing Mexican Americans, the more Americans' notions of their own racial and cultural superiority seemed self-evident. In a classic case of circular logic, the conquest and military occupation of the West and the subsequent social, political, and economic subordination of the region's indigenous populations seemed to "prove" to Americans that they were naturally superior to the people they displaced. And, as dispossessed Mexican Americans became more concentrated in segregated urban enclaves or isolated rural settlements, they seemed to disappear from the social landscape of the West. Thus, within twenty-five years of the annexation of the Southwest it seemed that Indians and Mexicans had in fact "melted away" before the advance of a superior civilization, just as the proponents of Manifest Destiny had predicted they would.

Had this been the extent of the social subordination of ethnic Mexicans in the West, the damage done them would have been bad enough. But just as their superior military might and control of economic resources had enabled Americans to consolidate their control over the West, such disparities in power also bestowed upon them the ability to rewrite its history from their own point of view. Freed from the necessity of viewing Mexicans as any kind of military or political threat, Westerners began to spin romanticized versions of the not-too-distant history of the region.

The most important catalyst was the publication in 1884 of Helen Hunt Jackson's famous novel *Ramona*. Set in southern California, it told the story of two star-crossed lovers—an Indian named Alessandro and a beautiful Mexican-Indian maiden, Ramona—during the tumultuous transfer of California from Mexico to the United States. Jackson, a prominent champion of Native American rights, spent several months in 1882 and 1883 touring southern California's impoverished Mexican barrios and isolated Indian settlements, then resolved to expose the horrible conditions she had seen in a novel that she hoped would stimulate the sort of concern for Indians and Mexican Americans that Harriet Beecher Stowe's *Uncle Tom's Cabin* had elicited for African-American slaves.

Jackson's historical romance was an overnight success, the most popular American novel of its time, but much to Jackson's chagrin, the public reacted to *Ramona* very differently than she had anticipated. Missing entirely Jackson's implicit calls for reform, readers were transfixed instead by the novel's depictions of a magical, bygone age in which gentle, contented Indians worked a bountiful land under the benevolent supervision of saintly Spanish missionaries and a wise and generous landed gentry.

Many came to accept Ramona's story as the "true history" of "Spanish California" and, by extension, of the Spanish Southwest. Within months of the novel's publication, tourists began turning up in California eager to see "Ramona's country" for themselves. Some Westerners at first attacked Jackson for her critical portrayal of the American takeover of the region, but it didn't take long for local entrepreneurs to recognize the commercial possibilities growing out of the craze she had inspired. Within two years of publication an entire cottage industry had sprung up around *Ramona*: railroads and local chambers of commerce promoted elaborate tours, promoters ground out tens of thousands of postcards allegedly depicting "Ramona's birthplace," "Ramona's school," and "the bed in which Ramona slept."

Eventually, promoters all over the Southwest were busily publicizing the region's Hispanic past. There were parades, rodeos, and cultural exhibitions; elaborate historical extravaganzas like the Los Angeles Fiesta, San Gabriel's "Mission Play," "Old Spanish Days" in Santa Barbara, and similar festivals in Santa Fe, Taos, and other towns in the newly named "Land of Enchantment."

The creation of what the writer Carey McWilliams called the "Spanish fantasy heritage" ultimately had a powerful effect on the public's imagination.

Virtually overnight, aspects of the Hispanic past that had been portrayed just ten or twenty years earlier as distasteful remnants of a primitive and backward culture were transformed into icons of romantic and nostalgic fascination. The Spanish and Mexican Franciscan missionaries, who had long been painted by American travelers as tyrannical, even sadistic exploiters of Indians, were now re-created in the Anglo imagination as benevolent, patient friars who not only converted the primitive Indians, but as the Los Angeles booster Charles E. Lummis wrote in 1903, "taught them to read and write, to sing, to play musical instruments, to spin, weave, and make clothing, . . . to dwell in houses instead of brush hovels, . . . and otherwise trained them in all the handicrafts necessary for a self-supporting community."

Ruins, too, took on new meanings. "Looked at with the cold eye of one indifferent to material," Gertrude Atherton had written after visiting what was left of California's Mission San Antonio de Padua at mid-century, "it is doubtful if there is any structure on earth colder, barer, uglier, dirtier, less picturesque, less romantic than a California mission; so cheap are they; so tawdry, so indescribably common, so suggestive of mules harbored within, and chattering unshorn priests, and dirty Mexicans, with their unspeakable young." By the early 1890s, the missions had been transmuted into potent positive symbols of both the state of California and the greater "Spanish Southwest" itself, "embodiments," as one contemporary writer put it, "not only of the purposes of their founders, but of the faith which built the great cathedrals of Europe."

And it didn't end there. Organizations like the Association for the Preservation of the Missions sprang up everywhere because, as Charles Lummis wrote, "[the missions] are as a group by far the most imposing, the most important, and the most romantic landmarks in the United States, architecturally and historically." A regional architectural renaissance known as the Mission Revival brought to life in adobe, stucco, and concrete the fantastic images Jackson, Lummis, and subsequent promoters had imagined. Ranging from monumental projects such as the synthetic Romanesque–Spanish Mission design of Stanford University to more utilitarian structures, the Mission Revival style was well on its way to becoming a southwestern cliché by the 1910s; by the 1930s, nearly a million "Spanish-style" homes had been built in California alone. "Who would live in a structure of wood and brick if they could get a palace of mud?" wrote one eastern journalist of buildings modeled more or less after those the pioneers had deprecated as hovels unworthy of civilized people. "The adobes to me [make] the most picturesque and comfortable [homes] . . . and harmonize . . . with the whole nature of the landscape."

. . .

Although invisible to most Anglos, the growth of the West's Hispanic population shaped the social, cultural, and political evolution of the region in important ways. Mexicans had to walk a very fine line in their efforts to survive and assert themselves in the midst of the American society that was growing around them, but just as they had learned to survive under the harsh conditions of Mexico's northern frontier over the previous two centuries, they now quietly worked to adapt to life under the Americans. Ironically, in some ways, social isolation and residential segregation worked as a kind of perverse guarantee that Mexicans would continue to follow traditional Mexican cultural practices as central components of their everyday lives. Since most Mexicans had little contact with Anglo-Americans and received little formal schooling, the overwhelming majority naturally continued to speak Spanish as their primary (or only) language throughout the nineteenth century. For similar reasons, local architectural styles utilizing adobe and roughly hewn lumber, popular forms of entertainment, traditional Mexican cuisine, and music, dance, and other forms of expressive culture remained the norm in ethnic Mexican enclaves across the region.

. . .

The growth of the Spanish-speaking population in enforced isolation from the mainstream of western American life had other important consequences. Anglo control of politics, ownership of much of the best land, and a virtual monopoly on skilled jobs placed clearly defined upper limits on what Mexicans reasonably could expect to achieve in the nineteenth-century West, but they doggedly filled whatever economic niche they could carve out. In areas where lines of social and economic discrimination were particularly harsh, such as in South Texas, ethnic Mexicans were often forced by circumstance to provide for their own needs. Thus, over time, they developed an informal economy, selling goods and services otherwise difficult to acquire: they offered agricultural products grown on their own small plots and prepared foods such as tamales, tacos, and *pan dulces* (sweet baked goods); ran *carnicerías* (butcher shops), *tienditas* (small grocery or dry goods stores), or cantinas in Mexican neighborhoods. Although few made much, ethnic Mexican entrepreneurs nevertheless built a resilient alternative economic and social infrastructure composed of local networks of religious confraternities, mom-and-pop stores, restaurants, saloons, barbershops, boardinghouses, bordellos, Spanish-language newspapers, even informal rotating credit and mutual life insurance companies. In the process, they created a parallel Hispanic society in the West that was largely unnoticed by Anglo-Americans.

Of course, social isolation exacted its costs from the first generation of Mexican Americans and their children. Systematically barred from most of the best-paid and highest-skilled occupations, ethnic Mexicans were slowly but surely forced to take the most arduous and lowest-paid jobs. And having been socially erased from the landscape, Spanish-speaking Westerners faced extremely painful challenges when it came to making decisions about their future—and their children's future—in the United States. Although life in urban barrios and rural ranch communities provided them with a relatively safe social space in which to foster cultural cohesion and solidarity, exclusion from the American mainstream also meant that ethnic Mexicans had very few ways to articulate political or legal grievances. Thus, they learned early on that before they could even take the first tentative steps toward regaining a political voice as citizens (or at least as potential citizens) they first had to get other Americans to recognize that they actually existed.

. . .

For all the concrete gains that ethnic Mexican civil rights leaders ultimately achieved in the century after annexation, their most important contribution may have been their insistence on challenging the mythology Americans had constructed about what had happened to Mexicans in the West. By demanding not only that they be "seen" but that they at long last be extended their full rights as U.S. citizens, ethnic Mexican activists took the first steps toward reclaiming their suppressed history. The ultimate legacy of their efforts may lie in their success in gaining belated recognition from other Americans that the "real" West is much more complicated, culturally diverse, and interesting than the distorted picture painted by promoters of the Spanish fantasy heritage could ever be.

Still, one does not have to look long to recognize that Americans' historical myopia about Hispanics continues to color their perceptions, and it is difficult not to view the recent debate over Mexican immigration as another case in which Americans' inability to "see" a process that has unfolded over the past century has blinded them to the fact that the resident ethnic Mexican population has grown from the approximately one-half million people who lived in the United States when my grandfather was born to a population estimated in 1990 to be more than 14 million. The current spate of blaming Mexican immigrants for all the Southwest's ills—and the severe restrictions on immigration that may soon follow—may slow the growth of the United States' ethnic Mexican population, but it will also allow westerners—and Americans in general—the dangerous luxury of avoiding the reality that they already live in an extremely diverse, multiethnic, and multicultural society, and will eventually have to deal with the political and social consequences of that fact.

As any visitor knows who has sipped a Margarita or otherwise lingered in the restored missions or "Old Town" sections of present-day Santa Fe, San Antonio, Los Angeles, San Diego, or Santa Barbara, despite the current hysteria over the increasing "Mexicanization" of the American West, the romantic image of the West's Hispanic past remains alive and well as a highly visible component of the region's historical mythology and tourist industry. And while the hundreds of thousands of tourists who travel through the Old Spanish Southwest each year to experience a taste of "Hispanic culture" may have a more sophisticated understanding of that complex culture than did their counterparts in the late nineteenth century, one need only think about the huge gulf between such popular attractions and the increasingly violent rhetoric concerning immigration, the poverty and violence of segregated inner-city barrios, and the general persistence of anti-Mexican sentiment in American life to recognize the extent to which American images of Hispanics remain polarized.

Discussion Questions

1. What does Gutiérrez claim is the continuing problem with the Anglo vi-
    sion of Hispanics? What is his main argument in this essay? Do you agree
    with Gutiérrez? Discuss in groups your previous perceptions about His-
    panics and their role in the West.

2. Map out the way Gutiérrez organizes his argument. Where does his the-
    sis occur and reoccur? What kinds of strategies does he use in organizing
    this essay? What variety of techniques and writing variations does he
    add? Discuss whether or not you liked the way this essay was organized,
    using specific examples in your discussion.

Writing Suggestions

1. Gutiérrez quotes, at the beginning of his essay, some of the remarkably
    racist early reports about the Mexican character, such as New York Sena-
    tor Daniel Dickenson's statement that Mexicans were part of

    > the fated aboriginal races who can neither uphold government or be re-
    > strained by it; who flourish only amid the haunts of savage indolence, and
    > perish under, if they do not recede before, the influence of civilization. . . .
    > Like their doomed brethren, who were once spread over the several States of
    > the union, they are destined by laws above human agency to give way to a
    > stronger race from this continent or another.

    Write an essay in which you reflect upon the purpose and impact of Dick-
    enson's rhetoric, comparing it to the rhetoric used to justify the displace-
    ment of the Indians and the enslavement of blacks. For example, you
    could refer to the speeches of Presidents Jackson and Jefferson (Chapter
    2) and to the writings of Fitzhugh (Chapter 4) or Custer (Chapter 3). In
    your essay, reflect upon the motives and political environment of the
    speakers, the goals of the speakers, and the intended effect on the various
    audiences. What do these speakers have in common in their use of lan-
    guage and argument? What kinds of differences do you find? What as-
    sumptions about nonwhite peoples are reflected in each speech or essay?

2. Gutiérrez writes, "Although invisible to most Anglos, the growth of the
    West's Hispanic population shaped the social, cultural, and political evo-
    lution of the region in important ways." Research one of these aspects in
    which Hispanics shaped the West, and write a paper in which you ex-
    pand upon Gutiérrez's argument. If you can, you may want to use specific
    examples from your personal experience, in addition to secondary sources
    and Internet sources. You might want to consider examples of Hispanic
    influence on Western architecture, food, music, immigration policies, pol-
    itics, and so on.

Ramona

HELEN HUNT JACKSON

Helen Hunt Jackson (1830–1885) overcame the loss of both her children to illness and the death of her husband during the Civil War to become a well-known author and one of the staunchest defenders of Indian rights. After the death of her husband in 1863, Jackson decided to pursue a writing career, a career that eventually led her to social and political activism. In 1872 she traveled to California, and in the winter of 1873–1874 she lived in Colorado Springs, Colorado, where she met and married William Jackson, a wealthy banker. In 1879 Hunt met Chief Standing Bear and heard his lecture about the federal government's forced removal of the Ponca Indians in Nebraska. Jackson became very interested in the plight of all Indians, and in 1881 she published *A Century of Dishonor*, which she hoped would force Congress to improve the conditions of the remaining Indian tribes. Although she sent a copy of her book to every congressman, her work failed to spur government reform. In 1882 she was named Special Commissioner of Indian Affairs, and she continued to lobby for aid to the Indians. Disappointed that *A Century of Dishonor* had not brought about the changes she desired, she wrote another book, *Ramona*, in an effort to highlight the plight of California Indians. The work was overly romantic and portrayed the life of Indians under the Spanish in a sentimental light; ironically, *Ramona* became a huge novelistic success but failed to draw attention to the plight of the Indians and instead attracted tourists in search of the lost days of Mission California. The following selection is from *Ramona*.

II

The Señora Moreno's house was one of the best specimens to be found in California of the representative house of the half barbaric, half elegant, wholly generous and free-handed life led there by Mexican men and women of degree in the early part of this century, under the rule of the Spanish and Mexican viceroys, when the laws of the Indies were still the law of the land, and its old name, "New Spain," was an everpresent link and stimulus to the warmest memories and deepest patriotisms of its people.

It was a picturesque life, with more of sentiment and gayety in it, more also that was truly dramatic, more romance, than will ever be seen again on those sunny shores. The aroma of it all lingers there still; industries and inventions have not yet slain it; it will last out its century,—in fact, it can never be quite lost, so long as there is left standing one such house as the Señora Moreno's.

When the house was built, General Moreno owned all the land within a radius of forty miles,—forty miles westward, down the valley to the sea; forty miles eastward, into the San Fernando Mountains; and good forty miles more or less along the coast. The boundaries were not very strictly defined; there was no occasion, in those happy days, to reckon land by inches. It might be asked, perhaps, just how General Moreno owned all this land, and the question might not be easy to answer. It was not and could not be answered to the satisfaction of the United States Land Commission, which, after the surrender of California, undertook to sift and adjust Mexican land-titles; and that was the way it had come about that the Señora Moreno now called herself a poor woman. Tract after tract, her lands had been taken away from her; it looked for a time as if nothing would be left. Every one of the claims based on deeds of gift from Governor Pio Pico, her husband's most intimate friend, was disallowed. They all went by the board in one batch, and took away from the Señora in a day the greater part of her best pasturelands. They were lands which had belonged to the Bonaventura Mission, and lay along the coast at the mouth of the valley down which the little stream which ran past her house went to the sea, and it had been a great pride and delight to the Señora, when she was young, to ride that forty miles by her husband's side, all the way on their own lands, straight from their house to their own strip of shore. No wonder she believed the Americans thieves, and spoke of them always as hounds. The people of the United States have never in the least realized that the taking possession of California was not only a conquering of Mexico, but a conquering of California as well; that the real bitterness of the surrender was not so much to the empire which gave up the country, as to the country itself which was given up. Provinces passed back and forth in that way, helpless in the hands of great powers, have all the ignominy and humiliation of defeat, with none of the dignities or compensations of the transaction.

Mexico saved much by her treaty, in spite of having to acknowledge herself beaten; but California lost all. Words cannot tell the sting of such a transfer. It is a marvel that a Mexican remained in the country; probably none did, except those who were absolutely forced to it.

Luckily for the Señora Moreno, her title to the lands midway in the valley was better than to those lying to the east and the west, which had once belonged to the missions of San Fernando and Bonaventura; and after all the claims, counter-claims, petitions, appeals, and adjudications were ended, she still was left in undisputed possession of what would have been thought by any new-comer into the country to be a handsome estate, but which seemed to the despoiled and indignant Señora a pitiful fragment of one. Moreover, she declared that she should never feel secure of a foot of even this. Any day, she said, the United States Government might send out a new Land Commission to examine the decrees of the first, and revoke such as they saw fit. Once a thief, always a thief. Nobody need feel himself safe under American rule. There was no knowing what might happen any day; and year by year the lines of sadness, resentment, anxiety, and antagonism deepened on the Seño-ra's fast aging face.

It gave her unspeakable satisfaction, when the Commissioners, laying out a road down the valley, ran it at the back of her house instead of past the front. "It is well," she said. "Let their travel be where it belongs, behind our kitchens; and no one have sight of the front doors of our houses, except friends who have come to visit us." Her enjoyment of this never flagged. Whenever she saw, passing the place, wagons or carriages belonging to the hated Americans, it gave her a distinct thrill of pleasure to think that the house turned its back on them. She would like always to be able to do the same herself; but whatever she, by policy or in business, might be forced to do, the old house, at any rate, would always keep the attitude of contempt,—its face turned away.

One other pleasure she provided herself with, soon after this road was opened,—a pleasure in which religious devotion and race antagonism were so closely blended that it would have puzzled the subtlest of priests to de-cide whether her act were a sin or a virtue. She caused to be set up, upon every one of the soft rounded hills which made the beautiful rolling sides of that part of the valley, a large wooden cross; not a hill in sight of her house left without the sacred emblem of her faith. "That the heretics may know, when they go by, that they are on the estate of a good Catholic," she said, "and that the faithful may be reminded to pray. There have been miracles of conversion wrought on the most hardened by a sudden sight of the Blessed Cross."

There they stood, summer and winter, rain and shine, the silent, solemn, outstretched arms, and became landmarks to many a guideless traveller who had been told that his way would be by the first turn to the left or the right, after passing the last one of the Señora Moreno's crosses, which he couldn't miss seeing. And who shall say that it did not often happen that the crosses bore a sudden message to some idle heart journeying by, and thus justified the pious half of the Señora's impulse? Certain it is, that many a good Catholic halted and crossed himself when he first beheld them, in the lonely places, standing out in sudden relief against the blue sky; and if he said a swift short prayer at the sight, was he not so much the better?

The house was of adobe, low, with a wide veranda on the three sides of the inner court, and a still broader one across the entire front, which looked to the south. These verandas, especially those on the inner court, were supplemen-tary rooms to the house. The greater part of the family life went on in them. No-body stayed inside the walls, except when it was necessary. All the kitchen work, except the actual cooking, was done here, in front of the kitchen doors and windows. Babies slept, were washed, sat in the dirt, and played, on the ve-randa. The women said their prayers, took their naps, and wove their lace there. Old Juanita shelled her beans there, and threw the pods down on the tile floor, till towards night they were sometimes piled up high around her, like corn-husks at a husking. The herdsmen and shepherds smoked there, lounged there, trained their dogs there; there the young made love, and the old dozed; the benches, which ran the entire length of the walls, were worn into hollows, and shone like satin; the tiled floors also were broken and sunk in places, making little wells, which filled up in times of hard rains, and were then an invaluable addition to the children's resources for amusement, and also to the comfort of the dogs, cats, and fowls, who picked about among them, taking sips from each.

The arched veranda along the front was a delightsome place. It must have been eighty feet long, at least, for the doors of five large rooms opened on it. The two western-most rooms had been added on, and made four steps higher than the others; which gave to that end of the veranda the look of a balcony, or loggia. Here the Señora kept her flowers; great red water-jars, hand-made by the Indians of San Luis Obispo Mission, stood in close rows against the walls, and in them were always growing fine geraniums, carnations, and yellow-flowered musk. The Señora's passion for musk she had inherited from her mother. It was so strong that she sometimes wondered at it; and one day, as she sat with Father Salvierderra in the veranda, she picked a handful of the blossoms, and giving them to him, said, "I do not know why it is, but it seems to me if I were dead I could be brought to life by the smell of musk."

"It is in your blood, Señora," the old monk replied. "When I was last in your father's house in Seville, your mother sent for me to her room, and under her window was a stone balcony full of growing musk, which so filled the room with its odor that I was like to faint. But she said it cured her of diseases, and without it she fell ill. You were a baby then."

"Yes," cried the Señora, "but I recollect that balcony. I recollect being lifted up to a window, and looking down into a bed of blooming yellow flowers; but I did not know what they were. How strange!"

"No. Not strange, daughter," replied Father Salvierderra. "It would have been stranger if you had not acquired the taste, thus drawing it in with the mother's milk. It would behoove mothers to remember this far more than they do."

Besides the geraniums and carnations and musk in the red jars, there were many sorts of climbing vines,—some coming from the ground, and twining around the pillars of the veranda; some growing in great bowls, swung by cords from the roof of the veranda, or set on shelves against the walls. These bowls were of gray stone, hollowed and polished, shining smooth inside and out. They also had been made by the Indians, nobody knew how many ages ago, scooped and polished by the patient creatures, with only stones for tools.

Among these vines, singing from morning till night, hung the Señora's canaries and finches, half a dozen of each, all of different generations, raised by the Señora. She was never without a young bird-family on hand; and all the way from Bonaventura to Monterey, it was thought a piece of good luck to come into possession of a canary or finch of Señora Moreno's raising.

Between the veranda and the river meadows, out on which it looked, all was garden, orange grove, and almond orchard; the orange grove always green, never without snowy bloom or golden fruit; the garden never without flowers, summer or winter; and the almond orchard, in early spring, a fluttering canopy of pink and white petals, which, seen from the hills on the opposite side of the river, looked as if rosy sunrise clouds had fallen, and become tangled in the tree-tops. On either hand stretched away other orchards,—peach, apricot, pear, apple, pomegranate; and beyond these, vineyards. Nothing was to be seen but verdure or bloom or fruit, at whatever time of year you sat on the Señora's south veranda.

A wide straight walk shaded by a trellis so knotted and twisted with grapevines that little was to be seen of the trellis wood-work, led straight down from the veranda steps, through the middle of the garden, to a little brook at the foot of it. Across this brook, in the shade of a dozen gnarled old willow-trees, were set the broad flat stone washboards on which was done all the family washing. No long dawdling, and no running away from work on the part of the maids, thus close to the eye of the Señora at the upper end of the garden; and if they had known how picturesque they looked there, kneeling on the grass, lifting the dripping linen out of the water, rubbing it back and forth on the stones, sousing it, wringing it, splashing the clear water in each other's faces, they would have been content to stay at the washing day in and day out, for there was always somebody to look on from above. Hardly a day passed that the Señora had not visitors. She was still a person of note; her house the natural resting-place for all who journeyed through the valley; and whoever came, spent all of his time, when not eating, sleeping, or walking over the place, sitting with the Señora on the sunny veranda. Few days in winter were cold enough, and in summer the day must be hot indeed to drive the Señora and her friends indoors. There stood on the veranda three carved oaken chairs, and a carved bench, also of oak, which had been brought to the Señora for safe keeping by the faithful old sacristan of San Luis Rey, at the time of the occupation of that Mission by the United States troops, soon after the conquest of California. Aghast at the sacrilegious acts of the soldiers, who were quartered in the very church itself, and amused themselves by making targets of the eyes and noses of the saints' statues, the sacristan, stealthily, day by day and night after night, bore out of the church all that he dared to remove, burying some articles in cottonwood copses, hiding others in his own poor little hovel, until he had wagon-loads of sacred treasures. Then, still more stealthily, he carried them, a few at a time, concealed in the bottom of a cart, under a load of hay or of brush, to the house of the Señora, who felt herself deeply honored by his confidence, and received everything as a sacred trust, to be given back into the hands of the Church again, whenever the Missions should be restored, of which at that time all Catholics had good hope. And so it had come about that no bedroom in the Señora's house was without a picture or a statue of a saint or of the Madonna; and some had two; and in the little chapel in the garden the altar was surrounded by a really imposing row of holy and apostolic figures, which had looked down on the splendid ceremonies of the San Luis Rey Mission, in Father Peyri's time, no more benignly than they now did on the humbler worship of the Señora's family in its diminished estate. That one had lost an eye, another an arm, that the once brilliant colors of the drapery were now faded and shabby, only enhanced the tender reverence with which the Señora knelt before them, her eyes filling with indignant tears at thought of the heretic hands which had wrought such defilement. Even the crumbling wreaths which had been placed on some of these statues' heads at the time of the last ceremonial at which they had figured in the mission, had been brought away with them by the devout sacristan, and the Señora had replaced each one, holding it only a degree less sacred than the statue itself.

This chapel was dearer to the Señora than her house. It had been built by the General in the second year of their married life. In it her four children had been christened, and from it all but one, her handsome Felipe, had been buried while they were yet infants. In the General's time, while the estate was at its best, and hundreds of Indians living within its borders, there was many a Sunday when the scene to be witnessed there was like the scenes at the Missions,— the chapel full of kneeling men and women; those who could not find room inside kneeling on the garden walks outside; Father Salvierderra, in gorgeous vestments, coming, at close of the services, slowly down the aisle, the close-packed rows of worshippers parting to right and left to let him through, all looking up eagerly for his blessing, women giving him offerings of fruit or flowers, and holding up their babies that he might lay his hands on their heads. No one but Father Salvierderra had ever officiated in the Moreno chapel, or heard the confession of a Moreno. He was a Franciscan, one of the few now left in the country; so revered and beloved by all who had come under his influence, that they would wait long months without the offices of the Church, rather than confess their sins or confide their perplexities to any one else. From this deep-seated attachment on the part of the Indians and the older Mexican families in the country to the Franciscan Order, there had grown up, not unnaturally, some jealousy of them in the minds of the later-come secular priests, and the position of the few monks left was not wholly a pleasant one. It had even been rumored that they were to be forbidden to continue longer their practice of going up and down the country, ministering everywhere; were to be compelled to restrict their labors to their own colleges at Santa Barbara and Santa Inez. When something to this effect was one day said in the Señora Moreno's presence, two scarlet spots sprang on her cheeks, and before she bethought herself, she exclaimed, "That day, I burn down my chapel!"

Luckily, nobody but Felipe heard the rash threat, and his exclamation of unbounded astonishment recalled the Señora to herself.

"I spoke rashly, my son," she said. "The Church is to be obeyed always; but the Franciscan Fathers are responsible to no one but the Superior of their own order; and there is no one in this land who has the authority to forbid their journeying and ministering to whoever desires their offices. As for these Catalan priests who are coming in here, I cannot abide them. No Catalan but has bad blood in his veins!"

There was every reason in the world why the Señora should be thus warmly attached to the Franciscan Order. From her earliest recollections the gray gown and cowl had been familiar to her eyes, and had represented the things which she was taught to hold most sacred and dear. Father Salvierderra himself had come from Mexico to Monterey in the same ship which had brought her father to be the commandante of the Santa Barbara Presidio; and her best-beloved uncle, her father's eldest brother, was at that time the Superior of the Santa Barbara Mission. The sentiment and romance of her youth were almost equally divided between the gayeties, excitements, adornments of the life at the Presidio, and the ceremonies and devotions of the life at the Mission. She was famed as the most beautiful girl in the country. Men of the army, men of the navy, and men of the Church, alike adored her. Her name was a toast from Monterey to San Diego. When at last she was wooed and won by Felipe Moreno, one of the most distinguished of the Mexican generals, her wedding ceremonies were the most splendid ever seen in the country. The right tower of the Mission church at Santa Barbara had been just completed, and it was arranged that the consecration of this tower should take place at the time of her wedding, and that her wedding feast should be spread in the long outside corridor of the Mission building. The whole country, far and near, was bid. The feast lasted three days; open tables to everybody; singing, dancing, eating, drinking, and making merry. At that time there were long streets of Indian houses stretching eastward from the Mission; before each of these houses was built a booth of green boughs. The Indians, as well as the Fathers from all the other Missions, were invited to come. The Indians came in bands, singing songs and bringing gifts. As they appeared, the Santa Barbara Indians went out to meet them, also singing, bearing gifts, and strewing seeds on the ground, in token of welcome. The young Señora and her bridegroom, splendidly clothed, were seen of all, and greeted, whenever they appeared, by showers of seeds and grains and blossoms. On the third day, still in their wedding attire, and bearing lighted candles in their hands, they walked with the monks in a procession, round and round the new tower, the monks chanting, and sprinkling incense and holy water on its walls, the ceremony seeming to all devout beholders to give a blessed consecration to the union of the young pair as well as to the newly completed tower. After this they journeyed in state, accompanied by several of the General's aids and officers, and by two Franciscan Fathers, up to Monterey, stopping on their way at all the Missions, and being warmly welcomed and entertained at each.

General Moreno was much beloved by both army and Church. In many of the frequent clashings between the military and the ecclesiastical powers he, being as devout and enthusiastic a Catholic as he was zealous and enthusiastic a soldier, had had the good fortune to be of material assistance to each party. The Indians also knew his name well, having heard it many times mentioned with public thanksgivings in the Mission churches, after some signal service he had rendered to the Fathers either in Mexico or Monterey. And now, by taking as his bride the daughter of a distinguished officer, and the niece of the Santa Barbara Superior, he had linked himself anew to the two dominant powers and interests of the country.

When they reached San Luis Obispo, the whole Indian population turned out to meet them, the Padre walking at the head. As they approached the Mission doors the Indians swarmed closer and closer and still closer, took the

General's horse by the head, and finally almost by actual force compelled him to allow himself to be lifted into a blanket, held high up by twenty strong men; and thus he was borne up the steps, across the corridor, and into the Padre's room. It was a position ludicrously undignified in itself, but the General submitted to it good-naturedly.

"Oh, let them do it, if they like," he cried, laughingly, to Padre Martinez, who was endeavoring to quiet the Indians and hold them back; "Let them do it. It pleases the poor creatures."

On the morning of their departure, the good Padre, having exhausted all his resources for entertaining his distinguished guests, caused to be driven past the corridors, for their inspection, all the poultry belonging to the Mission. The procession took an hour to pass. For music, there was the squeaking, cackling, hissing, gobbling, crowing, quacking of the fowls, combined with the screaming, scolding, and whip-cracking of the excited Indian marshals of the lines. First came the turkeys, then the roosters, then the white hens, then the black, and then the yellow; next the ducks, and at the tail of the spectacle long files of geese, some strutting, some half flying and hissing in resentment and terror at the unwonted coercions to which they were subjected. The Indians had been hard at work all night capturing, sorting, assorting, and guarding the rank and file of their novel pageant. It would be safe to say that a droller sight never was seen, and never will be, on the Pacific coast or any other. Before it was done with, the General and his bride had nearly died with laughter; and the General could never allude to it without laughing almost as heartily again.

At Monterey they were more magnificently fêted; at the Presidio, at the Mission, on board Spanish, Mexican, and Russian ships lying in harbor, balls, dances, bullfights, dinners, all that the country knew of festivity, was lavished on the beautiful and winning young bride. The belles of the coast, from San Diego up, had all gathered at Monterey for these gayeties; but not one of them could be for a moment compared to her. This was the beginning of the Señora's life as a married woman. She was then just twenty. A close observer would have seen even then, underneath the joyous smile, the laughing eye, the merry voice, a look thoughtful, tender, earnest, at times enthusiastic. This look was the reflection of those qualities in her, then hardly aroused, which made her, as years developed her character and stormy fates thickened around her life, the unflinching comrade of her soldier husband, the passionate adherent of the Church. Through wars, insurrections, revolutions, downfalls, Spanish, Mexican, civil, ecclesiastical, her standpoint, her poise, remained the same. She simply grew more and more proudly, passionately, a Spaniard and a Moreno; more and more stanchly and fierily a Catholic, and a lover of the Franciscans.

During the height of the despoiling and plundering of the Missions, under the Secularization Act, she was for a few years almost beside herself. More than once she journeyed alone, when the journey was by no means without danger, to Monterey, to stir up the Prefect of the Missions to more energetic action, to implore the governmental authorities to interfere, and protect the Church's property. It was largely in consequence of her eloquent entreaties that Governor Micheltorena issued his bootless order, restoring to the Church all the Missions south of San Luis Obispo. But this order cost Micheltorena his political head, and General Moreno was severely wounded in one of the skirmishes of the insurrection which drove Micheltorena out of the country.

In silence and bitter humiliation the Señora nursed her husband back to health again, and resolved to meddle no more in the affairs of her unhappy country and still more unhappy Church. As year by year she saw the ruin of the Missions steadily going on, their vast properties melting away, like dew before the sun, in the hands of dishonest administrators and politicians, the Church powerless to contend with the unprincipled greed in high places, her beloved Franciscan Fathers driven from the country or dying of starvation at their posts, she submitted herself to what, she was forced to admit, seemed to be the inscrutable will of God for the discipline and humiliation of the Church. In a sort of bewildered resignation she waited to see what farther sufferings were to come, to fill up the measure of the punishment which, for some mysterious purpose, the faithful must endure. But when close upon all this discomfiture and humiliation of her Church followed the discomfiture and humiliation of her country in war, and the near and evident danger of an English-speaking peoples possessing the land, all the smothered fire of the Señora's nature broke out afresh. With unfaltering hands she buckled on her husband's sword, and with dry eyes saw him go forth to fight. She had but one regret, that she was not the mother of sons to fight also.

"Would thou wert a man, Felipe," she exclaimed again and again in tones the child never forgot. "Would thou wert a man, that thou might go also to fight these foreigners!"

Any race under the sun would have been to the Señora less hateful than the American. She had scorned them in her girlhood, when they came trading to post after post. She scorned them still. The idea of being forced to wage a war with pedlers was to her too monstrous to be believed. In the outset she had no doubt that the Mexicans would win in the contest.

"What!" she cried, "shall we who won independence from Spain, be beaten by these traders? It is impossible!"

When her husband was brought home to her dead, killed in the last fight the Mexican forces made, she said icily, "He would have chosen to die rather than to have been forced to see his country in the hands of the enemy." And she was almost frightened at herself to see how this thought, as it dwelt in her mind, slew the grief in her heart. She had believed she could not live if her husband were to be taken away from her; but she found herself often glad that he was dead,—glad that he was spared the sight and the knowledge of the things which happened; and even the yearning tenderness with which her imagination pictured him among the saints, was often turned into a fierce wondering whether indignation did not fill his soul, even in heaven, at the way things were going in the land for whose sake he had died.

Out of such throes as these had been born the second nature which made Señora Moreno the silent, reserved, stern, implacable woman they knew, who knew her first when she was sixty. Of the gay, tender, sentimental girl, who danced and laughed with the officers, and prayed and confessed with the Fathers, forty years before, there was small trace left now, in the low-voiced, white-haired, aged woman, silent, unsmiling, placid-faced, who manœuvred with her son and her head shepherd alike, to bring it about that a handful of Indians might once more confess their sins to a Franciscan monk in the Moreno chapel.

Discussion Questions

1. *Ramona*, as a piece of fiction, brought to thousands of readers the picture of a peaceful and beautiful California under the rule of Spanish missionaries. From the selection you have just read, isolate and discuss the sort of details Jackson uses to portray the peaceful pre-American world. How does she describe Señora Moreno's early life? Does the narration of Señora Moreno's life work to deliver Jackson's antigovernment stance?

2. If this were your only source of information about life in California in the mid-nineteenth century, what opinions would you draw about the relationship between the Indians and the Church? About the Americans and the missions? How is Helen Hunt Jackson's perspective different from Richard White's view of the Spanish and the Catholic Church in California? How is it different from David Gutiérrez's account of Mexicans in California?

Writing Suggestions

1. Write a personal essay or journal entry reflecting on the different accounts of life in California under the mission rule that we have read in this chapter. What are your personal responses to these different authors? What do you find reassuring or disturbing? What information is new to you, and what have you learned before? Respond to the writings of Junipero Serra, Richard White, David Gutiérrez, and Helen Hunt Jackson in your reflection, and use specific details from each author in your essay.

2. Research the life of Helen Hunt Jackson, using both the Internet and the library. Write a paper about her original intentions in writing *Ramona*, and about her previous body of work, *A Century of Dishonor*. Discuss both her efforts to inform the U.S. Congress about the plight of the Native Americans in California and the results of her writing. Also research the pageantry and tourism that grew up around the story of *Ramona*, and search on the Web for information about the town of Ramona and the Ramona Days festivals. In your paper, answer the following research question: Was Helen Hunt Jackson successful in her attempt to draw attention to and aid the plight of Native Americans in California?

Americans and the California Dream

Beyond Eldorado

KEVIN STARR

Kevin Starr is the state librarian of California at the California State Library in Sacramento. He holds graduate degrees from Harvard and The University of California at Berkeley and is the author of nine books, including the five that make up the *Americans and the California Dream* series. Starr is a renowned author and historian and has won both the Guggenheim Fellowship and the Gold Medal of the Commonwealth Club of California. In this selection from the chapter entitled "Beyond Eldorado," from *Americans and the California Dream*, Starr describes vividly the ups and downs of life in Gold Rush California.

II

As epic experience, the Gold Rush was both Iliad and Odyssey. It was an Odyssey in that it was a wandering away from home, a saga of resourcefulness, a poem of sea, earth, loyalty, and return. It was an Iliad in that it was a cruel foreign war, a saga of communal ambition and collective misbehavior, a poem of expatriation, hostile gods, and betrayal. At first impression, the years 1849–1851 seem more burdened with suffering than victory, more Iliad than Odyssey. From the day sails were set for the voyage around the Horn or oxen goaded on the first step of the transcontinental trek, the hardships of the enterprise were overwhelming.

Of the more than 500 vessels that left Eastern ports for California in 1849, the majority sailed around the Horn. Americans traveling thus faced a voyage of 15,000 miles which took five months—and which could take as long as eight—in crowded ships hastily fitted out and most likely past their best sailing days. If the Forty-niner could afford to take a steamer from New York to Chagres, cross the Isthmus of Panama by dugout canoe up the Chagres River and by mule go over the mountains to Panama City, then sail by steamer to San Francisco, he could cut the time of the voyage by two-thirds, providing that he was willing to take his chances with the cholera, malaria, and dysentery of the Panama crossing. He might lie moaning in his bunk the first weeks out, spend terror-filled days and nights in the Straits of Magellan, or in later months limp with sore joints and swollen feet; yet seasickness, shipwreck, and scurvy seemed but obvious hardships compared to the psychological stresses of spending half a year in a floating tenement, squeezed into dark and fetid cabins, eating bad food, and never being alone. There were signs of psychic strain: ugly incidents, persecutions, assaults. Somewhere off the south-eastern coast of South America burials at sea began, of those too weak to stand the mounting hardships. Further on, off the southwestern coast of South America, a ship could lie becalmed for weeks. Empty sky and horizon, waveless sea, unbearable heat, not even the solace of motion—the monotony escalated into torture. Men paced the decks in desperation, climbed the rigging, or lay prostrate in their bunks staring at the bulkhead. They began to gamble and to drink. Some went insane and had to be shackled in a storeroom for the remainder of the voyage, their California adventure, over before it started, reduced to years in the Stockton Asylum or a merciful death in San Francisco. Grudges which would have been insignificant on land grew into violent hatreds and were settled with fists and knives. Tainted meat, wormy biscuit, foul water, the conviction that every corner was being cut in the matter of provisions, set passengers against crew. Passengers on the *Osceola* accused one steward of making their duff with dirty bath water. Unused to the customs of the sea, passengers found the captain a tyrant, which he often was. Committees of grievances met with profanity and the threat of irons.

The journey overland was no better. "Any man who makes a trip by land to California," observed Alonzo Delano in October 1849, after having himself done so, "deserves to find a fortune."

Rufus Porter, a scientific writer, proposed the feasibility of constructing steam-driven dirigibles to take passengers to California at 100 miles per hour, and he went so far as to float stock in an airship company. Emigrants in covered wagons, family people for the most part, farmers and mechanics, had to be content with twelve miles a day. A migration now celebrated in national myth as the westering trek of the American people, the crossing of the continent seemed to those who walked it to be a weary succession of prairies, deserts, mountains, painfully measured out in the plod of hooves and the creak of wheels. One could die in a variety of ways: from fever, poisoning, the accidental discharge of guns, gangrene. A wagon could roll backward down a mountain grade and crush those behind it. An oak tree camped under during a stormy night, struck by lightning, could fall and destroy a sleeping family. Men, even good men, under stress, might resort to gun and bowie knife—and be shot or skewered by someone more adept. If one were dying, and things were bad for the others, he could be left on the trailside to die alone. Children lost both parents. Women sat sobbing on the side of the trail as men trekked off to reach water or tried to repair an axle before the main caravan got too far ahead. Gravesites lined the overland trail ("may he rest peaceably in this savage unknown country"), becoming more and more frequent along the banks of the Humboldt River, where progress became most difficult. Animal carcasses littered the Humboldt Sink, together with broken wagons, abandoned furniture, trunks of clothes, cases of books. Men quarreled and made bad decisions, striking off on erroneous routes. One diarist felt that he had witnessed the nadir of human malice when he discovered signs left behind deliberately giving false information about cut-offs so that parties a day or two ahead might not be overtaken and forced to share grazing and water.

Descending the formidable Sierras just ahead of the winter snows, overland emigrants arrived in California tattered, weatherbeaten, emaciated. Many were too exhausted to take to the mines. Many died from the lingering effects of the journey. When it came down to it, what had they and those arriving by sea come to? Further hardship and squalor. For all their swaggering names and later aura of romance, mining camps were foul collections of tents and shacks, and mining was a back-breaking labor whose discomforts included heat prostration, pneumonia, rheumatism, and hernia.

Again, there were the usual frontier ways of dying from diseases carried by rats, fleas, and lice, and kept persistent by contaminated water: cholera, malaria, dysentery, typhoid. (William Stephen Hamilton, son of Alexander Hamilton, having crossed the plains and worked in the mines, died of cholera in Sacramento on 6 or 7 August 1850 and was buried in a trench alongside other victims.) Exhausted from work in the mines and from a just completed sea voyage or transcontinental journey, miners had little resistance once they became ill. If they were not as lucky as Edward Gould Buffum, who found some sprouting beans dropped along the trail, they could die of scurvy, after a painful illness. A more distinctly Californian end was met by those mauled to death by grizzly bears. As mining grew more complicated it grew more dangerous. There were landslides and cave-ins. "Indeed, it always seemed to me," noted one writer, "strange and unaccountable that men should die in California—they came there for so short a time, and for so different a purpose; unless it should be thought they had gone twenty thousand miles simply for that."

But die they did, by the thousands. Before they could even get to the mines, they died in San Francisco. "Early this morning the body of a dead man was found near our tent," observed Enos Christman on the evening of 24 February 1849, camping out in the Happy Valley area south of the city— "no unusual occurrence." An obituary in *The Pacific* for 8 October 1852 dramatized better than statistics the nightmare which could be Eldorado. "Died," it read, "on Wednesday morning, September 6th, a daughter of Mr. and Mrs. Wise, lately deceased, aged about three years. The family came to California some months ago from some part of South America. The marriage certificate of the parents, found among their papers, is dated in Clay, Onondaga County, New York. On arriving here they went to the mines. Being unfortunate, they returned to the vicinity of Sacramento and commenced preparations for cultivating some land. But they were soon taken sick and weak and exhausted; they returned to this city, where they arrived some three weeks ago. A kind friend, learning of their destitution and distress, secured their admission into the hospital. They had been there but a few days when they wrote a note to him saying that if they were left there they must certainly die of want. Upon seeing their condition, he immediately removed them to his own dwelling, where one child soon died. Shortly the father followed, and soon the mother also, and this poor little sick girl was brought to the [San Francisco Orphan] Asylum, too sick and exhausted to be able to speak. Medical attendance was immediately called, and everything was done that could be to restore her, but she was too weak. She survived only three days and fell asleep. Thus a whole family was cut down in the space of a few days, and now lie side by side in their last resting place."

Incidents of lonely deaths fill Gold Rush journals, men discovered dead in their tents after being missed for a week or so from the diggings, or dead in their bunks after a night in a Stockton or Marysville flophouse. "It is an everyday occurrence," wrote Garrett Low from Nevada City on 29 August 1851, "to see a coffin carried on the shoulders of two men, who are the only mourners and only witnesses of the burial of some stranger whose name they do not know." Delirium tremens carried off more than its share of Argonauts. John Steele, age eighteen, spent a night of horrors in a flophouse in the Feather River area in 1851. Drunken curses from a number of bunks kept him awake all night. One may lay shrieking and writhing in delirium tremens. About dawn he died. "A well dressed young man was seen, very drunk, lying on the ground," ran an entry by J. D. B. Stillman in November 1850 at Sacramento, "and a couple of boys we have with us took him to a shelter and medical aid was rendered him, but he died and was buried." Each squalid death—and there were thousands—turned California's golden fleece into a vomit-stained shroud.

As if such deaths were not enough, men killed each other. A truly Homeric number of homicides fills the literature of the Gold Rush, a catalogue of slit throats, gunshot wounds, and crushed skulls. Murder, especially from the latter part of 1850 through 1851, became a way of life. Howard C. Gardiner witnessed eight deliberate killings, so horrible that forty years later he could not bear to recollect them in detail. In the course of working his diggings near Downieville, John Steele uncovered the corpse of a young man shot through the head. Both the anonymous man's death and Steel's grisly discovery were not uncommon occurrences. In a saloon at Nevada City, listening with a hushed crowd to a tenor, accompanied by the violin, singing the plaintive notes of Robert Burns's "Highland Mary," Steele found himself dropping to the floor as shots rang out. Seconds later three men lay dead. At another camp where Steele was working, a miner in a fit of drunken rage killed his wife. He was lynched almost at once, leaving a one-year-old child where yesterday there had been a family. To his horror Steele found the atmosphere of violence infectious. He quarreled with his partner, with whom he had crossed the plains, over a minor matter. Within seconds both had drawn weapons. Luckily they both came to their senses; upon most such occasions Americans began to blaze away. "Yesterday one American shot another in the street," Enos Christman noted from Sonora in 1850, "and the occurrence was not noticed as much as a dog fight at home."

Sonora, in Tuolumne County, was among the most violent of mining camps. For the third week of June 1850 William Perkins listed four killings: two Massachusetts men were robbed and had their throats slit as they slept in their tent; a Chilean was shot to death in a gun fight; and a Frenchman stabbed a Mexican. Two weeks later, there were six murders within seven days. Coming home one evening, Perkins, who lived on the main street, tripped over the body of a man stabbed to death on his doorstep. The gambling hardly stopped, he noted one evening, when a man shot another dead at the bar of the saloon. "It is surprising," noted Perkins, "how indifferent people become to the sight of violence and bloodshed in this country."

In reaction, lynch law could be equally capricious and violent. An innocent French sailor was kicked to death in San Francisco as a suspected arsonist. At Weber in 1849 William Kelly saw "one lad shorn of the rims of his ears, and seared deeply in the cheek with a red-hot iron, for the theft of a small coffee-tin." Josiah Royce would later comment at length upon how the lynching habit brought out the most vicious side of the American character. Certainly one sees his point when reading accounts of mob justice. At Weaver's Creek Edward Gould Buffum mounted a stump and pleaded with a mob "in the name of God, humanity, and law" not to lynch three Spanish-speaking men who did not know enough English to understand what they were being charged with. Buffum was told to keep quiet or he would swing with them. Horrified, Buffum watched as the three pleading men were hoisted to their doom. No wonder diarists speculated that the Gold Rush might represent a communal relapse into barbarism on the part of Americans! "Whatever depravity there is in man's heart," observed J. D. B. Stillman, "now shows itself without fear and without restraint."

Men who had come in hope now slid into depression and defeat. Realizing, as most did, that they would not strike it rich, they brooded over what they had become and what they had failed to do. A sense of aborted effort undercut the continual attempts at rollicking good humor in Gold Rush songs. Men grew tired of themselves, tired of the ambitions and petty hopes which had brought them to such desperate ends. "Suicides, caused by disappointment," wrote home an adventurer of 1849, "are as numerous as the deaths resulting from natural causes."

Was it worth it? Forty-niners asked themselves, beholding broken dreams and dragging about broken bodies, seeing months of digging yield barely a living wage, seeing men killed and going mad and weeping like confused children. Was it worth it? Even as he landed in San Francisco, Enos Christman knew that "thousands will curse the day that brought them to this golden land." Even as they ascended into the foothills of the Sierras, they beheld deserted clusters of shacks where mining had proven futile, or encountered emaciated men coming down the trails of the Mother Lode, warning them not to waste their time, to go back. Young men, they came with the hopes of youth. "This country is no doubt a great place to give a young man a fair start in the world," Jasper Hill wrote to his parents, "as he can make money quite fast by being industrious and economical." Hill failed, as did George W. B. Evans, an attorney from Defiance, Ohio, who left family and practice to make the journey across the parched and bandit-infested Mexican route. Hill's journal, kept in the Mariposa mines, is a record of one misery after another. No mail reached him. He suffered from scurvy and rheumatism. He spent dreary days confined to a rude cabin. He found no gold. After a year, he went to Sacramento and died. "It was heart-rending," wrote John Hale of such disappointed miners, "to see stout-hearted men shedding tears over their horrible situation, not knowing what to do."

Those who survived did what they could. They dug for wages, did day labor on the docks of San Francisco, Sacramento, and Stockton, hauled freight—anything to keep alive and perhaps earn the price of a ticket home. In diaries and journals and letters they admitted that it all had not amounted to much. "A residence here at present," Franklin Langworthy felt of his California sojourn, "is a pilgrimage in a strange land, a banishment from good society, a living death, and a punishment of the worst kind, and the time spent here ought to be considered as a blank period in existence, and accordingly struck from the record of one's days." Alonzo Delano felt very bitter toward promotional writers and propagandists and all their exaggerated claims for the territory. "I think when the sufferings of the emigrants both on the plains and after their arrival is known at home," he wrote, "our people will begin to see California stripped of her gaudy robes, her paint and outward adornments, which have been so liberally heaped upon her by thoughtless letter-writers and culpable editors, and they will be content to stay at home and reap their own grain, and enjoy the comforts which they really possess, rather than come here to starve or pick up what would be thrown from their own tables at home to satisfy the cravings of hunger. The greatness of California! Faugh! Great for what and for whom? Great at present as an outlet to a portion of the surplus wheat, pork and clothes, blacklegs, prostitutes and vicious at home, and for the would-be politicians of the country and the ultras who quarrel over us in Washington."

III

This was the Gold Rush as Iliad, as a disastrous expedition to foreign shores. Had Helen been worth it to Trojan or Greek? After the fall of Troy, Odysseus went home and there was a new poem, an Odyssey, soaked through with the consolations of sensation and consciousness which keep men alive and coping and, no matter what is suffered, able to affirm. The Gold Rush had its Odyssey, its times when experience invigorated and the gods were good.

Hope gave zest to the long sea voyage. "California, the El Dorado of our hopes," intoned the toastmaster during Fourth of July festivities aboard the

Henry Lee as it sailed down the lower southeast coast of South America in the year 1849. "May we not be disappointed, but find stores of golden treasures to gladden our hearts, and make ample amends for the ills and trials of acquisition. May our families and friends be enabled to rejoice in our success, and all end well." Pleasant hours were passed on deck overhauling gear, talking of gold and the second chance they thought they might be finding. Ships returning from California with gold aboard, which they encountered at sea or at anchor in the harbors of Rio de Janeiro or Valparaiso, intensified their expectancy to an exquisite pitch. Sailing at last through the Golden Gate, Americans drank in every detail of the Republic's new Pacific harbor, spectacular in its spaciousness, mountain-guarded and Mediterranean. They were almost ready to swim ashore, to feel earth under foot, and to get moving to the mines.

The voyage had not been without its pleasures. The sea could be beautiful, clear and bracing days, nights radiant with the stars of the Southern Hemisphere. Tropical sunsets delighted Americans with a range of color unknown in northern latitudes. Porpoises played about the prow. A sailfish leapt in the distance. An albatross soared overhead. Whales and sea turtles surfaced, then returned to unknown depths. Beauty, the sense of being in a world apart, the rhythmic rocking of the ship, prompted recollection. There was time for reading and for thought, for reflection upon past life and present purposes. Harold Gardiner of Sag Harbor, Long Island, trained himself to brave the maintop. Roped to mast and spar he would gaze by the hour at the sea and the sky, or read—three times—*The Three Musketeers*. He never again enjoyed a book so much. Gardiner and other young landsmen with time on their hands learned the craft of the sea. They helped the crew, hoping to pass the time and hasten the voyage. Standing the test of deck and rigging in storms off Cape Horn, they felt they were preparing for California. In one case, the captain proving incompetent, the crew elected a passenger to take command.

The monotony which drove men to madness could also be a challenge to ingenuity and cooperation. Men formed debating societies, musical ensembles, and dramatic groups. They attended lectures. "In the evening," wrote John Stone of Friday, 1 June 1849, aboard the *Robert Bowne*, "we had a lecture on Phrenology by Mr. Abbott, who examined several heads." Two weeks later Stone "went with a few others at the evening hour to hear Wm. Hamilton—the irrepressible dandy in tight boots and straps, wig and dyed whiskers both on sea and land—read some original sketches about London and its surroundings or suburbs." Washington's Birthday, Thanksgiving, and the Fourth of July called for day-long celebrations, with sermons, speeches, military marching, and banquets followed by the grandiloquent toasts of the American nineteenth century. Men did not entirely lose their sense of humor. A group of young passengers secretly lowered a boat one night from the *James W. Paige* and simulated a piratical boarding. Another night on the same ship an excellent mimic walked out on the deck attired like the captain and in the captain's voice gave a string of contradictory orders to a baffled crew.

Sharing laughter at such capers, talking together of the future, men felt a solidarity with their fellows. "We are fast becoming a united family," wrote one diarist. "It is easily seen that our common interests are causing us to become necessary to one another, and when the time comes to disband it, it will be with many regrets that we are forced to separate."

The disruption of daily life for overland travelers was less dramatic than for those who sailed. Caravans of prairie schooners kept the organization and rhythms of village life. There were courtings, marriages, births, and there was more to do. At night men sat talking around campfires, planning for the next day, and women saw to the care of the household. Pleasures were less contrived than those aboard ship, more part of frontier life. "Sunday we had preaching by the Rev. Mr. Donleavy," Charles F. Putnam wrote home to his parents, as his wagon train rested twenty-five miles outside of Independence, Missouri; "our tent was crowded with young ladies. We set our table and spread a table cloth and they eat and drank as much milk as any ladies I ever saw set down to a table. We are now on a Prairie it is the most beautiful sight I ever saw they are filled with beautiful flowers and they cover over a space as far as the eye can reach."

As they did against the sea, young men tested themselves against the continent. Lorenzo Sawyer, a lawyer from Wisconsin, felt that crossing the plains had expanded his imagination and strengthened his grip on life. Whether he found gold or not, remained in California or not, it had been worth it. "I have crossed the broad continent of America from shore to shore," Sawyer exulted, "have seen its magnificent lakes and rivers, have traversed its almost illimitable plains, have stood upon the Rocky, and other mountains, where the eye could take in a circle of perhaps three hundred miles diameter. I have been upon the desert and again upon the Sierra Nevada, have seen human nature under a great variety of circumstances, and in every stage of development from the most degraded specimens of the American savage to the intellectual and polished European race. I feel that I have a more enlarged, a more comprehensive view of the works of nature, a more accurate conception, and a nicer appreciation of their beauty and grandeur. I am sensible that I have obtained a more thorough knowledge of mankind, of their character, their energies and capabilities, of the motives and springs that govern human actions. In short, I feel that I am better acquainted with the world, my fellow man and myself, and I am thus far satisfied with my enterprise, though, in some respects it may not turn out as favorable as I could wish."

Sawyer's sense of release, of excitement and high drama expanding his self-image and self-possession, was typical of an elation often felt during the Gold Rush. Tearing themselves free from routines of farm and city, from dull professions, stores, and clerkships, Americans threw themselves, indeed staked their lives upon, an unprecedented hope, a way, in striking it rich, of pushing instantaneously into the possession of human happiness. In time they learned better. The lesson broke some and deepened others. But for the moment it was liberating to be in pursuit of a golden dream, to be escaping the destiny of circumstance. Standing on the deck of a steamer as it sailed from New York in March 1849, Howard Gardiner, who had led an ordinary life, envisioned himself another Childe Harold, bound for adventure on a distant coast. "Adieu, Adieu," Gardiner quoted to himself,

> My native shore
> Fades o'er the waters blue;
> The night winds sigh, the breakers roar,
> And shrieks the wild sea mew.
> Yon sun that sets upon the sea,
> We follow in his flight;
> Farewell awhile to him and thee,
> My Native Land—Good Night!

Would Gardiner ever again have a chance to feel such a Byronic glow?

There was a gaudy freedom to California. "The very air," wrote Bayard Taylor of San Francisco in the year 1849, "is pregnant with the magnetism of bold, spirited, unwearied action, and he who but ventures into the outer circle of the whirlpool, is spinning ere he has time for thought, in its dizzy vortex." At the Parker House or the El Dorado women dealt the cards, a brass band or banjo music played, and gold nuggets were piled high on the tables. One could take a brandy-smash at the bar, then stroll the crowded streets rakish in hussar boots, corduroy pants, sash, red flannel shirt, and sombrero. Costume was posturing and romantic. Daguerreotypists did a good business in portraits of young men in miner's dress. J. Douglas Borthwick, an English artist sensitive to social distinctions, noted that it was the gentlemen who insisted on posing in the most picturesque attire.

If there were quarrels, there was also a new intensity to companionship as men took each other's measure under difficult conditions. "There is more intelligence and generous good feeling than in any country I ever saw," believed J. D. B. Stillman. "Men are valued for what they are." William Perkins met a former dandy, who on the East Coast had resorted to padded clothing, hair dye, makeup, and a dental device for filling out the cheeks. In California he discarded all of this, delighted to find himself a gray-haired, hale and hearty man of middle age. "Thanks to California," he told Perkins, "I have broken my chains. I am fifty-two this year and I don't care who knows it!"

Under stress, men came to moral insight as well as to violence. Indians stole Charles Pancoast's supplies, upon which he depended for his life. "A few days after this," Pancoast wrote in his journal, "as I was walking up the shady path beside the River, I discerned three Indians sitting in the bushes on the opposite side. I raised my Rifle to shoot at them, when the thought came to me that I should be taking the life of a Human Being without necessity or adding to my own security, and I should perhaps regret the Murder. I dropped my aim, and I have ever since rejoiced that I did not pull the trigger of my Rifle that day." It was true that Americans indulged in an orgy of self-seeking. It was also true that there were times of pity. "Right below me, upon a root of our wide-spreading oak, is seated an old man of three-score and ten years," Daniel B. Woods entered into his journal at Weaver's Creek on 21 August 1849. "He left a wife and seven children at home, whose memory he cherishes with a kind of devotion unheard of before. He says when he is home-sick he can not cry, but it makes him sick at his stomach. He is an industrious old man, but has not made enough to buy his provisions, and we have given him a helping hand."

There were other experiences, ones which kept the Gold Rush on a human scale, kept it bearable. Letters came from home. ("So if you should not be among the fortunate," Ellen Apple wrote her fiancé Enos Christman, "be not discouraged but return to those who devoutly love you in good old West Chester and let well enough alone.") There were Sundays when one sat before his cabin mending clothes, writing letters, smoking a pipe, or turning the pages of a Bible. Were later diversions ever as satisfying to Luther Melancthon Schaeffer as the evenings spent after work in Grass Valley with other miners singing to banjo, violin, and harmonica? Or the nights at Swett's Bar when the boys would gather together for a reading aloud from Shakespeare or Dickens? Did any other food ever taste so good to Howard Gardiner as the salmon he caught in the American River near Horse Shoe Bar and broiled over a fire at his campsite? Or the tinned turkey, sweet potatoes, bread, butter, doughnuts, coffee, and Bass Ale with which he celebrated in his Sierra cabin the Christmas of 1851? "The appetite one acquires in California is something remarkable," believed Bayard Taylor. "For two months after my arrival, my sensations were like those of a famished wolf." Miners found time to note beauties of landscape, to marvel at valleys and foothills in the spring, "this now most fairy-like country, everything so smiling and beautiful, flowers of the smaller varieties by thousands."

When they began to see signs that the Gold Rush was the prologue to lasting settlement, Forty-niners solaced themselves that they had been pioneers. Borthwick, an Englishman, claimed that the Gold Rush gave Americans their first opportunity to develop a territory as a colony in the English manner, as opposed to a frontier. The Gold Rush, Borthwick pointed out, brought to California not just wild people, but the cultivated populations of the Atlantic states. California blended frontier and civilization, laying foundations for a regional culture which from its inception combined qualities of the East, the South, and the Far West. As colonists, Borthwick believed, Americans in California had held to a civilized center and not degenerated, although in the early years of the Gold Rush social chaos posed a real threat. Even rugged frontier types seemed to improve in civility after a period of California residence.

Even without the comfort of seeing himself as a pioneer, a miner could admit that, although he had not made his fortune, he had at times enjoyed himself, had found something to affirm amid so much that was wasted and inconsequential. "I have enjoyed myself," wrote Franklin Buck after three years in California, "and lived most of the time just as I wanted to."

Discussion Questions

1. Kevin Starr likens the Gold Rush to both the *Iliad* and the *Odyssey* in this selection from *Americans and the California Dream*. Why does he refer to the Gold Rush as "epic experience"? How does he use the *Iliad* and *Odyssey* as metaphor? How does he distinguish between the two epics in relation to the Gold Rush experience?
2. What kinds of conflicts and violence were specific to the Gold Rush experience? What kind of balance does Starr offer in the second half of the selection when he details some positive experiences? After reading this selection, do you feel that Starr wanted to portray the Gold Rush as positive or negative? Both? Explain your reasoning.

Writing Suggestions

1. Write a journal entry in which you reflect on the myths and realities of Gold Rush life as explained in *Americans and the California Dream*. What images and myths did you grow up with about the Gold Rush? What did you learn about the Gold Rush in school and from films? How does Starr's description of both the good and bad aspects of the 49ers' experiences change your understanding of the Gold Rush?
2. Write a three-page essay in which you analyze Starr's writing style in this selection. Include in your thesis whether or not you find his style effective, and then go on to explain how, for example, his diction, tone, sentence structure, use of quotations, evidence, and primary sources affect the experience of reading his work. Quote directly from the text in your paper, and be specific in your assertion and evidence.

The Gentle Tamers

The Great Female Shortage

DEE BROWN

Author Dee Brown (1908–2002) is most famous for his book *Bury My Heart at Wounded Knee*, which was published in 1971 and which shocked the American public with its detailed account of the destruction of the American Indian way of life and the slaughter of American Indians in the latter half of the nineteenth century. Brown wrote a number of other books about the American West, including *Fighting Indians of the West*, *The American West*, and *The Gentle Tamers: Women of the Old Wild West*, from which our selection was taken. In the following selection from Chapter 12, "The Great Female Shortage," Brown writes about the relationships between men and women in the West, discussing both interracial marriages and the effects of the shortage of women on male/female relationships.

1

When the first white males ventured into the West, they left their women behind in the East or in border settlements. For female companionship they turned naturally to women of Indian tribes, buying or bartering for "wives" whose status sometimes became permanent, more often was quite temporary. "The man is thought a decent wooer who comes with money in his pocket to an Indian lodge," said a contemporary traveler, who observed that squaws were sold as one would sell "a buffalo hide or catamount skin."

For twenty dollars a frontiersman could buy an Indian girl and claim, through her, adoption in the tribe. Sometimes the price was cheaper, one of George Custer's officers being offered a bride by a chief who asked only a cup of sugar in exchange. And sometimes it seemed too high, as fur trader Alexander Henry noted in his Fort George diary after his associate, Donald McDougall, purchased one of Chief Concomly's daughters. "He gave 5 new guns and 5 blankets, making a total of 15 guns and 15 blankets, besides a great deal of other property, as the total cost of this precious lady. This Concomly is a mercenary brute destitute of decency."

This same diarist declared that "for a few inches of twist tobacco a Gros Ventre will barter the person of a wife or daughter with as much sangfroid as he would bargain for a horse . . . all those tribes (Blackfoot, Blood, or Piegan) are a nuisance when they come to the forts with their women. They intrude upon every room and cabin in the place, followed by their women, and even though the trader may have a family of his own they insist upon his doing them the charity of accepting of the company of at least one woman for the night. It is sometimes with the greatest difficulty that we can get the fort clear of them in the evening and shut the gates; they hide in every corner, and all for the sake of gain, not from any regard for us, though some of the men tell us it is with a view of having a white child—which frequently is the case."

The white man's motives for uniting with Indian women included security as well as convenience. While traveling in the West in the 1830s, Gottfried Duden noted that Indian women often acted to protect white men, warning them of tribal treachery. "It is commonly stated here," said Duden, "that Indian women are easily seduced by Europeans. A white man who lives among the Indians for any length of time often takes an Indian girl as a temporary wife, and as a precaution for his safety . . . incidentally the Indian girls are not by any means all ugly to look at." Some thirty years after Duden's observations, a Kansas newspaper reported that "'Old Man Hathaway,' who lives on Drywood, near the state line, has, in order to save himself from being driven off by the Indians, been down to the Cherokee Nation and married a Cherokee woman. Unmarried men living on the Neutral Land, and who wish to remain there, can do so, by following Mr. Hathaway's example."

Many of the great names of western exploration and settlement were "squaw men"—Jim Bridger, Kit Carson, John McLoughlin, William Bent, Joe Meek, Peter Skene Ogden, Jim Beckwourth, Milton Sublette—and not all limited themselves to one wife. Jim Beckwourth admitted to owning eight wives, all of the Crow tribe, yet he came down to Denver in 1860 and proposed to and married Elizabeth Lettbetter, daughter of the town's first laundress. Some early fur trappers swapped, borrowed, or stole each other's squaws. Joe Meek and Milton Sublette, although partners, were rivals for the hand of a beautiful Shoshone girl named Mountain Lamb. Sublette won out because he owned more horses, but when he had to go east for surgical treatment of an ailing leg, Joe Meek "so insinuated himself into the good graces" of Mountain Lamb that she consented to join her fortunes with his.

"She was the most beautiful Indian woman I ever saw," said Meek, "and when she was mounted on her dapple gray horse, which cost me three hundred dollars, she made a fine show. She wore a skirt of beautiful blue broadcloth, and a bodice and leggins of scarlet cloth, of the very finest make. Her hair was braided and fell over her shoulders, a scarlet silk handkerchief, tied on hood fashion, covered her head; and the finest embroidered moccasins her feet. She rode like all the Indian women, astride, and carried on one side of the saddle the tomahawk for war, and on the other the pipe of peace."

In fairness to the mountain men and fur traders, it must be said that most of them limited themselves to one mate at a time. The numerous Scotchmen representing the North West and Hudson's Bay fur companies often settled down for years with one tribeswoman and raised respectable families. For example, Angus McDonald, stationed at Fort Colville, had ten children by the same woman and considered himself as solidly married as any *pater familias* of his native Scotland.

In 1850, a traveler en route to California stopped at Jim Bridger's fort, recording that Bridger "had a squaw and two children, a boy and girl, half casts, of whom he seemed to be very fond. Old Jim, as the lord of the castle was called, was anxious for us to hear them read, which we did. Madam Bridger, the squaw, cooked us a good supper, making some light biscuit . . . the best I had ever eaten."

One of the curious aspects of these relations between white men and Indian women was that there was no social reproach whatever to such unions until white women began arriving in the West in increasing numbers. Almost as soon as the first wagonloads of females arrived from the States—hardly before they could unpack their household goods—it was considered a disgrace for a white man to live with a squaw. For example, a reformed drunkard named Hauxhurst was living contentedly with an Indian girl in Oregon until the female missionaries arrived. Almost immediately, Hauxhurst's conscience began troubling him, and one morning he handed the girl some blankets and other farewell presents and sent her back to her people.

According to one of Hauxhurst's neighbors, who recorded the incident in a diary of 1845, the girl returned that night to the man's door, "beseeching him to let her in, averring her love to him and promising to be good to him if he would let her live with him; he let her in; and knowing it was wicked for them to live together as they had done, he, in a short time soon experienced religion, and is now a respectable man in the community, only he has a squaw for a wife. This, it is presumed, is the source for great mortification to himself and affliction to his friends."

The first white men coming into the wilderness, straight out of a nineteenth-century civilization which professed to abhor the human form, had to make abrupt adjustments to a people who regarded clothing merely as protection from sun and weather rather than as concealment for the natural state of nakedness. Costumes varied, of course, from tribe to tribe, but in general the first difference noted was the dress, or lack of it, of Indian females. Eighteen-year-old Lewis Garrard considered the costumes of southwestern Indian women "a pleasing and desirable change from the sight of the pinched waists and constrained motions of the women of the States, to see these daughters of the prairie dressed loosely—free to act, unconfined by the ligatures of fashion . . ."

Colonel W. H. Emory was fascinated by an Apache beauty of the same area: "She had on a gauzelike dress, trimmed with the richest and most costly Brussels lace, pillaged no doubt from some fandango-going belle of Sonora; she straddled a fine grey horse, and whenever her blanket dropped from her shoulders, her tawny form could be seen through the transparent gauze. After she had sold her mule, she was anxious to sell her horse, and careered about to show his qualities. At one time she charged at full speed up a steep hill. In this, the fastenings of her dress broke, and her bare back was exposed to the crowd, who ungallantly raised a shout of laughter. Nothing daunted, she wheeled short round with surprising dexterity, and seeing the mischief done, coolly slipped the dress from her arms and tucked it between her seat and the saddle. In this state of nudity she rode through camp, from fire to fire, until, at last, attaining the object of her ambition, a soldier's red flannel shirt, she made her adieu in that new costume."

Ernest de Massey, a Frenchman in the gold rush, was less appreciative of the types he saw on the West Coast. "When I first saw these Indian women walking around in the open, and talking and laughing in the most natural manner before strange men when wearing scarcely more than the proverbial fig-leaf, my only feelings were those of indifference for they were neither beautiful nor appealing. Every time I touched their rough, cold, oily skin I had a feeling of repulsion just as if I had put my hand on a toad, tortoise, or huge lizard."

As for Alexander Henry, he was equally repelled and tantalized by the abundance of feminine nudity around Fort George: "This afternoon I had an opportunity of observing the total want of modesty, or even decency, in the women on this coast. I was walking on the wharf, where several women were washing themselves, as is their daily custom, in the small ponds left on the beach at low water. They were perfectly naked, and my presence did not affect their operations in the least. The disgusting creatures were perfectly composed, and seemed not to notice me. Although they stood naked in different postures, yet so close did they keep their thighs together that nothing could be seen. The operation over, they used their cedar coverings as towels, and, after drying themselves, tied them around their waists and walked away."

Callous disregard for, and sometimes outright cruelty toward, Indian women increased in proportion with the deepening social disgrace accorded "squaw men" which had begun with the arrival of the first white woman. A California Indian agent received a report in 1855 from Klamath County referring to mistreatment of female natives by miners. "They have singled out all the squaws, compelling them to sleep with some man every night. This causes great excitement. The Bucks complain daily of it."

The low status of Indian females during this period is indicated by an account of a party traveling by horseback to Oregon. The travelers came upon a naked Indian girl, suffering from hunger and almost eaten up by flies. She had evidently become lost from her tribe. A council was held among the men as to what to do with her; some wanted to take her along, others thought it would be best to kill her and put her out of her misery. A vote was taken and it was decided to leave the girl where they had found her. The women of the party protested, but they were overruled. After the party had gone on a short distance, one of the men went back and "put a bullet through her head and put her out of her misery."

One other reason for the change in attitude toward Indian women was the high rate of venereal disease among many tribes, a disease introduced, of course, by white men. Alexander Henry's diary has several illuminating comments on the subject. "At 11 P.M. I went to bed; Mr. McTavish was inclined to sit up. Mr. J. Cartier discharged his lady, she being so far gone with the venereal disease that he already has two pimples, and on examination the doctor gives it as his opinion that he is in a very bad way. Mr. Bethune keeps his, though he is very dubious about her." On another day, Henry recorded the death of a girl from the disease. Her owner, a former Canadian *voyageur*, sent for her family to come and bury the body, "lest the hogs should devour it. They did so, but in a barbarous manner, by dragging it perfectly naked down to the water, tying a cord around the neck, and towing it along the beach for some distance; they then squeezed the body into a bole, pushed it down with a paddle, and covered it over with stones and dirt. The poor girl had died in a horrible condition, in the last stage of venereal disease, discolored and swollen, and not the least care was ever taken to conceal the parts from bystanders."

2

Any commodity that is both uncommon and universally desired becomes overvalued in the market place, and that was the situation applying to white women in the Far West during its earlier years. "Women were queens," was the comment of one observer during the spring of 1849 when there were but fifteen women in all San Francisco. And by October the number had increased to only fifty. The following year, when an official census was taken, females composed less than 8 per cent of the total inhabitants of California, a statistic which told only part of the story, for in many mining regions there were no women at all. It was no wonder that male passersby turned to salute every female stranger encountered on streets and roads.

This acute scarcity resulted in a goodly amount of full-blown, heart-bleeding prose on the part of some of the literate males. Walter Colton, alcalde of Monterey at the time of the gold strike, set down his feelings in this manner: "There is no land less relieved by the smiles and soothing caress of woman. If Eden with its ambrosial fruits and guiltless joys was still sad till the voice of woman mingled with its melodies, California, with all her treasured hills and streams, must be cheerless till she feels the presence of the same enchantress."

Caspar Hopkins, a less mellifluous writer, struck a more cynical note: "As yet the female part of our population is only about two per cent of the whole, and of these, including all nations, the proportion who are what women ought to be is not more than twenty per cent. To say nothing of the large number of French women who are imported, like other French frail manufactures, only to take their places among the bottles and decanters, a great many American women who have started to join their husbands here, have found the journey too much for their principles. The attentions of extempore gallants have rendered the husbands they set out to meet the last persons they wished to see on their arrivals. Happily, however, these instances are in the minority; though were it otherwise, the universal depravity of the male population would be sufficient explanation for it."

In the back country, the female-starved miners came to consider it a privilege just to look at a member of the opposite sex. A typical story concerns a young man who learned one evening that a woman had arrived at another mining camp some forty miles distant. The young man went to his uncle and asked: "Uncle, will you lend me your mule tomorrow?"

"What do you want with my mule?"

"I've heard there's a woman over at the next camp, and I want to go and see her."

The uncle lent his nephew the mule, and he was off at daybreak, and never stopped until he had covered the forty miles and had a good look at the lady.

As late as 1860, in the Colorado mining country, a similar condition prevailed. "We were all in the habit of running to our cabin doors in Denver, on the arrival of a lady, to gaze at her as earnestly as at any other rare natural curiosity."

Not since the days of knighthood had women been accorded such courtesy, respect, and unobtrusive chivalry. The miners even went so far as to flatter the vanity of fair visitors by "salting" their diggings, and as Dame Shirley observed, "the dear creatures go home with their treasures, firmly believing that mining is the prettiest pastime in the world."

And one winter when Downieville was snowed in with deep drifts and food became short, the entire male population was ordered to leave town in order that the few women in camp would have sufficient provisions.

"I never knew a miner to insult a woman," wrote an observer of the times, "but, on the other hand, I know a woman could visit among a camp of miners and be treated with higher consideration than many honorable wives, mothers, and sisters are treated by men in passing along the streets of our cities in the evening, or even in the day time. Every miner seemed to consider himself her sworn guardian, policeman and protector, and the slightest dishonorable word, action or look of any miner or other person, would have been met with a rebuke he would remember as long as he lived, if, perchance, he survived the chastisement."

A woman traveling in upper California during this period was astonished at the honors shown her by the miners. "I am afraid I should have had a very mistaken impression of my importance if I had lived long among them. At every stopping-place they made little fires in their frying pans, and set them around me, to keep off the mosquitoes, while I took my meal. As the columns of smoke rose about me I felt like a heathen goddess, to whom incense was being offered."

Weddings were both rare and costly. Two thousand dollars was expended on a wedding celebration in Marysville, though the bride may have shared part of the expense, she being described as "a fair widow of thirty who had been left a fortune by a former husband." A miner in Shasta decided to defray part of his expenses by selling admissions to his wedding at five dollars per ticket; so many guests came and paid that he took in enough extra to furnish a house.

The female shortage was felt most acutely at dances or other social gatherings where the gaiety depended upon an even number of partners of opposite sexes. In the cattle country of western Washington, one rancher recalled attending a dance where there were sixty cowboys and three women. They had to resort to the old trick of tying handkerchiefs to the arms of a number of cowboys to designate them as females. Because of the woman shortage in that area, "a man bringing one girl to a dance got a free ticket, and if he brought two girls he got 25 cents to boot."

A Montana cowboy of the 1880s complained that girls were so scarce up there that engagements for dances had to be made eight months ahead. He told of trying to arrange a dance with several other cowboys, but found it impossible to round up nearly enough women. "One of the boys went into the back room of the honky-tonky where they were staging the dance and came out with a pair of woman's white ruffled drawers pulled on over his pants. He was the attraction of the evening."

Eleanor Alice Richards, daughter of a Wyoming governor, recalled that during one winter when she was a girl of eleven living in the Bighorn Basin, there were a hundred men in the Basin and seven women, if she included herself. She attended the all-night dances with her parents. "The men were very respectful and well behaved. I remember at one dance that a couple of the boys who became intoxicated were taken out, placed on their horses and shown the way home. There were so many men and so few women, they knew they must behave if they wished to have a good time."

Westerners who could afford servants found it impossible to keep female help longer than a month or so. "The parlormaid or the kitchen maid," commented Janos Xandus in a letter from California in 1857, "who weeks ago had cooked, charred, and washed the laundry, has become the wife of a banker or a rich merchant, because she has a nice face." And it was not always necessary to have "a nice face." An Army wife told of deliberately selecting a homely nurse so she would not marry one of the soldiers in the fort and leave her service. "The girl was almost a grenadier in looks and manners, and although not absolutely hideous, was so far from pleasing that we were confident of retaining her services . . . She had not been in the fort three days before the man who laid our carpets proposed to her."

After Fort Lincoln was fitted up as a sort of frontier luxury station in 1876, and maids were imported to keep the officers' quarters clean, the Army command itself was forced to take cognizance of the servant problem. When experience showed that all the imported maids married soldiers within two to six weeks after arrival, the military instructed employment offices in Chicago and eastern cities to supply only the homeliest females obtainable. The agencies complied, shipping out a troop of knock-kneed, cross-eyed, buck-toothed females to Fort Lincoln. At the end of two months, however, every one of them had landed a man.

Thousands of women of all classes went west in those days with that single purpose in mind—to get married as quickly as possible. Loreta Velazquez, the incredible male impersonator who took her dead husband's place as a soldier in the Civil War, discarded her disguise as soon as the fighting stopped and headed west to find a new mate. Dressed in a most feminine manner, she reached Omaha almost penniless, but she charmed old General W. S. Harney into supplying her with a buffalo robe, a pair of blankets, and a revolver—which she needed to continue her journey into the Nevada mining regions. Two days after Loreta arrived in Austin, Nevada, she received her first proposal of marriage, but the gentleman was sixty years old and she waited a few days for a younger suitor. She married, settled down, and lived a full and happy life.

Wedding ceremonies in the West were as short and swift as the engagement periods. For example, a marrying squire of Kansas is said to have used this one:

Squire: Have him?
Bride: Yes.
Squire: Have her?
Bridegroom: Kinder.
Squire: Done. One dollar.

A young single woman just arrived in the West attended a funeral on horseback. As she turned to leave, the bereaved widower rode up beside her horse and "expressed a wish that she might be induced to consent to fill the place of the dear departed one whose mortal remains had just been laid in the grave." The young woman rejected the suitor for lack of emotional delicacy.

Sometimes husbands were acquired through unusual circumstances, as in the case of a woman arrested for vagrancy in Meade, Kansas. On that same day a man was arrested for disorderly conduct. Both were sentenced to jail, creating a dilemma for the court, because the jail had only one cell. The defendants, however, solved the quandary by offering to get married. A collection was taken up, a marriage license was procured, the justice performed the ceremony without charge, and the honeymoon was celebrated in the calaboose.

3

Too much adoration poured upon a minority of females was bound to have pernicious psychological effects upon even the more worthy of the creatures. Naturally, many of them took advantage of their scarcity, and for a time made life almost intolerable for the competitive males. Historian Hubert Howe Bancroft observed that the excessive attention paid them "made modest women uncomfortable, while others encouraged it by extravagant conduct. Loose characters flaunted costly attire in elegant equipages, or appeared walking or riding in male attire."

Special privileges accorded females annoyed some men; a few were highly critical because western juries would not convict a woman for any crime, not even murder. "A white woman is treated everywhere on the Pacific slope, not as man's equal and companion, but as a strange and costly creature, which by virtue of its rarity is freed from the restraints and penalties of ordinary law. In San Francisco there is a brisk demand for wives, a call beyond the market to supply. A glut of men is everywhere felt, and the domestic relation is everywhere disturbed."

The diaries of male gold seekers are filled with continuous entries decrying the shortage: "Would give my little finger to go to the theater or museum with some certain Baltimore girls, tonight—hush memory—or I'll go mad." This same young man complained that before he could induce a homely woman to wash his linen he had to pay court to her as well as the six dollars a dozen she charged for his laundered shirts.

Polyandry without benefit of formal marriage—quite common among Chinese emigrants—was probably more generally practiced among the whites than the records indicate. Ernest de Massey told of visiting a ranch in southern California where two men were living with one woman in a congenial *ménage à trois*. "Perhaps in California," he commented primly, "there is a sacrament that blesses such a union, but it does not meet with local approval."

The ease with which some women shifted from one husband to another is exemplified in the rocky marital adventures of Henry T. P. Comstock, discoverer of the rich Nevada lode which bore his name. Comstock fell in love at first sight with the wife of a Mormon who arrived one day in Nevada City riding upon a dilapidated wagon. The woman was plainly dressed in drab calico and poke bonnet, but the grizzled old miner could not resist her charms. He persuaded her to leave her husband and run away with him to Washoe Valley, where a preacher friend married them. Proceeding to Carson City for a honeymoon, Comstock and his bride had scarcely settled into a hotel when the original Mormon husband arrived in a state of high indignation.

Comstock blithely produced a marriage license and dared the Mormon to do the same. When the Mormon admitted he had no license, the old miner graciously agreed to give him a horse, a revolver, and sixty dollars to settle the matter with no hard feelings. Probably because there was nothing else he could do, the Mormon agreed to the bargain and went on his way.

A few days later, Comstock left his bride comfortably ensconced in the hotel and started out to San Francisco to attend to some business matters. He had gone no farther than Sacramento when he received a message from a friend informing him that his new bride had absconded with "a seductive youth of Carson City" and the pair were on their way to Placerville. Rushing to Placerville, Comstock intercepted the runaways, had a long private talk with his sixty-dollar wife, and apparently convinced her she had made a rash mistake. But when he left her for a few minutes and then returned to her room, she was gone again. She had climbed out the back window and was in flight once more with the "seductive young lover."

Comstock was not one to give up easily. He hired all the horses in the town's livery stables and sent riders out in all directions with a promise of one hundred dollars' reward to the one who captured the fleeing lovers. Next day one of the searchers came back into Placerville, walking the runaways in front of his six-shooter. Comstock paid the hundred-dollar reward, and this time he locked his wife up securely. In the meantime, his friends took charge of the young man, placing him under armed guard. As soon as night fell, the young man was told he was to be hanged. A little later a new guard, previously instructed by Comstock, came on duty. He whispered to the prisoner that he was opposed to hangings. "I'm going outside to take a drink," the guard said, "and if I find you here when I return, it will be your own fault." The young lover made good the arranged escape, and he was never seen around Placerville or Carson City again.

As for the wife, she stayed on with Comstock through the winter, but she kept an alert eye out for another chance. In the spring she ran away with "a long-legged miner who, with his blankets on his back, came strolling that way." The last known of the onetime Mrs. H. T. P. Comstock she was working in a beer cellar in Sacramento.

4

In the course of time, the West's dearth of females attracted the attention of a number of ingenious entrepreneurs and social theorists, including knaves, fanatics, and a few sincere philanthropists. One of the first to propose a solution to the problem was Catharine E. Beecher, sister of the famed Harriet and Henry Ward Beecher. As early as 1845, Catharine recognized the great need for schoolteachers in the West, as well as the increasing geographical displacement of the sexes. She wrote a book called *The Duty of American Women to Their Country*, advocating "Go West, Young Woman" long before Horace Greeley thought up the phrase for young men. One of the points she belabored was the vast excess of female population in New England and other eastern areas.

A frontier newspaper editor took note of Miss Beecher's manifesto with this comment: "To supply the bachelors of the West with wives, to furnish the pining maidens of the East with husbands, and to better equalize the present disposition of the sexes in these two sections of our country, has been one of the difficulties of the age. The remedy was simple; it was only for the girls to go West and get married; but to go expressly to get married, offended their ideas of delicacy. Miss Beecher, herself a Yankee girl, has ingeniously got over the whole difficulty. She is engaging the girls to go West as school teachers."

The first money-making schemes for delivering marriageable females to western males appear to have originated in Europe. In Paris—which had been the hatching place for numerous American promotions from the time of John Law's Mississippi Bubble—a project was organized to recruit young girls for shipment to western America. The company's income was to be derived from a percentage of the girls' marriage portions. This Parisian plan failed before it was fully developed, but a different system originating in Germany met with more success.

Upon this German scheme the *Alta California* leveled a scorching editorial blast: "It may hardly seem credible that a system of peonage of Anglo-Saxon flesh and blood is rife in California. The system of importing females from Germany, by contract, has been carried on with great profit to one or two parties in this city. Young girls are bought, sent out here in ships, and have to serve a term of years to their master—no matter what labor may be required." The editor went on to say that dance houses were being supplied with these girls to act as partners to male customers at rates of four dollars per evening up to midnight and seven dollars if retained until morning. "We are informed they are virtuous; though notions of propriety forbid that a female who can be fondled and clasped by every comer, be he drunk or sober, uncouth or comely, can be chaste; yet such a miracle may exist."

As anyone might have guessed, it was a woman who organized the first American effort to supply brides to the California gold miners. She was Elizabeth Farnham, a New York prison matron, whose husband, Thomas J. Farnham, had gone to San Francisco and died there in 1848. Farnham left his business affairs in such confusion that Elizabeth decided to leave New York and journey out by ocean vessel and collect what monies might be due the estate. From her late husband and other sources she had learned of the great demand for marriageable women in the West, and being of a practical turn of mind she decided to organize a company of prospective brides and take them along with her. She also needed money and hoped to profit from the venture.

On February 2, 1849, Mrs. Farnham published a circular to explain her purposes:

> It is proposed that the company shall consist of persons not under twenty-five years of age, who shall bring from their clergyman, or some authority of the town where they reside, satisfactory testimonials of education, character, capacity, etc., and who can contribute the sum of two hundred and fifty dollars, to defray the expenses of the voyage, make suitable provision for their accommodation after reaching San Francisco, until they shall be able to enter upon some occupation for their support, and create a fund to be held in reserve for the relief of any who may be ill, or otherwise need aid before they are able to provide for themselves.
>
> It is believed that such arrangement, with one hundred or one hundred and thirty persons, would enable the company to purchase or charter a vessel, and fit it up with everything necessary for comfort on the voyage, and that

the combination of all for the support of each, would give such security, both
as to health, person, and character, as would remove all reasonable hesitation from the minds of those who may be disposed and able to join such a mission. It is intended that the party shall include six or eight respectable married
men and their families . . .

   The New York built packet ship *Angelique* has been engaged to take out
this Association . . . She will be ready to sail from New York about the 12th
or 15th of April.

To lend her circular an air of respectability and authority, she appended
the endorsements of such leading figures as Horace Greeley, William Cullen
Bryant, and Henry Ward Beecher. During the next several weeks, about two
hundred women communicated with Mrs. Farnham, but unfortunately she
fell ill and was not able to work actively in organizing the expedition. In the
end, only three women agreed to go to California with her. Her plan, however, was widely publicized in the West, and the California miners undoubtedly were more disappointed than she was by its failure, as this miner's
diary entry of June 10, 1849, suggests: "Went to church 3 times today. A few
ladies present, does my eyes good to see a woman once more. Hope Mrs.
Farnham will bring 10,000."

Discussion Questions

1.   Dee Brown published *The Gentle Tamers* in 1958. What does the book title
     imply about the contents? What might readers assume about Dee Brown's
     beliefs about women? How would you describe Brown's tone in our se-
     lection? Find examples of diction that date this selection—how might we
     guess it was written almost fifty years ago?

2.   Ambivalence toward Indian women on the part of white males has been
     a recurring theme in our readings. Discuss in groups how Brown explains
     the variety of treatment and the changes in attitude toward Indian women
     over time. What does Brown claim caused this change? How do the atti-
     tudes of the western explorers of the nineteenth century compare to ear-
     lier eastern white male attitudes toward Indian women? (Review the
     readings in Chapter 1 about Pocahontas and John Smith.)

Writing Suggestions

1.   Using Brown's selection as a starting point, write a sample journal entry
     from 1850—you could choose the persona of a miner, shop owner, or priest,
     for example, or of a woman visiting the mines, or of a prostitute, teacher,
     or wife. Write an entry describing your day, your impressions, and your

emotions. Let your imagination lead you, and try to imagine what your response might have been if you had been in Gold Rush California.

2. Review your answers to the first discussion question for this selection. Then write your ideas in a three-page analysis of Brown's tone, style, and argument, in which you answer the following questions:

    What might readers assume about Brown's beliefs about women?

    Find examples of diction that date this chapter—how might we guess it was written almost fifty years ago? Which words and phrases would be considered outdated?

    What does the book title imply about the contents?

    How would you describe Brown's tone in the selection?

    How might a selection about this topic be written differently today?

3. Brown writes that "too much adoration poured upon a minority of females was bound to have pernicious psychological effects upon even the more worthy of the creatures. Naturally, many of them took advantage of their scarcity, and for a time made life almost intolerable for the competitive males." To verify Brown's assertions, research the role of women in the California Gold Rush. Answer some of the following research questions in your paper:

    What variety of roles did women play in California?

    Were most prostitutes successful financially? What variety of experiences did they have?

    Why was there such a shortage of women in California?

    Did women really have the advantage over men?

    You might start your research with Anne Butler's book *Sisters of Mercy, Daughters of Joy,* and you can also find more information in *The Shirley Letters from the California Mine,* by Dame Shirley.

The Luck of Roaring Camp

BRET HARTE

Bret Harte (1836–1902) was an easterner who came to California at the age of eighteen, following his widowed mother who remarried in San Francisco in 1854. He held a number of different jobs in Northern California, working as a druggist, stagecoach messenger, and schoolteacher. He began to write in 1857, and after working for two newspapers, the *Northern Californian* and the *Golden Era*, he made his name as a writer and journalist and was eventually made editor of *The Overland Monthly* in the late 1860s. He went on to publish his famous stories of the gold miners and their rough lives in the Sierras. Harte was an extremely popular writer because of his ability to portray the details, sights, and sounds of the West in stories such as "The Luck of Roaring Camp," the story that established Bret Harte as a major literary figure.

There was commotion in Roaring Camp. It could not have been a fight, for in 1850 that was not novel enough to have called together the entire settlement. The ditches and claims were not only deserted, but "Tuttle's grocery" had contributed its gamblers, who, it will be remembered, calmly continued their game the day that French Pete and Kanaka Joe shot each other to death over the bar in the front room.

The whole camp was collected before a rude cabin on the outer edge of the clearing. Conversation was carried on in a low tone, but the name of a woman was frequently repeated. It was a name familiar enough in the camp— "Cherokee Sal."

Perhaps the less said of her the better. She was a coarse and, it is to be feared, a very sinful woman. But at that time she was the only woman in Roaring Camp, and was just then lying in sore extremity, when she most needed the ministration of her own sex. Dissolute, abandoned, and irreclaimable, she was yet suffering a martyrdom hard enough to bear even when veiled by sympathizing womanhood, but now terrible in her loneliness. The primal curse had come to her in that original isolation which must have made the punishment of the first transgression so dreadful.

It was, perhaps, part of the expiation of her sin that, at a moment when she most lacked her sex's intuitive tenderness and care, she met only the half-contemptuous faces of her masculine associates. Yet a few of the spectators were, I think, touched by her sufferings. Sandy Tipton thought it was rough on Sal, and, in the contemplation of her condition, for a moment rose superior to the fact that he had an ace and two bowers in his sleeve.

It will be seen also that the situation was novel. Deaths were by no means uncommon in Roaring Camp, but a birth was a new thing. People had been dismissed from the camp effectively, finally, and with no possibility of return; but this was the first time that anybody had been introduced *ab initio*. Hence the excitement.

"You go in there, Stumpy," said a prominent citizen known as "Kentuck," addressing one of the loungers. "Go in there, and see what you kin do. You've had experience in them things."

Perhaps there was a fitness in the selection. Stumpy, in other climes, had been the putative head of two families; in fact, it was owing to some legal informality in these proceedings that Roaring Camp—a city of refuge—was indebted to his company. The crowd approved the choice, and Stumpy was wise enough to bow to the majority. The door closed on the extempore surgeon and midwife, and Roaring Camp sat down outside, smoked its pipe, and awaited the issue.

The assemblage numbered about a hundred men. One or two of these were actual fugitives from justice, some were criminal, and all were reckless. Physically they exhibited no indication of their past lives and character. The greatest scamp had a Raphael face, with a profusion of blonde hair; Oakhurst, a gambler, had the melancholy air and intellectual abstraction of a Hamlet; the coolest and most courageous man was scarcely over five feet in height, with a soft voice and an embarrassed, timid manner.

The term "roughs" applied to them was a distinction rather than a definition. Perhaps in the minor details of fingers, toes, ears, etc., the camp may have been deficient, but these slight omissions did not detract from their aggregate force. The strongest man had but three fingers on his right hand; the best shot had but one eye.

Such was the physical aspect of the men that were dispersed around the cabin. The camp lay in a triangular valley between two hills and a river. The only outlet was a steep trail over the summit of a hill that faced the cabin, now illuminated by the rising moon. The suffering woman might have seen it from the rude bunk whereon she lay—seen it winding like a silver thread until it was lost in the stars above.

A fire of withered pine boughs added sociability to the gathering. By degrees the natural levity of Roaring Camp returned. Bets were freely offered and taken regarding the result. Three to five that "Sal would get through with it"; even that the child would survive; side bets as to the sex and complexion of the coming stranger.

In the midst of an excited discussion an exclamation came from those nearest the door, and the camp stopped to listen. Above the swaying and moaning of the pines, the swift rush of the river, and the crackling of the fire rose a sharp, querulous cry—a cry unlike anything heard before in the camp. The pines stopped moaning, the river ceased to rush, and the fire to crackle. It seemed as if Nature had stopped to listen too.

The camp rose to its feet as one man! It was proposed to explode a barrel of gunpowder; but in consideration of the situation of the mother, better counsels prevailed, and only a few revolvers were discharged; for whether owing to the rude surgery of the camp, or some other reason, Cherokee Sal was sinking fast. Within an hour she had climbed, as it were, that rugged road that led to the stars, and so passed out of Roaring Camp, its sin and shame, forever.

I do not think that the announcement disturbed them much, except in speculation as to the fate of the child. "Can he live now?" was asked of Stumpy. The answer was doubtful. The only other being of Cherokee Sal's sex and maternal condition in the settlement was an ass. There was some conjecture as to fitness, but the experiment was tried. It was less problematical than the ancient treatment of Romulus and Remus, and apparently as successful.

When these details were completed, which exhausted another hour, the door was opened, and the anxious crowd of men, who had already formed themselves into a queue, entered in single file. Beside the low bunk or shelf, on which the figure of the mother was starkly outlined below the blankets, stood a pine table. On this a candle-box was placed, and within it, swathed in staring red flannel, lay the last arrival at Roaring Camp.

Beside the candle-box was placed a hat. Its use was soon indicated. "Gentlemen," said Stumpy, with a singular mixture of authority and *ex officio* complacency—"gentlemen will please pass in at the front door, round the table, and out at the back door. Them as wishes to contribute anything toward the orphan will find a hat handy." The first man entered with his hat on; he uncovered, however, as he looked about him, and so unconsciously set an example to the next.

In such communities good and bad actions are catching. As the procession filed in comments were audible—criticisms addressed perhaps rather to Stumpy in the character of showman: "Is that him?" "Mighty small specimen"; "Hasn't more'n got the color"; "Ain't bigger nor a derringer."

The contributions were as characteristic: A silver tobacco box; a doubloon; a navy revolver, silver mounted; a gold specimen; a very beautifully embroidered lady's handkerchief, from Oakhurst the gambler; a diamond breastpin; a diamond ring, suggested by the pin, with the remark from the giver that he "saw that pin and went two diamonds better"; a slung-shot; a Bible, contributor not detected; a golden spur; a silver teaspoon, the initials, I regret to say, were not the giver's; a pair of surgeon's shears; a lancet; a Bank of England note for £5; and about $200 in loose gold and silver coin.

During these proceedings Stumpy maintained a silence as impassive as the dead on his left, a gravity as inscrutable as that of the newly born on his right. Only one incident occurred to break the monotony of the curious procession. As Kentuck bent over the candlebox half curiously, the child turned, and, in a spasm of pain, caught at his groping finger, and held it fast for a moment. Kentuck looked foolish and embarrassed. Something like a blush tried to assert itself in his weather-beaten cheek. "The d——d little cuss!" he said, as he extricated his finger, with perhaps more tenderness and care than he might have been deemed capable of showing.

He held that finger a little apart from its fellows as he went out, and examined it curiously. The examination provoked the same original remark in regard to the child. In fact, he seemed to enjoy repeating it. "He rastled with my finger," he remarked to Tipton, holding up the member, "the d——d little cuss!"

It was four o'clock before the camp sought repose. A light burnt in the cabin where the watchers sat, for Stumpy did not go to bed that night. Nor did Kentuck. He drank quite freely, and related with great gusto his experience, invariably ending with his characteristic condemnation of the newcomer. It seemed to relieve him of any unjust implication of sentiment, and Kentuck had the weaknesses of the nobler sex.

When everybody else had gone to bed, he walked down to the river and whistled reflectingly. Then he walked up the gulch past the cabin, still whistling with demonstrative unconcern. At a large redwood tree he paused and retraced his steps, and again passed the cabin. Halfway down to the river's bank he again paused, and then returned and knocked at the door. It was opened by Stumpy.

"How goes it?" said Kentuck, looking past Stumpy toward the candle-box.

"All serene!" replied Stumpy.

"Anything up?"

"Nothing."

There was a pause—an embarrassing one—Stumpy still holding the door. Then Kentuck had recourse to his finger, which he held up to Stumpy. "Rastled with it—the d——d little cuss," he said, and retired.

The next day Cherokee Sal had such rude sepulture as Roaring Camp afforded. After her body had been committed to the hillside, there was a formal meeting of the camp to discuss what should be done with her infant. A resolution to adopt it was unanimous and enthusiastic. But an animated discussion in regard to the manner and feasibility of providing for its wants at once sprang up. It was remarkable that the argument partook of none of those fierce personalities with which discussions were usually conducted at Roaring Camp.

Tipton proposed that they should send the child to Red Dog—a distance of forty miles—where female attention could be procured. But the unlucky suggestion met with fierce and unanimous opposition. It was evident that no plan which entailed parting from their new acquisition would for a moment be entertained. "Besides," said Tom Ryder, "them fellows at Red Dog would swap it, and ring in somebody else on us." A disbelief in the honesty of other camps prevailed at Roaring Camp, as in other places.

The introduction of a female nurse in the camp also met with objection. It was argued that no decent woman could be prevailed to accept Roaring Camp as her home, and the speaker urged that "they didn't want any more of the other kind." This unkind allusion to the defunct mother, harsh as it may seem, was the first spasm of propriety—the first symptom of the camp's regeneration. Stumpy advanced nothing. Perhaps he felt a certain delicacy in interfering with the selection of a possible successor in office. But when questioned, he averred stoutly that he and "Jinny"—the mammal before alluded to—could manage to rear the child.

There was something original, independent, and heroic about the plan that pleased the camp. Stumpy was retained. Certain articles were sent for to Sacramento. "Mind," said the treasurer, as he pressed a bag of gold dust into the expressman's hand, "the best that can be got—lace, you know, and fili-gree-work and frills—d——n the cost!"

Strange to say, the child thrived. Perhaps the invigorating climate of the mountain camp was compensation for material deficiencies. Nature took the foundling to her broader breast. In that rare atmosphere of the Sierra foothills—that air pungent with balsamic odor, that ethereal cordial at once bracing and exhilarating—he may have found food and nourishment, or a subtle chemistry that transmuted ass's milk to lime and phosphorus. Stumpy inclined to the belief that it was the latter and good nursing. "Me and that ass," he would say, "has been father and mother to him! Don't you," he would add, apostrophizing the helpless bundle before him, "never go back on us."

By the time he was a month old the necessity of giving him a name became apparent. He had generally been known as "The Kid," "Stumpy's Boy," "The Coyote" (an allusion to his vocal powers), and even by Kentuck's endearing diminutive of "The d——d little cuss." But these were felt to be vague and un-satisfactory, and were at last dismissed under another influence. Gamblers and adventurers are generally superstitious, and Oakhurst one day declared that the baby had brought "the luck" to Roaring Camp. It was certain that of late they had been successful.

"Luck" was the name agreed upon, with the prefix of Tommy for greater convenience. No allusion was made to the mother, and the father was un-known. "It's better," said the philosophical Oakhurst, "to take a fresh deal all round. Call him Luck, and start him fair."

A day was accordingly set apart for the christening. What was meant by this ceremony the reader may imagine who has already gathered some idea of the reckless irreverence of Roaring Camp. The master of ceremonies was one "Boston," a noted wag, and the occasion seemed to promise the greatest face-tiousness. This ingenious satirist had spent two days in preparing a burlesque of the Church service, with pointed local allusions. The choir was properly trained, and Sandy Tipton was to stand godfather.

But after the procession had marched to the grove with music and ban-ners, and the child had been deposited before a mock altar, Stumpy stepped before the expectant crowd. "It ain't my style to spoil fun, boys," said the lit-tle man, stoutly eying the faces around him, "but it strikes me that this thing ain't exactly on the squar. It's playing it pretty low down on this yer baby to ring in fun on him that he ain't goin' to understand. And ef there's goin' to be any godfathers round, I'd like to see who's got any better rights than me."

A silence followed Stumpy's speech. To the credit of all humorists be it said that the first man to acknowledge its justice was the satirist thus stopped of his fun. "But," said Stumpy, quickly following up his advantage, "we're here for a christening, and we'll have it. I proclaim you Thomas Luck, according to the laws of the United States and the State of California, so help me God."

It was the first time that the name of the Deity had been otherwise uttered than profanely in the camp. The form of christening was perhaps even more ludicrous than the satirist had conceived; but strangely enough, nobody saw it and nobody laughed. "Tommy" was christened as seriously as he would have been under a Christian roof, and cried and was comforted in as orthodox fashion.

And so the work of regeneration began in Roaring Camp. Almost imperceptibly a change came over the settlement. The cabin assigned to "Tommy Luck"—or "The Luck," as he was more frequently called—first showed signs of improvement. It was kept scrupulously clean and whitewashed. Then it was boarded, clothed, and papered. The rosewood cradle, packed eighty miles by mule, had, in Stumpy's way of putting it, "sorter killed the rest of the furniture." So the rehabilitation of the cabin became a necessity.

The men who were in the habit of lounging in at Stumpy's to see "how 'The Luck' got on" seemed to appreciate the change, and in self-defense the rival establishment of "Tuttle's grocery" bestirred itself and imported a carpet and mirrors. The reflections of the latter on the appearance of Roaring Camp tended to produce stricter habits of personal cleanliness.

Again Stumpy imposed a kind of quarantine upon those who aspired to the honor and privilege of holding The Luck. It was a cruel mortification to Kentuck—who, in the carelessness of a large nature and the habits of frontier life, had begun to regard all garments as a second cuticle, which, like a snake's, only sloughed off through decay—to be debarred this privilege from certain prudential reasons. Yet such was the subtle influence of innovation that he thereafter appeared regularly every afternoon in a clean shirt and face still shining from his ablutions.

Nor were moral and social sanitary laws neglected. "Tommy," who was supposed to spend his whole existence in a persistent attempt to repose, must not be disturbed by noise. The shouting and yelling, which had gained the camp its infelicitous title, were not permitted within hearing distance of Stumpy's. The men conversed in whispers or smoked with Indian gravity. Profanity was tacitly given up in these sacred precincts, and throughout the camp a popular form of expletive, known as "D——n the luck!" and "Curse the luck!" was abandoned, as having a new personal bearing.

Vocal music was not interdicted, being supposed to have a soothing, tranquilizing quality; and one song, sung by "Man o' War Jack," an English sailor from her Majesty's Australian colonies, was quite popular as a lullaby. It was a lugubrious recital of the exploits of "the Arethusa, Seventy-four," in a muffled minor, ending with a prolonged dying fall at the burden of each verse, "On b-oo-o-ard of the Arethusa." It was a fine sight to see Jack holding The Luck, rocking from side to side as if with the motion of a ship, and crooning forth this naval ditty. Either through the peculiar rocking of Jack or the length of his song—it contained ninety stanzas, and was continued with conscientious deliberation to the bitter end—the lullaby generally had the desired effect.

At such times the men would lie at full length under the trees in the soft summer twilight, smoking their pipes and drinking in the melodious utterances. An indistinct idea that this was pastoral happiness pervaded the camp. "This 'ere kind o' think," said the Cockney Simmons, meditatively reclining on his elbow, "is 'evingly." It reminded him of Greenwich.

On the long summer days The Luck was usually carried to the gulch from whence the golden store of Roaring Camp was taken. There, on a blanket spread over pine boughs, he would lie while the men were working in the ditches below. Latterly there was a rude attempt to decorate this bower with flowers and sweet-smelling shrubs, and generally someone would bring him a cluster of wild honeysuckles, azaleas, or the painted blossoms of Las Mariposas.

The men had suddenly awakened to the fact that there were beauty and significance in these trifles, which they had so long trodden carelessly beneath their feet. A flake of glittering mica, a fragment of variegated quartz, a bright pebble from the bed of the creek, became beautiful to eyes thus cleared and strengthened, and were invariably put aside for The Luck. It was wonderful how many treasures the woods and hillsides yielded that "would do for Tommy." Surrounded by playthings such as never child out of fairyland had before, it is to be hoped that Tommy was content. He appeared to be serenely happy, albeit there was an infantine gravity about him, a contemplative light in his round gray eyes, that sometimes worried Stumpy.

He was always tractable and quiet, and it is recorded that once, having crept beyond his corral—a hedge of tessellated pine boughs, which surrounded his bed—he dropped over the bank on his head in the soft earth, and remained with his mottled legs in the air in that position for at least five minutes with unflinching gravity. He was extricated without a murmur. I hesitate to record the many other instances of his sagacity, which rest, unfortunately, upon the statements of prejudiced friends. Some of them were not without a tinge of superstition.

"I crep' up the bank just now," said Kentuck one day, in a breathless state of excitement, "and dern my skin if he wasn't a-talking to a jaybird as was a-sittin' on his lap. There they was, just as free and sociable as anything you please, a-jawin' at each other just like two cherrybums."

Howbeit, whether creeping over the pine boughs or lying lazily on his back blinking at the leaves above him, to him the birds sang, the squirrels chattered, and the flowers bloomed. Nature was his nurse and playfellow. For him she would let slip between the leaves golden shafts of sunlight that fell just within his grasp; she would send wandering breezes to visit him with the balm of bay and resinous gum; to him the tall redwoods nodded familiarly and sleepily, the bumblebees buzzed, and the rooks cawed a slumbrous accompaniment.

Such was the golden summer of Roaring Camp. They were "flush times," and the luck was with them. The claims had yielded enormously. The camp was jealous of its privileges and looked suspiciously on strangers. No encouragement was given to immigration, and, to make their seclusion more perfect, the land on either side of the mountain wall that surrounded the camp they duly pre-empted.

This, and a reputation for singular proficiency with the revolver, kept the reserve of Roaring Camp inviolate. The expressman—their only connecting link with the surrounding world—sometimes told wonderful stories of the camp. He would say, "They've a street up there in 'Roaring' that would lay over any street in Red Dog. They've got vines and flowers round their houses, and they wash themselves twice a day. But they're mighty rough on strangers, and they worship an Injin baby."

With the prosperity of the camp came a desire for further improvement. It was proposed to build a hotel in the following spring, and to invite one or two decent families to reside there for the sake of The Luck, who might perhaps profit by female companionship. The sacrifice that this concession to the sex cost these men, who were fiercely skeptical in regard to its general virtue and usefulness, can only be accounted for by their affection for Tommy. A few still held out. But the resolve could not be carried into effect for three months, and the minority meekly yielded in the hope that something might turn up to prevent it. And it did.

The winter of 1851 will long be remembered in the foothills. The snow lay deep on the Sierras, and every mountain creek became a river, and every river a lake. Each gorge and gulch was transformed into a tumultuous watercourse that descended the hillsides, tearing down giant trees and scattering its drift and débris along the plain. Red Dog had been twice under water, and Roaring Camp had been forewarned.

"Water put the gold into them gulches," said Stumpy. "It's been here once and will be here again!" And that night the North Fork suddenly leaped over its banks and swept up the triangular valley of Roaring Camp.

In the confusion of rushing water, crashing trees, and crackling timber, and the darkness which seemed to flow with the water and blot out the fair valley, but little could be done to collect the scattered camp.

When the morning broke, the cabin of Stumpy, nearest the riverbank, was gone. Higher up the gulch they found the body of its unlucky owner; but the pride, the hope, the joy, The Luck, of Roaring Camp had disappeared. They were returning with sad hearts when a shout from the bank recalled them.

It was a relief-boat from down the river. They had picked up, they said, a man and an infant, nearly exhausted, about two miles below. Did anybody know them, and did they belong here?

It needed but a glance to show them Kentuck lying there, cruelly crushed and bruised, but still holding The Luck of Roaring Camp in his arms. As they bent over the strangely assorted pair, they saw that the child was cold and pulseless. "He is dead," said one.

Kentuck opened his eyes, "Dead?" he repeated feebly.

"Yes, my man, and you are dying too."

A smile lit the eyes of the expiring Kentuck. "Dying!" he repeated; "he's a-taking me with him. Tell the boys I've got The Luck with me now," and the strong man, clinging to the frail babe as a drowning man is said to cling to a straw, drifted away into the shadowy river that flows forever to the unknown sea.

Discussion Questions

1. Compare Harte's essay with Kevin Starr's description of the Gold Rush. How realistic do you think Harte's portrayal was of the mining camps? How do the details he uses work to bring the story alive? Do you think realism is necessary for the success of this story?

2. In this story Harte portrays the miners' care of the baby and their nurturing abilities as linked to their "luck." What gender roles has Harte reversed in the story? What role do women play in the story? Do you think Harte was suggesting the possibility of a male-only "utopia," or do you think the death of the child at the end of the story makes a different statement about the possibilities of an all-male world?

Writing Suggestions

1. Write a personal response to this story in your journal. Did you find the story moving, disturbing, entertaining? What impression of the Gold Rush did you take away from the story? Did Harte's style and tone appeal to you? Why or why not?

2. Review your answers to the second discussion question for this selection. Then write your ideas in an essay in which you answer the following questions:

    What gender roles has Harte reversed in the story?

    What role do women play in the story?

    Do you think Harte was suggesting the possibility of a male-only "utopia," or do you think the death of the child at the end of the story makes a different statement about the possibilities of an all-male world?

Be sure to use specific examples and quotes from the story.

Closing the Gate
The Very Recklessness of Statesmanship

ANDREW GYORY

Andrew Gyory received his Ph.D. in American history from the University of Massachusetts at Amherst in 1991, and has taught at Hunter College and Montclair State University. Currently, he is the executive editor of *Sharpe Reference* in Armonk, New York. Gyory is well-known for his studies of the Chinese in America, and his book *Closing the Gate: Race, Politics, and the Chinese Exclusion Act* won the Theodore Saloutos Award from the Immigration and Ethnic History Association. In the following selection from *Closing the Gate*, Gyory traces different historical interpretations of the Chinese Exclusion Act and proposes his own theory for understanding how politicians played such an important role in "the first law ever passed by the United States banning a group of immigrants solely on the basis of race or nationality."

I feel and know that I am pleading the cause of the free American laborer and of his children and of his children's children.

—James G. Blaine, February 24, 1879

"Ought we to exclude them?" asked Senator James G. Blaine on February 14, 1879. "The question lies in my mind thus: either the Anglo-Saxon race will possess the Pacific slope or the Mongolians will possess it." Championing the Fifteen Passenger Bill, a measure aimed at limiting Chinese immigration, Blaine declared on the Senate floor: "We have this day to choose . . . whether our legislation shall be in the interest of the American free laborer or for the servile laborer from China. . . . You cannot work a man who must have beef and bread, and would prefer beer, alongside of a man who can live on rice. It cannot be done."

With this speech, James Blaine became the nation's foremost politician to vigorously advocate Chinese exclusion. In a widely reprinted letter to the *New York Tribune* a week later, he elaborated his position, calling Chinese immigration "vicious," "odious," "abominable," "dangerous," and "revolting. . . . If as a nation we have the right to keep out infectious diseases, if we have the right to exclude the criminal classes from coming to us, we surely have the right to exclude that immigration which reeks with impurity and which cannot come to us without plenteously sowing the seeds of moral and physical disease, destitution, and death." Leaving no doubt as to where he stood, the Maine Republican concluded, "I am opposed to the Chinese coming here; I am opposed to making them citizens; I am opposed to making them voters."

As the most prominent statesman of the Gilded Age, Blaine single-hand-edly made racist attacks on Chinese immigrants an honorable act. His racist words in 1879 elevated the issue nationally from the streets of San Francisco to the Senate of the United States and made the cries of demagogues respectable. Blaine's polemic broadened the issue from one affecting only the West, where 97 percent of the nation's 105,000 Chinese immigrants lived, to one that sup-posedly affected the entire country, from one that generated political support from all classes on the Pacific Coast to one that might attract a single class na-tionwide—the working class. "There is not a laboring man from the Penob-scot [River in Maine] to the Sacramento [River in California] who would not feel aggrieved, outraged, burdened, crushed, at being forced into competition with the labor and the wages of the Chinese cooly. For one, I would never con-sent, by my vote or my voice, to drive the intelligent workingmen of America to that competition and that degradation." But Chinese immigration, Blaine said, involved more than the issue of class. It also affected racial harmony: "I supposed if there was any people in the world that had a race trouble on hand it was ourselves. I supposed if the admonitions of our own history were any-thing to us we should regard the race trouble as the one thing to be dreaded and the one thing to be avoided. . . . To deliberately sit down and . . . permit an-other and far more serious trouble seems to be the very recklessness of states-manship." As Blaine concluded, "It is a good deal cheaper . . . to avoid the trouble by preventing the immigration." Chinese exclusion could thus mini-mize further racial conflict and preclude another civil war. It could also reduce class tensions. Citing the divisive national railroad strike of 1877 when "un-employed thousands . . . manifested a spirit of violence," Blaine envisioned Chinese exclusion as a palliative measure giving working people what they wanted. "I feel and know that I am pleading the cause of the free American la-borer and of his children and of his children's children."

As the front-runner for his party's nomination for president in 1880, Blaine aimed his message at two constituencies—the West Coast and workers na-tionwide. During three days of debate, he was the only Republican senator east of the Rocky Mountains to speak out against Chinese immigration. But he was hardly alone in his party. When the Senate passed the Fifteen Passenger Bill, which would have limited to fifteen the number of Chinese passengers on any ship coming to the United States, 11 Republicans east of the Rockies supported the measure, and in the House of Representatives, 51 Republicans joined 104 Democrats to pass the bill by a comfortable margin. By 1879, con-gressional support for Chinese immigration restriction was becoming broad and bipartisan. But for a presidential veto it would have become law.

Three years later, in 1882, Congress debated the Chinese Exclusion Act, a measure far more extreme than the Fifteen Passenger Bill of 1879. Although Blaine had lost the Republican nomination to James A. Garfield in 1880, his racial and class arguments against Chinese immigration carried the day. Re-publican after Republican denounced the Chinese with a firmness and venom once the preserve of Westerners. "Alien in manners, servile in labor, pagan in religion, they are fundamentally un-American," thundered Representative Addison McClure (R-Ohio). "There is no common ground of assimilation," Senator George F. Edmunds (R-Vt.) asserted, to which Senator John Sherman (R-Ohio) added, the Chinese "are not a desirable population. . . . They are not good citizens." Invoking visceral racist images, eastern and midwestern Republicans echoed former senator Blaine. Representative George Hazelton (R-Wisc.) called the Chinese immigrant a "loathsome . . . revolting . . . monstrosity . . . [who] lives in herds and sleeps like packs of dogs in kennels." Other congressmen likened the Chinese to rats and swarming insects whose "withering and blighting effect," in the words of Representative Benjamin Butterworth (R-Ohio), "leave in their trail a moral desert." They "spread mildew and rot throughout the entire community," concluded Representative William Calkins (R-Ind.). Permit them to enter and "you plant a cancer in your own country that will eat out its life and destroy it."

Although condemning the Chinese on racial, cultural, and religious grounds, congressmen across the country emphasized that they favored Chinese exclusion because they favored the working person. "My chief reason for supporting such a measure:" said Representative Edwin Willits (R-Mich.), "is, that I believe it is in the interest of American labor." Likewise, Representative Stanton Peelle (R-Ind.) backed the law "upon the ground of protection to American labor as distinguished from protection to American society." As Edward K. Valentine (R-Nebr.) argued, "It is our opportunity to do justice to the American laborer, and injustice to no one." Senator Henry M. Teller (R-Colo.) was blunter: "I see no other way to protect American labor in this country." Lest anyone doubt that workers demanded the law, Representative John Sherwin (R-Ill.) declared that Chinese exclusion "is a question which comes home after all to the men and women who labor with their hands, more than to anyone else. And I think we can trust them in determining it better than we can trust anyone else."

Senator Blaine's endorsement of the Fifteen Passenger Bill in 1879 had given anti-Chinese racism legitimacy, and within three years a strong bipartisan consensus emerged to outlaw Chinese immigration. Scurrying to take credit for the Chinese Exclusion Act, politicians echoed Blaine in claiming to have passed the measure in response to workers' needs and long-stated demands. Although congressional opposition to Chinese immigration had actually begun forming in the mid-1870s, its swiftness amazed many observers. "If such a bill had been proposed in either House of Congress twenty years ago," Senator Sherman noted in 1882, "it would have been the death warrant of the man who offered it." Indeed, when Congress first debated Chinese citizenship in 1870, virtually no one suggested tampering with the nation's century-old policy of open immigration. During the next twelve years, however, Chinese exclusion would become an article of faith in both parties that would dictate political platforms and shape presidential campaigns.

The creation of Chinese immigration as a national issue and the passage of the Chinese Exclusion Act on May 6, 1882, mark a turning point in American history. It was the first immigration law ever passed by the United States barring one specific group of people because of their race or nationality. By changing America's traditional policy of open immigration, this landmark legislation set a precedent for future restrictions against Asian immigrants the late nineteenth and early twentieth centuries and against European immigrants in the 1920s. Despite the broad significance of the Chinese Exclusion Act, it has received remarkably little attention from historians. And much of what has been written is wrong.

Historians have ascribed two theories to explain the origins of the Chinese Exclusion Act: the California thesis and the national racist consensus thesis. The California thesis, advanced by Mary Roberts Coolidge in 1909, posits California and its working people as the key agents of Chinese exclusion. The Chinese first emigrated to America in large numbers in 1849, when, like thousands of people the world over, they joined the gold rush and raced to California. By 1852, about twenty-five thousand Chinese had arrived in Gam Saan, or Gold Mountain, as they called California, some staking claims in the mines, others working as cooks, launderers, and laborers. During the first three years, Coolidge argued, white Californians welcomed the Chinese. Called "one of the most worthy [classes] of our newly adopted citizens" by the state's second governor, the Chinese took part in services commemorating President Zachary Taylor's death in 1850 and marched in the parade celebrating California's admission to the union later that year. "The China Boys will yet vote at the same polls, study at the same schools, and bow at the same altar as our own countrymen," the *San Francisco Alta California* predicted in 1852. Yet long before this newspaper rolled off the press, racial hostilities had erupted in the mining camps when whites tried to drive all "foreigners"—Mexican, South American, and Chinese—from the region. Some Chinese immigrants had signed contracts in their native land to work for a set period of time at substandard wages. Miners and other Californians targeted them for abuse, and politicians exploited the situation for their own benefit. Several officials, such as Governor John Bigler and State Senator Philip Roach, denounced the Chinese and urged restrictions on their entry as early as 1852. Which came first—the anti-Chinese sentiment in the mining camps or the anti-Chinese rhetoric in the state capital—Coolidge did not say, but each fed on the other, and with miners a key voting bloc in the new state, politicians eagerly courted their support. In the course of the decade, the California legislature passed numerous discriminatory laws against the Chinese, culminating with an 1858 exclusion act. Most of these laws and others passed subsequently were declared unconstitutional by state or federal courts.

Despite bigotry and violence directed at them by whites, Chinese immigrants kept coming to Gam Saan, their numbers augmented when the Central Pacific Railroad Company imported thousands of workers directly from China in the 1860s to build the western portion of the transcontinental railroad. "They are very trusty, they are very intelligent, and they live up to their contracts," railroad president Charles Crocker observed, praising their "reliability and steadiness, and their aptitude and capacity for hard work." By 1870, the census counted 49,310 Chinese in California, making up 8.5 percent of the state's population. In San Francisco, the state's largest city, they composed one-fourth of the population; because most Chinese immigrants were single men, they were a third of the workforce. With the decline of mining, the Chinese entered a variety of occupations, including agriculture, manufacturing, and construction, often accepting wages below those of white workers. Combined with racism—the Chinese looked different, practiced a different religion, and seemed reluctant to "assimilate" into American society—this economic competition, Coolidge argued, led white workers to oppose the Chinese, and abetted by politicians, a revived labor movement in San Francisco after the Civil War mobilized against them. Because the courts had ruled that only Congress possessed the power to restrict immigration, western politicians turned to Washington, where as early as 1867 they began introducing bills aimed at limiting Chinese immigration.

In 1876, Democrats and Republicans locked horns in the most competitive presidential election since the Civil War and believed that the electoral votes of the West Coast could make the difference. Both parties embraced the Chinese issue and pushed for immigration restriction. Labor militancy in San Francisco kept the issue in the forefront in the late 1870s, Coolidge maintained, and the same dynamic recurred nationally in the election of 1880. By advocating anti-Chinese legislation to attract votes, national politicians pursued the identical strategy local politicians had used in California in the 1850s and 1860s. "The struggle on the part of both parties . . . to carry California became fiercer and fiercer," Coolidge wrote, "and gave her demands for legislation a prominence in the national legislature out of all proportion to their normal value." Coolidge blamed workers, and particularly Irish immigrants, for fanning the flames of racial hatred. "The clamor of an alien class in a single State— taken up by politicians for their own ends—was sufficient to change the policy of a nation and to commit the United States to a race discrimination at variance with our professed theories of government."

Although marred by class prejudice, numerous inaccuracies, and a polemical tone, Coolidge's presentation of the California thesis has remained the dominant explanation for Chinese exclusion. Succeeding generations of historians have refined but not overturned her argument. In *The Anti-Chinese Movement in California* (1939), Elmer Clarence Sandmeyer offered a more scholarly and balanced account, stressing that anti-Chinese sentiment on the West Coast was not confined to workers but crossed all classes. By 1876, middle-class and conservative Californians vied with workers in opposing Chinese immigration, Sandmeyer contended, while Chinese exclusion "found strong support in the growing labor organizations of the country." Despite these important additions, Sandmeyer essentially reaffirmed Coolidge's thesis.

Three decades later, Alexander Saxton provided the most sophisticated study of anti-Chinese politics. In *The Indispensable Enemy: Labor and the*

Anti-Chinese Movement in California (1971), Saxton traces the roots of anti-Chinese sentiment to working-class ideology of the Jacksonian era. As the franchise spread to propertyless white men in the early 1800s, northern Democrats embraced an egalitarian philosophy that appealed to workers wary of class hierarchy and special privilege. In the South, Democrats (like virtually all white Southerners) possessed a proslavery outlook that necessarily implied black inferiority. To win presidential elections, the Democratic Party needed both sections of the country, and northern Democrats of all classes readily accepted southern positions on slavery and race. "Workingmen alone of the northern white population came into direct competition with free Negroes," Saxton argues, and spurred on by this economic imperative, they incorporated racial supremacy into their ideology. Republicans, on the other hand, descended from a Federalist-Whig tradition that accepted divisions in society based on class and property and, by implication, race. This acceptance of social and class distinctions contributed to a distrust of the poor and a fear of immigrants. Although seemingly patrician in origin, nativism appealed to workers who believed that foreigners threatened their jobs. As the nation expanded westward during the 1840s and 1850s, Whigs and many Democrats wanted to keep the territories free of slavery and free of blacks. Defending his proviso to ban slavery from the vast region soon to be acquired from Mexico, Representative David Wilmot (D-Pa.) stated in 1847: "I plead the cause and the rights of white freemen. I would preserve to free white labor a fair country . . . where the sons of toil, of my own race and own color, can live without the disgrace which association with negro slavery brings upon free labor." This free-soil impulse, Saxton contends, was as much antiblack as antislavery. When these three forces—"whiggishness," nativism, and free soil—converged in the early 1850s to create the Republican Party, the goal of abolishing slavery played a small role. Only during the Civil War, when emancipation became necessary to win the war and preserve the union, did abolitionism become central to Republicans. But these changes during the Civil War and Reconstruction, Saxton claims, had little impact on white workers' racism: "Meanwhile, thousands of Americans, including workingmen and immigrants, passed through the free-soil and unionist phases of anti-slavery without modifying their previously held attitudes toward the Negro. Not much of abolition rubbed off on them." Saxton argues that despite their political differences, Democratic and Republican workers—the pioneers who headed west to California during and after the gold rush—carried with them a nearly identical ideological baggage steeped in racism. In California, however, they encountered not blacks but Chinese, and the transfer of their hostile attitudes from the former to the latter was a logical step, especially when they believed the Chinese posed an economic threat. In the anti-Chinese movement, Saxton concludes, racist white workers found a common foe—an indispensable enemy—that would unite them for generations.

Like Coolidge and Sandmeyer, Saxton pinpoints 1867 as the inauguration of labor's campaign in California against Chinese immigration. By 1870, workers and politicians statewide had made the cause their own, with Democrats and Republicans united on the issue. Saxton elaborates Sandmeyer's claim that 1876 saw a major diffusion of anti-Chinese sentiment across class lines, as most of California's labor organizations had collapsed during the depression in the mid-1870s. "Trade unionism in San Francisco . . . almost ceased to exist during the depression years," Saxton writes, leaving workers "leaderless, embittered, and disorganized." A bipartisan establishment of "respectable" citizens—employers, manufacturers, and business leaders—took the reins of the anti-Chinese movement in the centennial year. Saxton agrees with Sandmeyer that by 1870, organized labor nationally had adopted the issue of Chinese exclusion. Although Saxton's account is by far the most complete, the most textured, and the most persuasive explanation of the origins of the anti-Chinese movement in California, he scarcely connects it to the national debate over Chinese immigration. Like Coolidge and Sandmeyer of generations past, Saxton offers virtually no explanation of how Congress and the rest of the nation came to support Chinese exclusion.

The only serious challenge to the California thesis came in 1969 from Stuart Creighton Miller in *The Unwelcome Immigrant: The American Image of the Chinese, 1785–1882*. Examining thousands of books, magazines, and newspapers from the nineteenth century, Miller finds relentlessly negative stereotypes of the Chinese, a negative image that long preceded their arrival in North America. Merchants, diplomats, and missionaries—the only Americans in the first half of the century to interact with the Celestial Empire, as China was often called—sent back images of "Chinese deceit, cunning, idolatry, despotism, xenophobia, cruelty, infanticide, and intellectual and sexual perversity." This racist image, Miller writes, coincided with the emerging scientific controversy over racial origins and differences and whether human beings constituted one or multiple species. Because scientists on both sides accepted the inferiority of the "Mongolian" and "Ethiopian" races, the debate provided a solid basis for "Caucasian" superiority and "heightened American consciousness of racial differences." Racist iconography of the Chinese gained broad currency during the Opium War (1839–1842), the first major event involving the Celestial Empire covered by American newspapers, and this negative imagery read more widely in following decades with the rise of the penny press. "The important point to keep in mind," Miller argues, "is that the unfavorable image of the Chinese is discernible among American opinion makers long before the first Celestial gold seeker set foot upon California soil." It is this unfavorable image, Miller maintains, that served as the key agent of Chinese exclusion: "The accepted interpretation of the Chinese exclusion laws, referred to . . . as the 'California thesis,' does not stand up under close scrutiny and should be substantially modified, if not completely altered. To view the policy of exclusion simply as a victory for the obsessive prejudice of Californians is neither accurate nor fair. Although that state unquestionably catalyzed and spearheaded the movement for exclusion, there were much more potent national and historical forces at work than the mere accident of evenly balanced political parties."

Although Miller effectively illustrates the prevalence of anti-Chinese imagery in nineteenth-century America, his explanation for Chinese exclusion possesses a fundamental flaw: it is entirely intellectual. Racist thought does not necessarily produce racist action, and by leaving the politics out, Miller fails to make the connection of how racist imagery—or racism itself—gained expression in national legislation. Anti-Chinese imagery provided a climate conducive to exclusion but did not in itself cause it. In tracing causation, Miller repeats and magnifies earlier assumptions on working-class agency: "It would not be difficult to indict organized labor as the backbone of the anti-Chinese movement on a national level. Labor leaders in every section of the country attacked the coolie issue with the monomania of men whose backs are to the wall. . . . Virtually every labor newspaper and organization opposed Chinese immigration after 1870."

In emphasizing the role of the national labor movement, Miller joined the ranks of nearly every labor historian who has treated the subject. In 1918, John R. Commons, founder of the Wisconsin school of labor history and dean of labor historians, wrote that as early as 1870, the "national labour movement consistently" supported the exclusion of Chinese immigrants. His student Selig Perlman later called the Chinese Exclusion Act "the most important single factor in the history of American labor." These two set the tone for future labor historiography on the subject. Historians Philip Taft, Joseph G. Rayback, and Gerald N. Grob stressed the national labor movement's opposition to Chinese immigration in the 1870s, a point echoed by Herbert Hill, who has argued that nationally, "organized labor took up the anti-Chinese litany after 1870" and formed "the vanguard of the anti-Asian campaign" during the decade and that "the great effort generated in the ranks of labor" contributed to the Chinese Exclusion Act in 1882. Labor and immigration historians Robert D. Parmet and A. T. Lane, as well as Roger Daniels and Ronald Takaki, leading scholars of the Asian American experience, have also accepted this interpretation. As David R. Roediger writes, "Rare is the modern labor historian who does not recoil from regarding Chinese exclusion as *the* historic victory of the American working class."

The historian who most forcefully connects the national labor movement with the Chinese Exclusion Act is Gwendolyn Mink. In her 1986 study, *Old Labor and New Immigrants in American Political Development: Union, Party, and State, 1875–1920*, Mink argues that after the Civil War, "immigration, rather than immigrants, played the decisive role in formulating an American version of labor politics." Squeezed from below by newcomers from abroad, "the trade-union response to this pressure was to mobilize, and then to lobby, for immigration restriction." The overriding force galvanizing the labor movement and driving it toward this xenophobic goal was anti-Chinese hostility. "From the mid-1870s a profound racial and nativist strain would be at the political core of trade unionism," Mink writes, "Although the 'Chinese menace' was geographically contained, the anti-Chinese movement must be viewed in a national context. It invigorated national union solidarity." In providing "a peculiar bridge between unionism and national politics," she adds, Chinese exclusion became the dominant issue uniting the labor movement after the Civil War.

By placing anti-Chinese politics at the heart of the national labor movement and the national labor movement at the heart of the anti-Chinese campaign, Mink profoundly distorts the evolution of working-class ideology and organized labor after the Civil War. Like countless historians before and after, she misunderstands the positions of workers and working-class leaders nationwide toward Chinese immigration in the late 1860s and 1870s. One reason for Mink's faulty interpretation stems from her heavy reliance on secondary sources—many of which she misreads. She claims, for example, that as a result of working-class militancy in San Francisco in 1877–1878, Republicans included an anti-Chinese plank in their national platform in 1880—ignoring completely that Republicans had included an anti-Chinese plank in 1876, well before this labor militancy erupted. Her assertion that in 1882 Chinese exclusion was "a Democratic issue" overlooks the many prominent Republicans such as Blaine who strongly supported the Chinese Exclusion Act, vigorously campaigned on it, and took credit for it. Mink also errs by stating that in 1885, "Congress passed the Foran Act, repealing Republican Civil War legislation that had authorized the recruitment of European contract labor." Congress had actually repealed this legislation seventeen years earlier, in 1868. This fact debunks her conclusion that organized labor's successful campaign against Chinese immigration "prodded" the labor movement to oppose contract labor. The labor movement needed no such prodding. As the historical record makes clear, the fight to outlaw contract labor long preceded any effort by the national labor movement to restrict Chinese immigration. Perhaps Mink's most egregious error lies in repeatedly stressing, with virtually no original evidence, that workers in the eastern United States backed the cries of their brethren in California and that their support for Chinese exclusion thereby "nationalized labor politics." By misrepresenting workers' attitudes toward Chinese immigration, Mink seriously skews the development of the labor movement after the Civil War and presents a thesis on the origin of the Chinese Exclusion Act that is patently invalid.

In placing race at the core of white working-class formation, Mink echoes the work of Saxton and Hill and anticipates that of Roediger. No one has analyzed this theme more brilliantly than Saxton himself. In *The Rise and Fall of the White Republic: Class Politics and Mass Culture in Nineteenth-Century America* (1990), he dissects images and themes in popular culture to show how white racism evolved in the 1800s from a vague construct to a vital ideological force that helped justify slavery, American Indian extermination, and Chinese exclusion. Saxton's genius rests in portraying multiple racisms—Republicans could be "soft" on blacks but "hard" on Native Americans (and a little of both on the Chinese)—and in identifying politics as the conduit for crystallizing and propagating racial discourse. Whether dealing with slavery, westward expansion, or industrialization, politics served as the crucible for racism to be defined, refined, and perpetuated. Stressing the importance of American Indian

removal to the ideological formation of both political parties, Saxton argues
that for Democrats, strong proponents of slavery and manifest destiny, extermination of American Indians reinforced white superiority, whereas for Republicans, driven more by industrialization than by antislavery or territorial
growth, extermination helped harden racial attitudes and legitimize racist policies. As class boundaries solidified after the Civil War, racial identification became more central to working-class ideology, and white workers effortlessly
transferred antiblack and anti-Indian hostility to the Chinese. Although Saxton
convincingly traces the evolution of Democratic racial thought, he is less persuasive and less comprehensive in his analysis of Republican racial attitudes.
He claims that Free-Soilers, while virulently anti-Indian, remained silent on
blacks, a silence he doesn't explain. As a result, a key strand of Republican ideology—abolitionism and racial equality—remains unexplored and uncon-
nected to the party's Reconstruction policies. To Saxton, Reconstruction was a
momentary blip in the nation's history with little lasting impact on party policy or working-class ideology. This failure to analyze the antislavery, free-labor
heritage with the same rigor he applies to other forces leads Saxton to discount
the significance of this heritage and obscures the manner in which workers
adapted it to their ideology after the Civil War.

One of Saxton's major contributions is his emphasis on the complexity of
racism, his assertion that neither economic competition nor psychological
needs can explain the prevalence and pervasiveness of racism in American
history. Racism, he argues, is ultimately an ideological construct that has
served different functions for different groups and classes in different eras.
As he contends, "neither trade unionists nor anyone else in nineteenth-century
America arrived at conclusions involving matters of race simply through
processes of economic reasoning." There is a corollary, however, that Saxton
does not explore: white workers, like other white Americans, could be deeply
racist and possess a deeply racist ideology, but that does not mean they necessarily acted on this racist ideology or pursued or supported racist policies.
Thought is not action; ideology is not policy. Workers could be racist and still
oppose exclusion.

Saxton's failure to integrate the abolitionist legacy undercuts his analysis
of working-class attitudes toward Chinese immigration. By endorsing the
view that eastern workers united with western workers in support of Chinese exclusion after the Civil War, Saxton and all his predecessors miss a key
development and a key moment in working-class history. Racist as white
workers may have been in this era, they were neither much more nor much
less racist than other segments of American society. And although they were
the only group with a distinct economic motive to favor Chinese exclusion,
eastern workers—who made up the vast bulk of the working classes and the
national labor movement—were largely indifferent to Chinese exclusion and
played practically no role in the passage of the Chinese Exclusion Act.

One other historian bears noting. In *The Wages of Whiteness: Race and
the Making of the American Working Class* (1991), David Roediger stresses the

concept of whiteness as the signal force unifying workers before the Civil War. Whiteness provided psychological distance from blacks and elevated white workers, especially Irish immigrants, to a common equality as American citizens. Although Roediger offers numerous examples of working-class racism, his survey is ultimately impressionistic, giving little sense of working-class policies or working-class demands. He acknowledges but minimizes workers' roles as Free-Soilers and abolitionists and yet contends, unlike Saxton, that the war transformed workers' attitudes. Quoting Karl Marx, Roediger writes: "There was . . . a stunning 'moral impetus' . . . injected into the working-class movement by the Civil War and emancipation. Anti-slavery luminaries were not just welcomed onto labor platforms but courted by workers' organizations." Attempts at interracial unity "set it [the postwar labor movement] dramatically apart from the antebellum labor movement." But such unity had its limits, Roediger argues, citing as evidence the "tremendous working-class response in areas such as Chicago and Massachusetts . . . [to] the anti-Chinese movement." Much like Mink, Roediger relies heavily on secondary sources. Consequently, despite his careful attention to the meanings of working-class terminology (such as "wage slavery" and "white slavery"), he misses some of the nuances of that terminology and thus misconstrues working-class attitudes toward Chinese immigration. "Race is constructed differently across time by people in the same social class," Roediger argues, "and differently at the same time by people whose class positions differ." But to go one step further, race is also constructed differently at the same time by people in the *same* social class. Workers' myriad attitudes toward Chinese immigration demonstrate this point and reveal the dangers of generalizing too broadly about the extent and uniformity of racism in any single group.

Both the California thesis of Coolidge and Sandmeyer and the national racist consensus thesis of Miller provide valid insights into the origins of the Chinese Exclusion Act, but neither thesis explains the process by which Chinese exclusion came to be enacted. Nor does either thesis explain how national politicians appropriated and packaged the issue. The California thesis, in which West Coast activists agitated for Chinese exclusion and national politicians then picked up the issue for their own personal gain, remains accurate, but the emphasis on agency should be reversed. The single most important force behind the Chinese Exclusion Act was national politicians of both parties who seized, transformed, and manipulated the issue of Chinese immigration in the quest for votes. In an era of almost perfectly balanced party strength, presidential elections pivoted on a few thousand ballots, and candidates flailed desperately to capture them. Chinese immigrants, powerless and voteless, became pawns in a political system characterized by legislative stalemate and presidential elections decided by razor-thin margins. Politicians also used Chinese immigration as a smoke screen. In a period of rising class conflict, they aimed both to propitiate working-class voters and to deflect attention from genuine national problems—economic depression, mass poverty, and growing unemployment—by magnifying and distorting a side issue of paltry signifi- cance into one of seemingly overriding national importance. Chinese immi- grants became the indispensable enemy not to workers but to politicians, who, in a period of converging political consensus, needed a safe, nonideological cause to trumpet. Politicians—not California, not workers, and not national racist imagery—ultimately supplied the agency for Chinese exclusion.

The Chinese Exclusion Act provides a classic example of top-down poli- tics and opens a unique window for viewing the political system of the Gild- ed Age. The act also illustrates the transformation of the Republican Party from an antislavery force to a mere electoral apparatus. This transformation was neither swift nor sudden. Nor was it complete. As late as 1882, many principled Republicans fought exclusion adamantly. The difference, howev- er, was that in 1870 this idealistic wing of the party, the wing that had fought for emancipation and civil rights for freed slaves, was still influential and re- spected even by its enemies. But by 1882, this once prominent force had been relegated to the party's fringe. Formerly revered as the conscience of the na- tion, these altruistic leaders were now considered a nuisance and portrayed as doddering sentimentalists, "humanitarian half thinkers." The passage of the Chinese Exclusion Act reflects the passing of an era, revealing this funda- mental change in both the Republican Party and the nation at large.

The Chinese Exclusion Act marks the coda of Reconstruction, with North, South, and West uniting to usher in a new era of state-sponsored segregation. After a brief period of federal efforts to protect civil rights and promote inte- gration, politicians found restrictive, racist legislation a simpler and easier way to handle the nation's race problems. With antiblack bigotry temporari- ly in eclipse (at least among many) in the late 1860s and 1870s, anti-Chinese racism filled the vacuum and provided a convenient alternative in the hunt for scapegoats amid a sputtering economy. Anti-Chinese racism served as a bridge from the antebellum era to the rise of Jim Crow in the 1880s when racism again became fashionable. The Chinese Exclusion Act, by which Con- gress and the United States government legitimized racism as national poli- cy, remains a key legacy of the nineteenth century, and its lingering impact of anti-Asian bigotry remains to this day.

The origins of Chinese exclusion are neither simple nor direct. They in- volve numerous twists and turns through a decade and a half of industrial up- heaval and mounting class tensions. While Chinese immigrants flocked to Gam Saan in the nineteenth century, Californians, workers, and the national labor movement put the Chinese question on the map, but Gilded Age politi- cians redrew the map's boundaries and recast the issue. Abetted by the press, politicians such as James Blaine and countless others convinced the nation that American workers demanded Chinese exclusion and would be better off without Chinese immigrants. Nationally, however, workers remained gener- ally uninterested in Chinese exclusion. This, then, is the double tragedy of the Chinese Exclusion Act: not only did politicians close the gate on an entire race of people, but they also blamed this act on a group that did not seek it. Historians should no longer be misled by their arguments.

Discussion Questions

1. According to Gyory, what are the differences between the California thesis and the national racist thesis in explaining the Chinese Exclusion Act? Discuss in groups the major differences between each of the theories Gyory presents. What theory does Gyory offer for the passage and popularity of the Chinese Exclusion Act?
2. Do you think that the Chinese Exclusion Act resulted from racism or from the struggle for economic power and land acquisition? Discuss Gyory's assertions about racism, economics, and politics.

Writing Suggestions

1. Gyory presents a detailed analysis of the political forces behind the Exclusion Act. Write a well-analyzed summary of the major points in this selection. Organize your essay so that a reader unfamiliar with the selection could read your essay and come away with a clear sense of the political influences at work before the passage of the Chinese Exclusion Act.
2. Gyory claims that "in their quest for votes" the single most important force behind the Chinese Exclusion Act was the quest for power of "national politicians of both parties." Gyory has written elsewhere that he "detected a direct connection from the 1880s to the 1990s" concerning politicians and the "ongoing debate over race and immigration." Consider the role of politicians in immigration legislation today, and write a paper in which you trace and analyze the impact of political influence on immigration policies affecting those wishing to come to America from Haiti, Cuba, and Mexico. Analyze the arguments, for example, of a recent U.S. governor, senator, or congressperson, or of Presidents Bush or Clinton. How do immigration policies fit into the politician's party politics? What kinds of arguments has the politician made? What language and rhetoric appear in speeches about immigration? Refer to Gyory and the Chinese Exclusion Act in your paper, noting similarities or differences in political influence on immigration policies.

The Chinese Exclusion Act

Numbers of Chinese workers began to arrive in California after the news of the Gold Rush reached China, and by 1865 these Chinese workers were actually being recruited to work on the construction of the transcontinental railroad. However, the Chinese found themselves facing increasing hostility after the completion of the railroad, and by 1882 the first of four exclusion laws was passed by the U.S. government, barring laborers from entering the United States. The following text of the first of the exclusion laws bars all Chinese laborers from entering the United States; the ban also included their wives, who were considered laborers.

Forty-Seventh Congress. Session I. 1882

Chapter 126.—An act to execute certain treaty stipulations relating to Chinese.

Preamble.

Whereas, in the opinion of the Government of the United States the coming of Chinese laborers to this country endangers the good order of certain localities within the territory thereof: Therefore,

Be it enacted by the Senate and House of Representatives of the United States of America in Congress assembled, That from and after the expiration of ninety days next after the passage of this act, and until the expiration of ten years next after the passage of this act, the coming of Chinese laborers to the United States be, and the same is hereby, suspended; and during such suspension it shall not be lawful for any Chinese laborer to come, or, having so come after the expiration of said ninety days, to remain within the United States.

SEC. 2. That the master of any vessel who shall knowingly bring within the United States on such vessel, and land or permit to be landed, any Chinese laborer, from any foreign port of place, shall be deemed guilty of a misdemeanor, and on conviction thereof shall be punished by a fine of not more than five hundred dollars for each and every such Chinese laborer so brought, and may be also imprisoned for a term not exceeding one year.

SEC. 3. That the two foregoing sections shall not apply to Chinese laborers who were in the United States on the seventeenth day of November, eighteen hundred and eighty, or who shall have come into the same before the expiration of ninety days next after the passage of this act, and who shall produce to such master before going on board such vessel, and shall produce to the collector of the port in the United States at which such vessel shall arrive, the evidence hereinafter in this act required of his being one of the laborers in this section mentioned; nor shall the two foregoing sections apply to the case of any master whose vessel, being bound to a port not within the United States by reason of being in distress or in stress of weather, or touching at any port of the United States on its voyage to any foreign port of place: *Provided*, That all Chinese laborers brought on such vessel shall depart with the vessel on leaving port.

SEC. 4. That for the purpose of properly identifying Chinese laborers who were in the United States on the seventeenth day of November, eighteen hundred and eighty, or who shall have come into the same before the expiration of ninety days next after the passage of this act, and in order to furnish them with the proper evidence of their right to go from and come to the United States of their free will and accord, as provided by the treaty between the United States and China dated November seventeenth, eighteen hundred and eighty, the collector of customs of the district from which any such Chinese laborer shall depart from the United States shall, in person or by deputy, go on board each vessel having on board any such Chinese laborer and cleared or about to sail from his district for a foreign port, and on such vessel make a list of all such Chinese laborers, which shall be entered in registry-books to be kept for that purpose, in which shall be stated the name, age, occupation, last place of residence, physical marks or peculiarities, and all facts necessary for the identification of each of such Chinese laborers, which books shall be safely kept in the custom-house; and every such Chinese laborer so departing from the United States shall be entitled to, and shall receive, free of any charge or cost upon application therefor, from the collector or his deputy, at the time such list is taken, a certificate, signed by the collector or his deputy and attested by his seal of office, in such form as the Secretary of the Treasury shall prescribe, which certificate shall contain a statement of the name, age, occupation, last place of residence, personal description, and fact of identification of the Chinese laborer to whom the certificate is issued, corresponding with the said list and registry in all particulars. In case any Chinese laborer after having received such certificate shall leave such vessel before her departure he shall deliver his certificate to the master of the vessel, and if such Chinese laborer shall fail to return to such vessel before her departure from port the certificate shall be delivered by the master to the collector of customs for cancellation. The certificate herein provided for shall entitle the Chinese laborer to whom the same is issued to return to and re-enter the United States upon producing and delivering the same to the collector of customs of the district at which such Chinese laborer shall seek to re-enter; and upon delivery of such certificate by such Chinese laborer to the collector of customs at the time of re-entry in the United States, said collector shall cause the same to be filed in the custom house and duly canceled.

SEC. 5. That any Chinese laborer mentioned in section four of this act being in the United States, and desiring to depart from the United States by land, shall have the right to demand and receive, free of charge or cost, a certificate of identification similar to that provided for in section four of this act to be issued to such Chinese laborers as may desire to leave the United States by water; and it is hereby made the duty of the collector of customs of the district next adjoining the foreign country to which said Chinese laborer desires to go to issue such certificate, free of charge or cost, upon application by such Chinese laborer, and to enter the same upon registry-books to be kept by him for the purpose, as provided for in section four of this act.

SEC. 6. That in order to the faithful execution of articles one and two of the treaty in this act before mentioned, every Chinese person other than a laborer who may be entitled by said treaty and this act to come within the United States, and who shall be about to come to the United States, shall be identified as so entitled by the Chinese Government in each case, such identity to be evidenced by a certificate issued under the authority of said government, which certificate shall be in the English language or (if not in the English language) accompanied by a translation into English, stating such right to come, and which certificate shall state the name, title, or official rank, if any, the age, height, and all physical peculiarities, former and present occupation or profession, and place of residence in China of the person to whom the certificate is issued and that such person is entitled conformably to the treaty in this act mentioned to come within the United States. Such certificate shall be prima-facie evidence of the fact set forth therein, and shall be produced to the collector of customs, or his deputy, of the port in the district in the United States at which the person named therein shall arrive.

SEC. 7. That any person who shall knowingly and falsely alter or substitute any name for the name written in such certificate or forge any such certificate, or knowingly utter any forged or fraudulent certificate, or falsely personate any person named in any such certificate, shall be deemed guilty of a misdemeanor; and upon conviction thereof shall be fined in a sum not exceeding one thousand dollars, and imprisoned in a penitentiary for a term of not more than five years.

SEC. 8. That the master of any vessel arriving in the United States from any foreign port or place shall, at the same time he delivers a manifest of the cargo, and if there be no cargo, then at the time of making a report of the entry of vessel pursuant to the law, in addition to the other matter required to be reported, and before landing, or permitting to land, any Chinese passengers, deliver and report to the collector of customs of the district in which such vessels shall have arrived a separate list of all Chinese passengers taken on board his vessel at any foreign port or place, and all such passengers on board the vessel at that time. Such list shall show the names of such passengers (and if accredited officers of the Chinese Government traveling on the business of that government, or their servants, with a note of such facts), and the name and other particulars, as shown by their respective certificates; and such list shall be sworn to by the master in the manner required by law in relation to the manifest of the cargo. Any willful refusal or neglect of any such master to comply with the provisions of this section shall incur the same penalties and forfeiture as are provided for a refusal or neglect to report and deliver a manifest of cargo.

SEC. 9. That before any Chinese passengers are landed from any such vessel, the collector, or his deputy, shall proceed to examine such passengers, comparing the certificates with the list and with the passengers; and no passenger shall be allowed to land in the United States from such vessel in violation of law.

SEC. 10. That every vessel whose master shall knowingly violate any of the provisions of this act shall be deemed forfeited to the United States, and shall be liable to seizure and condemnation on any district of the United States into which such vessel may enter or in which she may be found.

SEC. 11. That any person who shall knowingly bring into or cause to be brought into the United States by land, or who shall knowingly aid or abet the same, or aid or abet the landing in the United States from any vessel of any Chinese person not lawfully entitled to enter the United States, shall be deemed guilty of a misdemeanor, and shall, on conviction thereof, be fined in a sum not exceeding one thousand dollars, and imprisoned for a term not exceeding one year.

SEC. 12. That no Chinese person shall be permitted to enter the United States by land without producing to the proper officer of customs the certificate in this act required of Chinese persons seeking to land from a vessel. And any Chinese person found unlawfully within the United States shall be caused to be removed therefrom to the country from whence he came, by direction of the United States, after being brought before some justice, judge, or commissioner of a court of the United States and found to be one not lawfully entitled to be or remain in the United States.

SEC. 13. That this act shall not apply to diplomatic and other officers of the Chinese Government traveling upon the business of that government, whose credentials shall be taken as equivalent to the certificate in this act mentioned, and shall exempt them and their body and household servants from the provisions of this act as to other Chinese persons.

SEC. 14. That hereafter no State court or court of the United States shall admit Chinese to citizenship; and all laws in conflict with this act are hereby repealed.

SEC. 15. That the words "Chinese laborers," whenever used in this act, shall be construed to mean both skilled and unskilled laborers and Chinese employed in mining.

Approved, May 6, 1882.

Discussion Questions

1.   The wording of the Chinese Exclusion Act is at times quite complicated and difficult to follow. In discussion groups, take one paragraph each and try to condense that paragraph into a single sentence. Then come back together as a group and see if you can distill the important rules and restrictions in this document into one paragraph of clear sentences. Then discuss how the writing in this document might have affected those Chinese laborers who would have had to understand the legalities involved. Who would have had to interpret these rules and regulations? What second language problems would be involved? Why might the document be worded in this kind of language?

2.   What is so important about Section 14 of this document? How would Section 14 hurt the Chinese who were allowed to stay in the United States?

Writing Suggestions

1.   Review your ideas from the first discussion question for this selection. Then write your findings in a clearly worded paragraph distilling the meaning of the Exclusion Act. Next, freewrite a response to the following questions:

     How might the writing in this document have affected those Chinese laborers who would have had to understand the legalities involved?

     Who would have had to interpret these rules and regulations?

     What second language problems would be involved?

     Why might the document be worded in this kind of language?

     Finally, write a two-page essay in which you discuss your ideas about the language of the Chinese Exclusion Act and its effect on Chinese laborers.

2.   Gyory wrote, "At the dawn of a new century, the Chinese Exclusion Act still casts a long, dark shadow over American society and our nation's treatment of immigrants." Using a search engine such as Google, research the latest immigration controversies and policies under discussion in the United States. Then write an essay in which you agree or disagree with Gyory, using specific examples from the Exclusion Act and from recent U.S. immigration policies. Do recent immigration policies reflect policies implemented during Chinese Exclusion? Or do you feel that our policies have evolved for the better since that time? Use specific examples of current laws and current immigration decisions by the U.S. government in your argument.

3.   Research the exclusion of the Chinese from the United States, and write a paper in which you follow the fates of those Chinese who did stay in California and other states. How did they cope with the restrictions against them? What kind of work did they find? Which businesses were they allowed to keep? What happened to these workers over the next 100 years? How and when did they regain their rights to work and live and vote in America?

The Chinese Question

THOMAS NAST

Thomas Nast (1849–1902), who immigrated from Bavaria to New York at an early age, studied art as a child and eventually worked as an artist at a variety of newspapers. After working as a freelance artist for *Harper's Weekly* for several years, in 1862 he became a member of the staff and began his flourishing career as a political cartoonist. Much of Nast's work was made into wood engravings, which were then printed in *Harper's Weekly*. One of his most famous campaigns was against the Tammany Hall Democrat, "Boss" Tweed, whom he depicted as a corrupt and ruthless politician. Nast also is credited with the symbol of the Democratic Party donkey and the Republican Party elephant. Nast had strong political opinions, and was staunchly in support of the Union, an end to slavery, and fair treatment of the Chinese workers. Nast's opinion about fair treatment of the Chinese is reflected in his cartoon "The Chinese Question."

When *Harper's Weekly* ran Thomas Nast's political cartoon "The Chinese Question" (see page 414) in 1871, the debate about Chinese immigration had become an important political topic, especially on the West Coast of the United States. In 1865, Chinese workers had been desperately needed to complete the Central Pacific Railroad, making up 80 percent of the workforce that blasted through tunnels and worked through terrible conditions in the Sierra Nevada. However, once the railroad was finished in 1869, the Chinese became scapegoats for any economic hardships or unemployment faced by white workers; white farmers in the West were particularly threatened by the industriousness of the Chinese farmers, who had already been banned from mining by whites who feared their competition. The first of the exclusion laws, barring any additional Chinese laborers from entering the country, were passed in 1882. As the political cartoon on page 414 suggests, animosity toward the Chinese workers was already very strong by 1871.

THE CHINESE QUESTION

"Hands off, gentlemen! America means fair play for all men!"

Thomas Nast, in Harper's Weekly/General Research Division,
The New York Public Library, Astor, Lenox and Tilden Foundations

Discussion Questions

1. Consider the illustration on page 414 carefully, and then write a new caption below it that sums up the argument in one simple sentence.

2. Now discuss the ways in which Thomas Nast makes his main argument. How do the details work to make his point? How does he use diction, symbolism, and fine detail to get the argument across?

Writing Suggestions

1. Write a two- to three-page analysis detailing how Nast argues his point of view; which rhetorical strategies does he pursue? Answer some of the following questions in your essay:

   What is the main argument of the political cartoon? What is the central position that the artist is trying to convey?

   Look closely at the details of the illustration. Which details serve to persuade? How many different details, and what kinds of details, make the artist's point?

   How does the artist consider the audience for this piece—how are the tone and purpose of the piece reflected in the artist's choice of images? How is the opposition represented?

   What kind of words or diction accompany this illustration? How are words used in addition to the illustration to persuade the audience?

   Use very specific examples from the illustration—do a close reading and then use the details to make your points.

2. Design your own political cartoon, and use a caption and drawing to take a stand on one of the immigration issues you have read about in this chapter. Use both illustration and words in the body of the illustration, clarifying your point of view through the use of sarcasm, exaggeration, or irony.

In the Land of the Free

SUI SIN FAR

Sui Sin Far (1865–1914) was the pseudonym adopted by Edith Maude Eaton, the daughter of a Chinese mother and an English father, who was the first Asian American to have her fiction published in the United States. Her work appeared in a variety of magazines, including *The Overland Monthly*, *Century*, and *Good Housekeeping*. In the following story, "In the Land of the Free," Sui Sin Far portrays the helplessness of Chinese families in the face of U.S. immigration policies and dramatizes the exploitation of the Chinese by Christian missionaries.

I

"See Little One—the hills in the morning sun. There is thy home for years to come. It is very beautiful and thou wilt be very happy there."

The Little One looked up into his mother's face in perfect faith. He was engaged in the pleasant occupation of sucking a sweetmeat; but that did not prevent him from gurgling responsively.

"Yes, my olive bud; there is where thy father is making a fortune for thee. Thy father! Oh, wilt thou not be glad to behold his dear face. 'Twas for thee I left him."

The Little One ducked his chin sympathetically against his mother's knee. She lifted him on to her lap. He was two years old, a round, dimple-cheeked boy with bright brown eyes and a sturdy little frame.

"Ah! Ah! Ah! Ooh! Ooh! Ooh!" puffed he, mocking a tugboat steaming by.

San Francisco's waterfront was lined with ships and steamers, while other craft, large and small, including a couple of white transports from the Philippines lay at anchor here and there off shore. It was some time before the *Eastern Queen* could get docked, and even after that was accomplished, a lone Chinaman who had been waiting on the wharf for an hour was detained that much longer by men with the initials U.S.C. on their caps, before he could board the steamer and welcome his wife and child.

"This is thy son," announced the happy Lae Choo.

Hom Hing lifted the child, felt of his little body and limbs, gazed into his face with proud and joyous eyes; then turned inquiringly to a customs officer at his elbow.

"That's a fine boy you have there," said the man. "Where was he born?"

"In China," answered Hom Hing, swinging the Little One on his right shoulder, preparatory to leading his wife off the steamer.

"Ever been to America before?"

"No, not he," answered the father with a happy laugh.

The customs officer beckoned to another.

"This little fellow," said he, "is visiting America for the first time."

The other customs officer stroked his chin reflectively.

"Good day," said Hom Hing.

"Wait!" commanded one of the officers. "You cannot go just yet."

"What more now?" asked Hom Hing.

"I'm afraid," said the customs officer, "that we cannot allow the boy to go ashore. There is nothing in the papers that you have shown us—your wife's papers and your own—having any bearing upon the child."

"There was no child when the papers were made out," returned Hom Hing. He spoke calmly; but there was apprehension in his eyes and in his tightening grip on his son.

"What is it? What is it?" quavered Lae Choo, who understood a little English.

The second customs officer regarded her pityingly.

"I don't like this part of the business," he muttered.

The first officer turned to Hom Hing and in an official tone of voice, said:

"Seeing that the boy has no certificate entitling him to admission to this country you will have to leave him with us."

"Leave my boy!" exclaimed Hom Hing.

"Yes; he will be well taken care of, and just as soon as we can hear from Washington, he will be handed over to you."

"But," protested Hom Hing, "he is my son."

"We have no proof," answered the man with a shrug of his shoulders; "and even if so we cannot let him pass without orders from the Government."

"He is my son," reiterated Hom Hing, slowly and solemnly. "I am a Chinese merchant and have been in business in San Francisco for many years. When my wife told to me one morning that she dreamed of a green tree with spreading branches and one beautiful red flower growing thereon, I answered her that I wished my son to be born in our country, and for her to prepare to go to China. My wife complied with my wish. After my son was born my mother fell sick and my wife nursed and cared for her; then my father, too, fell sick, and my wife also nursed and cared for him. For twenty moons my wife care for and nurse the old people, and when they did they bless her and my son, and I send for her to return to me. I had no fear of trouble. I was a Chinese merchant and my son was my son."

"Very good, Hom Hing," replied the first officer. "Nevertheless, we take your son."

"No, you not take him, he my son too."

It was Lae Choo. Snatching the child from his father's arms she held and covered him with her own.

The officers conferred together for a few moments; then one drew Hom Hing aside and spoke in his ear.

Resignedly Hom Hing bowed his head, then approached his wife. "'Tis the law," said he, speaking in Chinese, "and 'twill be but for a little while—until tomorrow's sun arises."

"You, too," reproached Lae Choo in a voice eloquent with pain. But accustomed to obedience she yielded the boy to her husband, who in turn delivered him to the first officer. The Little One protested lustily against the transfer; but his mother covered her face with her sleeve and his father silently led her away. Thus was the law of the land complied with.

II

Day was breaking. Lae Choo, who had been awake all night, dressed herself, then awoke her husband.

"'Tis the morn," she cried. "Go, bring our son."

The man rubbed his eyes and arose upon his elbow so that he could see out of the window. A pale star was visible in the sky. The petals of a lily in a bowl on the windowsill were unfurled.

"'Tis not yet time," said he, laying his head down again.

"Not yet time. Ah, all the time that I lived before yesterday is no so much as the time that has been since my Little One was taken from me."

The mother threw herself down beside the bed and covered her face.

Hom Hing turned on the light, and touching his wife's bowed head with a sympathetic hand inquired if she had slept.

"Slept!" she echoed, weepingly. "Ah, how could I close my eyes with my arms empty of the little body that has filled them every night for more than twenty moons! You do not know—man—what it is to miss the feel of the little fingers and the little toes and the soft round limbs of your little one. Even in the darkness his darling eyes used to shine up to mine, and often have I fallen into slumber with his pretty babble at my ear. And now, I see him not; I touch him not; I hear him not. My baby, my little fat one!"

"Now! Now! Now!" consoled Hom Hing, patting his wife's shoulder reassuringly; "there is no need to grieve so; he will soon gladden you again. There cannot be any law that would keep a child from its mother!"

Lae Choo dried her tears.

"You are right, my husband," she meekly murmured. She arose and stepped about the apartment, setting things to rights. The box of presents she had brought for her California friends had been opened the evening before; and silks, embroideries, carved ivories, ornamental lacquer-ware, brasses, camphor-wood boxes, fans, and chinaware were scattered around in confused heaps. In the midst of unpacking the thought of her child in the hands of strangers had overpowered her, and she had left everything to crawl into bed and weep.

Having arranged her gifts in order she stepped out on to the deep balcony.

The star had faded from view and there were bright streaks in the western sky. Lae Choo looked down the street and around. Beneath the flat occupied by her and her husband were quarters for a number of bachelor Chinamen, and she could hear them from where she stood, taking their early morning breakfast. Below their dining-room was her husband's grocery store. Across the way was a large restaurant. Last night it had been resplendent with gay colored lanterns and the sound of music. The rejoicings over "the completion of the moon," by Quong Sum's firstborn, had been long and loud, and had caused her to tie a handkerchief over her ears. She, a bereaved mother, had it not in her heart to rejoice with other parents. This morning the place was more in accord with her mood. It was still and quiet. The revellers had dispersed or were asleep.

A roly-poly woman in black sateen, with long pendant earrings in her ears, looked up from the street below and waved her a smiling greeting. It was her old neighbor, Kuie Hoe, the wife of the gold embosser, Mark Sing. With her was a little boy in yellow jacket and lavender pantaloons. Lae Choo remembered him as a baby. She used to like to play with him in those days when she had no child of her own. What a long time ago that seemed! She caught her breath in a sigh, and laughed instead.

"Why are you so merry?" called her husband from within.

"Because my Little One is coming home," answered Lae Choo. "I am a happy mother—a happy mother."

She pattered into the room with a smile on her face.

The noon hour had arrived. The rice was steaming in the bowls and a fragrant dish of chicken and bamboo shoots was awaiting Hom Hing. Not for one moment had Lae Choo paused to rest during the morning hours; her activity had been ceaseless. Every now and again, however, she had raised her eyes to the gilded clock on the curiously carved mantelpiece. Once, she had exclaimed:

"Why so long, oh! why so long?" Then, apostrophizing herself. "Lae Choo, be happy. The Little One is coming! The Little One is coming!" Several times she burst into tears, and several times she laughed aloud.

Hom Hing entered the room; his arms hung down by his side.

"The Little One!" shrieked Lae Choo.

"They bid me call tomorrow."

With a moan the mother sank to the floor.

The noon hour passed. The dinner remained on the table.

III

The winter rains were over: the spring had come to California, flushing the hills with green and causing an ever-changing pageant of flowers to pass over them. But there was no spring in Lae Choo's heart, for the Little One remained away from her arms. He was being kept in a mission. White women were caring for him, and though for one full moon he had pined for his mother and refused to be comforted he was now apparently happy and contented. Five moons or five months had gone by since the day he had passed with Lae Choo through the Golden Gate; but the great Government at Washington still delayed sending the answer which would return him to his parents.

Hom Hing was disconsolately rolling up and down the balls in his aba-
cus box when a keen-faced young man stepped into his store.

"What news?" asked the Chinese merchant.

"This!" The young man brought forth a typewritten letter. Hom Hing read
the words:

"Re Chinese child, alleged to be the son of Hom Hing, Chinese merchant,
doing business at 425 Clay Street, San Francisco.

"Same will have attention as soon as possible."

Hom Hing returned the letter, and without a word continued his manipulation of the counting machine.

"Have you anything to say?" asked the young man.

"Nothing. They have sent the same letter fifteen times before. Have you
not yourself showed it to me?"

"True!" The young man eyed the Chinese merchant furtively. He had
a proposition to make and was pondering whether or not the time was
opportune.

"How is your wife?" he inquired solicitously—and diplomatically.

Hom Hing shook his head mournfully.

"She seems less every day," he replied. "Her food she takes only when I
bid her and her tears fall continuously. She finds no pleasure in dress or flowers and cares not to see her friends. Her eyes stare all night. I think before another moon she will pass into the land of spirits."

"No!" exclaimed the young man, genuinely startled.

"If the boy not come home I lose my wife sure," continued Hom Hing
with bitter sadness.

"It's not right," cried the young man indignantly. Then he made his
proposition.

The Chinese father's eyes brightened exceedingly.

"Will I like you to go to Washington and make them give you the paper
to restore my son?" cried he. "How can you ask when you know my heart's
desire?"

"Then," said the young fellow, "I will start next week. I am anxious to see
this thing through if only for the sake of your wife's peace of mind."

"I will call her. To hear what you think to do will make her glad," said
Hom Hing.

He called a message to Lae Choo upstairs through a tube in the wall.

In a few moments she appeared, listless, wan, and hollow-eyed; but when
her husband told her the young lawyer's suggestion she became electrified;
her form straightened, her eyes glistened; the color flushed to her cheeks.

"Oh," she cried, turning to James Clancy. "You are a hundred man good!"

The young man felt somewhat embarrassed; his eyes shifted a little under
the intense gaze of the Chinese mother.

"Well, we must get your boy for you," he responded. "Of course"—turning to Hom Hing—"it will cost a little money. You can't get fellows to hurry
the Government for you without gold in your pocket."

Hom Hing stared blankly for a moment. Then: "How much do you want, Mr. Clancy?" he asked quietly.

"Well, I will need at least five hundred to start with."

Hom Hing cleared his throat.

"I think I told to you the time I last paid you for writing letters for me and seeing the Custom boss here that nearly all I had was gone!"

"Oh, well then we won't talk about it, old fellow. It won't harm the boy to go stay where he is, and your wife may get over it all right."

"What that you say?" quavered Lae Choo.

James Clancy looked out of the window.

"He says," explained Hom Hing in English, "that to get our boy we have to have much money."

"Money! Oh, yes."

Lae Choo nodded her head.

"I have not got the money to give him."

For a moment Lae Choo gazed wonderingly from one face to the other; then, comprehension dawning upon her, with swift anger, pointing to the lawyer, she cried: "You not one hundred man good; you just common white man."

"Yes, ma'am," returned James Clancy, bowing and smiling ironically.

Hom Hing pushed his wife behind him and addressed the lawyer again: "I might try," said he, "to raise something; but five hundred—it is not possible."

"What about four?"

"I tell you I have next to nothing left and my friends are not rich."

"Very well!"

The lawyer moved leisurely toward the door, pausing on its threshold to light a cigarette.

"Stop, white man; white man, stop!"

Lae Choo, panting and terrified, had started forward and now stood beside him, clutching his sleeve excitedly.

"You say you can go to get paper to bring my Little One to me if Hom Hing give you five hundred dollars?"

The lawyer nodded carelessly; his eyes were intent upon the cigarette which would not take the fire from the match.

"Then you go get paper. If Hom Hing not can give you five hundred dollars—I give you perhaps what more that much."

She slipped a heavy gold bracelet from her wrist and held it out to the man. Mechanically he took it.

"I go get more!"

She scurried away, disappearing behind the door through which she had come.

"Oh, look here, I can't accept this," said James Clancy, walking back to Hom Hing and laying down the bracelet before him.

"It's all right," said Hom Hing, seriously, "pure China gold. My wife's parent give it to her when we married."

"But I can't take it anyway," protested the young man.

"It is all same as money. And you want money to go to Washington," replied Hom Hing in a matter-of-fact manner.

"See, my jade earrings—my gold buttons—my hairpins—my comb of pearl and my rings—one, two, three, four, five rings; very good—very good—all same much money. I give them all to you. You take and bring me paper for my Little One."

Lae Choo piled up her jewels before the lawyer.

Hom Hing laid a restraining hand upon her shoulder. "Not all, my wife," he said in Chinese. He selected a ring—his gift to Lae Choo when she dreamed of the tree with the red flower. The rest of the jewels he pushed toward the white man.

"Take them and sell them," said he. "They will pay your fare to Washington and bring you back with the paper."

For one moment James Clancy hesitated. He was not a sentimental man; but something within him arose against accepting such payment for his services.

"They are good, good," pleadingly asserted Lae Choo, seeing his hesitation.

Whereupon he seized the jewels, thrust them into his coat pocket, and walked rapidly away from the store.

IV

Lae Choo followed after the missionary woman through the mission nursery school. Her heart was beating so high with happiness that she could scarcely breathe. The paper had come at last—the precious paper which gave Hom Hing and his wife the right to the possession of their own child. It was ten months now since he had been taken from them—ten months since the sun had ceased to shine for Lae Choo.

The room was filled with children—most of them wee tots, but none so wee as her own. The mission woman talked as she walked. She told Lae Choo that little Kim, as he had been named by the school, was the pet of the place, and that his little tricks and ways amused and delighted every one. He had been rather difficult to manage at first and had cried much for his mother; "but children so soon forget, and after a month he seemed quite at home and played around as bright and happy as a bird."

"Yes," responded Lae Choo. "Oh, yes, yes!"

But she did not hear what was said to her. She was walking in a maze of anticipatory joy.

"Wait here, please," said the mission woman, placing Lae Choo in a chair. "The very youngest ones are having their breakfast."

She withdrew for a moment—it seemed like an hour to the mother—then she reappeared leading by the hand a little boy dressed in blue cotton overalls and white-soled shoes. The little boy's face was round and dimpled and his eyes were very bright.

"Little One, ah, my Little One!" cried Lae Choo.

She fell on her knees and stretched her hungry arms toward her son.

But the Little One shrunk from her and tried to hide himself in the folds of the white woman's skirt.

"Go 'way, go 'way!" he bade his mother.

Discussion Questions

1. Discuss in groups the ways in which Sui Sin Far's story brings to life the Chinese Exclusion laws discussed by Gyory, whose text you have seen earlier in this chapter. Consider the story's title. What message is the author trying to convey about the experience of Chinese immigration? How does she portray the cultural differences between the white and the Chinese characters? Does she show sympathy for the goals of both white and Chinese characters?

2. This story offers just one example of how bureaucracy can affect individuals—think of other circumstances and individuals who would have been affected by the Exclusion Laws, but whose individual sufferings the document itself never addresses. What other scenarios can you think of that are not immediately apparent when you read the text of the Laws? What ramifications would the Laws have had for other family groupings?

Writing Suggestions

1. Write an essay in which you examine the implied arguments that Sui Sin Far is making in this story. Go beyond the most obvious arguments, and look for a variety of points she is making about the Chinese immigration experience in America. Consider the different individuals in conflict in this story—the Chinese family, the white lawyer, the white officers, and the missionary women. How does Sui Sin Far arrange the tale to emphasize her points? What kinds of details and images does she use to make her arguments convincing? How does she use dialogue to further her argument?

2. Current immigration laws can also separate mothers and children. Research the problem of illegal immigrant mothers from Mexico, for example, who are deported after they give birth to children in California (who are by rights U.S. citizens). Write an argument paper agreeing or disagreeing with current U.S. policies. What happens to the children of deportees? What numbers of people are involved in this situation? What policies have been instituted by individual states to deal with this problem? You will find your most recent information on this issue in current journals, magazines, and newspapers. (You can research this topic in newspapers using the database Lexis Nexis, also called Academic Universe.)

Chapter 5: Writing Suggestions

1. California letter sheets were a popular means for miners to show their families at home what life in California was really like. Look closely at the letter sheet below, and then go to the California Historical Association's Web page on letter sheets: <http://www.calhist.org/frost1/lettersheets/lettersheets.html>. After you have read more about letter sheets, analyze the letter sheet below, and then write an essay in which you link the pictures to the information you have gained from Kevin Starr's selection. What kinds of hopes and dreams are depicted on the sheet? Are different races portrayed on the sheet? What does the elephant symbolize on the letter sheets? Does this letter sheet portray California as a land of dreams or disillusionment?

Department of Special Collections, Stanford University Archives

2. The Vigilance Committees of California were formed in response to the lawlessness, murder, and arson that were rampant in San Francisco during and after the big Gold Rush in 1849. Research more about the Vigilance Committees, and write a paper in which you address some of the

controversies about the Vigilance Committees, who took the trial and punishment of the accused into their own hands.

What evidence can you find to support or condemn the Vigilance Committees' fairness?

What impact did the Vigilance Committees have on local government's response to crime?

Were the Vigilance Committees necessary for law enforcement or did they overstep the bounds of civilian rights?

3.   Bret Harte is one of the most famous authors who wrote about California and the Gold Rush. Research his life and other prose, poetry, and literary criticism, including his work for the *Overland Monthly*, and write a paper in which you discuss Harte's contribution to both the mythology and the realistic portrayal of the West. You might answer some of the following questions in your paper:

How did Harte's writings affect Easterners' perceptions about the West?

What were Harte's feelings about the whites' treatment of Native Americans?

What political risks did Harte take in his editorials about race relations in the West?

How has Harte influenced a lasting vision of the Gold Rush era?

Chapter 5: Further Research on the Web

To pursue your research on the Internet, explore some of the following sites:

Transcontinental Railroad
http://www.sfmuseum.org/hist1/rail.html
http://cprr.org/Museum/Chinese.html

Gold Rush
http://www.acusd.edu/~jross/goldrush.html

Junipero Serra and the California Missions
http://www.cmp.ucr.edu/exhibitions/missions

California State Library and Kevin Starr
http://www.library.ca.gov/
http://www.library.ca.gov/html/starr.html

6

Poverty, Wealth, and the American Dream

The last quarter of the nineteenth century saw not only a vast increase in industrialization, but also the growth of railroads that could transfer goods to a national market. With the growth of cities and factories came the need for more workers and the subsequent flow of immigrants from Europe, Russia, and Turkey. While the owners of steel mills, factories, and railroads became rich, the new immigrants who came to America in the 1880s found that life was much harder than they had expected. Their poverty contrasted sharply with the luxurious lives of their employers. Lured by reports of rich farmlands and easy money, immigrants continued to pour into America, searching for the "life, liberty, and pursuit of happiness" that they believed to be the attainable American dream.

Gradually, as these newer immigrants became more and more disenchanted with life in America, they became more vocal, began to go on strike, and eventually helped form the labor unions that remain such an important component of American labor today. At the same time, American women began to assert themselves and to call for equality with men. The primary and secondary sources included in this chapter have been chosen to give you more insight into the range of conflicts in America at the end of the nineteenth century. As you read the selections in this chapter, think about the following questions:

How does your own family history reflect the immigration history of the United States?

How has the goal of wealth informed the American character since the nineteenth century?

How did immigrants from different eras assimilate and make their way in American society?

How do labor unions in the United States today reflect the struggles and concerns of laborers at the turn of the century?

How did the fight for women's rights evolve, and what recurring themes do you see in the women's movement today?

The selections in this chapter will give you a picture of the philosophies and beliefs of those Americans who immigrated in the early 1800s to America and who believed they were entitled to their wealth and all that came with it. This chapter will also show you the experiences of those newer Americans who had to struggle through the horrors of the Ellis Island landing and the subsequent exhausting and inhumane conditions of the sweatshops and factories.

The first selection in the chapter is from Andrew Carnegie's essay "Wealth," in which he explains his beliefs that wealth in the hands of the few is not only moral but beneficial, since wise and wealthy men who give their money away while they are alive to institutions such as libraries, universities, parks, and other public forums will greatly help the poorer members of society. John D. Rockefeller, Jr.'s essay from *The Personal Relation in Industry* suggests that men of money and those who work for them must work together for the common good, and that labor and capitol can and must develop fair working conditions. The lofty goals of Rockefeller and Carnegie are challenged by historian Howard Zinn, who judges the wealthy of the Gilded Age harshly, writing not only about the terrible working conditions of those in the coal mines, but also about the details of the Rockefeller-owned Ludlow mines, where a massacre took place after miners went on strike to protest outrageously difficult and dangerous working conditions. In the selection from his book *Declarations of Independence: Cross-Examining American Ideology*, Zinn raises the question of the accuracy of history books and the importance of knowing the full story—he finds that incidents like the Ludlow massacre are rarely included in American texts, and he encourages students to look at both "orthodox" and "unorthodox" texts to see which accounts are "most important and most useful."

The contrast between the ideal and the reality of "the American dream" becomes clearer when you read Emma Lazarus's poem "The New Colossus," which is inscribed on the base of the Statue of Liberty. Lazarus came from a family of immigrants who were well-established and wealthy by the end of the nineteenth century, and she wrote the poem to raise money for the building of the Statue of Liberty pedestal. Her lines, "Give me your tired, your poor, your huddled masses yearning to breathe free," have come to represent an idealized version of American opportunities, a "truth" that Howard Zinn would encourage us to probe further.

One way to look more closely at the immigrant experience is to explore the writings of the immigrants themselves, such as those selected from letters written to an editor of the *Jewish Daily Forward* in New York. An early twentieth-century version of *Dear Abby*, these letters and answers from the editor reveal a remarkable range of problems that the immigrants experienced on a daily basis, from homesickness to religious confusion to rape to labor discrimination. This genre of letters sheds new light on our perception of the daily conflicts and trials of immigrant men and women.

Another source that provides more shocking information about the suffering of the immigrants is Samuel Gomper's testimony before the Senate Committee on Relations between Capitol and Labor in 1883. Gomper's testimony details the horrors of the sweatshops, the crowded living and working conditions, and the difficult lives of children who worked long days in factories alongside their parents. Gomper's firsthand testimony is a good example of the value of primary sources in researching any topic, and Gomper's testimony is also an interesting study of style, argument, and tone.

A recurrent theme in both primary and secondary sources about immigrant labor in American cities is the prevalence of dangerous, crowded sweatshops in the garment industry. Most workers were young female immigrants, many of whom spoke no English and had few choices about the kinds of work available to them. The Triangle Shirtwaist Company fire, which took place in New York City in 1911, is one of the most famous and deadly examples of the dangers faced by those who had few resources with which to implement reforms. Although the factory of the Triangle Shirtwaist Company had been identified as a fire danger, all exit doors were locked to make sure the workers stayed on throughout the day. When the fire broke out, the workers were locked in, and 146 employees died in the fire. Many of the young girls jumped from the upper stories to avoid death by fire, and the resulting scene horrified New York police, firemen, and civilians alike. In the investigation that followed, the owners of the factory were never punished for the locked doors, but the fire did draw attention to the need for more reforms and to the unfairness of the class and labor issues that lay beneath the surface of the garment industries. Leon Stein's chapters from *The Triangle Fire* explain what happened and why, and lead us through the maze of evidence and testimony that followed, providing an interesting model of a researched essay that relies on written, visual, and oral sources.

At the end of the nineteenth century, women, both recent immigrants and those from more established families, faced political, cultural, and economic hardships. While many women labored at low-paying jobs and suffered in sweatshops, there were those whose successful careers led them to economic triumphs, as Maxine Seller describes in "Beyond the Stereotype." Women began to find their own voices and to organize themselves to fight for better lives. Despite the promises of liberty and justice for all, American women were not allowed to vote, and in Elizabeth Cady Stanton's lively and outspoken speech "The Subjection of Woman" she decries the philosophy that women should be protected from political affairs and asks that women have "the same advantages, opportunities, and code of laws man claims for himself . . . ." Virginia Minor took the fight for the right to vote to the courts in *Minor v. Happersett*; you can see the legal justification for the refusal of her request in Justice Waite's majority opinion of the court. Not until 1920 did women win the right to vote, but these sources show us how the struggle began and how long these issues of equality and gender struggles have been a part of American culture.

The readings, discussion questions, and writing suggestions in this chapter will help you think about the struggles of men and women from previous centuries in relationship to the same struggles we encounter today in our search for security, education, political power, and happiness.

In addition, the reading selections will offer information and insight into the early beginnings of the women's rights movement, as women fought to make more money, earn the right to vote, and work under safe, reasonable conditions.

Before You Read

1. What are your feelings about current immigration laws in the United States? Do you think we should have a more lenient or a more strict policy toward immigrants from all over the world? How has immigration been part of your family history?

2. What role does the acquisition of wealth play in your plans? Are you committed to making a lot of money, or are you more interested in pursuing other dreams?

3. Write in your journal about your right to vote at the age of eighteen. Are you excited by this privilege, or are you nonchalant? Do you plan to vote in all elections open to you, or do you feel that your vote does not matter? Explain your reasoning.

Wealth

ANDREW CARNEGIE

Andrew Carnegie was born in Scotland in 1835, but a struggling economy in Scotland encouraged the Carnegie family to emigrate to Pittsburgh in 1848. After working in a variety of jobs, Carnegie invested in the steel business, and his company, U.S. Steel, grew into the largest steel and iron works in America. Carnegie felt it was important to give his wealth back to the public: His writings "Wealth" and "The Gospel of Wealth" discuss Carnegie's strong belief in philanthropy. His writings were widely read by other wealthy industrialists, including John D. Rockefeller, Jr. Carnegie created parks, schools, and libraries, and in fact vowed to buy a library for every town that could afford to support one. He contributed millions of dollars to public institutions in both the United States and the United Kingdom. In his old age, Carnegie retired from the steel business and moved to Skibo Castle in Sutherland, Scotland, where he died in 1925. In the selection that follows, Carnegie explains his beliefs about the importance of donating money during one's lifetime, and asserts his belief that "it is in the best interest of the race for wealth to be in the hands of the few."

The problem of our age is the proper administration of wealth, so that the ties of brotherhood may still bind together the rich and poor in harmonious relationship. The conditions of human life have not only been changed, but revolutionized, within the past few hundred years. In former days there was little difference between the dwelling, dress, food, and environment of the chief and those of his retainers. The Indians are today where civilized man then was. When visiting the Sioux, I was led to the wigwam of the chief. It was just like the others in external appearance, and even within the difference was trifling between it and those of the poorest of his braves. The contrast between the palace of the millionaire and the cottage of the laborer with us today measures the change which has come with civilization.

This change, however, is not to be deplored, but welcomed as highly beneficial. It is well, nay, essential for the progress of the race, that the houses of some should be homes for all that is highest and best in literature and the arts, and for all the refinements of civilization, rather than that none should be so. Much better this great irregularity than universal squalor. Without wealth there can be no Maecenas. The "good old times" were not good old times. Neither master nor servant was as well situated then as today. A relapse to old conditions would be disastrous to both—not the least so to him who serves—and would sweep away civilization with it. But whether the change be for good or ill, it is upon us, beyond our power to alter, and therefore to be accepted and made the best of. It is a waste of time to criticize the inevitable.

It is easy to see how the change has come. One illustration will serve for almost every phase of the cause. In the manufacture of products we have the whole story. It applies to all combinations of human industry, as stimulated and enlarged by the inventions of this scientific age. Formerly articles were manufactured at the domestic hearth or in small shops which formed part of the household. The master and his apprentices worked side by side, the latter living with the master, and therefore subject to the same conditions. When these apprentices rose to be masters, there was little or no change in their mode of life, and they, in turn, educated in the same routine succeeding apprentices. There was, substantially, social equality, and even political equality, for those engaged in industrial pursuits had then little or no political voice in the State.

But the inevitable result of such a mode of manufacture was crude articles at high prices. Today the world obtains commodities of excellent quality at prices which even the generation preceding this would have deemed incredible. In the commercial world similar causes have produced similar results, and the race is benefited thereby. The poor enjoy what the rich could not before afford. What were the luxuries have become the necessaries of life. The laborer has now more comforts than the farmer had a few generations ago. The farmer has more luxuries than the landlord had, and is more richly clad and better housed. The landlord has books and pictures rarer, and appointments more artistic, than the King could then obtain.

The price we pay for this salutary change is, no doubt, great. We assemble thousands of operatives in the factory, in the mine, and in the counting-house, of whom the employer can know little or nothing, and to whom the employer is little better than a myth. All intercourse between them is at an end. Rigid Castes are formed, and, as usual, mutual ignorance breeds mutual distrust. Each Caste is without sympathy for the other, and ready to credit anything disparaging in regard to it. Under the law of competition, the employer of thousands is forced into the strictest economies, among which the rates paid to labor figure prominently, and often there is friction between the employer and the employed, between capital and labor, between rich and poor. Human society loses homogeneity.

The price which society pays for the law of competition, like the price it pays for cheap comforts and luxuries, is also great; but the advantages of this law are also greater still, for it is to this law that we owe our wonderful material development, which brings improved conditions in its train. But, whether the law be benign or not, we must say of it, as we say of the change in the conditions of men to which we have referred: It is here; we cannot evade it; no substitutes for it have been found; and while the law may be sometimes hard for the individual, it is best for the race, because it insures the survival of the fittest in every department. We accept and welcome, therefore, as conditions to which we must accommodate ourselves, great inequality of environment, the concentration of business, industrial and commercial, in the hands of a few, and the law of competition between these, as being not only beneficial, but essential for the future progress of the race. Having accepted these, it follows that there must be great scope for the exercise of special ability in the merchant and in the manufacturer who has to conduct affairs upon a great scale. That this talent for organization and management is rare among men is proved by the fact that it invariably secures for its possessor enormous rewards, no matter where or under what laws or conditions. The experienced in affairs always rate the *man* whose services can be obtained as a partner as not only the first consideration, but such as to render the question of his capital scarcely worth considering, for such men soon create capital; while, without the special talent required, capital soon takes wings. Such men become interested in firms or corporations using millions; and estimating only simple interest to be made upon the capital invested, it is inevitable that their income must exceed their expenditures, and that they must accumulate wealth. Nor is there any middle ground which such men can occupy, because the great manufacturing or commercial concern which does not earn at least interest upon its capital soon becomes bankrupt. It must either go forward or fall behind: to stand still is impossible. It is a condition essential for its successful operation that it should be thus far profitable, and even that, in addition to interest on capital, it should make profit. It is a law, as certain as any of the others named, that men possessed of this peculiar talent for affairs, under the free play of economic forces, must, of necessity, soon be in receipt of more revenue than can be judiciously expended upon themselves; and this law is as beneficial for the race as the others.

Objections to the foundations upon which society is based are not in order, because the condition of the race is better with these than it has been with any others which have been tried. Of the effect of any new substitutes proposed we cannot be sure. The Socialist or Anarchist who seeks to overturn present conditions is to be regarded as attacking the foundation upon which civilization itself rests, for civilization took its start from the day that the capable, industrious workman said to his incompetent and lazy fellow, "If thou dost not sow, thou shalt not reap," and thus ended primitive Communism by separating the drones from the bees. One who studies this subject will soon be brought face to face with the conclusion that upon the sacredness of property civilization itself depends—the right of the laborer to his hundred dollars in the savings bank, and equally the legal right of the millionaire to his millions. To those who propose to substitute Communism for this intense Individualism the answer, therefore, is: The race has tried that. All progress from that barbarous day to the present time has resulted from its displacement. Not evil, but good, has come to the race from the accumulation of wealth by those who have the ability and energy that produce it. But even if we admit for a moment that it might be better for the race to discard its present foundation, Individualism,—

that it is a nobler ideal that man should labor, not for himself alone but in and for a brotherhood of his fellows, and share with them all in common, realizing Swedenborg's idea of Heaven, where, as he says, the angels derive their happiness, not from laboring for self, but for each other,—even admit all this, and a sufficient answer is, This is not evolution, but revolution. It necessitates the changing of human nature itself—a work of aeons, even if it were good to change it, which we cannot know. It is not practicable in our day or in our age. Even if desirable theoretically, it belongs to another and long-succeeding sociological stratum. Our duty is with what is practicable now; with the next step possible in our day and generation. It is criminal to waste our energies in endeavoring to uproot, when all we can profitably or possibly accomplish is to bend the universal tree of humanity a little in the direction most favorable to the production of good fruit under existing circumstances. We might as well urge the destruction of the highest existing type of man because he failed to reach our ideal as to favor the destruction of Individualism, Private Property, the Law of Accumulation of Wealth, and the Law of Competition; for these are the highest results of human experience, the soil in which society so far has produced the best fruit. Unequally or unjustly, perhaps, as these laws sometimes operate, and imperfect as they appear to the Idealist, they are, nevertheless, like the highest type of man, the best and most valuable of all that humanity has yet accomplished.

We start, then, with a condition of affairs under which the best interests of the race are promoted, but which inevitably gives wealth to the few. Thus far, accepting conditions as they exist, the situation can be surveyed and pronounced good. The question then arises,—and, if the foregoing be correct, it is the only question with which we have to deal,—What is the proper mode of administering wealth after the laws upon which civilization is founded have thrown it into the hands of the few? And it is of this great question that I believe I offer the true solution. It will be understood that *fortunes* are here spoken of, not moderate sums saved by many years of effort, the returns from which are required for the comfortable maintenance and education of families. This is not *wealth*, but only *competence*, which it should be the aim of all to acquire.

There are but three modes in which surplus wealth can be disposed of. It can be left to the families of the descedents; or it can be bequeathed for public purposes; or, finally, it can be administered during their lives by its possessors. Under the first and second modes most of the wealth of the world that has reached the few has hitherto been applied. Let us in turn consider each of these modes. The first is the most injudicious. In monarchical countries, the estates and the greatest portion of the wealth are left to the first son, that the vanity of the parent may be gratified by the thought that his name and title are to descend to succeeding generations unimpaired. The condition of this class in Europe today teaches the futility of such hopes or ambitions. The successors have become impoverished through their follies or from the fall in the value of land. Even in Great Britain the strict law of entail has been found inadequate to maintain the status of an hereditary class. Its soil is rapidly passing into the hands of the stranger. Under republican institutions the division of property among the children is much fairer, but the question which forces itself upon thoughtful men in all lands is: Why should men leave great fortunes to their children? If this is done from affection, is it not misguided affection? Observation teaches that, generally speaking, it is not well for the children that they should be so burdened. Neither is it well for the state. Beyond providing for the wife and daughters moderate sources of income, and very moderate allowances indeed, if any, for the sons, men may well hesitate, for it is no longer questionable that great sums bequeathed oftener work more for the injury than for the good of the recipients. Wise men will soon conclude that, for the best interests of the members of their families and of the state, such bequests are an improper use of their means.

It is not suggested that men who have failed to educate their sons to earn a livelihood shall cast them adrift in poverty. If any man has seen fit to rear his sons with a view to their living idle lives, or, what is highly commendable, has instilled in them the sentiment that they are in a position to labor for public ends without reference to pecuniary considerations, then, of course, the duty of the parent is to see that such are provided for *in moderation*. There are instances of millionaires' sons unspoiled by wealth, who, being rich, still perform great services in the community. Such are the very salt of the earth, as valuable as, unfortunately, they are rare; still it is not the exception, but the rule, that men must regard, and, looking at the usual result of enormous sums conferred upon legatees, the thoughtful man must shortly say, "I would as soon leave to my son a curse as the almighty dollar," and admit to himself that it is not the welfare of the children, but family pride, which inspires these enormous legacies.

As to the second mode, that of leaving wealth at death for public uses, it may be said that this is only a means for the disposal of wealth, provided a man is content to wait until he is dead before it becomes of much good in the world. Knowledge of the results of legacies bequeathed is not calculated to inspire the brightest hopes of much posthumous good being accomplished. The cases are not few in which the real object sought by the testator is not attained, nor are they few in which his real wishes are thwarted. In many cases the bequests are so used as to become only monuments of his folly. It is well to remember that it requires the exercise of not less ability than that which acquired the wealth to use it so as to be really beneficial to the community. Besides this, it may fairly be said that no man is to be extolled for doing what he cannot help doing, nor is he to be thanked by the community to which he only leaves wealth at death. Men who leave vast sums in this way may fairly be thought men who would not have left it at all, had they been able to take it with them. The memories of such cannot he held in grateful remembrance, for there is no grace in their gifts. It is not to be wondered at that such bequests seem so generally to lack the blessing.

The growing disposition to tax more and more heavily large estates left at death is a cheering indication of the growth of a salutary change in public opinion. The State of Pennsylvania now takes—subject to some exceptions—one-tenth of the property left by its citizens. The budget presented in the British Parliament the other day proposes to increase the death duties; and, most significant of all, the new tax is to be a graduated one. Of all forms of taxation, this seems the wisest. Men who continue hoarding great sums all their lives, the proper use of which for public ends would work good to the community, should be made to feel that the community, in the form of the state, cannot thus be deprived of its proper share. By taxing estates heavily at death the state marks its condemnation of the selfish millionaire's unworthy life.

It is desirable that nations should go much further in this direction. Indeed, it is difficult to set bounds to the share of a rich man's estate which should go at his death to the public through the agency of the state, and by all means such taxes should be graduated, beginning at nothing upon moderate sums to dependents, and increasing rapidly as the amounts swell, until of the millionaire's hoard, as of Shylock's, at least

——The other half
Comes to the privy coffer of the state.

This policy would work powerfully to induce the rich man to attend to the administration of wealth during his life, which is the end that society should always have in view, as being that by far most fruitful for the people. Nor need it be feared that this policy would sap the root of enterprise and render men less anxious to accumulate, for to the class whose ambition it is to leave great fortunes and be talked about after their death, it will attract even more attention, and, indeed, be a somewhat nobler ambition to have enormous sums paid over to the state from their fortunes.

There remains, then, only one mode of using great fortunes; but in this we have the true antidote for the temporary unequal distribution of wealth, the reconciliation of the rich and the poor—a reign of harmony—another ideal, differing, indeed, from that of the Communist in requiring only the further evolution of existing conditions, not the total overthrow of our civilization. It is founded upon the present most intense individualism, and the race is prepared to put it in practice by degrees whenever it pleases. Under its sway we shall have an ideal state, in which the surplus wealth of the few will become, in the best sense, the property of the many, because administered for the common good, and this wealth, passing through the hands of the few, can be made a much more potent force for the elevation of our race than if it had been distributed in small sums to the people themselves. Even the poorest can be made to see this, and to agree that great sums gathered by some of their fellow citizens and spent for public purposes, from which the masses reap the principal benefit, are more valuable to them than if scattered among them through the course of many years in trifling amounts.

If we consider what results flow from the Cooper Institute, for instance, to the best portion of the race in New York not possessed of means, and compare these with those which would have arisen for the good of the masses from an equal sum distributed by Mr. Cooper in his lifetime in the form of wages, which is the highest form of distribution, being for work done and not for charity, we can form some estimate of the possibilities for the improvement of the race which lie embedded in the present law of the accumulation of wealth. Much of this sum, if distributed in small quantities among the people, would have been wasted in the indulgence of appetite, some of it in excess, and it may be doubted whether even the part put to the best use, that of adding to the comforts of the home, would have yielded results for the race, as a race, at all comparable to those which are flowing and are to flow from the Cooper Institute from generation to generation. Let the advocate of violent or radical change ponder well this thought.

We might even go so far as to take another instance, that of Mr. Tilden's bequest of five millions of dollars for a free library in the city of New York, but in referring to this one cannot help saying involuntarily, How much better if Mr. Tilden had devoted the last years of his own life to the proper administration of this immense sum; in which case neither legal contest nor any other cause of delay could have interfered with his aims. But let us assume that Mr. Tilden's millions finally became the means of giving to this city a noble public library, where the treasures of the world contained in books will be open to all forever, without money and without price. Considering the good of that part of the race which congregates in and around Manhattan Island, would its permanent benefit have been better promoted had these millions been allowed to circulate in small sums through the hands of the masses? Even the most strenuous advocate of Communism must entertain a doubt upon this subject. Most of those who think will probably entertain no doubt whatever.

Poor and restricted are our opportunities in this life; narrow our horizon; our best work most imperfect; but rich men should be thankful for one inestimable boon. They have it in their power during their lives to busy themselves in organizing benefactions from which the masses of their fellows will derive lasting advantage, and thus dignify their own lives. The highest life is probably to be reached, not by such imitation of the life of Christ as Count Tolstoi gives us, but, while animated by Christ's spirit, by recognizing the changed conditions of this age, and adopting modes of expressing this spirit suitable to the changed conditions under which we live; still laboring for the good of our fellows, which was the essence of his life and teaching, but laboring in a different manner.

This, then, is held to be the duty of the man of Wealth: First, to set an example of modest, unostentatious living, shunning display or extravagance; to provide moderately for the legitimate wants of those dependent upon him; and after doing so to consider all surplus revenues which come to him simply as trust funds which he is called upon to administer, and strictly bound as a matter of duty to administer in the manner which, in his judgment, is best calculated to produce the most beneficial results for the community—the man of wealth thus becoming the mere agent and trustee for his poorer brethren, bringing to their service his superior wisdom, experience, and ability to administer, doing for them better than they would or could do for themselves. . . .

The best uses to which surplus wealth can be put have already been indicated. Those who would administer wisely must, indeed, be wise, for one of the serious obstacles to the improvement of our race is indiscriminate charity. It were better for mankind that the millions of the rich were thrown into the sea than so spent as to encourage the slothful, the drunken, the unworthy. Of every thousand dollars spent in so called charity today, it is probable that $950 is unwisely spent; so spent, indeed, as to produce the very evils which it proposes to mitigate or cure. A well-known writer of philosophic books admitted the other day that he had given a quarter of a dollar to a man who approached him as he was coming to visit the house of his friend. He knew nothing of the habits of this beggar; knew not the use that would be made of this money, although he had every reason to suspect that it would be spent improperly. This man professed to be a disciple of Herbert Spencer; yet the quarter-dollar given that night will probably work more injury than all the money which its thoughtless donor will ever be able to give in true charity will do good. He only gratified his own feelings, saved himself from annoyance—and this was probably one of the most selfish and very worst actions of his life, for in all respects he is most worthy.

In bestowing charity, the main consideration should be to help those who will help themselves; to provide part of the means by which those who desire to improve may do so; to give those who desire to rise the aids by which they may rise; to assist, but rarely or never to do all. Neither the individual nor the race is improved by alms-giving. Those worthy of assistance, except in rare cases, seldom require assistance. The really valuable men of the race never do, except in cases of accident or sudden change. Everyone has, of course, cases of individuals brought to his own knowledge where temporary assistance can do genuine good, and these he will not overlook. But the amount which can be wisely given by the individual for individuals is necessarily limited by his lack of knowledge of the circumstances connected with each. He is the only true reformer who is as careful and as anxious not to aid the unworthy as he is to aid the worthy, and, perhaps, even more so, for in alms-giving more injury is probably done by rewarding vice than by relieving virtue.

The rich man is thus almost restricted to following the examples of Peter Cooper, Enoch Pratt of Baltimore, Mr. Pratt of Brooklyn, Senator Stanford, and others, who know that the best means of benefiting the community is to place within its reach the ladders upon which the aspiring can rise—parks, and means of recreation, by which men are helped in body and mind; works of art, certain to give pleasure and improve the public taste, and public institutions of various kinds, which will improve the general condition of the people;—

in this manner returning their surplus wealth to the mass of their fellows in the forms best calculated to do them lasting good.

Thus is the problem of Rich and Poor to be solved. The laws of accumulation will be left free; the laws of distribution free. Individualism will continue, but the millionaire will be but a trustee for the poor; intrusted for a season with a great part of the increased wealth of the community, but administering it for the community far better than it could or would have done for itself. The best minds will thus have reached a stage in the development of the race in which it is clearly seen that there is no mode of disposing of surplus wealth creditable to thoughtful and earnest men into whose hands it flows save by using it year by year for the general good. This day already dawns. But a little while, and although, without incurring the pity of their fellows, men may die sharers in great business enterprises from which their capital cannot be or has not been withdrawn, and is left chiefly at death for public uses, yet the man who dies leaving behind him millions of available wealth, which was his to administer during life, will pass away "unwept, unhonored, and unsung," no matter to what uses he leaves the dross which he cannot take with him. Of such as these the public verdict will then be: "The man who dies thus rich dies disgraced."

Such, in my opinion, is the true Gospel concerning Wealth, obedience to which is destined some day to solve the problem of the Rich and the Poor, and to bring "Peace on earth, among men Good-Will."

Discussion Questions

1. Carnegie states that a man who is wealthy should first take care of his dependents, and then should spend his wealth, while he is alive, on projects for the general good. He holds in contempt the man who dies rich, whom he predicts will die "unwept, unhonored, and unsung." Discuss whether or not you agree with Carnegie when he says, "The public verdict will then be: 'The man who dies thus rich dies disgraced.'" Do you feel that wealthy individuals have a public duty to spend money while they are alive?

2. Carnegie believed that his "Gospel of Wealth" would solve "the problem of the Rich and the Poor," and that it would some day bring "Peace on earth, among men Good-Will." However, Carnegie also believed strongly in individualism, and that this "reign of harmony" would therefore be "put into practice by degrees," whenever individuals chose to do so. Discuss whether or not Carnegie's ideals have materialized in present-day society. Do you feel that philanthropic giving to parks, libraries, and schools has worked to promote harmony and to share the wealth of the few? Consider the immigrants' writings that we have read. How do you think they would have responded to Carnegie's theories?

Writing Suggestions

1. Carnegie believed that giving small amounts of money to needy individuals was not as effective as giving those same individuals the means to improve their lives through education, park lands, the establishment of libraries, and so on. Write an essay in which you explain what you would do for the benefit of humanity if you won the state lottery—a sum of 150 million dollars. First explain what you would do for close friends and family, and then design a plan to put your money to use for the common good. Would you follow Carnegie's principles, or would you donate to needy individuals? What kinds of programs or institutes would you fund? To which types of programs would you give the highest priority? Be sure to give your reasons for the decisions you make.

2. Different political parties have differing views on the distribution of funds to help needy people, and the U.S. welfare laws reflect the different views of Republicans and Democrats concerning funds for the poor. Research the current status of welfare laws in your state or in the United States, and write an essay about a specific controversial aspect of the law, such as increased or decreased aid to unwed mothers, more or less stringent food stamp requirements, shrinking or expanding welfare benefits, and so on. Referring to Carnegie's belief that aid to individuals is often wasted, agree or disagree with current policy, and use specific evidence to back up your arguments about a specific policy. Use the Internet to search for the most recent policies regarding welfare laws. You can begin your search at the Social Security Administration Web page: <http://www.uncle-sam.com/ssa.html> or at the Web site for the U.S. Department of Health and Human Services: <http://www.acf.dhhs.gov>.

The Personal Relation in Industry

JOHN D. ROCKEFELLER, JR.

John D. Rockefeller, Jr. (1874–1960) was the only son of John D. Rockefeller, Sr., and carried on many of his father's business and philanthropic interests. After graduating from Brown University in 1897, he went to work with his father in New York. The younger Rockefeller was instrumental in the running of both the Rockefeller Foundation and the Rockefeller Institute for Medical Research (now Rockefeller University). After World War I, Rockefeller turned all of his attention to the philanthropic side of the Rockefeller interests and also became very involved with the League of Nations, to which he contributed millions of dollars for the purchase of the land for the permanent home of the United Nations in New York. Rockefeller believed strongly in the value of the Protestant Church and contributed generously to many different religious organizations. In the selection that follows, excerpted from Rockefeller's *The Personal Relation in Industry*, he urges cooperation between both "men of muscle" and "men of money," and explains his efforts to improve the conditions of miners at the Colorado Fuel and Iron Company.

II

Capital cannot move a wheel without Labor, nor Labor advance beyond a mere primitive existence without Capital. But with Labor and Capital as partners, wealth is created and ever greater productivity made possible. In the development of this partnership, the greatest social service is rendered by that man who so cooperates in the organization of industry as to afford to the largest number of men the greatest opportunity for self-development, and the enjoyment by every man of those benefits which his own work adds to the wealth of civilization. This is better than charity or philanthropy; it helps men to help themselves and widens the horizon of life.

Through such a process the laborer is constantly becoming the capitalist, and the accumulated fruits of present industry are made the basis of further progress. The world puts its richest prizes at the feet of great organizing ability, enterprise, and foresight, because such qualities are rare and yet indispensable to the development of the vast natural resources which otherwise would lie useless on the earth's surface or in its hidden depths.

It is one of the noteworthy facts of industrial history that the most successful enterprises have been those which have been so well organized and so efficient in eliminating waste, that the laborers were paid high wages, the consuming public—upon whose patronage the success of every enterprise depends—enjoyed declining prices, and the owners realized large profits.

The development of industry on a large scale brought the corporation into being, a natural out-growth of which has been the further development of organized Labor in its various forms. The right of men to associate themselves together for their mutual advancement is incontestable; and under our modern conditions, the organization of Labor is necessary just as is the organization of Capital; both should make their contribution toward the creation of wealth and the promotion of human welfare.

The labor union, among its other achievements, has undoubtedly forced public attention upon wrongs which employers of to-day would blush to practice. But employers as well as workers are more and more appreciating the human equation, and realizing that mutual respect and fairness produce larger and better results than suspicion and selfishness.

We are all coming to see that there should be no stifling of Labor by Capital, or of Capital by Labor; and also that there should be no stifling of Labor by Labor, or of Capital by Capital.

While it is true that the organization of Labor has quite as important a function to perform as the organization of Capital, it cannot be gainsaid that evils are liable to develop in either of these forms of association.

Because evils have developed and may develop as a result of these increasing complexities in industrial conditions, shall we deny ourselves the maximum benefit which may be derived from using the new devices of progress? We cannot give up the corporation and industry on a large scale; no more can we give up the organization of labor; human progress depends too much upon them. Surely there must be some avenue of approach to the solution of a problem on the ultimate working out of which depends the very existence of industrial society.

To say that there is no way out except through constant warfare between Labor and Capital is an unthinkable counsel of despair; to say that progress lies in eventual surrender of everything by one factor or the other, is contrary, not only to the teachings of economic history, but also to our knowledge of human nature.

III

Most of the misunderstanding between men is due to a lack of knowledge of each other. When men get together and talk over their differences candidly, much of the ground for dispute vanishes.

In the days when industry was on a small scale, the employer came into direct contact with his employees, and the personal sympathy and understanding which grew out of that contact made the rough places smooth.

However, the use of steam and electricity, resulting in the development of large-scale industry with its attendant economies and benefits, has of necessity erected barriers to personal contact between employers and men, thus making it more difficult for them to understand each other.

In spite of the modern development of Big Business, human nature has remained the same, with all its cravings, and all its tendencies toward sympathy when it has knowledge and toward prejudice when it does not understand. The fact is that the growth of the organization of industry has proceeded faster than the adjustment of the interrelations of men engaged in industry.

Must it not be, then, that an age which can bridge the Atlantic with the wireless telephone, can devise some sort of social X-ray which shall enable the vision of men to penetrate the barriers which have grown up between men in our machine-burdened civilization?

IV

Assuming that Labor and Capital are partners, and that the fruits of industry are their joint product, to be divided fairly, there remains the question: What is a fair division? The answer is not simple—the division can never be absolutely just; and if it were just to-day, changed conditions would make it unjust to-morrow; but certain it is that the injustice of that division will always be greater in proportion as it is made in a spirit of selfishness and shortsightedness.

Indeed, because of the kaleidoscopic changes which the factors entering into the production of wealth are always undergoing, it is unlikely that any final solution of the problem of the fair distribution of wealth will ever be reached. But the effort to devise a continually more perfect medium of approach toward an ever fairer distribution must be no less energetic and unceasing.

For many years my father and his advisers had been increasingly impressed with the importance of these and other economic problems, and with a view to making a contribution toward their solution, had had under consideration the development of an institution for social and economic research.

While this general subject was being studied, the industrial disturbances in Colorado became acute. Their many distressing features gave me the deepest concern. I frankly confess that I felt there was something fundamentally wrong in a condition of affairs which made possible the loss of human lives, engendered hatred and bitterness, and brought suffering and privation upon hundreds of human beings. I determined, therefore, that in so far as it lay within my power I would seek some means of avoiding the possibility of similar conflicts arising elsewhere or in the same industry in the future. It was in this way that I came to recommend to my colleagues in the Rockefeller Foundation the instituting of a series of studies into the fundamental problems arising out of industrial relations. Many others were exploring the same field, but it was felt that these were problems affecting human welfare so vitally than an institution such as the Rockefeller Foundation, whose purpose, as stated in its charter, is "to promote the well-being of mankind throughout the world," could not neglect either its duty or its opportunity.

This resulted in securing the services of Mr. W. L. Mackenzie King, formerly Minister of Labor in Canada, to conduct an investigation "with a special view," to quote the language of an official letter, "to the discovery of some mutual relationship between Labor and Capital which would afford to Labor the protection it needs against oppression and exploitation, while at the same time promoting its efficiency as an instrument of economic production."

In no sense was this inquiry to be local or restricted; the problem was recognized to be a world-problem, and in the study of it the experience of the several countries of the world was to be drawn upon. The purpose was neither to apportion blame in existing or past misunderstandings, nor to justify any particular point of view; but solely to be constructively helpful, the final and only test of success to be the degree to which the practical suggestions growing out of the investigation actually improved the relations between Labor and Capital.

V

With reference to the situation which had unfortunately developed in Colorado, it became evident to those responsible for the management of one of the large coal companies there—the Colorado Fuel and Iron Company, in which my father and I are interested—that matters could not be allowed to remain as they were. Any situation, no matter what its cause, out of which so much bitterness could grow, clearly required amelioration.

It has always been the desire and purpose of the management of the Colorado Fuel and Iron Company that its employees should be treated liberally and fairly.

However, it became clear that there was need of some more efficient method whereby the petty frictions of daily work might be dealt with promptly and justly, and of some machinery which, without imposing financial burdens upon the workers, would protect the rights, and encourage the expression of the wants and aspirations of the men—not merely of those men who were members of some organization, but of every man on the company's payroll.

The problem was how to promote the well-being of each employee; more than that, how to foster at the same time the interest of both the stockholders and the employees through bringing them to realize the fact of their real partnership.

Long before the Colorado strike ended, I sought advice with respect to possible methods of preventing and adjusting such a situation as that which had arisen; and in December, 1914, as soon as the strike was terminated and normal conditions were restored, the officers of the Colorado Fuel and Iron Company undertook the practical development of plans which had been under consideration.

The men in each mining camp were invited to choose, by secret ballot, representatives to meet with the executive officers of the company to discuss matters of mutual concern and consider means of more effective cooperation in maintaining fair and friendly relations.

That was the beginning, merely the germ, of a plan which has now been developed into a comprehensive "Industrial Constitution." The scheme embodies practical operating experience, the advice and study of experts, and an earnest effort to provide a workable method of friendly consideration, by all concerned, of the daily problems which arise in the mutual relations between employer and employees.

The plan was submitted to a referendum of the employees in all the company's coal and iron mines, and adopted by an overwhelming vote. Before this general vote was taken, it had been considered and unanimously approved by a meeting of the employees' elected representatives. At that meeting I outlined the plan, which is described below, as well as the theory underlying it, which theory is in brief as follows:

Every corporation is composed of four parties: the stockholders, who supply the money with which to build the plant, pay the wages, and operate the business; the directors, whose duty it is to select executive officers carefully and wisely, plan the larger and more important policies, and generally see to it that the company is prudently administered; the officers, who conduct the current operations; and the employees, who contribute their skill and their work.

The interest of these four parties is a common interest, although perhaps not an equal one; and if the result of their combined work is to be most successful, each must do its share. An effort on the part of any one to advance its own interest without regard to the rights of the others, means, eventually, loss to all.

The problem which confronts every company is so to interrelate its different elements that the best interests of all will be conserved.

VI

The industrial machinery which has been adopted by the Colorado Fuel and Iron Company and its employees is embodied in two written documents, which have been printed and placed in the hands of each employee. One of these documents is a trade agreement signed by the representatives of the men and the officers of the company, setting forth the conditions and terms under which the men agree to work until January 1, 1918, and thereafter, subject to revision upon ninety days' notice by either side.

This agreement guarantees to the men that for more than two years, no matter what reductions in wages others may make, there shall be no reduction of wages by this company; furthermore, that in the event of an increase in wages in any competitive field, this company will make a proportional increase.

The agreement provides for an eight-hour day for all employees working underground and in coke ovens; it insures the semi-monthly payment of wages; it fixes charges for such dwellings, light, and water, as are provided by the company; it stipulates that the rates to be charged for powder and coal used by the men shall be substantially their cost to the company.

To encourage employees to cultivate flower and vegetable gardens, the company agrees to fence free of cost each house-lot owned by it. The company also engages to provide suitable bath houses and club houses for the use of employees at the several mining camps.

The other document is an "Industrial Constitution," setting forth the relations of the company and its men. The Constitution stipulates, among other things, that "there shall be a strict observance by management and men of the Federal and State laws respecting mining and labor," and that "the scale of wages and the rules in regard to working conditions shall be posted in a conspicuous place at or near every mine."

Every employee is protected against discharge without notice, except for such offenses as are posted at each mine. For all other misconduct the delinquent is entitled to receive warning in writing that a second offense will cause discharge, and a copy of this written notice must be forwarded to the office of the president of the company at the same time it is sent to the employee.

The constitution specifically states that "there shall be no discrimination by the company or any of its employees on account of membership or non-membership in any society, fraternity, or union." The employees are guaranteed the right to hold meetings on company property, to purchase where they choose, and to employ check-weighmen, who, on behalf of the men, shall see to it that each gets proper credit for his work.

Besides setting forth these fundamental rights of the men, the Industrial Constitution seeks to establish a recognized means for bringing the management and the men into closer contact for two general purposes:

First, to promote increased efficiency and production, to improve working conditions and to further the friendly and cordial relations between the company's officers and employees; and,

Second, to facilitate the adjustment of disputes and the redress of grievances.

In carrying out this plan, the wage-earners at each camp are to be represented by two or more of their own number chosen by secret ballot, at meetings especially called for the purpose, which none but wage-earners in the employ of the company shall be allowed to attend. The men thus chosen are to be recognized by the company as authorized to represent the employees for one year, or until their successors are elected, with respect to terms of employment, working and living conditions, adjustment of differences, and such other matters as may come up.

A meeting of all the men's representatives and the general officers of the company will be held once a year to consider questions of general importance.

The Industrial Constitution provides that the territory in which the company operates shall be divided into a number of districts based on the geographical distribution of the mines. To facilitate full and frequent consultation between representatives of the men and the management in regard to all matters of mutual interest and concern, the representatives from each district are to meet at least three times a year—oftener if need be—with the president of the company, or his representative, and such other officers as the president may designate.

The district conferences will each appoint from their number certain joint committees on industrial relations, and it is expected that these committees will give prompt and continuous attention to the many questions which affect the daily life and happiness of the men as well as the prosperity of the company. Each of these committees will be composed of six members, three designated by the employees' representatives and three by the president of the company.

A joint committee on industrial cooperation and conciliation will consider matters pertaining to the prevention and settlement of industrial disputes, terms and conditions of employment, maintenance of order and discipline in the several camps, policy of the company stores, and so forth. Joint committees on safety and accidents, on sanitation, health and housing, on recreation and education, will likewise deal with the great variety of topics included within these general designations.

Prevention of friction is an underlying purpose of the plan. The aim is to anticipate and remove in advance all sources of possible irritation. With this in view a special officer, known as the President's Industrial Representative, is added to the personnel of the staff as a further link between the president of the corporation and every workman in his employ. This officer's duty is to respond promptly to requests from employees' representatives for his presence at any of the camps, to visit all of them as often as possible, to familiarize himself with conditions, and generally to look after the well-being of the workers.

It is a fundamental feature of the plan, as stated in the document itself, that "every employee shall have the right of ultimate appeal to the president of the company concerning any condition or treatment to which he may be subjected and which he may deem unfair." For the adjustment of all disputes, therefore, the plan provides carefully balanced machinery.

If any miner has a grievance, he may himself, or preferably through one of the elected representatives in his camp, seek satisfaction from the foreman or mine superintendent. If those officials do not adjust the matter, appeal may be had to the president's industrial representative. Failing there, the employee may appeal to the division superintendent, assistant manager, or general manager, or the president of the company, in consecutive order.

Yet another alternative is that, after having made the initial complaint to the foreman or mine superintendent, the workman may appeal directly to the joint committee on industrial cooperation and conciliation in his district, which, itself failing to agree, may select one or three umpires whose decision shall be binding upon both parties to the dispute.

If all these methods of mediation fail the employee may appeal to the Colorado State Industrial Commission, which is empowered by law to investigate industrial disputes and publish its findings.

So as adequately to protect the independence and freedom of the men's representatives, the Constitution provides that in case any one of them should be discharged or disciplined, or should allege discrimination, he may resort to the various methods of appeal open to the other employees, or he may appeal directly to the Colorado State Industrial Commission, with whose findings in any such case the company agrees to comply.

The company is to pay all expenses incident to the administration of the plan, and to reimburse the miners' representatives for loss of time from their work in the mines.

Discussion Questions

1. Write out a list of Rockefeller's major arguments about capital and labor. Which of these ideas do you find to be realistic? Which seem idealistic? Discuss Rockefeller's ideals about the partnership between labor and capital. How do you think these ideals would stand up to discussion in today's economic climate in the United States?

2. Analyze Rockefeller's account of the Colorado Coal strike. What kind of diction and tone do you find in his statements? What image of the strike does he represent? How does he appeal to his audience in recounting the story of the strike?

Writing Suggestions

1. Write a personal response to Rockefeller's statement about labor, taken from his 1941 statement of principles that was first heard on a radio broadcast on behalf of the War Fund:

    I believe in the dignity of labor, whether with head or hand; that the world owes no man a living but that it owes every man an opportunity to make a living.

    Respond to this statement in a personal essay, agreeing or disagreeing with Rockefeller's statement and responding to his aversion to giving donations to individuals. Be sure to use specific examples from your life and from current events to back up your points. Answer some of the questions at the top of page 448 in your essay:

What does the phrase "dignity of labor" mean to you?

What, if anything, do you feel the world, or the government, or wealthy individuals owe you?

What would you consider a fair "opportunity to make a living," as opposed to receiving welfare or charitable donations from wealthy individuals?

2. Rockefeller eventually left the business world and devoted himself entirely to philanthropy. Research the Rockefeller Foundation at the Web site <http://www.rockfound.org/display.asp?Context=1&Collection=1> and compare the original mission statement with the latest mission statement, both of which can be found on the Web site. Consider which areas of funding you agree with and which you would like to see changed.

    Then write a paper in which you answer the following question: If you could be on the board of directors of the Rockefeller Foundation, which areas specifically would you like to add or delete from the many programs now funded? Be specific about your reasons for adding or deleting programs, and be sure to research the Web site carefully before you write.

Declarations of Independence

The Use and Abuse of History

HOWARD ZINN

Howard Zinn was born in 1922 and grew up, as he writes in *Declarations of Independence*, "in the dirt and dankness of New York tenements," the child of blue-collar workers. He worked in a shipyard and was a bombardier during World War II, which allowed him to see the violence of war firsthand. He received a Ph.D. from Columbia and went on to become a professor, scholar, and activist. He is perhaps most famous for his book *A People's History of the United States* (1995), which tells the history of the United States from the point of view of blacks, Indians, women, and poor laborers, and includes many aspects of American history that are often left out of more mainstream texts. The following selection comes from Chapter 4, "The Use and Abuse of History," from *Declarations of Independence: Cross-Examining American Ideology*. In this selection, Zinn argues that history texts too often leave out the darker side of American labor and the growth of the American economy, and he argues for a more honest telling of history.

Before I became a professional historian, I had grown up in the dirt and dankness of New York tenements, had been knocked unconscious by a policeman while holding a banner in a demonstration, had worked for three years in a shipyard, and had participated in the violence of war. Those experiences, among others, made me lose all desire for "objectivity," whether in living my life, or writing history.

This statement is troubling to some people. It needs explanation.

I mean by it that by the time I began to study history formally I knew I was not doing it because it was simply "interesting" or because it meant a solid, respectable career. I had been touched in some way by the struggle of ordinary working people to survive, by the glamour and ugliness of war, and by the reading I had done on my own trying to understand fascism, communism, capitalism, and socialism. I could not possibly study history as a neutral. For me, history could only be a way of understanding and helping to change (yes, an extravagant ambition!) what was wrong in the world.

That did not mean looking only for historical facts to reinforce the beliefs I already held. It did not mean ignoring data that would change or complicate my understanding of society. It meant asking questions that were important for social change, questions relating to equality, liberty, peace, and justice, but being open to whatever answers were suggested by looking at history.

I decided early that I would be biased in the sense of holding fast to certain fundamental values: the equal right of all human beings—whatever race, nationality, sex, religion—to life, liberty, and the pursuit of happiness, Jefferson's ideals. It seemed to me that devoting a life to the study of history was worthwhile only if it aimed at those ideals.

But I wanted to be flexible in arriving at the *means* to achieve those ends. Scrupulous honesty in reporting on the past would be needed, because any decision on means (tactics, avenues, and instruments) had to be tentative and had to be open to change based on what one could learn from history. The values, ends, and ideals I held need not be discarded, whatever history disclosed. So there would be no incentive to distort the past, fearing that an honest recounting would hurt the desired ends.

Does this mean that our values, our most cherished ideals, have no solid basis in *fact*, that desires for freedom and justice have the lightness of personal whims and subjective desires? On the contrary, our powerful impulses for freedom and community come from deep, dependable internal drives (these too are *facts*), often deflected or overcome by terrible pressures in our culture, but never extinguished. Does this not account for the way peoples long oppressed and apparently beaten into silence, suddenly rebel, demanding their freedom?

Professional philosophers refer to the "fact-value" problem. That is, do your basic values depend on certain facts, so that if you discover your facts are wrong, you are compelled to change your values? I am arguing here for holding on to certain basic values—and insisting that whatever facts you discover in history may change your means without dislodging your ends.

I can illustrate that with my own experience. At seventeen or eighteen, I was reading lots of novels. Some were pure entertainment. Others were novels of social criticism, like Upton Sinclair's *The Jungle*, and John Steinbeck's *The Grapes of Wrath*.

I don't know exactly when I decided that I believed in the socialism described by Sinclair in the last pages of *The Jungle*. Or that I wouldn't be afraid of the epithet "Communist," because, as someone said (I recall it approximately) in *The Grapes of Wrath*, "A Communist is anyone who asks for twenty cents an hour when the boss is paying fifteen."

When I encountered young Communists in my working-class neighborhood and they bombarded me with literature on the Soviet Union, I was persuaded (like many Americans in the Depression years) that here was a model for a future society of equality and justice, the rational planning of production and distribution, the creation of a "workers' state." But while flying bombing missions in World War II, I became friends with a young gunner on another crew who, like me, was a constant reader. He gave me a book I had never heard of, by a writer I had never heard of. It was *The Yogi and the Commissar* by Arthur Koestler.

That book, written by a former Communist who had fought against fascism in Spain, was a powerful, eloquent denunciation of the Soviet Union, seeing what happened there as a betrayal of Communist ideals. Its historical data seemed irrefutable. I trusted the author's commitment and his intelligence. That was the beginning of my own move away from acceptance of the Soviet Union as a socialist or Communist model.

When Khrushchev gave his astounding speech in 1956 acknowledging Stalin's crimes (which involved, although Khrushchev did not stress this, the complicity of so many other members of the Soviet hierarchy), he was affirming what Koestler and other critics of the Soviet Union had been saying for a long time. When Soviet troops invaded Hungary and then Czechoslovakia to crush rebellions, it was clear to me that the Soviet Union was violating a fundamental Marxist value—really, a universal principle, beyond Marxism—of international solidarity.

My faith in the ideal of an egalitarian society, a cooperative commonwealth, in a world without national boundaries, remained secure. My idea that the Soviet Union represented that new world was something I could discard. I had to be willing to call the shots as I saw them in reading the history of the Soviet Union, just as I wanted those who had a romanticized view of the United States to be willing to call the shots as they saw them in the American past. I knew also that it was a temptation to hold onto old beliefs, to ignore uncomfortable facts because one had become attached to ideals, and that I must guard myself against that temptation and be watchful for it in reading other historians.

A historian's strong belief in certain values and goals *can* lead to dishonesty or to distortions of history. But that is avoidable if the historian understands the difference between solidity in ultimate values and openness in regard to historical fact.

There is another kind of dishonesty that often goes unnoticed. That is when historians fail to acknowledge their own values and pretend to "objectivity," deceiving themselves and their readers.

Everyone is biased, whether they know it or not, in possessing fundamental goals, purposes, and ends. If we understand that, we can be properly skeptical of all historians (and journalists and anyone who reports on the world) and check to see if their biases cause them to emphasize certain things in history and omit or give slight consideration to others.

Perhaps the closest we can get to objectivity is a free and honest marketplace of subjectivities, in which we can examine both orthodox accounts of the past and unorthodox ones, commonly known facts and hitherto ignored facts. But we need to try to discover (which is not easy) what items are missing from that marketplace and insist that they be available for scrutiny. We can then decide for ourselves, based on our own values, which accounts are most important and most useful.

Anyone reading history should understand from the start that there is no such thing as impartial history. All written history is partial in two senses. It is partial in that it is only a tiny *part* of what really happened. That is a limitation that can never be overcome. And it is partial in that it inevitably takes sides, by what it includes or omits, what it emphasizes or deemphasizes. It may do this openly or deceptively, consciously or subconsciously.

The chief problem in historical honesty is not outright lying. It is omission or deemphasis of important data. The definition of *important*, of course, depends on one's values.

An example is the Ludlow Massacre.

I was still in college studying history when I heard a song by folksinger Woody Guthrie called "The Ludlow Massacre," a dark, intense ballad, accompanied by slow, haunting chords on his guitar. It told of women and children burned to death in a strike of miners against Rockefeller-owned coal mines in southern Colorado in 1914.

My curiosity was aroused. In none of my classes in American history, in none of the textbooks I had read, was there any mention of the Ludlow Massacre or of the Colorado coal strike. I decided to study the history of the labor movement on my own.

This led me to a book, *American Labor Struggles*, written not by a historian but an English teacher named Samuel Yellen. It contained exciting accounts of some ten labor conflicts in American history, most of which were unmentioned in my courses and my textbooks. One of the chapters was on the Colorado coal strike of 1913–1914.

I was fascinated by the sheer drama of that event. It began with the shooting of a young labor organizer on the streets of Trinidad, Colorado, in the center of the mining district on a crowded Saturday night, by two detectives in the pay of Rockefeller's Colorado Fuel & Iron Corporation. The miners, mostly immigrants, speaking a dozen different languages, were living in a kind of serfdom in the mining towns where Rockefeller collected their rent, sold them their necessities, hired the police, and watched them carefully for any sign of unionization.

The killing of organizer Gerry Lippiatt sent a wave of anger through the mine towns. At a mass meeting in Trinidad, miners listened to a rousing speech by an eighty-year-old woman named Mary Jones—"Mother Jones"— an organizer for the United Mine Workers: "What would the coal in these mines and in these hills be worth unless you put your strength and muscle in to bring them. . . . You have collected more wealth, created more wealth than they in a thousand years of the Roman Republic, and yet you have not any."

The miners voted to strike. Evicted from their huts by the coal companies, they packed their belongings onto carts and onto their backs and walked through a mountain blizzard to tent colonies set up by the United Mine Workers. It was September 1913. There they lived for the next seven months, enduring hunger and sickness, picketing the mines to prevent strikebreakers from entering, and defending themselves against armed assaults. The Baldwin-Felts Detective Agency, hired by the Rockefellers to break the morale of the strikers, used rifles, shotguns, and a machine gun mounted on an armored car, which roved the countryside and fired into the tents where the miners lived.

They would not give up the strike, however, and the National Guard was called in by the governor. A letter from the vice president of Colorado Fuel & Iron to John D. Rockefeller, Jr., in New York explained,

> You will be interested to know that we have been able to secure the cooperation of all the bankers of the city, who have had three or four interviews with our little cowboy governor, agreeing to back the State and lend it all funds necessary to maintain the militia and afford ample protection so our miners could return to work. . . . Another mighty power has been rounded up on behalf of the operators by the getting together of fourteen of the editors of the most important newspapers in the state.

The National Guard was innocently welcomed to town by miners and their families, waving American flags, thinking that men in the uniform of the United States would protect them. But the guard went to work for the operators. They beat miners, jailed them, and escorted strikebreakers into the mines.

The strikers responded. One strikebreaker was murdered, another brutally beaten, four mine guards killed while escorting a scab. And Baldwin-Felts detective George Belcher, the killer of Lippiatt, who had been freed by a coroner's jury composed of Trinidad businessmen ("justifiable homicide"), was killed with a single rifle shot by an unseen gunman as he left a Trinidad drugstore and stopped to light a cigar.

The miners held out through the hard winter, and the mine owners decided on more drastic action. In the spring, two companies of National Guardsmen stationed themselves in the hills above the largest tent colony, housing a thousand men, women, and children, near a tiny depot called Ludlow. On the morning of April 20, 1914, they began firing machine guns into the tents. The men crawled away to draw fire and shoot back, while the women and children crouched in pits dug into the tent floors. At dusk, the soldiers came down from the hills with torches, and set fire to the tents. The countryside was ablaze. The occupants fled.

The next morning, a telephone linesman, going through the charred ruins of the Ludlow colony, lifted an iron cot that covered a pit dug in the floor of one tent, and found the mangled, burned bodies of two women and eleven children. This became known as the Ludlow Massacre.

As I read about this, I wondered why this extraordinary event, so full of drama, so peopled by remarkable personalities, was never mentioned in the history books. Why was this strike, which cast a dark shadow on the Rockefeller interests and on corporate America generally, considered less important than the building by John D. Rockefeller of the Standard Oil Company, which was looked on as an important and positive event in the development of American industry?

I knew that there was no secret meeting of industrialists and historians to agree to emphasize the admirable achievements of the great corporations and ignore the bloody costs of industrialization in America. But I concluded that a certain unspoken understanding lay beneath the writing of textbooks and the teaching of history: that it would be considered bold, radical, perhaps even "communist" to emphasize class struggle in the United States, a country where the dominant ideology emphasized the oneness of the nation "We the People, in order to . . . etc., etc." and the glories of the American system.

Not long ago, a news commentator on a small radio station in Madison, Wisconsin, brought to my attention a textbook used in high schools all over the nation, published in 1986, titled *Legacy of Freedom*, written by two high-school teachers and one university professor of history and published by a division of Doubleday and Company, one of the giant publishers in the United States. In a foreword "To the Student" we find,

> *Legacy of Freedom* will aid you in understanding the economic growth and development of our country. The book presents the developments and benefits of our country's free enterprise economic system. You will read about the various ways that American business, industry, and agriculture have used scientific and technological advances to further the American free market system. This system allows businesses to generate profits while providing consumers with a variety of quality products from which to choose in the marketplace, thus enabling our people to enjoy a high standard of living.

In this overview one gets the impression of a wonderful, peaceful development, which is the result of "our country's free enterprise economic system." Where is the long, complex history of labor conflict? Where is the human cost of this industrial development, in the thousands of deaths each year in industrial accidents, the hundreds of thousands of injuries, the short lives of the workers (textile mill girls in New England dying in their twenties, after starting work at twelve and thirteen)?

The Colorado coal strike does not fit neatly into the pleasant picture created by most high-school textbooks of the development of the American economy. Perhaps a detailed account of that event would raise questions in the minds of young people as it raised in mine, questions that would be threatening to the dominant powers in this country, that would clash with the dominant orthodoxy. The questioners—whether teachers or principals, or school boards—might get into trouble.

For one thing, would the event not undermine faith in the neutrality of government, the cherished belief (which I possessed through my childhood) that whatever conflicts there were in American society, it was the role of government to mediate them as a neutral referee, trying its best to dispense, in the words of the Pledge of Allegiance, "liberty and justice for all"? Would the Colorado strike not suggest that governors, that perhaps all political leaders, were subject to the power of wealth, and would do the bidding of corporations rather than protect the lives of poor, powerless workers?

A close look at the Colorado coal strike would reveal that not only the state government of Colorado, but the national government in Washington—under the presidency of a presumed liberal, Woodrow Wilson—was on the side of the corporations. While miners were being beaten, jailed, and killed by Rockefeller's detectives or by his National Guard, the federal government did nothing to protect the constitutional rights of its people. (There is a federal statute—Title 10, Section 333—which gives the national government the power to defend the constitutional rights of citizens when local authorities fail to do so.)

It was only after the massacre, when the miners armed themselves and went on a rampage of violence against the mine properties and mine guards, that President Wilson called out the federal troops to end the turmoil in southern Colorado.

And then there was an odd coincidence. On the same day that the bodies were discovered in the pit at Ludlow, Woodrow Wilson, responding to the jailing of a few American sailors in Mexico, ordered the bombardment of the Mexican port of Vera Cruz, landed ten boatloads of marines, occupied the city, and killed more than a hundred Mexicans.

In that same textbook the foreword "To the Student" says: "*Legacy of Freedom* will aid you in understanding our country's involvement in foreign affairs, including our role in international conflicts and in peaceful and cooperative efforts of many kinds in many places." Is that not a benign, misleading, papering over of the history of American foreign policy?

A study of the Ludlow Massacre, alongside the Mexican incident, would also tell students something about our great press, the comfort we feel when picking up, not a scandal sheet or a sensational tabloid, but the sober, dependable *New York Times*. When the U.S. Navy bombarded Vera Cruz, the *Times* wrote in an editorial:

> We may trust the just mind, the sound judgment, and the peaceful temper of President Wilson. There is not the slightest occasion for popular excitement over the Mexican affair; there is no reason why anybody should get nervous either about the stock market or about his business.

There is no *objective* way to deal with the Ludlow Massacre. There is the subjective (biased, opinionated) decision to omit it from history, based on a value system that doesn't consider it important enough. That value system may include a fundamental belief in the beneficence of the American industrial system (as represented by the passage quoted above from the textbook *Legacy of Freedom*) or it may just involve a complacency about class struggle and the intrusion of government on the side of corporations. In any case, a certain set of values has dictated the ignoring of an important historical event.

It is also a subjective (biased, opinionated) decision to tell the story of the Ludlow Massacre in some detail (as I do, in a chapter in my book *The Politics of History*, or in several pages in *A People's History of the United States*). My decision was based on my belief that it is important for people to know the extent of class conflict in our history, to know something about how working people had to struggle to change their conditions, and to understand the role of the government and the mainstream press in the class struggles of our past.

One must inevitably omit large chunks of what is available in historical information. But *what* is omitted is critical in the kind of historical education people get; it may move them one way or another or leave them motionless—passive passengers on a train that is already moving in a certain direction, which they by their passivity seem to accept. My own intention is to select subjects and emphasize aspects of those subjects that will help move citizens into activity on behalf of basic human rights: equality, democracy, peace, and a world without national boundaries. Not by hiding factors from them, but by adding to the orthodox store of knowledge, opening wider the marketplace of information.

The problem of selection in history is strikingly shown in the story of Christopher Columbus, which appears in every textbook of American history on every level from elementary school through college. It is a story, always, of skill and courage, leading to the discovery of the Western Hemisphere.

Something is omitted from that story, in almost every textbook in every school in the United States. What is omitted is that Columbus, in his greed for gold, mutilated, enslaved, and murdered the Indians who greeted him in friendly innocence, and that this was done on such a scale as to deserve the term "genocide"—the destruction of an entire people.

This information was available to historians. In Columbus's own log he shows his attitude from the beginning. After telling how he and his men landed on that first island in the Bahamas and were greeted peaceably by the Arawak Indians, who seemed to have no knowledge of weapons and gave the strangers gifts, Columbus says, "They would make fine servants. . . . With fifty men we could subjugate them all and make them do whatever we want."

The closest we have to a contemporary source on what happened after that first landing is the account by Bartolomeo de las Casas, who as a young priest participated in the conquest of Cuba. In his *History of the Indies*, las Casas wrote, "Endless testimonies . . . prove the mild and pacific temperament of the natives. . . . But our work was to exasperate, ravage, kill, mangle, and destroy. . . . The admiral . . . was so anxious to please the King that he committed irreparable crimes against the Indians."

The "admiral" was Columbus. One of the few historians even to mention the atrocities committed by Columbus against the Indians was Samuel Eliot Morison, who wrote the two-volume biography of Columbus, *Admiral of the Ocean Sea*. In his shorter book, written for a wider audience in 1954, *Christopher Columbus, Mariner*, Morison says, "The cruel policy initiated by Columbus and pursued by his successors resulted in complete genocide."

But this statement is on one page, buried in a book that is mostly a glowing tribute to Columbus.

In my book *A People's History of the United States* I commented on Morison's quick mention of Columbus's brutality:

> Outright lying or quiet omission takes the risk of discovery which, when made, might arouse the reader to rebel against the writer. To state the facts, however, and then to bury them in a mass of other information is to say to the reader with a certain infectious calm: yes, mass murder took place, but it's not that important—it should weigh very little in our final judgements; it should affect very little what we do in the world.

Is my own emphasis on Columbus's treatment of the Indians biased? No doubt. I won't deny or conceal that Columbus had courage and skill, was an extraordinary sailor. But I want to reveal something about him that was omitted from the historical education of most Americans.

My bias is this: I want my readers to think twice about our traditional heroes, to reexamine what we cherish (technical competence) and what we ignore (human consequences). I want them to think about how easily we accept conquest and murder because it furthers "progress." Mass murder for "a good cause" is one of the sicknesses of our time. There were those who defended Stalin's murders by saying, "Well, he made Russia a major power." As we have seen, there were those who justified the atom bombing of Hiroshima and Nagasaki by saying "We had to win the war."

Discussion Questions

1. Zinn writes, "The chief problem in historical honesty is not outright lying. It is omission or de-emphasis of important data. The definition of *important*, of course, depends on one's values." How does Zinn go on to use the Ludlow massacre as an example of a lack of historical honesty? What would Zinn say, in your opinion, about Rockefeller's piece from *The Personal Relation in Industry*? Discuss the ways in which Rockefeller and Zinn are reporting so differently on the same coal strike, considering Zinn's assertions about historical dishonesty.

2. Zinn quotes from the foreword to the textbook *Legacy of Freedom*, and objects to the fact that it omits "the long, complex history of labor conflicts." Discuss whether or not you agree with Zinn's criticism of the foreword. Do you think this foreword, and high school texts in general, should be more concerned with the darker side of history, or do you think the foreword and the optimistic tone of "wonderful, peaceful development" is appropriate for a high school text? What, for example, would you like your high school texts to have said about the Ludlow Massacre? What did they say?

Writing Suggestions

1. Zinn writes that he feels it is important for "people to know the extent of
    class conflict in our history, to know something about how working peo-
    ple had to struggle to change their conditions, and to understand the role
    of government and the mainstream press in the class struggles of our
    past." Write a personal response to this assertion, considering what you
    learned or did not learn about class struggles in your high school text-
    books. How did your high school textbooks treat the subject of class con-
    flict, industrialists, and working people? Do you feel that what you have
    learned supports or conflicts with Zinn's belief that most high school text-
    books do not go past "a pleasant picture . . . of the development of the
    American economy"?

2. Research the Ludlow Massacre and the Colorado coal strike more thor-
    oughly, and write a research paper in which you evaluate the role of the
    government and the press in supporting the Rockefellers' interests. Does
    your research support Zinn's claim that "not only the state government
    of Colorado, but the national government in Washington was on the side
    of the corporations"? State your thesis early in your paper, and use spe-
    cific examples to support or disagree with Zinn's argument.

The New Colossus

EMMA LAZARUS

Emma Lazarus (1849–1887) was born into a wealthy, fourth-generation Jewish-American family. She was well-educated by tutors and exposed to literature, music, and language training as a child. Lazarus died at the young age of 38, but she began writing early in her life and produced drama, poems, essays, short stories, and a novel. She was also an outspoken believer in the settlement of Palestine by Jews, and she worked in a number of organizations that helped Jewish immigrants settle in America. In 1883 she wrote her famous poem "The New Colossus" for a literary auction whose purpose was to raise funds to build the pedestal for the Statue of Liberty. Ironically, Lazarus never saw her work inscribed on the plaque at the base of the Statue of Liberty because she died some years before it was placed there in 1903.

The New Colossus[1]

Not like the brazen giant of Greek fame,[2]
With conquering limbs astride from land to land;
Here at our sea-washed, sunset gates shall stand
A mighty woman with a torch, whose flame
Is the imprisoned lightning,[3] and her name
Mother of Exiles.[4] From her beacon-hand
Glows world-wide welcome; her mild eyes command
The air-bridged harbor that twin cities frame.[5]
"Keep, ancient lands, your storied pomp!" cries she
With silent lips. "Give me your tired, your poor,
Your huddled masses yearning to breathe free,
The wretched refuse of your teeming shore.
Send these, the homeless, tempest-tost to me,
I lift my lamp beside the golden door!"

---

[1] Written in aid of Bartholdi Pedestal Fund, 1883 [Lazarus's note].

[2] The Colossus of Rhodes, a giant bronze statue of Helios, the sun god, created by the ancient Greek sculptor Chares of Lindos in the early 3d century B.C.E., is said to have straddled the harbor of Rhodes. It was destroyed by an earthquake in 225 B.C.E.

[3] Barak was the general who the prophetess Deborah urged to fight the Canaanite Sisera; his name means "lightning" in Hebrew (Judges 4.4–7). "Woman with a torch": the Hebrew phrase *eshet lapidot*, referring to the prophetess Deborah, "wife of Lappidoth," also means "woman of the torch."

[4] Deborah is called a "mother in Israel" (Judges 5.7).

[5] The Statue of Liberty stands in New York Harbor between New York City and Jersey City.

Discussion Questions

1. Carefully read the poem and the notes included by the editors. Then discuss how Lazarus's Jewish identity is woven into the poem. How does she frame the poem into a contrast between the Greek statue of Rhodes and Deborah of the Israelites? What differences is Lazarus stressing by contrasting these two figures? What other contrast does she draw in the second half of the poem? What is the purpose of this comparison?

2. The Statue of Liberty was a gift to the American people from France; it was designed by sculptor Frederic Auguste Bartholdi and was originally supposed to commemorate the centennial of the American Declaration of Independence. After various financial problems and construction delays, the statue was finally completed and assembled in 1886. Consider what the Statue of Liberty has meant to you personally. Has it been a part of your family history or not? Do you find it an appropriate symbol of liberty and freedom? Why or why not?

Writing Suggestions

1. Consider your answers to the first discussion question for this selection, and then write an explication of the poem, answering some of the questions below. Use specific quotes from the poem to back up your interpretations.

    What is the central argument in the poem?

    How does Lazarus shape the poem into a contrast between the Greek statue of Rhodes and Deborah of the Israelites? What differences is Lazarus stressing by contrasting these two figures?

    What other contrast does she draw in the second half of the poem? What is the purpose of this comparison?

    Do you find the poem powerful? Why or why not?

2. The image of the Statue of Liberty and the poem by Emma Lazarus have both come under attack in recent years by those who feel that the promises offered by the Statue and the poem are hollow or hypocritical, given the often very difficult experience of immigrants and minorities who have come to America. Others argue that the American dream is alive and well, and that the Statue of Liberty represents a fitting and idealistic image for the opportunities awaiting newcomers to America. Write a personal response to the poem by Lazarus, addressing the following questions:

    Do you find the poem appropriate for the plaque at the entrance to New York Harbor?

    Do you feel the poem is idealistic or hypocritical?

    Be specific in your praise or criticism of this plaque and what it represents to Americans and immigrants from other countries.

A Bintel Brief

Sixty Years of Letters from the Lower East Side to the Jewish Daily Forward

ISAAC METZKER

"A Bintel Brief" was the name of the *Jewish Daily Forward*'s advice column, which gave practical and straightforward advice to its readers, mainly Eastern European immigrants. They sought help for a range of problems, including spiritual dilemmas, family problems, sexual harassment, and even hate crimes. The letters, taken as a whole, offer a remarkable picture of life and its various struggles for Jewish immigrants in the early twentieth century. Editor Isaac Metzker compiled these letters into a book entitled *A Bintel Brief: Sixty Years of Letters from the Lower East Side to the Jewish Daily Forward*. Isaac Metzker was an immigrant himself, who came to America in 1924 after stowing away on a ship from Bremen, Germany. Metzker came to New York and eventually found a job writing for the *Daily Forward*. The following selections represent just a few examples of the many letters found in Metzker's book.

1907

Worthy Editor,

I am eighteen years old and a machinist by trade. During the past year I suffered a great deal, just because I am a Jew.

It is common knowledge that my trade is run mainly by the Gentiles and, working among the Gentiles, I have seen things that cast a dark shadow on the American labor scene. Just listen:

I worked in a shop in a small town in New Jersey, with twenty Gentiles. There was one other Jew besides me, and both of us endured the greatest hardships. That we were insulted goes without saying. At times we were even beaten up. We work in an area where there are many factories, and once, when we were leaving the shop, a group of workers fell on us like hoodlums and beat us. To top it off, we and one of our attackers were arrested. The hoodlum was let out on bail, but we, beaten and bleeding, had to stay in jail. At the trial, they fined the hoodlum eight dollars and let him go free.

After that I went to work on a job in Brooklyn. As soon as they found out that I was a Jew they began to torment me so that I had to leave the place. I have already worked at many places, and I either have to leave, voluntarily, or they fire me because I am a Jew.

Till now, I was alone and didn't care. At this trade you can make good wages, and I had enough. But now I've brought my parents over, and of course I have to support them.

Lately I've been working on one job for three months and I would be satisfied, but the worm of anti-Semitism is beginning to eat at my bones again. I go to work in the morning as to Gehenna, and I run away at night as from a fire. It's impossible to talk to them because they are common boors, so-called "American sports." I have already tried in various ways, but the only way to deal with them is with a strong fist. But I am too weak and they are too many.

Perhaps you can help me in this matter. I know it is not an easy problem.

Your reader,
E.H.

Answer:

In the answer, the Jewish machinist is advised to appeal to the United Hebrew Trades and ask them to intercede for him and bring up charges before the Machinists Union about this persecution. His attention is also drawn to the fact that there are Gentile factories where Jews and Gentiles work together and get along well with each other.

Finally it is noted that people will have to work long and hard before this senseless racial hatred can be completely uprooted.

1907

Dear Editor,

I am one of those unfortunate girls thrown by fate into a dark and dismal shop, and I need your counsel.

Along with my parents, sisters and brothers, I came from Russian Poland where I had been well educated. But because of the terrible things going on in Russia we were forced to emigrate to America. I am now seventeen years old, but I look younger and they say I am attractive.

A relative talked us into moving to Vineland, New Jersey, and here in this small town I went to work in a shop. In this shop there is a foreman who is an exploiter, and he sets prices on the work. He figures it out so that the wages are very low, he insults and reviles the workers, he fires them and then takes them back. And worse than all of this, in spite of the fact that he has a wife and several children, he often allows himself to "have fun" with some of the working girls. It was my bad luck to be one of the girls that he tried to make advances to. And woe to any girl who doesn't willingly accept them.

Though my few hard-earned dollars mean a lot to my family of eight souls, I didn't want to accept the foreman's vulgar advances. He started to pick on me, said my work was no good, and when I proved to him he was wrong, he started to shout at me in the vilest language. He insulted me in Yiddish and then in English, so the American workers could understand too. Then, as if the Devil were after me, I ran home.

I am left without a job. Can you imagine my circumstances and that of my parents who depend on my earnings? The girls in the shop were very upset over the foreman's vulgarity but they don't want him to throw them out, so they are afraid to be witnesses against him. What can be done about this? I beg you to answer me.

Respectfully,
A Shopgirl

Answer:

Such a scoundrel should be taught a lesson that could be an example to others. The girl is advised to bring out into the open the whole story about the foreman, because there in the small town it shouldn't be difficult to have him thrown out of the shop and for her to get her job back.

1908

My dearest friends of the *Forward*,

I appeal to you for help, since I have no better comrades than the workers.

I have been jobless for six months now. I have eaten the last shirt on my back and now there is nothing left for me but to end my life. I have struggled long enough in the dark world. Death is better than such a life. One goes about with strong hands, one wants to sell them for a bit of bread, and no one wants to buy. They tell you cold-bloodedly: "We don't need you." Can you imagine how heartsick one gets?

I get up at four in the morning to hunt a job through the newspaper. I have no money for carfare, so I go on foot, but by the time I get to the place there are hundreds before me. Then I run wherever my eyes lead me. Lately I've spent five cents a day on food, and the last two days I don't have even that. I have no strength to go on.

I am an ironworker. I can work a milling machine and a drill press. I can also drive horses and train colts. In Russia I served in the cavalry, and there I once hit my superior. For that I was sent to prison for forty days. Then I was returned to my squadron and my case was transferred to the military court in Kiev. Then orders came for me to be brought to Kiev.

When I learned of this I fled at three o'clock in the morning. I gave my gun and sword to the Bund organization and they gave me passage money to America.

If I had known it would be so bitter for me here, I wouldn't have come. I didn't come here for a fortune, but where is bread? What can I do now? I ask you, comrades. I beg you to help me in my dire need. Do not let a man die a horrible death.

Your friend,
G.B.
[Full name and address were given]

Poverty, Wealth, and the American Dream

Answer:

This is one of hundreds of heartrending pleas for help, cries of need, that we receive daily. The writer of this letter is told to go first to the Crisis Conference at 133 Eldridge Street, New York, and they will not let him starve. And further we ask our readers to let us know if someone can create a job for this unemployed man.

1908

Worthy Editor,

I have been in America almost three years. I came from Russia where I studied at a *yeshiva*. My parents were proud and happy at the thought that I would become a rabbi. But at the age of twenty I had to go to America. Before I left I gave my father my word that I would walk the righteous path and be good and pious. But America makes one forget everything.

Here I became an operator, and at night I went to school. In a few months I entered a preparatory school, where for two subjects I had a Gentile girl as teacher. I began to notice that the teacher paid more attention to me than to the others in the class and in time she told me I would be better off taking private lessons from her for the same price I paid to the school.

I agreed, and soon realized that her lessons with me were not ordinary. For example, I was to pay five dollars a month for two hours a week, but she gave me three lessons a week, each lasting two and sometimes three hours. Then I had to stop the lessons because I had no money to pay her. However, she wanted to teach me without pay, explaining that she taught not only for money but also because teaching gave her pleasure.

In short, I began to feel at home in her house and not only she but also her parents welcomed me warmly. I ate there often and they also lent me money when I was in need. I used to ask myself, "What am I doing? but I couldn't help myself. There was a depression at the time, I had no job and had to accept their aid.

I don't know what I would have done without her help. I began to love her, but with mixed feelings of respect and anguish. I was afraid to look her in the eyes. I looked at her like a Russian soldier looks at his superior officer and I never imagined she thought of marrying me.

A few weeks ago I took the Regents examinations for entering college. After the exams, my teacher told me not to look for work for a few weeks, but to eat and drink at their home. I didn't want to but she insisted and I couldn't refuse.

Many times upon leaving her house, I would decide not to return, but my heart drew me to her, and I spent three weeks in her house. Meanwhile I received the report on my examinations which showed that I had passed with the highest grades. I went directly to her to show her the report and she asked me what I planned to do. I answered that I didn't know as yet, because I had no money for college. "That's a minor problem," she said, and asked if I didn't know that she was not indifferent toward me. Then she spoke frankly of her love for me and her hope that I would love her.

"If you are not against it, my parents and I will support you while you study. The fact that I am a Gentile and you a Jew should not bother us. We are both, first of all, human beings and we will live as such." She told me she believed that all men and all nations were equal.

I was confused and I couldn't answer her immediately. In Europe I had been absorbed in the *yeshiva*, here with my studies, and I knew little of practical life. I do agree with her that we are first of all human beings, and she is a human being in the fullest sense of the word. She is pretty, intelligent, educated, and has a good character. But I am in despair when I think of my parents. What heartaches they will have when they learn of this!

I asked her to give me a few days to think it over. I go around confused and yet I am drawn to her. I must see her every day, but when I am there I think of my parents and I am torn by doubt.

I wait impatiently for your answer.

Respectfully,
Skeptic from Philadelphia

Answer:

We can only say that some mixed marriages are happy, others unhappy. But then many marriages between Jew and Jew, Christian and Christian, are not successful either. It is true, however, that in some mixed marriages the differences between man and wife create unhappiness. Therefore we cannot take it upon ourselves to advise the young man regarding this marriage. This he must decide for himself.

1911

Dear Editor,

I am writing to you here about a serious matter because I need your advice.

My husband and I were married for nineteen years and we have two sons, seventeen and fifteen years old. We were divorced three months ago because we hadn't been getting along.

But now we have reconsidered and realize we made a grave mistake, and we want to correct it. We wanted to remarry but we have difficulties. My husband is a *kohen*, and no rabbi will perform a religious ceremony for us. The rabbis we went to explained that it is against the Jewish law for a *kohen* to marry a divorced woman.

Therefore I ask you for advice, because we don't know what to do now. We aren't religious fanatics, but we want to handle this so that it will be proper in people's eyes.

We await your answer and will accept your advice.

Thank you in advance,
Mrs. R.D.K.

Answer:

Handling this problem in a way that would be proper and suit everyone is impossible. If they decide to live together, without being married by a rabbi, it would be considered proper by freethinkers but not by religious people.

If they obey the Jewish law and remain separate, it would be in accord with the Orthodox tradition. However, they don't have to ask anyone's advice, but should act according to their own convictions.

1923

Worthy Mr. Editor,

I was born in a small town in Russia and my mother brought me up alone, because I had lost my father when I was a child. My dear mother used all her energies to give me a proper education.

A pogrom broke out and my mother was the first victim of the blood bath. They spared no one, and no one was left for me. But that wasn't enough for the murderers, they robbed me of my honor. I begged them to kill me instead, but they let me live to suffer and grieve.

After that there were long days and nights of loneliness and grief. I was alone, despondent and homeless, until relatives in America brought me over. But my wounded heart found no cure here either. Here I am lonely, too, and no one cares. I am dejected, without a ray of hope, because all my former dreams for the future are shattered.

A few months ago, however, I met a young man, a refined and decent man. It didn't take long before we fell in love. He has already proposed marriage and he is now waiting for my answer.

I want to marry this man, but I keep putting off giving him an answer because I can't tell him the secret that weighs on my heart and bothers my conscience. I have no rest and am almost going out of my mind. When my friend comes to hear my answer, I want to tell him everything. Let him know all; I've bottled up the pain inside me long enough. Let him hear all and then decide. But I have no words and can tell him nothing.

I hope you will answer and advise me what I can do.

I thank you,
A Reader

Answer:

In the pogroms, in the great Jewish disasters, this misfortune befell many Jewish girls like you. But you must not feel guilty and not be so dejected, because you are innocent. A man who can understand and sympathize can be told everything. If your friend is one of these people and he really loves you, he will cherish you even after he learns your secret.

Since we do not know your friend, it is hard for us to advise you whether to tell him everything now, or not. In this matter you must take more responsibility on yourself. You know the man, and you must know, more or less, if he will be able to understand.

1909

Dear Editor,

Please print my letter and give me an answer. You might possibly save my life with it. I have no peace, neither day nor night, and I am afraid I will go mad because of my dreams.

I came to America three years ago from a small town in Lithuania, and I was twenty years old at that time. Besides me, my parents had five more unmarried daughters. My father was a Hebrew teacher. We used to help out by plucking chickens, making cigarettes, washing clothes for people, and we lived in poverty. The house was like a Gehenna. There was always yelling, cursing, and even beating of each other. It was bitter for me till a cousin of mine took pity on me. He sent a steamship ticket and money. He wrote that I should come to America and he would marry me.

I didn't know him, because he was a little boy when he left our town, but my delight knew no bounds. When I came to him, I found he was a sick man, and a few weeks later he died.

Then I began to work on ladies' waists. The "pleasant" life of a girl in the dreary shop must certainly be familiar to you. I toiled, and like all shopgirls, I hoped and waited for deliverance through a good match.

Landsleit and matchmakers were busy. I met plenty of prospective bridegrooms, but though I was attractive and well built, no one grabbed me. Thus a year passed. Then I met a woman who told me she was a matchmaker and had many suitors "in stock." I spilled out all my heartaches to her. First she talked me out of marrying a work-worn operator with whom I would have to live in poverty, then she told me that pretty girls could wallow in pleasure if they made the right friends. She made such a connection for me. But I had not imagined what that meant.

What I lived through afterwards is impossible for me to describe. The woman handed me over to bandits, and when I wanted to run away from them they locked me in a room without windows and beat me savagely.

Time passed and I got used to the horrible life. Later I even had an opportunity to escape, because they used to send me out on the streets, but life had become meaningless for me anyway, and nothing mattered any more. I lived this way for six months, degraded and dejected, until I got sick and they drove me out of that house.

I appealed for admission into several hospitals, but they didn't want to take me in. I had no money, because the rogues had taken everything from me. I tried to appeal to *landsleit* for help, but since they already knew all about me, they chased me away. I had decided to throw myself into the river, but wandering around on the streets, I met a richly dressed man who was quite drunk. I took over six hundred dollars from him and spent the money on doctors, who cured me.

Then I got a job as a maid for fine people who knew nothing about my past, and I have been working for them quite a while. I am devoted and diligent, they like me, and everything is fine.

A short time ago the woman of the house died, but I continued to work there. In time, her husband proposed that I marry him. The children, who are not yet grown up, also want me to be their "mother." I know it would be good for them and for me to remain there. The man is honest and good; but my heart won't allow me to deceive him and conceal my past. What shall I do now?

Miserable

Answer:

Such letters from victims of "white slavery" come to our attention quite often, but we do not publish them. We are disgusted by this plague on society, and dislike bringing it to the attention of our readers. But as we read this letter we felt we dare not discard it, because it can serve as a warning for other girls. They must, in their dreary lives, attempt to withstand these temptations and guard themselves from going astray.

This letter writer, who comes to us with her bitter and earnest tears, asking advice, has sufficient reason to fear that if the man finds out about her past he will send her away. But it is hard to conceal something that many people know. Such a thing cannot be kept secret forever. When the man finds out about it from someone else, he would feel that she had betrayed him and it would be worse.

Therefore, "Honesty is the best policy." She should tell him the truth, and whatever will be, will be.

1917

Dear Editor,

Four years ago, because of my activity in the revolutionary movement in Russia, I was forced to leave the country and come to America. I had no trade, because I was brought up in a wealthy home, so I struggled terribly at first. Thanks to my education and my ability to adjust, I am now a manager of a large wholesale firm and earn good wages. In time I fell in love with an intelligent, pretty American girl and married her.

America was my new home, and my wife and I tried to live in a way that would be most interesting and pleasant. From time to time, however, I had the desire to visit Russia to see what was going on there. But in America one is always busy and there is no time to be sentimental so I never went.

But now everything is changed. The Russian freedom movement, in which I took part, has conquered Czarism. The ideal for which I fought has become a reality, and my heart draws me there more than ever now. I began to talk about it to my wife, but her answer is that she hasn't the least desire to go to Russia. My revolutionary fire has cooled down here in the practical America, but it is not altogether extinguished, and I'm ready to go home now.

The latest events in Russia do not let me rest, and my mind is not on my job. But my wife and her parents tell me it would be foolish to leave such a good job and ruin everything. My wife doesn't want to go, and she holds me back. I can't leave my wife, whom I love very much, but it's hard to turn my back on my beloved homeland. I don't know how to act and I beg you to advise me what to do.

I will be very thankful for this.

Respectfully,
A.

Answer:

Many of those who took part in the freedom struggle are drawn to take a look at liberated Russia. But not everyone can do so. This is also the position of the writer, who has obligations to his wife. She is an American, she has her family here, so how can she leave her home and go to a strange country? The writer must take this into consideration. Besides, while the terrible battles are still raging, there can be no discussion about visiting Russia.

Discussion Questions

1. Review these letters in discussion groups and list the variety of conflicts and problems that appear in these letters. How are the women's problems different from the men's? And how are the younger generation's problems different from the older generation's?
2. Consider the other selections you have read about the immigrant experience. What picture of immigration emerges for Jewish immigrants and other immigrants? How can you reconcile the images of hope and promise expressed in Lazarus's poem with the experiences of the letter writers?

Writing Suggestions

1. Assume the identity of a Jewish immigrant, male or female, old or young, and then write your own letter to the editor of *A Bintel Brief* asking for advice about a particular problem. Your letter should reflect some reality of immigrant life, such as problems with work, religion, gender issues, the loss of the old country, intergenerational problems, and so on.
2. Research an aspect of immigrant life that appears in these letters, and then write a paper in which you explore the topic you have chosen. Sample research topics might include the following:

    Political and religious reasons for leaving Russia and Eastern Europe
    Labor issues in America for immigrant men and women
    The garment industry and immigrant labor
    Sexual harassment of immigrant women
    Religious harassment of immigrants
    Religious communities in newly adopted cities

Testimony of Samuel Gompers

SAMUEL GOMPERS

In 1883 the Senate Committee on Relations between Capital and Labor convened to examine the causes of recent labor strikes and the conditions of industrial workers. The committee listened to the testimony of Samuel Gompers (1850–1924), who was at the time active in the Cigar Makers Union and was employed by one of the larger cigar-making shops. As an immigrant to New York from London, Gompers had experienced firsthand the sweatshops where children often worked with their parents to make a small living. In 1886 Gompers became the first president of the American Federation of Labor, which within four years represented 250,000 workers. He worked to unify workers into strong trade unions, which he felt would be more effective than strikes in improving labor conditions. Gomper's testimony below comes from editor John A. Garraty's compilation of testimony from hearings of the Senate Committee in *Labor and Capital in the Gilded Age: Testimony Taken by the Senate Committee upon the Relations between Labor and Capital—1883*.

Testimony of Samuel Gompers

The Witness: . . . I will not start with the organizations. I would rather speak first of the general condition of labor as I find it, as I know it and believe it to be.

Sen. Blair: Well, take up the subject in your own way, but before you get through I would like you to answer the question I have put with regard to the extent and the actual objects and results of these organizations.—*A.* Oh, certainly; I shall endeavor to give you that to the best of my ability. The condition of the working people appears to be coming to what may rightly be termed a focus. On the one hand it would be well to note the underlying motives that frequently break out in what are generally termed strikes. Strikes are the result of a condition, and are not, as is generally or frequently understood, the cause. For instance, in the State of Massachusetts they have a ten-hour law, intended to benefit the female and child operatives there, yet the employers (and the same is true in Cohoes, in this State, and other places where the hours of labor are recognized as settled) or their agents start up the mills several minutes, sometimes seven, eight, nine, or ten minutes, before the time for commencing to work according to rule and law. In other instances they close them at "noon" several minutes after twelve o'-clock and open them again several minutes before the hour, or half hour rather, has elapsed, closing again for the day several minutes after the rule requires. These employers are pretty well described by some of the English economists and labor advocates—not labor advocates, but men who have made economic questions a study; they call them "minute thieves." . . .

In the branch of industry in which I work we have a bane to contend with, a curse, known as the manufacturing of cigars in tenement houses, in which the employer hires a row of tenements four or fives stories high, with two, three, or four families living on each floor, occupying a room and bedroom, or a room, bedroom, and an apology for a kitchen. The tobacco for the work is given out by the manufacturer or his superintendent to the operatives who work there, the husband and wife, and they seldom work without one or more of their children, if they have any. Even their parents, if they have any, work also in the room, and any indigent relative that may live with them also helps along. I myself made an investigation of these houses about two years ago; went through them and made measurements of them, and found that however clean the people might desire to be they could not be so. The bedroom is generally dark, and contains all the wet tobacco that is not intended for immediate use, but perhaps for use on the following day; while in the front room (or back room, as the case may be) the husband and wife and child, or any friend or relative that works with them, three or four or five persons are to be found. Each has a table at which to work. The tobacco which they work and the clippings or cuttings, as they are termed, are lying around the floor, while the scrap or clip that is intended to be used immediately for the making of cigars is lying about to dry. Children are playing about, as well as their puny health will permit them, in the tobacco. I have found, I believe, the most miserable conditions prevailing in those houses that I have seen at any time in my life.

Q. How many families are thus engaged in the manufacture of cigars in this city?—A. Between 1,900 and 2,000. The lowest ascertained number was 1,920 families. That was about five or six months ago.

Q. About 10,000 people, taking the average to a family of five?—A. Probably. These rooms I found to be, the main room, in which they work, about 12 feet by 8 or 9; the height of ceiling generally about 7 feet 6 inches to 8 feet 2 inches. It may probably be in order for me to state how I ascertained the height of these places. If I had gone in my true character as an investigator of the conditions pervading these houses I would not have been admitted into them. I, however, assumed the character of a book agent, and endeavored to sell Charles Dickens's works; and, by a practice of calculating the dimensions of small rooms, that I had undertaken and continued for several weeks, I found that the rooms in those tenements varied so very little that the differences between the different rooms could easily be estimated.

Sen. George: What was the size of the bedrooms?—A. The bedrooms were generally 6 feet by 8, or, in some instances, less. The kitchen was generally what is known in New York tenements as "dark"—an intermediate room. There is, first, the front or back room, as the case may be, then the kitchen, which has no light, and then another room in the back, which has no ventilation whatever except an aperture about 2 feet square in the side, and leading into a hall which leads into the street or the yard.

Q. The kitchen is not so large as the front room?—*A.* Not so long; it is as wide, generally.

Q. There is a narrow hall, making four families on each floor?—*A.* Four families on each floor.

Q. In what condition were the yards?—*A.* I made an investigation into that also, and found that the yards were all dirty. The halls were kept very dirty with tobacco stems and refuse that accumulates from the tobacco. In one instance it bordered on the ludicrous. There was a sign, "Keep off the grass!" The only "grass" that I could see was the green paint on the walls and the tobacco stems lying around by the hundred weight. The water closets are all vaults, in very few places connected with sewers, vaults in the backyard, around which a few boards have been nailed and the places termed "water closets." The water supply is very meager indeed.

Q. How many stories high are the buildings?—*A.* Four, generally; sometimes higher.

Q. Is there a water closet for each family?—*A.* No; there are generally two or three private closets, which are locked and keys given to, probably, one closet for two, three, or four families, there being not more than three or four water closets for all the families in the building. On the lower floor or basement generally in those houses there are stores, sometimes grocery stores or lager-beer saloons, or second-hand furniture stores, or Chinese laundries.

Q. Do you mean to say that about 1,900 families, engaged in the manufacture of cigars, live in the manner which you have just described?—*A.* Four-fifths of them, I think. Within this last year one of the manufacturers has endeavored to build a row of houses that are an improvement upon the old ones; but notwithstanding all attempts to keep these places clean, that is impossible, in consequence of the long hours of toil and the fact that all of the family are employed right at the work of cigar-making. . . .

The Cigar-makers' International Union adopted a system of agitation against the tenement-house cigar manufacture some years ago, believing that it was a public nuisance, and the press of the city of New York, together with that of the entire country, took this matter in hand, discussed it ably, exposed the iniquity of the system and the greed and avarice to which many men will resort in unfair competition, even with their fairer rivals in the trade. The opinions of the press, several of them, were extracted and printed by us and spread broadcast. I do not know that they may be of any importance, but this one from the *New York Sun* says, speaking of certain of these tenements:

> From cellar to attic the business carried on is the stripping of tobacco or the manufacture of cigars; women as well as men, girls as well as boys, toiling for life in an atmosphere thick with tobacco dust and reeking with odors too foul to be described. All this illustrates how one may start an extensive cigar and tobacco factory without investing in buildings and appliances.

The New York *Staats Zeitung* said:

The manufacture of cigars is one of the most important industries in our city, and tens of thousands of our working population make, directly or indirectly, their living in the tobacco industry. Circumstances impeding this industry must therefore affect also the prosperity of the city in general.

That the manufacturer in tenement houses can underbid other tobacco manufacturers is in the first place possible by compelling their workmen to pay the rent for factory rooms. Every other manufacturer has to pay high rents, taxes, etc., for his factory rooms; while the manufacturer in tenement houses not only pays nothing therefor, but the subletting of the rooms yields him perhaps a surplus income. In addition to saving his expense he makes additional extra profits by means of low wages. He is not, like other manufacturers, confined to certain working hours; the law against the employment of children under fourteen years of age is a dead letter for his tenement-house factories; the workingman, whose landlord he is at the same time, is much more dependent upon him. The workingman cannot quit work without being thrown into the street when he is refractory, the manufacturer raises the rent, or assigns him to poorer rooms; in short, he has a great many more means to oppress the workingman. The wages are so regulated that the whole family must assist in working; that women, young girls, and children, without regard to age, bodily development, mental education, must year after year, on Sunday and weekday, work hard in an atmosphere pestered by poisonous tobacco dust to earn the money necessary for the high rent and the direct necessities of life.

The manufacturer is getting rich, though he sells cheaper than his competitors. But he obtains his favorable position at the expense of the health, morals, and manliness of his workingmen, and the system thereby becomes an aggravated nuisance. The system is not only a pecuniary injury to a great many; to enrich a few it is a social as well as an economical evil. Hundreds of medical testimonials prove the injurious effects which the work has in ill-ventilated factories upon workingmen, and all these consequences are much stronger in tenement houses where the working room is at the same time used for dwelling purposes. This kind of work is especially injurious to the health of women. Out of 100 girls of the age of twelve to sixteen years, 72 in the average become sick after six months' work. In tenement houses where cigars are manufactured there are only 1.09 to 1.63 children to every married couple, and the mortality is about twenty per cent greater than in other tenement houses. Surely this evil ought to be remedied. It endangers the whole society, inasmuch as infectious diseases, as scarlet fever, etc., when occurring in such houses, may be spread all over the city by means of cigars manufactured in the room of sick cigar-makers. One physician states from his own experience that in the same room where persons were suffering from small-pox the manufacture of cigars was continued until the board of health interfered. Other physicians have seen that persons suffering from diphtheria continue to make cigars. This is a direct danger to all citizens.

Furthermore, the children in such houses grow up without sufficient education; the dense population, the working in dwelling rooms, the unreasonable extension of the working hours, the working on Sundays, endangers the morals and the education of adult persons. Low wages and insufficient control induces to smaller or greater embezzlements and evasions of the revenue laws.

Continually dirty surroundings prove also in this case to be detrimental to good morals. These evils are so apparent that, as the House-owners' Association has demonstrated, a tenement house in which cigars are manufactured decreases the value of the adjoining real estate. . . .

Q. What is your personal observation as compared with that statement?—*A*. I think there are a larger number of children to a family, and that this is rather an underestimate. . . .

I visited Cohoes, N.Y., during the strike there, about a year ago. That strike was organized against a proposed reduction of 10 percent in the operatives' wages. There were certain conditions surrounding the people in Cohoes that struck me very forcibly. On meeting the committee who received me (as I had been invited to attend), I made inquiries as to an immense building which I saw in the town, that being the first time I had visited Cohoes, and upon all hands was I informed, "That belongs to the Harmony Mills." Inquiring further as to another building, I was told, "That belongs to the Harmony Company." Everything belonged to the Harmony Company. The hotel was the Harmony Hotel. The boardinghouses were Harmony boardinghouses; the tenements in which the people lived belonged to the Harmony Company. The water is controlled by the Harmony Company. The waterpower by which the mills are run, the water which the people drink, the water which the other manufacturers are compelled to use, all is under the control of the Harmony Company.

Sen. Pugh: How many persons are there in the employ of that company?—*A*. Over 5,000.

Q. Where is Cohoes?—*A*. It is within an hour's travel from Albany, on the Mohawk River. As to the church there, I am informed that the minister in that church is a brother-in-law of the superintendent of the Harmony Mills. When the Harmony Company are in want of water to run their mills, and the people want water to drink, they have to go thirsty and the mills are run.

Sen. Blair: Is the water supply of the town taken from the river?—*A*. From the river; supplied through works first constructed by the Harmony Company.

Q. Are the city and the Harmony Company substantially identical? Does the company own the city pretty much?—*A*. Pretty much.

Q. Has not the city, the municipality, any reasonable opportunity of freeing itself of this dependence for water upon the Harmony Company? Can they not get a supply of water elsewhere?—*A*. Not very easily. I think it would require a great outlay, more than the people of Cohoes would be able to bear, outside of the interest of the Harmony Company. I was informed while there that several attempts had been made to start competitive mills in Cohoes, but that in consequence of the ownership by the Harmony Company, and their control of the water supply of Cohoes, competition was strangled at once; and while I have not traveled very extensively, I have seen some mills, and I am of the opinion that no greater water facilities exist in this country than in Cohoes for the running of mills.

Q. I interrupted your statement to draw closer attention to your assertion that when water was scarce the people went thirsty in order that the mills might run. You, perhaps, were never thirsty in that city yourself, but you may know of the complaints of people who reside there. I would like to know what your information is on that point.—A. The complaints were general. Of course scarcity of water in a place of so few inhabitants is not apt to occur very frequently, but when it does occur, and it has occurred several times, then complaint is general.

Q. Then the dearth is of water for purposes of cleanliness and ablution, rather than for drinking?—A. Sometimes it is.

Q. But still you do understand that the corporation restricts the people in the necessary amount of water for sanitary purposes?—A. No, sir, I do not; but I say that when there is a natural drought or scarcity of water they do. I do not wish to be understood as saying that the Harmony Company are willfully depriving the people of water, but that when there is a natural scarcity of water they first run the mills, even though the people have to go dirty and thirsty.

Q. That you understand from common conversation and from complaints that you have heard yourself?—A. Yes, sir.

Q. Complaints that you have heard on the ground?—A. Yes, sir; during my visit there.

Q. Was that a time of scarcity of water or not?—A. I could not answer that question.

Q. Do you believe that statement?—A. If I did not believe it, if I did not place some credit in it, I would not mention it.

Q. You think it is a fact?—A. Yes, sir.

Q. It satisfied your own judgment as a true statement?—A. Yes, sir; I believe it to be a truth; I have no reason to doubt it; I made inquiries after the persons told me that, and the statements were verified. I will say, by the way, that so much was I impressed with the information continually given that this and that and the other thing belonged to Harmony Mills, that although I am not on a poetical turn of mind I paraphrased Tennyson's "Charge of the Light Brigade," so that instead of "cannon to right of them, cannon to left of them," it was "Harmony to right of them, Harmony to left of them." The operatives there were striking against a reduction of 10 percent in wages which was proposed, notwithstanding the fact that during that period we had had the greatest era of prosperity that this country had known. . . .

I will proceed now to another branch of inquiry, in reference to one of the most hardworked class of people under the sun, the freight-handlers of the city of New York. They are a body of men, very sinewy, working for $.17 an hour for the railroad corporations. Last year they had the hardihood to ask for three cents more an hour, making $.20 an hour, when the railroads informed them that they would not pay it. The freighthandlers were, after a struggle, starved into submission, and are working now for $.17 an hour.

Q. Now, you are here and see these people: what sort of life does a freight-handler have on $.17 an hour?—*A.* He generally lives in very poor quarters; his home is but scantily furnished; he can eat only of the coarsest food; his children, like too many others, are frequently brought into the factories at a very tender age; in some instances his wife takes in sewing and does chores for other people, while in other instances that I know of they work in a few of the remaining laundries where women are still engaged, the work not having been absorbed by the Chinese. By this means the home, of course, is broken up; indeed there is hardly the semblance of a home, and in these instances where the wife goes out to work no meal is cooked. Many of the stores have for sale dried meats or herrings, cheese, or some other article which does not require any cooking. Of course, when the wife is at home although the living is very poor, it is cooked; she cooks what can be purchased with the portion of the $.17 per hour remaining after the payment of rent, and the cost of light, fuel, etc. . . .

The car-drivers of the city of New York are working from fourteen to sixteen hours a day in all weathers, and receive $1.75 a day.

Q. Now, why is not that enough?—*A.* Because it will not purchase the commonest necessaries of life.

Q. You understand, of course, that my question is designed to draw you out fully in regard to that class of workmen, their condition, etc. I understand your assertion to be that it is not enough; it does not seem to me, either, that it is enough; but I want to know from you what chance a man has to live on $1.75 a day?—*A.* He has this chance: his meals are served to him by his wife or friend or child, as the case may be, in a kettle, while he is driving his team, and at the end of the route he may possibly have two or three minutes to swallow his food. It is nothing more than swallowing it, and when he comes home he is probably too tired or perhaps too hungry to eat.

Q. There is no cessation in his work during the day of any consequence, then?—*A.* If there is, that which is termed relays or switches, he has still the same number of hours to work.

Q. Do you mean that that is deducted from his fourteen or sixteen hours?—*A.* Yes, sir.

Q. Then, if the relays amounted to an hour, he would be absent from his home seventeen hours?—*A.* Yes, sir.

Q. And if two hours, eighteen?—*A.* Yes, sir. And in the matter of these relays, in some instances men who do not and cannot live, on account of the meagerness of their wages, on the route of the railroad, are compelled to live at some distance, and when they have these relays or switches it takes them sometimes twenty or thirty minutes to reach their homes, and to return again takes another half or three-quarters of an hour.

Q. Then, do I understand you that these relays and the time occupied morning and evening going to and returning from their work are to be added to the fourteen or sixteen hours of actual service required?—*A.* The actual service is from fourteen to fifteen hours. Then there is the looking after their horses and cleaning the car besides.

Q. From the time that a car-driver leaves home in the morning until he returns for the night how much of the twenty-four hours will ordinarily be consumed?—*A.* I cannot tell you exactly as to how long a time they have at home, for the reason that it depends to some extent upon how far they live from the route of travel.

Q. State it approximately as near as you can.—*A.* Well, I do not believe that they have more than seven and a half hours out of the twenty-four.

Sen. Call: At what hour in the morning do they commence ordinarily, and what time do they quit?—*A.* Several of the street railroads of this city run all day and night; and on those, of course, the men commence at various hours. During the day the traffic on some routes is not so much as on others, and then they will be relayed; and, although they may go on to work at five o'clock in the morning, they probably would not get off before eleven or twelve o'-clock at night, or probably later still. I would not say later still positively, but I think in some instances later.

Sen. Pugh: Have they ever been paid higher wages?—*A.* Yes, sir. About two years ago they were on a strike to obtain, I think, $2.00 a day, but were starved into submission.

Q. What do they get now?—*A.* One dollar and seventy-five cents.

Sen. George: Does the conductor get the same wages, or more?—*A.* I think he gets $.25 more, by reason of his position of trust.

Sen. Blair: Have you any knowledge with regard to those who operate the elevated railways?—*A.* The men who work at ticket collecting or at the boxes where the tickets are deposited receive $1.25 a day, I think. I would rather wait until I can give you information definitely. I think I can do so now, but I prefer to wait.

Sen. George: Are the car-drivers allowed to have seats?—*A.* They are not. They have to stand all the time.

Sen. Call: How many hours do they stand?—*A.* Fourteen or fifteen.

Q. Do you mean fourteen hours' standing without intermission?—*A.* Very little intermission. They sometimes rest back against the door of the car for a while. They also, in some instances, have to act as conductors; that is, give change, count the passengers, and register the number of passengers on an indicator. And then they are sometimes held responsible when somebody is run over on account, perhaps, of their having to perform two men's work. The greed of the horse-railroad companies has been such that they have introduced on several lines what is known as the bobtailed car, and have dispensed with the services of a conductor.

Sen. Blair: Don't you think that is because they cannot afford to pay any more?—*A.* I hardly believe that. Judging from the traffic, they are capable of paying it, and judging from what is currently reported as their dividends, they are more than capable of paying it. I must acknowledge, though, that so far as their dividends are concerned, I am personally uninformed. I take merely current rumor and the appearance of the traffic, the number of passengers I see on the cars.

Among some of the tailoresses in the city I have made a personal investigation. They make a regular heavy pantaloon, working pants, for $.07 a pair. They are capable of making ten pairs per day of twelve hours. Boys' pantaloons they make for $.05 to $.06 per pair, making fourteen to sixteen pairs per day of twelve hours. They work mostly seven full days in the week; sometimes they will stop on Sunday afternoon, but all work on Sunday, and their average weekly wages is about $3.81, providing no time is lost.

They are compelled to provide their own cotton out of this, and their own needles and thimbles, and other small things that are necessary in the work. Overalls and jumpers (a kind of calico jacket used by laborers in warm weather sometimes, to prevent the dirt getting to the shirt or underclothing) they make for $.30 to $.35 per dozen. They generally work in "teams" of two, and they make about three dozen per day, or in a working day of thirteen to fifteen hours they earn from $.45 to $.52 1/2 each. They work generally in the shop, but usually finish some work at home on Sunday.

In the manufacture of cigars in shops there is a branch termed "stripping." I am not sure as to these statistics that I am going to give you, but I believe them to be correct. Nine-tenths of these strippers, or about that proportion, are females. Their average hours of labor are ten per day. Their wages range between $3 and $7 a week when at work. About one-half of these girls are employed at the former wage, but two-thirds at $5 a week, and the remaining third at a higher wage.

They lose days and weeks' work frequently, or have lost them in the past more than at present, and in very rare instances are they paid for loss of time, even when it is caused by national or other holidays. In the shops, more especially the larger ones, they are prohibited from holding any conversation under pain of fine or dismissal. Even if they were disposed to converse they could not. The very positions in which they work, or are placed to work (which are not necessary to the work), in long rows, in which each faces the back of the girl in front of her, precludes them from holding conversation. They suffer in every way the disciplinary measures of imprisonment at hard labor. They cannot hold conversation. One sits with her face to the back of the other, and that is the rule in almost all the factories. Where there are only a few of them of course it makes very little difference. It is believed that this plan of placing them gets more work out of them. . . .

Q. Now, about the newsboys and the other little fellows that we see around the streets, the bootblacks. Those little waifs seem to be pretty busy doing something all the time. What pay do they get out of their labors—how do they live?—*A.* Well, the newsboys earn very small sums. I do not believe more than one-half of them live at home with their parents. The others, out of the papers they sell or earn, try to purchase a ticket for some variety show, and buy cigarettes, of course, and keep just sufficient to get a meal in a five-cent restaurant and to pay their lodging in a newsboys' lodging-house, which costs about half a dollar a week.

Q. What chance is there of their attending school?—*A.* Without answering that question I would like to make a statement that I read in one of the papers (and the paper said that the superintendent of the Newsboys' Home acknowledged it to be true) that the newsboys were required to pay for one week's lodging in advance; that one boy was taken sick while in the lodging-house, and sent to the hospital after the second night of the week for which he had paid, and when he came out of the hospital he thought that he had five nights good yet to sleep in the lodging-house, but when he came there he was informed that he had forfeited that money by not sleeping in the lodging-house during the week. . . .

Q. Are the newsboys employed by the newspapers, or do they just get so much for every paper they sell?—A. They get so much for every paper they sell, and sometimes a man can buy two-cent papers for a penny. Some will offer you two papers for a cent.

Q. When they have a supply left which they do not sell what becomes of it?—A. It is their own loss.

Sen. George: They buy the papers themselves and make what they can?—A. Yes, sir; and it is quite a sight to see some of the boys running after the wagons that contain the papers, the evening papers more especially; to see one hundred or two hundred of them, and as one drops off that has been served with his papers another one takes his place, the others coming up continually and keeping up the crowd. If the poor boys were on the point of starvation and their only hope of life was in that wagon I do not believe they could run much faster or risk their lives much more than they do sometimes.

Q. How about the bootblacks?—A. How the bootblacks do I cannot say, any more than their position in life is very hard.

Q. Does the newsboy get a chance for school at all?—A. I do not see where that comes in, except that possibly one here and there may have an opportunity of going to a night school, and that, I think, is not generally taken advantage of by them. The boy fails to see the importance of an education himself, and there are very few who are willing to lend a hand to guide him. . . .

Sen. Pugh: What is your opinion as to whether that idea of regarding the laborer as a machine exists more now than it has existed in the past?—A. I think it exists now in a greater degree than it did formerly. Not only do I think that, but I am forced to the opinion that it is increasing and intensifying even as we go along.

Q. Anyhow, that, you say, is the view that the employees take of the sentiments entertained towards them by their employers?—A. Yes. sir. They find that employers are no longer—when I speak of employers I speak of them generally—that they are no longer upon the same footing with them that they were on formerly. They find that where a man who may have worked at the bench with them employs one or two hands they and he may have full social intercourse together, but as that man increases his business and employs a larger number of hands they find that his position has been removed so far above that of his old friends that they meet no more socially. Probably they may meet occasionally in the factory, when there will be a passing remark of "Good morning" or "Good day"; and then, after a while, the employer fails to see the employees at all; the superintendent does all the business and the employer does not bother himself any more about the men. That is how the position of the two has been changed since both were workingmen at the bench. The difference is considerably greater when the employer and the employee did not know each other before, and when the employer's resources are already large. In such cases he and the men do not know each other at all, and in most such instances the employees are not known as men at all, but are known by numbers—"1," "2," "3," or "4," and so on. . . .

Discussion Questions

1. Make a list of the broad range of information Gompers manages to convey in his testimony. About how many different occupations does he testify? What groups of individuals does he mention? How does his tone add to or detract from the range of information he gives the senators questioning him?

2. Analyze both the tone of Senator Blair's questions and the range of questions he asks. Do you feel he is sincerely interested in Gomper's information or not? Were his questions pertinent to his task of examining the working conditions of laborers? Note any diction you can find which might indicate how Gomper's testimony was affecting Blair emotionally. After reading this testimony, what would you guess Blair felt about the information Gompers gave him?

Writing Suggestions

1. Based on your own experiences and those of your family and friends, freewrite about how much the life of the American worker has evolved since the late nineteenth and early twentieth century. Do you see remnants of labor problems similar to those of an earlier time, or do you think American workers are protected by unions and laws that prevent labor abuses similar to those Gompers describes? What about the lives of immigrant workers in the United States today? Do you know of any abuses of labor concerning these immigrants?

2. Gompers mentions again and again the problem of child laborers who are overworked in dark and dirty tenements and whose health is badly compromised by the working conditions. Research the question of child labor in the United States, and write an essay analyzing the gradual institution of child labor laws in the twentieth century. Research the existing state and federal child labor laws today, and argue in your paper whether or not these current laws do enough to protect children from abusive working conditions.

The Triangle Fire

LEON STEIN

In 1962 Leon Stein published *The Triangle Fire*, an account of the 1911 factory fire in which 146 employees (primarily young, immigrant women) of the Triangle Shirtwaist Company in New York City either jumped to their deaths or were killed by fire. Most of the building's exit doors were illegally locked to keep workers inside during working hours. On March 26, the day after the fire, the *New York Times* reported, "The victims—mostly Italians, Russians, Hungarians, and Germans—were girls and men who had been employed by the firm of Harris & Blanck, owners of the Triangle Shirtwaist Company .... The building had experienced four recent fires and had been reported by the Fire Department to the Building Department as unsafe on account of the insufficiency of its exits." Stein himself was a garment cutter and pattern maker, and returned to the industry after his graduation from City College in New York in 1934. In 1939, Stein began to write for *Justice*, the publication of the International Ladies' Garment Workers' Union. Eventually he became copy editor, assistant editor, and finally, in 1952, editor. He also wrote *Out of the Sweatshop: The Struggle for Industrial Democracy*, and edited an anthology of writing from the labor press. In order to write *The Triangle Fire*, Stein used newspapers, interviews with survivors and witnesses, and official documents. His book not only documents the appalling working conditions common before the fire, but also details the efforts of reformers after the fire to institute safety reforms and enforce laws to protect workers' lives.

Chapter 1: Fire

I intend to show Hell.

    —Dante, *Inferno*, canto xxix:96

The first touch of spring warmed the air.

It was Saturday afternoon—March 25, 1911—and the children from the teeming tenements to the south filled Washington Square Park with the shrill sounds of youngsters at play. The paths among the old trees were dotted with strollers.

Genteel brownstones, their lace-curtained windows like drooping eyelids, lined two sides of the 8-acre park that formed a sanctuary of green in the brick and concrete expanse of New York City. On the north side of the Square rose the red brick and limestone of the patrician Old Row, dating back to 1833.

Only on the east side of the Square was the almost solid line of homes broken by the buildings of New York University.

The little park originally had been the city's Potter's Field, the final resting place of its unclaimed dead, but in the nineteenth century Washington Square became the city's most fashionable area. By 1911 the old town houses stood as a rear guard of an aristocratic past facing the invasions of industry from Broadway to the east, low-income groups from the crowded streets to the south, and the first infiltration of artists and writers into Greenwich Village to the west.

Dr. D. C. Winterbottom, a coroner of the City of New York, lived at 63 Washington Square South. Some time after 4:30, he parted the curtains of a window in his front parlor and surveyed the pleasant scene.

He may have noticed Patrolman James P. Meehan of Traffic B proudly astride his horse on one of the bridle paths which cut through the park.

Or he may have caught a glimpse of William Gunn Shepherd, young reporter for the United Press, walking briskly eastward through the Square.

Clearly visible to him was the New York University building filling half of the eastern side of the Square from Washington Place to Waverly Place. But he could not see, as he looked from his window, that Professor Frank Sommer, former sheriff of Essex County, New Jersey, was lecturing to a class of fifty on the tenth floor of the school building, or that directly beneath him on the ninth floor Professor H. G. Parsons was illustrating interesting points of gardening to a class of forty girls.

A block east of the Square and parallel to it, Greene Street cut a narrow path between tall loft buildings. Its sidewalks bustled with activity as shippers trundled the day's last crates and boxes to the horse-drawn wagons lining the curbs.

At the corner of Greene Street and Washington Place, a wide thoroughfare bisecting the east side of the Square, the Asch building rose ten floors high. The Triangle Shirtwaist Company, largest of its kind, occupied the top three floors. As Dr. Winterbottom contemplated the peaceful park, 500 persons, most of them young girls, were busily turning thousands of yards of flimsy fabric into shirtwaists, a female bodice garment which the noted artist Charles Dana Gibson had made the sartorial symbol of American womanhood.

One block north, at the corner of Greene Street and Waverly Place, Mrs. Lena Goldman swept the sidewalk in front of her small restaurant. It was closing time. She knew the girls who worked in the Asch building well for many of them were her customers.

Dominick Cardiane, pushing a wheelbarrow, had stopped for a moment in front of the doors of the Asch building freight elevator in the middle of the Greene Street block. He heard a sound "like a big puff," followed at once by the noise of crashing glass. A horse reared, whinnied wildly, and took off down Greene Street, the wagon behind it bouncing crazily on the cobblestones.

Reporter Shepherd, about to cross from the park into Washington Place, also heard the sound. He saw smoke issuing from an eighth-floor window of the Asch building and began to run.

Patrolman Meehan was talking with his superior, Lieutenant William Egan. A boy ran up to them and pointed to the Asch building. The patrolman put spurs to his horse.

Dr. Winterbottom saw people in the park running toward Washington Place. A few seconds later he dashed down the stoop carrying his black medical bag and cut across the Square toward Washington Place.

Patrolman Meehan caught up with Shepherd and passed him. For an instant there seemed to be no sound on the street except the urgent tattoo of his horse's hoofbeats as Meehan galloped by. He pulled up in front of 23 Washington Place, in the middle of the block, and jumped from the saddle.

Many had heard the muffled explosion and looked up to see the puff of smoke coming out of an eighth-floor window. James Cooper, passing by, was one of them. He saw something that looked "like a bale of dark dress goods" come out of a window.

"Some one's in there all right. He's trying to save the best cloth," a bystander said to him.

Another bundle came flying out of a window. Halfway down the wind caught it and the bundle opened.

It was not a bundle. It was the body of a girl.

Now the people seemed to draw together as they fell back from where the body had hit. Nearby horses struggled in their harnesses.

"The screams brought me running," Mrs. Goldman recalled. "I could see them falling! I could see them falling!"

John H. Mooney broke out of the crowd forming on the sidewalk opposite the Asch building and ran to Fire Box 289 at the corner of Greene Street. He turned in the first alarm at 4:45 P.M.

Inside the Asch building lobby Patrolman Meehan saw that both passenger elevators were at the upper floors. He took the stairs two steps at a time.

Between the fifth and sixth floors he found his way blocked by the first terrified girls making the winding descent from the Triangle shop. In the narrow staircase he had to flatten himself against the wall to let the girls squeeze by.

Between the seventh and eighth floors he almost fell over a girl who had fainted. Behind her the blocked line had come to a stop, the screaming had increased. He raised her to her feet, held her for a moment against the wall, calming her, and started her once again down the stairs.

At the eighth floor, he remembers that the flames were within 8 feet of the stairwell. "I saw two girls at a window on the Washington Place side shouting for help and waving their hands hysterically. A machinist—his name was Brown—helped me get the girls away from the window. We sent them down the stairs."

The heat was unbearable. "It backed us to the staircase," Meehan says.

Together with the machinist, he retreated down the spiral staircase. At the sixth floor, the policeman heard frantic pounding on the other side of the door facing the landing. He tried to open the door but found it was locked. He was certain now that the fire was also in progress on this floor.

"I braced myself with my back against the door and my feet on the nearest step of the stairs. I pushed with all my strength. When the door finally burst inward, I saw there was no smoke, no fire. But the place was full of frightened women. They were screaming and clawing. Some were at the windows threatening to jump.

These were Triangle employees who had fled down the rear fire escape. At the sixth floor, one of them had pried the shutters open, smashed the window and climbed back into the building. Others followed. Inside, they found themselves trapped behind a locked door and panicked.

As he stumbled back into the street, Meehan saw that the first fire engines and police patrol wagons were arriving. Dr. Winterbottom, in the meantime, had reached Washington Place. For a moment he remained immobilized by the horror. Then he rushed into a store, found a telephone, and shouted at the operator, "For God's sake, send ambulances!"

The first policemen on the scene were from the nearby Mercer Street Station House of the 8th Precinct. Among them were some who had used their clubs against the Triangle girls a year earlier during the shirtwaist makers' strike.

First to arrive was Captain Dominick Henry, a man inured to suffering by years of police work in a tough, two-fisted era. But he stopped short at his first view of the Asch building. "I saw a scene I hope I never see again. Dozens of girls were hanging from the ledges. Others, their dresses on fire, were leaping from the windows."

From distant streets came piercing screams of fire whistles, the nervous clang of fire bells. Suddenly, they were sounding from all directions.

In the street, men cupped their hands to their mouths, shouting, "Don't jump! Here they come!" Then they waved their arms frantically.

Patrolman Meehan also shouted. He saw a couple standing in the frame of a ninth-floor window. They moved out onto the narrow ledge. "I could see the fire right behind them. I hollered, 'Go over!'"

But nine floors above the street the margin of choice was as narrow as the window ledge. The flames reached out and touched the woman's long tresses. The two plunged together.

In the street, watchers recovering from their first shock had sprung into action. Two young men came charging down Greene Street in a wagon, whipping their horses onto the sidewalk and shouting all the time, "Don't jump!" They leaped from the wagon seat, tore the blankets from their two horses, and shouted for others to help grip them. Other teamsters also stripped blankets, grabbed tarpaulins to improvise nets.

But the bodies hit with an impact that tore the blankets from their hands. Bodies and blankets went smashing through the glass deadlights set into the sidewalk over the cellar vault of the Asch building.

Daniel Charnin, a youngster driving a Wanamaker wagon, jumped down and ran to help the men holding the blankets. "They hollered at me and kicked me. They shouted, 'Get out of here, kid! You want to get killed?'"

One of the first ambulances to arrive was in the charge of Dr. D. E. Keefe of St. Vincent's Hospital. It headed straight for the building. "One woman fell so close to the ambulance that I thought if we drove it up to the curb it would be possible for some persons to strike the top of the ambulance and so break their falls."

The pump engine of Company 18, drawn by three sturdy horses, came dashing into Washington Place at about the same time. It was the first of thirty-five pieces of fire-fighting apparatus summoned to the scene. These included the Fire Department's first motorized units, ultimately to replace the horses but in 1911 still experimental.

Another major innovation being made by the Fire Department was the creation of high-water-pressure areas. The Asch building was located in one of the first of these. In such an area a system of water-main cutoffs made it possible to build up pressure at selected hydrants. At Triangle, the Gansevoort Street pumping station raised the pressure to 200 pounds. The most modern means of fighting fires were available at the northwest corner of Washington Place and Greene Street.

A rookie fireman named Frank Rubino rode the Company 18 pump engine, and he remembers that "we came tearing down Washington Square East and made the turn into Washington Place. The first thing I saw was a man's body come crashing down through the sidewalk shed of the school building. We kept going. We turned into Greene Street and began to stretch in our hoses. The bodies were hitting all around us."

When the bodies didn't go through the deadlights, they piled up on the sidewalk, some of them burning so that firemen had to turn their hoses on them. According to Company 18's Captain Howard Ruch the hoses were soon buried by the bodies and "we had to lift them off before we could get to work."

Captain Ruch ordered his men to spread the life nets. But no sooner was the first one opened than three bodies hit it at once. The men, their arms looped to the net, held fast.

"The force was so great it took the men off their feet," Captain Ruch said. "Trying to hold the nets, the men turned somersaults and some of them were catapulted right onto the net. The men's hands were bleeding, the nets were torn and some caught fire."

Later, the Captain calculated that the force of each falling body when it struck the net was about 11,000 pounds.

"Life nets?" asked Battalion Chief Edward J. Worth. "What good were life nets? The little ones went through life nets, pavement, and all. I thought they would come down one at a time. I didn't know they would come down with arms entwined—three and even four together." There was one who seemed to have survived the jump. "I lifted her out and said, 'Now go right across the street.' She walked ten feet—and dropped. She died in one minute."

The first hook and ladder—Company 20—came up Mercer Street so fast, says Rubino, "that it almost didn't make the turn into Washington Place."

The firemen were having trouble with their horses. They weren't trained for the blood and the sound of the falling bodies. They kept rearing on their hind legs, their eyes rolling. Some men pulled the hitching pins and the horses broke loose, whinnying. Others grabbed the reins and led them away.

The crowd began to shout: "Raise the ladders!"

Company 20 had the tallest ladder in the Fire Department. It swung into position, and a team of men began to crank its lifting gears. A hush fell over the crowd.

The ladder continued to rise. One girl on the ninth floor ledge slowly waved a handkerchief as the ladder crept toward her.

Then the men stopped cranking. The ladder stopped rising.

The crowd yelled in one voice: "Raise the ladders!"

"But the ladder had been raised," Rubino says. "It was raised to its fullest length. It reached only to the sixth floor."

The crowd continued to shout. On the ledge, the girl stopped waving her handkerchief. A flame caught the edge of her skirt. She leaped for the top of the ladder almost 30 feet below her, missed, hit the sidewalk like a flaming comet.

Chief Worth had arrived at the scene at 4:46 1/2, had ordered the second alarm to be transmitted at 4:48. Two more alarms were called, one at 4:55 and a fourth at 5:10.

In the first two minutes after his arrival, the Chief had assessed the situation. He directed his men to aim high water pressure hoses on the wall above the heads of those trapped on the ledge. "We hoped it would cool off the building close to them and reassure them. It was about the only reassurance we could give. The men did the best they could. But there is no apparatus in the department to cope with this kind of fire."

The crowd watched one girl on the ledge inch away from the window through which she had climbed as the flames licked after her. As deliberately as though she were standing before her own mirror at home, she removed her wide brimmed hat and sent it sailing through the air. Then slowly, carefully, she opened her handbag.

Out of it she extracted a few bills and a handful of coins—her pay. These she flung out into space. The bills floated slowly downward. The coins hit the cobblestones, ringing as she jumped.

Three windows away one girl seemed to be trying to restrain another from jumping. Both stood on the window ledge. The first one tried to reach her arm around the other.

But the second girl twisted loose and fell. The first one now stood alone on the ledge and seemed oblivious to everything around her. Like a tightrope walker, she looked straight ahead and balanced herself with her hands on hips hugging the wall.

Then she raised her hands. For a moment she gestured, and to the staring crowd it seemed as if she were addressing some invisible audience suspended there before her. Then she fell forward.

They found her later, buried under a pile of bodies. She was Celia Weintraub and lived on Henry Street. Life was still in her after two hours in which she had lain among the dead.

William Shepherd, the United Press reporter and the only newspaperman on the scene at the height of the tragedy, had found a telephone in a store and dictated his story as he watched it happen through a plate-glass window. He counted sixty-two falling bodies, less than half the final total.

"Thud—dead! Thud—dead! Thud—dead!" Shepherd began his story. "I call them that because the sound and the thought of death came to me each time at the same instant."

As he watched, Shepherd saw "a love affair in the midst of all the horror.

"A young man helped a girl to the window sill on the ninth floor. Then he held her out deliberately, away from the building, and let her drop. He held out a second girl the same way and let her drop.

"He held out a third girl who did not resist. I noticed that. They were all as unresisting as if he were helping them into a street car instead of into eternity. He saw that a terrible death awaited them in the flames and his was only a terrible chivalry."

Then came the love affair.

"He brought another girl to the window. I saw her put her arms around him and kiss him. Then he held her into space—and dropped her. Quick as a flash, he was on the window sill himself. His coat fluttered upwards—the air filled his trouser legs as he came down. I could see he wore tan shoes.

"Together they went into eternity. Later I saw his face. You could see he was a real man. He had done his best. We found later that in the room in which he stood, many girls were burning to death. He chose the easiest way and was brave enough to help the girl he loved to an easier death."

Bill Shepherd's voice kept cracking. But he was first of all a newspaper reporter, and he steeled himself to see and to report what untrained eyes might miss.

He noticed that those still in the windows watched the others jump. "They watched them every inch of the way down." Then he compared the different manner in which they were jumping on the two fronts of the Asch building.

On the Washington Place side they "tried to fall feet down. I watched one girl falling. She waved her arms, trying to keep her body upright until the very instant she struck the sidewalk."

But on the Greene Street side "they were jammed into the windows. They were burning to death in the windows. One by one the window jams broke. Down came the bodies in a shower, burning, smoking, flaming bodies, with disheveled hair trailing upward. These torches, suffering ones, fell inertly.

"The floods of water from the firemen's hoses that ran into the gutter were actually red with blood," he wrote. "I looked upon the heap of dead bodies and I remembered these girls were the shirtwaist makers. I remembered their great strike of last year in which these same girls had demanded more sanitary conditions and more safety precautions in the shops. These dead bodies were the answer."

At 4:57 a body in burning clothes dropped from the ninth floor ledge, caught on a twisted iron hook protruding at the sixth floor. For a minute it hung there, burning. Then it dropped to the sidewalk. No more fell.

Chapter 2: Trap

With sad announcement of impending doom.
                                              —Dante, *Inferno*, canto xiii:12

"My building is fireproof," Joseph J. Asch insisted.

He talked to reporters in the sitting room of his suite in the Hotel Belmont, a grave-looking man of fifty, sun-tanned and sporting a white mustache. He and his wife had just arrived in the city en route from St. Augustine, Florida, to their home in Saugatuck, Connecticut. He first learned of the fire when he read about it in the Sunday morning papers.

"I was overcome by the horror of it," he emphasized for the reporters. "The architects claimed my building was ahead of any other building of its kind which had previously been constructed."

First plans for the construction of a building at Greene Street and Washington Place were filed in April, 1900, by an architect named John Wooley. He was acting for Ole H. Olsen of the Bronx who owned a 25- by 100-foot lot on the site and had acquired from Asch the adjoining 75- by 100-foot lot.

But Asch changed his mind, took over the combined site from Olsen, and decided to build for himself. His architect, Julius Franke, filed new plans with the Building Department on April 28, 1900. The plans were finally approved on July 13 of that year. The Asch building, representing a cost of about $400,000, was completed January 15, 1901.

The structure was 135 feet high. At 150 feet—or with one additional story—it would have had, as required by law, metal trim, metal window frames, and stone or concrete floors. At 135 feet its wooden trim, wooden window frames, and wooden floors were legal.

The law required only a single staircase in a building in which the floor space at each level was less than 2,500 square feet; if the single floor measured more than that but less thin 5,000 square feet the building was required to have two staircases; there would be an additional stairway for each additional 5,000 square feet.

By this measure, the Asch building with an interior area of 10,000 square feet per floor should have had three staircases. This flaw was noted by Rudolph P. Miller, then an inspector for the Building Department over which he had risen to be director by 1911. On May 7, 1900, he wrote to architect Franke that "an additional continuous line of stairway should be provided."

The architect asked for an exception because "the staircases are remote from each other and, as there is a fire escape in the court, it practically makes three staircases, which in my opinion is sufficient."

Miller also insisted that the "fire escape in the rear must lead down to something more substantial than a skylight." The architect replied with the promise that "the fire escape will lead to the yard and an additional balcony will be put in where designated on the plan."

Both staircases were in vertical wells with their steps winding once around a center between floors. The steps were of slate set in metal and measured 2 feet 9 inches in width but were tapered at the turns. The walls were of terra cotta.

Only the Greene Street staircase, with windows between floors facing the backyard, had an exit to the roof. The windowless Washington Place stairs ended at the tenth floor.

At each floor, a wooden door with a wired glass window, opened into the loft. Section 80 of the State Labor Law required that factory doors "shall be so constructed as to open outwardly, where practicable, and shall not be locked, bolted or fastened during working hours."

But in the Asch building, the last step at each landing was only one stair's width away from the door. Therefore it was not "practicable" for the doors to open outward. Therefore all of them opened in.

The Asch building's "third staircase"—its single fire escape—ended at the second floor, despite Miller's requests. But, as Manhattan Borough President George McAneny pointed out after the fire, the law "doesn't compel any sort of building to have fire escapes. It leaves enormous discretionary power with the Building Department."

The dangers implicit in this situation were underscored by Arthur E. Mc-Farlane, an expert in fire prevention and fire insurance. He charged that in many instances speculative builders "decided to build their loft buildings without any fire escapes at all. Others put them in the air shaft which, in case of fire, becomes its natural flue. Others bolted on the antique, all but vertical, 18-inch ladder escapes such as could not legally have been placed upon even a three-story tenement house."

The City's Board of Aldermen was aware of the danger. In 1909 it spent time studying the problem and ended up with proposed revisions of the building code, one of which would have required street-side fire escapes on buildings of the Asch type.

The entire effort, however, was tripped up by a fight that started with rival interests controlling the production and sale of fireproof materials. The Board divided along parallel lines and stalemated all action on the matter.

"I have never received any request or demand from any department or bureau for alteration to the building nor has any request or demand been received by me for additional fire escapes nor has the fire escape on the building ever been unfavorably criticized to me by any official," Mr. Asch continued in his Belmont Hotel suite. And, slicing the air with his right hand, he added, "I never gave the matter any thought."

There was no law requiring fire sprinklers in New York City factory buildings.

Fire Chief Edward F. Croker argued that there had never been a loss of life in a sprinkler-equipped building. These devices, attached to the ceiling, had heat fuses which automatically could set off an alarm and at the same time release heavy sprays of water in the area where heat from a fire had accumulated.

Chief Croker admitted that installation of sprinklers would add about 4 per cent to construction costs. But he stressed his opinion that "sprinklers increase the renting value of a building and so decrease the price of insurance as to pay for themselves within five years."

Sharing this opinion, and on the basis of his own investigations, Fire Commissioner Rhinelander Waldo had ordered sprinklers to be installed in a number of warehouses. Three weeks before the Triangle conflagration, the Protective League of Property Owners held an indignation meeting. The League's counsel, Pendleton Dudley, then issued a statement charging that the Fire Department was seeking to force the use of "cumbersome and costly" apparatus.

The League insisted that the order was arbitrary and imposed a burden of unnecessary expense and that the action was unreasonable, mischievous, and misleading, the *Tribune* reported. And the *Herald* noted that the owners claimed the order amounted to "a confiscation of property and that it operates in the interest of a small coterie of automatic sprinkler manufacturers to the exclusion of all others."

Chief Croker restrained his anger. "If the manufacturers of certain sprinkler systems have formed a combination," he replied, "there are other sprinkler systems that are not controlled by a combination. Nine sprinklers in all have been tested and approved by the National Board of Underwriters."

There was no law requiring fire drills to be held in New York City factory buildings.

In the fall of 1910, the New York Joint Board of Sanitary Control, a labor-management group that included a number of cooperating public-spirited citizens, investigated work conditions in 1,243 coat and suit shops in the city. The Board had been created after a strike by the International Ladies' Garment Workers' Union in the summer of 1910.

Nine days before the Triangle fire—on March 16—the New York *Call* published excerpts from the report of Dr. George M. Price, the Board's director. Copies of the full report on the investigation had already been sent to the Building, Fire, and Police Departments. In addition, the Board's secretary, Henry Moskowitz, had sent a long list of shops with hazards to Mayor William J. Gaynor.

Dr. Price noted that the coat and suit shops were not the worst offenders in the matter of safety. "Yet," he declared, "our investigation into the conditions in these shops clearly shows that fire prevention facilities are very much below even the most indispensable precautions necessary."

Ninety-nine per cent of the shops were found to be defective in respect to safety: 14 had no fire escapes; 101 had defective drop ladders; 491 had only one exit; 23 had locked doors during the day; 58 had dark hallways; 78 had obstructed approaches to fire escapes; and 1,172, or 94 per cent, had doors opening in instead of out.

Only one had ever had a fire drill.

But at Triangle there had been a warning. In 1909, when the firm was adding to its insurance coverage, P. J. McKeon, an expert and lecturer on fire prevention at Columbia University, was commissioned to make an inspection of the shop.

He was concerned immediately with the crowding of so many people into the top three floors of the building. Upon inquiring, he learned that the firm had never held a fire drill. He noted that without previous instruction on how to handle themselves in such an emergency a fire would panic the girls.

McKeon found that the door to the Washington Place stairway was "usually kept locked," and was told this was because "it was difficult to keep track of so many girls." He thought he had impressed management with the need to hold fire drills. Accordingly, he recommended that Mr. H. F. J. Porter, one of the ablest fire prevention experts in the city, be called in to set up the drills.

On June 19, 1909, Porter wrote to Triangle at McKeon's suggestion, offering to call at management's convenience. He never received a reply to his letter.

There were other portents.

Exactly four months before the Triangle tragedy—on November 25, 1910—fire broke out in an old four-story building at Orange and High Streets in Newark, New Jersey. In minutes, twenty-five factory workers, most of them young women, were dead. Of these, six were burned to death, nineteen jumped to death.

The disaster just across the Hudson River shocked New York and the next day Chief Croker warned:

"This city may have a fire as deadly as the one in Newark at any time. There are buildings in New York where the danger is every bit as great as in the building destroyed in Newark. A fire in the daytime would be accompanied by a terrible loss of life."

Professor Francis W. Aymar of the New York University Law School read Chief Croker's warning. He immediately wrote a letter to the city Building Department saying that from the windows of his classroom he could see the crowded and dangerous conditions in the Asch building across the yard. His letter was acknowledged and assurance of an investigation was given.

Following the Newark fire, the Women's Trade Union League assigned Miss Ida Rauh to study the disaster and draw up a set of conclusions and recommendations. This she did and then, on behalf of the League, Miss Rauh wrote to the January Grand Jury asking to be heard.

Her hearing was short, and fruitless. She was practically dismissed by the foreman of the Grand Jury when she had identified herself. He warned her that "unless you have a complaint of criminal negligence on the part of an official, you had better take your stories to the Corporation Counsel and have him prosecute for violations."

The lesson of the Newark fire was not lost on Alderman Ralph Folks. He introduced a resolution in the Board calling on the Superintendent of the Building Department to investigate and determine if additional legislation were needed to protect the lives of factory workers in New York. Four months before the Triangle fire the resolution was passed.

The day after the Asch building disaster, the *Times* sought out Alderman Folks and asked him what had come of the investigation he had requested in his resolution.

"I don't know. I never heard of it again," he replied.

The *Times* also found Mr. H. F. J. Porter, who had written to Triangle for an appointment on the matter of fire drills.

"There are only two or three factories in the city where fire drills are in use," he declared ruefully. "In some of them where I have installed the system myself, the owners have discontinued it."

"The neglect of factory owners in the matter of safety of their employees is absolutely criminal. One man whom I advised to install a fire drill replied to me: 'Let 'em burn. They're a lot of cattle, anyway.'"

On October 15, 1910—a little more than five months before the tragedy—Fireman Edward F. O'Connor of Engine Company 72 made a routine inspection of the Asch building. Under the definitions of the existing codes, he had to report that the fire escape was "good," the stairways were "good," the building was "fireproof." He noted that an 8- by 10-foot tank on the roof had a capacity of 5,000 gallons of water and that there were 259 water pails distributed over the building's ten floors for emergency use.

In the decade since the construction of the Asch building, about $150,000,000 had gone into the building of similar structures in lower Manhattan. Greater height meant greater returns on land values.

By September, 1909, the greater city had 612,000 employees in 30,000 factories—50,000 more workers than in all of Massachusetts at that time. And, early in 1911, the Women's Trade Union League reported that about half the total number was employed above the seventh floor.

That was just about the height beyond which the finest fire-fighting force in the country could not deal successfully with a fire.

Yet so strong was the feeling of safety in the new buildings that not a single new building or factory law was enacted in the entire decade. Even the number of required stairways, for example, continued to be geared to the area of a single floor with no regard to the number of floors in the structure or the number of workers in the building.

Indeed, the day after the Triangle fire, Albert G. Ludwig, Chief Inspector and Deputy Superintendent of the Building Department, inspected the Asch building. Then he declared: "This building could be worse and come within the requirements of the law."

Joseph J. Asch was right. In his hotel suite, he leaned forward and assured the reporters: "I have obeyed the law to the letter. There was not one detail of the construction of my building that was not submitted to the Building and Fire Departments. Every detail was approved and the Fire Marshal congratulated me."

And that is why, high above the city's streets, beyond the reach of fire-fighting equipment, without benefit of fire sprinklers, proper fire escapes, or fire drills, 500 employees of the Triangle Shirtwaist Company on that March 25, having heard the bell marking the end of their work day, began to rise from their machines and their work tables with the utmost confidence in their own security and safety.

Discussion Questions

1. Compare Stein's writing style in Chapters 1 and 2 of his book. What is the tone and narrative style of Chapter 1? How does this compare to the tone of Chapter 2? Why do you think Stein chose to write these two chapters in this order, with varying tones? What kind of contrast is he drawing?

2. Look at the political and labor issues introduced in Chapter 2. Make a list of the various *implied* arguments found in the narrative. Look at the arguments implied in Stein's choice of quotes from the owner of the building, the Fire Chief, the director of the New York Joint Board of Sanitary Control, Professor Aymar of New York University Law School, and Ida Rauh from the Women's Trade Union League. How does this variety of quotes from primary sources affect Stein's argument? Do you find his strategy effective or not?

Writing Suggestions

1. Cornell University has created an on-line multimedia exhibit about the Triangle Shirtwaist Company fire, including oral interviews, official documents, newspaper accounts, and book reviews of works written about the fire. You can find the site at <http://www.ilr.cornell.edu/trianglefire>. Read through the site, looking at a variety of links, documents, interviews, and information, and then write a journal essay responding to Stein's chapters and the Web site. Ask yourself how the presentation of different kinds of information affected you. How did you respond to the Web site offerings in comparison to reading the narrative written in Chapter 1 of Stein's book? What did you find especially helpful about the reading? About the Web site? And finally, what impact did Stein's writing have on you, as a modern reader? What impact did the Web site have on you? What kind of information touched you the most?

2. The garment industry today remains a focus of investigation for labor law infractions and poor working conditions for workers, both abroad and in the United States. Modern garment industry factories and sweatshops in U.S. cities have recently been spotlighted in the media; conditions show a shocking similarity to the unsafe and unsanitary working conditions found in the early 1900s. Research the problem of labor conditions in the garment industry today, and write a paper in which you compare current labor issues in U.S. garment industries to those issues in the garment industries in the early twentieth century.

   On-line you can use Academic Universe to get the most up-to-date information about this issue, and you can also read more about current problems in the most recent Cornell University Press edition of *The Triangle Fire*, which has an introduction by William Greider, national affairs correspondent for *The Nation* magazine, where he discusses the ongoing nature of dangerous working conditions in U.S. factories. In addition, your school libraries will have more information about this topic.

Beyond the Stereotype

A New Look at the Immigrant Woman, 1880–1924

MAXINE S. SELLER

Maxine S. Seller is a professor in the Department of Educational Organization, Administration, and Policy at the State University of New York at Buffalo, and is also an adjunct professor in the History department. She was born in Wilmington, North Carolina in 1935, attended Bryn Mawr college, and then received her doctorate from the University of Pennsylvania in 1965. Seller is an established authority on immigration history and ethnic life, and has written extensively on these subjects. She is the author of many books about American history, including *Immigrant Women . . . Women Educators in the United States 1820–1993,* and *Identity, Community, and Pluralism in American Life.* In the essay that follows, "Beyond the Stereotype: A New Look at the Immigrant Woman, 1880–1924," Sellers examines the ways in which immigrant women's roles have been stereotyped and describes the lives of three immigrant women as examples of the kind of powerful and active women whom history has largely ignored.

Much has been written about the achievements and experiences of the men who came to the United States from Southern and Eastern Europe between 1880 and 1924. Much less has been written, however, about the achievements and experiences of the immigrant women of this period. It is my opinion that the relative lack of material about immigrant women is not the result of a lack of activity on the part of these women. Rather, it is the result of the persistence of old, negative stereotypes, stereotypes making it appear that women did little worth writing about.

According to her native born contemporaries, the immigrant woman from Southern or Eastern Europe spent her life "confined within the four walls of her home and chained to her household routine." According to a librarian, "(Immigrant) women are left behind in intelligence by the father and children. They do not learn English; they do not keep up with other members of the family." The political influence of the foreign born woman was supposedly nil, both before and after the passage of the Women's Suffrage Amendment. As one observer put it, "The foreign born woman plays directly in American politics a part somewhat, but not much, more important than that played by snakes in the zoology of Ireland." In summary, the native born who saw all immigrants as a threat to the American way of life, saw the immigrant woman in particular as backward, ignorant, and degraded. She was

5

considered excellent raw material for the "uplift" programs of social workers and home missionary societies, but good for little else. To fervent advocates of Americanization the immigrant mother was a "natural obstructionist" whose eventual death would enable the family to "move on much more victoriously to Americanization."

These negative stereotypes from the early twentieth century have continued to influence our view of the immigrant woman. The second or third generation ethnic comedian romanticizes her as Super-Mom, a domestic wonder woman who solved the problems of the world with steaming bowls of chicken soup, spaghetti, or other appropriate ethnic food. Those less steeped in nostalgia are likely to think of her, if at all, as a shadowy, kerchiefed figure absorbed in the not very efficient care of a cluttered tenement apartment and an unending stream of offspring. If she had ambition, it was for her children, never for herself. Her own horizons were limited to the corner grocery and the parish church.

Historians, like others, have been influenced by these stereotypes. They have also been influenced by the knowledge that Southern and Eastern European immigrant groups usually had, and still have, a patriarchal family structure. Many share the general bias of our society that the activities of women are less important than those of men. Even in recent works on ethnic history far fewer women than men are mentioned by name, and women's organizations and activities are rarely treated as fully as the corresponding organizations and activities of men.

Is the stereotyped picture of the immigrant woman an accurate reflection of reality? There were women who did conform to the stereotype, but significant numbers did not. Women of energy and ability stepped outside the traditionally feminine spheres of home and child care to make a variety of contributions to their ethnic communities and to American life in general. Immigrant women built social, charitable, and educational institutions that spanned the neighborhood and the nation. They established day care centers, restaurants, hotels, employment agencies, and legal aid bureaus. They wrote novels, plays, and poetry. They campaigned for a variety of causes, from factory legislation to birth control, from cleaner streets to cleaner government.

To illustrate the range of these activities, I will begin this paper with case studies of three non-traditional women, each from a different ethnic background, each making her contribution in a different area: Antonietta Pisanelli Alessandro, a founder of professional Italian theater in the United States; Josephine Humpel Zeman, Bohemian journalist, lecturer, and feminist; and Rose Pesotta, Russian Jewish labor organizer. After sketching the career of each of these undeservedly obscure women, I will explore how, coming from patriarchal ethnic cultures, they were able to achieve what they did. Then, by discussing briefly the activities of other immigrant women, I will show that these three were not unique. So many women's lives, traditional as well as non-traditional, departed from the stereotype in so many ways that much more research in this area is needed. As ethnic historian Rudolph Vecoli recently observed, the history of the immigrant woman remains to be written.

Antonietta Pisanelli Alessandro came from Naples to New York as a child. As a young woman, she made her living singing, dancing, and acting in the major eastern cities. She made her New York debut at an Italian benefit in Giambelli Hall. Then, as there were no professional Italian theaters in New York, she and some colleagues organized several. Personal tragedy marred her career, however; first her mother died, then her husband, then one of her two children.

With her remaining young son and few other resources but her ingenuity, she arrived in San Francisco in 1904. She assembled a group of amateur performers, rented a ramshackled hall, and opened an Italian theater. According to an early patron, the settings were so crude they were liable to fall apart at any moment—as were the actors. But the performance earned $150. By the time the fire department closed the building, Pisanelli was able to open the more substantial Cafe Pisanelli Family Circle, a combination theater, club, opera house, and cafe. Featuring the finest actors and singers imported from Italy, the Circle was soon known as the liveliest theater in San Francisco. Through road tours as well as home performances, Antonietta Pisanelli Alessandro and her company brought Italian drama and Italian music, from folk songs to opera, to Italian Americans and others throughout the country.

Josephine Humpel Zeman was born in Bohemia (Czechoslovakia) in 1870 and immigrated to Chicago as a young girl. There she met Mary Ingersoll, a social worker at Hull House who became, in Humpel's words, "my second mother." Recognizing the young girl's ability, Mary Ingersoll helped her learn English and get an education. In 1895 Josephine Humpel Zeman was a member of the staff of Hull House, devoting her time to the study of the Bohemian community of Chicago. She was especially sensitive to the problems of women. In a published Hull House paper she complained that "nothing whatsoever has been done for the Bohemian working woman. No one has deemed her worthy of any effort. This is an interesting fact; for as long as these hundreds of thousands of girls shall be unorganized and uninformed, they will always be a great stumbling block in the path of the working women of Chicago."

As social worker, author, journalist, and lecturer (both in her native language and in English) Josephine Zeman showed her concern for the welfare of immigrants, of women, and of all who were at the bottom of the nation's socioeconomic pyramid. She wrote articles for the ethnic press, for American magazines such as *Commons*, and for the United States Industrial Commission on Immigration and Education. According to the Library of Congress catalog, a Josephine Zeman, presumably Josephine Humpel Zeman, wrote two novels, *The Victim Triumphs: A Panorama of Modern Society* published by Dillingham in 1903, and *My Crime*, published by Ogelvie in 1907. Thomas Capek, who described Zeman's career in his *History of the*

Czechs in the United States, did not mention these novels, however, raising the question of whether she did in fact write them. He does mention her social critique of the United States, *America in Its True Light,* published in Prague in 1903. The book contained lectures she delivered on a tour to some thirty towns in Bohemia, and Silesia. Zeman's most important work was the founding of the Chicago-based Bohemian feminist journal *Zemske Listy, The Woman's Gazette,* in 1894. Written, edited, and even printed by an exclusively female staff, the paper circulated throughout the United States. Avoiding the household hints and beauty advice common to most women's publications, the paper stressed the need to improve the lot of the working woman and campaigned for the adoption of the Women's Suffrage Amendment.

Rose Pesotta was born in 1896 in the Ukraine, in the pale of settlement where Russian Jews were forced by law to live. At the age of seventeen she came to New York City, where her older sister, who had emigrated earlier, got her a job in a garment factory. Familiar with the ideas of various peasant and worker revolutionary groups in Russia, Pesotta joined Waistmakers Local 25 of the International Ladies Garment Workers Union almost immediately. On May Day, 1914 she marched with her co-workers in a mass parade past the scene of the Triangle Waist Factory fire—an industrial disaster in which 126 garment workers, mostly immigrant girls like herself, burned to death.

Inspired by stories of the great labor battles of the recent past and by the distress of working people she saw all around her, Pesotta became actively involved in the organizational work of her union. She learned English at night school and continued her education, under the auspices of the Union, at Brookwood Labor College and at the Bryn Mawr Summer School for Working Girls. According to Pesotta, the aim of the latter institution was "to stimulate an active and continuous interest in the problems of our economic life which vitally concern industrial women as wage earners."

The Bryn Mawr Summer School realized its aim: Pesotta began by working to organize her fellow workers in New York, many of whom, like herself, were Jewish immigrants. Soon she was also organizing Italians and other workers of a wide variety of ethnic backgrounds. She traveled from coast to coast, unionizing garment workers in Los Angeles, San Francisco, Montreal, San Juan, and wherever else her services were needed. During the Great Depression of the 1930s she helped organize automobile and rubber workers also. She traveled in Europe and, upon her return, rallied aid for the cause of the Spanish Loyalists. In recognition of her valuable services, she was elected a vice president of the International Ladies Garment Workers Union for three consecutive terms. Rejecting the suggestion of a fourth term in 1944, she pointed out that a union with 300,000 members, 85 percent of whom were women, should have more than one token woman, herself, on its executive committee.

The lives of Antonietta Pisanelli Alessandro, Josephine Humpel Zeman, and Rose Pesotta were not confined within the limits of customary women's activities. Why did these three women break with tradition? In the first place, like millions of other working women, immigrant and native born, they could not afford the luxury of full-time domesticity. Alessandro was a widow with a child to support when she opened her first theater in San Francisco. An "unfortunate" marriage made it necessary for Zeman to support herself. Pesotta, too, worked throughout her life to earn her own living.

For all three of these women, however, economic necessity was a less important motivating force than their inner drives to do meaningful and challenging work in the larger world. Antoinetta Alessandro began organizing theaters in New York while her first husband was still alive and continued to run her theater in San Francisco after a second marriage relieved her of the necessity to earn her living. Even before she left Russia, Rose Pesotta had decided that the traditional woman's life would not meet her needs. In her own words, "I can see no future for myself except to marry some young man returned from his four years of military service and be a housewife. That is not enough. . . . In America things are different. A decent middle class girl can work without disgrace."

In each of these women motivation was matched by energy and ability. Alessandro impressed all who met her with her business acumen and resourcefulness, as well as with her unfailing charm. A fellow journalist dubbed Zeman "Mrs. General," a derisive acknowledgement of her forceful manner. A colleague and former teacher described Pesotta as "possessing built-in energy . . . talk with her a few minutes as casually as you may and strength is poured into you, as when a depleted battery is connected to a generator."

All three of these women came from ethnic backgrounds in which men were the dominant sex and women were relegated to domestic duties. Why, then, despite their obvious abilities, did they aspire to non-traditional careers in the first place? The journey to America opened new possibilities to these women, as it did to all immigrants. Still, early twentieth century America was scarcely more liberal than Europe in the roles it assigned to women. Also, by the time these three women arrived in the United States, their personalities and aspirations had already been shaped by old world environments. Undoubtedly there must be intensive investigation on the status of women in the mother countries if the immigrant woman is to be fully understood. Even a cursory investigation reveals, however, that there were cross currents in European ethnic cultures that supported the achievements of women like Alessandro, Zeman, and Pesotta.

Alessandro grew up in Southern Italy, where women were taught to be subservient to their fathers, husbands, uncles, brothers, even their male cousins. Still, Southern Italian women were respected, even revered, in their roles as mothers—perhaps because of the religious veneration of Mary as the mother of Jesus, or perhaps because of the critical economic importance of their work in a society where livelihood was marginal. Whatever the reasons, an Italian family could survive the death of the father, but not that of the mother.

Alessandro was not above utilizing the respect due her as an Italian mother when it was to her advantage to do so. On one occasion, a road tour audience in St. Louis threatened to riot in the theater because of a misunderstanding about the program. (They had expected the opera *Carmen* instead of the folk song with a similar name that was actually presented.) Alessandro restored peace and probably saved the building from being torn apart by putting her young son on stage to sing "Wait Til the Sun Shines, Nellie"—while her husband slipped out of the back door to safety carrying with him the evening's cash receipts.

According to an old Slavic proverb, "the man who does not beat his wife is not a man." According to another, "one man is worth more than ten women." Women in the more remote areas of the Balkans were used, along with the animals, to carry the heavy burdens. The Slavic societies of Eastern Europe were far from monolithic, however, in their views on religion, sex, or anything else. Josephine Humpel Zeman was from Bohemia, an area with a long tradition of opposition to established religious and political institutions. The rationalism of Bohemian "free thinkers" was notorious both in the United States and in Europe, and provided a hospitable atmosphere for the radical social ideas and non-traditional behavior of someone like Josephine Zeman. Indeed, her lectures on feminism and social reform may have seemed less shocking in Bohemia than in Chicago.

Rose Pesotta, too, could find support for her chosen life work from within her own ethnic tradition. Sex roles were sharply defined in East European Jewish society, but not in precisely the same way as in Anglo Saxon society. In theory at least, the Jewish man was most admired for his religious scholarship rather than for his physical prowess or his economic achievement. It was not uncommon for a pious Jewish man to spend all his time in religious study, while his wife assumed full responsibility for earning the family livelihood. Thus, many East European Jewish women from religious backgrounds were at home in the world of the marketplace.

In addition, by the turn of the century some young women had come under the influence of two new secular philosophies, socialism and zionism, both of which emphasized the equality of the sexes and offered a new range of roles for women. In 1880 Russia opened its universities to women. Although the government allowed few Jewish women to take advantage of this opportunity, increasing numbers found their way to some secular education. The "new" Jewish woman, intellectual, aggressive, and self-sufficient, brought her new lifestyle with her to the United States. According to journalist Hutchins Hapgood, who described the Jewish quarter of New York City in 1902,

> there are successful female dentists, physicians, writers, and even lawyers
> by the score in East Broadway who have attained financial independence
> through their industry and intelligence. They are ambitious to a degree and
> often direct the careers of their husbands. . . . There is more than one case
> on record where a girl has compelled her recalcitrant lover to learn law,

medicine, or dentistry, or submit to being jilted by her. . . . The description of this type of woman seems rather cold and forbidding in the telling, but such an impression is misleading. . . . The women . . . are strikingly interesting because of their warm temperaments. . . .

Certainly the old, limiting stereotypes of immigrant women do not apply to Alessandro, Zeman, and Pesotta. These three women were unusually able, but, as already suggested, they were not unique. The same combination of talents, motivations, necessities, and opportunities that turned these three to activities outside the traditional woman's sphere acted upon other immigrant women as well.

As many historians have noted, more men than women immigrated to the United States between 1880 and 1924, husbands often coming first and then sending for their wives and children. Still, surprisingly large numbers of single women did immigrate independently. Between 1912 and 1917, half a million single women under the age of thirty entered the United States. Many, like Rose Pesotta, were in their teens. Of 120,000 Polish women who came during this period, 84,000 were under the age of twenty-one. Undoubtedly some came to join fiancés, but others came entirely on their own. For them, the act of immigration itself was a breach of the stereotype.

In a family unit or on their own, immigrant women frequently became part of the labor force. In 1910 about a million and a quarter foreign born women were gainfully employed. Thus, contrary to the stereotype of the homebound immigrant woman, large numbers spent the greater part of their time somewhere other than in their own homes. Nor was this necessarily a new experience. The economic pressures that stimulated immigration had already forced tens of thousands of East European women into day labor fields or in the homes of the large landowners. Thus, even before immigration, many women were working outside the traditional family unit, beyond the immediate supervision of father or husband.

The women of Southern Italy were kept closer to home than their Slavic counterparts, but here too, economic pressures were causing breaks in the traditional patterns even before immigration. In the United States most Italian families preferred to have their women work at home, but the need to earn more money drove increasing numbers into the garment factories. So many entered the clothing industry that the Women's Trade Union League of New York found it worthwhile to establish a special Italian committee to organize Italian working women.

Working outside the home did not always—or even often—lead to a new lifestyle. But the ability to earn money could be a first step toward change. New economic power among women caused an enormous change in the lifestyle of at least one immigrant group—those from the Middle East. Arabic immigrant men, who often earned their living peddling lace, underwear, and notions from door to door, discovered that their wives had easier access to

American homes than they did. Arabic wives learned English quickly by peddling with or for their husbands. As the family fortunes advanced, some became active partners in large commercial enterprises. Such women moved in one generation from a subordinate, almost cloistered life in the old country to economic and social equality with their husbands in the United States and positions of importance in their communities.

Whether an immigrant woman worked outside of her home or not, other aspects of life in the United States tended to break up traditional patterns. American courts could be appealed to prevent some of the abuses, such as repeated wife beating, against which there was no legal redress in many old world cultures. According to male Ukrainian immigrants, "the laws here are made for women." In Middle Eastern societies the education and even the social life of the children had been controlled by their father. In the United States teachers, doctors, and social workers supported the mother in assuming control of these areas.

Neighborhood problems pulled immigrant women into activities not traditionally associated with their homemaking and childbearing roles—politics, for example. An Italian woman, newly arrived in a Chicago neighborhood, was appalled at the presence of open ditches, a hazard to her young children. At the suggestion of a settlement worker, she canvassed the neighborhood to see how many other children were similarly endangered. Her survey led to a formal complaint to city hall, and the offending ditches were covered.

Nor was this an isolated case. In Chicago Bohemian women organized to protest the use of open garbage wagons in their neighborhood. After the passing of the Nineteenth Amendment, Poles, Bohemians, and other immigrant women in Chicago helped organize a women's civic league, which registered five thousand women voters and campaigned against corrupt city administration. J. Joseph Huthmacher suggests that the success of Progressive Era reforms in urban states like Massachusetts and New York was at least partly the result of immigrant political pressure. More investigation is needed on the role of immigrant women in these reforms.

In a study of today's working-class women, Nancy Seifer suggests that "When a wife comes home after testifying at a City Council hearing, from a meeting of the local school or hospital board, or from helping to out-maneuver a local politician or win a vote for day care in her union, she is changing the balance of power in her marriage in the most fundamental way, often without realizing it." Did the pioneering ventures of immigrant women into the public life of their day have a similar effect on their marriages?

Immigrant women created a great variety of local organizations, sometimes with the aid of second generation women of their own ethnic group or sympathetic social workers from nearby settlements and sometimes entirely on their own. Singing societies and other cultural associations were common, but there were many others. In New York City a group of Finnish domestic servants pooled their money to rent a small apartment for use on their days off.

Within a few years the Finnish Women's Cooperative Home, as it was called, grew into a four story building with sleeping accommodations for forty, lounges, clubrooms, a library, a restaurant, and an employment bureau—still owned and operated by the women themselves. In Buffalo an immigrant Jewish women's club based on a settlement house bought and remodeled an old home where they established a day care center for their own children and the children of others.

Slovenes, Lithuanians, Poles, Ukrainians, Lebanese, Syrians, Jews, and other immigrant women formed organizations that often expanded to include regions, or even the entire nation, to pursue charitable and educational work among the women of their own communities. Some of these groups functioned as auxiliaries to men's organizations. Others were independent. The Polish National Alliance, for example, was organized as one unit in which men and women were to be equal members. In practice, however, the Polish women discovered themselves an ineffective minority in a male dominated organization. A group of women decided, therefore, to establish a completely independent organization, The Polish Women's Alliance, so that Polish women could develop their own self-confidence and leadership ability.

The varied and wide ranging activities of ethnic women's organizations are an appropriate subject for more intensive investigation. The Polish Women's Protective League gave free legal advice and other aid to Polish working women. The Ukrainian Women's Alliance published a magazine offering its members information on homemaking, childcare, and women's suffrage. The Lithuanian Women's Alliance provided insurance policies as well as social and educational programs. Syrian, Lebanese, and Armenian women's groups had a virtual monopoly of social and charitable services within their communities. Another group of immigrant women whose contributions were great, and often overlooked, are the members of religious orders. Among these women were capable organizers and administrators of badly needed schools, hospitals, orphanages, and other social service institutions.

Contrary to the view expressed in the old stereotypes, then, many immigrant women had interests and commitments that extended beyond the care of their own homes and families. But what of those who did not? What of the very traditional wife and mother who had neither the time, the energy, the self-assurance, nor perhaps even the desire to participate in public life. The negative stereotypes are unfair to her too. They are unfair because they confuse illiteracy with ignorance and poverty with personal degradation. The woman who fed and clothed a large family on five dollars a week—to the astonishment of the social worker trained in home economics—may have been illiterate, but she was certainly not ignorant. The woman who worked a twelve hour night shift in a foundry and cared for her family and several boarders during the day had no time for the so-called "finer" things in life, but she was not therefore a degraded human being. To survive at all she must have possessed enormous inner resources.

Nor was the uneducated, homebound immigrant woman necessarily politically naive. While many women, like many men, sold their votes or did not vote at all, others were remarkably conscientious and astute. According to Jane Addams, Italian women who came in to vote knew more about the city's problems than their husbands, who were often away on construction or railroad jobs six months of the year. Addams writes of an illiterate Irish woman whom she was allowed to help at the voting booth in a Chicago municipal election. "The first proposition was about bonds for a new hospital. The Irish woman said, 'Is the same bunch to spend the money that run the hospital we have now? Then I am against it'. . . . There were ten propositions to be acted upon. I was scrupulous not to influence her: Yet on nine of them she voted from her own common sense just as the Municipal League and the City Club had recommended as the result of painstaking research."

Undoubtedly life was too much for some immigrant women. Broken homes, physical and mental illness, despair, even suicide were all too often present in the ethnic ghetto. The amazing thing is that, given the cultural shock of immigration and the problems of poverty, and discrimination, and survival in urban slums, so many women were able to keep themselves and their families from being defeated. An early social worker, Katherine Anthony, described one such woman, a Hungarian immigrant, Mrs. Mary Grubinsky. Mr. Grubinsky worked in a furniture factory. The couple had seven children. Mrs. Grubinsky worked "a day here, half a day there" returning to her jobs within a month after the birth of each of her children.

> In addition she helps her husband with chair caning, makes the children's clothes, mends for her own family and also for hire, cooks, washes, irons, scrubs, tends her window boxes, minds the children of a neighbor who is doing a day's work, fetches ice from the brewery where it is thrown away, forages for kindling around warehouses, runs to the school when the teacher summons her—but a list of all that Mrs. Grubinsky does in the course of a week would be quite impossible. In her home nothing is lost. Even the feathers from a Thanksgiving turkey were made into cushions and dust brushes.

It would be understandable if such a busy woman would lag behind the rest of her family in learning English and adjusting to the United States. But according to Katherine Anthony, this was not the case with Mary Grubinsky.

> She takes the lead in Americanizing her husband and family. She insisted they move from a two to a three room apartment to have a sitting room. . . . Sees to it the girls have proper clothes, white shoes for confirmation. In these matters Mrs. Grubinsky feels that she must decide and that Martin must accommodate himself.

Like Alessandro, Humpel, and Pesotta, Mary Grubinsky was unusually capable. But also like them, she was not unique.

In conclusion, the current interest in ethnicity occurring simultaneously with the new interest in the history of women makes this an opportune time for scholars to take a new look at the immigrant woman. "Forgotten" women, who like Alessandro, Humpel, and Pesotta, played an important role in the public life of their communities can be rediscovered by a careful study of the ethnic press and the papers of ethnic institutions (especially women's groups), labor unions, settlement houses, and political parties. The experiences of these women should become an integral part of our understanding of immigration history.

So, too, should the experiences of the more traditional women whose lives, like that of Mary Grubinsky, were centered around care of the home and the family. These women constituted too varied and complex a group to be ignored or dismissed with an inherited negative stereotype. More can be learned about them from their letters and diaries (where these exist), from the records of charities, hospitals, courts and other institutions, and from demographic sources such as census tracts and school surveys. Letters-to-the-editor columns in the ethnic press can be useful, as can the short stories, novels, and poetry of immigrant writers. Research is needed on the impact of immigration and acculturation on the lives of all immigrant women, on the institution of marriage, and on child-rearing practices.

In conclusion, sources are available for the study of the Southern and Eastern European immigrant women. With the use of some ingenuity on the part of historians, many more can probably be uncovered. It is time to begin writing the story of the immigrant woman—beyond the stereotype.

Discussion Questions

1. Seller believes that ". . . the relative lack of material about immigrant women is not the result of a lack of activity on the part of these women. Rather, it is the result of the persistence of old, negative stereotypes, stereotypes making it appear that women did little worth writing about." First, list some of the negative stereotypes Seller discusses in her essay. Then, discuss in groups whether or not you, in fact, did or did not hold these negative stereotypes about immigrant women. What associations and beliefs did you have about immigrant women before reading Seller's article? Did the article surprise you with its information? Why or why not?

2. How does Seller relate the achievements of Alessandro, Zeman, and Pesotta in America to their "mother countries?" What aspects of life in Southern Italy, the Balkans, and Eastern European Jewish communities contributed to the women's success in America? Which aspects of life in America contributed to immigrant women's abilities to succeed?

Writing Suggestions

1. After reading Seller's essay, consider the strategies of the immigrant women who were determined to improve their lives and the lives of their families in America. Then consider the efforts of both black and white women, in the West and in the South, and write a personal essay in which you reflect on struggles and successes of women in the last half of the nineteenth century and the early twentieth century. What has surprised you or moved you? What do you admire about these women? If you are a woman, how do you think you would have responded to the challenges and political and social obstacles faced by women during that time? And what do you feel women today have gained from the struggles of these women of earlier centuries?

2. Seller points out that this is "an opportune time for scholars to take a new look at the immigrant woman." Take one aspect of the history of immigrant women and research both primary and secondary sources. The Web sites at the end of this chapter will help you begin your research on the Web. You can also look at Maxine Seller's book *Immigrant Women*, which is a collection of essays by many authors about the experiences of immigrant women. Below are some possible research questions for your paper:

   How did immigrant women contribute to the fight to obtain the vote for women?

   What kinds of businesses did immigrant women start and own?

   What role did immigrant women play in local politics?

   How did immigrant women from different backgrounds break free of the expectations of women in their countries of origin?

   What role did immigrant women play in educational reform?

   How did immigrant women survive and flourish in the settling of the West?

   What political, legal, and economic improvements were won by immigrant women's organizations such as the Polish Women's Protective League?

   When you and your classmates have finished your research papers, you can create a class Web site and post your papers so that other students interested in the topic of immigrant women will have access to your findings.

The Subjection of Woman

ELIZABETH CADY STANTON

Elizabeth Cady Stanton (1815–1902) promised her father at the death of his only son, "I will try to be all my brother was." She was educated not only by her early exposure to her father's law practice and political career in New York, but also by her attendance at Troy Female Seminary in New York, one of the few schools that offered advanced education to women. Stanton went on to become involved with the abolitionist movement, and traveled with her husband, Henry Stanton, to London to attend the World Anti-Slavery Convention. The convention refused to allow women to be recognized as delegates and they were forced to sit in the balcony. Stanton and her friend Lucretia Mott, whom she met at the convention, came back to the United States determined to sponsor a women's rights convention of their own. Eight years later, in 1848, five women met to discuss the rights of women, and Stanton wrote the *Seneca Falls Declaration of Sentiments*, which included a women's bill of rights and demanded suffrage for women. In 1851 she met Susan B. Anthony, who would remain her lifelong friend and colleague. In 1868 they founded the National Woman Suffrage Association, and began publishing the *Revolution*, an outspoken newspaper championing women's rights. Stanton became an eloquent speaker and writer; her publications included the three-volume *History of Woman Suffrage*, and the very controversial *Woman's Bible*, which she published in 1895. This work lost her the support of a number of women because it attacked specific scriptures that she felt were demeaning to women's rights, and it questioned the Church's authority over women. The selection that follows, "The Subjection of Woman," was written as a speech but never delivered in its final form. In this piece she responds to remarks made by Mr. O. B. Frothingham in his book *The Religion of Humanity*, in which he suggests that women deserve to be protected and that this protection is not a form of subjugation.

O. B. Frothingham in his late work on the "Religion of Humanity" tells us that "some of the deepest students into the melancholy history of woman's subjection bring back the cheerful report" that her multiplied wrongs and oppressions have their origin not in the tyranny and selfishness of man, but in "an unintelligent and well-meaning kindness." In rude times of strife, pillage and lust woman's condition was necessarily one of perpetual guardianship in order to preserve her purity and social position. Her family were her protectors. Her Father's authority was her shield, his power her defence, his wealth her provision, insult to her was affront to him, wrong to her brought down his vengeance. She was rooted in the family, could not be detached, in passing from the guardianship of parents, she passed into the guardianship of a second parent. Her husband was in law her Father. It was in his capacity of Father that he acquired rights over her person and property. She was not his slave but daughter, his own blood as it were, part and parcel of himself. The worst injustices, the worst indignities against woman, had this kindly root. True he says, "this root is so deep down under the ground that none but the keenest sighted naturalists suspect it," but we shall accept the assertion and see how well the facts of our times prove its truthfulness.

It is pleasant for those of us who can trace relationship to some of those sons of Adam to know that men are not as bad as they seem to be. "If in things most evil there is a soul of goodness, our faith in the moral constitution of things is justified." Without however going centuries back to analyze the component elements of man's chivalry, let us glance at his successive acts of goodness in our own day and generation, in the full faith that however bad his deeds may seem on the surface, all injustices and oppressions have been perpetrated against woman, from the highest motives of kindness and protection. If this is true of the Hebrews, Egyptians, Persians, Greeks and Romans, it must hold true of the German, French, English and Americans. When the heroes of 76 made their constitution, for the protection of men only, it was not from indifference, or design that they made no mention of woman, but because they knew her natural delicacy would revolt at having her name hawked about in constitutions and declarations, booming at the mouth of the cannon round the globe. When they incorporated the old English laws, by which a wife to day, is there, an actual bond slave, into our codes, they were moved by no feelings of selfishness or tyranny, but a tender sense of her need of guardianship or protection. They legislated her property into their own pockets, that she need not lumber her brain with our complicated systems of finance, with stocks, mortgages, tariffs, and taxes. And they spent her money too, to save her the degradation of bartering on the street corners, in the market place, or exchange; they understood her wants and needs far better than she possibly could herself. True the man on whom this particular woman depended was oftimes ignorant and incompetent himself, or suddenly translated to another sphere, leaving the wife all unprepared to depend on herself, but then that extra sense with which God in his mercy has endowed all women, namely "intuition" came in, enabling her to do things of which she had never dreamt before, changing her in one hour from a helpless dependent to a self reliant will power.

Thus finding herself ever and anon her own guardian and protector, some women thought it would be wise, by a thorough education, to prepare themselves for the emergencies of life, and begged the privilege of entering the colleges of law, medicine and divinity. But these excellent men said no, not because they desired to keep woman ignorant and dependent, and feared her competition with themselves, for they all assert that there is nothing in the universe they so much admire as a highly educated woman, and that for the offices of wife and mother woman needs all knowledge; but they feared lest the sciences of physics, jurisprudence, and theology, and contact with the men who fill those temples of learning might demoralize these ideal beings, who are supposed to live in the clouds, to gaze on the stars and the sons of earth from a lofty distance, quite forgetting that the actual woman digs and delves by the side of man all through the hum drum of life. But in the face of all this "unintelligent and well-meaning kindness" on the part of these good men, women have steadily taken possession of one stronghold after another, and are destined to conquer many more. The good men are frightened from their propriety with each new step of aggression, but as the root of all their opposition is based on love, it gracefully yields in time to the inevitable. When women held their first convention, the men laughed good naturedly from Maine to California, knowing a rebellion against their best friends must die out in sixty days. But it has gone on twenty five years. In this quarter of a century of work woman has worked her way into the schools, colleges, hospitals, pulpits and editorial chair, into many branches of trade, and commerce, and into the telegraph, printing, and post offices. This has been done by argument and assertion, by persistent work, and by taking the positions she claimed. When girls first went into the printing offices, the men laid down their type and walked off. According to Mr. Frothingham they meant no indignity, but feeling their own unworthiness to stand beside such exalted beings they reverently veiled their faces and retired. When Theodore Cuyler's church was thrown into convulsions by the preaching of Sarah Smiley in their pulpit, it was not because they respected woman less but Paul more. "Good men" are apt to be governed more by authorities and precedents than reason and those Brooklyn deacons feared that while Miss Smiley's preachings might turn sinners to repentance, it would also turn the Roman Apostle with horror in his grave. For the same reason women are solemnly warned to keep silent in the Fulton street prayer meeting. It matters not that American women in the 19th century can pray and preach acceptably to God, and man, so long as Corinthian women, who could do neither, were forbidden to try 1800 years ago. I wish all deacons would remember, that while each generation makes its own history, it must make its own laws and customs also. And what shall we say of the lawyers, judges, statesmen and politicians, who deny women the rights of citizenship and compel them to discharge its duties. They must obey the laws; they are forbidden to study in the universities to practise in the courts or to discuss and pass in the legislative assemblies. After all these years of discussion can these gentlemen be "unintelligent" on all the interests involved in this question? The resolution passed at the Massachusetts state convention, pledging the republican party squarely to woman's suffrage, and the 14th plank in the national platform solemnly promising "a respectful consideration of the rights of women["] show plainly that the men of our day thoroughly understand the situation, and that no well-meaning kindness coats the bitter pills of insult and ridicule the women of this republic are daily compelled to swallow. Myra Bradwell is denied the right to practise law in the state of Illinois, because she is a married woman. I wonder if she thinks the roots of this decision are based deep down in love. Catharine Stebbins is denied the right to vote in Michigan because she is a married woman, while Annette Gardner at the same time is allowed to vote because she is a widow. Are these men blind that they do not see they are offering bounties on sending husbands off at pack horse speed to heaven? We might think these thrusts at marriage were a premium on celibacy, but lo! Susan B. Anthony, a republican spinster in Rochester N.Y. having duly registered her name and voted, is arrested by U.S. republican officers for voting a clean republican ticket. Carrie Burnham spinster in Philadelphia, offers her vote and is refused. Whereupon the United States sues the former and the latter sues the United States.

What! a labyrinth of difficulties! with these "unintelligent and well-meaning kindnesses." Where is all this to end? In the triumph of woman, in her individual sovereignty, in the grand march of progress, her turn has come. Perhaps in the coming centennial celebration of our nation's birth, as women are called to help in the busy preparations, the century may round out with her enfranchisement and the old Liberty bell ring in equality for all. She has already conquered so many difficulties, so many places in the trades and professions, in art, science, and literature, that she has earned the crown of American citizenship, and in all its rights, honors, and dignities she should be now secured.

As by persistent demand we have gained the heights we hold to day, so by our own self assertion must we achieve the rights we are still denied. Susan B. Anthony whom we have long jocosely called the Napoleon of our movement is leading off in the right direction. Being a citizen of the United States, she is determined to exercise the rights of a citizen. The authorities say she shall not. Thus she found herself at war with the United States and on the 17th of June her rights as a belligerent were tried and decided. On the anniversary of the Battle of Bunker Hill, she was denied the sacred right of trial by Jury, as Judge Hunt ordered a verdict of guilty and sentenced her as a criminal to pay a fine of one hundred dollars for exercising a citizen's right of suffrage. It must have been a great consolation to Miss Anthony to know that her sentence was "rooted in love"; a ray of sunshine in that dark hour to remember that the arbitrary form of trial was owing to the "unintelligent and well-meaning kindness" of the Judiciary of the United States. Though guilty of the grossest outrage on the constitutional liberties of a citizen, yet the Judge behaved like a well bred gentleman. The polite way in which he robbed Miss Anthony of her most sacred rights reminded me of a remark of Charles O'Conor. Some one asked him what he thought of Judge Hunt. "Judge Hunt, said he, why I think he is a very lady like Judge."

The case of Carrie S. Burnham decided in the Supreme court of Pennsylvania about the same time is interesting as showing that "this unintelligent and well-meaning kindness" is apparent in all latitudes. I have just reread the very able argument of Miss Burnham before the court and the opinion of the Hon. George Sharswood the presiding judge, and I must say I should rather be the author of the argument, than the opinion. In the Pennsylvania Constitution the word "freeman" is substituted for "white male." As the women of that state pay taxes, and the penalty of their crimes, Carrie S. Burnham inferred they were "freemen" and had the right to vote, but according to the Judge the word "freeman" had a pickwickian sense, not quite broad enough to include women. Reading the able arguments of Miss Anthony, and Miss Burnham, in pleading a right for themselves, already secured to every type of degraded manhood in the nation, remembering the youth of the one, and the age of the other, and seeing how little effect in both cases, the ablest arguments, and highest moral considerations seemed to produce on the opinions of these stolid courts, I felt afresh the mockery of this boasted chivalry of man towards woman. As I read history old and new the subjection of woman may be clearly traced to the same cause that subjugated different races and nations to one another, the law of force, that made might right, and the weak the slaves of the strong. Men mistake all the time their reverence for an ideal womanhood, for a sense of justice towards the actual being, that shares with them the toils of life. Man's love and tenderness to one particular woman for a time is no criterion for his general feeling for the whole sex for all time. The same man that would die for one woman, would make an annual holocaust of others, if his appetites or pecuniary interests required it. Kind husbands and Fathers that would tax every nerve and muscle to the uttermost to give their wives and daughters every luxury, would grind multitudes of women to powder in the world of work for the same purpose.

The subjection of woman to man in the best conditions is rooted in selfishness and sensuality, so insidious is its tyranny that I can liken it only to the subjection of the higher faculties, sentiments, and affections of the individual to the gross animal propensities. Of all kinds of slavery the most hopeless and pitiful is that of an individual of genius, power, ambition, bound to the earth by an appetite. Many of our greatest men have been victims of intemperance, gluttony or licentiousness. If man will thus abuse himself, subjugate his whole moral and spiritual nature, will he not make woman his victim, impelled by the strongest appetite in his being? Does he not need all the restraints of law and gospel, custom, and constitution to teach him justice to woman, and should not the state and the church throw round her every shield to make her self reliant and independent, instead of making as now, by their creeds and codes, the strong stronger and the weak more helpless? We have arrived at that point in civilization when woman demands a union with man higher and more enduring than that of the chivalry based on sex. The great lesson, the reform we press, teaches, *sex* in mind. A recognition of the masculine and feminine element in art, science, philosophy, and literature will give new force and zest to life and love and lift the race from the animal plane, where woman's degradation holds it to day. In this higher civilization woman must lead. In demanding political equality, we do not begin with the soul of the question. The ballot box is but one of the outposts of progress, a victory that all orders of men can see and understand. Only the few can grasp the metaphysics of this question, in all its social, religious, and political bearings and appreciate the moral effect of according all outward honor and dignity to woman.

We must educate in every way woman's self respect, and show man the momentous responsibilities that rest on her elevation, that all the best interests of the race are at stake in her ignorance and degradation. Let good men in high places remember that their words and sentiments, find expression in the acts of the ignorant masses. So long as the press and pulpit of a country teach the subjection of woman, so long will our Journals be compelled to chronicle the outrages on womanhood so rife to day. Thieves and robbers seldom enter churches, to desecrate the altars or sacramental service, because they are taught from childhood to reverence these temples and emblems of sacred mysteries. They care not for the theologies, the doctrines, the catechisms or the discipline, but they see the great and good pay deference to the externals of religion and they are awed to respect. But who alas! teaches honor and reverence for woman. And yet does not the mother of the race hold a more important place in civilization than golden goblets, altars, and cathedral walls? Does not the growth of generations, in goodness wisdom and power depend more on the status of womanhood, than the church? We all hesitate to undermine another's religious faith however hedged about with superstitions knowing the need of every soul, for some Gibralter rock on which to stand. But who fears to undermine the faith of sons and daughters in her who gave them birth? No holy influence held so light! The church tells them, the woman is the weaker vessel, unworthy to enter the presence of God, to preach and pray in the assemblies of the people. The heaven ordained condition of the wife is in subjection to the husband drunk or sober, a failure, or success.

The laws and the customs of society echo the same ideas. I will not stop now to quote the insulting laws that degrade every statute book in the union, but I recommend every woman to read a tract just prepared by Carrie Burnham, a digest of the laws of Pennsylvania for the women of that state. These laws have a two fold influence, they not only cripple and oppress woman in every civil action, but they lower the moral tone of society and woman herself in her own estimation. We cannot estimate the far reaching demoralization of training the best minds in our country, the expounders of the science of jurisprudence, and constitutional law in a one sided justice, that violates the first principles of republican government. No matter how noble the women of their households, what must be the impression on the minds of young men in our law schools, when they first read the codes for women, and the opinions of Judges as to their status in law and nature.

Charles Sumner in his able speeches made on the passage of the 13th 14th and 15th amendments clearly traces the evil effects of slavery on the law, religion and public sentiment of the entire nation. From the standpoint of the slaveholder, constitutions were interpreted, and decisions of the supreme courts of the United States, given in violation of every principle of natural rights. If the slavery of 4,000,000 Africans on southern plantations could thus make the eternal principles of justice in their administration as uncertain as the sands on the sea shore and poison the fountains of our political, religious, commercial, and social life, throughout the union must not the violation of the same principles in the case of 20,000,000 women in every state of the union cause equal judicial blindness, clerical hypocrisy and social demoralization? In the case of the slave, statesmen saw that emancipation was a mockery, without the power to legislate for himself, and from the highest moral considerations they gave him the ballot for his protection. Politicians saw their party success depended on the votes of the slave, and from humbler motives they said give him the right of suffrage. We ask statesmen to apply the same principles for woman's protection. We ask politicians to use the same policy for their own success in the reorganization of parties.

Do you think the women on this platform have persistently demanded the right of suffrage for twenty five years, merely to enjoy the pleasure of going to the polls to vote for a Gov. Dix or Mayor Havemeyer or to get some picayune office for themselves, or some male relation?

I ask to exercise this right 1st because it is my right, and all women need this power for their protection, dignity and moral influence. With man's chivalry for the one woman he loves, he feels it must be safe to trust the rights of all women, to all men, but the experience of life teaches us a different lesson. Brutal men kill wives, daughters, sisters, mothers. Respectable men cheat the women of their households out of their substance. Lawyers can tell of cases on their calendars of Fathers defrauding daughters, brothers sisters, husbands wives, of their rights of property. Look how women are treated in the world of work crowded into a few employments and half paid there. When a girl is prospective heir to a crown in the old world, every advantage of education is accorded her. She is trained to higher dignity of speech and manner, fitting the station for which she is destined. Our throne is self government, our crown equality, our sceptre the ballot, and when American girls are heirs to these, the colleges will open wide their doors and vie with each other for the honor of educating these heirs apparent to the rights of American citizens. They will be honored in the world of work! expurgated editions of the creeds and codes will be speedily issued, and party, pulpit, and press will treat women citizens with as much respect as they now do the new made southern freeman and the unlettered foreigner just landed on our shores.

To save the nation from the demoralization openly confessed in every branch of our government, noble women should be willing to use their influence to elevate the tone of our politics, and ensure a wiser policy on many questions. History is full of incidents of woman's wisdom and heroism in hours of distress and danger. What a Florence Nightingale, a Clara Barton, a Grace Darling, an Ida Lewis have done for wounded soldiers and drowning sailors, women who study the political horoscope may now do for the nation's life, and save our ship of state now drifting for Lambro light. A page of German history in 1140 tells us of the Duke of Guelph besieged in Weisburgh by Conrad III and being hard pressed he capitulated on the terms that the women should be allowed to depart in safety taking with them all they could carry. Accordingly the Duchess came forth bearing the Duke on her shoulders and all the women of the city with their husbands. The conquerors were so surprized and pleased with this manifestation of woman's strength and devotion that they watched the exodus in silence and inaction. If the hope of family safety could thus nerve faint hearts and make feeble arms so strong, cannot a nation's safety, the triumph of those great principles of republican government so dearly bought, and oftimes redeemed, rouse the women of our day to action.

Great as our country is in her boundless acres, majestic forests, mighty lakes and rivers and inexhaustible mines of wealth, she has hidden treasures in the undeveloped powers of her women, that if employed would add more to the wealth of the state, than all our other revenues together. The white man's "wards" have all alike, Africans, Indians, women and Labor been crippled by his guardianship and protection, and have alike avenged themselves, by art and stratagem outside the rules of war, because denied fair action and debate. His protection has been like that of the Eagle to the lamb he carries to his eyrie. I think we should all be willing to forego such protection and stand on our own feet. I often wonder in reading the able articles of The New York World on Free trade, that it so seldom touches on this most odious form of "protection." We have thrown the African race on its own responsibility and it does not crave the old guardianship again. The best policy we can inaugurate for the Indian is to treat him the same way. Make no discrimination for or against him, hunger and taxation and the just penalty for individual crime would soon settle the problem of work, property and law. He will stay at home and raise cattle instead of ponies when he provides his own beef and flour. And this is all we ask for woman, the same advantages, opportunities, and code of laws man claims for himself, no discriminations on the ground of sex, no "protection," but justice liberty equality and as these are the corner stones of national life peace prosperity. All partial reforms wait woman's enfranchisement.

The cry of "peace" is mockery so long as its fundamental principles are scouted as glittering generalities. With 20,000,000 women in chains, with labor ground to powder between the upper and nether millstones of avarice and ignorance, with the church endorsing poverty as a divine ordination, and the state enforcing it by cunning legislation, our jails and prisons crowded with helpless victims waiting for the tardy justice that seldom comes, the cry of peace from our leaders is as vain and guilty as it would have been from the watchtower of the *Atlantic* in that awful hour when 700 souls went down.

Let those who preach temperance, who urge prohibitory law review the situation, look deep down for the causes of these overpowering animal appetites. Feeble desponding sons of sickly low spirited mothers will crave stimulants for mind and body alike, and no legislation can quench the thirst, or destroy the means of gratification, so long as our chosen rulers belong to the whiskey rings. Labor wretchedly housed, fed and clothed, when it can purchase Paradise for a few hours by a dram, will not resist the temptation. Luxury in its palace home, satiated with the good things of life, with nothing to hope, and nothing to do, if it can lighten its ennui with a sparkling glass, who can wonder? The radical steps towards peace and temperance are these: equality before the law; a generation of healthy happy scientific mothers; educated labor, well housed, fed, clothed, an inviolable homestead; luxury driven to work, by a system of graduated taxation. Temperance in the present diseased condition of the race, with the extremes and antagonisms of its conditions, the risks and strain of competition, the anxieties and disappointments of success and failure, is impossible. Those who are overtaxed with work and those who are enervated for lack of it will alike seek stimulants.

They who do most to equalize the conditions of society, will do the best work for all reforms. If we trace all questions of national interest we shall find that they run in parallel lines together, and that each demands a more radical work than yet done by any government. Let the people now awake to their duty. That our rulers are lamentably neglecting their duty all admit. In a recent editorial in The Christian Union, the question "is this a well governed nation" is thus answered.

> What has Congress or any of our Legislatures done toward meeting the labor difficulty? We readily admit that this class of subjects is full of perplexity, and that it is doubtful how far legislative action is called for upon them. But they are of great and growing importance, and certainly not to be ignored by any wise government. What have our governments done? Massachusetts alone has taken action for getting light upon the matter by official statistics, though this is the least that should be done. In general, our politicians have confined themselves to buncombe resolutions. Often they have done worse than that. Congress has passed an eight-hour law for the national workmen. The law was a sheer piece of demagogism. It was not based on any intelligent conviction that eight hours was a fair day's work, and should receive the old ten hours' wages. It was a sop to voters, and, as far as it went, it said to the laboring class, "Anything you want; only keep us in office!" We do not undertake to say what legislative action is needed in regard to labor; but we do say this; if in any State a hundred intelligent and disinterested men met daily for three months to consult for the welfare of the community, "labor questions" would come in for a large share of their attention. Why do our governing bodies so entirely ignore this class of subjects? Is it lack of intelligence or of disposition?

Political government is the highest and most difficult of all social arts. The Government is the organ of the entire people in their collective capacity. In the governing power, therefore—which with us is really the legislative assembly—should be found not only pureness of purpose, but the best practical sagacity, the most intelligent consideration of common interests, that the community can afford.

In what degree do our Congress and our average Legislatures display these qualities? We have lately had startling evidence of the want among them of even average honesty. But, waiving for the present any discussion as to the amount of positive corruption in our governing bodies, there is another indictment to be brought against most of them, which is serious enough. We find everywhere the radical trouble that our legislators do not intelligently attend to their proper work. In theory, their business is to take care of the whole community. In practice, to a great extent, their business is to take care for themselves and their party—terms which to a politician generally mean the same thing. We see, continually, our Congress and our Legislatures slighting the gravest public interests, and devoting themselves to squabbles in which the people is only the goose to be plucked. And the plucking is not the worst the goose has to suffer. What we complain of is, not chiefly that these gentlemen at Washington and Albany and Harrisburg and elsewhere, make us pay so heavily for their services. It is that we get so little in return. The matters most vital to the community—questions of finance, of labor, of social order, of public morals—are left untouched, or bunglingly patched up, while it is being settled who shall have the custom-house or the post-office or the next seat in Congress.

Carl Schurz in a late speech in the Senate said

> Do we not see and understand what is going on around us? What is it that attracts to the capital of the nation that herd of monopolists and speculators and their agents who so assiduously lay siege to the judgment and also to the consciences of those who are to give to the country its laws? What is it that fills the lobbies of these halls with the atmosphere of temptation? What is it that brings forth such melancholy, such deplorable exhibitions as the American people have been beholding this winter, and which we would have been but too glad to hide from the eyes of the world abroad? It is that policy which uses the power of this great Government for the benefit of favored interests; that policy which takes money out of the pockets of the people to put it into the pockets of a few; that policy which in every country where it prevailed has poisoned the very fountain of legislation. Do you think that the consequences can be different here? Are not your great railroad kings and monopolists boasting that they can buy whole State Legislatures to do their bidding? Have we not seen some of them stalking around in this very Capitol like the sovereign lords of creation? Are not some of them vaunting themselves already that they have made and can make profitable investments in Congressmen and United States Senators? Have we not observed the charming catholicity of their operations and the breadth of their cosmopolitanism, as shown before the Crédit Mobilier Committee of the House, when Dr. Durant said that he did not care whether the man he supported for election was a Republican or a Democrat, provided he was a good man? And now if you let them know that a man who has purchased his seat here, or for whom it has been purchased, with money, will be secure in the enjoyment of the property so bought, I ask you, Will not their enterprise be limited only by their desires? And will not their rapacious desires, from which the country has already suffered so much pecuniarily and morally, grow with their opportunities? As long as

such evils are permitted to exercise their influences, they will spread with the power of contagion, and nothing but the most unflinching resistance can check them. Such is our condition. Everybody sees and feels it.

It is time that we should face the dangers which threaten this Republic. It has no monarchial traditions, no pretenders of historic right to disturb its repose and to plot its overthrow. It is not likely to succumb to the shock of force. But there have been republics whose original Constitution was as healthy as ours, but which died after all of the slower disease of corruption and demoralization, and that decay of constitutional life and anarchy of power which always go hand in hand with them. It is time for us to keep in mind that it requires more to make and preserve a Republic than the mere absence of a king, and that when a Republic decays its soul is apt to die first, while its outward form may still be lasting.

One good effect of a Presidential campaign is that the rogues all betray each other. And what an unearthing of fraud and corruption we have had! enough it seems to me to warn the women of this republic that they cannot trust the interest of 40,000,00 of people and the wealth of a continent to spendthrift and unprincipled legislators. Have the women of property in the state of New York no interest in the heavy taxes enforced by these rings, in bank defalcations, in the public school fund, whether used for good teachers, buildings, and sanitary conditions, or by a dishonest ring? Have women no interest in the accidents by land [or] sea, the result of imperfect rails, sleepers, bridges, boilers, vessels, and incompetent captains and conductors? All this comes from just that want of caution and care that woman with her greater love of life possesses and would sacredly guard if she had a word in the legislation on these matters.

Poets find great beauty in woman's blind faith in man's capacity to do not only his own work but hers also. It may do to turn a stanza but not for the emergencies of life. Had the passengers of the ill fated *Atlantic* trusted less in their Captain and organized a police of their own to watch at night, how little care and time from each one might have saved that multitude from a watery grave.

Women of America we are all passengers in the ship [of] state, to share its dangers and delays. We are sailing fast towards an unknown shore, there are breakers ahead, the watchmen on the towers are sleeping. Man's skill in battling with the waves, suspended mid ropes and sails will avail us nothing. In the hour of danger without courage and strength in ourselves we must one and all be sacrificed.

Discussion Questions

1. Stanton mentions many areas in which she feels women's rights need to be expanded. Make a list of the various arguments she makes in this speech, and then consider the questions at the top of page 518.

What are the major rights that women are denied, according to Stanton?
What fallacy does she point out in the logic of men who claim they are just "protecting" women from unsavory elements of the world?
What is Stanton's attitude toward the Church?
What is Stanton's attitude toward men in government?
What specific rights does Stanton ask for in this speech?

2. Isolate particular phrases in which you can see Stanton's use of sarcasm, and discuss how this sarcasm works for or against her. Consider her audience: If she had ever given this speech publicly, how might the men in the audience have reacted differently from the women? Would women like the sarcasm in the speech or not? Do you think it was a good tactic on her part? How do you think her speech would be viewed by women who classify themselves as "feminists" today?

Writing Suggestions

1. Write an essay in which you analyze Stanton's feelings toward men as evidenced in this speech:

   What kinds of examples does she use to make her points against men who refuse to extend women's rights?
   What tone does she use when she refers to men?
   How does she use sarcasm?
   How does she weave history into her discussion of men and women?
   How does she use humor in her discussion of men?
   What range of male figures does she include in her speech?
   Does her overall representation of and attitude toward men help or hinder her cause, in your opinion?

2. Referring to Susan B. Anthony's attempts to vote, Stanton writes that "Susan B. Anthony whom we have long jocosely called the Napoleon of our movement is leading off in the right direction." Research the partnership of Stanton and Anthony, and then write a paper about their work together. What did each contribute to the suffrage and women's rights movement? How did they differ in their contributions to the movement? How did they divide the work in their collaborative efforts at writing and organizing? And finally, how effective were these two women together in gaining the rights for women that they fought for so strongly?

Minor v. Happersett

In 1872, Virginia Minor, president of the Woman Suffrage Association of Missouri, tried to vote in a general election in St. Louis, but was turned away at the polls. Happersett, the registrar for voters, claimed that she was not a lawful voter because she was a woman. Minor and her husband then sued Happersett in one of the lower state courts of Missouri, which ruled in favor of Happersett. The case finally made its way to the Supreme Court. Below is the excerpted version of the final Supreme Court decision that ruled that the Fourteenth Amendment, while guaranteeing that no state or law could "abridge the privileges or immunities of citizens," did not include women's right to vote as one of those privileges. As a result, women continued to rally for an amendment to the Constitution that would allow them to vote; the Nineteenth Amendment granting suffrage to women citizens was finally passed in 1920.

WAITE, C. J., Opinion of the Court

The CHIEF JUSTICE delivered the opinion of the court.

The question is presented in this case, whether, since the adoption of the fourteenth amendment, a woman, who is a citizen of the United States and of the State of Missouri, is a voter in that State, notwithstanding the provision of the constitution and laws of the State, which confine the right of suffrage to men alone. We might, perhaps, decide the case upon other grounds, but this question is fairly made. From the opinion we find that it was the only one decided in the court below, and it is the only one which has been argued here. The case was undoubtedly brought to this court for the sole purpose of having that question decided by us, and in view of the evident propriety there is of having it settled, so far as it can be by such a decision, we have concluded to waive all other considerations and proceed at once to its determination.

It is contended that the provisions of the constitution and laws of the State of Missouri which confine the right of suffrage and registration therefor to men, are in violation of the Constitution of the United States, and therefore void. The argument is, that as a woman, born or naturalized in the United States and subject to the jurisdiction thereof, is a citizen of the United States and of the State in which she resides, she has the right of suffrage as one of the privileges and immunities of her citizenship, which the State cannot by its laws or constitution abridge.

There is no doubt that women may be citizens. They are persons, and by the fourteenth amendment "all persons born or naturalized in the United States and subject to the jurisdiction thereof" are expressly declared to be "citizens of the United States and of the State wherein they reside." But, in our opinion, it did not need this amendment to give them that position. Before its adoption the Constitution of the United States did not in terms prescribe who should be citizens of the United States or of the several States, yet there were necessarily such citizens without such provision. There cannot be a nation without a people. The very idea of a political community, such as a nation is, implies an association of persons for the promotion of their general welfare. Each one of the persons associated becomes a member of the nation formed by the association. He owes it allegiance and is entitled to its protection. Allegiance and protection are, in this connection, reciprocal obligations. The one is a compensation for the other; allegiance for protection and protection for allegiance.

For convenience it has been found necessary to give a name to this membership. The object is to designate by a title the person and the relation he bears to the nation. For this purpose the words "subject," "inhabitant," and "citizen" have been used, and the choice between them is sometimes made to depend upon the form of the government. Citizen is now more commonly employed, however, and as it has been considered better suited to the description of one living under a republican government, it was adopted by nearly all of the States upon their separation from Great Britain, and was afterwards adopted in the Articles of Confederation and in the Constitution of the United States. When used in this sense it is understood as conveying the idea of membership of a nation, and nothing more.

To determine, then, who were citizens of the United States before the adoption of the amendment it is necessary to ascertain what persons originally associated themselves together to form the nation, and what were afterwards admitted to membership.

Looking at the Constitution itself we find that it was ordained and established by "the people of the United States," and then going further back, we find that these were the people of the several States that had before dissolved the political bands which connected them with Great Britain, and assumed a separate and equal station among the powers of the earth, and that had by Articles of Confederation and Perpetual Union, in which they took the name of "the United States of America," entered into a firm league of friendship with each other for their common defence, the security of their liberties and their mutual and general welfare, binding themselves to assist each other against all force offered to or attack made upon them, or any of them, on account of religion, sovereignty, trade, or any other pretence whatever.

Whoever, then, was one of the people of either of these States when the Constitution of the United States was adopted, became ipso facto a citizen— a member of the nation created by its adoption. He was one of the persons associating together to form the nation, and was, consequently, one of its original citizens. As to this there has never been a doubt. Disputes have arisen as to whether or not certain persons or certain classes of persons were part of the people at the time, but never as to their citizenship if they were.

Additions might always be made to the citizenship of the United States in two ways: first, by birth, and second, by naturalization. This is apparent from the Constitution itself, for it provides that "no person except a natural-born citizen, or a citizen of the United States at the time of the adoption of the Constitution, shall be eligible to the office of President," and that Congress shall have power "to establish a uniform rule of naturalization." Thus new citizens may be born or they may be created by naturalization.

The Constitution does not, in words, say who shall be natural-born citizens. Resort must be had elsewhere to ascertain that. At common-law, with the nomenclature of which the framers of the Constitution were familiar, it was never doubted that all children born in a country of parents who were its citizens became themselves, upon their birth, citizens also. These were natives, or natural-born citizens, as distinguished from aliens or foreigners. Some authorities go further and include as citizens children born within the jurisdiction without reference to the citizenship of their parents. As to this class there have been doubts, but never as to the first. For the purposes of this case it is not necessary to solve these doubts. It is sufficient for everything we have now to consider that all children born of citizen parents within the jurisdiction are themselves citizens. The words "all children" are certainly as comprehensive, when used in this connection, as "all persons," and if females are included in the last they must be in the first. That they are included in the last is not denied. In fact the whole argument of the plaintiffs proceeds upon that idea.

Under the power to adopt a uniform system of naturalization Congress, as early as 1790, provided "that any alien, being a free white person," might be admitted as a citizen of the United States, and that the children of such persons so naturalized, dwelling, within the United States, being under twenty-one years of age at the time of such naturalization, should also be considered citizens of the United States, and that the children of citizens of the United States that might be born beyond the sea, or out of the limits of the United States, should be considered as natural-born citizens. These provisions thus enacted have, in substance, been retained in all the naturalization laws adopted since. In 1855, however, the last provision was somewhat extended, and all persons theretofore born or thereafter to be born out of the limits of the jurisdiction of the United States, whose fathers were, or should be at the time of their birth, citizens of the United States, were declared to be citizens also.

As early as 1804 it was enacted by Congress that when any alien who had declared his intention to become a citizen in the manner provided by law died before he was actually naturalized, his widow and children should be considered as citizens of the United States, and entitled to all rights and privileges as such upon taking the necessary oath; and in 1855 it was further provided that any woman who might lawfully be naturalized under the existing laws, married, or who should be married to a citizen of the United States, should be deemed and taken to be a citizen.

From this it is apparent that from the commencement of the legislation upon this subject alien women and alien minors could be made citizens by naturalization, and we think it will not be contended that this would have been done if it had not been supposed that native women and native minors were already citizens by birth.

But if more is necessary to show that women have always been considered as citizens the same as men, abundant proof is to be found in the legislative and judicial history of the country. Thus, by the Constitution, the judicial power of the United States is made to extend to controversies between citizens of different States. Under this it has been uniformly held that the citizenship necessary to give the courts of the United States jurisdiction of a cause must be affirmatively shown on the record. Its existence as a fact may be put in issue and tried. If found not to exist the case must be dismissed. Notwithstanding this the records of the courts are full of cases in which the jurisdiction depends upon the citizenship of women, and not one can be found, we think, in which objection was made on that account. Certainly none can be found in which it has been held that women could not sue or be sued in the courts of the United States. Again, at the time of the adoption of the Constitution, in many of the States (and in some probably now) aliens could not inherit or transmit inheritance. There are a multitude of cases to be found in which the question has been presented whether a woman was or was not an alien, and as such capable or incapable of inheritance, but in no one has it been insisted that she was not a citizen because she was a woman. On the contrary, her right to citizenship has been in all cases assumed. The only question has been whether, in the particular case under consideration, she had availed herself of the right.

In the legislative department of the government similar proof will be found. Thus, in the pre-emption laws, a widow, "being a citizen of the United States," is allowed to make settlement on the public lands and purchase upon the terms specified, and women, "being citizens of the United States," are permitted to avail themselves of the benefit of the homestead law.

Other proof of like character might be found, but certainly more cannot be necessary to establish the fact that sex has never been made one of the elements of citizenship in the United States. In this respect men have never had an advantage over women. The same laws precisely apply to both. The fourteenth amendment did not affect the citizenship of women any more than it did of men. In this particular, therefore, the rights of Mrs. Minor do not depend upon the amendment. She has always been a citizen from her birth, and entitled to all the privileges and immunities of citizenship. The amendment prohibited the State, of which she is a citizen, from abridging any of her privileges and immunities as a citizen of the United States; but it did not confer citizenship on her. That she had before its adoption.

If the right of suffrage is one of the necessary privileges of a citizen of the United States, then the constitution and laws of Missouri confining it to men are in violation of the Constitution of the United States, as amended, and consequently void. The direct question is, therefore, presented whether all citizens are necessarily voters.

The Constitution does not define the privileges and immunities of citizens. For that definition we must look elsewhere. In this case we need not determine what they are, but only whether suffrage is necessarily one of them.

It certainly is nowhere made so in express terms. The United States has no voters in the States of its own creation. The elective officers of the United States are all elected directly or indirectly by State voters. The members of the House of Representatives are to be chosen by the people of the States, and the electors in each State must have the qualifications requisite for electors of the most numerous branch of the State legislature. Senators are to be chosen by the legislatures of the States, and necessarily the members of the legislature required to make the choice are elected by the voters of the State. Each State must appoint in such manner, as the legislature thereof may direct, the electors to elect the President and Vice-President. The times, places, and manner of holding elections for Senators and Representatives are to be prescribed in each State by the legislature thereof, but Congress may at any time, by law, make or alter such regulations, except as to the place of choosing Senators. It is not necessary to inquire whether this power of supervision thus given to Congress is sufficient to authorize any interference with the State laws prescribing the qualifications of voters, for no such interference has ever been attempted. The power of the State in this particular is certainly supreme until Congress acts.

The amendment did not add to the privileges and immunities of a citizen. It simply furnished an additional guaranty for the protection of such as he already had. No new voters were necessarily made by it. Indirectly it may have had that effect, because it may have increased the number of citizens entitled to suffrage under the constitution and laws of the States, but it operates for this purpose, if at all, through the States and the State laws, and not directly upon the citizen.

It is clear, therefore, we think, that the Constitution has not added the right of suffrage to the privileges and immunities of citizenship as they existed at the time it was adopted. This makes it proper to inquire whether suffrage was coextensive with the citizenship of the States at the time of its adoption. If it was, then it may with force be argued that suffrage was one of the rights which belonged to citizenship, and in the enjoyment of which every citizen must be protected. But if it was not, the contrary may with propriety be assumed.

When the Federal Constitution was adopted, all the States, with the exception of Rhode Island and Connecticut, had constitutions of their own. These two continued to act under their charters from the Crown. Upon an examination of those constitutions we find that in no State were all citizens permitted to vote. Each State determined for itself who should have that power.

Thus, in New Hampshire, "every male inhabitant of each town and parish with town privileges, and places unincorporated in the State, of twentyone years of age and upwards, excepting paupers and persons excused from paying taxes at their own request," were its voters; in Massachusetts "every male inhabitant of twenty-one years of age and upwards, having a freehold estate within the commonwealth of the annual income of three pounds, or any estate of the value of sixty pounds;" in Rhode Island "such as are admitted free of the company and society" of the colony; in Connecticut such persons as had "maturity in years, quiet and peaceable behavior, a civil conversation, and forty shillings freehold or forty pounds personal estate," if so certified by the selectmen; in New York "every male inhabitant of full age who shall have personally resided within one of the counties of the State for six months immediately preceding the day of election . . . if during the time aforesaid he shall have been a freeholder, possessing a freehold of the value of twenty pounds within the county, or have rented a tenement therein of the yearly value of forty shillings, and been rated and actually paid taxes to the State;" in New Jersey "all inhabitants . . . of full age who are worth fifty pounds, proclamation-money, clear estate in the same, and have resided in the county in which they claim a vote for twelve months immediately preceding the election;" in Pennsylvania "every freeman of the age of twenty-one years, having resided in the State two years next before the election, and within that time paid a State or county tax which shall have been assessed at least six months before the election;" in Delaware and Virginia "as exercised by law at present;" in Maryland "all freemen above twenty-one years of age having a freehold of fifty acres of land in the county in which they offer to vote and residing therein, and all freemen having property in the State above the value of thirty pounds current money, and having resided in the county in which they offer to vote one whole year next preceding the election;" in North Carolina, for senators, "all freemen of the age of twenty-one years who have been inhabitants of any one county within the State twelve months immediately preceding the day of election, and possessed of a freehold within the same county of fifty acres of land for six months next before and at the day of election," and for members of the house of commons "all freemen of the age of twenty-one years who have been inhabitants in any one county within the State twelve months immediately preceding the day of any election, and shall have paid public taxes;" in South Carolina "every free white man of the age of twenty-one years, being a citizen of the State and having resided therein two years previous to the day of election, and who hath a freehold of fifty acres of land, or a town lot of which he hath been legally seized and possessed at least six months before such election, or (not having such freehold or town lot), hath been a resident within the election district in which he offers to give his vote six months before said election, and hath paid a tax the preceding year of three shillings sterling towards the support of the government;" and in Georgia such "citizens and inhabitants of the State as shall have attained to the age of twenty-one years, and shall have paid tax for the year next preceding the election, and shall have resided six months within the county."

In this condition of the law in respect to suffrage in the several States it cannot for a moment be doubted that if it had been intended to make all citizens of the United States voters, the framers of the Constitution would not have left it to implication. So important a change in the condition of citizenship as it actually existed, if intended, would have been expressly declared. . . .

But if further proof is necessary to show that no such change was intended, it can easily be found both in and out of the Constitution. By Article 4, section 2, it is provided that "the citizens of each State shall be entitled to all the privileges and immunities of citizens in the-several States." If suffrage is necessarily a part of citizenship, then the citizens of each State must be entitled to vote in the several States precisely as their citizens are. This is more than asserting that they may change their residence and become citizens of the State and thus be voters. It goes to the extent of insisting that while retaining their original citizenship they may vote in any State. This, we think, has never been claimed. And again, by the very terms of the amendment we have been considering (the fourteenth), "Representatives shall be apportioned among the several States according to their respective numbers, counting the whole number of persons in each State, excluding Indians not taxed. But when the right to vote at any election for the choice of electors for President and Vice-President of the United States, representatives in Congress, the executive and judicial officers of a State, or the members of the legislature thereof, is denied to any of the male inhabitants of such State, being twenty-one years of age and citizens of the United States, or in any way abridged, except for participation in the rebellion, or other crimes, the basis of representation therein shall be reduced in the proportion which the number of such male citizens shall bear to the whole number of male citizens twenty-one years of age in such State." Why this, if it was not in the power of the legislature to deny the right of suffrage to some male inhabitants? And if suffrage was necessarily one of the absolute rights of citizenship, why confine the operation of the limitation to male inhabitants? Women and children are, as we have seen, "persons." They are counted in the enumeration upon which the apportionment is to be made, but if they were necessarily voters because of their citizenship unless clearly excluded, why inflict the penalty for the exclusion of males alone? Clearly, no such form of words would have been selected to express the idea here indicated if suffrage was the absolute right of all citizens.

And still again, after the adoption of the fourteenth amendment, it was deemed necessary to adopt a fifteenth, as follows: "The right of citizens of the United States to vote shall not be denied or abridged by the United States, or by any State, on account of race, color, or previous condition of servitude." The fourteenth amendment had already provided that no State should make or enforce any law which should abridge the privileges or immunities of citizens of the United States. If suffrage was one of these privileges or immunities, why amend the Constitution to prevent its being denied on account of race, &c.? Nothing is more evident than that the greater must include the less, and if all were already protected why go through with the form of amending the Constitution to protect a part?

It is true that the United States guarantees to every State a republican form of government. It is also true that no State can pass a bill of attainder, and that no person can be deprived of life, liberty, or property without due process of law. All these several provisions of the Constitution must be construed in connection with the other parts of the instrument, and in the light of the surrounding circumstances.

The guaranty is of a republican form of government. No particular government is designated as republican, neither is the exact form to be guaranteed, in any manner especially designated. Here, as in other parts of the instrument, we are compelled to resort elsewhere to ascertain what was intended.

The guaranty necessarily implies a duty on the part of the States themselves to provide such a government. All the States had governments when the Constitution was adopted. In all the people participated to some extent, through their representatives elected in the manner specially provided. These governments the Constitution did not change. They were accepted precisely as they were, and it is, therefore, to be presumed that they were such as it was the duty of the States to provide. Thus we have unmistakable evidence of what was republican in form, within the meaning of that term as employed in the Constitution.

As has been seen, all the citizens of the States were not invested with the right of suffrage. In all, save perhaps New Jersey, this right was only bestowed upon men and not upon all of them. Under these circumstances it is certainly now too late to contend that a government is not republican, within the meaning of this guaranty in the Constitution, because women are not made voters.

The same may be said of the other provisions just quoted. Women were excluded from suffrage in nearly all the States by the express provision of their constitutions and laws. If that had been equivalent to a bill of attainder, certainly its abrogation would not have been left to implication. Nothing less than express language would have been employed to effect so radical a change. So also of the amendment which declares that no person shall be deprived of life, liberty, or property without due process of law, adopted as it was as early as 1791. If suffrage was intended to be included within its obligations, language better adapted to express that intent would most certainly have been employed. The right of suffrage, when granted, will be protected. He who has it can only be deprived of it by due process of law, but in order to claim protection he must first show that he has the right.

But we have already sufficiently considered the proof found upon the inside of the Constitution. That upon the outside is equally effective.

The Constitution was submitted to the States for adoption in 1787, and was ratified by nine States in 1788, and finally by the thirteen original States in 1790. Vermont was the first new State admitted to the Union, and it came in under a constitution which conferred the right of suffrage only upon men of the full age of twenty-one years, having resided in the State for the space of one whole year next before the election, and who were of quiet and peaceable behavior. This was in 1791. The next year, 1792, Kentucky followed with a constitution confining the right of suffrage to free male citizens of the age of twenty-one years who had resided in the State two years or in the county in which they offered to vote one year next before the election. Then followed Tennessee, in 1796, with voters of freemen of the age of twenty-one years and upwards, possessing a freehold in the county wherein they may vote, and being inhabitants of the State or freemen being inhabitants of any one county in the State six months immediately preceding the day of election. But we need not particularize further. No new State has ever been admitted to the Union which has conferred the right of suffrage upon women, and this has never been considered a valid objection to her admission. On the contrary, as is claimed in the argument, the right of suffrage was withdrawn from women as early as 1807 in the State of New Jersey, without any attempt to obtain the interference of the United States to prevent it. Since then the governments of the insurgent States have been reorganized under a requirement that before their representatives could be admitted to seats in Congress they must have adopted new constitutions, republican in form. In no one of these constitutions was suffrage conferred upon women, and yet the States have all been restored to their original position as States in the Union.

Besides this, citizenship has not in all cases been made a condition precedent to the enjoyment of the right of suffrage. Thus, in Missouri, persons of foreign birth, who have declared their intention to become citizens of the United States, may under certain circumstances vote. The same provision is to be found in the constitutions of Alabama, Arkansas, Florida, Georgia, Indiana, Kansas, Minnesota, and Texas.

Certainly, if the courts can consider any question settled, this is one. For nearly ninety years the people have acted upon the idea that the Constitution, when it conferred citizenship, did not necessarily confer the right of suffrage. If uniform practice long continued can settle the construction of so important an instrument as the Constitution of the United States confessedly is, most certainly it has been done here. Our province is to decide what the law is, not to declare what it should be.

We have given this case the careful consideration its importance demands. If the law is wrong, it ought to be changed; but the power for that is not with us. The arguments addressed to us bearing upon such a view of the subject may perhaps be sufficient to induce those having the power, to make the alteration, but they ought not to be permitted to influence our judgment in determining the present rights of the parties now litigating before us. No

Poverty, Wealth, and the American Dream

argument as to woman's need of suffrage can be considered. We can only act upon her rights as they exist. It is not for us to look at the hardship of withholding. Our duty is at an end if we find it is within the power of a State to withhold.

Discussion Questions

1. What does Chief Justice Waite establish about the definition of the word "citizen" in relationship to suffrage for women? Why does he take so much time in the opinion to define the word? What is the logic behind the organization of his opinion? How does he use the wording of the Fourteenth Amendment to show that suffrage was not included in the rights of citizenship?

2. Waite writes that ". . . sex has never been made one of the elements of citizenship in the United States. In this respect men have never had an advantage over women. The same laws precisely apply to both. The Fourteenth Amendment did not affect the citizenship of women any more that it did of men." Waite then goes on to say that since women have never been guaranteed suffrage by their rights of citizenship, it is not for the Supreme Court to change the laws because "the power for that is not with us." What do you think of this reasoning? Do you find it logical or not? Do you find it persuasive?

Writing Suggestions

1. At the time of this ruling, most male citizens of the United States, including ex-slaves, could vote, but women citizens could not. Imagine you are a man or a woman in America in 1875; write an editorial to the local paper expressing your views on the Supreme Court ruling on *Minor v. Happersett*. Be specific in your reference to the Fourteenth Amendment and the Supreme Court language, and make it clear why you do or do not agree with the decision. Sign your name and your occupation at the end of the letter.

2. Women now have the right to vote, to hold and inherit property, and to enjoy all rights of citizenship equally with men. However, many topics, such as equal pay for equal work, inequality in hiring practices, sexual harassment on the job, and other gender-related issues continue to be important to those who live and work in America, male or female. Write a researched essay exploring one of the topics above, reporting on the status of women in America today. Focus your paper on one specific issue, and use specific examples from current newspapers and periodicals to inform your paper.

Chapter 6: Writing Suggestions

1. Write a personal history of how you and your family came to be in America. If you came from another country, write about that experience and about how you came to America. If your parents, grandparents, great-grandparents, or other known relatives came as immigrants, interview family members and try to piece together the story of the family immigration. And if your family is Native American, write your own family history—describe your tribe and your origins, going back as far as you can. The story of immigration and assimilation often involves intermarriage between peoples of different races, faiths, and geographical backgrounds—be sure to include these details of your family history, too, and reflect on how your family history has helped shape the person you are today. If any members of your family came through Ellis Island, you can try the site <www.ellisisland.org> to trace your family's immigration history. Write about the process and the results of your search, and reflect on the experience of finding your family history on this site.

2. Research the immigration policies of other countries. Find out what your rights would be in a variety of countries, such as countries in Europe, Africa, and South America. Could you vote? Could you own land? Could you hold a permanent job? Could you become a citizen? Are other countries more or less strict than the United States about immigration laws and policies? You can contact local embassies and consulates and the United Nations for more information. Then write a research paper comparing the policies of one or more of these countries to America's immigration policies.

3. Write an essay comparing the labor struggles of the immigrants and poor workers in the Gilded Age with the struggles of other groups who fought to obtain better working conditions, such as the black freedmen in the South, or the Chinese laborers who worked for the railroads. Compare and contrast some of the issues that have occurred and reoccurred in the history of labor in nineteenth- and twentieth-century America.

4. Look in four or five high school history texts to further research Zinn's assertions that our educational textbooks do not tell the darker side of American economic growth in the nineteenth and twentieth centuries. Then write your findings in an essay, agreeing or disagreeing with Zinn, using specific examples from the textbooks you surveyed.

5. To read Elizabeth Cady Stanton's Seneca Falls Declaration (1848), visit the Web site <http://www.ukans.edu/carrie/docs/texts/seneca.htm>. Then write an essay discussing which of Stanton's rights for women have been achieved and which rights are still not available for modern women. Use specific examples from both the Seneca Falls Declarations and from your own life and current events, comparing and contrasting Stanton's goals with your perception of women's position in society today.

Chapter 6: Further Research on the Web

To pursue your research on the Internet, explore some of the following sites:

Immigration
http://www.umn.edu/ihrc
http://www.nara.gov/genealogy/immigration/immigrat.html
http://www.ins.usdoj.gov

Ellis Island
http://www.cmp.ucr.edu/exhibitions/immigration_id.html
http://www.ellisisland.com

Triangle Shirtwaist Fire
http://www.ilr.cornell.edu/trianglefire

History of Early Women's Rights Movement
http://www.lib.rochester.edud/rbk/women/women.htm

7

The Depression
and the Two World Wars
on the Home Front

The selections in this chapter represent some of the conflicts and issues in America in the first half of the twentieth century. World War I, the Great Depression, and World War II presented new challenges to all Americans. While we cannot cover these large events in American history completely, these selections will give you a sense of the importance of the conflicts between rich and poor, politicians and farmers, men and women, and Americans of different races during these times. We begin the chapter with a study of Woodrow Wilson's *War Message to Congress* in 1917, in which Wilson explains his belief that the United States must go to war "to keep the world safe for democracy." In your study of Wilson's speech, bear in mind that Wilson was reelected president in 1916 in part because of his determination to keep America out of World War I.

The war, which had been raging in Europe since 1914, aligned the Allied Powers of Great Britain, Japan, France, Russia, and Italy against the Central Powers: Germany, Austria-Hungary, Turkey, and Bulgaria. In the face of this global war, isolationism remained a popular sentiment in America, and Wilson's strong belief in neutrality was key in determining his foreign policy decisions. However, after the sinking of the Luisitania in 1915, in which many American lives were lost, and after Germany openly stated in 1917 that unrestricted submarine attacks would begin on all American ships, including those supplying goods to Allied forces, Wilson convened Congress to ask for war. Although Congress voted to declare war, the vote was mixed and reflected the political ambivalence about entering the conflict. Many politicians had already spoken urgently against U.S. involvement in the war, and thus Wilson's speech was key in persuading Congress to back his declaration of war and to send U.S. troops "over there."

When the United States entered the war and the ongoing need for military personnel, money, and ammunition became urgent, the U.S. government created propaganda posters and newspaper advertisements encouraging women and men to do their part in supporting the war, and, later, in supporting the postwar economy by purchasing "Victory" Liberty Loan bonds. This chapter offers a small selection of these posters and advertisements, along with political cartoons, so that you can study and understand some of the persuasive techniques used to rally the country.

You can also look at the visual arguments addressing some of the gender conflicts that Americans had to overcome if they were to rally as one nation. As you look at the World War I political cartoons, propaganda posters, and newspaper advertisements, ask yourselves what you can learn about American society from the depiction of women and men in these illustrations. For example, to what emotions did the illustrations appeal? What strategies did the artists use in both text and art? And after the armistice was signed on November 11, 1918, how did these strategies change to rally support for the postwar economy?

One of the next great challenges to Americans lay in surviving the Great Depression, which came as a surprise to most Americans who were enjoying the post–World War I economic boom and stock-market highs. In the years that followed World War I, stock market prices had surged, and many Americans had invested in "sure bets" that they felt sure would bring them wealth and security. Prices on stocks became highly inflated in 1928 and 1929, and many buyers bought stocks on margin, borrowing up to 75 percent of the stock price from banks. The stock market prices began to slide in September of 1929, and on "Black Tuesday," October 29, 1929, panic-selling took over as frantic investors tried to get their money out of banks. Most banks were uninsured at the time, and when they failed, investors lost their life savings. The Stock Market crash alone did not cause the ensuing Great Depression; in fact, it was caused by a number of factors, including the U.S. economic relationship to the worldwide economic instability. Farmers in America were particularly hard hit by the Depression, and had suffered losses throughout the 1920s and 1930s due to surpluses, overproduction, low prices, and, finally, drought. In his chapter "The American People on the Eve of the Great Depression," from *Freedom from Fear*, historian David M. Kennedy clarifies the political, economic, and social conditions of life in America just before the Great Depression, and models for us the use of primary and secondary sources in research.

The role of the media in portraying crises and great events is key to our understanding of the relationship of language to national conflict, and to this end a study of the media's depiction of Herbert Hoover proves instructive. Herbert Hoover, as president during the Great Depression, has since come under a great deal of criticism for the events of the Depression era, but in the early days after the crash Hoover's optimism and refusal to interfere with the stock market were treated kindly by the press. However, Hoover's policies, including his belief that the government should not support individuals with government handouts during the Depression, failed to stop the economic slide, and while Hoover did make efforts to reverse the economic nightmare gripping the county, conditions did not improve until Franklin Delano Roosevelt beat Hoover in the 1932 election and began to institute the New Deal reforms.

While he was in office, Herbert Hoover had both supporters and enemies in the ranks of the nation's newspaper owners, and in this chapter we will look at two very different reports of events that many feel ended Hoover's political career—the veterans' Bonus Expeditionary Force march on Washington, D.C., and the subsequent riots in July of 1932. Veterans who had been promised bonuses upon returning from service in World War I marched on Washington to demand their money—money desperately needed to stave off the poverty and starvation that many of the veterans and their families were facing. The media selections in this chapter will give you a chance to see the power of the media in interpreting events and portraying political figures in different lights. The first selection is from Republican Henry Luce's *Time Newsmagazine* coverage of the riots, and the second selection is from William Randolph Hearst's paper, the *San Francisco Examiner*. As you read these selections, think about the tone, diction, and point of view that each writer uses to convey strong support or condemnation of Hoover. These selections should help you sharpen your critical eye when reading current media selections about contemporary national and international events.

The final selections in this chapter concern the events on the home front during World War II, events that are key to any discussion of race, culture, and conflict in the United States. When the Japanese attacked Pearl Harbor on December 7, 1941, President Roosevelt reacted swiftly, asking Congress in his *Pearl Harbor Speech* to declare war to avenge "the day of infamy." Comparing the strategies and rhetorical devices Roosevelt used to justify the U.S. declaration of war on Japan to those used by President Wilson in his *War Message to Congress*, we can see the importance of tone, audience awareness, and imagery in political arguments.

The lives of the Japanese in America, citizens and noncitizens alike, changed forever after the bombing of Pearl Harbor, and some of the selections in this chapter detail the experiences of those persons of Japanese ancestry and of the government officials who sought to move all Japanese and Japanese Americans to relocation camps during the war. First, however, we look at a piece that appeared in *Time Magazine*: "How to Tell Your Friends from the Japs" further clarifies popular sentiment about the Japanese in America after Pearl Harbor, and allows us to view the results of fear and prejudice when applied to "logical" definitions of differences in racial characteristics.

In his address to the Commonwealth Club of San Francisco, "The Story of Pacific Coast Japanese Evacuation," Colonel Karl R. Bendetsen offers the government rationale for the evacuation of thousands of Japanese Americans to hastily constructed barracks and camps in desolate areas all over the western United States. This speech gives us the opportunity to examine Bendetsen's evidence, his understanding of his audience and of the political climate of the time, and his subsequent appeals to the emotions of fear and pride. An alternative view of the Japanese evacuation appears in one of the internment camp's censored newspapers, the *Manzanar Free Press*. This selection offers us new perspectives on the racial struggles and injustices faced by the evacuees. Together these readings also allow us to study implied arguments, the ironic use of understatement, and the power of language to convey many different views of one event.

Another group of Americans whose lives on the home front were dramatically altered by World War II were women, married or single, whom the U.S. government aggressively recruited for war work. With the need for ships and ammunition so great, and with so many of the men fighting overseas, the American government mounted a campaign to convince women not only that it was their duty to work in the factories, but also that they could do so and still be feminine. As some of the World War II posters at the end of this chapter show, the government appealed to women in many different ways. As students of argument, you can compare the World War II posters at the end of the chapter to the World War I posters that appear earlier in the chapter. But first you can read the selection from Sherna Berger Gluck's book *Rosie the Riveter Revisited*, which was based on many oral interviews she conducted with women who had worked during the war. As you read the selection, which is a compilation of the oral histories of Fanny Christina (Tina) Hill, Juanita Loveless, Charlcia Neuman, and Beatrice (Bea) Morales Clifton, consider the range of cultural and racial factors that impacted the motivations and experiences of women who went to work in factories and shipyards. How were these women's experiences similar and how were they different according to their race and social position? How did men take to the women's arrival in the shipyards, and how were the women treated when the war was over? How did their perceptions of themselves as Americans and as women alter during the war? How did their work change the role of women in the workforce in the ensuing decades?

The next selection in this chapter concerns a group of people in America whose experience with race and language during World War II played a key part in the U.S. victory, but whose contributions, until recently, have been largely ignored. The Navajo Code Talkers were instrumental in Allied victories in the Pacific Theater because the code they developed based on the Navajo language was unbreakable. Code talkers served in the Marines, both in combat and as translators, as Bruce Watson explains in his article "Navajo Code Talkers." Watson pays tribute to the enormous contribution the Navajo made to the victory in the Pacific, in spite of prejudice and racism that haunted them even as they fought on foreign shores and risked their lives to help their country.

The selection of World War II propaganda posters at the end of this chapter will give you just an idea of the rich variety of posters you can study on your own. While posters are not often used by the U.S. government today, during World War II these posters were a very important component of government propaganda.

As you reflect on the selections in this chapter, look for the lasting impact of the changes that occurred in American society as a result of the Depression and the two world wars. How did these events and the changes they brought about in American culture manifest themselves over the following decades? How did conflicts of race, gender, and class change because of these events? How does contemporary American society reflect the influence of the economic, racial, and social conflicts represented in these readings?

Before You Read

1. Make a list of your associations with American patriotism in World War I and World War II. What images of the home front come to mind? What film or documentary images of patriotism have you seen? How do you think patriotism is expressed in America today?

2. What do you know about the reasons for and the results of the internment of the Pacific Coast Japanese Americans? What have you learned in history classes about the relocation camps?

3. What kind of propaganda does the U.S. government use today to attract recruits to the Armed Forces? Which persuasive techniques are used today to promote enlistment?

War Message to Congress

WOODROW WILSON

Woodrow Wilson (1856–1924), although born in Virginia, lived as a child in Georgia during the Civil War. Wilson went to Princeton University, the University of Virginia Law School, and Johns Hopkins University, where he earned a Ph.D. He began his academic career as a professor of political science at Princeton, where he quickly moved up the ranks to become president of the University. Although he had no previous political experience, he was convinced by Democratic Party members to run for governor of New Jersey. As governor of New Jersey he then ran for president of the United States and won both the 1912 and 1916 elections. Although Wilson ran on a platform of isolationism and was reelected in 1916 partly because he kept the nation out of war, by April of 1917 he was convinced that the United States must enter the war to "keep the world safe for democracy." In the excerpt that follows from Wilson's *War Message to Congress* on April 2, 1917, he urges Congress to declare war on Germany; four days later Congress passed the War Resolution by an overwhelming majority.

2 April, 1917

Gentlemen of the Congress:

I have called the Congress into extraordinary session because there are serious, very serious, choices of policy to be made, and made immediately, which it was neither right nor constitutionally permissible that I should assume the responsibility of making.

On the 3d of February last I officially laid before you the extraordinary announcement of the Imperial German Government that on and after the 1st day of February it was its purpose to put aside all restraints of law or of humanity and use its submarines to sink every vessel that sought to approach either the ports of Great Britain and Ireland or the western coasts of Europe or any of the ports controlled by the enemies of Germany within the Mediterranean. That had seemed to be the object of the German submarine warfare earlier in the war, but since April of last year the Imperial Government had somewhat restrained the commanders of its undersea craft in conformity with its promise then given to us that passenger boats should not be sunk and that due warning would be given to all other vessels which its submarines might seek to destroy, when no resistance was offered or escape attempted, and care taken that their crews were given at least a fair chance to save their lives in their open boats. The precautions taken were meagre and haphazard enough, as was proved in distressing instance after instance in the progress of the cruel and unmanly business, but a certain degree of restraint was observed. The new policy has swept every restriction aside. Vessels of every kind, whatever their flag, their character, their cargo, their destination, their errand, have been ruthlessly sent to the bottom without warning and without thought of help or mercy for those on board, the vessels of friendly neutrals along with those of belligerents. Even hospital ships and ships carrying relief to the sorely bereaved and stricken people of Belgium, though the latter were provided with safe-conduct through the proscribed areas by the German Government itself and were distinguished by unmistakable marks of identity, have been sunk with the same reckless lack of compassion or of principle.

I was for a little while unable to believe that such things would in fact be done by any government that had hitherto subscribed to the humane practices of civilized nations. International law had its origin in the attempt to set up some law which would be respected and observed upon the seas, where no nation had right of dominion and where lay the free highways of the world. By painful stage after stage has that law been built up, with meagre enough results, indeed, after all was accomplished that could be accomplished, but always with a clear view, at least, of what the heart and conscience of mankind demanded. This minimum of right the German Government has swept aside under the plea of retaliation and necessity and because it had no weapons which it could use at sea except these which it is impossible to employ as it is employing them without throwing to the winds all scruples of humanity or of respect for the understandings that were supposed to underlie the intercourse of the world. I am not now thinking of the loss of property involved, immense and serious as that is, but only of the wanton and wholesale destruction of the lives of noncombatants, men, women, and children, engaged in pursuits which have always, even in the darkest periods of modem history, been deemed innocent and legitimate. Property can be paid for; the lives of peaceful and innocent people can not be. The present German submarine warfare against commerce is a warfare against mankind.

It is a war against all nations. American ships have been sunk, American lives taken, in ways which it has stirred us very deeply to learn of, but the ships and people of other neutral and friendly nations have been sunk and overwhelmed in the waters in the same way. There has been no discrimination. The challenge is to all mankind. Each nation must decide for itself how it will meet it. The choice we make for ourselves must be made with a moderation of counsel and a temperateness of judgment befitting our character and our motives as a nation. We must put excited feeling away. Our motive will not be revenge or the victorious assertion of the physical might of the nation, but only the vindication of right, of human right, of which we are only a single champion.

When I addressed the Congress on the 26th of February last, I thought that it would suffice to assert our neutral rights with arms, our right to use the seas against unlawful interference, our right to keep our people safe against unlawful violence. But armed neutrality, it now appears, is impracticable. Because submarines are in effect outlaws when used as the German submarines have been used against merchant shipping, it is impossible to defend ships against their attacks as the law of nations has assumed that merchantmen would defend themselves against privateers or cruisers, visible craft giving chase upon the open sea. It is common prudence in such circumstances, grim necessity indeed, to endeavour to destroy them before they have shown their own intention. They must be dealt with upon sight, if dealt with at all. The German Government denies the right of neutrals to use arms at all within the areas of the sea which it has proscribed, even in the defense of rights which no modern publicist has ever before questioned their right to defend. The intimation is conveyed that the armed guards which we have placed on our merchant ships will be treated as beyond the pale of law and subject to be dealt with as pirates would be. Armed neutrality is ineffectual enough at best; in such circumstances and in the face of such pretensions it is worse than ineffectual; it is likely only to produce what it was meant to prevent; it is practically certain to draw us into the war without either the rights or the effectiveness of belligerents. There is one choice we can not make, we are incapable of making: we will not choose the path of submission and suffer the most sacred rights of our nation and our people to be ignored or violated. The wrongs against which we now array ourselves are no common wrongs; they cut to the very roots of human life.

With a profound sense of the solemn and even tragical character of the step I am taking and of the grave responsibilities which it involves, but in unhesitating obedience to what I deem my constitutional duty, I advise that the Congress declare the recent course of the Imperial German Government to be in fact nothing less than war against the Government and people of the United States; that it formally accept the status of belligerent which has thus been thrust upon it, and that it take immediate steps not only to put the country in a more thorough state of defense but also to exert all its power and employ all its resources to bring the Government of the German Empire to terms and end the war.

What this will involve is clear. It will involve the utmost practicable cooperation in counsel and action with the governments now at war with Germany, and, as incident to that, the extension to those governments of the most liberal financial credits, in order that our resources may so far as possible be added to theirs. It will involve the organization and mobilization of all the material resources of the country to supply the materials of war and serve the incidental needs of the nation in the most abundant and yet the most economical and efficient way possible. It will involve the immediate full equipment of the Navy in all respects, but particularly in supplying it with the best means of dealing with the enemy's submarines. It will involve the immediate addition to the armed forces of the United States already provided for by law in case of war at least 500,000 men, who should, in my opinion, be chosen upon the principle of universal liability to service, and also the authorization of subsequent additional increments of equal force so soon as they may be needed and can be handled in training. It will involve also, of course, the granting of adequate credits to the Government, sustained, I hope, so far as they can equitably be sustained by the present generation, by well conceived taxation. . . .

While we do these things, these deeply momentous things, let us be very clear, and make very clear to all the world what our motives and our objects are. My own thought has not been driven from its habitual and normal course by the unhappy events of the last two months, and I do not believe that the thought of the nation has been altered or clouded by them. I have exactly the same things in mind now that I had in mind when I addressed the Senate on the 22d of January last; the same that I had in mind when I addressed the Congress on the 3d of February and on the 26th of February. Our object now, as then, is to vindicate the principles of peace and justice in the life of the world as against selfish and autocratic power and to set up amongst the really free and self-governed peoples of the world such a concert of purpose and of action as will henceforth ensure the observance of those principles. Neutrality is no longer feasible or desirable where the peace of the world is involved and the freedom of its peoples, and the menace to that peace and freedom lies in the existence of autocratic governments backed by organized force which is controlled wholly by their will, not by the will of their people. We have seen the last of neutrality in such circumstances. We are at the beginning of an age in which it will be insisted that the same standards of conduct and of responsibility for wrong done shall be observed among nations and their governments that are observed among the individual citizens of civilized states.

We have no quarrel with the German people. We have no feeling towards them but one of sympathy and friendship. It was not upon their impulse that their Government acted in entering this war. It was not with their previous knowledge or approval. It was a war determined upon as wars used to be determined upon in the old, unhappy days when peoples were nowhere consulted by their rulers and wars were provoked and waged in the interest of dynasties or of little groups of ambitious men who were accustomed to use their fellow men as pawns and tools. Self-governed nations do not fill their neighbour states with spies or set the course of intrigue to bring about some critical posture of affairs which will give them an opportunity to strike and make conquest. Such designs can be successfully worked out only under cover and where no one has the right to ask questions. Cunningly contrived plans of deception or aggression, carried, it may be, from generation to generation, can be worked out and kept from the light only within the privacy of courts or behind the carefully guarded confidences of a narrow and privileged class. They are happily impossible where public opinion commands and insists upon full information concerning all the nation's affairs.

A steadfast concert for peace can never be maintained except by a partnership of democratic nations. No autocratic government could be trusted to keep faith within it or observe its covenants. It must be a league of honour, a partnership of opinion. Intrigue would eat its vitals away; the plottings of inner circles who could plan what they would and render account to no one would be a corruption seated at its very heart. Only free peoples can hold their purpose and their honour steady to a common end and prefer the interests of mankind to any narrow interest of their own.

Does not every American feel that assurance has been added to our hope for the future peace of the world by the wonderful and heartening things that have been happening within the last few weeks in Russia? Russia was known by those who knew it best to have been always in fact democratic at heart, in all the vital habits of her thought, in all the intimate relationships of her people that spoke their natural instinct, their habitual attitude towards life. The autocracy that crowned the summit of her political structure, long as it had stood and terrible as was the reality of its power, was not in fact Russian in origin, character, or purpose; and now it has been shaken off and the great, generous Russian people have been added in all their native majesty and might to the forces that are fighting for freedom in the world, for justice, and for peace. Here is a fit partner for a league of honour.

One of the things that has served to convince us that the Prussian autocracy was not and could never be our friend is that from the very outset of the present war it has filled our unsuspecting communities and even our offices of government with spies and set criminal intrigues everywhere afoot against our national unity of counsel, our peace within and without our industries and our commerce. Indeed it is now evident that its spies were here even before the war began; and it is unhappily not a matter of conjecture but a fact proved in our courts of justice that the intrigues which have more than once come perilously near to disturbing the peace and dislocating the industries of the country have been carried on at the instigation, with the support, and even under the personal direction of official agents of the Imperial Government accredited to the Government of the United States. Even in checking these things and trying to extirpate them we have sought to put the most generous interpretation possible upon them because we knew that their source lay, not in any hostile feeling or purpose of the German people towards us (who were, no doubt, as ignorant of them as we ourselves were), but only in the selfish designs of a Government that did what it pleased and told its people nothing. But they have played their part in serving to convince us at last that that Government entertains no real friendship for us and means to act against our peace and security at its convenience. . . .

We are accepting this challenge of hostile purpose because we know that in such a government, following such methods, we can never have a friend; and that in the presence of its organized power, always lying in wait to accomplish we know not what purpose, there can be no assured security for the democratic governments of the world. We are now about to accept gage of battle with this natural foe to liberty and shall, if necessary, spend the whole force of the nation to check and nullify its pretensions and its power. We are glad, now that we see the facts with no veil of false pretence about them, to fight thus for the ultimate peace of the world and for the liberation of its peoples, the German peoples included: for the rights of nations great and small and the privilege of men everywhere to choose their way of life and of obedience. The world must be made safe for democracy. Its peace must be planted upon the tested foundations of political liberty. We have no selfish ends to serve. We desire no conquest, no dominion. We seek no indemnities for ourselves, no material compensation for the sacrifices we shall freely make. We are but one of the champions of the rights of mankind. We shall be satisfied when those rights have been made as secure as the faith and the freedom of nations can make them.

Just because we fight without rancour and without selfish object, seeking nothing for ourselves but what we shall wish to share with all free peoples, we shall, I feel confident, conduct our operations as belligerents without passion and ourselves observe with proud punctilio the principles of right and of fair play we profess to be fighting for.

I have said nothing of the governments allied with the Imperial Government of Germany because they have not made war upon us or challenged us to defend our right and our honour. The Austro-Hungarian Government has, indeed, avowed its unqualified endorsement and acceptance of the reckless and lawless submarine warfare adopted now without disguise by the Imperial German Government, and it has therefore not been possible for this Government to receive Count Tarnowski, the Ambassador recently accredited to this Government by the Imperial and Royal Government of Austria-Hungary; but that Government has not actually engaged in warfare against citizens of the United States on the seas, and I take the liberty, for the present at least, of postponing a discussion of our relations with the authorities at Vienna. We enter this war only where we are clearly forced into it because there are no other means of defending our rights.

It will be all the easier for us to conduct ourselves as belligerents in a high spirit of right and fairness because we act without animus, not in enmity towards a people or with the desire to bring any injury or disadvantage upon them, but only in armed opposition to an irresponsible government which has thrown aside all considerations of humanity and of right and is running amuck. We are, let me say again, the sincere friends of the German people, and shall desire nothing so much as the early reestablishment of intimate relations of mutual advantage between us—however hard it may be for them, for the time being, to believe that this is spoken from our hearts. We have borne with their present government through all these bitter months because of that friendship—exercising a patience and forbearance which would otherwise have been impossible. We shall, happily, still have an opportunity to prove that friendship in our daily attitude and actions towards the millions of men and women of German birth and native sympathy, who live amongst us and share our life, and we shall be proud to prove it towards all who are in fact loyal to their neighbours and to the Government in the hour of test. They are, most of them, as true and loyal Americans as if they had never known any other fealty or allegiance. They will be prompt to stand with us in rebuking and restraining the few who may be of a different mind and purpose. If there should be disloyalty, it will be dealt with with a firm hand of stern repression; but, if it lifts its head at all, it will lift it only here and there and without countenance except from a lawless and malignant few.

It is a distressing and oppressive duty, gentlemen of the Congress, which I have performed in thus addressing you. There are, it may be, many months of fiery trial and sacrifice ahead of us. It is a fearful thing to lead this great peaceful people into war, into the most terrible and disastrous of all wars, civilization itself seeming to be in the balance. But the right is more precious than peace, and we shall fight for the things which we have always carried nearest our hearts—for democracy, for the right of those who submit to authority to have a voice in their own governments for the rights and liberties of small nations, for a universal dominion of right by such a concert of free peoples as shall bring peace and safety to all nations and make the world itself at last free. To such a task we can dedicate our lives and our fortunes, everything that we are and everything that we have, with the pride of those who know that the day has come when America is privileged to spend her blood and her might for the principles that gave her birth and happiness and the peace which she has treasured. God helping her, she can do no other.

Discussion Questions

1. President Wilson stresses repeatedly in his speech that he does not hold the German people responsible for the actions of the German government, and states that "we have no feeling towards them but one of sympathy and friendship." Discuss the reason for Wilson's profession of friendship toward the German people. Why does he make such a distinction between the German government and the German populace? Where in his speech does he return to this theme? How might this theme of friendship be effective in persuading the American people that his decision to go to war is correct?

2. Discuss the variety of arguments that appear in this speech regarding international relations, freedom, and democracy. How does Wilson extend his argument for declaring war on Germany to an argument for the American way of life? Why does Wilson refer to the overthrow of the "Prussian autocracy" in this message to Congress?

Writing Suggestions

1. Analyze Wilson's speech as a persuasive argument and discuss the strategies he uses to convince the isolationist Congress that the time has finally come to end neutrality and to declare war on Germany. Consider the outline of the speech, the chronological arrangement of its contents, the tone and diction used, and the variety of evidence Wilson presents to Congress in his appeal for war. In your analysis, you can also include your personal opinion of this speech—did you find it convincing and moving, or not?

2. Woodrow Wilson had long been opposed to entering the war, but he eventually became convinced that America had to join the war to make the world "safe for democracy." Research the pre-war period in America, and write a paper discussing the reasons for and political climate of isolationism. What were the roots of this national trend, and how did economic forces play a part in isolationism? How did Woodrow Wilson argue for isolationism before the war? What other political figures supported or disagreed with isolationism? What kind of popular support did Americans give the idea of isolationism, and why?

World War I Propaganda

The political cartoons, propaganda posters, and newspaper advertisements presented on the following pages are just a sampling of the
great variety of recruitment and propaganda materials that appeared
in the nation's media once President Wilson declared war on Germany in April of 1917. Throughout the war, the armistice (November 11, 1918), and the postwar occupation period, Americans were
bombarded by visual and written texts urging them to do their part,
to buy bonds, to buy Victory buttons, and to support the war effort in
every way possible. Artists appealed to a wide variety of emotions
to persuade Americans to participate in the war effort and to mobilize Americans on the home front.

The New York Times Magazine, January 27, 1918
Hoover Institution Archives Collection

Food for Thought

The New York Times Magazine, February 3, 1918
Hoover Institution Archives Collection

The Loreley

The New York Times Magazine, April 14, 1918
Hoover Institution Archives Collection

One Front They Did Not Mean to Break

The New York Times Magazine, June 9, 1918
Hoover Institution Archives Collection

circa 1918, Hoover Institution Archives Collection

circa 1918, Hoover Institution Archives Collection

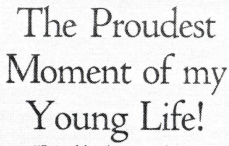

The Proudest Moment of my Young Life!

"I would rather wear this Button than a hundred dollar diamond ring! It gives me more 'class' than any jewelry or clothing. It puts me in line with those who have sacrificed for the freedom of mankind; who are rebuilding the shattered and healing the sick. It gets for me the approval of all because they see I have done what they either have done or ought to do."

The "Victory" Liberty Loan

is the highest type of investment for the savings of the wage-earner—of professional men and women, or of those in business. They combine sentiment and income, saving and service.

Those who own Liberty Bonds command more steady employment, enjoy a basis for credit, and receive the approval of the people with whom they live. These are worth striving for.

Subscribe: Wear the Button

Finish the Job
Subscribe to the
'Victory'Liberty
Loan

Patriotically Save for a Prosperous Peace

Keep the Habit Going

Buy Today

At any Bank—Cash or Instalments

Liberty Loan Committee of New England

1919, Hoover Institution Archives Collection

Oh! My Boy! My Boy!!

—

We welcome the home-comers

But more than one million soldiers are still over there. We must maintain, victual and clothe them until a prosperous and durable peace is a secured fact. Subscribe to the "Victory" Liberty Loan, —the "Victorious Fifth." We must pay our honorable debts incurred to carry us to a victorious finish. We must rebuild the maimed and restore the sick and wounded to health. We must keep faith with the world!

The "Victory" Liberty Loan will do it

Patriotically Save for a Prosperous Peace

Buy Early

At any Bank — Cash or Instalments

Liberty Loan Committee of New England

1919, Hoover Institution Archives Collection

Can You Look this Man in the Eye with Pride?

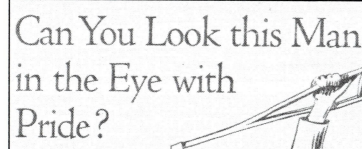

Or do you avoid his gaze?

You were a staunch American when the Country was at war, and you bought First, Second, Third and Fourth Liberty Bonds. You could meet him upstanding then. Now that we are striving to gather the sweet fruits of Victory, to pay our honest war debts, and maintain military strength to enforce a righteous peace,

How do you feel?

Not all the men who fought for you and who returned alive have been maimed. Many grievous wounds are hidden. Suffering and sacrifice are not measurable by a yardstick, nor can you recognize the veterans now in "civies." You will meet them unawares.

They will judge you!

If this little "Victory" Liberty Loan button is pinned on your coat, then you are the *American* that you were while your country was at war.

And you can look this boy *in the eye*.

But if the button is not there, you will shrink from his gaze.

For you are not *what you were* a year ago.

Subscribe and wear a button!

We cannot sully the brightness of our victory by failing in our financial obligations, by refusing to maintain our army or declining to restore our wounded, crippled and sick fighting men.

This Button, worn with pride, is the sign that you have again taken your place in the army of savers for patriotic purposes.

Patriotically Save for a Prosperous Peace.   Keep the Habit Going

Buy Today

At any Bank — Cash or on Instalments

Liberty Loan Committee of New England

This Advertisement is Dedicated by us to New England's Heroic Soldiers and Sailors

Finish the Job Subscribe to the Victory Liberty Loan

1919, Hoover Institution Archives Collection

Dear New England Folks:

This is what the war did to me.

Am I downhearted?

No!

If I could only be sure you would support the "Victory" Liberty Loan to a finish I wouldn't care.

But if New England falls down on its quota I will be sore and I wont care if I never come back.

Buddie

Can we folks, safe and sound in mind and limb, look this boy in the eye if the loan fails?

Come on!
Help finish the job

The Victory Liberty Loan is our last chance to put our patriotism to the acid test.

Subscribe early and Wear the Button

At any Bank—Cash or Instalments   Patriotically Save for a Prosperous Peace

Liberty Loan Committee of New England

1919, Hoover Institution Archives Collection

Discussion Questions

1. Look at the World War I poster on page 545 (bottom right) and the one on page 546. Both these posters use women as the centerpiece, but their strategies are very different. Discuss the different strategies of the artists in urging women to do their part. How does the poster on page 545 use the central female figure? What emotions is the artist appealing to? What is the central argument? Then look at the poster on page 546. Ask yourself the same questions about this poster, and discuss the differences and similarities in the arguments and strategies of the two posters. Which do you find more appealing, and why?

2. Look through the cartoons, posters, and advertisements in this section and discuss the various strategies and techniques used to persuade Americans to do their part for the war and the occupation period. Then design your own cartoon, poster, or advertisement, mapping out both the illustration and the words that would have been typical for propaganda of the World War I era, seeking support both for the war and for the postwar economic stability of the United States.

Writing Suggestions

1. Review your answers to the first discussion question for this selection. Then write a comparison essay, looking at the similarities and differences in the World War I poster on page 545 (bottom right) and the one on page 546. Discuss the different strategies of the artists in urging women to do their part. How does the poster on page 545 use the central female figure? What emotions is the artist appealing to? What is the central argument? Then look at the poster on page 546. Ask yourself the same questions about this poster, and in your essay discuss the differences and similarities in the arguments and strategies of the two posters. Which do you find more appealing, and why?

2. Write an analysis of the four "Victory" Liberty Loan advertisements (see pages 547–550) that ran in the *New York Times* from March 31 to May 10, 1919, during the American occupation of Germany. Look for the political issues and events that are reflected in the text of the advertisements. What strategies do the different artists use to persuade Americans to buy these bonds? How does the text change in order to appeal to different emotions? How do the illustrations represent these different appeals? Which of these advertisements do you think would be most effective in persuading the American public to buy Liberty Loan bonds? Why?

Freedom from Fear

The American People on the Eve of the Great Depression

DAVID M. KENNEDY

David M. Kennedy is the Donald J. McLachlan Professor of History at Stanford University. Educated at Stanford (B.A., 1963) and Yale (Ph.D., 1968), he is the author of numerous books and articles about American history, including the Pulitzer Prize winning book *Freedom from Fear: The American People in Depression and War, 1929–1945*, which also won the Society of American Historians' Francis Parkman Prize for "literary distinction in the writing of history." Kennedy has written extensively on American social and political history, including a study of American involvement in World War I, *Over Here: The First World War and American Society*, and *Birth Control in America: The Career of Margaret Sanger*. In the following excerpt from *Freedom from Fear*, from Chapter 1, "The American People on the Eve of the Great Depression," Kennedy describes the social, political, and economic conditions in America just before the crash of the stock market in 1929.

We in America today are nearer to the final triumph over poverty than ever before in the history of any land.

—Herbert Hoover, August 11, 1928

Like an earthquake, the stock market crash of October 1929 cracked startlingly across the United States, the herald of a crisis that was to shake the American way of life to its foundations. The events of the ensuing decade opened a fissure across the landscape of American history no less gaping than that opened by the volley on Lexington Common in April 1775 or by the bombardment of Sumter on another April four score and six years later.

The ratcheting ticker machines in the autumn of 1929 did not merely record avalanching stock prices. In time they came also to symbolize the end of an era. The roaring industrial expansion that had boomed since the Civil War hushed to a near standstill for half a generation. The tumult of crisis and reform in the ten depression years massively enlarged and forever transformed the scanty Jeffersonian government over which Herbert Hoover had been elected to preside in 1928. And even before the battle against the Great Depression was won, the American people had to shoulder arms in another even more fearsome struggle that wreathed the planet in destruction and revolutionized America's global role.

None of this impending drama could have been foreseen by the tweedy group of social scientists who gathered at the White House for dinner with President Hoover on the warm, early autumn evening of September 26, 1929. The Crash, still four weeks away, was unimagined and almost unimaginable. Nearly three decades of barely punctuated economic growth, capped by seven years of unprecedented prosperity, gave to the mood in the room, as in the entire country, an air of masterful confidence in the future. The president personified the national temper. Attired as always in starched high collar and immaculate business suit, he greeted his guests with stiff, double-breasted dignity. He exuded the laconic assurance of a highly successful executive. He was arguably the most respected man in America, a man, said the novelist Sherwood Anderson, who had "never known failure." A wave of popular acclamation had lifted him to the White House just six months earlier, after a famously distinguished career as a mining engineer, international businessman, relief and food administrator in the Great War of 1914–1918, and exceptionally influential secretary of commerce in the Republican administrations of Warren G. Harding and Calvin Coolidge.

Hoover was no mossback conservative in the Harding-Coolidge mold, and the men gathered in the White House dining room knew it. "[T]he time when the employer could ride roughshod over his labor is disappearing with the doctrine of '*laissez-faire*' on which it is founded," he had written as early as 1909. Long sympathetic to the progressive wing of his party, Hoover as secretary of commerce had not only supported the cause of labor but also urged closer business-government cooperation, established government control over the new technology of radio, and proposed a multibillion-dollar federal public works fund as a tool to offset downswings in the business cycle. As president, he meant to be no passive custodian. He dreamt the progressive generation's dream of actively managing social change through informed, though scrupulously limited, government action. "A new era and new forces have come into our economic life and our setting among nations of the world," he said in accepting the Republican presidential nomination in 1928. "These forces demand of us constant study and effort if prosperity, peace, and contentment shall be maintained."

Organizing that study was the dinner meeting's agenda. The little assemblage around the president's dining table symbolized, in a sense, the core progressive faith in knowledge as the servant of power. Hoover intended to possess knowledge, and with it to rule responsibly. After methodically interrogating each of his guests over the coffee cups as the table was cleared, Hoover explained his ambitious project. He meant to recruit the best brains in the country, he said, to compile a body of data and analysis about American society that would be more comprehensive, more searching, and more useful than anything ever before attempted. Their findings, he went on, would serve as "a basis for the formulation of large national policies looking to the next phase in the nation's development."

The following month's upheavals in the financial markets, and their aftershocks, rendered ironic Hoover's confident anticipation of "the next phase in the nation's development." Underscoring the irony, Hoover eventually disowned the study he so confidently commissioned on that Indian summer evening. In the four years between its conception and its publication—the four years of Herbert Hoover's presidency—the world changed forever. Among the casualties of that violent mutation was Hoover's research project and the hope of an orderly command of the future that it represented—not to mention his own reputation. A massive dreadnought of scholarship, its pages barnacled with footnotes, it was launched at last in 1933 onto a Sargasso Sea of presidential and public indifference.

Useless to Hoover in 1933, the scholars' work has nevertheless provided historians ever since with an incomparably rich source of information about the pre-Depression period. Entitled *Recent Social Trends*, it ran to some fifteen hundred pages densely packed with data about all aspects of American life. It ranged from an inventory of mineral resources to analyses of crime and punishment, the arts, health and medical practice, the status of women, blacks, and ethnic minorities, the changing characteristics of the labor force, the impact of new technologies on productivity and leisure, and the roles of federal, state, and local governments. From its turgid prose and endless tables emerged a vivid portrait of a people in the throes of sweeping social, economic, and political change, even before they were engulfed by the still more wrenching changes of the Depression era.

President Hoover's charge to the assembled scholars at that hopeful supper registered his commitment to what Walter Lippmann in 1914 had called mastery, not drift, in the nation's affairs and to government as the instrument of that mastery. Hoover's dinner-table speech to the social scientists also accurately reflected their shared sense—indeed the sense of most Americans in pre-Crash 1929—that they dwelt in a land and time of special promise. "A new era," Hoover called it, one that was witnessing breathtaking transformations in traditional ways of life and that demanded commensurate transformations in the institutions and techniques of government.

This sense of living through a novel historical moment pervaded commentaries on American society in the 1920s. Even the sober academic authors of *Recent Social Trends* marveled at the social and economic forces that "have hurried us dizzily away from the days of the frontier into a whirl of modernisms which almost passes belief." The same sense of astonishment suffused the pages of the decade's most famous sociological inquiry, Robert and Helen Merrell Lynd's *Middletown*, drawn from an exhaustive examination of Muncie, Indiana, in 1925. Measuring from the baseline of 1890, the Lynds found dramatic alterations in every conceivable aspect of the Middletowners' lives. "[W]e today," they concluded, are probably living in one of the eras of greatest rapidity of change in the history of human institutions."

The list of changes in the generation since the close of the nineteenth century seemed endlessly amazing. *Recent Social Trends* began with a brief recital of some of the "epoch-making events" that had filled the first third of the twentieth century: the Great War, mass immigration, race riots, rapid urbanization, the rise of giant industrial combines like U.S. Steel, Ford, and General Motors, new technologies like electrical power, automobiles, radios, and motion pictures, novel social experiments like Prohibition, daring campaigns for birth control, a new frankness about sex, women's suffrage, the advent of mass-market advertising and consumer financing. "These," the researchers declared, "are but a few of the many happenings which have marked one of the most eventful periods of our history."

The sheer scale of America in the 1920s was impressive, and its variety was downright astonishing. The nation's population had nearly doubled since 1890, when it had numbered just sixty-three million souls. At least a third of the increase was due to a huge surge of immigrants. Most of them had journeyed to America from the religiously and culturally exotic regions of southern and eastern Europe. Through the great hall in the immigrant receiving center on New York's Ellis Island, opened in 1892, streamed in the next three decades almost four million Italian Catholics; half a million Orthodox Greeks; half a million Catholic Hungarians; nearly a million and a half Catholic Poles; more than two million Jews, largely from Russian-controlled Poland, Ukraine, and Lithuania; half a million Slovaks, mostly Catholic; millions of other eastern Slavs from Byelorussia, Ruthenia, and Russia, mostly Orthodox; more millions of southern Slavs, a mix of Catholic, Orthodox, Muslim, and Jew, from Rumania, Croatia, Serbia, Bulgaria, and Montenegro. The waves of arrivals after the turn of the century were so enormous that of the 123 million Americans recorded in the census of 1930, one in ten was foreign born, and an additional 20 percent had at least one parent born abroad.

Immigrants settled in all regions, though only scantily in the South and heavily in the sprawling industrial zone of the Northeast. To an overwhelming degree they were drawn not to the land but to the factories and tenements of the big cities. They turned urban America into a kind of polyglot archipelago in the predominantly Anglo-Protestant American sea. Almost a third of Chicago's 2.7 million residents in the 1920s were foreign born; more than a million were Catholic, and another 125,000 were Jews. New Yorkers spoke some thirty-seven different languages, and only one in six worshiped in a Protestant church.

Everywhere immigrant communities banded together in ethnic enclaves, where they strove, not always consistently, both to preserve their old-world cultural patrimony and to become American. They were strangers in a strange land, awkwardly suspended between the world they had left behind and a world where they were not yet fully at home. They naturally looked to one another for reassurance and strength. The Jewish ghettoes and Little Italys and Little Polands that took root in American cities became worlds unto themselves. Immigrants read newspapers and listened to radio broadcasts in their native languages. They shopped at stores, patronized banks, and dealt with insurance companies that catered exclusively to their particular ethnic group. They chanted their prayers in synagogues, or, if they were Catholic, often in "national" churches where sermons were preached in the old-world tongue. They educated their children in parish schools and buried their dead with the help of ethnic funeral societies. They joined fraternal organizations to keep alive the old traditions and paid their dues to mutual aid societies that would help when bad times came.

Times were often hard. Huddled on the margins of American life, immigrants made do with what work they could find, typically low-skill jobs in heavy industry, the garment trades, or construction. Isolated by language, religion, livelihood, and neighborhood, they had precious little ability to speak to one another and scant political voice in the larger society. So precarious were their lives that many of them gave up altogether and went back home. Nearly a third of the Poles, Slovaks, and Croatians returned to Europe; almost half the Italians; more than half the Greeks, Russians, Rumanians, and Bulgarians. Old-stock Americans continued to think of the foreigners who remained in their midst as alien and threatening. Many immigrants wondered if the fabled promise of American life was a vagrant and perhaps impossible dream.

The flood of newcomers, vividly different from earlier migrants in faiths, tongues, and habits, aroused powerful anxieties about the capacity of American society to accommodate them. Some of that anxiety found virulent expression in a revived Ku Klux Klan, reborn in all its Reconstruction-era paraphernalia at Stone Mountain, Georgia, in 1915. Klan nightriders now rode cars, not horses, and they directed their venom as much at immigrant Jews and Catholics as at blacks. But the new Klan no less than the old represented a peculiarly American response to cultural upheaval. By the early 1920s the Klan claimed some five million members, and for a time it dominated the politics of Indiana and Oregon. The nativist sentiment that the Klan helped to nurture found statutory expression in 1924, when Congress choked the immigrant stream to a trickle, closing the era of virtually unlimited entry to the United States. The ethnic neighborhoods that had mushroomed in the preceding generation would grow no more through further inflows from abroad. America's many ethnic communities now began to stabilize. Millions of immigrants awaited the day when they might become American at last.

From peasant plots in the basins of the Volga and Vistula, from rough pastures high in the Carpathians and Apennines, as well as from the cotton South and the Midwestern corn belt, new Americans as well as old flowed to the throbbing industrial centers in the northeastern quadrant of the United States. The region of settlement defined as the "frontier" had officially closed in 1890. By 1920, for the first time in the nation's history, a majority of Americans were city dwellers. In the following decade, some six million more American farmers quit the land and moved to the city.

Yet the urbanization of early twentieth-century America can be exaggerated. More than one in five working Americans still toiled on the land in the

1920s. Forty-four percent of the population was still counted as rural in 1930. Well over half the states of the Union remained preponderantly rural in population, economy, political representation, and ways of life.

In many respects, those country ways of life remained untouched by modernity. The fifty million Americans who dwelt in what F. Scott Fitzgerald called "that vast obscurity beyond the city" still moved between birth and death to the ancient rhythms of sun and season. More than forty-five million of them had no indoor plumbing in 1930, and almost none had electricity. They relieved themselves in chamber pots and outdoor latrines, cooked and heated with wood stoves, and lit their smoky houses with oil lamps. In the roadless Ozark mountains, future Arkansas governor Orval Faubus's mother could not do the family laundry until she had first boiled the guts of a freshly butchered hog to make lye soap. In the isolated Texas Hill Country, future president Lyndon Johnson's mother grew stoop-shouldered lugging buckets of water from well to kitchen. As it had for most of mankind for all of human memory, sunset routinely settled a cloak of darkness and silence over that immense domain where the fields of the republic rolled on under the night. Another Texas Hill Country woman remembered from her girlhood the scary after-dark trips to the outhouse: "I had a horrible choice of either sitting in the dark and not knowing what was crawling on me or bringing a lantern and attracting moths, mosquitoes, nighthawks and bats."

The widening gap between country and city life had helped to fuel the Populist agitation of the late nineteenth century and had prompted Theodore Roosevelt to appoint a Commission on Country Life in 1908. By the 1920s a stubborn agricultural depression, the product of war and technological change, badly exacerbated the problems of the countryside. When the guns of August 1914 announced the outbreak of fighting in Europe, American farmers had scrambled to supply the world's disrupted markets with foodstuffs. They put marginal lands under the plow, and they increased yields from all acreage with more intensive cultivation, aided especially by the advent of the gasoline-engine tractor. The number of motorized farm vehicles quintupled in the war years, to some eighty-five thousand. With the return of peace this trend accelerated. By the end of the 1920s nearly a million farmers chugged along their furrows mounted atop self-propelled tractors. And as tractor-power substituted for horse- and mule-power, some nine million work animals were destroyed, releasing an additional thirty million acres of pastureland for the planting of wheat or cotton or for the grazing of dairy animals.

After the armistice of November 1918, however, world agricultural production returned to its familiar prewar patterns. American farmers found themselves with huge surpluses on their hands. Prices plummeted. Cotton slumped from a wartime high of thirty-five cents per pound to sixteen cents in 1920. Corn sank from $1.50 per bushel to fifty-two cents. Wool slid from nearly sixty cents per pound to less than twenty cents. Although prices improved somewhat after 1921, they did not fully recover until war resumed in

1939. Farmers suffocated under their own mountainous surpluses and under the weight of the debts they had assumed to expand and to mechanize. Foreclosures increased, and more and more freeholders became tenants. The depopulation of the countryside proceeded ever more rapidly.

Congress tried repeatedly to find a remedy for the ills of farmers in the 1920s. As the agricultural depression persisted through the decade, the federal government assumed regulatory control over commodity markets and eventually established a modestly funded federal agency to provide financing for agricultural cooperatives. Congress twice passed, and President Coolidge twice vetoed, the McNary-Haugen Bill. It proposed that the federal government should become the buyer of last resort of surplus farm products, which it should then dispose of—or "dump"—in overseas markets.

Herbert Hoover needed no comprehensive study to know that the farm issue was urgent. Virtually his first act as president, even before he commissioned his wide-ranging examination of recent social trends, was to convene a special congressional session to resolve the farm crisis. It produced the Agricultural Marketing Act of 1929, which created several government-sponsored "stabilization corporations" authorized to buy surpluses and hold them off the market in order to maintain price levels. But as the agricultural depression of the 1920s merged with the general depression of the 1930s, the corporations quickly exhausted both their storage capacity and their funds. The misery of rural America knew no relief. As the decade of the Great Depression opened, the already reeling farmers would be its hardest-hit victims.

The South in the 1920s was the nation's most rural region. Not a single southern state met the superintendent of the census's modest definition of "urban" in 1920—having a majority of its population in cities of twenty-five hundred or more souls. From the Potomac to the Gulf the land looked little different than it had at the end of Reconstruction in the 1870s. Inhabiting a region of scarce capital and abundant labor, Southerners planted and picked their traditional crops of cotton, tobacco, rice, or sugarcane with mules and muscle, just as their ancestors had done for generations. And like their forebears, they bled not only against the blade of chronic agricultural depression but also against the uniquely American thorn of race.

The Great War had drawn some half a million blacks out of the rural South and into the factories of the North. With the throttling of immigration in 1924, northern industry needed to find new sources of fresh labor. Southern blacks (as well as some half a million Mexicans, who were exempted from the new immigration quotas) seized the opportunity. By the end of the 1920s another million African-Americans had left the old slave states to take up employment in the Northeast and upper Midwest (only about a hundred thousand blacks dwelt west of the Rockies). There they found jobs in metalworking shops, automobile factories, and packing houses. The political implications of this migration were vividly illustrated in 1928 when Chicago alderman Oscar De Priest, a Republican loyal to the party of the Great Emancipator, became the first black elected to Congress since Reconstruction and the first ever from a northern district.

Yet as late as 1930 more than four out of five American blacks still lived in the South. There they tortuously made their daily way through what the historian C. Vann Woodward has called an "anthropological museum of Southern folkways," which history knows as the Jim Crow system. Despite its antiquated and grotesquely burdensome character, that system was deeply entrenched in southern life. Indeed, as Woodward notes, it "reached its perfection in the 1930s."

Jim Crow meant, above all, that blacks could not vote. They had been almost universally disfranchised throughout the South in the post-Reconstruction decades. In the eleven states of the former Confederacy, fewer than 5 percent of eligible African-Americans were registered to vote as late as 1940. Jim Crow also meant social and economic segregation. Blacks sat in separate waiting rooms in railroad and bus stations, drank from separate drinking fountains, worshiped in separate churches, and attended strictly segregated and abysmally inferior schools. The South's few industrial jobs were largely barred to them. Southern blacks thus constituted an extreme case of rural poverty in a region that was itself a special case of economic backwardness and isolation from modern life. Hoover's social scientists discovered that infant mortality rates for blacks were nearly double those for whites in 1930 (10 percent and 6 percent respectively) and that blacks had an average life expectancy fifteen years shorter than whites (forty-five years compared with sixty). African-Americans in the South were bound as fast to the land by debt, ignorance, and intimidation as they had been by slavery itself. As for the white folk of the South, declared the eminent southern historian Ulrich B. Phillips in 1928, they shared "a common resolve indomitably maintained—that it shall be and remain a white man's country."

To Americans who were white and lived in the city, blacks were nearly invisible and the complaints of the farmers seemed a distant annoyance, the mewlings of laughably untutored hayseeds as modernity passed them by. Urban sophisticates snickered with approval when H. L. Mencken lampooned the South as the "Sahara of the Bozart." They nodded knowingly when Sinclair Lewis, in books like *Main Street* (1920) and *Babbitt* (1922), satirized the same midwestern small towns from which many of them had fled to the metropolis. They clucked appreciatively when Lewis unmasked the tawdry hypocrisy of rural America's fundamentalist faiths in *Elmer Gantry* (1927). They smirked at the biblical literalism of the "yokels" who swarmed out of the east Tennessee hills in 1925 to gape at the trial of John T. Scopes, indicted for violating Tennessee law by teaching Darwinian evolution to high school students. They smiled with satisfaction when street-smart Chicago attorney Clarence Darrow humiliated rural America's historic paladin, William Jennings Bryan, in the course of that trial.

Bryan's mortification symbolized for many the eclipse of rural fundamentalism and the triumphant ascendancy of the metropolis as the fount and arbiter of modern American values. New national magazines, like *Time*, first published in 1923, Mencken's *American Mercury* in 1924, and the *New Yorker*, whose first issue appeared in 1925, catered to the "caviar sophisticates" and testified to the new cultural power of the great urban centers. Urban America was confident that the city—like Darrow's and Carl Sandburg's Chicago, "stormy, husky, brawling . . . proud to be Hog Butcher, Tool Maker, Stacker of Wheat, Player with Railroads and Freight Handler to the Nation"—was the big-shouldered master to whom rural America must pay tribute.

But to thoughtful observers and policymakers the contrast between country and city life was a matter for neither laughter nor poetry. They worried obsessively about "balance" between rural and urban America, which *Recent Social Trends* called "the central problem" of the economy. Politicians sought interminably for ways to solve it.

The economic disparities between the agricultural and industrial sectors were gaping. Both areas of the economy had grown since the turn of the century, but the urban-based manufacturing sector had expanded far more robustly. While American farmers brought about 50 percent more product to market in 1930 than they had in 1900, manufacturing output had doubled and redoubled again over the same period, to four times its earlier level. Factory workers had achieved remarkable productivity improvements of nearly 50 percent, thanks largely to more efficient means of industrial organization and to the revolutionary introduction of electrically driven machinery on the shop floor. Fully 70 percent of American industry was powered by electricity in 1929, much of it from generating plants fueled by oil from newly developed fields in Texas, Oklahoma, and California. By 1925 a completely assembled Model T Ford rolled off the continuously moving assembly line at Henry Ford's Highland Park plant every ten seconds. Just a dozen years earlier it had taken fourteen hours to put together a single car.

Shrinking export markets, along with the dampening of American population growth after the closure of immigration, spelled stable or even declining demand for American agricultural products. Yet the capacity of Americans to buy ever more industrial goods seemed limitless, as the automobile revolution vividly illustrated. Essentially a cottage industry when the century opened, automobile manufacturing accounted for 10 percent of the nation's income two decades later and employed some four million workers. The motorcar in 1900 had been the plaything of the rich, who purchased some four thousand vehicles. By 1929 ordinary Americans were driving more than twenty-six million motor vehicles, one for every five people in the country. They bought nearly five million vehicles in that year alone, and they paid far less for them than they had a generation earlier.

In a stunning demonstration of the fruitful marriage of innovative technologies to mass markets, the effective price of an automobile fell steeply from the century's opening onward. A car that cost the average worker the equivalent of nearly two years' wages before the First World War could be purchased for about three months' earnings by the late 1920s. This low-price, high-volume marketing strategy was among the miracles of mass production—or "Fordism," as it was sometimes called in honor of its most famous pioneer. Largely an American invention, the technique of mass-producing standardized products was in a sense an American inevitability, as, in its time, would be the revolution in consumer electronics: a means to tap the economic potential of a democratic society whose wealth was nearly as widely diffused as its formal political power.

Yet even this fabulously successful strategy had limits. Mass production made mass consumption a necessity. But as Hoover's investigators discovered, the increasing wealth of the 1920s flowed disproportionately to the owners of capital. Workers' incomes were rising, but not at a rate that kept pace with the nation's growing industrial output. Without broadly distributed purchasing power, the engines of mass production would have no outlet and would eventually fall idle. The automobile industry, where Fordism had begun, was among the first to sense the force of this logic. A spokesman for General Motors Corporation acknowledged in 1926 that

> while the industry has been subject to an unusually rapid rate of expansion in the past, the volume has now reached such large proportions that it seems altogether unlikely that tremendous annual increases will continue. The expectation is rather for a healthy growth, in line with the increase in population and wealth of the country, and the development of the export market.

Here was among the first recognitions that even a youthful industry like automobile manufacturing might rapidly grow to "maturity." The carmakers had apparently saturated available domestic markets. The introduction of consumer credit, or "installment buying," pioneered at General Motors in 1919 with the creation of the General Motors Acceptance Corporation, constituted one attempt to stretch those markets still further by relieving buyers of the need to pay full cash for cars at the moment of sale. The explosive growth of advertising, an infant industry before the 1920s, provided further sign of the fear that the limits of "natural" demand were being reached. General Motors alone annually spent some $20 million on advertising in the 1920s in an effort to nurture consumer desires that transcended consumer needs. Together, credit and advertising sustained automobile sales for a time, but without new foreign outlets or a significant redistribution of domestic purchasing power—especially to the impoverished rural half of the country— the boundaries of consumer demand were apparently being approached.

Yet in the pulsing industrial cities, virtually all Americans dramatically improved their standards of living over the course of the post–World War I decade. While farmers' living standards eroded through the 1920s, real wages for industrial workers rose by nearly 25 percent. By 1928 average per capita income among nonagricultural employees had reached four times the average level of farmers' incomes. For urban workers, prosperity was wondrous and real. They had more money than ever before, and they enjoyed an amazing variety of new products on which to spend it: not only automobiles but also canned foods, washing machines, refrigerators, synthetic fabrics, telephones, motion pictures (with sound after 1927), and—along with the automobile the most revolutionary of the new technologies—radios. In the unelectrified countryside, of course, many of these modern conveniences were nowhere to be found.

The authors of *Recent Social Trends* found that thirty-eight million male and ten million female workers produced and distributed this abundance of goods in 1930. Agricultural laborers had constituted the largest category of employment as recently as 1910, but by 1920 the number of workers in manufacturing and mechanical industries eclipsed the number in farming. The workweek of the typical nonfarm employee had shortened since the turn of the century, but the regimen of virtually continuous labor long familiar on the farm had been imported onto the factory floor in the earliest days of industrialization and had only slowly relaxed. Not until 1923 did United States Steel Corporation grudgingly abandon the twelve-hour day, its grinding human damage made worse by the periodic "turnover" of the night and day gangs, when the men were required to stand a continuous twenty-four-hour shift. Most industrial workers in 1930 put in forty-eight hours a week. The two-day "weekend" was not yet a fixture of American life, and paid vacations for workers were almost unknown. "Retirement," too, was still an elusive fantasy for the average American worker, whose days of toil extended virtually to the end of the life cycle.

. . .

The ten million women who worked for wages in 1929 were concentrated in a small handful of occupations including teaching, clerical work, domestic service, and the garment trades. As the service sector of the economy had expanded, so had women's presence in the labor force. Women made up about 18 percent of all workers in 1900 and 22 percent in 1930, when about one of every four women was gainfully employed. The typical woman worker was single and under the age of twenty-five. Once she married, as almost every woman did, typically before the age of twenty-two, she was unlikely to work again for wages, particularly while she had children at home. Only one mother in ten worked outside the household, and the numbers of older women workers, with or without children, were few. Even in this late phase of the industrial era, the traditional division of family labor that the industrial revolution had introduced a century earlier—a husband working for wages outside the home, and a wife working without wages within it—still held powerful sway in American culture.

Yet traditional definitions of the family, and of women's place within it, were weakening. Married women might remain a distinct minority of all women workers, but their numbers were increasing at a rate nearly triple the rate of growth in female employment as a whole. Here, well before the century's midpoint, the dynamic changes in women's employment patterns that would transform the very fabric of family life by the century's end were already visible, however faintly.

Other evidences of changes in women's status were more immediately apparent. The legendary "flapper" made her debut in the postwar decade, signaling with studied theatrical flourishes a new ethos of feminine freedom and sexual parity. The Nineteenth Amendment, enacted just in time for the 1920 presidential election, gave women at least formal political equality. The Equal Rights Amendment, first proposed by Alice Paul of the National Women's Party in 1923, sought to guarantee full social and economic participation to women. An organized movement for the promotion of birth control, founded by Margaret Sanger in 1921 as the American Birth Control League, heralded a growing feminine focus on reproductive control and erotic liberation. Countless women, especially if they were urban, white, and affluent, now used the new technologies of spermicidal jelly and the Mensinga-type diaphragm, both first manufactured in quantity in the United States in the 1920s, to limit the size of their families. This development worried the authors of *Recent Social Trends*, who feared that the old-stock, white, urban middle class would be demographically swamped by the proliferation of the rural and immigrant poor, as well as blacks.

Many of these developments unsettled the guardians of traditional values, but others they found pleasing. The exploitation of child labor, a practice that had outraged critics from Charles Dickens in Victorian England to Jane Addams in early twentieth-century America, had slowly receded as rising wages enabled a single wage-earner to support a family. While almost one in five ten- to-fifteen-year-olds was employed in 1890, fewer than one in twenty was in 1930, though the Supreme Court repeatedly struck down federal efforts to legislate a total ban on child labor.

Fewer children working meant more children in school. The authors of *Recent Social Trends* saw grounds for celebration in their finding that in the 1920s, for the first time, a near majority of high school–age students remained in school—constituting an eightfold increase in high school enrollments since 1900. This, they concluded, was "evidence of the most successful single effort which government in the United States has ever put forth."

. . .

The conservative Republicans who recaptured the Congress in 1918 and the White House in 1920 had small use for any form of government activism. The Republican administrations of the 1920s abandoned or reversed many progressive policies and eviscerated most others. Harding's attorney general, Harry M. Daugherty, extinguished a railroad workers' strike in 1922 by successfully petitioning a federal judge for the most stifling antilabor injunction ever issued. In the same year, Congress reverted to traditional Republican protectionism, as the Fordney-McCumber Tariff raised import duties to the forbidding levels that obtained before the World War. Coolidge appointed to the chairmanship of the Federal Trade Commission in 1925 a man who believed the commission was "an instrument of oppression and disturbance and injury," a statement that only slightly exaggerated conservative opinion about all regulatory agencies. Both the Harding and Coolidge administrations resisted progressive proposals for federal development of hydroelectric generating stations on the Tennessee River, notably at Muscle Shoals, Alabama. And Harding's minions displayed their rapacious regard for the nation's environmental endowment in the Teapot Dome and Elk Hills scandals, when they tried to lease the U.S. Navy's oil reserves in Wyoming and California to private interests with which they were associated.

No one better represented the hoary precepts of laissez-faire that were now reenshrined in policy than the unfortunate Harding's phlegmatic successor, Calvin Coolidge. "Mr. Coolidge was a real conservative, probably the equal of Benjamin Harrison," said Herbert Hoover, who was frequently at odds with his chief. "He was a fundamentalist in religion, in the economic and social order, and in fishing," added Hoover, who had a fly fisherman's disdain for Coolidge's artless reliance on worms. Famously mum, Coolidge occasionally emitted pithy slogans that summarized conservative Republican orthodoxy. "The chief business of the American people is business," he legendarily pronounced in 1925. He declared only somewhat more expansively on another occasion that "the man who builds a factory builds a temple; the man who works there worships there."

Coolidge's epigrams faithfully reflected the principles of frugality and laissez-faire that informed federal policies in the 1920s. The few, frail organs of the positive state spawned by the prewar Progressives withered from inanition. Coolidge personally quashed Herbert Hoover's ambitious plans for federally financed river-control projects, especially in the parched West, because he deemed them too expensive. On similar grounds, he vetoed proposals for farm relief and for accelerated "bonus" payments to veterans of the World War. He resisted all efforts to restructure the $10 billion in Allied war debts owed to the U.S. Treasury. ("They hired the money, didn't they?" he declared in another pellet of policy summary.) Content with "Coolidge prosperity," he napped peacefully and often. He played pranks on the White House servants. He stayed silent. ("If you don't say anything, you won't be called on to repeat it," he reportedly said.) He believed, Hoover later recounted, that nine out of ten troubles "will run into the ditch before they reach you" and could therefore be safely ignored. "The trouble with this philosophy," Hoover commented, "was that when the tenth trouble reached him he was wholly unprepared, and it had by that time acquired such momentum that it spelled disaster. The outstanding instance was the rising boom and orgy of mad speculation which began in 1927, in respect to which he rejected or sidestepped all our anxious urgings and warnings to take action." For his part, Coolidge said of Hoover in 1928: "That man has offered me unsolicited advice for six years, all of it bad."

Fortune smiled on the recumbent Coolidge until he made his somnambulatory exit from the White House in early 1929. (A wit allegedly greeted the news that Coolidge was dead in 1933 by asking: "How can you tell?") "In the domestic field there is tranquility and contentment," he serenely informed the Congress in his last State of the Union message on December 4, 1928. The country should "regard the present with satisfaction and anticipate the future with optimism."

Prosperity lasted long enough for Coolidge to sound plausible in 1928. But deep down in the bowels of the economy, small but fateful contractions had already set in. The agonies of agriculture had long been apparent. Now other sectors began to feel similar pain. Automobile manufacturing slowed its prodigious rate of growth as early as 1925. Residential construction turned down in the same year. A boom in Florida real estate drowned in a devastating hurricane in September 1926. Bank clearings in Miami sank from over a billion dollars in 1925 to $143 million in 1928, a chilling adumbration of the financial clotting that would soon choke the entire banking system. Business inventories began to pile up in 1928, nearly quadrupling in value to some $2 billion by midsummer of 1929.

Most ominous of all was what Hoover bluntly labeled the "orgy of mad speculation" that beset the stock market beginning in 1927. Theory has it that the bond and equity markets reflect and even anticipate the underlying realities of making and marketing goods and services, but by 1928 the American stock markets had slipped the bonds of surly reality. They catapulted into a phantasmagorical realm where the laws of rational economic behavior went unpromulgated and prices had no discernible relation to values. While business activity steadily subsided, stock prices levitated giddily. By the end of 1928, John Kenneth Galbraith later wrote, "the market began to rise, not by slow, steady steps, but by great vaulting leaps." Radio Corporation's stock, symbolic of the promise of new technologies that helped to feed the speculative frenzy, gyrated upward in ten-and twenty-point jumps. By the summer of 1929, Frederick Lewis Allen recorded, even as unsold inventories accumulated in warehouses, stock prices "soared . . . into the blue and cloudless empyrean."

Money to fuel the skyrocketing stock market flowed from countless spigots. It flowed so copiously, according to Galbraith, that "it seemed as though Wall Street were by way of devouring all the money of the entire world." Some of the money flowed directly from the pocketbooks of individual investors, though their resources were generally meager and their numbers surprisingly few. More money poured from big corporations. Their healthy profits in the 1920s endowed them with lavish cash reserves, a good share of which they began to divert from productive investment in plant and machinery to stock market speculation. Still more money came from the banking system. It, too, was flush with funds that found fewer and fewer traditional outlets. By 1929 commercial bankers were in the unusual position of loaning more money for stock market and real estate investments than for commercial ventures. The Federal Reserve Board flooded the banks with more liquidity in 1927 by lowering its rediscount rate to 3.5 percent and undertaking heavy purchases of government securities.

This easy-money policy was due largely to the influence of Benjamin Strong, the stern and influential governor of the New York Federal Reserve Bank. Strong's policy was meant to support the imprudent decision Chancellor of the Exchequer Winston Churchill had made in 1925 to return Britain to the prewar gold standard at the old exchange rate of $4.86 to the pound. That unrealistically high rate crimped British exports, boomed imports, and threatened to drain the Bank of England of its gold reserves. Strong reasoned, not incorrectly, that lower interest rates and cheaper money in America would stanch the hemorrhage of gold from London to New York, thus stabilizing an international financial system that was still precariously recovering from the strains of the World War. The same policies, of course, facilitated vast speculative borrowing in the United States. It was that disastrous consequence that prompted Herbert Hoover's contemptuous description of Strong as "a mental annex to Europe"—a remark that also hinted at Hoover's conception of where the blame for the ensuing depression should be laid.

Significantly, much of the money lent by banks for stock purchases went not directly into stocks but into brokers' call loans. Call loans enabled purchasers to buy stocks on margin, leveraging a cash payment (sometimes as little as 10 percent, but more typically 45 or 50 percent, of the stock's price) with a loan secured by the value of the stock purchased. The lender could theoretically "call" for repayment if the stock price dropped by an amount equal to its collateral value. Though some of the larger brokerage houses shunned the call-loan device, most made profligate use of it. The practice became so popular that brokers at the height of the boom could charge prodigious interest rates on their stock-secured loans to customers. Thanks to the Federal Reserve System's low rediscount rate, member banks could and did borrow federal funds at 3.5 percent and relend them in the call market for 10 percent and more. When the demand for call loans overwhelmed even the abundantly liquid resources of the banking system, corporations stepped in. They accounted for roughly half the call-loan monies in 1929. Standard Oil of New Jersey was then loaning some $69 million a day; Electric Bond and Share, over $100 million.

All of this extravagantly available credit did not in itself cause the boom, just as fuel alone does not make a fire. Combustion in the financial world, no less than in the physical, requires not only fuel but also oxygen and ignition. No observer has succeeded in pinpointing the spark that set off the roaring conflagration that swept and eventually consumed the securities markets in 1928 and 1929. Clearly, however, its sustaining oxygen was a matter not only of recondite market mechanisms and traders' technicalities but also of simple atmospherics—specifically, the mood of speculative expectation that hung feverishly in the air and induced fantasies of effortless wealth that surpassed the dreams of avarice.

Much blame has been leveled at a feckless Federal Reserve System for failing to tighten credit as the speculative fires spread, but while it is arguable that the easy-money policies of 1927 helped to kindle the blaze, the fact is that by late 1928 it had probably burned beyond controlling by orthodox financial measures. The Federal Reserve Board justifiably hesitated to raise its rediscount rate for fear of penalizing nonspeculative business borrowers. When it did impose a 6 percent rediscount rate in the late summer of 1929, call loans were commanding interest of close to 20 percent—a spread that the Fed could not have bridged without catastrophic damage to legitimate borrowers. Similarly, the board had early exhausted its already meager ability to soak up funds through open-market sales of government securities. By the end of 1928, the system's inventory of such securities barely exceeded $200 million—a pittance compared to the nearly $8 billion in call loans then outstanding. By ordinary measures, in fact, credit was tight after 1928. Mere money was not at the root of the evil soon to befall Wall Street; men were—men, and women, whose lust for the fast buck had loosed all restraints of financial prudence or even common sense.

The first rumbles of distress were heard in September 1929, when stock prices broke unexpectedly, though they swiftly recovered. Then on Wednesday, October 23, came an avalanche of liquidation. A huge volume of more than six million shares changed hands, wiping out some $4 billion in paper values. Confusion spread as the telegraphic ticker that flashed transactions to traders across the country fell nearly two hours behind.

In this atmosphere of anxiety and uncertainty the market opened on "Black Thursday," October 24, with a landslide of sell orders. A record-shattering 12,894,650 shares were traded. By noon, losses had reached some $9 billion. The ticker ran four hours late. Yet when it cracked off the day's last transaction at 7:08 in the evening, it appeared that a small recovery in prices had contained the session's losses to about a third of the previous day's.

If Thursday was black, what could be said of the following Tuesday, October 29, when 16,410,000 shares were bought and sold—a record that stood for thirty-nine years? "Black Tuesday" pulled down a cloak of gloom over Wall Street. Traders abandoned all hope that the frightful shake-out could somehow be averted. For two more ghastly weeks stock prices continued to plummet freely down the same celestial voids through which they had recently and so wondrously ascended. The stark truth was now revealed that leverage worked two ways. The multiplication of values that buying on margin made possible in a rising market worked with impartial and fearful symmetry when values were on the way down. Slippage of even a few points in a stock's price compelled margin loans to be called. The borrower then had to put up more cash or accept forced sale of the security. Millions of such sales occurring simultaneously blew the floor out from under many stocks. The mercilessly downward slide went on for three weeks after Black Tuesday. By mid-November some $26 billion, roughly a third of the value of stocks recorded in September, had evaporated.

Much mythology surrounds these dramatic events in the autumn of 1929. Perhaps the most imperishable misconception portrays the Crash as the cause of the Great Depression that persisted through the decade of the 1930s. This scenario owes its durability, no doubt, to its intuitive plausibility and to its convenient fit with the canons of narrative, which require historical accounts to have recognizable beginnings, middles, and ends and to explain events in terms of identifiable origins, development, and resolution. These conventions are comforting; they render understandable and thus tolerable even the most terrifying human experiences. The storyteller and the shaman sometimes feed the same psychic needs.

The disagreeable truth, however, is that the most responsible students of the events of 1929 have been unable to demonstrate an appreciable cause-and-effect linkage between the Crash and the Depression. None assigns to the stock market collapse exclusive responsibility for what followed; most deny it primacy among the many and tangled causes of the decade-long economic slump; some assert that it played virtually no role whatsoever. One authority states flatly and summarily that "no causal relationship between the events of late October 1929 and the Great Depression has ever been shown through the use of empirical evidence."

Certainly contemporaries took this view of the matter in the immediate aftermath of the Crash, as 1929 gave way to 1930. They could scarcely do otherwise, since in point of fact there was as yet no evident depression, "Great" or otherwise, to be explained. Some writers later made much sport of Herbert Hoover for pronouncing on October 25, 1929, that "the fundamental business of the country, that is, production and distribution of commodities, is on a sound and prosperous basis." Yet in retrospect that statement appears reasonably and responsibly accurate. To be sure, a business slowdown was detectable by midsummer 1929, but as yet there was little reason to consider it anything more than a normal dip in the business cycle.

What was clearly abnormal was the explosive near doubling of stock prices since 1928. Hoover had long warned against speculative excesses and could now credibly regard the Crash as the long-predicted correction, one that would at last purge the economic system of unhealthy toxins. In this view he had abundant company, much of it distinguished. John Maynard Keynes opined from England that Black Thursday had been a healthy development that would redirect funds from speculative to productive uses. The respected *New York Times* financial writer Alexander Dana Noyes called the Crash "a reaction from an orgy of reckless speculation" and echoed Hoover's appraisal by adding that "no such excesses had been practiced by trade and industry."

The American Economic Association in December 1929 predicted recovery by June 1930. Early in 1930 the *New York Times* obliquely indicated contemporary assessment of the significance of the Crash when it declared that the most important news story of 1929 had been Admiral Byrd's expedition to the South Pole.

The behavior of the financial markets themselves confirmed these sentiments in the weeks following the Crash. By April 1930 stock prices had regained some 20 percent of their losses of the previous autumn. The *New York Times* average of industrial stocks then stood about where it had at the beginning of 1929, which was approximately double the level of 1926. Unlike previous panics on Wall Street, this one had thus far seen the failure of no major company or bank. As the last moments of 1929 slipped away, the great crash could be plausibly understood as an outsized but probably freakish event. For many individual stockholders, the Crash had assuredly constituted a calamity, but the calamity was not a depression. Not yet.

Another of the fables that has endured from that turbulent autumn—thanks largely to the immense popularity of Frederick Lewis Allen's nostalgic essay of 1931, *Only Yesterday*—portrays legions of slap-happy small stockholders, drunk with the dreams of the delirious decade, suddenly wiped out by the Crash and cast en masse into the gloom of depression. This familiar picture, too, is grossly distorted. Allen probably relied on an estimate by the New York Stock Exchange in 1929 that some twenty million Americans owned stocks. That figure was later shown to be wildly exaggerated. The chief actuary of the Treasury Department calculated that only about three million Americans—less than 2.5 percent of the population—owned securities in 1928, and brokerage firms reported a substantially lower number of 1,548,707 customers in 1929.

So, legend to the contrary, the average American—a description that in this case encompasses at least 97.5 percent of the population—owned no stock in 1929. Even indirect ownership of stock must have been minimal, in this age before the creation of pension funds gave millions of workers a financial stake in capitalism. Accordingly, the Crash in itself had little direct or immediate economic effect on the typical American. The Depression, however, would be another story.

As 1930 opened, the investigators compiling *Recent Social Trends* were just beginning their researches. Taking their presidential mission seriously, they were much interested in that typical American. His age, they determined, was twenty-six. (He would have been a male, this hypothetically abstracted individual, as men continued to outnumber women in the United States until 1950, when the effects of declining immigration, heavily male, and rising maternal survival rates made women for the first time a numerical majority in the American population.) He had been born during the first term of Theodore Roosevelt's presidency, in the midst of the progressive reform ferment. His birth occurred about the time that Japan launched a surprise attack on the Russian fleet at Port Arthur, China—an attack that led to war, Russian defeat, and the first Russian revolution (in 1905) and that heralded Japan's ambition to play the great-power game.

About a million immigrants—virtually none of them Japanese, thanks to a distasteful "gentlemen's agreement" by which the Japanese government grudgingly agreed to limit its export of people—entered the United States in every year of his early childhood. He had reached the age of ten when World War I broke out in 1914, and he had just become a teenager—a term, indeed a concept, not yet in wide use—when President Woodrow Wilson took the United States into the war. By the time the fighting ended, in 1918, he had left the eighth grade and completed his formal schooling. (He would have completed it some three years earlier if he had been black.)

He was too young to have seen battle, but he soon concluded that the whole business of sending American troops to Europe was a useless, colossal blunder and an inexcusable departure from the venerable American doctrine of isolation. The spectacle of wretched Europeans going bankrupt in Germany, knuckling under to a fascist dictator in Italy, welcoming Bolsheviks—Bolsheviks!—in Russia, and then, to top it off, refusing to pay their war debts to the United States confirmed the wisdom of traditional isolationism, so far as he was concerned.

Raised in the country without flush toilets or electric lighting, as the 1920s opened he moved to the city, to an apartment miraculously plumbed and wired. In the streets he encountered the abundant and exotic offspring of all those immigrants who had arrived when he was a baby. Together they entered the new era when their country was transiting, bumpily, without blueprints or forethought, from an agricultural to an industrial economy, from values of simple rural frugality to values of flamboyant urban consumerism, and, however much the idea was resisted, from provincial isolationism to inevitable international involvement.

Jobs were plentiful for the moment and paid good wages. With hard work he was making a little more than a hundred dollars a month. He had been laid off several times in the preceding years but had built a small cushion of savings at his bank to tide him over when unemployment hit again, as he knew it must. The stock market had just crashed, but it seemed to be recovering, and in any case he owned no stocks—for that matter, neither did anybody he knew. Evenings he "radioed." Weekends he went to the movies, better now that they had sound. Sometimes he broke the law and lifted a glass. On his one day a week off, he took a drive in the car that he was buying on the installment plan.

He was living better than his parents had ever dreamed of living. He was young and vigorous; times were good, and the future promised to be still better. He had just cast his first presidential vote, in 1928, for Herbert Hoover, the most competent man in America, maybe in the world. In that same year he married a girl three years younger than he. She gave up her job to have their first baby. They started to think of buying a house, perhaps in one of the new suburbs. Life was just beginning.

And their world was about to come apart.

Discussion Questions

1. Make a list of the different trends in American society that Kennedy relates in this selection—what different groups, issues, and economic trends does he cover to inform the audience about life right before the Great Depression? Discuss how this overview of society in 1929 relates to what you have read about the race, gender, and class conflicts in previous chapters; review, for example, readings on racial issues in Chapter 4 and readings on wealth, poverty, and immigration in Chapter 6. How does Kennedy's selection shed light on the selections you read earlier?

2. Kennedy won the Pulitzer prize for *Freedom from Fear*. Discuss Kennedy's tone, diction, use of examples, use of primary sources, and other writing techniques, and consider how his skill in relating history helped him win the Pulitzer prize. Does his writing make history accessible? Did you like his style? Why or why not?

Writing Suggestions

1. Kennedy writes that Hoover's *Recent Social Trends* profile, which was never published, described the average American as a 26-year-old male. Review the description of this average American at the end of Kennedy's selection, and then write a corresponding version of what you think the average American profile would be today if the government tried to produce another *Recent Social Trends* profile. This is not a fact-based essay but a personal essay that explains your perception of the "average American." If you cannot develop a profile of an average American, explain why you feel there is no average American. If you do have an image of the "average American," remember to delineate his or her age, education level, political affiliations, economic status, and leisure activities.

2. Review your answers to the second discussion question for this selection. Then write an analysis of Kennedy's style, examining tone, diction, use of examples, use of primary sources, and other writing techniques. In your essay, discuss whether or not you found his style accessible and interesting, and give specifics from the text to support your assertions.

Herbert Hoover and the Bonus Expeditionary Force

The role of the media in the career of Herbert Hoover and his presidency greatly impacted the public perception of the man who had once been heralded as a great humanitarian and successful secretary of commerce under President Coolidge. However, after the crash of the stock market in 1929 and the subsequent and continuing financial crisis that evolved into a full-scale Depression, Hoover began to suffer at the hands of the press, whether controlled by Republican or Democratic publishers. While some large national newspapers and magazines supported Hoover throughout his presidency, many eventually turned on him and lambasted his policies openly. In the selections that follow, you can compare coverage about the same event from two points of view: The first article is from staunch Republican Henry Luce's very successful *Time Newsmagazine*, a publication that generally spared Hoover from the harshest criticism. The second article is from William Randolph Hearst's paper, the *San Francisco Examiner*, and you can see from the coverage of the same incident that Hearst was fiercely and openly derisive of President Hoover.

The incident covered by the *Time Newsmagazine* and the *San Francisco Examiner* is the expulsion of thousands of World War I veterans and their families who had marched on Washington, D.C. in April of 1932, hoping to pressure Congress into paying them a promised and long-overdue bonus for their service in the Armed Forces. Out of work, hungry, and often homeless, the veterans formed the Bonus Expeditionary Force and set up camp along the Anacostia River near the Capitol. Hoover refused to meet with the veterans and was convinced that their ranks were heavily infiltrated by criminals and communists. As time passed the fear of crime and rioting began to grow, and when D.C. police were involved in a brick-throwing incident that injured six officers, the police asked Hoover for help. Hoover ordered cavalry troops to clear the entire area of encampments; the troops not only used tanks and tear gas to scatter the Bonus Expeditionary Force, but also used bayonets to drive the marchers out of Washington, D.C. While most members of the press treated Hoover mildly in the days immediately following this incident and even supported his rout of the veterans, this incident nonetheless eventually marked a decline in Hoover's support from both the press and the public, ending in his loss to Roosevelt in the upcoming election.

Time / The Weekly Newsmagazine / August 8, 1932

Heroes: Battle of Washington

When War came in 1917 William Hushka, 22-year-old Lithuanian, sold his St. Louis butcher shop, gave the proceeds to his wife, joined the Army. He was sent to Camp Funston, Kan. where he was naturalized. Honorably discharged in 1919, he drifted to Chicago, worked as a butcher, seemed unable to hold a steady job. His wife divorced him, kept their small daughter. Long jobless, in June he joined a band of veterans marching to Washington to fuse with the Bonus Expeditionary Force. "I might as well starve there as here," he told his brother. At the capital he was billeted in a Government-owned building on Pennsylvania Avenue. One of thousands, he took part in the demonstration at the Capitol the day Congress adjourned without voting immediate cashing of the Bonus.

Last week William Hushka's Bonus for $528 suddenly became payable in full when a police bullet drilled him dead in the worst public disorder the capital has known in years.

Prelude to Washington's bloody battle was a third march toward the White House by some 200 Reds, led by Communist John Pace, Michigan contractor. It was a routine performance which the police efficiently squelched with much pate-thwacking and the nine arrests. One veteran climbed a tree, kept shouting "We want our Bonus!" until police dragged him down, gagged him. This radical demonstration, outlawed by the regular B. E. F., was important only in that it gave Administration officials the idea of blaming Communists for all that followed.

More serious trouble was presented by the Treasury's attempt to repossess Government property on the south side of Pennsylvania Avenue, three blocks west of the Capitol. Wholesale warehouses, a cheap hotel, automobile showrooms, a Chinese restaurant and an undertaking shop occupied the row of old ugly brick buildings on this site. The U. S. had bought up the land as part of its plan to beautify the Federal City (*Time*, May 6, 1929). The plot was to be converted into a park. Wreckers had knocked the walls out of the buildings when the B. E. F. began to arrive last May. Brigadier General Pelham Glassford, Washington's long-legged, kindly police chief, arranged to halt demolition, have veterans quartered in the skeletonized buildings. With Congress gone and the Bonus fight over, the Treasury sought to evict the veterans and start work again. Four times 200-odd veterans were ordered out. Four times they refused to budge.

One morning last week General Glassford finally persuaded Walter W. Waters, the B. E. F.'s curly-headed commander, to evacuate his men on the promise of new quarters elsewhere. Treasury agents arrived at 10 A.M. to clear the buildings. Most of the veterans refused to leave. Police helped the Federal men do their job. Hundreds of veterans swelled to thousands as men flocked from other B. E. F. camps to the scene to watch the eviction. By noon the buildings had been practically cleared when a trio of veterans carrying a U. S. flag tried to march back in. Police blocked them. Somebody tossed a brick. "There's a fight!" went up the cry. More bricks flew.

"Give the cops hell!" a veteran shouted. His massed companions pressed in upon the police, now flailing with their clubs. The fighting spread with quick contagion. One policeman had his head bashed in. Veterans trampled him. Blood streamed down others' faces. Veterans swung scrap iron, hunks of concrete, old boards. General Glassford rushed into the mêlée, was knocked flat by a brick. Before he could get up, a veteran snatched off his gold police badge. A riot call brought 800 extra police to battle several thousand of the B. E. F.

"Be peaceful, men! Be calm!" shouted General Glassford. "Let's not throw any more bricks. They're mighty hard and hurt. You've probably killed one of my best officers."

"Hell, that's nothing," a veteran flung back. "Lots of us were killed in France."

Meanwhile hot-headed veterans had seeped back into their old quarters to tussle with police amid the rubble. Officers George Shinault and Miles Zamanezck were cornered on the second floor. "Let's get 'em!" someone shouted. The two policemen pulled their revolvers. A half dozen shots banged out. William Hushka keeled over with a bullet in his heart (1:25 P.M.). Two other veterans were wounded. One of them, Eric Carlson, 38, of Oakland, Cal., died later.

The street fighting gradually subsided. A legless veteran inside the Government building loudly challenged the police to remove him. He was ignored. General Glassford withdrew his forces. The B. E. F. cooled off, recovered its head. Commander Waters, who had kept out of the fray, nervously declared: "The men got out of control. There's nothing I can do."

But there was something the three District of Columbia Commissioners governing the city could do and they did it. President Hoover was lunching when the Commissioners called to ask him for Federal troops. "Tell them to put their request in writing," said the President. They wrote:

"A serious riot occurred. . . . This area contains thousands of brickbats and these were used by the rioters in their attack upon the police. . . . It will be impossible to maintain law & order except by the free use of firearms which will make the situation a dangerous one. The presence of Federal troops will result in far less violence and bloodshed."

Without declaring martial law (he did not have to because Washington is Federal territory), President Hoover ordered Secretary of War Hurley to call out the Army from Fort Myer in nearby Virginia. Secretary Hurley passed the command along to handsome, well-tailored General Douglas MacArthur, Chief of Staff, in the following crisp dispatch (2:55 P.M.):

"You will have United States troops proceed immediately to the scene of the disorder. Surround the affected area and clear it without delay. . . . Any women and children should be accorded every consideration and kindness. Use all humanity consistent with the execution of this order."

Six minutes later cavalry and infantry, to the number of 1,000 men began moving into Washington for an encounter with the B. E. F. for which the War Department had long been preparing. In their wake came five small tanks, a fleet of trucks. Bayonets glittered in the sun, equipment clanked over the pavement as the force marched slowly up Pennsylvania Avenue. Reaching the "affected area" (4.45 P.M.) troopers rode straight into the hooting, booing ranks of the B. E. F. Veterans scrambled out of the way of swinging sabres, trampling hoofs. Steel-helmeted infantrymen with drawn revolvers advanced 20 abreast. Behind them came others with rifles lowered, bayonets prodding.

Suddenly tear gas bombs began to pop on the streets. The soldiers put on their masks, pushed slowly on while the heavy grey fumes cut great gaps in the retreating throng of veterans. Citizen spectators tangled with the soldiers, were ordered to "get the hell out of the way." The Government buildings were methodically gassed. A huge Negro sat in a crotch of a tree, waving a U. S. flag and sonorously chanting: "God that gave us this h'yar country, h'ep us now."

The unarmed B. E. F. did not give the troopers a real fight. They were too stunned and surprised that men wearing their old uniform should be turned against them. Here & there veterans would toss back gas bombs with half-forgotten skill, kick the troopers' horses,throw a few bricks, swear bitter oaths at the impassive regulars, most of them youngsters. But resistance was wholly unorganized.

General MacArthur directed the military operation, tears streaming down his cheeks, not from emotion but from the fumes of the bombs. When his cavalry rode down a group of veterans with a U. S. flag, a spectator sang out: "The American flag means nothing to me after this." General MacArthur snapped: "Put that man under arrest if he opens his mouth again."

The rout of the B. E. F. from Pennsylvania Avenue broke its back. But the military was not yet through. It "gassed" small scattered camps in the vicinity of the Capitol, shoved out their occupants, left smoking ruins behind. By 9 P.M. the troopers had advanced to the Anacostia bridge, beyond which on the mudflats lay Bonus City, the B. E. F.'s main encampment. The camp commander rushed out waving a white shirt for a truce, asked for time to evacuate the several hundred women and children. He got an hour's grace.

As the infantry moved into Bonus City (10:14 P.M.) gassing each wretched shack and shanty, veterans by the thousands trudged off into the night. Some carried their belongings wrapped in bundles on their backs. One drunk went lurching away bearing only a large oil lamp. A few sang old War songs. Women carried babies in their arms. Huts and lean-tos were set afire, partly by the departing veterans, partly by the soldiers. By midnight Bonus City, once the home of 10,000 jobless hungry men & women, was a field of roaring bonfires. President Hoover could see its fiery glow on the Eastern sky from his

White House window. At dawn the place was a charred & blackened ruin. The B. E. F. was gone. Not a shot had been fired by the victorious Army.

The Day's Toll: Dead, 2; injured, 55; arrested, 135, including Charles P. Ruby, D. S. C., first to greet the President at the New Year's day reception at the White House in 1931 (*Time*, Jan. 12, 1931).

In France Joe Angelo of Camden, N. J. was decorated for saving the life of Major George O. Patton. At Anacostia Major Patton headed the cavalry that drove Joe Angelo out of his B. E. F. quarters.

"Challenge Met." During the two months the B. E. F. was in Washington President Hoover silently ignored them. But after he had summoned troops, he also summoned the Press and explained:

"Congress made provision for the return home of the so-called Bonus marchers. . . . Some 5,000 took advantage of the arrangement. . . . An examination of a large number of names discloses the fact that a considerable part of those remaining are not veterans. . . . Many are Communists and persons with criminal records."

Next day, when the B. E. F. had left, the President more fully expressed his indignation. Said he: "A challenge to the authority of the Untied States Government has been met, swiftly and firmly. . . . Government cannot be coerced by mob rule. . . . It is my sincere hope that those agitators who inspired yesterday's attack upon Federal authority may be brought speedily to trial. . . . There can be no safe harbor in the U. S. for violence. . . . Order and civil tranquility are the first requisites in the great task of economic reconstruction."

General MacArthur observed that the B. E. F. "was a bad looking mob animated by the essence of revolution." A week's delay by the President, he thought "would have threatened the institution of our Government." According to the General, not one man out of ten in the B. E. F. was a "real veteran."

"Damned Lie!" Commander Waters raged against President Hoover's assertion that the B. E. F. was Red and criminal. "A damned lie!" he shouted. "Every man is a veteran. We examined the discharge papers of everyone."

Communists, flattered at drawing White House fire, gladly took all credit for the Washington disturbance. Most impartial observers, however, doubted if the rioting could be really attributed to them. John Pace was in jail at the time and his handful of Red followers were not identified as actively participating in the fracas.

Gertrude Mann, two months, involuntary B. E. F. camp follower, died of malnutrition in Washington's Gallinger Hospital. In the same hospital lay Bernard Myers, 11 weeks, affected by tear gas.

The government buried Veteran William Hushka in Arlington National Cemetery with full military honors.

On to Johnstown. While the Army "mopped up" the Capital of all B. E. F. stragglers, Virginia blocked the veterans on the South. Maryland supplied trucks to carry thousands of them to the Pennsylvania line. The Red Cross handled the women & children. Red-headed Mayor Eddie McCloskey of

Johnstown, Pa., onetime pants-presser and prizefighter, invited B. E. F. leaders to his city to reorganize their force. Johnstown citizens protested loudly when veterans began to straggle in and bivouac in a fly-ridden amusement park outside town, where another B. E. F. baby was born.

"Khaki Shirts." Commander Waters, in Washington, announced the B. E. F. would become the nucleus of a political organization to be known as the "Khaki Shirts," open to all who want "to clean out the high places in government." "Loyal Americanism" was heavily accented in his declaration. For $1 he purchased 25 wooded acres in Maryland from a Mrs. Maude Edgell, proprietor of a nursing home, who felt "very bitter" about the Battle of Washington. Major L. J. H. Herwig, U. S. A., retired, of Washington, offered them his 400-acre Virginia farm. On these plots Commander Waters proposed to establish "Khaki Shirts" colonies, warned: "If they try to burn us out again, damn 'em we'll kill 'em." Brigadier General Smedley Darlington Butler, retired, flirted with the idea of consolidating the "Khaki Shirts."

Comment. Most of the nation's Press approved the manner in which the President had dealt with its B. E. F. Public blame, if any, was placed less on members of the B. E. F. than upon those Representatives & Senators who by agitating full and immediate Bonus payments had lured veterans to Washington and kept them there with false hopes and promises.

When the troops were withdrawn from Washington, Secretary Hurley exulted: "It was a great victory. . . . Mac [General MacArthur] did a great job. He is the man of the hour. (*A thoughtful pause.*) But I must not make any heroes just now."

Examiner / The Dailies / Saturday, July 30, 1932

Troops again Attack Vets with Gas; Thousands of Hungry Men, Women, and Children Flee before Fixed Bayonets

Maryland, Virginia Police Harass Refugees / Camps Sacked / Homeless Hordes' Food Supplies Burned

By Fraser Edwards / Staff Correspondent Universal Service.

WASHINGTON, July 29—A beaten and bewildered "army without a country," which still marched under the Stars and Stripes, was on the move today, but knew not where to go.

Thousands of bedraggled, hungry, sleepless men, women and children of the bonus army were driven from the nation's capital by the police and soldiers with fixed bayonets, only to be harassed by the police and sheriffs of Maryland and Virginia, the adjoining States.

Until saner orders were issued, the Maryland State police stationed along the District of Columbia line refused to allow the weary veterans and their families to enter the State. After hundreds had run the gauntlet, the police began assisting them across the State.

Police Blockade

Despite a denial from Governor Pollard of Virginia, that he had issued orders to bar the veterans from the Old Dominion, the State police mobilized a strong force at Alexandria, across the Potomac River from Washington, to block those who attempted to enter.

As a consequence, these unwelcome wanderers were shunted from one spot to another for hours before the Federal, district and State authorities formed any plan to rid the city of the veterans who were driven from their temporary homes by tear gas and bayonets.

Late this afternoon, the War Department took steps to remedy the hopeless situation. Arrangements were made with the Red Cross to furnish transportation and subsistence for veterans with families to their homes, the cost to be ultimately deducted from the men's adjusted service certificates.

Assistance Asked

The War Department also sent telegrams to the adjutant generals of all States, sheriffs and other responsible authorities requesting them to assist the veterans home in the same way they assisted them to reach Washington.

Through McConnellsburg, Pa., and nearby towns, the main body of the Bonus Expeditionary Force, retreating to a new base of operations, straggled today and tonight.

They were footsore and weary. They were not downhearted. They had obtained food at several Maryland towns and villages along the road from Washington. They halted frequently to rest. Most of them carried small packs. Some had heavy bedding. A few lugged suitcases. One pushed a wheelbarrow.

The police in the Maryland towns and the farmers along the highway were not hostile. Officials appeared inclined to expedite the migration of the veterans. Feeding the marchers and treating them civilly was viewed as the best means of having them move along to their new encampment at Johnstown.

"Well, boys, guess you had a tough time down in Washington," was the most familiar greeting.

Most of the veterans still had red eyes from the tear gas bombing in Washington yesterday.

Meanwhile, the Army—cavalry, infantry and tanks—retracted the battle line of yesterday and completed the sack of the bonus city of shacks with torch and tear gas, routing the last of the defenseless straggles from the various camps.

Starting with Camp Marks, the soldiers razed to ashes the few remaining shanties on the Anacostia Flats, which once "housed" 12,000 bonus seekers. Leaving the smoke curling from the smouldering hovels, the troops moved on to a billet behind the Congressional Library, but found it deserted.

Tear-gas was hurled into a crowd made up largely of Government employees returning to their homes from work at Third and Maryland avenue, Northwest, when a few lingering veterans jeered the soldiers and called them "Hoover rats." All shacks in that area were burned.

The deserted shacks at Thirteenth and B, C and D streets, Southwest, which had been occupied by the so-called Communists, next went up in flames. War-equipped soldiers with steel-helmets and bayonets fixed, were left to guard all camps.

The concentration of 3,500 troops at Fort Myer continued despite the fact that no emergency exists any longer. Both bridges over the Anacostia River to Washington, also remained under guard of the troops. The homeless hordes that tried to pass through the city proper to take the road were driven to the east.

The only camp passed up by the Army was Camp Bartlett, near the District line and situated on private property. No evacuation order from the police was needed there, for some 2,000 veterans and their families left voluntarily. They apparently decided to brave the open road rather than face the bayonets.

The most pitiful sight among the bonus marchers was the "lost battalion of women and children," this hapless group of eighty-five children, some babies in arms, and fifty-seven mothers, were driven out of the old Department of Agriculture Building this morning and their meager effects dumped on the sidewalks. The women sat for hours on bundles and tried to comfort crying, hungry children, while the men looked on disconsolately.

Otto Green of Nashville, Tenn., leader of the "lost battalion," said the soldiers burned their food supplies last night and most of the children went supperless to bed and were without food until late in the day. Some were taken in by families in the neighborhood, while others who became ill were taken to Gallinger Hospital. Others left town.

Green, who had his ear slashed by a cavalryman's sabre in the charge at Third and Pennsylvania avenue yesterday, was bitter about the treatment of the women and children. He said:

"Sherman was no more ruthless in his march through Georgia than the soldiers were to us."

When the remnants of the radical band, under John Pace of Detroit, tried to stage a meeting this afternoon, the police rounded up forty-three and held them under a charge of "investigation."

Police furnished trucks to escort many of the veterans leaving the city. This was done in the case of 200 veterans driven back from Virginia by deputy sheriffs. They were taken to Rockville, Md., ten miles from the District, where they evaded the Maryland police and began their trek westward. Later the Maryland authorities furnished trucks to speed the veterans across the state.

Discussion Questions

1. Split discussion groups into two parts, with each group looking at one of the two newspaper accounts in this selection. Each group can answer some of the following questions:

    Does the article give both sides of the story? What kinds of primary sources does the article include?

    What is the article's attitude toward the Federal government?

    Are President Hoover and General MacArthur glorified or cast as villains?

    How does the article represent the likelihood of communist involvement in the conflict?

    What is the dominant tone of the article?

    When you come back together as a large group, discuss the following questions:

    What kinds of details are added to or omitted from each article's story of the Bonus Expeditionary Force?

    How do the headlines, large and small, cast different angles on the story?

    At the end of each article, how does the reader feel about the government? How does the reader feel about the Bonus Expeditionary Force?

    How would a reader react differently to the story, depending on which article he or she had read?

2. What variety of conflicts are represented in both newspaper articles? How do these conflicts reflect the period of history both before and during the veterans' march on Washington? What elements of race are reflected in the articles? How are women and children represented in the two articles? What elements of class conflict appear in these articles? What kind of picture of life in 1932 can you piece together from the two articles?

Writing Suggestions

1. Consider your answers to the first discussion question for this selection, and then write a comparison essay analyzing the reporting in the two newspaper articles about Herbert Hoover and the Bonus Expeditionary Force, addressing the central question: How would a reader react differently to the story of Hoover and the Bonus Expeditionary Force, depending on which article he or she had read? You will want to answer some of the following questions in developing support for your thesis:

    What is the dominant tone of each article?

    What kinds of details are added to or omitted from each article's story of the Bonus Expeditionary Force?

    How does each article portray General MacArthur and Herbert Hoover?

What is each article's attitude toward the Federal government?

How does each article represent the likelihood of communist involvement in the conflict?

How do the headlines, large and small, cast different angles on the story?

At the end of each article, how does the reader feel about the government and about the Bonus Expeditionary Force?

2. Research an important current news story in at least three different national newspapers. For example, you might look at the same story in the *New York Times*, the *Wall Street Journal*, and the *Los Angeles Times*, or pick any combination of three large city newspapers across the country. Look at the questions you answered in the first discussion question about the two different reports of the Bonus Expeditionary Force. Then apply the same fine reading to the three newspaper articles you have selected, and write an analysis of the different reporting strategies and techniques, detailing the ways in which different reporting informs you as a reader. How does each article impact your knowledge and ideas about the subject? What does each article add to the other? How well-informed would you have been if you had only read one of the articles? Which aspects appear in all three articles? Which aspects of the story have been left out? Use specific quotes from the articles, and use details to back up your assertions.

Pearl Harbor Address

FRANKLIN DELANO ROOSEVELT

Franklin Delano Roosevelt (1882–1945), president of the United States from 1933 to 1945, was born in 1882 in Hyde Park, New York. As a member of an affluent family, he attended Harvard University and the Columbia University School of Law. He served under President Wilson as Assistant Secretary of the Navy, and was nominated for vice-president in 1920. In 1921 Roosevelt was stricken with polio, but he refused to let the disease stop his political career. He used a wheelchair that he tried to keep hidden from view in pictures printed in the media. He became governor of New York in 1928, and in 1932 in the midst of the Depression he defeated Herbert Hoover by a wide margin to become president. He served four terms as president, during which time, as part of the New Deal, he instituted various government programs to overcome the Depression. Roosevelt led America into World War II after the bombing of Pearl Harbor, but he did not live to see the end of the war—he died in 1945, just a few months before VE Day. In the selection below, Roosevelt addresses Congress and asks them to declare war on Japan after the Pearl Harbor bombing, the day that would "live in infamy."

(December 8, 1941)

To the Congress of the United States:

Yesterday, Dec. 7, 1941—a date which will live in infamy—the United States of America was suddenly and deliberately attacked by naval and air forces of the Empire of Japan.

The United States was at peace with that nation and, at the solicitation of Japan, was still in conversation with the government and its emperor looking toward the maintenance of peace in the Pacific.

Indeed, one hour after Japanese air squadrons had commenced bombing in Oahu, the Japanese ambassador to the United States and his colleagues delivered to the Secretary of State a formal reply to a recent American message. While this reply stated that it seemed useless to continue the existing diplomatic negotiations, it contained no threat or hint of war or armed attack.

It will be recorded that the distance of Hawaii from Japan makes it obvious that the attack was deliberately planned many days or even weeks ago. During the intervening time, the Japanese government has deliberately sought to deceive the United States by false statements and expressions of hope for continued peace.

The attack yesterday on the Hawaiian islands has caused severe damage to American naval and military forces. Very many American lives have been lost. In addition, American ships have been reported torpedoed on the high seas between San Francisco and Honolulu.

Yesterday, the Japanese government also launched an attack against Malaya.

Last night, Japanese forces attacked Hong Kong.

Last night, Japanese forces attacked Guam.

Last night, Japanese forces attacked the Philippine Islands.

Last night, the Japanese attacked Wake Island.

This morning, the Japanese attacked Midway Island.

Japan has, therefore, undertaken a surprise offensive extending throughout the Pacific area. The facts of yesterday speak for themselves. The people of the United States have already formed their opinions and well understand the implications to the very life and safety of our nation.

As commander in chief of the Army and Navy, I have directed that all measures be taken for our defense.

Always will we remember the character of the onslaught against us.

No matter how long it may take us to overcome this premeditated invasion, the American people in their righteous might will win through to absolute victory.

I believe I interpret the will of the Congress and of the people when I assert that we will not only defend ourselves to the uttermost, but will make very certain that this form of treachery shall never endanger us again.

Hostilities exist. There is no blinking at the fact that our people, our territory and our interests are in grave danger.

With confidence in our armed forces—with the unbounding determination of our people—we will gain the inevitable triumph—so help us God.

I ask that the Congress declare that since the unprovoked and dastardly attack by Japan on Sunday, Dec. 7, a state of war has existed between the United States and the Japanese empire.

Discussion Questions

1. How does Roosevelt's diction stress the element of surprise in the Japanese attack on Pearl Harbor? List the words that he uses to reinforce the idea of a surprise attack. Why would Roosevelt want to emphasize this aspect in his declaration of war on Japan?

2. Analyze the organization of the speech—how does Roosevelt use sentence structure, repetition, and diction to reach out to his audience, clarify the goals of the United States, and maintain a sense of authority?

Writing Suggestions

1. Calling on your responses to the discussion questions for this selection, compare President Roosevelt's declaration of war on the Empire of Japan with President Wilson's address to Congress calling for America's entrance into World War I. Compare the structure of both speeches, and the tone, diction, imagery, and pattern of explanation for the declaration of war. Which elements of the speeches are similar, and which are different? Which did you find more effective, and why?

2. The 2001 release of the movie *Pearl Harbor*, starring Ben Affleck, set off a wave of controversy concerning the depiction of the Japanese in the film. Some Asian-American groups felt that the movie was unfair in portraying the Japanese as overly militaristic and evil, and many officials were afraid that the release of the movie would set off a new round of hate crimes against Japanese Americans. Rent the movie, and then write a movie review answering the following questions: Did *Pearl Harbor* portray the Japanese unfairly? Did the movie do justice to the historical importance of the attack? Or was it, as some critics claimed, too much of a love story? Use specific details and incidents from the movie to back up your assertions.

How to Tell Your Friends from the Japs

TIME MAGAZINE

After the bombing of Pearl Harbor, both the media and the U.S. government stressed the importance of knowing the difference between Japanese and Chinese people. The article below from *Time Magazine,* December 22, 1941, attempts to describe "a few rules of thumb—not always reliable" for telling "your friends from the Japs." Chinese-Americans were anxious to differentiate themselves from Japanese-Americans, and often wore buttons or put up signs saying "I am not a Jap!" In its 75th anniversary issue, *Time* addressed the racist overtones of the piece, under the title "Regrets, We Have a Few." *Time* went on to say: "As with most publications, *Time's* approach to questions of ethnicity and gender wasn't always what it should have been."

. . . There is no infallible way of telling [the Chinese and the Japanese] apart, because the same racial strains are mixed in both. Even an anthropologist, with calipers and plenty of time to measure heads, noses, shoulders, hips, is sometimes stumped. A few rules of thumb—not always reliable:

- Some Chinese are tall (average: 5 ft. 5 in.). Virtually all Japanese are short (average: 5 ft. 2 1/2 in.).
- Japanese are likely to be stockier and broader-hipped than short Chinese.
- Japanese—except for wrestlers—are seldom fat; they often dry up and grow lean as they age. The Chinese often put on weight, particularly if they are prosperous (in China, with its frequent famines, being fat is esteemed as a sign of being a solid citizen).
- Chinese, not as hairy as Japanese, seldom grown an impressive mustache.
- Most Chinese avoid horn-rimmed spectacles.
- Although both have the typical epicanthic fold of the upper eyelid (which makes them look almond-eyed), Japanese eyes are usually set closer together.
- Those who know them best often rely on facial expression to tell them apart: the Chinese expression is likely to be more placid, kindly, open; the Japanese more positive, dogmatic, arrogant.

In Washington, last week, Correspondent Joseph Chiang made things much easier by pinning on his lapel a large badge reading "Chinese Reporter—NOT *Japanese*—Please."

- Some aristocratic Japanese have thin, aquiline noses, narrow faces and, except for their eyes, look like Caucasians.
- Japanese are hesitant, nervous in conversation, laugh loudly at the wrong time.
- Japanese walk stiffly erect, hard-heeled. Chinese, more relaxed, have an easy gait, sometimes shuffle.

Discussion Questions

1. Most modern audiences would find this comparison of Japanese and Chinese people absurd and offensive. However, after the bombing of Pearl Harbor, the political climate in the United States was uniquely anti-Japanese. Discuss the reasons *Time Magazine* would have run such a piece, and try to consider the political times, the date of publication, the audience, and the reasoning behind this article. What was the motivation for trying to teach the audience to differentiate between Chinese and Japanese? How do you think the reading public of 1941 might have responded to this article? What is the implied argument in this article?

2. Review the selections in Chapter 5 about the treatment of the Chinese in America. Then discuss some of the ironies found in the description of the Chinese in this 1941 article, compared to the descriptions of the Chinese by politicians in the 1880s in the Gyory article, for example. List the descriptions offered by spokesmen from the two eras, and discuss the way the changes in political and economic affairs impacted the representation of the Chinese.

Writing Suggestions

1. Write an essay analyzing the persuasive strategies of this article. Define the implied argument of the piece, and then look at the supposed "logic" and the supposed "rational" definitions this article claims to make. What kinds of appeals to emotion does it make? What kinds of scientific claims does it use? Does the article's author make any apology for the generalizations he or she draws? Quote from the article and make use of specifics in your analysis.

2. Write a research paper about American anti-Japanese propaganda during World War II. You can research posters, documentaries, editorials, and government pamphlets for this paper. You can look on the Web sites listed at the end of this chapter for on-line posters from World War II, and you can also find many good books about the subject in your college libraries. A good source to start with is Peter Paret's book on World War II posters, *Powers of Persuasion.* For your paper, consider some of the following research questions:

   How were the Japanese soldiers and leaders portrayed on posters?

   What kinds of animals were used to symbolize the Japanese?

   What character traits did U.S. propaganda-makers emphasize in portraying the Japanese?

   What appeals to emotion did the propaganda-makers use to portray the Japanese as the enemy?

The Story of Pacific Coast Japanese Evacuation

KARL R. BENDETSEN

Colonel Karl R. Bendetsen (1908–1989) attended Stanford University, where he received both a B.A. and a law degree. He worked as a lawyer both before and after World War II and was an officer of Field Artillery of the U.S. Army, also serving as Special Representative of the Secretary of War to General Douglas MacArthur in the Philippines. Bendetsen was assigned to the Western Defense Command and Fourth Army as Assistant Chief of Staff and Commanding Officer of the Wartime Civil Control Administration, which put him in charge of the evacuation and relocation of the persons of Japanese ancestry on the Pacific Coast. On May 20, 1942, Bendetsen gave a speech entitled "The Story of Pacific Coast Japanese Evacuation" to the Commonwealth Club of San Francisco. In the following excerpt from that speech, Bendetsen explains his views on the dangers of a "fifth-column" and explains why he believed it was so necessary to remove "all persons of Japanese ancestry from the coastal frontier."

The problem of evacuation of all persons of Japanese ancestry from the Pacific coastal frontier is one that interests the people of the United States. Especially is it one that interests members of the Commonwealth Club, as well as all persons resident in this coastal area.

First, I should like to tell you something of the reasoning behind the evacuation of all persons of Japanese ancestry from this coastal frontier.

There are three principal dangers—hence, three principal problems bearing upon internal security in time of war. These problems, and the methods used to combat them, are described, ordinarily, in these terms: Anti-sabotage, counter-espionage and counter-fifth column. By the latter is meant action in concert by well-organized groups under raid or invasion conditions.

The relationship of the Japanese population to these dangers, following the outbreak of war, became a problem peculiar to the West Coast. The Japanese community presented a group with a high potential for action against the national interest—I will comment more fully on this in a moment. To approach the problem as one involving only alien enemies would be to suggest, first, that the danger, if any, would emanate from alien Japanese alone, a group of persons whose average age is well above sixty years. Also, it would be to suggest that every alien Japanese is a potential saboteur or espionage agent; and, perforce, to suggest the converse.

By design, or by accident, substantial numbers of the Japanese coastal frontier communities were deployed through very sensitive and very vital areas.

Now, if you and I had settled in Japan, raised our families there and if our children and grandchildren were raised there, it is most improbable that during a period of war between Japan and the United States, if we were not interned, that we would commit any overt acts of sabotage acting individually. Doubtless, in the main, and irrespective of our inner emotions, you and I would be law abiding.

But when the final test of loyalty came, if United States forces were engaged in launching an attack on Japan, I believe it is extremely doubtful whether we could withstand the ties of race and the affinity for the land of our forebears, and stand with the Japanese against United States forces.

To withstand such pressure seems too much to expect of any national group, almost wholly unassimilated and which has preserved in large measure to itself, its customs and traditions—a group characterized by strong filial piety.

It is doubtless true that many persons of Japanese ancestry are loyal to the United States. It is also true that many are not loyal. We know this. Contrary to other national or racial groups, the behavior of Japanese has been such that in not one single instance has any Japanese reported disloyalty on the part of another specific individual of the same race.

There has been no substantial evidence of manifestation of nationalistic fervor exhibited by any Japanese group in the United States since the outbreak of the war. Even on the Emperor's birthday there was no visible evidence that the day was remembered in evacuee centers.

This attitude—well illustrated, I think, by the fact that there has not been a single instance when any Japanese has reported disloyalty on the part of another of the same race—may be, and can be a most ominous thing. Chasing specters of fear is merely exhausting. It accomplishes nothing. The Army least of all will expend its energies in that direction. But it must be realistic—the nation must be realistic. The real contingencies must be taken into account. The contingency that under raid or invasion conditions there might be widespread action in concert—well-regulated, well-disciplined and controlled—a fifth column, is a real one. As such, it presented a threat to the national security and therefore a problem which required solution.

. . .

The evacuation program itself consisted of three interim steps and a final solution.

The first step was designation of military areas from which the Japanese were to be excluded and the voluntary migration which followed. Encouragement was given to the voluntary migration from Military Areas and an effort was made on the part of some groups of Japanese to locate in other states. Altogether about 6000 Japanese moved inland, but voluntary migration, on the whole, proved to be impractical because it was not accepted. The Army had in mind from the beginning that the major extent of the movement of the Japanese from military areas would have to be undertaken as a completely organized, controlled and supervised operation. The Army's job, however, called for the evacuation of 113,000 people and this involved development of means to assist evacuees in the disposition of homes and businesses, farms and crops, equipment and property and innumerable problems of personal adjustment as well as finding and preparing temporary locations for the evacuees.

The second interim step was a plan for immediate evacuation if developments required. The Army needed time to prepare a permanent program and the situation called for an emergency plan. It was impossible, of course, at this time for the Army to reveal the fact that it was prepared to affect a complete evacuation, practically overnight, in the event of an emergency. Plans were made to move the 113,000 Japanese into already established Army cantonments in a Mass Movement which could have been undertaken immediately. Prepared in this way against the possibility of fifth column activity, or for any outbreaks of anti-Japanese feeling, the Army continued with its plans for a permanent program.

The third interim step was the selection and preparation of eighteen temporary Assembly Centers to which the Japanese could be quickly removed for later transfer to permanent locations. The decision to remove the Japanese to temporary Assembly Centers was based upon several important considerations. In the first place, the use of fairgrounds, race tracks and other public properties which provided installations of utilities as well as convenient locations, contributed to greater speed in the evacuation program. The use of these properties also made it easier to protect the evacuees' welfare and property. Moreover, evacuation through these centers could be accomplished with the use of a minimum number of soldiers.

The final step in the program is the settlement of evacuees in the permanent centers operated by the War Relocation Authority. This is the phase of the program that has taken more time than was available considering the necessity for early evacuation. It was primarily to prepare for this concluding phase of the evacuation program that the methods described were employed in the preliminary or interim steps.

. . .

In addition to the military, the Wartime Civil Control Administration includes representatives of all Federal departments and civilian agencies involved in the evacuation job.

The Federal Reserve Bank of San Francisco, has assisted Japanese in the disposition of their property including leases, transfers, merchandise, automobiles and household furnishings.

The Department of Agriculture through the Farm Security Administration has undertaken a program of resettlement of evacuated lands and the protection of growing crops.

The Federal Security Agencies, through the United States Employment Service, the Social Security Board, and the United States Public Health Service, have given important assistance at several stages of the evacuation centers.

The Department of Justice has had difficult legal problems and its Federal Bureau of Investigation has made an important contribution.

The Works Progress Administration has provided civilian personnel to handle under army direction the management and operation of the evacuation centers.

The Department of Commerce through the Bureau of Census has provided highly qualified statistical and research personnel and service.

The Office of Emergency Management has assisted in administrative operations.

So far we have considered the problem that confronted the government and the nation, the time table of important developments in meeting the problem, the major step in the evacuation program, and the administrative authority and organization in charge of the program. This brings me to the actual details of how the evacuation is carried on.

There are 64 W. C. C. A. stations on the coast through which the Japanese are given necessary assistance. In each station there are representatives of each Federal agency directly involved. For example, the Federal Security Administration provides a receptionist; a social worker who is prepared to assist in family problems and in preliminary plans for housing. The Federal Reserve Bank provides consultants to advise on property protection, auto and truck transportation, household goods, storage, etc. Representatives of Farm Security Administration advise on crop loans, handling of farm equipment and matters relating to the purchase or management of farm lands.

The exclusion order is the first step in actual evacuation procedure. It has required careful advance planning down to the smallest detail by the Army staff comprising the Wartime Civil Control Administration. The task of each agency, whether civil or military is carefully prescribed to fit the evacuation project involved. Careful synchronizing must be assured by this advance planning. Following this, the order for the evacuation of a given, desirable area is given and the team starts functioning.

Notices are posted advising the Japanese population of the limits of the area to be evacuated and advising them to report to a Civil Control Station and to be prepared to move by a given date.

Each civil control station functions about five days in a particular evacuation area. The team which makes up a given "station" then moves on to its next assignment—it spends about 4 days in advance reconnaissance. Such a team comprises civilian agency representatives including a medical examiner from the U. S. Public Health Service and a team captain from the U. S. Employment Service. They have been trained in advance for the job by the Wartime Civil Control Administration.

The next major phase of the evacuation procedure is the transportation of evacuees to the Assembly Centers.

On the date of moving the Army takes full charge of the movement and determines whether the evacuation is accomplished by train, bus or automobile caravan. Evacuees may sell their automobiles to the Government or have them stored temporarily.

Upon arrival at the center the evacuees are registered and assigned living quarters by the civilian personnel. Much of the detail work connected with re-settlement in the Assembly Centers is carried on with the assistance of the Japanese themselves. A small Army contingent guards the camp but the Army has no other personnel involved in the operation of the Assembly Centers after the evacuees have been brought into the grounds.

The accommodations at each of the Assembly Centers include living quarters for family units, group dining halls, milk stations, shower baths, toilets and laundries. A post exchange is in operation at each center and a modest program of recreational activities to supplement work projects is being provided. Each center has its own hospital and staff.

The evacuees are supplied with food housing, hospitalization, medical and dental care and necessary clothing. During their temporary residence in the Assembly Centers, Japanese are given nominal allowances for incidentals. Upon application the evacuees may secure coupon books which may be used for the purchase of merchandise at the center exchanges or stores. These books entitle a single adult to $2.50 merchandise per month, a couple to $4.00., an individual under 16 years $1.00. The maximum allowance for any family is $7.50.

Compensation is given to those evacuees who work in the Assembly Centers upon this basis: unskilled workers $8.00 a month; skilled workers $12.00; professional and technical workers $16.00 a month. No wage schedule for evacuees who are assigned to administrative and maintenance work has been determined. The wage schedules in Assembly Centers are based on a 44-hour week. The compensation to which I refer is provided only for work done in connection with the operation of the Assembly Centers.

The eighteen temporary Assembly Centers were selected for the accommodation of all Japanese in the Western States. These centers are located in four states as follows:

Arizona: Mayer.

California: Fresno, Marysville, Merced, Pinedale, Pomona, Sacramento, Salinas, Arcadia, Stockton, Tanforan, Tulare, Turlock, Tule Lake, Manzanar.

Oregon: Portland.

Washington: Puyallup.

The largest is at the Santa Anita race track in Arcadia, with a capacity of 17,000. Next come Manzanar and Tule Lake with a capacity of 10,000 each and Puyallup and Tanforan, each with 8,000.

Fresno, Merced, Pinedale, Pomona, Sacramento, Stockton and Tulare have capacities of 5,000 each, Salinas and Turlock 4,000 each, Marysville and Portland 3,000 each, and the more or less isolated Mayer center, 250.

The complete job of preparing the Assembly Centers and actual removal of the Japanese to these centers will have been accomplished during a period of about two months. During this time housing for 112,000 people has been erected, supplied and equipped. The construction, equipping and supplying of the eighteen Assembly Centers and the whole evacuation procedure have been accomplished under the direction of only 35 Army officers.

We have referred to Assembly Centers as temporary locations. It is definitely understood that the Japanese who have been removed to the Assembly Centers will be transferred at a later date to the permanent Relocation Centers which are now being prepared.

The machinery for this final phase of the program was established under executive order on March 18th in the creation of the War Relocation Authority as a civilian agency under the direction of Mr. Milton Eisenhower. The War Relocation Authority works in cooperation with the War Department and is charged with the responsibility for locating and operating Relocation Centers in which the Japanese may live for the duration of the war. The Army will have no part in this phase of the program except for the actual transfer of evacuees from Assembly Centers to Relocation Centers and the maintenance of protective military guards outside the centers, although the Army does actually construct and equip the permanent Centers which War Relocation Authority is to operate.

Many people have asked about the extent to which the Japanese will be available to contribute to the nation's production of agricultural and other products.

This matter lies solely within the jurisdiction and responsibility of the War Relocation Authority, the separate agency charged with the permanent handling of the whole program.

Therefore, I can only answer the question in part directly and in part by quoting from a statement of policy just issued by War Relocation Authority.

War Relocation Authority has created a War Relocation Work Corps in which all Japanese over 16 years of age may voluntarily enlist. The following is quoted from War Relocation Authority's booklet on the subject:

"Enlistment in the work corps is entirely voluntary and all evacuees over sixteen years of age who are employable, both men and women, may apply. Among the obligations which the enlistee assumes are these:

1. He agrees to serve as a member of the corps until two weeks after the end of the war.
2. He swears loyalty to the United States and agrees to perform faithfully all tasks assigned to him by the Corps authority.
3. He may be granted furloughs for work in agricultural, industrial or other private employment under the following conditions:
   a. Since the Army cannot provide protective services for groups or communities of less than 5,000, each State and local community where enlistees are to work must give assurance that they are in a position to maintain law and order.

    b. Transportation to the place of private employment and return must be arranged without cost to the Federal Government.

    c. Employers must, of course, pay prevailing wages to enlistees without displacing other labor and must provide suitable living accommodations.

    d. For the time enlistees are privately employed, they will pay the Government for expenses incurred in behalf of their dependents who may remain at Relocation Centers.

Upon application from War Relocation Authority, and statement that the conditions just quoted have been met to the satisfaction of War Relocation Authority, the Army will permit Japanese to leave Assembly Centers for private employment providing the location of such Japanese is to be outside the boundaries of Military Area No. 1. The Army will grant no permits for work within Military Area No. 1 under any circumstances. So far as the Army is concerned then, evacuees are now in Assembly Centers—virtually all of them. Soon all of them will be. While there, they are the Army's full responsibility. It accepts that. When the permanent centers are built it will transport evacuees to such centers under Army convoy. It will also provide military guard around such established centers. It accepts that responsibility, too. But it cannot accept the responsibility when evacuees are released to be employed privately because it does not have the men or the equipment to spare. On the other hand if state, local and private interests ask War Relocation Authority for evacuees labor, and agree to be responsible for the maintenance of law and order, knowing that the Army cannot provide supervision, the Army cannot and will not stand in the way of permitting such labor to be made available by War Relocation Authority.

Prospective employers seeking to arrange for the private employment of Japanese under the conditions I have outlined should consult Mr. E. R. Fryer, Regional Director of the War Relocation Authority, Whitcomb Hotel, San Francisco.

I have tried—and I hope—succeeded—in making clear the distinction between *relocation* which is being handled by War Relocation Authority with our cooperation, and *evacuation* which has been the Army's job, and which I have described in detail.

Discussion Questions

1.   Bendetsen is faced with the task of explaining to his audience at the Commonwealth Club of San Francisco why Japanese Americans, including citizens, had to be relocated to camps for the duration of World War II. Look at his strategies of persuasion, and try to answer some of the following questions:

    How does Bendetsen appeal to his audience?

    What emotions does he try to appeal to in his speech?

How does he try to refute any opposition his audience might have?

How does he establish the government authority behind the decision?

What kinds of evidence does he offer for his assertions of the dangers of a well-organized fifth-column of spies?

2.   Bendetsen claims that because "there has been no substantial evidence of manifestation of nationalistic fervor exhibited by any Japanese group in the United States since the outbreak of the war," this "may be, and can be a most ominous thing." Discuss Bendetsen's logic and argumentation in this sentence. What would he have said if the Japanese had exhibited militaristic fervor? Compare this argument with the arguments of those who favored Chinese exclusion (see Gyory's article in Chapter 5). What similar appeals to emotion do you find in these arguments?

Writing Suggestions

1.   Newspaper reports about the relocation of Japanese Americans in 1942 paint a vivid picture of the political climate of the time. To read a variety of these articles and to see political cartoons, go to the San Francisco Museum of History page at <http://www.sfmuseum.org/war/evactxt.html>. Then write an essay in which you analyze Bendetsen's speech in relationship to the public atmosphere of suspicion and anger surrounding the relocation of Japanese Americans. Compare the major points that Bendetsen makes with corresponding items in the newspaper articles or political cartoons you find. How does Bendetsen's speech mirror the tone of the editorials and articles in the San Francisco newspapers? What kinds of assumptions do Bendetsen and the newswriters make? Can you infer from the newspaper articles what kinds of assumptions Bendetsen might have made about his audience? Be sure to quote directly from Bendetsen's speech and from the newspaper articles, and mention the dates and the titles of the newspaper articles in the body of your text.

2.   Bendetsen states that the use of fairgrounds and racetracks at Assembly Centers "made it easier to protect the evacuees' welfare and property." Research the question of the safety of Japanese American citizens and noncitizens in California after the bombing of Pearl Harbor in January and February of 1942, before the relocation was enforced. How serious was the threat to the safety of Japanese Americans along the coast of California? Were there any incidents of looting of Japanese American homes, or were there incidents of violence against Japanese American civilians? Then write a response to Bendetsen's claim, either refuting or supporting his assertion. You might start your research with a microfiche search of the index of the *San Francisco Chronicle*.

Manzanar Free Press

The *Manzanar Free Press* was a newsletter put out by the inhabitants of Manzanar under the supervision of the camp authorities. Because the contents were censored and under the control of the authorities, the tone and content of the *Manzanar Free Press* do not necessarily reflect the true feelings of the inhabitants, but the paper nonetheless offers a remarkable portrait of the challenges of daily life in the camp. Many of the relocation camps did allow the detainees to put out newspapers, and these original newspapers are now collected together in several bound volumes located in the Hoover Institution Archives at Stanford University.

Free Press / Vol. 1, No. 3 / Manzanar, California / April 18, 1942

FIRST BABY COMES TO MANZANAR

Editorial Board

City Editor	Joe Blamey
Feature Editor	Sam Hohri
News Editor	Chiye Mori
Editorial	Tom Yamazaki

Staff Members

Paul Aino, Tetsuko Fujii, Yoichi Hara, Jimmy Hashimoto, Emily Higuchi, John Hohri, Roy Hoshizaki, Yoshio Katayama, Miyo Kikuchi, Minoru Koba, Yoshio Kusayanagi, Emi Meeda, Roy Nakama, James Oda, Satoru Sakuma, Chiyoko Shiba, Robert Toyama, Dan Tsurutani, Julia Yamada, Harry Yamashita.

You Can't Leave Camp for Jobs, Says Army

In response to inquiries about the possibility of leaving Manzanar to take up job offers in the interior areas, assistant camp manager, H. L. Black stated that under army orders, no Japanese may leave this camp, once he has come in from a restricted area.

Explaining that this is not a regulation of the camp management but a decree handed down from the Fourth Army Command under which Manzanar is operated, he stated that no provision had been made for any individual reallocation to new work areas.

However, in due time, Milton C. Eisenhower, who has been put in charge of further resettlement, is expected to make arrangements for the transfer of workers to needed areas in adequately authorized employment.

Wedding Ceremonies for Camp Pair Due Sunday: Hundred Invites Sent

Of keen interest to the public will be the first local nuptial ceremonies uniting Miss Kimiko Wakamura to Howard Kumagai which will be held in 9-16 this coming Sunday afternoon at 3 P.M. with the Rev. Preston officiating.

A hundred invitations are being issued to friends, but the public is invited to fill the remainder of the hall. A reception will be held after the rituals.

A blue dress suit will be worn by the bride; while her fiance wears a business suit. The couple will be given separate quarters, it was indicated by the administration. A honeymoon trip isn't contemplated for the present.

The bridegroom will be represented by his parents, Mr. and Mr. Kichisaburo Kumagai. The parents of the bride are in Japan.

Baishakunin were Mr. & Mrs. Fred Tayama of Los Angeles; Mr. & Mrs. Kiyoshi Higashi, of Terminal Island. The marriage culminates a five year friendship.

Kumagai, a former mechanical engineer, is now employed as a sanitation inspector.

New Arrival Thursday Increases Camp Population

Heralded by a lusty wail, Manzanar's first bouncing baby boy arrived early Thursday morning in Manzanar emergency hospital, tipping the scales at 6 lbs. 4 ozs.

The proud young parents are Mr. & Mrs. Hatsuji Ogawa, formerly of Los Angeles.

The stork which had been hovering over the village for several days decided to alight April 16, and was ably assisted by Dr. Yoshiye Togasaki, who made the delivery; Dr. Masako Kusayanagi, anesthetist, and Miss Fumi Gohata, nurse.

The slender young father, waiter in Mess 12, was beaming excitedly as he dished out extra helpings of hash. Disappointing those local residents who had hoped that the first baby would be called Owen, the child's name is to be Kenji.

A contribution box had been placed in the canteen to receive donations for the expected first baby.

Everyone Register

Everyone without exception who has failed to register, please do so immediately at 1-2-1. Deadline is Monday at 5 P.M.

Vote by Absentee Ballots

All eligible voters presiding in Camp Manzanar will be permitted to cast their votes by absentee ballots during any election, it was learned from Harry L. Black, as camp manager.

It will be necessary to have the voter write to the registrar of voters in his home county precinct and send for the absentee ballot.

As this absentee voting is a privilege that can be exercised, all registered nisei should feel that it is their responsibility to avail themselves of it. Those who have reached voting majority age are in a group now being mooted.

Police Department Expansion Announced

Seventy-five men were enrolled on the staff of the police department this week, according to reports from the police office.

Ken Ozaki, desk sergeant, stated that the department will later add detectives to its staff. A few cars will be added and horses for the sergeants are contemplated, he said.

Of interest to the general public were the penalties which may be inflicted on miscreants. Chief of Police Horton said it depends entirely on the individual case: "Major crimes may be carried to the court at Lone Pine," he said "although we are trying to keep all activities here as self-governing as possible." Minor crimes will be under the jurisdiction of block leaders.

Seek Books for Library

An appeal for books and magazines for the proposed Manzanar library, to be at 7-15, has been made.

Life, Readers Digest, Time, Saturday Evening Post, Hygeia, and Parents Magazine, are some of the magazines now being sought.

Quiet games, such as checkers and card games will also be made accessible to library users.

Shower Curtains Coming; Also Police Uniforms

Uniforms for the police force and curtains for the women's showers will be the first assignment for the projected sewing program now being planned by Robert Harrison, supervisor of the production department.

Flag Ceremonies

Colors of the United States fluttered in the spring breeze as flag raising ceremonies took place Friday afternoon in front of the Administration Building. Five Boy Scouts and four buglers participated. Assistant Camp Manager Harry L. Black delivered the dedication address.

Vainly attempting to break coca cola bottles in lieu of champagne Camp Manager Triggs officially christened the two brown and white burros, Mervin and Bill. These little burros are camp mascots and will be allowed to roam at large.

New Life

As symbolic as the cheerful apple blossoms that cluster on the sear old boughs and young shoots on the trees among the houses is the lot of some thirty-three hundred residents at Manzanar. It is significant that our life here should start with the visit of Spring in the Valley when the calendar of nature points to rebirth of the world around us.

Because the keynote of our community here is: New Life.

True, it is hard to obliterate the past; the memories of men linger on. We have come from all walks of life, from different places on the map, from different trades and professions, from different levels on the economic scale.

But here at Manzanar we meet on a common ground; we have one common denominator—we are all plain citizens of Manzanar Reception Center. And, because we start from this fundamental promise, which circumstances have given us, it is easy to arrive at a logical conclusion that there should be no special class or privilege among us. Every person here should fit into the new community life according to his ability and not to his past.

Of such stuff is democracy made.

Weather Forecast

"No dust or wind after April" is the welcome forecast given by the old-timers in this region. Reports that the winds abate by May will encourage Owens Valley's newest population who were becoming perturbed by the continuous dust storms that have been scourging the valley.

According to those same experts the snow will remain on the peaks until September, assuring Manzanar of a view during the summer months. Snows melt in September but reappear in December, it was reported.

Garbage Collection to Be Installed

Grounds and apartments of the Japanese in Manzanar will be kept in first-class sanitary condition as more than 2000 garbage cans were brought in and distributed to each barrack last Thursday morning.

The crew for the distribution and collection of garbage will be manned entirely by Japanese and supervised by Mr. Thorne of the food and sanitation department.

No Shipments Admitted

Further shipments of freight to village residents were banned by the Fourth Army Command office in San Francisco.

Pending further orders from Gen. DeWitt's headquarters, radios in particular—even those being sent thru parcel post—are not being allowed in.

However, aside from radios, goods which have already been delivered by truck lines are ready to be called for by the consignee.

Children's Center

Pre-school Recreational Centers opened April 15, in bungalows 3–15 and 11–15 for 68 children between the ages of 3 and 6, much to the delight of all.

The second day brought more than seventy-five children gleefully storming the doors of the nursery classes long before the opening hour at 9:00, demonstrating enthusiasm for this new project.

An efficient staff in charge include Michi Amamatsu, Chiyeko Oyama, and Michi Nishi of Bainbridge, and May Oshizaki and Takai Kaneda of Los Angeles headed by the able Mrs. Florence Ikobata, formerly of New York.

Police Vigilance

As evidence of their vigilance in selecting its staff members, the Police Office announced that one of its members had been dismissed. Negligence of duty and disorderly conduct was given as the reason for the action.

Dance Notice

Dances will be held this Saturday, tonight, from 7:30 to 10 P.M. at the community recreation centers, 1-5 and 6-15. Everyone welcome.

C-a-l-l f-o-r-r-r Typewriter Serviceman

One of the most urgently needed people so far unfound is someone experienced in servicing typewriters. If there is anyone who can do this job, he'll be welcomed with wide open arms—and the offices seem to have a corner on comely girls. . . .

Don't Give up the Fight; Plenty of Mops and Water

There are ample supplies of house cleaning equipment to go around, and what's more, they are being given to householders free of charge by the army, was the statement issued by H. A. Nelson, head of the supply department.

"Don't spare the mop and water in fighting the dust in your room," advised this office, as Manzanar experienced one of the worst dust and sand storms Thursday and Friday.

Haircuts

It's possible to control the voluntary behavior of human beings, but there are some aspects in which Dame Nature gives the merry "ha-ha" to these homo saps. Chief among these pranks is the way the cranial fur keeps growing 'n growing.

Tho one of these days, those familiar peppermint sticks will dot Manzanar landscape, time nor growing hair cannot wait for that day.

So to meet this emergency, hand-clippers and shears are snipping away in many a village apartment as amateur and semi-pro barbers do their bit to keep the crowning glory of mankind respectable and presentable to their fellows.

In some instances, the whir of electric clippers gives an almost professional air. The deft wielding of a razor adds the ultimate metropolitan nicety.

Some of the young fellas have taken this new life spirit really to heart and taken unto themselves "butch" haircuts, variously known as "victory," "military," or—oh, horrible implications—"german" style.

Seeing this streamlined trend in hair mode, some of the girls, who have been taking an awful beating in having their raven tresses take on that "tattle-tale gray" tinge, have enviously threatened to follow suit.

On the other hand, the call of the rugged wild—or maybe it's the difficulty of getting hot water, have encouraged our manlier specimens to develop facial accessories that were supposed to have eloped with hoop-skirts. They now sport flowing locks from around their jowls that would be the envy of many a member of the House of David.

With several licensed and professional barbers here already and others expected in future contingents, designated barber shops as well as beauty salons for the girls are anticipated to provide a better solution to this need.

Discussion Questions

1. As a group, make a list of the different aspects of life in Manzanar that you can glean from the *Manzanar Free Press*. Then try to describe life in the camps as it might have been, describing the physical and emotional condition of the inhabitants from the various articles in the newsletter. What were the major physical hardships revealed by the *Manzanar Free Press*? What kinds of freedoms were lost? What racial misunderstandings are alluded to? What general picture of life in the camps can you put together from this publication?

2. What is the tone of this piece? Who were the different audiences for the *Manzanar Free Press*? How did the existence of different audiences affect the writers' tone, diction, and style?

Writing Suggestions

1. There are a number of places where careful reading of the text can show you that this censored paper reveals more about the Japanese relocation camps than first meets the eye. Using your responses to the second discussion question for this selection, analyze the text carefully and write a paper exploring how the writers of the paper let their feelings show while at the same time producing a document that is careful to be pro-American, cooperative, and polite. Read between the lines, and look carefully at the headings and the subtext of the writing.

2. Make a list of the headings and components of this edition of the *Manzanar Free Press*. Then, matching the format of the paper, write what you think would be an uncensored edition of the *Manzanar Free Press* on April 18, 1942, using information from this edition and from research you can do on the Internet about Manzanar. (See the Web site listings at the end of this chapter.)

Rosie the Riveter Revisited

Women, the War, and Social Change

SHERNA BERGER GLUCK

Sherna Berger Gluck is director of the Oral History Program at California State University, Long Beach, and professor of Women's Studies. In addition to her book *Rosie the Riveter Revisited: Women, the War, and Social Change,* from which our selection is taken, she has written *From Parlor to Prison: Five American Suffragists Talk about Their Lives.* Gluck is one of the founders of the Feminist History Research Project, and she was part of the Rosie the Riveter Revisited oral history project funded by the Rockefeller Foundation and the National Endowment for the Humanities. For *Rosie the Riveter Revisited,* she and her colleagues interviewed forty-five women and recorded oral histories of their war work experiences. The selection below includes a sampling of the oral histories on which Gluck based her book.

It wasn't difficult for Tina to find an aircraft job. By 1943, when she returned to Los Angeles, the Negro Victory Committee, led by the Reverend Clayton Russell, had organized a march on the local U.S. Employment Office and had forced an expansion of training and job opportunities for blacks. The Los Angeles group used the pages of the California Eagle to inform and mobilize the community. Women were especially targeted, and advice was regularly offered, especially to former domestic workers, who were not accustomed to the industrial setting or to the ways in which the unions could help them.

The goal of the wartime black organizations went beyond the short-range objective of opening up jobs. The National Council of Negro Women, for example, mobilized a "Hold Your Job Campaign." They hoped to ensure that the inroads made during the war years were not lost. The council offered its services to employers and workers alike in an effort to integrate women workers into these new jobs. A series of wartime employment clinics were set up, primarily in the Washington, D.C., area. The inclusion of charm clinics and classes on behavior and attitude indicates that the black woman was being trained how to fit in and be accepted—how to be white, as it were. It is no wonder that Tina Hill and many other black women were conscious of the historic role they were playing. One of the pamphlets issues by the National Council of Negro Women contained a War Workers' Pledge: "I shall never for a moment forget that thirteen million Negroes believe in me and depend on me. . . . I am a soldier on the Home Front and I shall keep the faith."

Tina didn't want to work at Douglas Aircraft, where her sister had a job, and instead applied at North American Aviation, which was located closer to the heart of the black community. Both because of its location and because of the pressure placed on it by the United Auto Workers union and the local civil rights groups, North American had a higher proportion of black workers than any other aircraft plant.

[TINA:] I don't remember what day of the week it was, but I guess I must have started out pretty early that morning. When I went there, the man didn't hire me. They had a school down here on Figueroa and he told me to go to the school. I went down and it was almost four o'clock and they told me they'd hire me. You had to fill out a form. They didn't bother too much about your experience because they knew you didn't have any experience in aircraft. Then they give you some kind of little test where you put the pegs in the right hole.

There were other people in there, kinda mixed. I assume it was more women than men. Most of the men was gone, and they weren't hiring too many men unless they had a good excuse. Most of the women was in my bracket, five or six years younger or older. I was twenty-four. There was a black girl that hired in with me. I went to work the next day, sixty cents an hour.

I think I stayed at the school for about four weeks. They only taught you shooting and bucking rivets and how to drill the holes and to file. You had to use a hammer for certain things. After a couple of whiles, you worked on the real thing. But you were supervised so you didn't make a mess.

When we went into the plant, it wasn't too much different than down at the school. It was the same amount of noise; it was the same routine. One difference was there was just so many more people, and when you went in the door you had a badge to show and they looked at your lunch. I had gotten accustomed to a lot of people and I knew if it was a lot of people, it always meant something was going on. I got carried away: "As long as there's a lot of people here, I'll be making money." That was all I could ever see.

I was a good student, if I do say so myself. But I have found out through life, sometimes even if you're good, you just don't get the breaks if the color's not right. I could see where they made a difference in placing you in certain jobs. They had fifteen or twenty departments, but all the Negroes went to Department 17 because there was nothing but shooting and bucking rivets. You stood on one side of the panel and your partner stood on this side, and he would shoot the rivets with a gun and you'd buck them with the bar. That was about the size of it. I just didn't like it. I didn't think I could stay there with all this shooting and a'bucking and a'jumping and a'bumping. I stayed in it about two or three weeks and then I just decided I did *not* like that. I went and told my foreman and he didn't do anything about it, so I decided I'd leave.

While I was standing out on the railroad track, I ran into somebody else out there fussing also. I went over to the union and they told me what to do. I went back inside and they sent me to another department where you did bench work and I liked that much better. You had a little small jig that you would work on and you just drilled out holes. Sometimes you would rout them or you would scribe them and then you'd cut them with a cutters.

I must have stayed there nearly a year, and then they put me over in another department, "Plastics." It was the tail section of the B-Bomber, the Billy Mitchell Bomber. I put a little part in the gun-sight. You had a little ratchet set and you would screw it in there. Then I cleaned the top of the glass off and put a piece of paper over it to seal it off to go to the next section. I worked over there until the end of the war. Well, not quite the end, because I got pregnant, and while I was off having the baby the war was over.

Tina stayed at North American for almost two years during the war. Her description of housing and daily life underscores wartime conditions and is also a reminder of the extent to which northern cities, too, were still segregated in the 1940s.

[TINA:] Negroes rented rooms quite a bit. It was a wonderful thing, 'cause it made it possible for you to come and stay without a problem. My sister and I was rooming with this lady and we was paying six dollars a week, which was good money, because she was renting the house for only twenty-six dollars a month. She had another girl living on the back porch and she was charging her three dollars. So you get the idea.

We were accustomed to shacking up with each other. We had to live like that because that was the only way to survive. Negroes, as a rule, are accustomed to a lot of people around. They have lived like that from slavery time on. We figured out how to get along with each other.

In the kitchen everybody had a little place where he kept his food. You had a spot in the icebox; one shelf was yours. You bought one type of milk and the other ones bought another type of milk, so it didn't get tangled up. But you didn't buy too much to have on hand. You didn't overstock like I do today. Of course, we had rationing, but that didn't bother me. It just taught me a few things that I still do today. It taught me there's a lot of things you can get along without. I liked cornbread a lot—and we had to use Cream of Wheat, grits, to make cornbread. I found out I liked that just as well. So, strange as it may seem, I didn't suffer from the war thing.

I started working in April and before Thanksgiving, my sister and I decided we'd buy a house instead of renting this room. The people was getting a little hanky-panky with you; they was going up on the rent. So she bought the house in her name and I loaned her some money. The house only cost four thousand dollars with four hundred dollars down. It was two houses on the lot, and we stayed in the little small one-bedroom house in the back. I stayed in the living room part before my husband came home and she stayed in the bedroom. I bought the furniture to go in the house, which was the stove and refrigerator, and we had our old bedroom sets shipped from Texas. I worked the day shift and my sister worked the night shift. I worked ten hours a day for five days a week. Or did I work on a Saturday? I don't remember, but I know it was ten hours a day. I'd get up in the morning, take a bath, come to the kitchen, fix my lunch—I always liked a fresh fixed lunch—get my breakfast, and then stand outside for the ride to come by. I always managed to get someone that liked to go to work slightly early. I carried my crocheting and knitting with me.

You had a spot where you always stayed around, close to where you worked, because when the whistle blew, you wanted to be ready to get up and go to where you worked. The leadman always come by and give you a job to do or you already had one that was a hangover from the day before. So you had a general idea what you was going to do each day.

Then we'd work and come home. I was married when I started working in the war plant, so I wasn't looking for a boyfriend and that made me come home in the evening. Sometimes you'd stop on the way home and shop for groceries. Then you'd come home and clean house and get ready for bed so you can go back the next morning. Write letters or what have you. I really wasn't physically tired.

Recreation was Saturday and Sunday. But my sister worked the swing shift and that made her get up late on Saturday morning, so we didn't do nothing but piddle around the house. We'd work in the garden, and we'd just go for little rides on the streetcar. We'd go to the parks, and then we'd go to the picture show downtown and look at the newsreel: "Where it happens, you see it happen." We enjoyed going to do that on a Sunday, since we was both off together.

We had our little cliques going; our little parties. Before they decided to break into the white nightclubs, we had our own out here on Central Avenue. There were a ton of good little nightclubs that kept you entertained fairly well. I don't know when these things began to turn, because I remember when I first came to Los Angeles, we used to go down to a theater called the Orpheum and that's where all the Negro entertainers as well as whites went. We had those clip joints over on the east side. And the funniest thing about it, it would always be in our nightclubs that a white woman would come in with a Negro man, eventually. The white man would very seldom come out in the open with a black woman. Even today. But the white woman has always come out in the open, even though I'm sure she gets tromped on and told about it.

Joseph Hill had been stationed in northern California and returned home in January 1944. Tina became pregnant the following September.

[TINA:] Some weeks I brought home twenty-six dollars, some weeks sixteen dollars. Then it gradually went up to thirty dollars, then it went up a little bit more and a little bit more. And I learned somewhere along the line that in order to make a good move you gotta make some money. You don't make the same amount everyday. You have some days good, sometimes bad. Whatever you make you're supposed to save some. I was also getting that fifty dollars a month from my husband and that was just saved right away. I was planning on buying a home and a car. And I was going to go back to school. My husband came back, but I never was laid off, so I just never found it necessary to look for another job or to go to school for another job.

I was still living over on Compton Avenue with my sister in this small little back house when my husband got home. Then, when Beverly was born, my sister moved in the front house and we stayed in the back house. When he came back, he looked for a job in the cleaning and pressing place, which was just plentiful. All the people had left these cleaning and pressing jobs and every other job; they was going to the defense plant to work because they was paying good. But in the meantime he was getting the same thing the people out there was getting, $1.25 an hour. That's why he didn't bother to go out to North American. But what we both weren't thinking about was that they did have better benefits because they did have an insurance plan and a union to back you up. Later he did come to work there, in 1951 or 1952.

I worked up until the end of March and then I took off. Beverly was born the twenty-first of June. I'd planned to come back somewhere in the last of August. I went to verify the fact that I did come back, so that did go on my record that I didn't just quit. But they laid off a lot of people, most of them, because the war was over.

It didn't bother me much—not thinking about it jobwise. I was just glad that the war was over. I didn't feel bad because my husband had a job and he also was eligible to go to school with his GI bill. So I really didn't have too many plans—which I wish I had had. I would have tore out page one and fixed it differently; put my version of page one in there.

I went and got me a job doing day work. That means you got to a person's house and clean up for one day out of the week and then you go to the next one and clean up. I did that a couple of times and I discovered I didn't like that so hot. Then I got me a job downtown working in a little factory where you do weaving—burned clothes and stuff like that. I learned to do that real good. It didn't pay too much but it paid enough to get me going, seventy-five cents or about like that.

When North American called me back, was I a happy soul! I dropped that job and went back. That was a dollar an hour. So, from sixty cents an hour, when I first hired in there, up to one dollar. That wasn't traveling fast, but it was better than anything else because you had hours to work by and you had benefits and you come home at night with your family. So it was a good deal.

It made me live better. I really did. We always say that Lincoln took the bale off of the Negroes. I think there is a statue up there in Washington, D.C., where he's lifting something off the Negro. Well, my sister always said—that's why you can't interview her because she's so radical—"Hitler was the one that got us out of the white folks' kitchen."

Tina acknowledged what the job at North American Aircraft meant to black women like herself, but she was also adamant about the discrimination that black workers faced. Because she worked there for almost forty years, it was sometimes difficult for her to pinpoint the precise time frame. During the war years, ironically, the prevailing cultural attitudes about women's proper role might have benefited black women. If women were only temporarily taking these jobs, then placing black women in production jobs would not pose a permanent threat to the racial status quo. As a result, the black women were more often given production jobs, whereas the black men were more frequently placed in janitorial positions.

[TINA:] But they had to fight. They fought hand, tooth, and nail to get in there. And the first five or six Negroes who went in there, they were well educated, but they started them off as janitors. After they once got their foot in the door and was there for three months—you work for three months before they say you're hired—then they had to start fighting all over again to get off of that broom and get something decent. And some of them did.

But they'd always give that Negro man the worst part of everything. See, the jobs have already been tested and tried out before they ever get into the department, and they know what's good about them and what's bad about them. They always managed to give the worst one to the Negro. The only reason why the women fared better was they just couldn't quite give the woman as tough a job that they gave the men. But sometimes they did.

I can't exactly tell you what a tough job would be, but it's just like putting that caster on that little stand there. Let's face it, now you know that's light and you can lift that real easy, but there are other jobs twice as heavy as that. See, the larger the hole is, the thicker the drill, which would take you longer. So you know that's a tougher job. Okay, so they'd have the Negro doing that tough drilling. But when they got to the place where they figured out to get a drill press to drill that with—which would be easier—they gave it to a white person. So they just practiced that and still do, right down to this day. I just don't know if it will ever get straight.

There were some departments, they didn't even allow a black person to walk through there let alone work in there. Some of the white people did not want to work with the Negro. They had arguments right there. Sometimes they would get fired and walk on out the door, but it was one more white person gone. I think even to this very day in certain places they still don't want to work with the Negro. I don't know what their story is, but if they would try then they might not knock it.

But they did everything they could to keep you separated. They just did not like for a Negro and a white person to get together and talk. Now I am a person that you can talk to and you will warm up to me much better than you can a lot of people. A white person seems to know that they could talk to me at ease. And when anyone would start—just plain, common talk, everyday talk—they didn't like it.

I know I had several leadmen—it's a lot of work if you're a lead; a lot of paperwork to do. You know yourself if anybody catches on and learns good, you kinda lean towards that person and you depend on them. If you step out for a few minutes, you say, "If anybody come in here looking for me, find out what they want and if you can, help them." You start doing like that and if you find out he's doing a good job at it, you leave that work for them to do. But they didn't like that at all. Shoot, they'd get rid of that leadman real quick.

And they'd keep you from advancing. They always manage to give the Negroes the worst end of the deal. I happened to fall into that when they get ready to transfer you from one department to the next. That was the only thing that I ever ran into that I had to holler to the union about. And once I filed a complaint downtown with the Equal Opportunity.

The way they was doing this particular thing—they always have a lean spot where they're trying to lay off or go through there and see if they can curl out a bunch of people, get rid of the ones with the most seniority, I suppose. They had a good little system going. All the colored girls had more seniority in production than the whites because the average white woman did not come back after the war. They thought like I thought: that I have a husband now and I don't have to work and this was just only for the war and blah, blah, blah. But they didn't realize they was going to need the money. The average Negro was glad to come back because it meant more money than they was making before. So we always had more seniority in production than the white woman.

All the colored women in production, they was just one step behind the other. I had three months more than one, the next one had three months more than me, and that's the way it went. So they had a way of putting us all in Blueprint. We all had twenty years by the time you got in Blueprint and stayed a little while. Here come another one. He'd bump you out and then you went out the door, because they couldn't find nothing else for you to do—so they said. They just kept doing it and I could see myself: "Well, hell, I'm going to be the next one to go out the door!"

So I found some reason to file a grievance. I tried to get several other girls: "Let's get together and go downtown and file a grievance" [a discrimination complaint with the Equal Opportunities Employment Commission]. I only got two girls to go with me. That made three of us. I think we came out on top, because we all kept our jobs and then they stopped sending them to Blueprint, bumping each other like that. So, yeah, we've had to fight to stay there.

Joseph Hill had resisted Tina's suggestions that he get a job at North American— partially because of Tina's assessment of how the black men were treated. But in the early 1950s he relented and went to work there until his death in 1972. Between their two earnings, the Hills were able to enjoy the life-style to which Tina had aspired, and they were among the one-third of urban blacks who were becoming home owners after the war. With the perfect timing of a born storyteller, Tina recounted her experience of moving into a predominantly white neighborhood.

[TINA:] When I bought my house in '49 or '48, I went a little further on the other side of Slauson, and I drove up and down the street a couple of times. I saw one colored woman there. I went in and asked her about the neighborhood. She said there was only one there, but there was another one across the street. So I was the third one moved in there. I said, "Well, we's breaking into the neighborhood."

I don't know how long we was there, but one evening, just about dusk, here comes this woman banging on my door. I had never seen her before. She says, "I got a house over here for sale, you can tell your friends that they can buy it if they want to." I thought to myself, "What in the hell is that woman thinking about?" She was mad because she discovered I was there. Further down, oh, about two streets down, somebody burned a cross on a lawn.

Then, one Sunday evening, I don't know what happened, but they saw a snake in the yard next door to us. Some white people were staying there and the yard was so junky, I tell you. Here come the snake. We must have been living there a good little while, because Beverly was old enough to bring the gun. Everybody was looking and they had a stick or something. I don't know how, but that child came strutting out there with the gun to shoot the snake. My husband shot the snake and from that point on, everybody respected us— 'cause they knew he had a gun and could use it.

I was talking to a white person about the situation and he said, "Next time you get ready to move in a white neighborhood, I'll tell you what you do. The first thing you do when you pull up there in the truck, you jump out with your guns. You hold them up high in the air." He says, "If you don't have any, borrow some or rent 'em, but be sure that they see you got a gun. Be sure one of them is a shotgun and you go in there with it first. They going to be peeping out the window, don't you worry about it. They going to see you. But if they see those guns going in first, they won't ever bother you."

I did like he said, moved in here with some guns, and nobody come and bothered me. Nobody said one word to me.

. . .

[JUANITA:] My mother left my father in '36, after the last girl was born. She moved from the farm to town and taken some of the kids and left some of them out at the farm with my dad. She went to work for the Sewing Room, a project that they had during the depression. I was out on the farm with all the boys. Some boy in town was coming out and was fresh with me. When I told my dad about it, he said, "Well, I guess you'd better go in and live with your mother. You're getting too old to be around all these boys."

My mother wasn't too square then, wasn't too honorable. She had some guy move in with her, a young kid almost half her age, and it just seemed like she went bad. She was having men coming and going to the house all the time. My dad came around a couple of times, and I guess she got scared. Once he came over with a shotgun. He'd heard about her partying, and he came over to get the kids.

Then she took us all one night. I don't know how she did it. I went to sleep in Childress and woke up at 3:00 or 4:00 in the morning at a truck stop with music blaring, in Oklahoma. I'd never seen neon lights. Hell, in Childress we had little lights strung up with bare bulbs, and that was only on a special occasion—for example, when Roosevelt was re-elected. And I'd never heard jukebox music. I said to myself, "My God! What is this?" That was the spring of '37.

My mother moved into the community camp in Oklahoma City, like a refugee camp. They took old cars and old pieces of cardboard and wood and they built shacks. They got their water from the faucet at the city park, and they camped under bridges like hoboes. Hobo camps is really what it was. She was working for someone who was making bootleg whiskey. She would give me and one of my brothers a certain amount of bottles, and we packed these pints in a satchel and made deliveries.

I was in what they called a honky-tonk, a beer bar, making a delivery when this woman saw me. She started questioning me, "How old are you?" "I'm thirteen." "Well, are you working?" I said, "Well, I work for my mother." Then she said, "I am a police officer. You tell me everything."

She was a big heavyset woman with authority like a big bull. I'm young and I didn't know the difference and I don't know Oklahoma. All I know is the community camp and a few slummy honky-tonks around it. So I take her down to this camp. She says to Mama, "Well, I want to hire your girl off of you. My daughter is having a baby and she's got a couple little kids and she's married to a lawyer. We live on the north side of town and we need the girl to do the housework." Mama said, "Take her." Just like that.

I walked out of there with a ragged pair of my brother's overalls, no shoes, and one of my brother's shirts. The first thing she did was cut my hair and de-lice me. I walk into this beautiful home and I can't believe it. It's a home with rugs and a radio. It was a mansion to me. But it didn't remain a mansion very long because the first thing she did was tell me what I had to do.

I washed and ironed and cooked and sewed. Then they would wake me up in the middle of the night right after she breast-fed to put the baby back to bed. Then the mother-in-law would come over when it was supposed to be my free time, and she'd say, "You can't sit around. Get those cabinets washed." I wondered what the hell is this? I was with those people six months. But, oh, my god, they almost killed me. Day and night. There was never any rest.

Juanita left that job when she met another family who took her in and found her a job as a carhop. They bought her clothes and taught her how to spend money. In 1940, she came to California with another Oklahoma family and worked in the fields picking dates, oranges, and avocados. At the end of the season, they all returned to Oklahoma, and Juanita went to Fort Sill to join the friends with whom she had lived earlier.

[JUANITA:] I got a job in the post exchange. That was in 1941. I was there about six months before the war started. All hell broke loose on the seventh of December. We were told to evacuate the barracks and find quarters in town. It was general confusion. Everybody was leaving to go to Seattle or California.

I came out here. In those days they had drivers' cars who came back and forth. You'd pay something like ten dollars or fifteen dollars. There were six or seven passengers and we were stacked on top of each other. They dropped us off in a hotel downtown and we were to wait in the lobby. We waited and he never came back. I had four or five dollars, a coat and the clothes on my back, and that was it. He took my luggage, my pictures, everything—the little souvenirs a young girl has. But every place I'd turn, someone was there to help me. Maybe it was my youth.

I came to Hollywood and got a room. That first time I was in California, when we were working in Indio, we came into the city a couple of times, and to Hollywood. Real tourists. I liked the weather and the smell of orange blossoms and gardenias. The palm trees impressed me. So it just seemed the logical place for me.

The name of the hotel—I'm sure it will bring back a lot of memories to anyone who was in California in 1940 or '41, or even before—was the Studio Hotel. It's in Hollywood, nestled almost within two or three blocks of Hollywood and Vine Street. It was a small hotel with three floors, nice little singles with a bath. Prior to the war it had been for studio people, actors and actresses. The manager was a lovely woman. You could only stay in a hotel for X amount of days and you had to move. This was a wartime thing. So she'd put me on the first floor, then she'd put me on the second floor, then I'd go to the third floor, and I'd register each time.

I sent my dad a telegram and told him I was in California, and I was going to get a job but I don't have any money. That was the first time in my life I ever asked him for anything. He sent me a blank check. I think I wrote a check for seven dollars. My landlady accepted it and that was my week's rent. He sent me another check about a week later, a blank check again, and he kept doing that for about three months until I told him I didn't need money anymore. A year later I sent him a couple of hundred dollars. That is one memory I have of him. Although I never asked him for anything before or after that again, I never forgot that.

So that's how I really got started in that first crucial two weeks. Then for food, I went to Thrifty Drugs and got a grilled cheese sandwich and a Coke for a dime, or an egg salad sandwich and a Coke. I lived on one meal a day for a week. That's my first early memory of being totally and completely alone in California.

I didn't know what to do: no experience and I was under age. So I walked to the bowling alley and I got a job as a pinsetter. I was working for tips, setting up pins, but I couldn't take that. It was too noisy. I stayed two days. Then I went to work at a gas station.

The first gas station I worked at was paying me sixteen dollars a week, Mueller Brothers, on Sunset Boulevard. They had a black comedian who greeted everyone. It was a gimmick. I walked over there and said I was interested in working. Fifteen minutes later I was filling tanks with gas. I had no experience, but I learned as I went along. They didn't want to pay me very much money. Then someone came into the gas station and recruited me: "Look, we'd like to have you. How much are you making here?" And I said, "Sixteen dollars," and they said, "We'll give you eighteen dollars. Come work for us."

So I went to work for Kreager Oil Company, which was better. They gave me a uniform everyday and soap to wash the grease off my hands, and they taught me how to do batteries. It was very simple, very easy: check the oil, wipe the windshield, put the gas in, get the money, get the coupon.

I worked for six months and everyday someone came in saying, "Do you want a job?" My head was going crazy. They were recruiting for any kind of work you wanted. Newspapers, just splashed everywhere: "Help Wanted," "Help Wanted," "Jobs," "Jobs," "Jobs." Propaganda on every radio station: "If you're an American citizen, come to gate so-and-so"—at Lockheed or at the shipyards in San Pedro. And they did it on the movie screens when they'd pass the collection cans. You were bombarded.

They were begging for workers. They didn't care whether you were black, white, young, old. They didn't really care if you could work. It got even worse in '43. I worked two jobs for a long time. I had so much work offered to me and I was not even qualified—I just had the capability of learning very fast. Within three weeks of coming to California my mind was dazzled with all the offers I had. Before the war, in Oklahoma City and in California, I'd ask people if I could get a job and they'd say: "Well, you're not old enough." But here I didn't even have to look. I was having people approach me six to ten times a day—RCA Victor wanted me to come work for them; Technicolor said they'd train me.

Actually what attracted me—it was not the money and it was not the job because I didn't even know how much money I was going to make. But the ads—they had to be bombardments: "Do Your Part," "Uncle Sam Needs You," "V for Victory." I got caught up in that patriotic "win the war," "help the boys." The patriotism that was so strong in everyone then.

Anyhow, Vega Aircraft was the first one I learned about. Someone came in two or three times to the station to get me to come to the application office. One day I said, "I'll be off tomorrow and I'll go and fill out papers." I called this girl I had met and we went together. We both went for the same job, but she was immediately hired for a more educated job because she had finished high school. I went on the assembly line.

I already had something to wear. When I was recruited for Kreager Oil Company, they made me a jumpsuit which was absolutely stunning. It was in khaki color, made of gabardine or wool and cotton. When I first went in, I wore that. Then went into boys' blue jeans and a plaid shirt. Jeans were sturdy and their little shirts were made of a heavy, tough material, and the heavier and tougher the material the better for me, because it kept me from getting hurt.

I wore some kind of a cap that had a net and a bill and you put your goggles on. Some women wore bandanas. Most of us eventually ended up with our hair cut short. That's another reason they say the women became very masculine during the war. I disagree. Your hair would slip down and you'd try to get it up, and your hands were filthy with chemicals and little bits of metal. It was like rubbing salt into a wound. We didn't wear earrings or necklaces or rings, obviously, because we were working with tools.

Let me see if I can describe my first impression—which later wasn't the truth. It was like you were walking into a big, huge cavernous barn, just like a huge hangar; dead white from the huge, tremendous lights. On platforms—saw-jacks I would call them—they had poles and shelves and pieces and parts of planes. The first thing I noticed was that all the men were instructors. Most of the workers were men. I saw very few women. Even the bench I worked on, there were six or eight young boys, eighteen or nineteen years old, and myself, and two or three middle-aged women.

It was very dull, very boring. The first day I thought, "Oh, this is ridiculous. I have to set here for three weeks on this bench?" What we did was we learned to buck and then we learned to rivet. I set there for three or four hours that first day and I picked up the rivet gun: "You show me once and I'll do it for you." The bucking, you have a bar. I said, "What's to learn here? Look at my hands. I've been working as a grease monkey. I could do this. I don't have to set here and train." I learned very fast.

I went into the shell the next day. First I went inside and I bucked, and then I went outside and I riveted. I was working with real seasoned workable men and it was so easy. We did strip by strip, the whole hull. We used strips of like cheesecloth and paste that had to go on the inside and across the seam. I had to do that. Then, as the riveter outside riveted, I was inside bucking. It would be like a sewing machine, you just sort of have to go along with them.

I stayed there maybe six weeks, and I worked on all parts of it, up in the wings. One by one, day by day, new faces. I would say within six months there were maybe twenty or thirty men left in Department 16 where maybe there had been fifteen hundred. One by one they disappeared. I'd have a group leader one day and two or three days later he was gone. Leadman, two or three days later he was gone. There were men in the tool crib and one by one they disappeared.

As they recruited more and more women, men with deferments were the ones that actually remained to work. Even a lot of the young women working would disappear, going into the service. I made friends with four or five girls that became WACS and WAVES and nurses. It was very more difficult to keep friends, because they came and they went so fast.

By late '42 we had very few men left. They were gradually replaced by women and blacks. When the blacks started coming in, suddenly I was jerked off my nice little wing section and I was sent over to the training area, which was at the far end of the huge plant. The first day I picked a young man who was nineteen years old, Stan—I can't remember his full name, but today he is a musician and you see him on television in the Les Brown Orchestra—and four or five other blacks, men and women. I worked with training them the first day, the second day, the third day. They just couldn't get it. Stan, he'd fall asleep, he wouldn't work. I gave up. I went to my group leader and said, "I have to either transfer or I'm quitting."

So I got out of that assembly and went into final assembly, thank God, or I would never have stayed. I thought, "I really have got it made now." Only it was just as bad or worse, in a sense, because the heat and my getting up into those wings. I used to carry a crawl light with me, and I'd lay up there and I'd wait and wait for my partner on the outside. I had no way of knowing what was going on outside. I can't tell you how many times I'd lay there, and a drill or something would come through and nick me in the leg. Carelessness on the outside part and they'd missed the mark. Two or three of my very vivid experiences was climbing out of the wings of those planes, sweating, hot and dirty, finding whoever was supposed to be working with me sound asleep. I'd give them a good kick in the ass.

Then I transferred again. I went into the wiring and cockpit section and I loved it. But sometime during this work with chemicals and metals I got a skin disease. It started out on my arm.

The war activity transformed communities from a relaxed, small-town atmosphere to frenetic, bustling centers. Where jobs and money had been so scarce just a few years before, they were now plentiful. Because of the wartime shortages, war workers were often earning more money than they could spend. It was a time to recoup from the hardships of the depression, and many civilians held several different jobs. Businessmen left their white-collar jobs at five to put in a half shift at the local war plant; high school students spent half days in school and half days assembling planes; even servicemen on leave often put in half shifts at the defense plants.

The daily pace of life was hectic, but there was also time for play, especially among the young single war workers. The excitement of the period, the activity, the social interactions were the up side. But there were also bitter reminders of the war as casualties mounted.

[JUANITA:] At the same time I worked in the aircraft, I also worked for a record-cutting company; we'd cut records and make tape recordings for the servicemen to send back home. I also worked for a fellow in Glendale who had a storage garage. As the young men were going to war, they would store their cars with him. He hired me to come over and take each car out every other day or so and put a few miles on it to keep up the engine, and I'd check the water, check the tires, check the oil, and sometimes lubricate them. He wasn't paying me very much, but I got gas coupons and I'd take a car occasionally to work.

I had so much work sometimes, I wouldn't even go back for my money. Sometimes they'd just mail me a check and I'd think, "Gee, now where was this?" At one period of time I had six or eight checks laying in my dresser drawer that I hadn't even cashed. I simply didn't know how to handle money. The first paycheck I got in aircraft was more money than I'd ever seen in my life. I didn't even know what to do with it. I didn't have a bank account. You couldn't buy anything much.

But we'd hang out in drive-ins or the bowling alleys. And we went to places like the Hangover, Tropics, Knickerbocker Hotel, Blackouts, Garden of Allah, Har 'O Mar, the Haig on Wilshire. I was going into bars and drinking. One of my favorites was the Jade on Hollywood Boulevard. Another was the Merry-Go-Round on Vine Street. When Nat King Cole sat at the piano and sang, he wasn't even known and the piano bar went round. This was long before I ever reached twenty-one.

We found places like the beach, the pier, on our day off. I think that was on Sunday, 'cause some of us were on a six-day schedule. But we hung out, we read poetry, we discussed books that were current and popular. One book was passed from one to another. It was word of honor, really; you'd pass your book on to the next person and it would eventually get back to you. And movies, mainly movies. We'd sit in the lobbies.

Young people got together in harmless, easy companion ways. Dancing was great. You got rid of your energy by dancing. You'd get a little radio and put it out on the back porch or the lawn where you were living and had everybody come over. That was it. There were no cars racing around. We had a lot of blackouts so you couldn't have outdoor picnics or beach parties.

Oh, I'll tell you where we met, workers and their relatives, brothers, sisters, boyfriends, soldiers, sailors, families. At the Biltmore Hotel. They had a tea dance in the afternoon and when my brother would come in with his friends, we'd go there. We'd bring girlfriends to dance with our brother's boyfriends or our boyfriends would bring in friends and we'd get the girls together. It really didn't make any difference, but years later I found out a lot of these friends were homosexuals. At that time I didn't even know what it meant. They were "in the closet," so to speak. I don't think many of the gays realized they were gay.

During the war there was a lot of homosexuality. Straight people became very friendly with homosexual people, more so the women. I'm not a homosexual, but I had a great many friends who were, like the bus driver, Margaret. She was very tall. And there was one girl from aircraft. She and Margaret were always riding the bus, even when she wasn't working, and I'd say, "Don't you ever get off this bus?" I sensed there was something different about them when I would show a picture of a boyfriend or I would talk about some fellow I knew who was going into service. You'd exchange pictures in wallets, and you'd see a picture of a WAC or a WAVE.

We met one time at the beach, and there they were together. I said to them, "Hey, you guys act like you're married or something." They handed me a book, all wrapped up in a nice package with a ribbon on it, and they said, "You know you have a lot of friends. We want you to read this book and then if you have any questions, you talk to us and if you don't ever want to talk to us anymore, it's all right too." The name of the book was *The Well of Loneliness*. It introduced me to the fact that there were people who were different from me. It didn't make a damn bit of difference to me. I still liked them; they were still friends.

We accepted people then. People were more respectful of each other, too. They respected each other's privacy, and when you had conversations you weren't noisy [sic]. You talked about the weather, a book, a movie, what are we going to do next week, how many were shot down, who lost a friend or a brother. It was innocent. I think the end of innocence came after the Second World War. By the time the Korean War ended, we were hardened and tough.

I think people just clung together. They were closer. Even in aircraft, the friends you made, even though you didn't really know them very well, you were concerned. When you said good-bye to them, you said, "Well, I'll see you again soon, I hope," and you really meant it. Today you meet someone and you say, "I'll see you later," and you don't even remember their names five minutes later.

Most of the fellows that I knew, by 1943 were gone in three days or a week. I mean they were just gone! The next thing you'd get a letter with just a PO number. "Can't tell you where I am, but will see you when I come back." The song that was very popular then "I'll Be Seeing You." I think it was symbolic of that time. "I'll Be Seeing You," not when, where, how, or if.

Then I began to see boys coming back. One fellow I'd gone with in 1942, I got off the bus and I'm walking home and I heard: "tap, tap, tap." I turned around and looked and I thought: "Gee, a soldier in uniform with a cane." I turned back again and I said, "My God, it's Dick." Still in uniform. He came home blind. That was my very first shock, seeing him come back blind. He could see just a little, but later became totally blind—at twenty-three years! There were two or three other fellows I had known at the bowling alley who I went with, my age. When I began to see them coming back like this, it really did something to me.

You know, this is the first time I ever talked about this. I've never actually admitted to boyfriends that I worked in aircraft. A lot of the fellows coming home thought we were pretty frivolous—gum popping, silly, flowers in our hair, working and looking for men and roaming the streets looking for soldiers. It's not true. By the time you got out of work, you were so damned tired you didn't want to do anything. In my case, the first thing I wanted was a bath.

By mid-1944, the country had been at war for over three and a half years. The fervent patriotism that had been the driving force in the beginning of the war was beginning to wear thin. People were getting tired, and the strain of long hours of work at noisy jobs was beginning to show. High turnover and absenteeism rates reflected declining morale.

[JUANITA:] I quit because I'd look around me on the outside and I saw people not working in aircraft living an easy life. Women I had known, some that had worked and quit right away, went in and worked three or four weeks and said, "This is not for me. Forget it. To hell with it." This is touchy. I don't know how to bring this up. The morale was not that strong at the end. On our day off, we saw our friends in the neighborhood that were not working in aircraft: "I know this fellow that owns this store and I can get you anything you want"; "I can get it for you wholesale." You heard stories of people buying up the Japanese stores and of hoards of supplies in warehouses. Soap was rationed, butter, Kleenex, toilet paper, toothpaste, cigarettes, clothing, shoes. And you saw these people making a lot of money and not doing anything for the war effort, even bragging: "I kept my son out of it." You thought here are these special, privileged types of people and here I am working and sweating and eating our hearts out for the casualty lists that are coming in.

By 1944 a lot of people were questioning the war. "Why the hell are we in it?" We were attacked by the Japanese and were fighting to defend our honor. But still, this other side had the Cadillacs and the "I can get it for you wholesale." They suddenly owned all the mom-and-pop stores and suddenly owned all the shoe factories. The rumblings began with that—and the discontent.

. . .

Until the war began, Charlcia's life revolved around her family, her neighborhood, and her Eastern Star activities. She and her daughter were very close and the family did everything together, though Charlcia did not participate very much in her daughter's school activities.

Charlcia and her husband often played cards with the next-door neighbors, but most of her friends were members of Eastern Star. It was in that organization that she was able to express some of her artistic abilities. She decorated the tables for their events and on several occasions decorated large halls. She took this work very seriously and enjoyed the challenge, even studying various techniques from books. With the onset of the war, the pace of her daily life changed—at least temporarily.

[CHARLCIA:] Pearl Harbor. I remember that very definitely. I was standing at the sink. The man next door, he was a captain in the reserves. I remember opening the window and calling to him and telling him to go in and turn the radio on. I didn't like it, naturally—no one did—they came in with no warning at all and bombed Pearl Harbor. It was a terrible thing.

The patriotic feeling was so strong that anyone would have done anything to help. You never had any of this protest type of thing. There were a great many things that were wrong, especially what they did to the Japanese people that lived here. I knew one family that because the grandmother was Japanese, they had to leave their home. This was terrible. On the other hand, my husband had worked on Terminal Island in the schools there and amongst those people there were Japanese that were spies. Because of that, everybody suffered and it was wrong.

I started defense work in '42. I think a lot of it was because one of my neighbors found out about it, and she wanted me to go with her. I thought, "Well, now, this would take care of the situation." I still was getting along on next to nothing; it was still difficult. And my husband was talking about whether he should quit the school board or not. In those days, they didn't belong to any union, and they were paid a very small amount. As prices were going up it wasn't enough to cover our expenses. So I said, "No, I'll go see what I can do."

My husband didn't like it. He was one of these men that never wanted his wife to work. He was German and was brought up with the idea that the man made the living; the woman didn't do that. But he found that it was a pretty good idea at the time. It was a necessity, because he would have had to do something else. We couldn't live on what he was making, so that's the way it goes.

And my brother, especially my youngest brother, he thought it was terrible. My father, oh, he was very upset. He said, "You can't work amongst people like that." They were people just like me, but they thought it was people that were rough and not the same type I'm used to being with. They just couldn't see me going over and working in a factory and doing that type of work. And they were trying to protect me, I'm sure. Well, there again, I had quite a bit of arthritis and they felt that it would just be a bad thing to get in there.

But I wasn't trained for just any type of work. See, most of the women I knew, they went into stores and into that type of work. It was easier to do. They wouldn't go into the war plants. My oldest sister worked at Lockheed and she was a drill press operator, but the sister right next to me, she was a waitress. When she looked at my wages and what she collected, she said, "No, no part of that." She was making more money by the time she figured her tips.

So, my family thought I was a little off for doing it. But if that's what I wanted to do, that's what I did. And my husband got used to the fact that his wife worked.

I went over and took tests to see about getting a job at Vultee. When I took the test, as far as using the hands and the eye and hand movements, I passed just about the highest. See, anything using my hands—I could take a little hand drill and go up and down these holes as fast as you could move, just go like that, where most people would break a drill. It was a very simple thing. The riveting is the same way. It's just a matter of rhythm. So it was easy to do.

They had a school set up in Downey to show us how to do assembly work and riveting and the reasons for things—what was a good rivet and what wasn't. We went there about two weeks before we started to work. It was mostly women on these jobs. See, so many young men were in the service that it didn't leave very many of them to do these types of jobs; the ones that were kept out of the service could do the more specialized work. They had to have men to make these jigs and to make the forms for the ribs. That was beyond us.

I was started on this jig. The P-38 that Lockheed put out was a twin engine, and we worked on the center part between the two hulls. It was a much heavier rivet that went into this. It was what they call cold riveting; you took them out of the icebox real cold and riveted it. That was harder work.

Well, the jig would be empty, see, so the first job would be to mark your ribs. We took a red pencil and just put a line right down through the center. That was so that when we pushed it into position, then we could be sure we were hitting the center of the rib when we drilled. You'd ruin the whole rib if you've got too much in the curve or something like that. So we fastened the ribs in; then we put the skin on and fastened the Cleco clamps on it. The jig was in place so we could drill it. We marked along the edges so we could trim it, and then we took it off and trimmed the excess piece. We put it back together again and riveted up, and then we'd loosen the whole thing and take it off and put it in a special holder to be inspected for bad rivets. After inspection, it went to the next two girls and they added the next part.

Sometimes I had someone working with me and that made it a little faster, because otherwise I'd have to reach to the back and be sure it's in place. The person in the back would drill and you'd drill in the front, and then they'd be there all ready to rivet. My partner was better at the bucking than I was. She could hold it steadier. I wasn't strong enough. You had to hold that square bar on the other side while the gun was shooting on this side. It was quite a force on it. It was hard to do—but that didn't mean I didn't buck on some things.

618 *The Depression and the Two World Wars on the Home Front*

For the traditional homemakers, especially, the defense plant widened their social world. Charlcia had a sense of history and was proud of the fact that she was partici-pating in a turning point in the relationship between the races.

[CHARLCIA:] Vultee was the first plant of this type in the area to hire a black girl. She was a very nice person. Wilhelmina was her first name, but I can't remember her last name. Her mother was a schoolteacher and she was from Los Angeles.

The girls that worked together became quite friendly. If someone hap-pened to quit and went in the WACS, we would have a party. I remember this one time, we thought, "No, we're not going to have it at the restaurant; we'll have it in one of our homes and ask Willie to come, too." We didn't want to leave her out. About seven o'clock that night, we got a telegram from Willie saying she was so sorry she couldn't come, but that she appreciated us ask-ing her. She didn't want to break the color line, but those things wouldn't happen anymore today.

But she was among the first blacks in our department. In that three years that I was there, then they began coming from the South. You could really tell the difference. The ones coming from the South were shy. It was very hard for them to mix with people. It was a very hard situation for them, but they were treated nice.

When these black people were beginning to come in pretty steadily, I went over to show them how to do smaller types of assembly work, get them used to working with people and like that. The only difference that I could see was that they were inclined to get very angry at things. Maybe they hadn't under-stood something and they would get very upset. But they didn't do that to me. There was something about the way I worked with them that they didn't get so upset with me. So that was my job for a while and that was a good experience.

Then there were the Mexican girls. They were treated just like we were. There was no such thing as brown; they were white as far as we were con-cerned. There again, they were very nice. They couldn't pronounce my name, and they always called me Charli. I remember this one, when I would walk up toward them, she would say, "Now you speak English; you know Charli can't speak Spanish." This one particular group was clustered in that area, but there were others scattered through the plant. It wasn't that they were separating this group; it just happened. I couldn't see that they were being discriminated against in any way. But at that time, the Negroes were just treated very badly. Here again, I've always been different, where things like this was concerned. I could see the wrong.

But the women on my crew were a bit like me. One girl lived in San Pedro. I think her folks were fishermen down there. And another one lived over in Huntington Park, just a plain ordinary family. At thirty-one, thirty-two, I was considered fairly old. There was one woman that I think was forty-eight when they hired her, and she was an old lady! But these girls were mostly younger; they were in their early twenties. I don't think any of them had children.

GLUCK / *Rosie the Riveter Revisited*

We kept pretty busy working all the time, and there wasn't much personal talk. We sat down as a group at lunchtime, though. We would just find some spot to sit and eat and talk about different things. We didn't have any close connections, so there wasn't very much that we could talk about. I just knew where they lived.

But the one who was bucking rivets for me, she talked more because she was trying to make me a communist. She was very active with this group downtown and it was a communist group. Of course, I was telling her, "No, I'd never join a communist group." I said, "You wouldn't either if you knew what they were like." There was one other man that worked around there and he was a Republican, too. Of course, this was quite noticeable. We would stand out like sore thumbs because the majority of people that you met in a plant at this time were all Democrats. I never said anything about my affiliations because they were so—almost radical. But this other man was talking about it, and I said, "Sure, you can talk, look how big you are." He was saying to her, too, that if she ever had a chance to go to Russia and live under the conditions there, she would change her mind in a hurry.

I talked to her quite a bit. She owned property up in San Fernando Valley. She felt that things should be divided with other people, that one person shouldn't have everything and somebody else have nothing. Her beliefs, when she was talking, were for socialism, but she couldn't see the difference between socialism and communism.

Despite the enjoyable aspects of the job, the pace was hard and fast and the working conditions, particularly the noise level, were unpleasant. Charlcia described how noticeable this was at lunchtime, when the motors were all turned off. In fact, if anyone broke the relative calm by turning on a motor, the others would all rebel. Industrial accidents were not uncommon.

[CHARLCIA:] Most of the time when you have an accident, it's your own fault. The first one, I was working when the jig was moving; they had a moving line in one section. I was doing some safety wiring and I wanted to move. I just hopped down off of where I was onto one of those stools and it flipped. I had the blackest fanny for a long time. But nothing broke. I went to the first aid station and a report was made out.

The second one, I was working with this one girl on a section where it was sort of blind for me in the back. I had to put my hand in. She was working along the edge. Well, there's a guard that goes over the spring on the rivet gun so when the gun shoots that can't possibly come out—'cause they come out with quite a force. Well, she couldn't get into what she was trying to shoot, so she took the guard off. I was on the other side, see. I remember that it hit me at quite a blow, right next to the nose. Luckily, it hit the one spot that it could hit and the bone was solid enough that it didn't break it and kept from going on through. I was taken to the infirmary. I thought the fellows would take her apart. They were so upset with her. That was a definite thing that you don't do. Had it hit me in the eye I would have been dead. I think there's a little mark still someplace.

At the time of her accident, Charlcia was working with the heavier rivets and had the higher rating of assemblyman A. She was quick to point that it was assemblyman, not assemblyperson.

[CHARLCIA:] We paid off the house then, is what we were doing. We had a horror of being in debt—for anything. The depression left that feeling with us, that we had to get out of debt. We saved. Well, we didn't have time to spend very much then, anyhow, and with the two of us working, it made it easier.

But, of course, it was hard. I worked six days all the time and sometimes seven days—which was terrible. If I didn't have a family that supported me so much, I couldn't have managed it. I had a daughter that was very capable. She did all the shopping. See, by the time I got home from work, the shops were closed. She took the ration books and she figured that all out. The shop owners all knew her, and they'd let her have things that they wouldn't let me have if I did have time to go. She was in junior high school at the time. It helped make her a stronger person, I'm sure.

My husband helped me a lot with the housework; he was always good about helping. He was very strong and could do his work and then help me with some of mine, too. So whoever had time to do that did it. Typically, what I'd do, I'd get up before 6:00 and get things going. I was ready to leave at 7:00 and I was picked up. Then we got off at 4:00 P.M. and came home. I had dinner to fix and what could be done around the place. So it was a full day. If it hadn't been for my family, though, it would have been much harder for me.

Then things began to slow down. We knew the war was about over. For that matter, I think the bomb had been dropped already and we were just kind of waiting. You could see the difference; it wasn't that push and the trying to do more all the time.

I was laid off in September of '45. I just got a slip of paper saying that I wouldn't be needed again. Most of us went at the same time; it was just a matter that there was no more work. There were a few jobs that they kept open, but most of the women were off then—and men, too. It wasn't discriminatory; it was what they happened to have left.

The idea was for the women to go back home. The women understood that. And the men had been promised their jobs when they came back. I was ready to go home. I was tired. I had looked forward to it because there were too many things that I wanted to do with my daughter. I knew that it would be coming and I didn't feel any letdown. The experience was interesting, but I couldn't have kept it up forever. It was too hard.

So, I just had to sort of try to get myself straightened up again and get back in the groove. My daughter became more busy in different things, so there was always something to do then. She belonged to the Civil Air Patrol for a while and she belonged to the Rainbow Girls, the teenage group sponsored by the Masons and Eastern Star. So that kept me busy doing things. And I did a lot of Eastern Star work again that I couldn't do while I was working.

And I had a mother at home that needed different things, and I helped do things for her and my own daughter and my husband. I was kept very busy.

And it wasn't a bad word to say you were a housewife, either. You know, it was considered a job that needed to be done, too.

But I always felt that if married women needed to work, then that was their choice. I felt with my own daughter that if she wanted to work, she should be trained to do something where she would be paid good money, not that type of physical work. After I worked, I realized that if I had to work all the time, I would be very limited in what I could do. It's not that I couldn't learn to do something else. I think I would be capable of doing that. But with her, I told her there was no use spending her time and not really studying to do something that would be good. We talked of college as just being a part of what she would be doing. That way she kept through high school with the idea that she would go on to college.

She had one advantage. After the war, the government sent out people to examine students to see what they were most capable of doing, what their qualifications could be and what they would like. She had always thought she wanted to be a scientist. This man talking to her when she took the test, he told her that she was just a natural teacher and that she should follow through with that. So she did and it has proven to be right. She never had any problem with her job. They just offered her jobs wherever she was. Then she kept going into psychology—just taking extra courses—and they kept pushing her into higher classes because she had a natural trend toward that. So that's what she ended up doing. She is married, but she doesn't have children.

Charlcia thinks she herself would have liked to have become a teacher, although it was difficult for her to conceive of other options for herself in her own day. As she reflected on my question of what she would do differently if she were a young woman today, she seemed almost embarrassed to fantasize about it, and laughed self-consciously. But she was not at all self-conscious about her pride in her wartime work and her mechanical abilities.

[CHARLCIA:] The women got out and worked because they wanted to work. And they worked knowing full well that this was for a short time. We hoped the war would be over in a very short time and that we could go back home and do what we wanted to do. So that was what I felt. And my friend that worked in the smaller assembly work, she was the same way. She went to work during the war because there was a need for workers, but she wanted to go back home. So that was the main thing. We knew when we went to work that it was not for all the time.

But it was a very good experience for me because of the challenge of doing something like that, to prove to myself that I could do it. And working with all the different types of people—I'd always been very shy about meeting people. Actually, I was afraid of going out and asking for a job because I didn't think I could do it. So I found out I could do it; it was the type of thing that I could do, that I liked to do. I had a natural knack. There again, the rhythm of riveting is natural. You know if you're good at tools and good in using your hands, your eye and hand coordination is good then. And riveting is a very easy thing for a woman to do.

Of course, my father was a mechanic and I was always around with him. And we didn't have boughten toys. If we wanted anything, we made it. If we wanted a scooter, you took an old pair of skates and you put it on a couple of boards and you made yourself a scooter. If you wanted a dollhouse, you took an old box and put it up on a tree. So I was used to using tools, but it probably made me a little more efficient in using tools. I could always use any kind of tools I wanted to up until about three years ago when my hands began going bad with arthritis. That was one of the worst things because I can hardly cut out a dress now. In the kitchen, when we're through, I'll show you over my stove one type of work I did with tools. I took a class in jewelry making and, oh, just anything. I've done everything from wire sculpture to paper sculpture. Just everything.

But it was very important, yes. I'm very glad I did it. Of course, it was also selfish on my part. I went out of necessity, but also to help. Whether I would have gone just to help, I'm not too sure. You see, it was an effort for me to go. It was not something that was real easy to do. But I'm glad I did it. I'm sure it helped the arthritis. Shook them all loose.

. . .

[BEA:] I'd never thought about working. My brother at that time had separated from his wife, and he had an adopted girl. His wife remarried and the stepfather didn't like the girl. We considered that girl like ours because my mother had gotten her when I was a kid. She used to take care of children from the Welfare, and she got that baby when she was six months old. She gave it to my brother because he didn't have no children. He brought that girl to me and says, "I'll have her stay with you and I'll give you some money every week." She was sixteen or fifteen and she wanted a job.

They had these offices everywhere in Pasadena, of aircraft. I went in there to try and get her something, but they said, "We've got aircraft work right now for everybody, except she's too young." He says, "Why don't you get it?" I said, "Me?" He said, "Yeah, why don't you get the job?" I said, "Well, I don't know." But the more I kept thinking about it, the more I said, "That's a good idea." So I took the forms and when I got home and told my husband, oh! he hit the roof. He was one of those men that didn't believe in the wife ever working; they want to be the supporter. I said, "Well, I've made up my mind. I'm going to go to work regardless of whether you like it or not." I was determined.

My family and everybody was surprised—his family. I said, "Well, yeah, I'm going to work." "And how does Julio feel?" "He doesn't want me to, but I'm going anyway." When he saw that, he just kept quiet; he didn't say no more. My mother didn't say nothing because I always told her, "Mother, you live your life and I live mine." We had that understanding. When I decided to go to work, I told her, "I'm going to go to work and maybe you can take care of the children." She said, "Yeah."

The intensity of emotions Bea felt on that day some forty years ago when she first walked through the doors of Lockheed was communicated through her demeanor as well as her words. She crouched in mock meekness and whispered hesitatingly, feigning fear.

[BEA:] I filled out the papers and everything and I got the job. Why I took Lockheed, I don't know, but I just liked that name. Then they asked me, "Do you want to go to Burbank, to Los Angeles?" I said, "I don't know where Burbank is." I didn't know my way around. The only way that I got up to Los Angeles was with Julio driving me there. I said, "Well, Los Angeles. The streetcar passes by Fair Oaks, close to where I live, and that drops me off in front."

To me, everything was new. They were doing the P-38s at that time. I was at Plant 2, on Seventh and Santa Fe. It was on the fifth floor. I went up there and saw the place, and I said, "Gee—." See, so many parts and things that you've never seen. Me, I'd never seen anything in my whole life. It was exciting and scary at the same time.

They put me way up in the back, putting little plate nuts and drilling holes. They put me with some guy—he was kind of a stinker, real mean. A lot of them guys at the time resented women coming into jobs, and they let you know about it. He says, "Well, have you ever done any work like this?" I said, "No." I was feeling just horrible. Horrible. Because I never worked with men, to be with men alone other than my husband. So then he says "You know what you've got in your hand? That's a rivet gun." I said, "Oh." What could I answer? I was terrified. So then time went on and I made a mistake. I messed up something, made a ding. He got so irritable with me, he says, "You're not worth the money Lockheed pays you."

He couldn't have hurt me more if he would have slapped me. When he said that, I dropped the gun and I went running downstairs to the restroom, with tears coming down. This girl from Texas saw me and she followed me. She was real good. She was one of these "toughies"; dressed up and walked like she was kind of tough. She asked me what was wrong. I told her what I had done and I was crying. She says, "Don't worry." She started cussing him. We came back up and she told them all off.

I was very scared because, like I say, I had never been away like that and I had never been among a lot of men. Actually, I had never been out on my own. Whenever I had gone anyplace, it was with my husband. It was all building up inside of me, so when that guy told me that I wasn't worth the money Lockheed paid me, it just came out in tears.

At the end of that first day, I was so tired. I was riding the streetcar and I had to stand all the way from Los Angeles clear to Pasadena. When I got home, the kids just said, "Oh, Mom is here." My husband, he didn't have very much to say, 'cause he didn't approve from the beginning. As time went on, his attitude changed a little, but I don't think he ever really, really got used to the idea of me working. But he was a very reserved man. He wasn't the type of guy that you'd sit down and you'd chatter on. Like me, I'm a chatterbox. You had to pull the words out of him.

As Bea described her initiation to her sixty-five-cents-an-hour assembly job, her tone of voice slowly changed. The hesitancy that had reflected her sense of awe and fear as she faced this new experience was replaced with a more forceful delivery that displayed her increased confidence and pride.

[BEA:] They had a union, but it wasn't very strong then. It wasn't like it is now. But I joined. I joined everything that they told me. Buck of the Month, everything. And they gave me a list of the stuff that I would be needing. At that time they used to sell you your tools and your toolboxes through Lockheed. So I bought a box. I bought the clothing at Sears. It was just a pair of pants and a blouse. To tell you the truth, I felt kind of funny wearing pants. Then at the same time, I said, "Oh, what the heck." And those shoes! I wasn't used to low shoes. Even in the house, I always wore high heels. That's how I started.

As time went on, I started getting a little bit better. I just made up my mind that I was going to do it. I learned my job so well that then they put me to the next operation. At the very first, I just began putting little plate nuts and stuff like that. Then afterwards I learned how to drill the skins and burr them. Later, as I got going, I learned to rivet and buck. I got to the point where I was very good.

I had a Mexican girl, Irene Herrera, and she was as good a bucker as I was a riveter. She would be facing me and we'd just go right on through. We'd go one side and then we'd get up to the corner and I'd hand her the gun or the bucking bar or whatever and then we'd come back. Her and I, we used to have a lot of fun. They would want maybe six or five elevators a day. I'd say, "let's get with it." We worked pretty hard all day until about 2:00. Then we would slack down.

I had a lot of friends there. We all spoke to each other. Most of them smoked, and we'd sit in the smoking areas out there in the aisle. Then, some of the girls—on the next corner there was a drugstore that served lunches. There was a white lady, she used to go, and Irene would go. We'd talk about our families and stuff like that.

Irene stayed on that same operation. I don't know why I got a chance to learn all the other jobs, but I learned the whole operation until I got up to the front, the last step. They used to put this little flap with a wire, with a hinge. I had to have that flap just right so that it would swing easy without no rubbing anywhere. I used to go with a little hammer and a screwdriver and knock those little deals down so that it would be just right. That guy that I used to work with helped me, teached me how to do it, and I could do it just like him.

New people would come in, and they would say, "You teach them the job. You know all the jobs." Sometimes it would make me mad. I'd tell them, "What the heck, you get paid for it. You show them the job." But I would still show them.

Then, like that leadperson, they'd say, "Look at her now. You should have seen her a year ago when she first came in. You'd go boo and she'd start crying. Now she can't keep her mouth shut." I figured this is the only way you're going to survive, so I'm going to do it.

I was just a mother of four kids, that's all. But I felt proud of myself and felt good being that I had never done anything like that. I felt good that I could do something, and being that it was war, I felt that I was doing my part.

I went from 65 cents to $1.05. That was top pay. It felt good and, besides, it was my own money. I could do whatever I wanted with it because my husband, whatever he was giving to the house, he kept on paying it. I used to buy clothes for the kids; buy little things that they needed. I had a bank account and I had a little saving at home where I could get ahold of the money right away if I needed it. Julio never asked about it. He knew how much I made; I showed him. If there was something that had to be paid and I had the money and he didn't, well, I used some of my money. But he never said, "Well, you have to pay because you're earning money." My money, I did what I wanted.

I started feeling a little more independent. Just a little, not too much, because I was still not on my own that I could do this and do that. I didn't until after. Then I got really independent.

Although Julio had originally opposed her going to work, he and the children pitched in to do the household chores, along with Bea's mother, who also provided child care during Bea's work hours. Still, Bea, like most working mothers, was ultimately responsible for keeping her household running smoothly and caring for her children.

Like so many homemakers, Bea was able to deviate from her traditional role because her work was viewed within the context of patriotic duty. Few of these working mothers, however, were ready to openly challenge conventional values. When there was a family crisis, they were likely to quit their job in order to take charge at home. As a result, the absenteeism and turnover rates were high among such women.

[BEA:] I got home and my mother told me, she says, "Gerry is very sick. He's got a lot of fever and it won't go down." I never thought of having a family doctor, so I had to call the police station and they sent me this doctor that was real nice. He started giving him shots and that's what brought him out. It was pneumonia and he was very sick for quite a long time.

My husband, right away, he jumped: "You see, the kids are like this because you're not here." My mother was there, but he blamed everything on me. We got into a little bit of an argument on account of that, and then I said, "Okay, I'll quit." I didn't want to, but I said my boy comes first. Afterwards, I realized I could have gone on a leave of absence. But I wasn't too familiar with all that, so I just panicked and quit.

When I quit, I just took over the same as I was before—taking care of my kids. Well, it was kind of quiet and I wasn't too satisfied. That's why I started looking to go to work. I had already tasted that going-out business and I wasn't too satisfied. I stayed home about a year or so, and then I took a little job at Joyce; they used to make shoes. It was walking distance from where I lived. I would get the packages of leather already cut and mark the shoes with a marking machine and put them in pairs and put them on the belt so the stitchers could sew them.

I worked there about a year. Then my husband told me, "Well, if you're going to be working, why don't you work with me?" There was this man that got sick—he was a janitor—so they gave me his theater. My husband would help me. He would get the biggest mopping and the windows. I would do mostly the auditorium—sweep it and vacuum. We would do his job and my job together. They were giving me a hassle. It was union and they didn't want me to join the union. I would be working on a permit with the union, and I said, "Well, if I can work on a permit, why can't I work as a member?" I finally said, "Look, go jump in the lake." So I quit.

I was already thinking of Lockheed. I wasn't satisfied. I felt myself alone and I said, "Oh, I can't do this; I can't stay here." In 1950 I wrote to Lockheed asking them if they had a job for me because I knew that they were still taking people. They wrote and told me that they weren't taking any women, but that they would the following year. The next year, the minute I received that telegram, I headed for Lockheed.

I went to the office all ready. This was in Burbank. They give you a list of rides and stuff and that's how I started—riding with people from Pasadena. I think they started me at $1.65, or something like that. Riveting. We were working on the side panels of the T-33.

It wasn't like it was before because I already knew a little of it, so it wasn't as hard. I was working two months when they told me, being that I was new I had to either go on nights or I'd be laid off. So I told them, "I'll go on nights!"

Discussion Questions

1. Based on the oral histories you have just read, discuss the impact of World War II on race relations and prejudice. Discuss the ways in which each woman's oral history sheds light on racial attitudes and changes in attitude and opportunity during World War II. How did the experiences of black, white, and Latino women differ?

2. First look at the World War II posters at the end of this chapter. Then, in groups, design a poster aimed at recruiting women for factory work during World War II. Sketch out the poster, and discuss what might or might not have worked to attract women to jobs during the era when women either worked in the home or worked primarily in secretarial, teaching, or nursing jobs.

Writing Suggestions

1. In her oral history, Juanita Loveless stated that what really attracted her to working in the aircraft industry was not the money but the advertisements that were circulating at the time: "The ads—they had to be

bombardments: 'Do Your Part,' 'Uncle Sam Needs You,' 'V for Victory.' I got caught up in that patriotic 'win the war. . . .'" Write an analysis of the war-time "calls to work" that appeared in women's magazines. Focus your analysis on advertisements from the manufacturers of women's products. For your research, use old copies of *Ladies Home Journal*, the *Saturday Evening Post*, or other magazines you find from the war years. Answer some of the following questions in your analysis:

How did product advertisements entice women to work while assuring them that they would remain feminine? Consider both visual and textual arguments here.

How did the advertisements appeal to patriotism at the same time that they appealed to women's desire to remain feminine?

What kind of art was used in the advertisements? How did they use live models and photographs?

How did the advertisements keep the war at the forefront of every piece?

2. Consider your responses to the first discussion question, and then write an analytical paper in which you discuss the impact of World War II on race relations and prejudice. Using specific details from the oral histories, discuss the ways in which each woman's oral history sheds light on racial attitudes and changes in attitude and opportunity during World War II. Discuss how the experiences of black, white, and Latino women differed.

3. Research what happened to women in the labor force after the war, when the men returned home and women were encouraged to return to their homes. Consider some of the following questions for your analysis:

How many women were able to stay in the workforce?

What kinds of jobs remained available to women, and which jobs were no longer offered?

Did most women want to return home, or did they want to continue working?

What happened to childcare after the war?

What kind of propaganda did the government issue to get women back into their homes?

Navajo Code Talkers

BRUCE WATSON

The Navajo Code Talkers were members of the U.S. Marines who not only encoded, decoded, and transmitted messages in an unbreakable Navajo code, but also participated in warfare in the Pacific from 1942 to 1945. Although their contribution to the war remained secret for many years, since 1968 they have begun to receive some publicity and public acclaim for developing an unbreakable code that mystified the Japanese military completely; today a permanent exhibit in the Pentagon honors their contributions. In the article below from the August 1993 issue of *Smithsonian Magazine*, "Navajo Code Talkers," writer Bruce Watson explains how the Navajo were recruited and trained, and he also explores the suspicion they encountered during their participation in the war in the Pacific and the lasting psychological effects of the war on the Navajo soldiers.

Cloaked in secrecy and syntax, code machines were the pride of World War II cryptographers. State-of-the-art devices with cryptic names like "Enigma," "Purple" and "The Bomb," these black boxes used rotors and ratchets to shroud messages in a thick alphabet soup. But U.S. marines storming Pacific beaches used a different kind of code machine. Instead of rotors, each Marine Corps cryptograph had two arms, two legs, an M-1 rifle and a helmet. Their code name was *Dineh*—"The People." In English, they were called "Navajos."

As marines fought cave to cave on Iwo Jima, a foreign language crackled over field radios. Bombers were called *jaysho*—buzzards—and bombs were *ayeshi*—eggs. The commanding officer was *bihkehhe*—war chief—and each platoon was a *hasclishnih*—mud clan. On the morning of February 23, 1945, when six soldiers on a mountaintop hoisted the Stars and Stripes for all the world to see, the word went out in code: *"Naastsosi Thanzie Dibeh Shida Dahnestsa Tkin Shush Wollachee Moasi Lin Achi."* Marine cryptographers translated the Navajo words for *"Mouse Turkey Sheep Uncle Ram Ice Bear Ant Cat Horse Intestines,"* then told their fellow marines in English: the American flag flew over Mount Suribachi.

In most movies, the Navajos speak in a primitive pidgin and they still fight on horseback. But long after the West was won and lost, a group of Navajo patriots sharpened speech into a precise weapon and went to war for the nation that surrounded their own. They hit every Pacific beach from Guadalcanal to Okinawa, but their story is at best a footnote in war chronicles. They are the Navajo Code Talkers, and theirs is one of the few unbroken codes in military history.

More than 3,600 Navajos served in World War II but only 420 were Code Talkers. Members of all six Marine Corps divisions in the Asian-Pacific theater, they coded and decoded messages faster than any black box, baffling the Japanese with a hodgepodge of everyday Navajo and some 400 code words of their own devising. In early Pacific invasions their code was barely used by skeptical officers, but Marine commanders came to see it as "indispensable for the rapid transmission of classified dispatches." For three critical years, these Navajo polyglots proved that when it came to heroism, The People, too often known for their silence, spoke volumes.

Like all Americans of his generation, Keith Little remembers exactly where he was when he heard the news of Pearl Harbor (*SMITHSONIAN*, December 1991). Now a robust, rugged man in his 60s, Little recalls the boarding school on the reservation of Ganado, Arizona. He and his fellow students had some choice words for the cafeteria gruel, Little remembers. So on Sunday afternoon, December 7, "Me and a bunch of guys were out hunting rabbits with a .22. We had a rabbit cooking down in the wash, and somebody went to the dorm, came back and said, 'Hey, Pearl Harbor was bombed!' One of us asked, 'Where's Pearl Harbor?'

"'In Hawaii.'

"'Who did it?'

"'Japan.'

"'Why'd they do it?'

"'They hate Americans. They want to kill all Americans.'

"'Us, too?'

"'Yeah, us too.'

"Then and there, we all made a promise. We were, most of us, 15 or 16, I guess. We promised each other we'd go after the Japanese instead of hunting rabbits."

The next morning, the superintendent of the Navajo reservation looked out his office window. There stood dozens of ponytailed men in red bandanas, carrying hunting rifles, ready to fight. A year earlier the Navajo Tribal Council, taking cognizance of a world at war, had unanimously resolved to defend the United States against invasion. "There exists no purer concentration of Americanism than among the First Americans," the council declared. But the Navajo volunteers were sent home. No official call to arms had been issued, and besides, most of the men spoke only Navajo.

When the war broke out, Philip Johnston was a civil engineer with wire-rimmed glasses, a buttoned-down mind and a fluency in Navajo. The son of missionaries, Johnston grew up on the reservations. Reading about an Army test of Native American languages in combat maneuvers, Johnston had a mousetrap of an idea. During World War I, Indians in the American and Canadian armies had sent messages in their native languages. But lacking words like "machine gun" and "grenade," their use was limited. Early in 1942, when Johnston visited the Marine Corps' Camp Elliott, north of San Diego, he proposed an up-to-date code, guaranteed unbreakable. The Marines were skeptical at first, but Johnston returned with a few Navajo friends. For 15 minutes, while the iron jaws of Marine brass went slack, messages metamorphosed from English to Navajo and back. In April 1942, as the Japanese sent American prisoners on the Bataan Death March, Marine recruiters came to the land of "Changing Woman," the Navajo fertility goddess.

Though the Marines had been from the halls of Montezuma to the shores of Tripoli, they had never seen a place like the Navajo Nation. Scattered across the mile-high Southwest desert, fewer than 40,000 Navajos lived in a territory the size of West Virginia. The reservation had few paved roads, no electricity or plumbing, only a handful of schools. Nearly all Navajos herded sheep, lived in houses called hogans and bought what little they could not grow or make at the nearest trading post. Recruiters set up tables in the sagebrush and sandstone, called them enlistment offices and began looking for a few good men fluent in Navajo and English.

Fewer than 80 years had passed since the Navajo Nation had fought *against* the U.S. military. In 1864, following Kit Carson's scorched-earth campaign against them, a band of starving, ragged Navajos was marched 350 miles across New Mexico. Navajos call the relocation "The Long Walk." Though they returned four years later, the sad story was still being told when white men in uniform came seeking soldiers. President Franklin Roosevelt's Administration was then destroying Navajo sheep to reduce soil erosion and overgrazing. Why would men volunteer to fight for a nation that had humbled their ancestors, killed their herds and wouldn't even let them vote? (Voting rights for Navajos were restricted until 1948 in Arizona, 1953 in New Mexico and 1957 in Utah.) "Why do you have to go?" asked one mother. "It's not your war. It's the white man's war."

From nation to nation, soldiers enlist for reasons that lose nothing in translation, including jobs, adventure, family tradition and patriotism. "What happened to the Navajos in the past were social conflicts," explained Albert Smith, a soft-spoken, highly spiritual man who now serves as president of the Navajo Code Talkers' Association in Gallup, New Mexico. "But this conflict involved Mother Earth being dominated by foreign countries. It was our responsibility to defend her."

The Navajo creation story tells how The People emerged through a series of imperfect worlds. From a First World "black as wool" to a second, third and fourth realm, First Man and First Woman led Navajos to this world where beauty surrounds them. Not all the boys boarding the train for boot camp in San Diego believed the old story. Nevertheless, the Code Talkers, switching from hogans to Quonset huts, stood at the rim of one world looking into another.

Few had ever been off the reservation. They had met "Anglos" only on trading posts. Soon they would fight across an ocean they'd never seen, against an enemy they'd never met. So much mystery demanded ceremony, and recruits hired medicine men to perform a ritual called "The Blessing Way." The devout carried sacred corn pollen for protection. Unarmed but guarded by the ritual, 29 Navajos got their first glimpse of the Pacific and entered the world of drill instructors and *Semper Fi.*

Marines called the Navajos "Chief" and "Geronimo," and expected them to be eagle-eyed with a bow and arrow. But while the Navajos had long ago put aside bow and arrow, they proved to be model marines. Accustomed to walking miles each day in the high desert, they marched on with full packs after others balked and buckled. Only once did they falter. A drill instructor ordered his Chiefs to march in cadence to their language. But Navajo numbers lack the rhythm of "Hup, two, three, four," and the marchers added colloquial remarks about the D.I. The unit dissolved in disorder and hysterics. Toughened with the usual grit and gristle, the first group of Navajos became the 382d Platoon, USMC, and was ordered to make a code.

In 1942, it was mostly anthropologists and linguists who wrote Navajo. On the reservation the language was primarily oral, and the Code Talkers were told to keep it that way. There would be no code books, no cryptic algorithms. Navajo itself was puzzling enough. Germans deciphering English codes could tap common linguistic roots. Japanese eavesdropping on G.I.'s were often graduates of American universities. But Navajo, rooted in Athabaskan tongues probably brought across the land bridge from Asia, is a tonal language. Its vowels rise and fall, changing meaning with pitch. A single Navajo verb, containing its own subjects, objects and adverbs, can translate into an entire English sentence. In Navajo, one speaker noted, words "paint a picture in your mind."

To paint pictures at an exhibition of war, the Code Talkers turned not to math and machines but to nature. They named planes after birds: *gini*—chicken hawk (dive bomber); *neasjah*—owl (observation plane); *taschizzie*—swallow (torpedo plane). They named ships after fish: *lotso*—whale (battleship); *calo*—shark (destroyer); *beshlo*—iron fish (submarine). To spell out proper names, the Code Talkers made a Navajo bestiary, turning the Marines' Able Baker Charlie into *Wollachee Shush Moasi* . . . Ant Bear Cat. Finished with flora and fauna, they played word games. "District" became the Navajo words for "deer ice strict," and "belong" became "long bee." The enemy was christened by characteristic: Japanese—*Behnaalitsosie* (slant eyes); Hitler—*Daghailchiih* (Mustache Smeller); and Mussolini—*Adee 'yaats'iin Tsoh* (Big Gourd Chin). Soon a message like "Jap sniper by fortification at Bloody Ridge" became: "Slant eye kill 'em all by cliff dwelling at Badger Lamb Owl Onion Deer Yucca Rabbit Ice Dog Goat Elk." Once the message was translated, some brave "One Silver Bar" (lieutenant) could lob a few "potatoes" (grenades) into the "cliff dwelling," sending the "kill 'em all" to the place "among devils" (a cemetery).

Instant Coding and Decoding—Like Magic

When the code was finished, Navy intelligence officers spent three weeks trying, and failing, to decipher a single message. New Navajo recruits untrained in the code could not break it. Yet it still seemed too simple to be trusted. Since 1940, U.S. intelligence had routinely intercepted and translated every message from the Japanese "Purple" code. The process, code-named "Magic," took hours. But these Indians were encoding and decoding sensitive military information almost instantly. What kind of magic was this?

"Well, in Navajo everything is in memory," said William McCabe, one of the code's designers. "From the songs, prayers, everything, it's all in memory. So we didn't have no trouble. That's the way we was raised up."

Two Code Talkers stayed behind to teach the next group. The rest were shipped overseas. The Navajo cosmology does not include a hell, but the Navajo recruits were about to enter one called Guadalcanal.

Assigned to four separate regiments on "the Canal," Code Talkers met skepticism in the flesh. One colonel agreed to use them only if they won a man-versus-machine test against a cylindrical gizmo that disguised words and broadcast in coded clicks. The Code Talkers won handily. When another officer gave them a trial on a common frequency, frantic Marine radio operators elsewhere on the island thought the Japanese were jamming the airwaves. After the lieutenant answered that the jabber came from fellow marines, the word came back: "What's going on over there at Division? You guys drunk?" Despite the Code Talkers' undeniable speed and mystifying language, officers were reluctant to trust lives to a code still untested in combat. Instead, the Code Talkers were used as everyday soldiers, fighting both the Japanese and the jungle.

For sons of the high desert, Guadalcanal, infested with leeches and crocodiles, drenched by torrential rains, recalled horrors from the Navajos' dark "First World." But, while ordinary marines survived on C-rations, the Code Talkers lived off the land, making stew from chickens picked off with a slingshot, hunting, skinning and dining on goats and horses. Other marines stumbled in the dark and recoiled from the wild terrain, but the Navajos proved adept night scouts and natural guerrilla fighters.

Back on the reservation, while medicine men performed rituals to protect sons overseas, Navajo instructors led by Sgt. Philip Johnston kept searching for the best and brightest volunteers. In boot camp, Keith Little was just another Chief, and few knew or cared from which tribe. Then a D.I. took him aside and asked, "By any chance, are you a Navajo?" Sent to Code Talkers' school, Little memorized 25 words a day. Tests weeded out about 5 percent of the recruits, who returned to regular duty. The rest were shipped to island infernos where the code had begun to convince the doubters.

An Urgent Plea: "Do You Have a Navajo?"

On Rabaul, Code Talkers loaned to the Navy kept Japanese from learning of impending air attacks. On Saipan, an advancing American battalion was shelled from behind by "friendly fire." Desperate messages called "Hold your fire!" but the Japanese had imitated Marine broadcasts all day, and the mortar crews weren't sure what to believe. The shelling continued. Finally headquarters asked, "Do you have a Navajo?" A single Navajo sent the same message back to his buddy, and the shelling stopped.

"When you started sending messages and everything was correct, they started treating you like a king," Harold Foster recalled. "They'd say 'Chief, let me carry your radio for you. Let me carry your rifle for you.' " Code Talkers were given their own bodyguards, often to protect them from marines who couldn't tell a Navajo from a Japanese.

On Saipan, Samuel Holiday joined his buddies skinny-dipping in a shell hole filled with rainwater. He made the mistake of being the last man out of the pool. An MP saw the short, black-haired man wearing his birthday suit instead of a private's stripe. "I turned around and they had the bayonet right between my eyes," Holiday recalled. Marched back to camp, he became one of many Navajos glad to hear a familiar face call him "Chief."

Ethnicity fools soldiers but not bullets. Wading ashore in a hail of fire, two Code Talkers were killed on New Britain, three on Bougainville, one on Guam, another on Peleliu. The bodies came home but not the top secret. To conceal the code's origin, Code Talkers' letters home were not delivered. A year after their sons left the reservation, families still had no word from them. When an anxious Navajo superintendent asked Johnston about the recruits, the by-the-book sergeant couldn't contain his pride. They were involved in a secret code project, he wrote. Soon an article, "Navajo Indians at War," appeared in an Arizona magazine. After the Marines traced the source, Johnston was booted out of the Corps. Before he left, fearing the story would be forgotten, he took some Code Talker documents and later gave them to the Code Talkers' Association.

The Special Horrors of a Corpse-Strewn Beach

As U.S. forces closed in on Japan, the word was that this new code could not be broken, not even when the Japanese captured an ordinary Navajo soldier. "They ordered him to translate," Code Talker James Nahkai recalled. "The poor guy couldn't do it. 'It's their own code,' he told the Japs. 'I don't understand.' This was in a POW camp back in Japan, in winter, and they stripped his clothes off and his feet froze to the ground."

Between invasions, Code Talkers convened to update the code. Then it was back to the beachheads. There may be no atheists in foxholes, but for a devout Navajo in battle, faith brought as much terror as comfort. Believing that the living can be harmed by the presence of the dead, unless protected by ceremony, some Code Talkers were especially horrified at seeing a corpse-strewn beach.

"We went right directly to the Marshall Islands first," remembered Dan Akee. I saw some dead Japanese. And the Navajos usually fear that, you know. I tried not to glance at it, but I just couldn't help it. I just had to be among all those deads. That was one of the hardest things to get over."

The carnage of battle continues to haunt Code Talkers who can scarcely find words for what they saw. Asked "What did you do in the war, Daddy?" most World War II vets summon tales from the jungle of memory. But even 50 years later many Code Talkers respond with a deadly pause. Ask Sidney Bedoni, veteran of Guadalcanal, Saipan, Iwo Jima and Okinawa. "No. No. Uh, well, it really . . . I could tell a lot of stories about that, but I just don't . . . don't have the time to talk about it." Ask Lewis Ayze, veteran of Saipan and Guam: "These stories I don't care to relate." George Kirk, survivor of ten Pacific bloodbaths, rummages through photographs in his Arizona home. One shows him a baby-faced rookie at the radio on Bougainville. Another taken only months later shows a war-weary veteran seated beside a helmet with a hole through the top. "Shrapnel," Kirk says. He doesn't say much more.

The Code Talkers have reason to be proud of their work on Iwo Jima, but their words paint mere impressions: "It just seemed like the island was burning early in the morning," one recalled. "This shelling was just coming down just like rain." Approaching "Iwo," a teardrop with a volcano on one end, most marines bowed their heads with the chaplain. Code Talkers sprinkled corn pollen and recalled their "Blessing Way" ritual.

George Kirk remembered, "Some of the guys didn't believe in a church, either Anglo or Navajo religion, but on Iwo Jima I heard them pray. I heard them cry."

Teddy Draper grew up at the site of a Navajo "day of infamy," a canyon where Spanish invaders slaughtered 125 Navajos in 1804. But not even the legends of Canyon del Muerto (Canyon of Death) prepared him for Iwo Jima. As Draper hit the beach, the tide washed back the dead. "There were a lot of machine guns going along all the way around Suribachi about 50 feet apart from the bottom to the top," he said. "Just flying shells, all over. You couldn't see." A shell tore through Draper's pants, just missing his leg. "And I thought, 'I don't know if I'm going to live or not.' "

Working around the clock during the first two days on Iwo, six networks of Code Talkers transmitted more than 800 messages without an error. In the monthlong battle, three Code Talkers were killed. But by the time their code spelled out "Mt. Suribachi," they had at last convinced all skeptics. Signal officer Maj. Howard Conner recalled, "Without the Navajos the Marines would never have taken Iwo Jima."

With human code machines churning out messages, the Marines went on to take Okinawa. Many Code Talkers were practicing street fighting, preparing for the invasion of Japan, when the war ended. "I kind of wanted to see Japan," George Kirk said. But the Navajos were headed home to their high country.

Decades after he exchanged his .22 for an M-1, Keith Little, a successful logger representing the National Inter-tribal Timber Council, visited Washington, D.C. and dropped by the Pentagon. The burly Iwo Jima veteran wandered the halls, looking at war photographs, searching for some mention of Navajos or Native Americans. "It finally hit home," Little remembered. "I realized we had lost our own country to foreigners and they were still getting all the recognition. Native Americans were getting nothing."

After the war some Code Talkers accompanied their divisions to China and stood on the Great Wall. In Japan, some saw the ashes of the atomic age at Nagasaki. But once back on the reservation, they were Indians again. Utah, Arizona and New Mexico still limited their voting rights. The government's livestock reduction plan had killed a third of all Navajo sheep, leaving the grass to grow, fertilized by resentment. Boys who had upped their ages to see the world and defend Mother Earth went back to high school. Others worked where they could, returned to their hogans and had nightmares.

When George Kirk began dreaming of enemy soldiers leaping into his foxhole, his wife sent him to a medicine man. "The Enemy Way," a three-day ceremonial slaying of the "enemy presence," cured Kirk and many other Navajo veterans. Samuel Smith told his medicine man the whole story. "Now my son," the healer answered, "don't tell it no more to nobody, anywhere. That way you won't be bothered in the future."

The code remained top secret. Asked about the war, Code Talkers simply said, "I was a radioman." War movies and histories poured forth without mentioning them. But by linking The People to the world beyond the reservation, the Navajo vets had changed the Nation forever. A few remained in the Marines and fought in Korea and Vietnam, but the code was never used again. It was finally declassified in 1968. Only then did the secret come out.

The first Code Talker reunion in 1969 brought nation-wide attention. In 1982, President Ronald Reagan named August 14 "National Navaho Code Talkers Day." Ten years later, Keith Little was invited to the Pentagon. There he translated a prayer for peace phoned in by a Code Talker in Arizona. Simple but efficient, the code still worked. Then Little and other Navajo vets helped dedicate a permanent exhibit on the Code Talkers.

Today a small, proud corps of silver-haired Code Talkers, as loyal to *Semper Fi* as they are to Navajo tradition, march in symbolic uniforms, wearing both turquoise beads and military medals. But mindful of Navajo caveats against glorifying war, most of the remaining few hundred avoid all ceremonies and parades. Only a handful will even discuss the war. "Talking about war contaminates the minds of those who should not hear about the bloodshed," explained Albert Smith. "There is always the danger of enticement for the young." So, like the stern photographs of young men in Marine uniforms framed in homes scattered across the sparse Navajo Nation, the Code Talkers are silent again.

Still their phones keep ringing, "a constant barrage," Smith said. History students seek details for dissertations. Hollywood wants a Native American Rambo. Already, a dime-store novel, *The Code Talkers*, tells of one Johnny Redhawk who leaves the reservation to become "America's secret weapon in the South Pacific." Keith Little shook his head. "Most of us are common men," he said. "We don't get in the front line and wave our arms. We know what we did and can tell it as it was without having to wave it on a TV screen."

But at the Window Rock Elementary School on the Arizona-New Mexico border, students are in search of a few good heroes. Children in the Navajo capital live in houses or trailers, often with a hogan out back beside the TV satellite dish. In school, young Navajos well versed in American pop culture learn Native Studies from teacher Isidore Begay. They read about the Navajo ascent through the four worlds. They study Changing Woman. And they read about the Code Talkers.

"Are they heroes?" Begay asks a fourth-grade class.

Students nod. "We could have lost the war," one says. "Then we'd be slaves to Japan."

Students send messages in Navajo code and find Iwo Jima on a map, trying to imagine how far the Code Talkers traveled. The chasm between countries and cultures has been closed by men who crossed the border between different traditions. In code, they spoke of snipers and fortifications, but their real message needed no interpreter. They spoke about surmounting stereotypes and vendettas for a higher cause. They spoke about blending tradition into the modern world. They spoke Navajo.

Discussion Questions

1. Discuss the method the Navajo Code Talkers used to send messages. How did the Navajo use their language and the English language together to create messages that were undecipherable? What aspects of the Navajo language made it particularly appropriate for the needs of the government for an unbreakable code?

2. Watson mentions a number of instances in which Navajo culture made the experience of war in the Pacific particularly difficult for the Code Talkers. Discuss the variety of specific problems faced by the Navajo relevant to their race and their culture.

3. In the government Indian schools in the 1920s and 1930s, the Navajo were forbidden to use their own language and were punished if they did so. Discuss the irony of the loyalty of the Japanese, Navajo, and black soldiers who fought so hard despite the history of racism against them in the United States.

Writing Suggestions

1. Bruce Watson wrote this article for the *Smithsonian Magazine*; he did not write the article as a research paper, although it contains a great deal of research. Write an essay in which you analyze Watson's style—what makes this essay more appropriate for a magazine than for a research journal? How has he geared his organization, tone, and style toward a magazine article? Consider his sentences, paragraphs, introduction, and conclusion as you analyze his essay.

2. Research the story of the Navajo Code Talkers more fully and write an analysis of the code itself, its uses, and the training involved for the Navajo who used it. You can begin your research with the Navy and Marine Corps World War II Committee article on the Web at <http//www.wae.com/webcat/navajos.htm>. You can also find more information on other sites on the Internet and in books on the Code Talkers in your library.

World War II Propaganda

The propaganda posters presented on the following pages are just a sampling of the variety of recruitment and propaganda materials that appeared in the nation's media during World War II. Artists appealed to a wide variety of emotions to encourage women to join the workforce and to persuade all Americans, male and female, to participate in the war effort and to exceed production quotas in the workplace.

Hoover Institution Archives Collection

Hoover Institution Archives Collection

Hoover Institution Archives Collection

Hoover Institution Archives Collection

Hoover Institution Archives Collection

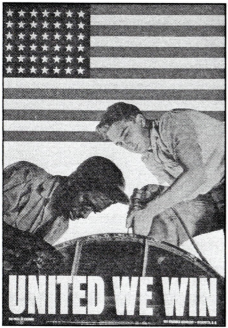

Hoover Institution Archives Collection

Hoover Institution Archives Collection

Hoover Institution Archives Collection

Chapter 7: Writing Suggestions

1. Write an essay about your perceptions of the U.S. relocation camps in comparison to the concentration camps of Nazi Germany. Some writers have claimed that the American camps were in fact concentration camps, since the inhabitants were segregated by race, had lost many personal freedoms, and were surrounded by barbed wire and forbidden to leave. Respond to this point of view, arguing your position about whether or not the relocation camps could in fact be called concentration camps.

2. Rent the movie *Tora, Tora, Tora,* produced in 1970 by Twentieth Century Fox, and write a comparison paper looking at the similarities and differences between this movie and the 2001 movie *Pearl Harbor.* How did the producers stress different aspects of Pearl Harbor? How were the Japanese portrayed in each movie? What political elements were stressed in each movie? Which movie do you feel portrayed the events of Pearl Harbor more accurately? Use specifics from each movie to back up your assertions.

3. Look at the World War II posters on page 639 that depict the Japanese enemy. Write an analysis of how the enemy is portrayed. How might the propaganda from the government have affected the lives of the Japanese Americans who were in the internment camps? How do you think these posters affected the civilian population's attitude toward the Japanese Americans once they were released from the internment camps?

4. This chapter presents many topics for an interesting research paper. Choose one of the controversial topics below or develop one of your own, and write an argumentative research paper, taking a stand with a strong thesis, examining opposing points of view, and using additional evidence to back up your argument.

   Woodrow Wilson's isolationism and late entrance into World War I

   World War I propaganda

   The American occupation of Germany after the armistice

   The terms of the Treaty of Versailles

   Government programs to halt the Depression

   President Hoover's approach to public aid during the depression

   Woody Guthrie's depression-era music and its effect on morale

   The conflict between the farmers and the migrant workers in the 1930s

   The contributions of blacks, Native Americans, Philippine Americans, Hawaiians, and other minority groups in World War II

   President Roosevelt's foreknowledge or lack of knowledge about the Pearl Harbor attack

   The U.S. government's handling of the relocation of Japanese Americans

   The dropping of the atomic bomb on Hiroshima and Nagasaki

   American involvement in the Black Market in Germany

   The American occupation of Germany and Japan and subsequent changes to their school texts

5.　Kennedy writes that "the disagreeable truth, however, is that the most responsible students of the events of 1929 have not been able to demonstrate
an appreciable cause-and-effect linkage between the Crash and the Depression." Research the causes of the Depression further, and then write a paper
agreeing or disagreeing with Kennedy's assertion. What variety of factors
caused the Depression? What do modern historical scholars propose in lieu
of the stock-market crash as the determining factor for the Depression? Use
at least five sources in addition to Kennedy's *Freedom from Fear*, and try to
use books and articles that have been published within the past twenty years.

6.　Look at the World War II propaganda posters (on pages 637–638) that
were primarily aimed at women on the home front, and also look at the
posters in the National Archives on-line poster collection: <http://
www.nara.gov/exhall/powers/powers.html>. You can also find a collection of World War II posters at Northwestern University's site: <http://
www.library.northwestern.edu/govpub/collections/wwii-posters>. Then
write an analysis of the posters on pages 637–638 or of the posters you
found on-line, discussing the different appeals used to attract women to
war jobs. What emotions did government posters target? How did they
vary the symbols and slogans used in the posters? What kind of written
texts accompanied the posters? How was design used, and what patterns
did you find? How did the posters appeal specifically to women?

Chapter 7: Further Research on the Web

To pursue your research on the Internet, explore some of the following sites:

World War I
http://www.lib.byu.edu/~rdh/wwi
http://www.pbs.org/greatwar

Great Depression and Dust Bowl
http://lcweb2.loc.gov/ammem/afctshtml/tshome.html

World War Two
http://www.yale.edu/lawweb/avalon/wwii/wwii.htm
http://history.rutgers.edu/oralhistory/orlhom.htm
http://www.nara.gov/exhall/people/people.htm

World War Two Posters
http://www.nara.gov/exhall/powers/powers.html
http://www.library.northwestern.edu/govpub/collections/wwii-posters

Manzanar Relocation Camp
http://www.nps.gov/manz

Pearl Harbor
http://www.nationalgeographic.com/pearlharbor
http:www.nps.gov.usar

Civil Rights, Protest, and Foreign Wars

The selections in this chapter have been chosen to give you a sense of the conflicts that dominated the postwar era in the United States, from the women's movement, to the civil rights movement, to the Chicano farm workers' movement, and finally to U.S. involvement in Vietnam. All of these conflicts had vocal representatives—writers and speakers who sought to influence the political, economic, racial, and gender-related issues of the day. As you read the following selections, ask yourself how language, written and oral, can influence the trends of social change. How do the speeches of political leaders sway the public? How do protesters use words and essays to begin to effect massive changes in society? How can research and writing be tools for reflection on past, present, and future conflicts in American society?

The period of economic prosperity after the end of World War II was accompanied by a more disturbing trend in the United States—the beginning of the hunt for communists within the United States, a hunt that victimized thousands of innocent people who lost their jobs and reputations, often because of an unsubstantiated rumor or because of a political affiliation with left-wing labor groups that conservatives deemed dangerous. The House Un-American Activities Committee, formed in the 1930s, took on new life in the late 1940s as it began to institute judicial hearings to weed out possible communists or subversives. The Hollywood film industry was viewed with particular suspicion by the HUAC; anyone who was suspected of communist sympathies was "blacklisted," although the existence of a blacklist was denied by industry personnel. The Truman administration also took extreme steps to investigate the loyalty of federal employees, running extensive security checks and investigations by the FBI. Universities, state and local governments, and even churches followed suit, firing or expelling those who would not take a loyalty oath or who were somehow considered too "left-wing" in their politics. After the 1950 conviction of Alger Hiss, a former State Department official who was suspected of spying for the Russians, the stage was set for Senator Joseph McCarthy to deliver his famous speech at Wheeling, West Virginia, on February 9, 1950. McCarthy claimed to hold in his hand "a list of 205 card-carrying Communists who worked in the State Department." In his speech he made claims that he could never substantiate, but the political climate at the time supported his accusations, and from 1950 to 1954 McCarthy spearheaded the anticommunist movement that swept the country. In the speech, which you can study both as a historical document and as a rhetorical argument, you will find appeals to fear, patriotism, and pride, but few facts that could support a strong argument. McCarthy finally lost support when he accused the U.S. Army of harboring communists, and the country began to see his smear tactics and complete lack of factual evidence. He was eventually censured by the Senate for conduct unbecoming to a senator. McCarthy's speech at Wheeling represents a period of American history in which conflicts of international and national dimensions blinded Americans to common sense and the tenets of democracy they claimed to hold so dear.

The period after the war was especially prosperous for whites, who increasingly moved to suburbs and bought homes that were mass produced all over the country to make up for the shortage of housing for young families and returning war veterans. Financed by the government, highways and housing developments sprang up from coast to coast. Many of the new housing developments openly stated that they were for whites only, and urban blacks and minorities enjoyed none of the affluence that characterized life in the suburbs. In the 1950s, black people could not ride at the front of buses, and they could not sit at the same lunch counters, use the same public toilets, or even use the same drinking fountains as white people. The decay of the inner cities and the continuing racism and segregation eventually gave way to a more vocal opposition and a rallying of forces in the South.

Black activism slowly drew attention to the lack of equality for blacks, and in 1954 the Supreme Court ruled in *Brown v. Board of Education* that public schools could not segregate blacks from whites on the basis of race, and the National Association for the Advancement of Colored People (NAACP) began to file suits to overturn segregation in other areas of public life, such as transportation, housing, and recreational areas. However, these changes did not come easily, and some white Southerners fought back with a fierce resistance to granting blacks rights that they had been fighting for since the Civil War. Reverend Martin Luther King, Jr. emerged as the leader of the nonviolent protest movement that sought to continue integration despite the mobs, violence, and riots that accompanied the end of segregation. President John F. Kennedy supported King and his civil rights activists, and when mobs in Alabama attacked a peaceful protest in the spring of 1963, Kennedy authorized the use of the National Guard to restore order. In June of that year, when black students attempted to register at the University of Alabama, Kennedy again had to order the use of troops to ensure the students' safety. On June 11, after ordering the Alabama National Guard to the campus, Kennedy delivered his Civil Rights Announcement on television and radio, explaining his rationale for the use of the National Guard, and outlining his goals for civil rights in America. Later that summer, King shared his vision of an integrated America with thousands of supporters in Washington, D.C., in his famous 1963 speech, "I Have a Dream." King's speech not only clarified the kinds of racial conflicts individual blacks had already endured, but also served as a model of persuasive rhetoric, infused with King's passion and masterful use of imagery, diction, and rhythm. You can compare the speeches of Kennedy and King with the speeches of other important national figures we have looked at in this text, from Thomas Jefferson to Abraham Lincoln to Franklin Roosevelt to Joseph McCarthy. What makes each speech unique? What similar strategies do the speakers use to persuade their audiences? Which rhetorical devices seem most effective to you?

Women, too, began to speak up for their rights by the end of the 1950s. The 1950s were a time when the common belief propagated by advertisements, television, and conventional wisdom was that women were delighted to be back at home after their stint in the world of work during World War II, and that the role of housewife and mother was the greatest delight a woman could aspire to. Although a surprising number of women did hold jobs outside the home, society clearly expected them to remain at home in charge of domestic responsibilities. Accordingly, most television shows popular in the 1950s showed women only as mothers who wouldn't or couldn't hold a job, such as the mothers in *Leave It to Beaver, Father Knows Best,* and *I Love Lucy.* However, women were beginning to organize politically and to rally for nuclear disarmament, racial integration, rights for nurses and teachers, and paid maternity leave for those women who were working. By the time Betty Friedan published her book *The Feminine Mystique,* enough women were aware of their feelings of boredom and unfulfilled desires that Friedan was able to interview and talk to many women who felt that the mystique of femininity was beginning to grow stale. Friedan was one of the first women to speak openly of the need for women to find fulfillment in their work as well as in their homes, and in her first chapter, "The Problem That Has No Name," Friedan begins to identify both the societal pressures and the internal longings of women who were feeling stifled at home.

Gloria Steinem was another important leader of the women's rights movement. She began her feminist career in the 1960s, when she founded the National Organization for Women, and then in the early 1970s she published *Ms. Magazine.* Steinem toured the country speaking on behalf of women's rights, legalization of abortion, and the problems of low self-esteem in women. In our selection, "Men and Women Talking," which is taken from Steinem's first book, *Outrageous Acts and Everyday Rebellions,* Steinem identifies the psychological patterns men and women find acceptable and encourages a fuller mode of expression for both sexes. Her article remains relevant today, when women and men still have trouble articulating their feelings and finding a common language with which to communicate.

Before we leave the civil rights movement, we need to consider another important groups of activists whose voices began to be heard more loudly in the late 1960s. In 1953 Congress passed a resolution that sought to remove Native Americans from reservations and to open Indian lands for mining, timber, and agricultural interests. Once again, Native Americans were forced out of familiar territory, this time encouraged to assimilate and become part of the melting pot. However, Native Americans did not necessarily want to move to relocation centers in big cities like San Francisco, Denver, and Chicago, and once again many felt the burden of poverty and hopelessness. During the civil rights era, Indian activists began to come together in the Pan Indian movement, and in the San Francisco Bay Area a group of activists from different tribes decided to call attention to the needs of Native Americans by temporarily occupying Alcatraz Island in the San Francisco Bay. Although originally the activists had not thought they would be allowed to stay on the island for long, in fact they remained there from 1969 to 1971, in varying numbers, and they were supported by well-wishers from all walks of life who dropped food from helicopters and boats, and who engaged the media's attention so that the desires of Native Americans would be heard. Although the activists were not granted the cultural center and educational site on Alcatraz that they demanded, most Native American historians today agree that the occupation of Alcatraz was an unprecedented turning point for Native American activism. As Troy Johnson, Duane Champagne, and Joane Nagel point out in their article "American Indian Activism and Transformation," the spirit of tribal unity and the will to organize and protest increased dramatically after the Alcatraz occupation.

Another group of Americans who found their voice during the civil rights era and afterward were the Chicano farm workers who came together under the leadership of Cesar Chavez. Chavez believed strongly in nonviolent protest, and with his persuasive speeches and gentle nature he was able to rally tremendous support for the farm workers in their battle for better pay and better working conditions with the growers. In his "Address to the Commonwealth Club of California," Chavez explains in powerful, concrete language the sufferings, triumphs, and challenges of the lives of farmworkers in the 1980s.

While the 1960s and 1970s saw the growth of civil rights protests for changes at home, the greatest demonstrations of civil unrest developed because of the U.S. involvement in Vietnam. Although the United States had backed the French and then the South Vietnamese governments under the presidencies of Truman, Eisenhower, Nixon, and Kennedy, the increased number of U.S. troops in Vietnam and the commencement of bombing in North

Vietnam during Lyndon Johnson's presidency mobilized Americans to mass protests. As President Johnson ordered bombing attacks on North Vietnam and sent ever-larger numbers of ground troops into battle, students, peace groups, church leaders, and citizens from every walk of life began to join together in rallies, sit-ins, and sometimes violent demonstrations against the war. In 1965 the Department of State released its famous *White Paper on Vietnam*, in which the government tried to justify the need for further troops and U.S. involvement in Vietnam. Unconvinced, thousands of protesters gathered in Washington, D.C., in April of 1965, where Paul Potter, leader of the powerful Students for a Democratic Society (SDS) delivered his well-received protest speech, "The Incredible War." What are we to make of this period of American history? How can we understand the vastly differing points of view of the U.S. government and the millions who chose to burn their draft cards, flee to Canada, or go to prison rather than serve? How did the war in Vietnam permanently affect American culture and society?

The last selection in this chapter offers us a chance to see how politicians justified and explained the need to enter the Gulf War. When Saddam Hussein's troops entered Kuwait in 1990, President George H. Bush responded by sending U.S. troops to "assist the Saudi Arabian government in the defense of its homelands." In President Bush's "Address to the Nation" in August of 1990, you can analyze once again the strategies of persuasion a U.S. president uses to explain why American men and women will be sent into combat. As you read President Bush's speech, consider the changes in political climate from the Vietnam era. How does the president clarify our role in Kuwait? What justifications does he offer? How does his speech compare to the 1965 *White Paper on Vietnam* or to President Roosevelt's speech announcing the beginning of World War II?

The selections in this chapter should give you a better understanding of an era closely linked to your own. As you read the selections, try to see how these conflicts from previous decades have left their mark on contemporary society.

Before You Read

1. Jot down your impressions of the civil rights movement in the 1960s, and then write your impressions of the struggle for civil rights today.

2. Think about opportunities for women and minorities in the job market today. What is your impression of the reality of the goal of equal opportunity for all?

3. What images of Vietnam have you seen in films, media articles, or your history books? What is your general impression about the war and the impact it had on America as a country?

Speech at Wheeling, West Virginia

JOSEPH McCARTHY

Joseph McCarthy (1908–1957) entered politics in 1946 after working as a lawyer and a circuit-court judge. Before winning his Republican seat, he fought in World War II as a marine in the Pacific Theatre, and then came home to Wisconsin to campaign for the senate seat. Mc-Carthy's fame as a communist hunter began in 1950 when he delivered his famous speech, reprinted below, at Wheeling, West Virginia, where he claimed that he had a list in his hand "of the names of 205 men that were known to the Secretary of State as being members of the Communist Party and who nevertheless are still working and shaping the policy of the State Department." His speech further fueled the government attacks on communists, attacks that had already caused many innocent people to lose their jobs in state and local governments, universities, businesses, and the Hollywood film industry. Against a backdrop of widespread fear of the "Communist menace," McCarthy's accusations about the State Department were readily accepted, although he never provided the names of the people on his list, and in fact later lowered the number of people to 57. While President Truman openly accused McCarthy of slander, when Eisenhower was elected president he did not make any public statements against McCarthy. It was not until 1954 that McCarthy finally went too far, when he accused the U.S. Army of harboring subversives. During televised hearings, lawyer Joseph Welch, who represented the Army, finally accused McCarthy of ruining lives and using smear tactics lacking any true evidence. By the end of 1954 the Senate voted to censure McCarthy for unbecoming conduct, and he died three years later at the young age of forty-eight, discredited and dishonored.

Five years after a world war has been won, men's hearts should anticipate a long peace, and men's minds should be free from the heavy weight that comes with war. But this is not such a period—for this is not a period of peace. This is a time of the "cold war." This is a time when all the world is split into two vast, increasingly hostile armed camps—a time of a great armaments race. . . .

Today we are engaged in a final, all-out battle between communistic atheism and Christianity. The modern champions of communism have selected this as the time. And, ladies and gentlemen, the chips are down—they are truly down. . . .

Six years ago, at the time of the first conference to map out the peace—Dumbarton Oaks—there was within the Soviet orbit 180,000,000 people. Lined up on the antitotalitarian side there were in the world at that time roughly 1,625,000,000 people. Today, only 6 years later, there are 800,000,000 people under the absolute domination of Soviet Russia—an increase of over 400 percent. On our side, the figure has shrunk to around 500,000,000. In other words, in less than 6 years the odds have changed from 9 to 1 in our favor to 8 to 5 against us. This indicates the swiftness of the tempo of Communist victories and American defeats in the cold war. As one of our outstanding historical figures once said, "When a great democracy is destroyed, it will not be because of enemies from without, but rather because of enemies from within." . . .

The reason why we find ourselves in a position of impotency is not because our only powerful potential enemy has sent men to invade our shores, but rather because of the traitorous actions of those who have been treated so well by this Nation. It has not been the less fortunate or members of minority groups who have been selling this Nation out, but rather those who have had all the benefits that the wealthiest nation on earth has had to offer—the finest homes, the finest college education, and the finest jobs in Government we can give.

This is glaringly true in the State Department. There the bright young men who are born with silver spoons in their mouths are the ones who have been the worst. . . . In my opinion the State Department, which is one of the most important government departments, is thoroughly infested with Communists.

I have in my hand 57 cases of individuals who would appear to be either card carrying members or certainly loyal to the Communist Party, but who nevertheless are still helping to shape our foreign policy. . . .

I know that you are saying to yourself, "Well, why doesn't the Congress do something about it?" Actually, ladies and gentlemen, one of the important reasons for the graft, the corruption, the dishonesty, the disloyalty, the treason in high Government positions—one of the most important reasons why this continues is a lack of moral uprising on the part of the 140,000,000 American people. In the light of history, however, this is not hard to explain.

It is the result of an emotional hang-over and a temporary moral lapse which follows every war. It is the apathy to evil which people who have been subjected to the tremendous evils of war feel. As the people of the world see mass murder, the destruction of defenseless and innocent people, and all of the crime and lack of morals which go with war, they become numb and apathetic. It has always been thus after war.

However, the morals of our people have not been destroyed. They still exist. This cloak of numbness and apathy has only needed a spark to rekindle them. Happily, this spark has finally been supplied.

As you know, very recently the Secretary of State proclaimed his loyalty to a man guilty of what has always been considered as the most abominable of all crimes—of being a traitor to the people who gave him a position of great trust. The Secretary of State in attempting to justify his continued devotion to the man who sold out the Christian world to the atheistic world, referred to Christ's Sermon on the Mount as a justification and reason therefore, and the reaction of the American people to this would have made the heart of Abraham Lincoln happy.

When this pompous diplomat in striped pants, with a phony British accent, proclaimed to the American people that Christ on the Mount endorsed communism, high treason, and betrayal of a sacred trust, the blasphemy was so great that it awakened the dormant indignation of the American people.

He has lighted the spark which is resulting in a moral uprising and will end only when the whole sorry mess of twisted, warped thinkers are swept from the national scene so that we may have a new birth of national honesty and decency in government.

Discussion Questions

1. McCarthy's speech was written to make his audience fearful, and he uses many techniques to make sure fear carries his message of Communist infiltration. Discuss specific words and "facts" McCarthy produces to scare his audience. Consider also these questions: How does he appeal to religion to persuade his audience of his correctness? How does he appeal to moderate-income Americans who might be listening to his speech?

2. Compare McCarthy's speech to current speeches by politicians who support or oppose government proposals to combat terrorism inside the United States. Do you find in these speeches any similarities to McCarthy's appeals to fear, or are today's politicians more subtle in their persuasive techniques when they are arguing about internal threats to American security?

Writing Suggestions

1. Research the career of Joseph McCarthy, including his censure by the U.S. Senate in 1954. Then write an analysis of the rise and fall of McCarthy, looking at political, national, and international issues that contributed first to his power and then to his diminished stature in the Senate. How did he gain the attention of the media and the nation, and how did he finally push his anti-Communist scare too far? Address the change in international events between 1950 and 1954, and discuss the influence of world issues on the career of Senator McCarthy.

2. Write an essay in which you compare the proceeding at the Salem Witch Trials with the Senate hearings run by Senator McCarthy. Review the selections in Chapter 1 concerning Salem's witch trials, and then research on the Internet and in your library to learn more about the McCarthy hearings in which he accused a large number of Army personnel and government officials of being "card-carrying" Communists. Referring to the transcripts of Sarah Good (Chapter 1) and of McCarthy, compare the types of questions and evidence used in both trials. What similarities and differences in questioning do you find? What similarities in motivation do you find between the accusers? What kind of evidence was provided at both trials?

Civil Rights Announcement

JOHN F. KENNEDY

John F. Kennedy was the nation's first Catholic president and the youngest president, elected when he was 46. He served only from 1961 to 1963, when he was assassinated in Dallas, Texas, on November 22. Although Kennedy was in the White House for a short period of time, his presidency and his personality had an enormous impact on the American public. Kennedy presented a youthful, energetic, and hopeful image to America, and he is perhaps best known for his development of the Peace Corps, his diplomacy during the Cuban missile crisis involving the Soviet Union, and the nuclear weapons test ban treaty.

During Kennedy's presidency, civil rights became an increasingly urgent national problem. In the South, blacks were still commonly banned from eating in the same restaurants as whites, using the same restrooms and water fountains, and attending the same colleges and universities. Under the leadership of Martin Luther King, Jr., civil rights demonstrators had begun anew the long and arduous task of fighting for equality for all Americans. Despite his strong verbal support of civil rights, Kennedy needed the white Southern vote for re-election in 1964, and he acted slowly in actually creating and pushing new legislation for civil rights. However, in the spring of 1963 when violence and rioting broke out in Alabama during a peaceful demonstration and later when black students tried to register at the University of Alabama, Kennedy sent in the National Guard to restore order. On June 11, 1963, Kennedy gave the radio and television news report that follows. Kennedy did not pass a comprehensive civil rights bill while he was alive, but President Lyndon Johnson took up the cause after Kennedy's death. Addressing the nation on November 27, 1963, Johnson promised to pursue meaningful civil rights legislation, so that "the ideas and the ideals which [Kennedy] so nobly represented must and will be translated into effective action." Johnson did in fact pursue this legislation, and on July 2, 1964, President Johnson signed the Civil Rights Act into law.

June 11, 1963

This afternoon, following a series of threats and defiant statements, the presence of Alabama National Guardsmen was required on the University of Alabama to carry out the final and unequivocal order of the United States District Court of the Northern District of Alabama. This order called for the admission of two clearly qualified young Alabama residents who happen to have been born Negro.

That they were admitted peacefully on the campus is due in good measure to the conduct of the students of the University of Alabama, who met their responsibilities in a constructive way.

I hope that every American, regardless of where he lives, will stop and examine his conscience about this and other related incidents. This nation was founded by men of many nations and backgrounds. It was founded on the principle that all men are created equal, and that the rights of every man are diminished when the rights of one man are threatened.

Today we are committed to a worldwide struggle to promote and protect the rights of all who wish to be free. When Americans are sent to Vietnam or West Berlin, we do not ask for whites only. It ought to be possible, therefore, for American students of any color to attend any public institution they select without having to be backed up by troops.

It ought to be possible for American consumers of any color to receive equal service in places of public accommodation, such as hotels and restaurants and theaters and retail stores, without being forced to resort to demonstration in the street. It ought to be possible for American citizens of any color to register and to vote in a free election without interference or fear of reprisal.

It ought to be possible, in short, for every American to enjoy the privileges of being American without regard to his race or his color. In short, every American ought to have the right to be treated as he would wish to be treated, as one would wish his children to be treated. But this is not the case today.

The Negro baby born in America today, regardless of the section of the nation in which he is born, has about one half as much chance of completing high school as a white baby born in the same place on the same day, one third as much chance of completing college, one third as much chance of becoming a professional man, twice as much chance of becoming unemployed, about one seventh as much chance of earning $10,000 a year or more, a life expectancy which is seven years shorter, and the prospects of earning only half as much.

This is not a sectional issue. Difficulties over segregation and discrimination exist in every city, in every state of the Union, producing in many cities a rising tide of discontent that threatens the public safety. Nor is this a partisan issue. In a time of domestic crisis men of goodwill and generosity should be able to unite regardless of party or politics. This is not even a legal or legislative issue alone. It is better to settle these methods in the courts than on the streets, and new laws are needed at every level, but law alone cannot make men see right.

We are confronted primarily with a moral issue. It is as old as the Scriptures and is as clear as the American Constitution.

The heart of the question is whether all Americans are to be afforded equal rights and equal opportunities, whether we are going to treat our fellow Americans as we want to be treated. If an American, because his skin is dark, cannot eat lunch in a restaurant open to the public, if he can not send his children to the best public school available, if he cannot vote for the public officials who represent him, if, in short, he cannot enjoy the full and free life which all of us want, then who among us would be content to have the color of his skin changed and stand in his place? Who among us would be content with the counsels of patience and delay?

One hundred years have passed since President Lincoln freed the slaves, yet their heirs, their grandsons, are not fully free. They are not yet freed from the bonds of injustice. They are not yet freed from social and economic oppression. And this nation, for all its hopes and all its boasts, will not be fully free until all its citizens are free.

We preach freedom around the world, and we mean it, and we cherish our freedom here at home; but are we to say to the world, and, much more importantly, to each other, that this is a land of the free except for the Negroes; that we have no second-class citizens except Negroes; that we have no class or caste system, no ghettos, no master race, except with respect to Negroes?

Now the time has come for this nation to fulfill its promise. The events in Birmingham and elsewhere have so increased the cries for equality that no city or state or legislative body can prudently choose to ignore them.

The fires of frustration and discord are burning in every city, North and South, where legal remedies are not at hand. Redress is sought in the streets, in demonstrations, parades, and protests which create tensions and threaten violence and threaten lives.

We face, therefore, a moral crisis as a country and as a people. It cannot be met by repressive police action. It cannot be left to increased demonstrations in the streets. It cannot be quieted by token moves or talk. It is a time to act in the Congress, in your state and local legislative bodies and, above all, in all of our daily lives.

It is not enough to pin the blame on others, to say this is a problem of one section of the country or another, or deplore the facts that we face. A great change is at hand, and our task, our obligation, is to make that revolution, that change, peaceful and constructive for all.

Those who do nothing are inviting shame as well as violence. Those who act boldly are recognizing right as well as reality.

Next week I shall ask the Congress of the United States to act, to make a commitment it has not fully made in this century to the proposition that race has no place in American life or law. The federal judiciary has upheld that proposition in the conduct of its affairs, including the employment of federal personnel, the use of federal facilities, and the sale of federally financed housing.

But there are other necessary measures which only the Congress can provide, and they must be provided at this session. The old code of equity law under which we live commands for every wrong a remedy, but in too many communities, in too many parts of the country, wrongs are inflicted on Negro citizens and there are no remedies at law. Unless the Congress acts, their only remedy is in the streets.

I am, therefore, asking the Congress to enact legislation giving all Americans the right to be served in facilities which are open to the public—hotels, restaurants, theaters, retail stores, and similar establishments.

This seems to me to be an elementary right. Its denial is an arbitrary indignity that no American in 1963 should have to endure. But many do.

I have recently met with scores of business leaders urging them to take voluntary action to end this discrimination, and I have been encouraged by their response. In the last two weeks over seventy-five cities have seen progress made in desegregating these kinds of facilities. But many are unwilling to act alone, and for this reason, nationwide legislation is needed if we are to move this problem from the streets to the courts.

I am also asking Congress to authorize the federal government to participate more fully in lawsuits designed to end segregation in public education. We have succeeded in persuading many districts to desegregate voluntarily. Dozens have admitted Negroes without violence. Today, a Negro is attending a state-supported institution in every one of our fifty states. But the pace is very slow.

Too many Negro children entering segregated grade schools at the time of the Supreme Court's decision nine years ago will enter segregated high schools this fall, having suffered a loss which can never be restored. The lack of an adequate education denies the Negro a chance to get a decent job.

The orderly implementation of the Supreme Court decision, therefore, cannot be left solely to those who may not have the economic resources to carry the legal action or who may be subject to harassment.

Other features will also be requested, including greater protection for the right to vote. But legislation, I repeat, cannot solve this problem alone. It must be solved in the homes of every American in every community across our country.

In this respect, I want to pay tribute to those citizens, North and South, who have been working in their communities to make life better for all. They are acting not out of a sense of legal duty but out of a sense of human decency. Like our soldiers and sailors in all parts of the world, they are meeting freedom's challenge on the firing line, and I salute them for their honor and courage.

My fellow Americans, this is a problem which faces us all—in every city of the North as well as the South. Today there are Negroes, unemployed—two or three times as many compared to whites—with inadequate education, moving into the large cities, unable to find work, young people particularly out of work and without hope, denied equal rights, denied the opportunity to eat at a restaurant or lunch counter or go to a movie theater, denied the right to a decent education. It seems to me that these are matters which concern us all, not merely presidents or congressmen or governors, but every citizen of the United States.

This is one country. It has become one country because all the people who came here had an equal chance to develop their talents. . . .

We have a right to expect that the Negro community will be responsible and will uphold the law; but they have a right to expect that the law will be fair, that the constitution will be color blind, as Justice Harlan said at the turn of the century.

This is what we are talking about. This is a matter which concerns this country and what it stands for, and in meeting it I ask the support of all our citizens.

Discussion Questions

1. How does Kennedy appeal to his audience on a personal level in this report? How does he share the focus between a call for governmental action and a call for individual action against racism? How does he take his audience into account when choosing his diction and tone?

2. What kinds of details does Kennedy use to support his argument that racism is far too prevalent in the United States? What kinds of examples does he give of racism? Did you find his speech effective? Why or why not?

Writing Suggestions

1. Compare the style of Kennedy's speech to the style of the speech that follows—Martin Luther King, Jr.'s "I Have a Dream" speech—and then write a paper in which you analyze each writer's audience, tone, diction, and use of evidence. Discuss the rhetorical elements in each speech when comparing the effectiveness of the two speeches.

2. Research the year 1963 and write a report in which you give context to Kennedy's speech. What happened in civil rights in America before and after this speech? What impact did Kennedy's call for action have on Congress? What kinds of changes resulted from this speech? How effective was Kennedy in the field of civil rights?

I Have a Dream

MARTIN LUTHER KING, JR.

Martin Luther King, Jr. (1929–1968) was one of the most beloved civil rights leaders of the late 1950s and early- to mid-1960s. King received a Ph.D. in Divinity from Boston University in 1956 and then became active in leading nonviolent, peaceful protests for civil rights. King was jailed along with 2,400 other civil rights workers in Alabama in 1963 and wrote his famous letter to the clergy, "Letter from Birmingham Jail," at that time. That same year he delivered his stirring address, "I Have a Dream," at the base of the Lincoln Monument in Washington, D.C. In 1964 King was awarded the Nobel Peace Prize for his nonviolent leadership in the quest for social change. He was assassinated in Memphis, Tennessee, on April 4, 1968.

Five score years ago, a great American, in whose symbolic shadow we stand, signed the Emancipation Proclamation. This momentous decree came as a great beacon light of hope to millions of Negro slaves who had been seared in the flames of withering injustice. It came as a joyous daybreak to end the long night of captivity.

But one hundred years later, we must face the tragic fact that the Negro is still not free. One hundred years later, the life of the Negro is still sadly crippled by the manacles of segregation and the chains of discrimination. One hundred years later, the Negro lives on a lonely island of poverty in the midst of a vast ocean of material prosperity. One hundred years later, the Negro is still languishing in the comers of American society and finds himself an exile in his own land. So we have come here today to dramatize an appalling condition.

In a sense we have come to our nation's capital to cash a check. When the architects of our republic wrote the magnificent words of the Constitution and the declaration of Independence, they were signing a promissory note to which every American was to fall heir. This note was a promise that all men would be guaranteed the inalienable rights of life, liberty, and the pursuit of happiness.

It is obvious today that America has defaulted on this promissory note insofar as her citizens of color are concerned. Instead of honoring this sacred obligation, America has given the Negro people a bad check which has come back marked "insufficient funds." But we refuse to believe that the bank of justice is bankrupt. We refuse to believe that there are insufficient funds in the great vaults of opportunity of this nation. So we have come to cash this check—a check that will give us upon demand the riches of freedom and the security of justice. We have also come to this hallowed spot to remind America of the fierce urgency of now. This is no time to engage in the luxury of cooling off or to take the tranquilizing drug of gradualism. Now is the time to rise from the dark and desolate valley of segregation to the sunlit path of racial justice. Now is the time to open the doors of opportunity to all of God's children. Now is the time to lift our nation from the quicksands of racial injustice to the solid rock of brotherhood.

It would be fatal for the nation to overlook the urgency of the moment and to underestimate the determination of the Negro. This sweltering summer of the Negro's legitimate discontent will not pass until there is an invigorating autumn of freedom and equality. Nineteen sixty-three is not an end, but a beginning. Those who hope that the Negro needed to blow off steam and will now be content will have a rude awakening if the nation returns to business as usual. There will be neither rest nor tranquility in America until the Negro is granted his citizenship rights. The whirlwinds of revolt will continue to shake the foundations of our nation until the bright day of justice emerges.

But there is something that I must say to my people who stand on the warm threshold which leads into the palace of justice. In the process of gaining our rightful place we must not be guilty of wrongful deeds. Let us not seek to satisfy our thirst for freedom by drinking from the cup of bitterness and hatred.

We must forever conduct our struggle on the high plane of dignity and discipline. We must not allow our creative protest to degenerate into physical violence. Again and again we must rise to the majestic heights of meeting physical force with soul force. The marvelous new militancy which has engulfed the Negro community must not lead us to distrust of all white people, for many of our white brothers, as evidenced by their presence here today, have come to realize that their destiny is tied up with our destiny and their freedom is inextricably bound to our freedom. We cannot walk alone.

And as we walk, we must make the pledge that we shall march ahead. We cannot turn back. There are those who are asking the devotees of civil rights, "When will you be satisfied?" We can never be satisfied as long as our bodies, heavy with the fatigue of travel, cannot gain lodging in the motels of the highways and the hotels of the cities. We cannot be satisfied as long as the Negro's basic mobility is from a smaller ghetto to a larger one. We can never be satisfied as long as a Negro in Mississippi cannot vote and a Negro in New York believes he has nothing for which to vote. No, no, we are not satisfied, and we will not be satisfied until justice rolls down like waters and righteousness like a mighty stream.

I am not unmindful that some of you have come here out of great trials and tribulations. Some of you have come fresh from narrow cells. Some of you have come from areas where your quest for freedom left you battered by the storms of persecution and staggered by the winds of police brutality. You have been the veterans of creative suffering. Continue to work with the faith that unearned suffering is redemptive.

Go back to Mississippi, go back to Alabama, go back to Georgia, go back to Louisiana, go back to the slums and ghettos of our northern cities, knowing that somehow this situation can and will be changed. Let us not wallow in the valley of despair.

I say to you today, my friends, that in spite of the difficulties and frustrations of the moment, I still have a dream. It is a dream deeply rooted in the American dream.

I have a dream that one day this nation will rise up and live out the true meaning of its creed: "We hold these truths to be self-evident: that all men are created equal."

I have a dream that one day on the red hills of Georgia the sons of former slaves and the sons of former slaveowners will be able to sit down together at a table of brotherhood.

I have a dream that one day even the state of Mississippi, a desert state, sweltering with the heat of injustice and oppression, will be transformed into an oasis of freedom and justice.

I have a dream that my four children will one day live in a nation where they will not be judged by the color of their skin but by the content of their character.

I have a dream today.

I have a dream that one day the state of Alabama, whose governor's lips are presently dripping with the words of interposition and nullification, will be transformed into a situation where little black boys and black girls will be able to join hands with little white boys and white girls and walk together as sisters and brothers.

I have a dream today.

I have a dream that one day every valley shall be exalted, every hill and mountain shall be made low, the rough places will be made plain, and the crooked places will be made straight, and the glory of the Lord shall be revealed, and all flesh shall see it together.

This is our hope. This is the faith with which I return to the South. With this faith we will be able to hew out of the mountain of despair a stone of hope. With this faith we will be able to transform the jangling discords of our nation into a beautiful symphony of brotherhood. With this faith we will be able to work together, to pray together, to struggle together, to go to jail together, to stand up for freedom together, knowing that we will be free one day.

This will be the day when all of God's children will be able to sing with a new meaning, "My country, 'tis of thee, sweet land of liberty, of thee I sing. Land where my fathers died, land of the pilgrim's pride, from every mountainside, let freedom ring."

And if America is to be a great nation this must become true. So let freedom ring from the prodigious hilltops of New Hampshire. Let freedom ring
from the mighty mountains of New York. Let freedom ring from the heightening Alleghenies of Pennsylvania!

Let freedom ring from the snowcapped Rockies of Colorado!

Let freedom ring from the curvaceous peaks of California!

But not only that; let freedom ring from Stone Mountain of Georgia!

Let freedom ring from Lookout Mountain of Tennessee!

Let freedom ring from every hill and every molehill of Mississippi. From
every mountainside, let freedom ring.

When we let freedom ring, when we let it ring from every village and
every hamlet, from every state and every city, we will be able to speed up that
day when all of God's children, black men and white men, Jews and Gentiles,
Protestants and Catholics, will be able to join hands and sing in the words of
the old Negro spiritual, "Free at last! free at last! thank God Almighty, we are
free at last!"

Discussion Questions

1. Martin Luther King, Jr.'s powerful "I Have a Dream" speech contains
   many allusions, both overt and subtle, to the diction and the oratorical
   style of Abraham Lincoln. Review Lincoln's "Gettysburg Address" in
   Chapter 4. Then, as a group, make a list of the ideas, stylistic devices, and
   diction that mirror Lincoln's speech and ideals. Discuss the ways in which
   King's use of Lincoln's rhetorical style and language added to the power
   of "I Have a Dream."

2. After you have analyzed the speech, view the video of Martin Luther
   King, Jr. giving the address at the Lincoln Memorial. (This video is available in your library or on the Internet.) Discuss the differences between
   your impressions after reading the speech and after hearing the speech.
   What additional impact, if any, did the speech have when you viewed
   Martin Luther King, Jr. on film? Imagine his audience of 250,000 civil
   rights protesters that day. What aspects of the speech might they miss?
   What aspects of the speech would be clearer in person? Where do you
   find the most power in this speech—the words or the delivery? How do
   King's words and delivery interact to help him reach his audience?

3. Discuss your perceptions about the state of the civil rights movement
   today. Consider the goals King mentions in his speech. How much
   progress do you feel has been made in America since King gave this
   speech in 1963? Which aspects of his "dream" have come true? Which remain elusive? Which rights are now widespread and which rights are still
   withheld from African Americans?

Writing Suggestions

1. Martin Luther King, Jr. has used a wide variety of rhetorical devices to give power and depth to his "I Have a Dream" speech. Write an essay in which you analyze this speech and King's rhetorical style, addressing some of the following stylistic and persuasive strategies:

    The use of parallel sentence structure
    The use of repetition in diction and structure
    The use of historical references
    The use of song lyrics
    The tone of the speech
    The awareness of his audience
    The use of imagery and metaphor
    The use of personal references
    The acknowledgement of his opposition
    The construction of his conclusion

    For each point you cover, use several examples from the text to back up your assertion about the impact of each of the above strategies on the forcefulness of his argument.

2. Research the life and times of Martin Luther King, Jr., and write a research essay in which you evaluate King's contribution to the civil rights movement and his role in context of the early 1960s in America. What kinds of racial conflicts came in the years before and after his "I Have a Dream" speech? To what incidents was King alluding when he mentioned the Alabama governor, the jailings and beatings that his audience may have suffered, and the "new militancy" that had "engulfed the Negro people"? What were King's greatest triumphs and failures before the assassination that cut short his life? Use secondary sources from your library and references to the text of this speech in your paper.

The Feminine Mystique

The Problem That Has No Name

BETTY FRIEDAN

Betty Friedan, born in 1921, was one of the earliest leaders of the feminist movement. She published *The Feminine Mystique* in 1963, in an effort to publicize the problems and unhappiness of women whose lives were controlled by the popular 1950s notion that women's happiness could only come from being good mothers and good homemakers. Friedan was educated at Smith College and the University of California, but dropped out of graduate school, not wanting to "become an old maid college teacher," a move in retrospect that she said made her one of the victims of "the feminine mystique." After marrying and raising three children in the suburbs, where she was very unhappy, she began to write *The Feminine Mystique*. She began the research for the book when she started to see a pattern of the "problem that has no name," the unhappiness and dissatisfaction she recognized in herself and other women who were not using their education and talents outside the home. Friedan went on to become one of the founders of NOW, the National Organization for Women, serving as its president until 1970. She also helped start the National Women's Caucus (1971) and wrote two more books, *The Second Stage* (1981) and *The Fountain of Age* (1993). Friedan has worked not only for women's rights but also for the rights of senior citizens, whose treatment in this country she has strongly criticized. In the selection below, Chapter 1 ("The Problem That Has No Name") of *The Feminine Mystique*, Friedan discusses the postwar social expectations for women to stay at home and raise large families, and she also discusses the intense unhappiness of women that began to surface in the late 1950s and early 1960s.

The problem lay buried, unspoken, for many years in the minds of American women. It was a strange stirring, a sense of dissatisfaction, a yearning that women suffered in the middle of the twentieth century in the United States. Each suburban wife struggled with it alone. As she made the beds, shopped for groceries, matched slipcover material, ate peanut butter sandwiches with her children, chauffeured Cub Scouts and Brownies, lay beside her husband at night—she was afraid to ask even of herself the silent question—"Is this all?"

For over fifteen years there was no word of this yearning in the millions of words written about women, for women, in all the columns, books and articles by experts telling women their role was to seek fulfillment as wives and mothers. Over and over women heard in voices of tradition and of Freudian sophistication that they could desire no greater destiny than to glory in their own femininity. Experts told them how to catch a man and keep him, how to breastfeed children and handle their toilet training, how to cope with sibling rivalry and adolescent rebellion; how to buy a dishwasher, bake bread, cook gourmet snails, and build a swimming pool with their own hands; how to dress, look, and act more feminine and make marriage more exciting; how to keep their husbands from dying young and their sons from growing into delinquents. They were taught to pity the neurotic, unfeminine, unhappy women who wanted to be poets or physicists or presidents. They learned that truly feminine women do not want careers, higher education, political rights—the independence and the opportunities that the old-fashioned feminists fought for. Some, women, in their forties and fifties, still remembered painfully giving up those dreams, but most of the younger women no longer even thought about them. A thousand expert voices applauded their femininity, their adjustment, their new maturity. All they had to do was devote their lives from earliest girlhood to finding a husband and bearing children.

By the end of the nineteen-fifties, the average marriage age of women in America dropped to 20, and was still dropping, into the teens. Fourteen million girls were engaged by 17. The proportion of women attending college in comparison with men dropping from 47 per cent in 1920 to 35 per cent in 1958. A century earlier, women had fought for higher education; now girls went to college to get a husband. By the mid-fifties, 60 per cent dropped out of college to marry, or because they were afraid too much education would be a marriage bar. Colleges built dormitories for "married students," but the students were almost always the husbands. A new degree was instituted for the wives—"Ph.T." (Putting Husband Through).

Then American girls began getting married in high school. And the women's magazines, deploring the unhappy statistics about these young marriages, urged that courses on marriage, and marriage counselors, be installed in the high schools. Girls started going steady at twelve and thirteen, in junior high. Manufacturers put out brassieres with false bosoms of foam rubber for little girls of ten. And an advertisement for a child's dress, sizes 3–6x, in the *New York Times* in the fall of 1960, said: "She Too Can Join the Man-Trap Set."

By the end of the fifties, the United States birthrate was overtaking India's. The birth-control movement, renamed Planned Parenthood, was asked to find a method whereby women who had been advised that a third or fourth baby would be born dead or defective might have it anyhow. Statisticians were especially astounded at the fantastic increase in the number of babies among college women. Where once they had two children, now they had four, five, six. Women who had once wanted careers were now making careers out of having babies. So rejoiced *Life* magazine in a 1956 paean to the movement of American women back to the home.

In a New York hospital, a woman had a nervous breakdown when she found she could not breastfeed her baby. In other hospitals, women dying of cancer refused a drug which research had proved might save their lives: its side effects were said to be unfeminine. "If I have only one life, let me live it as a blonde," a larger-than-life-sized picture of a pretty, vacuous woman proclaimed from newspaper, magazine, and drugstore ads. And across America, three out of every ten women dyed their hair blonde. They ate a chalk called Metrecal, instead of food, to shrink to the size of the thin young models. Department-store buyers reported that American women, since 1939, had become three and four sizes smaller. "Women are out to fit the clothes, instead of vice-versa," one buyer said.

Interior decorators were designing kitchens with mosaic murals and original paintings, for kitchens were once again the center of women's lives. Home sewing became a million-dollar industry. Many women no longer left their homes, except to shop, chauffeur their children, or attend a social engagement with their husbands. Girls were growing up in America without ever having jobs outside the home. In the late fifties, a sociological phenomenon was suddenly remarked: a third of American women now worked, but most were no longer young and very few were pursuing careers. They were married women who held part-time jobs, selling or secretarial, to put their husbands through school, their sons through college, or to help pay the mortgage. Or they were widows supporting families. Fewer and fewer women were entering professional work. The shortages in the nursing, social work, and teaching professions caused crises in almost every American city. Concerned over the Soviet Union's lead in the space race, scientists noted that America's greatest source of unused brainpower was women. But girls would not study physics: it was "unfeminine." A girl refused a science fellowship at Johns Hopkins to take a job in real-estate office. All she wanted, she said, was what every other American girl wanted—to get married, have four children and live in a nice house in a nice suburb.

The suburban housewife—she was the dream image of the young American women and the envy, it was said, of women all over the world. The American housewife—freed by science and labor-saving appliances from the drudgery, the dangers of childbirth and the illnesses of her grandmother. She was healthy, beautiful, educated, concerned only about her husband, her children, her home. She had found true feminine fulfillment. As a housewife and mother, she was respected as a full and equal partner to man in his world. She was free to choose automobiles, clothes, appliances, supermarkets; she had everything that women ever dreamed of.

In the fifteen years after World War II, this mystique of feminine fulfillment became the cherished and self-perpetuating core of contemporary American culture. Millions of women lived their lives in the image of those pretty pictures of the American suburban housewife, kissing their husbands goodbye in front of the picture window, depositing their stationwagonsful of children at school, and smiling as they ran the new electric waxer over the spotless kitchen floor. They baked their own bread, sewed their own and their children's clothes, kept their new washing machines and dryers running all day. They changed the sheets on the beds twice a week instead of once, took the rug-hooking class in adult education, and pitied their poor frustrated mothers, who had dreamed of having a career. Their only dream was to be perfect wives and mothers; their highest ambition to have five children and a beautiful house, their only fight to get and keep their husbands. They had no thought for the unfeminine problems of the world outside the home; they wanted the men to make the major decisions. They gloried in their role as women, and wrote proudly on the census blank: "Occupation: housewife."

For over fifteen years, the words written for women, and the words women used when they talked to each other, while their husbands sat on the other side of the room and talked shop or politics or septic tanks, were about problems with their children, or how to keep their husbands happy, or improve their children's school, or cook chicken or make slipcovers. Nobody argued whether women were inferior or superior to men; they were simply different. Words like "emancipation" and "career" sounded strange and embarrassing; no one had used them for years. When a Frenchwoman named Simone de Beauvoir wrote a book called *The Second Sex,* an American critic commented that she obviously "didn't know what life was all about," and besides, she was talking about French women. The "woman problem" in America no longer existed.

If a woman had a problem in the 1950s and 1960s, she knew that something must be wrong with her marriage, or with herself. Other women were satisfied with their lives, she thought. What kind of a woman was she if she did not feel this mysterious fulfillment waxing the kitchen floor? She was so ashamed to admit her dissatisfaction that she never knew how many other women shared it. If she tried to tell her husband, he didn't understand what she was talking about. She did not really understand it herself. For over fifteen years women in America found it harder to talk about this problem than about sex. Even the psychoanalysts had no name for it. When a woman went to a psychiatrist for help, as many women did, she would say, "I'm so ashamed," or "I must be hopelessly neurotic." "I don't know what's wrong with women today," a suburban psychiatrist said uneasily. "I only know something is wrong because most of my patients happen to be women. And their problem isn't sexual." Most women with this problem did not go to see a psychoanalyst, however. "There's nothing wrong really," they kept telling themselves. "There isn't any problem."

But on an April morning in 1959, I heard a mother of four, having coffee with four other mothers in a suburban development fifteen miles from New York, say in a tone of quiet desperation, "the problem." And the others knew, without words, that she was not talking about a problem with her husband, or her children, or her home. Suddenly they realized they all shared the same problem, the problem that has no name. They began, hesitantly, to talk about it. Later, after they had picked up their children at nursery school and taken them home to nap, two of the women cried, in sheer relief, just to know they were not alone.

Gradually I came to realize that the problem that has no name was shared by countless women in America. As a magazine writer I often interviewed women about problems with their children, or their marriages, or their houses, or their communities. But after a while I began to recognize the telltale signs of this other problem. I saw the same signs in suburban ranch houses and split-levels on Long Island and in New Jersey and Westchester County; in colonial houses in a small Massachusetts town; on patios in Memphis; in suburban and city apartments; in living rooms in the Midwest. Sometimes I sensed the problem, not as a reporter, but as a suburban housewife, for during this time I was also bringing up my own three children in Rockland County, New York. I heard echoes of the problem in college dormitories and semi-private maternity wards, at PTA meetings and luncheons of the League of Women Voters, at suburban cocktail parties, in station wagons waiting for trains, and in snatches of conversation overheard at Schrafft's. The groping words I heard from other women, on quiet afternoons when children were at school or on quiet evenings when husbands worked late, I think I understood first as a woman long before I understood their larger social and psychological implications.

Just what was this problem that has no name? What were the words women used when they tried to express it? Sometimes a woman would say "I feel empty somehow . . . incomplete." Or she would say, "I feel as if I don't exist." Sometimes she blotted out the feeling with a tranquilizer. Sometimes she thought the problem was with her husband, or her children, or that what she really needed was to redecorate her house, or move to a better neighborhood, or have an affair, or another baby. Sometimes, she went to a doctor with symptoms she could hardly describe: "A tired feeling . . . I get so angry with the children it scares me . . . I feel like crying without any reason." (A Cleveland doctor called it "the housewife's syndrome.") A number of women told me about great bleeding blisters that break out on their hands and arms. "I call it the housewife's blight," said a family doctor in Pennsylvania. "I see it so often lately in these young women with four, five and six children who bury themselves in their dishpans. But it isn't caused by detergent and it isn't cured by cortisone."

Sometimes a woman would tell me that the feeling gets so strong she runs out of the house and walks through the streets. Or she stays inside her house and cries. Or her children tell her a joke, and she doesn't laugh because she doesn't hear it. I talked to women who had spent years on the analyst's couch, working out their "adjustment to the feminine role," their blocks to "fulfillment as a wife and mother." But the desperate tone in these women's voices, and the look in their eyes, was the same as the tone and the look of other women, who were sure they had no problem, even though they did have a strange feeling of desperation.

A mother of four who left college at nineteen to get married told me:

> I've tried everything women are supposed to do—hobbies, gardening, pickling, canning, being very social with my neighbors, joining committees, running PTA teas. I can do it all, and I like it, but it doesn't leave you anything to think about—any feeling of who you are. I never had any career ambitions.

All I wanted was to get married and have four children. I love the kids and Bob and my home. There's no problem you can even put a name to. But I'm desperate. I begin to feel I have no personality. I'm a server of food and put-ter-on of pants and a bedmaker, somebody who can be called on when you want something. But who am I?

A twenty-three-year-old mother in blue jeans said:

I ask myself why I'm so dissatisfied. I've got my health, fine children, a lovely new home, enough money. My husband has a real future as an electronics en-gineer. He doesn't have any of these feelings. He says maybe I need a vaca-tion, let's go to New York for a weekend. But that isn't it. I always had this idea we should do everything together. I can't sit down and read a book alone. If the children are napping and I have one hour to myself I just walk through the house waiting for them to wake up. I don't make a move until I know where the rest of the crowd is going. It's as if ever since you were a little girl, there's always been somebody or something that will take care of your life: your par-ents, or college, or falling in love, or having a child, or moving to a new house. Then you wake up one morning and there's nothing to look forward to.

A young wife in a Long Island development said:

I seem to sleep so much. I don't know why I should be so tired. This house isn't nearly so hard to clean as the cold-water flat we had when I was work-ing. The children are at school all day. It's not the work. I just don't feel alive.

In 1960, the problem that has no name burst like a boil through the image of the happy American housewife. In the television commercials the pretty housewives still beamed over their foaming dishpans and *Time's* cover story on "The Suburban Wife, an American Phenomenon" protested: "Having too good a time . . . to believe that they should be unhappy." But the actual un-happiness of the American housewife was suddenly being reported—from the *New York Times* and *Newsweek* to *Good Housekeeping* and CBS Television ("The Trapped Housewife"), although almost everybody who talked about it found some superficial reason to dismiss it. It was attributed to incompetent appli-ance repairmen (*New York Times*), or the distances children must be chauffeured in the suburbs (*Time*), or too much PTA (*Redbook*). Some said it was the old problem—education: more and more women had education, which naturally made them unhappy in their role as housewives. "The road from Freud to Frigidaire, from Sophocles to Spock, has turned out to be a bumpy one," re-ported the *New York Times* (June 28, 1960). "Many young women—certainly not all—whose education plunged them into a world of ideas feel stifled in their homes. They find their routine lives out of joint with their training. Like shut-ins, they feel left out. In the last year, the problem of the educated house-wife has provided the meat of dozens of speeches made by troubled presidents of women's colleges who maintain, in the face of complaints, that sixteen years of academic training is realistic preparation for wifehood and motherhood."

There was much sympathy for the educated housewife. ("Like a two-headed schizophrenic . . . once she wrote a paper on the Graveyard poets;

now she writes notes to the milkman. Once she determined the boiling point of sulphuric acid; now she determines her boiling point with the overdue repairman. . . . The housewife often is reduced to screams and tears. . . . No one, it seems, is appreciative, least of all herself, of the kind of person she becomes in the process of turning from poetess into shrew.")

Home economists suggested more realistic preparation for housewives, such as high-school workshops in home appliances. College educators suggested more discussion groups on home management and the family, to prepare women for the adjustment to domestic life. A spate of articles appeared in the mass magazines offering "Fifty-eight Ways to Make Your Marriage More Exciting." No month went by without a new book by a psychiatrist or sexologist offering technical advice on finding greater fulfillment through sex.

A male humorist joked in *Harper's Bazaar* (July, 1960) that the problem could be solved by taking away woman's right to vote. ("In the pre-19th Amendment era, the American woman was placid, sheltered and sure of her role in American society. She left all the political decisions to her husband and he, in turn, left all the family decisions to her. Today a woman has to make both the family *and* the political decisions, and it's too much for her.")

A number of educators suggested seriously that women no longer be admitted to the four-year colleges and universities: in the growing college crisis, the education which girls could not use as housewives was more urgently needed than ever by boys to do the work of the atomic age.

The problem was also dismissed with drastic solutions no one could take seriously. (A woman writer proposed in *Harper's* that women be drafted for compulsory service as nurses' aides and baby-sitters.) And it was smoothed over with the age-old panaceas: "love is their answer," "the only answer is inner help," "the secret of completeness—children," "a private means of intellectual fulfillment," "to cure this toothache of the spirit—the simple formula of handing one's self and one's will over to God."

The problem was dismissed by telling the housewife she doesn't realize how lucky she is—her own boss, no time clock, no junior executive gunning for her job. What if she isn't happy—does she think men are happy in this world? Does she really, secretly, still want to be a man? Doesn't she know yet how lucky she is to be a woman?

The problem was also, and finally, dismissed by shrugging that there are no solutions: this is what being a woman means, and what is wrong with American women that they can't accept their role gracefully? As *Newsweek* put it (March 7, 1960):

> She is dissatisfied with a lot that women of other lands can only dream of. Her discontent is deep, pervasive, and impervious to the superficial remedies which are offered at every hand. . . . An army of professional explorers have already charted the major sources of trouble. . . . From the beginning of time, the female cycle has defined and confined woman's role. As Freud was credited with saying: "Anatomy is destiny." Though no group of women has ever

pushed these natural restrictions as far as the American wife, it seems that she still cannot accept them with good grace. . . . A young mother with a beautiful family, charm, talent and brains is apt to dismiss her role apologetically. "What do I do?" you hear her say. "Why nothing. I'm just a housewife." A good education, it seems, has given this paragon among women an understanding of the value of everything except her own worth . . .

And so she must accept the fact that "American women's unhappiness is merely the most recently won of women's rights," and adjust and say with the happy housewife found by *Newsweek*: "We ought to salute the wonderful freedom we all have and be proud of our lives today. I have had college and I've worked, but being a housewife is the most rewarding and satisfying role. . . . My mother was never included in my father's business affairs . . . she couldn't get out of the house and away from us children. But I am an equal to my husband; I can go along with him on business trips and to social business affairs."

The alternative offered was a choice that few women would contemplate. In the sympathetic words of the *New York Times*: "All admit to being deeply frustrated at times by the lack of privacy, the physical burden, the routine of family life, the confinement of it. However, none would give up her home and family if she had the choice to make again." *Redbook* commented: "Few women would want to thumb their noses at husbands, children and community and go off on their own. Those who do may be talented individuals, but they rarely are successful women."

The year American women's discontent boiled over, it was also reported (*Look*) that the more than 21,000,000 American women who are single, widowed, or divorced do not cease even after fifty their frenzied, desperate search for a man. And the search begins early—for seventy per cent of all American women now marry before they are twenty-four. A pretty twenty-five-year-old secretary took thirty-five different jobs in six months in the futile hope of finding a husband. Women were moving from one political club to another, taking evening courses in accounting or sailing, learning to play golf or ski, joining a number of churches in succession, going to bars alone, in their ceaseless search for a man.

Of the growing thousands of women currently getting private psychiatric help in the United States, the married ones were reported dissatisfied with their marriages, the unmarried ones suffering from anxiety and, finally, depression. Strangely, a number of psychiatrists stated that, in their experience, unmarried women patients were happier than married ones. So the door of all those pretty suburban houses opened a crack to permit a glimpse of uncounted thousands of American housewives who suffered alone from a problem that suddenly everyone was talking about, and beginning to take for granted, as one of those unreal problems in American life that can never be solved—like the hydrogen bomb. By 1962 the plight of the trapped American housewife had become a national parlor game. Whole issues of magazines, newspaper columns, books learned and frivolous, educational conferences and television panels were devoted to the problem.

Even so, most men, and some women, still did not know that this problem was real. But those who had faced it honestly knew that all the superficial remedies, the sympathetic advice, the scolding words and the cheering words were somehow drowning the problem in unreality. A bitter laugh was beginning to be heard from American women. They were admired, envied, pitied, theorized over until they were sick of it, offered drastic solutions or silly choices that no one could take seriously. They got all kinds of advice from the growing armies of marriage and child-guidance counselors, psychotherapists, and armchair psychologists, on how to adjust to their role as housewives. No other road to fulfillment was offered to American women in the middle of the twentieth century. Most adjusted to their role and suffered or ignored the problem that has no name. It can be less painful for a woman, not to hear the strange, dissatisfied voice stirring within her.

It is no longer possible to ignore that voice, to dismiss the desperation of so many American women. This is not what being a woman means, no matter what the experts say. For human suffering there is a reason; perhaps the reason has not been found because the right questions have not been asked, or pressed far enough. I do not accept the answer that there is no problem because American women have luxuries that women in other times and lands never dreamed of; part of the strange newness of the problem is that it cannot be understood in terms of the age-old material problems of man: poverty, sickness, hunger, cold. The women who suffer this problem have a hunger that food cannot fill. It persists in women whose husbands are struggling interns and law clerks, or prosperous doctors and lawyers; in wives of workers and executives who make $5,000 a year or $50,000. It is not caused by lack of material advantages; it may not even be felt by women preoccupied with desperate problems of hunger, poverty or illness. And women who think it will be solved by more money, a bigger house, a second car, moving to a better suburb, often discover it gets worse.

It is no longer possible today to blame the problem on loss of femininity: to say that education and independence and equality with men have made American women unfeminine. I have heard so many women try to deny this dissatisfied voice within themselves because it does not fit the pretty picture of femininity the experts have given them. I think, in fact, that this is the first clue to the mystery: the problem cannot be understood in the generally accepted terms by which scientists have studied women, doctors have treated them, counselors have advised them, and writers have written about them. Women who suffer this problem, in whom this voice is stirring, have lived their whole lives in the pursuit of feminine fulfillment. They are not career women (although career women may have other problems); they are women whose greatest ambition has been marriage and children. For the oldest of these women, these daughters of the American middle class, no other dream was possible. The ones in their forties and fifties who once had other dreams gave them up and threw themselves joyously into life as housewives. For the youngest, the new wives and mothers, this was the only dream. They are the ones who quit high school and college to marry, or marked time in some job in which they had no real interest until they married. These women are very "feminine" in the usual sense, and yet they still suffer the problem.

Are the women who finished college, the women who once had dreams beyond housewifery, the ones who suffer the most? According to the experts they are, but listen to these four women:

> My days are all busy, and dull, too. All I ever do is mess around. I get up at eight—I make breakfast, so I do the dishes, have lunch, do some more dishes, and some laundry and cleaning in the afternoon. Then it's supper dishes and I get to sit down a few minutes, before the children have to be sent to bed. . . . That's all there is to my day. It's just like any other wife's day. Humdrum. The biggest time, I am chasing kids.

> Ye Gods, what do I do with my time? Well, I get up at six. I get my son dressed and then give him breakfast. After that I wash dishes and bathe and feed the baby. Then I get lunch and while the children nap, I sew or mend or iron and do all the other things I can't get done before noon. Then I cook supper for the family and my husband watches TV while I do the dishes. After I get the children to bed, I set my hair and then I go to bed.

> The problem is always being the children's mommy, or the minister's wife and never being myself.

> A film made of any typical morning in my house would look like an old Marx Brothers' comedy. I wash the dishes, rush the older children off to school, dash out in the yard to cultivate the chrysanthemums, run back in to make a phone call about a committee meeting, help the youngest child build a blockhouse, spend fifteen minutes skimming the newspapers so I can be well-informed, then scamper down to the washing machines where my thrice-weekly laundry includes enough clothes to keep a primitive village going for an entire year. By noon I'm ready for a padded cell. Very little of what I've done has been really necessary or important. Outside pressures lash me through the day. Yet I look upon myself as one of the more relaxed housewives in the neighborhood. Many of my friends are even more frantic. In the past sixty years we have come full circle and the American housewife is once again trapped in a squirrel cage. If the cage is now a modern plate-glass-and-broadloom ranch house or a convenient modern apartment, the situation is no less painful than when her grandmother sat over an embroidery hoop in her gilt-and-plush parlor and muttered angrily about women's rights.

The first two women never went to college. They live in developments in Levittown, New Jersey, and Tacoma, Washington, and were interviewed by a team of sociologists studying workingmen's wives. The third, a minister's wife, wrote on the fifteenth reunion questionnaire of her college that she never had any career ambitions, but wishes now she had. The fourth, who has a Ph.D. in anthropology, is today a Nebraska housewife with three children. Their words seem to indicate that housewives of all educational levels suffer the same feeling of desperation.

The fact is that no one today is muttering angrily about "women's rights," even though more and more women have gone to college. In a recent study of all the classes that have graduated from Barnard College, a significant minority of earlier graduates blamed their education for making them want "rights," later classes blamed their education for giving them career dreams, but recent graduates blamed the college for making them feel it was not enough simply to be a housewife and mother; they did not want to feel guilty if they did not read books or take part in community activities. But if education is not the cause of the problem, the fact that education somehow festers in these women may be a clue.

If the secret of feminine fulfillment is having children, never have so many women, with the freedom to choose, had so many children, in so few years, so willingly. If the answer is love, never have women searched for love with such determination. And yet there is a growing suspicion that the problem may not be sexual, though it must somehow be related to sex. I have heard from many doctors evidence of new sexual problems between man and wife—sexual hunger in wives so great their husbands cannot satisfy it. "We have made women a sex creature," said a psychiatrist at the Margaret Sanger marriage counseling clinic. "She has no identity except as a wife and mother. She does not know who she is herself. She waits all day for her husband to come home at night to make her feel alive. And now it is the husband who is not interested. It is terrible for the women, to lie there, night after night, waiting for her husband to make her feel alive." Why is there such a market for books and articles offering sexual advice? The kind of sexual orgasm which Kinsey found in statistical plenitude in the recent generations of American women does not seem to make this problem go away.

On the contrary, new neuroses are being seen among women—and problems as yet unnamed as neuroses—which Freud and his followers did not predict, with physical symptoms, anxieties, and defense mechanisms equal to those caused by sexual repression. And strange new problems are being reported in the growing generations of children whose mothers were always there, driving them around, helping them with their homework—an inability to endure pain or discipline or pursue any self-sustained goal of any sort, a devastating boredom with life. Educators are increasingly uneasy about the dependence, the lack of self-reliance, of the boys and girls who are entering college today. "We fight a continual battle to make our students assume manhood," said a Columbia dean.

A White House conference was held on the physical and muscular deterioration of American children: were they being over-nurtured? Sociologists noted the astounding organization of suburban children's lives: the lessons, parties, entertainments, play and study groups organized for them. A suburban housewife in Portland, Oregon, wondered why the children "need" Brownies and Boy Scouts out here. "This is not the slums. The kids out here have the great outdoors. I think people are so bored, they organize the children, and then try to hook everyone else on it. And the poor kids have no time left just to lie on their beds and daydream."

Can the problem that has no name be somehow related to the domestic routine of the housewife? When a woman tries to put the problem into words, she often merely describes the daily life she leads. What is there in this recital of comfortable domestic detail that could possibly cause such a feeling of desperation? Is she trapped simply by the enormous demands of her role as modern housewife: wife, mistress, mother, nurse, consumer, cook, chauffeur; expert on interior decoration, child care, appliance repair, furniture refinishing, nutrition, and education? Her day is fragmented as she rushes from dishwasher to washing machine to telephone to dryer to station wagon to supermarket, and delivers Johnny to the Little League field, takes Janey to dancing class, gets the lawnmower fixed and meets the 6:45. She can never spend more than 15 minutes on any one thing; she has no time to read books, only magazines; even if she had time, she has lost the power to concentrate. At the end of the day, she is so terribly tired that sometimes her husband has to take over and put the children to bed.

Thus terrible tiredness took so many women to doctors in the 1950s that one decided to investigate it. He found, surprisingly, that his patients suffering from "housewife's fatigue" slept more than an adult needed to sleep—as much as ten hours a day—and that the actual energy they expended on housework did not tax their capacity. The real problem must be something else, he decided—perhaps boredom. Some doctors told their women patients they must get out of the house for a day, treat themselves to a movie in town. Others prescribed tranquilizers. Many suburban housewives were taking tranquilizers like cough drops. "You wake up in the morning, and you feel as if there's no point in going on another day like this. So you take a tranquilizer because it makes you not care so much that it's pointless."

It is easy to see the concrete details that trap the suburban housewife, the continual demands on her time. But the chains that bind her in her trap are chains in her own mind and spirit. They are chains made up of mistaken ideas and misinterpreted facts, of incomplete truths and unreal choices. They are not easily seen and not easily shaken off.

How can any woman see the whole truth within the bounds of her own life? How can she believe that voice inside herself, when it denies the conventional, accepted truths by which she has been living? And yet the women I have talked to, who are finally listening to that inner voice, seem in some incredible way to be groping through to a truth that has defied the experts.

I think the experts in a great many fields have been holding pieces of that truth under their microscopes for a long time without realizing it. I found pieces of it in certain new research and theoretical developments in psychological, social and biological science whose implications for women seem never to have been examined. I found many clues by talking to suburban doctors, gynecologists, obstetricians, child-guidance clinicians, pediatricians, high-school guidance counselors, college professors, marriage counselors, psychiatrists and ministers—questioning them not on their theories, but on their actual experience in treating American women. I became aware of a

growing body of evidence, much of which has not been reported publicly because it does not fit current modes of thought about women—evidence which
throws into question the standards of feminine normality, feminine adjustment, feminine fulfillment, and feminine maturity by which most women are
still trying to live.

I began to see in a strange new light the American return to early marriage
and the large families that are causing the population explosion; the recent
movement to natural childbirth and breastfeeding; suburban conformity, and
the new neuroses, character pathologies and sexual problems being reported
by the doctors. I began to see new dimensions to old problems that have long
been taken for granted among women: menstrual difficulties, sexual frigidi-
ty, promiscuity, pregnancy fears, childbirth depression, the high incidence of
emotional breakdown and suicide among women in their twenties and thirties, the menopause crises, the so-called passivity and immaturity of American men, the discrepancy between women's tested intellectual abilities in
childhood and their adult achievement, the changing incidence of adult sexual orgasm in American women, and persistent problems in psychotherapy
and in women's education.

If I am right, the problem that has no name stirring in the minds of so many
American women today is not a matter of loss of femininity or too much education, or the demands of domesticity. It is far more important than anyone
recognizes. It is the key to these other new and old problems which have been
torturing women and their husbands and children, and puzzling their doctors
and educators for years. It may well be the key to our future as a nation and a
culture. We can no longer ignore that voice within women that says: "I want
something more than my husband and my children and my home."

Discussion Questions

1. How does Friedan marshal her evidence in this first chapter of *The Fem-
    inine Mystique* to build to her last line in the chapter: "We can no longer
    ignore that voice within women that says: 'I want something more than
    my husband and my children and my home?'" How does she organize her
    chapter in terms of presentation of materials? What variety of sources
    does she use? When does she first introduce her argument? Do you find
    her organization and evidence compelling or not?

2. Freewrite about the following question: From your personal experience,
    the experience of your mother, aunts, friends, and peers, what do you
    think women want today? Do they want to be mothers, wives, and ca-
    reer women all at once? Do they want to be career women instead of moth-
    ers? Or do they want to stay at home with children instead of trying to
    juggle both career and home? Freewrite on this topic for about ten min-
    utes, and then come back as a group to discuss your answers. Did the
    men in your group tend to answer differently than the women? Was there

any consensus about what people think women want today? What conclusions can you come to from your discussion? How did the group writings reflect Friedan's belief that women who stay home will be filled with a sense of loss and emptiness?

Writing Suggestions

1. Review what you have written in your response to the second discussion question: From your personal experience, the experience of your mother, aunts, friends, and peers, explain what you think women want today. Do they want to be mothers, wives, and career women all at once? Do they want to be career women instead of mothers? Or do they want to stay at home with children instead of trying to juggle both career and home? Now use your freewriting notes to develop a well-organized personal essay, using specific examples and colorful anecdotes to bring your points to life.

2. Friedan discusses the role that was described for women by all the "columns, books, and articles by experts telling women their role was to seek fulfillment as wives and mothers." By 1956, she reports, women were "making a career out of having babies" instead of choosing their own careers. During this time, advertisements and magazine articles supported this role of women, and so did television programs like *I Love Lucy*, one of the all-time favorite shows in America. Review Friedan's discussion of women's roles in the 1950s, and then watch at least six episodes of *I Love Lucy* on television. (*I Love Lucy* reruns are often run on daytime television; you can also rent episodes at a video store.) Then write a paper, referring to Friedan's description of what women were told they should like, and discuss the plots and characters of *I Love Lucy* as a reflection of the life of women in the 1950s. You might answer some of the following questions in your analysis:

   How do Lucy and Ethel use their time? What kinds of pursuits occupy their minds? What are their goals?

   What is their relationship to their husbands, Ricky and Fred?

   What happens when Lucy and Ethel try to get jobs or raise money?

   How do the men treat their wives?

   What is the humor of the show based on?

   How do the two married couples resolve their problems?

   How well do Lucy and Ethel match Friedan's analysis of what women thought they should like in the 1950s?

   When you write your analysis, quote directly from Friedan and use specific quotes and examples from the *I Love Lucy* episodes you watched. Discuss whether or not the answers to the above questions corroborate Friedan's descriptions of the 1950s media portrayal of the perfect housewife.

Outrageous Acts and Everyday Rebellions

Men and Women Talking

GLORIA STEINEM

Gloria Steinem, born in 1934, has been one of the most influential feminist leaders since the late 1960s. Educated at Smith, where she graduated Phi Beta Kappa in 1956, Steinem went to India for two years and then returned to New York, hoping to find a job as a reporter. She experienced firsthand the "glass ceiling" for women, and she discovered that women were rarely given real reporting jobs. She persevered, writing freelance articles for *Help! Magazine, Esquire, Glamour,* and other magazines. Eventually she was hired by *New York Magazine,* where she was able to write about her political and activist interests. Steinem became more and more involved in the women's movement in the 1970s, and published the first issue of *Ms. Magazine,* a magazine for and about women's issues, in 1972. She led the battle to legalize abortion and spoke publicly about her own abortion. She published her first book, *Outrageous Acts and Everyday Rebellions,* in 1983. She has also written *Revolution from Within: A Book of Self-Esteem* (1992) and *Moving beyond Words* (1994). Steinem has continued to work at *Ms. Magazine* and as a political activist, writing, speaking, and touring the country. In "Men and Women Talking," from *Outrageous Acts and Everyday Rebellions,* Steinem analyzes the different patterns of speech men and women find acceptable and urges a "full human circle of expression" for both men and women.

Once upon a time (that is, just a few years ago), psychologists believed that the way we chose to communicate was largely a function of personality. If certain conversational styles turned out to be more common to one sex than the other (more abstract and aggressive talk for men, for instance, more personal and equivocal talk for women), then this was just another tribute to the influence of biology on personality.

Consciously or otherwise, feminists have challenged this assumption from the beginning. Many of us learned a big lesson in the sixties when our generation spoke out on the injustices of war, as well as of race and class; yet women who used exactly the same words and style as our male counterparts were less likely to be listened to or to be taken seriously. When we tried to talk about this and other frustrations, the lack of listening got worse, with opposition and even ridicule just around every corner. Only women's own meetings and truth telling began to confirm what we had thought each of us was alone in experiencing.

It was also those early consciousness-raising groups that began to develop a more cooperative, less combative way of talking, an alternative style that many women have maintained and been strengthened by ever since.

The problem is that this culturally different form has remained an almost totally female event. True, it has helped many, many women arrive at understanding each other and working out strategies for action. But as an influence on the culturally male style of public talking, it has remained almost as removed as its more domestic versions of the past.

One reason for our decade or so of delay in challenging existing styles of talking makes good tactical sense. Our first task was to change the words themselves. We did not feel included (and usage studies showed that, factually, we were not) in hundreds of such supposedly generic terms as *mankind* and *he*, *the brotherhood of man* and *statesman*. Nor could we fail to see the racial parallels to being identified as "girls" at advanced ages, or with first names only, or by our personal connection (or lack of one) to a member of the dominant group.

Hard as it was (and still is), this radical act of seizing the power to name ourselves and our experience was easier than taking on the politics of conversation. Documenting society-wide patterns of talking required expensive research and surveys. Documenting the sexism in words, and even conjuring up alternatives, took only one courageous woman scholar and a dictionary (for instance, *Guidelines for Equal Treatment of the Sexes*, the pioneering work of Alma Graham for McGraw-Hill). That was one good economic reason why such works were among the first and best by feminist scholars.

In retrospect, the second cause for delay makes less feminist sense—the long popularity of assertiveness training. Though most women needed to be more assertive (or even more aggressive, though that word was considered too controversial), many of these courses taught women how to play the existing game, not how to change the rules. Unlike the feminist assault on sexist language, which demanded new behavior from men, too, assertiveness training was more reformist than revolutionary. It pushed one-way change for women only, thus seeming to confirm masculine-style communication as the only adult model or the most effective one. Certainly, many individual women were helped, and many men were confronted with the educational experience of an assertive woman, but the larger impact was usually to flatter the existing masculine game of talk-politics by imitating it.

Since then, however, a few feminist scholars have had the time and resources to document conversational patterns of mixed- and single-sex groups, both here and in Europe. Traditional scholarship, influenced by feminism, has also begun to look at conversational styles as functions of power and environment. For instance employees pursue topics raised by their employers more than the reverse, older people feel free to interrupt younger ones, and subordinates are more polite than bosses. Since women share all those conversational habits of the less powerful, even across the many lines of class and status that divide us, how accidental can that be?

Even the new feminist-influenced research has a long way to go in neutralizing the masculine bias of existing studies. For instance, *talking* is assumed to be the important and positive act, while *listening*, certainly a productive function, is the subject of almost no studies at all.

Nonetheless, there is enough new scholarship to document different styles, to point out some deficiencies in the masculine model of communicating, and to give us some ideas on how to create a synthesis of both that could provide a much wider range of alternatives for women *and* for men.

I

Have you assumed that women talk more than men—and thus may dominate in discussion if nowhere else? If so, you're not alone. Researchers of sex differences in language started out with that assumption. So did many feminists, who often explained women's supposedly greater penchant for talking as compensation for a lack of power to act.

In fact, however, when Dale Spender, an English feminist and scholar, surveyed studies of talkativeness for her recent book, *Man Made Language*, she concluded that "perhaps in more than any other research area, findings were in complete contradiction with the stereotype. . . . There has not been one study which provides evidence that women talk more than men, and there have been numerous studies which indicate that men talk more than women."

Her conclusion held true regardless of whether the study in question asked individuals to talk into a tape recorder with no group interaction; or compared men and women talking on television; or measured amounts of talk in mixed groups (even among male and female state legislators); or involved group discussions of a subject on which women might be expected to have more expertise. (At a London workshop on sexism and education, for instance, the five men present managed to talk more than their thirty-two female colleagues combined.)

Some studies of male silence in heterosexual couples might seem to counter these results, but Spender's research supports their conclusion that a major portion of female talk in such one-to-one situations is devoted to drawing the man out, asking questions, introducing multiple subjects until one is accepted by him, or demonstrating interest in the subjects he introduces. Clearly, male silence (or silence from a member of any dominant group) is not necessarily the same as listening. It might mean a rejection of the speaker, a refusal to become vulnerable through self-revelation, or a decision that this conversation is not worthwhile. Similarly, talking by the subordinate group is not necessarily an evidence of power. Its motive may be a Scheherazade-like need to intrigue and thus survive, or simply to explain and justify one's actions.

In addition to a generally greater volume of talk, however, men interrupt women more often than vice versa. This is true both in groups and in couples. Male interruptions of women also bring less social punishment than female interruptions of men. Men also interrupt women more often than women interrupt each other.

Moreover, males are more likely to police the subject matter of conversation in mixed-sex groups. One study of working-class families showed that women might venture into such "masculine" topics as politics or sports, and men might join "feminine" discussions of domestic events, but in both cases, it was the men who ridiculed or otherwise straightened out nonconformers who went too far. Even in that London workshop on sexism, for instance, the concrete experiences of the female participants were suppressed in favor of the abstract, general conclusions on sexism that were preferred by the men. The few males present set the style for all the females.

How did the myth of female talkativeness and conversational dominance get started? Why has this supposed female ability been so accepted that many sociologists, and a few battered women themselves, have even accepted it as a justification for some men's violence against their wives?

The uncomfortable truth seems to be that the amount of talk by women has been measured less against the amount of men's talk than against the expectation of female silence.

Indeed, women who accept and set out to disprove the myth of the talkative woman may pay the highest price of all. In attempting to be the exceptions, we silence ourselves. If that is so, measuring our personal behavior against real situations and real studies should come as a relief, a confirmation of unspoken feelings.

We are not crazy, for instance, if we feel that, when we finally do take the conversational floor in a group, we are out there in exposed verbal flight, like fearful soloists plucked from the chorus. We are not crazy to feel that years of unspoken thoughts are bottled up inside our heads, and come rushing out in a way that may make it hard to speak calmly, even when we finally have the chance.

Once we give up searching for approval by stifling our thoughts, or by imitating the male norm of abstract, assertive communicating, we often find it easier to simply say what needs to be said, and thus to earn respect and approval. Losing self-consciousness and fear allows us to focus on the content of what we are saying instead of on ourselves.

Women's well-developed skill as listeners, perhaps the real source of our much-vaunted "intuition," should not be left behind. We must retain it for ourselves and teach it to men by bringing it with us into our work and daily lives, but that will only happen if we affirm its value. Female culture does have a great deal to contribute to the dominant one. Furthermore, women might feel better about talking equally, selecting subjects, and even interrupting occasionally if we took the reasonable attitude that we are helping men to become attentive and retentive listeners, too. We are paying them the honor of communicating as honestly as we can and treating them as we would want to be treated. After all, if more men gained sensitive listening skills, they would have "intuition," too.

These are practical exercises for achieving a change in the balance of talk. Try tape-recording a dinner-table conversation or meeting (in the guise of record-ing facts, so participants don't become self-conscious about their talk poli-tics), then play the tape back to the same group, and ask them to add up the number of minutes talked, interruptions, and subject introductions for each gender. Or give a dozen poker chips to each participant in a discussion, and require that one chip be given up each time a person speaks. Or break the si-lence barrier for those who rarely talk by going around the room once at the beginning of each meeting, consciousness-raising-style, with a question that each participant must answer personally, even if it's only a self-introduction. (It is said that the British Labour party was born only after representatives of its warring factions spent an hour moving their conference table into a larg-er room. That one communal act broke down individual isolation, just as one round of communal speaking helps break the ice.)

If such methods require more advance planning or influence on the group than you can muster, or if you're trying to sensitize just one person, try some individual acts. Discussing the results of studies on who talks more can pro-duce some very healthy self-consciousness in both women and men. If one group member speaks rarely, try addressing more of your own remarks to her (or him) directly. On the other hand, if one man (or woman) is a domi-neering interrupter, try objecting directly, interrupting in return, timing the minutes of his or her talk, or just being inattentive. If someone cuts you off, say with humor, "That's one," then promise some conspicuous act when the interruptions get to three. Keep score on "successful" topic introductions, add them up by gender, and announce them at the discussion's end.

If questions and comments following a lecture come mostly from men, stand up and say so. It may be a learning moment for everyone. The preva-lence of male speakers in mixed audiences has caused some feminist lectur-ers to reserve equal time for questions from women only.

To demonstrate the importance of listening as a positive act, try giving a quiz on the content of female and male speakers. Hopefully you *won't* dis-cover the usual: that men often remember what male speakers say better than they remember female speakers' content; that women often remember male content better, too, but that women listen and retain the words of *both* sexes somewhat better than men do.

Check the talk politics concealed in your own behavior. Does your anxi-ety level go up (and your hostess instincts quiver) when women are talking and men are listening, but not the reverse? For instance, men often seem to feel okay about "talking shop" for hours while women listen, but women seem able to talk in men's presence for only a short time before feeling anxious, apologizing, and encouraging the men to speak. If you start to feel wrongly uncomfortable about making males listen, try this exercise: *keep on talking*, and encourage your sisters to do the same. Honor men by treating them as honestly as you treat women. You will be allowing them to learn.

II

Here are three popular assumptions: (1) Women talk about themselves, personalize, and gossip more than men do. (2) Men would rather talk to groups of men than to mixed groups, and women prefer mixed groups to all-female ones. (3) Women speakers and women's issues are hampered by the feminine style of their presentation. As you've probably guessed by now, most evidence is to the contrary of all three beliefs.

After recording the conversational themes of single-sex and mixed-sex groups, for instance, social psychologist Elizabeth Aries found that men in all-male groups were also more likely to use self-mentions to demonstrate superiority or aggressiveness, while women used them to share an emotional reaction to what was being said by others.

Phil Donahue, one of the country's most experienced interviewers, capsulizes the cultural difference between men and women this way: "If you're in a social situation, and women are talking to each other, and one woman says, 'I was hit by a car today,' all the other women will say, 'You're kidding! What happened? Where? Are you all right?' In the same situation with males, one male says, 'I was hit by a car today.' I guarantee you that there will be another male in the group who will say, 'Wait till I tell you what happened to *me*.'"

If quantity of talking about oneself is a measure of "personalizing," and self-aggrandizement through invoking the weakness of others is one characteristic of gossip, then men may be far more "gossipy" than women—especially when one includes sexual bragging.

In addition, subjects introduced by males in mixed groups are far more likely to "succeed" than subjects introduced by women, and, as Aries concluded, women in mixed groups are more likely to interact with men than with other women. Thus, it's not unreasonable to conclude that mixed groups spend more time discussing the lives and interests of male participants than of female ones.

On the other hand, research by Aries and others shows that women are more likely to discuss human relationships. Since "relationships" often fall under "gossip" in men's view, this may account for the frequent male observation that women "personalize" everything. Lecturers often comment, for instance, that women in an audience ask practical questions about their own lives, while men ask abstract questions about groups or policies. When the subject is feminism, women tend to ask about practical problems. Men are more likely to say something like, "But how will feminism impact the American family?"

To quote Donahue, who deals with mostly female audiences: "I've always felt a little anxious about the possibility of a program at night with a male audience. The problem as I perceive it—and this is a generalization—is that men tend to give you a speech, whereas women will ask a question and then listen for the answer and make another contribution to the dialogue. In countless situations I have a male in my audience stand up and say in effect, 'I don't know what you're arguing about; here's the answer to this thing.' And then proceed to give a mini-speech."

Aries also documented the more cooperative, rotating style of talk and leadership in women-only groups: the conscious or unconscious habit of "taking turns." As a result, women actually prefer talking in their own single-sex groups for the concrete advantages of both having a conversational turn and being listened to. On the other hand, she confirmed research that shows male-only groups to have more stable hierarchies, with the same one or several talkers dominating most of the time.

As Aries points out, no wonder men prefer the variation and opportunity of mixed-sex audiences. They combine the seriousness of a male presence with more choice of styles—and, as Spender adds caustically, the assurance of at least some noncompetitive listeners.

Women's more gentle delivery, "feminine" choice of adjectives, and greater attention to grammar and politeness have been heavily criticized. Linguist Robin Lakoff pioneered the exposure of "ladylike" speech as a double bind that is both required of little girls, and used as a reason why, as adults, they may not be seen as forceful or serious. (Even Lakoff seems to assume, however, that female speech is to be criticized as the deficient form, while male speech is the norm and thus escapes equal comment.) Sociologist Arlie Hochschild also cites some survival techniques of racial minorities that women of all races seem to share: playing dumb and dissembling, for instance, or expressing frequent approval of others.

But whether this criticism of female speech patterns is justified or not, there is also evidence that a rejection of the way a woman speaks is often a way of blaming or dismissing her without dealing with the content of what she is saying.

For instance, women speakers are more likely to hear some version of "You have a good point, but you're not making it effectively," or "Your style is too aggressive/weak/loud/quiet." It is with such paternalistic criticisms that male politicians often dismiss the serious message of a female colleague, or that husbands turn aside the content of arguments made by their wives.

It is also such criticisms that allow women candidates to be rejected without dealing with the substance of the issues they raise. When Bella Abzug of New York and Gloria Schaeffer of Connecticut both ran for political office in one recent year, each was said to have a personal style that would prevent her from being an effective senator: Abzug because she was "too abrasive and aggressive," and Schaeffer because she was "too ladylike and quiet." Style was made the central issue by the press, and thus became one in the public-opinion polls. Both were defeated.

There are three anomalies that give away this supposedly "helpful" criticism. First, it is rarely used when a woman's message is not challenging to male power. (How often are women criticized for being too fierce in defense of their families? How often was Phyllis Schlafly criticized for being too aggressive in her opposition to the Equal Rights Amendment?) Second, the criticism is rarely accompanied by real support, even when the critic presents himself (or herself) as sympathetic. (Women political candidates say they often get critiques of their fund-raising techniques instead of cash, even from people who agree with them on issues.) Finally, almost everyone, regardless of status, feels a right to criticize. (Women professors report criticism of their teaching style from young students, as do women bosses from their employees.)

Just as there is a conversational topic that men in a group often find more compelling than any introduced by a woman (even when it's exactly the same topic, but *re*introduced by a man), or a political issue that is "more important" than any of concern to women, so there is usually a better, more effective style than the one a woman happens to be using.

Men *would* support us, we are told, if only we learned how to ask for their support in the right way. It's a subtle and effective way of blaming the victim.

. . .

III

Women's higher-pitched voices and men's lower ones are the result of physiology. Because deep voices are more pleasant and authoritative, women speakers will always have a problem. Besides, female facial expressions and gestures aren't as forceful . . . and so on. It's true that tone of voice is partly created by throat-construction and the resonance of bones. Though there is a big area of male-female overlap in voice tone, as well as in size, strength, and other physical attributes, we assume that all men will have a much deeper pitch than all women.

In fact, however, no one knows exactly how much of our speaking voices are imitative and culturally produced. Studies of young boys before puberty show that their vocal tones may deepen *even before physiological changes can account for it.* They are imitating the way the males around them speak. Dale Spender cites a study of males who were not mute, but who were born deaf and thus unable to imitate sound. Some of them never went through an adolescent voice change at all.

Whatever the mix of physiological and cultural factors, however, the important point is that the *acceptance* of vocal tone is definitely cultural and therefore subject to change.

In Japan, for instance, a woman's traditionally high-pitched, soft speaking voice is considered a very important sexual attribute. (When asked in a public-opinion poll what attribute they found most attractive in women, the majority of Japanese men said "voice.") Though trained to speak in upper registers, Japanese women, like many of their sisters around the world, often speak in lower tones when men are not present. They may even change their language as well. (A reporter's tapes of Japanese schoolgirls talking among themselves caused a scandal. They were using masculine word endings and verbs in a country where the language is divided into formally masculine and feminine forms.) Thus Japanese men may find a high voice attractive not for itself but for its tribute to a traditional subservience.

. . .

The point is not that one gender's cultural style is superior to the other's. The current "feminine" style of communicating may be better suited to, say, the performing arts, medical diagnosis, and conflict resolution. It has perfected emotional expressiveness, careful listening, and a way of leaving an adversary with dignity intact. The current "masculine" style may be better suited to, say, procedural instruction, surgical teams and other situations requiring hierarchical command, and job interviews. It has perfected linear and abstract thinking, quick commands, and a willingness to speak well of oneself or present views with assertiveness. But we will never achieve this full human circle of expression if women imitate the male "adult" style. We have to teach as well as learn.

A feminist assault on the politics of talking, and listening, is a radical act. It's a way of transforming the cultural vessel in which both instant communication and long-term anthropological change are carried. Unlike the written word, or visual imagery, or any form of communication divorced from our presence, talking and listening won't allow us to hide. There is no neutral page, image, sound, or even a genderless name to protect us. We are demanding to be accepted and understood by all the senses and for our whole selves.

That's precisely what makes the change so difficult. And so crucial.

Discussion Questions

1. What are Steinem's major goals for women and men talking? What does she want women to be able to do? What does she want men to be able to do? After you have listed these goals, discuss in groups whether or not men and women in your classes, dorms, seminars, or social gatherings meet these goals today. Do you find the same patterns Steinem presents, or do you feel that the patterns have changed in the past twenty years? If so, how have they changed?

2. What differences do you perceive about male versus female silence? Do you agree with Steinem that male silence "... might mean a rejection of the speaker, a refusal to become vulnerable through self-revelation, or a

decision that this conversation is not worthwhile?" What do you assume when a man is silent in conversation? What do you assume when a woman is silent in conversation?

Writing Suggestions

1. Referring to your responses to the second discussion question for this selection, write a personal response to Steinem's article. What differences do you perceive about male silence versus female silence? Do you agree with Steinem that male silence ". . . might mean a rejection of the speaker, a refusal to become vulnerable through self-revelation, or a decision that this conversation is not worthwhile?" What do you assume when a man is silent in conversation? What do you assume when a woman is silent in conversation?

2. Conduct your own primary source analysis of patterns of male and female conversation. At a group meeting, a dorm discussion, or in a seminar or other class, gather your data. After you receive permission from your interview subjects, use either a tape recorder or a notebook to record the number of times men speak versus the number of times women speak. Design your own chart to record interruptions, topic choices, types of questions, types of assertions, "successful topic introductions," as Steinem calls them, and length of speaking time for men and women. You can add your own variants to this experiment too. Try to record your results in at least three different settings, and then write a paper analyzing your findings, referring to Steinem's article, agreeing with or disagreeing with her assertions.

American Indian Activism and Transformation

Lessons from Alcatraz

TROY JOHNSON / DUANE CHAMPAGNE / JOANE NAGEL

In 1969, a small group of Native Americans landed on the island of Alcatraz in San Francisco Bay to protest government relocation policies for American Indians. Native Americans from many different tribes remained on the island from 1969 to 1971, supplied by food drops from helicopters and boats, supported by thousands who rallied behind their cause. What started as a small protest movement attracted tremendous media attention, and although the original requests made by the Native Americans to turn Alcatraz into a cultural center were never met, many American Indians today feel that the unity and pride that resulted from the Alcatraz occupation mark a turning point in the civil rights movement of Native Americans. After the occupation of Alcatraz ended, Native American activism rose to new heights, as Troy Johnson, Duane Champagne, and Joane Nagel explain in their article "American Indian Activism and Transformation: Lessons from Alcatraz," from which the following selection is taken. Troy Johnson teaches American history and Indian studies at California State University, Long Beach; Duane Champagne is director of the American Indian Studies Center at the University of California, Berkeley; and Joane Nagel is a professor of sociology at the University of Kansas.

The Alcatraz Occupations

In actuality, there were three separate occupations of Alcatraz Island. The first was a brief, four-hour occupation on 9 March 1964 by five Sioux Indians representing the urban Indians of the Bay Area. The event was planned by Belva Cottier, the wife of one of the occupiers. The federal penitentiary on the island had been closed in 1963, and the government was in the process of transferring the island to the city of San Francisco for development purposes. But Belva Cottier and her Sioux cousin had plans of their own. They recalled having heard of a provision in the 1868 Sioux treaty with the federal government that stated that ownership of all abandoned federal lands that once belonged to the Sioux reverted to the Sioux people. Using this interpretation of the treaty, they encouraged five Sioux men to occupy Alcatraz Island and issued press releases claiming the island in accordance with the treaty and demanding better treatment for urban Indians. Richard McKenzie, the most outspoken of the group, pressed the claim for title to the island through the court system, only to have the courts rule against him. More important, however, the Indians of the Bay Area were becoming vocal and united in their efforts to improve their lives.

The 1964 occupation of Alcatraz Island foreshadowed the unrest that was fomenting, quietly but surely, among the urban Indian population. Prior to the occupation, Bay Area newspapers contained a large number of articles about the federal government's abandonment of the urban Indian and the refusal of state and local governments to meet Indian people's needs. The Indian social clubs that had been formed for support became meeting places at which to discuss discrimination in schools, housing, employment, and health care. Indian people also talked about the police, who, like law officers in other areas of the country, would wait outside Indian bars at closing time to harass, beat up, and arrest Indian patrons. Indian centers began to appear in all the urban relocation areas and became nesting grounds for new pan-Indian, and eventually activist, organizations.

The second Alcatraz occupation had its beginning on Bay Area and other California college and university campuses when young, educated Indian students joined with other minority groups during the 1969 Third World Liberation Front Strike and began demanding courses relevant to Indian students. Indian history written and taught by non-Indian instructors was no longer acceptable to these students, awakened as they were to the possibility of social protest to bring attention to the shameful treatment of Indian people. Anthropologist Luis S. Kemnitzer has described the establishment of the country's first Native American Studies Program at San Francisco State College in 1969—the spring before the occupation. The students involved in that program went on to plan the Alcatraz occupation:

> . . . a non-Indian graduate student in social science at San Francisco State who was tutoring young Indian children in the Mission District came to know a group of young Indians who . . . all had some contact with college and had come to San Francisco either on vocational training, relocation, or on their own. . . . Conversation with the student tutor led them to become interested in the strike and in exploring the possibility of working toward a Native American studies department.
>
> . . . the university and the Third World Liberation Front had started negotiations, and there was limited room for movement. . . . [LaRaza] agreed to represent the Indians in negotiations, and there was close collaboration between representatives of LaRaza and the future Native American studies students. I was one of the faculty members on strike, and, although I was not involved in the negotiations with the university administration, I was informally recruited by other striking faculty to help plan and negotiate with LaRaza.

Richard Oakes was one of the students in the program. He came from the St. Regis Reservation, had worked on high steel in New York, and had traveled across the United States, visiting various Indian reservations. He eventually wound up in California, where he married a Kashia Pomo woman, Anne Marufo, who had five children from a previous marriage. Oakes worked in an Indian bar in Oakland for a period of time and eventually was admitted to San Francisco State College. In September 1969, he and several other Indian students began discussing the possibility of occupying Alcatraz Island as a symbolic protest, a call for Indian self-determination. Preliminary plans were made for the summer of 1970, but other events led to an earlier takeover. During the fall term, Oakes and his fellow Indian students and friends caught the attention of a nation already engrossed in the escalating protest and conflict of the civil rights movement as they set out across the San Francisco Bay for Alcatraz Island.

The catalyst for the occupation was the destruction of the San Francisco Indian Center by fire in late October 1969. The center had become the meeting place for the Bay Area Indian organizations and the newly formed United Bay Area Indian Council, which had brought the thirty private clubs together into one large council headed by Adam Nordwall (later to be known as Adam Fortunate Eagle). The destruction of the center united the council and the American Indian student organizations as never before. The council needed a new meeting place and the students needed a forum for their new activist voice. The date for the second occupation of Alcatraz Island was thus moved up to 9 November 1969. Oakes and the other students, along with a group of people from the San Francisco Indian Center, chartered a boat and headed for Alcatraz Island. Since many different tribes were represented, the occupiers called themselves "Indians of All Tribes."

The initial plan was to circle the island and symbolically claim it for all Indian people. During the circling maneuver, however, Oakes and four others jumped from the boat and swam to the island. They claimed Alcatraz in the name of Indians of All Tribes and then left the island at the request of the caretaker. Later that evening, Oakes and fourteen others returned to the island with sleeping bags and food sufficient for two or three days but left the next morning, again without incident, when asked to do so.

In meetings following the 9 November occupation, Oakes and his fellow students realized that a prolonged occupation was possible. It was clear that the federal government had only a token force on the island and that so far no physical harm had come to anyone involved. A new plan began to emerge. Oakes traveled to UCLA, where he met with Ray Spang and Edward Castillo and asked for their assistance in recruiting Indian students for what would become the longest Indian occupation of any federal facility. Spang, Castillo, and Oakes met in UCLA's Campbell Hall, now the home of the American Indian Studies Center and the editorial offices of the *American Indian Culture and Research Journal*, in private homes, and in Indian bars in Los Angeles. When the third takeover of Alcatraz Island began, seventy of the eighty-nine Indian occupiers were students from UCLA.

In the early morning hours of 20 November 1969, eighty-nine American Indians landed on Alcatraz Island in San Francisco Bay. These Indians of All Tribes claimed the island by "right of discovery" and by the terms of the 1868

Treaty of Fort Laramie, which gave Indians the right to unused federal property that had previously been Indian land. Except for a small caretaker staff, the island had been abandoned by the federal government since 1963, when the federal penitentiary was closed. In a press statement, Indians of All Tribes set the tone of the occupation and the agenda for negotiations during the next nineteen months:

> We, the native Americans, re-claim the land known as Alcatraz Island in the name of all American Indians. . . . [W]e plan to develop on this island several Indian institutions: 1. A center for Native American studies . . . 2. An American Indian spiritual center . . . 3. An Indian center of Ecology . . . 4. A great Indian Training School . . . [and] an American Indian Museum . . . In the name of all Indians, therefore, we reclaim this island for our Indian nations. . . . We feel this claim is just and proper, and that this land should rightfully be granted to us for as long as the rivers shall run and the sun shall shine. Signed, Indians of all Tribes.

The occupiers quickly set about organizing themselves. An elected council was put into place, and everyone was assigned a job: security, sanitation, day-care, housing, cooking, laundry. All decisions were made by unanimous consent of the people. Sometimes meetings were held five, six, or seven times per day to discuss the rapidly developing events. It is important to remember that, while the urban Indian population supported the concept of an occupation and provided the logistical support, the Alcatraz occupation force itself was made up initially of young, urban Indian students from UCLA, UC Santa Cruz, San Francisco State College, and UC Berkeley.

The most inspiring person, if not the recognized leader, was Richard Oakes, described as handsome, charismatic, a talented orator, and a natural leader. The casting of Oakes as the person in charge, a title he himself never claimed, quickly created a problem. Not all the students knew Oakes, and, in keeping with the concepts underlying the occupation, many wanted an egalitarian society on the island, with no one as their leader. Although this may have been a workable form of organization on the island, it was not comprehensible to the non-Indian media. Newspapers, magazines, and television and radio stations across the nation sent reporters to the island to interview the people in charge. They wanted to know who the leaders were. Oakes was the most knowledgeable about the landing and the most often sought out, and he was therefore identified as the leader, the "chief," the "mayor of Alcatraz." He was strongly influenced by the White Roots of Peace, which had been revitalized by Ray Fadden, and Mad Bear Anderson. Before the Alcatraz occupation, in the autumn of 1969, Jerry Gambill, a counselor for the White Roots of Peace, had visited the campus of San Francisco State and inspired many of the students, none more than Oakes.

By the end of 1969, the Indian organization on the island began to change, and two Indian groups rose in opposition to Oakes. When many of the Native

American students left the island to return to school, they were replaced by Indian people from urban areas and reservations who had not been involved in the initial planning. Where Oakes and the other students claimed title to the island by right of discovery, the new arrivals harked back to the rhetoric of the 1964 occupation and the Sioux treaty, a claim that had been pressed through the court system by Richard McKenzie and had been found invalid. Additionally, some non-Indians took up residence on the island, many of them from the San Francisco hippie and drug culture. Drugs and liquor had been banned from the island by the original occupiers, but they now became commonplace.

The final blow to the nascent student occupation occurred on 5 January 1970 when Oakes's thirteen-year-old stepdaughter, Yvonne, who was apparently playing unsupervised with some other children, slipped and fell three floors to her death down an open stairwell. The Oakes family left the island, and the two groups began maneuvering for leadership roles. Despite these changes, the demands of the occupiers remained consistent: title to Alcatraz Island, the development of an Indian university, and the construction of a museum and cultural center that would display for and teach non-Indian society the valuable contributions of Indian people.

In the months that followed, thousands of protesters and visitors spent time on Alcatraz Island. They came from a large number of Indian tribes, including the Sioux, Navajo, Cherokee, Mohawk, Puyallup, Yakima, Hoopa, and Omaha. The months of occupation were marked by proclamations, news conferences, powwows, celebrations, "assaults" with arrows on passing vessels, and negotiations with federal officials. In the beginning months, workers from the San Francisco Indian Center gathered food and supplies on the mainland and transported them to Alcatraz. However, as time went by, the occupying force, which fluctuated but generally numbered around one hundred, confronted increasing hardships as federal officials interfered with delivery boats and cut off the supply of water and electricity to the island. Tensions on the island grew.

The federal government, for its part, insisted that the Indian people leave, and it placed an ineffective Coast Guard barricade around the island. Eventually, the government agreed to the Indian council's demands for formal negotiations. But, from the Indian people's side, the demands were nonnegotiable. They wanted the deed to the island, they wanted to establish an Indian university, a cultural center, and a museum; and they wanted the necessary federal funding to meet their goals. Negotiations collapsed for good when the government turned down these demands and insisted that the Indians of All Tribes leave the island. Alcatraz Island would never be developed in accordance with the goals of the Indian protesters.

In time, the attention of the federal government shifted from negotiations with the island occupants to restoration of navigational aids that had been discontinued as the result of a fire that shut down the Alcatraz lighthouse.

The government's inability to restore these navigational aids brought criticism from the Coast Guard, the Bay Area Pilot's Association, and local newspapers. The federal government became impatient, and on 11 June 1971, the message went out to end the occupation of Alcatraz Island. The dozen or so remaining protesters were removed by federal marshals, more than a year and a half after the island was first occupied. Some members of Indians of All Tribes moved their protest to an abandoned Nike missile base in the Beverly Hills, overlooking San Francisco Bay. While that occupation lasted only three days, it set in motion a pattern of similar occupations over the next several years.

The events that took place on Alcatraz Island represented a watershed moment in Native American protest and caught the attention of the entire country, providing a forum for airing long-standing Indian grievances and for expressing Indian pride. Vine Deloria noted the importance of Alcatraz, referring to the occupation as a "master stroke of Indian activism." He also recognized the impact of Alcatraz and other occupations on Indian ethnic self-awareness and identity: "Indian[n]ess was judged on whether or not one was present at Alcatraz, Fort Lawson, Mt. Rushmore, Detroit, Sheep Mountain, Plymouth Rock, or Pitt River. . . . The activists controlled the language, the issues, and the attention." In 1993, Deloria reflected on the longer-term impact of the Red Power movement: "This era will probably always be dominated by the images and slogans of the AIM people. The real accomplishments in land restoration, however, were made by quiet determined tribal leaders. . . . In reviewing the period we should understand the frenzy of the time and link it to the definite accomplishments made by tribal governments."

The Alcatraz occupation and the activism that followed offer firm evidence to counter commonly held views of Indians as powerless in the face of history, as weakened remnants of disappearing cultures and communities. Countless events fueled American Indian ethnic pride and strengthened Indian people's sense of personal empowerment and community membership. Wilma Mankiller, now principal chief of the Cherokee Nation of Oklahoma, visited Alcatraz many times during the months of occupation. She described it as an awakening that "ultimately changed the course of my life." This was a recurrent theme in our interviews with Native Americans who participated in or observed the protests of that period:

> George Horse Capture: In World War II, the marines were island-hopping; they'd do the groundwork, and then the army and the civilians would come in and build things. Without the first wave, nothing would happen. Alcatraz and the militants were like that. They put themselves at risk, could be arrested or killed. You have to give them their due. We were in the second wave. In the regular Indian world, we're very complacent; it takes leadership to get things moving. But scratch a real Indian since then, and you're going to find a militant. Alcatraz tapped into something. It was the lance that burst the boil.

John Echohawk: Alcatraz just seemed to be kind of another event—what a lot of people had been thinking, wanting to do. We were studying Indian law for the first time. We had a lot of frustration and anger. People were fed up with the status quo. That's just what we were thinking. Starting in 1967 at the University of New Mexico Law School, we read treaties, Indian legal history. It was just astounding how unfair it was, how wrong it was. It [Alcatraz] was the kind of thing we needed.

Leonard Peltier: I was in Seattle when Alcatraz happened. It was the first event that received such publicity. In Seattle, we were in solidarity with the demands of Alcatraz. We were inspired and encouraged by Alcatraz. I realized their goals were mine. The Indian organizations I was working with shared the same needs: an Indian college to keep students from dropping out, a cultural center to keep Indian traditions. We were all really encouraged, not only those who were active, but those who were not active as well.

Frances Wise: The Alcatraz takeover had an enormous impact. I was living in Waco, Texas, at the time. I would see little blurbs on TV. I thought, these Indians are really doing something at Alcatraz. . . . And when they called for the land back, I realized that, finally, what Indian people have gone through is finally being recognized. . . . It affected how I think of myself. If someone asks me who I am, I say, well, I have a name, but Waco/Caddo—that's who I am. I have a good feeling about who I am now. And you need this in the presence of all this negative stuff, for example, celebrating the Oklahoma Land Run.

Rosalie McKay-Want: In the final analysis, however, the occupation of this small territory could be considered a victory for the cause of Indian activism and one of the most noteworthy expressions of patriotism and self-determination by Indian people in the twentieth century.

Grace Thorpe: Alcatraz was the catalyst and the most important event in the Indian movement to date. It made me put my furniture into storage and spend my life savings.

These voices speak to the central importance of the Alcatraz occupation as the symbol of long-standing Indian grievances and increasing impatience with a political system slow to respond to native rights. They also express the feelings of empowerment that witnessing and participating in protest can foster. Loretta Flores, an Indian women, did not become an activist herself until several years after the events on Alcatraz, but she has eloquently described the sense of self and community that activism can produce: "The night before the protest, I was talking to a younger person who had never been in a march before. I told her, 'Tomorrow when we get through with this march, you're going to have a feeling like you've never had before. It's going to change your life.' Those kids from Haskell (Indian Nations University) will never forget this. The spirits of our ancestors were looking down on us smiling."

Discussion Questions

1. Reread the primary source interviews included in this article, and then discuss with your peers the difference between the information you received from the secondary and primary sources in the article. How do the two kinds of sources work together to bring you a different picture of the importance of the Native American occupation of Alcatraz? What do the primary sources add in particular to your understanding? What does the secondary source material in the article add that the primary sources could not?

2. Reread Luther Standing Bear's selection in Chapter 2. How do you think he might have reacted to the occupation of Alcatraz? Do you think he would have supported the occupation or cautioned against it? What similarities in philosophy do you find between Luther Standing Bear's feelings and the feelings of those Native Americans who participated in or were inspired by the occupation of Alcatraz?

Writing Suggestions

1. Imagine that you were a student in San Francisco when the Native Americans occupied Alcatraz. Write an editorial to the *San Francisco Chronicle* responding to the statement from the All Tribes Indians asking the government for the Center for Native American Studies, a spiritual center and center of ecology, a training school, and an American Indian Museum. In your editorial, argue for or against the Native American requests, and be specific in your reasons for or against granting these requests.

2. Research the Red Power movement that was formed in part as a result of growing Native American activism after the occupation of Alcatraz. In addition to sit-ins and other protest activities, Native American activists took over the Bureau of Indian Affairs headquarters in 1972 and participated in an armed siege at the Pine Ridge Reservation that became known as Wounded Knee II. Then write a paper in which you discuss the goals, successes, and failures of the Red Power movement. How is the history of American Indian activism during the 1970s reflected in the struggle for Native American rights today? How far have Native American rights movements come since the 1970s? What kinds of activism is prevalent today?

Address to the Commonwealth Club of California

CESAR CHAVEZ

Cesar Chavez (1927–1993) began work as a migrant farm worker when his family lost its farm in Arizona during the Depression. Chavez and his family were forced to travel throughout the Southwest, picking in fields or vineyards wherever they could find work. After serving in the navy in World War II, Chavez returned to pick apricots in San Jose, California, and here he began his fight for farm laborer rights. In 1962, after working for many years with the Community Service Organization to support Chicano issues, he moved to Delano, California, to found the National Farm Worker Association (NFWA). With the help of the AFL/CIO, he formed the United Farm Worker's Association and led a five-year boycott against the table- and wine-grape growers. By 1970, the success of the boycott forced growers to sign contracts with the UFW, but another grape boycott was necessary in 1975 to force growers to work with Governor Brown's 1975 Agricultural Labor Relations Act. Chavez was devoted to nonviolent protest, and modeled his leadership on Martin Luther King, Jr. and Ghandi. Although farm workers were able to achieve higher pay, better health coverage, and pensions, in 1982 farm workers began to have trouble once again—the law was not being enforced and they were not obtaining their rightful benefits. In 1984, Chavez led another grape boycott, and in 1988 he endured a "Fast for Life" to protest the use of pesticides that gravely endangered the health of farm workers and their families. Chavez died in 1993 at the age of 66; he was posthumously awarded the Presidential Medal of Freedom by President Clinton, who spoke of Chavez's "faith and discipline" and "humility and inner strength" in leading others in the struggle for equality and fair working conditions. In the selection below, from a speech to the Commonwealth Club of California in 1984, Chavez addresses the continuing abuses of farm laborers and protests California Governor George Deukmajian's favoritism toward growers, stating that Deukmajian "has paid back his debt to the growers with the blood and sweat of California farm workers."

November 9, 1984—San Francisco

Twenty-one years ago last September, on a lonely stretch of railroad track paralleling U.S. Highway 101 near Salinas, 32 Bracero farm workers lost their lives in a tragic accident.

692

The Braceros had been imported from Mexico to work on California farms. They died when their bus, which was converted from a flatbed truck, drove in front of a freight train.

Conversion of the bus had not been approved by any government agency. The driver had "tunnel" vision.

Most of the bodies lay unidentified for days. No one, including the grower who employed the workers, even knew their names.

Today, thousands of farm workers live under savage conditions—beneath trees and amid garbage and human excrement—near tomato fields in San Diego County, tomato fields which use the most modern farm technology.

Vicious rats gnaw on them as they sleep. They walk miles to buy food at inflated prices. And they carry in water from irrigation pumps.

Child labor is still common in many farm areas.

As much as 30 percent of Northern California's garlic harvesters are under-aged children. Kids as young as six years old have voted in state-conducted union elections since they qualified as workers.

Some 800,000 under-aged children work with their families harvesting crops across America. Babies born to migrant workers suffer 25 percent higher infant mortality than the rest of the population.

Malnutrition among migrant worker children is 10 times higher than the national rate.

Farm workers' average life expectancy is still 49 years—compared to 73 years for the average American.

All my life, I have been driven by one dream, one goal, one vision: To overthrow a farm labor system in this nation which treats farm workers as if they were not important human beings.

Farm workers are not agricultural implements. They are not beasts of burden—to be used and discarded.

That dream was born in my youth. It was nurtured in my early days of organizing. It has flourished. It has been attacked.

I'm not very different from anyone else who has ever tried to accomplish something with his life. My motivation comes from my personal life—from watching what my mother and father went through when I was growing up; from what we experienced as migrant farm workers in California.

That dream, that vision, grew from my own experience with racism, with hope, with the desire to be treated fairly and to see my people treated as human beings and not as chattel.

It grew from anger and rage—emotions I felt 40 years ago when people of my color were denied the right to see a movie or eat at a restaurant in many parts of California.

It grew from the frustration and humiliation I felt as a boy who couldn't understand how the growers could abuse and exploit farm workers when there were so many of us and so few of them.

Later, in the '50s, I experienced a different kind of exploitation. In San Jose, in Los Angeles and in other urban communities, we—the Mexican American people—were dominated by a majority that was Anglo.

I began to realize what other minority people had discovered: That the only answer—the only hope—was in organizing. More of us had to become citizens. We had to register to vote. And people like me had to develop the skills it would take to organize, to educate, to help empower the Chicano people.

I spent many years—before we founded the union—learning how to work with people.

We experienced some successes in voter registration, in politics, in battling racial discrimination—successes in an era when Black Americans were just beginning to assert their civil lights and when political awareness among Hispanics was almost non-existent.

But deep in my heart, I knew I could never be happy unless I tried organizing the farm workers. I didn't know if I would succeed. But I had to try.

All Hispanics—urban and rural, young and old—are connected to the farm workers' experience. We had all lived through the fields—or our parents had. We shared that common humiliation.

How could we progress as a people, even if we lived in the cities, while the farm workers—men and women of our color—were condemned to a life without pride?

How could we progress as a people while the farm workers—who symbolized our history in this land—were denied self-respect?

How could our people believe that their children could become lawyers and doctors and judges and business people while this shame, this injustice was permitted to continue?

Those who attack our union often say, 'It's not really a union. It's something else: A social movement. A civil rights movement. It's something dangerous.'

They're half right. The United Farm Workers is first and foremost a union. A union like any other. A union that either produces for its members on the bread and butter issues or doesn't survive.

But the UFW has always been something more than a union—although it's never been dangerous if you believe in the Bill of Rights.

The UFW was the beginning! We attacked that historical source of shame and infamy that our people in this country lived with. We attacked that injustice, not by complaining; not by seeking hand-outs; not by becoming soldiers in the War on Poverty.

We organized!

Farm workers acknowledged we had allowed ourselves to become victims in a democratic society—a society where majority rule and collective bargaining are supposed to be more than academic theories or political rhetoric. And by addressing this historical problem, we created confidence and pride and hope in an entire people's ability to create the future.

The UFW's survival—its existence—was not in doubt in my mind when the time began to come—after the union became visible—when Chicanos started entering college in greater numbers, when Hispanics began running for public office in greater numbers—when our people started asserting their rights on a broad range of issues and in many communities across the country.

The union's survival—its very existence—sent out a signal to all Hispanics that we were fighting for our dignity, that we were challenging and overcoming injustice, that we were empowering the least educated among us—the poorest among us.

The message was clear: If it could happen in the fields, it could happen anywhere—in the cities, in the courts, in the city councils, in the state legislatures.

I didn't really appreciate it at the time, but the coming of our union signaled the start of great changes among Hispanics that are only now beginning to be seen.

I've travelled to every part of this nation. I have met and spoken with thousands of Hispanics from every walk of life—from every social and economic class.

One thing I hear most often from Hispanics, regardless of age or position—and from many non-Hispanics as well—is that the farm workers gave them hope that they could succeed and the inspiration to work for change.

From time to time you will hear our opponents declare that the union is weak, that the union has no support, that the union has not grown fast enough. Our obituary has been written many times.

How ironic it is that the same forces which argue so passionately that the union is not influential are the same forces that continue to fight us so hard.

The union's power in agriculture has nothing to do with the number of farm workers under union contract. It has nothing to do with the farm workers' ability to contribute to Democratic politicians. It doesn't even have much to do with our ability to conduct successful boycotts.

The very fact of our existence forces an entire industry—unionized and non-unionized—to spend millions of dollars year after year on improved wages, on improved working conditions, on benefits for workers.

If we're so weak and unsuccessful, why do the growers continue to fight us with such passion?

Because so long as we continue to exist, farm workers will benefit from our existence—even if they don't work under union contract.

It doesn't really matter whether we have 100,000 members or 500,000 members. In truth, hundreds of thousands of farm workers in California—and in other states—are better off today because of our work.

And Hispanics across California and the nation who don't work in agriculture are better off today because of what the farm workers taught people about organization, about pride and strength, about seizing control over their own lives.

Tens of thousands of the children and grandchildren of farm workers and the children and grandchildren of poor Hispanics are moving out of the fields and out of the barrios—and into the professions and into business and into politics. And that movement cannot be reversed!

Our union will forever exist as an empowering force among Chicanos in the Southwest. And that means our power and our influence will grow and not diminish.

Two major trends give us hope and encouragement.

First, our union has returned to a tried and tested weapon in the farm workers' non-violent arsenal—the boycott!

After the Agricultural Labor Relations Act became law in California in 1975, we dismantled our boycott to work with the law.

During the early- and mid-'70s, millions of Americans supported our boycotts. After 1975, we redirected our efforts from the boycott to organizing and winning elections under the law.

The law helped farm workers make progress in overcoming poverty and injustice. At companies where farm workers are protected by union contracts, we have made progress in overcoming child labor, in overcoming miserable wages and working conditions, in overcoming sexual harassment of women workers, in overcoming dangerous pesticides which poison our people and poison the food we all eat.

Where we have organized, these injustices soon pass into history.

But under Republican Governor George Deukmejian, the law that guarantees our right to organize no longer protects farm workers. It doesn't work anymore.

In 1982, corporate growers gave Deukmejian one million dollars to run for governor of California. Since he took office, Deukmejian has paid back his debt to the growers with the blood and sweat of California farm workers.

Instead of enforcing the law as it was written against those who break it, Deukmejian invites growers who break the law to seek relief from the governor's appointees.

What does all this mean for farm workers?

It means that the right to vote in free elections is a sham. It means that the right to talk freely about the union among your fellow workers on the job is a cruel hoax. It means the light to be free from threats and intimidation by growers is an empty promise.

It means the right to sit down and negotiate with your employer as equals across the bargaining table—and not as peons in the field—is a fraud. It means that thousands of farm workers—who are owed millions of dollars in back pay because their employers broke the law—are still waiting for their checks.

It means that 36,000 farm workers—who voted to be represented by the United Farm Workers in free elections—are still waiting for contracts from growers who refuse to bargain in good faith.

It means that, for farm workers, child labor will continue. It means that infant mortality will continue. It means malnutrition among our children will continue. It means the short life expectancy and the inhuman living and working conditions will continue.

Are these make-believe threats? Are they exaggerations?

Ask the farm workers who are still waiting for growers to bargain in good faith and sign contracts. Ask the farm workers who've been fired from their jobs because they spoke out for the union. Ask the farm workers who've been threatened with physical violence because they support the UFW.

Ask the family of Rene Lopez, the young farm worker from Fresno who was shot to death last year because he supported the union.

These tragic events forced farm workers to declare a new international boycott of California table grapes. That's why we are asking Americans once again to join the farm workers by boycotting California grapes.

The Louis Harris poll revealed that 17 million American adults boycotted grapes. We are convinced that those people and that good will have not disappeared.

That segment of the population which makes our boycotts work are the Hispanics, the Blacks, the other minorities and our allies in labor and the church. But it is also an entire generation of young Americans who matured politically and socially in the 1960s and '70s—millions of people for whom boycotting grapes and other products became a socially accepted pattern of behavior.

If you were young, Anglo and on or near campus during the late '60s and early '70s, chances are you supported farm workers.

Fifteen years later, the men and women of that generation are alive and well. They are in their mid-30s and 40s. They are pursuing professional careers. Their disposable income is relatively high. But they are still inclined to respond to an appeal from farm workers. The union's mission still has meaning for them.

Only today we must translate the importance of a union for farm workers into the language of the 1980s. Instead of talking about the right to organize, we must talk about protection against sexual harassment in the fields. We must speak about the right to quality food—and food that is safe to eat.

I can tell you that the new language is working; the 17 million are still there. They are responding—not to picketlines and leafletting alone, but to the high-tech boycott of today—a boycott that used computers and direct mail and advertising techniques which have revolutionized business and politics in recent years.

We have achieved more success with the boycott in the first 11 months of 1984 that we achieved in the 14 years since 1970.

The other trend that gives us hope is the monumental growth of Hispanic influence in this country and what that means in increased population, increased social and economic clout, and increased political influence.

South of the Sacramento River in California, Hispanics now make up more than 25 percent of the population. That figure will top 30 percent by the year 2000.

There are 1.1 million Spanish-surnamed registered voters in California; 85 percent are Democrats; only 13 percent are Republicans.

In 1975, there were 200 Hispanic elected officials at all levels of government. In 1984, there are over 400 elected judges, city council members, mayors and legislators.

In light of these trends, it is absurd to believe or suggest that we are going to go back in time—as a union or as a people!

The growers often try to blame the union for their problems—to lay their sins off on us—sins for which they only have themselves to blame.

The growers only have themselves to blame as they begin to reap the harvest from decades of environmental damage they have brought upon the land—the pesticides, the herbicides, the soil fumigants, the fertilizers, the salt deposits from thoughtless irrigation—the ravages from years of unrestrained poisoning of our soil and water.

Thousands of acres of land in California have already been irrevocably damaged by this wanton abuse of nature. Thousands more will be lost unless growers understand that dumping more poisons on the soil won't solve their problems—on the short term or the long term.

Health authorities in many San Joaquin Valley towns already warn young children and pregnant women not to drink the water because of nitrates from fertilizers which have contaminated the groundwater.

The growers only have themselves to blame for an increasing demand by consumers for higher quality food—food that isn't tainted by toxics; food that doesn't result from plant mutations or chemicals which produce red, luscious-looking tomatoes—that taste like alfalfa.

The growers are making the same mistake American automakers made in the '60s and '70s when they refused to produce small economical cars—and opened the door to increased foreign competition.

Growers only have themselves to blame for increasing attacks on their publicly-financed hand-outs and government welfare: Water subsidies; mechanization research; huge subsidies for not growing crops.

These special privileges came into being before the Supreme Court's one-person, one-vote decision—at a time when rural lawmakers dominated the Legislature and the Congress. Soon, those hand-outs could be in jeopardy as government searches for more revenue and as urban taxpayers take a closer look at farm programs—and who they really benefit.

The growers only have themselves to blame for the humiliation they have brought upon succeeding waves of immigrant groups which have sweated and sacrificed for 100 years to make this industry rich. For generations, they have subjugated entire races of dark-skinned farm workers.

These are the sins of the growers, not the farm workers. We didn't poison the land. We didn't open the door to imported produce. We didn't covet billions of dollars in government hand-outs. We didn't abuse and exploit the people who work the land.

Today, the growers are like a punch-drunk old boxer who doesn't know he's past his prime. The times are changing. The political and social environment has changed. The chickens are coming home to roost—and the time to account for past sins is approaching.

I am told, these days, why farm workers should be discouraged and pessimistic: The Republicans control the governor's office and the White House. They say there is a conservative trend in the nation.

Yet we are filled with hope and encouragement. We have looked into the future and the future is ours!

History and inevitability are on our side. The farm workers and their children—and the Hispanics and their children—are the future in California. And corporate growers are the past!

Those politicians who ally themselves with the corporate growers and against the farm workers and the Hispanics are in for a big surprise. They want to make their careers in politics. They want to hold power 20 and 30 years from now.

But 20 and 30 years from now—in Modesto, in Salinas, in Fresno, in Bakersfield, in the Imperial Valley, and in many of the great cities of California—those communities will be dominated by farm workers and not by growers, by the children and grandchildren of farm workers and not by the children and grandchildren of growers.

These trends are part of the forces of history that cannot be stopped. No person and no organization can resist them for very long. They are inevitable.

Once social change begins, it cannot be reversed.

You cannot uneducate the person who has learned to read. You cannot humiliate the person who feels pride. You cannot oppress the people who are not afraid anymore.

Our opponents must understand that it's not just a union we have built. Unions, like other institutions, can come and go.

But we're more than an institution. For nearly 20 years, our union has been on the cutting edge of a people's cause—and you cannot do away with an entire people; you cannot stamp out a people's cause.

Regardless of what the future holds for the union, regardless of what the future holds for farm workers, our accomplishments cannot be undone. "La Causa"—our cause—doesn't have to be experienced twice.

The consciousness and pride that were raised by our union are alive and thriving inside millions of young Hispanics who will never work on a farm!

Like the other immigrant groups, the day will come when we win the economic and political rewards which are in keeping with our numbers in society. The day will come when the politicians do the right thing by our people out of political necessity and not out of charity or idealism.

That day may not come this year. That day may not come during this decade. But it will come, someday!

And when that day comes, we shall see the fulfillment of that passage from the Book of Matthew in the New Testament, "That the last shall be first and the first shall be last."

And on that day, our nation shall fulfill its creed—and that fulfillment shall enrich us all.

Thank you very much.

Discussion Questions

1. Consider the organization of Chavez's speech to the members of the Commonwealth Club of California. How does he keep his audience in mind as he argues against the wine growers? How does he pay attention to the arguments of those who oppose his goals? What kinds of evidence does he provide for his audience in order to convince them to believe his statements? And finally, what tone does Chavez take at the end of his speech? Discuss whether or not you found the speech effective, and then consider whether or not the predominantly white, professional male members of the Commonwealth Club would have been moved by this speech.

2. Chavez uses historical references throughout his speech to give context to the struggles of the farm workers in California. Discuss his strategies: To which periods of history does he refer? How does he use past labor issues to appeal to his audience?

Writing Suggestions

1. Review your answers to the first discussion question for this selection, and then write an analysis of Chavez's speech, answering some of the following questions:

    How does he keep his audience in mind as he argues against the wine growers?
    How does he pay attention to the arguments of those who oppose his goals?
    What kinds of evidence does he provide for his audience in order to convince them to believe his statements?
    What tone does he take at the end of his speech?

    In your analysis, discuss whether or not you found the speech effective and explain your answers with specific examples from the text.

2. Chavez writes that farm workers are not "beasts of burden—to be used and discarded." He also writes that the Farm Worker's Union has "never been dangerous if you believe in the Bill of Rights." Find the text of the Bill of Rights on the Internet or in a library, and then write an analysis of Chavez's demands in this speech in light of the guarantees of the Bill of Rights. How do his demands and goals for the farm workers conform to the promises of the Bill of Rights? How does Chavez use diction and imagery to support his claim that the farm workers' goals are supported by the Bill of Rights? Compare his specific examples with the broad principles outlined in the Bill of Rights, and be sure to quote from both texts in your analysis.

White Paper on Vietnam

DEPARTMENT OF STATE

By 1965, U.S. troops were involved in a full-scale conflict in Vietnam, U.S. soldiers were dying, and the U.S. public was growing increasingly critical of U.S. involvement in a war that had already dragged on longer than expected and to which the U.S. government was committing more and more troops. The Students for a Democratic Society (SDS) had already organized a number of "teach-ins" at universities across the country, and the first large anti-war march on Washington was soon to take place. Because the Vietnam War was not officially called a war but a foreign policy initiative, the Department of State issued the *White Paper on Vietnam* in February of 1965 as an explanation and defense of its policies and plans in Vietnam.

February 27, 1965 (*Department of State Bulletin*, March 22, 1965)

South Vietnam is fighting for its life against a brutal campaign of terror and armed attack inspired, directed, supplied, and controlled by the Communist regime in Hanoi. This flagrant aggression has been going on for years, but recently the pace has quickened and the threat has now become acute.

The war in Vietnam is a new kind of war, a fact as yet poorly understood in most parts of the world. Much of the confusion that prevails in the thinking of many people, and even governments, stems from this basic misunderstanding. For in Vietnam a totally new brand of aggression has been loosed against an independent people who want to make their way in peace and freedom.

Vietnam is not another Greece, where indigenous guerrilla forces used friendly neighboring territory as a sanctuary.

Vietnam is not another Malaya, where Communist guerrillas were, for the most part, physically distinguishable from the peaceful majority they sought to control.

Vietnam is not another Philippines, where Communist guerrillas were physically separated from the source of their moral and physical support.

Above all, the war in Vietnam is not a spontaneous and local rebellion against the established government.

There are elements in the Communist program of conquest directed against South Vietnam common to each of the previous areas of aggression and subversion. But there is one fundamental difference. In Vietnam a Communist government has set out deliberately to conquer a sovereign people in a neighboring state. And to achieve its end, it has used every resource of its own government to carry out its carefully planned program of concealed aggression. North Vietnam's commitment to seize control of the South is no less total than was the commitment of the regime in North Korea in 1950. But knowing the consequences of the latter's undisguised attack, the planners in Hanoi have tried desperately to conceal their hand. They have failed and their aggression is as real as that of an invading army.

This report is a summary of the massive evidence of North Vietnamese aggression obtained by the Government of South Vietnam. This evidence has been jointly analyzed by South Vietnamese and American experts.

The evidence shows that the hard core of the Communist forces attacking South Vietnam were trained in the North and ordered into the South by Hanoi. It shows that the key leadership of the Vietcong (VC), the officers and much of the cadre, many of the technicians, political organizers, and propagandists have come from the North and operate under Hanoi's direction. It shows that the training of essential military personnel and their infiltration into the South is directed by the Military High Command in Hanoi. In recent months new types of weapons have been introduced in the VC army, for which all ammunition must come from outside sources. Communist China and other Communist states have been the prime suppliers of these weapons and ammunition, and they have been channeled primarily through North Vietnam.

The directing force behind the effort to conqueror South Vietnam is the Communist Party in the North, the Lao Dong (Workers) Party. As in every Communist state, the party is an integral part of the regime itself. North Vietnamese officials have expressed their firm determination to absorb South Vietnam into the Communist world.

Through its Central Committee, which controls the Government of the North, the Lao Dong Party directs the total political and military effort of the Vietcong. The Military High Command in the North trains the military men and sends them into South Vietnam. The Central Research Agency, North Vietnam's central intelligence organization, directs the elaborate espionage and subversion effort. . .

Under Hanoi's overall direction the Communists have established an extensive machine for carrying on the war within South Vietnam. The focal point is the Central Office for South Vietnam with its political and military subsections and other specialized agencies. A subordinate part of this Central Office is the liberation Front for South Vietnam. The front was formed at Hanoi's order in 1960. Its principle function is to influence opinion abroad and to create the false impression that the aggression in South Vietnam is an indigenous rebellion against the established Government.

For more than 10 years the people and the Government of South Vietnam, exercising the inherent right of self-defense, have fought back against these efforts to extend Communist power south across the 17th parallel. The United States has responded to the appeals of the Government of the Republic of Vietnam for help in this defense of the freedom and independence of its land and its people.

In 1961 the Department of State issued a report called A Threat to the Peace. It described North Vietnam's program to seize South Vietnam. The evidence in that report had been presented by the Government of the Republic of Vietnam to the International Control Commission (ICC). A special report by the ICC in June 1962 upheld the validity of that evidence. The Commission held that there was "sufficient evidence to show beyond reasonable doubt" that North Vietnam had sent arms and men into South Vietnam to carry out subversion with the aim of overthrowing the legal Government there. The ICC found the authorities in Hanoi in specific violation of four provisions of the Geneva Accords of 1954.

Since then, new and even more impressive evidence of Hanoi's aggression has accumulated. The Government of the United States believes that evidence should be presented to its own citizens and to the world. It is important for free men to know what has been happening in Vietnam, and how, and why. That is the purpose of this report. . .

The record is conclusive. It establishes beyond question that North Vietnam is carrying out a carefully conceived plan of aggression against the South. It shows that North Vietnam has intensified its efforts in the years since it was condemned by the International Control Commission. It proves that Hanoi continues to press its systematic program of armed aggression into South Vietnam. This aggression violates the United Nations Charter. It is directly contrary to the Geneva Accords of 1954 and of 1962 to which North Vietnam is a party. It is a fundamental threat to the freedom and security of South Vietnam.

The people of South Vietnam have chosen to resist this threat. At their request, the United States has taken its place beside them in their defensive struggle.

The United States seeks no territory, no military bases, no favored position. But we have learned the meaning of aggression elsewhere in the post-war world, and we have met it.

If peace can be restored in South Vietnam, the United States will be ready at once to reduce its military involvement. But it will not abandon friends who want to remain free. It will do what must be done to help them. The choice now between peace and continued and increasingly destructive conflict is one for the authorities in Hanoi to make.

Discussion Questions

1. The Department of State was charged with the task of explaining to the American people why a full-scale military operation was underway in Vietnam, although the United States had not declared war. The *White Paper on Vietnam* sought to clarify the distinction between viewing the conflict between the South and the North as a rebellion in South Vietnam against the government, and viewing it as a planned, armed aggression

by the North in order to take over "a sovereign people in a neighboring state." Discuss the strategy of the *White Paper*'s argument. How does the paper use the threat of Communism to make its arguments? How does it appeal to past historical events to confirm the danger from Communism? What kind of diction did the Department of State writers use to describe the U.S. actions? The South Vietnamese people? The North Vietnamese government? How convincing would this paper have been to you as a student in the United States in 1965?

2. Look back to the speeches of Wilson and Roosevelt when they declared war on Germany and Japan in 1917 and 1941. These speeches addressed the Congress and explained why it was necessary for America to protect its interests and its citizens. How does the *White Paper* differ in its emphasis, considering that we were not at war with North Vietnam? What similar appeals do the writers of the *White Paper* use to justify U.S. military action in Vietnam? What aspects of the previous declarations of war are missing from the *White Paper* strategies? How persuasive a document is the *White Paper* when compared to Wilson's and Roosevelt's speeches?

Writing Suggestions

1. Consider your answers to the first discussion question for this selection. Then write an analysis of the *White Paper*, addressing its strengths and weaknesses as a persuasive document, discussing the same issues you considered in responding to the first discussion question. Also consider more carefully the kinds of details and evidence the *White Paper* offers, and how it appeals to the ideals of U.S. citizens. Use specific examples from the text, and include in your paper what you feel your response to this document would have been if you had been a student in 1965.

2. Search the Internet for presidential speeches and White House publications about U.S. involvement in foreign conflicts since Vietnam. You can search each president's library for papers, and you can also look at the White House Home page, at <www.whitehouse.gov> for current speech texts. For example, you might look at speeches by President George W. Bush when he decided to send U.S. troops to Iraq. In addition, you can find President George H. Bush's speech about sending troops to the Gulf War at the end of this chapter, and President George W. Bush's speech about war on terrorism in Chapter 9. Analyze whichever speech you select in light of the history of public protest about Vietnam, and look at the way the president presented the need for U.S. troops to go overseas. Do you see any indirect or direct mention of Vietnam in the speech? What kinds of reassurances does the president give about contained involvement? Where in the speech do you see awareness that overseas intervention will be a difficult concept to sell to the U.S. public?

The Incredible War

PAUL POTTER

Paul Potter gave the following speech in 1965 when he was president of the Students for a Democratic Society, a group that organized students and other citizens to protest civil rights infractions, the threat of nuclear war, the lack of equality for women, the Vietnam war, and other problems in American society. Paul Potter was educated at Oberlin College and was a student there when he joined the SDS in 1962, when it was still a relatively small organization. Galvanized by SDS, approximately 25,000 people gathered for a March on Washington, where, on April 17, 1965, Potter gave the following speech to an enthusiastic crowd. The march is credited with the enormous rise in the numbers of chapters of SDS across the country, and Potter's speech served as a rallying point for an increasingly large number of students involved in sit-ins, teach-ins, and nonviolent protests across the country.

(April 17, 1965)

The incredible war in Vietnam has provided the razor, the terrifying sharp cutting edge that has finally severed the last vestiges of illusion that morality and democracy are the guiding principles of American foreign policy. The saccharine, self-righteous moralism that promises the Vietnamese a billion dollars of economic aid at the very moment we are delivering billions for economic and social destruction and political repression is rapidly losing what power it might ever have had to reassure us about the decency of our foreign policy. The further we explore the reality of what this country is doing and planning in Vietnam the more we are driven toward the conclusion of Senator Morse that the United States may well be the greatest threat to peace in the world today. . . .

The president says that we are defending freedom in Vietnam. Whose freedom? Not the freedom of the Vietnamese. The first act of the first dictator (Diem) the United States installed in Vietnam was to systematically begin the persecution of all political opposition, non-Communist as well as Communist. . . .

The pattern of repression and destruction that we have developed and justified in the war is so thorough that it can only be called "cultural genocide." I am not simply talking about napalm or gas or crop destruction or torture hurled indiscriminantly on women and children, insurgent and neutral, upon the first suspicion of rebel activity. That in itself is horrendous and incredible beyond belief. But it is only part of a large pattern of destruction to the very fabric of the country. We have uprooted the people from the land and imprisoned them in concentration camps called "sunrise villages." Through conscription and direct political intervention and control we have broken or destroyed local customs and traditions, trampled upon those things of value which give dignity and purpose to life. . . .

Not even the president can say that this is war to defend the freedom of the Vietnamese people. Perhaps what the president means when he speaks of freedom is the freedom of the Americans.

What in fact has the war done for freedom in America? It has led to even more vigorous governmental efforts to control information, manipulate the press, and pressure and persuade the public through distorted or down-right dishonest documents such as the white paper on Vietnam. . . .

In many ways this is an unusual march, because the large majority of the people here are not involved in a peace movement as their primary basis of concern. What is exciting about the participants in this march is that so many of us view ourselves consciously as participants as well in a movement to build a more decent society. There are students here who have been involved in protest over the quality and kind of education they are receiving in growingly bureaucratized, depersonalized institutions called universities; there are Negroes from Mississippi and Alabama who are struggling against the tyranny and repression of those states; there are poor people here—Negro and white—from Northern urban areas who are attempting to build movements that abolish poverty and secure democracy; there are faculty who are beginning to question the relevance of their institutions to the critical problems facing the society. . . .

The president mocks freedom if he insists that the war in Vietnam is a defense of American freedom. Perhaps the only freedom that this war protects is the freedom of the warhawks in the Pentagon and the State Department to "experiment" with "counterinsurgency" and guerrilla warfare in Vietnam. Vietnam, we may say is a "laboratory" run by a new breed of gamesmen who approach war as a kind of rational exercise in international power politics.

Thus far the war in Vietnam has only dramatized the demand of ordinary people to have some opportunity to make their own lives, and of their unwillingness, even under incredible odds, to give up the struggle against external domination. We are told however that that struggle can be legitimately suppressed since it might lead to the development of a Communist system—and before that menace, all criticism is supposed to melt.

This is a critical point and there are several things that must be said here—not by way of celebration, but because I think they are the truth. First, if this country were serious about giving the people of Vietnam some alternative to a Communist social revolution, that opportunity was sacrificed in 1954 when we helped to install Diem and his repression of non-Communist movements. There is no indication that we were serious about that goal—that we were ever willing to contemplate the risks of allowing the Vietnamese to choose their own destinies. Second, those people who insist now that Vietnam can be neutralized are for the most part looking for a sugar coating to cover the bitter pill. We must accept the consequences that calling for an end of the war in Vietnam is in fact allowing for the likelihood that a Vietnam without war will be a self-styled Communist Vietnam. Third, this country must come to understand that the creation of a Communist country in the world today is not an ultimate defeat. If people are given the opportunity to choose their own lives it is likely that some of them will choose what we have called "Communist systems." . . . And yet the war that we are creating and escalating in Southeast Asia is rapidly eroding the base of independence of North Vietnam as it is forced to turn to China and the Soviet Union.

But the war goes on; the freedom to conduct that war depends on the dehumanization not only of Vietnamese people but of Americans as well; it depends on the construction of a system of premises and thinking that insulates the president and his advisers thoroughly and completely from the human consequences of the decisions they make. I do not believe that the president or Mr. Rusk or Mr. McNamara or even McGeorge Bundy are particularly evil men. If asked to throw napalm on the back of a ten-year-old child they would shrink in horror—but their decisions have led to mutilation and death of thousands and thousands of people.

What kind of system is it that allows "good" men to make those kinds of decisions? What kind of system is it that justifies the United States or any country seizing the destinies of the Vietnamese people and using them callously for our own purpose? What kind of system is it that disenfranchises people in the South, leaves millions upon millions of people throughout the country impoverished and excluded from the mainstream and promise of American society, that creates faceless and terrible bureaucracies and makes those the place where people spend their lives and do their work, that consistently puts material values before human values—and still persists in calling itself free and still persists in finding itself fit to police the world? . . .

We must name that system. We must name it, describe it, analyze it, understand it, and change it. For it is only when that system is changed and brought under control that there can be any hope for stopping the forces that create a war in Vietnam today or a murder in the South tomorrow. . . .

If the people of this country are to end the war in Vietnam, and to change the institutions which create it, then, the people of this country must create a massive social movement—and if that can be built around the issue of Vietnam, then that is what we must do. . . .

But that means that we build a movement that works not simply in Washington but in communities and with the problems that face people throughout the society. That means that we build a movement that understands Vietnam, in all its horror, as but a symptom of a deeper malaise, that we build a movement that makes possible the implementation of the values that would have prevented Vietnam, a movement based on the integrity of man and a belief in man's capacity to determine his own life; a movement that does not exclude people because they are too poor or have been held down; a movement that has the capacity to tolerate all of the formulations of society that men may choose to strive for; a movement that will build on the new and creative forms of protest that are beginning to emerge, such as the teach-in, and extend their efforts and intensify them; a movement that will not tolerate the escalation or prolongation of this war but will, if necessary, respond to the administration war effort with massive civil disobedience all over the country that will wrench the country into a confrontation with the issues of the war; a movement that must of necessity reach out to all those people in Vietnam or elsewhere who are struggling to find decency and control for their lives.

For in a strange way the people of Vietnam and the people on this demonstration are united in much more than a common concern that the war be ended. In both countries there are people struggling to build a movement that has the power to change their condition. The system that frustrates these movements is the same. All our lives, our destinies, our very hopes to live depend on our ability to overcome that system. . . .

Discussion Questions

1. Consider Potter's audience as he gave "The Incredible War" speech to a large crowd gathered in Washington, D.C. in 1965 at the first anti-war march. How does Potter broaden his argument to include more issues than U.S. involvement in Vietnam? How does he appeal to a broader segment of his audience? How does he approach the discussion of the men in government who have made the decisions he so strongly criticizes? Discuss the different strategies he uses to appeal to his audience, considering his use of specific examples, his appeals to American ideals, and the link he creates to the civil rights movement.

2. Potter claims that to understand the system that has allowed the government and "good men" to enter into this war in Vietnam we must "name the system, describe it, analyze it, understand it, and change it." Discuss the system Potter criticizes and detail the different aspects of this system. Then consider whether or not this "system" still exists today. Do you feel that the "president and his advisers" still are insulated "thoroughly and completely from the human consequences of the decisions they make?" Consider a number of different decisions our current president has made recently: You could discuss Bush's responses to September 11, recent military actions in Iraq, changes in health care, policies regarding the environment, canceling of social programs, and so on.

Writing Suggestions

1. Consider your responses to the second discussion question for this selection. Then write your thoughts about Potter's claim that to understand the system that has allowed the government and "good men" to enter into this war in Vietnam we must "name the system, describe it, analyze it, understand it, and change it." In your paper, discuss the system Potter criticizes and detail the different aspects of this system. Then consider whether or not this "system" still exists today. Do you feel that the "president and his advisers" still are insulated "thoroughly and completely from the human consequences of the decisions they make?" Discuss in your paper a number of different decisions our current president has made recently: You could discuss Bush's responses to September 11, recent military actions in Iraq, changes in health care, policies regarding the environment, canceling of social programs, and so on. Use specific examples from current affairs to back up your arguments.

2. Research the role of the Students for Democratic Society in the civil rights movement and the anti-war movement of the 1960s. What were the stated goals of this group? How effective was the group in mobilizing student protest? What were the methods of protest the SDS encouraged? Assess the movement's successes and failures, and then write a fact-based argument paper about the SDS's role in the protest movement, supporting your representation of the SDS with specific facts from at least five different sources.

Address to the Nation

Announcing the Deployment of U.S. Armed Forces to Saudi Arabia

GEORGE H. BUSH

George H. Bush was the forty-first President of the United States, serving in the White House from 1989 to 1993. Born in Massachusetts in 1924, he served as a navy pilot in World War II and then returned to complete his studies at Yale University. After entering the oil business in West Texas, Bush decided to run for Congress and served two terms as a Representative from Texas. Bush also went on to serve as Ambassador to the United Nations, Chairman of the Republican National Committee, and Director of the Central Intelligence Agency. Bush served as vice-president for eight years under Ronald Reagan and then ran for president himself in 1988 and won. In 1990, Bush responded to Iraqi President Saddam Hussein's invasion of Kuwait by sending 425,000 American troops to Saudi Arabia. In the "Address to the Nation" below, Bush explains why he feels it is important "to assist the Saudi Arabian Government in the defense of its homeland."

August 8, 1990

In the life of a nation, we're called upon to define who we are and what we believe. Sometimes these choices are not easy. But today as President, I ask for your support in a decision I've made to stand up for what's right and condemn what's wrong, all in the cause of peace.

At my direction, elements of the 82d Airborne Division as well as key units of the United States Air Force are arriving today to take up defensive positions in Saudi Arabia. I took this action to assist the Saudi Arabian Government in the defense of its homeland. No one commits America's Armed Forces to a dangerous mission lightly, but after perhaps unparalleled international consultation and exhausting every alternative, it became necessary to take this action. Let me tell you why.

Less than a week ago, in the early morning hours of August 2d, Iraqi Armed Forces, without provocation or warning, invaded a peaceful Kuwait. Facing negligible resistance from its much smaller neighbor, Iraq's tanks stormed in blitzkrieg fashion through Kuwait in a few short hours. With more than 100,000 troops, along with tanks, artillery, and surface-to-surface missiles, Iraq now occupies Kuwait. This aggression came just hours after Saddam Hussein specifically assured numerous countries in the area that there would be no invasion. There is no justification whatsoever for this outrageous and brutal act of aggression.

A puppet regime imposed from the outside is unacceptable. The acquisition of territory by force is unacceptable. No one, friend or foe, should doubt our desire for peace; and no one should underestimate our determination to confront aggression.

Four simple principles guide our policy. First, we seek the immediate, unconditional, and complete withdrawal of all Iraqi forces from Kuwait. Second, Kuwait's legitimate government must be restored to replace the puppet regime. And third, my administration, as has been the case with every President from President Roosevelt to President Reagan, is committed to the security and stability of the Persian Gulf. And fourth, I am determined to protect the lives of American citizens abroad.

Immediately after the Iraqi invasion, I ordered an embargo of all trade with Iraq and, together with many other nations, announced sanctions that both freeze all Iraqi assets in this country and protected Kuwait's assets. The stakes are high. Iraq is already a rich and powerful country that possesses the world's second largest reserves of oil and over a million men under arms. It's the fourth largest military in the world. Our country now imports nearly half the oil it consumes and could face a major threat to its economic independence. Much of the world is even more dependent upon imported oil and is even more vulnerable to Iraqi threats.

We succeeded in the struggle for freedom in Europe because we and our allies remain stalwart. Keeping the peace in the Middle East will require no less. We're beginning a new era. This new era can be full of promise, an age of freedom, a time of peace for all peoples. But if history teaches us anything, it is that we must resist aggression or it will destroy our freedoms. Appeasement does not work. As was the case in the 1930s, we see in Saddam Hussein an aggressive dictator threatening his neighbors. Only 14 days ago, Saddam Hussein promised his friends he would not invade Kuwait. And 4 days ago, he promised the world he would withdraw. And twice we have seen what his promises mean: His promises mean nothing.

In the last few days, I've spoken with political leaders from the Middle East, Europe, Asia, and the Americas; and I've met with Prime Minister Thatcher, Prime Minister Mulroney, and NATO Secretary General Woerner. And all agree that Iraq cannot be allowed to benefit from its invasion of Kuwait.

We agree that this is not an American problem or a European problem or a Middle East problem: It is the world's problem. And that's why, soon after the Iraqi invasion, the United Nations Security Council, without dissent, condemned Iraq, calling for the immediate and unconditional withdrawal of its troops from Kuwait. The Arab world, through both the Arab League and the Gulf Cooperation Council, courageously announced its opposition to Iraqi aggression. Japan, the United Kingdom, and France, and other governments around the world have imposed severe sanctions. The Soviet Union and China ended all arms sales to Iraq.

And this past Monday, the United Nations Security Council approved for the first time in 23 years mandatory sanctions under chapter VII of the United Nations Charter. These sanctions, now enshrined in international law, have the potential to deny Iraq the fruits of aggression while sharply limiting its ability to either import or export anything of value, especially oil.

I pledge here today that the United States will do its part to see that these sanctions are effective and to induce Iraq to withdraw without delay from Kuwait.

But we must recognize that Iraq may not stop using force to advance its ambitions. Iraq has massed an enormous war machine on the Saudi border capable of initiating hostilities with little or no additional preparation. Given the Iraqi government's history of aggression against its own citizens as well as its neighbors, to assume Iraq will not attack again would be unwise and unrealistic.

And therefore, after consulting with King Fahd, I sent Secretary of Defense Dick Cheney to discuss cooperative measures we could take. Following those meetings, the Saudi Government requested our help, and I responded to that request by ordering U.S. air and ground forces to deploy to the Kingdom of Saudi Arabia.

Let me be clear: The sovereign independence of Saudi Arabia is of vital interest to the United States. This decision, which I shared with the congressional leadership, grows out of the longstanding friendship and security relationship between the United States and Saudi Arabia. U.S. forces will work together with those of Saudi Arabia and other nations to preserve the integrity of Saudi Arabia and to deter further Iraqi aggression. Through their presence, as well as through training and exercises, these multinational forces will enhance the overall capability of Saudi Armed Forces to defend the Kingdom.

I want to be clear about what we are doing and why. America does not seek conflict, nor do we seek to chart the destiny of other nations. But America will stand by her friends. The mission of our troops is wholly defensive. Hopefully, they will not be needed long. They will not initiate hostilities, but they will defend themselves, the Kingdom of Saudi Arabia, and other friends in the Persian Gulf.

We are working around the clock to deter Iraqi aggression and to enforce U.N. sanctions. I'm continuing my conversations with world leaders. Secretary of Defense Cheney has just returned from valuable consultations with President Mubarak of Egypt and King Hassan of Morocco. Secretary of State Baker has consulted with his counterparts in many nations, including the Soviet Union, and today he heads for Europe to consult with President Ozal of Turkey, a staunch friend of the United States. And he'll then consult with the NATO Foreign Ministers.

I will ask oil-producing nations to do what they can to increase production in order to minimize any impact that oil flow reductions will have on the world economy. And I will explore whether we and our allies should draw down our strategic petroleum reserves. Conservation measures can also help;

Americans everywhere must do their part. And one more thing: I'm asking the oil companies to do their fair share. They should show restraint and not abuse today's uncertainties to raise prices.

Standing up for our principles will not come easy. It may take time and possibly cost a great deal. But we are asking no more of anyone than of the brave young men and women of our Armed Forces and their families. And I ask that in the churches around the country prayers be said for those who are committed to protect and defend America's interests.

Standing up for our principle is an American tradition. As it has so many times before, it may take time and tremendous effort, but most of all, it will take unity of purpose. As I've witnessed throughout my life in both war and peace, America has never wavered when her purpose is driven by principle. And in this August day, at home and abroad, I know she will do no less.

Thank you, and God bless the United States of America.

Discussion Questions

1. George H. Bush states, "No one, friend or foe, should doubt our desire for peace; and no one should underestimate our determination to confront aggression." Compare his words and actions in the Gulf War with the current post–9/11 U.S. foreign policy decisions and George W. Bush's attitudes toward involvement in foreign wars or conflicts. Has the United States become more cautious or more aggressive? Do you think U.S. foreign policy is more or less ready to commit troops overseas than it was during the presidency of George H. Bush? Do you approve or disapprove of either Bush's actions? What are your feelings about the current administration's approach to overseas military interventions?

2. Reread Woodrow Wilson's "War Message to Congress" and Franklin Roosevelt's "Pearl Harbor Speech" in Chapter 7. Then discuss the similarities and differences you find when comparing these speeches to George H. Bush's "Address to the Nation." Consider some of the following aspects of all three speeches:

   How does each president begin his address?

   How does each president describe the enemy?

   Which justifications for war does each president use?

   Which presidents refer to international allies in their speeches?

   What do the presidents ask from the American people?

   Which American values are mentioned in all three speeches?

   Which speech do you find most convincing, and why?

   Discuss the similarities and differences in the speeches, and try to come up with a list of common themes and devices used to explain the commencement of war or military action.

Writing Suggestions

1. Operation Desert Storm created an outpouring of both intense Ameri-
    can patriotism and intense American criticism of Bush's decision to de-
    ploy the air and ground troops that inflicted tremendous casualties on
    the Iraqis. Research this topic more thoroughly, starting with some of
    the Web sites listed at the end of this chapter, and researching the edi-
    torials of major newspapers in August 1990. (You can use the Academ-
    ic Universe site to search for these editorials.) Then, with the benefit of
    hindsight, write a personal essay arguing for or against the American
    military Operation Desert Storm. Do you agree or disagree with Presi-
    dent Bush's actions? Do you agree or disagree with his decision to pull
    out the troops before Saddam Hussein had been caught? Do you agree
    or disagree with the reasons and explanations Bush offered in his "Ad-
    dress to the Nation" regarding the reasons for deploying the Armed
    Forces? Clarify your thesis early in your essay, and then use specifics to
    back up your opinions.

2. George Lakoff, Professor of Linguistics at the University of California
    at Berkeley, sent a widely distributed e-mail on December 31, 1990 dis-
    cussing the danger of the use of metaphor in war to justify military ac-
    tions. Lakoff wrote that in the Gulf War "it is vital . . . to understand just
    what role metaphorical thought played in bringing us in this war."
    Lakoff went on to say that a broad "panorama" of metaphors was pre-
    sent during the entry into the Gulf War, and that Bush eventually set-
    tled for the "Rescue Scenario: Iraq is villain, the US is hero, Kuwait is
    victim, the crime is kidnap and rape." Lakoff then went on to say that
    Bush rejected the other metaphor, that of a "Self-Defense Scenario," in
    which the "United States and other industrialized nations are victims,
    and the crime is . . . a threat to economic health," because this scenario
    "amounted to trading lives for oil," and polls showed that the U.S. pub-
    lic would not support this approach. (If you would like to read Lakoff's
    entire essay, you can go to <http://lists.village.virginia.edu/sixties/
    HTML_docs/Texts/Scholarly>.)

    Now write an essay in which you analyze Bush's speech in light of
    Lakoff's theory about the "Rescue Scenario." Look closely at Bush's words
    and choices in the speech, and then discuss the ways in which you feel
    Lakoff does or does not accurately describe the use of metaphor in the
    speech. Be sure to assess the effectiveness of this metaphor in rallying the
    American public behind the war.

    Alternatively, rewrite Bush's speech, in a shortened version, in which
    you utilize the "Self-Defense Scenario," depicting the United States as vic-
    tim and the crime as the threat to our oil supply.

Chapter 8: Writing Suggestions

1. Consider Martin Luther King, Jr.'s speech "I Have a Dream," and then write a journal entry about your own dream for America. Let yourself imagine the picture of America that you would find ideal, for example, in terms of class, race, gender, educational opportunities, health care, and economic opportunities. Describe life in this America of your dreams, either imitating King's style or writing in your own style.

2. Research the role of President Kennedy, President Johnson, or President Nixon in the Vietnam War. Write an analysis of the period of involvement in Vietnam under one of these presidencies, looking at the political, moral, and economic forces that affected the president's choices involving U.S. policy in Vietnam. Consider the president's political party, the international developments under his presidency, the role of public opinion in his decisions about Vietnam policy, and the role of advisors to the president in determining that policy.

3. Rent one of the movies made about Vietnam since the end of the war, such as *Full Metal Jacket, Born on the Fourth of July,* or *Apocalypse Now.* Then write a review of the movie in light of the selections about Vietnam that you have read in this chapter. Discuss the way the movie affected you, and also discuss how realistic the movie appears in terms of public perception of the war, the protest movements, and the role of the United States in Vietnam itself. Include in your review not only an assessment of the film's realism, but also a review of its artistic merit.

4. Write a personal essay in which you examine the progress or lack of progress you perceive in your own world of school, family, or community in relationship to the activism of the civil rights movement in the 1960s. Which aspects of your world today reflect the efforts of public protest? Which aspects reflect a lack of progress despite the efforts of civil rights leaders, feminists, and student protesters? Be specific in your examples from your own life.

5. Research the roles of Betty Friedan and Gloria Steinem, leaders of the early feminist movement. Write a researched essay in which you answer the following questions:

   What were the goals of the early leaders?

   What kinds of contributions did these women make?

   What similarities and differences did you find in their styles and stated goals for women?

   What lasting changes did they bring about in political or economic circles?

   What debt do you feel women today owe these early outspoken feminists?

716   *Civil Rights, Protest, and Foreign Wars*

Chapter 8: Further Research on the Web

To pursue your research on the Internet, explore some of the following sites:

Senator McCarthy and Army Hearings
http://www.nara.gov/education/cc/mccarthy.html
http://usinfo.state.gov/usa/infousa/facts/democrac/60.htm

Civil Rights
http://www.cr.nps.gov/nr/travel/civilrights
http://www.pbs.org/wgbh/amex/presidents

Martin Luther King Papers
http://www.stanford.edu/group/king

Women and the Civil Rights Movement
www.yale.edu/ynhti/curriculim/units/1997/3/97.03.10.x.htm

Betty Friedan
www.radcliffe.edu/schles/libcolls/mssarch/findaids/Friedan/71-
/Friedan71.62.htm

Vietnam War
http://www.pbs.org/wgbh/amex/vietnam
http:www.pbs.org/pov/stories/
http://www.ford.utexas.edu/library/guides/vietnam.htm

George Bush Presidential Library
http://bushlibrary.tamu.edu

9

Conflicts Past
and Conflicts Present

The issue of conflict in contemporary American society remains absolutely central to our national awareness. The selections in this chapter and their accompanying discussion questions and writing suggestions ask you to look back to the origins and roots of these conflicts, and to develop a greater understanding of the arc of events that links the past to the present. You can read each of the selections in this chapter without reading selections from previous chapters, but you will benefit more from these readings if you also look at previous selections in this text that address race, immigration, gender, and class conflicts from earlier centuries and decades.

To begin this chapter, we look at the ongoing issues surrounding the West:

What American ideals do the frontier and the history of "settling of the West" represent?

How are those ideals cherished today?

How can we come to terms with the romance and the violence that are both part of the history of western expansion?

In her essay "At the Buffalo Bill Museum, June 1988," Jane Tompkins considers these questions as she tries to acknowledge both her love for Buffalo Bill as a man and her horror at the genocide and destruction of natural resources his era represents. Tompkins not only discusses issues of race and conquest, but also reflects on the roles of museums and museum goers. To understand Tompkin's essay from more than one perspective, read it along with Frederick Jackson Turner's essay on the frontier and Scott Momaday's assessment of Buffalo Bill (both in Chapter 3). Reread Luther Standing Bear's essay (Chapter 2) and look at Custer's writings about the Indians (Chapter 3). Then consider the ways in which the West is still portrayed today in film, media, museums, and advertisements. Which Western qualities are still romanticized? Which Western ideals remain alive and well as part of the American dream?

Another continuing conflict in American society is the battle for gender equality. Women in America have struggled since the days of the Salem Witch Trials to assert their independence and to ensure that their voices are heard above the din of others contending for rights and equality. Although women have made great strides at home and in the workplace, Susan Faludi's assessment of the status of American women shows that women's rights still have a long way to go in American society. In her book *Backlash: The Undeclared War against American Women*, Faludi examines the "backlash" against feminism in recent years, and refutes the claims of those who feel that women cannot handle the freedom and choices available now. Other important women's issues continue to surface, as women speak out more forcefully against sexual harassment and domestic violence. Estelle B. Freedman, in her recent book *No Turning Back: The History of Feminism and the Future of Women*, examines the continuing struggles of women against sexual harassment in the workplace and violence in the home. When you read the selections from Faludi's book and Freedman's book in the context of Elizabeth Cady Stanton's speech (Chapter 6), the experiences of women in World War II on the home front (Chapter 7), and the writings of Betty Friedan and Gloria Steinem from the 1960s and 1970s (Chapter 8), the struggle for women's rights will take on a sharper focus as a result of the historical context these additional readings provide.

Conflicts about immigration, citizenship, and assimilation have remained central in America, as Leslie Marmon Silko illustrates in her essay "Fences against Freedom." Silko describes her feelings of being an outsider of mixed race, and decries the policies of the U.S. government regarding the regulation of U.S. borders with Mexico. Silko's essay relates not only to the essays on Native American struggles (Chapter 2), but also to the essays on exclusionist government policies and the conflicts of the dominant culture and Mexican Americans throughout the history of American expansionism and changeable U.S. immigration policies (Chapters 3 and 5). A more recent essay, "Fresh off the Boat" (by an anonymous author), addresses the process of naturalization with irony and humor; we can see how the naturalization process has or has not changed by comparing this essay with the readings in Chapter 6.

The next two selections in this chapter address ongoing issues of race and prejudice in American society. Addressing the problem of the "racial divide" that still separates too many Americans, Ronald Takaki suggests in his book *A Different Mirror: A History of Multicultural America* that we develop a new metaphor for multiculturalism, leaving the "melting pot" metaphor behind in favor of "a different mirror"—a mirror that more accurately reflects the roots of racial diversity in America. Brent Staples also tackles the problem of the "racial divide," describing in "Black Men and Public Space" the need to shake off the stereotype of black men as dangerous night stalkers. His personal, academic, and professional achievements reflect the great gains blacks have made in American society since the days of slavery and the Civil War, but his inability to walk in the city at night without becoming an object of fear and suspicion highlights the problems blacks continue to face in America today. If you read the selections by Takaki and Staples along with the writings of Sojourner Truth in Chapter 4, and of Martin Luther King, Jr. and John F. Kennedy in Chapter 8, you can begin to see the complex cultural and historical roots of racial conflicts still existing today.

While ongoing struggles for equality are central to contemporary American society, the events of September 11, 2001 have required Americans to take a new look at the very meaning of the words "race, culture, and conflict." Not only do these events demand that Americans rethink the way other countries perceive the United States, but also they offer us an opportunity to look closely at the way in which we, as a nation, respond to the experience of an attack on American soil. The selections in this chapter can only give you a glimpse of the many American voices that emerged in response to the attacks of September 11: Phillip Lopate, writer and New York City resident, shares his anguished response to the attack on his city in his essay "Ashes," and President George W. Bush addresses a Joint Session of Congress and the American people, promising a war on terror that will not end "until every terrorist group of global reach has been found, stopped, and defeated." In response to President Bush and the American news media, Susan Sontag (in *The New Yorker*) writes a blistering attack on the "self-righteous drivel and outright deceptions being peddled on the public." And editorial cartoonists Joe Heller, Steve Lindstrom, Mike Thompson, Marty Riskin, and Rick McKee use visual rhetoric to express their feelings and convey their arguments about the terrorist attacks.

As you read the selections in this chapter, revisit the roots of the many conflicts in our country. At the same time, look at contemporary society as evolving and fluid, moving toward a new future, where our current world will become the past. What kind of progress will your generation achieve in resolving conflicts of race, gender, class, and equality? What role will written, visual, and oral arguments play in interpreting and directing the shape of the future? And what role will you play in creating the new America to come?

Before You Read

1. Jot down your impressions of America's multicultural population. What metaphor would you choose to describe American society today, other than the "melting pot" metaphor?
2. How do you feel that past accomplishments of women are reflected in women's opportunities today? Do you feel that women have equal opportunities in the workplace today or not? What strides do you feel women still need to make, if any?
3. How have the events of September 11 affected your life? Jot down a brief journal entry discussing how your life has or has not changed since September 11, 2001.

At the Buffalo Bill Museum, June 1988

JANE TOMPKINS

Jane Tompkins received her Ph.D. from Yale University in 1966, taught for some years as professor of English at Duke University, and is now a professor of education at the University of Illinois at Chicago. She is the author of a number of books, including *Sensational Designs: The Cultural Work of American Fiction, 1790–1870* (1985), *West of Everything: The Inner Life of Westerns* (1992), from which our selection is taken, and *A Life in School: What the Teacher Learned.* She wrote the essay below, "At the Buffalo Bill Museum, June 1988," in response to her own visits to the four museums housed in the Buffalo Bill Historical Center, each of which elicited strong and varied reactions from Tompkins. In this essay she writes about her ambivalence about the museum, describing it as ". . . one of the most disturbing places" she has ever visited, and offers her reflections on violence and its relationship to individual "human intentionality."

The video at the entrance to the Buffalo Bill Historical Center says that Buffalo Bill was the most famous American of his time, that by 1900 more than a billion words had been written about him, and that he had a progressive vision of the West. Buffalo Bill had worked as a cattle driver, a wagoneer, a Pony Express rider, a buffalo hunter for the railroad, a hunting guide, an army scout and sometime Indian fighter; he wrote dime novels about himself and an autobiography by the age of thirty-four, by which time he was already famous; and then he began another set of careers, first as an actor, performing on the urban stage in wintertime melodramatic representations of what he actually earned a living at in the summer (scouting and leading hunting expeditions), and finally becoming the impresario of his great Wild West show, a form of entertainment he invented and carried on as actor, director, and all-around idea man for thirty years. Toward the end of his life he founded the town of Cody, Wyoming, to which he gave, among other things, two hundred thousand dollars. Strangely enough, it was as a progressive civic leader that Bill Cody wanted to be remembered. "I don't want to die," the video at the entrance quotes him as saying, "and have people say—oh, there goes another old showman. . . . I would like people to say—this is man who opened Wyoming to the best of civilization."

"The best of civilization." This was the phrase that rang in my head as I moved through the museum, which is one of the most disturbing places I have ever visited. It is also a wonderful place. It is four museums in one: the Whitney Gallery of Western Art, which houses artworks on Western subjects;

the Buffalo Bill Museum proper, which memorializes Cody's life; the Plains Indian Museum, which exhibits artifacts of American Indian civilization; and the Winchester Arms Museum, a collection of firearms historically considered.

The whole operation is extremely well designed and well run, from the video program at the entrance that gives an overview of all four museums, to the fresh-faced young attendants wearing badges that say "Ask Me," to the museum shop stacked with books on Western Americana, to the ladies room—a haven of satiny marble, shining mirrors, and flattering light. Among other things, the museum is admirable for its effort to combat prevailing stereotypes about the "winning of the West," a phrase it self-consciously places in quotation marks. There are placards declaring that all history is a matter of interpretation, and that the American West is a source of myth. Everywhere, except perhaps in the Winchester Arms Museum, where the rhetoric is different, you feel the effort of the museum staff to reach out to the public, to be clear, to be accurate, to be fair, not to condescend—in short, to educate in the best sense of the term.

On the day I went, the museum was featuring an exhibition of Frederic Remington's works. Two facts about Remington make his work different from that of artists usually encountered in museums. The first is that Remington's paintings and statues function as a historical record. Their chief attraction has always been that they transcribe scenes and events that have vanished from the earth. The second fact, related to this, is the brutality of their subject matter. Remington's work makes you pay attention to what is happening in the painting or the piece of statuary. When you look at his work you cannot escape from the subject.

Consequently, as I moved through the exhibit, the wild contortions of the bucking broncos, the sinister expression invariably worn by the Indians, and the killing of animals and men made the placards discussing Remington's use of the "lost wax" process seem strangely disconnected. In the face of unusual violence, or implied violence, their message was: what is important here is technique. Except in the case of paintings showing the battle of San Juan Hill, where white Americans were being killed, the material accompanying Remington's works did not refer to the subject matter of the paintings and statues themselves. Nevertheless, an undertone of disquiet ran beneath the explanations; at least I thought I detected one. Someone had taken the trouble to ferret out Remington's statement of horror at the slaughter on San Juan Hill; someone had also excerpted the judgment of art critics commending Remington for the lyricism, interiority, and mystery of his later canvasses—pointing obliquely to the fascination with bloodshed that preoccupied his earlier work.

The uneasiness of the commentary, and my uneasiness with it, were nothing compared to the blatant contradictions in the paintings themselves. A pastel palette, a sunlit stop-action haze, murderous movement arrested under a lazy sky, flattened onto canvas and fixed in azure and ochre—two opposed impulses nestle here momentarily. The tension that keeps them from splitting apart is what holds the viewer's gaze.

The most excruciating example of what I mean occurs in the first painting in the exhibit. Entitled *His First Lesson*, it shows a horse standing saddled but riderless, the white of the horse's eye signaling his fear. A man using an instrument to tighten the horse's girth, at arm's length, backs away from the reaction he clearly anticipates, while the man who holds the horse's halter is doing the same. But what can they be afraid of? For the horse's right rear leg is tied a foot off the ground by a rope that is also tied around his neck. He can't move. That is the whole point.

His First Lesson. Whose? And what lesson, exactly? How to stand still when terrified? How not to break away when they come at you with strange instruments? How to be obedient? How to behave? It is impossible not to imagine that Remington's obsession with physical cruelty had roots somewhere in his own experience. Why else, in statue after statue, is the horse rebelling? The bucking bronco, symbol of the state of Wyoming, on every licence plate, on every sign for every bar, on every belt buckle, mug, and decal—this image Remington cast in bronze over and over again. There is a wild diabolism in the bronzes; the horse and rider seem one thing, not so much rider and ridden as a single bolt of energy gone crazy and caught somehow, complicatedly, in a piece of metal.

In the paintings, it is different—more subtle and bizarre. The cavalry on its way to a massacre, sweetly limned, softly tinted, poetically seized in mid-career, and gently laid on the two-dimensional surface. There is about these paintings of military men in the course of performing their deadly duty an almost maternal tenderness. The idealization of the cavalrymen in their dusty uniforms on their gallant horses has nothing to do with patriotism; it is pure love.

Remington's paintings and statues, as shown in this exhibition, embody everything that was objectionable about his era in American history. They are imperialist and racist; they glorify war and the torture and killing of animals; there are no women in them anywhere. Never the West as garden, never as pastoral, never as home. But in their aestheticization of violent life, Remington's pictures speak (to me, at least) of some other desire. The maternal tenderness is not an accident, nor is the beauty of the afternoons or the warmth of the desert sun. In them Remington plays the part of the preserver, as if by catching the figures in color and line he could save their lives and absorb some of that life into himself.

In one painting that particularly repulsed and drew me, a moose is outlined against the evening sky at the brink of a lake. He looks expectantly into the distance. Behind him and to one side, hidden from his view and only just revealed to ours, for it is dark there, is a hunter poised in the back of a canoe, rifle perfectly aimed. We took closer; the title of the picture is *Coming to the Call*. Ah, now we see. This is a sadistic scene. The hunter has lured the moose to his death. But wait a moment. Isn't the sadism really directed at us? First we see the glory of the animal; Remington has made it as noble as he knows how. Then we see what is going to happen. The hunter is one up on the moose, but Remington is one up on us. He makes us feel the pain of the anticipated killing, and makes us want to hold it off, to preserve the moose, just as he has done. Which way does the painting cut? Does it go against the hunter—who represents us, after all—or does it go against the moose who came to the call? Who came, to what call? Did Remington come to the West in response to it—to whatever the moose represents or to whatever the desire to kill the moose represents? But he hasn't killed it; he has only preserved an image of a white man about to kill it. And what call do we answer when we look at this painting? Who is calling whom? What is being preserved here?

That last question is the one that for me hung over the whole museum.

The Whitney Gallery is an art museum proper. Its allegiance is to art as academic tradition has defined it. In this tradition, we come to understand a painting by having in our possession various bits of information. Something about the technical process used to produce it (pastels, watercolors, and color and movement); something about the artist's life (where born, how educated, by whom influenced, which school belonged to or revolted against); something about the artist's relation to this particular subject, such as how many times the artist painted it or whether it contains a favorite model. Occasionally there will be some philosophizing about the themes or ideas the paintings are said to represent.

The problem is, when you're faced with a painter like Remington, these bits of information, while nice to have, don't explain what is there in front of you. They don't begin to give you an account of why a person should have depicted such things. The experience of a lack of fit between the explanatory material and what is there on the wall is one I've had before in museums, when, standing in front of a painting or a piece of statuary, I've felt a huge gap between the information on the little placard and what it is I'm seeing. I realize that works of art, so-called, all have a subject matter, are all engaged with life, with some piece of life no less significant, no less compelling than Remington's subjects are, if we could only see its force. The idea that art is somehow separate from history, that it somehow occupies a space that is not the same as the space of life, seems out of whack here.

I wandered through the gallery thinking these things because right next to it, indeed all around it, in the Buffalo Bill Museum proper and in the Plains Indian Museum, are artifacts that stand not for someone's expertise or skill in manipulating the elements of an artistic medium, but for life itself; they are the residue of life.

The Buffalo Bill Museum is a wonderful array of textures, colors, shapes, sizes, forms. The fuzzy brown bulk of a buffalo's hump, the sparkling diamonds in a stickpin, the brilliant colors of the posters—the mixture makes you want to walk in and be surrounded by it, as if you were going into a child's adventure story. For a moment you can pretend you're a cowboy too; it's a museum where fantasy can take over. For a while.

As I moved through the exhibition, with the phrase "the best of civilization" ringing in my head, I came upon certain objects displayed in a section that recreates rooms from Cody's house. Ostrich feather fans, peacock feather fans, antler furniture—a chair and a table made entirely of antlers—a bearskin rug. And then I saw the heads on the wall: Alaska Yukon Moose, Wapiti American Elk, Muskox (the "Whitney," the "DeRham"), Mountain Caribou (the "Hyland"), Quebec Labrador Caribou (the "Elbow"), Rocky Mountain Goat (the "Haase," the "Kilto"), Woodland Caribou (world's record, "DeRham"), the "Rogers" freak Wapiti, the "Whitney" bison, the "Lord Rundlesham" bison. The names that appear after the animals are the names of the men who killed them. Each of the animals is scored according to measurements devised by the Boone and Crockett Club, a big-game hunters' organization. The Lord Rundlesham bison, for example, scores 124 6/8, making it number 25 in the world for bison trophies. The "Reed" Alaska Yukon Moose scores 247. The "Witherbee" Canada moose holds the world's record.

Next to the wall of trophies is a small enclosure where jewelry is displayed. A buffalo head stickpin and two buffalo head rings, the heads made entirely of diamonds, with ruby eyes, the gifts of the Russian crown prince. A gold and diamond stickpin from Edward VII; a gold, diamond, and garnet locket from Queen Victoria. The two kinds of trophies—animals and jewels—form an incongruous set; the relationship between them compelling but obscure.

If the rest of the items in the museum—the dime novels with their outrageous covers, the marvelous posters, the furniture, his wife's dress, his daughter's oil painting—have faded from my mind it is because I cannot forget the heads of the animals as they stared down, each with an individual expression on its face. When I think about it I realize that I don't know why these animal heads are there. Buffalo Bill didn't kill them; perhaps they were gifts from the famous people he took on hunts. A different kind of jewelry.

After the heads, I began to notice something about the whole exhibition. In one display, doghide chaps, calfskin chaps, angora goathide chaps, and horsehide chaps. Next to these a rawhide lariat and a horsehair quirt. Behind me, boots and saddles, all of leather. Everywhere I looked there was tooth or bone, skin or fur, hide or hair, or the animal itself entire—two full-size buffalo (a main feature of the exhibition) and a magnificent stone sheep (a mountain sheep with beautiful curving horns). This one was another world's record. The best of civilization.

In the literature about Buffalo Bill you read that he was a conservationist, that if it were not for the buffalo in his Wild West shows the species would probably have become extinct. (In the seventeenth century 40 million buffalo roamed North America; by 1900 all the wild buffalo had been killed except for one herd in northern Alberta.) That the man who gained fame first as a buffalo hunter should have been an advocate for conservation of the buffalo is not an anomaly but typical of the period. The men who did the most to preserve America's natural wilderness and its wildlife were big-game hunters. The Boone and Crockett Club, founded by Theodore Roosevelt, George Bird Grinnell, and Owen Wister, turns out to have been one of the earliest organizations to devote itself to environmental protection in the United States. *The*

Reader's Encyclopedia of the American West says that the club "supported the national park and forest reserve movement, helped create a system of national wildlife refuges, and lobbied for the protection of threatened species, such as the buffalo and antelope." At the same time, the prerequisites for membership in the club were "the highest caliber of sportsmanship and the achievement of killing 'in fair chase' trophy specimens [which had to be adult males] from several species of North American big game."

The combination big-game hunter and conservationist suggests that these men had no interest in preserving the animals for the animals' sake but simply wanted to ensure the chance to exercise their sporting pleasure. But I think this view is too simple; something further is involved here. The men who hunted game animals had a kind of love for them and a kind of love for nature that led them to want to preserve the animals they also desired to kill. That is, the desire to kill the animals was in some way related to a desire to see them live. It is not an accident, in this connection, that Roosevelt, Wister, and Remington all went west originally for their health. Their devotion to the West, their connection to it, their love for it are rooted in their need to reanimate their own lives. The preservation of nature, in other words, becomes for them symbolic of their own survival.

In a sense, then, there is a relationship between the Remington exhibition in the Whitney Gallery and the animal memorabilia in the Buffalo Bill Museum. The moose in *Coming to the Call* and the mooseheads on the wall are not so different as they might appear. The heads on the wall serve an aesthetic purpose; they are decorative objects, pleasing to the eye, which call forth certain associations. In this sense they are like visual works of art. The painting, on the other hand, has something of the trophy about it. The moose as Remington painted it is about to become a trophy, yet in another sense it already is one. Remington has simply captured the moose in another form. In both cases the subject matter, the life of a wild animal, symbolizes the life of the observer. It is the preservation of that life that both the painting and the taxidermy serve.

What are museums keeping safe for us, after all? What is it that we wish so much to preserve? The things we put in safekeeping, in our safe-deposit boxes under lock and key, are always in some way intended finally as safeguards of our own existence. The money and jewelry and stock certificates are meant for a time when we can no longer earn a living by the sweat of our brows. Similarly, the objects in museums preserve for us a source of life from which we need to nourish ourselves when the resources that would normally supply us have run dry.

The Buffalo Bill Historical Center, full as it is of dead bones, lets us see more clearly than we normally can what it is that museums are for. It is a kind of charnel house that houses images of living things that have passed away but whose life force still lingers around their remains and so passes itself on to us. We go and look at the objects in the glass cases and at the paintings on the wall, as if by standing there we could absorb into ourselves some of the energy that flowed once through the bodies of the live things represented. A museum, rather than being, as we normally think of it, the most civilized of places, a place most distant from our savage selves, actually caters to the urge to absorb the life of another into one's own life.

If we see the Buffalo Bill Museum in this way, it is no longer possible to separate ourselves from the hunters responsible for the trophies with their wondering eyes or from the curators who put them there. We are not, in essence, different from Roosevelt or Remington or Buffalo Bill, who killed animals when they were abundant in the Wild West of the 1880s. If in doing so those men were practicing the ancient art of absorbing the life of an animal into their own through the act of killing, realizing themselves through the destruction of another life, then we are not so different from them, as visitors to the museum, we stand beside the bones and skins and nails of beings that were once alive, or stare fixedly at their painted images. Indeed our visit is only a safer form of the same enterprise as theirs.

So I did not get out of the Buffalo Bill Museum unscathed, unimplicated in the acts of rapine and carnage that these remains represent. And I did not get out without having had a good time, either, because however many dire thoughts I may have had, the exhibits were interesting and fun to see. I was even able to touch a piece of buffalo hide displayed especially for that purpose (it was coarse and springy). Everyone else had touched it too. The hair was worn down, where people's hands had been, to a fraction of its original length.

After this, the Plains Indian Museum was a terrible letdown. I went from one exhibit to another expecting to become absorbed, but nothing worked. What was the matter? I was interested in Indians, had read about them, taught some Indian literature, felt drawn by accounts of native religions. I had been prepared to enter this museum as if I were going into another children's story, only this time I would be an Indian instead of a cowboy or a cowgirl. But the objects on display, most of them behind glass, seemed paltry and insignificant. They lacked visual presence. The bits of leather and sticks of wood triggered no fantasies in me.

At the same time, I noticed with some discomfort that almost everything in those glass cases was made of feathers and claws and hide, just like the men's chaps and ladies' fans in the Buffalo Bill Museum, only there was no luxury here. Plains Indian culture, it seemed, was made entirely from animals. Their mode of life had been even more completely dedicated to carnage than Buffalo Bill's, dependent as it was on animals for food, clothing, shelter, equipment, everything. In the Buffalo Bill Museum I was able to say to myself, well, if these men had been more sensitive, if they had had a right relation to their environment and to life itself, the atrocities that produced these trophies would never have occurred. They never would have exterminated the Indians and killed off the buffalo. But the spectacle before me made it impossible to say that. I had expected that the Plains Indian Museum would show me how life in nature ought to be lived: not the mindless destruction of nineteenth-century America but an ideal form of communion with animals and the land. What the museum seemed to say instead was that cannibalism was universal. Both colonizer and colonized had had their hands imbrued with blood. The Indians had lived off animals and had made war against one another. Violence was simply a necessary and inevitable part of life. And a person who, like me, was horrified at the extent of the destruction was just the kind of romantic idealist my husband sometimes accused me of being. There was no such thing as the life lived in harmony with nature. It was all bloodshed and killing, an unending cycle, over and over again, and no one could escape.

But perhaps there was a way to understand the violence that made it less terrible. Perhaps if violence was necessary, a part of nature, intended by the universe, then it could be seen as sacramental. Perhaps it was true, what Calvin Martin had said in *Keepers of the Game*: that the Indians had a sacred contract with the animals they killed, that they respected them as equals and treated their remains with honor and punctilio. If so, the remains of animals in the Plains Indian Museum weren't the same as those left by Buffalo Bill and his friends. They certainly didn't look the same. Perhaps. All I knew for certain was that these artifacts, lifeless and shrunken, spoke to me of nothing I could understand. No more did the life-size models of Indians, with strange featureless faces, draped in costumes that didn't look like clothing. The figures, posed awkwardly in front of tepees too white to seem real, carried no sense of a life actually lived, any more than the objects in the glass cases had.

The more I read the placards on the wall, the more disaffected I became. Plains Indian life apparently had been not only bloody but exceedingly tedious. All those porcupine quills painstakingly softened, flattened, dyed, then appliqued through even more laborious methods of stitching or weaving. Four methods of attaching porcupine quills, six design groups, population statistics, patterns of migration. There wasn't any glamour here at all. No glamour in the lives the placards told about, no glamour in the objects themselves, no glamour in the experience of looking at them. Just a lot of shriveled things accompanied by some even drier information.

Could it be, then, that the problem with the exhibitions was that Plains Indian culture, if representable at all, was simply not readable by someone like me? Their stick figures and abstract designs could convey very little to an untrained Euro-American eye. One display in particular illustrated this. It was a piece of cloth, behind glass, depicting a buffalo skin with some marks on it. The placard read: "Winter Count, Sioux ca. 1910, after Lone Dog's, Fort Peck, Montana, 1877." The hide with its markings had been a calendar, each year represented by one image, which showed the most significant event in the life of the tribe. A thick pamphlet to one side of the glass case explained each image year by year: 1800–1801, the attack of the Uncapoo on a Crow Indian Fort; 1802–1803, a total eclipse of the sun. The images, once you knew what they represented, made sense, and seemed poetic interpretations of the experiences they stood for. But without explanation they were incomprehensible.

The Plains Indian Museum stopped me in my tracks. It was written in a language I had never learned. I didn't have the key. Maybe someone did, but

I wasn't too sure. For it may not have been just cultural difference that made the text unreadable. I began to suspect that the text itself was corrupt, that the architects of this museum were going through motions whose purpose was, even to themselves, obscure. Knowing what event a figure stands for in the calendar doesn't mean you understand an Indian year. The deeper purpose of the museum began to puzzle me. Wasn't there an air of bad faith about preserving the vestiges of a culture one had effectively extinguished? Did the museum exist to assuage our guilt and not for any real educational reason? I do not have an answer to these questions. All I know is that I felt I was in the presence of something pious and a little insincere. It had the aura of a failed attempt at virtue, as though the curators were trying to present as interesting objects whose purpose and meaning even they could not fully imagine.

In a last-ditch attempt to salvage something, I went up to one of the guards and asked where the movie was showing which the video had advertised, the movie about Plains Indian life. "Oh, the slide show, you mean," he said. "It's been discontinued." When I asked why, he said he didn't know. It occurred to me then that that was the message the museum was sending, if I could read it, that that was the bottom line. Discontinued, no reason given.

The movie in the Winchester Arms Museum, *Lock, Stock, and Barrel*, was going strong. The film began with the introduction of cannon into European warfare in the Middle Ages, and was working its way slowly toward the nineteenth century when I left. I was in a hurry. Soon my husband would be waiting for me in the lobby. I went from room to room, trying to get a quick sense impression of the objects on display. They were all the same: guns. Some large drawings and photographs on the walls tried to give a sense of the context in which the arms had been used, but the effect was nil. It was case after case of rifles and pistols, repeating themselves over and over, and even when some slight variation caught my eye the differences meant nothing to me.

But the statistics did. In a large case of commemorative rifles, I saw the Antlered Game Commemorative Carbine. Date of manufacture: 1978. Number produced: 19,999. I wondered how many antlered animals each carbine had killed. I saw the Canadian Centennial (1962): 90,000; the Legendary Lawman (1978): 19,999; the John Wayne (1980–1981): 51,600. Like the titles of the various sections of the museum, these names had a message. The message was: guns are patriotic. Associated with national celebrations, law enforcement, and cultural heroes. The idea that firearms were inseparable from the march of American history came through even more strongly in the titles given to the various exhibits: Firearms in Colonial America; Born in America: The Kentucky Rifle; The Era of Expansion and Invention; The Civil War: Firearms of the Conflict; The Golden Age of Hunting; Winning the West. The guns embodied phases of the history they had helped to make. There were no quotation marks here to indicate that expansion and conquest might not have been all they were cracked up to be. The fact that firearms had had a history seemed to consecrate them; the fact that they had existed at the time when certain famous events had occurred seemed to make them not only worth preserving but worth studying and revering. In addition to the exhibition rooms, the museum housed three "study galleries": one for hand arms, one for shoulder arms, one for U.S. military firearms.

As I think back on the rows and rows of guns, I wonder if I should have looked at them more closely, tried harder to appreciate the workmanship that went into them, the ingenuity, the attention. Awe and admiration are the attitudes the museum invites. You hear the ghostly march of military music in the background; you imagine flags waving and sense the implicit reference to feats of courage in battle and glorious death. The place had the air of an expensive and well-kept reliquary, or of the room off the transept of a cathedral where the vestments are stored. These guns were not there merely to be seen or even studied; they were there to be venerated.

But I did not try to appreciate the guns. They were too technical, too foreign. I didn't have their language, and, besides, I didn't want to learn. I rejoined my husband in the lobby. The Plains Indian Museum had been incomprehensible, but in the Winchester Arms Museum I could hardly see the objects at all, for I did not see the point. Or, rather, I did see it and rejected it. Here in the basement the instruments that had turned live animals into hides and horns, had massacred the Indians and the buffalo, were being lovingly displayed. And we were still making them: 51,600 John Waynes in 1980–1981. Arms were going strong.

As I bought my books and postcards in the gift shop, I noticed a sign that read "Rodeo Tickets Sold Here," and something clicked into place. So that was it. *Everything* was still going strong. The whole museum was just another rodeo, only with the riders and their props stuffed, painted, sculpted, immobilized and put under glass. Like the rodeo, the entire museum witnessed a desire to bring back the United States of the 1880s and 1890s. The American people did not want to let go of the winning of the West. They wanted to win it all over again, in imagination. It was the ecstasy of the kill, as much as the life of the hunted, that we fed off here. The Buffalo Bill Historical Center did not repudiate the carnage that had taken place in the nineteenth century. It celebrated it. With its gleaming rest rooms, cute snack bar, opulent museum shop, wooden Indians, thousand rifles, and scores of animal trophies, it helped us all reenact the dream of excitement, adventure, and conquest that was what the Wild West meant to most people in this country.

This is where my visit ended, but it had a sequel. When I left the Buffalo Bill Historical Center, I was full of moral outrage, an indignation so intense it made me almost sick, though it was pleasurable too, as such emotions usually are. But the outrage was undermined by the knowledge that I knew nothing about Buffalo Bill, nothing of his life, nothing of the circumstances that led him to be involved in such violent events. And I began to wonder if my reaction wasn't in some way an image, however small, of the violence I had been objecting to. So when I got home I began to read about Buffalo Bill, and a whole new world opened up. I came to love Buffalo Bill.

"I have seen him the very personification of grace and beauty . . . dashing over the free wild prairie and riding his horse as though he and the noble animal were bounding with one life and one motion." That is the sort of thing people wrote about Buffalo Bill. They said "he was the handsomest man I ever saw." They said "there was never another man lived as popular as he was." They said "there wasn't a man woman or child that he knew or ever met that he didn't speak to." They said "he was handsome as a god, a good rider and a crack shot." They said "he gave lots of money away. Nobody ever went hungry around him." They said "he was way above the average, physically and every other way."

These are quotes from people who knew Cody, collected by one of his two most responsible biographers, Nellie Snyder Yost. She puts them in the last chapter, and by the time you get there they all ring true. Buffalo Bill was incredibly handsome. He was extremely brave and did things no other scout would do. He would carry messages over rugged territory swarming with hostile Indians, riding all night in bad weather and get through, and then take off again the next day to ride sixty miles through a blizzard. He was not a proud man. He didn't boast of his exploits. But he did do incredible things, not just once in a while but on a fairly regular basis. He had a great deal of courage; he believed in himself, in his abilities, in his strength, and endurance and knowledge. He was very skilled at what he did—hunting and scouting—but he wasn't afraid to try other things. He wrote some dime novels, he wrote his autobiography by age thirty-four, without very much schooling; he wasn't afraid to try acting, even though the stage terrified him and he knew so little about it that, according to his wife, he didn't even know you had to memorize lines.

Maybe it was because he grew up on the frontier, maybe it was just the kind of person he was, but he was constantly finding himself in situations that required resourcefulness and courage, quick decisions and decisive action and rising to the occasion. He wasn't afraid to improvise.

He liked people, drank a lot, gave big parties, gave lots of presents, and is reputed to have been a womanizer! When people came to see him in his office tent on the show grounds, to shake his hand or have their pictures taken with him, he never turned anyone away. "He kept a uniformed doorman at the tent opening to announce visitors," writes a biographer. "No matter who was outside, from a mayor to a shabby woman with a baby, the Colonel would smooth his mustache, stand tall and straight, and tell the doorman to 'show 'em in.' He greeted everyone the same."

As a showman, he was a genius. People don't say much about *why* he was so successful; mostly they describe the wonderful goings-on. But I get the feeling that Cody was one of those people who was connected to his time in an uncanny way. He knew what people wanted, he knew how to entertain them, because he *liked* them, was open to them, felt his kinship with them, or was so much in touch with himself at some level that he was thereby in touch with almost everybody else.

He liked to dress up and had a great sense of costume (of humor, too, they say). Once he came to a fancy dress ball, his first, in New York, wearing white tie and tails and a large Stetson. He knew what people wanted. He let his hair grow long and wore a mustache and beard, because, he said, he wouldn't be believable as a scout otherwise. Hence his Indian name, Pahaska, meaning "long hair," which people loved to use. Another kind of costume. He invented the ten-gallon hat, which the Stetson company made to his specifications. Afterward, they made a fortune from it. In the scores of pictures reproduced in the many books about him, he most often wears scout's clothes—usually generously fringed buckskin, sometimes a modified cavalryman's outfit—though often he's impeccably turned out in a natty-looking three-piece business suit (sometimes with overcoat, sometimes not). The photographs show him in a tuxedo, in something called a "Mexican suit" which looks like a cowboy outfit, and once he appears in Indian dress. In almost every case he is wearing some kind of hat, usually the Stetson, at exactly the right angle. He poses deliberately, and with dignity, for the picture. Cody didn't take himself so seriously that he had to pretend to be less than he was.

What made Buffalo Bill so irresistible? Why is he still so appealing even now, when we've lost, supposedly, all the illusions that once supported his popularity? There's a poster for one of his shows when he was traveling in France that gives a clue to what it is that makes him so profoundly attractive a figure. The poster consists of a huge buffalo galloping across the plains, and against the buffalo's hump, in the center of his hump, is a cutout circle that shows the head of Buffalo Bill, white-mustachioed and bearded now, in his famous hat, and beneath, in large red letters, are the words "Je viens."

Je viens ("I am coming") are the words of a savior. The announcement is an annunciation. Buffalo Bill is a religious figure of a kind who makes sense within a specifically Christian tradition. That is, he comes in the guise of a redeemer, of someone who will save us, who will through his own actions do something for us that we ourselves cannot do. He will lift us above our lives, out of the daily grind, into something larger than we are.

His appeal on the surface is to childish desires, the desire for glamour, fame, bigness, adventure, romance. But these desires are also the sign of something more profound, and it is to something more profound in us that he also appeals. Buffalo Bill comes to the child in us, understood not as that part of ourselves that we have outgrown but as the part that got left behind, of necessity, a long time ago, having been starved, bound, punished, disciplined out of existence. He promises that that part of the self can live again. He has the power to promise these things because he represents the West, that geographical space of the globe that was still the realm of exploration and discovery, that was still open, that had not yet quite been tamed, when he began to play himself on the stage. He not only represented it, he *was* it. He brought the West itself with him when he came. The very Indians, the very buffalo, the very cowboys, the very cattle, the very stagecoach itself which had been memorialized in story. He performed in front of the audience the feats that had made him famous. He shot glass balls and clay pigeons out of the air with amazing rapidity. He rode his watersmooth silver stallion at full gallop. "Jesus he was a handsome man," wrote e. e. cummings in "Buffalo Bill's Defunct."

"I am coming." This appearance of Buffalo Bill, in the flesh, was akin to the apparition of a saint or of the Virgin Mary to believers. He was the incarnation of an ideal. He came to show people that what they had only imagined was really true. The West really did exist. There really were heroes who rode white horses and performed amazing feats. e. e. cummings was right to invoke the name of Jesus in his poem. Buffalo Bill was a secular messiah.

He was a messiah because people believed in him. When he died, he is reputed to have said, "Let my show go on." But he had no show at the time, so he probably didn't say that. Still, the words are prophetic because the desire for what Buffalo Bill had done had not only not died but would call forth the countless reenactments of the Wild West, from the rodeo—a direct descendant of his show—to the thousands of Western novels, movies, and television programs that comprise the Western genre in the twentieth century, a genre that came into existence as a separate category right about the time that Cody died. Don Russell maintains that the way the West exists in our minds today is largely the result of the way Cody presented it in his show. That was where people got their ideas of what the characters looked like. Though many Indian tribes wore no feathers and fought on foot, you will never see a featherless, horseless Indian warrior in the movies, because Bill employed only Sioux and other Plains tribes which had horses and traditionally wore feathered headdresses. "Similarly," he adds, "cowboys wear ten-gallon Stetsons, not because such a hat was worn in early range days, but because it was part of the costume adopted by Buffalo Bill for his show."

But the deeper legacy is elsewhere. Buffalo Bill was a person who inspired other people. What they saw in him was an aspect of themselves. It really doesn't matter whether Cody was as great as people thought him or not, because what they were responding to when he rode into the arena, erect and resplendent on his charger, was something intangible, not the man himself, but a possible way of being. William F. Cody and the Wild West triggered the emotions that had fueled the imaginative lives of people who flocked to see him, especially men and boys, who made up the larger portion of the audience. He and his cowboys played to an inward territory; a Wild West of the psyche that hungered for exercise sprang into activity when the show appeared. *Je viens* was a promise to redeem that territory, momentarily at least, from exile and oblivion. The lost parts of the self symbolized by buffalo and horses and wild men would live again for an hour while the show went on.

People adored it. Queen Victoria, who broke her custom by going to see it at all (she never went to the theater, and on the rare occasions when she wanted to see a play she had it brought to her), is supposed to have been lifted out of a twenty-five-year depression caused by the death of her husband after she saw Buffalo Bill. She liked the show so much that she saw it again, arranging for a command performance to be given at Windsor Castle the day before her Diamond Jubilee. This was the occasion when four kings rode in the Deadwood stagecoach with the Prince of Wales on top next to Buffalo Bill, who drove. No one was proof against the appeal. Ralph Blumenfeld, the London correspondent for the New York *Herald*, wrote in his diary while the show was in London that he'd had two boyhood heroes, Robin Hood and Buffalo Bill, and had delighted in Cody's stories of the Pony Express and Yellow Hand:

> Everything was done to make Cody conceited and unbearable, but he remained the simple, unassuming child of the plains who thought lords and ladies belonged in the picture books and that the story of Little Red Riding Hood was true. I rode in the Deadwood coach. It was a great evening in which I realized a good many of my boyhood dreams, for there was Buffalo Bill on his white rocking horse charger, and Annie Oakley behind him.

Victor Weybright and Henry Blackman Sell, from whose book on the Wild West some of the foregoing information has come, dedicated their book to Buffalo Bill. It was published in 1955. Nellie Snyder Yost, whose 1979 biography is one of the two scholarly accounts of Cody's life, dedicates her book "to all those good people, living or dead, who knew and liked Buffalo Bill." Don Russell's *The Lives and Legends of Buffalo Bill* (1960), the most fact-filled scholarly biography, does not have a dedication, but in the final chapter, where he steps back to assess Cody and his influence, Russell ends by exclaiming, "What more could possibly be asked of a hero? If he was not one, who was?"

Let me now pose a few questions of my own. Must we throw out all the wonderful qualities that Cody had, the spirit of hope and emulation that he aroused in millions of people, because of the terrible judgment history has passed on the epoch of which he was part? The kinds of things he stands for— courage, daring, strength, endurance, generosity, openness to other people, love of drama, love of life, the possibility of living a life that does not deny the body and the desires of the body—are these to be declared dangerous and delusional although he manifested some of them while fighting Indians and others while representing his victories to the world? And the feelings he aroused in his audiences, the idealism, the enthusiasm, the excitement, the belief that dreams could become real—must these be declared misguided or a sham because they are associated with the imperialistic conquest of a continent, with the wholesale extermination of animals and men?

It is not so much that we cannot learn from history as that we cannot teach history how things should have been. When I set out to discover how Cody had become involved in the killing of Indians and the slaughter of buffalo, I found myself unable to sustain the outrage I had felt on leaving the museum. From his first job as an eleven-year-old herder for an army supply outfit, sole wage earner for his ailing widowed mother who had a new baby and other children to support, to his death in Colorado at the age of seventy-one, there was never a time when it was possible to say, there, there you went wrong, Buffalo Bill, you should not have killed that Indian. You should have held your fire and made your living some other way and quit the army and gone to work in the nineteenth-century equivalent of the Peace Corps. You should have known how it would end. My reading made me see that you cannot prescribe for someone in Buffalo Bill's position what he should have done, and it made me reflect on how eager I had been to get off on being angry at the museum. The thirst for moral outrage, for self-vindication, lay pretty close to the surface.

I cannot resolve the contradiction between my experience at the Buffalo Bill Historical Center with its celebration of violent conquest and my response to the shining figure of Buffalo Bill as it emerged from the pages of books— on the one hand, a history of shame; on the other, an image of the heart's desire. But I have reached one conclusion that for a while will have to serve.

Major historical events like genocide and major acts of destruction are not simply produced by impersonal historical processes or economic imperatives or ecological blunders; human intentionality is involved and human knowledge of the self. Therefore, if you're really, truly interested in not having any more genocide or killing of animals, no matter what else you might do, if you don't first, or also, come to recognize the violence in yourself and your own anger and your own destructiveness, whatever else you do won't work. It isn't that genocide doesn't matter. Genocide matters, and it starts at home.

Buckaroo Using Snaffle Bit and Mecate Reins. (*Arthur Black, 2001*)

Discussion Questions

1. How does Tompkins arrange her essay, and how does this organization work to support her major points? Why does she go into detail about the four museums before she begins her own study of Buffalo Bill and her own assessment of "the contradiction between [her] experience at the Buffalo Bill Historical Center with its celebration of violent conquest and [her] response to the shining figure of Buffalo Bill as it emerged from the pages of books—on the one hand, a history of shame; on the other, an image of the heart's desire"? What conclusions does she reach at the end of her explorations? How does she expand her essay to reach a wider audience?

2. Read N. Scott Momaday's article "The American West and the Burden of Belief" in Chapter 3. Then discuss in groups the different points of view Momaday and Tompkins bring to the question of Buffalo Bill's role in the national perceptions of the West. How do the two authors differ in their responses to Buffalo Bill? What kinds of conflicts do both authors mention? How do both authors treat the issue of genocide and destruction? Which author do you feel more closely represents your own opinions about Buffalo Bill as a person and as a mythological figure?

Writing Suggestions

1. Tompkins writes, "Therefore, if you're really, truly interested in not having any more genocide or killing of animals, no matter what else you might do, if you don't first, or also, come to recognize the violence in yourself and your own anger and your own destructiveness, whatever else you do won't work." Write a response to this statement, considering your own anger and destructive feelings. Do you agree with Tompkins that each individual must face the demons in his or her heart? Do you feel that individual anger will be played out in larger social contexts, as Tompkins implies about the "human intentionality" and the violence that manifested themselves in the "taming" of the West?

2. Visit a museum in your city or state capitol. Look for displays that deal with issues of race, war, gender, or other conflicts in American society. Then read the descriptions next to each piece of art, and, like Tompkins, try to discover how the museum curators have cast a certain light on the display. Have the curators highlighted specific aspects of the display? Are social or racial conflicts highlighted or minimized? Does one point of view dominate the display, or are a number of points of view explained? Does the exhibit do justice to the topic, or does the exhibit shortchange the depth and complexity of the topic? Write a review of the exhibit you chose to study, including your responses to the arrangement of the exhibit, the details of the writing and labeling that accompany the exhibit, and the breadth or narrowness of the exhibit's scope.

Backlash

Blame It on Feminism

SUSAN FALUDI

Susan Faludi graduated from Harvard University in 1981 with a B.A. in history and literature, and began her career writing for a variety of magazines, such as the *New York Times*, the *Miami Herald*, the *Atlanta Journal-Constitution*, and the *Wall Street Journal*. Faludi's article "The Reckoning," about the leveraged buyout of the Safeway chain of supermarkets, won her a Pulitzer Prize in 1981. In 1992 she published *Backlash: The Undeclared War against American Women*, for which she was awarded the National Book Critics Circle Award in 1991. In *Backlash*, Faludi disputes the notion that American women are unhappy because they have gained equality and refutes the claim that women would rather return to the lifestyle of those women who stayed home in the 1950s. In the following selection, "Blame It on Feminism," from *Backlash*, Faludi explores the recent trend in American media and culture of linking women's unhappiness to feminism.

To be a woman in America at the close of the twentieth century—what good fortune. That's what we keep hearing, anyway. The barricades have fallen, politicians assure us. Women have "made it," Madison Avenue cheers. Women's fight for equality has "largely been won," *Time* magazine announces. Enroll at any university, join any law firm, apply for credit at any bank. Women have so many opportunities now, corporate leaders say, that we don't really need equal opportunity policies. Women are so equal now, lawmakers say, that we no longer need an Equal Rights Amendment. Women have "so much," former President Ronald Reagan says, that the White House no longer needs to appoint them to higher office. Even American Express ads are saluting a woman's freedom to charge it. At last, women have received their full citizenship papers.

And yet . . .

Behind this celebration of the American woman's victory, behind the news, cheerfully and endlessly repeated, that the struggle for women's rights is won, another message flashes. You may be free and equal now, it says to women, but you have never been more miserable.

This bulletin of despair is posted everywhere—at the newsstand, on the TV set, at the movies, in advertisements and doctors' offices and academic journals. Professional women are suffering "burnout" and succumbing to an "infertility epidemic." Single women are grieving from a "man shortage."

The *New York Times* reports: Childless women are "depressed and confused" and their ranks are swelling. *Newsweek* says: Unwed women are "hysterical" and crumbling under a "profound crisis of confidence." The health advice manuals inform: High-powered career women are stricken with unprecedented outbreaks of "stress-induced disorders," hair loss, bad nerves, alcoholism, and even heart attacks. The psychology books advise: Independent women's loneliness represents "a major mental health problem today." Even founding feminist Betty Friedan has been spreading the word: she warns that women now suffer from a new identity crisis and "new 'problems that have no name.'"

How can American women be in so much trouble at the same time that they are supposed to be so blessed? If the status of women has never been higher, why is their emotional state so low? If women got what they asked for, what could possibly be the matter now?

The prevailing wisdom of the past decade has supported one, and only one, answer to this riddle: it must be all that equality that's causing all that pain. Women are unhappy precisely *because* they are free. Women are enslaved by their own liberation. They have grabbed at the gold ring of independence, only to miss the one ring that really matters. They have gained control of their fertility, only to destroy it. They have pursued their own professional dreams— and lost out on the greatest female adventure. The women's movement, as we are told time and again, has proved women's own worst enemy.

"In dispensing its spoils, women's liberation has given my generation high incomes, our own cigarette, the option of single parenthood, rape crisis centers, personal lines of credit, free love, and female gynecologists," Mona Charen, a young law student, writes in the *National Review*, in an article titled "The Feminist Mistake." "In return it effectively robbed us of one thing upon which the happiness of most women rests—men." The *National Review* is a conservative publication, but such charges against the women's movement are not confined to its pages. "Our generation was the human sacrifice" to the women's movement, *Los Angeles Times* feature writer Elizabeth Mehren contends in a *Time* cover story. Baby-boom women like her, she says, have been duped by feminism: "We believed the rhetoric." In *Newsweek*, writer Kay Ebeling dubs feminism "the Great Experiment That Failed" and asserts "women in my generation, its perpetrators, are the casualties." Even the beauty magazines are saying it: *Harper's Bazaar* accuses the women's movement of having "lost us [women] ground instead of gaining it."

In the last decade, publications from the *New York Times* to *Vanity Fair* to the *Nation* have issued a steady stream of indictments against the women's movement, with such headlines as WHEN FEMINISM FAILED, OR THE AWFUL TRUTH ABOUT WOMEN'S LIB. They hold the campaign for women's equality responsible for nearly every woe besetting women, from mental depression to meager savings accounts, from teenage suicides to eating disorders to bad complexions. The "Today" show says women's liberation is to blame for bag ladies. A guest columnist in the *Baltimore Sun* even proposes that feminists produced the rise in slasher movies. By making the "violence" of abortion more acceptable, the author reasons, women's rights activists made it all right to show graphic murders on screen.

At the same time, other outlets of popular culture have been forging the same connection: in Hollywood films, of which *Fatal Attraction* is only the most famous, emancipated women with condominiums of their own slink wild-eyed between bare walls, paying for their liberty with an empty bed, a barren womb. "My biological clock is ticking so loud it keeps me awake at night," Sally Field cries in the film *Surrender*, as, in an all too common transformation in the cinema of the '80s, an actress who once played scrappy working heroines is now showcased groveling for a groom. In prime-time television shows, from *thirtysomething* to *Family Man*, single, professional, and feminist women are humiliated, turned into harpies, or hit by nervous breakdowns; the wise ones recant their independent ways by the closing sequence. In popular novels, from Gail Parent's *A Sign of the Eighties* to Stephen King's *Misery*, unwed women shrink to sniveling spinsters or inflate to fire-breathing she-devils; renouncing all aspirations but marriage, they beg for wedding bands from strangers or swing axes at reluctant bachelors. We "blew it by waiting," a typically remorseful careerist sobs in Freda Bright's *Singular Women*; she and her sister professionals are "condemned to be childless forever." Even Erica Jong's high-flying independent heroine literally crashes by the end of the decade, as the author supplants *Fear of Flying*'s saucy Isadora Wing, a symbol of female sexual emancipation in the '70s, with an embittered careerist-turned-recovering-"co-dependent" in *Any Woman's Blues*—a book that is intended, as the narrator bluntly states, "to demonstrate what a deadend the so-called sexual revolution had become, and how desperate so-called free women were in the last few years of our decadent epoch."

Popular psychology manuals peddle the same diagnosis for contemporary female distress. "Feminism, having promised her a stronger sense of her own identity, has given her little more than an identity *crisis*," the best-selling advice manual *Being a Woman* asserts. The authors of the era's self-help classic *Smart Women/Foolish Choices* proclaim that women's distress was "an unfortunate consequence of feminism," because "it created a myth among women that the apex of self-realization could be achieved only through autonomy, independence, and career."

In the Reagan and Bush years, government officials have needed no prompting to endorse this thesis. Reagan spokeswoman Faith Whittlesey declared feminism a "straitjacket" for women, in the White House's only policy speech on the status of the American female population—entitled "Radical Feminism in Retreat." Law enforcement officers and judges, too, have pointed a damning finger at feminism, claiming that they can chart a path from rising female independence to rising female pathology. As a California sheriff explained it to the press, "Women are enjoying a lot more freedom now, and as a result, they are committing more crimes." The U.S. Attorney General's Commission on Pornography even proposed that women's professional advancement might be responsible for rising rape rates. With more women in college and at work now, the commission members reasoned in their report, women just have more opportunities to be raped.

Some academics have signed on to the consensus, too—and they are the "experts" who have enjoyed the highest profiles on the media circuit. On network news and talk shows, they have advised millions of women that feminism has condemned them to "a lesser life." Legal scholars have railed against "the equality trap." Sociologists have claimed that "feminist-inspired" legislative reforms have stripped women of special "protections." Economists have argued that well-paid working women have created "a less stable American family." And demographers, with greatest fanfare, have legitimated the prevailing wisdom with so-called neutral data on sex ratios and fertility trends; they say they actually have the numbers to prove that equality doesn't mix with marriage and motherhood.

Finally, some "liberated" women themselves have joined the lamentations. In confessional accounts, works that invariably receive a hearty greeting from the publishing industry, "recovering Superwomen" tell all. In *The Cost of Loving: Women and the New Fear of Intimacy*, Megan Marshall, a Harvard-pedigreed writer, asserts that the feminist "Myth of Independence" has turned her generation into unloved and unhappy fast-trackers, "dehumanized" by careers and "uncertain of their gender identity." Other diaries of mad Superwomen charge that "the hard-core feminist viewpoint," as one of them puts it, has relegated educated executive achievers to solitary nights of frozen dinners and closet drinking. The triumph of equality, they report, has merely given women hives, stomach cramps, eye-twitching disorders, even comas.

But what "equality" are all these authorities talking about?

If American women are so equal, why do they represent two-thirds of all poor adults? Why are more than 80 percent of full-time working women making less than $20,000 a year, nearly double the male rate? Why are they still far more likely than men to live in poor housing and receive no health insurance, and twice as likely to draw no pension? Why does the average working woman's salary still lag as far behind the average man's as it did twenty years ago? Why does the average female college graduate today earn less than a man with no more than a high school diploma (just as she did in the '50s)— and why does the average female high school graduate today earn less than a male high school dropout? Why do American women, in fact, face the worst gender-based pay gap in the developed world?

If women have "made it," then why are nearly 80 percent of working women still stuck in traditional "female" jobs—as secretaries, administrative "support" workers and salesclerks? And, conversely, why are they less than 8 percent of all federal and state judges, less than 6 percent of all law partners, and less than one half of 1 percent of top corporate managers? Why are there only three female state governors, two female U.S. senators, and two Fortune 500 chief executives? Why are only nineteen of the four thousand corporate officers and directors women—and why do more than half the boards of Fortune 500 companies still lack even one female member?

If women "have it all," then why don't they have the most basic requirements to achieve equality in the work force? Unlike virtually all other industrialized nations, the U.S. government still has no family-leave and child care programs—and more than 99 percent of American private employers don't offer child care either. Though business leaders say they are aware of and deplore sex discrimination, corporate America has yet to make an honest effort toward eradicating it. In a 1990 national poll of chief executives at Fortune 1000 companies, more than 80 percent acknowledged that discrimination impedes female employees' progress—yet, less than 1 percent of these same companies regarded *remedying* sex discrimination as a goal that their personnel departments should pursue. In fact, when the companies' human resource officers were asked to rate their department's priorities, women's advancement ranked last.

If women are so "free," why are their reproductive freedoms in greater jeopardy today than a decade earlier? Why do women who want to postpone childbearing now have fewer options than ten years ago? The availability of different forms of contraception has declined, research for new birth control has virtually halted, new laws restricting abortion—or even *information* about abortion—for young and poor women have been passed, and the U.S. Supreme Court has shown little ardor in defending the right it granted in 1973.

Nor is women's struggle for equal education over; as a 1989 study found, three-fourths of all high schools still violate the federal law banning sex discrimination in education. In colleges, undergraduate women receive only 70 percent of the aid undergraduate men get in grants and work-study jobs—and women's sports programs receive a pittance compared with men's. A review of state equal-education laws in the late '80s found that only thirteen states had adopted the minimum provisions required by the federal Title IX law—and only seven states had anti-discrimination regulations that covered all education levels.

Nor do women enjoy equality in their own homes, where they still shoulder 70 percent of the household duties—and the only major change in the last fifteen years is that now middle-class men *think* they do more around the house. (In fact, a national poll finds the ranks of women saying their husbands share equally in child care shrunk to 31 percent in 1987 from 40 percent three years earlier.) Furthermore, in thirty states, it is still generally legal for husbands to rape their wives; and only ten states have laws mandating arrest for domestic violence—even though battering was the leading cause of injury of women in the late '80s. Women who have no other option but to flee find that isn't much of an alternative either. Federal funding for battered women's shelters has been withheld and one third of the 1 million battered women who seek emergency shelter each year can find none. Blows from men contributed far more to the rising numbers of "bag ladies" than the ill effects of feminism. In the '80s, almost half of all homeless women (the fastest growing segment of the homeless) were refugees of domestic violence.

The word may be that women have been "liberated," but women themselves seem to feel otherwise. Repeatedly in national surveys, majorities of women say they are still far from equality. Nearly 70 percent of women polled by the *New York Times* in 1989 said the movement for women's right had only just begun. Most women in the 1990 Virginia Slims opinion poll agreed with the statement that conditions for their sex in American society had improved "a little, not a lot." In poll after poll in the decade, overwhelming majorities of women said they needed equal pay and equal job opportunities, they needed an Equal Rights Amendment, they needed the right to an abortion without government interference, they needed a federal law guaranteeing maternity leave, they needed decent child care services. They have none of these. So how exactly have we "won" the war for women's rights?

Seen against this background, the much ballyhooed claim that feminism is responsible for making women miserable becomes absurd—and irrelevant. . . . The afflictions ascribed to feminism are all myths. From "the man shortage" to "the infertility epidemic" to "female burn-out" to "toxic day care," these so-called female crises have had their origins not in the actual conditions of women's lives but rather in a closed system that starts and ends in the media, popular culture, and advertising—an endless feedback loop that perpetuates and exaggerates its own false images of womanhood.

Women themselves don't single out the women's movement as the source of their misery. To the contrary, in national surveys 75 to 95 percent of women credit the feminist campaign with *improving* their lives, and a similar proportion say that the women's movement should keep pushing for change. Less than 8 percent think the women's movement might have actually made their lot worse.

What actually is troubling the American female population, then? If the many ponderers of the Woman Question really wanted to know, they might have asked their subjects. In public opinion surveys, women consistently rank their own *inequality*, at work and at home, among their most urgent concerns. Over and over, women complain to pollsters about a lack of economic, not marital, opportunities; they protest that working men, not working women, fail to spend time in the nursery and the kitchen. The Roper Organization's survey analysts find that men's opposition to equality is "a major cause of resentment and stress" and "a major irritant for most women today." It is justice for their gender, not wedding rings and bassinets, that women believe to be in desperately short supply. When the *New York Times* polled women in 1989 about "the most important problem facing women today," job discrimination was the overwhelming winner; none of the crises the media and popular culture had so assiduously promoted even made the charts. In the 1990 Virginia Slims poll, women were most upset by their lack of money, followed by the refusal of their men to shoulder child care and domestic duties. By contrast, when the women were asked where the quest for a husband or the desire to hold a "less pressured" job or to stay at home ranked on their list of concerns, they placed them at the bottom.

As the last decade ran its course, women's unhappiness with inequality only mounted. In national polls, the ranks of women protesting discriminatory treatment in business, political, and personal life climbed sharply. The proportion of women complaining of unequal employment opportunities jumped more than ten points from the '70s, and the number of women complaining of unequal barriers to job advancement climbed even higher. By the end of the decade, 80 percent to 95 percent of women said they suffered from job discrimination and unequal pay. Sex discrimination charges filed with the Equal Employment Opportunity Commission rose nearly 25 percent in the Reagan years, and charges of general harassment directed at working women climbed 208 percent. In the decade, complaints of sexual harassment jumped 70 percent. At home, a much increased proportion of women complained to pollsters of male mistreatment, unequal relationships, and male efforts to, in the words of the Virginia Slims poll, "keep women down." The share of women in the Roper surveys who agreed that men were "basically kind, gentle, and thoughtful" fell from almost 70 percent in 1970 to 50 percent by 1990. And outside their homes, women felt more threatened, too: in the 1990 Virginia Slims poll, 72 percent of women said they felt "more afraid and uneasy on the streets today" than they did a few years ago. Lest this be attributed only to a general rise in criminal activity, by contrast only 49 percent of men felt this way.

While the women's movement has certainly made women more cognizant of their own inequality, the rising chorus of female protest shouldn't be written off as feminist-induced "oversensitivity." The monitors that serve to track slippage in women's status have been working overtime since the early '80s. Government and private surveys are showing that women's already vast representation in the lowliest occupations is rising, their tiny presence in higher-paying trade and craft jobs stalled or backsliding, their minuscule representation in upper management posts stagnant or falling, and their pay dropping in the very occupations where they have made the most "progress." The status of women lowest on the income ladder has plunged most perilously; government budget cuts in the first four years of the Reagan administration alone pushed nearly 2 million female-headed families and nearly 5 million women below the poverty line. And the prime target of government rollbacks has been one sex only: one-third of the Reagan budget cuts, for example, came out of programs that predominantly serve women—even more extraordinary when one considers that all these programs combined represent only 10 percent of the federal budget.

The alarms aren't just going off in the work force. In national politics the already small numbers of women in both elective posts and political appointments fell during the '80s. In private life, the average amount that a divorced man paid in child support fell by about 25 percent from the late '70s to the mid '80s (to a mere $140 a month). Domestic-violence shelters recorded a more than 100 percent increase in the numbers of women taking refuge in their quarters between 1983 and 1987. And government records chronicled a spectacular rise in sexual violence against women. Reported rapes more than doubled from the early '70s—at nearly twice the rate of all other violent crimes and four times the overall crime rate in the United States. While the homicide rate declined, sex-related murders rose 160 percent between 1976 and 1984. And these murders weren't simply the random, impersonal byproduct of a violent society; at least one-third of the women were killed by their husbands or boyfriends, and the majority of that group were murdered just after declaring their independence in the most intimate manner—by filing for divorce and leaving home.

By the end of the decade, women were starting to tell pollsters that they feared their sex's social status was once again beginning to slip. They believed they were facing an "erosion of respect," as the 1990 Virginia Slims poll summed up the sentiment. After years in which an increasing percentage of women had said their status had improved from a decade earlier, the proportion suddenly shrunk by 5 percent in the last half of the '80s, the Roper Organization reported. And it fell most sharply among women in their thirties—the age group most targeted by the media and advertisers—dropping about ten percentage points between 1985 and 1990.

Some women began to piece the picture together. In the 1989 *New York Times* poll, more than half of black women and one-fourth of white women put it into words. They told pollsters they believed men were now trying to retract the gains women had made in the last twenty years. "I wanted more autonomy," was how one woman, a thirty-seven-year-old nurse, put it. And her estranged husband "wanted to take it away."

The truth is that the last decade has seen a powerful counterassault on women's rights, a backlash, an attempt to retract the handful of small and hard-won victories that the feminist movement did manage to win for women. This counterassault is largely insidious: in a kind of culture version of the Big Lie, it stands the truth boldly on its head and proclaims that the very steps that have elevated women's position have actually led to their downfall.

The backlash is at once sophisticated and banal, deceptively "progressive" and proudly backward. It deploys both the "new" findings of scientific research and the dime-store moralism of yesteryear; it turns into media sound bites both the glib pronouncements of pop-psych trend-watchers and the frenzied rhetoric of New Right preachers. The backlash has succeeded in framing virtually the whole issue of women's rights in its own language. Just as Reaganism shifted political discourse far to the right and demonized liberalism, so the backlash convinced the public that women's "liberation" was the true contemporary American scourge—the source of an endless laundry list of personal, social, and economic problems.

But what has made women unhappy in the last decade is not their "equality"—which they don't yet have—but the rising pressure to halt, and even reverse, women's quest for that equality. The "man shortage" and the "infertility epidemic" are not the price of liberation; in fact, they do not even exist. But these chimeras are the chisels of a society-wide backlash. They are part of a relentless whittling-down process—much of it amounting to outright propaganda—that has served to stir women's private anxieties and break their political wills. Identifying feminism as women's enemy only furthers the ends of a backlash against women's equality, simultaneously deflecting attention from the backlash's central role and recruiting women to attack their own cause.

Some social observers may well ask whether the current pressures on women actually constitute a backlash—or just a continuation of American society's long-standing resistance to women's rights. Certainly hostility to female independence has always been with us. But if fear and loathing of feminism is a sort of perpetual viral condition in our culture, it is not always in an acute stage; its symptoms subside and resurface periodically. And it is these episodes of resurgence, such as the one we face now, that can accurately be termed "backlashes" to women's advancement. If we trace these occurrences in American history . . . , we find such flare-ups are hardly random; they have always been triggered by the perception—accurate or not—that women are making great strides. These outbreaks are backlashes because they have always arisen in reaction to women's "progress," caused not simply by a bedrock of misogyny but by the specific efforts of contemporary women to improve their status, efforts that have been interpreted time and again by men—especially men grappling with real threats to their economic and social well-being on other fronts—as spelling their own masculine doom.

The most recent round of backlash first surfaced in the late '70s on the fringes, among the evangelical right. By the early '80s, the fundamentalist ideology had shouldered its way into the White House. By the mid '80s, as resistance to women's rights acquired political and social acceptability, it passed into the popular culture. And in every case, the timing coincided with signs that women were believed to be on the verge of breakthrough.

Just when women's quest for equal rights seemed closest to achieving its objectives, the backlash struck it down. Just when a "gender gap" at the voting booth surfaced in 1980, and women in politics began to talk of capitalizing on it, the Republican party elevated Ronald Reagan and both political parties began to shunt women's rights off their platforms. just when support for feminism and the Equal Rights Amendment reached a record high in 1981, the amendment was defeated the following year. Just when women were starting to mobilize against battering and sexual assaults, the federal government stalled funding for battered-women's programs, defeated bills to fund shelters, and shut down its Office of Domestic Violence—only two years after opening it in 1979. Just when record numbers of younger women were supporting feminist goals in the mid '80s (more of them, in fact, than older women) and a majority of all women were calling themselves feminists, the media declared the advent of a younger "postfeminist generation" that supposedly reviled the women's movement. Just when women racked up their largest percentage ever supporting the right to abortion, the U.S. Supreme Court moved toward reconsidering it.

In other words, the antifeminist backlash has been set off not by women's achievement of full equality but by the increased possibility that they might win it. It is a preemptive strike that stops women long before they reach the finish line. "A backlash may be an indication that women really have had an effect," feminist psychiatrist Dr. Jean Baker Miller has written, "but backlashes occur when advances have been small, before changes are sufficient to help many people. . . . It is almost as if the leaders of backlashes use the fear of change as a threat before major change has occurred." In the last decade, some women did make substantial advances before the backlash hit, but millions of others were left behind, stranded. Some women now enjoy the right to legal abortion—but not the 44 million women, from the indigent to the military workforce, who depend on the federal government for their medical care. Some women can now walk into high-paying professional careers—but not the more than 19 million still in the typing pools or behind the department store sales counters. (Contrary to popular myth about the "have-it-all" baby-boom women, the largest percentage of women in this generation remain typists and clerks.)

As the backlash has gathered force, it has cut off the few from the many—and the few women who have advanced seek to prove, as a social survival tactic, that they aren't so interested in advancement after all. Some of them parade their defection from the women's movement, while their working-class peers founder and cling to the splintered remains of the feminist cause. While a very few affluent and celebrity women who are showcased in news articles boast about having "found my niche as Mrs. Andy Mill" and going home to "bake bread," the many working-class women appeal for their economic rights—flocking to unions in record numbers, striking on their own for pay equity and establishing their own fledgling groups for working women's rights. In 1986, while 41 percent of upper-income women were claiming in the Gallup poll that they were not feminists, only 26 percent of low-income women were making the same claim.

Women's advances and retreats are generally described in military terms; battles won, battles lost, points and territory gained and surrendered. The metaphor of combat is not without its merits in this context and, clearly, the same sort of martial accounting and vocabulary is already surfacing here. But by imagining the conflict as two battalions neatly arrayed on either side of the line, we miss the entangled nature, the locked embrace, of a "war" between women and the male culture they inhabit. We miss the reactive nature of a backlash, which, by definition, can exist only in response to another force.

In times when feminism is at a low ebb, women assume the reactive role—privately and most often covertly struggling to assert themselves against the dominant cultural tide. But when feminism itself becomes the tide, the opposition doesn't simply go along with the reversal: it digs in its heels, brandishes its fists, builds walls and dams. And its resistance creates countercurrents and treacherous undertows.

The force and furor of the backlash churn beneath the surface, largely invisible to the public eye. On occasion in the last decade, they have burst into view. We have seen New Right politicians condemn women's independence, antiabortion protesters fire-bomb women's clinics, fundamentalist preachers damn feminists as "whores" and "witches." Other signs of the backlash's wrath, by their sheer brutality, can push their way into public consciousness for a time—the sharp increase in rape, for example, or the rise in pornography that depicts extreme violence against women.

More subtle indicators in popular culture may receive momentary, and often bemused, media notice, then quickly slip from social awareness: A report, for instance, that the image of women on prime-time TV shows has suddenly degenerated. A survey of mystery fiction finding the numbers of female characters tortured and mutilated mysteriously multiplying. The puzzling news that, as one commentator put it, "So many hit songs have the B-word [bitch] to refer to women that some rap music seems to be veering toward rape music." The ascendancy of virulently misogynist comics like Andrew Dice Clay—who called women "pigs" and "sluts" and strutted in films in which women were beaten, tortured, and blown up—or radio hosts like Rush Limbaugh, whose broadsides against "femi-Nazi" feminists made his syndicated program the most popular radio talk show in the nation. Or word that in 1987, the American Women in Radio & Television couldn't award its annual prize for ads that feature women positively: it could find no ad that qualified.

These phenomena are all related, but that doesn't mean they are somehow coordinated. The backlash is not a conspiracy, with a council dispatching agents from some central control room, nor are the people who serve its ends often aware of their role: some even consider themselves feminists. For the most part, its workings are encoded and internalized, diffuse and chameleonic. Not all of the manifestations of the backlash are of equal weight or significance either; some are mere ephemera, generated by a culture machine that is always scrounging for a "fresh" angle. Taken as a whole, however, these codes and cajolings, these whispers and threats and myths, move overwhelmingly in one direction: they try to push women back into their "acceptable" roles—whether as Daddy's girl or fluttery romantic, active nester or passive love object.

Although the backlash is not an organized movement, that doesn't make it any less destructive. In fact, the lack of orchestration, the absence of a single string-puller, only makes it harder to see—and perhaps more effective. A backlash against women's rights succeeds to the degree that it appears not to be political, that it appears *not* to be a struggle at all. It is most powerful when it goes private, when it lodges inside a woman's mind and turns her vision inward, until she imagines the pressure is all in her head, until she begins to enforce the backlash, too—on herself.

In the last decade, the backlash has moved through the culture's secret chambers, traveling through passageways of flattery and fear. Along the way, it has adopted disguises: a mask of mild derision or the painted face of deep "concern." Its lips profess pity for any woman who won't fit the mold, while it tries to clamp the mold around her ears. It pursues a divide-and-conquer strategy: single versus married women, working women versus homemakers, middle- versus working-class. It manipulates a system of rewards and punishments, elevating women who follow its rules, isolating those who don't. The backlash remarkets old myths about women as new facts and ignores all appeals to reason. Cornered, it denies its own existence, points an accusatory finger at feminism, and burrows deeper underground.

Backlash happens to be the title of a 1947 Hollywood movie in which a man frames his wife for a murder he's committed. The backlash against women's rights works in much the same way: its rhetoric charges feminists with all the crimes it perpetrates. The backlash line blames the women's movement for the "feminization of poverty"—while the backlash's own instigators in Washington pushed through the budget cuts that helped impoverish millions of women, fought pay equity proposals, and undermined equal opportunity laws. The backlash line claims the women's movement cares nothing for children's rights—while its own representatives in the capital and state legislatures have blocked one bill after another to improve child care, slashed billions of dollars in federal aid for children, and relaxed state licensing standards for day care centers. The backlash line accuses the women's movement of creating a generation of unhappy single and childless women—but its purveyors in the media are the ones guilty of making single and childless women feel like circus freaks.

To blame feminism for women's "lesser life" is to miss entirely the point of feminism, which is to win women a wider range of experience. Feminism remains a pretty simple concept, despite repeated—and enormously effective—efforts to dress it up in greasepaint and turn its proponents into gargoyles. As Rebecca West wrote sardonically in 1913, "I myself have never been able to find out precisely what feminism is: I only know that people call me a feminist whenever I express sentiments that differentiate me from a doormat."

The meaning of the word "feminist" has not really changed since it first appeared in a book review in the *Athenaeum* of April 27, 1895, describing a woman who "has in her the capacity of fighting her way back to independence." It is the basic proposition that, as Nora put it in Ibsen's *A Doll House* a century ago, "Before everything else I'm a human being." It is the simply worded sign hoisted by a little girl in the 1970 Women's Strike for Equality: I AM NOT A BARBIE DOLL. Feminism asks the world to recognize at long last that women aren't decorative ornaments, worthy vessels, members of a "special-interest group." They are half (in fact, now more than half) of the national population, and just as deserving of rights and opportunities, just as capable of participating in the world's events, as the other half. Feminism's agenda is basic: It asks that women not be forced to "choose" between public justice and private happiness. It asks that women be free to define themselves—instead of having their identity defined for them, time and again, by their culture and their men.

The fact that these are still such incendiary notions should tell us that American women have a way to go before they enter the promised land of equality.

Discussion Questions

1. Faludi wrote her book about the backlash against feminism over ten years ago. Discuss with your peers where you think the movement is now. Are you aware of a continuing backlash? Do you think women in America are pushing ahead despite the backlash? What evidence do you find for a continued backlash or for an increased interest in feminism in political, economic, or social developments?

2. Faludi discusses the increasing number of movies that portray emancipated women as they slink "wild-eyed between bare walls, paying for their liberty with an empty bed, a barren womb." Discuss recent movies you have seen and write down a list of the movies that individual members of your class have seen—then consider the ways in which women are emerging on the silver screen today. How have emancipated women been portrayed in recent movies? How have housewives and mothers been portrayed in recent movies? Do you find that ambitious working women are portrayed favorably or unfavorably? Do you see any trend to support Faludi's statement?

Writing Suggestions

1. Faludi writes that the idea that feminism is responsible for making women miserable has its origin in "a closed system that starts and ends in the media, popular culture, and advertising . . . ." Analyze the portrayal of women in advertisements in at least five magazines, ranging from sports magazines to fashion magazines to news magazines. Consider at least

fifty advertisements targeting women, and then use your analysis to answer the following questions:

How do current advertisements that target female audiences approach the idea of the liberated, equal woman?

How do advertisements address the Superwoman concept?

Do advertisements show women working in a serious manner, or do they make fun of women at work?

How do advertisers portray working women? Are women at work sexualized in advertisements, or are women made to look more masculine?

How do advertisers portray women who are homemakers and mothers? Who looks happier in advertisements—working women or stay-at-home mothers?

Do you see evidence of a backlash against women's equality in advertisements, or do you see progress in the portrayal of women in advertising?

Remember that advertisers are trying to persuade women to buy their products, so the advertisements will display what advertisers think women want to see. Write an analysis of the advertisements, formulating your thesis after you have done your research and after you have written and thought about the questions above.

2. One of Faludi's concerns is the increasing violence against women and the increase in battered women since the women's movement began in the 1960s and 1970s. Research the current statistics and evidence about violence against women, and write a report in which you analyze current statistics of violence against women. Also look for recent legislation that seeks to control this problem. Report in your paper not only on recent trends in violence but also on any political progress or lack of progress in dealing with this issue. Discuss the evolution of this problem in the past twenty years, tracing the amelioration or deterioration of women's struggles against violence.

No Turning Back

Expanding the Definition: Sexual Harassment and Domestic Violence

ESTELLE B. FREEDMAN

Estelle B. Freedman teaches at Stanford University in the Department of History, specializing in women's history and feminist studies; she has received a number of undergraduate teaching awards for service to undergraduate education and for excellence in teaching. Freedman, who holds a B.A. from Barnard College and a Ph.D. from Columbia University, has recently published *No Turning Back: The History of Feminism and the Future of Women* (2002), from which our selection below is taken. Freedman has long been interested in the history of women's rights and social change, both in the United States and abroad, and has studied women's roles in social reform, women's prison reform, and the history of sexuality and sexual violence. In the selection below, Freedman discusses the history of sexual harassment and domestic violence both in the United States and abroad.

Feminists have named all forms of unwanted sexual and physical acts as a source of gender inequality, including behaviors once taken for granted as woman's lot to suffer. In 1974, for example, Carmita Wood, a U.S. wage-earning mother of four, resigned from her job after her supervisor made repeated sexual advances toward her. In her claim for unemployment benefits, she used the phrase "sexual harassment." Courts had never ruled on this concept, but at least half of all working women had experienced it. The phrase would soon come to national and then international attention. In 1979 feminist legal theorist Catharine MacKinnon argued in *The Sexual Harassment of Working Women* that sexual pressures on women workers enforced women's economic disadvantage in the labor market. Sexual harassment, she held, was therefore a form of sex discrimination prohibited under Title VII of the U.S. Civil Rights Act of 1964. Serving as cocounsel before the U.S. Supreme Court, MacKinnon contributed to a 1986 ruling that made sexual harassment illegal in the United States. The court's narrow ruling, however, permitted a woman's speech or dress to be cited as relevant "sexual provocation."

In her book MacKinnon identified two ways in which the imposition of unwanted sexual requirements in the context of a relationship of unequal power could disadvantage women at work or in school. The first, quid pro quo, involved the promise of some form of advancement, such as a job, a raise, or better grades, in exchange for sex. The second, a hostile work environment, meant that sexual advances made the workplace or classroom unbearable, even if the worker refused the advances and no exchange of favors occurred. Both forms left psychological scars and undermined job or academic performance. While women who have advanced professionally can also harass their subordinates, as many as 90 percent of reported cases involve male workers who use sexual language and gestures to harass women. According to MacKinnon, sexual harassment is not simply about sex; rather, it rests at the intersection of the economic and the sexual control of women. Harassment often dissuades women from persisting in higher-paying blue-collar or managerial jobs or in professional education.

Like women who report rape, those who name sexual harassment often face disbelief and questioning about their sexual histories, as former Equal Employment Opportunity Commission employee Anita Hill learned in 1991 when she testified about harassment at the confirmation hearings for Supreme Court Justice nominee Clarence Thomas. Commentators discredited her testimony because she had remained in her job despite the offensive behavior of her supervisor, even though Hill explained that she had feared retribution in her career if she revealed his unwanted advances and crude comments. Moreover, her status as a single African American woman made his behavior seem acceptable to some.

Anita Hill's painful testimony riveted the American public and the hostile response of male legislators unleashed a powerful female political force. African American women organized a defense of Hill in the press; after the hearings, sexual harassment complaints increased by 50 percent at the EEOC; membership in the National Organization for Women surged the following year; and 1992 became known as the Year of the Woman in U.S. politics, with 117 women candidates for congress. During the 1990s more women took employers and schools to court for not controlling sexual harassment, with major victories won by U.S. workers at Mitsubishi Motors and by public school students in Georgia and Texas who demanded protection from harassment by peers or teachers.

Tolerance for sexual harassment has declined outside the United States as well. In 1989, for example, Spain outlawed sexual harassment, while lawyers in Japan organized a hotline for women workers who felt they had been harassed. By the end of the 1990s countries such as Israel, Korea, and Venezuela had outlawed the practice, and the Indian Supreme Court ruled that sexual harassment violated a woman's right not only when manifested by physical touching but also through verbal offenses. As with rape, legal reform could achieve only limited progress toward changing cultural practices. Feminists have insisted on broader measures, including educational workshops for teachers and managers to explain the costs of inappropriate sexual advances and the procedures for complaining of them.

While institutions struggle to change practices that once intimidated women, feminists have disagreed about the extent and importance of sexual harassment. Some fear that highlighting sex as the source of a hostile work environment could produce a climate that constrains free speech about sexuality in the name of protecting women. For instance, a teacher or worker could elicit charges of sexual harassment for discussing sex in any form. In addition, the law itself is vulnerable to abuse through false charges. In the "he said/she said" scenarios, one party claims that the other either misunderstood or misrepresented the encounter, finding hostile intent in allegedly innocent behaviors. Like the controversy over date rape, the line between sexual play and sexual harassment creates a blurred legal and ethical space that fosters dissent among feminists. Most can agree, however, that learning to communicate clearly about sexual desire and respect for women's right to say no are common goals.

Domestic Violence

Sexual harassment occurs in public work and educational settings, so it is subject to antidiscrimination laws. In contrast, violence against women in the home has long been protected by the privacy accorded to the family and the implicit right permitted to husbands to rule over their wives and children. Behind closed doors, battery, verbal abuse, and life-threatening assaults take place regularly. "I can't remember a time when my mother wasn't physically abused by my father," a woman recalled in 1991. "I learned at an early age," another woman wrote, "that a man has the right to beat his wife and if he abstains, she should be grateful."

In patriarchal cultures, husbands had the right to chastise their wives physically. From the Greeks through the Reformation, European husbands ruled over their wives and children and could correct them, as St. Augustine wrote, "by word or blow." The "rule of thumb" in Anglo-American law held that a husband could beat his wife as long as he used a stick that was no thicker than his thumb. The legitimacy of the practice persisted in the English-speaking world even after courts began to reject the legality of wife beating in the 1800s. In other cultures, husbands meted out physical punishment of wives, whether in China (where mothers-in-law also beat daughters-in-law), Africa, or the Middle East.

Early European feminists challenged the right of husbands to punish their wives. In England, Harriet Martineau and John Stuart Mill fought for the right to divorce in part so that wives could leave abusive husbands. In the United States social purity reformers and the Women's Christian Temperance Union blamed liquor for making men brutish husbands. Historian Elizabeth Pleck has shown that by the 1890s women's organizations provided social services, encouraged victims to bring charges in court, and established the first safe houses for abused wives. By the twentieth century a new legal concept of marital cruelty provided grounds for divorce. For mothers, however, it was difficult to apply these grounds if divorce left women either without custody of their children or economically unable to support them.

Although abuse of wives in Europe and the Americas has been publicly portrayed as a lower-class phenomenon, estimates of its incidence reveal a more extensive social problem. At the end of the twentieth century, each year between 10 and 20 percent of North American women were beaten by a man with whom they had an intimate relationship. One-fourth to one-half of all North American women could expect to experience domestic violence at some point in their lives. In the United States a woman is battered every fifteen seconds, and domestic violence is a major cause of injuries to women, including one-third of their murders. The Federal Bureau of Investigation notes that four women die every day in the United States from domestic assaults. In one Canadian study 62 percent of the murderers of women had been their intimate partners. One-third of all U.S. calls for police assistance concern domestic violence, yet until recently no police training existed and police departments typically advised officers not to interfere with private family matters. For years a "stitch rule" held that perpetrators should be charged with a crime only if the violence required stitches.

Internationally, the figures are equally disturbing. A 1985 survey in Thailand found that 50 percent of respondents had experienced domestic abuse. While the figures emphasized lower-class violence, they probably reflected underreporting among other social groups. United Nations figures for the proportion of adult women who had been physically assaulted by an intimate partner ranged in 1995 from about one-fourth in northern Europe and some Latin American countries, such as Chile, to three-fourths of the lower-caste women in Indian villages. An Egyptian study found that domestic violence was the major reason women were treated for physical trauma. Unique forms of family violence lead to injury and death in India. Dowry deaths and dowry burnings refer to the harassment of a wife who is either pressured to commit suicide or murdered so that her husband's family can extract and keep her dowry, the price paid at marriage. During the 1980s one or two women were burned to death a day in each of several Indian cities. Estimates during the 1990s ranged from five thousand to fifteen thousand Indian women killed annually in dowry-related incidents.

Contemporary feminists analyze domestic violence as a problem shared by women across class, race, and national lines. While social science studies show that patterns of abuse are passed from parents to children in families of any background, feminists move beyond a purely psychological argument based on family dynamics. Rather, they emphasize the economic problem of female dependency as a contributing factor to domestic violence. As Zimbabwe's deputy health minister, Tsungirirai Hungwe, explains, "Those leaving violent relationships often have limited options to support themselves and their children, and face poverty and isolation. Each year, a number of women try to commit suicide to escape such difficult situations." A survey of Thai women found that those who worked in the low-paid informal sector and those who considered divorce a stigma for their families often remained in abusive relationships. Women who cannot be economically self-supporting may become trapped in cycles of "learned helplessness." Most battered women in North America are homemakers, many of whom have internalized blame for a husband's violence. When a wife depends on her husband for economic support she may feel both financially and psychologically dependent. Whether in Africa, India, Iran, or the United States, women who feel trapped within their families fear that they may be beaten or killed if they attempt to leave.

Throughout the world feminists have responded to domestic violence by naming the problem, providing services, and empowering women to claim their rights. In India protest marches began in 1979 to call attention to dowry burnings, making the once-personal issue a public one. Refusing the stories that deaths by fire were suicides, Indian women rallied with signs reading Down with Dowry. They also demanded police investigations and pressed for laws to punish cruelty to wives. In Latin America Brazilian women formed the Committee on Violence Against Women, which became the most active feminist organization in the country at the end of the 1970s. After a series of murders of Brazilian women, feminists staged public demonstrations that paralleled the Take Back the Night marches that protested rape.

Along with protests and services feminists insist on adequate police protection from domestic violence. Pop singer Tracy Chapman captured well the way law enforcement once handled domestic disputes: "The police always come too late if they come at all." In 1976 feminist lawyers brought a class action suit against the Oakland, California, police department because of its weak response to calls about domestic violence. A court settlement required special training for officers who intervene in domestic disputes. By 1986 almost half of the large urban police departments in the United States had adopted the policy of arresting perpetrators of domestic violence, compared to only 10 percent just two years earlier. Laws mandating the arrest of batterers have also become more common—twenty-six U.S. states had enacted them by 1994. The process of obtaining a judicial restraining order against an abusive partner has been simplified in the United States, and hospitals have also changed their responses. Since the American Medical Association declared the physical abuse of women a major health issue in 1991, emergency room staff have become more sensitive to the signs of domestic abuse.

International movements to protect women from abuse and to prosecute batterers expanded rapidly after 1980. Between 1985 and 1995 a hundred special police stations for women opened in Brazil, with feminist monitoring so that women could report violence and find their way to shelters. Women's courts hear cases of abuse in the Indian capital, New Delhi. In 1995 the Association of Women's Organizations in Jamaica succeeded in obtaining the passage of the Domestic Violence Act, which allows courts to remove abusive partners.

Feminists around the world have established shelters for battered women. First founded in England, the movement spread internationally after 1970. By 1990 there were over 1,250 shelters in the United States and Canada. The Women's Shelter Programme in Bangkok, founded in the 1980s, serves poor women in a neighborhood where up to half of them had been attacked by husbands. Some of these women fought back; some had killed their attackers. The founders of the shelter recognized that "the issue of battered women is not merely one of 'bad Karma' or a private matter of each individual woman. We see it as a problem embedded in our social structure, which neglects the fundamental rights of women." In response they provided a temporary refuge from abuse, group therapy for residents, and a campaign to raise public consciousness "of battered wives as another form of violence which any woman, regardless of status or class, can fall prey to." Run by volunteers who have survived abuse themselves, the Ambassador One-Stop Drop-in Advice Centre in England, established in 1998, provides a range of services to women fleeing domestic violence. In both Great Britain and the United States law enforcement agencies sometimes cooperate with shelters, directing women to them when they report abuse. By the 1990s specialized agencies reached out to immigrants. South Asian women living in the United States had organized shelters in New York, New Jersey, and California.

Most of these shelters rely on private funding, although some governments have provided help. The Netherlands, for example, subsidized forty-eight shelters in the 1990s, while Spain offered a toll-free hotline advising women about shelters. To fund its shelter, one city used a marriage license tax, while in the Basque area of Spain, battered women receive a "salary" to encourage them to leave their abusers. In 1994 the U.S. Violence Against Women Act provided funding for grants to shelters, as well as for research on violence and its prevention. Despite conservative opposition, the funding was renewed in 2000. Much of the funding for shelters continues to be raised by the feminist community, however. In the United States young women take wilderness hikes to raise funds for the Elizabeth Stone House in Boston, founded in 1974. In California a shelter solicits funds by sending Mother's Day cards created by children who reside there with their mothers.

Shelters offer a variety of services, including a safe house (a location kept secret from an abusive husband), group therapy, child care, and legal counseling to let women know their rights and options. In some cases consciousness-raising or support groups are critical elements. As one woman explained, the shelter helped her forget her husband and her fears. "They listened when I told my story . . . I felt safe." As in the cases of rape and incest, part of the resistance to violence is to break down silence and isolation.

Shelters and restraining orders cannot always protect women, some of whom have been murdered while under court protection. Fear of continued abuse has driven some women to strike back. A large proportion of women serving prison sentences for murder in the United States have killed their batterers, often in self-defense. Lawyers have turned to the psychological theory of "battered woman syndrome" to explain why these women remained in abusive relationships to the point that they became violent themselves.

Women can be violent against partners or children as well as in response to abusive husbands. Studies of violence suggest that those who feel most entitled to social power are most likely to use violence to achieve or enforce it. Since power, not simply masculinity, produces violence, the solution is not just for women to achieve greater power. Rather, as theorists such as Nancy Hartsock have argued, feminists must reexamine the very concept of power. One kind of power, self-determination, is critical to full citizenship in democratic societies; another form, power over others, can legitimate violence as a means to enforce it. Thus, for African American feminist bell hooks, "Feminist efforts to end male violence against women must be expanded into a movement to end all forms of violence."

Discussion Questions

1. Considering sexual harassment court cases, Freedman states that some feminists "fear that highlighting sex as the source of a hostile work environment could produce a climate that constrains free speech about sexuality in the name of protecting women. For instance, a teacher or worker could elicit charges of sexual harassment for discussing sex in any form." Comment on this idea, and discuss your own opinions and the pros and cons of lawsuits intended to protect women from harassment.

2. Although this excerpt is primarily concerned with American women, Freedman extends the context of the discussion by bringing in examples of sexual harassment and domestic violence in other countries. According to Freedman, how does America compare to other countries in terms of the prevalence of harassment and domestic violence? How does Freedman's writing benefit from this extended context? What did you learn about the extent of domestic violence at home and abroad?

Writing Suggestions

1. Freedman states that "studies of violence suggest that those who feel most entitled to social power are most likely to use violence to achieve or enforce it." Freedman also quotes African American feminist bell hooks: "Feminist efforts to end male violence against women must be expanded into a movement to end all forms of violence." Write a journal entry commenting on the relationship of power and violence, agreeing or disagreeing with this assessment of the relationship between the two.

2. Research the "battered woman syndrome" and write a report analyzing the causes and proposed remedies for women who suffer from this syndrome. What kinds of shelters and programs seem to be effective? What kinds of problems do these women encounter when they try to change their life patterns? What kinds of success stories did you find when researching this problem? How has the law helped or hindered battered women?

Fences against Freedom

LESLIE MARMON SILKO

Leslie Marmon Silko, born in 1948, grew up outside of Albuquerque, New Mexico, in the Laguna Pueblo. She was aware of race and racial discrimination from an early age; her ancestry was part white, part Mexican, and part Pueblo, and she has written that "we of mixed ancestry belonged on the outer edge of the circle between the world of the Pueblo and the outside world." Silko is the author of poems, stories, and two novels, *Ceremony* (1977) and *Almanac of the Dead* (1992). In 1996 she published *Yellow Woman and the Beauty of the Spirit*, from which our selection, "Fences against Freedom" is taken. In this essay she examines the role of the government and of politicians in the effort "to control our borders," and describes her own terrifying experiences with the Border Patrol.

As a person of mixed ancestry, I have always been very sensitive to the prevailing attitudes toward people of color. I remember a time around 1965 when the term *race* was nearly replaced with the term *ancestry* on government forms and applications. For a short time questions about one's ancestry and religion were even deleted from paperwork. During this time, concerted efforts were made by public officials and media people to use the term *ancestry* instead of *race*. Geneticists had scientific evidence that there is only one race, the human race; there is only one species to which all people belong: *Homo sapiens*. This period of conscientious education of the public to eradicate misinformation about "race" grew out of the civil rights movement of the 1950s and from key decisions from the U.S. Supreme Court. Presidents Kennedy and Johnson spoke explicitly about the blot on the honor of the United States made by centuries of prejudice; even the U.S. Congress, with the exception of a few senators and congressmen from southern states, joined them in asserting equality for all human beings.

In 1967 I chose "race" as my topic for a paper in one of my college honors seminars. I had taken two semesters of anthropology in my freshman year, and I already knew that "race" had been a hot topic among the physical anthropologists for decades. I understood that the "one race, human race" theorists like Ashley Montagu had finally assembled incontrovertible biological proofs that had swept away the nineteenth-century theories of distinct "races." But I wanted to see exactly how this shift had come about, because I knew that many people still were under the influence of nineteenth-century notions concerning race.

I went to the University of New Mexico library and checked out all the books I could find on the topic of "race." As a person of mixed ancestry, I could not afford to take my anthropology professor or Ashley Montagu's word for it. Segregationists implied that liberals had seized power on campuses and that to mollify blacks and other "racial" minorities these liberals had concocted false data to prove human equality. My parents and the people of the Laguna Pueblo community who raised me taught me that we are all one family—all the offspring of Mother Earth—and no one is better or worse according to skin color or origin. My whole life I had believed this, but now I had to test what I had been taught as a child because I had also been taught that the truth matters more than anything, even more than personal comfort, more than one's own vanity. It was possible that my parents and the people at home, along with people like Ashley Montagu, had deluded themselves just as the segregationists had alleged. I was determined to know the truth even if the truth was unpleasant.

I don't remember all the books I read, but I do remember that Carleton Coon was the name of the leading physical anthropologist whose books and articles argued the "racial superiority" of some "races" over others. I wondered then if Mr. Coon's vehemence about the superiority of the white race had anything to do with his name, which I knew was a common slur used against African Americans. Had the other children teased him about his name in the school yard? Was that why Coon had endured censure by his peers to persist in his "race" research in physical anthropology long after the Nuremberg trials?

I once read an article whose author stated that racism is the only form of mental illness that is communicable. Clever but not entirely true. Racism in the United States is learned by us beginning at birth.

As a person of mixed ancestry growing up in the United States in the late 1950s, I knew all of the cruel epithets that might be hurled at others; the knowledge was a sort of solace that I was not alone in my feelings of unease, of not quite belonging to the group that clearly mattered most in the United States.

Human beings need to feel as if they "belong"; I learned from my father to feel comfortable and happy alone in the mesas and hills around Laguna. It was not so easy for me to learn where we Marmons belonged, but gradually I understood that we of mixed ancestry belonged on the outer edge of the circle between the world of the Pueblo and the outside world. The Laguna people were open and accepted children of mixed ancestry because appearance was secondary to behavior. For the generation of my great-grandmother and earlier generations, anyone who had not been born in the community was a stranger regardless of skin color. Strangers were not judged by their appearances—which could deceive—but by their behavior. The old-time people took their time to become acquainted with a person before they made a judgment. The old-time people were very secure in themselves and their identity; and thus they were able to appreciate differences and to even marvel at personal idiosyncrasies so long as no one and nothing was being harmed.

The cosmology of the Pueblo people is all-inclusive; long before the arrival of the Spaniards in the Americas, the Pueblo and other indigenous communities knew that the Mother Creator had many children in faraway places. The ancient stories include all people of the earth, so when the Spaniards marched into Laguna in 1540, the inclination still was to include rather than to exclude the strangers, even though the people had heard frightening stories and rumors about the white men. My great-grandmother and the people of her generation were always very curious and took delight in learning odd facts and strange but true stories. The old-time people believed that we must keep learning as much as we can all of our lives. So the people set out to learn if there was anything at all *good* in these strangers; because they had never met any humans who were completely evil. Sure enough, it was true with these strangers too; some of them had evil hearts, but many were good human beings.

Similarly, when my great-grandfather, a white man, married into the Anaya family, he was adopted into the community by his wife's family and clans. There always had been political factions among these families and clans, and by his marriage, my great-grandfather became a part of the political intrigues at Laguna. Some accounts by anthropologists attempt to portray my great-grandfather and his brother as instigators or meddlers, but the anthropologists have overestimated their importance and their tenuous position in the Pueblo. Naturally, the factions into which the Marmon brothers had married incorporated these new "sons" into their ongoing intrigues and machinations. But the anthropologists who would portray the Marmon brothers as dictators fool themselves about the power of white men in a pueblo. The minute the Marmon brothers crossed over the line, they would have been killed.

Indeed, people at Laguna remember my great-grandfather as a gentle, quiet man, while my beloved Grandma A'mooh is remembered as a stern, formidable woman who ran the show. She was also a Presbyterian. Her family, the Anayas, had kept cattle and sheep for a long time, and I imagine that way back in the past, an ancestor of hers had been curious about the odd animals the strangers brought and decided to give them a try.

I was fortunate to be reared by my great-grandmother and others of her generation. They always took an interest in us children and they were always delighted to answer our questions and to tell us stories about the old days. Although there were very few children of mixed ancestry in those days, the old folks did not seem to notice. But I could sense a difference from younger people, the generation that had gone to the First World War. On rare occasions, I could sense an anger that my appearance stirred in them, although I sensed that the anger was not aimed at me personally. My appearance reminded them of the outside world, where racism was thriving.

I learned about racism firsthand from the Marmon family. My great-grandfather endured the epithet Squaw Man. Once when he and two of his young sons (my Grandpa Hank and his brother Frank) walked through the lobby of Albuquerque's only hotel to reach the café inside, the hotel manager stopped my great-grandfather. He told my great-grandfather that he was welcome to walk through the lobby, but when he had Indians with him, he should use the back door. My great-grandfather informed him that the "Indians" were his sons, and then he left and never went into the hotel again.

There were branches of the Marmon family that, although Laguna, still felt they were better than the rest of us Marmons and the rest of the Lagunas as well. Grandpa Hank's sister, Aunt Esther, was beautiful and vain and light skinned; she boarded at the Sherman Institute in Riverside, California, where my grandfather and other Indian students were taught trades. But Aunt Esther did not get along with the other Indian girls; she refused to speak to them or to have anything to do with them. So she was allowed to attend a Riverside girls school with white girls. My grandfather, who had a broad nose and face and "looked Indian," told the counselor at Sherman that he wanted to become an automobile designer. He was told by the school guidance counselor that Indians weren't able to design automobiles; they taught him to be a store clerk.

I learned about racism firsthand when I started school. We were punished if we spoke the Laguna language once we crossed onto the school grounds. Every fall, all of us were lined up and herded like cattle to the girls' and boys' bathrooms, where our heads were drenched with smelly insecticide regardless of whether we had lice or not. We were vaccinated in both arms without regard to our individual immunization records.

But what I remember most clearly is the white tourists who used to come to the school yard to take our pictures. They would give us kids each a nickel, so naturally when we saw tourists get out of their cars with cameras, we all wanted to get in the picture. Then one day when I was older, in the third grade, white tourists came with cameras. All of my playmates started to bunch together to fit in the picture, and I was right there with them maneuvering myself into the group when I saw the tourist look at me with a particular expression. I knew instantly he did not want me to be in the picture; I stayed close to my playmates, hoping that I had misread the man's face. But the tourist motioned for me to move away to one side, out of his picture. I remember my playmates looked puzzled, but I knew why the man did not want me in his picture: I looked different from my playmates. I was part white and he didn't want me to spoil his snapshots of "Indians." After that incident, the arrival of tourists with cameras at our school filled me with anxiety. I would stand back and watch the expressions on the tourists' faces before trying to join my playmates in the picture. Most times the tourists were kindly and did not seem to notice my difference, and they would motion for me to join my classmates; but now and then there were tourists who looked relieved that I did not try to join in the group picture.

Racism is a constant factor in the United States; it is always in the picture even if it only forms the background. Now as the condition of the U.S. economy continues to deteriorate and the people grow restive with the U.S. Congress and the president, the tactics of party politicians sink deeper in corruption. Racism is now a trump card, to be played again and again shamelessly by both major political parties. The U.S. government applications that had used the term *ancestry* disappeared; the fiction of "the races" has been reestablished. Soon after Nixon's election the changes began, and racism became a key component once more in the U.S. political arena. The Republican Party found the issue of race to be extremely powerful, so the Democrats, desperate for power, have also begun to pander racism to the U.S. electorate.

Fortunately, the people of the United States are far better human beings than the greedy elected officials who allegedly represent them in Congress and the White House. The elected officials of both parties currently are trying to whip up hysteria over immigration policy in the most blatantly racist manner. Politicians and media people talk about the "illegal aliens" to dehumanize and demonize undocumented immigrants, who are for the most part people of color. The Cold War with the Communist world is over, and now the military defense contractors need to create a new bogeyman to justify U.S. defense spending. The U.S.–Mexico border is fast becoming a militarized zone. The army and marine units from all over the United States come to southern Arizona to participate in "training exercises" along the border.

When I was growing up, U.S. politicians called Russia an "Iron Curtain" country, which implied terrible shame. As I got older I learned that there wasn't really a curtain made of iron around the Soviet Union; I was later disappointed to learn that the wall in Berlin was made of concrete, not iron. Now the U.S. government is building a steel wall twelve feet high that eventually will span the entire length of the Mexican border. The steel wall already spans four-mile sections of the border at Mexicali and Naco; and at Nogales, sixty miles south of Tucson, the steel wall is under construction.

Immigration and Naturalization Services, or the Border Patrol, has greatly expanded its manpower and checkpoint stations. Now when you drive down Interstate 10 toward El Paso, you will find a check station. When you drive north from Las Cruces up 1-25 about ten miles north of Truth or Consequences, all interstate highway traffic is diverted off the highway into an INS checkpoint. I was detained at that checkpoint in December 1991 on my way from Tucson to Albuquerque for a book signing of my novel *Almanac of the Dead*. My companion and I were detained despite the fact that we showed the Border Patrol our Arizona driver's licenses. Two men from California, both Chicanos, were being detained at the same time, despite the fact that they too presented an ID and spoke English without the thick Texas accents of the Border Patrolmen. While we were detained, we watched as other vehicles were waved through the checkpoint. The occupants of those vehicles were white. It was quite clear that my appearance—my skin color—was the reason for the detention.

The Border Patrol exercises a power that no highway patrol or county sheriff possesses: the Border Patrol can detain anyone they wish for no reason at all. A policeman or sheriff needs to have some shred of probable cause, but not the Border Patrol. In fact, they stop people with Indio-Hispanic characteristics, and they target cars in which white people travel with brown people. Recent reports of illegal immigration by people of Asian ancestry mean that the Border Patrol now routinely detain anyone who looks Asian. Once you have been stopped at a Border Patrol checkpoint, you are under the control of the Border Patrol agent; the refusal to obey any order by the Border Patrol agent means you have broken the law and may be arrested for failure to obey a federal officer. Once the car is stopped, they ask you to step out of the car; then they ask you to open the trunk. If you ask them why or request a search warrant, they inform you that it will take them three or four hours to obtain a search warrant. They make it very clear that if you "force" them to get a search warrant, they will strip-search your body as well as your car and luggage. On this particular day I was due in Albuquerque, and I did not have the four hours to spare. So I opened my car trunk, but not without using my right to free speech to tell them what I thought of them and their police state procedures. "You are not wanted here," I shouted at them, and they seemed astonished. "Only a few years ago we used to be able to move freely within our own country," I said. "This is our home. Take all this back where you came from. You are not wanted here."

Scarcely a year later, my friend and I were driving south from Albuquerque, returning to Tucson after a paperback book promotion. There are no Border Patrol detention areas on the southbound lanes of 1-25, so I settled back and went to sleep while Gus drove. I awakened when I felt the car slowing to a stop. It was nearly midnight on New Mexico State Road 26, a dark lonely stretch of two-lane highway between Hatch and Deming. When I sat up, I saw the headlights and emergency flashers of six vehicles—Border Patrol cars and a Border Patrol van blocked both lanes of the road. Gus stopped the car and rolled down his window to ask what was wrong. But the Border Patrolman and his companion did not reply; instead the first officer ordered us to "step out of the car." Gus asked why we had to get out of the car. His question seemed to set them off—two more Border Patrolmen immediately approached the car and one of them asked, "Are you looking for trouble?" as if he would relish the opportunity.

I will never forget that night beside the highway. There was an awful feeling of menace and of violence straining to break loose. It was clear that they would be happy to drag us out of the car if we did not comply. So we both got out of the car and they motioned for us to stand on the shoulder of the road. The night was very dark, and no other traffic had come down the road since they had stopped us. I thought how easy it would be for the Border Patrolmen to shoot us and leave our bodies and car beside the road. There were two other Border Patrolmen by the van. The man who had asked if we were looking for trouble told his partner to "get the dog," and from the back of the white van another Border Patrolman brought a small female German shepherd on a leash. The dog did not heel well enough to suit him, and I saw the dog's handler jerk the leash. They opened the doors of our car and pulled the dog's head into the car, but I saw immediately from the expression in her eyes that the dog hated them, and she would not serve them. When she showed no interest in the inside of the car, they brought her around back to the trunk, near where we were standing. They half-dragged her up into the trunk, but still she did not indicate stowed-away humans or illegal drugs.

Their mood got uglier; they seemed outraged that the dog could not find any contraband, and they dragged her over to us and commanded her to sniff our legs and feet. To my relief, the strange anger the INS agents had focused at us now had shifted to the dog. I no longer felt so strongly that we would be murdered. We exchanged looks—the dog and I. She was afraid of what they might do, just as I was. The handler jerked the leash violently as she sniffed us, as if to make her perform better, but the dog refused to accuse us. The dog had an innate dignity, an integrity that did not permit her to serve those men. I can't forget the expression in her eyes; it was as if she was embarrassed to be associated with them. I had a small amount of medicinal marijuana in my purse that night, but the dog refused to expose me. I am not partial to dogs, but I can't forget the small German shepherd. She saved us from the strange murderous mood of the Border Patrolmen that night.

In February of 1993, I was invited by the Women's Studies Department at UCLA to be a distinguished visiting lecturer. After I had described my run-ins with the Border Patrol, a professor of history at UCLA related her story. It seems she had been traveling by train from Los Angeles to Albuquerque twice each month to work with an informant. She had noticed that the Border Patrol officers were there each week to meet the Amtrak trains to scrutinize the passengers, but since she is six feet tall and of Irish and German ancestry, she was not particularly concerned. Then one day when she stepped off the train in Albuquerque, two Border Patrolmen accosted her. They wanted to know what she was doing, why she was traveling between Los Angeles and Albuquerque. This is the sort of police state that has developed in the southwest United States. No person, no citizen is free to travel without the scrutiny of the Border Patrol. Because Reverend Fife and the sanctuary movement bring political refugees into the United States from Central America, the Border Patrol is suspicious of and detains white people who appear to be clergy, those who wear ethnic clothing or jewelry, and women who wear very long hair or very short hair (they could be nuns). Men with beards and men with long hair are also likely to be detained because INS agents suspect "those sorts" of white people may help political refugees.

In Phoenix the INS agents raid public high schools and drag dark-skinned students away to their vans. In 1992, in El Paso, Texas, a high school football coach driving a vanload of his players in full uniform was pulled over on the freeway and INS agents put a cocked revolver to the coach's head through the van window. That incident was one of many similar abuses by the INS in the El Paso area that finally resulted in a restraining order against the Border Patrol issued by a federal judge in El Paso.

At about the same time, a Border Patrol agent in Nogales shot an unarmed undocumented immigrant in the back one night and attempted to hide the body; a few weeks earlier the same Border Patrol agent had shot and wounded another undocumented immigrant. His fellow agent, perhaps realizing Agent Elmer had gone around the bend, refused to help in the cover-up, so Agent Elmer threatened him. Agent Elmer was arrested and tried for murder, but his southern Arizona jury empathized with his fear of brown-skinned people; they believed Agent Elmer's story that he feared for his life even though the victim was shot in the back trying to flee. Agent Elmer was also cleared of the charges of wounding in the other case. For years, undocumented immigrant women have reported sexual assaults by Border Patrol agents. But it wasn't until Agent Elmer was tried for murder that another Nogales INS agent was convicted of the rape of a woman he had taken into custody for detainment. In the city of South Tucson, where 80 percent of the respondents were Chicano or Mexicano, a research project by the University of Wisconsin recently revealed that one out of every five persons living there had been stopped by INS agents in the past year.

I no longer feel the same about driving from Tucson to Albuquerque via the southern route. For miles before I approach the INS check stations, I can feel the anxiety pressing hard against my chest. But I feel anger too, a deep, abiding anger at the U.S. government, and I know that I am not alone in my hatred of these racist immigration policies, which are broadcast every day, teaching racism, demonizing all people of color, labeling indigenous people from Mexico as "aliens"—creatures not quite human.

The so-called civil wars in El Salvador and Guatemala are actually wars against the indigenous tribal people conducted by the white and mestizo ruling classes. These are genocidal wars conducted to secure Indian land once and for all. The Mexican government is buying Black Hawk helicopters in preparation for the eradication of the Zapatistas after the August elections.

I blame the U.S. government—congressmen and senators and President Clinton. I blame Clinton most of all for playing the covert racism card marked "Immigration Policy." The elected officials, blinded by greed and ambition, show great disrespect to the electorate they represent. The people, the ordinary people in the street, evidence only a fraction of the racist behavior that is exhibited on a daily basis by the elected leaders of the United States and their sluttish handmaidens, the big television networks.

If we truly had a representative democracy in the United States, I do not think we would see such a shameful level of racism in this country. But, so long as huge amounts of money are necessary in order to run for office, we will not have a representative democracy. The form of government we have in the United States right now is not representative democracy but "big capitalism"; big capitalism can't survive for long in the United States unless the people are divided among themselves into warring factions. Big capitalism wants the people of the United States to blame "foreigners" for lost jobs and declining living standards so the people won't place the blame where it really belongs: with our corrupt U.S. Congress and president.

As I prepare to drive to New Mexico this week, I feel a prickle of anxiety down my spine. Only a few years ago, I used to travel the highways between Arizona and New Mexico with a wonderful sensation of absolute freedom as I cruised down the open road and across the vast desert plateaus in southern Arizona and southern New Mexico. We citizens of the United States grew up believing this freedom of the open road to be our inalienable right. The freedom of the open road meant we could travel freely from state to state without special papers or threat of detainment; this was a "right" citizens of Communist and totalitarian governments did not possess. That wide open highway was what told us we were U.S. citizens. Indeed, some say, this freedom to travel is an integral part of the American identity.

To deny this right to me, to some of us who because of skin color or other physical characteristics appear to fit fictional profiles of "undesirables," is to begin the inexorable slide into further government-mandated "race policies" that can only end in madness and genocide. The slaughters in Rwanda and Bosnia did not occur spontaneously—with neighbor butchering neighbor out of the blue; no, politicians and government officials called down these maelstroms of blood on their people by unleashing the terrible irrational force that racism is.

Take a drive down Interstate 8 or Interstate 10, along the U.S.–Mexico border. Notice the Border Patrol checkpoints all vehicles must pass through. When the Border Patrol agent asks you where you are coming from and where you are going, don't kid around and answer in Spanish—you could be there all afternoon. Look south into Mexico and enjoy the view while you are still able, before you find yourself behind the twelve-foot steel curtain the U.S. government is building.

Discussion Questions

1. Leslie Marmon Silko has organized her essay by beginning with her own experiences of racism, but she soon moves to a larger assessment of the role of the government and "big capitalism" in promoting and institutionalizing racism. Why has she begun this essay with personal stories about her family and her life? What does her use of personal anecdotes add to the essay? Did you like the mixture of personal and analytical styles? Why or why not?

2. Silko describes the difference between the Laguna people's approach to strangers and the racism she encountered in the outside world. What philosophy informed the Laguna people's treatment of strangers? How does Silko compare this philosophy later in the essay with the attitudes of civilians in the world outside the Pueblo and the behavior of the Border Patrol?

Writing Suggestions

1. Part of Silko's essay deals with the danger of traveling near the border of Mexico and the United States and with her experience of not feeling safe in the hands of the Border Patrol or the INS. Write a personal essay about a time when you traveled either in a foreign country or in America and felt out of your "comfort zone," whether due to discrimination, racism, or a sense of differentness from the people you were around. If you have had an experience with a border crossing, write an essay about that experience, especially considering your feelings at the point of crossing the border. Remember that a good personal essay will allow the audience to see, feel, hear, and imagine clearly your environment and the details of your experience, so be sure to use concrete details and strong verbs.
2. Watch the film *El Norte*, which came out in 1983 and was nominated for an Academy Award for Best Original Screenplay. Then write an essay in which you respond to the portrayal of the U.S. government's attitude toward illegal immigrants, referring also to Silko's essay as a basis for comparison. Consider some of the following questions in your paper:

    How did the film influence you?
    Did the film change your attitude toward illegal immigrants?
    Did the film (or Silko's essay) surprise you in the depiction of the INS?
    Would you consider the film a convincing argument or not?

Fresh off the Boat

An Immigrant's Tale

This article by an anonymous author appeared in the July 7, 2001 edition of *The Economist*. The writer, who has just received American citizenship, recounts the long, arduous, and ironic process of becoming a legal citizen.

Tired? Sometimes. Poor? Certainly. Huddled, homeless, or tempest-tossed? Not a bit. Your correspondent, a scrap of wretched refuse from the shores of India, became a citizen of the United States last month, alongside 1,500 other new citizens at a ceremony in San Francisco. Given the unexpectedly bizarre mingling of cant and ritual, it made more than practical sense that the event took place in the city's Masonic Centre.

The citizenship oath represents the culmination of a bleak obstacle course set by the Immigration and Naturalisation Service (INS). During the two years while your application is being processed, you have to send your fingerprints to the FBI, you are questioned on American history and asked to declare a willingness to serve in the American armed forces. On entering the hall, you have to state whether you have become a communist, a drunkard, a panderer or a wife-beater in the ten weeks since your last interview. (Deny everything; after the ceremony, head for Vegas.)

Once the oath has crossed your lips, though, the INS lays down the welcome mat with gusto. An opera singer, recently Chinese, is requisitioned from the crowd to sing the national anthem; a woman from Iraq (strongly emphasised by the master of ceremonies) is asked to recite the pledge of allegiance. Finally, in ringing tones, an official points out that as a newly minted citizen you can now sponsor the applications of your family members.

Despite the Kafkaesque delays created by INS bureaucracy, in 1993–2000 more than 6.9m immigrants applied for citizenship, a number that exceeds the total in the previous 40 years combined. Many of those are now trying to bring in their relatives. And on the very day when your correspondent was finally clasped to America's hunky breast, the House Judiciary Committee was fretting through a hearing on "guest" visas for Mexican workers.

There are now at least 5m illegal immigrants in America. Many of the participants in San Francisco were one once. One reason why America's immigration law is a mess is that illegal immigrants beget legal ones, both literally and figuratively. Most parts of the government try to fudge the differences between the two sorts. Welfare officials, for instance, scratch their heads over how to provide care to (legal) children but not their (illegal) parents.

But the INS's purpose is to maintain a sharp distinction between legal and illegal, and between citizen and "alien." Before the ceremony, you are brusquely handed yet another set of forms. After the oath, with beaming faces and irony-free applause, the same officials congratulate applicants whom they and their sort have tortured for years.

These muddled messages carry on right until the finish, when a local politician and former colonel bellows his advice on cultivating American values. The listeners receive his exhortations—to vote faithfully, attend church and seize opportunities—in respectful silence. That may be misleading. When your correspondent asked her neighbours for a pen, nobody understood English.

At the end the colonel issued what was perhaps the most basically American instruction of the lot: he told his audience to rise and greet the total stranger in the neighbouring seat. After a pregnant pause, sheepish handshakes and the occasional hug were traded, and the colonel beamed benevolently from the podium. He then bade his listeners to go forth and "engage with" their new country. He did not, as he might have done, bid them to go forth and multiply. But don't worry: we will.

Discussion Questions

1. What do you think the author's purpose is in telling this "immigrant's tale"? How would you describe her tone? Is she trying to make an argument? What do you think that argument is? Is she happy or not about becoming an American citizen? How does she use humor to bring out her points?

2. How does this author imply a comparison to the nineteenth-century immigration process? What similarities in attitude toward immigrants do you see in the experiences of recent immigrants and immigrants who came to America in the nineteenth century? Do you know of new changes to the process of immigration since the September 11 terrorist attacks?

Writing Suggestions

1. Consider the use of humor, colorful and concrete details, character descriptions, and quotations in this piece. Then write your own essay about a time when you felt you were in a situation that was somewhat serious, yet somehow ironic and silly, too. Describe the situation, use concrete details, and add interesting quotations to make the experience real for your readers. Be sure that you have one main feeling you want to convey to your audience, and drop your audience right into the action of the piece, as this author has done in the first paragraph of her story.

2. The author brings up the controversial issue of welfare assistance to illegal immigrant parents who have children who were born in the United States and are therefore citizens. She claims that "most parts of the government try to fudge the differences between the two sorts" of immigrants, so that they do not have to confront the legal and moral dilemmas of giving welfare assistance to children but not to their parents. Research the current immigration regulations about health and welfare benefits for illegal aliens. You can begin your search on Lexis Nexis Academic Universe, reading recent articles about welfare assistance for illegal immigrants, many of whom pay taxes. Write an informed opinion essay on this topic, answering the following questions: Do you think that the government agencies should help illegal aliens with benefits if they have children who are citizens? What if they do not have children who are citizens—should illegal aliens receive health and welfare benefits anyway? Why or why not?

A Different Mirror

A History of Multicultural America

RONALD TAKAKI

Ronald Takaki, professor of ethnic studies at the University of California, Berkeley, is the author of numerous books, including *Strangers from a Different Shore; Pau Hana: Plantation Life and Labor in Hawaii; Iron Cages; A Pro-Slavery Crusade;* and *Violence in the Black Imagination.* In his book *A Different Mirror: A History of Multicultural America,* Takaki writes that he has chosen in this book to look closely at America's "racial and cultural diversity—Native Americans as well as peoples from different 'points of departure' such as England, Africa, Ireland, Mexico, Asia, and Russia." In this selection, taken from *A Different Mirror,* Takaki reflects on the history of race relations in America, and urges us to consider American multiculturalism through a "different mirror," a mirror that reflects all of the many races and peoples who make up the American identity.

I had flown from San Francisco to Norfolk and was riding in a taxi to my hotel to attend a conference on multiculturalism. Hundreds of educators from across the country were meeting to discuss the need for greater cultural diversity in the curriculum. My driver and I chatted about the weather and the tourists. The sky was cloudy, and Virginia Beach was twenty minutes away. The rearview mirror reflected a white man in his forties. "How long have you been in this country?" he asked. "All my life," I replied, wincing. "I was born in the United States." With a strong southern drawl, he remarked, "I was wondering because your English is excellent!" Then, as I had many times before, I explained: "My grandfather came here from Japan in the 1880s. My family has been here, in America, for over a hundred years." He glanced at me in the mirror. Somehow I did not look "American" to him; my eyes and complexion looked foreign.

Suddenly, we both became uncomfortably conscious of a racial divide separating us. An awkward silence turned my gaze from the mirror to the passing landscape, the shore where the English and the Powhatan Indians first encountered each other. Our highway was on land that Sir Walter Raleigh had renamed "Virginia" in honor of Elizabeth I, the virgin Queen. In the English cultural appropriation of America, the indigenous peoples themselves would become outsiders in their native land. Here, at the eastern edge of the continent, I mused, was the site of the beginning of multicultural America. Jamestown, the English settlement founded in 1607, was nearby: the first twenty Africans were brought here a year before the Pilgrims arrived at Plymouth Rock. Several hundred miles offshore was Bermuda, the "Bermoothes" where William Shakespeare's Prospero had landed and met the native Caliban in *The Tempest*. Earlier, another voyager had made an Atlantic crossing and unexpectedly bumped into some islands to the south. Thinking he had reached Asia, Christopher Columbus mistakenly identified one of the islands as "Cipango" (Japan). In the wake of the admiral, many peoples would come to America from different shores, not only from Europe but also Africa and Asia. One of them would be my grandfather. My mental wandering across terrain and time ended abruptly as we arrived at my destination. I said good-bye to my driver and went into the hotel, carrying a vivid reminder of why I was attending this conference.

Questions like the one my taxi driver asked me are always jarring, but I can understand why he could not see me as American. He had a narrow but widely shared sense of the past—a history that has viewed American as European in ancestry. "Race," Toni Morrison explained, has functioned as a "metaphor" necessary to the "construction of Americanness": in the creation of our national identity, "American" has been defined as "white."

But America has been racially diverse since our very beginning on the Virginia shore, and this reality is increasingly becoming visible and ubiquitous. Currently, one-third of the American people do not trace their origins to Europe; in California, minorities are fast becoming a majority. They already predominate in major cities across the country—New York, Chicago, Atlanta, Detroit, Philadelphia, San Francisco, and Los Angeles.

This emerging demographic diversity has raised fundamental questions about America's identity and culture. In 1990, *Time* published a cover story on "America's Changing Colors." "Someday soon," the magazine announced, "white Americans will become a minority group." How soon? By 2056, most Americans will trace their descent to "Africa, Asia, the Hispanic world, the Pacific Islands, Arabia—almost anywhere but white Europe." This dramatic change in our nation's ethnic composition is altering the way we think about ourselves. "The deeper significance of America's becoming a majority nonwhite society is what it means to the national psyche, to individuals' sense of themselves and their nation—their idea of what it is to be American."

Indeed, more than ever before, as we approach the time when whites become a minority, many of us are perplexed about our national identity and our future as one people. This uncertainty has provoked Allan Bloom to reaffirm the preeminence of Western civilization. Author of *The Closing of the American Mind*, he has emerged as a leader of an intellectual backlash against cultural diversity. In his view, students entering the university are "uncivilized," and the university has the responsibility to "civilize" them. Bloom claims he knows what their "hungers" are and "what they can digest." Eating is one of his favorite metaphors. Noting the "large black presence" in major universities, he laments the "one failure" in race relations—black students have proven to be "indigestible." They do not "melt as have *all* other groups." The problem, he contends, is that "blacks have become blacks": they have become "ethnic." This separatism has been reinforced by an academic permissiveness that has befouled the curriculum with "Black Studies" along with "Learn Another Culture." The only solution, Bloom insists, is "the good old Great Books approach."

Similarly, E. D. Hirsch worries that America is becoming a "tower of Babel," and that this multiplicity of cultures is threatening to rend our social fabric. He, too, longs for a more cohesive culture and a more homogeneous America: "If we *had* to make a choice between the *one* and the *many*, most Americans would choose the principle of unity, since we cannot function as a nation without it." The way to correct this fragmentization, Hirsch argues, is to acculturate "disadvantaged children." What do they need to know? "Only by accumulating shared symbols, and the shared information that symbols represent," Hirsch answers, "can we learn to communicate effectively with one another in our national community." Though he concedes the value of multicultural education, he quickly dismisses it by insisting that it "should not be allowed to supplant or interfere with our schools' responsibility to ensure our children's mastery of American literate culture." In *Cultural Literacy: What Every American Needs to Know*, Hirsch offers a long list of terms that excludes much of the history of minority groups.

While Bloom and Hirsch are reacting defensively to what they regard as a vexatious balkanization of America, many other educators are responding to our diversity as an opportunity to open American minds. In 1990, the Task Force on Minorities for New York emphasized the importance of a culturally diverse education. "Essentially," the *New York Times* commented, "the issue is how to deal with both dimensions of the nation's motto: 'E pluribus unum'— 'Out of many, one.'" Universities from New Hampshire to Berkeley have established American cultural diversity graduation requirements. "Every student needs to know," explained University of Wisconsin's chancellor Donna Shalala, "much more about the origins and history of the particular cultures which, as Americans, we will encounter during our lives." Even the University of Minnesota, located in a state that is 98 percent white, requires its students to take ethnic studies courses. Asked why multiculturalism is so important, Dean Fred Lukermann answered: As a national university, Minnesota has to offer a national curriculum—one that includes all of the peoples of America. He added that after graduation many students move to cities like Chicago and Los Angeles and thus need to know about racial diversity. Moreover, many educators stress, multiculturalism has an intellectual purpose. By allowing us to see events from the viewpoints of different groups, a multicultural curriculum enables us to reach toward a more comprehensive understanding of American history.

What is fueling this debate over our national identity and the content of our curriculum is America's intensifying racial crisis. The alarming signs and symptoms seem to be everywhere—the killing of Vincent Chin in Detroit, the black boycott of a Korean grocery store in Flatbush, the hysteria in Boston over the Carol Stuart murder, the battle between white sportsmen and Indians over tribal fishing rights in Wisconsin, the Jewish–black clashes in Brooklyn's Crown Heights, the black–Hispanic competition for jobs and educational resources in Dallas, which *Newsweek* described as "a conflict of the have-nots," and the Willie Horton campaign commercials, which widened the divide between the suburbs and the inner cities.

This reality of racial tension rudely woke America like a fire bell in the night on April 29, 1992. Immediately after four Los Angeles police officers were found not guilty of brutality against Rodney King, rage exploded in Los Angeles. Race relations reached a new nadir. During the nightmarish rampage, scores of people were killed, over two thousand injured, twelve thousand arrested, and almost a billion dollars' worth of property destroyed. The live televised images mesmerized America. The rioting and the murderous melee on the streets resembled the fighting in Beirut and the West Bank. The thousands of fires burning out of control and the dark smoke filling the skies brought back images of the burning oil fields of Kuwait during Desert Storm. Entire sections of Los Angeles looked like a bombed city. "Is this America?" many shocked viewers asked. "Please, can we get along here," pleaded Rodney King, calling for calm. "We all can get along. I mean, we're all stuck here for a while. Let's try to work it out."

But how should "we" be defined? Who are the people "stuck here" in America? One of the lessons of the Los Angeles explosion is the recognition of the fact that we are a multiracial society and that race can no longer be defined in the binary terms of white and black. "We" will have to include Hispanics and Asians. While blacks currently constitute 13 percent of the Los Angeles population, Hispanics represent 40 percent. The 1990 census revealed that South Central Los Angeles, which was predominantly black in 1965 when the Watts rebellion occurred, is now 45 percent Hispanic. A majority of the first 5,438 people arrested were Hispanic, while 37 percent were black. Of the fifty-eight people who died in the riot, more than a third were Hispanic, and about 40 percent of the businesses destroyed were Hispanic-owned. Most of the other shops and stores were Korean-owned. The dreams of many Korean immigrants went up in smoke during the riot: two thousand Korean-owned businesses were damaged or demolished, totaling about $400 million in losses. There is evidence indicating they were targeted. "After all," explained a black gang member, "we didn't burn our community, just *their* stores."

"I don't feel like I'm in America anymore," said Denisse Bustamente as she watched the police protecting the firefighters. "I feel like I am far away." Indeed, Americans have been witnessing ethnic strife erupting around the world—the rise of neo-Nazism and the murder of Turks in Germany, the ugly "ethnic cleansing" in Bosnia, the terrible and bloody clashes between Muslims and Hindus in India. Is the situation here different, we have been nervously wondering, or do ethnic conflicts elsewhere represent a prologue for America? What is the nature of malevolence? Is there a deep, perhaps primordial, need for group identity rooted in hatred for the other? Is ethnic pluralism possible for America? But answers have been limited. Television reports have been little more than thirty-second sound bites. Newspaper articles have been mostly superficial descriptions of racial antagonisms and the current urban malaise. What is lacking is historical context; consequently, we are left feeling bewildered.

How did we get to this point, Americans everywhere are anxiously asking. What does our diversity mean, and where is it leading us? *How* do we work it out in the post–Rodney King era?

Certainly one crucial way is for our society's various ethnic groups to develop a greater understanding of each other. For example, how can African Americans and Korean Americans work it out unless they learn about each other's cultures, histories, and also economic situations? This need to share knowledge about our ethnic diversity has acquired new importance and has given new urgency to the pursuit for a more accurate history.

More than ever before, there is a growing realization that the established scholarship has tended to define America too narrowly. For example, in his prize-winning study *The Uprooted*, Harvard historian Oscar Handlin presented—to use the book's subtitle—"the Epic Story of the Great Migrations That Made the American People." But Handlin's "epic story" excluded the "uprooted" from Africa, Asia, and Latin America—the other "Great Migrations" that also helped to make "the American People." Similarly, in *The Age of Jackson*, Arthur M. Schlesinger, Jr., left out blacks and Indians. There is not even a mention of two marker events—the Nat Turner insurrection and Indian removal, which Andrew Jackson himself would have been surprised to find omitted from a history of his era.

Still, Schlesinger and Handlin offered us a refreshing revisionism, paving the way for the study of common people rather than princes and presidents. They inspired the next generation of historians to examine groups such as the artisan laborers of Philadelphia and the Irish immigrants of Boston. "Once I thought to write a history of the immigrants in America," Handlin confided in his introduction to *The Uprooted*. "I discovered that the immigrants *were* American history." This door, once opened, led to the flowering of a more inclusive scholarship as we began to recognize that ethnic history was American history. Suddenly, there was a proliferation of seminal works such as Irving Howe's *World of Our Fathers: The Journey of the East European Jews to America*, Dee Brown's *Bury My Heart at Wounded Knee: An Indian History of the American West*, Albert Camarillo's *Chicanos in a Changing Society*, Lawrence Levine's *Black Culture and Black Consciousness*, Yuji Ichioka's *The Issei: The World of the First Generation Japanese Immigrants*, and Kerby Miller's *Emigrants and Exiles: Ireland and the Irish Exodus to North America*.

But even this new scholarship, while it has given us a more expanded understanding of the mosaic called America, does not address our needs in the post–Rodney King era. These books and others like them fragment American society, studying each group separately, in isolation from the other groups and the whole. While scrutinizing our specific pieces, we have to step back in order to see the rich and complex portrait they compose. What is needed is a fresh angle, a study of the American past from a comparative perspective.

While all of America's many groups cannot be covered in one book, the English immigrants and their descendants require attention, for they possessed inordinate power to define American culture and make public policy. What men like John Winthrop, Thomas Jefferson, and Andrew Jackson thought as well as did mattered greatly to all of us and was consequential for everyone. A broad range of groups has been selected: African Americans, Asian Americans, Chicanos, Irish, Jews, and Indians. While together they help to explain general patterns in our society, each has contributed to the making of the United States.

African Americans have been the central minority throughout our country's history. They were initially brought here on a slave ship in 1619. Actually, these first twenty Africans might not have been slaves; rather, like most of the white laborers, they were probably indentured servants. The transformation of Africans into slaves is the story of the "hidden" origins of slavery. How and when was it decided to institute a system of bonded black labor? What happened, while freighted with racial significance, was actually conditioned by class conflicts within white society. Once established, the "peculiar institution" would have consequences for centuries to come. During the nineteenth century, the political storm over slavery almost destroyed the nation. Since the Civil War and emancipation, race has continued to be largely defined in relation to African Americans—segregation, civil rights, the underclass, and affirmative action. Constituting the largest minority group in our society, they have been at the cutting edge of the Civil Rights Movement. Indeed, their struggle has been a constant reminder of America's moral vision as a country committed to the principle of liberty. Martin Luther King clearly understood this truth when he wrote from a jail cell: "We will reach the goal of freedom in Birmingham and all over the nation, because the goal of America is freedom. Abused and scorned though we may be, our destiny is tied up with America's destiny."

Asian Americans have been here for over one hundred and fifty years, before many European immigrant groups. But as "strangers" coming from a "different shore," they have been stereotyped as "heathen," exotic, and unassimilable. Seeking "Gold Mountain," the Chinese arrived first, and what happened to them influenced the reception of the Japanese, Koreans, Filipinos, and Asian Indians as well as the Southeast Asian refugees like the Vietnamese and the Hmong. The 1882 Chinese Exclusion Act was the first law that prohibited the entry of immigrants on the basis of nationality. The Chinese condemned this restriction as racist and tyrannical. "They call us 'Chink,'" complained a Chinese immigrant, cursing the "white demons." "They think we no good! America cuts us off. No more come now, too bad!" This precedent later provided a basis for the restriction of European immigrant groups such as Italians, Russians, Poles, and Greeks. The Japanese painfully discovered that their accomplishments in America did not lead to acceptance, for during World War II, unlike Italian Americans and German Americans, they were placed in internment camps. Two-thirds of them were citizens by birth. "How could I as a six-month-old child born in this country," asked Congressman Robert Matsui years later, "be declared by my own Government to be an enemy alien?" Today, Asian Americans represent the fastest-growing ethnic group. They have also become the focus of much mass media attention as "the Model Minority" not only for black and Chicanos, but also for whites on welfare and even middle-class whites experiencing economic difficulties.

Chicanos represent the largest group among the Hispanic population, which is projected to outnumber African Americans. They have been in the United States for a long time, initially incorporated by the war against Mexico. The treaty had moved the border between the two countries, and the people of "occupied" Mexico suddenly found themselves "foreigners" in their "native land." As historian Albert Camarillo pointed out, the Chicano past is an integral part of America's westward expansion, also known as "manifest destiny." But while the early Chicanos were a colonized people, most of them today have immigrant roots. Many began the trek to El Norte in the early twentieth century. "As I had heard a lot about the United States," Jesus Garza recalled, "it was my dream to come here." "We came to know families from Chihuahua, Sonora, Jalisco, and Durango," stated Ernesto Galarza. "Like ourselves, our Mexican neighbors had come this far moving step by step, working and waiting, as if they were feeling their way up a ladder." Nevertheless, the Chicano experience has been unique, for most of them have lived close to their homeland—a proximity that has helped reinforce their language, identity, and culture. This migration to El Norte has continued to the present. Los Angeles has more people of Mexican origin than any other city in the world, except Mexico City. A mostly mestizo people of Indian as well as African and Spanish ancestries, Chicanos currently represent the largest minority group in the Southwest, where they have been visibly transforming culture and society.

The Irish came here in greater numbers than most immigrant groups. Their history has been tied to America's past from the very beginning. Ireland represented the earliest English frontier: the conquest of Ireland occurred before the colonization of America, and the Irish were the first group that the English called "savages." In this context, the Irish past foreshadowed the Indian future. During the nineteenth century, the Irish, like the Chinese, were victims of British colonialism. While the Chinese fled from the ravages of the Opium Wars, the Irish were pushed from their homeland by "English tyranny." Here they became construction workers and factory operatives as well as the "maids" of America. Representing a Catholic group seeking to settle in a fiercely Protestant society, the Irish immigrants were targets of American nativist hostility. They were also what historian Lawrence J. McCaffrey called "the pioneers of the American urban ghetto," "previewing" experiences that would later be shared by the Italians, Poles, and other groups from southern and eastern Europe. Furthermore, they offer contrast to the immigrants from Asia. The Irish came about the same time as the Chinese, but they had a distinct advantage: the Naturalization Law of 1790 had reserved citizenship for "whites" only. Their compatible complexion allowed them to assimilate by blending into American society. In making their journey successfully into the mainstream, however, these immigrants from Erin pursued an Irish "ethnic" strategy: they promoted "Irish" solidarity in order to gain political power and also to dominate the skilled blue-collar occupations, often at the expense of the Chinese and blacks.

Fleeing pogroms and religious persecution in Russia, the Jews were driven from what John Cuddihy described as the "Middle Ages into the Anglo-American world of the *goyim* 'beyond the pale.'" To them, America represented the Promised Land. This vision led Jews to struggle not only for themselves but also for other oppressed groups, especially blacks. After the 1917 East St. Louis race riot, the Yiddish *Forward* of New York compared this anti-black violence to a 1903 pogrom in Russia: "Kishinev and St. Louis—the same soil, the same people." Jews cheered when Jackie Robinson broke into the Brooklyn Dodgers in 1947. "He was adopted as the surrogate hero by many of us growing up at the time," recalled Jack Greenberg of the NAACP Legal Defense Fund. "He was the way we saw ourselves triumphing against the forces of bigotry and ignorance." Jews stood shoulder to shoulder with blacks in the Civil Rights Movement: two-thirds of the white volunteers who went south during the 1964 Freedom Summer were Jewish. Today Jews are considered a highly successful "ethnic" group. How did they make such great socioeconomic strides? This question is often reframed by neoconservative intellectuals like Irving Kristol and Nathan Glazer to read: if Jewish immigrants were able to lift themselves from poverty into the mainstream through self-help and education without welfare and affirmative action, why can't blacks? But what this thinking overlooks is the unique history of Jewish immigrants, especially the initial advantages of many of them as literate and skilled. Moreover, it minimizes the virulence of racial prejudice rooted in American slavery.

Indians represent a critical contrast, for theirs was not an immigrant experience. The Wampanoags were on the shore as the first English strangers arrived in what would be called "New England." The encounters between Indians and whites not only shaped the course of race relations, but also influenced the very culture and identity of the general society. The architect of Indian removal, President Andrew Jackson told Congress: "Our conduct toward these people is deeply interesting to the national character." Frederick Jackson Turner understood the meaning of this observation when he identified the frontier as our transforming crucible. At first, the European newcomers had to wear Indian moccasins and shout the war cry. "Little by little," as they subdued the wilderness, the pioneers became "a new product" that was "American." But Indians have had a different view of this entire process. "The white man," Luther Standing Bear of the Sioux explained, "does not understand the Indian for the reason that he does not understand America." Continuing to be "troubled with primitive fears," he has "in his consciousness the perils of this frontier continent. . . . The man from Europe is still a foreigner and an alien. And he still hates the man who questioned his path across the continent." Indians questioned what Jackson and Turner trumpeted as "progress." For them, the frontier had a different "significance": their history was how the West was lost. But their story has also been one of resistance. As Vine Deloria declared, "Custer died for your sins."

By looking at these groups from a multicultural perspective, we can comparatively analyze their experiences in order to develop an understanding of their differences and similarities. Race, we will see, has been a social construction that has historically set apart racial minorities from European immigrant groups. Contrary to the notions of scholars like Nathan Glazer and Thomas Sowell, race in America has not been the same as ethnicity. A broad comparative focus also allows us to see how the varied experiences of different racial and ethnic groups occurred within shared contexts.

During the nineteenth century, for example, the Market Revolution employed Irish immigrant laborers in New England factories as it expanded cotton fields worked by enslaved blacks across Indian lands toward Mexico. Like blacks, the Irish newcomers were stereotyped as "savages," ruled by passions rather than "civilized" virtues such as self-control and hard work. The Irish saw themselves as the "slaves" of British oppressors, and during a visit to Ireland in the 1840s, Frederick Douglass found that the "wailing notes" of the Irish ballads reminded him of the "wild notes" of slave songs. The U.S. annexation of California, while incorporating Mexicans, led to trade with Asia and the migration of "strangers" from Pacific shores. In 1870, Chinese immigrant laborers were transported to Massachusetts as scabs to break an Irish immigrant strike; in response, the Irish recognized the need for interethnic working-class solidarity and tried to organize a Chinese lodge of the Knight of St. Crispin. After the Civil War, Mississippi planters recruited Chinese immigrants to discipline the newly freed blacks. During the debate over an immigration exclusion bill in 1882, a senator asked: If Indians could be located on reservations, why not the Chinese?

Other instances of our connectedness abound. In 1903, Mexican and Japanese farm laborers went on strike together in California: their union officers had names like Yamaguchi and Lizarras, and strike meetings were conducted in Japanese and Spanish. The Mexican strikers declared that they were standing in solidarity with their "Japanese brothers" because the two groups had toiled together in the fields and were now fighting together for a fair wage. Speaking in impassioned Yiddish during the 1909 "uprising of twenty thousand" strikers in New York, the charismatic Clara Lemlich compared the abuse of Jewish female garment workers to the experience of blacks: "[The bosses] yell at the girls and 'call them down' even worse than I imagine the Negro slaves were in the South." During the 1920s, elite universities like Harvard worried about the increasing number of Jewish students, and new admissions criteria were instituted to curb their enrollment. Jewish students were scorned for their studiousness and criticized for their "clannishness." Recently, Asian-American students have been the targets of similar complaints: they have been called "nerds" and told there are "too many" of them on campus.

Indians were already here, while blacks were forcibly transported to America, and Mexicans were initially enclosed by America's expanding border. The other groups came here as immigrants: for them, America represented liminality—a new world where they could pursue extravagant urges and do things they had thought beyond their capabilities. Like the land itself, they found themselves "betwixt and between all fixed points of classification." No longer fastened as fiercely to their old countries, they felt a stirring to become new people in a society still being defined and formed.

These immigrants made bold and dangerous crossings, pushed by political events and economic hardships in their homelands and pulled by America's demand for labor as well as by their own dreams for a better life. "By all means let me go to America," a young man in Japan begged his parents. He had calculated that in one year as a laborer here he could save almost a thousand yen—an amount equal to the income of a governor in Japan. "My dear Father," wrote an immigrant Irish girl living in New York, "Any man or woman without a family are fools that would not venture and come to this plentiful Country where no man or woman ever hungered." In the shtetls of Russia, the cry "To America!" roared like "wild-fire." "America was in everybody's mouth," a Jewish immigrant recalled. "Businessmen talked [about] it over their accounts; the market women made up their quarrels that they might discuss it from stall to stall; people who had relatives in the famous land went around reading their letters." Similarly, for Mexican immigrants crossing the border in the early twentieth century, El Norte became the stuff of overblown hopes. "If only you could see how nice the United States is," they said, "that is why the Mexicans are crazy about it."

The signs of America's ethnic diversity can be discerned across the continent—Ellis Island, Angel Island, Chinatown, Harlem, South Boston, the Lower East Side, places with Spanish names like Los Angeles and San Antonio or Indian names like Massachusetts and Iowa. Much of what is familiar in America's cultural landscape actually has ethnic origins. The Bing cherry was developed by and early Chinese immigrant named Ah Bing. American Indians were cultivating corn, tomatoes, and tobacco long before the arrival of Colombus. The term *okay* was derived from the Choctaw word *oke*, meaning "it is so." There is evidence indicating that the name *Yankee* came from Indian terms for the English—from *eankke* in Cherokee and *Yankwis* in Delaware. Jazz and blues as well as rock and roll have African American origins. The "Forty-Niners" of the Gold Rush learned mining techniques from the Mexicans; American cowboys acquired herding skills from Mexican *vaqueros* and adopted their range terms—such as *lariat* from *la reata*, *lasso* from *lazo*, and *stampede* from *estampida*. Songs like "God Bless America," "Easter Parade," and "White Christmas" were written by a Russian-Jewish immigrant named Israel Baline, more popularly known as Irving Berlin.

Furthermore, many diverse ethnic groups have contributed to the building of the American economy, forming what Walt Whitman saluted as "a vast, surging, hopeful army of workers." They worked in the South's cotton fields, New England's textile mills, Hawaii's canefields, New York's garment factories, California's orchards, Washington's salmon canneries, and Arizona's copper mines. They built the railroad, the great symbol of America's industrial triumph. Laying railroad ties, black laborers sang:

> Down the railroad, um-hum
> Well, raise the iron, um-huh
> Raise the iron, um-huh

Irish railroad workers shouted as they stretched an iron ribbon across the continent:

> Then drill, my Paddies, drill—
> Drill, my heroes, drill,
> Drill all day, no sugar in your tay
> Workin' on the U.P. railway.

Japanese laborers in the Northwest chorused as their bodies fought the fickle weather:

> A railroad worker—
> That's me!
> I am great.
> Yes, I am a railroad worker.
> Complaining:
> "It is too hot!"
> "It is too cold!"
> "It rains too often!"
> "It snows too much!"
> They all ran off,
> I alone remained.
> I am a railroad worker!

Chicano workers in the Southwest joined in as they swore at the punishing work:

> Some unloaded rails
> Others unloaded ties,
> And others of my companions
> Threw out thousands of curses.

Moreover, our diversity was tied to America's most serious crisis: the Civil War was fought over a racial issue—slavery. In his "First Inaugural Address," presented on March 4, 1861, President Abraham Lincoln declared: "One section of our country believes slavery is *right* and ought to be extended, while the other believes it is *wrong* and ought not to be extended." Southern secession, he argued, would be anarchy. Lincoln sternly warned the South that he had a solemn oath to defend and preserve the Union. Americans were one people, he explained, bound together by "the mystic chords of memory, stretching from every battlefield and patriot grave to every living heart and hearthstone all over this broad land." The struggle and sacrifices of the War for Independence had enabled Americans to create a new nation out of thirteen separate colonies. But Lincoln's appeal for unity fell on deaf ears in the South. And the war came. Two and a half years later, at Gettysburg, President Lincoln declared that "brave men" had fought and "consecrated" the ground of this battlefield in order to preserve the Union. Among the brave were black men. Shortly after this bloody battle, Lincoln acknowledged the military contribution of blacks. "There will be some black men," he wrote in a letter to an old friend, James C. Conkling, "who can remember that with silent tongue, and clenched teeth, and steady eye, and well-poised bayonet, they have helped mankind on to this great consummation. . . ." Indeed, 186,000 blacks served in the Union Army, and one-third of them were listed as missing or dead. Black men in blue, Frederick Douglass pointed out, were "on the battlefield mingling their blood with that of white men in one common effort to save the country." Now the mystic chords of memory stretched across the new battlefields of the Civil War, and black soldiers were buried in "patriot graves." They, too, had given their lives to ensure that the "government of the people, by the people, for the people shall not perish from the earth."

Like these black soldiers, the people in our study have been actors in history, not merely victims of discrimination and exploitation. They are entitled to be viewed as subjects—as men and women with minds, wills, and voices.

> In the telling and retelling
>   of their stories,
> They create communities
>   of memory.

They also re-vision history. "It is very natural that the history written by the victim," said a Mexican in 1874, "does not altogether chime with the story of the victor." Sometimes they are hesitant to speak, thinking they are only "little people." "I don't know why anybody wants to hear my history," an Irish maid said apologetically in 1900. "Nothing ever happened to me worth the tellin'."

But their stories are worthy. Through their stories, the people who have lived America's history can help all of us, including my taxi driver, understand that Americans originated from many shores, and that all of us are entitled to dignity. "I hope this survey do a lot of good for Chinese people," an immigrant told an interviewer from Stanford University in the 1920s. "Make American people realize that Chinese people are humans. I think very few American people really know anything about Chinese." But the remembering is also for the sake of the children. "This story is dedicated to the descendants of Lazar and Goldie Glauberman," Jewish immigrant Minnie Miller wrote in her autobiography. "My history is bound up in their history and the generations that follow should know where they came from to know better who they are." Similarly, Tomo Shoji, an elderly Nisei woman, urged Asian Americans to learn more about their roots: "We got such good, fantastic stories to tell. All our stories are different." Seeking to know how they fit into America, many young people have become listeners; they are eager to learn about the hardships and humiliations experienced by their parents and grandparents. They want to hear their stories, unwilling to remain ignorant or ashamed of their identity and past.

The telling of stories liberates. By writing about the people on Mango Street, Sandra Cisneros explained, "the ghost does not ache so much." The place no longer holds her with "both arms. She sets me free." Indeed, stories may not be as innocent or simple as they seem to be. Native American novelist Leslie Marmon Silko cautioned:

> I will tell you something about stories . . .
> They aren't just entertainment.
> 　　Don't be fooled.

Indeed, the accounts given by the people in this study vibrantly re-create moments, capturing the complexities of human emotions and thoughts. They also provide the authenticity of experience. After she escaped from slavery, Harriet Jacobs wrote in her autobiography: "[My purpose] is not to tell what I have heard but what I have seen—and what I have suffered." In their sharing of memory, the people in this study offer us an opportunity to see ourselves reflected in a mirror called history.

In his recent study of Spain and the New World, *The Buried Mirror*, Carlos Fuentes points out that mirrors have been found in the tombs of ancient Mexico, placed there to guide the dead through the underworld. He also tells us about the legend of Quetzalcoatl, the Plumed Serpent: when this god was given a mirror by the Toltec deity Tezcatlipoca, he saw a man's face in the mirror and realized his own humanity. For us, the "mirror" of history can guide the living and also help us recognize who we have been and hence are. In *A Distant Mirror*, Barbara W. Tuchman finds "phenomenal parallels" between the "calamitous 14th century" of European society and our own era. We can, she observes, have "greater fellow-feeling for a distraught age" as we painfully recognize the "similar disarray," "collapsing assumptions," and "unusual discomfort."

But what is needed in our own perplexing times is not so much a "distant" mirror, as one that is "different." While the study of the past can provide collective self-knowledge, it often reflects the scholar's particular perspective or view of the world. What happens when historians leave out many of America's peoples? What happens, to borrow the words of Adrienne Rich, "when someone with the authority of a teacher" describes our society, and "you are not in it"? Such an experience can be disorienting—"a moment of psychic disequilibrium, as if you looked into a mirror and saw nothing."

Through their narratives about their lives and circumstances, the people of America's diverse groups are able to see themselves and each other in our common past. They celebrate what Ishmael Reed has described as a society "unique" in the world because "the world is here"—a place "where the cultures of the world crisscross." Much of America's past, they point out, has been riddled with racism. At the same time, these people offer hope, affirming the struggle for equality as a central theme in our country's history. At its conception, our nation was dedicated to the proposition of equality. What has given concreteness to this powerful national principle has been our coming together in the creation of a new society. "Stuck here" together, workers of different backgrounds have attempted to get along with each other.

People harvesting
Work together unaware
Of racial problems,

wrote a Japanese immigrant describing a lesson learned by Mexican and Asian farm laborers in California.

Finally, how do we see our prospects for "working out" America's racial crisis? Do we see it as through a glass darkly? Do the televised images of racial hatred and violence that riveted us in 1992 during the days of rage in Los Angeles frame a future of divisive race relations—what Arthur Schlesinger, Jr., has fearfully denounced as the "disuniting of America"? Or will Americans of diverse races and ethnicities be able to connect themselves to a larger narrative? Whatever happens, we can be certain that much of our society's future will be influenced by which "mirror" we choose to see ourselves. America does not belong to one race or one group, the people in this study remind us, and Americans have been constantly redefining their national identity from the moment of first contact on the Virginia shore. By sharing their stories, they invite us to see ourselves in a different mirror.

Discussion Questions

1. Discuss Takaki's central argument that we need to look at history through a "different mirror," a mirror that reflects the way in which "Americans have been constantly redefining their national identity from the moment

of first contact on the Virginia shore." How does this metaphor differ from a metaphor that describes America as a "melting pot"? Why does Takaki consider it so important to listen to and study the stories that show how "Americans originated from many shores"?

2. In this selection, Takaki includes stories from Irish Americans, Chinese Americans, Japanese Americans, African Americans, and other racial groups. Read some of the primary sources presented earlier in this book, such as the selections by Sojourner Truth (Chapter 4), Luther Standing Bear (Chapter 2), and the Powhatan Nation (Chapter 1). Do you agree with Takaki that these stories all help to create a clearer sense of the variety of American population? Do these stories support Takaki's point? Why or why not?

Writing Suggestions

1. One of the arguments Takaki makes in his book is that "the established scholarship has tended to define America too narrowly," and that recent revisionist historians are beginning to examine a larger variety of people who have helped to write American history. Write an argument paper in which you respond to Takaki's call for a comparative analysis "to develop an understanding" of the "differences and similarities" of these groups. Outline which stories and voices should be included in American textbooks. Do you feel that historical and literary texts about America should include the stories of the many different groups Takaki refers to? If so, how would you encourage writers to change textbooks for high school students, for example? If not, argue for a more compact and less multicultural representation of the American experience. You can use your own experiences with college and high school texts as a basis for your argument.

2. Takaki discusses the way that the English language reflects the ethnic diversity of American society. Research the impact of one or two languages from different ethnic groups on "Standard English" words. Discuss not only the roots of these words but also what they tell us about American society. For example, Takaki explains that "American cowboys acquired herding skills from Mexican vaqueros and adopted their range terms— such as *lariat* from *la reata*, *lasso* from *lazo*, and *stampede* from *estampida*." In this example, you might research the interrelationship between Mexican and American cowboys, and explain the historical and cultural background that led to the integration of the Spanish words. You can use the Oxford English dictionary to find the roots of many words, and you can also research this topic by looking in libraries for books about the origins of the English language.

Black Men and Public Space

BRENT STAPLES

Brent Staples grew up in Chester, Pennsylvania, where he saw first-hand the effects of street violence, drug dealing, and gang violence. Staples's younger brother was a drug dealer who was shot to death at the age of twenty-two; this incident, in part, caused Staples to "remain a shadow—timid, but a survivor," as he writes in "Black Men and Public Space," an essay that was published first in *Ms. Magazine* in 1986 and later in *Harper's Magazine* in revised form. Staples went to Widener University as an undergraduate, completing his studies in 1973. He then went on to study at the University of Chicago, where he received a Ph.D. in psychology in 1982. He worked as a reporter at the *Chicago Sun Times* and then the *New York Times*. In 1994 he published a memoir about his life in Chester, *Parallel Time: Growing Up in Black and White*. In the essay that follows, "Black Men and Public Space," Staples writes about his sudden awareness, at the age of twenty-two, of "the lethality nighttime pedestrians attributed" to him, and he discusses the effects of "being ever the suspect."

My first victim was a woman—white, well dressed, probably in her early twenties. I came upon her late one evening on a deserted street in Hyde Park, a relatively affluent neighborhood in an otherwise mean, impoverished section of Chicago. As I swung onto the avenue behind her, there seemed to be a discreet, uninflammatory distance between us. Not so. She cast back a worried glance. To her, the youngish black man—a broad six feet two inches with a beard and billowing hair, both hands shoved into the pockets of a bulky military jacket—seemed menacingly close. After a few more quick glimpses, she picked up her pace and was soon running in earnest. Within seconds she disappeared into a cross street.

That was more than a decade ago, I was twenty-two years old, a graduate student newly arrived at the University of Chicago. It was in the echo of that terrified woman's footfalls that I first began to know the unwieldy inheritance I'd come into—the ability to alter public space in ugly ways. It was clear that she thought herself the quarry of a mugger, a rapist, or worse. Suffering a bout of insomnia, however, I was stalking sleep, not defenseless wayfarers. As a softy who is scarcely able to take a knife to a raw chicken—let alone hold one to a person's throat—I was surprised, embarrassed, and dismayed all at once. Her flight made me feel like an accomplice in tyranny. It also made it clear that I was indistinguishable from the muggers who occasionally seeped into the area from the surrounding ghetto. That first encounter, and those that followed, signified that a vast, unnerving gulf lay between night-time pedestrians—particularly women—and me. And I soon gathered that being perceived as dangerous is a hazard in itself. I only needed to turn a corner into a dicey situation, or crowd some frightened, armed person in a foyer somewhere, or make an errant move after being pulled over by a policeman. Where fear and weapons meet—and they often do in urban America—there is always the possibility of death.

In that first year, my first away from my hometown, I was to become thoroughly familiar with the language of fear. At dark, shadowy intersections, I could cross in front of a car stopped at a traffic light and elicit the *thunk, thunk, thunk, thunk* of the driver—black, white, male, or female—hammering down the door locks. On less traveled streets after dark, I grew accustomed to but never comfortable with people crossing to the other side of the street rather than pass me. Then there were the standard unpleasantries with policemen, doormen, bouncers, cabdrivers, and others whose business it is to screen out troublesome individuals *before* there is any nastiness.

I moved to New York nearly two years ago and I have remained an avid night walker. In central Manhattan, the near-constant crowd cover minimizes tense one-on-one street encounter. Elsewhere—in SoHo, for example, where sidewalks are narrow and tightly spaced buildings shut out the sky—things can get very taut indeed.

After dark, on the warrenlike streets of Brooklyn where I live, I often see women who fear the worst from me. They seem to have set their faces on neutral, and with their purse straps strung across their chests bandolier-style, they forge ahead as though bracing themselves against being tackled. I understand, of course, that the danger they perceive is not a hallucination. Women are particularly vulnerable to street violence, and young black males are drastically overrepresented among the perpetrators of that violence. Yet these truths are no solace against the kind of alienation that comes of being ever the suspect, a fearsome entity with whom pedestrians avoid making eye contact.

It is not altogether clear to me how I reached the ripe old age of twenty-two without being conscious of the lethality nighttime pedestrians attributed to me. Perhaps it was because in Chester, Pennsylvania, the small, angry industrial town where I came of age in the 1960s, I was scarcely noticeable against a backdrop of gang warfare, street knifings, and murders. I grew up one of the good boys, had perhaps a half-dozen fistfights. In retrospect, my shyness of combat has clear sources.

As a boy, I saw countless tough guys locked away; I have since buried several, too. They were babies, really—a teenage cousin, a brother of twenty-two, a childhood friend in his mid-twenties—all gone down in episodes of bravado played out in the streets. I came to doubt the virtues of intimidation early on. I chose, perhaps unconsciously, to remain a shadow—timid, but a survivor.

The fearsomeness mistakenly attributed to me in public places often has a perilous flavor. The most frightening of these confusions occurred in the late 1970s and early 1980s, when I worked as a journalist in Chicago. One day, rushing into the office of a magazine I was writing for with a deadline story in hand, I was mistaken for a burglar. The office manager called security and, with an ad hoc posse, pursued me through the labyrinthine halls, nearly to my editor's door. I had no way of proving who I was. I could only move briskly toward the company of someone who knew me.

Another time I was on assignment for a local paper and killing time before an interview. I entered a jewelry store on the city's affluent Near North Side. The proprietor excused herself and returned with an enormous red Doberman pinscher straining at the end of a leash. She stood, the dog extended toward me, silent to my questions, her eyes bulging nearly out of her head. I took a cursory look around, nodded, and bade her good night.

Relatively speaking, however, I never fared as badly as another black male journalist. He went to nearby Waukegan, Illinois, a couple of summers ago to work on a story about a murderer who was born there. Mistaking the reporter for the killer, police officers hauled him from his car at gunpoint and but for his press credentials would probably have tried to book him. Such episodes are not uncommon. Black men trade tales like this all the time.

Over the years, I learned to smother the rage I felt at so often being taken for a criminal. Not to do so would surely have led to madness. I now take precautions to make myself less threatening. I move about with care, particularly late in the evening. I give a wide berth to nervous people on subway platforms during the wee hours, particularly when I have exchanged business clothes for jeans. If I happen to be entering a building behind some people who appear skittish, I may walk by, letting them clear the lobby before I return, so as not to seem to be following them. I have been calm and extremely congenial on those rare occasions when I've been pulled over by the police.

And on late-evening constitutionals I employ what has proved to be an excellent tension-reducing measure: I whistle melodies from Beethoven and Vivaldi and the more popular classical composers. Even steely New Yorkers hunching toward nighttime destinations seem to relax, and occasionally they even join in the tune. Virtually everybody seems to sense that a mugger wouldn't be warbling bright, sunny selections from Vivaldi's *Four Seasons*. It is my equivalent of the cowbell that hikers wear when they know they are in bear country.

Discussion Questions

1. Staples mentions in his essay that both black and white drivers lock their doors when he walks by their cars, and he also concedes that "young black males are drastically overrepresented among the perpetrators of

... violence." Given that the purpose of this essay is not to blame those who are afraid of him, what do you think Staples wants his audience to understand from this piece? What is the purpose of this essay and who is his intended audience? Why did he include the idea of "public space" in both his title and his essay? What did you learn from Staples's essay?

2. Discuss Staples's experience in light of Martin Luther King, Jr.'s essay, "I Have a Dream" (Chapter 8), considering the changes the civil rights movement tried to make in the lives of blacks, women, and other minorities. Does Staples's essay make King's dream seem hopeless, or are there positive signs of progress for blacks in this essay, too? Which details show some improvement in the lives of blacks since the Civil Rights movement began? How does the end of the piece change the tone and the impact of the essay?

Writing Suggestions

1. Write a personal essay about a time you felt threatened by a stranger who meant you no harm, or about a time when you felt that you inadvertently frightened someone else just by your presence. Discuss your feelings of fear and your attempts to cope with that fear, or your feelings when you realized that you were the cause of another's fear. Was race an element of your fear or not? What did you learn from that experience? How did you resolve the tension of that moment? How would you handle the situation differently if you could do it all over again? Would you change your responses or respond in the same way?

2. Staples points out in his essay that "black men trade tales" of being mistaken for criminals. Research the current problem of "racial profiling" by police who stop and search the cars of people of color more often than those of white people. You can read newspaper or magazine articles about this problem, searching the index of magazines, the *Los Angeles Times*, the *New York Times*, or Academic Universe under the term "racial profiling." Then write an editorial about racial profiling, agreeing or disagreeing with the statements of the many law officers who claim that they need the freedom to stop and search anyone they perceive as a threat to public safety, whether that person has committed any crime or not. In your paper, discuss whether or not you feel that stopping these drivers is in violation of their rights, and be specific in your reasons for supporting or condemning this practice.

Ashes

PHILLIP LOPATE

Phillip Lopate is a well-known New York writer and the Adams Professor of the Humanities at Hofstra University. Lopate is also the recipient of Guggenheim and National Endowment for the Arts fellowships and has published two novels in addition to his collections of essays. Lopate wrote the essay below for inclusion in a New York City Web site entitled *Mr. Beller's Neighborhood*, a site conceived before September 11 by writer Thomas Beller, who wanted to create an Internet site where people from all walks of life could post essays about living and working in New York, a site that could provide "a venue for pieces with no pitch, no angle." After September 11, Beller writes that "stories and accounts began to pour in," and that the site became another kind of memorial to those who had died in the September 11 terrorist attacks. Phillip Lopate's essay "Ashes" is now published in the 2002 book version of the Web site essays, entitled *Mr. Beller's Neighborhood, Before and After Stories from New York*. In the essay that follows, Lopate describes his personal response to the tragedy, and details some of his emotions and thoughts in the days directly following the attacks.

Sackett St., Brooklyn

My first inkling of an attack on the Twin Towers came from the Fed Ex man delivering a packet. He rang the doorbell around 9:15, and when I started to sign for it, he said, shaken, "Did you hear what happened? A plane crashed into the World Trade Center. You can see the black smoke from here." Indeed, looking down Sackett Street toward the river on that infamously sunny day, I did see a plume of grayish black cloud at the end of my block. My first response was So what? Planes do crash. I went inside, the phone rang and it was my mother-in-law, telling me to turn on the television. My mother-in-law is something of TV addict, especially if bad weather threatens; she'll keep the tube on day and night to track a rainstorm.

I had been looking forward to writing all day, now that my seven-year-old daughter Lily was back in school, and so I said rather testily that I couldn't turn the television on now, and hung up.

But something urgent in her voice disturbed me, and so, against my practice, I did put on the television, and saw the footage of the second plane crashing into the World Trade Center. Now I was gripped, shocked, queasy, realized something unprecedented was happening. Still, I wandered by habit over to my desktop computer, and tried to punch in a few sentences for my book about the New York waterfront. Maybe because I have been so fixated on this subject, I began to think this horrifying event was directly connected to the geography of the waterfront: Manhattan's slender, lozenge shape, surrounded by rivers, made it easier for the hijacking pilots to hug the shore and spot the towers. My concentration, needless to say, was poor but I resisted giving myself up entirely to this (so it yet seemed) public event. I am the kind of person who can write, and does, as a consoling escape from anxiety, in the midst of carpenters or other distractions. Around 10:30 I had the television turned on in my office when my wife Cheryl called me from Lily's Montessori class and said she was sticking around the school, in case they decided to close it. I replied—the resolve had suddenly formed in me, I needed to be out in the streets—that I was going for a walk down by the waterfront, to see what I could. "Why don't you stop by the school afterwards, and look in on us?" she asked. I said I doubted I would, not adding that suddenly I felt a sharp urge to be alone.

The tragedy had registered on me, exactly the same way as after my mother had died: a pain in the gut, the urge to walk and walk through the city, and a don't-touch-me reflex, *noli me tangere*. I made my way down to Columbia Street, which feeds into the Brooklyn Promenade: the closer I got to the waterfront, the harder it was to breathe. The smoke was blowing directly across the East River, into Brooklyn. There were not many people on Columbia Street, but most of those I passed had surgical masks on (I wondered if they got them from nearby Long island Community Hospital). I was choking, without a mask. Cinders and poisonous-smelling smoke thickened the air, and ash fell like snowflakes on the parked cars and on one's clothing, constantly.

It was exactly what I had imagined war to be like. An Arabic-looking delivery man had pulled over and was talking worriedly into a cell phone. It was two hours after the attack, and you could no longer make out the Manhattan skyline, all you could see was a billowing black cloud. Later, my wife told me she had actually glimpsed the top of one of the Twin Towers in flames. I found myself envying everyone who had actually witnessed the buildings on fire or collapsing. Of course I had no one to blame but myself, having secreted myself indoors for the first few hours. I can't imagine running into Manhattan to get a closer look, but I should have gone up to my roof and looked. At the moment it didn't occur to me; I was terrified. Now I saw thousands of people on foot crossing over the bridges into downtown Brooklyn. When I reached Atlantic Avenue I turned east, away from the water, and began to encounter hordes of office workers, released early from their jobs. Not all of them seemed upset; there was a sort of holiday mood, in patches, of unexpected free time. Some younger people behind me, two men and a woman in their twenties, were even laughing as they recounted to each other the morning's events, how they had been stopped on their way out of the subway. The middle-aged and elderly, on the other hand, seemed profoundly disturbed. They had not expected anything so terrible as an attack on America to happen in the last quarter of their lives. Just as there is something unseemly when a young person dies, so the natural order of things seems wronged when the elderly, braced for their own diminishment, illness and death, must absorb the bitter, shocking knowledge of how vulnerable and perishable their society is—the world they had expected to outlast them. I myself felt, at only fifty-eight, that the attack was a personal affront to one's proper autobiographical arc, as though a messy and unnecessarily complicated subplot had been introduced too late in the narrative.

I went by the Arab shops and cafes on Atlantic Avenue, wondering foolishly if I would detect any mood of celebration. In fact, many of the Arab-owned stores had taken the precaution to close for the day; in several of the shops left open, the proprietors had retreated to the back room. To the degree that expressions among the Brooklyn-Islamic community could be made out, they looked grim, no one was wreathed in smiles, though I did not rule out the possibility that some were rejoicing inwardly. All at once, I wanted to be with my family. My cocoa-colored shirt was flecked with white ash, like residual bird shit, when I turned into the Brooklyn Heights Montessori School. The lobby was crowded with parents, many picking up their children to take them home. School seemed as safe a place for Lily to be as our house; I saw no reason to take her out prematurely. My wife, Cheryl, was standing by the door of the multipurpose room, waiting for Lily to exit with her class. They were on their way to or from dance. Lily seemed happily surprised to see me in midday; I hugged her. She trooped off to her next activity. Cheryl milled around with the mothers and some of the fathers returning from the financial district; they were all comparing accounts, and engaging in that compulsively repetitious dialogue by which an enormity is made real.

A few days later, my wife reproached me for having shown up with ash-laden clothing, the shirttails left outside my pants; she said I could have frightened the children. I said I did not think anyone noticed me. But on some level, her reproach was justified: I was indulging the fantasy that I was invisible, not being a team player. Some sort of communal bonding was taking place, foreign to me, beautiful in many respects, scary in others.

My wife and I both felt anguished all week, but it was an anguish we could not share. The fault was mine: selfishly, I wanted to nurse my grief at what had been done to my city. I mistrusted any attempt to co-opt me into group-think, even conjugal-think.

Later that day, I went with two friends to give blood. These two gentlemen, Kent Jones and James Harvey, both fine film critics who live in my neighborhood, met me on the corner of Sackett and Henry Streets and we walked toward the hospital together. James Harvey is in his seventies, a veteran of World War II, and I expected him to have a special insight into the attack, to compare it to Pearl Harbor, say, but he just shook his head and said this was different. When we arrived at the blood donor station we were turned away; apparently so many people had volunteered that the medical technicians had run out of blood bags. (As the city learned in the days that followed, we had been optimistic in thinking that that many wounded could be pulled from the wreckage and would need transfusions.) Kent, James and I repaired to the Harvest Café, which was unusually crowded with diners. The owner and waiters seemed harried, forgetting to give us silverware. The TV was on, the volume turned so loud that it was difficult to talk. Normally, when these friends and I get together, the conversation flows, we have endless things to say; but this time we could derive no nourishment from each other's company.

Our language had dried up. Embarrassed, being writers, to say the obvious, we said little. Kent kept consulting his cell phone. James held his head and stared at the floor. I turned around and looked up at the self-same television which I resented being on in the first place, yet was hypnotized by.

When I got home, my wife was glued to the television. Uneasy about joining her in this electronic vigil, yet feeling I had no choice, nothing else mattered, I joined her. Our daughter said, "Why do you keep watching that? They just keep saying the same things. We know that already. Two planes crashed into the building." Blasé, not at all traumatized, Lily, the customary center of our universe, was annoyed that her parents were not paying attention to her. She was right: there was something punitive about the same information, the same pictures, over and over. I realize that this has become our modern therapy in catastrophic events, the hope that by immersing ourselves in the news media, its thoughtful anchorpersons and interviews with pundits, by the numbing effect of repetition if nothing else, we will work through our grief. But for me it doesn't work: I get a kind of sugar buzz and feel nauseous afterwards.

The first day there was a bit more unexpected quality, especially shots of people running away from the explosion, stampeding, the camera flailing about. The footage's amateurism seemed to signal its authenticity. In succeeding days, I felt sickened by the slick, unending interviews with relatives of missing persons and back-stories about the victims, the same technique used for coverage of the Olympics, now applied to this Olympics of Thanatos. We must not forget the politicians' parade, their eloquence and competence inversely proportionate to their office. Most impressive was the local mayor, Rudy Giuliani, who seemed always to know what he was talking about; then came New York State's Governor Pataki, who graciously deferred to the mayor; Senator Hilary Clinton, who blustered unconvincingly, all the way up to President Bush, whose bellicosity and syntactical tentativeness embarrassed all educated liberals like myself. Most incredible were the efforts of the President to say kind things about New York, a city which he and the country at large have so often mistrusted and disliked.

That this was primarily an attack on New York I had no doubt. I feel so identified with my native city that it took a mental wrenching to understand all of America considered itself a target. I knew the Pentagon had been hit as well, but the attack on a low-rise, suburban military complex did not seem as significant, as humanly interesting. Urbanism, density, verticality, secular humanism, skepticism, popular culture, mass transit, commerce, these were the threatened values, in my view. The American flags that started appearing everywhere seemed to me entirely fitting, especially if they were taken to honor the heroic local firemen and police who died trying to rescue victims. But if they were a nationalistic statement about America as the greatest nation, then, no, I could not join that sentiment. The only banner I wanted to fly from our brownstone window was the orange, green and white flag of New York City, with its clumsy Dutchman and beaver.

All the talk in the media that we were attacked because we were a free nation, and the terrorists who went after us hated freedom, frankly, disgusted me. Why could we not accept that an awful thing had happened to us without patting ourselves on the back and asserting it was a sign of our superior virtue? Awful things happened in the Iran-Iraq war, terrorist attacks, germ warfare, and neither country was a beacon of freedom. Awful things happened to Afghanistan.

It was quickly established that the plane hijackings had been done by Osama bin Laden's followers, and were intended in part as chastisement for the U.S. support of Israel. As a Jew, I felt hot, exposed, implicated, frightened by the re-approach of anti-Semitism; I felt angry at the fundamentalist Muslim terrorists, even as I knew the majority of Muslims would condemn the slaughter; I felt angry at the Israeli government for all their past rigidities and missed opportunities, and especially at the Sharon-Netanyahu faction for having the audacity to gloat, "Now you know the pain we live under;" I felt angry at Arafat and the Palestinian people for not having accepted the concessions offered by Ehud Barat, however inadequate, and gone on to build something better from there; and I felt angry at the United States for having supported and grown bin Laden, the Taliban and Saddam Hussein as anti-Communist forces. Confused and chagrined as my thinking was, the one thing I felt sure, with thousands of innocent people blown apart, was that I did not want to hear the old argument of my radical-left friends: "When you are an oppressed people fighting a hegemonic power like the United States, you have to use the means at your disposal, and 'terrorism' is merely a label the American Empire applies to its opponents."

To be honest, we did not hear that argument, though one of my friends smugly quoted Malcolm X: "The chickens have come home to roost." People claim that New York will be changed forever by this attack. It is easy to say that, less easy to understand exactly how. A few days after September 11th, I noticed subway riders being unnaturally polite to each other, whether out of greater communal solidarity and respect for human life, or more wariness of the Other's potential rage, I am unable to say. No New Yorker expects the rest of America's warm feelings toward the city to last very long; it is like getting licked by a large, forgetful St. Bernard dog. Meanwhile, the towers that had anchored lower Manhattan are gone, pfft. I ask myself how I will be changed personally. On the morning of September 12

I awoke and remembered immediately what had happened, like a murderer returning to the horror of his altered moral life. I sensed I would never be the same. I have never bought the idea that suffering ennobles people. Rather, I expect that this dreadful experience will add to the scar tissue left by other atrocities of life, like the death of one's parents, the illness of one's children, or the shame of one's nation (My Lai), sorrows over which one has no control but that cause, for all that, the deepest regrets.

Discussion Questions

1. Lopate writes that he felt so "identified with [his] native city that it took a mental wrenching to realize all of America considered itself a target." Discuss this idea with your peers—how did September 11 impact New Yorkers differently from the way it impacted those who live in the Midwest, the South, or the West? How did you react in your part of the country?

2. How does being Jewish factor into Lopate's feelings? How does he include his prejudices in this essay, while at the same time candidly acknowledging his own misperceptions?

3. What did reading this primary source essay add to your understanding of the experience of September 11 in New York? How does this primary source offer information that a secondary source could not?

Writing Suggestions

1. Most Americans will always remember where they were when they learned of the terrorist attacks on September 11. Write a personal essay in which you detail how you heard about the attacks, how you reacted, what feelings and emotions you experienced, and what you did on that day. Use specific details and concrete images to help us understand your feelings and experiences.

2. Lopate describes his feelings about the American flags that appeared all over New York City, stating that "they were entirely fitting, especially if they were taken to honor the local firemen and police." However, he writes that if the flags "were a nationalistic statement about America as the greatest nation, then no, I could not join that sentiment." Write a response to Lopate, expressing your feelings about the flying of flags that took place all over America. Did you and your friends or family fly a flag? Why or why not? What did flying the flag mean to you—what did the flag represent? How do you respond to Lopate's statement?

Address to a Joint Session of Congress and the American People

GEORGE W. BUSH

George W. Bush, 43rd president of the United States, was elected to the White House in 2000 after serving as governor of Texas. Bush received a B.A. from Yale University and an M.B.A. from Harvard Business School. After serving in the Texas Air National Guard, he worked in the oil and gas industry from 1975 to 1986. In 1989 he went on to be the managing general partner of the Texas Rangers baseball team until he won the election for governor of Texas in 1994. In office for less than a year before the terrorist attacks of September 11, Bush was charged with the task of addressing a Congress and nation stunned by the realization that America was not invulnerable to foreign attacks on domestic soil. Bush's *Address to a Joint Session of Congress and the American People* (September 20, 2001) was hailed by some as his most powerful and unifying address, while others criticized the speech as inflammatory and jingoistic.

United States Capitol
Washington, D.C.
September 20, 2001

Mr. Speaker, Mr. President Pro Tempore, members of Congress, and fellow Americans:

In the normal course of events, Presidents come to this chamber to report on the state of the Union. Tonight, no such report is needed. It has already been delivered by the American people.

We have seen it in the courage of passengers, who rushed terrorists to save others on the ground—passengers like an exceptional man named Todd Beamer. And would you please help me to welcome his wife, Lisa Beamer, here tonight.

We have seen the state of our Union in the endurance of rescuers, working past exhaustion. We have seen the unfurling of flags, the lighting of candles, the giving of blood, the saying of prayers—in English, Hebrew, and Arabic. We have seen the decency of a loving and giving people who have made the grief of strangers their own.

My fellow citizens, for the last nine days, the entire world has seen for itself the state of our Union—and it is strong.

Tonight we are a country awakened to danger and called to defend freedom. Our grief has turned to anger, and anger to resolution. Whether we bring our enemies to justice, or bring justice to our enemies, justice will be done.

I thank the Congress for its leadership at such an important time. All of America was touched on the evening of the tragedy to see Republicans and Democrats joined together on the steps of this Capitol, singing "God Bless America." And you did more than sing; you acted, by delivering $40 billion to rebuild our communities and meet the needs of our military.

Speaker Hastert, Minority Leader Gephardt, Majority Leader Daschle and Senator Lott, I thank you for your friendship, for your leadership and for your service to our country.

And on behalf of the American people, I thank the world for its outpouring of support. America will never forget the sounds of our National Anthem playing at Buckingham Palace, on the streets of Paris, and at Berlin's Brandenburg Gate.

We will not forget South Korean children gathering to pray outside our embassy in Seoul, or the prayers of sympathy offered at a mosque in Cairo. We will not forget moments of silence and days of mourning in Australia and Africa and Latin America.

Nor will we forget the citizens of 80 other nations who died with our own: dozens of Pakistanis; more than 130 Israelis; more than 250 citizens of India; men and women from El Salvador, Iran, Mexico and Japan; and hundreds of British citizens. America has no truer friend than Great Britain. Once again, we are joined together in a great cause—so honored the British Prime Minister has crossed an ocean to show his unity of purpose with America. Thank you for coming, friend.

On September the 11th, enemies of freedom committed an act of war against our country. Americans have known wars—but for the past 136 years, they have been wars on foreign soil, except for one Sunday in 1941. Americans have known the casualties of war—but not at the center of a great city on a peaceful morning. Americans have known surprise attacks—but never before on thousands of civilians. All of this was brought upon us in a single day—and night fell on a different world, a world where freedom itself is under attack.

Americans have many questions tonight. Americans are asking: Who attacked our country? The evidence we have gathered all points to a collection of loosely affiliated terrorist organizations known as al Qaeda. They are the same murderers indicted for bombing American embassies in Tanzania and Kenya, and responsible for bombing the USS Cole.

Al Qaeda is to terror what the mafia is to crime. But its goal is not making money; its goal is remaking the world—and imposing its radical beliefs on people everywhere.

The terrorists practice a fringe form of Islamic extremism that has been rejected by Muslim scholars and the vast majority of Muslim clerics—a fringe movement that perverts the peaceful teachings of Islam. The terrorists' directive commands them to kill Christians and Jews, to kill all Americans, and make no distinction among military and civilians, including women and children.

This group and its leader—a person named Osama bin Laden—are linked to many other organizations in different countries, including the Egyptian

Islamic Jihad and the Islamic Movement of Uzbekistan. There are thousands of these terrorists in more than 60 countries. They are recruited from their own nations and neighborhoods and brought to camps in places like Afghanistan, where they are trained in the tactics of terror. They are sent back to their homes or sent to hide in countries around the world to plot evil and destruction.

The leadership of al Qaeda has great influence in Afghanistan and supports the Taliban regime in controlling most of that country. In Afghanistan, we see al Qaeda's vision for the world.

Afghanistan's people have been brutalized—many are starving and many have fled. Women are not allowed to attend school. You can be jailed for owning a television. Religion can be practiced only as their leaders dictate. A man can be jailed in Afghanistan if his beard is not long enough.

The United States respects the people of Afghanistan—after all, we are currently its largest source of humanitarian aid—but we condemn the Taliban regime. It is not only repressing its own people, it is threatening people everywhere by sponsoring and sheltering and supplying terrorists. By aiding and abetting murder, the Taliban regime is committing murder.

And tonight, the United States of America makes the following demands on the Taliban: Deliver to United States authorities all the leaders of al Qaeda who hide in your land. Release all foreign nationals, including American citizens, you have unjustly imprisoned. Protect foreign journalists, diplomats and aid workers in your country. Close immediately and permanently every terrorist training camp in Afghanistan, and hand over every terrorist, and every person in their support structure, to appropriate authorities. Give the United States full access to terrorist training camps, so we can make sure they are no longer operating.

These demands are not open to negotiation or discussion. The Taliban must act, and act immediately. They will hand over the terrorists, or they will share in their fate.

I also want to speak tonight directly to Muslims throughout the world. We respect your faith. It's practiced freely by many millions of Americans, and by millions more in countries that America counts as friends. Its teachings are good and peaceful, and those who commit evil in the name of Allah blaspheme the name of Allah. The terrorists are traitors to their own faith, trying, in effect, to hijack Islam itself. The enemy of America is not our many Muslim friends; it is not our many Arab friends. Our enemy is a radical network of terrorists, and every government that supports them.

Our war on terror begins with al Qaeda, but it does not end there. It will not end until every terrorist group of global reach has been found, stopped and defeated.

Americans are asking, why do they hate us? They hate what we see right here in this chamber—a democratically elected government. Their leaders are self-appointed. They hate our freedoms—our freedom of religion, our freedom of speech, our freedom to vote and assemble and disagree with each other.

They want to overthrow existing governments in many Muslim countries, such as Egypt, Saudi Arabia, and Jordan. They want to drive Israel out of the Middle East. They want to drive Christians and Jews out of vast regions of Asia and Africa.

These terrorists kill not merely to end lives, but to disrupt and end a way of life. With every atrocity, they hope that America grows fearful, retreating from the world and forsaking our friends. They stand against us, because we stand in their way.

We are not deceived by their pretenses to piety. We have seen their kind before. They are the heirs of all the murderous ideologies of the 20th century. By sacrificing human life to serve their radical visions—by abandoning every value except the will to power—they follow in the path of fascism, and Nazism, and totalitarianism. And they will follow that path all the way, to where it ends: in history's unmarked grave of discarded lies.

Americans are asking: How will we fight and win this war? We will direct every resource at our command—every means of diplomacy, every tool of intelligence, every instrument of law enforcement, every financial influence, and every necessary weapon of war—to the disruption and to the defeat of the global terror network.

This war will not be like the war against Iraq a decade ago, with a decisive liberation of territory and a swift conclusion. It will not look like the air war above Kosovo two years ago, where no ground troops were used and not a single American was lost in combat.

Our response involves far more than instant retaliation and isolated strikes. Americans should not expect one battle, but a lengthy campaign, unlike any other we have ever seen. It may include dramatic strikes, visible on TV, and covert operations, secret even in success. We will starve terrorists of funding, turn them one against another, drive them from place to place, until there is no refuge or no rest. And we will pursue nations that provide aid or safe haven to terrorism. Every nation, in every region, now has a decision to make. Either you are with us, or you are with the terrorists. From this day forward, any nation that continues to harbor or support terrorism will be regarded by the United States as a hostile regime.

Our nation has been put on notice: We are not immune from attack. We will take defensive measures against terrorism to protect Americans. Today, dozens of federal departments and agencies, as well as state and local governments, have responsibilities affecting homeland security. These efforts must be coordinated at the highest level. So tonight I announce the creation of a Cabinet-level position reporting directly to me—the Office of Homeland Security.

And tonight I also announce a distinguished American to lead this effort, to strengthen American security: a military veteran, an effective governor, a true patriot, a trusted friend—Pennsylvania's Tom Ridge. He will lead, oversee and coordinate a comprehensive national strategy to safeguard our country against terrorism, and respond to any attacks that may come.

These measures are essential. But the only way to defeat terrorism as a threat to our way of life is to stop it, eliminate it, and destroy it where it grows.

Many will be involved in this effort, from FBI agents to intelligence operatives to the reservists we have called to active duty. All deserve our thanks, and all have our prayers. And tonight, a few miles from the damaged Pentagon, I have a message for our military: Be ready. I've called the Armed Forces to alert, and there is a reason. The hour is coming when America will act, and you will make us proud.

This is not, however, just America's fight. And what is at stake is not just America's freedom. This is the world's fight. This is civilization's fight. This is the fight of all who believe in progress and pluralism, tolerance and freedom.

We ask every nation to join us. We will ask, and we will need, the help of police forces, intelligence services, and banking systems around the world. The United States is grateful that many nations and many international organizations have already responded—with sympathy and with support. Nations from Latin America, to Asia, to Africa, to Europe, to the Islamic world. Perhaps the NATO Charter reflects best the attitude of the world: An attack on one is an attack on all.

The civilized world is rallying to America's side. They understand that if this terror goes unpunished, their own cities, their own citizens may be next. Terror, unanswered, can not only bring down buildings, it can threaten the stability of legitimate governments. And you know what—we're not going to allow it.

Americans are asking: What is expected of us? I ask you to live your lives, and hug your children. I know many citizens have fears tonight, and I ask you to be calm and resolute, even in the face of a continuing threat.

I ask you to uphold the values of America, and remember why so many have come here. We are in a fight for our principles, and our first responsibility is to live by them. No one should be singled out for unfair treatment or unkind words because of their ethnic background or religious faith.

I ask you to continue to support the victims of this tragedy with your contributions. Those who want to give can go to a central source of information, libertyunites.org, to find the names of groups providing direct help in New York, Pennsylvania, and Virginia.

The thousands of FBI agents who are now at work in this investigation may need your cooperation, and I ask you to give it.

I ask for your patience, with the delays and inconveniences that may accompany tighter security; and for your patience in what will be a long struggle.

I ask your continued participation and confidence in the American economy. Terrorists attacked a symbol of American prosperity. They did not touch its source. America is successful because of the hard work, and creativity, and enterprise of our people. These were the true strengths of our economy before September 11th, and they are our strengths today.

And, finally, please continue praying for the victims of terror and their families, for those in uniform, and for our great country. Prayer has comforted us in sorrow, and will help strengthen us for the journey ahead.

Tonight I thank my fellow Americans for what you have already done and for what you will do. And ladies and gentlemen of the Congress, I thank you, their representatives, for what you have already done and for what we will do together.

Tonight, we face new and sudden national challenges. We will come together to improve air safety, to dramatically expand the number of air marshals on domestic flights, and take new measures to prevent hijacking. We will come together to promote stability and keep our airlines flying, with direct assistance during this emergency.

We will come together to give law enforcement the additional tools it needs to track down terror here at home. We will come together to strengthen our intelligence capabilities to know the plans of terrorists before they act, and find them before they strike.

We will come together to take active steps that strengthen America's economy, and put our people back to work.

Tonight we welcome two leaders who embody the extraordinary spirit of all New Yorkers: Governor George Pataki, and Mayor Rudolph Giuliani. As a symbol of America's resolve, my administration will work with Congress, and these two leaders, to show the world that we will rebuild New York City.

After all that has just passed—all the lives taken, and all the possibilities and hopes that died with them—it is natural to wonder if America's future is one of fear. Some speak of an age of terror. I know there are struggles ahead, and dangers to face. But this country will define our times, not be defined by them. As long as the United States of America is determined and strong, this will not be an age of terror; this will be an age of liberty, here and across the world.

Great harm has been done to us. We have suffered great loss. And in our grief and anger we have found our mission and our moment. Freedom and fear are at war. The advance of human freedom—the great achievement of our time, and the great hope of every time—now depends on us. Our nation—this generation—will lift a dark threat of violence from our people and our future. We will rally the world to this cause by our efforts, by our courage. We will not tire, we will not falter, and we will not fail.

It is my hope that in the months and years ahead, life will return almost to normal. We'll go back to our lives and routines, and that is good. Even grief recedes with time and grace. But our resolve must not pass. Each of us will remember what happened that day, and to whom it happened. We'll remember the moment the news came—where we were and what we were doing. Some will remember an image of a fire, or a story of rescue. Some will carry memories of a face and a voice gone forever.

And I will carry this: It is the police shield of a man named George Howard, who died at the World Trade Center trying to save others. It was given to me by his mom, Arlene, as a proud memorial to her son. This is my reminder of lives that ended, and a task that does not end.

I will not forget this wound to our country or those who inflicted it. I will not yield; I will not rest; I will not relent in waging this struggle for freedom and security for the American people.

The course of this conflict is not known, yet its outcome is certain. Freedom and fear, justice and cruelty, have always been at war, and we know that God is not neutral between them.

Fellow citizens, we'll meet violence with patient justice—assured of the rightness of our cause, and confident of the victories to come. In all that lies before us, may God grant us wisdom, and may He watch over the United States of America.

Thank you.

Discussion Questions

1. Analyze and discuss the way Bush has structured his speech to appeal to a wide audience. How does he extend his audience past the Congress and the American people? Why does he extend his audience this way?
2. Consider Bush's use of symbols and concrete images—look through the speech and discuss how the diction and choice of imagery impacts the effectiveness of this address.
3. Did you find the speech powerful and unifying or overly-militaristic? Discuss with your peers your various responses to the speech.

Writing Suggestions

1. Bush's speech is a declaration of war on terrorism, although not a formal declaration of war against any one country. Write a comparison of this speech with Roosevelt's declaration of war after the Pearl Harbor attack (Chapter 7). How do these speeches parallel each other? What kinds of similarities in diction, imagery, structure, and appeal to emotion do you find? What are the major differences in the two speeches? Did you find one more effective than the other? Why or why not?
2. Write an essay about how this speech affected you personally, whether you saw it live on television or read it later. How did you feel about America and the war on terrorism after the speech? Did you find it to be moving, successful, militaristic, or comforting? Did you feel that Bush did a good job of uniting the country or not? Which elements do you think Bush should have added or left out? Why?

from *The New Yorker*

SUSAN SONTAG

Susan Sontag, born in 1933, is a well-known writer and critic who won the National Book Award in 2000 for her novel *In America*. Sontag became a formidable presence in the literary world in the 1960s, when she began to publish essays in magazines like *The Nation*, *Harper's Weekly*, and the *New York Review of Books*. She first published a collection of her essays in *Against Interpretation and Other Essays* (1968) and went on to publish *On Photography* (1977), *Illness as Metaphor* (1979), *Under the Sign of Saturn* (1980), and *Aids and Its Metaphors* (1988). Sontag is well known for her outspoken opinions and strong, critical voice, as illustrated by the essay below, which appeared in *The New Yorker* on September 24, 2001.

September 24, 2001

The disconnect between last Tuesday's monstrous dose of reality and the self-righteous drivel and outright deceptions being peddled by public figures and TV commentators is startling, depressing. The voices licensed to follow the event seem to have joined together in a campaign to infantilize the public. Where is the acknowledgement that this was not a "cowardly" attack on "civilization" or "liberty" or "humanity" or "the free world" but an attack on the world's self-proclaimed super-power, undertaken as a consequence of specific American alliances and actions? How many citizens are aware of the ongoing American bombing of Iraq? And if the word "cowardly" is to be used, it might be more aptly applied to those who kill from beyond the range of retaliation, high in the sky, than to those willing to die themselves in order to kill others. In the matter of courage (a morally neutral virtue): whatever may be said of the perpetrators of Tuesday's slaughter, they were not cowards.

Our leaders are bent on convincing us that everything is O.K. America is not afraid. Our spirit is unbroken, although this was a day that will live in infamy and America is now at war. But everything is not O.K. And this was not Pearl Harbor. We have a robotic president who assures us that America stands tall. A wide spectrum of public figures, in and out of office, who are strongly opposed to the policies being pursued abroad by this Administration apparently feel free to say nothing more than that they stand united behind President Bush. A lot of thinking needs to be done, and perhaps is being done in Washington and elsewhere, about the ineptitude of American intelligence and counter-intelligence, about options available to

American foreign policy, particularly in the Middle East, and about what constitutes a smart program of military defense. But the public is not being asked to bear much of the burden of reality. The unanimously applauded, self-congratulatory bromides of a Soviet Party Congress seemed contemptible. The unanimity of the sanctimonious, reality-concealing rhetoric spouted by American officials and media commentators in recent days seems, well, unworthy of a mature democracy.

Those in public office have let us know that they consider their task to be a manipulative one: confidence-building and grief management. Politics, the politics of a democracy—which entails disagreement, which promotes candor—has been replaced by psychotherapy. Let's by all means grieve together. But let's not be stupid together. A few shreds of historical awareness might help us to understand what has just happened, and what may continue to happen. "Our country is strong," we are told again and again. I for one don't find this entirely consoling. Who doubts that America is strong? But that's not all America has to be.

Discussion Questions

1. Sontag's language in this piece is particularly forceful. Make a list of her adjectives and verbs, and then discuss the impact on you, as a reader, of this language. Do you feel more or less drawn to her argument? Do you take what she has to say more or less seriously because of her language? Consider the variety of opinions and discuss with your peers your agreement or disagreement with Sontag's approach to argument.

2. When Sontag states that "strong" is not all that America has to be, what is she arguing for? How does she want America to be? Do you agree or disagree with her assessment of the "manipulative" task of "those in public office"?

Writing Suggestions

1. Review your answers to the second discussion question for this selection. Then write an analysis of Sontag's style—consider the impact of her language, descriptions, imagery, and sentence structure. Argue for or against her style as a persuasive piece—did the style sway you or alienate you? Use specific examples from her essay.

2. Write a personal response to Susan Sontag, as many readers did when her piece was published in *The New Yorker*. Using specific ideas and phrases, write an agreement or a rebuttal to Sontag's argument, and use specific details from current events to back up your point of view.

Editorial Cartoons

Although propaganda posters are no longer common in the United States, editorial cartoons remain an important genre of visual rhetoric in all major newspapers and magazines in America. Symbols, drawings, and in some cases, captions, capture the national experience and argue forcefully for the artists' own interpretation of events. Each year numerous awards, including a Pulitzer Prize, are awarded to cartoonists and, since 1973, Charles Brooks, past president of the Association of American Editorial Cartoonists, has edited the annual volume of *Best Editorial Cartoons of the Year*. The cartoons on the following pages, taken from the 2002 edition of *Best Editorial Cartoons of the Year*, are the work of cartoonists Joe Heller, Steve Lindstrom, Mike Thompson, Marty Riskin, and Rick McKee.

Joe Heller / Green Bay Press Gazette

Steve Lindstrom / Duluth News Tribune

Mike Thompson / Detroit Free Press

Marty Riskin / Georgetown Record

Rick McKee / Augusta Chronicle

Discussion Questions

1. Look closely at the political cartoons by Risken and McKee (page 805), which show the U.S. response to terrorism in two very different ways. Discuss the arguments implied in both cartoons—what caption would you place under each? What symbols does each artist use to convey his message? What emotions does each cartoon express? What commentary on conflict does each make?

2. Look back at the World War II posters in Chapter 7. Then compare the imagery from the post–September 11 Lindstrom (page 804) and McKee (page 805) cartoons in this chapter with the imagery found in the World War II posters. What kinds of similar imagery do you find? What differences do you notice? How do the appeals to patriotism differ, and how are they similar?

3. Discuss the cartoon by Mike Thompson (page 805) that appeared in the *Detroit Free Press*. What criticism of American society does it express? Do you agree or disagree with the sentiments of the cartoonist?

Writing Suggestions

1. Consider your answers to the second discussion question for this selection, and then write an argumentative essay explaining which cartoon you find more effective and why. Use specific details from each cartoon in your analysis, and explain how the images and captions work to deliver a political argument in the cartoon you prefer.

2. Design your own political cartoon, with captions and drawings, arguing your point of view about the current war on terrorism in the cartoon. Then write a one-page essay explaining why you chose the images and words you did to make your point. What were your strategies, and what were you trying to argue?

Chapter 9: Writing Suggestions

1. The opportunities for African Americans in American society have increased tremendously since Lincoln's emancipation of the slaves, but many African Americans are not entirely positive about the political, economic, and social possibilities for African Americans in America. Write a researched argument about one aspect of African American life in America today, looking for statistical, legal, and primary source materials to examine one of the following topics:

    The recent increase or decline of African American graduates from college, graduate school, law school, and medical school

    The per capita income of blacks compared to whites in America

    The ratio of blacks in jail to whites in jail

    The percentage of blacks with AIDS compared to whites with AIDS

    African American involvement in politics on state, local, and federal levels

    The status of African American families, marriages, and divorces

    In your paper, look for a positive or negative trend in these areas in the past twenty years, and argue your points with specific quotations and statistics. U.S. government statistics are available on the Internet at <http://www.census.gov> and you can also browse through recent articles on Academic Universe to get a feel for the most recent studies and statistics about African Americans in America.

2. Read Susan Faludi's selection in this chapter and Elizabeth Cady Stanton's selection in Chapter 6. Then write an essay in which you reflect on the current state of women's rights and relationships to men, using your personal opinions but responding to Faludi's and Stanton's assertions. Make a list of those points you wish to respond to in each essay, and then evaluate the current state of women's rights in relation to both essays. Quote specifically from Faludi and Stanton, and use personal anecdotes to back up your own opinions.

3. Consider the Treaty of Guadalupe Hidalgo (Chapter 3) and Richard White's and David G. Gutiérrez's essays (Chapter 5) about the treatment of Mexicans and Mexican Americans under the U.S. government. Write an essay in which you discuss the ways in which the previous history of Mexican immigrants and Mexican American citizens informs Silko's essay in this chapter. How does the material in the three previous selections add to your understanding of Silko's experiences? Which ideas are mirrored in all of the writings? How can you trace Silko's experiences with racism back to the Treaty of Guadalupe Hidalgo, the early treatment of Hispanics in California and the Southwest, and the attitude of the U.S. government toward Hispanics in the nineteenth century?

4. *Mr. Beller's Neighborhood* began not as a book but as a community Web site. Start your own class Web site, and post your own essays about your feelings and experiences on September 11 and in the months following.

5. Search the Internet for "Political Cartoons September 11" or "Editorial Cartoons September 11," and extend your study of visual rhetoric that you began with the editorial cartoons in this chapter. Look for cartoons published not only in the American media but also in foreign newspapers. Then write a comparison of the editorial cartoonists' interpretations of the terrorist attacks, George Bush's response, and the visual portrayal of September 11. Analyze the different arguments and emotions you find in at least five American editorial cartoons and five foreign editorial cartoons.

Chapter 9: Further Research on the Web

To pursue your research on the Internet, explore some of the following sites:

Minority Census Information and Minority Issues
www.census.gov/pubinfo/www/afamhot1.htm
http://www.inform.umd.edu/CampusInfo/Departments/PRES/PCEM1

Bureau of Labor Statistics
http://stats.bls.gov

Women's Rights
http://usinfo.state.gov/usa/womrts

Buffalo Bill Museum
http://www.bbhc.org
http://groups.colgate.edu/aarislam/response.htm#Editorialpiecesandarticles
http://www.thenation.com/special/wtc/index.mhtml
http://www.andover.edu/library/weblinks.htm

Political Cartoons
http://dailynews.yahoo.com/fc/US/Terrorism/political_cartoons.html

Credits

RONALD TAKAKI, "The 'Tempest' in the Wilderness," from *A Different Mirror: A History of Multicultural America*. Copyright © 1993 Ronald Takaki. Reprinted by permission of Little, Brown & Company, Inc.

RAYNA GREEN, "The Pocahontas Perplex: The Image of Indian Women in American Culture," from *The Massachusetts Review* 16, no. 4. Copyright © 1975 The Massachusetts Review. Reprinted by permission.

JACQUELYN KILPATRICK, "Disney's 'Politically Correct' Pocahontas," from *Cineaste Magazine*. Reprinted by permission.

CHIEF ROY CRAZY HORSE, Powhatan Nation Response, "The Pocahontas Myth," from <www.powhatan.org>. Reprinted by permission.

DAVID LEVIN, "Introduction" to *What Happened in Salem?* 2nd edition. Copyright © 1960. Reprinted by permission of a division of Thomson Learning. (Fax: 800-730-2215)

ELAINE G. BRESLAW, "The Reluctant Witch: Fueling Puritan Fantasies," from *Tituba, Reluctant Witch of Salem*. Copyright © 1996 New York University Press. Reprinted by permission.

RICHARD HOFSTADTER, "Black Slavery," from *America at 1750: A Social Portrait*. Copyright © 1971 by Beatrice Hofstadter. Reprinted by permission of Alfred A. Knopf, a division of Random House, Inc.

MICHAEL PAUL ROGIN, "Liberal Society and the Indian Question," from *Fathers and Children: Andrew Jackson and the Subjugation of the American Indian*. Copyright © 1975 by Michael Paul Rogin. Reprinted by permission.

FREDERICK W. TURNER III, Introduction to *I Have Spoken: American History through the Voices of the Indians* by Virginia Irving Armstrong. Copyright © 1981 by Virginia Irving Armstrong. Introduction © 1971 by Frederick W. Turner III. Athens, OH: Swallow Press. Reprinted by permission.

LUTHER STANDING BEAR, "What the Indian Means to America," from *Land of the Spotted Eagle*. Copyright © 1933 Houghton Mifflin Company.

MARY ROWLANDSON, "The Twentieth Remove," from *The Sovereignty and Goodness of God, Together with the Faithfulness of His Promises Displayed*. Copyright © 1997 Bedford Books, a division of St. Martin's Press, Inc.

RUTH ROSEN, "The War to Control the Past." Copyright © *San Francisco Chronicle*, September 29, 2000. Reprinted by permission.

JANE TOMPKINS, "At the Buffalo Bill Museum, June 1988," from *West of Everything: The Inner Life of Westerns*. Copyright © 1992 Jane Tompkins. Reprinted by permission of Oxford University Press.

SUSAN FALUDI, "Blame It on Feminism," from *Backlash*. Copyright © 1991 by Susan Faludi. Reprinted by permission of Crown Publishers, a division of Random House, Inc.

ESTELLE B. FREEDMAN, from *No Turning Back*. Copyright © 2002 Estelle B. Freedman. Reprinted by permission of Ballantine Books, a division of Random House, Inc.

LESLIE MARMON SILKO, "Fences against Freedom," from *Yellow Woman and a Beauty of the Spirit*. Reprinted by permission of Simon & Schuster Adult Publishing Group. Copyright © 1996 Leslie Marmon Silko.

ANONYMOUS, "Fresh Off the Boat," from *The Economist*, July 7, 2001. Copyright © 2001 The Economist Newspaper Ltd. All rights reserved. Reprinted with permission. Further reproduction prohibited. www.economist.com

RONALD TAKAKI, from *A Different Mirror: A History of Multicultural America*. Copyright © 1993 Ronald Takaki. Reprinted by permission of Little, Brown & Company, Inc.

BRENT STAPLES, "Black Men and Public Space," first appeared as "Just Walk on By" in *Ms. Magazine*, September 1986. Copyright © 1986 Brent Staples. Reprinted by permission of the author.

PHILLIP LOPATE, "Ashes," from *Before and After: Stories from New York*. Copyright © 2002 Thomas Beller. Reprinted by permission of Mr. Beller's Neighborhood Books.

SUSAN SONTAG, originally published in *The New Yorker*, September 24, 2001. Reprinted by permission of The Wylie Agency, Inc.